INTERNATIONAL ENCYCLOPEDIA OF

Marriage
and
Family

INTERNATIONAL ENCYCLOPEDIA OF

Marriage and Family

SECOND EDITION

Volume 2: Ea–Ju

James J. Ponzetti, Jr
Editor in Chief

**MACMILLAN
REFERENCE
USA™**

THOMSON

GALE

New York • Detroit • San Diego • San Francisco • Cleveland • New Haven, Conn. • Waterville, Maine • London • Munich

International Encyclopedia of Marriage and Family
James J. Ponzetti, Jr.

LIBRARY OF CONGRESS CATALOGING-IN-PUBLICATION DATA

International encyclopedia of marriage and family / James J. Ponzetti, Jr.,
editor in chief. — 2nd ed.
   p. cm.
Rev. ed. of: Encyclopedia of marriage and the family. c1995.
Includes bibliographical references and index.
   ISBN 0-02-865672-5 (set : alk. paper) — ISBN 0-02-865673-3 (v. 1 : alk.
paper) — ISBN 0-02-865674-1 (v. 2 : alk. paper) — ISBN 0-02-865675-X
(v. 3 : alk. paper) — ISBN 0-02-865676-8 (v. 4 : alk. paper)
   1. Marriage—Encyclopedias. 2. Family—Encyclopedias. I. Ponzetti,
James J. II. Encyclopedia of marriage and family.

   HQ9 .E52 2003
   306.8'03—dc21

2002014107

Printed in the United States of America
10 9 8 7 6 5 4 3 2 1

EATING DISORDERS

Eating disorders have become a major health problem in Western society, and there is evidence of their emergence in most parts of the world. The most common eating disorders are *anorexia nervosa* and *bulimia nervosa,* with a number of variations on these, including *binge eating disorder.* What they have in common, besides an excess preoccupation with weight and shape, is poor self-esteem. Indeed, they might equally be called disorders of self-esteem because self-esteem in this population is based on weight and shape.

In anorexia nervosa, people refuse to maintain a minimally normal body weight, engage in a relentless pursuit of thinness, have a distorted body image, and suffer physical side effects such as *amenorrhoea* (loss of menstrual cycle), poor blood circulation, low blood pressure, muscle wasting, and *osteoporosis.*

People with bulimia nervosa tend to maintain a normal weight, but engage in overeating (bingeing) and purging (use of laxatives, self-induced vomiting, and diuretics). Bulimia also results in serious medical complications such as cardiac abnormalities, gastro- and intestinal problems, tooth erosion, and damage to the ovaries.

Binge eating disorder is characterized by consuming an excessive amount of food, accompanied by a lack of control and marked distress, but no purging or distortion of body image.

In each of these conditions, eating gives rise to shame, disgust, fear, and self-loathing. Purging leads to a sense of relief.

Individuals with anorexia nervosa or bulimia nervosa have an intense preoccupation with shape and weight. A distorted body image is characteristic of anorexia. OSCAR BURRIEL/LATIN STOCK/SCIENCE PHOTO LIBRARY. CUSTOM MEDICAL STOCK PHOTO.

In childhood and early adolescence, other eating disorders may occur in addition to anorexia nervosa and bulimia nervosa. These include *food avoidance emotional disorder* (FAED) in which there is determined food avoidance but without the intense preoccupation with weight and shape seen in anorexia and bulimia; *selective eating,* in which there is a very limited number of foods consumed, although the total calorie intake is sufficient to maintain a normal weight; and *functional dyspha-gia,* in which the child is frightened of swallowing for fear of vomiting or choking.

Who Develops Eating Disorders

The majority of eating disorders are far more likely to occur in females than males, the ratio being around 10:1. Conservative estimates suggest that between 1 and 4 percent of older adolescent females and young women in Western society suffer from anorexia nervosa or bulimia nervosa (Brownell and Fairburn 2001). Food avoidance emotional disorder, selective eating, and functional dysphagia affect boys and girls equally (Lask and Bryant-Waugh 2000).

Previously, eating disorders were most likely to occur in white middle-class young women. However, incidence patterns are now changing and eating disorders may be found in any race, ethnicity, social class, culture, age, or sex, although prevalence data are not available.

Specific risk factors for the development of eating disorders include:

(1) Poor self-esteem;

(2) Family history of eating disorders;

(3) Participation in sports or other pursuits that emphasize low body weight, for example, modeling, ballet, gymnastics, cheerleading, athletics;

(4) Past history of sexual abuse; and

(5) Perfectionist and conscientious personality types, who have a need to please others and have difficulty in expressing negative feelings.

How Culture Contributes

Although eating disorders are clearly multifactorial in their origin—in other words, there are many different components to their development including genetic predisposition, biological vulnerability, entry into puberty, and stress (Lask and Bryant-Waugh 2000)—cultural influences do seem to be particularly important (Wolf 1991). The barrage of social and cultural messages about maintaining a low weight, and equating thinness with beauty, exerts enormous pressure on young women (Fallon, Katzman, and Wooley 1993). For those who have particularly low self-esteem, one means of feeling

better about themselves is to conform to what society maintains as "looking good." This is exemplified by the fact that in the 1970s the average fashion model weighed 8 percent less than the average U.S. woman. In the 1990s the difference rose to 23 percent. In the twenty-first century, images of models are computer modified to the point where the idealized body shape and size is virtually impossible to achieve. Nonetheless, the vulnerable strive to do so.

The Family's Role

The role of the family in eating disorders is complex and unclear. There is increasing evidence that genetic factors play a major part (Brownell and Fairburn 2001). The emphasis within a family upon the value of thinness exerts strong temptations upon young females to maintain a low body weight. The tendency to overemphasize the importance of appearance at the cost of other features such as kindness, intelligence, and creativity enhances the risk. Furthermore, what family members do is as important as what they say. Thus, mothers who diet or who have eating disorders are more likely to have children who ultimately develop eating disorders.

Families can also set the stage for how children relate to food, regardless of issues related to weight. For example, parents may use food to reward, punish, placate, or distract. Children then learn that food is more than a substance of nourishment. It can also be a source of comfort or a source of distress. Some parents ignore their children's cues and feed them according to parental needs, schedules, or beliefs about how much the child should eat. This does not allow the individual to develop an awareness of appetite, hunger, or fullness, thus setting the tone for the development of eating disorders.

Pre-teenage girls often have a very close relationship with their fathers. As they progress into puberty, fathers may have difficulty in coping with their daughters' emerging sexuality, and consequently reduce their closeness. Alternatively, they may try to maintain the same level of contact as previously. Either of these can be a source of distress for the teenage girl, who may subconsciously start trying to return to an earlier stage of development by dieting (Maine 1991).

Regardless of whether or not a family may have contributed in some inadvertent way to the development of an eating disorder, the way in which they manage the problem can be extremely influential. A positive approach can quickly resolve the problem whilst confused, inconsistent, or negative approaches can exacerbate it. Arguments between parents about how best to proceed when their child or teenage daughter develops an eating disorder can exacerbate the problem. The teenager becomes caught up in parental conflict, feels worse, and delves deeper into the eating disorder. Sometimes the individual with the eating disorder can serve as a peacemaker, best friend, or confidante to one or both parents. Although the eating disorder symptoms may emerge for a number of different reasons, it may ultimately serve the purpose of helping family stability. As the individual becomes increasingly ill, parents often pay attention to the individual in a way that is reassuring and comforting. A couple in conflict may work together to try to help their child, especially when they see how serious are the side effects of the illness. This can exacerbate the illness by giving the subconscious message that illness equates with parental harmony.

Treatment

Because the eating disorders are complex, serious and varied, there can be no one simple approach to treatment (Lask and Bryant-Waugh 2000; Brownell and Fairburn 2001). For children and adolescents who live at home, working with the parents as well as the child is essential. Focusing on the factors that appear to maintain the problem is an essential part of the treatment program. Whether this is achieved through parental counseling and individual therapy for the child, or family therapy, or a combination of these, matters less than the family's involvement. For young adults, individual therapy/counseling is of undoubted help, so long as it focuses on the "here and now" problems that the individual is experiencing. There is no evidence that therapy focused on "subconscious" material or the distant past is of particular value. A problem-solving approach that looks at why it is necessary to maintain an eating disorder and that helps to enhance self-esteem is far more likely to work.

Many of these comments also apply to the treatment of bulimia nervosa, although in addition,

medication can be valuable. *Fluoxetine* or related drugs do seem to reduce the urge to binge and can improve mood. Antidepressants can also be useful when there is marked mood lowering.

For the other eating disorders that occur in childhood, a combination of working through the parents and various individual approaches is usually helpful (Lask and Bryant-Waugh 2000). Medication that is chosen judiciously and monitored carefully may also have value.

Whichever condition is being treated, the involvement of family members and open exploration of issues and problems that contribute to and maintain the eating disorder will help people with eating disorders to feel less guilty, less abnormal, and will enhance their self-worth and self-confidence. Thus, although families may be part of the problem, they are equally part of the solution. A number of self-help and parent guides are available (Bryant-Waugh and Lask 1999; Schmidt and Treasure 1993; Siegel, Brisman, and Weinshel 1988).

Conclusion

Eating disorders are potentially life threatening, resulting in death for as many as 10 percent of those who develop them. They can also cause considerable psychological distress and major physical complications. Important relationships are eroded as the eating disorder takes up time and energy, brings about self-absorption, and impairs self-esteem. Treatment should be initiated as quickly as possible, focus upon the immediate distress experienced by the individual, and aim to help the patient and family become powerful enough to overcome the eating disorder.

See also: CHILDHOOD, STAGES OF: ADOLESCENCE; DEPRESSION: CHILDREN AND ADOLESCENTS; FOOD; HEALTH AND FAMILIES; SELF-ESTEEM; SEXUALITY IN ADOLESCENCE; THERAPY: FAMILY RELATIONSHIPS; THERAPY: PARENT-CHILD RELATIONSHIPS

Bibliography

Brownell, K., and Fairburn, C. (2001). *Eating Disorders and Obesity: A Comprehensive Handbook,* 2nd edition. New York: Guilford Press.

Bryant-Waugh, R., and Lask, B. (1999). *Eating Disorders: A Parent's Guide.* London: Penguin.

Fallon, P.; Katzman, M.; and Wooley, S. (1993). *Feminist Perspective on Eating Disorders*. New York: Guilford Press.

Lask, B., and Bryant-Waugh, R. (2000). *Anorexia Nervosa and Related Eating Disorders in Childhood and Adolescence*. Hove, UK: Psychology Press.

Maine, M. (1991). *Father Hunger: Fathers, Daughters and Food*. Carlsbad, CA: Gurze Books.

Pate, J. E.; Pumariega, A. J.; Hester, C.; and Garner, D. M. (1992). "Cross-Cultural Patterns in Eating Disorders: A Review." *Journal of the American Academy of Child and Adolescent Psychiatry* 31:802–808.

Schmidt, U., and Treasure, J. (1993). *Getting Better Bit(e) by Bit(e): A Survival Guide for Sufferers of Bulimia Nervosa and Binge Eating Disorders*. Hove, UK: Psychology Press.

Siegel, M.; Brisman, J.; and Weinshel, M. (1988). *Surviving an Eating Disorder: Strategies for Families and Friends*. New York: Harper and Row.

Wolf, N. (1991). *The Beauty Myth: How Images of Beauty are Used against Women*. New York: William Morrow.

BRYAN LASK

ECUADOR

See LATIN AMERICA

EDUCATION

See ACADEMIC ACHIEVEMENT; CHILDHOOD, STAGES OF: ADOLESCENCE; FAMILY LIFE EDUCATION; FAMILY LITERACY; HOMESCHOOLING; PARENTING EDUCATION; SCHOOL; SCHOOL PHOBIA AND SCHOOL REFUSAL; SEXUALITY EDUCATION

EGYPT

For most contemporary Egyptians, the family remains the central and most important institution in their everyday lives. Few individuals live independently from their immediate family or kin, and single-person households are almost unheard of. Individuals of all classes constantly articulate and defend the importance of family within the community and the nation. Issues relating to family relations, gender roles, and authority are pervasive throughout the society, as evidenced by conversations in homes, on the street, and in the media. Further, the proper functioning of families is part of a religious dialogue that is increasingly heard in all sectors of the society.

Egypt's estimated population in 1999 was 66,050,004, with 36.1 percent of the population under age fifteen, 60 percent between ages fifteen and sixty-five, and 3.7 over age sixty-five. Ninety-five percent of the country's population is Muslim, and approximately 5 percent is Coptic. Approximately 98 percent of the population between twenty-five and sixty-five is or has been married, indicating the continuing primacy of founding a family through marriage for Egyptians of all classes.

Defining Family in Egypt

Linguistic issues. In Egypt, the widely recognized importance of family stands in direct contrast to the ambiguity of linguistic terms dealing with the institution. When referring to their families, Egyptians tend to use the Arabic word *ahl*, a broad term that encompasses various relationships, including immediate family related through blood ties, members of the household, and individuals related through marriage, and can, therefore, refer to up to 100 to 200 people. Another term, *a'ila*, is also commonly used, and can refer to either a nuclear or extended group of people, depending on context. The term *a'ila* carries with it the connotation of close relationship and mutual obligation.

The smallest family unit specified by Egyptian terminology is the word *bait*, which means "house." Bait is used to specify the actual residence of a family or the group of people who live under the same roof most of the time. Although this usually refers to the nuclear family, it can also include a spinster aunt, a widowed parent, or any other member of the extended family who is a part of the residential group. Egyptian family terms seem to be even more ambiguous than those of other Arab countries such as Saudi Arabia, for example, where individuals have a stronger sense of specificity of genealogy (Rugh 1984).

The Egyptian linguistic ambiguity about kinship terms allows individuals to manipulate the concept of family to fit the context and situation.

Family is the most important institution in most Egyptians' lives. Few people live apart from their immediate family or kin.
CORY LANGLEY

Constant references to family and family name allow individuals to place one another within the society and to identify important ties and reciprocal obligations. The honor, social standing, and wealth of a family are all interconnected, making the identification with family a primary social marker for every Egyptian.

Social class and family.   Class divisions within society play a vital role in Egyptian life. Egyptians have an incredibly fine-tuned sense of class, and this plays a part in every aspect of an individual's life. Primarily, these divisions are based on family, wealth, education, and experiences and/or education abroad. In addition, reputation, religious piety,

and foreign ancestry (for example, having a Turkish mother, grandmother, etc.) may raise a family's social status in the eyes of others. The division by class is a distinctive but complex dividing line in the society that is constantly reflected in the written and oral media.

Furthermore, even though the major cities of Cairo and Alexandria are divided into newer and older, as well as richer and poorer sections, it is not customary for Egyptians to move, even if their financial situation improves substantially. As a result, older, well-to-do Egyptians are often found living in sections of the city that are considered middle class or, at times, even lower-middle class. Among these families, it is common for the older generation to buy apartments in their buildings for their children as they marry, thereby keeping them close. Among low-income communities, all family members routinely continue to live in the same apartment, and as the children marry, their spouses move in with the extended families. Among this group, individuals rely even more heavily on their families because they have fewer ties to other structures of power in the society.

The role of the natal family. In Cairo, the importance of family for women and men in all arenas can hardly be overestimated. Although women, upon marriage, become incorporated into the household of their husbands, they remain members of their natal families. They retain their fathers' family names after marriage and, in case of divorce or widowhood, are expected to move back to their natal home. Men bear the financial responsibility of caring for all single women in their families, even if these women have been previously married. Thus, women are brought up with the expectation that their primary ties and ultimate sources of economic security will be in their relationships to their fathers, brothers, and sons. These relationships with both female and male members of the immediate family remain the strongest links in women's lives.

The role of extended families. Some version of the extended family is the ideal among all classes, and living in the same building or neighborhood as fathers, brothers, sisters, mothers, or cousins is still considered the best situation (Macleod 1991). The extended families that are often found in Egypt do not follow the traditional patterns in which genealogically related persons of two generations live together or in which married siblings form one household. Rather, extended families are based on the incorporation of unmarried relatives into a family. Widows, divorcees (especially those with no children), and bachelors do not live separately and would be stigmatized should they make this choice. Further, unmarried sons or daughters live with their parents until marriage, regardless of age. After divorce or the death of a spouse, both men and women, especially if they do not have children, are expected to return to their parents if they are still alive; otherwise, they are supposed to live with a brother, sister, or other relative. Another popular extended family pattern is the one in which a child is "borrowed" by a relative with no children of his or her own. Among lower-class people, one tends to find this phenomenon more often among grandparents who need the assistance of a child for housework. Among more well-to-do families, an uncle or aunt will offer to take care of a siblings' children for an extended time period, primarily for sentimental reasons or because the biological parents already have other pressing obligations such as an extended leave abroad.

Another common middle- and lower-class family pattern found in Egypt is the incorporation of nonrelatives, such as apprentices and work assistants, into a particular household. Such individuals have a special position, because although not all of them sleep in the house of their employer, their food and laundry is part of the household. Upper-middle and upper-class families employ domestic servants who may or may not live in the household. Often a domestic live-in servant will come from the family's natal village, even if the family has not lived there in several generations.

Migrants, a group often ignored, exhibit an alternative family pattern: they do not usually bring their families when they first enter the city from the countryside. When they arrive in the city, they tend to live in the same neighborhoods as others from their natal village. Each will live with other relatives in the local neighborhood until he becomes established and acquires a house of his own.

The continuing primacy of extended families can be explained by the fact that for most Egyptians, family provides a sense of place, a congenial setting, and a social network for financial and personal support. People often mention that life in the West, with its emphasis on individual needs and pursuits, looks very lonely and self-centered. Although the actual composition of a household may vary widely within the same class level or within a larger extended family, the structure and ideology of family remains crucial for the network of resources and sense of identity that it continues to provide.

Gender and Family

Egyptian society is organized on the principle that men and women simply have different natures, talents, and inherent tendencies. This becomes most apparent in the realm of the family where each gender has a different part to play. Men are created for going out in the world and are responsible for providing financially for the family. Women are suited for remaining within family boundaries, caring for the home, the children, and the husband. Further, women's inherent sexuality is believed to be constantly endangering the social harmony of society (specifically, men) and is, therefore, best controlled through women's modesty and women remaining as much as possible within the private sphere of the family. This belief is reinforced through cultural and religious norms that are increasingly advocating that family roles of both women and men are fundamental in maintaining societal structure; dominant gender constructions therefore support keeping women in the home and oppose women working and abandoning their primary roles (Macleod 1991). Nonetheless, contemporary images of women as economic assets and providers are rapidly coming into conflict with what are perceived as divinely inspired roles.

Gender roles in Egypt derive much of their legitimacy from the Qur'an. In particular, women are often the focus of quotes that supposedly refer to the appropriate roles and behaviors of women. At the same time, references to the role of women are scattered broadly throughout the Qur'an and are subject to interpretation.

Existing side by side and sometimes in contradiction to the reality of women's daily struggles in Egypt is the cultural and religious ideal of complementarity between the sexes. Within this concept, women are not devalued as persons, somehow considered to be inherently less valuable than men, or thought to be lacking in abilities. Instead, Egyptians tend to emphasize that everyone—men, women, and children—is thought to be part of an interrelated community, and that gender complementarity is part of the message of the religion. This concept of gender complementarity, particularly in the realm of the family, is an integral part of understanding the social structure of Egyptian society.

Marriage and Family

Marriage remains at the center of contemporary Egyptian social life. It is the primary focal point in the lives of both women and men, followed only by the birth of a child. The rights and obligations of husband and wife are defined by Islamic law, the division of labor by gender, and Egyptian cultural practice.

A Muslim marriage gives a wife the unconditional right to economic support from her husband regardless of her own financial resources. She also remains in control of her property, including inheritance or earned income. However, in case of divorce, the ex-wife is only entitled to three months' alimony and to those possessions that she brought with her at the beginning of her marriage or those that she acquired with her own income, as well as any portion of her *mahr* that is due her. Mahr is a sum of money or durable property that, according to Islamic practice, a husband agrees to pay to his bride at any time prior to or during the marriage or upon divorce.

In return for the unconditional economic support of his family, a husband has certain rights within the marriage, the most important of which is the right to restrict his wife's physical mobility, which is often interpreted as the right of a husband to prevent his wife from working outside the home. He also has the unilateral right to end the marriage without the consent of his wife. And in case of divorce, the husband legally receives custody of the children after they have reached the age of seven. It is, however, customary for girls to remain with their mothers after a divorce. Recently, changes in the law in favor of women have curtailed some of husbands' rights. Primarily, women are now able to file for divorce, especially in cases of domestic violence, and men must now legally file for divorce and cannot divorce a woman simply by uttering "I divorce thee" three times, as is permitted by the Qur'an. Cultural practices, such as cross-cousin marriages and sizable sums of money through the mahr, have evolved to protect women and counterbalance the unequal rights in cases of divorce. However, the relatively low incidence of divorce in Egypt (according to the last census at 2%), particularly after children are born, suggests that marriage is a stable institution.

The Marriage Negotiation

All Muslim Egyptian marriages are characterized by a formalized set of negotiations that begin once the suitability of the marriage partners has been determined. The prelude to the marriage contract is the betrothal, which is the request by the man for the hand of a certain woman in marriage. It is at this point that the man will approach her family with the view of describing his status and negotiating with them the marriage contract and their respective demands. For the betrothal to be valid, both parties should be aware of the circumstances of the other and should know the potential spouse's character and behavior. This information is obtained through inquiries, investigations, and the direct contact of the couple in the presence of a chaperon. Once the man's offer is accepted by the woman, or by those who are legally entitled to act on her behalf, the betrothal will have taken place. It is usual at the point of betrothal that the man offers his future bride a gift, which in Egypt is referred to as the *shabka*. In some instances, particularly if the man does not know the bride's family through previous contacts, or if he wants to make an extremely favorable impression on the young woman, the man will offer her the shabka before the *khutba*, thereby showing his good will, his good intentions, and, perhaps his good financial standing. The shabka is, by middle-class American standards, a very expensive gift of jewelry. Betrothal does not, however, constitute a marriage contract: It is merely a mutual promise of marriage between the two parties, and it is not legally binding for either. In practice, the khutba is easily dissolved.

Among Egyptians, the betrothal becomes a public acknowledgment of the couple's right to spend *chaperoned* time together. It is a general rule that now the prospective bridegroom will join the woman's family for dinner regularly, giving the couple an opportunity to get to know each other in the presence of others. In addition, other members of the two families will start visiting one another. In particular, the man's mother and sisters or female cousins will begin spending long periods of time with the prospective bride

The Islamic Marriage Contract

The key to understanding any Islamic marriage (and 95% of all marriages in Egypt are Islamic) is the contract that is formed by the two parties. From a legal standpoint, the marriage contract establishes a series of rights and obligations between a couple that have a long-lasting effect on many aspects of their lives. In all schools of Islamic law, marriage is seen as a contract, the main function of which is to make sexual relations between a man and a woman licit. A valid and effective marriage contract outlines certain respective legal rights and duties for wife and husband, together with other rights and duties common to both of them. This contract, however, represents more than a mere exchange of money or material goods. It is a form of social exchange and is thus a legal, religious, economic, and symbolic transaction. The contract is attended to with utmost seriousness and is preceded by a set of lengthy negotiations, almost all of which center around the material protection of the woman and her unborn children once she enters the state of matrimony. Nevertheless, the marriage contract may include conditions that are advantageous for either or both spouses. Conditions that are specified in the contract range from the woman's right to dissolve the marriage, to an agreement that neither party may leave the town they agree to live in, and even that the husband may not marry another woman. The contract, as a matter of course, also acts as a medium for bringing the various members of the two families together and provides them with the opportunity to discuss in detail the preliminary workings of the marriage. Most important, the marriage contract symbolizes the public acknowledgement of the formation of a lawful sexual partnership that will be sanctioned both religiously and socially, and that marks the beginning of a family and the care and upbringing of children. Marriage remains the focal point for channeling sexuality, founding a family, and joining two extended families into a reciprocal relationship of obligations.

Changing economic conditions and new perceptions of the relative value of education and of wage employment have led to new configurations of family strategies among all classes of Egyptian families. Today, even in the most patriarchal family contexts, decisions concerning education, employment, and spending are to a large extent collectively reached. Further, economic circumstances force many Egyptian families to depend on the earnings and contributions of women and children as well as adult males. Access to new opportunities in Egypt and abroad have been distributed unequally and have led to perceptions of relative economic disadvantage. Nevertheless, not all families, even those within a single class, have experienced these shifts in identical ways. Family strategies reflect this range of experience.

See also: ISLAM; KINSHIP

Bibliography

Abdel Kader, S. (1992). *The Situation Analysis of Women in Egypt*. Cairo: Central Agency for Population, Moblization and Statistics (CAPMAS) and UNICEF.

CAPMAS. (1986). National Census, Cairo.

CAPMAS. (1990). Labour Force Sample Survey (LFSS), Cairo.

CAPMAS and UNICEF. (1991). Women's Participation in the Labour Force. Cairo.

El-Nashif, H. (1994). *Basic Education and Female Literacy in Egypt*. Cairo: Third World Forum, Middle East Office.

Macleod, A. E. (1991). *Accommodating Protest: Working Women, and the New Veiling in Cairo*. New Haven, CT: Yale University Press.

Rugh, A. (1984). *Family in Contemporary Egypt*. Syracuse, NY: Syracuse University Press.

UNICEF (1993). *Report on the State of Women and Children in Egypt*. Cairo.

BAHIRA SHERIF

ELDER ABUSE

Although conflict in families has been a consistent theme in world literature since ancient times, elder abuse did not surface as a social problem until the mid-1970s, first identified in British literature, followed soon after in the United States and Canada. During the next decade several European countries and Australia began publishing reports on elder mistreatment. By the 1990s elder abuse research and programs, although still limited, were underway in many developed nations and emerging in developing countries as well.

Definition

Elder abuse has been used as an all-inclusive term representing types of abusive behavior against the elderly, or it can refer to a specific act of physical violence. Most experts agree that elder abuse can be an act of commission (abuse) or omission (neglect), intentional or unintentional, and of one of more types: physical, psychological (emotional and/or verbal aggression), and financial abuse and neglect that results in unnecessary suffering, injury, pain, loss, and/or violation of human rights and decreased quality of life. Whether the behavior is labelled as abusive, neglectful, or exploitative may depend on the frequency of the mistreatment, as well as the duration, intensity, severity, consequences, and cultural context. Some researchers have questioned the legal and professional basis of the current definitions and suggest that it is the older person's perception of the behavior that is meaningful. Others have noted the importance of cultural traditions in defining what is acceptable and unacceptable behavior.

An initial effort to elicit information about elder abuse directly from older persons in three historically "black" South African townships showed that in addition to the typical western schema of physical, verbal, financial, sexual, abuse and neglect, the focus group participants added loss of respect for elders, accusations of witchcraft, and systemic abuse (marginalization of older persons by the government).

Prevalence

So far, prevalence studies have been restricted to the developed world. Five community-based prevalence surveys conducted in five countries using different methods of data collection reported rates that ranged between 4 to 6 percent of the older population although the proportion of abuse types among the five varied. Two were national in scope, Canada and the UK (Podnieks 1992; Ogg and Bennett 1992); a third encompassed the retired population of a small Finnish town (Kivelä et al. 1992), and the other two utilized representative samples of cities in the United States (Boston) (Pillemer and Finkelhor 1988) and the Netherlands (Amsterdam) (Comijs et al. 1998). In the U.S. and Canadian studies, men and women were apt to be mistreated equally; in the Finnish and Dutch surveys, female victims outnumbered males. A later national Canadian survey on family violence reported older men (9%) were more likely than older women (6%) to report being victims of emotional or financial abuse (Bunge and Locke 2000). No systematic collection of abuse statistics or prevalence surveys has been conducted in the developing world but crime records, journalistic reports, social welfare records, and small scale studies contain evidence that mistreatment of elders is occurring.

Theoretical Explanations and Risk Factors

To explain the causes of elder abuse, some researchers in the developed countries have viewed it as a problem of an overburdened caregiver (situational model), a mentally disturbed abuser (intra-individual dynamics), or a dependent perpetrator and dependent victim (exchange theory). Others have used learned behavior (social learning theory), the imbalance of power within relationships (feminist theory), the marginalization of elders (political economy theory), or a lack of fit between the organism and the environment (ecological theory).

Without data to support the theories, the focus has been on determining the risk-factors or characteristics that increase the probability of victimization but are not necessarily causal agents. With the limited data available, the most likely risk factors seem to be (a) victim-perpetrator dependency, (b) perpetrator deviance, (c) victim disability, (d) caregiver stress, and (e) social isolation. While the developed nations have emphasized the individual and interpersonal attributes, the developing nations have given weight to societal and cultural factors, including poverty, ageism, sexism, and violence.

Consequences of Mistreatment

Few empirical studies have been conducted to determine the consequences of mistreatment on the physical and mental health of older victims, in part because of the difficulty in separating the effects of normal aging and chronic diseases from abusive behavior. To date, one study has reported the impact on physical status. Using two existing data bases (health survey data from a representative sample of 2,812 elders in a U.S. city and reports to the adult protective service agency [APS] collected over a nine year period), researchers found that those individuals who had been reported to APS and who were physically abused or neglected had a mortality rate three times those who had not been reported. After controlling for the possible factors that might affect mortality (e.g., age, gender, income, functional and cognitive status, diagnosis, and social supports) and finding no significant relationships, they speculated that mistreatment causes extreme interpersonal stress that may confer an additional death risk (Lachs et al. 1998).

Several studies have reported in an abuse sample a higher proportion of older victims with depression or psychological distress than in a nonabuse sample. Since these were cross-sectional in design, there is no way to know whether the condition was an antecedent or consequence of the abuse (Bristowe and Collins 1989; Phillips 1983; Pillemer and Prescott 1989; Comijs et al. 1999) Other suggested symptomatology associated with these cases include feelings of learned helplessness, alienation, guilt, shame, fear, anxiety, denial, and posttraumatic stress syndrome.

Intervention Strategies

Generally, countries delivering services to abused, neglected, and exploited elders have done so through existing health and social service systems. Because of the complexity of the cases, which often involve medical, legal, ethical, psychological, financial, criminal, and environmental issues, guidelines and protocols are used to assist the workers, and special training is made available to them. Multidisciplinary consulting teams are called upon to assist in planning the care. Telephone "helplines" to take reports are often the first component of an elder abuse system. Since much of elder abuse is spouse abuse, there is growing interest in providing services modeled after those developed for younger battered women, such as emergency shelters, support groups, the use of law enforcement, and the criminal justice system. Except for the United States, Israel, and four Canadian provinces, most countries have not passed specific elder abuse legislation but rely on civil rights, family violence, mental health, property rights, and criminal statutes to address the problem.

Conclusion

That family members can be abusive or neglectful toward their elders even in societies that emphasize *filial piety* and family harmony came as a revelation to the world. A quarter century of efforts to deal with the problem in the United States has built an infrastructure based on a model in which protective service personnel respond to reports of abuse by conducting investigations and devising follow-up treatment plans, but primary prevention techniques have received little attention in other developed countries. Families in the developing world face still more severe challenges, including forced emigration, economic recession, and changing characteristics. The process of industrialization has eroded long-standing patterns of interdependence between the generations, producing material and emotional hardships for elders. However, with increasing interest around the globe in human rights, gender equality, and violence prevention, the future augers well for bringing an end to this age old problem.

See also: CAREGIVING: INFORMAL; DEMENTIA; ELDERS; FILIAL RESPONSIBILITY; INTERGENERATIONAL RELATIONS; LATER LIFE FAMILIES; RESPITE CARE: ADULT; SPOUSE ABUSE: PREVALENCE; SPOUSE ABUSE: THEORETICAL EXPLANATIONS; STRESS; SUBSTITUTE CAREGIVERS

Bibliography

Bristowe, E., and Collins, J. B. (1989). "Family Mediated Abuse of Non-Institutionalized Elder Men and Women Living in British Columbia." *Journal of Elder Abuse and Neglect* 1(1):45–54.

Bunge, V. P., and Locke, D. (2000). *Family Violence in Canada: A Statistical Profile.* Ottawa: Canadian Centre for Justice Statistics, Statistics Canada.

Comijs, H. C.; Penninx, B. W. J. H.; Knipscheer, K. P. M.; and van Tilburg, W. (1999). "Psychological Distress in Victims of Elder Mistreatment: The Effects of Social Support and Coping." *Journal of Gerontology* 64B(4):240–245.

Comijs, H. C.; Pot, A. M.; Smit, J. H.; Bouter, L. M.; and Jonker, C. (1998). "Elder Abuse in the Community: Prevalence and Consequences." *Journal of the American Geriatrics Society* 46:885–888.

Kivelä, S. L.; Köngäs-Saviro, P.; Kesti, E.; Pahkala, K.; and Ijäs, M. L. (1992). "Abuse in Old Age: Epidemiological Data from Finland." *Journal of Elder Abuse and Neglect* 4(3):1–18.

Lachs, M. S.; Williams, E.; O'Brien, S.; Hurst, L.; Pillemer, K; and Charlson, M. (1998). "The Mortality of Elder Mistreatment." *Journal of the American Medical Association* 280(5):428–432.

Ogg, J., and Bennett, G. (1992). "Elder Abuse in Britain." *British Medical Journal* 305:998–999.

Phillips, L. R. (1983). "Abuse and Neglect of the Frail Elderly at Home: An Exploration of Theoretical Relationships." *Advanced Nursing* 8:379–382.

Pillemer, K., and Finkelhor, D. (1988). "Prevalence of Elder Abuse: A Random Sample Survey." *Gerontologist* 28(1):51–57.

Pillemer, K., and Prescott, D. (1989). "Psychological Effects of Elder Abuse: A Research Note." *Journal of Elder Abuse and Neglect* 1(1):65–74.

Podnieks, E. (1992). "National Survey on Abuse of the Elderly in Canada." *Journal of Elder Abuse and Neglect* 4(1/2):5–58.

ROSALIE S. WOLF

ELDER CARE

See ALZHEIMER'S DISEASE; CAREGIVING: FORMAL; CAREGIVING: INFORMAL; CHRONIC ILLNESS; DEMENTIA; DISABILITIES; DIVISION OF LABOR; RESPITE CARE: ADULT

ELDERS

Attempts to define *elders* reveal cultural variations about what it means to be an elder in different societies. In some traditional societies, to be old is to be respected, considered wise, and revered as a teacher of traditions. In postmodern society most definitions of elder have come to be related to chronological age, degrees of disability, accepted roles (especially those considered economically productive), and age discrimination.

There are three significant changes in demographics related to elders. The first is the increase in individual life expectancy. In the United States a child born in 1998 can expect to live about twenty-nine years longer than a child born in 1900 (American Association of Retired Persons 2000). Life expectancy in developing countries is expected to rise from forty-one years in 1950 to seventy years in 2020. Not only are individuals experiencing greater longevity, but societies as a whole are also aging. Worldwide, by 2020 there will be more than a billion people over sixty years of age. More than 700 million of them will live in developing countries (World Health Organization 1998). The proportion of the population aged sixty and over is expected to reach 23 percent in North America, 17 percent in East Asia, 12 percent in Latin America and 10 percent in South Asia (World Health Organization 1998). The percentage of seniors in U.S. society increased from 2 percent in 1790 to 12.7 percent in 1999 (Atchley 2000).

A second important demographic change is that the elderly population (people sixty-five or older) is itself aging. In the United States in 1999, the eighty-five and older group included 4.2 million elders (American Association of Retired Persons 2000). In 2020, the proportion of the population sixty and over who are among the oldest old (eighty and above) will reach over 20 percent in most of Europe and 21 percent in Japan.

A third important change in the population of elders in the United States is the increasing racial-ethnic diversity among this population. Minority populations are expected to represent 25 percent of the elderly population by 2030 (American Association for World Health 1999).

Many facets of U.S. life are affected by these three demographic trends. Most elders are experiencing better health than previous age cohorts (Atchley 2000; Moody 2000) and consequently can look forward to greater activity in later years. Families, as well as older individuals themselves, are challenged by the new phenomenon of twenty to thirty years of life after retirement. This extension of life raises issues about how individuals will use this time in later life and will maintain their quality of life. Care provision for elders who become disabled is an increasing challenge for families around the world (Administration on Aging 2001). The increase in numbers of elders eighty and older has raised concern about the availability of health care and social services, as well as the development of many such services since the 1960s (Morgan and Kunkel 2001).

Most elders continue to perform in roles as they always have while adding new and unexpected roles. As always, they are sexual beings. They continue to participate in hobbies and other activities. They are parents, spouses, and friends, and they maintain most of the patterns and characteristics of earlier times in the life-cycle. In addition, elders can have several careers; take many roles in families and the community; and maintain good health through disease prevention, healthy diet, exercise programs, and improved medical technology. New roles include expanded volunteer activities, nontraditional student roles, caring for grandchildren in parental roles, and pursuing creative, artistic, and athletic interests.

Sometimes, because of life situations, elders change in unexpected ways. They may begin to abuse alcohol to cope with difficulties. Their personality traits may seem to change because of medications or mental or physical changes in their bodies. They may become sad, angry, or depressed because of unexpected losses or changes in their lives. These situational changes are not an inevitable part of the aging process. They can be treated in many of the same ways as they are in younger persons.

What it means to be an elder varies by culture. New roles that many elders take on include volunteering, being a student, caring for grandchildren, and pursuing creative, artistic, and athletic interests. A/P WIDE WORLD PHOTOS

Many political and policy debates have emerged in response to the aging of society. The questions include the chronological age at which an individual should be considered an elder, the appropriateness of current patterns of retirement, the financing of health care, and other resource utilization issues (Moody 2000). In the 1980s and 1990s an intergenerational equity debate emerged that blamed elders for using an excessive amount of limited public resources. Meredith Minkler (2000) and other social policy analysts argue that society needs to look at inequality in distribution of resources among socioeconomic classes rather than focusing on generational inequality.

Robert Butler coined the word *ageism* in 1968 to describe the process of systematic stereotyping of people because they are old. Ageism is a term that parallels other *isms* in society, such as *racism, sexism, heterosexism,* and *classism.* "Ageism allows [other] generations to see older people as different from themselves; thus they subtly cease to identify with their elders as human beings" (Butler 1975, 12). All people, including adolescents and elders, can be discriminated against based on age. Common myths and stereotypes about elders that form the basis for ageism are often included in cartoons and jokes about *senility,* frailty, and disabilities. These result in invisibility, disrespect, and avoidance of older persons. The popular media can promote negative attitudes and images of elders based on ageism for young and old alike.

In sum, it is important to note that the context of the aging experience includes socioeconomic class position, amount of social support, gender, ethnicity, health status, and other factors (Dressel, Minkler, and Yen 2000). Younger members of society are socialized to the elder experience by cultures that structure social boundaries between generations, distribute power and resources between genders and ethnic populations over the life-cycle, and perpetuate stories and mythology (Sokolovsky 1993).

Overall, the opportunity to have a longer life with increasingly productive roles is, for the first time, possible. Societies around the world are challenged to change many of the negative attitudes toward the aging process. Jeanette Takamura (2002) notes that "the demographic revolution occurring will not by-pass the developing world" and suggests that "the strongest impetus for refocusing the international policy agenda to give heightened and timely attention to aging as a social and economic issue of significant resonance will continue to come from outside of the U.S. due to the critical demographic impact in such countries as Japan, Germany, France, and other countries that are aging more rapidly than the U.S." However, regardless of the immediacy of the aging population it is critical that all countries focus attention on structural integration of the elderly. This policy agenda must look for better ways to integrate the aging population as a strong and contributory force in future social structures and at the same time find new, compassionate ways to meet the needs of elderly individuals who require care.

See also: ADULTHOOD; ALZHEIMER'S DISEASE; CAREGIVING: FORMAL; CAREGIVING: INFORMAL; DEATH AND DYING; DEMENTIA; DISABILITIES; DIVORCE: EFFECTS ON PARENTS; ELDER ABUSE; FAMILY DEVELOPMENT THEORY; FILIAL RESPONSIBILITY; GRANDPARENTHOOD; GRANDPARENTS' RIGHTS; GRIEF, LOSS, AND BEREAVEMENT; INTERGENERATIONAL PROGRAMMING; INTERGENERATIONAL RELATIONS; INTERGENERATIONAL TRANSMISSION; LATER LIFE FAMILIES; MENOPAUSE; RESPITE CARE: ADULT; RETIREMENT; SEXUALITY IN ADULTHOOD; WIDOWHOOD

Bibliography

Administration on Aging. (2001). *Innovative Programs and Activities of National Significance under the National Family Caregiver Support Program.* Washington, DC: Author

American Association of Retired Persons. (2000). *A Profile of Older Americans: Based on Data from the U.S. Bureau of the Census.* Washington, DC: Author.

American Association for World Health. (1999). *Healthy Aging Healthy Living—Start Now!* Resource Booklet. Washington, DC: Author.

Atchley, R. C. (2000). *Social Forces and Aging,* 9th edition. Belmont, CA: Wadsworth.

Butler, R. (1975). *Why Survive?: Being Old in America.* New York: Harper and Row.

Dressel, P.; Minkler, M.; and Yen, I. (2000). "Gender, Race, Class, and Aging: Advances and Opportunities." In *Critical Gerontology: Perspectives from Political and Moral Economy,* ed. M. Minkler and C. Estes. Amityville, NY: Baywood.

Minkler, M. (2000). "New Challenges for Gerontology." In *Intersections in Aging: Readings in Social Gerontology,* ed. E. Markson and L. Hollis-Sawyer. Los Angeles: Roxbury.

Moody, H. (2000). *Aging Concepts and Controversies,* 3rd edition. Thousand Oaks, CA: Pine Forge Press.

Morgan, L., and Kunkel, S. (2001). *Aging: The Social Context,* 2nd edition. Thousand Oaks, CA: Pine Forge Press.

Sokolovsky, J. (1993). "Images of Aging: A Cross-Cultural Perspective." *Generations* 17:51–54.

Takamura, J. (in press). "Towards a New Era in Aging and Social Work." *Journal of Gerontological Social Work.*

World Health Organization. (1998). *Population Aging— A Public Health Challenge.* Geneva, Switzerland: Author.

ENID OPAL COX
PAMELA METZ

EMPTY NEST SYNDROME

See FAMILY DEVELOPMENT THEORY

ENCULTURATION

See SOCIALIZATION

ENGLAND

See GREAT BRITAIN

EQUITY

It is not surprising that in cultures founded on principles of individualism, equality, and capitalism, such as in the United States, theories concerned with fairness and exchange would develop regarding close relationships. A large body of relationship research has originated from a group of theories associated with social-exchange principles, which conceptualize relationships as based on principles of economics and behavioral psychology. One of the main principles of this research is the idea that a relationship is developed or ended based on partners' calculations regarding the costs and benefits of the relationship (Thibaut and Kelly 1959). For example, a person may rely on a friend for entertainment, occasional help such as getting a ride to the airport, and emotional support when a romantic relationship goes bad. These are types of benefits or rewards a person gets from the friendship. For the person giving the assistance and support, these behaviors can be perceived as personal costs associated with being in the friendship. Different social-exchange types of theories offer different insights into the possible ways relational partners compare their costs and benefits to determine whether or not the relationships is worth pursuing.

Equity theory proposes that relationship outcomes, such as satisfaction and continued involvement, are based upon evaluations of how just or fair the distribution of costs and benefits are for each partner (Walster, Walster, and Berscheid 1978). The four main propositions of equity theory indicate that partners judge the distribution of costs and benefits according to socially acceptable rules of fairness. When their calculations indicate they are in an inequitable arrangement, partners will become distressed and try to adjust the costs and benefits of the relationship to make the relationship equitable.

The Scope of Equity Theory and Close Relationships

Researchers using equity theory have examined close relationships like friendships and family relationships. By far, though, the most researched type of relationship has been the heterosexual romantic relationship and much of the research reported here reflects that bias. Changes in sex role expectations for men and women, an increased number of women in the workforce, and an increased expectation of companionship and emotional intimacy in marriage has resulted in a more egalitarian, or equality-oriented, marital ideal over the past few decades (VanYperen and Buunk 1994). Equity theory provides an excellent framework for researchers interested in studying marital equality because it specifically focuses on perceived fairness in relationships. Furthermore, psychologists and sociologists have long noted differing outcomes of marriage for men and women in regard to well-being. Equity theory can be used as a framework to help explain their findings.

Equity theory is occasionally used to study close relationships in families. For example, perceptions of fairness, particularly in conflict management between parents and children, have been found to affect how siblings interact with each other later in life (Handel 1986). Equity theory has also been used to examine how satisfied parents and children are with their relationships and how perceived equity or inequity relates to different ways of maintaining a satisfying relationship between parents and children (Vogl-Bauer, Kalbfleisch, and Beatty 1999). However, most current research on equity theory and families focuses on the family's relationship with other institutions, such as education, welfare, and health care (see, for example, Wells, Kataoka, and Asarnow 2001).

Relatively little research has examined cultural or racial differences in regard to equity in interpersonal relationships, although there is some evidence that these characteristics affect both perceptions of fairness about sharing housework and providing income to the family and the amount of housework men perform (Coltrane and Valdez 1993; John, Shelton, and Luschen 1995). Research has also indicated that race may affect levels of distress resulting from perceived inequities in household labor (Rogers and Bird 1998). Additionally, in a cross-cultural analysis, Nico VanYperen and Bram Buunk (1991) found that the qualities seen as positive contributions to a relationship were different for Dutch and U.S. study participants. The Dutch participants saw social qualities, such as having friends, as more of a contribution to the relationship than the U.S. participants did. Conversely, the U.S. participants valued qualities associated with status, such as attractiveness and ambition, more than the Dutch participants did. These findings indicate that a person's racial, ethnic, or cultural identity and values may affect the way they judge fairness in a relationship as well as the characteristics and behaviors they label as costs and benefits.

Most research regarding equity theory and cultural or racial variables also considers the affects of gender. Research on Dutch couples has shown that gender role ideologies affect the division of housework and financial contributions to the family economy. For example, couples who are concerned with gender equality are more likely to split the division of labor in a way that benefits both partners, whereas couples with a more gender-stereotypic ideology tend to divide contributions along gender lines with women providing more domestic work and men providing more financial support (Kluwer, Heesink, and Van de Vliert 1997). This same pattern has also been demonstrated in U.S. couples as well (Blaisure and Allen 1995).

Overview of Equity Theory

As noted above, equity theory is a theory about fairness. Its application to close relationships has been primarily advanced by Elaine Hatfield (previously known as Elaine Walster) and her colleagues in the book *Equity: Theory and Research* (Walster, Walster, and Berscheid 1978). The book outlines four interlocking propositions of equity theory and discusses the application of equity theory to different types of relationships, including intimate ones. The propositions are:

Proposition 1: Individuals will try to maximize their outcomes (where outcomes equal rewards minus costs).

Proposition 2a: Groups can maximize collective reward by evolving accepted systems for equitably apportioning resources among members. Thus, groups will evolve such systems of equity, and will attempt to induce members to accept and adhere to these systems.

Proposition 2b: Groups will generally reward members who treat others equitably, and generally punish (increase the costs for) members who treat others inequitably.

Proposition 3: When individuals find themselves participating in inequitable relationships, they become distressed. The more inequitable the relationship, the more distressed the individuals feel.

Proposition 4: Individuals who discover they are in an inequitable relationship attempt to eliminate their distress by restoring equity. The greater the inequity that exists, the more distress they feel, and the harder they try to restore equity.

As noted in *Proposition 1*, equity theory rests on the assumption that people are self-interested and will try to maximize their personal gains. This proposition has sometimes been questioned by researchers who believe that the nature of close relationships differs from other types of relationships. They argue that close relationships should not be based on individual calculations of costs and rewards and a self-interested focus on maintaining relationships solely for the personal profit they may provide. Instead, they argue that relationships should be based on a mutual concern for each others' welfare or needs (Clark and Chrisman 1994; Clark and Mills 1979).

Three primary ways of dealing with challenges to this assumption exist. One is to consider that individuals may vary in "exchange orientation" or the importance they give to monitoring equity in their relationships (Murstein, Cerreto, and Mac-Donald 1977). For example, some individuals may be high in exchange orientation, constantly keeping track of how much they and their partners put into or get out of a relationship. Other individuals may be low in exchange orientation, not paying attention to inputs, outputs, costs, and rewards of their relationships at all.

Measuring exchange orientation may be a way of measuring self-interest in relationships. Research by Susan Sprecher (1998) has supported this notion. Her findings suggest that different motivations for "keeping score" of costs and benefits in a relationship have different effects on relationship quality. People who keep track of inputs and outputs to make sure they are not underbenefited by the relationship seem to be less satisfied by their relationship whereas people who keep track of inputs and outputs to make sure they are not overbenefited by the relationship seem to be more satisfied by it.

A second way to account for differences in philosophies regarding self-interest in relationships is to include relational-level outcomes such as mutuality, sharing, and respect as types of benefits that individuals can receive from relationships. Relational partners may see themselves as a unit, with both of them maximally benefiting from the relationship. In this type of relationship, where identities of the individual partners have merged, what benefits one partner will also benefit the other. Relational-level outcomes have not regularly been considered in equity research, although similar concepts arise during discussions of entitlement processes (Desmarais and Lerner 1994) and fairness rules (Clark and Chrisman 1994) in close relationships.

Finally, equity in a relationship may be seen as its own reward. This idea is suggested by *Proposition 2* that attempts to account for the development of rules, or norms, that limit self-interest behavior. If individuals were to continually strive for the most resources, anarchy and violence would dominate society as each member tried to gain more. However, *Proposition 2* asserts that societies, groups, and couples will develop rules that foster fairness to each member in order to prevent such a condition. People who follow the rules of fairness will be rewarded, and people who do not will be punished. Thus, behaving equitably becomes a means to maximize one's outcomes, and fairness, more so than self-interest, becomes the norm.

Understanding the concept of *fairness* is essential to understanding equity theory. Elaine Hatfield (Walster) and her colleagues (Walster, Walster, and Berscheid 1978) argue that fairness rules are culturally bound, indicating that generally one of three rules of fairness can apply: proportionality, equality, or need. Rules based upon proportionality mean that individuals receive "equal *relative gains* from the relationship" (p. 10, emphasis in original). In other words, each person should get out of the relationship gains that are *in proportion* to what they have put into the relationship. The *equality rule,* on the other hand, means that regardless of how much each person has put into the relationship, they should each reap equal rewards. Finally, the *need-based rule* indicates that need should be the determining factor in what partners get from a relationship, regardless of their individual contributions to it (Deutsch 1985).

Understanding fairness rules is very important to students, scholars, and practitioners interested in equity theory because distinct bodies of research have developed based on the different fairness rules. Moreover, considerable scholarly debate centers around which fairness rule is best applied to close relationships. Finally, the term *equity* has become synonymous with the use of the *proportionality rule* (e.g., Clark and Chrisman 1994), and theorists seem to fall into two categories: proportionality researchers who are identified as equity theorists and equality researchers who are identified as social (or distributive) justice researchers. Work from researchers who examine other fairness rules, such as the need-based rule, can be found in both bodies of work. Because equity theory as outlined in the four principles above is primarily concerned with perceived fairness in relationships, the term *equity* as used here will apply to fairness. *Proportionality* and *equality* will be used to refer to research and findings based on their respective rules. However, one should note that in the majority of the literature, the term equity is synonymous with the term proportionality, and equity and equality are the two terms that one will find most fruitful when searching databases and libraries for information.

Equity theorist have realized the importance of fairness rules and have debated their application to the study of close relationships. Although Elaine Hatfield (Walster) and her colleagues (1978) propose proportionality as the appropriate fairness rule, Margaret Clark and K. Chrisman (1994) note "we could not find work clearly documenting that people actually do tend to follow an equity [proportionality] norm more often than other possible norms in their intimate relationships" (p. 67). After reviewing relevant research regarding all three fairness rules, they argue that the need-based fairness rule is the most appropriate for intimate relationships. They also suggest that certain factors, such as the stage of development of the relationship, may affect the application of fairness rules. The idea that people may invoke different rules under different circumstances has also been supported by other theorists. For example, Linda Keil and Charles McClintock (1983) review literature that indicates situational factors may interact with age-related cognitive and social process to make certain fairness rules salient. Serge Desmarais and Melvin Lerner (1994) propose that situational and contextual cues, such as strong feelings of "we-ness" in a relationship determine which fairness rules are appropriate, and Morton Deutsch (1975) contends that people choose the fairness rule they believe will be most effective for them in reaching their particular relational goals.

One situational variable that has received much attention in examining fairness in close relationships is power. Hatfield (Walster) and her colleagues (1978) address the role of power in equity theory by postulating that due to their self-interested nature, people will try to persuade others that their contributions are more valuable than the others' contributions. Those who successfully accomplish this will receive more benefits, will be able to persuade others that they are entitled to more benefits, and will develop ideologies that reinforce their right to receive more benefits. Over time, people will see this lopsided allocation of benefits as normal and acceptable. However, as Hatfield (Walster) and her colleagues note, a marked shift in social power would enable underbenefited individuals to feel entitled to more and encourage them to begin efforts to change the allocation of benefits. It is interesting to note that parallels can be drawn between this scenario, gender relations in the United States over the past few decades, and research regarding marital relationships.

Researchers across disciplines have noted changes in marital relationships over the past few decades. This is not surprising because marital relationships across time and cultures differ with the social circumstances in which they exist. Among other factors, the feminist movement in the 1960s and 1970s has influenced changes in the labor market, with more and more women entering the workforce. Research on intimate relationships has shown that higher income for one partner can be associated with increased relational power (Blumstein and Schwartz 1983), and researchers often cite the increased numbers of women in the workforce as having affected changes in women's power, in sex-role expectations, and in marital ideals (VanYperen and Buunk 1994). One particular change is that marital partners are striving for more equality in the distribution of domestic, economic, and emotional contributions to their relationships (Scanzoni and Scanzoni 1988).

Even with changes in social and relational power between men and women, many researchers suggest that judgements of fairness in heterosexual relationships should not be based on the proportionality rule but should be based on the equality rule. Reasons for this assertion come in two forms. First, it is argued that because we live in a social system that values men's contributions more than women's, proportionality-based evaluations of contributions to a relationship can never be fair; for even though men and women may contribute equally to a relationship, men's contributions will be valued more that would, therefore, entitle them to more (Steil 1997). Research examining the perceived value of different relational contributions has been sparse, and mixed results have been found. For example, Janice Steil and Karen Weltman (1991) found support for gender-based valuing of careers when their research showed that women's careers are often not perceived as important as men's. However, Pamela Regan and Susan Sprecher (1995) found that men and women valued their own and their partner's contributions similarly on sixteen of twenty-two characteristics such as having a prestigious and important career, being easy to get along with, being passionate, and taking care of inside chores.

The second reason for equality-based rules of fairness is rooted in research related to equity theory *Proposition 3* that focuses on the outcomes of inequitable relationships by asserting that individuals in inequitable relationships will become distressed. Researchers exploring the area of equitable outcomes in marital relationships often measure outcomes through reports or observations of behaviors rather than perceptions. This is because individuals' perceptions of their relationships can become skewed through gender-biased valuing of relational inputs, because an incongruence often exists between perception of one's behavior and the actual behavior itself, and because people in low-power positions often feel entitled to less that leads them to perceive an unfair situation as fair. Given this caveat, people do still report perceived inequity in their relationships, and it has been associated with negative outcomes, including less sexual intimacy, less sexual satisfaction, less commitment to the relationship, decreased happiness and satisfaction with the relationship, and relationship breakup (Sprecher 1995).

In 1972, Jesse Bernard published her book *The Future of Marriage* and argued that the outcome of marriage is unequal for men and women in terms of psychological well-being or distress. Well-being differences have been reported between married men and women in many studies, with women reporting more instances of psychosomatic illnesses, such as depression, distress, and headaches (Gove, Hughes, and Style 1983), even when they report satisfaction within their marriages (Steil and Turetsky 1987). According to *Proposition 3,* the presence of distress in a relationship can indicate the presence of inequity.

On the flip side of the coin, inequality is costly to men as well, although in different ways. Men become alienated from their families and do not participate in the domestic sphere or with their children. They have a reduced capacity for intimacy (Kaufman 1994). Furthermore, wives often resent their husbands' absence from the family (Schwartz 1994) and children become unhappy with their fathers' lack of emotional and physical participation in their lives (Kaufman 1994; Schwartz 1994; Silberstein 1992). Disconnection from the family often results in relational boredom and increases the potential for divorce (Schwartz 1994).

Support for the equality rule of fairness comes from researchers interested in close relationships and equality. Pepper Schwartz (1994; Blumstein and Schwartz 1983) and other researchers have found qualitative differences between couples who are able to create equality in their relationships and couples who are not or who come close but do not quite make it (Blaisure and Allen 1995; Hochschild and Machung 1989; Knudson-Martin and Mahoney 1998). Their findings show that equality is the essential ingredient for prevention of these negative outcomes. When marital equality is present, men are relieved of the pressures associated with the provider role and they have more intimate, more meaningful, and more satisfying relationships with their families (Steil 1997). Higher levels of marital satisfaction are related to equality in shared decision making and shared task control (Gray-Little and Burks 1983), and higher levels of wives' well-being have been associated with men's participation in housework (Steil 1997). Furthermore, husbands do not suffer from shouldering domestic duties. In fact, in marital relationships where economic and domestic responsibilities are shared equally, both husbands and children benefit from increased family time (Schwartz 1994); male empathy, understanding, and attentiveness (Coltrane 1996); more intimate and stable parent-child bonds; and more intimate and stable marital bonds (Schwartz 1994).

Given all the costs of relationship inequality, it is not surprising that *Proposition 4* states people involved in inequitable relationships will try to restore equity. Hatfield (Walster) and her colleagues (1978) provide two ways that a person can restore equity to a relationship: by restoring actual equity or by restoring psychological equity (the perception that equity actually exists when it does not). As noted earlier, researchers who use behavior to measure relational equity instead of perceptions may do so because they believe partners in an inequitable relationship do not see the inequity. This assumption is congruent with the concept of restoring psychological equity.

Research examining equity-restoring behaviors is scant but supportive of the proposition. In a study asking participants to imagine they were in an inequitable relationship, Sprecher (1992) found that participants expected that they would engage in equity-restoring behaviors, including increasing their partner's rewards, asking their partners to contribute more to the relationship, or changing their perceptions of the relationship so that it seemed fair. She also found that women were more likely to expect to engage in equity-restoring activities than men. Women in inequitable relationships have also reported engaging in or wanting to engage in extramarital sexual behavior. Engaging in sex outside of one's marriage may be a way of restoring perceived inequity (Sprecher 1995).

Proposition 4 of equity theory can provide an interesting framework for examining negative family behavior, such as extramarital relationships. Although it may be unpleasant to think about, the restoration of equity can help explain parent-child abuse. In this framework, abuse may be perceived as a way to restore equity to an inequitable parent-child relationship. Parents who feel exploited by their children may attempt to restore equity by retaliating against their children with verbal or physical abuse or by psychologically or physically abandoning their children (Walster, Walster, and Berscheid 1978). Furthermore, research regarding family violence has examined and supported a relationship between domestic violence and inequitable gender perceptions (Bryant 2001). Finally, the equitable or inequitable division of inheritance property may be another way for families to reestablish equity among its members (Stum 1999).

Conclusion

Equity theory has provided a solid framework for examining perceived fairness in close relationships. Research has focused mainly on heterosexual romantic relationships because of the close link between the development, implementation, and perpetuation of fairness rules in this type of relationship with expectations and perceptions of gender roles. Some theorists disagree with the assumption that close, personal relationships should be based upon calculated inputs and outcomes, whereas other researchers support the idea that, at least for marriages, partners should be vigilant to ensure that both spouses benefit equally from the relationship. Although equity theory has long been associated with the fairness rule of proportionality, the rule of equality is also compatible with equity theory, and research examining the use of this rule in close relationships provides a substantial body of literature in support of the theory.

Equity theory states that when inequity exists, relational parties become distressed. Support is mixed regarding whether participants in overbenefiting or underbenefiting relationships suffer the same type or extent of distress. Distress arising from perceived inequities in marital relationships has been the focus of researchers using the equality rule. In particular, women in inequitable marital relationships report more psychological and physical symptoms, such as headaches and depression, whereas men seem to suffer emotional detachment and relational boredom. Although equality researchers tend to assume victims of inequity will psychologically adjust their perceptions to believe that no injustice exists, little research exists to support this assumption. In fact, little research examines how partners set about reestablishing equity in their relationships at all, although negative relational behaviors such as extramarital affairs and violence have been explored.

Surprisingly, not much research has examined equity theory in family relationships, intercultural relationships, or other close relationships such as friendships. However, the research that has been conducted shows promising results for equity theory. As changes in society continue, their impact on close relationships will surely continue to affect expectations and perceptions of fairness. Beliefs about fairness are bound in cultural and political ideologies. As global communications become easier and international boundaries shrink, interpersonal relationships will become a greater focus for researchers. Fairness rules and their appropriateness and application to different types of relationships will no doubt continue to be a central theme.

See also: CONFLICT: COUPLE RELATIONSHIPS; DECISION MAKING; DIVISION OF LABOR; DUAL-EARNER FAMILIES; HOUSEWORK; MARITAL TYPOLOGIES; POWER: MARITAL RELATIONSHIPS; RELATIONSHIP DISSOLUTION; RELATIONSHIP MAINTENANCE; SOCIAL EXCHANGE THEORY; WORK AND FAMILY

Bibliography

Bernard, J. S. (1972). *The Future of Marriage*. New Haven, CT: Yale University Press.

Blaisure, K. R., and K. R. Allen. (1995). "Feminists and the Ideology and Practice of Marital Equity." *Journal of Marriage and the Family* 57(1):5–20.

Blumstein, P., and P. Schwartz. (1983). *American Couples: Money, Work, Sex*. New York: Morrow.

Bryant, A .S. (2001). Relationships Between Domestic Violence, Abuse, and Gender-Equity Perceptions: A Study of the Appalachian Region of Kentucky. Ed.D. diss., University of Louisville.

Clark, M. S., and K. Chrisman. (1994). "Resource Allocation in Intimate Relationships: Trying to Make Sense of a Confusing Literature." In *Entitlement and the Affectional Bond: Justice in Close Relationships,* ed. M. J. Lerner and G. Mikula. New York: Plenum Press.

Clark, M. S., and J. Mills. (1979). "Interpersonal Attraction in Exchange and Communal Relationships." *Journal of Personality and Social Psychology* 37:12–24.

Coltrane, S. (1996). *Family Man: Fatherhood, Housework, and Gender Equality.* New York: Oxford University Press.

Coltrane, S., and E. O. Valdez. (1993). "Reluctant Compliance: Work-Family Role Allocation in Dual-Earner Chicano Families." In *Men, Work, and Family,* ed. J. Hood. Newbury Park, CA: Sage Publications.

Desmarais, S., and M. J. Lerner. (1994). "Entitlements in Close Relationships: A Justice-Motive Analysis." In *Entitlement and the Affectional Bond: Justice in Close Relationships,* ed. M. J. Lerner and G. Mikula. New York: Plenum Press.

Deutsch, M. (1975). "Equity, Equality, and Need: What Determines which Value Will Be Used as the Basis of Distributive Justice?" *Journal of Social Issues* 31:137–149.

Deutsch, M. (1985). *Distributive Justice: A Social Psychological Perspective.* New Haven, CT: Yale University Press.

Gove, W. R.; Hughes, M.; and Style, C. B. (1983). "Does Marriage Have Positive Effects on the Psychological Well-Being of the Individual?" *Journal of Health and Social Behavior* 24:122–131.

Gray-Little, B., and N. Burks. (1983). "Power and Satisfaction in Marriage: A Review and Critique." *Psychological Bulletin* 93:513–538.

Handel, G. (1986). "Beyond Sibling Rivalry: An Empirically Grounded Theory of Sibling Relationships." *Sociological Studies of Child Development* 1:105–122.

Hochschild, A. (1989). *The Second Shift: Working Parents and the Revolution at Home.* New York: Viking.

John, D.; Shelton, B.A.; and Luschen, K. (1995). "Race, Ethnicity, Gender, and Perceptions of Fairness." *Journal of Family Issues* 16:357–379.

Kaufman, M. (1994). "Men, Feminism, and Men's Contradictory Experiences of Power." In *Theorizing Masculinity,* ed. H. Brod and M. Kaufman. Thousand Oaks, CA: Sage Publications.

Keil, L. J., and McClintock, C. G. (1983). "A Developmental Perspective on Distributive Justice." In *Equity Theory: Psychological and Sociological Perspectives,* ed.

D. M. Messick and K. S. Cook. New York: Praeger Publishers.

Kluwer, E.; Heeskink, J. A. M.; and Van de Vliert, E. (1996). "Marital Conflict about the Division of Household Labor and Paid Work." *Journal of Marriage and the Family* 58:958–969.

Knudson-Martin, C., and Mahoney, A. R. (1998). "Language and Processes in the Construction of Equality in New Marriages." *Family Relations* 47(1):81–92.

Murstein, B. I., Cerreto, M.; and MacDonald, M. G. (1977). "A Theory and Investigation of the Effect of Exchange-Orientation on Marriage and Friendships." *Journal of Marriage and the Family* 39:543–548.

Regan, P. C., and Sprecher, S. (1995). "Gender Differences in the Value of Contributions to Intimate Relationships: Egalitarian Relationships are Not Always Perceived to be Equitable." *Sex Roles* 33(3/4):221–238.

Rogers, M. L., and Bird, C. E. (1998). "Do Gender Differences in the Effects of Equity in Paid Work and Household Labor on Depression Hold across Ethnic and Racial Groups?" Paper read at Annual meeting of the American Sociological Association, San Francisco, California.

Scanzoni, L. D., and Scanzoni, J. (1988). *Men, Women and Change,* 3rd edition. New York: McGraw-Hill.

Schwartz, P. (1994). *Peer Marriage: How Love Between Equals Really Works.* New York: Free Press.

Silberstein, L. (1992). *Dual-Career Marriage: A System in Transition.* Hillsdale, NJ: Lawrence Erlbaum Associates.

Sprecher, S. (1992). "How Men and Women Expect to Feel and Behave in Response to Inequity in Close Relationships." *Social Psychology Quarterly* 55(1):57–69.

Sprecher, S. (1995). "Equity and Close Relationships." In *Encyclopedia of Marriage and the Family,* ed. D. Levinson. New York: Macmillan.

Sprecher, S. (1998). "The Effect of Exchange Orientation on Close Relationships." *Social Psychology Quarterly* 61(3):220–231.

Steil, J., and Weltman, K. (1991). "Marital Inequality: The Importance of Resources, Personal Attributes, and Social Norms on Career Valuing and the Allocation of Domestic Responsibilities." *Sex Roles* 24(3/4):161–179.

Steil, J. M. (1997). *Marital Equality: Its Relationship to the Well-Being of Husbands and Wives.* Thousand Oaks, CA: Sage Publications.

Steil, J. M., and Turetsky, B. A. (1987). "Is Equal Better? The Relationship between Marital Equality and Psychological Symptomatology." *Applied Social Psychology Annual* 7:73–97.

Stum, M. S. (1999). "'I Just Want to be Fair': Interpersonal Justice in Intergenerational Transfers of Non-Titled Property." *Family Relations* 48(2):159–166.

Thibaut, J. W., and Kelley, H. H. (1959). *The Social Psychology of Groups.* New York: Wiley.

VanYperen, N. W., and Buunk, B. P. (1991). "Equity Theory: Communal and Exchange Orientation in Cross-Cultural Perspective." *Journal of Social Psychology* 131:5–20.

VanYperen, N. W., and Buunk, B. P. (1994). "Social Comparison and Social Exchange in Marital Relationships." In *Entitlement and the Affectional Bond: Justice in Close Relationships,* edited by M. J. Lerner and G. Mikula. New York: Plenum Press.

Vogl-Bauer, S.; Kalbfleisch, P. J.; and Beatty, M. J. (1999). "Perceived Equity, Satisfaction, and Relational Maintenance Strategies in Parent-Adolescent Dyads." *Journal of Youth and Adolescence* 28(1):27–49.

Walster, E.; Walster, G. W.; and Berscheid, E. (1978). *Equity: Theory and Research.* Boston: Allyn and Bacon.

Wells, K. B.; Kataoka, S. H.; and Asarnow, J. R. (2001). "Affective Disorders in Children and Adolescents: Addressing Unmet Need in Primary Care Settings." *Biological Psychiatry* 49(12):1111–1120.

ALAINA M. WINTERS

ETHNIC VARIATION/ ETHNICITY

Ethnicity has been defined as a family's common ancestry through which identity develops as a result of evolved shared values and customs (McGoldrick, Giordano, and Pearce 1996). The definitions of *ethnicity,* or the more functional term, *ethnic group,* consist of individuals and families who are members of international, national, religious, cultural, and racial groups that do not belong to the dominant group in a society. They can be differentiated from both the dominant group and other ethnic groups by some combination of their values, expectations, geographic location, language, attitudes, customs, lifestyles, rituals, and celebrations. In addition, ethnicity and sense of *peoplehood* are recognized by themselves and by others.

A number of other terms, such as *minority, people of color,* and *racial groups* are related to the term ethnic group. Some minorities are differentiated on the basis of power and resources, so that

to be a member of a minority group is to share a status relationship dissimilar from the dominant group. To be a member of a racial group is to be defined by both physical and cultural characteristics. The same individuals can be a member of a minority group, a racial group, and an ethnic group (Mindel, Habenstein, and Wright 1988).

According to Nathan Glazer and Daniel P. Moynihan (1975), ethnicity (or, more commonly, ethnic groups) was relatively new to research and the media until the 1960s. The terms ethnicity, ethnic groups, *ethnic consciousness,* and *ethnic identity* now appear regularly in both social science writings and in the mass media. In fact, it is rare that one might witness an event or situation in which the consequences are not in some way related to the ethnic identity of the individuals involved. According to the *Harvard Encyclopedia of American Ethnic Groups* (Thernstrom, Orlov, and Handlin 1980), there are criteria for inclusion in an ethnic group. The following are the criteria most often associated with ethnic group membership: (1) economics or class; (2) geographic origin; (3) political position; (4) migratory statuses; (5) race; (6) language and dialect; (7) religious faiths or faiths; (8) ties that transcend kinship, neighborhood, and community boundaries; (9) shared traditions, values, and symbols; and (10) level of discrimination.

Origins and Importance of Ethnicity

According to early research, there are three dominant theoretical positions related to the understanding of ethnicity and its implications for daily family life. Glazer and Moynihan (1975) stated that the two earliest perspectives associated with ethnicity are the *primordialists* and *circumstantialists.* The *primordial approach* emphasizes history and experiences and may even include genetic transmission, so ethnicity is viewed as a base identity that may be both overt and latent. It implies the existence of a distinct culture or subculture, so that members feel themselves bound together by a number of commonalities, including history, geographic location, language, values, traditions, norms, and behaviors. Most individuals belonging to an ethnic group have a strong sense of ethnic identity and *peoplehood.* Society also recognizes the distinctiveness of the group (Gil-White 1999). The identity is more likely to be ascribed, rather than voluntary. For the individuals who fit into this particular category, ethnicity is inescapable.

The *circumstantialist* (or *instrumentalist*) view is a functional one, with ethnicity serving the economic and political interests of individuals. Ethnicity for this group of persons is more of a convenience. An ethnic group uses traditional beliefs, symbols, and ceremonies in order to develop an informal political organization as it struggles for power (Cohen 1969). As such, it is less permanent and may vary in terms of time, place, and situation. This particular group has the luxury of claiming ethnic identity when needed or desired and are usually only self-identified.

A third perspective (Bernal and Knight 1993) emphasizes the role of marginality in the development and maintenance of ethnicity. Groups that are placed on the fringes and labeled as *outsiders* (either through their own volition or through barriers such as prejudice, discrimination, and segregation) with seemingly little chance of ever being accepted by the dominant society without total assimilation (the act of conforming to the dominant culture) are most likely to develop an ethnic perspective. The more marginal the group is the higher the possibility of developing and maintaining a strong ethnic identity. Conversely, the more accepted a group, the less likely it is to develop a strong ethnic identity.

Ethnic groups can last over an extended period of time or they can change, merge, or disappear. One way in which change may occur is for ethnic minority individuals to assimilate. According to Milton Myron (1964), groups who assimilate tend to have weak or under developed ethnic identities. Researchers have also suggested that those individuals who are removed from both familiar surroundings and support systems may also assimilate to the dominant culture (Shorti and Kohls 2001). This type of assimilation is often most associated with individuals who live in predominantly majority environments or ethnic minorities who attend majority educational institutions.

Ethnic self-identification and membership in an ascribed ethnic group are important because they control, limit, and/or enhance opportunities for well being in society. Ethnic identification and membership have been linked to most aspects of human existence in the twentieth and twenty-first centuries. It is often said to predict educational and professional outcomes, networking opportunities, economic status, living conditions, partner selection, and marital success.

The diversity between and within ethnic families defies simple generalizations. The historical background, the gender role affiliation, the religion or spirituality, the availability of resources, and the educational and employment opportunities, often offers clues for understanding the ethnic family.

It is impossible to present the full spectrum of international ethnic groups and their families, but the following divisions provide useful categories. The divisions are (1) *African families,* (2) *Asian families,* (3) *Latino families,* and (4) *Middle Eastern families.*

African Families

The continent of Africa is slightly less than 12 million square miles and has several hundred ethnic groups and different languages. As a result of Africa's diversity, it is difficult to identify common family characteristics. Two of the African family forms often discussed include Jamaican (British West Indies) and Haitian families. African culture defines family as *immediate* or *nuclear* and includes individuals related by blood regardless of generation (*extended kin*). Traditional African families are close-knit and kinship groups were the foundations of the larger social structure of the tribe and the nation (McGoldrick, Giordano, and Pearce 1996). Extended family ensures support (such as childrearing, economic support, and housing) during times of crisis. Within the African community children and the elderly are highly regarded. Children are thought to carry family values and expected to provide economically for aging parents. Elders are appreciated for their life experiences and are, in most cases, considered wise.

African families are more accepting of women working outside the home than most other ethnic groups are. African history notes the importance of women's work and has long valued their contribution beyond childbearing and childrearing responsibilities. Women are traditionally responsible for organizing the community and gathering food, and many are leaders and rulers in their communities. Although families report practicing indigenous religions, Christianity and Islam were most often reported (Mbiti 1992). However, as previously stated, not every African family experience is the same.

Jamaican families. In the Jamaican family, young women are taught domestic and childrearing practices and given little freedom to explore opposite gender relationships. On many occasions, young women are only allowed to date males known well by the family. Womanhood is connected with motherhood and childrearing (socialization and discipline) and is the responsibility of the mother.

Young males are taught to be responsible. They are encouraged to obtain an education in order to secure respectable employment with upward mobility. Males are often asked to assume economic responsibility in the absence of the father. Single males are encouraged to experiment sexually; however, once married, although discouraged from having extramarital affairs, it is seen as successful if a male is able to provide economically for a mistress and any out-of-wedlock children.

Haitian families. Haitian family structure tends to follow class-system patterns. Middle- and upper-class families tend to follow a more Western structure (formalized marriages), whereas lower socio-economic status families were most often identified as common-law *(placage)* marriages. Although men may not be present in the household on a regular basis, they are expected to support the family financially.

Family roles are clearly delineated within the Haitian family. Men are financially responsible for any family they create in-wedlock or out-of-wedlock. Women are the domestic caretakers of the family. Children are taught unconditional respect for elders and family privacy and disrespectful behaviors are not tolerated. They are expected to care (financially) for their parents when they are no longer able to care for themselves. The elderly often provide childrearing assistance and are thought to have enormous amounts of wisdom as a result of age and overall years of experience.

Catholicism was the reported religion in Haiti for centuries. However, the early twenty-first century has seen an increase in various Protestant (charismatic and evangelical) groups (Nobles 1980). Haitians are also known to practice varying forms of voodoo. *Voodoo* (a religion derived from African ancestor worship involving sorcery), combined with religious beliefs, is often used to explain the incongruence between the supernatural and "real" worlds.

Asian Families

Asian families include the Chinese, Japanese, Korean, Vietnamese, Cambodian, and Indonesian families. There is remarkable diversity between and within the groups in terms of history, language, and demographic variables (including education, population, income, religion, and occupation). The most pronounced belief in Asian culture, except in Filipino culture, is the *Confucian* value system. This code of conduct determined relationships an individual had with people and their obligations to them (obey your parents, be a good citizen, take care of your family).

Chinese families. Morrison Wong (1988) indicates that the Chinese family is the product of social, legal, political, and economic factors interacting with culture through generations of families. The majority of Asian families can trace their roots to the traditional family structure of China, which included (1) *patriarchal rule,* with clearly defined roles of male dominance; (2) *patrilocal residence patterns,* where married couples lived with the husband's parents; and (3) *extended families*; in which many generations lived with their offspring under one roof.

Traditional Chinese family roles are governed by prescribed roles defined by hierarchy, obligation, and duty. The family is thought of as a collective unit and an individualistic perspective is seen as disruptive and disrespectful to the family. Marriages are commonly arranged and spousal relationships are secondary to parent-child relationships. Males within the Chinese culture are dominant and fathers handle familial disciplinarian responsibilities. On the other hand, women are affectionate, self-sacrificing, and caring as mothers; taught to assist with household responsibilities as daughters; and adhere to the *thrice-obeying* rule (comply with fathers/eldest brother in youth, husbands in marriage, and sons when widowed) as wives (Tung 2000).

Because ancestor worship is emphasized, having sons to carry on the family name and serving in-laws is also a cherished value. Another important value is *filial piety*; family relations are characterized by duty, obligation, importance of the family name, self-sacrifice for the good of the elders, and respect for status (Williams-Leon and Nakashima 2001).

Japanese families. Like many other Asian cultures, the Japanese family assigns responsibility according to gender. Women are considered the transmitters of tradition and handle most house-work and childcare. Men, on the other hand, provide financially for the family.

The Japanese are encouraged to think first of being part of a group. In other words, one is never fully independent; therefore, one must always be conscious of others. Examples of the Japanese *we* orientation include: (1) hiring practices, (2) decision making, (3) language, and (4) nonverbal expressions (Varley 2000).

Korean families. Korean families are hierarchical by gender, generation, age, and class. There is differentiation by gender and men and women have traditional gender roles. Parents support children and children are obligated to respect their parents.

Jip-an (*within the house*) identifies family membership, values, and traditions practiced within a particular family. Marriage is considered a union among families rather than individuals (Coleman and Steinhoff 1992). Prior to marriage, the family's community standing, as well as the specific credentials of the family members, is considered.

Vietnamese families. China has long influenced Vietnamese culture. Vietnam adopted Chinese Confucianism enthusiastically, and this code of conduct governed its society for centuries. Like many other Asian cultures, Vietnamese hold elders in high regard and respect their position in the family. Both adults and children are taught to remain quiet when in the midst of elders and to listen with great intent. Eye contact is seen as disrespectful and shaking hands with both hands is expected.

In most Vietnamese families rules of etiquette were followed. Couples wed through parental arrangement or by their own initiative. Once married, the union is considered permanent unless the woman committed adultery. Until the mid-1950s, adultery by men was overlooked unless the position of the wife was in jeopardy in the extended family or children were not guaranteed financial security.

In traditional Vietnamese families, the husband is the head of the family, chief financial provider, and the rest of the family looks to him for guidance. The wife is the caregiver and comforter of the family and only deals with the outside community by choice (Trinh 2002).

Cambodian families. Cambodian people are a racial mix of indigenous tribal people and people who came during the invasion from India and Indonesia in 1970. Unlike many of the neighboring countries, the majority of the people are Buddhists with a small Muslim following. The Cambodian family is based on close relationships (extended kin). Central values within the Cambodian family are built around harmony and balance (Sun-Him 1987).

The husband is considered the head of the household and expects to be consulted at all times prior to decision making. Women in Cambodian culture hold stereotypical gender roles within the family (Sun-Him 1987).

Indonesian families. Indonesia is one of the largest Muslim nations with over 90 percent of its people reporting it as their primary religion. There are over 100 distinct groups in Indonesia, each with its own cultural identity related to language, class, custom, and value. In the Indonesian family, family closeness and loyalty, obligation, and respect for parents is important (Collins and Bahar 1995).

Indonesian culture recognizes the responsibility of the male to be the economic provider for the family. Muslim men in Indonesia may have up to four wives, but few do, because the husband must secure the permission from previous wives and treat each equally.

Women are taught to respect their husbands and are the primary caretakers of the family; women are responsible for domestic maintenance. Children are taught to obey and respect both parents. It is also common for children to remain in the homes of their parents for extended lengths of time. In fact, it has been reported that most young Indonesian individuals live with either their parents or extended family until they marry (Collins and Bahar 1995).

Latino Families

Latino families include the Mexican, Cuban, Puerto Rican, Brazilian, and Central America families. The most extensive research relates to Mexican, Cuban, and Puerto Rican families. The background of each of these groups is that of foreign influences in their homelands, first by Europeans, primarily the Spanish, then by the United States.

Mexican families. Traditional Mexican families consist largely of unskilled workers in the low-wage sectors of the economy (Seymour and Stuart

1998). The traditional structure is based on the socioeconomic needs of the agrarian and craft economics of Mexico: an extended, multigenerational group of persons with special ascribed roles. The division of roles and functions, which include mutual support, enables the family to survive during difficult times. The family, in both work and leisure times, is the most important structure in traditional Mexican society (Hoobler and Hoobler 1998).

A popular stereotype concerning the role of the Mexican male was that of *machismo.* It was often equated with the absolute power of the male—including excessive aggression and sexual prowess—and a secondary role for women. Rafael Ramirez and Rosa Casper (1999) indicate that genuine machismo is characterized by bravery, valor, courage, generosity, and a concern for others. It serves to protect and provide for the family, and includes the use of just authority and a respect for wife and children.

Figures indicate the Mexican family income is low and fertility rates are high. Mexican families are less likely to have extended kin residing in the same household, and the traditional family system is characterized more by voluntary interaction than by the necessity of family survival.

Cuban families. The traditional Cuban nuclear family recognizes the importance of extended family relationships. The tightly knit nuclear family allows for the inclusion of relatives and godparents (*padrinos*). There is an emphasis on lineal family relations, and it is expected that children show absolute obedience to their parents, and wives to husbands (Perez 2001).

Puerto Rican families. The traditional Puerto Rican family is an extended family, with the primary responsibility for childrearing vested in the nuclear family. Although husbands are the traditional source of family authority, childrearing is the major responsibility of the wives (Steward 1956). Kinship bonds are strong, and interdependence is a major theme among family and kinship members. Co-parenthood (*compadrazgo*) and the practice of informal adoption of children (*hijos de crianza*) are two components of extended kinship (Sanchez-Ayendez 1988).

Middle Eastern Families

Until the late twentieth century, Middle Eastern family research focused on Arab, Iranian, Lebanese, and Armenian families. Of the Middle Eastern families studied, the best known is the Arab family. Arabs may be described as a heterogeneous group that is a "multicultural, multiracial, and multiethnic mosaic population" (Abudabbeth and Nydell 1993). The term *Arab* is based on the person's language and culture and is not an ethnic origin: as a result, there is a great deal of diversity among Arabs. One distinctive difference is religion.

Between the seventh and tenth centuries one of the most profound historical changes in the Arab world took place: the spread of Islam. The essence of Islam, as preached by the Prophet Mohammed, was transmitted through the Qur'an (believed to be the literal word of God). The Prophet's own sayings (*hadith*) and practices (*sunna*) were combined with the Qur'an to elaborate or extend the laws of society. Except by implication, the Qur'an does not contain explicit doctrines or instructions—basically, it provides guidance. However, the *hadith* and *sunna* provide concrete commands on issues related to the rights and responsibilities of marriage, the division of property, the daily habits of believers, and the manner in which people should treat one another (Ali 2001).

Although many Arabs report following the Islamic religion, there are approximately 14 million Arab Christians. Those following Christianity are primarily reported in Lebanon, Sudan, Syria, Egypt, Jordan, and Israel. The largest Christian congregation in the Middle East is the Coptic Orthodox Church with nearly 6 million believers.

Arabic is the official language of the Middle East. Arabs are extremely conscious of their language and consider it a great art and their greatest cultural achievement (Nydell 1987). Although spoken Arabic language is as varied as the different parts of the Arab world, classical Arabic and written Arabic are the same in all the Arab countries and are used for formal speech, broadcasting, and writing (Rouchdy 1992).

The Arab family is the dominant social institution through which persons inherit their religion, social class, and identity. The family is often thought of as a patriarchal, hierarchical pyramid (as far as age and sex are concerned) and what befell one member is thought to bring honor or shame to the entire family. The communication style of many Arabic families tends to be hierarchical in nature. This vertical style can lead to miscommunication between persons in authority (parents) and subordinates (children).

Marriage (*nikah*) is seen as a highly religious and sacred ceremony central to the growth and stability of society. It legalizes sexual intercourse and the procreation of children. *Hanafi* law allows a Muslim man to marry a non-Muslim woman as long as she belongs to the *people of the Book* (Jewish or Christianity). Women, however, are not allowed to marry a man who is not Muslim (Esposito 1982). Traditionally, Islamic law allows men to marry four wives. However, the Qur'an qualifies multiple marriages by suggesting a man not marry more than one woman unless he is able to treat them equally.

The traditional Iranian family is patriarchal. Fathers are considered the dominant force and completely control the family. No one questions his authority over his wife, children, and grandchildren (Hillman 1990). He is a strict disciplinarian and he demands respect and obedience from the family. Although seen as the enforcer of domestic rules, he is also affectionate and caring. When the father dies, the eldest son inherits the authority and accepts responsibility for his mother and any unmarried siblings.

Iranian families. In Iranian marriages, women are generally ten to fifteen years younger than their partner. Upon marriage, the two families unite to combine their wealth and increase their power. To marry, a woman must obtain permission from her father first. Generally, women reside with the family of their husbands. According to religious law, women are required to be submissive to their husband. They are taught to take care of the domestic responsibilities at home and to be ever cognizant of their actions publicly and privately. Women address men more formally in public and are taught to never openly disagree with a mate. In difficult situations, women often use children or in-laws to intercede on their behalf.

In Iran, an individual's life is dominated by the nuclear and extended family relationships. People rely on family connections for position, security, influence, and power. It is not uncommon to see an extended family that consists of a married couple and any of their children (both married and unmarried), and grandchildren. In the extended family, authority is almost always given to the oldest

male (Hillman 1990). He can discipline his siblings, as well as any nieces or nephews who reside in the household. The responsibility of the male head of household is to unify the family and to resolve internal conflict.

Lebanese families. The typical Lebanese views family as an extension of him or herself. The family is patrilineal, endogamous, and extended, with complex kin relationships that help sustain traditional functions of the culture (Hassan, Healy, and McKenna 1985). The extended family is a means of support and often provides financial resources, childrearing support, and assistance during medical emergencies.

Although other religions have been reported by Lebanese families, Christianity is the most represented religion. Lebanese Christians have a strong affiliation with the church and look to religion as a source of their identity (Abridge 1996).

Armenian families. The traditional Armenian family structure usually consists of several generations living together within the same household. The family is strongly patriarchal, with elder males dominating the affairs of the family. Most marriages are arranged, and a new bride is expected to live with her husband's family, where she is clearly subservient to the eldest female in the household (Miller and Miller 1993).

Conclusion

The late twentieth century has seen an increase in the research related to ethnicity, culture, custom, and tradition. According to research, the definition of family, ethnicity, and culture varies from one ethnic group and country to another. For example, for many Africans, the definition of family suggests the importance of extended family and community. The Chinese culture includes ancestors and descendents in their definition of family.

Research has also alluded to cultural differences in such aspects as gender roles, religion or spirituality, education, and celebrations. Studying family and ethnicity helps one appreciate differences in groups' attitudes and behaviors. As a result of these differences, it is imperative that one develop a sufficient level of cultural competency, a process of continuous learning that leads to an ability to effectively respond to the challenges and opportunities posed by the presence of social cultural diversity in a defined social system.

Finally, research related to the diversity of family form, structure, and obligations underscores the significance of a flexible social system with fluid boundaries—so that individuals are able to define themselves by their groupings that relate to their heritages and practices and go beyond labels such as *minority, Africans,* or *Latinos.*

See also: AFRICAN-AMERICAN FAMILIES; ASIAN-AMERICAN FAMILIES; CARIBBEAN FAMILIES; CHINA; FICTIVE KINSHIP; HISPANIC-AMERICAN FAMILIES; INDONESIA; INTERGENERATIONAL TRANSMISSION; IRAN; ISLAM; JAPAN; KOREA; LATIN AMERICA; MEXICO; VIETNAM

Bibliography

Abridge, L. (1996). "Sex and the Single Shi'ite: Mut'a Marriage in an American Lebanese Shi'ite Community." In *Family and Gender among American Muslims,* ed. B. C. Aswad and B. Bilge. Philadelphia: Temple University Press.

Abudabbeh, N., and Nydell, M. (1993). "Transcultural Counseling and Arab Americans." In *Transcultural Counseling: Bilateral and International Perspectives,* ed. J. McFadden. Alexandria, VA: American Counseling Association.

Akbar, N. (1985). "Nile Valley Origins of the Science of the Mind." In *Nile Valley Civilizations,* ed. I. Van Sertima. New York: Journal of African Civilization.

Bem, S. (1993). *The Lenses of Gender: Transforming the Debate on Sexual Inequality.* New Haven, CT: Yale University Press.

Bernal, M. and Knight, G. (1993). *Ethnic Identity: Formation and Transmission among Hispanics and Other Minorities.* Albany, NY: SUNY Press.

Chen, H. S. (1992). *Chinatown No More.* Ithaca, NY: Cornell University Press.

Cohen, A. (1969). *Custom and Politics in Urban Africa.* London: Routledge and Kegan Paul.

Coleman, S. J. and Steinhoff, P. G. (1992). *Family Planning in Japanese Society.* Princeton, NJ: Princeton University Press.

Collins, E. F. and Bahar, E. (1995). *Malu: Shame, Gender, Hierarchy, and Sexuality.* Athens, OH: Ohio University (unpublished).

Defeats, G. (1999). "The Emergence of the Hispanic American Labor Force." In *Rethinking the Color Line: Readings in Race and Ethnicity,* ed. C. Gallagher. Mountain View, CA: Mayfield.

Defeats, G. (2001). *Inequality and Work: Hispanics in the United States Labor Force.* La Vergne, TN: Lightning Source.

Dietz, J. (1986). *Economic History of Puerto Rico.* Princeton, NJ: Princeton University Press.

Esposito, J. L. (1982). *Women and the Family in the Middle East.* Austin: University of Texas Press.

Gerson, K. (1985). *Hard Choices: How Women Decide About Work, Career, and Motherhood.* Berkeley: University of California Press.

Gerson, K. (1993). *No Man's Land: Men's Changing Commitments to Work and Family.* New York: Basic Books.

Gil-White, F. S. (1999). "How Thick Is Blood? The Plot Thickens . . . : If Ethnic Actors are Primordialists, What Remains of the Circumstantialists/Primordialists Controversy?" *Ethnic and Racial Studies* 22(5):789–820.

Glazer, N., and Moynihan, P. (1975). *Ethnicity and Theory Experience.* Cambridge, MA: Harvard University Press.

Hassan, R., Healy, J., and McKenna, R. B. (1985). "Lebanese Families." in D. Stoner, ed., *Ethnic Family Values in America.* Englewood Cliffs, NJ: Prentice Hall.

Hillman, M. C. (1990). *Iranian Culture.* Lanham, MD: University Press of America.

Hoobler, D., and Hoobler, T. (1998). *The Mexican American Family Album.* New York: Oxford University Press.

Lips, H. (1997). *Sex and Gender,* 3rd edition. Mountain View, CA: Mayfield.

Mbiti, J. S. (1992). *African Religions and Philosophy,* 2nd edition. Portsmouth, NH: Heineman Press.

McGoldrick, M.; Giordano, J.; and Pearce, eds. (1996). *Ethnicity and Family Therapy,* 2nd edition. New York: Guilford Press.

Miller, D., and Miller, L. T. (1993). *Survivors: An Oral History of the Armenian Genocide.* Berkeley: University of California Press.

Mindel, C.; Habenstein, R.; and Wright, R., Jr., eds. (1988). *Ethnic Families in America.* New York: Elsevier.

Myron, M. (1964). *Assimilation in American Life: The Role of Race, Religion, and National Origins.* New York: Oxford University Press.

Nobles, W. (1980). "African Philosophy: Foundations of Black Psychology." In *Black Psychology,* 2nd edition, ed. R. Jones. New York: Harper and Row.

Nobles, W. (1985). *Africanicity and the Black Family: The Development of a Theoretical Model.* Oakland, CA: Black Family Institute Publishers.

Nydell, M. K. (1987). *Understanding Arabs: A Guide for Westerners.* Yarmouth, ME: Intercultural Press.

O'Brien, D. J., and Fugita, S. S. (1991). *The Japanese American Experience*. Bloomington: Indiana University Press.

Okamura, J. (1998). *Imagining the Filipino American Diaspora*. New York: Garland.

Perez, L. A. (2001). *On Becoming Cuban: Identity, Nationality, and Culture*. New York: Ecco Press.

Ramirez, R. L., and Casper, R. E. (1999). *What It Means to Be a Man: Reflections on Puerto Rican Masculinity*. Piscataway, NJ: Rutgers University Press.

Rouchdy, A. (1992). *The Arabic Language in America*. Detroit, MI: Wayne State University Press.

Sanchez-Ayendez, M. (1988). "The Puerto Rican Family." In *Ethnic Families in America,* ed. C. H. Mindel, R. W. Habenstein, and R. Wright, Jr. New York: Elsevier.

Seymour, I., and Stuart, L. (1998). *I Am Mexican American*. New York: Power Kids Press.

Shorti, C., and Kohls, R. (2001). *The Art of Crossing Cultures*. Memphis, TN: Nicholas Bradley Intercultural.

Shryock, A., and Abraham, N. (2000). "On Margins and Mainstreams." In *Arab Detroit,* ed. N. Abraham and A. Schrock. Detroit, MI: Wayne State University Press.

Steward, J. H. (1956). *The People of Puerto Rico*. Urbana: University of Illinois Press.

Sun-Him, C. (1987). *Introduction to Cambodian Culture*. San Diego: SDSU Multicultural Resource Center.

Thernstrom, S.; Orlov, A.; and Handlin, O. (1980). "Introduction." In *Harvard Encyclopedia of American Ethnic Groups*. Cambridge, MA: Harvard University Press.

Tung, M. P. M. (2000). *Chinese Americans and Their Immigrant Parents: Conflict, Identity, and Values*. Binghamton, NY: Haworth Press.

Varley, H. P. (2000). *Japanese Culture*. Honolulu: University of Hawaii Press.

Williams-Leon, T., and Nakashima, C. L. (2001). *The Sum of Our Parts: Mixed Heritage of Asian Americans*. Philadelphia: Temple University Press.

Wong, M. G. (1988). "The Chinese American Family." In *Ethnic Families in America,* ed. C. Mindel, R. W. Habenstein, and R. Wright, Jr. New York: Elsevier.

Other Resource
Trinh, T. N. L. (2002). "Vietnamese Traditional Family Values." Available from www.vietspring.org/values/tradionval.html.

DEBORALE RICHARDSON-BOUIE

EUTHANASIA

The passage from life to death should be serene and dignified, not an agonizing ordeal. This conception of *eu* (good) *thanasia* (death) is expressed in the term itself as it comes from Greek antiquity. A serene death might be achieved through skilled and compassionate care, as well as by the dying person's own sense of having lived a righteous life. There were circumstances, however, in which hastening the end of a life seemed the only apparent way to relieve suffering. A fatally injured or wounded individual might implore another person to put an end to the suffering. *Mercy killing,* as it became known, occurred on battlefields throughout the world. Animals with painful and fatal injuries would also be released from their suffering.

The root conception of euthanasia has divided itself into two branches. Prevention and reduction of suffering is the primary mission of the hospice or palliative care movement (Saunders 1997). State of the art medication, skilled nursing care, and family support enhance the possibilities of maintaining a meaningful quality of life until the end. The other branch advocates the principle and practice of avoiding suffering by foreshortening life. Health care professionals, ethicists, clergy, and the general public are all faced with the question of what guidelines should be used in attempting to help people to end their lives without pain and other distressing symptoms. Should people rely upon palliative care—and only palliative care—in every instance? Or is it acceptable—even obligatory—to terminate a life to prevent further suffering?

Euthanasia: History, Controversy, Facts

Objective discussion of euthanasia has become increasingly difficult since this term became associated with state-sponsored mass murder in Nazi Germany. Robert J. Lifton (1986) documents in *The Nazi Doctors* how these doctors took the lives of thousands of their fellow citizens on orders from the government. These unfortunates were institutional residents who required shelter and care but were neither terminally ill nor in pain. They were "useless eaters" whose murder was thinly disguised as euthanasia. The fact that this program could be carried out without effective protest became a stepping stone for the subsequent slaughter of Jews and Romi (Gypsies) in the Holocaust.

This cynical abuse of the euthanasia concept was itself encouraged by two previous movements (Pernick 1996). *Eugenics* had as its mission the weeding out of "inferior" genetic stock from the population in order to upgrade society with the finest human specimen. Sterilization of people deemed to have undesirable characteristics was to be the major tool, but other possibilities were also being considered. In the United States one of these other possibilities gained some influential advocacy: infants born with impairments should be allowed to perish or perhaps be "mercifully" put to death immediately. The Black Stork movement did not succeed in its aims, but raised enough clamor to attract the attention of people who would later become active in the Nazi movement.

Awareness of the Nazi mass murders has made many people wary of any movement that speaks favorably of euthanasia. It has generated the *slippery slope* argument: Permitting any action to end a person's life in any situation might lead to many more deaths. People who give high priority to the slippery slope argument often are sympathetic to the plight of a particular person who is suffering greatly. They might assent to some form of euthanasia in this instance, but fear that such a precedent would make it easier to end the life of somebody whose condition is less serious, and so on until one has slipped way down the slope. Proponents believe that adequate safeguards through legislation, regulation, and due process can limit euthanasia to the situations in which it is most appropriate.

One of the most controversial issues centers on the use of active versus passive euthanasia. *Active euthanasia* occurs when something is done with the specific intention of ending a person's life, such as injecting a lethal medication. *Passive euthanasia* occurs when interventions that might prolong life are withheld, such as deciding against connecting a dying person to a life support. This distinction, though, is not always so straightforward. Is "pulling the plug" a form of active or passive euthanasia? It might be considered active because it requires an intentional action to turn off life support services. However, the weight of opinion now considers withdrawal of interventions to be a passive form of euthanasia: one *stops* doing something.

The distinction is consequential because some people who reject active euthanasia do accept passive euthanasia as a practice that provides benefits to the dying person without violating ethical standards and religious values. Legislation and court decisions also tend to treat active and passive euthanasia differently. The situation is even more complicated. It can also be argued that it is an evasion to regard passive euthanasia as acceptable while condemning active interventions because both approaches result in an earlier death. Perhaps passive euthanasia is also sometimes unintentionally cruel because the person continues to suffer while life runs out (Rachels 1989). Whether or not we should continue to focus on the active versus passive distinction is a controversy that does not seem close to resolution.

Support has not come easily for even the more limited forms of euthanasia: withholding or withdrawing life support interventions. The *living will* was introduced in 1968 as a document expressing an individual's wish to avoid "artificial means and heroic measures" at the end of life (Scofield 1989). This document did not have the force of law, depending instead on the willingness of physicians to accept the patient's request. The landmark case of Karen Ann Quinlan in 1975 aroused enormous public and professional controversy in addition to the personal distress experienced by her parents (Kastenbaum 2001). The young woman lapsed into a coma after a party and never recovered consciousness. Physicians believed she would die if taken off the ventilator. Courts first ruled against and then in favor of the request to withdraw this intervention. To the astonishment of many, Quinlan lived another ten years, though without showing any signs of mental life. Courts have since made a variety of rulings with the overall effect of accepting withdrawing of treatment under specified circumstances. The significant principle of *informed consent* has also received support: a mentally competent person has the right to reject proposed treatments. *Advance directives*—more flexible and refined versions of the living will—now provide individuals with an improved opportunity to state their preferences for end-of-life care, thereby reducing the burden of decision making on the part of others (King 1996). Furthermore, most state legislatures have passed *natural death acts* that affirm a person's right to avoid the prolongation of suffering or a persistent vegetative state.

Very much still gripped by controversy is the proposition that society should honor "death on demand" (Baird and Rosenbaum 1989; Cohen

1988; Gomez 1991; Kevorkian 1991; Scherer and Simon 1999; Singer 1996). Should physicians be permitted—or even required—to end a terminally ill and suffering person's life by lethal injection or similar means? Proponents argue that the individual has the right to die as well as the right to live. Society fails dying people, consigning them to agony and despair. It is time to shake off outmoded tradition and provide a quick and merciful ending for those in terminal torment.

Opponents muster arguments from a variety of perspectives. "Thou shalt not kill" and "Man should not play God" are objections that are based on religious faith. "Doctors should not kill" expresses the view that the physician's reputation and role would be compromised by also becoming an agent of death. The prohibition against doctors providing lethal medicines is traced back to the Hippocratic Oath (fifth century B.C.E.), but in reality physicians have been divided on this subject since antiquity, and the Oath itself does not command as much power in the medical community as one might suppose (Edelstein 1943; Kevorkian 1991). Another objection has already been noted: the slippery slope is sure to become even more treacherous if physician-assisted death is countenanced. For every death that occurs after due process, many others will take place on whim and impulse.

Perhaps the most formidable criticism comes from people who are familiar with hospice care. Jack Kevorkian, M.D., the most conspicuous advocate and practitioner of physician-assisted death in the United States, has been charged with ignorance both of palliative care measures, depression, and family dynamics (Kaplan 2000). According to these criticisms, Kevorkian has performed and encouraged medical homicides on people who (1) could have found relief through competent management of their symptoms, (2) needed treatment for depression, and (3) were not terminally ill in the first place. Studies reported by Kalman J. Kaplan and his colleagues provide some support for these charges. After being associated with more than a hundred deaths, Kevorkian was found guilty and jailed on charges of second degree murder.

The world continues to observe, wonder, and dispute about the legalization of euthanasia in the Netherlands. The issue became salient in 1973 when a doctor obeyed her dying mother's request to end her life. Eventually the Dutch Supreme Court made a ruling that has remained confusing to those not familiar with that nation's justice system. Euthanasia was illegal, but it was also acceptable—if it involves a competent person who has had full access to information and an adequate time to decide, and is in a situation of intolerable and hopeless suffering without any acceptable alternative remaining. The physician must also consult another independent doctor with experience in end-of-life care. Over the years doctors practicing euthanasia in the Netherlands have either followed these guidelines conscientiously, or found ways around the guidelines whenever it suited the physician's interests—depending on whose version of the events and which study one cares to believe. The legal side of the issue was clarified when the Dutch parliament passed and the Senate confirmed a pro-euthanasia legislative act (April 11, 2001).

Other nations are also struggling with the euthanasia decision. Australia's Northern Territory, for example, approved physician-assisted suicide for the terminally ill, but it proved difficult to find doctors willing to perform this act, and the measure itself was subsequently overturned at the national level. A voter-approved bill is on the books in Oregon, but the future of legalized physician-assisted death in the United States, as in most other nations, remains an open question.

See also: DEATH AND DYING; GRIEF, LOSS, AND BEREAVEMENT; HOSPICE; INFANTICIDE; SUICIDE

Bibliography

Baird, Robert M., and Rosenbaum, Stuart E., eds. (1989). *Euthanasia. The Moral Issues.* Buffalo, NY: Prometheus Press.

Cohen, Cynthia B. (1988). *Casebook on the Termination of Life-Sustaining Treatment and the Care of the Dying.* Bloomington: Indiana University Press.

Edelstein, L. (1943). *The Hippocratic Oath: Text, Translation, and Interpretation.* Baltimore: Johns Hopkins University Press.

Gomez, C. (1991). *Regulating Death.* New York: Free Press.

Greenberg, S. I. (1997). *Euthanasia and Assisted Suicide.* Springfield, IL: Charles C. Thomas.

Kaplan, K. J., ed. (2000). *Right to Die Versus Sacredness of Life.* Amityville, NY: Baywood.

Kastenbaum, R. (2001). *Death, Society, and Human Experience,* 7th edition. Boston: Allyn & Bacon.

Kevorkian, J. (1991). *Prescription: Medicide*. Buffalo, NY: Prometheus Press.

King, N. M. P. (1996). *Making Sense of Advance Directives*. Rev. edition. Washington, DC: Georgetown University Press.

Lifton, R. J. (1986). *The Nazi Doctors*. New York: Basic Books.

Pernick, M. S. (1996). *The Black Stork*. New York: Oxford University Press.

Saunders, C. (1997). "Hospices Worldwide: A Mission Statement." In *Hospice Care on the International Scene*, ed. C. Saunders and R. Kastenbaum. New York: Springer.

Scherer, J. M., and Simon, R. J. (1999). *Euthanasia and the Right to Die*. Lanham, MD: Rowman & Littlefield.

Scofield, G. (1989). "The Living Will." In *Encyclopedia of Death*, ed. R. Kastenbaum and B. Kastenbaum. Phoenix, AZ: Oryx Press.

Singer, P. (1996). *Rethinking Life and Death*. New York: St. Martin's Griffith.

ROBERT KASTENBAUM

EVANGELICAL CHRISTIANITY

Evangelical Christianity entails being *born again* (John 3:3) and then experiencing a progressive conformity to the image of God in Christ over the lifespan. Evangelical Christianity understands marriage and the family in light of biblical understanding and Christian experience. It offers a normative vision of family life and relations aimed at embodying Christian convictions in everyday life. The family thus bears important theological and ethical significance as an arena where Christian beliefs seek daily expression and where future generations are raised and nurtured.

History and Overview

The origin of the term *religion*, however, can shed some light on its early history. It lies in two understandings of the Latin verb, *religio*. It denoted a binding or fastening together and eventually came to indicate a reverence and fear of deity. *Religio* also denoted a restraining or holding back. While the former points to the reverential aspects of religion, the latter points to the ethical restraint role of religion's bridling of human motives and impulses.

Hence, religion is seen etymologically as a force that reconnects human disjointedness, restrains errant impulses, and gives uniqueness, identity, and integrity to the individual.

Evangelical Christianity embodies these characteristics, and its understanding of the family exhibits a wide range of historical influences. From the ancient Jewish tradition, Christianity derives the convictions that sex is a good of creation ordained by God for procreation and pleasure; marriage and the family are human institutions and ordained by God and can be understood as a covenant; and women and men have dignified roles in marriage and family life. In addition to the themes from Hebrew scripture, the writings of the New Testament offer an abundance of thought on marriage and the family. As a result, the use of scripture can vary widely from one interpretation to the next and often depends on views of the authority and function of scripture developed independently from reflection on marriage and family life. Perhaps because it assumes an understanding of the Old Testament or because it is less predicated on the social structure of a single people, the New Testament has much less to say about the family as a sociological unit. Although not denying the value of strong internal ties in a traditional Jewish family (see Luke 1:17), Jesus would not permit such ties to stand in the way of one's decision to follow him (Matt. 10:35–36). Genesis 2:24 is cited with approbation twice in the Gospels (Matt. 19:5; Mark 10:8) and twice in the Pauline corpus (1 Cor. 6:16; Eph. 5:31) as indicating the close bonds between husband and wife and, therefore of the family unit. The Greco-Roman tradition influenced Christian thought through its contention that marriage is a secular contract entered by consent of the individuals and dissolvable by legal action and that any felt religious dimension to marriage and family life is a private matter.

The history of the church sheds more light on the construction of Christian belief as it relates to marriage and family. Augustine of Hippo, for example, proclaimed the family as a social institution ordained by God that helped to insure three goods: offspring, marital fidelity, and enduring commitment. Augustine's position greatly influenced later thought and is seen to have set the terms, if not the outcome, of theological debate. By the time of the Reformation, four criteria for a valid Christian marriage had emerged: consent, contract,

Evangelical Christians give praise during an evening service in Hato Rey, Puerto Rico. They believe that marriage and family are ordained by God and entered into as a covenant. PHILIP GOULD/CORBIS

church ceremony, and consummation. These were based chiefly on Augustine's synthesis and the laws and customs of medieval Europe. The foundational impact of the Reformation on the Protestant Christian understanding of marriage and family was to eliminate the requirement of a church ceremony and with it the sacramental (but not the symbolic) character of marriage. Family life was upheld by the Reformers as a secular reality especially blessed by God. From the sixteenth century onward, elements of romantic love involving personal fulfillment and physical pleasure became incorporated into a popular understanding shaping Christian thought to where it began to see the family as a means of self-expression. This became the precursor for modern psychology's influence on religion in general, Protestant Christianity specifically, and its shaping of Christianity's practice and view of marriage and the family.

Evangelical Views of Family Relations

Christian marriage and family life is regarded as a sacred and creative calling by all Christians. It is a basic biblical teaching. Marital union *in Christ* appeals to divine grace for support and fulfillment of a natural union of a man and a woman. Whereas the Orthodox teaching and practice of marriage is understood in sacramental terms, emphasizing the ecclesial, salvific, and eschatological dimensions of the married life, most Protestants find other expressions and concepts to describe the marital union. Although unwilling to formulate marriage and family life in precisely sacramental terms, Protestants generally stress that this union is a profound spiritual commitment and covenantal relationship. The biblical teaching and the church's participation in assisting the couple to preserve and complete their marriage are held as basic by all Christians. Most Protestants tend to limit the role of the clergy and the church in marriage, as contrasted with the Orthodox teaching, because for them marriage is not constituted by the marriage rite.

Biblical wisdom is paramount to the Evangelical faith in fulfilling God's direction for the family. However, the purpose of the scriptures is not to give a detailed description of the stages of family development or specific instructions for dealing with the diversity of challenges and tasks that face parents and their children. Still, there are specific commands and promises given to parents and children in the Bible. Subjects like discipline (Prov. 22:6), good communication (Eph. 6:4), and familial responsibilities (1 Tim. 3:1) are certainly addressed. But it would be a mistake to look at the Christian scriptures as a textbook on family functioning. Lewis Smedes (1976) observed that what Protestant Christians generally hold as true is that it would be more helpful to look to the Bible as informing us about human life as a whole, so that we as humans can increasingly understand and evaluate our experiences as people in our nuclear and extended families.

Protestant Christians see the family as a social institution entered into by a private contract that may be blessed by the church. Where explicitly religious dimensions are present, they are thought of as bolstering the couple's private consent. The spiritual foundation for the family is thus by choice and orders the physical, social, and personal foundations of the family covenant with God. Because of this, the Christian family relies heavily on the church and Evangelical community for nurturing family life through its understanding of Scripture, tradition, and experience. The pastoral care provided by the church assists this process by making accessible the social skills and psychological insights helpful to it, and by offering assistance in articulating the theological and cultural context within which a given Christian family seeks to live.

The Christian church is an advocate for the family. There has always been something like what is called *the family* to protect and nurture those who are young. In modern times, however, there has been an exploration into the ways in which the whole human story might be told in terms of household events. The history of Israel is often carried by family stories. Although the continuity of the church as the New Israel is not dependent on family lineage, the early Christian community is often described in family metaphors. The Bible everywhere assumes the significance of the family. The church has sought throughout its history to establish and maintain the sanctity of the home. It has taught that the family is the vehicle for God's continual creation and rule.

In contemporary times, the evangelical community has strongly supported *family values.* Although there is some divergence within this segment of the church on specific topics, this generally means that evangelicals share a common worldview—assumptions about the universe, about God, about human beings, about right and wrong, and about lifestyle. This evangelical worldview, for example, is often viewed as anti-divorce, pro-life, anti–gay marriages, and so on; in short, it is a conservative view dedicated to preserving the traditional family. Within this context, the evangelical community promotes family education. Marriage preparation and enrichment as well as child-rearing are clear examples of this. The evangelical community prizes opportunities to intentionally sponsor instruction in areas related to strong family values (Collins 1995).

Few would argue that the family is not of special concern to the Christian church. For Christians, it was the church that validated marriages and legitimated the birth of children. For most of its history, the church's care for families has centered on landmarks of birth, puberty, marriage, and death as primary modes of care that enable individuals and families to live through the stress that usually accompanies change and loss. Preparing for, sustaining, and nurturing the family in a normative vision, however, is nowhere more apparent than in moments of tragedy in family life. Divorce, abortion, death, adultery, suicide, depression, spouse and child abuse, and a host of other devastating moments in family life are not understandable for Christians apart from a sense of how the Christian faith would have us see and respond to them. In the absence of that vision, Christians lose sight of what the family is about, and thus it and its tragedies are governed by other beliefs and experiences.

The family is an organism of change. Some of that change is unexpected. Some of it is inevitable as individuals within the family grow up and grow older. Because the family is always changing, adaptability is one of its essential characteristics. To believe in a God who is always making something new means that change is an unavoidable dimension of each family structure.

Despite wide diversity of form and function throughout human history, the family has fulfilled God's intent to provide a context for creation and care in order to ensure the continuity of humankind. From the perspective of Evangelical Christianity, however, the family can never be an end in itself. In order to be a vital human organism, the family is always moving outside itself for the sake of justice, peace, and freedom in ever-widening human communities.

See also: FAMILY MINISTRY; FAMILY VALUES; INTERFAITH MARRIAGE; PROTESTANTISM; RELIGION

Bibliography

Collins, G. R. (1995). *Family Shock: Keeping Families Strong in the Midst of Earthshaking Change.* Wheaton, IL: Tyndale.

Smedes, L. B. (1976). *Sex for Christians.* Grand Rapids, MI: Eerdmans.

LES PARROTT

EXTENDED FAMILIES

All societies have a concept of extended family. Its relative importance, structure, and functions, however, vary according to the particular culture. Traditionally, the term *extended family* has been applied to the kinship network of social and economic ties composed of the nuclear family (parents and children) plus other, less immediate, relatives. Study of the extended family unites two independent concepts: the household and kinship ties. The former refers to co-residence, whereas the latter implies relationship. When extended families share a common household, those most likely to be residents are the household heads' brothers and sisters, grandparents and grandchildren, and depending on the society, aunts and uncles. The social and economic importance of extended family can most readily be seen when family members are living together; however, this does not discount the importance of kinship ties. Even in societies where extended families do not reside together and nuclear family households predominate, the nuclear family may rely on extended kin to assist with basic day-to-day activities such as child or elder care and may be emotionally and economically codependent on family members outside the household.

Extended Family Kinship

Although the extended family household as a cultural idea has been characterized in the majority of documented human history, it would be a mistake to believe that extended family households were characteristic of all historical societies or that all contemporary societies are dominated by the nuclear family. In truth, extended family households, even in societies where they were the ideal, may still have actually constituted only a minority of households; furthermore, the average amount of time the extended family spends under one roof is highly variable and often depends on factors such as economic need and the age of family members. Household formation is a cycle in which both nuclear and extended family households may appear and that these forms are not mutually exclusive. Contemporary Western models that herald the nuclear family household as ideal and minimize the importance of the extended family are relatively recent and have resulted from a number of factors, including: the Industrial Revolution, the associated rise of class influences in social networks, the increasing importance of individualism brought about by Western political change and education, the decline of kinship in defining social networks, and the replacement of government services for those traditionally associated with the family. Yet in the face of otherwise pervasive economic and social change toward Western cultural models, extended family households in non-Western societies have proved remarkably resilient.

Descent systems. Extended family ties that reach across households provide important social and economic advantages in terms of shared labor, socialization of children, and support for the elderly. In preindustrial societies, labor cooperation is often essential, and kinship is the primary means of defining the composition of groups. Extended family ties spread both risks and benefits—important especially in settings with scarce resources. In societies emphasizing descent as an organizing principle, extended family groups often form corporations of individuals who function in concert as a single social and economic unit. One traditional example is in contemporary hunter-gatherer societies, where resources are often uncertain, and individuals have minimal success in obtaining these resources. In these settings, highly elaborate rules, based on concepts of extended family, often govern the distribution of food and

The Lehmann family gathers for dinner with their extended family members. PHILIP GOULD/CORBIS

other resources. In this way, the success of an individual benefits the group.

Societies in which the extended family network is defined primarily through relationships between males are patrilineal. This type of descent system, where membership is passed from father to son, is most common cross-culturally. The Tiv of Nigeria, for example, live in extended polygynous family compounds consisting of the household head, several wives, and perhaps the household head's married brother, wives, and children. However, several such compounds linked by blood ties between males occupy a common contiguous territory and form a corporate economic unit more important than the household (Bohannan and Bohannan 1968). Patrilineal descent systems have dominated European and Chinese societies. Additional examples of these systems include the Juang of central India and Bedouin in Egypt (Stone 2001).

In matrilineal systems, membership in an extended family group is defined through women, and it is usually the son who moves to his wife's household. Matrilineal descent systems are most

often found in sedentary agricultural societies where women perform the majority of agricultural tasks. Both the Hopi Indians of North America and the Trobriand Islanders off eastern New Guinea are prominent examples of cultures with matrilineal systems. Matrilineal societies also occur in small pockets in lacustrine central Africa, parts of northeast and southeast India, and south-central Vietnam (Parkin 1997). Matrilineal systems, not usually definable as matriarchies, nonetheless provide women with a degree of control over property and politics that is not found elsewhere.

In cognatic, or bilateral, descent systems, any combination of male and female kin may be used to define who constitutes the extended family network. This type of descent system is the most flexible in allowing individuals to define their own universe of extended family members. One example of this system is the Maori of New Zealand. Still other systems exist that do not consider blood relations as the basis of decent such as the Zumbagua of Ecuador, who believe kinship is established through food.

If the extended family network relationships can all be traced through a common known ancestor, this network may be said to constitute a lineage, particularly if the members function together as a single corporate unit. For example, all the members of a Tiv patrilineage can trace their relationship to a single known ancestor. If such links are not exactly known, or if they are based less in fact than in myth, the extended family network constitutes a clan.

Household composition. The importance of extended family ties is most easily seen in settings where family members share a common residence. Extended family households may be constituted by affinals, collaterals, or people of common descent. Extended family households based on common descent continue to exist in Western culture and remain prevalent throughout Europe, Asia, and the Americas. Descent-based households may be extended in several ways. The stem household form, made up of at least two generations of related nuclear families, is sometimes considered a class by itself. Stem family households are common in agricultural societies in which the elderly control the resources, and inheritance is based on primogeniture, meaning that all land is passed from father to first-born son. One popular theory, although widely contested, is that stem family households resulted from land scarcity and were an adaptation for keeping landholdings intact (Verdon 1979). An alternative view is that stem family households provide secure retirement environments for the elderly. In much of Asia, the stem family household still represents an important cultural norm (De Vos and Lee 1993: Foster 1978; Tsui 1989).

Households may also be extended either lineally (e.g., containing grandparents or grandchildren), collaterally (e.g., aunts or uncles, nephews, and nieces), or affinially (e.g., marriage). Collaterals are people of the same generation tied by kinship, such as joint families of India in which all brothers along with their wives and children share a common household. Affinial relationships are premised on marriage or cohabitation; examples include polygynous households and group marriages. Despite lack of acceptance in the Western world, such households are extremely common elsewhere, particularly in Africa and India.

Although there is no steadfast rule, contemporary extended family households based on common descent tend to show more lineal than collateral extension. Research indicates that African and Asian Americans are more likely to participate in lineally extended family households, with the former emphasizing the inclusion of children and the latter emphasizing inclusion of the elderly.

Study of the Extended Family

Study of the extended family has been integrated into multiple disciplines; chief among them are anthropology, demography, history, sociology, and social work. Understanding of the extended family and extended family ties has been defined as essential to a wide array of policy concerns, including economic development policies, effective health-care delivery (e.g., Pilisuk and Froland 1978), and assimilation of immigrants (e.g., Benson 1990; Glick 2000). From a historical perspective, extended family households have been studied extensively for their role in shaping the direction of social, economic, and demographic change. From a sociological/anthropological orientation, extended family ties form much of the basis for understanding social networks in both traditional and contemporary societies.

Historical perspective. Critical to understanding the historical study of extended families is the distinction between extended family ties and extended family households. Historical study is almost exclusively limited to examining the form and function of extended family households whose structures can be determined from census records, tax lists, and other widely available written sources. Researching extended families from a social perspective is more difficult because scholars must obtain any surviving family diaries, journals, and letters in attempting to understand how extended family networks functioned across households. Oral traditional societies, nineteenth-century British colonies in Africa for example, often had surviving census and tax documents, but little other written data.

Interest in the history of the extended family households was kindled in the 1940s and 1950s as an aspect of population and development studies. At that time it was believed that the extended family household, prominent in many non-Western societies, stood as a barrier to economic modernization. One popular position suggested that women living in extended families were likely to marry earlier and have more children, the resultant large families being defined as an obstacle to economic and social development (Castillo, Wiesblat, and Villeral 1968). An alternative perspective held that

Western industrialization had, in effect, "caused" the emergence of the nuclear family household (Parsons and Bales 1955). Both perspectives made a better understanding of historical family forms important, although it now seems clear that neither position in its extreme adequately reflects the historical record.

Nuclear family households were prevalent prior to industrialization (Laslett and Wall 1972). Even in societies where large extended family households were the ideal, such households may have constituted only a minority or simple majority of households. Household formation is a process. Nuclear family households may mature into extended family households as children grow up and marry. This type of evolution is particularly evident in stem family household cycles. Conversely, an extended family household may disappear with the death of the grandparent. In short, it is rarely accurate to talk about the disappearance of extended family households. Instead, from a historical perspective, the issue is more often one of frequency and transformation of structure.

The Balkan *zadruga* is one well-documented example that demonstrates the ability of the extended family to transform rather than disappear (Byrnes 1976). The *zadruga,* or South Slavic rural extended family household, was important in shaping the central Serbian frontier during the nineteenth century. In its classic sense, the *zadruga* consisted of married brothers and their families living in a single household and functioning as a single agricultural economic unit. After World War II, the *zadruga* lost much of its historical economic importance with the increasing industrialization of the region. However, with increasing longevity, decreasing fertility, and increased nonagricultural economic opportunities, ties between brothers have been replaced by ties between grandfathers and grandsons, and laterally extended households have been replaced by lineally extended ones. Historical research shows that the number of households containing extended family members has varied little since the mid-nineteenth century, remaining constant at about 70 percent (Halpern and Anderson 1970).

Nevertheless, when researchers discuss the demise or evolution of the extended family, several factors are commonly cited. These include industrialization and the proliferation of Western political and education models over the last century. By

removing kinship from the economic arena, industrialization is said to have made the viability of nuclear family households possible. Likewise, Western education and politics are said to have produced value changes in direct opposition to extended family life since they emphasize individualism over collectivity (Parsons and Bales 1955).

Despite these factors, numerous examples remain of the resiliency of extended family networks. Extended family networks and households are still important in Taiwan (Stokes; Leclere; and Yeu 1987), Japan (Morgan and Kiyosi 1983), India (Ram and Wong 1994), and China (Tsui 1989), to cite a few examples. In Africa, researchers have portrayed the persistence of extended family networks as cultural bridges in modernization rather than impediments (Silverstein 1984).

Importantly, not all people considered kin have affinal or blood ties. Fictive kinship often elaborates the body of people considered to be extended family members. In much of Mexico and Latin America, *compadrazgo* (godparenthood) is as important a relationship as any tie of blood or marriage. Other examples occur in many diverse settings, including a comparable pattern of godfatherhood among Yugoslavs *(kumstvo).* In the United States, at the turn of the century, it was common for households to contain a lodger or boarder who paid rent for living space and over time came to be regarded as fictive kin.

Contemporary perspective. As noted, extended family ties and households have often proved remarkably adaptable to changing social conditions. It has been observed that the extended family is most likely to emerge in contemporary society when young adults face unemployment or divorce or when older adults become widowed and/or their health declines (Lee 1999). Modern day extended family networks are important in assisting immigrants to assimilate (Glick 2000). For example, support from the extended family has been portrayed as a significant factor in the successful integration of Vietnamese refugees into American life (Benson 1990). The importance of extended family households and networks has also been shown among low-income urban African Americans; considerable research points to the benefits of grandmothers in single-parent households and extrahousehold extended family networks as important mechanisms for coping with inadequate financial resources (e.g., Ford and Harris 1991; Pearson et al. 1990).

Government services have made extended family life less important for the care of the elderly, yet if programs such as social security and welfare continue to receive less funding, the extended family may become important in compensating for the lack of these services (Glick 2000; Goldstein and Warren 2000). Interestingly, the frequency of extended family households has begun to decline in some Asian societies (Ogawa and Retherford 1993), but has been shown to have increased for the first time in decades in the United States from 10 percent to 12 percent between 1980 and 1990 (Glick 1997).

The outlook for the extended family is unclear. At the same time, it is certain that as socioeconomic conditions, technology, and cultural values continue to change, so will the face of the extended family. New constructions of the extended family are inevitable in contemporary society. Recent family forms that pose a challenge as to who will be considered part of the extended family and the nature of these relationships include: same-sex couples with children living in extended family arrangements (Ainslie and Feltey 1991), the Israeli kibbutz (Talmon 1972), children of open adoption who remain in contact with their biological parent(s) (Silber and Dorner 1989), children conceived with reproductive technologies (e.g., surrogate motherhood) (Stone 2001), and the relationships between stepchildren and their extended stepfamily (Ganong and Coleman 1994).

See also: Asian-American Families; Caribbean Families; Family, Definition of; Fictive Kinship; Godparents; Grandparenthood; Hutterite Families; Intergenerational Relations; Kenya; Kinship; Latin America; New Zealand; Nuclear Family; South Africa; United States

Bibliography

Ainslie, J., and Feltey, K. M. (1991). "Definitions and Dynamics of Motherhood and Family in Lesbian Communities." *Marriage and Family Review* 17:63–85.

Benson, J. E. (1990). "Households, Migration, and Community Context." *Urban Anthropology* 19:9–29.

Bohannan, L., and Bohannan, P. (1968). *Tiv Economy.* Evanston, IL: Northwestern University Press.

Byrnes, R. F., ed. (1976). *Communal Families in the Balkans: The Zadruga.* Notre Dame, IN: University of Notre Dame Press.

Castillo, G. T.; Wiesblat, A. M.; and Villareal, F. R. (1968). "The Concept of the Nuclear and Extended Family." *International Journal of Comparative Sociology* 9:1–40.

Chen, X. (1985). "The One-Child Population Policy, Modernization, and the Extended Chinese Family." *Journal of Marriage and the Family* 47:193–202.

De Vos, S., and Lee, Y. J. (1993). "Change in Extended Family Living Among Elderly People in South Korea, 1970–80." *Economic Development and Cultural Change* 41:377–393.

Ford, D. Y., and Harris, J. J. (1991). "The Extended African-American Family." *Urban League Review* 14:71–83.

Foster, B. L. (1978). "Socioeconomic Consequences of Stem Family Composition in a Thai Village." *Ethnology* 17:139–156.

Ganong, L. H., and Coleman, M. (1994). *Remarried Family Relationships.* Thousand Oaks, CA: Sage Publications.

Glick, J. E. (2000). "Nativity, Duration of Residence and the Life Course Pattern of Extended Family Living in the USA." *Population Research and Policy Review* 19:179–198.

Glick, J. E., Bean, F. D., and Van Hook, J. V. W. (1997). "Immigration and Changing Patterns of Extended Household Structure in the United States: 1970-1990." *Journal of Marriage and the Family* 59:177–191.

Goldstein, J. R., and Warren, J. R. (2000). "Socioeconomic Research and Heterogeneity in the Extended Family: Contours and Consequences." *Social Science Research* 29:382–404.

Gunda, B. (1982). "The Ethnosociological Structure of the Hungarian Extended Family." *Journal of Family History* 7:40–51.

Halpern, J. M., and Anderson, D. (1970). "The Zadruga: A Century of Change." *Anthropologia* 12:83–97.

Laslett, P., and Wall, R., eds. (1972). *Household and Family in Past Time.* Cambridge, UK: Cambridge University Press.

Lee, G. R. (1999). "Comparative Perspectives." In *Handbook of Marriage and the Family,* 2nd edition, ed. M. B. Sussman, S. K. Steinmetz and G. W. Peterson. New York: Plenum Press.

Liu, W. T., and Yu, E. S. H. (1977). "Variations in Women's Roles and Family Life Under the Socialist Regime in

China." *Journal of Comparative Family Studies* 8:201–215.

Mere, A. A. (1976). "Contemporary Changes in Igbo Family System." *International Journal of Sociology of the Family* 6:155–160.

Morgan, S. P., and Hirosima, K. (1983). "The Persistence of Extended Family Residence in Japan: Anachronism or Alternative Strategy?" *American Sociological Review* 48:269–281.

Ogawa, N. and Retherford, R. D. (1993). "Care of the Elderly in Japan: Changing Norms and Expectations." *Journal of Marriage and the Family* 55:585–597.

Parkin, R. (1997). *Kinship: An Introduction to the Basic Concepts*. Oxford, UK: Blackwell Publishers.

Parsons, T. and Bales, R. F. (1955). *Family Socialization and Interaction Process*. Glencoe, IL: Free Press.

Pearson, J. L.; Hunter, A. G.; Ensminger, M. E.; and Kellam, S. G. (1990). "Black Grandmothers in Multigenerational Households: Diversity in Family Structure and Parenting Involvement in the Woodlawn Community." *Child Development* 61:434–442.

Pilisuk, M., and Froland, C. (1978). "Kinship, Social Networks, Social Support, and Health." *Social Science and Medicine* 12:273–280.

Ram, M., and Wong, R. (1994). "Covariates of Household Extension in Rural India: Change Over Time." *Journal of Marriage and the Family* 56:853–864.

Silber, K. and Dorner, P. M. (1989). *Children of Open Adoption*. San Antonio, TX: Corona Publishing.

Silverstein, S. B. (1984). "Igbo Kinship and Modern Entrepreneurial Organization: The Transportation and Spare Parts Business." *Studies in Third World Societies* 28:191–209.

Stokes, C. S.; LeClere, F. B.; and Yeu, S. H. (1987). "Household Extension and Reproductive Behavior in Taiwan." *Journal of Biosocial Science* 19:273–282.

Stone, L., ed. (2001). *New Directions in Anthropological Kinship*. Lanham, MD: Rowman and Littlefield.

Talmon, Y. (1972). *Family and Community in the Kibbutz*. Cambridge, MA: Harvard University Press.

Tsui, M. (1989). "Changes in Chinese Urban Family Structure." *Journal of Marriage and the Family* 51:737–747.

Verdon, M. (1979). "The Stem Family: Toward a General Theory." *Journal of Interdisciplinary History* 10:87–105.

Wall, R.; Robin, J.; and Laslett, P., eds. (1983). *Family Forms in Historic Europe*. New York: Social Science Research Council.

AMY E. WAGNER

F

FAILURE TO THRIVE

Failure to thrive is defined as poor growth in children during the first three years of life. A child's growth is evaluated by comparison with standard growth charts for normal children. Poor growth will sometimes be apparent because a child does not grow as fast as other children: Over time his or her position on the growth chart becomes lower. It may also be apparent because he or she is at the bottom of the chart in terms of weight, length, or weight in relation to length. There is no single definition on which everyone agrees. Interpretation of children's growth requires knowledge and care.

Failure to thrive commonly arises without medical causes. In such cases the family is often blamed for emotional or psychosocial deprivation. Because of the negative connotation of the term *failure to thrive,* many clinicians prefer to use more neutral terms such as *pediatric undernutrition.* The term *failure to thrive* is used in developed countries. In developing countries, on the other hand, the term more often used is *protein-energy malnutrition,* and the emphasis is on alleviating poverty and increasing food supplies. These two traditions could learn from each other.

Causative Factors

A basic lack—and maldistribution—of food is the major factor in undernutrition in developing countries. Even in wealthy countries, however, food may not be readily available to all people, especially the poor. Surveys in the United States have shown that as many as 12 percent of households experience inadequate access to food at some time during a year.

Cultural beliefs and practices around the world influence young children's nutritional intake. Cultures differ with respect to the nutritional value of foods given to children of different ages, prestige and status of food types, healing values that people attribute to food, religious customs such as fasting, who is responsible for feeding children, caregiver versus child control of eating, and toddler-weaning practices (Sturm and Gahagan 1999). Even in developing countries where poverty is widespread, nutrient intake can be affected by differences in cultural norms and parents' beliefs.

Families' choices of foods for their infants may impair their nutrition. For example, parents may give soda pop or too much fruit juice, so that infants take less milk and solid foods. Some parents, in an effort to be healthy by avoiding fat in their diet, unduly limit their infants' intake of fat, which is especially needed in the first two years for brain and bodily growth.

Infants may themselves have difficulties in feeding. These difficulties may be obvious in infants with problems in moving the body, like cerebral palsy, or they may be subtle in children who have trouble chewing and swallowing. Such children may, for example, lose excessive amounts of food or milk from the mouth, pocket food in the mouth, be unable to move their tongues well, or refuse foods with rough textures. Children's eating behavior can also contribute to poor intake and is often a focus of parental concern. Probably the most common behavioral problem is food refusal, in which children close their mouths, turn their faces away, and cry. All these factors can make meals take a long time.

During the first two years, infant-parent relationships change, and so does child feeding. During the first two months, parents help babies establish a regular schedule of eating and sleeping. If parents do not learn to tell when a baby wants to be awake or asleep, or is hungry or full, the baby many not get enough milk or formula. Between approximately three and eight months, babies look for more social interaction with their caretakers. If parents have trouble recognizing, interpreting, or responding appropriately to their cues, feeding may be affected. At the end of the first year and during the second year, babies seek more and more independence from their parents during feeding and other parts of everyday life. This process of psychological separation and individuation may lead to control struggles over the child's becoming an autonomous self-feeder (Birch 1999; Satter 1987).

Lack of daily structure can result in an absence of predictable mealtime and sleep routines, two processes intrinsically interrelated for babies and toddlers (Yoos, Kitzman, and Cole 1999). Toddlers who are allowed to snack and drink caloric beverages without a reliable schedule of mealtimes and snacks may not develop the internal cycles of hunger and satiety that are the basis for self-regulation of eating and good growth. Adequate amounts of sleep at night and daytime naps are necessary for the child to attend to the task of eating during meals. Appetite can be limited because of inappropriate timing and size of meals across the day (Kedesdy and Budd 1998).

Many aspects of family functioning can affect how much a child eats and the nutritional value of what is eaten. Within the family unit, general life stressors and worries can interfere with the primary caretakers' ability to monitor the child's nutritional intake, to provide regular meals, and to respond attentively and sensitively during meals (e.g., with encouragement and praise). Parental psychological disorders, family interaction problems such as marital conflict, and problems in parent-child relationships can impair caloric intake. Although research has been inconclusive as to whether there are more psychiatric problems in parents of babies with failure to thrive compared to parents of babies with normal growth, clinical case reports indicate that such problems can damage the feeding relationship. Maternal depression, social isolation, alcohol use and substance abuse, domestic violence, and a history of problematic parental childhood can make it harder for parents to have good relationships with their young children (Drotar and Robinson 2000).

Infants with low birth weight (less than 5.5 pounds or 2500 grams) start out life small and are more likely than others to be small later on. If their growth rate is normal, there may be no problem, although it is important to make sure they receive good nutrition. Many illnesses can impair children's growth. Most of those illnesses are common infectious diseases, such as repeated ear infections, respiratory infections, and diarrhea. Less commonly, infants may gain weight poorly because they have a cleft palate, their intestines fail to absorb nutrients, stomach contents slide up the esophagus (*gastroesophageal reflux*), or they have a long-term medical disorder like *Down's syndrome* or *fetal alcohol syndrome*.

Effects of Failure to Thrive

Studies in developing countries have shown that poor nutrition in early childhood leads to problems in cognitive functioning. Attention, self-regulatory skills for self-control, organizational skills, and performance on tests of cognitive functions and academic skills all appear to be vulnerable to the effects of malnutrition. The link between early, severe malnutrition and long-term deficits in emotional and cognitive development appears to extend into adolescence (Galler and Ramsey 1989). Research from industrialized countries where milder undernutrition is more typical suggests that it places young children at risk for developmental delays in all areas of development. At the time of the undernutrition, babies and toddlers typically score lower than well-nourished counterparts on tests of development, may have more behavioral feeding problems, are more likely to be insecurely attached to their mothers, and may show altered social responsiveness and irritability (Benoit 2000). Long-term effects of early failure to thrive have not been extensively studied, and the findings thus far are inconsistent. Some studies show little difference in cognitive and academic functioning between children with prior failure to thrive and well-nourished comparison children, whereas others indicate continued school-related difficulties and problems with behavior and personality development. It is important, in looking toward a child's future, to recognize that many other factors besides nutrition influence development (Shonkoff and Phillips 2000).

Undernutrition can limit long-term growth, which is why middle-aged and elderly people from developing countries are often short. In the United States, children from families below the federal poverty level are one to two centimeters shorter than children from families above it. Stunted children are likely to become stunted adults (Institute of Medicine 1996). Undernutrition can weaken the body's defense against infection; conversely, infection can impair nutrition. These effects are especially serious in developing countries, but in developed countries they are also important with certain chronic illnesses, such as cystic fibrosis and acquired immunodeficiency syndrome (AIDS).

Evaluation and Treatment

An initial assessment is important for planning treatment and is best accomplished by a multidisciplinary team that can continue to provide long-term follow-up care to the family (Frank and Drotar 1994). A detailed review of what the child eats and drinks provides basic information. Parent-child feeding interactions and the child's feeding behavior and oral-motor skills should be evaluated. Psychosocial evaluation should include information from all of the child's caretakers (e.g., child care staff, relatives), the family, and the child. Assessment of the family environment should include the caretakers' cultural beliefs, psychological functioning, family stressors, and social supports and community resources that can be used on the child's behalf.

Intervention should be guided by the family needs identified in the evaluation. Treatment is typically multifaceted and requires good interdisciplinary and interagency collaboration (Black 1995). Parents may obtain advice about increasing calories in the child's diet. They may be given iron or zinc supplements for their child if needed. Any medical or physical problems the child has are treated. Parents may get advice about managing children's behavior during mealtime; they can often benefit from coaching around viewing videotapes of feedings. Much of the treatment can be done in the home. Referral for early intervention

services may aid the child's general development. Helping families access community-based resources from government programs should be a priority with low-income families. In the United States those include the Special Supplemental Nutrition Program for Women, Infants, and Children (WIC), and the Food Stamp program (Baer 1999). In the event of severe malnutrition or failure of intensive outpatient intervention, pediatric hospitalization may be justified. Parental mental health and substance-abuse problems usually require individual attention. In the minority of cases that involve neglect or abuse, intervention by child protective services may be necessary to protect the child's physical and developmental well-being. With comprehensive evaluation and treatment, most undernourished children improve their nutritional status, growth, and development.

Public Policy

Governmental policies can improve maternal and child nutrition through public programs. In the United States, for example, in 2001 the WIC program served seven million participants at a cost of $4 billion. Programs to promote maternal nutrition and breast feeding can help to prevent undernutrition in children. Governmental policies can also help families buy food by providing money. All industrialized countries except the United States provide family allowances to parents to help with the costs of raising children. Many countries subsidize housing; cash benefits for maternity are available in more than 100 countries (Kamerman 1996). Such approaches indirectly help families feed their children. Provision of good nutrition to infants and young children is a basic responsibility of society. As Sir Winston Churchill said in 1943, "There is no finer investment for any community than putting milk into babies."

See also: CHILD ABUSE: PHYSICAL ABUSE AND NEGLECT; CHILDHOOD, STAGES OF: INFANCY; CHILDHOOD, STAGES OF: TODDLERHOOD; DEVELOPMENT: COGNITIVE; DEVELOPMENT: EMOTIONAL; FAMILY POLICY; FOOD; ORPHANS; POVERTY

Bibliography

Baer, M. T. (1999). "Community Food and Nutrition Programs." In *Failure to Thrive and Pediatric Undernutrition: A Transdisciplinary Approach,* ed. D. B. Kessler and P. Dawson. Baltimore, MD: Paul H. Brookes.

Benoit, D. (2000). "Feeding Disorders, Failure to Thrive, and Obesity." In *Handbook of Infant Mental Health,* 2nd edition, ed. C. H. Zeanah, Jr. New York: Guilford Press.

Birch, M. (1999). "Psychological Issues and Infant-Parent Psychotherapy." In *Failure to Thrive and Pediatric Undernutrition: A Transdisciplinary Approach,* ed. D. B. Kessler and P. Dawson. Baltimore, MD: Paul H. Brookes.

Black, M. (1995). "Failure to Thrive: Strategies for Evaluation and Intervention." *School Psychology Review* 24:171–185.

Churchill, W. (1943). Quoted in *The Oxford Dictionary of Quotations,* 4th edition, ed. A. Partington. Oxford, UK: Oxford University Press, 1992.

Corrales, K. M., and Utter, S. L. (1999). "Failure to Thrive." In *Handbook of Pediatric Nutrition,* 2nd edition, ed. P. Q. Samour, K. K. Helm, and C. E. Lang. Gaithersburg, MD: Aspen.

Drotar, D., and Robinson, J. (2000). "Developmental Psychopathology of Failure to Thrive." In *Handbook of Developmental Psychopathology,* 2nd edition, ed. A. J. Sameroff, M. Lewis, and S. M. Miller. New York: Kluwer Academic/Plenum.

Frank, D. A., and Drotar, D. (1994). "Failure to Thrive." In *Child Abuse: Medical Diagnosis and Management,* ed. R. Reece. Philadelphia: Lean and Febiger.

Frank, D. A.; Silva, M.; and Needlman, R. (1993). "Failure to Thrive: Mystery, Myth, and Method." *Contemporary Pediatrics* (February):114–133.

Galler, J. R., and Ramsey, F. (1989). "A Followup Study of the Influence of Early Malnutrition on Development: Behavior at Home and School." *Journal of the American Academy of Child and Adolescent Psychiatry* 28:254–261.

Institute of Medicine. (1996). *WIC Nutrition Risk Criteria: A Scientific Assessment.* Washington, DC: National Academy Press.

Kamerman, S. B. (1996). "Child and Family Policies: An International Overview." In *Children, Families, and Government: Preparing for the Twenty-First Century,* ed. E. F. Zigler, S. L. Kagan, and N. W. Hall. Cambridge, UK: Cambridge University Press.

Kedesdy, J. H., and Budd, K. S. (1998). *Childhood Feeding Disorders: Biobehavioral Assessment and Intervention.* Baltimore, MD: Paul H. Brookes.

Kessler, D. P., and Dawson, P. (1999). *Failure to Thrive and Pediatric Undernutrition: A Transdisciplinary Approach.* Baltimore, MD: Paul H. Brookes.

Lieberman, A. F.; Silverman, R.; and Pawl, J. H. (2000). "Infant-Parent Psychotherapy." In *Handbook of Infant Mental Health,* 2nd edition, ed. C. H. Zeanah, Jr. New York: Guilford Press.

Satter, E. (1987). *How to Get Your Kid to Eat . . . But Not Too Much.* Palo Alto, CA: Bull Publishing.

Shonkoff, J. P., and Phillips, D. A. (2000). *From Neurons to Neighborhoods: The Science of Early Childhood Development.* Washington, DC: National Academy Press.

Sturm, L., and Gahagan, S. (1999). "Cultural Issues in Provider-Parent Relationships." In *Failure to Thrive and Undernutrition: A Transdisciplinary Approach,* ed. D. B. Kessler and P. Dawson. Baltimore, MD: Paul H. Brookes.

Yoos, H. L.; Kitzman, H.; and Cole, R. (1999). "Family Routines and the Feeding Process." In *Failure to Thrive and Undernutrition: A Transdisciplinary Approach,* ed. D. B. Kessler and P. Dawson. Baltimore, MD: Paul H. Brookes.

PETER DAWSON
LYNNE STURM

FAMILISM

The term *familism* refers to a model of social organization, based on the prevalence of the family group and its well-being placed against the interests and necessities of each one of its members. It is part of a traditional view of society that highlights loyalty, trust, and cooperative attitudes within the family group. Although its origin is in the traditional family institution, it is also used as an analogy for characterizing different forms of organization and social relationships—those that are guided by group interest and well-being instead of the general interest and well-being.

From a psychological point of view, familism is a cluster of attitudes that emphasizes the relevance of the family for personal and social life, the development of a feeling of duty among the members of the family group, and the belief that to have children is a requirement for personal and social realization (Popenoe 1988; Gundelach and Riis 1994).

Familism is a concept that has evolved over time. Three main orientations can be distinguished: a classical social position; a sociopolitical formulation; and a psychological re-elaboration. The main antecedents of these orientations are, respectively, the disappearance of the Old Regime, the changes that have taken place around World War II, and the development of a culture of service characteristic of the postindustrial societies.

The Antecedents of Familism

The example of the familists. A Christian group who lived in small communities in sixteenth-century England could be considered to be one of the oldest antecedents for familism. They defended the spiritual unification of Christianity, giving up some of their more basic beliefs to accomplish this aim. The familists first appeared in 1540 in a small German town, where the political ideas of Johannes Althaus were widely accepted. In the book *Systematic Analysis of the Politics,* published in 1603, Althaus defends a new conception of the state as a federal entity composed of small basic units (family, economic associations, villages). A benevolent conception of an absolute monarchy was looked for in the intellectual atmosphere of this period. The existence of small communities, as those of the familists, helped with this renovated vision of the monarchy. The familists found great social acceptance in England. These communities spread between 1550 and 1650, but were accused of inspiring Puritanism. Their disappearance coincided with the restoration of English monarchy (1660).

The New Social Order of the Revolution

In political terms, familism can be associated with the new social order, inspired by the European Enlightenment in the eighteenth century—which stressed the ability of human reason to understand the world and to solve social and ethical problems, and citizens' right to participate in the process of governance—and the French Revolution. The new order broke with the old hierarchical and stratified ways of social organization, facilitating a democratic social model. However, the private domain, and, therefore, the family institution, remained within the old hierarchical pattern of relationships.

Alexis de Tocqueville, in *De la démocratie en Amérique* (*Democracy in America,* 1835), did not use the term familism specifically, but analyzed a tendency of general well-being and interest, remaining between the limits of the family and reference group. He called this feeling individualism.

Familism, as a double moral behavior (competition in the public domain and cooperation in the private domain), appears in Herbert Spencer's evolutionism. Spencer's concept of empathy could be seen as a tool for softening the competitive mechanism that governs social matters. In his theory, the family is the only social context where the behaviors of help and protection are expected.

Colonial economics. The colonial economic pattern of the nineteenth and the beginning of the twentieth centuries is another antecedent of the current concept of familism. Colonialism, as a way of political and economic organization, developed an economy of subsistence and one that tended to export, and at the same time maintained a traditional cultural pattern, which guaranteed social stability. In the process of economic growth and decolonization, this traditional culture became an obstacle for the modernization of those societies.

Briefly, in the development of the democratic Western societies and the experience of the colonial economic pattern, familism could be seen in the family, clan, or village as a conservative element that impeded the economic and democratic growth of modem societies.

Familism After World War II

The political, economic, and psychological impacts of the family were criticized in the 1930s and especially after World War II—for example, in the description of the authoritarian character by Wilhelm Reich, Erich Fromm, and Theodor W. Adorno. The principle of equality in modem societies did not modify the family. The internal structure of family still maintained a framework, based on the principle of authority and acceptance of its norms. Democratic and industrialized societies, focusing on the individual and his or her social achievements, collided with the traditional and hierarchical structure of the family.

The criticism of the family as a closed and traditional structure appears in three different contexts: psychology, sociology, and politics. These three contexts are represented by the German criticisms of the family, Edward C. Banfield's concept of amoral familism, and Gabriel A. Almond and Sidney Verba's concept of *civic culture.*

The German criticism of family. Fromm, Reich, and, later, Adorno (1950), in *The Authoritarian*

Personality, criticized the impact that the traditional family has on the social and political attitudes of individuals. They argued that the family stimulates the emergence of authoritarian adults, very susceptible to Fascist propaganda. On the other hand, in North America, Kurt Lewin (1948) developed group dynamics as a way to develop democratic attitudes in the family and in social groups to counteract the possible influences of the growing European authoritarianism.

Amoral familism. Banfield employs the concept of amoral familism in his book, *The Moral Basis to Backward Society* (1958), to describe a cultural pattern characterized by the absence of moral obligations to anyone who does not belong to the family group, together with a strong distrust toward social and political institutions. Banfield detected this phenomenon in a little community in southern Italy, as a contrary phenomenon to events in northern Italy. Amoral familism takes place when at least two elements combine: scarce economic development and ongoing foreign dominance. This situation reinforces social bonds and cooperation bonds exclusively among relatives. In *The Unheavenly City* (1970), Banfield applied his thesis of poverty's cultural bases to North American industrialized cities, where excluded and impoverished subcultures exist. From this point of view, the idea that economic development is rooted in cultural factors emerges again, emphasizing mainly the negative presence of basic groups in the social bonds of the society. This concept of the amoral familism was used later by Rafael López-Pintor and José Ignacio Ortega (1982) in the studies they carried out between 1968 and 1980 with the Spanish population.

The civic culture. The civic culture represents a postwar concern to study the conditions that favor the stability of democratic systems. The important decline of political participation—for example, in voting behavior—accompanied by high levels of distrust and political inefficiency justifies this concern. Almond and Verba in *The Civic Culture* (1963) assumed that interpersonal trust is a basic condition, although not the only one, for the development of secondary associations required for political participation. Interpersonal trust eliminates the barriers of the primary group, establishing bonds and duties with those who are different from one's own group. Interpersonal trust is the opposite of familism, which only establishes bonds

of loyalty and cooperation inside the family group. Verba in *The Civic Culture Revisited* (1980) highlights the importance of family's democratization for the development of social and political attitudes that are necessary for a democratic culture.

The New Familism

The new familism has emerged in postindustrial and services societies, which tend basically to satisfy the needs of personal realization. Many authors have labeled this new culture as hedonistic and narcissistic; some authors consider it a radical individualism (Seoane 1993).

The development in the 1970s of new forms of marriage, different from the traditional civil and religious forms, the rise of the divorce rates, and the decline in birth rates are clear examples of this new culture. Paternal authority, strict family morality, obligations to family members, and the sexual division of the domestic work were replaced by the principle of equality, the relaxation of traditional moral values, and the family opening to the outside world.

At the beginning of the 1980s, a turn to family values is evident (Inglehart 1998). However, this new familism is full of ambiguities. On the one hand, it means the resurgence of the family as an important force. At the same time, it supports an individualistic and narcissistic conception of the family relationships. The current importance given to the family is related to a defense of its affective and emotional functions and its help for personal development. From this new familism, the family group is used as a resource to satisfy the psychological needs of its members (Demo et a1. 2000).

The new familism moves away from the political and social context from which it originated. It can be considered as a psychologized familism, because it answers the concrete needs of personal and individual realization. This familism moves away from the traditional cultural pattern, in which the family was more important than the goals and aspirations of its members, and from the traditional definition of familism.

From the point of view of psychological needs, the ambiguity of the new familism allows very different family politics. Although some approaches defend alternative ways of families, other writers turn to the new familism to stop the advance of a radical individualism, or even to compensate the setback of the state of families' well-being (Popenoe 1988; Garzón 1998, 2000).

Conclusion

The future of the term *familism* is uncertain. Its religious, political, and economic roots, and elements of postindustrial societies, are implicit in its current meaning. However, it is used in an ongoing way to characterize a psychological syndrome caused by a combination of attitudes, beliefs, and values that evolved along with changes in our societies. Thereafter, familism is a term in transition, aside from its classic assumptions and well-established definitions. It illustrates the difficulties of ambiguity, but at the same time has all the advantages of being open to the changes of society of the twenty-first century.

See also: FAMILY LOYALTY; GRANDPARENTHOOD; IMMIGRATION; ISRAEL; LATIN AMERICA; PHILIPPINES, THE

Bibliography

Adorno, T. W.; Frenkel-Brunswik, E.; Levinson, D. J.; and Sanford, R. N. (1950). *The Authoritarian Personality.* New York: Harper & Row.

Almond, G. A., and Verba, S. (1963). *The Civic Culture.* London: Sage.

Banfield, E. C. (1958). *The Moral Basis of a Backward Society.* Chicago: Free Press.

Banfield, E. C. (1970). *The Unheavenly City; The Nature and Future of Our Urban Crisis.* Boston: Little, Brown.

Cooper, D. (1971). *The Death of the Family.* New York: Pantheon Books.

Demo, D. H.; Allen, K. R.; and Fine, M. A., eds. (2000). *Handbook of Family Diversity.* New York: Oxford University Press.

Flaquer, L. (1998). *El destino de la familia.* Barcelona: Ariel.

Garzón, A. (1998). "Familismo y creencias políticas." *Psicología Política* 17:101–128.

Garzón, A. (2000). "Cultural Change and Familism." *Psicothema* 12(1):45–54.

Gundelach, P., and Riis, O. (1994). "¿El retorno al familismo?". In *Tendencias mundiales de cambio en los valores sociales y políticos,* ed. J. Díez Nicolás and R. Inglehart. Madrid: Fundesco.

Inglehart, R. (1998). "Values and Beliefs. Political, Religious, Sexual, and Economic Norms in 43 Societies: Findings from the 1990–1993 World Values." In *Human Values and Beliefs: A Cross-Cultural Sourcebook,* ed. R. Inglehart, M. Basañez, and A. Moreno. Ann Arbor: University of Michigan Press.

Lewin, K. (1948). *Resolving Social Conflicts: Selected Papers on Group Dynamics.* New York: Harper.

López-Pintor, R., and Ortega, J. I. (1982). "La otra España: Insolidaridad e intolerancia en la tradición político-cultural española." *Investigaciones Sociológicas* 19:292–307.

Popenoe, D. (1988). *Disturbing the Nest: Family Change and Decline in Modern Societies.* New York: Aldine de Gruyter.

Seoane, J. (1993). "Las viejas creencias de la sociedad post." *Psicothema* 5:169–180.

Tocqueville, A. (1835-40). *De la démocratie en Amérique,* 2 vols. Madrid: Sarpe.

Verba, S. (1980). "On Revisiting the Civic Culture. A Personal Postscript." In *The Civic Culture Revisited,* ed. G. A. Almond and S. Verba. London: Sage.

ADELA GARZÓN PÉREZ

FAMILY, DEFINITION OF

Over the decades, social scientists have struggled in their efforts to define the multidimensional concept of family. Through her research Jan Trost (1990) confirmed this overwhelming definitional dilemma experienced not only by family researchers but also the general population. Specifically, she illustrated the difficulty and diversity with which people identify those who could or should be labeled family members. For some in her sample, family consisted of only closest family members, the *nuclear* family, while for others family included various other kin, friends, and even pets. This study highlights the difficulty in defining who is part of the family. However, the complexity of defining the family does not end with the determining of family membership. Family definitions are also linked to ideological differences.

For example, John Scanzoni and colleagues (1989, p. 27), in their attempt to expand the definition of the family in the 1980s, discussed the traditional family defined as two parents and a child or children as the prevailing paradigm of the family. They state, "All other family forms or sequencing tend to be labeled as deviant (as in research on minorities) or as 'alternatives' (when occurring among whites)." They challenged the view held by many early writers that the traditional family was the ideal family, the family type by which the success of other families may be evaluated. This statement illustrates how the definition of family is not only structurally focused but also oriented to both ideology and process. Katherine Allen (2000, p. 7) further defines the ideology and process when she states, "Our assumptions, values, feelings, and histories shape the scholarship we propose, the findings we generate, and the conclusions we draw. Our insights about family processes and structures are affected by our membership in particular families, by the lives of those we study, and by what we care about knowing and explaining." These inescapable ideological differences result in a definition of the family that is driven by theory, history, culture, and situation.

Is it possible to arrive at a definition of family that is universal? A universal definition would require that the definition be viable when applied to all situations and societies, historically, developmentally, and cross-culturally. Most argue that such a definition is either not possible (Settles 1987) or only possible to discuss in relation to categories of definitions (Trost 1990). The latter argues that the definition of family will vary based on situational requirements. Most experts in the field have concluded that "there is no single correct definition of what a family is" (Fine 1993, p. 235). Rather, the approaches that individuals have taken in attempting to define the family have ranged in meaning from very specific to very broad, from theoretical to practical, and from culturally specific to culturally diverse.

Related Constructs

Researchers have attempted to define the family based on constructs that are larger than the family. For example, the family has been viewed as a close relationship or a social group. Difficulty and theoretical problems related to defining family or families have led some to seek these broader constructs that transcend the definition of the family, from their view leading to a higher level of understanding (Goode 1959; Kelley et al., 1983; Scanzoni et al. 1989).

For example, a close relationship defined as "strong, frequent, and diverse, interdependence

that lasts over a considerable period of time" (Kelley 1983, p. 38) is a broader construct than family. This has been viewed as an encompassing term that would define most families. However, this generalizing concept, although applicable to most families, does not apply to all families—for example, the family where a parent is absent and does not want to be present. It also includes others who are not part of the family such as friends and co-workers.

The family has also been viewed as a form of social group, a group held together by a common purpose. Although the family is indeed a social group, it is a social group that is very distinct when compared to other social groups. Distinctions between a family and a group have been discussed by researchers (Day, Gilbert, Settles, and Burr 1995) and include the following: (1) family membership may be involuntary, and the connection may be more permanent; (2) actions of family members can be hidden and thus there is a safe environment provided for openness and honesty but also an environment for dark activities such as abuse, addictions, and neglect; (3) family members may be more intensely bonded through emotional ties; (4) there is often a shared family paradigm or world view; and (5) there is frequently a biological connectedness that is not present in other social groups.

The review of these two encompassing constructs makes it evident that although larger constructs are useful in understanding the family, they do not specifically define family. These broad constructs allow for the inclusion of those not part of the family and the exclusion those who are part of the family. To address the problem of excluding family members, some researchers have attempted to develop definitions of the family by accounting for any type of family.

Inclusive Definitions

Inclusive definitions are those that are so broad that no one's perception of family will be excluded. For example, James Holstein and Jaber Gubrium (1995) illustrate an inclusive definition of the family by utilizing a phenomenological and ethnomethodological theoretical perspective in an attempt to understand how individuals experience reality. *Family*, based on this perspective, is each individual's interpretation of who their kin are. The basic argument is that meanings and interpretations have no connection to rules, norms, or culture. Thus, the definition of family is based on the individual's local subculture and is his or her own reality. For example, Barbara Rothberg and Dan Weinstein illustrate an inclusive definition that can encompass all local subcultures by stating that: "the constellation of family is limited only by the limits of participants' creativity" (1966, p. 57).

Inclusive definitions are reasoned and scholarly attempts to deal with the increasing diversity of primary or close relationships in postmodern societies. According to David Cheal (1993), the 1980s and 1990s have brought a shift from defining the family as the modern family to defining it as the postmodern family. The family is no longer a fixed form; it is now more free form. The term family has been replaced by families and has become the embodiment of whatever the individual perceives to be family.

Based on this type of definition, the family becomes whatever the individual wants it to be. The definition of family is thus dependent on every feature of an individual's life, including beliefs, culture, ethnicity, and even situational experiences. Although this definition type is extremely universal, it is also very nebulous, thus making research on the family difficult. The researcher is confronted with the problem of no longer being able to define what family is, as it can become anything the individual wants it to be. For this reason, other researchers have proposed definitions of the family that focus on similarities among families and thus allow for theoretical as well as applied research.

Theoretical Definitions

Basing the definition of family on theoretical perspectives means that the definition of the family will vary based on the theoretical perspective that one takes. Multiple definitions of family have been formulated from particular theoretical perspectives (Doherty et al. 1993). Because of the variety of definitions that can be linked with specific theories, Suzanna Smith (1995) was able to create a different definition of the family for each of eight conceptual approaches.

For example, the definition of family for symbolic interaction theory is a unit of interacting personalities (Smith 1995). Those defining the family from a feminist perspective would assume that there are broad differences among marriages and families, and these differences are greater than the similarities. The traditional definition of the family would be rejected with emphasis on change and diversity (Thompson and Walker 1995).

However, most theories are not specifically directed at defining the family. David Klein and James White (1996) have pointed out that the family developmental theory is the only theory where the focus is specifically on the family. Other approaches can be and are used to study other social groups and institutions; in contrast, the developmental approach is microsystem oriented. According to this theory, family members occupy socially defined positions (e.g., daughter, mother, father, or son) and the definition of family changes over the family career.

Initially, the stages of change discussed in the literature related directly to the traditional nuclear family. According to Paul Mattessich and Reuben Hill (1987), some of the original theorists in the area, family life stage was based on changes in family size, age composition, and the occupational status of the breadwinner(s). The stages of family development identified were: childless couples, childbearing families, families with infants and preschool children, childbearing families with grade-school children, families with teenagers, families with young adults still at home, families in the middle years, and aging families.

In the 1990s, researchers updated this theory to include families defined in other ways over the family careers (Rodgers and White 1993; Klein and White 1996; White 1991). These authors specify the significance of change that is related to other transitions, such as cohabitation, births in later stages, separation, divorce, remarriage, or death. Thus, how one defines one's own family is not static, but changes with the addition of family members through close relationships, birth, adoption, and foster relationships or the loss of family members because of death or departure.

Talcott Parsons (1943), a structural-functionalist, discussed the development of the family by using more generic family definitions that apply to all members of society. According to Parsons, one is born into the biological family, or one's family of origin. If the individual is raised in this family, it becomes their family of orientation. However, if the marriage dissolves, or the child is given up for adoption, the new family of which the individual is part becomes the family of orientation. However, by leaving this family to marry or cohabitate, for example, the individual becomes part of the family of procreation. This term is somewhat dated because in several types of relationships such as childless or gay and lesbian relationships, procreation may not be a part of the relationship.

With the move from the family of origin or orientation to family of procreation, the individual's original nuclear family, or their closest family members, become part of their kinship group or their extended family, while their new partner or child become part of their new nuclear family. The North American family changes and develops with new members being added (e.g., new partners, birth, adoption) or replaced (e.g., foster parents, nonbiological parents, partners) over their lifetime (McGoldrick and Carter 1982). Thus, this terminology was developed to describe these family changes. It should be noted, however, that this theoretical terminology is most appropriate for the North American population. As has been pointed out by several writers, the basic family unit in non-North American and non-European countries is the extended family rather than the nuclear family (Ingoldsby and Smith 1995; Murdock 1949).

Thus, although theoretical definitions are important for research purposes, conceptual approaches are not in themselves true or false but are rather a set of assumptions with which to examine social phenomena. They may not apply to all situations or cultures. Although useful in doing research, definitions other than theoretical definitions may be more suitable in other situations. For example, practical or situational definitions of the family may be more appropriate in specific situations and circumstances.

Situational Definitions

Theoretical definitions direct research, whereas situational definitions are important in practical situations and thus are the working terminology. This terminology facilitates the training of professional caregivers. Situational definitions are used for special types of families and are utilized by individuals from social service agencies to deal with special situations in which family form is changed, and a new form of family must emerge to protect those within the family, often children (Hartman 1990;

McNeece 1995; Seligmann 1990). For example, Margaret Crosbie-Burnett and Edith Lewis (1993) utilize a situational definition of family in working with families where alcohol is abused. The term pedifocal, defined as "all those involved in the nurturance and support of an identified child, regardless of household membership [where the child lives]" (p. 244), expands the definition of the family from being only family members to include those working with the family. Thus, the child's interests are put above other needs to protect the child, despite the change in family structure and relationships. In this case, others who are not related to the child may become *fictive kin* who respond to the child's needs and contributing to his or her well-being.

Marci Hanson and Eleanor Lynch further illustrate the broader situational definitions of family. In their research with teachers they state, state (1992, p. 285) family is, "any unit that defines itself as a family including individuals who are related by blood or marriage as well as those who have made a commitment to share their lives." Perhaps the most explicit example of a situational definition of the family was given by Sally Bould (1993, p. 138) who defines family as "the informal unit where those who cannot take care of themselves can find care in the time of need." The family in this case is expanded to include anyone who helps an individual.

Another example would be the Israeli Kibbutz of the past, where children were cared for in a group setting by people other than their parents (i.e., the metaplot or caretaker). In this setting, although the children still have biological parents, they also have caretakers who become their parent figures (Broude 1994). Based on this definition, family is expanded to those who may be caretakers and thus may only be part of one's family for a short period of time. Although this is a useful definition in practical situations, more formal definitions exist that are based on societal rules and expectations.

Normative Definitions

Within the 1990s and into the early twenty-first century, the definition of family was no longer confined to the traditional family, but also included the normative family. Normative is a sociological concept that, according to Abu-Laban and Abu-Laban, "are agreed upon societal rules and expectations specifying appropriate and inappropriate ways to behave in a particular society" (1994, p. 53). These are terms and family types that are normative across most modern and postmodern societies.

Families with at least one parent and one child are viewed as a normative definition of the family in most if not all societies (Angus Reid Group 1996; Bibby 1995; Reiss 1965; Levin and Trost 1992; Rothberg and Weinstein 1966). For example, in a Swedish study done by Levin and Trost (1992), a majority of those surveyed identified as families married couples with children, nonmarried, separated, or divorced couples with children and single parents and their children.

The child in these cases is not necessarily biologically related to those providing care and nurturance. They may, for example, be adopted, grandchildren, products of other relationships, or perhaps children conceived through artificial insemination or a surrogate mother. Despite the lack of biological relationship these relationships can still be included as part of the normative definition of the family. All of these families would be considered examples of the nuclear family.

Also part of the normative family would be all others who are closest to the individual. Not only is the parent-child relationship a normative nuclear family in most societies, the definition of a normal family and nuclear families also includes couples in close relationships that lead to common-law relationships or marriage relationships. However, expectations of a legitimate and thus a normative family union may vary among and within various cultures, based on formal rules related to law, religious orientation, and cultural norms, as well as to informal expectations of family, friends, and associates.

Taking this one step further, intergenerational bonds are also normal if based on lineage or biological parentage are known as one's kinship group or extended family. These terms do not specify the number of parents or children. However, in most societies, the kinship group or the extended family includes one or two partners, their children, and a variety of involved relatives such as grandparents, aunts and uncles, and cousins.

Information on the intricacy and the cultural diversity of the extended family is discussed in the writings of many authours (e.g., Murdock 1949;

Stanton 1995). The reasons that families continue to live in an extended family situation vary greatly among cultures and generations. Some identified in the literature are for mutual assistance both for household work and income and also the inheritance of property or the perpetuation of kinship values viewed as important to the preservation of the family system.

Thus, these norms based on culture, religion, and ethnicity all influence the definition of the family. These norms may or may not be adhered to, and what is normative may change over the stages of the family.

Conclusion

No universal definition of the family exists, but rather many appropriate definitions do (Petzold 1998). Definitions are not only racially and intergenerationally diverse (Bedford and Blieszner 2000), but are also situationally diverse.

Functionally, arguments related to defining the family are most often dependent on one's paradigm of social interaction and one's purpose in defining the term. Thus, perspectives on what constitutes family vary greatly. The family becomes what the individual or the researcher perceives it to be based on the purpose for which the term is being used. In defining family, there is often vigorous discussion contrasting form or process. Beliefs, which frequently have an emotional cornerstone; bias, our perception of what family is, should be or could be.

In all of the complexity of defining family, however, there is a strong emerging international theme within the scientific community that is based on evidence. Variations in family form and process are extremely prevalent but must also acknowledge the dominant structures by which cultures define family. In contrast to the reactionary themes of the 1960s and 1970s to "traditional family," we have observed openness to family diversity in more recent literature. As a result of greater international networks, particularly in the research communities, we are growing increasingly aware of dominant family definitions that acknowledge its great variety.

See also: EXTENDED FAMILIES; FAMILY THEORY; INTENTIONAL
    COMMUNITIES; KINSHIP; NUCLEAR FAMILIES

Bibliography

Abu-Laban, S. M., and Abu-Laban, A. (1994). "Culture, Society, and Change." In *An Introduction to Sociology,* ed. W. A. Meloff and W. D. Pierce. Scarborough: Nelson Canada.

Allen, K. R. (2000). "Becoming More Inclusive of Diversity in Family Studies." *Journal of Marriage and the Family* 62(1):4–12.

Bibby, R. W. (1995). *The Bibby Report: Social Trends Canadian Style.* Toronto: Stoddart.

Bould, S. (1993). "Familial Caretaking: A Middle-Range Definition of Family in the Context of Social Policy." *Journal of Family Issues* 14(1):133–151.

Broude, G. J. (1994). *Marriage, Family, and Relationships: A Cross-Cultural Encyclopedia.* Santa Barbara, CA: ABC-CLIO.

Cheal, D. (1993). "Unity and Difference in Postmodern Families." *Journal of Family Issues* 14(1):5–19.

Crosbie-Burnett, M., and Lewis, E. A. (1993). "Theoretical Contributions from Social, Cognitive, and Behavioral Psychology." In *Sourcebook of Family Theories and Methods: A Contextual Approach,* ed. P. G. Boss, G. W. Doherty, R. LaRossa, W. R. Schumm, and S. K. Steinmetz. New York: Plenum Press.

Day, D.; Gilbert, K. R.; Settles, B. H.; and Burr, W. R. (1995). *Research and Theory in Family Science.* Pacific Grove, CA: Brooks/Cole Publishing.

Doherty, W. J.; Boss, P.G.; LaRossa, R.; Schumm, W.R.; and Steinmetz, S. K. (1993). "Family Theories and Methods: A Contextual Approach." In *Sourcebook of Family Theories and Methods: A Contextual Approach,* ed. P. G. Boss, G. W. Doherty, R. LaRossa, W. R. Schumm, and S. K. Steinmetz. New York: Plenum Press.

Fine, M. A. (1993). "Current Approaches to Understanding Family Diversity: An Overview of the Special Issue." *Family Relations* 42(3):235–237.

Goode, W. J. (1959). "The Sociology of the Family." In *Sociology Today,* ed. R. K. Merton, L. Broom, and L. S. Cotrell Jr. New York: Basic Books.

Hanson, M. J., and Lynch, E. W. (1992). "Family Diversity: Implications for Policy and Practice." *Topics in Early Childhood Special Education* 12(3):283–306.

Hartman, A. (1990). "Family Ties." *Social Work* 35:195–196.

Holstein, J. A., and Gubrium, J. F. (1995), "Deprivatiztion and the Construction of Domestic Life." *Journal of Marriage and the Family* 57(4):894–908.

Ingoldsby, B. B., and Smith, S. (1995). *Families in Multicultural Perspective.* New York: Guilford Press.

Kelley, H. H. (1983). "Epilogue: An Essential Science." In *Close Relationships: Perspectives on the Meaning of Intimacy,* ed. H. H. Kelley, E. Berscheid, A. Christensen, J. H. Harvey, T. L. Huston, G. Levinger, E. McClintock, L. A. Peplau, and D. R. Peterson. New York: Freeman.

Klein, D. M., and White, J. M. (1996). *Family Theories: An Introduction.* Thousand Oaks, CA: Sage.

McGoldrick, M., and Carter, E. (1982). "The Family Life Cycle." In *Normal Family Processes,* ed. F. Walsh. New York: Guilford Press.

McNeece, C. A. (1995). "Family Social Work Practice from Therapy to Policy." *Journal of Family Social Work* 1(1):3–17.

Mattessich, P., and Hill, R. (1987). "Life Cycle and Family Development," In *Handbook of Marriage and the Family,* ed. M. G. Sussman, and Suzanne K. Steinmetz. New York: Plenum.

Murdock, G. (1949). *Social Structure.* New York: Free Press.

Parsons, T. (1943). "The Kinship System of the Contemporary United States." *American Anthropologist* 45:22–28.

Reiss, I. (1965). "The Universality of the Family: A Conceptual Analysis." *Journal of Marriage and the Family* 27:443–453.

Rodgers, R. H., and White, J. M. (1993). "Family Development Theory." In *Sourcebook of Family Theories and Methods: A Contextual Approach,* ed. P. G. Boss, W. G. Doherty, R. LaRossa, W. R. Schumm, and S. K. Steinmetz. New York: Plenum.

Rothberg, B., and Weinstein, D. L. (1966). "A Primer on Lesbian and Gay Families." *Journal of Gay and Lesbian Social Services* 4(2):55–68.

Scanzoni, J.; Polonko, K.; Teachman, J.; and Thompson, L. (1989). *The Sexual Bond: Rethinking Families and Close Relationships.* Newbury Park, CA: Sage.

Settles, B. H. (1987). "A Perspective on Tomorrow's Families." In *Families in Multicultural Perspective,* ed. M. B. Sussman, and S. K. Steinmetz, New York: Plenum.

Smith, S. (1995). "Family Theory and Multicultural Family Studies." In *Families in Multicultural Perspective,* ed. B. B. Ingoldsby, and S. Smith. New York: Guildford Press.

Stanton M. E. (1995). "Patterns of Kinship and Residence." In *Families in Multicultural Perspective,* ed. B. B. Ingoldsby, and S. Smith. New York: Guildford Press.

Thompson, L., and Walker, A. J. (1995). "The Lace of Feminism in Family Studies." *Journal of Marriage and the Family* 57(4):847–865.

Trost, J. (1990). "Do We Mean the Same Thing by the Concept of the Family?" *Communication Research* 17(4):431.

White, J. (1991). *Dynamics of Family Development: A Theoretical Perspective.* New York: Guilford Press.

Other Resources

Angus Reid Group. (1996). "Canadians' Views on the Canada Pension Plan." Available from http://www.ipsos-reid.com/ca/index.cfm.

BRENDA MUNRO
GORDON MUNRO

FAMILY, HISTORY OF

The historical study of the family is generally regarded as a subfield of social history whose particular focus is the ways in which families live out histories of their own while participating actively in the larger arenas of national and international history. There is ultimately little historical space that family does not impinge upon. Family history, consequently, takes in such subjects and approaches as demography and household composition; childhood and other life stages; the life course; the family economy; family strategies, traditions and rituals; gender, class, race and generational relations; kinship; sexuality; and the varied forms of domesticity. Any adequate historical understanding of family must acknowledge its central role in social and political as well as personal relationships, in societal as well as biological reproduction. Although regularly classified as a *natural* or biological unit, *the family* is also very much a social construction. Despite its seemingly transhistorical elements, its meaning is grounded in specific cultures and their historical objectives.

Borrowing from the social sciences, historians use the term *family* to describe a kinship and legal unit based on relationships of marriage or biology (parent-child linkages). *Household* refers to a residential unit, and also to both kin and nonkin who share that residence. The *nuclear* or *conjugal* family is composed of a heterosexual marital couple and their dependent children, living in an independent household. *Extended families* are usually multigenerational, and include kin related by blood as well as by marriage. Even in using such definitions, historians are mindful that most people define *family* subjectively, according to their own experiences and the historical forces that have shaped them. Social groups also vary in conceptualizing *family*. Some trace descent through the paternal or maternal line; others give more weight to horizontal ties of kinship, as acquired through marriage, than to these vertical ones. If we tend to refer frequently and without particular reflection to the family, history shows that there are many identifiable forms of family in any culture, in any historical moment.

Given the varied meanings of *family,* finding ways to approach families historically is a complicated exercise. The development of family sociology did much to prepare the way for family history. By the second half of the nineteenth century, a consciously "scientific" approach to families was taking shape under the auspices of a developing European social science, influenced particularly by the ideas of Frédéric LePlay (1806–82) and the Société d'Economie Sociale de Paris (Howard 1981). LePlay posited that the family was not only the foundation, but the determining element of all social organization. Fuelled by a perceived "crisis in the family" that was seen to result directly from the rapid, intensive sociocultural change occurring in the wake of modernizing forces, European and North American social scientists began to probe the family's role in, and responses to, modernization (Lasch 1977). Early twentieth century attempts to historicize the family were thus produced by sociologists: Arthur W. Calhoun's three-volume *History of the American Family* (1919), for example, closely aligns familial change with economic change. During the 1920s, University of Chicago sociologists Robert Parks and Ernest Burgess devised a theory of family as process that emphasized a dialectical relationship between family. Their *interactionist* approach allowed for a range of stable family types, each relating in different ways to the larger society, with the nuclear family found to be most suited to the industrial capitalist order. Reinforcing the connections between familial and structural change, the functionalist model furthered by Chicago's Talcott Parsons during the 1940s and 1950s would dominate sociological ideas about the family for some thirty years (Howard 1981).

Although clearly an important research subject for early twentieth-century sociologists, family history became a distinct and acknowledged field of historical inquiry only during the 1960s, with the continued refinements to the "new social history" that emerged in that decade. Historians dedicated to recovering the experiences of common people invariably hit upon the bedrock of family, so embedded are all other social relations in those of domesticity. Initially, the surest way across the threshold of private homes appeared to be quantitative. French historical demographers such as Louis Henry and the *Annales* group working out of the Institut National des Etudes Démographiques devised a family reconstitution technique that would provide an enduring basis for family history. In England, the Cambridge Group for the History of Population and Social Structure, established in 1964 under the direction of Peter Laslett, used these tools to demonstrate that "the great family of Western nostalgia"—the three-generation household—was never more than a tiny minority in Western Europe since the sixteenth century, and that the nuclear or conjugal unit had actually preceded industrialization. This path-breaking work led to new questions about standard historical periodization and about the wider social impact of industrialization, especially in regard to demographic patterns (Laslett 1965; Wrigley 1966; Henry 1968; Laslett and Wall 1972; Rabb and Rotberg 1973; Katz 1975; Forster and Ranum 1976). Historians of Europe introduced the concept of *proto-industrialization* to explain how families prepared their members for factory labor through a transitional phase of household production in which they participated as laboring units (Mendels 1972). Reflecting this interdisciplinary exchange, the principal questions of early family history were those that lent themselves to numerical answers and were posed with a view to understanding the impact of structural change on families. The demographic approach has greatly expanded our knowledge about such important trends as declining family size and mortality rates, increasing childhood dependence, and the timing of life stages.

Building on these demographic foundations, a second group of family historians developed a more dynamic, relational approach by studying the life course of families. Life-course historians are concerned with the relationship between the life stages of individual family members and the larger family cycle. Family decisions and actions are viewed as adaptations to the changing ages and roles of members, and also to external social, economic, and political pressures. The community studies of the U.S. historian Tamara Hareven, which examine the intersections of *family time* and *industrial time,* identified the family as an active agent of change, and also the continued importance of kinship ties as adaptive strategies (Hareven 1978, 1982, 2000). Frequently used in combination with life-course analysis, the *family strategies* approach considers how families use their familial and kin resources to deal with their own needs and objectives as well as those imposed upon them by their society and culture. Life-course historians attend to the ways in which family members follow their own paths, but these individual life histories are examined as they converge with larger histories: those of the family itself, as well as those of generations, communities, regions, and nations. By getting a sense of how much or how little the phases of the life course have changed over time, historians can identify such developments as the increasing systematization of the life course itself over the twentieth century (Hareven 1977; Elder 1978; Modell 1989; Bradbury 1993).

Life-course analysis has been especially effective in historical studies on women and gender. Examinations of women's contributions to the family economy revealed the carryover of gender-typed labor from proto-industrial households into the factory and the sociopolitical realm, as demonstrated by Louise Tilly and Joan Wallach Scott in their seminal work in this area (Tilly and Scott 1978; Hudson and Lee 1990; Parr 1990; Zarnowska 1997). If their power was always kept within the sociocultural, economic, legal and political confines established by men, women have historically been the primary agents of familial adaptation to the forces of change (Hall 1992; Rose 1992). The *sentiments* or *emotions* approach to family history is perhaps methodologically closer to the history of ideas than to the social sciences (Anderson 1980). Highlighting sociocultural values, expectations, images and roles assigned to the family and its members, its practitioners study such topics as courtship, childrearing, sexual conduct, marriage practices, media and literary representations, social constructs and public discourses. They aim to reconstruct the complex and often contradictory aspects of family life and relations, and to integrate the study of individuals and families with the broader sociocultural phenomena grounding their experiences. Philippe Ariès' seminal work has been criticized for inferring broad patterns from a narrow upper-class source base, but his *Centuries of Childhood* (1962), which located an overall shift in societal perceptions of children in seventeenth century Europe, inspired an international scholarly interest in private lives and the emotional ties of family (Ariès 1962; Demos 1970; Stone 1977; Shorter and Sutherland 1976; Pollock 1987). Ariès also edited and contributed to the important multivolume *A History of Private Life* (Ariès and Duby 1987–91). Once it was recognized that childhood is specific to time and place, age joined the identifying categories of class, gender, and race that historians could no longer overlook in their forays into past societies.

Social reproduction and state formation are related issues that have recently interested family historians. The family is not only the main location of biologically and legally defined relationships between men and women, adults and children, but also where private and public spheres intersect. Families replicate values and belief systems, forging the links between personal identity and social role, individuals and society, home and nation. During the twentieth century, the state has increasingly regulated and supervised their efforts toward these ends. The French social theorist Jacques Donzelot's *The Policing of Families* (1979) is a landmark study in this regard. Inspired by the theories of Michel Foucault on the increasing moral regulation of modern society, Donzelot situated the nineteenth-century European family within an international context of shifting sociopolitical relations (Donzelot 1979). Other historians interested in the state's growing role in social reproduction have looked to models derived from materialist and feminist theories (Coontz 1988; Skocpol 1992; Seccombe 1993).

As the twentieth century closed, historical analysis reflected the growing importance of poststructuralist concepts and tools of analysis, notably Derridian deconstructive reading, Lacanian psychoanalysis, and Foucault's emphasis on the discourses of power. Foucault's influence has been paramount. Placing power at the center of social relations, he emphasized its compulsory, disciplinary, and exclusionary elements through public discourses. By making language an active element in "constructing" reality, discourse analysis encourages interrogation of concepts long presumed to be timeless, universal, and definitive. Since the family is a multidimensional symbol system, the insights permitted by poststructuralist approaches have been valuable in its historical understanding, especially in regard to the impact on family and familial relations of such identifying marks as those inscribed by class, "race," ethnicity, sexuality, religion, and culture. Just as they differentiate both individual and family experiences, they serve to distinguish the norm. Examinations of the social construction of gender have demonstrated how motherhood developed as a self-conscious vocation within the context of changing feminine roles and prescribed ideals, while work on masculinity has led to critical reappraisals of how masculine roles fit with larger patriarchal structures and the public status ascribed to "breadwinning." "Race" as a social construct is also increasingly significant to studies of the historic relations of family, state, and society (Bederman 1995; Sonbol 1996).

Having contributed much to the wider field of social history by examining private lives in relation to the larger processes of social change—even leading to a critical rethinking of the timing and impact of those processes—family history was healthy and vibrant as the twenty-first century opened. Two major scholarly journals in the English language—*Journal of Family History* and *History of the Family*—and an expanding and welcome contribution by historians outside the dominant North American/Western European purview, testify to its continued dynamism (Lardinois 1996; Potthast-Jutkeit 1997; Romero 1997; Wang 2000). While interest in family reconstitution remains strong (Bouchard 1996; Wrigley, Davies, Oeppen, and Schofield 1997), interdisciplinary approaches derived from cultural anthropology have made memory, family "stories," and ritual important keys to family history (Sutherland 1997; Gillis 1997). As Hareven remarked, the field's evolution over the past thirty years has effectively laid the basis for cross-cultural research that promises to bring historians closer to grasping the local, cultural foundations of historic changes and continuities as manifested in "the family" (Hareven 2000; Hareven, Wall, Ehmer, and Cerman 2001).

See also: CHILDHOOD; FAMILY SCIENCE; FAMILY
  THEORY; PROTESTANTISM

Bibliography

Anderson, M. (1980). *Approaches to the History of the Western Family, 1500–1914.* London: Macmillan.

Ariès, P. (1962). *Centuries of Childhood: A Social History of Family Life,* trans. R. Baldick. New York: Knopf.

Ariès, P. and G. Duby, eds. (1987–91). *A History of Private Life,* 5 vols, trans. A. Goldhammer. Cambridge, MA: Belknap Press.

Bederman, Gail. (1995). *Manliness and Civilization: A Cultural History of Gender and Race in the United States, 1880–1917.* Chicago: University of Chicago Press.

Bouchard, G. (1996). *Quelques arpents d'Amérique: Population, économie, famille au Saguenay, 1838–1971.* Montréal: Boréal.

Bradbury, B. (1993). *Working Families: Age, Gender and Daily Survival in Industrializing Montreal.* Toronto: McClelland and Stewart.

Coontz, S. (1988). *The Social Origins of Private Life: A History of American Families, 1600–1900.* New York: Verso.

Demos, J. (1970). *A Little Commonwealth: Family Life in Plymouth Colony.* New York: Oxford University Press.

Donzelot, J. (1979). *The Policing of Families,* trans. R. Hurley. New York: Pantheon.

Elder, G. (1978). "Family History and the Life Course." In *Transitions: The Family and the Life Course in Historical Perspective,* ed. T. Hareven. New York: Academic Press.

Forster, R. and O. Ranum. eds. (1976). *Family and Society: Selections from the Annales: économies, sociétés, civilisations,* trans. E. Forster and P. M. Ranum. Baltimore, MD.: Johns Hopkins University Press.

Foucault, M. (1972). *The Archaeology of Knowledge,* trans. A. M. Sheridan. New York: Pantheon.

Gillis, J. (1997). *A World of Their Own Making: A History of Myth and Ritual in Family Life.* New York: Oxford University Press.

Hall, C. (1992). *White, Male and Middle Class: Explorations in Feminism and History.* London: Routledge.

Hareven, T. ed. (1977). *Family and Kin in American Urban Communities, 1780–1940.* New York: Franklin and Watts.

Hareven, T. (1982). *Family Time and Industrial Time: The Relationship Between the Family and Work in a New England Industrial Community.* New York: Cambridge University Press.

Hareven, T. (2000). *Families, History and Social Change.* Boulder, CO: Westview Press.

Hareven, T.; Wall, R.; Ehmer, J.; and Cerman, M., eds. (2001). *Family History Revisited: Comparative Perspectives.* Newark, NJ: University of Delaware Press.

Henry, L. (1968). "Historical Demography." *Daedalus* 97:385–396.

Howard, R. L. (1981). *A Social History of American Family Sociology, 1865–1940.* Westport, CT: Greenwood Press.

Hudson, P., and Lee, W. (1990). *Women's Work and the Family Economy in Historical Perspective.* Manchester, U.K.: Manchester University Press.

Katz, M. (1975). *The People of Hamilton, Canada West: Family and Class in a Mid-Nineteenth Century City.* Cambridge, MA: Harvard University Press.

Lardinois, R. (1996). "Histoire de la Famille en Inde a L'Epoque Moderne" (History of the Family in Modern India). *Historiens et Geographes* [France] 87(353):177–188.

Lasch, C. (1977). *Haven in a Heartless World: The Family Besieged.* New York: Basic Books.

Laslett, P. (1965). *The World We Have Lost.* London: Methuen.

Laslett, P., and Wall, R., eds. (1973). *Household and Family in Past Times.* Cambridge: Cambridge University Press.

Mendels, F. (1972). "Proto-Industrialization: The First Phase of the Industrialization Process." *Journal of Economic History* 32:241–261.

Modell, J. (1989). *Into One's Own: From Youth to Adulthood in the United States, 1920–1975.* Berkeley: University of California Press.

Parr, J. (1990). *The Gender of Breadwinners: Women, Men and Change in Two Industrial Towns, 1880–1950.* Toronto: University of Toronto Press.

Potthast-Jutkeit, B. (1997). "The History of Family and Colonialism: Examples from Africa, Latin America, and the Caribbean." *History of the Family* 2(2):115–121.

Rabb, T. K., and Rotberg, R. I., eds. (1973). *The Family in History: Interdisciplinary Essays.* New York: Harper and Row.

Romero, P. W. (1997). *Lamu: History, Society, and Family in an East African Port City.* New York: Markus Wiener.

Rose, S. (1992). *Limited Livelihoods: Gender and Class in Nineteenth-Century England.* Berkeley, CA: University of California Press.

Seccombe, W. (1993). *Weathering the Storm: Working-Class Families from the Industrial Revolution to the Fertility Decline.* New York: Verso.

Shorter, E. (1975). *The Making of the Modern Family*. New York: Basic Books.

Skocpol, T. (1992). *Protecting Soldiers and Mothers: The Political Origins of Social Policy in the United States*. Cambridge, MA: Belknap Press.

Sonbol, A. El Azhary, ed. (1996). *Women, the Family, and Divorce Laws in Islamic History*. Syracus, NY: Syracuse University Press.

Stone, L. (1977). *The Family, Sex, and Marriage in England, 1500–1800*. New York: Harper and Row.

Sutherland, N. (1976). *Children in English Canadian Society, 1880–1920: Framing the Twentieth-Century Consensus*. Toronto: University of Toronto Press.

Sutherland, N. (1997). *Growing Up: Childhood in English Canada from the Great War to the Age of Television*. Toronto: University of Toronto Press.

Tilly, L., and Wallach Scott, J. (1978). *Women, Work, and Family*. New York: Holt, Rinehart and Winston.

Wang, Y. (2000). "Zhongguo Jiating Shi Yanjiu Chuy" (Opinions on historical studies of the Chinese family). *Lishi Yanjiu* [China](3):165–172.

Wrigley, E. (1966). "Family Reconstitution." In *An Introduction to English Historical Demography*, ed. P. Laslett, et.al. New York: Basic Books.

Wrigley, E. A.; Davies, R. S.; Oeppen, J. E.; and Schofield R. S. (1997). *English Population History from Family Reconstitution, 1580-1837*. Cambridge, UK: Cambridge University Press.

Wrigley, E., and Schofield, R. (1981). *The Population History of England, 1541–1871*. Cambridge, MA: Harvard University Press.

Zarnowska, A. (1997). "Social Change, Women and the Family in the Era of Industrialization: Recent Polish Research." *Journal of Family History* 22(2):191–203.

CYNTHIA COMACCHIO

FAMILY AND RELATIONAL RULES

Think about your own family for a moment. Is it expected that you will eat dinner together as a family? Are there certain chores you must do? Are there topics you cannot talk about? These questions address specific rules your family may have. According to Virginia Satir (1996) every significant relationship develops rules. Most relationship rules can be identified by looking at the redundancies or repetitive behaviors of the relational partners (Yerby, Buerkel-Rothfuss, and Bochner 1990).

Rules are defined as a "followable prescription that indicates what behavior is obligated, preferred, and prohibited in certain contexts" (Shimanoff 1980, p. 57). Because rules enable the relationship members to predict the others' behaviors (Satir 1996) they are important for the survival and maintenance of one's relationship. This predictability leads to comfort and helps family members understand what topics are acceptable to discuss, how difficult topics are dealt with, and whom to include. Rules deal with the concept of what one should and/or should not do, and identify what types of actions define one as a member of the group (Satir 1996). Rules contribute to relational self-definition, development, and satisfaction (Satir 1996).

Rule Transmission

Most romantic and family relationships have many different rules. There are rules about how to handle money, show affection, divide the chores, and how to deal with someone who breaks the rules. "Rules exist for all other contributing factors that make it possible for people to live together in the same house and grow or not grow" (Satir 1996, p. 168). Because rules are typically unique to the family and romantic relationship, the types of rules are discussed in the ways in which they are transmitted.

Most scholars discuss types of rules and transmission of rules using the *continuum of awareness*. This continuum ranges from direct, *explicit* relationship agreements that may have been negotiated to *implicit*, unspoken rules. These end points (i.e., explicit vs. implicit) address rule transmission.

Although it is difficult to predict when relational members might use explicit versus implicit means of establishing rules, there is a body of literature on taboo topics that lends some insight into this decision. Michael Roloff and Danette Ifert (1998) found that in new romantic relationships, individuals reported that they and their partner made explicit agreements about which topics were taboo when (1) the couple determined the topic was not important to their relationship, (2) one member of the relationship determined the topic was too personal to discuss, or (3) the members of the relationship had different opinions regarding the topic and felt their differences could not be resolved. More specifically, a prolonged discussion about a topic prior to declaring it taboo leads to a more explicit statement that the topic is off limits (Roloff and Ifert 1998).

At the other end of the awareness continuum are *implicit* or unspoken rules. These rules often emerge from repeated interactions or experiences (e.g., never mention Mike's mother when he is sad) (Satir 1996). Implicit rules are typically communicated nonverbally (Turner and West 1998) but may also be transmitted through stories. A relational member may tell a story in which someone followed the rule and was rewarded or did not follow the rule and was punished. Implicit rules can also be set by redirecting the undesirable behavior. Amy Jordan (1990), in her study of television viewing and VCR use, tells the story of a mother who came home and found her daughter and babysitter watching a shoot out on the television. This violated her rule of no violence on television. Rather than telling them that, the mother redirected the viewing by suggesting the daughter watch *Dumbo*.

Implicit rules can have more importance than explicit rules (Turner and West 1998). Roloff and Ifert (1998) found that a topic is declared taboo implicitly when the members of the relationship feel a discussion of the topic might harm the relationship. "Perhaps partners sense the relational danger associated with discussing a particular topic and, therefore, avoid frequent confrontations about it" (Roloff and Ifert 1998, p. 202).

Regardless of how the rule is transmitted, being able to identify family rules can be important. Virginia Satir talks about family counseling methods in which families or individuals try to identify all the family rules. Although the explicit rules are easily identified, often the implicit rules are not. In her counseling sessions, she tries to have the family or individual identify the implicit rules so that they can better understand their own behavior. Moreover, by naming the implicit rules, the family members can decide if they want to challenge these rules or not. It is important to point out that many critical communication rules are learned in childhood and carried into adult relationships without much thought unless the rule is challenged by a relational partner (Satir 1988). Challenging rules is important. Satir argues that to

deepen certain relationships, someone has to challenge a rule; this challenge enables the relationship to reach a new level.

What Affects the Rules

There is little research on how people decide which type of rule to set, whereas there is a plethora of research on what affects the number of rules, the subject of the rule, adherence to the rules, and flexibility of the rules. Individual and family demographics can affect the frequency, focus, adherence, and flexibility of the rules.

Cultural norms can affect what rules families hold. Mario Mikulincer and his colleagues (1993) collected data from 350 Israeli-Jewish and 504 Israeli-Arab high school students. They found that Arab youths recounted more rules restricting their conduct compared with their Jewish counterparts. When looking at taboo topics among friends, Robin Goodwin and Iona Lee (1994) found that Chinese respondents had a greater level of taboo topics (thus more rules regarding what could not be discussed) than the British respondents.

Sex of the rule recipient can also affect the number of rules. In both the Israeli-Arab and Israeli-Jewish cultures, adolescent girls reported more restrictions on dating and leaving home than boys (Mikulincer, Weller, and Florian 1993). The sex of the person making the rule can also influence the number of rules. The Chinese and British males in Goodwin and Lee's (1994) study reported a higher number of topics that they could not discuss than the females in the study.

Most rules also change over time. In her two-year study on African-American adolescents, Judith Smetana (2001) found African-American middle-class families were less restrictive at Time 1 (when the average age was 13.14 years) than at Time 2 (when the average age was 15.05 years).

In addition to impact of demographics on the number and focus of the rules, there is research on what impacts rule flexibility and perceptions of parental authority. Smetana (2001) found that income affects perceptions of parents' legitimate authority. African-American adolescents from upper income families rejected parents' legitimate authority to regulate personal issues more than those from middle-income families. Elliott A. Medrich and his colleagues (1982) and Amy Jordan (1990) both found that families with two working parents typically impose fewer rules on television viewing.

How Rules Affect Behavior and Attitudes

The task of identifying the outcome of family and relational rules is as important as identifying predictors of rules. Rules provide a guideline for behavior and a set of expectations. These guidelines often impact the children in families. For example, parental rules about smoking has been linked to lower levels of adolescent smoking (Proeschold-bell, Chassin, MacKinnon 2000) whereas the absence of rules about the use of smokeless tobacco resulted in greater use by U.S. middle-school boys (Brubaker, Fowler, and Kinder 1989). Elaine Rodney and her colleagues (1999) studied the home environment and delinquency for African-American adolescents. They found that family rules—as well as time spent with the child—and home discipline were significantly related to incidents of conduct disorder (e.g., getting into fights, destroying property).

Family and relational rules also provide a sense of predictability and can impact relationship maintenance and satisfaction. The number of rules has been linked to the level of closeness between children and their parents. Mikulincer and his colleagues (1993) reported that Israeli-Arab adolescents who had more rules felt closer to their parents. This is not true for every culture or every family however. Mikulincer and his colleagues also reported that no such pattern was evident among Israeli-Jewish youth.

Family secrets. Perhaps the most profound impact of family and relational rules centers on the rules of communication. A majority of the research on relational and family rules has centered on communication rules. This is because a majority of the research on family rules is centered in family counseling. Satir, a family counselor, specifically addresses the freedom to comment. *Freedom to comment* rules address what can you say, to whom can you say it, how you go about handling disagreements or disapproval of someone or something, and how you ask a question when you do not understand.

Satir argues that fear on part of the family members has much to do with rules about taboos and secrets. Anita Vangelisti's (1994) research on

family secrets supported this idea. Vangelisti identified three types of family secrets: *taboo, rule violations,* and *conventional secrets.* Taboo topics were activities that is often condemned and stigmatized by both family members and larger society (e.g., sexual preferences, extramarital affairs) and were often secrets kept by the whole family. Rule violations were activities that broke rules families typically try and enforce (e.g., premarital pregnancy, drinking, partying) and were often secrets kept by an individual family member. Conventional secrets included information that is not usually wrong but is considered inappropriate to talk about with non-intimate others (e.g., health problems, traditions). Each of these types is associated with fear on the family member's part.

Satir also argues that family secrets can be detrimental to the health of the family. She specifically argues that family rules about taboo topics can hurt the child later. Families who avoid discussing a "fault" in a family member (e.g., a relative is in jail) often have children who "grow up to be adults who see themselves as versions of saints or devils instead of living human [beings] who *feel*" (Satir 1996, p. 170). Satir believes an individual's and family's health is a result of the freedom to comment on rules. This belief is supported by communication research that found secrets impact family and relational satisfaction. Vangelisti found the families with more secrets were less satisfied than families with fewer secrets. This was especially true when family members held secrets from other family members. Roloff and Ifert (1998) also found that relationship partners who had more taboo topics were less satisfied.

See also: COMMUNICATION: FAMILY RELATIONSHIPS; CONFLICT: FAMILY RELATIONSHIPS; DISCIPLINE; FAMILY RITUALS; FAMILY STORIES AND MYTHS; FAVORITISM/DIFFERENTIAL TREATMENT; HEALTH AND FAMILIES; HOUSING; POWER: FAMILY RELATIONSHIPS; RELATIONSHIP METAPHORS; SELF-DISCLOSURE

Bibliography

Goodwin, R., and Lee, I. (1994). "Taboo Topics Among Chinese and English Friends: A Cross-Cultural Comparison." *Journal of Cross-Cultural Psychology* 25:325–338.

Jordan, A. B. (1990). "A Family Systems Approach to the VCR." In *Social and Cultural Aspects of VCR Use,* ed. J. R. Dobrow. Hillsdale, NJ: Erlbaum.

Medrich, E. A.; Roizen, J.; Rubin, V.; and Buckelyl, S. (1982). *The Serious Business of Growing Up.* Berkeley: University of California Press.

Mikulincer, M.; Weller, A.; and Florian, V. (1993). "Sense of Closeness to Parents and Family Rules: A Study of Arab and Jewish Youth in Israel." *International Journal of Psychology* 28:323–335.

Proescholdbell, R. J.; Chassin, L.; and MacKinnon, D. P. (2000). "Home Smoking Restrictions and Adolescent Smoking." *Nicotine and Tobacco Research* 2:159–167.

Rodney, H. E.; Tachia, H. R.; and Rodney L. W. (1999). "The Home Environment and Delinquency: A Study of African American Adolescents." *Families in Society* 80:551–559.

Roloff, M. E., and Ifert, D. (1998). "Antecedents and Consequences of Explicit Agreements to Declare a Topic Taboo in Dating Relationships." *Personal Relationships* 5:191–205.

Satir, V. (1988). *The New Peoplemaking.* Palo Alto, CA: Science and Behavior Books.

Satir, V. (1996). "The Rules You Live By." In *Making Connections: Readings in Relational Communication,* ed. K. Galvin and P. Cooper. Los Angeles: Roxbury Publishing.

Shimanoff, S. (1980). *Communication Rules: Theory and Research.* Beverly Hills, CA: Sage.

Smetana, J. G. (2001). "Middle-Class African American Adolescents' and Parents' Conceptions of Parental Authority and Parenting Practices: A Longitudinal Investigation." *Child Development* 71:1672–1686.

Turner, L. H., and West, R. (1998). *Perspectives on Family Communication.* Mountain View, CA: Mayfield Publishing.

Vangelisti, A. (1994). "Family Secrets: Forms, Functions, and Correlates." *Journal of Social and Personal Relationships* 11:113–135.

Yerby, J.; Buerkel-Rothfuss, N.; and Bochner, A. P. (1990). *Understanding Family Communications,* 2nd edition. Scottsdale, AZ: Gorsuch Scarisbuck.

YVONNE KELLAR-GUENTHER

FAMILY ASSESSMENT

Since the last half of the twentieth century there has been a growing interest in the empirical study of the family. Family assessment has been undertaken by social scientists who examine various dimensions of family life. Assessment may also be undertaken by mental health professionals with the goal of obtaining information about the families who seek their assistance in order to determine the necessary interventions and the methods of evaluating their outcomes.

Many of the objectives of family assessment are similar to assessment of individuals and their personalities. Issues about what is being assessed may be primary but when, where, how, and why the assessment is taking place may all be relevant.

Why a Family Assessment?

The whole family is not equivalent to the sum of its individual and dyadic parts. Adults in intimate relationships may consider each other as their "whole" family. But with the birth of a child, a mother-father-child triad transforms the adult dyad into a larger family system with new and multiple role demands. For even young children, being with both parents together means coping with the dynamics of the marital relationship, and family (including marital) life after the birth of a second child may change even more profoundly. Further, family cohesiveness, warmth, and flexibility may be essential for optimal child as well as adult development, and serve as resources and buffers against stressful life events. Assessment of the many family subsystems may be necessary but each may be understood best only in the context of the family as a whole.

What, Where, and How of Family Assessment

Questionnaires, structured and unstructured interviews and tasks, descriptions of observations in naturalistic settings and in the laboratory, and scoring systems have been developed to assess family life and describe the family along many different dimensions. One dimension could be a global one, for example, placing the family along a continuum of *competence.* Is this family functioning optimally, is it functioning adequately, or is it severely dysfunctional (Beavers and Hampson 1993)? Descriptions and reviews of the reliability, validity, and in some cases, clinical utility of a large number of these methods and scoring manuals can be found in the following books: W. Robert Beavers and Robert B. Hampson (1990); Anne E. Copeland and Kathleen M. White (1991); Harold D. Grotevant and Cindy I. Carlson (1989); Theodore Jacob and

Daniel L. Tennenbaum (1988); Patricia K. Kerig and Kristin M. Lindahl (2001); Luciano L'Labate and Dennis A. Bagarozzi (1993); Richard H. Mikesell, Don-David Lusterman, and Susan H. McDaniel (1995); David H. Olson, Candyce S. Russell, and Douglas H. Sprenkle (1989); Barry F. Perlmutter, John Touliatos, and Murray A. Straus (2000); Irving E. Sigel and Gene H. Brody (1990); and Froma Walsh (1993).

Social scientists and mental health professionals often study the dimension of *family structure*. Family structure is characterized by the roles and relationships among the individual members of the family. Who disciplines the children? Who provides leadership and helps in problem solving? Who does one turn to for support and encouragement? The family may include one or several male and/or female adults of various ages, in varying biological relationships with one or several male and/or female children of various ages from infancy through adulthood. Each child and adult has varying physical, cognitive, emotional, and social characteristics and possible problems in living that he or she brings to daily family life. Assessment of family structure and its changes over time may be made to understand, for example, general and specific effects of age, education, marital status, socioeconomic and other social conditions, developmental processes, roles, culture and the acculturation process, and religious beliefs and practices.

Assessment may be made of the dimension *family dynamics*. Family dynamics consist of the sequence of interactions (parent-child exchanges) and transactions (parent$A$-child-parent$B$-child-parent$A$ exchanges); their synchrony, reciprocity, and patterns of mutual influence. When a child hits a sibling, does the mother or father respond first or not at all until one of the sibling cries? What does mother say and do? If the father is present, what does he say or do after watching? Is he silent throughout the encounter? What does each of the children say or do next in response to their mother and/or father? What does the mother and/or father say or do in response to the children's next words or actions? Is there a pattern, across parent-child or sibling-sibling conflicts, especially over time, in how the family acts? Study also may be made of how these interactions and transactions affect family structure and the family subsystem relationships. These patterns may affect individual child, marital, and family characteristics, and these, too,

may change over time. These analyses may provide information about family cohesion and intimacy, distribution of power in the family, decision making, family flexibility, and family competence and adjustment.

A wide variety of chronic or acute stresses may affect family structure and dynamics including, for example, violence between the adults in the home, separation and/or divorce of the parents, and the illness, injury, or death of a child, parent, grandparent, or animal companion.

The assessor decides whether the focus should be on the whole family or one or more of its subsystems: parental, marital, or sibling. One or more family members' individual attitudes, values, and perceptions of family life and relationships may be the focus. Description and ratings of family life may also be made after whole family interviews. Family behavior may also be observed, described, and scored in the home (e.g., at dinner); or coded from videotapes made of the family dinner or in a laboratory (e.g., planning a menu); or by a mental health professional after, for example, hearing an hour-long argument about the lack of manners or a child's refusal to eat at the dinner table. The information obtained from different persons (inside or outside the family), from different methods (objective or subjective), and in different social contexts may be similar, but each may be unique, and all may be relevant for more complete and useful understanding (Hayden et al. 1998; Snyder et al. 1995).

Selection of Assessment Methods

The choice of tasks reflects the purposes of the assessment. A family member's responses to sentences in a questionnaire may provide the necessary and sufficient information about perceptions of a wide spectrum of family dimensions and characteristics. But if the main interest is studying conflict resolution strategies, for example, observation may be necessary. In addition, observing a number of interactions in naturalistic, laboratory, and office settings may allow the assessor to obtain more valid and representative samples of behavior.

There are, of course, significant differences between infants, school-age children, and adolescents. The child's as well as the adult's ages, developmental stages, and cognitive, linguistic, and physical abilities and limitations affect role and task assignments in the family and the ability to complete questionnaires and engage in discussions and tasks.

Self-Report Questionnaires

Questionnaires may be completed at home, in a school or college classroom, or in a waiting room. (For example, the Family Adaptability and Cohesion Evaluation Scale [FACES III: Gorall and Olson 1995; Olson 1986], the McMaster Family Assessment Device [FAD: Epstein, Baldwin, and Bishop 1983], the Family Environment Scale [FES: Moos and Moss 1994], and the Self-Report Family Inventory [SFI: Beavers and Hampson 1995; Hampson, Hulgus, and Beavers 1991].)

Questionnaires have been created to assess a wide variety of family dimensions including:

Family cohesion: Items that refer to the degree of emotional bonding, closeness, and togetherness. For example, "There is closeness in my family but each person is allowed to be special and different." Responses to sentences may lead to hypotheses about whether the family is perceived as *disengaged, separated, connected,* or *enmeshed.*

Family flexibility/adaptability: Items that refer to the amount of or degree of change occurring in family leadership, role relationships, and relationship rules especially under stress. For example, "It is hard to know who is the leader in my family." Answers may lead to hypotheses about whether the family is perceived as *rigid, structured, flexible,* or *chaotic.*

Family problem solving: Items that refer to the ability to resolve both instrumental and affective issues to the level that maintains effective family functioning. For example, "We argue a lot and never solve problems."

Family roles: Items that refer to the current or changing roles and patterns of behavior that facilitate family functioning, including those that meet basic needs, that designate responsibilities for household tasks, maintain appropriate family boundaries, provide nurturance to family members, and assess the existence of alliances and coalitions in the family. For example, "We usually blame one person in our family when things aren't going right."

Affective responsiveness: Items that refer to the family's ability to experience and express an appropriate range, quantity, and quality of feeling.

For example, "Family members pay attention to each other's feelings."

Affective involvement: Items that refer to the extent to which family members are perceived to be interested, be concerned, and to value each other. For example, "In our home, we feel loved."

Behavior control: Items that refer to the perceived rules and standards for behavior maintained by the family for all its members. For example, "It is hard to know what the rules are in our family because they always change."

Family conflict: Items that refer to the presence of stressful encounters and styles and strategies for resolving them. For example, "When things go wrong we blame each other."

Family warmth: Items that refer to the overt and explicit presence and expression of affection and nurturance. For example, "Our family members touch and hug each other."

Communication: Items that refer to listening and speaking skills with each other including variations in the clarity and directness of messages in both instrumental and affective exchanges of information among family members. For example, "Family members pay attention to each other and listen to what is said."

Overall family functioning: Items that ask for a global assessment of the family's ability to accomplish its basic everyday tasks across domains. For example, "On a scale of 1–5, I would rate my family as (1) My family functions very well together . . . (5) My family does not function well together at all. We really need help."

Questionnaires may be completed twice, first with the instructions "Describe your family now" and then "Ideally, how would you like your family to be." The discrepancy between scores has been used as an indicator of satisfaction and the reduction of the discrepancy as an indicator of successful intervention (Gorall and Olson 1995). Scoring of responses can also allow the assessor to place the family into different categories or typologies, for example, *centrifugal or centripetal; balanced or unbalanced; severely disturbed, borderline, midrange, adequate, optimal* (Beavers and Hampson 1990) or *rigidly enmeshed* or *flexibly connected* (Olson 1993). Different family members may view the family differently and these differences may need to be confronted during interventions.

Focused Interviews and Discussion Tasks

Focused interviews are designed to obtain information about specific issues of interest. The whole family may be asked to fill out the questionnaire together—after or instead of individual completions—to come up with one family answer to each of the items, and then asked, as a whole, to provide details of events that led to the family answer. Similar kinds of information may also be obtained by having every family member complete a child behavior checklist with respect to a specific child—including individual administration to a child too young to read. The family is then asked, as a whole, to come up with one answer for each sentence and then to discuss specific events leading to the family answer. Again, differences in perceptions of child behavior and its possible causes, correlates, and consequences may become the focus of interventions.

Focused family interviews may also be conducted by behavioral scientists to obtain information related to theoretically important dimensions related to child and family development and not necessarily related to possible child or family problems. For example, to assess family cohesion and family flexibility the family may be asked to discuss such general issues as time, space, friends, and interests; what a typical day, evening, or week is like; how they handle their daily routines; and family strengths (Epstein, Baldwin, and Bishop 1982; Hayden et al. 1998; Thomas and Olson 1993). More clinically relevant, a family may be asked to identify what they believe to be the most important problems for their family from among a list of common areas of conflict (e.g., bedtime, homework, television, chores, allowances, sibling or peer fighting, drinking, or school). From these lists, the assessor could choose the highest-ranking area of conflict that all members identify as a problem for their family. The family is then asked to discuss this problem and attempt to come to a solution. Many of the discussion tasks are similar to those described by Michael S. Robbins and his colleagues (2001):

- "Each of you tell about the things everyone does in the family: the things that please you the most and make you feel good, and also the things each one does that make you unhappy or mad. Everyone try to give her or his own ideas about this. Go ahead."

- "In every family things happen that cause a fuss now and then. Discuss and talk together about an argument you had, a fight or argument at home that you can remember. Talk together about it, like what started it, who was in on it. See if you can remember what it was all about. Take your time. Go ahead."

- "Suppose all of you had to work out a menu for dinner tonight and would all like to have your favorite foods for dinner, but you can only have one meat, two vegetables, one drink, and one dessert. Talk together about it, but you must decide on one meal you would all enjoy and that has one meat, two vegetables, one drink, and one dessert. Remember you must end up agreeing on just one meal that everyone would enjoy. Okay, go ahead."

Tasks for Families with Very Young Children

With children who do not have the ability to complete a questionnaire because of their age or other factors, other family tasks may be completed. During these tasks, these children's words and actions—including those of an infant—on family behavior may be illuminating. A wide variety of family tasks, especially in a playroom with many age-appropriate toys, can be found in Gary E. Stollak, Anat Barlev, and Ioanna D. Kalogiros (2000) and Kerig and Lindahl (2001). Free play for a period of time allows all family members (which may include a toddler and school-aged and adolescent children) to group themselves as they wish, interact with and/or avoid whomever they choose, and address any topic they want, all without the direction of the assessor. After a period of time, the parents receive instructions to cease free play and to begin other tasks. For example, they are given pencils and crayons and asked to create a family drawing with instructions such as: "Please draw a picture of your family doing something. Try to draw whole people, not cartoon or stick people. Remember, make a picture of your family doing something—some kind of action."

Karen S. Wampler and her colleagues (1989) described several construction tasks including asking the family to build two houses out of various materials (for example, *Lincoln Logs* and *Legos*); the first to match a model house and the second, any other structure they wanted to build.

Other activities could include family reading of a story book, playing simple musical instruments or dancing together to recorded music, and playing board games (such as *Chutes and Ladders* or *Candyland*) in which parents and child roll dice or turn over cards, move pieces according to directions on each card or space, and attempt to reach a goal. Families with very young children are asked to play "peek-a-boo" and blow up and pop soap bubbles. As noted above, mealtime provides an excellent opportunity to observe the family, and if home observation is not practical, observation of mealtime dynamics and family structure are made in the playroom. After completion of the family drawing or other tasks, the family is offered food, and asked to spend some time eating together before proceeding with the assessment. Or, refreshments are simply left on a table in the playroom before the family enters and no further instructions given. Finally, a clean-up task provides a good conclusion to a play session.

Rating Family Behavior

At the conclusion of family interviews or observations of the family in the home, in the laboratory or playroom, or in an office, ratings can be made of the same dimensions of family functioning assessed by questionnaires as well as of many other characteristics (Kerig and Lindahl 2001). Such ratings of family dynamics from family insiders and outsiders and in different social contexts can, of course, be similar in one or more ways and divergent and conflicting in significant ways. These similarities and differences may have great significance for determining and evaluating interventions that would reduce complaints by individuals within and outside the family.

Limitations and Cautions

The multitude of empirical methods and ratings made from standardized family assessments has increased our understanding of important dimensions of family life. Using the results of standardized theoretically and empirically based methods of assessment to determine and implement specific interventions is difficult but ongoing (Beavers and Hampson 1990; Olson, Russell, and Sprenkle 1989; Snyder et al. 1995).

Caution is always needed in interpreting information from the use of any method of assessment when families are from different structures (e.g.,

single parent, gay, lesbian, foster, or blended families) and cultures, especially applying norms derived from assessment of families in majority cultures and from traditional families. Although questionnaires have been translated into languages other than English and completed by persons of various cultures (Olson 1995), observation, description, and empirical scoring of family life across different cultures has not received equal attention.

Assessors must become as knowledgeable as possible of the values and attitudes unique to the family being encountered and informed of their individual life histories, family traditions, and culture—before and even during the assessment. For example, such variables may affect willingness and ease of parents' talking about family (and any marital) matters with the children present, discussing family secrets, accepting the advice from someone from another culture or religion, or accepting the need for the family to change. Behavioral scientists and therapists have become increasingly aware that each family must be viewed as "a unique system and assessed and treated with regard to its unique conditions and relationships" (Olson 1995, p. 231).

The diversity of family life across communities and nations and the importance of understanding culture and minority status has increasingly affected judgments about family structure and dynamics, family psychopathology, and family therapy (Boyd-Franklin 1989; Flores and Carey 2000; McGoldrick, Giordano, and Pearce 1996; Pedersen 1997; Szapocznik and Kurtines 1993).

Empirical study of the similarities and differences of diverse families across the multitude of the world's cultures will lead to greater understanding of human and social development and provide clearer guidelines for those attempting to change family life and educate those who will become parents.

See also: FAMILY DIAGNOSIS/DSM-IV; FAMILY
 DIAGRAMMATIC ASSESSMENT: ECOMAP; FAMILY
 DIAGRAMMATIC ASSESSMENT: GENOGRAM;
 RESEARCH: FAMILY MEASUREMENT; THERAPY:
 FAMILY RELATIONSHIPS; THERAPY: PARENT-CHILD
 RELATIONSHIPS

Bibliography

Beavers, W. R., and Hampson, R. B. (1990). *Successful Families: Assessment and Intervention.* New York: Norton.

Beavers, W. R., and Hampson, R. B. (1993). "Measuring Family Competence." In *Normal Family Processes,* 2nd edition, ed. F. Walsh. New York: Guilford.

Boyd-Franklin, N. (1989). *Black Families in Therapy: A Multisystems Approach.* New York: Guilford.

Copeland, A. P., and White, K. M. (1991). *Studying Families.* Newbury Park, CA: Sage.

Epstein, N. B.; Baldwin, L. M.; and Bishop, D. S. (1982). *McMaster Clinical Rating Scale.* Providence, RI: Brown/Butler Family Research Program.

Epstein, N. B.; Baldwin, L. M.; and Bishop, D. S. (1983). "The McMaster Family Assessment Device." *Journal of Marital and Family Therapy* 9: 171–180.

Flores, M. T., and Carey, G. (2000). *Family Therapy with Hispanics: Toward Appreciating Diversity.* Needham Heights, MA: Allyn and Bacon.

Gorall, D. M., and Olson, D. H. (1995). "Circumplex Model of Family Systems: Integrating Ethnic Diversity and Other Social Systems." In *Integrating Family Therapy: Handbook of Family Psychology and Systems Theory,* ed. R. H. Mikesell, D. D. Lusterman, and S. H. McDaniel. Washington, DC: American Psychological Association.

Grotevant, H. D., and Carlson, C. I. (1989). *Family Assessment: A Guide to Methods and Measurements.* New York: Guilford.

Hampson, R. B., and Beavers, W. R. (1996). "Measuring Family Therapy Outcome in a Clinical Setting: Families that Do Better or Do Worse in Therapy." *Family Process* 35:347–361.

Hampson, R. B.; Hulgus, Y. F.; and Beavers, W. R. (1991). "Comparisons of Self-Report Measures of the Beavers Systems Model and Olson's Circumplex Model." *Journal of Family Psychology* 4:326–340.

Hayden, L. C.; Schiller, M.; Dickstein, S.; Seifer, R.; Sameroff, A. J.; Miller, I.; Keitner, G.; and Rasmussen, S. (1998). "Levels of Family Assessment: I. Family, Marital, and Parent-Child Interaction." *Journal of Family Psychology* 12:7–22.

Jacob, T., and Tennenbaum, D. L. (1988). *Family Assessment: Rationale, Methods, and Future Directions.* New York: Plenum.

Kerig, P. K., and Lindahl, K. M., eds. (2001). *Family Observational Coding Systems: Resources for Systemic Research.* Mahway, NJ: Erlbaum.

L'Labate, L., and Bagarozzi, D. A. (1993). *Sourcebook of Marriage and Family Evaluation.* New York: Brunner/Mazel.

McGoldrick, M.; Giordano, J.; and Pearce, J. K. (1996). *Ethnicity and Family Therapy,* 2nd edition. New York: Guilford.

Mikesell, R. H.; Lusterman, D.; and McDaniel, S. H., eds. (1995). *Integrating Family Therapy: Handbook of Family Psychology and Systems Theory.* Washington, DC: American Psychological Association.

Moos, R. H., and Moos, B. S. (1994). *Family Environment Scale Manual,* 3rd edition. Palo Alto, CA: Consulting Psychologists Press.

Olson, D. H. (1986). "Circumplex Model VII: Validation Studies and FACES III." *Family Process* 25:337–351.

Olson, D. H. (1993). "Circumplex Model of Marital and Family Systems: Assessing Family Functioning." In *Normative Family Processes,* 2nd edition, ed. F. Walsh. New York: Guilford.

Olson, D. H.; Russell, C.; and Sprenkle, D., eds. (1989). *Circumplex Model: Systemic Assessment and Treatment of Families,* 2nd edition. New York: Haworth.

Pedersen, P. B. (1997). "Recent Trends in Cultural Theory." *Applied and Preventive Psychology* 6:221–231.

Perlmutter, B. F.; Touliatos, J.; and Straus, M. A., eds. (2000). *Handbook of Family Measurement Techniques.* Newbury Park, CA: Sage.

Robbins, M. S.; Hervis, O.; Mitrani, V. B.; and Szapocznik, J. (2001). "Assessing Changes in Family Interaction: Structural Family Systems Ratings." In *Family Observational Coding Systems: Resources for Systemic Research,* ed. P. K. Kerig and K. M. Lindahl. Mahway, NJ: Erlbaum.

Sigel, I. E., and Brody, G. H., eds. (1990). *Normal Families,* Vol. I of *Methods of Family Research: Biographies of Research Projects.* Hillsdale, NJ: Erlbaum.

Snyder, K. D.; Cavell, T. A.; Heffer, R. W.; and Mangrum, L. F. (1995). "Marital and Family Assessment: A Multifaceted, Multilevel Approach." In *Integrating Family Therapy: Handbook of Family Psychology and Systems Theory,* ed. R. H. Mikesell, D. D. Lusterman, and S. H. McDaniel. Washington, DC: American Psychological Association.

Stollak, G. E.; Barlev, A.; and Kalogiros, I. D. (2000). "Assessment of the Child and Family in Play Contexts." In *Play Diagnosis and Assessment,* ed. by K. Gitlin, C. E. Schaefer, and A. Sandgrund. New York: Wiley.

Szapocznik, J., and Kurtines, W. M. (1993). "Family Psychology and Cultural Diversity." *American Psychologist* 48:400–407.

Thomas, V., and Olson, D. H. (1993). "Problem Families and the Circumplex Model: Observational Assessment

Using the Clinical Rating Scale (CRS)." *Journal of Marital and Family Therapy* 19:159–175.

Walsh, F., ed. (1993). *Normal Family Processes,* 2nd edition. New York: Guilford.

Wampler, K. S.; Halverson, C. F., Jr.; Moore, J. J.; and Walters, L. H. (1989). "The Georgia Family Q-sort: An Observational Measure of Family Functioning." *Family Process* 28:223–238.

GARY E. STOLLAK

FAMILY BUSINESS

The family business has arrived into its own as a distinct enterprise with unique concerns and issues. In the broadest sense, a family business is an enterprise where family members have influence over strategy and major policies, maintain the intention of keeping the business in the family, own significant portions of stock, and sit on the board (Shanker and Astrachan 1996). Other criteria for a family business include that the founder, or the descendants of the founder, still run the company on a daily basis, and where multiple generations participate in daily operations, and have significant management responsibilities (Holland and Boulton 1984).

Employee-owned businesses vary in their size and type. Sole proprietorships as family businesses represent upwards of 17 million organizations in the United States, 10 percent of which are family farms (Shanker and Astrachan 1996). A sole proprietorship is owned by a single person with other family members likely to help out. Partnerships owned by two or more people represent 1.5 million organizations in the United States (Neubauer and Lank 1998). Private corporations owned by three or more people in the family represent 3.8 million organizations in the U.S., and employ numerous family members with multiple generations (Shanker and Astrachan 1996). Of more than 21 million family-operated companies, over 11,300 have publicly traded stock (Shanker and Astrachan 1996). Examples of family-owned international businesses abound: Tetra Laval, the Wallenberg group, and H&M (Sweden), Hermès, Michelin, Bic, Marie Brizard, and L'Oréal (France), Tata (India), Kuok Group (Hong Kong), Seagram and Bata

(Canada), Fiat, Ferrero, Barillo, Beretta and Benetton (Italy), Lego (Denmark), Caran d'Ache, SGS, and André (Switzerland), C&A (Netherlands), Bahlesen (Germany), Kikkoman (Japan), Claroen Pokphmd (Thailand), and the Rothschild banking family. Estimates of contribution to the global Gross Domestic Product (GDP) from international family businesses is up to 70 percent throughout the non-communist world (Neubauer and Lank 1998). Thus, family businesses can range from a "mom and pop" enterprise with fewer than twenty employees to one that is significantly larger, such as the Coors Brewing Company, to even larger multinational corporations. Perhaps more importantly, these businesses also have a significant impact on the global economy.

Among the most emotionally wrought issues in a family enterprise is who will be the successor to the business. Succession is the transfer of ownership and control to the next generation (Churchill and Hatten 1987; Ward 1987; Goldberg 1991). Succession planning involves efficiently and fairly distributing assets from older to younger generations, passing control of the business in a way that will ensure effective business leadership, and maintaining and promoting family harmony. An assumption of succession is that all parties to the process are satisfied with the outcomes of the process itself (Stempler 1988). Because the rate of succession for family businesses is low—30 percent of family firms are passed from the first generation to the second and 10 percent survive to be passed onto the third generation—it is important to understand how the family business works and what will determine whether or not the business will be successfully passed onto the next generation. Of particular interest to those who study family business succession is how family members who have a business manage conflict, as this is considered to be a key to surviving the succession process.

Because continuity is a unifying concern among all members, succession is considered the ultimate test of a family business (Gersick et al. 1997; Le Van 1999). Thus, conflict can be perceived either as the ultimate threat or ultimate opportunity for a family enterprise. Conflict is a disagreement between two or more interdependent parties who perceive incompatible goals, scarce resources, and interference from others in achieving their goals. Therefore, as part of the succession process, family businesses need to be aware of the five points in which conflict is most likely to occur: (1) the mutual acceptance of roles; (2) the agreement to continue the business; (3) the propensity of a successor to take over; (4) the propensity of an incumbent to step aside; and (5) succession planning.

Mutual Acceptance of Roles

The mutual acceptance of roles is the extent to which family members accept their own and others' relative levels of involvement (Barach 1984; Crane 1982; Post 1993; Sharma 1997; Ward 1988). Involvement means mutual acceptance of the amount of control associated with each family member's role. Research has shown that the family members' mutual acceptance of individual roles is positively related to perceived family harmony (Handler, 1989). Roles can be defined by the number of heirs in line for succession (Bork 1986; Rutigliano 1986; Scranton 1992), the relative position of each heir in the family and the business (Barnes 1988; Kaye 1992), and the clarification of roles and responsibilities of family members in the context of the business (Handler 1989; Rosenberg 1991). For example, due to birth order older siblings with more experience in the family business may hold managerial positions in the firm expecting to be in line as successor to the enterprise, while younger siblings who have gone to college to obtain knowledge badly needed by the enterprise may expect to take over the business. If family members do not mutually accept their and others' roles within the business, they may attempt to undermine the efforts of others in order to achieve what they perceive to be a more equitable distribution of power. This in turn may slow decision making regarding the succession process (Dyer 1986). Thus, managing perception during conflict regarding the mutual acceptance of roles is of key importance to each family business member's satisfaction.

Conflict over the mutual acceptance of roles is also an opportunity to enhance mutual respect, trust, and understanding among family members. In the conflict between the younger and older siblings vying for the role of successor, the incumbent can view disagreements as opportunities for siblings to learn from one another (developing their relationships), exchange information that will enhance the business for all (everyone brings necessary knowledge, skills, and abilities to the table), and create respect for what each sibling has to offer the family business without privileging one experience over the other. Thus, managing conflict effectively means viewing disagreements as opportunities rather than threats, and seeing conflict as an opportunity to learn rather than the destruction of important family relationships. Opportunity is an important view of conflict because when the aforementioned relational features are present in the family business (e.g. mutual respect, trust, and understanding) the level of satisfaction with decision outcomes increases (Dyer 1986; Sharma 1997). Family business members need to be sensitive to the mutual acceptance of roles during the succession process, and utilize disagreements and conflict as a means to clarify perceptions of incompatibility, negotiate the amount of influence each family member has in the business relationship, and promote win-win, mutually satisfying relationships.

Agreement to Continue the Business

Agreement to continue the business occurs when family members are committed to the perpetuation of the business and are willing to work together to ensure its future (Handler 1989). Research has shown that the agreement to continue the business is positively related to perceived family harmony (Babicky 1987) and payoffs from the business (e.g. financial gains, increased market share and growth) (Alexrod 1984). Although the agreement to continue the business is not correlated with any negative aspects, the decision to continue the family business is not a simple one. Family members must unanimously agree regarding the future of the business, what constitutes continuity, and what opportunities for the future are possible. Thus, the decision to continue the business must be one of consensus with clear gains for those involved in the agreement. Additionally, each member of the family business must be willing to put forth what is necessary to perpetuate the enterprise.

Propensity of a Successor to Take Over

Propensity of a successor to take over is the inclination of a successor to take over the leadership of a business (Christensen 1953). Taking over the leadership of the business entails influence, authority, and control. Research has shown that the propensity of a successor to take over is positively related to the acceptance of individual roles, career interests (Handler 1992), and payoffs from the business (Malone 1989). Conflict may occur when anyone voices or displays the interest in taking over the business. This display of interest may lead to resentment from other family members who feel they are being forced to accept roles among family members. Such is the case from the earlier example where both the older siblings who worked in the family business "learning the ropes" as managers and the younger siblings who went to college express interest in becoming successor. Will siblings who expect to become the successor mutually accept another as successor and their (unexpected) subordinated role?

Other family members may also be upset because there is a perceived lack of financial reward for the potential successor. If the enterprise itself has matured or if there is the perception that profits cannot be enhanced or sustained or the market share cannot grow, then a potential successor may not come forward. Thus, without the perception of monetary financial gains, the family enterprise may not succeed to the next generation. Other family members may also believe the potential successor lacks continuity between his or her career interests and the opportunities available in the family enterprise or that the potential successor does not have the type of leadership style needed. Managed effectively, conflict can serve to define terms and clarify needs, expectations, and goals, leading to productive and positive outcomes.

Propensity of an Incumbent to Step Aside

Propensity of an incumbent to step aside is the ability of the present family member manager to let go of the leadership of a family business and hand it over to a successor (Davis 1992). Thorelli (1986) has shown that the propensity of an incumbent to step aside is positively related to how much the incumbent trusts the successor's abilities to run the business and how much faith the incumbent has in the successor's intentions, as well as the incumbent's own interests outside the business. Thus it is important not only that the successor have a high desire to take over and a high level of confidence in his or her own ability to take over the business, but also that the present manager be involved in activities outside the enterprise and look forward to pursuing new activity outside the business.

Conflict can arise when the incumbent endangers the long-term vitality or existence of the enterprise by not adequately addressing continuity issues in turning over the business. If the older and younger siblings cannot reach an agreement regarding their roles following a selection of the new successor, the incumbent may not step down or choose to dissolve the enterprise, and the business will not succeed to the next generation. Without a smooth transition, the incumbent may continue to work as long as possible and then end the family business with retirement and/or death.

Additionally, issues of trust in the successor's capabilities and intentions, and what the incumbent will do next, are often the crux of conflict perceptions. Conflict regarding the propensity of an incumbent to step aside provides the opportunity to make expectations explicit regarding the work, and prepare both the incumbent and successor for a satisfying personal life in the family itself. However, if the incumbent perceives that the older and younger siblings will not work effectively together for the good of the business, or if their family relationships will erode, leading to family members no longer speaking to one another, then the incumbent may choose to not have the business succeed.

Succession Planning

Succession planning is the process for the transfer of management control from one family member to the next (Christensen 1953). Research has shown that succession planning is positively related to the propensity of the incumbent to step aside, the presence of an active advisory board (Christensen 1953), and the agreement to continue the business (Wong, McReynolds, and Wong 1992). Conflict during succession planning can arise when no written plan exists, and when the stockholders connected with the enterprise, including the founder, the family members, the managers, suppliers, and customers, are uncertain of the significant changes associated with the impending shift in power and authority. Additionally, conflict in succession planning may involve disagreements about the knowledge, skills, and abilities of the successor, the educational level, experience, and background of the successor, and the level of trust, faith, and goodwill the successor can generate. Conflict during succession planning can also include disputes over whether family members should take over the enterprise or not, whether the incumbent has accomplished everything desired and possible during his or her reign of the enterprise, whether the incumbent was ready to give up power, what criteria would be used to identify the successor, and how decision outcomes are communicated.

International Family Business Succession

Research on international family business and conflict is incomplete because most studies focus on United States–based family enterprises. There are, however, studies that may shed light on conflict and family business succession in an international context. Differences in ethnic background may influence the expectations of family business members in a succession process (Sharma, 1997). For example, Chau (1991), McGoldrick and Troast (1993), and Wong (1993) suggest that there are differences in the basic philosophy and underlying assumptions of the family members of different ethnic backgrounds with regards to the way succession is handled. For example, while Chinese family enterprises divide the family assets equally among the male members, Japanese family enterprises often have one male heir who is the successor and receives all the assets. Other succession issues that vary across cultures are patterns of communication (e.g. face-saving/confrontation), modes of conflict resolution (e.g. direct/indirect), value given to education, and the position of women in the culture (Chau 1991; Fruin 1980; Lansberg and Perrow 1991; Rothstein 1992; McGoldrick and Troast 1993; Dean 1992; Stallings 1992). For example, in Japan, succession is viewed as a foundation for the professionalism of the children and not a priority, and in China, succession is viewed as a family legacy and a top priority (Dean 1992; Wong, McReynolds, and Wong 1992). Additionally, in Japan women have been denied a visibly prominent role in the family business; however, recent findings have reported that women own 23 percent of all family businesses in Japan (Wild, Wild, and Han 2000). In Australia women own 33 percent of the family businesses, in Canada 31 percent, in Mexico 16 percent, and in the Netherlands women own 15 percent of the family businesses (Wild, Wild, and Han 2000).

Conclusion

The family enterprise continues to be an important element of the world economy and a location for understanding conflict in family relationships internationally. Managing conflict effectively in the process of succession is crucial to preserving the impact family enterprise has on our economy and families themselves. Therefore, whether the family business is based in the United States or across the world, one needs to be aware of the five points in which conflict is most likely to occur: (1) the mutual acceptance of roles; (2) the agreement to continue the business; (3) the propensity of a successor to take over; (4) the propensity of an incumbent to step aside; and (5) succession planning because conflict in family succession is universal.

See also: COMMUNICATION: FAMILY RELATIONSHIPS; CONFLICT: FAMILY RELATIONSHIPS; CONFLICT: PARENT-CHILD RELATIONSHIPS; DECISION MAKING; RICH/WEALTHY FAMILIES; SIBLING RELATIONSHIPS; WORK AND FAMILY

Bibliography

Alexrod, R. (1984). *The Evolution of Cooperation.* New York: Basic Books.

Babicky, J. (1987). "Consulting to the Family Business." *Journal of Management Consulting* 3:25–42.

Barach, J. A. (1984). "Is There a Cure for Paralyzed Family Boards?" *Sloan Management Review* 25:3–12.

Barnes, L. B. (1988). "Incongruent Hierarchies: Daughters and Younger Sons as Company CEOs." *Family Business Review* 1:9–21.

Bork, D. (1986). *Family Business: Risky Business: How to Make It Work.* New York: AMACOM Books.

Chau, T. T. (1991). "Approaches to Succession in East Asian Business Organizations." *Family Business Review* 4:161–179.

Christensen, C. (1953). *Management Succession in Small and Growing Enterprises.* Boston: Division of Research, Harvard Business School.

Churchill, N. C., and Hatten, K. J. (1987). "Non-Market Based Transfers of Wealth and Power: A Research Framework for Family Business." *Journal of Small Business Management* 25:51–64.

Crane, M. (1982). "How to Keep Families from Feuding." *Inc.,* (February):73–79.

Dean, S. M. (1992). "Characteristics of African American Family-Owned Businesses in Los Angeles." *Family Business Review* 5:373–395.

Dyer, Jr., W. G. (1986). *Cultural Change in Family Firms: Anticipating and Managing Business and Family Transitions.* San Francisco: Jossey Bass.

Fruin, W. M. (1980). "The Family as a Firm and the Firm as a Family in Japan: The Case of Kikkoman Shoyo

Company Limited." *Journal of Family History* 5:432–449.

Gersick, K. E.; Davis, J. A.; Hampton, M. M.; and Lansberg, I. (1997). *Generation to Generation: Life Cycles of the Family Business.* Boston: Harvard Business School Press.

Goldberg, S. D. (1991). "Factors Which Impact Effective Succession in Small Family-Owned Businesses: An Empirical Study." Ph.D. dissertation. Amherst: University of Massachusetts.

Handler, W. C. (1989). "Methodological Issues and Considerations in Studying Family Businesses." *Family Business Review* 2:257–276.

Handler, W. C. (1992). "The Succession Experience of the Next Generation." *Family Business Review* 5:283–307.

Holland, P. G., and Boulton, W. R. (1984). "Balancing the 'Family' and the 'Business' in Family Business." *Business Horizons* 27:16–21.

Kaye, K. (1992). "'The Kid Brother.'" *Family Business Review* 5:237–256.

Lansberg, I., and Perrow, E. (1991). "Understanding and Working with Leading Family Businesses in Latin America." *Family Business Review* 4:127–147.

Le Van, G. (1999). *The Survival Guide for Business Families.* London: Routledge.

Malone, S. C. (1989). "Selected Correlates of Business Continuity Planning in the Family Business." *Family Business Review* 2:341–353.

McGoldrick, M., and Troast, J. G. (1993). "Ethnicity, Families, and Family Businesses: Implications For Practitioners." *Family Business Review* 2:401–411.

Neubauer, F., and Lenk, A. G. (1998). *The Family Business: Its Governance for Sustainability.* New York: Routledge.

Post, J. E. (1993). "The Greening of the Boston Park Plaza Hotel." *Family Business Review* 6:131–148.

Rosenberg, C. F. (1991). "Entrepreneurial Couples: Organizational, Marital, and Spouse/Personal Factors that Influence the Quality of Their Working Relationship." Ph.D. dissertation. Philadelphia: Temple University.

Rothstein, J. (1992). "Don't Judge a Book by Its Cover: A Reconstruction of Eight Assumptions about Jewish Family Businesses." *Family Business Review* 5:397–411.

Rutigliano, A. J. (1986). "Family Businesses Need Help From Outside." *Management Review,* February, 26–27.

Scranton, P. (1992). "Learning Manufacture: Education and Shop Floor Schooling in the Family Firm." *Family Business Review* 5:323–342.

Shanker, M. C., and Astrachan, J. (1996). "Your Impact on the Economy." *Family Business Review* 9:25–30.

Sharma, P. (1997). "Determinants of the Satisfaction of the Primary Stakeholders with the Succession Process in Family Firms." Ph.D. dissertation. Calgary: University of Calgary.

Sonnefeld, J. A., and Spence, P. L. (1989). "The Parting Patriarch of a Family Firm." *Family Business Review* 2:355–375.

Stallings, S. L. A. (1992). "Research Note: The Emergence of American-Indian Enterprise." *Family Business Review* 5:413–416.

Stempler, G. L. (1988). "A Study of Succession in Family Owned Businesses." Ph.D. dissertation. Washington, DC: George Washington University.

Thorelli, H. (1986). "Networks: Between Markets and Hierarchies." *Strategic Management Journal* 7:37–51.

Ward, J. L. (1988). "The Special Role of Strategic Planning for Family Businesses." *Family Business Review* 1:105–117.

Wild, J. J.; Wild, K. L.; and Han, J. C. Y. (2000). *International Business: An Integrated Approach.* Upper Saddle River, NJ: Prentice Hall

Wong, B.; McReynolds, S.; and Wong, W. (1992). "Chinese Family Firms in the San Francisco Bay Area." *Family Business Review* 5:355–372.

Wong, S. L. (1993). "The Chinese Family: A Model." *Family Business Review* 6:327–340.

MICHAEL A. GROSS

FAMILY DEVELOPMENT THEORY

Family development theory focuses on the systematic and patterned changes experienced by families as they move through their life course. The term *family* as used here represents a social group containing at least one parent-child relationship. The family group is organized and governed by social norms. The general notion of a family life-cycle has a long history that dates back to 1777 (Mattessich and Hill 1987). A more conscious formulation known as family development theory began after World War II with work on family stress by Reuben Hill (1949) and a later textbook by Evelyn Duvall (1957). The first systematic statement of the approach characterized family development as proceeding through life-cycle stages (family stages) such as early marriage, families with young children, the launching of children out of the home, and the empty nest (Hill and Rodgers 1964). These family stages can be studied on three levels of analysis: the individual-psychological, the interactional-associational, and the societal-institutional.

In the decades following the initial formulation of family development theory, there has been a conscious departure from the life-cycle concept. Roy H. Rodgers (1973) suggests abandoning the family life-cycle concept in favor of a more life-course-oriented concept that he calls *the family career*. Joan Aldous (1978) argues that the family career contains subcareers, most notably the sibling career, the marital career, and the parental career. These, in turn, are strongly influenced by careers external to the family, such as educational and occupational careers. Paul Mattessich and Reuben Hill (1987) maintain that family development unfolds through invariant, universal stages, a conception that is very similar to the aging process. However, the conception of invariant and universal family stages continues to attract criticism (e.g., White 1991; Bengston and Allen 1993). Aldous (1990) believes that the major difference between the life-course and family development perspectives is that the life-course perspective focuses on the individual, whereas the family developmental approach focuses on the family as a group. She maintains that neither approach can properly be called a scientific theory.

In contrast to Aldous's position, James M. White (1991) proposes that family development is a scientific theory because it offers general propositions and can be formulated as a mathematical model that describes the process of family development. Rodgers and White (1993) suggest that the old perspective of families moving through deterministic, invariant stages invites a stagnant and less-productive understanding of family dynamics. Family development theorists Rodgers and White have revised and simplified some of the following key concepts.

Basic Concepts and Propositions

Position is a term denoting a person's place in the kinship structure that is defined by gender, marriage or blood relations, and generational relations. The basic positions within the family are husband, wife, father, mother, son, daughter, brother, and sister.

Norms are social rules that govern group and individual behavior. For example, the incest taboo is a strong and pervasive social rule forbidding mating between family members.

Role is defined as all the norms attached to one of the kinship positions. For instance, in most societies the role of mother entails the norm of nurturing of the young. However, because the positions are defined structurally, the content of a role (the norms) may change from society to society or ethnic subculture to subculture.

Family stage is defined as the period of time in which the structure and interactions of role relationships are noticeably distinct from other periods. The stage is usually inferred from the events that indicate a change in the membership of the family or the way in which members of the family are spatially and interactionally organized. For example, launching a child does not mean the end of the parental role but a change based on the spatial and interactional organization of the family members.

Transitions from one family stage to another are indicated by the events between stages. Family stages are experienced as *on time* or *off time* in terms of the expected timing for these events. For instance, having another child when postadolescent children are leaving home would be "off time."

Family career (family life course) is composed of all the events and periods of time (stages) between events traversed by a family. At the societal level, the stage-graded norms are indicated by the sequence of events followed by most families. For example, a premarital birth is considered *out of sequence* for most people. Variations in families indicate the strength of the norms within any given birth cohort and historical period.

Deviation by large numbers of families from a career sequence is viewed as a source of social change. Social change comes about because families seek to align their sequencing of stages with the sequencing and timing norms of nonfamily institutions (e.g., education and occupation). For instance, as the time required for education rises, the age at which a person marries rises, and the period of fertility available to a couple is reduced. Cross-institutional norms, such as finishing one's education before marriage, create the need for systemic deviation in family career and, hence, social change.

Basic propositions proposed by Aldous (1978) lead to the definition of the process of family development. Rodgers and White (1993), in defining the process, claim the probability for a family to move to a new stage of family development is dependent on the old stage they were in and how long they had been in that stage. They further suggest that the process can be mathematically modeled as a semi-Markov process (Coleman 1981; Tuma and Hannan 1984). Two examples of propositions derived by Rodgers and White are that "normative demands of any given institution must be in line with the stage of the family, otherwise the family is strained" and "institutional normative adaptation is preceded by systematic behavioral deviance" (1993, p. 244).

Critiques

Debate continues as to the usefulness of concepts such as *developmental tasks* and the amount of emphasis on structure rather than interaction. Family researchers using family development concepts have produced only modest empirical correlations with dependent variables such as marital satisfaction. Developmental scholars argue that these disappointing results are due to a lack of appropriate measurement of the concepts. Critics respond that this is because the concepts are too vague or ambiguous. In addition, the focus on the modal (center point of all variations) career has been criticized as concealing variations that are due to age cohort, ethnicity, race, and gender.

Research

Despite criticisms, family development theory and its associated concept of family life-cycle stages remains one of the most internationally popular academic approaches to the study of the families. Researchers have applied this theory to such diverse topics as work-family interface (White 1999), family computer uses (Watt and White 1999), blended families (Baxter; Braithewaite; and Nicholson 1999), and sexual orientation (Friedman 1998). This approach has also proved useful to international researchers; examples include the study of German families (Vaskovics 2000), Eastern European families (Judge 1999), and families of India (Desai 1993).

In addition to the academic research, this theory has been useful to practitioners and therapists in several areas. For example, applications of the theory have been undertaken in the study of stress (e.g., Klein and Aldous 1988), traumatic brain injury (Moore, Stambrook, and Peters 1993), alcoholism (Rotunda; Scherer; and Imm 1995), and schizophrenia (Stromwall and Robinson 1998). The practical applicability of this theory has greatly benefited from the substantial literature on using family development theory as a therapeutic tool to assist in the analysis of on-time careers and events (Carter and McGoldrick 1988; Falicov 1987).

Conclusion

Future improvements of family development theory may bring the possibility of integration between the life-course perspective and family development theory (Aldous 1990; Bengston and Allen 1993). White (2000) suggested that such integration might pave the way for ever-wider scope and application and explanatory power for this popular approach. There is little doubt that international scholars will continue to use the family development approach to assist in descriptive and cross-cultural comparative analysis of family stages and the family life course.

See also: ADULTHOOD; CHILDHOOD; ELDERS; FAMILY LIFE EDUCATION; FAMILY SYSTEM THEORY; FAMILY THEORY; RETIREMENT; STRESS; TRANSITION TO PARENTHOOD

Bibliography

Aldous, J. (1978). *Family Careers*. New York: John Wiley & Sons.

Aldous, J. (1990). "Family Development and the Life Course: Two Perspectives." *Journal of Marriage and the Family* 52:571–583.

Baxter, L. A.; Braithewaite, D. O.; and Nicholson, J. H. (1999). "Turning Points in the Development of Blended Families." *Journal of Social and Personal Relationships* 16:291–313.

Bengston, V. L., and Allen, K. R. (1993). "The Life Course Perspective Applied to Families over Time." In *Sourcebook of Family Theories and Methods: A Contextual Approach,* ed. P. Boss; W. Doherty; R. LaRossa; W. Schumm; and S. Steinmetz. New York: Plenum.

Carter, E. A., and McGoldrick, M., eds. (1988). *The Changing Family Cycle: A Framework for Family Therapy.* 2nd edition. New York: Gardner Press.

Coleman, J. S. (1981). *Longitudinal Data Analysis*. New York: Basic Books.

Duvall, E. M. (1957). *Family Development*. Philadelphia: Lippincott.

Falicov, C., ed. (1987). *Family Transitions*. New York: Guilford.

Friedman, R. C. (1998). "On Sexual Orientation and Family Development." *American Journal of Orthopsychiatry* 68:653–653.

Hill, R. (1949). *Families Under Stress*. New York: Harper & Row.

Hill, R., and Rodgers, R. H. (1964). "The Developmental Approach." In *Handbook of Marriage and the Family*, ed. H. T. Christensen. Chicago: Rand McNally.

Judge, S. L. (1999). "Eastern European Adoptions: Current Status and Implications for Intervention." *Topics in Early Childhood Special Education* 19:244–252.

Klein, D. M., and Aldous, J., eds. (1988). *Social Stress and Family Development*. New York: Guildford.

Mattessich, P., and Hill, R. (1987). "Life Cycle and Family Development." In *Handbook of Marriage and the Family*, ed. M. B. Sussman and S. K. Steinmetz. New York: Plenum.

Moore A.; Stambrook, M.; and Peters, L. (1993). "Centripetal and Centrifugal Family-Life Cycle Factors in Long-Term Outcome Following Traumatic Brain Injury." *Brain Injury* 7:247–255.

Rodgers, R. H. (1973). *Family Interaction and Transaction: The Development Approach*. Englewood Cliffs, NJ: Prentice Hall.

Rodgers, R. H., and White J. H. (1993). "Family Development Theory." In *Sourcebook of Family Theories and Methods: A Contextual Approach*, ed. P. Boss; W. Doherty; R. LaRossa; W. Schumm; and S. Steinmetz. New York: Plenum.

Stromwall, L. K., and Robinson, E. A. R. (1998). "When a Family Member Has a Schizophrenic Disorder: Practice Issues Across the Family Life Cycle." *American Journal of Orthopsychiatry* 68:580–589.

Tuma, N. B., and Hannan, M. T. (1984). *Social Dynamics*. New York: Academic Press.

Vaskovics, L. A. (2000). "Family Development in Germany—Socio-demographic Processes, Theory, Law, and Politics with Respect to the GDR." *Kolner Z. Soziologie* 52:383-385.

Watt, D., and White, J. M. (1999). "Computers and the Family: A Family Development Perspective." *Journal of Comparative Family Studies* 30:1–15.

White, J. M. (1991). *Dynamics of Family Development: A Theoretical Perspective*. New York: Guilford.

White, J. M. (1999). "Work-Family Stage and Satisfaction with Work-Family Balance." *Journal of Comparative Family Studies* 30:163–175.

White, J. M. (2000). "The Future of Theory in the Study of Families: A Programmatic Essay." Paper presented at the plenary Session, Theory Construction and Research Methodology Workshop, National Council on Family Relations, Mineapolis, MN, November.

JAMES M. WHITE

FAMILY DIAGNOSIS/ DSM-IV

Family therapy is based on the theory that healthy systems prevent psychological maladjustment. When the family system functions properly, adequate support is available for individuals in the family to make necessary adjustments to most stressors in life. If the stressors are extreme when self, family, and community resources are weak, symptoms are likely to develop in at least one member of the family system. When resources are sufficiently strengthened, symptoms generally disappear, as the individual is now able to respond effectively to stress and/or demands for change. Intervening to strengthen family functioning resources is the most efficient access point because family members then continue on a daily basis to provide the needed support for the individual(s) under stress. If the cause of the stress is within the family functioning, such as family violence, the patterns of dysfunction must be interrupted and displaced with healthy patterns. Family therapists believe that focusing only on the external symptoms caused by internal system stress is misleading and ineffective.

The association of family functioning and individual symptoms has been defined on four levels (Kaslow 1996):

- The problem is solely in the family functioning and is not manifesting individual symptoms in family members.

- The problem is primarily in the family functioning but individual symptoms are clearly resulting from the family problem.

- The problem is primarily individual but does have critical family functioning components to effectively understand and treat.

- The problem is primarily individual but treating the family functioning component greatly enhances the treatment outcome.

Even if the family functioning is not the cause of the problem, it is a vital component to planning effective treatment. Insurance companies authorizing treatment have not yet understood this. They still require diagnoses based on individual symptoms described in the *Diagnostic and Statistical Manual of Mental Disorders*.

Understanding the DSM-IV Classification System

The *Diagnostic and Statistical Manual of Mental Disorders* (DSM) classification system of the American Psychiatric Association (APA) attempts to unify language about mental disorders. This classification system developed from the need to collect statistical information. Roots of the DSM reach back before the publication of the first DSM in 1952 as a clinical parallel of the International Classification of Diseases (ICD-6) adopted by the World Health Organization (WHO) in 1948. Nineteenth-century census data did not have adequate categories to describe mental illnesses. In 1917, the APA expanded the classification concept to gathering uniform statistics across mental hospitals. After World War II, the Veterans Administration expanded the nomenclature developed by the APA to include more outpatient presentations of servicemen and veterans. This clinical utility focus continued and incorporated more research with each publication: DSM-I in 1952, DSM-II in 1968, DSM-III in 1980, DSM-III-R in 1987, DSM-IV in 1994, and DSM-IV-TR in 2000. Unfortunately, the wide acceptance of the DSM as the full and complete picture of mental illness overlooks the value of family therapy theories regarding the underlying diagnosis and treatment of symptomatic behavior.

DSM-IV is designed to facilitate clinical and research shared language. Special efforts have been made to address the impact of culture: where relevant, a special paragraph is devoted to cultural variations within the text describing each diagnosis; the appendix includes a description of culturally related syndromes that have not been included

in the DSM classification system; and the appendix includes a brief discussion of steps the clinician can take in determining impact of culture on the diagnosis. The DSM-IV is organized for making diagnoses using the following guidelines:

- Axis I: Clinical disorders and other conditions that may be a focus of clinical attention (including V codes);

- Axis II: Personality disorders and mental retardation;

- Axis III: General medical conditions;

- Axis IV: Psychosocial and environmental problems; and

- Axis V: Global assessment of functioning scale (GAF).

Perhaps because of the DSM's roots in the medical model and its wide acceptance as the standard, current insurance coverage of behavioral health/mental illness as a medical problem, and the relatively new systems theory and research, a true family systems model of understanding mental illness has not yet been included in the DSM classification. Axis IV identifies psychosocial and environmental problems that may affect diagnosis and treatment, but insurance companies will not provide coverage without an Axis I diagnosis. Family problems are identified on Axis IV in the category *Problems with Primary Support Group*. Family functioning problems can be identified on Axis I with diagnoses under the category *Other Conditions That May Be a Focus of Clinical Attention*; however, the V codes V61.20 (*Parent-Child Relational Problem*), V61.1 (*Partner Relational Problem*), V61.8 (*Sibling Relational Problem*), V61.21 (*Child Abuse*), and V61.1 (*Adult Abuse*) alone are generally not considered to be medical problems covered by insurance. The policies of insurance companies tend to shape the thinking of clinicians and consequently researchers. Thus, a linear medical model of simplistic static answers to complex dynamic problems is reinforced.

In preparation for the DSM-IV, work began among professionals (Group for the Advancement of Psychiatry (GAP) Committee on the Family 1996; Kaslow 1993) to construct new classification schemas for family functioning. Work begun by the 1986 GAP Committee on the Family—later joined by the Coalition on Family Diagnosis (with members from fourteen different organizations)—resulted in the *Global Assessment of Relational Functioning* (GARF) being included in the DSM-IV appendix under the category *Criteria Sets and Axes Provided for Further Study*. The two new schemas for family functioning were a rated comprehensive range of functioning (the GARF as a dimensionalized rating parallel to the GAF individual functioning now used on Axis V) and a categorical identification of functioning (*Classification of Relational Diagnoses* [CORD]) parallel to the discrete descriptive diagnoses of individual disorders now used on Axes I and II). (For more on GARF and these classification schemas, see next section, below.) However, work on the CORD was not completed in time for DSM-IV. Recommendations in the DSM-IV note that the GARF can be included along with the GAF on Axis V. This inclusion was a significant change in attitude of the APA; professionals recognized the need for the development of a systems method for understanding mental illness. However, the challenge has fallen to family therapists to provide the necessary research to verify the concepts in systemic diagnosis/assessment and treatment/intervention before DSM-V is published.

GARF Development

As the only truly systemic family relations diagnostic tool to be included in the DSM-IV, the GARF was developed by leaders in the field of family assessment. It was intended to be simple to learn and use. However, a basic understanding of family systems functioning seems to be necessary in order to accurately interpret the rating. In the DSM-IV (1996) appendix describing the GARF, the dimensionalized scale (1–100) is grouped into five twenty-point categories ranging from, at the top of the scale, "81–100 Overall. Relational unit is functioning satisfactorily from self-report of participants and from perspectives of observers" (p. 758) to "1–20 Overall. Relational unit has become too dysfunctional to retain continuity of contact and attachment" (p. 759) at the bottom. These ratings are based on three basic variables that describe system functioning (DSM-IV 1994, p. 758):

- Problem solving—skills in negotiating goals, rules, and routines; adaptability to stress; communication skills; ability to resolve conflict.

- Organization—maintenance of interpersonal roles, subsystem boundaries, and hierarchical functioning; coalitions and distribution of power, control, and responsibility.

- Emotional climate—tone and range of feelings; quality of caring, empathy, involvement, and attachment/commitment; sharing of values; mutual affective responsiveness, respect, and regard; quality of sexual functioning.

These variables may be considered the *organizational structure* of a system with certain rules about who does what, when, where, and why; the *communication processes* that develop, sustain, and adapt those structural guidelines; and the *emotional result* of family members feeling safe, supported, heard, and understood. Lynelle Yingling and her colleagues (1998) helped pilot test the GARF for the DSM-IV, and continued research on the GARF in the doctoral clinic for Ph.D. interns in family therapy at Texas A&M University-Commerce. Clinical experience indicated that the GARF had greater usefulness when the three variables were measured separately rather than being combined as a global rating as directed in the DSM-IV. Models of family therapy intervention strategies can be correlated with each of the variables. When the organizational structure is unstable or rigidly distorted, working to get the structure realigned and stabilized is the goal of therapy. Examples of distortion are the parentification of children, unequal spousal power resulting in overt or covert power struggles, and adults still being tied to their biological parents in a child role rather than free to act as adults. When the structure is functioning normally but the communication skills are weak, focusing on learning to communicate effectively is the therapeutic goal. Several models have been developed to enhance open, clear, understandable, and accepted communication among family members. When both of those system dimensions are in need of help, all relevant goals for system change are integrated into the therapy. When the system is functioning normally, the Axis I symptoms of depression/substance abuse (from not being able to communicate fears and feel heard), anxiety (from organizational instability), and conduct disorder/family violence (from organizational distortion) will likely disappear. Axis II personality disorders (possibly from being raised in a chaotic family system) are much more difficult to eliminate because the relational patterns have been deeply engrained in the developmental process during childhood.

Family Therapy Theorists' Concerns About Using the DSM Diagnosis System

Because family therapists provide services for clients covered by insurance contracts, family therapy effectiveness is limited by the requirements of the insurance company to assign an individual diagnosis in order to be paid. In family therapy theory, a primary goal is to reframe the presenting individual symptom as a family system problem that takes the blame off the individual and creates a team approach for solving the problem. Placing an individual diagnosis on the insurance claim runs counter to successfully depathologizing and reframing the problem. If the family therapist tries to explain the reason for an individual diagnosis, the communication does not make logical sense to the client, thus creating dysfunctional communication in the therapist-client system. If an individual in the family does not meet criteria for an individual DSM diagnosis but the therapy will not be covered without a diagnosis, what is the therapist to do?

The courts are another payer requiring the use of DSM in order to be accepted as a professional. Scientific evidence is required to substantiate expert testimony in legal cases. The DSM system has the most scientific evidence of any classification system used. Thus, it is the preferred evidence resource in court.

Even if insurance companies and courts were enlightened about the efficiency of family therapy and accepted family functioning diagnoses as sufficient, many family therapists would see using a family diagnosis as unethical (Becvar and Becvar 2000; Denton 1989; Denton 1990; Strong 1993). According to the constructivist philosophy of family therapy, classifying human behavior is seen as limiting the possibilities for growth, and consequently harmful. Using a pathology-based medical model—such as the DSM—is even more limiting in effect. Another dilemma is the lack of consensus among family therapists on how to diagnose family functioning. One goal of the GARF development was to create a consensus in the field concerning an accepted model of family assessment.

Continuous Improvement Options

If there is an inherent tension between family therapists and the current DSM-IV requirements, how can the tension be resolved? One option is to work within the DSM system to incorporate family assessment using the GARF and the CORD, as well as enhancement of Axis IV psychosocial stressor definitions. A unified effort will be required to achieve this goal in DSM-V. Another option is to develop a separate, parallel classification system. Several options are discussed in Florence Kaslow's (1996) *Handbook of Relational Diagnosis and Dysfunctional Family Patterns.* Perhaps a third option is for family therapists to abandon the use of diagnosing and participation in the current insurance and court testimony requirements (Becvar and Becvar 2000). Professionals could make a greater effort to educate insurance companies and courts about the efficiency of family therapy without diagnosis; some Employee Assistance Programs (EAP) accept this premise. If education were unsuccessful, moving away from payment by insurance and/or courts and accepting the financial risk of serving only self-paying clients would be a dramatic way for family therapists to make a statement consistent with systemic beliefs.

See also: CHILDREN OF ALCOHOLICS; CONDUCT DISORDER; DEVELOPMENTAL PSYCHOPATHOLOGY; FAMILY ASSESSMENT; FAMILY SYSTEMS THEORY; RESEARCH: FAMILY MEASUREMENT; THERAPY: FAMILY RELATIONSHIPS

Bibliography

American Psychiatric Association. (1994). *Diagnostic and Statistical Manual of Mental Disorders,* 4th edition. Washington, DC: American Psychiatric Association.

American Psychiatric Association. (2000). *Diagnostic and Statistical Manual of Mental Disorders-Text Revision,* 4th edition, rev. edition. Washington, DC: American Psychiatric Association.

Becvar, D. S., and Becvar, R. J. (2000). *Family Therapy: A Systemic Integration,* 4th edition. Boston: Allyn and Bacon.

Denton, W. H. (1989). "DSM-III-R and the Family Therapist: Ethical Considerations." *Journal of Marital and Family Therapy* 15(4):367–378.

Denton, W. H. (1990). "A Family Systems Analysis of DSM-III-R." *Journal of Marital and Family Therapy* 16(2):113–126.

Group for the Advancement of Psychiatry Committee on the Family. (1996). "Global Assessment of Relational Functioning Scale (GARF): I. Background and Rationale." *Family Process* 35(2):155–190.

Kaslow, F. W. (1993). "Relational Diagnosis: An Idea Whose Time Has Come?" *Family Process* 32(June):255–259.

Kaslow, F. W., ed. (1996). *Handbook of Relational Diagnosis and Dysfunctional Family Patterns*. New York: Wiley.

Strong, T. (1993). "DSM-IV and Describing Problems in Family Therapy." *Family Process* 32(June):249–253.

World Health Organization. (1948) Manual of the International Statistical Classification of Diseases, Injuries, and Causes of Death. Sixth Revision of the International Lists of Diseases and Causes of Death. Geneva: Author.

Yingling, L. C.; Miller, W. E.; McDonald, A. L.; and Galewaler, S. T. (1998). *GARF Assessment Sourcebook: Using the DSM-IV Global Assessment of Relational Functioning*. Philadelphia: Brunner/Mazel.

LYNELLE C. YINGLING

FAMILY DIAGRAMMATIC ASSESSMENT

ECOMAP *T. Laine Scales, Renee H. Blanchard*

GENOGRAM *J. Phillip Stanberry*

ECOMAP

The ecomap, also called a sociogram, is a visual assessment tool depicting the relationships between a family and its social network. As the name signifies, therapist and client together map out connections between the family and its ecological environment. Identifying these connections clarifies and organizes data on a family's environment; highlights energy that flows into and out of the family; and raises issues such as network size and stability, reciprocity of relationships, and access to or deprivation of available resources.

The ecomap diagram consists of circles, lines, and arrows (see Figure 1). Standard symbols are used to express energy that flows from a person or family to other important people and institutions. For example, a solid line may indicate a strong and healthy relationship, while a diffused line represents a weaker tie. Arrows indicated direction of energy flow and conflicted or broken relationships may be represented by interrupted lines. Using the ecomap, the therapist and family can identify the external relationships that are nourishing, as well as those that are wounded. This empowers families to know where to begin making changes.

The social worker Ann Hartman first introduced the ecomap in 1978 in her article "Diagrammatic Assessment of Family Relations." Hartman's work evolves from the school of family theories known as family systems theory, which grew out of the general systems theory applied to sciences such as physics, biology, and anthropology. The concept quickly became popular with family therapists in the United States and the United Kingdom.

Since its creation, the ecomap has been used in a variety of practice settings. Other social workers who have joined Hartman in refining the ecomap include Joan Laird and Mark Mattaini. Although originating in social work, the use of this tool spans disciplinary boundaries; literature on nursing, psychology, law, and other disciplines salutes the usefulness of family diagrammatic tools. In recent years, new computer software allows professional helpers to develop computer-generated diagrammatic assessments such as ecomaps and genograms. Two such resources are "Ecotivity" by Wonderware and Mattaini's software companion to "Visual Ecoscan for Clinical Practice."

Helping professionals from the United States, Canada, the United Kingdom, and New Zealand have written about the value of utilizing family diagrammatic tools with families. However, virtually no literature exists on the usefulness of the ecomap with non-Western cultures. The ecomap may be an effective cross-cultural tool, especially in situations when language differences may impede therapeutic process. The graphic may be shared with and interpreted for others in the family who may not speak the language of the therapist. In addition, the ecomap promotes the value of communal relationships, highly valued in non-Western cultures, and highlights the strength of a family's ability to connect with those around them. However, practitioners must carefully consider the cultural context before using the ecomap and be

FIGURE 1

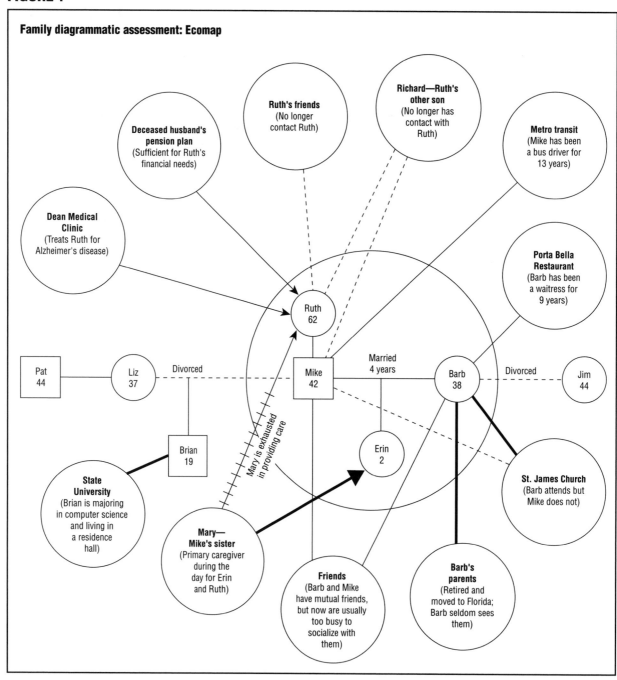

Family diagrammatic assessment: Ecomap

Source: Redrawn from Zastrow and Kirst-Ashman. (2001).

prepared to adapt its use. For example, when gathering information from a Middle Eastern or Asian family, clients are not likely to be sitting in the helping professional's office answering pointed questions. It will be the responsibility of the helping professional to listen closely to the family's stories, however they are revealed, and then be willing to piece together the information in a diagrammatic format for further use.

See also: FAMILY ASSESSMENT; FAMILY DIAGRAMMATIC ASSESSMENT: GENOGRAM; FAMILY SYSTEMS THEORY

Bibliography

Hartman, A. (1995). "Diagrammatic Assessment of Family Relationships." *Families in Society* 76(2):111–122.

Hartman, A., and Laird, J. (1983). *Family-Centered Social Work Practice*. New York: Free Press.

Mattaini, M. A. (1993). *Visual EcoScan for Clinical Practice*. Washington, DC: NASW Press.

Mattaini, M. A. (1993). *More than a Thousand Words: Graphics for Clinical Practice*. Washington, DC: NASW Press.

Zastrow, C. and Kirst-Ashman, K. K. (2001). *Understanding Human Behavior and the Social Environment*, 5th edition. Pacific Grove, CA: Brooks/Cole.

Other Resource

Wonderware. "Ecotivity." Available from http://www.clark.net/pub/wware/wware.html.

T. LAINE SCALES
RENEE H. BLANCHARD

GENOGRAM

The *genogram* is a map of family process. It can be described as a graphic representation of families that charts the interactional processes over three generations (McGoldrick, Gerson, and Shellenberger 1999). With its lines, boxes, circles, and symbols, the genogram records important facts, life-changing events, and complex relationships of a family system. These deceptively simple explanations capture the essence of a complex clinical and consulting instrument that depicts nuances of description and relationship that may be lost in larger narratives or omitted in an overly intense focus upon self.

The construction of a genogram is an interpersonal event in which an individual, couple, or family collaborate with a consulting professional in the gathering, recording, and interpreting of data about family relationships. Data are initially drawn from clients' memories as they report and interpret events. These are recorded with standardized symbols that indicate dates, descriptions of events, perceived relationships between family members, pertinent information about deaths, births, addictions, and illnesses, and family secrets known to the client. An example of a four-generation genogram with significant relational and sociological data is presented in Figure 2.

The meaning of events and relationships within the family is a function of individual memory and is of equal importance with objective facts, because memory intrudes itself into one's interpretation of present events. The role of memory in present events has long been debated in professional circles but, nevertheless, is still taken seriously by investigators from varied and diverse fields of study including anthropology, psychology, sociology, and philosophy.

Many clinical observers relate the genogram to the theory of Murray Bowen (Becvar and Becvar 2000) because it easily communicates the intergenerational transmission of anxiety that is focused around closeness/distance issues of relationships; these dynamics are the centerpieces of his theory. The genogram's depiction of dates, sequences of nodal events, and descriptions of relationships, together with the evolved context of family history, provides a picture where marital and family problems can be readily identified (Guerin and Pendagast 1976; Titelman 1998).

Though similar to the ecomap, the genogram can also identify community and other systems that interact with the family as well as beliefs, rituals, and customs of culture. This function is particularly important because the cultural diversity is a reality for everyone. Family professionals must therefore be sensitive to the contours of cultural practice.

Culturally, the genogram is also used to chart the uniqueness of families. Using the genogram, culturally sensitive professionals can recognize both the strengths and vulnerabilities of minority families—as represented by diverse family forms and relationships—and therefore avoid harmful labeling. For example, African-American families often include blood and non-blood members, informally adopted children, and varied support arrangements (Boyd-Franklin 1989). Asian and other immigrant families may live in multigenerational households in which the opinions of senior members are revered and respected in ways unfamiliar to western family practice (Tseng and Hsu 1991). While nontraditional by some standards, family professionals now find evidence that varying cultural traditions of family life can and do provide the nurturance, care, and respect attributed to healthy family relationships and a place where children can grow to responsible adulthood.

Personal genograms help sensitize family professionals and consultants to their own multigenerational issues and the differences between their clients' values and cultures and their own (Hardy

FIGURE 2

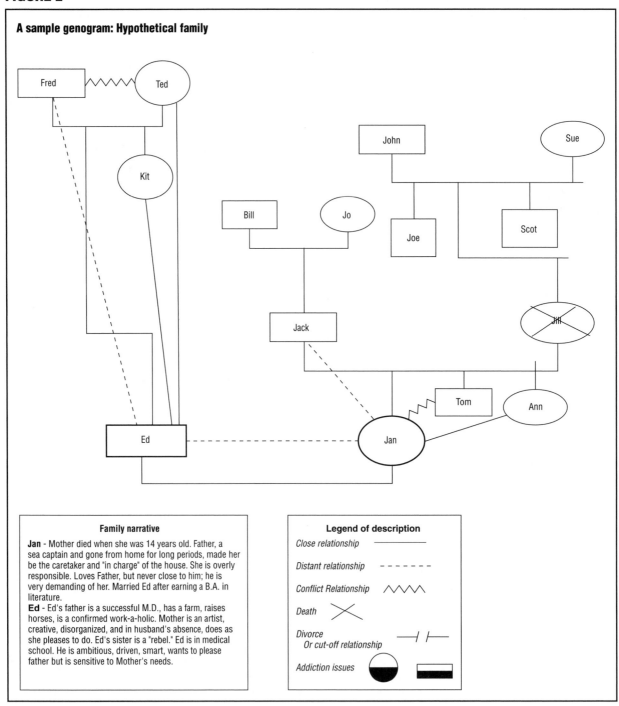

A sample genogram: Hypothetical family

Family narrative

Jan - Mother died when she was 14 years old. Father, a sea captain and gone from home for long periods, made her be the caretaker and "in charge" of the house. She is overly responsible. Loves Father, but never close to him; he is very demanding of her. Married Ed after earning a B.A. in literature.

Ed - Ed's father is a successful M.D., has a farm, raises horses, is a confirmed work-a-holic. Mother is an artist, creative, disorganized, and in husband's absence, does as she pleases to do. Ed's sister is a "rebel." Ed is in medical school. He is ambitious, driven, smart, wants to please father but is sensitive to Mother's needs.

Legend of description

Close relationship ——————

Distant relationship - - - - - -

Conflict Relationship ∧∧∧∧

Death ✕

Divorce
Or cut-off relationship

Addiction issues

With its lines, boxes, circles, and symbols, the genogram records important facts, life-changing events, and complex relationships of a family system.

and Laszloff 1995). Therapists, consultants, and educators can construct a three-part genogram that records demographics (dates, places, absences, and relocations), relationships (conflicted, close, or disconnected), and cultural contexts (coping strategies, loss, grief, or community resources). When this personal narrative is in focus, the family professional's experience of cultural difference can be made clearer and can therefore obtain an uncluttered view of diversity and its meaning.

The genogram has multiple applications. A selected literature review reveals its use in assessment of belief systems, serious illness and aging issues, career choices, family developmental issues, sexual attitudes, women's issues, organizational assessment, and consultation.

Thus, the genogram is widely used for assessing family dynamics, either in general or focused around specific issues. This versatile instrument is used in both consultation and research. Its value resides in objective and subjective evaluation as well as the collaborative development of a family narrative.

See also: FAMILY ASSESSMENT; FAMILY DIAGRAMMATIC ASSESSMENT: ECOMAP; TRIANGULATION

Bibliography

Becvar, D. S., and Becvar, R. J. (2000). *Family Therapy: A Systemic Integration,* 4th edition. Boston: Allyn and Bacon.

Boyd-Franklin, N. (1989). *Black Families in Therapy: A Multisystems Approach.* New York: Guilford Press.

Guerin, P. J., and Pendagast, E. G. (1976). "Evaluation of Family System and Genogram." In *Family Therapy: Theory and Practice,* ed. P. J. Guerin. New York: Gardner Press.

Hardy, K. V., and Laszloff, T. A. (1995). "The Cultural Genogram: Key to Training Culturally Competent Family Therapists." *Journal of Marital and Family Therapy* 21:227–238.

Hargrave, T. D., and Anderson, W. T. (1997). "Finishing Well: A Contextual Family Therapy Approach to the Aging Family." In *The Aging Family: New Visions in Theory, Practice, and Reality,* ed. T. D. Hargrave and S. M. Hanna. Philadelphia: Brunner/Mazel.

McGoldrick, M.; Gerson, R.; and Shellenberger, S. (1999). *Genograms in Family Assessment,* 2nd edition. New York: Norton.

Milewski-Hertlein, K. A. (2001). "The Use of a Socially Constructed Genogram in Clinical Practice." *American Journal of Family Therapy* 29:23–38.

Titelman, P. (1998). "Family Systems Assessment Based on Bowen Theory." In *Clinical Applications of Bowen Family Systems Theory,* ed. P. Titelman. New York: Haworth Press.

Tseng, W-S., and Hsu, J. (1991). *Culture and Family: Problems and Therapy.* New York: Haworth Press.

Walsh, F. (1993). "Conceptualization of Normal Family Processes." In *Normal Family Processes,* 2nd edition, ed. F. Walsh. New York: Guilford Press.

J. PHILLIP STANBERRY

FAMILY FOLKLORE

Family folklore encompasses the traditional expressions that people make, say, and do in the constitution of family life and in consideration of family members, events, and history. Traditional expressive behavior helps members identify themselves as a family group over space and time and provides knowledge about appropriate actions and ways to find meaning in the world. Material culture connected with family life may include the vernacular architecture of homes and other arts learned in families. Folklorists are increasingly interested in the production or display of items significant to the family, including heirlooms, quilts, crafts, photographs, home videos, and other memory objects. Traditional verbal expressions important to families include names, songs, stories, sayings, proverbs, riddles, and inside jokes. Customary expressions play an essential part in family life and often incorporate verbal and material traditions also. These customs may occur as daily and weekly routines as well as annual, seasonal, or life-cycle events. Some customs practiced by families move members through the day from songs in the morning, to games at midday, and to bedtime stories or lullabies before a night's rest. Customary actions can help family members assign household chores and responsibilities, maintain gardens and animals, prepare and consume food, and negotiate shared living space. Life-cycle events mark changes and transformations in the family involving birth, puberty, marriage, migrations, reunions, and death. Holidays and festivals unite the family with wider communities.

The identification of three major types of family folklore matches the categories of material, verbal, and customary lore that folklorists in the United States have used to study their field since the 1970s. The role of folklore in family life can be better understood by considering some specific forms of folklore in each major category. Material culture has been overlooked by some folklorists interested in customs and spoken traditions, whereas other folklorists have noted the significance of artifacts in understanding a group's way of life. Many families around the world still live in structures constructed with traditional designs and local materials, and most families manipulate their built environment to match their needs. The arrangement of objects and of domestic living space can both reflect and influence the values and identities of family members. In *The Dynamics of Folklore,* Barre Toelken (1996) describes the initial worldview of a baby in Anglo or European cultures who lives in a home with flat, painted ceilings, a crib with sharp angles, and distance from other family members. He compares this with a Navajo child in a traditional hogan, surrounded by a domed roof of mud and stones, a cradleboard that allows an upright view, and integration with family activities. Folklorist Henry Glassie (1999) includes photographs and drawings of family dwellings in Sweden, Turkey, England, Wales, Ireland, Bangladesh, and several areas of the United States in *Material Culture.* Glassie indicates that the structure, materials, interior layout, and decoration of houses reflect and influence the knowledge and culture of individuals, families, and their communities.

Physical buildings and their interior furnishings may or may not identify residents as family members, but dwelling places often provide physical and symbolic shelter for families. Many cultures divide living space and attendant duties according to gender or age; some cultures by economic necessity or by deeply held beliefs minimize divisions of public and private space. Therefore, the production and arrangement of objects and space can play an important role in how a family signifies and understands relationships among members, between the genders, and with other community members. Many folklorists interested in material culture value objects made by hand using traditional methods and materials. Skills for making these items are often learned and shared in families. Some of these arts include weaving, welding, pottery, woodworking, quilting, basketry, cooking, and painting. Sometimes the artifacts actually make up the home, whereas at other times the objects are used functionally for household chores or for decoration. Michael Owen Jones (1987), a folklorist interested in material culture, points out that even home remodeling allows for the personalization of space. Jones discusses ways that people change suburban homes to serve better the needs and values of the residents. Folklorist Barbara Kirshenblatt-Gimblett (1989) writes how everyday objects inside houses, such as a wooden kitchen spoon, can be material companions from childhood to old age, whereas souvenirs and collections can be acquired and displayed in a home to evoke memories and reflection. The artifacts that family members make, use, or display can be an unseen backdrop to the duties and demands of family life. Alternatively, they might be carefully crafted statements about the values and expectations of family tradition bearers. Family stories, photos, and memories often can be associated with the decorations and details of family dwelling places and ancestral homes.

The verbal art of family life also has an early and lasting impact on families. Naming traditions, courtship stories, songs, sayings, and inside jokes identify individual family members and explain how the family came to be. Oral traditions connect the family to ancestors or to other significant groups such as religious or ethnic communities. Most cultures have preferences for what names are acceptable, who selects the name, and how the name is given. Families that adhere to certain religions may follow conventions of naming children for saints or prophets. Parents also may select names to remind children of their ethnic heritage. Jacqueline Thursby (1999) notes that third-generation Basque Americans often select ancestral or mythic Basque names, such as *Argia* (meaning light), to perpetuate their cultural heritage. Other families tell stories of ancestors whose names were anglicized upon migration. Elizabeth Stone's (1988) grandmother was Annunziata Bongiorno in Sicily and became known as Nancy Bonney after emigration to the United States. Because she knew a story about Annunziata's mother running away to marry the postman, Stone associates her great-grandmother with the founding of her family. Although she has other great-grandparents and ancestors, Stone believes her family started with the strong-willed act of the first Annunziata. Families can include great diversity in personalities and historical circumstances; the possibilities of closeness and unity are challenged exponentially by the past and the future. Names, stories, sayings, and songs can be a resource to maintain coherence and to recognize or construct continuities in family history.

Although not every family has lengthy stories about ancestors or important happenings, many families have stores of stories, sayings, songs, and humorous incidents that can be alluded to with key phrases. Children in many cultures are taught values, reasoning skills, and appropriate behavior through proverbs and riddles. These verbal expressions deal with recurring human experiences such as humorous predicaments or hardships, and they teach family members values and attitudes for responding to life events. However, each family knows and understands a unique repertoire. Folklorist William A. Wilson (1991) explains that these stories and sayings are comparable to a family novel that requires knowing the contexts of family events and the various character traits of family members to fully understand and appreciate. Steven J. Zeitlin, Amy J. Kotkin, and Holly Cutting Baker (1992) include family expressions in their collection of U.S. family folklore; these expressions demonstrate the creativity and useful shorthand of allusions in family life. Families use phrases such as "easy hands" and "my shoes are too big" to allude to inside jokes about making excuses for poor behavior. Some families attuned to the power of music use songs to accompany household duties, as well as to mark transitions and celebrations. The combination of words and music makes particularly strong memories that often are eagerly shared over generations.

Customary practices can be significant in daily family life and throughout the human life-cycle. With the invention and availability of cameras and other forms of documentation, families have tended to capture and preserve images of their celebration of holidays and festivals. Zeitlin (1992) quotes Carol Maas, who notes that family pictures in the United States document the same recurring images, including Christmas trees and families behind a birthday cake. Cakes and Christmas trees or other appropriate objects assume significance in celebrations; usually stories, songs, and sayings are repeated among family members during these events as well. The presence of the camera also demonstrates that technology can be embraced by families to document and perpetuate traditions. Larry Danielson (1996), a folklorist, has noted that technology and the media affect but do not necessarily displace family traditions. Often families use technology and transportation to gather physically or to share images across distances. Some families in a cultural or religious diaspora, or affected in other ways by migrations, may make pilgrimages to distant sites important to their heritage. Anthropologist Arjun Appadurai (1996) discusses the *transnational ironies* and different meanings that he and family members experienced on a pilgrimage to Meenaksi Temple in South India. Participating in and documenting customs allows family members to identify changes and continuities in the family structure. Traditions provide images and symbols that members use to find or question their place in the family and the world.

Folklorists have considered traditional daily practices and the religious observances and occupational traditions that may affect families in significant ways. Folklore archives contain many examples of family customs, some gathered by students. "Valuing, Preserving, and Transmitting Family Traditions," by folklorists Jill Terry Rudy, Eric Eliason, and Kristi Bell (2000), includes family customs from an archives collection. In the collection, students note that parents wake them up by singing lines from the Brigham Young University fight song, "Rise and shout, the Cougars are out!" Other parents sing, "Good Morning, Mary Sunshine," or "You Are My Sunshine." Siblings in a variety of locations claim to have invented games like "Hot Lava," where they jump from item to item and avoid touching the floor because it is hot lava. Most students admit that these games are created and played out of boredom, but stories about them later bring happy memories. Many families maintain mealtimes not only to eat together but to exchange stories and riddles; some families share ways of preparing and serving food that are important everyday, on weekends, or for holidays. Janet Goode, Janet Theophano, and Karen Curtis (1984) note that food is used by families to maintain, negotiate, and display ethnic identity. From carpet weaving and musical performance to firefighting and medical professions, families occasionally establish occupational traditions as well. Occupational traditions can inform a person's daily activities, leisure, and many aspects of identity. Religious commitment also can affect identity and stem from and contribute to family traditions. Grace at meals, prayer, and religious devotions promote gratitude and instill a sense of the sacred in family life. Religious traditions can serve families in times of adversity and struggle as well. Traditions mark the spaces and bridge the times of family life. Traditional artifacts, sayings, and customs identify family members as part of a group and help confirm or adjust values and behaviors.

Functions and Values of Folklore for Family Relationships

Margaret Yocom (1997) mentions that L. Karen Baldwin called families the social base for folklore. There is a difference, however, between families as the social base for folklore and folklore as the social and expressive base for families. The Zeitlin collection of U.S. family folklore and other works suggest that traditional expressions serve key functions in establishing and maintaining family relationships and values. Zeitlin and his colleagues (1992) indicate that families select images and traits that match their beliefs to perpetuate as traditions. Families use these traditions to present themselves to themselves, to characterize each other, and to note important transitional events as they memorialize the family. Selecting who can and cannot appear in a family photograph, for example, demonstrates the boundaries of the group. Both Danielson (1994) and Yocom (1997) emphasize defining family is variable and that dysfunctional and untraditional families, households, and *committed relationships* should be included in family lore studies. Toelken (1996) discusses *immediate families*; *horizontal families* of cousins, aunts, uncles, grandparents; *vertical families* of ancestors; and *ethnic families* from larger dynamic units that family members affiliate with. Toelken also asserts that traditional expressions develop a family sense of "us" that is distinguishable from other groups. Because family often is the first group a person knows, the habits and assumptions acquired through family traditions shape perception and experience in profound ways. Most people require belonging to a group and the stability of the familiar and the intrigue of the unfamiliar as traditions are repeated and altered.

Folklorist William Bascom (1965) identifies four functions of folklore that also work in the family folk group. He asserts that folklore serves to (1) amuse, (2) validate culture, (3) educate, and (4) maintain conformity. Families retell stories and celebrate holidays and events because they are entertained by their lore and by each other. Bascom notes that there usually is more than amusement going on when folklore is being performed. He acknowledges that some traditions invite fantasy and creativity, allowing people to imagine living in a better situation or escaping the limitations of life and death. However, these fantasies often release tension to prepare group members to accept or adapt to their life situations. Moreover, if family members question how things actually are, often there is a tradition to validate what the family stands for and to indicate how members should behave. Stone recounts the story of a blond, blue-eyed family that told stories about failed marriages with dark-haired men. To perpetuate the family as a unit over space and time, often traditions will validate previous behaviors and attitudes even if other options are appealing or even more viable. Traditions thus have a function to educate, primarily to instruct on how to act and live. Bascom notes from his research in Africa that children in nonliterate societies primarily are taught by stories, sayings, and ceremonies. Families can use traditions to teach appropriate behavior and to gently or openly reprimand members for making unacceptable decisions. Finally, Bascom asserts that folklore will be used as an "internalized check on behavior" to encourage conformity to group values. Although Bascom sees folklore performances as maintaining the status quo, traditions also can be altered to allow families to recognize themselves in spite of new attitudes or circumstances.

Family members come to know each other as performers of particular stories or customs, and they often relate to each other by deferring to the person who best knows the tradition. Toelken (1996) calls this "traditional deference," noting that often many family members know how to perform a tradition but allow or expect one person to be the primary performer. Although seldom a formal process of selection, traditional deference occurs with respect for age, ability, interest, or custom itself. Sometimes when the primary performer becomes incapable of continuing the tradition, others can readily step in to make the baskets, organize the holiday celebration, or tell the joke. Other times, the tradition has become so associated with one person that it must be radically altered or can no longer be practiced when that person is no longer available. The willing and easy sharing of traditions among family members can be a source of pride and unity, but disagreements over heirlooms or other invisible traits may indicate strained areas of family relationships. Although associating stories or artifacts with particular family members may cause contention, the informal distribution of traditional performances among family members can enhance identity, esteem, and bonding. Family folklore helps members relate to each other, know each other's moods and talents, and learn how to adapt relationships when changes occur.

International Scholarship and Applications of Family Folklore

Obviously folklorists find many elements of family life under the rubric of traditional expressive behavior. Jacob and Wilhelm Grimm, two brothers with a keen interest in their German language and traditions, encouraged collecting lore in the nineteenth century through their publication of household tales and legends. Scholars around the world became inspired to find and publish traditional materials. With brothers and other father-son or husband-wife pairs as founding figures, family has been an important aspect of folklore studies. However, family lore was not an early interest of scholars. Often folklorists collected tales, ballads, or games that belonged to a particular national group, or they tried to trace international similarities and differences. The focus on larger groups throughout the early twentieth century tended to obscure the traits and talents of individuals and specific families. Even when folklorists collected from family members, they focused on the songs, stories, or artifacts rather than on the function of lore in family life. Folklorist Mody Boatright has been identified by Yocom (1997) as one of the first to focus specifically on family folklore in his 1958 study of family sagas. By the 1970s, more folklorists studied and considered the family as the primary and essential group for the perpetuation and performance of folklore.

The traditional expressive behaviors studied by folklorists also have been researched as family ritual in other disciplines and presented in museum exhibits and web sites. Folklorists emphasize the description, function, and aesthetics of traditional behaviors, whereas family studies scholars tend to investigate the analytic, evaluative, and therapeutic elements. Family studies scholars may come to their study through clinical work with families, such as those dealing with *alcoholism,* and folklorists often study families who focus on artistic elements of family traditions. The folkloric approach can be enhanced by efforts to assess the efficacy of traditions in creating healthy family life, and the family studies approach can be enriched by attention to the artful and symbolic aspects of traditional behaviors. Folklorists teach community members how to document family lore through web sites, community organizations, and museums. The web site *My History is America's History,* sponsored by the National Endowment for the Humanities, includes ways to document family traditions and artifacts. A traveling exhibit of the Vermont Folklife Center, *Family Stories, Family Sagas,* features six New England families from a variety of ethnic and religious affiliations. Units on family folklore, such as Louisiana Voices and FOLKPATTERNS, help school and community groups teach children how to interview family members and preserve artifacts and photos. Radio programs and scholarly research focus on family stories, on African-American family reunions, and on family, childhood, and material culture in Europe. Although family historian John Gillis (1996) asserts that families are a world of their own making, increasingly important and fragile in contemporary society, family folklore reminds that families connect with wider communities such as ethnic, religious, or occupational groups. Family traditions are performed as practical responses to daily demands of family life as well as hopeful bridges between generations of time and space.

See also: FAMILY RITUALS; FAMILY STORIES AND MYTHS; FOOD; HOUSING; INTERGENERATIONAL TRANSMISSION

Bibliography

Appadurai, A. (1996). *Modernity at Large: Cultural Dimensions of Globalization.* Minneapolis: University of Minnesota Press.

Bascom, W. R. (1965). "Four Functions of Folklore." In *The Study of Folklore,* ed. A. Dundes. Englewood Cliffs, NJ: Prentice Hall.

Danielson, L., ed. (1994). "Family Folklore: Special Issue." *Southern Folklore* 51.

Danielson, L. (1996). "Family Folklore." In *American Folklore: An Encyclopedia,* ed. J. Brunvand. New York: Garland.

Gillis, J. R. (1996). *A World of Their Own Making: Myth, Ritual, and the Quest for Family Values.* New York: Basic Books.

Glassie, H. (1999). *Material Culture.* Bloomington: Indiana University Press.

Goode, J.; Theophano, J.; and Curtis, K. (1984). "A Framework for the Analysis of Continuity and Change in Shared Sociocultural Rules for Food Use: The Italian-American Pattern." In *Ethnic and Regional Foodways of the United States: The Performance of Group Identity,* ed. L. K. Brown and K. Mussell. Knoxville: University of Tennessee Press.

Jones, M. O. (1987). "L. A. Re-dos and Add-ons: Private Space vs. Public Policy." In *Exploring Folk Art.* Logan: Utah State University Press.

Kirshenblatt-Gimblett, B. (1989). "Objects of Memory: Material Culture as Life Review." In *Folk Groups and Folklore Genres: A Reader,* ed. E. Oring. Logan: Utah State University Press.

Rudy, J. T.; Eliason, E.; Bell, K. (2000). "Valuing, Preserving, and Transmitting Family Traditions." In *Strengthening Our Families: An In-Depth Look at the Proclamation on the Family,* ed. D. Dollahite. Salt Lake City, UT: Bookcraft.

Stone, E. (1988). *Black Sheep and Kissing Cousins: How Our Family Stories Shape Us.* New York: Times Books.

Thursby, J. (1999). *Mother's Table, Father's Chair: Cultural Narratives of Basque American Women.* Logan: Utah State University Press.

Toelken, B. (1996). *The Dynamics of Folklore,* revised and expanded edition. Logan: Utah State University Press.

Wilson, W. A. (1991). "Personal Narratives: The Family Novel." *Western Folklore* 50:127–149.

Yocom, M. (1997). "Family Folklore." In *Folklore: An Encyclopedia of Beliefs, Customs, Tales, Music, and Art,* Vol. I, ed. T. A. Green. Santa Barbara, CA: ABC-CLIO.

Zeitlin, S. J.; Kotkin, A. J.; Baker, H. C., eds. (1992). *A Celebration of American Family Folklore: Tales and Traditions from the Smithsonian Collection,* new edition. Cambridge, MA: Yellow Moon Press.

Other Resources

Louisiana Division of the Arts, National Endowment for the Arts. (2002). "Louisiana Voices." Available from http://www.crt.state.la.us/folklife/edu_home.html.

National Endowment for the Humanities. (2002). "My History is America's History." Available from http://www.myhistory.org.

Smithsonian Institution. (2002). "Family Folklore: How to Collect Your Own Family Folklore." Available from http://educate.si.edu/migrations/seek2/family.html.

JILL TERRY RUDY

FAMILY LAW

Most Western legal systems have a body of law known as *family law.* This body of law concerns itself with defining familial relations, attaching and defining of legal consequences to those relationships and their dissolution, and the transition of individuals into new family formations. In concrete terms, this translates into marriage and its effects, divorce, the law of the parent-child relationship, including postseparation parenting and child support, and the *recognition* of nonmarital relationships. Other matters often included in family law, but depending on the local distribution of legislative powers and not discussed here, include domestic violence, adoption, and child protection.

The Eras of Family Law: From Form to Function

Before turning to examine some of the specific tasks confronting family law, it may be helpful to sketch the larger background against which these tasks are undertaken. That background is one of significant changes, or transitions, in the objectives, assumptions and techniques of family law systems (Glendon 1989). It has been suggested (Dewar and Parker 2000) that family law has passed through a number of eras—a *formal era* (which was in place from the introduction of judicial divorce in the mid-nineteenth century until the late 1960s and early 1970s), a *functionalist era* (which began when the formal era ended), and the *complex era* (which started towards the late 1980s and early 1990s).

In the formal era, family law rested on an identifiable legal-conceptual structure. Marriage was a contract in the sense of being a set of voluntarily assumed rights and obligations, but in the nature of a contract of adhesion and thus not freely negotiable. Under this model, spouses had identifiable rights and obligations, and remedies were available for breach of marital entitlements. Thus, divorce was available only on proof of commission by a spouse of one of a carefully defined list of matrimonial offences; innocence or guilt of matrimonial misconduct affected the consequences of a divorce in terms of money and children. This model of marriage also affected the civil status of the parties to it, especially the wife. For example, a husband could not be prosecuted for raping his wife; spouses could not be compelled to testify against one another in a court of law; and spouses could not sue each other for personal injuries.

The introduction of *no-fault divorce* marked the shift to a functionalist era. Marriage could be ended without proof of fault, but instead with proof of irretrievable breakdown, usually evidenced by a period of separation. The functionalist era of family law was one in which the task of the legal system was to assist parties in negotiating transitions, and employ judicial order-making power to achieve certain welfare-defined outcomes, rather than allocating punishment or blame. This functionalist model was seen to be supportive of family life—and of the institution of marriage in general—because it enabled individuals to move on from bad marriages to more satisfying ones. It thus marked a shift in techniques of family governance, from control through restriction to control through managed change (Smart 2000).

The Era of Complexity

The functionalist era has now been displaced by the complex era. It will become apparent that there is no single set of ideas or explanations lying behind the trends characteristic of the complex era, although there may be some loose connections between them. Instead, the patterns are diverse, fragmented, and sometimes contradictory.

The shift from functionalism to complexity can be seen in the following aspects of modern family law. First, marriage has been displaced as the central concept linking law to families. Instead, legislation increasingly *recognizes* other relationships, such as unmarried cohabitation, or attaches greater significance to existing ones, such as parenthood. Some jurisdictions have gone further and have created new forms of marriage or legal partnership to accommodate those who cannot enter marriage in its conventional sense (Barron 2000). At the same time, concerns about the instability of marriage have led to calls for a return to fault-based divorce laws, or for offering couples the option of entering marriages that are harder to exit than normal ones (Wardle 1999). Ironically, perhaps, these seem to offer a return to an older—prefunctionalist—mode of family governance.

Second, there has been a retreat from the discretionary legislation that was the core of the functionalist model. Family law legislation is increasingly drafted in more specific, rule-like, terms. For example, child support legislation, whether drafted as judicial guidelines or as legislation creating a separate agency charged with assessment and enforcement of child support, is drafted in terms of fixed entitlements rather than discretionary awards. Rules on property adjustment are similarly debated in terms of increasingly clearer rules rather than broad discretions (Blumberg 2000), whereas legislation on postseparation parenting often includes statements of principles of equality between parents, or of rights of children, in mandatory rather than discretionary terms. The explanation for this lies in governmental desire to control the costs of family breakdown to the welfare state and the legal system; an increased tendency to conceive of parties in family law disputes as bearers of rights rather than as objects of welfarist interventions; and a perceived need to offer a clearer set of principles for law in this area, so that parties are more easily able to arrive at their own agreements rather than having to litigate.

Third, there is a greater emphasis on family autonomy in decision making, through promotion of binding prenuptial agreements, and nonjudicial forms of dispute resolution for those who have no ready-made agreements to fall back on. Once again, this trend is informed by a wish to remove family disputes from costly judicial arenas as much as possible, while at the same time drawing on the concepts of *individual, empowerment, responsibility,* and *autonomy* as self-sufficient justifications for parties to agree without court or professional involvement. Indeed, it seems that the role of law itself—or, at any rate, of lawyers—is sometimes in question.

A final shift of emphasis has been in the area of postdivorce parenting. Under the functionalist model, the emphasis was on assisting parties to move on from one relationship, and household, to the next. The language was that of the clean break, of "looking to the future." In this context, little prominence was given to the issue of how ongoing relationships were to be maintained or managed between children and their nonresident parent. That issue has now moved to center stage, with policy makers increasingly concerned to respond to demands from nonresident parents, often framed in terms of fathers' rights, for greater participation and involvement in the lives of children. Indeed, much attention is focused on how best to manage postseparation relationships centered on children, including (perhaps especially) those relationships characterized by high conflict.

Relationship Definition: Entries and Exits

A central concern of modern family law is how familial relationships should be defined, and for what purpose (Diduck 2001). Under the functionalist model, as we have seen, marriage was the chief means by which families were linked to law. Marriage conferred a status, in the sense of rights not available to others, in private and public law. There was only limited recognition of other forms of family organization as having legal significance. Marriage is a convenient conceptual device for making families visible in law, provided that most family life is conducted within marriage. The difficulty facing legal policy in this area, however, has been the dramatic shift in attitudes and social practices in relation to nonmarital cohabitation and other family forms. This leads to two consequences, both of which have reduced the centrality of marriage as a legal concept.

The first is growing practical and political pressure to grant nonmarital relationships some form of legal recognition (Graycar and Millbank 2000). The terms and consequences of that recognition, however, are not settled (Polikoff 1993). For example, should such recognition be a matter of choice by the parties, or is it to be imposed; and in either case, how far should recognition extend and with what consequences? In some cases, it is argued that marriage itself, or something like it, should be extended to embrace couples previously excluded from it (e.g., same-sex couples). Indeed, in some jurisdictions there has been explicit judicial or legislative recognition of a right to marry for same-sex couples, by entering either marriage itself or something similar to it (Barron 2000). In most jurisdictions, however, legislation is confined to involuntary recognition of unmarried cohabitation, with consequences less far-reaching than those attaching to marriage.

The second is an increased prominence for the legal status of *parenthood*—if relationships between adults are increasingly fragile and transitory, at least the parent-child relationship is susceptible of clear proof, and is enduring. Indeed, in many jurisdictions, the legal consequences of being a parent are of far greater practical significance (especially in terms of child support) than are the consequences of marriage. The net result is that there is no privileged legal perspective on families—instead, the law now offers a variety of lenses through which family relations may be understood, whether between adults or between adults and children.

The most obvious evidence of this is the growth in child support schemes, which impose significant financial obligations on separated parents, whether they are married to the other parent or not. One consequence of this is that for many couples, especially those with few capital assets, the financial consequences of a separation will be the same whether they are married or not—it is the presence or absence of children that will make the biggest difference.

The increased significance of parenthood can be seen as the function of three separate developments. First, it is a necessary consequence of a policy of removing any distinction in the legal treatment of marital and nonmarital children, and of eradicating the common law concept of *illegitimacy*. One effect of this is that, from the child's point of view, the marital status of the parents is, or should be, irrelevant—what matters, in other words, is parenthood, not marriage.

Second, the decline in marriage as a social practice has meant that some other legal technique was needed to link men to children, and to impose parental obligations on men, especially obligations of support. Parenthood is a way of tying men into the nonmarital family. As Richard Collier (1995) has suggested, the rise of parenthood can be seen as a "widening of the net of paternal authority through facilitating the making of links between men and children just at the time when rising trends of divorce, cohabitation, step-parenthood and serial marriage might appear to have been breaking down the traditional family unit."

Third, parenthood has become a means by which family law maintains a notional set of links between family members after separation. That family law is increasingly emphasizing the maintenance of economic and legal ties between parents and children after separation, as if to create the illusion of permanence in the face of instability, is discussed below. Because, by definition, neither marriage nor cohabitation is available for the purpose, these continuing links are founded on parenthood.

Parenthood: Meaning and Effects

If it is the case that parenthood is an increasingly important legal status, then what does it mean? It is easy to assume that parenthood is a simple question of biology—that a child's parents are those who have provided the genetic material that created the embryo that grew into the child. Yet there are at least two reasons why this may not be as straightforward as it appears.

The first is that the creation of embryos is increasingly a matter of human intervention and one consequence of this is that a focus on nature or biology may be at odds with the social arrangements one wishes to reproduce. For example, a woman who has had a fertilized egg created from donated genetic material implanted in her womb, which she then carries to term, will usually wish to do so because she (and, often, her partner) wants to be considered the resulting child's parents, legally and otherwise. The legislative regimes governing assisted reproduction in most jurisdictions (where it exists) are happy to assist in maintaining this fictive parenthood, by specifying that the woman carrying the child to term will be deemed the child's mother, whereas her husband—or (male) partner—will be the father. Donors of genetic material will be exonerated from parenthood, and would no doubt be alarmed if it were otherwise.

The second complicating factor stems from the culturally specific nature of biological understandings of parenthood (Dewar 2000). A child has two biological parents, and this mirrors the social expectation that childrearing will be discharged in a nuclear, two-parent household. To that extent, biology underpins notions of kinship, and much of the legal structure of parenthood shares this two-parent premise. Yet this sits uneasily with the childrearing practices of, for example, indigenous or ethnic communities, for whom parenthood may be indistinguishable from subtle and extended notions of kinship, so that a child may be regarded as having many parents, and parenting regarded as a communal rather than individual responsibility. There is a danger that a shift towards parenthood in its crude biological sense will amount to the imposition of one set of cultural values on another.

Family Finances

Empirical research almost invariably finds that women and children are most adversely affected economically by divorce and separation. Because of the uneven distribution of childrearing tasks and wage inequalities in the labor market, women tend to bear the costs of failed marriages more heavily than men; and because women continue to bear a disproportionate share of childrearing tasks after divorce, those costs are passed onto the children. In addition, the parties' greatest asset is usually earning capacity rather than tangible assets, and it is also one to which the other party perhaps has the strongest claim; yet the law has only limited means to capture and redistribute this. Child support regimes, which seek to correct unfairness to children by guaranteeing children a portion of their parents' incomes, could be seen as a form of splitting future earning potential; and legislation splitting superannuation and pension entitlements is another, depending on how it is framed. Their effectiveness in achieving this aim is yet to be proven, however.

Many jurisdictions rely on a combination of the concepts of *contribution* and *need* in the distribution of assets on divorce. Under such regimes, the spouses' property is divided in accordance with their contributions to property and, more generally, to the family, and then adjusted in the light of disparities in their future needs. Sometimes *need* is the governing or dominant criterion. There are numerous variations on this theme, including regimes that apply presumptions of equal division only to property defined as *marital* as distinct from separate, before applying some form of needs-based adjustment. Yet there is a growing consensus that these conceptual tools are inadequate to explain or justify what is taking place (Ellman 1989; Brinig 2000). At the same time, most jurisdictions include provision for spousal maintenance, but evidence suggests that these powers are rarely used. For that reason, many couples are unable to divide what may be their most significant asset—namely, their future earning capacity.

Contractualization

Although there is a trend toward the public enunciation of more detailed and prescriptive rules for financial adjustment, there is a parallel trend towards greater contractualization of marriage and divorce. *Contractualization* refers to the use of private contracting as a way of ordering domestic relationships, both while they are on-going and when they end. As a legal technique, it has long been available to unmarried couples (subject to issues of enforceability, long since resolved—see, for example, *Marvin v. Marvin* [557 P.2d 106 Cal. 1976]); but legislators now seem keen to extend its possibilities to married couples as well, pointing to the control that enforceable contracts provide parties over their own affairs. Each relationship may potentially acquire its own *proper law,* determined by the parties themselves rather than by an outsider armed with discretionary powers of distribution. In this way, private contracting is set to become an autonomous, or semiautonomous, source of legal norms.

Sustaining the Postdivorce Family

A prominent feature of the complex era of family law is the increased emphasis on maintaining relationships between parents and children after separation. What form does this emphasis take? One obvious form is the creation of child support liabilities by statute (discussed above). Another is the increased legislative emphasis on postseparation contact between a child and the parent with which it is not living, and on the sharing of parenting responsibilities. This finds expression in different ways—joint-custody laws, legal presumptions of access, visitation or contact, and more funding for community agencies involved in supervising or supporting contact arrangements.

Postseparation childcare arrangements, and in particular visitation or contact, has become a key issue for feminist engagement with family law. Apparent attempts to shift the balance away from mothers towards fathers has attracted opposition and heightened attention. Research in Australia has suggested that the new regime has led to contact being ordered in inappropriate circumstances, and to women being harassed by men through abuse of court processes, thereby confirming the worst fears of its detractors (Rhoades, Graycar, and Harrison 2000). Legislation of this sort is said to grant power without responsibility, and to place women at the mercy of former partners.

The significance of this lies in the fact that divorce no longer represents the effective termination of parent-child relationships. As Carol Smart and Bren Neale (1999) have put it, "fragments of families are to be found in various households linked by biological and economic bonds, but not necessarily by affection or shared life prospects. We might say that family law is trying to hold the fragments together through the imposition of a new normative order based on genetics and finances, but not on a state-legitimated heterosexual union with its roots in the ideal of Christian marriage."

A Future Direction? Giving Children a Say

Much of the policy debate around postseparation parenting has been conducted as if it consisted of a zero-sum game of gains and losses to be distributed between mothers and fathers. The metaphor of the shifting balance between mothers and fathers, employed above, exemplifies this way of thinking. Researchers, though, suggest that one way to break out of this seemingly intractable debate is to focus more on the expressed needs and desires of the children involved (e.g., Lowe and Murch 2001; Smart, Neale, and Wade 2001; Woodhouse 2000).

See also: ADOPTION; CHILD CUSTODY; CHILDREN'S RIGHTS; DIVORCE: EFFECTS ON COUPLE; GRANDPARENTS' RIGHTS; GUARDIANSHIP; MARRIAGE, DEFINITION OF; PREMARITAL AGREEMENTS; PROTESTANTISM; SEXUAL ORIENTATION

Bibliography

Barron, J. (2000). "The Constitutionalisation of American Family Law: The Case of the Right to Marry." In *Cross-Currents: Family Law and Policy in the U.S. and England,* ed. S. Katz, J. Eekelaar, and M. Maclean. Oxford, UK: Oxford University Press.

Blumberg, G. (2000). "The Financial Incidents of Family Dissolution." In *Cross-Currents: Family Law and Policy in the U.S. and England,* ed. S. Katz, J. Eekelaar, and M. Maclean. Oxford, UK: Oxford University Press.

Brinig, M. (2000). *From Contract to Covenant: Beyond the Law and Economics of the Family.* Cambridge, MA: Harvard University Press.

Collier, R. (1995). *Masculinity, Law and the Family.* London: Routledge.

Dewar, J. (2000). "Family Law and Its Discontents." *International Journal of Law, Policy and the Family* 14: 59–85.

Dewar, J., and Parker, S. (2000). "English Family Law since WW II: From Status to Chaos." In *Cross-Currents: Family Law and Policy in the U.S. and England,* ed. S. Katz, J. Eekelaar, and M. Maclean. Oxford, UK: Oxford University Press.

Diduck, A. (2001). "A Family by Any Other Name . . . or Starbucks (tm) Comes to England." *Journal of Law and Society* 28:290–310.

Ellman, M. (1989). "The Theory of Alimony." *California Law Review* 77:3–81.

Glendon, M-A. (1989). *The Transformation of Family Law: State, Law and Family in the United States and Western Europe.* Chicago: University of Chicago Press.

Graycar, R., and Millbank, J. (2000). "The Bride Wore Pink . . . to the Property (Relationships) Legislation Amendment Act 1999: Relationships Law Reform in New South Wales." *Canadian Journal of Family Law* 17:227–282.

Lowe, N., and Murch, M. (2001). "Children's Participation in the Family Justice System—Translating Principles into Practice." *Child and Family Law Quarterly* 13: 137–158.

Polikoff, N. (1993). "We Will Get What We Ask for: Why Legalising Gay and Lesbian Marriage Will Not 'Dismantle the Structure of Gender in Every Marriage.'" *Virginia Law Review* 79:1535–1550.

Rhoades, H., Graycar, R., and Harrison, M. (2000). *The Family Law Reform Act 1995: The First Three Years.* Sydney: University of Sydney/Family Court of Australia.

Smart, C. (2000). "Divorce in England 1950–2000: A Moral Tale?" In *Cross-Currents: Family Law and Policy in the U.S. and England,* ed. S. Katz, J. Eekelaar, and M. Maclean. Oxford, UK: Oxford University Press.

Smart, C., and Neale, B. (1999). *Family Fragments?* Cambridge, UK: Polity Press.

Smart, C.; Neale, B.; and Wade, A. (2001). *The Changing Experience of Childhood: Families and Divorce.* Cambridge, UK: Polity Press.

Wardle, L. (1999). "Divorce Reform at the Turn of the Millennium: Certainties and Possibilities." *Family Law Quarterly* 33:783–800.

Woodhouse, B. (2000). "The Status of Children: A Story of Emerging Rights." In *Cross-Currents: Family Law and Policy in the U.S. and England,* ed. S. Katz, J. Eekelaar, and M. Maclean. Oxford, UK: Oxford University Press.

JOHN DEWAR

FAMILY LIFE EDUCATION

Preparing individuals and families for the roles and responsibilities of family living is nothing new. Because knowledge about human development, interpersonal relationships, and family living is not innate, societies have needed to develop ways through which they may transmit the wisdom and the experience of family living from one generation to succeeding ones. Some societies transmit this knowledge through formal means such as puberty or initiation rites. For the most part, however, individuals learn about family living in the family setting itself as they observe and participate in family activities and interactions in their own and other families.

As societies change and become more complex, this pattern of informal learning about living in families becomes inadequate. The development of new knowledge, advances in technology, and changing social and economic conditions create situations where the teachings of previous generations are no longer appropriate or sufficient. In these circumstances, societies must find or create new ways to prepare individuals for their family roles and responsibilities. One of these new ways is *family life education.*

An Overview of Family Life Education

In North America, family life education developed as an educational specialty around the turn of the twentieth century in response to the changing social conditions of the time (Lewis-Rowley et al. 1993). Changes such as urbanization, industrialization, and the changing roles of women commonly resulted in family and societal difficulties, including increased parent-child strife, juvenile delinquency, shifts in marital roles, and an increased divorce rate. Families were inadequately prepared to deal with these changes, and the founders of family life education believed that providing educational programs in family life education would help to ameliorate or reduce these and other family-related social problems and thus improve family living and social well-being.

By the end of the twentieth century, the family life education movement in North America had experienced considerable growth in the number and kinds of programs available and in the scholarship underlying these programs (Arcus 1995). These developments were not unique to North America, however, as other countries throughout the world have sought ways to help families deal with social and economic changes. Some examples of international family life education initiatives include the Marriage Encounter movement, founded in Spain but present in other countries; the International

Family Life Education Institute, Taiwan; Marriage Care (formerly Catholic Marriage Guidance), United Kingdom; the Australian Family Life Institute; and family planning and sexuality education programs throughout the world. The United Nations named 1994 as the International Year of the Family, further attesting to the importance of providing support for families globally.

The purpose of family life education is to strengthen and enrich individual and family well-being (Thomas and Arcus 1992). Major objectives include (1) gaining insight into one's self and others; (2) acquiring knowledge about human development and behavior in the family setting over the life course; (3) understanding marital and family patterns and processes; (4) acquiring interpersonal skills for present and future family roles; and (5) building strengths in individuals and families (Arcus and Thomas 1993). It is assumed that if these and other similar objectives are met through family life education, then families will be better able to deal with or prevent problems and will be empowered to live their family lives in ways that are both personally satisfying and socially responsible. Family life education programs are preventative, intended to *equip* individuals for their family roles rather than to *repair* family dysfunction.

The Framework for Family Life Education, developed under the auspices of the National Council on Family Relations, specifies nine broad content areas deemed essential for family life education: families in society; internal dynamics of families; human growth and development; human sexuality; interpersonal relationships; family resource management; parent education and guidance; family law and public policy; and ethics (Bredehoft 1997). The Framework lists the most important knowledge, attitudes, and skills relevant to each area, with the focus and complexity differing for people of different ages (children, adolescents, adults, and older adults). Key processes of communication, decision making, and problem solving are incorporated into each area. Other terms sometimes used to describe the same general content include sex education, human relations education, personal development, and life skills education.

An underlying assumption of family life education is that it is relevant to individuals of all ages and to all families whatever their structure, stage of the life course, or special circumstances (Arcus, Schvaneveldt, and Moss 1993). Some programs are related to normative developments for individuals and families, such as getting married, becoming a parent, or the death of a parent (Hennon and Arcus 1993). Other programs are based on non-normative developments or the special needs and transitions that affect some but not all individuals and families (parenting children with special needs, prevention of elder abuse). The response of the family life education movement to both the normative and nonnormative needs of families has resulted in a diverse range of family life programs, some well established (parent education, sexuality education, marriage preparation) and others emerging (parent education for adolescent parents, sexual abuse education/prevention, marriage the second time around).

Family Life Education During Childhood

Basic family life concepts, attitudes, and skills that need to be learned during childhood include developing a sense of self, learning right from wrong, learning about family roles and responsibilities, making and keeping friends, respecting similarities and differences in individuals and families, and learning to make choices (Bredehoft 1997). Although these may be learned within the family, they also receive attention in family life programs because some families may be unable or unwilling to educate their children about these concepts or their efforts may be unsuccessful or may not happen at the right time.

In the United States, most family life education programs for children are provided in school settings (Hennon and Arcus 1993). Programs are typically organized around individual rather than family development, that is, children of the same age or developmental stage are taught the same things regardless of their particular family situations. This approach may be appropriate for many children, but it also may fail to address the important family life education needs of children in nonnormative family situations, such as being raised by a grandparent or dealing with the premature death of a parent.

In 1947, the Japanese Ministry of Education mandated education for both boys and girls to help prepare them for their family roles and responsibilities, and this education, offered through Home Economics departments, continues to be

In this Japanese home economics class students learn the fundamental skill of sewing. Such education programs seek to strengthen families by providing training in roles and responsibilities. BOHEMIAN NOMAD PICTUREMAKERS/CORBIS

mandated for grades five and six. The curriculum revision implemented in 2002 emphasized learning knowledge, gaining skills, increasing interest in daily family life, and improving family life as a family member (Ministry of Education 2000). Textbooks approved by the Ministry of Education typically focus on normative family needs and *ideal family life,* and thus may not reflect the reality of the daily lives of some students.

A review of policies and practices in Human Relations in Australian schools found that most of the human relations content at the primary school level was integrated into Health or Social Studies units (Wolcott 1987), including topics such as self-esteem, interpersonal relationships, family life, family roles in child care, different family types, male/female differences, and aspects of physical growth. Curriculum guidelines were recognized as guidelines only, with the specific content to be taught subject to local school interpretation and teacher modification.

Educational reforms in schools in Jamaica in the 1990s (Hodelin 1999) incorporated education

for family betterment and the promotion of family health into several subject areas in the core curriculum for grades seven through nine, including social studies, guidance, and counseling and religious studies. This family education is now required for all students, both males and females, entering secondary schools in Jamaica.

Sexuality education is a controversial area in family life education, especially at the elementary or primary level, with many adults believing that sexuality education is a family rather than a school responsibility. A U.S. nationwide poll found that 93 percent of adults surveyed supported sexuality education for adolescents, but fewer than half approved of sexuality education in elementary school (Advocates for Youth 1999). A survey of U.S. fifth- and sixth-grade teachers found that a majority of schools were doing little to prepare students for puberty and for dealing with pressures and decisions regarding sexual activity (Landry, Singh, and Darroch 2000).

One area of sexuality education that does receive attention in elementary or primary schools is that of child sexual abuse. Concerns about sexual abuse have resulted in the development of sexual-abuse prevention programs for young children that teach concepts of personal safety such as good and bad touch, saying no, and telling someone you trust about the abuse. Some evidence indicates that sexual-abuse education increases knowledge, but acquiring knowledge *per se* may not prevent abuse or change behaviors (Engel, Saracino, and Bergen 1993). There is no evidence that these programs increase children's fears or damage their relationships with parents or other significant adults, but in the absence of positive sexuality education, it is of concern that children may learn only negative messages about sexuality.

Family Life Education During Adolescence

Family life education for adolescents addresses two important kinds of needs: (1) their current normative needs associated with changing physical, sexual, cognitive, social, and emotional developments, and (2) their anticipatory or future family-related needs to help prepare them for adult roles and responsibilities in marriage and parenting. Important family life content includes understanding one's self and others; building self-esteem; making choices about sexuality; forming, maintaining, and ending relationships; taking responsibility for one's actions; understanding family roles and responsibilities; and improving communication skills (Hennon and Arcus 1993). Programs differ in the emphasis placed on this content, with some focusing on personal development themes and others giving greater attention to marriage and family relationships.

The assumption underlying anticipatory family education is that if adolescents are prepared for their potential future family roles, then their adult life experiences in these roles will be more successful (Hennon and Arcus 1993). As most adolescents have not yet selected a marital partner, anticipatory education for marriage emphasizes acquiring knowledge about marriage and intimate relationships, improving relationship skills, and exploring personal attitudes and values regarding marriage, marital expectations, and marital roles (Stahmann and Salts 1993). Anticipatory education for parenthood helps adolescents acquire knowledge about child development and different patterns of child rearing and sometimes includes the study and observation of children (Brock, Oertwein, and Coufal 1993). These programs are most

successful when they also include the *precursors* of successful parenting—self-understanding and the development of interpersonal relationship skills (de Lissovoy 1978).

In the United States and Canada, most family life education programs for adolescents are found in schools, although some may also be offered through youth organizations, community agencies, and churches. Programs vary considerably in their content and approach, in whether they are required or elective, and in which department they may be offered (typically Home Economics, Guidance and Counseling, Social Studies, or Health). Information about program effectiveness is limited but suggests that programs may be successful in helping students acquire knowledge and skills but have little impact on attitudes and values (Hennon and Arcus 1993). Many programs are hampered by the lack of time allocated to them, the lack of educational resources, and limitations in preparing family life teachers.

In Japan, family life goals at the upper-secondary level include understanding human development and daily life, understanding the meaning of families, family and community connections, learning knowledge and skills for daily life, and creating family and community life cooperatively between men and women (Ministry of Education 2000). This content, taught in the Home Economics department, has been mandated for girls since 1960 and for both girls and boys since 1989. Secondary school subjects called *Life Environment Studies* and *Morals* may also teach content related to human development, interpersonal relationships, family interaction, ethics, and family and society.

Human relations topics in Australian secondary schools may either be integrated into established subject areas (typically Health Education, Social Studies, or Home Economics) or presented as an independent subject such as Personal Development, Life Skills, or Human Relations (Wolcott 1987). Curriculum guidelines vary among the states and territories, and because these guidelines are "suggestive," some family life topics may receive little if any attention.

Beginning in 2002, *citizenship,* which includes respecting individual differences and the development of good relationships, will become a statutory subject taught in all state schools in the United

Kingdom (Blunkett 1999). For the first time, relationship skills and different kinds of relationships, such as marriage and parenthood, will be taught to all students from age eleven on. Although citizenship is a statutory subject, each individual school will determine how the content is to be taught and by whom. This curricular development is being supported by other U.K. agencies such as Marriage Care, which provides flexible-use teaching units emphasizing good communication skills for use with twelve- to twenty-year-olds through their project *Foundations for a Good Life.*

In Jamaica, education for family in secondary schools has typically been offered by Home Economics (Hodelin 1999). Originally, this education was based on nineteenth-century educational views exported from the United Kingdom to the English-speaking Caribbean and, depending on social class, tended to emphasize either preparation for domestic responsibilities as wife/mother or preparation for vocational domestic service. A reconceptualization of the Home Economics Curriculum in the 1990s emphasized the betterment of family life and provides a Caribbean-relevant curriculum relevant for both male and female secondary students.

The biological onset of puberty highlights the universal need for sexuality education for adolescents, and sexuality education/family planning education receives considerable attention worldwide, prompted by global concerns about adolescent pregnancy and parenthood and the emergence of HIV/AIDS as a health and social issue. A comparative study of family life education, sex education, and human sexuality conducted by UNESCO identified the need to broaden traditional population education to include topics such as reproductive health, the status and empowerment of women, intergenerational relationships, and problem-solving skills in order to improve family and social welfare (Blanchard 1995). In the United States and Canada, most schools provide some form of sexuality education for adolescents, although many curricular guides are out-of-date and programs are not comprehensive, omitting topics such as communication and decision making, personal values and responsibility, and reducing risk-taking behaviors (Engel, Saracino, and Bergen 1993). Efforts to expand and improve family life/sexuality education have been reported in many countries and regions, including Russia (Popova 1996), India (Sathe 1994; Nayak and Bose 1997), Africa (Centre for Development and Population Activities 1997), and New Zealand (Duncan and Bergen 1997). Despite many differences in these programs, educators promote a broad rather than narrow approach to sexuality education, although implementation may be difficult because of resistance from parents and from political and religious leaders.

Family Life Education for Adults

Two characteristics distinguish family life education for adults from that for children and adolescents: first, it is more complex and more varied, as adults must not only meet their own needs for family living but may also bear some responsibility for the family socialization of the next generation(s); second, it is more likely to be related to family life tasks and transitions than to age or developmental level, that is, getting married or becoming parents is more important than the age at which these transitions might occur (Hennon and Arcus 1993).

The earliest family life education for adults was *parent education,* provided for mothers who met in groups specifically organized to improve parent understanding and parenting practices (Lewis-Rowley et al. 1993). Fathers are increasingly involved, but most parent education is still provided to mothers. Important outcomes of parent education include more positive child behaviors, more positive perceptions of child behaviors, and improved parent-child interactions (Brock, Oertwein, and Coufal 1993). Early generic programs have been adapted to specific target groups, including parents with different backgrounds, different parenting needs, and children of different ages. Despite the diversity of programs available, research indicates that no one parent education program is more effective than the others (Medway 1989). The two most widely used programs, *Systematic Training for Effective Parenting* (STEP) (Dinkmeyer and McKay 1989) and *Parent Effectiveness Training* (PET) (Gordon 1975), were developed in the United States, but are available in many countries throughout the world.

Concern for the potential negative impact of divorce on children has led to the development of special parenting education for divorcing parents (Geasler and Blaisure 1998). First documented in 1978, these programs have proliferated since then and are now mandated in some U.S. states. Most are relatively short-term (single, two-hour sessions), and are designed to help parents understand and moderate the effects of divorce on children and to improve their coparenting skills. There has been little systematic evaluation of these programs (McKenry, Clark, and Stone 1999), but exit questionnaires suggest that participant satisfaction is high (Geasler and Blaisure 1998).

ParentLink, an innovative coalition of agencies and organizations in Missouri (U.S.), facilitates access to a wide range of parenting information, services, and support throughout the state (Mertensmeyer and Fine 2000). In addition to a library loan service and community resource lists, ParentLink provides assistance through a toll-free 1–800 number, development of an Internet site, review and evaluation of other websites, a monthly electronic newsletter, and access to consultants (both face-to-face and through listservs). This statewide initiative helps overcome the typically fragmented and piecemeal nature of much family life/parent education for adults.

Marriage education has been a focus of family life education for adults since the earliest programs were developed in the 1930s and 1940s in the United States and Great Britain (Stahmann and Salts 1993; Mace and Mace 1986). Since then, different marriage education programs have been developed to provide premarital couples with opportunities to gain knowledge about and discuss the critical issues and tasks of marriage, to acquire behavioral skills and problem-solving strategies to enhance their relationships, and to evaluate their relationships, including any romanticism, untested assumptions, and/or unrealistic expectations (Stahmann and Salts 1993). Premarital programs appear effective in meeting at least some of their goals, but they may not be equally effective for all participants (Fowers, Montel, and Olson 1996; Gottman et al. 1998). Little is known about the long-term effects of these programs.

Originally, marriage preparation was provided primarily for young adult couples; however, variations of these programs have been developed for couples marrying for the second time, for those marrying during later years, and for those in committed relationships other than marriage. Because premarital education is based on a companionate view of marriage, these programs may not be relevant to all cultural or religious groups. Websites on

the Internet can help to disseminate program information to interested persons throughout the world.

Another form of marriage education—*marriage enrichment*—emerged during the 1960s in Spain and the United States, designed to help people maintain and improve significant interpersonal relationships (Stahmann and Salts 1993). Programs emphasize the strengths of relationships and help participants increase their awareness of self and others, explore and express thoughts and feelings, and improve and use relationship skills. Enrichment programs are typically delivered either through a series of weekly meetings or in intensive weekend retreats. Reviews indicate that marriage enrichment programs are effective, although their effects appear to diminish over time (Stahmann and Salts 1993).

During later adulthood, special family life education needs emerge related to the impact of developmental and health changes on one's self-esteem and sexuality, the loss of significant others such as parents or partners, changes in work roles, and the impact of changing family structure on roles and relationships (addition/loss of family members) (Arcus 1993). Family life education for this age group is limited, but examples include *Becoming a Better Grandparent* (Strom, Strom, and Collinsworth 1990), designed to increase satisfaction and performance as a grandparent, and *Survival KIT for the Holidays* (Wood 1987), designed to help adults deal with loss and grief through educational experiences and the development of support systems. Preretirement programs typically focus on financial planning (Riker and Myers 1990), but they may not include important topics such as later-life transitions and changes in family roles. Because transportation and mobility may be issues for older adults, innovative approaches such as a correspondence course in human sexuality (Engel 1983) and disseminating gerontological information through interactive television (Riekse, Holstege, and Faber 2000) have promise for later-life family life education.

Challenges in Family Life Education

Qualified educators are central to the success of family life education, as it is these individuals who bear major responsibility for shaping the educational experience and interacting with participants. Despite their importance, however, few guidelines are available to help prepare family educators. In 1985, the National Council on Family Relations established a certificate program to help improve the training and qualifications of family life educators (Davidson 1989; National Council on Family Relations 1984). Through this program, recognition is given to individuals who hold a baccalaureate or advanced degree in specified fields of study, have a minimum level of postsecondary education in the content areas of the Framework for Family Life Education, and have completed a specified level of related work experience. The *Certificate in Family Life Education* (CFLE) is a voluntary credential, and has been granted to individuals in the United States, Canada, Puerto Rico, Japan, Korea, the Philippines, and Singapore. An important outcome of the CFLE program has been its influence on the content of the college/university programs that prepare family life educators.

The Internet and the World Wide Web present new challenges for family life education. Information technologies make it possible to provide family-related information twenty-four hours a day, every day, and may help facilitate the preparation of professionals through online courses and chatrooms (Hughes, Ehata, and Dollahite 1999). Although it is likely that these technologies will enhance rather than replace more traditional family life education approaches, important issues that will require attention include the reliability and validity of the information available and the effectiveness of this form of family education. As well, the emergence of such things as computer-mediated relationships (cyber-relationships) and sexualized Internet use requires rethinking the content and strategies of family life education (Merkle and Richardson 2000; Sanders, Deal, and Myers-Bowman 2000).

Family life education is an important means to help ameliorate family issues and problems, but in many situations these programs by themselves may not be sufficient unless their development and implementation are supported by social and educational policies and political decisions. School boards and community interest groups may place restrictions on the content taught in schools, thereby failing to meet some important needs of this age group. Inadequate financial support often means that programs are available primarily to those who can afford to pay registration fees, not necessarily to those who may want or need the

programs the most. And, as seen at the beginning of the twenty-first century, resolving the AIDS (Acquired immunodeficiency syndrome) crisis in Africa and elsewhere will not only require adequate family education and governmental support to make this education widely available but also political decisions that will ensure that medications are available to those who need it at a reasonable cost.

Underlying the practice of family life education is a basic belief in the importance of family living and a basic respect for persons that recognizes their ability to take charge of their own lives in satisfying ways. Through educational programs, family life education makes an important contribution toward strengthening families to fulfill their significant role as the basic unit of society.

See also: BIRTH CONTROL: SOCIOCULTURAL AND HISTORICAL ASPECTS; CHILDHOOD; CHILDHOOD, STAGES OF: ADOLESCENCE; COMMUNICATION: FAMILY RELATIONSHIPS; COPARENTING; DECISION MAKING; DEVELOPMENT: SELF; FAMILY DEVELOPMENT THEORY; FAMILY MINISTRY; FAMILY ROLES; FAMILY SCIENCE; FAMILY STRENGTHS; FATHERHOOD; MARRIAGE ENRICHMENT; MARRIAGE PREPARATION; MATE SELECTION; MOTHERHOOD; PARENTING EDUCATION; PARENTING STYLES; POWER: MARITAL RELATIONSHIPS; PROBLEM SOLVING; RESOURCE MANAGEMENT; SEXUALITY EDUCATION; SEXUALITY IN ADOLESCENCE; TIME USE

Bibliography

Advocates for Youth and Sexuality Information and Education Council of the United States. (1999). "Public Support for Sexuality Education Reaches Highest Level." News Release, June 1, 1999. Washington, DC: Advocates for Youth and New York: SIECUS.

Arcus, M. E. (1993). "Family Life Education for Mid-life and Later Life Families." In *Handbook of Family Life Education,* Vol. 2: *The Practice of Family Life Education,* ed. M. E. Arcus, J. D. Schvaneveldt, and J. J. Moss. Newbury Park, CA: Sage.

Arcus, M. E. (1995). "Advances in Family Life Education: Past, Present, and Future." *Family Relations* 45:336–344.

Arcus, M. E.; Schvaneveldt, J. D.; and Moss, J. J. (1993). "The Nature of Family Life Education." In *Handbook of Family Life Education,* Vol. 1: *Foundations of Family Life Education,* ed. M. E. Arcus, J. D. Schvaneveldt, and J. J. Moss. Newbury Park, CA: Sage.

Arcus, M. E., and Thomas, J. (1993). "The Nature and Practice of Family Life Education." In *Handbook of Family Life Education,* Vol. 2: *The Practice of Family Life Education,* ed. M. E. Arcus, J. D. Schvaneveldt, and J. J. Moss. Newbury Park, CA: Sage.

Blanchard, J. (1995). *Comparative Study on Family Life Education, Sex Education, and Human Sexuality: Mandate, Concepts, Activities.* Paris: UNESCO.

Blunkett, D. (1999). *The National Curriculum Handbook for Secondary Teachers.* London: Department of Education and Employment.

Bredehoft, D. J. (2001). "The Framework for Life Span Family Life Education Revisited and Revised." *The Family Journal: Counseling and Therapy for Couples and Families* 9(2):134–139.

Brock, G. W.; Oertwein, M.; and Coufal, J. D. (1993). "Parent Education: Theory, Research, and Practice." In *Handbook of Family Life Education,* Vol. 2: *The Practice of Family Life Education,* ed. M. E. Arcus, J. D. Schvaneveldt, and J. J. Moss. Newbury Park, CA: Sage.

Centre for Development and Population Activities. (1997). *African Forum on Adolescent Reproductive Health: United Nations Population Fund.* Washington, DC: Author.

Davidson, J. K., Sr. (1989). "The Certification of Family Life Educators: A Quest for Professionalism." *Family Science Review* 2:125–136.

de Lissovoy, V. (1978). "Parent Education: White Elephant in the Classroom." *Youth and Society* 9:315–338.

Dinkmeyer, D., and McKay, G. D. (1989). *The Parent's Handbook. STEP: Systematic Training for Effective Parenting,* 3rd edition. Circle Pines, MN: American Guidance Service.

Duncan, D., and Bergen, M. B. (1997). "Knowledge of New Zealand Youth Regarding Sexuality and AIDS." *Journal of Sex and Marital Therapy* 23:47–51.

Engel, J. (1983). "Sex Education of Adults: An Evaluation of a Correspondence Course." *Family Relations* 32:123–128.

Engel, J. S.; Saracino, M.; and Bergen, M. B. (1993). "Sexuality Education." In *Handbook of Family Life Education,* Vol. 2: *The Practice of Family Life Education,* ed. M. E. Arcus, J. D. Schvaneveldt, and J. J. Moss. Newbury Park, CA: Sage.

Fowers, B. J.; Montel, K. H.; and Olson, D. H. (1996). "Predicting Marital Success for Premarital Couple Types Based on PREPARE." *Journal of Marital and Family Therapy* 22:103–119.

Geasler, M. J., and Blaisure, K. R. (1998). "A Review of Divorce Education Program Materials." *Family Relations* 47:167–175.

Gordon, T. (1975). *Parent Effectiveness Training.* Berkenfield, NJ: Penguin.

Gottman, J. M.; Coan, J.; Carrere, S.; and Swanson, C. (1998). "Predicting Marital Happiness and Stability from Newlywed Interactions." *Journal of Marriage and the Family* 60:5–22.

Hennon, C. B., and Arcus, M. (1993). "Lifespan Family Life Education." In *Family Relations: Challenges for the Future,* ed. T. H. Brubaker. Newbury Park, CA: Sage.

Hodelin, G. B. (1999). "The Legacy of Education for Family in the Caribbean." *Caribbean Journal of Home Economics* 1:2–14.

Hughes, R., Jr.; Ebata, A. T.; and Dollahite, D. C. (1999). "Family Life in the Information Age." *Family Relations* 48:5–6.

Landry, D. J.; Singh, S.; and Darroch, J. E. (2000). "Sexuality Education in Fifth and Sixth Grades in U.S. Public Schools, 1999." *Family Planning Perspectives* 32:212–219.

Lewis-Rowley, M.; Brasher, R. E.; Moss, J. J.; Duncan, S. F.; and Stiles, R. J. (1993). "The Evolution of Education for Family Life." In *Handbook of Family Life Education,* Vol. 1: *Foundations of Family Life Education,* ed. M. E. Arcus, J. D. Schvaneveldt, and J. J. Moss. Newbury Park, CA: Sage.

Mace, D., and Mace, V. (1986). "The History and Present Status of the Marriage and Family Enrichment Movement." In *Marriage and Family Enrichment,* ed. W. Denton. New York: Haworth Press.

McKenry, P. C.; Clark, K. A.; and Stone, G. (1999). "Evaluation of a Parent Education Program for Divorcing Parents." *Family Relations* 48:129–137.

Medway, F. (1989). "Measuring the Effectiveness of Parent Education." In *The Second Handbook on Parent Education,* ed. M. J. Fine. San Diego, CA: Academic Press.

Merkle, E. R., and Richardson, R. A. (2000). "Digital Dating and Virtual Relating: Conceptualizing Computer Mediated Romantic Relationships." *Family Relations* 49:187–192.

Mertensmeyer, C., and Fine, M. (2000). "ParentLink: A Model of Integration and Support for Parents." *Family Relations* 49:257–265.

Ministry of Education, Science, Sports, and Culture. (2000). *Education in Japan,* 13th edition. Tokyo: Gyosei.

National Council on Family Relations. (1984). *Standards and Criteria for the Certification of Family Life Educators, College/University Curriculum Guidelines, and*

Content Guidelines for Family Life Education: A Framework for Planning Programs Over the Lifespan. Minneapolis, MN: Author.

Nayak, J., and Bose, R. (1997). "Making Sense, Talking Sexuality: India Reaches Out to its Youth." *SIECUS Report* 25(2):19–21.

Popova, V. J. (1996). "Sexuality Education Moves Forward in Russia." *SIECUS Report* 24(3):14–15.

Riekse, R. J.; Holstege, H.; and Faber, M. (2000). "Using Interactive Television Technology to Disseminate Applied Gerontological Information." *Educational Gerontology* 26:751–760.

Riker, H., and Myers, J. (1990). *Retirement Counseling: A Practical Guide for Action.* New York: Hemisphere.

Sanders, G.; Deal, J.; and Myers-Bowman, K. (2000). "Sexually Explicit Material on the Internet: Implications for Family Life Educators." *Journal of Family and Consumer Sciences* 91:112–116.

Sathe, A. G. (1994). "Introduction of Sex Education in Schools: Perceptions of Indian Society." *Journal of Family Welfare* 40:30–37.

Stahmann, R. F., and Salts, C. J. (1993). "Education for Marriage and Intimate Relationships." In *Handbook of Family Life Education,* Vol 2: *The Practice of Family Life Education,* ed. M. E. Arcus, J. D. Schvaneveldt, and J. J. Moss. Newbury Park, CA: Sage.

Strom, R.; Strom, S.; and Collinsworth, P. (1990). "Improving Grandparent Success." *Journal of Applied Gerontology* 9:480–491.

Thomas, J., and Arcus, M. (1992). "Family Life Education: An Analysis of theConcept." *Family Relations* 41:3–8.

Wolcott, I. (1987). "Human Relations Education in Australian Schools: A Review of Policies and Practices." Policy Background paper No. 6. Melbourne, Australia: Australian Institute of Family Studies.

Wood, B. (1987). "Survival KIT for the Holidays: A Grief Workshop Approach." *Family Relations* 36:235–241.

Other Resources
Parentlink. (2002). Available from http://outreach.missouri.edu/parentlink/.

Smart Marriages. (2002). Available from http://www.smartmarriages.com.

MARGARET EDWARDS ARCUS
(WITH ASSISTANCE FROM D. CASSIDY [UNITED STATES],
M.J. CZAPLEWSKI [UNITED STATES], K. MAKINO [JAPAN],
A. UENO [JAPAN], AND R. WHITFIELD [UNITED KINGDOM])

FAMILY LITERACY

In 1983, Denny Taylor coined the term *family literacy* to describe the ways in which reading and writing were embedded in the daily lives of the middle-class families with whom she worked. Taylor's ethnographic study documented young children's early attempts at reading and writing for a variety of purposes, including writing lists and notes, and reading product labels, notices, and traffic signs. Taylor concluded that these parents did not deliberately set out to teach their children literacy skills. Rather, by encouraging children to participate in different literacy activities, parents and other family members supported early literacy development.

Family Literacy Programs

The recognition that children begin to learn literacy prior to formal schooling, and that family contexts shape literacy development, had profound implications for the field of early literacy. Since 1983, family literacy has emerged as a new and distinct field of inquiry. Although it originated as a concept describing the rich and varied ways that families use literacy in home and community settings, family literacy has increasingly become associated with formal programs aimed at improving the literacy of parents and their young children.

Some of the most common programs in the United States, Canada, and the United Kingdom are short-term, weekly sessions involving parents and young children in storybook reading and school readiness. One such program in Canada is *Parent-Child Mother Goose,* which aims to help parents support their children's oral language development. A slightly more structured program in Canada is the *Home Spun* model, which consists of a series of workshops on topics such as storybook reading, school readiness, oral language development, and parenting. The aims of such programs vary from teaching parents how to get their children ready for school, to drawing parents into discussions about family life, concerns about their own learning needs, and ways to make relationships between families and schools more democratic.

In the United States, family literacy legislation has allowed for more intensive programming known as the *comprehensive* or the *four component* family literacy model (NIFL 2001). The four components entail academic upgrading for parents, an early childhood development program, parenting and early literacy development, and a parent-child together (PACT) time, in which parents spend quality time with their children and try out new literacy ideas with them. The Even Start program in the United States is an example of such a program.

The programs described above vary in design and philosophy. Elsa Auerbach (1995) offers a conceptual framework that divides family literacy programs into three broad philosophical approaches: intervention/prevention, multiple literacies, and social change. In practice, these approaches are not mutually exclusive.

Family literacy programs reflecting an intervention/prevention approach aim to compensate for perceived inadequacies in parenting behaviors and home literacy activities, believed to negatively affect children's readiness for school (Darling 1993). The theoretical roots for this approach are in behavioral psychology, which conceptualizes reading and writing as sets of observable and measurable behaviors that can be regulated through appropriate interventions (Teale 1995). Such programs commonly target minority children and those from families with low socioeconomic status (SES) and families most *at risk* for school failure. Curricula include teaching English literacy and parenting skills and literacy behaviors believed to promote success in school literacy, such as storybook reading.

A second broad approach to family literacy programming is known as *multiple literacies,* which is informed by anthropological, sociolinguistic, and sociocultural studies. Here, literacy is seen not as a single skill, but rather as a set of practices grounded in social contexts and social roles (Barton 1994). This research shows how people are proficient in many or multiple literacies (such as media literacy, mathematical literacy, and technological literacy), including, but not limited to, the forms of literacy most strongly associated with schools. Programs reflecting a multiple-literacies perspective affirm cultural and linguistic diversity by conceptualizing home and school literacies as culturally specific ways of knowing. Curricula include investigating home and school literacy practices, integrating culturally familiar content and pedagogical practices into instruction and teaching, and maintaining home languages.

A third broad approach is associated with critical literacy and social change theories, informed by the work of Paulo Freire (1987) and Henri Giroux (1988). These programs present family literacy within a broader context of social inequities that shape power relationships among families, schools, and the broader society. The aim of social change approaches in family literacy programs is to transform social conditions that negatively affect family life through participant control of the programs, dialogue, and solution-oriented learning and teaching processes (Auerbach 1995).

Issues

Several debates have emerged in family literacy research and practice that stem from the varied philosophical approaches described above. With the growing popularity of family literacy, these debates have taken on new importance. These are described below.

Family-School Relationships

A key issue in family literacy is the relationship between home and school, and, more specifically, between literacy as valued and practiced in homes and literacy as valued and practiced in schools. For example, Shirley Brice Heath (1983) studied the literacy practices of three communities in the Carolina Piedmonts and found that the ways that white, middle-class families used literacy at home were most strongly associated with the forms of literacy taught in school. Consequently, these children tended to succeed in school. However, the literacy practices of African-American middle-class and working-class communities at home differed from the forms of literacy valued and taught in school. These children were less successful in school. Heath intended to demonstrate the need for more diverse and inclusive literacy teaching strategies in schools. However, the mismatch between home and school literacy has remained a topic of ongoing concern and debate. That is, many children from low-income homes, and for whom English is a second language, continue to score below their more privileged peers on standardized tests and in overall academic performance (Gunderson and Clarke 1998).

It is here that family literacy programs and research are best understood within a broader social and economic policy context. Scholars have linked the growth in family literacy programs with a concern over what is termed the literacy crisis, high dropout rates, and low academic achievement (Auerbach 1989). National studies and policies in North America and the United Kingdom (e.g., the International Adult Literacy Survey, OECD, 1996, and the United States' Equipped for the Future initiative, 2000) increasingly look beyond schools to families as the source of both the problem of and the solution to the low school achievement of minority and low-income children.

The understanding of *family* in these policies seems to be limited to mothers and primary caregivers and their young children. This phenomenon prompted Jane Mace to comment:

> The evidence of the literacy problem in industrialized countries with mass schooling systems has revealed that schools cannot alone meet this need. Families must therefore be recruited to do their bit, too. This is where the spotlight falls on the mother. She it is who must ensure that the young child arrives at school ready for school literacy, and preferably already literate. (1998, p. 5)

Another concern related to family literacy policies is the lack of longitudinal studies documenting their impact over time. Adele Thomas describes much of the research in family literacy as "testimonials" (1998, p. 20), suggesting that little attention has been paid to broad measures of program effectiveness.

Focus on Storybook Reading

Although ethnographic research with families reveals myriad forms and functions of reading and writing in daily life, many family literacy programs focus on reading story books to children as the way (Pellegrini 1991) to support children's literacy development. This emphasis on storybook reading apparently emanates from early research with precocious readers (Clarke 1976). This research, conducted mainly with white, middle-class families, indicates that reading to children was a common factor.

Several criticisms, however, have been raised about the emphasis on storybook reading. First, clear evidence shows that young children's literacy development is supported in many different ways in addition to storybook reading (Taylor 1983). Second, storybook reading is not common across all cultures and social classes; by emphasizing it, the literacy practices of minority and other groups are devalued. Third, not all children enjoy being read to, and the implication that it is necessary in order for children to learn to read causes some parents to insist on their children's participation. Hollis Scarborough and Wanda Dobrich (1994) cautioned that some children consequently develop negative attitudes toward reading. Finally, despite the importance placed on storybook reading, the empirical evidence suggests that it plays a less significant role in learning to read than is commonly believed (Scarborough and Dobrich 1994).

Early Childhood Focus

Another area of debate in the family literacy field is the wisdom of designing family literacy programs mainly for children from birth to five years old and their primary caregiver—usually the mother or grandmother. This has raised concerns about ignoring the literacy and learning needs of alternative families, as well as of older children, youth, and adults. Allan Luke and Carmen Luke (2001) make the case that the needs of adolescents experiencing literacy difficulties and their families are largely ignored, and resources are directed almost exclusively to young children.

Conclusion

In spite of the focus on early childhood, educators are beginning to develop family literacy programs for older children and their families. One such program is Effective Partners in Secondary Literacy Learning (EPISLL) developed by Trevor Cairney (1995). He reported success in helping parents, who themselves had not completed secondary school, to support their adolescent children's literacy learning.

Such initiatives point to positive aspects of family literacy programs and research, particularly those that aim to empower families to take an active and equitable role in their children's learning, as well as addressing broader social issues that shape literacy. For example, in Canada, PALS (Parents as Literacy Supporters) is a program where parents of kindergarten children in British Columbia identify that which they want to learn and help design sessions. Sessions vary from one community to the next, depending on parents' interests. The most powerful aspect of this program is that it lowers barriers between schools and parents because parents spend time working with their children in classrooms.

Increasingly, community partnerships are seen as a central part of family literacy provisions with the potential to address broader social issues that affect families. For example, rural and northern communities in Canada have formed a network of partnerships among community health organizations, schools, childcare centers, community colleges, universities, and family support programs to offer families seamless services that meet needs for learning opportunities, social support, and health care. Parents also have opportunities to spend time in their older children's schools, and to meet with health care professionals in informal settings. This promotes the formation of social support networks among families, contributes to community building, and builds the capacity of community partners to address the broader issues related to literacy, such as unemployment, parents' fear of schools, and social isolation.

Inner-city writing projects, such as the *Journal of Ordinary Thought*'s writing workshops in Chicago, Illinois, similarly provide a context for families to address important social issues, personal goals, and connections to their communities.

Family literacy programs are not a magic bullet for the complex issues facing families and schools in the twenty-first century. However, ideas associated with family literacy, such as holistic approaches to family support, the recognition of the importance of informal learning, and the vital role of families in shaping social change, can contribute to a vision of education that values diversity. The family literacy field continues to evolve, and the direction in which it goes will depend on the extent to which policies promote all, regardless of gender, culture, race, and class.

See also: ACADEMIC ACHIEVEMENT; COMPUTERS AND FAMILIES; HOMESCHOOLING; PARENTING EDUCATION; POVERTY; SCHOOL

Bibliography

Auerbach, E. (1989). "Toward a Social-Contextual Approach to Family Literacy." *Harvard Educational Review* 59:165–181.

Auerbach, E. (1995). "Deconstructing the Discourse of Strengths in Family Literacy." *Journal of Reading Behaviour* 27:643–61.

Barton, D. (1994)."Exploring Family Literacy." *RAPAL Bulletin* 24: 2–5.

Cairney, T. (1995). "Effective Partners in Secondary Literacy Learning." *Journal of Reading* 38:520–526.

Clark, M. (1976). *Young Fluent Readers*. London: Heinemann Educational.

Daisey, P. (1991). "Intergenerational Literacy Programs: Rationale, Description, and Effectiveness." *Journal of Clinical Child Psychology* 20:11–17.

Darling, S. (1993). "Family Literacy: An Intergenerational Approach to Education." *Viewpoints* 15:2–5.

Freire, P. (1985). *The Politics of Education*. Cambridge, MA: Bergin-Garvey.

Gunderson, L., and Clarke, D. (1998). "An Exploration of the Relationship Between ESL Students' Backgrounds and Their English and Academic Achievement." In *Yearbook of the National Reading Conference, 47,* ed. T. Shanahan and F. Rodriguez-Brown .Chicago: National Reading Conference.

Heath, S. (1983). *Ways with Words*. New York: Cambridge University Press.

Luke, A., and Luke, C. (2001). "Adolescence Lost/ Childhood Regained: On Early Intervention and the Emergence of the Techno-Subject." *Journal of Early Childhood Literacy* 1:91–120.

Mace, J. (1998). *Playing with Time: Mothers and the Meanings of Literacy*. London: UCL Press Limited.

OECD and Statistics Canada (1996). *Literacy, Economy, and Society: Results of the First International Adult Literacy Survey*. Author.

Pellegrini, A. (1991). "A Critique of the Concept of At Risk as Applied to Emergent Literacy." *Language Arts* 68:380–385.

Scarborough, H., and Dobrich, W. (1994). "On the Efficacy of Reading to Preschoolers." *Developmental Review* 14:245–302.

Taylor, D. (1983). *Family Literacy: Young Children Learning to Read and to Write*. Portsmouth, NH: Heinemann.

Teale, W. (1995). "Young Children and Reading: Trends Across the Twentieth Century." *Journal of Education* 177:95–127.

Thomas, A., ed. (1998). *Family Literacy in Canada: Profiles of Effective Practice*. Welland, Ontario: Soleil Publications.

JIM ANDERSON
SUZANNE SMYTHE
JACQUELINE LYNCH

FAMILY LOYALTY

Family loyalty refers to the feelings of mutual obligation, commitment, and closeness that exist among family members (e.g., parents and children, grandparents and grandchildren, siblings). This devotion or allegiance to one's family has been examined primarily with reference to social support or assistance from children to parents in later life (Burr and Mutchler 1999; Stone 1991). Specifically, studies have focused on measures of filial obligation (Ishii-Kuntz 1997; Hamon and Blieszner 1990; McGrew 1991; Sung 1995) and intergenerational solidarity or reciprocity (Bengston and Roberts 1991; Bengtson and Schrader 1982) to further understandings of loyalty within the context of the family.

In addition, much of the research on loyalty has been undertaken with Hispanic or Asian families, both in North America and abroad (Cortes 1995; Li 1997; Montoro-Rodriguez and Kosloski 1998; Rogler and Cooney 1984; Sung 1998) The focus on these cultural groups makes sense given the central importance of family harmony and solidarity in the traditional value systems of ethnocultural groups within these two populations.

Filial Obligation as an Indicator of Family Loyalty

Filial obligation is a cultural concept that refers to an adult child's sense of duty and commitment to respect and care for his or her parents in later life. This level of commitment or loyalty may vary according to different variables, including cultural context (Burr and Mutchler 1999; Lee and Peek 1999), level of acculturation of the child (Montoro-Rodriguez and Kosloski 1998), the quality of the relationship or emotional closeness between parent and child (Kobayashi 2000), children's resources (Ishii-Kuntz 1997), gender of the child (McGrew 1991), and parent's expectations (Ujimoto 1987).

Adherence to the value of filial obligation, a key indicator of family loyalty, has been examined in the literature on intergenerational co-residence in later-life families. For example, research on the living arrangements of Asian immigrant older adults has fueled the notion that Asian North Americans are more likely to live with family members than are their white counterparts, due to stronger kin networks and stronger filial traditions (Chow 1983; Himes, Hogan, and Eggebeen 1996; Maeda 1983). This conception of Asian North Americans as having ideal or close-knit families is an offshoot of the model minority myth (Ishii-Kuntz 1997), a stereotype that attributes the educational and occupational success of Asian North Americans to their adherence to traditional cultural value systems (Takaki 1989). In the context of family loyalty, the ideal family myth assumes that Asian North Americans, regardless of group or generation, greatly revere older family members and, as such, feel strongly obligated to provide emotional, financial, and service support to their aging parents (Ishii-Kuntz 1997; Osako 1976; Osako and Liu 1986). One of the key ways in which children demonstrate this support is through co-resident living arrangements. Indeed, as recently as 1994, researchers have attributed the prevalence of intergenerational co-residence among married children and older parents to the strong influence of filial obligation (Kamo and Zhou 1994). Co-residence, however, is only an example of behaviorally oriented filial piety and obligation (Sung 1995), and does not provide support for the hypothesis that Asian North American adult children necessarily provide more love and affection (emotionally oriented filial piety/obligation) to their aging parents than adult children in other ethnic groups.

Recent studies examining supportive family networks, coupled with an increased research interest in the translation of filial obligation among younger generations of adult children in Asian countries, have given rise to investigations of the effects of traditional family values on adult children's provision of support to their parents in Asian North American families (Ishii-Kuntz 1997; Kobayashi 2000). Much of the research in this area has been comparative (across Asian-origin groups) and, thus, has not addressed the intracultural diversity in parent-child relationships due to generational differences and immigration experiences (Ishii-Kuntz 1997; Kurzeja et al. 1986). One exception has been

Karen Kobayashi's (2000) investigation into continuity and change in older *nisei* (second generation) parent-adult *sansei* (third generation) child relationships in Japanese-Canadian families. The study incorporates a life-course approach, with its emphasis on historical, social structural, and cultural influences on the life-course. This approach provides insights into the effects of adherence to traditional Asian value systems on adult children's provision of support to parents in later life and to their feelings of family loyalty.

Solidarity as an Indicator of Family Loyalty

The concept of family solidarity or cohesion, as proposed by Vern Bengtson and his colleagues (1985), has been the source of many intergenerational family relations studies on *familism* over the past two decades. This view of family relations provides an important framework for understanding the roots of familism—the factors that contribute to the maintenance and/or development of loyalty within families.

Emotional closeness between parents and children and its impact on the quality of the parent-child bond is explored in research into the "intergenerational stake" (Bengtson and Kuypers 1971; Bond and Harvey 1991) and "intergenerational solidarity" (Bengtson and Schrader 1982; Roberts and Bengtson 1990). For example, the intergenerational stake hypothesis explores the cross-generational nature of emotional closeness between parents and children. The hypothesis holds that: (1) parents' descriptions of the relationship will be more positive than children's; and (2) different levels of investment and development may account for these variances in relationship perceptions. The intergenerational solidarity model goes a step further, looking at emotional closeness or "affect" between parents and children as just one of six indicators of solidarity or integration between generations in a family.

In a study examining the relationship between acculturation and family solidarity in Hispanic-American families, Julian Montoro-Rodriguez and Karl Kosloski (1998) find that for two dimensions of attitudinal familism (familial obligation and support from relatives), acculturation is positively related to familism. This means, contrary to assimilationist perspectives on family ties, that as Hispanic Americans become acculturated to the dominant Anglo culture, they continue to maintain and further develop loyalty to their families. That is, familism persists over time despite changes in, for example, language proficiency and preference, and ethnic origin of friends.

Further, Jeff Burr and Jan Mutchler (1999), in a study on ethnic variations and changing norms of filial responsibility among older adults, conclude that older Blacks and Hispanics are more likely than their non-Hispanic white counterparts to concur with the statement that each generation should provide assistance with living arrangements (e.g., co-residence) when needed. The likelihood that this attitude, an indicator of family loyalty, will translate into actual behavior, however, may be, as the solidarity model points out, dependent on a number of other factors, such as the level of emotional closeness between parent and child and the ability of children or parents to provide such support.

Conclusion

Family loyalty is defined primarily in two different ways: (1) as adherence to norms of filial obligation; and (2) as the level of intergenerational solidarity or closeness between the generations in a family. Both of these definitions have been studied within ethnocultural family contexts. Specifically, much of the research on filial obligation has focused on Asian and Asian immigrant families, while other investigations into the development and maintenance of familistic attitudes and behaviors—the foundation for solidarity—have been done with Hispanic immigrants.

One shortcoming of the literature on family loyalty is that it fails to incorporate broader definitions or measures; that is, the research continues to define and measure loyalty according to adult children's levels of filial obligation or as attitudinal or behavioral congruence or similarity between parents and children. Clearly, other intragenerational measures, such as the quality of children's relationship with siblings and the quality of husband-wife relationships, can be used to measure familism.

Finally, to gain a better understanding of family loyalty across ethno-cultural groups, particularly in countries with large immigrant populations like Canada and the United States, it is important to explore the diversity that exists within each group.

Future research in this area then should examine the effects of ethnic identity, language spoken in the home, and immigrant status on measures of loyalty within families. Such analyses will provide valuable insights into the nature of loyalty in ethnic minority families.

See also: FAMILISM; FAMILY STRENGTHS; FILIAL RESPONSIBILITY

Bibliography

Bengtson, V. L., and Roberts, R. E. L. (1991). "Intergenerational Solidarity in Aging Families: An Example of Formal Theory Construction." *Journal of Marriage and the Family* 53:856–870.

Bengtson, V. L., and Schrader, S. S. (1982). "Parent-Child Relations." In *Handbook of Research Instruments in Social Gerontology,* ed. D. Mangen and W. Peterson. Minneapolis: University of Minnesota Press.

Bond, J. B., and Harvey, C. D. H. (1991). "Ethnicity and Intergenerational Perceptions of Family Solidarity." *International Journal of Aging and Human Development* 33:33–44.

Burr, J. A., and Mutchler, J. E. (1999). "Race and Ethnic Variation in Norms of Filial Responsibility among Older Persons." *Journal of Marriage and the Family* 61:674–687.

Chow, N. W-S. (1983). "The Chinese Family and Support of the Elderly in Hong Kong." *The Gerontologist* 23:584–588.

Cortes, D. E. (1995). "Variations in Familism in Two Generations of Puerto Ricans." *Hispanic Journal of Behavioral Sciences* 17:249–255.

Hamon, R. R., and Blieszner, R. (1990). "Filial Responsibility Expectations among Adult Child-Older Parent Pairs." *Journal of Gerontology* 45:P110–P112.

Himes, C. L.; Hogan, D. P.; and Eggebeen, D. J. (1996). "Living Arrangements of Minority Elders." *Journal of Gerontology* 51B:S42–48.

Ishii-Kuntz, M. (1997). "Intergenerational Relationships among Chinese, Japanese, and Korean Americans." *Family Relations* 46:23–32.

Kamo, Y., and Zhou, M. (1994). "Living Arrangements of Elderly Chinese and Japanese in the United States." *Journal of Marriage and the Family* 56:544–558.

Kobayashi, K. M. (2000). "The Nature of Support from Adult Sansei (Third Generation) Children to Older Nisei (Second Generation) Parents in Japanese Canadian Families." *Journal of Cross-Cultural Gerontology* 15:185–205.

Kurzeja, P. L.; Koh, S. D.; Koh, T.; and Liu, W. T. (1986). "Ethnic Attitudes of Asian American Elderly." *Research on Aging* 8:110–127.

Lee, G. R.; Netzer, J. K.; and Coward, R. T. (1994). "Filial Responsibility Expectations and Patterns of Intergenerational Assistance." *Journal of Marriage and the Family* 56:559–565.

Lee, G. R.; Peek, C. W.; and Coward, R. T. (1998). "Race Differences in Filial Responsibility: Expectations among Older Parents." *Journal of Marriage and the Family* 60:404–12.

Li, C. (1997). "Shifting Perspectives: Filial Mortality Revisited." *Philosophy East and West* 47:211–232.

Maeda, D. (1983). "Family Care in Japan." *The Gerontologist* 23:579–583.

McGrew, K. B. (1991). *Daughters' Decision-Making about the Nature and Level of Their Participation in the Long-Term Care of Their Dependent Elderly Mothers: A Qualitative Study.* Oxford, OH: Scripps Gerontology Centre.

Montoro-Rodriguez, J. M., and Kosloski, K. (1998). "The Impact of Acculturation on Attitudinal Familism in a Community of Puerto Rican Americans." *Hispanic Journal of Behavioural Sciences* 20:375–391.

Osako, M. M. (1979). "Aging and Family among Japanese Americans: The Role of the Ethnic Tradition in the Adjustment to Old Age." *The Gerontologist* 5:448–455.

Osako, M. M., and Liu, W. T. (1986). "Intergenerational Relations and the Aged among Japanese Americans." *Research on Aging* 8:128–155.

Rogler, L. H., and Cooney, T. (1984). *Puerto Rican Families in New York City: Intergenerational Processes.* Maplewood, NJ: Waterfront.

Stone, R. (1991). "Familial Obligation: Issues for the 1990s." *Generations* 15:47–50.

Sung, K. (1995). "Measures and Dimensions of Filial Piety in Korea." *The Gerontologist* 35:240–247.

Takaki, R. (1989). *Strangers from a Different Shore.* New York: Penguin Books.

Ujimoto, K. V. (1987). "Organizational Activities, Cultural Factors, and Well-Being of Aged Japanese Canadian." In *Ethnic Dimensions of Aging,* ed. D. E. Gelfand and C. Barresi. New York: Springer.

KAREN M. KOBAYASHI

FAMILY MINISTRY

Family ministry is a term used to describe the many and diverse activities of religious congregations in support of family relationships. Although congregations of many different religious traditions worldwide have activities and programs for families, the term *family ministry* has been used predominantly in the Roman Catholic Church internationally and in other Christian churches in the United States, including mainline and evangelical Protestant denominations and their congregations, and congregations organized independently of any denomination.

Family ministry often takes the shape of family-targeted educational programs, such as parent and marriage education programs, support groups for families dealing with various life issues (illness, disability, divorce), and counseling services for families in crisis. Family ministry can also refer to all the programs and services that take place in a particular location; a congregation's *Family Life Center* can include a wide assortment of programs and services: exercise and fitness programs, sports activities, stress management seminars, childcare, and emergency assistance for families in crisis, for example. Finally, congregations collaborate to provide services to families through other agencies, supporting these agencies financially and with volunteers: community family and children's service agencies, residential treatment programs for children with mental illness or behavioral disorders, residential programs for older adults, counseling centers, community centers, agencies providing emergency assistance to families in need, foster care and adoption agencies, and so on.

Family ministry refers not only to family-targeted programs, however, but also to the ways congregations support and strengthen families simply by being a supportive community. Intergenerational friendships develop as people worship, share fellowship meals, serve others, do the business of the congregation, and play together. These friendships can encourage and sustain members of families in the celebrations, challenges, and crises that family living presents. Congregations often support families by providing celebrations of births and marriages, informal mentoring to new parents or spouses, friendly visiting to families in grief or crisis, meals and other tangible support in times of illness and death in the family, and the support of prayer and concern across many life circumstances.

Finally, family ministry targets not only families who are members of the congregation but also families in the larger community and world. Family ministry includes congregations volunteering to serve as mentors to families in their community seeking to escape poverty and welfare, providing after-school activity programs to keep neighborhood children safe and help them succeed in school while their parents are working, providing transportation and support to children of incarcerated parents who want to visit their parents in prison, or collecting funds and supplies to send to families in distant places who have been impoverished by war or natural disaster.

Why Congregations Do Family Ministry

Families are one of the most significant contexts in which people attempt to live the principles of their religious faith. The Roman Catholic Church officially declared at Vatican II, "The family is not merely like the Church, but is truly Church." Learning to live justly and lovingly with family members is a challenging daily discipline. When congregations provide education and support programs for families, they are, in essence, providing spiritual guidance. Learning to discipline children wisely, lovingly, and effectively is not simply a way that parents can be more effective parents, but is also an expression of their religious beliefs about what it means to be parents. In short, congregations do family ministry in order to help people live their faith, even and especially in their most intimate relationships.

Second, religious congregations have a mission of service. For Christians, serving people who live in poverty or are otherwise in need is one of the most significant ways of expressing love for God. In the words of Jesus Christ, "whoever welcomes a children like this in my name welcomes me" (Matthew 18:5 *New International Version*); those who welcome strangers, provide clothing and food to those in need, and visit the sick and imprisoned are doing these thing for Jesus himself (see Matthew 25:31–46).

For centuries, religious congregations were often the only places that families in poverty or in crisis could find help. Members of congregations often informally adopted children orphaned by war and disease. In the aftermath of the American Civil War, so many children were orphaned that individual families could not absorb them, and churches began opening children's homes, especially in the South.

In the early twentieth century, the social work profession began as middle-class women volunteers from congregations started to serve as *friendly visitors,* visiting poor women and their families, often immigrants, to offer encouragement and support. Many of the first settlement houses designed to serve as community centers in slums were staffed and supported by members of congregations who served as an expression of religious vocation. Although not called family ministry, all of these efforts, and many others, had the same purpose—to encourage and strengthen families, and to care for children when their families could not.

In the mid-twentieth century, a second impetus arose for the flurry of programs that came to be called family ministry, however. There has been increasing concern over the growing fragility of family relationships not only in the larger culture, but also within congregations. Since the 1940s, American congregational leaders have been sounding a warning. The Christian family magazine *Home Life* was first published in 1947 by the largest Protestant denomination in the United States, the Southern Baptist Convention. In introducing this new publication, Clifton J. Allen, executive secretary of the Southern Baptist Sunday School Board, wrote:

> Your heart beats with the conviction, "There's no place like home." But one out of five homes crashes on the rocks of divorce. Family life is being blighted by strong drink, lust, and worldly pleasure. Happiness is driven from literally millions of homes by misunderstanding, selfishness, irreligion, and ignorance. The home front is under siege. This peril is a call to action. Fathers and mother must awake to their God-given privilege and responsibility. Churches must grasp their supreme opportunity to help parents build virile Christian homes. . . . Our homes demand and deserve our best. They are at the center of God's plan. . . . They are the fountain of our nation's life. They are set to preserve

the heritage of civilization and to perpetuate the ideals of godliness. (p. 1)

Similar alarms were sounded in other Christian denominations as well. In the mid-twentieth century, when the divorce rate rose to almost one out of two marriages, denominations and congregations began a number of initiatives to shore up family life: publications, marriage preparation, marriage enrichment, parent education programs, and family counseling.

The first marriage enrichment and encounter programs began in Spain in the Roman Catholic Church and rapidly spread to the United States. From Rome, Catholic leaders began advocating taking a family perspective in planning, implementing, and evaluating policies, programs, ministries, and services of the church.

Finally, some congregations have used family ministry programs as marketing tools—a way of reaching out and bringing others into the congregation. People who will not come to a worship service will come to a course that addresses the stresses of living. People will come use the church gymnasium when they will not come to a Bible study.

Congregational Family Ministry and Public Family Service Programs

The community mental health center movement of the 1960s in the United States provided interesting parallels and opportunities for professional collaboration between congregational leaders developing family ministries and community social service professionals. Sometimes, the same people were involved in both movements. Community mental health was a new government initiative supported by the social service professions. The federal government provided major funding to develop centers whose purpose was to lower the incidence of mental illness in a community through prevention programs, and to treat those with mental illness and developmental disabilities in their own families and communities rather than in large state mental hospitals and institutions. Because theory of the day suggested that family processes caused or at least contributed to mental illness, developing healthy families was a significant focus of these centers. Both family ministry and the community mental health movement emphasized prevention of family problems when possible and crisis intervention to keep existing problems from worsening.

Government funding for community mental health centers was time-limited and never fully adequate, however. Increasingly, social service professionals looked to other institutions to provide prevention and family life education services. Both public schools and churches are located in virtually every community and touch the lives of many community families. Consequently, many community leaders, with the support of social service professionals, began to advocate for these institutions to take on responsibility for providing the prevention, education, and counseling services for families.

Who Leads Family Ministry?

The parallel developments of community mental health services and church family ministry programs have shaped the leadership of family ministry. During the 1960s and 1970s, research and theory in family sociology and psychology were mushrooming. Family therapy was developing into a profession. Seminary degree programs that educated church clergy were increasingly providing content in their basic ministry degree programs in pastoral care and family counseling. That content drew directly from the social sciences and the professional literature of psychology, psychiatry, social work, and family therapy. Larger seminaries began offering specialized degree programs in psychology, social work, and family therapy. Pastoral care was also becoming recognized as a ministry specialization, and many came to seminary to prepare for church positions as pastoral counselors. Grounded in the social science literature of research and professional practice, these new church leaders saw the significant role that congregations could play in providing professional services to families through premarital preparation, educational programs, and family counseling. Although churches had historically been involved in these activities, now professionally educated social workers, psychologists, and pastoral counselors were offering leadership and writing resources in family ministry for congregations.

Most congregations, however, have small professional staffs and cannot afford to have someone identified as the official family minister. Family ministry often is the responsibility of a congregation's clergy leaders who are not themselves family professionals or family ministry specialists. Family ministry is also often led by a committee of lay persons designated to be advocates for families in all the programs of the congregation. In some large congregations or congregations with a special emphasis in family ministry, family professionals serve as congregational leaders, whether as full-time, part-time, or volunteer staff in congregational life. At the end of the twentieth century, many congregations had begun employing family counselors or at least providing counselors with use of the congregations' buildings as places to conduct private counseling practices. These counselors were variously trained as social workers, pastoral counselors, psychologists, and marriage and family therapists.

In order to provide a resource to congregational leaders in family ministry, a group of family professionals began publishing *The Journal of Family Ministry* in 1987, later renamed *Family Ministry: Empowering Through Faith*. A second professional publication in family ministry was launched in 1999, the *Audio-Magazine in Family Ministry (AM/FM)*. Many denominations publish guidebooks for congregations in doing annual program planning in family ministry, and such writers as Diana Garland, Don Hebbard, Ben Freudenberg and Rick Lawrence, and Merton Strommen and Richard Hardel are providing resources for congregations across denominations and Christian traditions.

Methods of Family Ministry

There are four methods of family ministry: (1) developing a congregational life that supports and nurtures all families; (2) organizing and facilitating support groups and networks; (3) providing educational resources and programs; and (4) counseling (Garland 1999).

Developing a congregational life that supports and nurtures all family relationships. The fundamental and essential method of family ministry is congregational development as a supportive and nurturing community. The other three methods of family ministry, which are more overtly focused specifically on family issues, depend on the existence of this supportive congregational life. Community life is particularly important as a context for helping families deal with specific life stressors and situations, whether they are common to all kinds of families or are characteristic of particular kinds of family structures and experiences.

Some faith groups become havens, communities that counter the values of mainstream society. They may have ways of living designed to protect members from negative cultural influences. The Amish continue to live a lifestyle that sets them apart from the surrounding social world. Less radically, some congregations choose to provide their children with day care and schools as a means of controlling what they are taught and protecting them from unwanted influences. Others provide support to parents who choose to homeschool their children.

A few communities of faith may use communal principles, sharing cars and other expensive items, making it less necessary for so many family members to work outside their homes or to make choices about fewer work hours and less demanding careers. In one congregation, a number of families have intentionally bought homes in the same block of an inner-city community, using their presence to bring new stability and safety to the neighborhood. They share evening meals, each household taking a turn in feeding the others. The church may be intentional in guiding and supporting families in making these choices and in using their presence as a means of creating positive social change.

Even congregations that do not go so far as to develop physical communities still often serve as significant social communities in the lives of families. There families find others who share and support their values and family culture, who provide advice and resources for family living, and who help them with life challenges.

Being an advocate for families is an essential part of being a supportive and nurturing community. Congregations have voices that need to be used in behalf of the needs not only of their own members, but also of their neighbors, whomever and wherever they may be. A congregation can be the leaven that raises the consciousness of the whole community about needs and vulnerabilities of families. Advocacy can range from encouraging members to run for posts on the local school board to contacting national government representatives concerning government policies that affect families. It can be as simple as writing letters to the local television stations applauding their family programming and discouraging the broadcasting of shows with violent content. Or it can be much more hands-on, such as organizing families in a poor community to find ways to clean their neighborhoods of gang violence and drugs.

Organizing and facilitating support groups and networks. Supporting and advocating for families is the foundation for family ministry. In addition, congregations may develop specific programs and services to address particular issues in family life. These programs and services can be conceptualized as a continuum from the most general to more specialized forms of family ministry. Families are helped by being with other families who share their life situations—parents of teenagers, caregivers of people with Alzheimer's disease, mentors of single parents, parents of young adults who are troubled by substance addiction, grandparents raising their grandchildren. Together, families learn from and support one another. This support may be formalized in a group, or it may be a more loosely structured network of families who are in touch with one another as they choose. The role of the church leader is primarily helping families find and become linked with one another, and helping them, if needed, to identify resources that can be helpful to them. The families themselves provide any leadership needed for their group or network, although professional staff persons can help equip them and support them in this role.

Providing educational programs and resources. Some families want or need to learn new information or skills that will help them with their particular situation in life. Educational groups or seminars such as parent education or premarital education are common in congregations. Congregational leaders take more visible leadership roles in providing this kind of ministry, either providing the educational content themselves or securing other knowledgeable educators. Congregational leaders may also provide families with educational resources such as books or videotapes for families to use individually.

Counseling. Finally, some families have barriers to learning information or skills they need. These barriers need to be addressed in individual, family, or group counseling. For example, a marital couple may be so angry with one another that they cannot learn in a group setting about anger and conflict management until they have been guided through their current crisis. Families face a variety of crises that need the individual attention provided in a counseling relationship. Congregational leaders may either provide this counseling or refer to community professionals who can do so.

Family counseling thus plays a supportive, not a central, role to the family ministries of congregations. Counseling is like tutoring, preparing people who need help in overcoming obstacles to their full participation in the mutual relationships of a community. Some families are dealing with crises beyond the capabilities of the congregation to respond. They need the loving support of the congregation, but they may also need a professional counselor to help them deal with such issues as post-traumatic stress syndrome after the death of a family member, a deep disappointment in life, and other difficult life circumstances.

See also: CATHOLICISM; EVANGELICAL CHRISTIANITY; FAMILY LIFE EDUCATION; MARRIAGE ENRICHMENT; MARRIAGE PREPARATION; PARENTING EDUCATION; PROTESTANTISM; RELIGION

Bibliography

AM/FM: Audio-Magazine in Family Ministry. Waco, TX: Baylor University Center for Family and Community Ministries.

Browning, D. S.; Miller-McLemore, B. J.; Couture, P. D.; Lyon, K. B.; and Franklin, R. M. (1997). *From Culture Wars to Common Ground: Religion and the American Family Debate.* Louisville, KY: Westminster John Knox Press.

Family Ministry: Empowering Through Faith. Louisville, KY: Louisville Presbyterian Theological Seminary.

Freudenburg, B., and Lawrence, R. (1998). *The Family-Friendly Church.* Loveland, CO: VitalMinistry.

Garland, D. R. (1994). *Church Agencies: Caring for Children and Families in Crisis.* Washington, DC: Child Welfare League of America.

Garland, D. R. (1999). *Family Ministry: A Comprehensive Guide.* Downers Grover, IL: InterVarsity Press.

Hebbard, D. W. (1995). *The Complete Handbook for Family Life Ministry in the Church.* Nashville, TN: Thomas Nelson Publishers.

Lyon, K. B., and Smith, A., Jr., eds. (1998). *Tending the Flock: Congregations and Family Ministry.* Louisville, KY: Westminster John Knox Press.

Strommen, M. P., and Hardel, R. A. (2000). *Passing On the Faith: A Radical New Model for Youth and Family Ministry.* Winona, MN: Saint Mary's Press.

DIANA R. GARLAND

FAMILY PLANNING

Family planning is both a descriptive term and an organizational one. It was originally conceived as a public relations effort to emphasize the broadened scope of those involved in the struggle to spread the concept of birth control. The term achieved popularity in England before it did in the United States, and in May 1939, various British birth control groups amalgamated into the Family Planning Association, including in their program treatment for infertility and minor gynecological problems, child spacing, and contraceptive instruction and equipment. In the United States the name of the American Birth Control League was changed to the Planned Parenthood Federation in 1941 to emphasize the broad focus of family planning. The Planned Parenthood name was also adopted by the international federation that formed after the end of World War II, and family planning or *planned parenthood* became universal descriptors.

Broadly defined, family planning is the act of making a conscious plan about the number and timing of children's births. Timing may include the time of the first birth, the amount of space between births, and when to stop having children. It can include abortion, a discussion of the various means of contraception, and fertility testing and even treatment. Family planning involves not only the individual or couple, but society as well.

Methods and Effectiveness

People have consciously or unconsciously engaged in family planning throughout history. Abstinence, either lifelong or temporary, and prohibitions forbidding intercourse during certain times of the year or during certain festivals effectively curtail the fertility rate (the number of live births for each women during her lifetime). Separation of husbands and wives for long periods of time by war or business trips also curtails the fertility rate.

Abortion has often been used to limit family size, and descriptions of abortifacients, or agents that cause abortion, can be found in the herbal and other folklore of women and midwives of most societies. The deliberate abandonment of infants and young children, even killing of newborns, has not been uncommon in the past or even in some areas of the world today. Although the early Christian Church outlawed infanticide, it emphasized the stigma of illegitimacy, which meant that out-of-wedlock infants were brought to overcrowded orphanages and monasteries, where the majority of them died of starvation or disease within a few months.

Prolonged lactation is also a factor in spacing births. Lactation and the stimulus of the infant sucking ordinarily suppresses ovulation and menstruation, but it is highly effective as a birth control mechanism only when the infant consumes nothing but breast milk or when couples normally abstain from intercourse during lactation. As partial weaning takes place—as early as four to six months—the menstrual cycle returns in most women who are adequately nourished, and pregnancy is again possible.

Numerous devices such as condoms and IUDS (intrauterine devices) have been and still are used in family planning. Alternate methods of intercourse, including withdrawal and anal intercourse, also lessen the chance of pregnancy. One of the earliest results of the use of broad-scale methods sufficient to affect national fertility was the decline in the French birth rate from the end of the eighteenth century, a decline attributed to the widespread use of coitus interruptus (Van de Walle 1978). The continuing search for means of controlling contraception emphasizes an almost universal desire for humans to gain some control over the number and spacing of births.

The effectiveness of family planning is measured by the fertility rate, the total number of live births a woman at age fifty would have had. The replacement rate for a stable population is over two and under three. In the twentieth century, many countries had fertility rates below the replacement ratio but still gained population because people were living longer and several generations of a family were alive at the same time. In determining potential rates of increase without any family planning, demographers traditionally have used Hutterite women as their maximum standard for potential. The Hutterites are members of a religious denomination (in the northern United States and Southern Canada) who in the past did not use any method of family planning, although evidence suggests that this is changing. Their living standard is not luxurious, but their food supply is more than adequate, and they are regarded as very healthy.

Hutterite women bore an average of twelve children in the early part of the twentieth century (Coale 1971), and this has been considered the maximum for a totally uninhibited rate of fertility that only could reached under the best possible conditions. Current fertility rates in some countries of the Third World, such as Saudi Arabia, Malawi, and Rwanda, were between seven and eight at the beginning of the 1990s, but even these had dropped to between six and seven at the end of the decade (International Planned Parenthood Federation 2002), indicating the growing influence of family planning.

Social Regulation

Organized efforts at family planning began to appear in the nineteenth century although, as in the case of France, some forces were at work earlier. The nineteenth-century efforts were started by individuals concerned with the poverty and malnutrition that seemed to be endemic among large families. Governmental bodies initially paid little attention to such efforts, and when they did they often opposed the advocates of family planning. In the United States, for example, governmental agencies such as the post office in the last part of the nineteenth century classified family planning materials as pornography. At the beginning of the twentieth century, President Theodore Roosevelt compared women who avoided pregnancy to men who refused to serve in the armed services in time of great national emergency. He argued that U.S. women had a patriotic duty to have children. Not until the last part of the twentieth century did governments in general take direct or indirect action to encourage family planning. This concern came primarily because of a growing concern about overpopulation, but it also reflected the growing influence of women on national policy.

At the beginning of the Industrial Revolution in the eighteenth century, the world population was estimated at 750 million. With growing urbanization and industrialization, growth escalated rapidly, reaching one billion in 1830, two billion in 1930, three billion in 1960, five billion by 1990, and six billion in 2000. It will probably continue to grow—unless there is radical change in trends—until 2020, after which a slow decline will begin. The growth, as indicated above, is due to declining mortality as the standard of living and sanitation have improved and communicable diseases controlled. The most rapid growth has not been in the highly industrialized countries but in those that have not yet industrialized. As the standard of living has risen in Western Europe, the United States, and similar countries, the fertility rate by 1990 had already fallen below two and in some as low as one and three-tenths (Green 1992).

Most countries have relied on education in family planning to lower fertility rates, although more drastic means have also been used. In India, for example, the government of the late Indira Gandhi was forced to cut back on their program because it was alleged that sterilization was being forced on the less educated peasants. The problem of overpopulation is compounded in many of the underdeveloped countries because the largest segment of their population is in the childbearing years. In these places, even with the more or less drastic lowering of fertility ratios, population will continue to grow. The People's Republic of China in the 1980s became the first country in the world to embark on a deliberate and comprehensive course to reach zero population growth by the end of 2000 or as soon after that as possible. In spite of drastic efforts to limit families to one child, forcing families in the cities to get permission to even try to get pregnant, and the use of drastic sterilization and abortion programs, the country failed to meet its goal, and its population in 2001 was nearly 1,300,000,000. It is, however, well on its way to doing so, and soon it will be surpassed as the country with the largest population by India (which stands at 1,034,000,000).

The Chinese policy uses, on the one hand, the carrot and stick, with promises of better schooling and other rewards for families who have only one child, and on the other hand, forced abortions or sterilizations for those who have more. In 1993 the government approved a bill to forbid marriages of persons with hepatitis and other sexually transmitted diseases, mental illness, and congenital disabilities, but the Chinese experiment emphasizes the difficulty that even authoritarian states have in encouraging family planning. In the United States, where the fertility rate is under two, in the year 2000 more than 30 percent of the women did not use any modern mechanical or chemical method of contraception. Half of the U.S. pregnancies are believed to be unplanned or unwanted, a rate that is higher than in most other industrial countries. This is one reason for the high—although declining—abortion rate in the United States. Most of the pregnancies in the United States occurred among women who came from disadvantaged backgrounds and were under twenty-five. This suggests that in general, not everyone in the United States has fully changed to the belief in an overpopulated world. How much they should change their beliefs is a matter of public discussion. That fact that not all the U.S. states gave people access to contraception until 1965, and that abortions were prohibited until 1973, emphasizes the difficulty family planning had in being accepted.

Evidence suggests that about 600 million people use contraception, and millions more would do so if they had access to high-quality services. To reach them, family planning advocates have adopted an educational four-point program that points out what family planning does: First, it saves women's lives. Avoiding unintended pregnancies could prevent about one-fourth of all maternal deaths in developing countries. Using contraceptives helps women avoid unsafe abortions, limit birth to their healthiest childbearing years, and prevent giving birth more times than is good for their health. Second, family planning saves children's lives. Spacing pregnancies at least two years apart helps women have healthier children and improves the odds of infants' survival by about 50 percent. Limiting births to a woman's healthiest childbearing years also improves her children's chances of surviving and remaining healthy. Third, women are given more choices. Controlling their own childbearing by using effective contraception can open the door to education, employment, and community involvement. Couples who have fewer children are more likely to send their daughters as well as sons to schools. Fourth, family planning encourages the adoption of safer sexual behavior. All sexually active people need to protect themselves against sexually transmitted infections (STIs), including HIV/AIDS. Using condoms or avoiding sex except in a mutually monogamous relationship are the best ways to do so. Advocates also emphasize that effective family planning helps protect the environment and aids economic development by slowing population growth.

Although governments increasingly have taken an active role in pushing family planning, many professionals believe that the keys to success are also encouraging individual advocacy—presenting

A poster promoting the "One-Child Family" policy in the People's Republic of China. China was the first country in the world to embark on a deliberate and comprehensive course to reach zero population growth by the end of 2000. OWEN FRANKEN/CORBIS

stories of people's personal experiences showing how family planning improves individual lives—and encouraging nongovernmental organized groups to carry out educational campaigns. Several published guides on advocacy are available, including International Planned Parenthood Federation's *Advocacy Guide* and the Population Information Program at Johns Hopkins University, *A Frame for Advocacy*. The optimal situation for family planning involves a discussion between both members of the couple before they begin to have sexual relations and includes a sharing of mutual hopes and desires to make sure they are sufficiently congruent to achieve a good marriage or partnership. These discussions should include all aspects of planning (whether marriage will occur and when, whether children are planned and when, and the number and spacing of children). They should consider early in the discussion whether the individual man or woman wants to have children. Most young people want at least one child, although they may change their minds over time. If a couple decides to have children, they must then plan the number of children. People make these decisions in the context of the norms of their individual groups, although it is good to keep in mind that such norms can also change, which emphasizes the need for ongoing discussion.

Infertility

Perhaps the best indicator of the North American and increasingly worldwide desire for children is the growing ongoing concern with infertility, something that is also part of family planning. Somewhere between 10 and 15 percent of all couples have difficulty conceiving, with the causes about equally divided between men and women. Major causes include venereal infections, failure to ovulate, low sperm count, obstructions in either the male or female reproductive organs, and impenetrable cervical mucus. Sometimes these problems can be treated with antibiotics, surgery, or hormones. If these methods fail, couples may also try artificial insemination or in vitro fertilization—approaches that have have been successful for many couples. The down side to their use, however, is that now that these technological approaches to conception are available, some couples feel obligated to try to have a baby. The complex approaches, including in vitro fertilizations, are expensive, time consuming, and often disappointing.

Conclusion

Ideal family planning includes consideration of the timing of marriage, number and spacing of children, and when the first and last births will occur. It requires that couples discuss sexuality, contraception, and other long-range plans such as schooling or work plans that affect births. North Americans still do little of this planning, and teenagers receive insufficient instruction about these topics. Family planning should be an important part of the modern lifestyle. If individuals do not take on this responsibility, there is always the potential that government, as in the case of China, will see a need to intervene.

See also: ABORTION; ACQUIRED IMMUNODEFICIENCY SYNDROME (AIDS); ABSTINENCE; ASSISTED

REPRODUCTIVE TECHNOLOGIES; BIRTH CONTROL: CONTRACEPTIVE METHODS; BIRTH CONTROL: SOCIOCULTURAL AND HISTORICAL ASPECTS; CHILDCARE; CHILDLESSNESS; CIRCUMCISION; FERTILITY; HUTTERITE FAMILIES; INFANTICIDE; PREGNANCY AND BIRTH; SEXUALITY; SEXUALITY EDUCATION; SEXUALLY TRANSMITTED DISEASES; SINGLE-PARENT FAMILIES

Bibliography

Bullough, B., and Bullough, V. (1998). *Contraception.* Buffalo, NY: Prometheus Books.

Bullough, V. (2001). *Encyclopedia of Birth Control.* Santa Barbara, CA: ABC-Clio.

Bullough, V., and Bullough, B. (1983–84). "Population Control vs. Freedom in China." *Free Inquiry* 3:12–15.

Bullough, V., and Bullough, B. (1995) *Sexual Attitudes: Myths and Realities.* Buffalo, NY: Prometheus.

Central Intelligence Agency. (1998). *The World Factbook 1997–98.* Washington, DC: Brassey.

Cleland, J., and Hobcraft, J., eds. (1985) *Reproductive Change in Developing Countries: Insights from the World Fertility Survey.* Oxford, UK: Oxford University Press.

Coale, A. J. (1971). "The Decline of Fertility in Europe from the French Revolution to World War II." In *Fertility and Family Planning: A World View,* ed. S. J. Behrman, L. Cors, Jr., and R. Freedman. Ann Arbor: University of Michigan Press.

Freeman, S., and Bullough, V. (1993). *The Complete Guide to Fertility Planning.* Buffalo, NY: Prometheus.

Green, C. P. (1992). *The Environment and Population Growth: Decade for Action.* Supplement to *Population Reports,* Series M., No. 10, Vol. 20. Baltimore: Population Information Program, The Johns Hopkins University.

McKeown, T. (1976). *The Modern Rise of Population.* New York: Academic Press.

Van de Walle, E. (1978). "Alone in Europe, The French Fertility Decline Until 1850." In *Historical Studies of Changing Fertility,* ed. C. Tilly. Princeton, NJ: Princeton University Press.

"Why Family Planning Matters." *Population Reports,* Series J., Number 49, 2000.

Other Resources

International Planned Parenthood Federation. (2002). Available from http://www.ippf.org.

VERN L. BULLOUGH

FAMILY POLICY

All social and economic policies affect families, but the term *family policy* usually refers to social programs, laws, and public directives designed to promote and enhance marriage, reproduction, and raising children. Family policy also ensures child protection and child and spousal support and attempts to resolve conflicts between work and family. The state usually initiates such policies, but employers or voluntary organizations may also establish them. Legislatures and governments that create laws and policy, as well as the agencies mandated and financed to enforce them, such as child welfare agencies, will be referred to as *the state.* This entry focuses on policies and social programs initiated by governments. It investigates how academics have studied these policies and how they have explained variations among nations.

Until the 1980s, many governments saw *the family* as the basic unit of social support and respected family privacy unless children were flagrantly neglected or abused, discipline problems were apparent, or parents were clearly impoverished. Nevertheless, the state in industrialized countries has regulated some aspects of family life for more than a century, requiring the registration of marriages, births, and deaths. It has also legalized marriage, adoption, and separation, and tried to ensure that men support their wives and children. The state has also provided income security and social services for families in need (Ursel 1992).

Many nations never develop social benefits for families because they cannot acquire sufficient fiscal resources or because their governments are too unstable to sustain the development of social programs. Developing nations often spend scarce public resources on defense or debt repayment, but may also provide retirement pensions for the army or civil service. Civilian families are expected to fend for themselves. Birth rates in less developed nations are typically high because many parents rely on their children to help support the family and to provide financial security for aging parents. Family policies often focus on reducing overpopulation, child malnutrition, infant and maternal mortality, and child labor, as well as finding homes for orphans and abandoned children.

Some industrialized countries have not developed explicit family policies because they cannot gain consensus about what the family is or how to encourage its development and cohesion. Two broad opinions exist among the lobby groups pressuring governments, especially in English-speaking countries. One contends that family structure and behavior reflect individual preferences as well as the trends and tensions in the broader society. Therefore, governments cannot easily modify personal behavior through social programs or legislation, but they need to acknowledge that parents make an important social contribution in producing children. Parents also need ongoing public support, especially when they raise children under difficult circumstances. The contrasting view is that the family is deteriorating and declining as the major institution in society. As a result, social legislation needs to bolster the family (or a preferred version of family) in the fight against the intrusion of alternative and unhealthful (or immoral) lifestyles. The political left, feminist organizations, and gay and lesbian groups express the first view; the second view is more prevalent among political and social conservatives and the Christian right.

Welfare State Development

From the 1940s to the 1970s, governments in industrialized countries developed a broad range of social programs to guarantee citizens and their families at least a minimal level of income in the event of unemployment, accidents, sickness, pregnancy, childbirth, disability, and retirement. The development of the welfare state was based on the assumption that governments (as well as employers, employees, and community groups) have a role to play in maintaining income security and well-being. Welfare states were also premised on the idea that governments should assist families at certain stages of life (such as childbirth and retirement) or during family crises (such as marital breakdown or disciplinary problems with children) (Baker and Tippin 1999).

Much of the theorizing and research about social policy relates to the development of welfare states. Postwar prosperity enabled many nations to establish or expand their social programs, although some created more generous programs than others. During the 1960s, many people expected welfare states to eliminate hunger and poverty, reinforce the social value of child rearing, and reward a lifetime of paid work or care giving.

Yet widespread poverty and inequality continued to exist while government social expenditures increased throughout the 1960s and 1970s. The political consensus that supported generous social benefits in the 1960s began to fracture by the 1980s, especially in the English-speaking countries. Growing unemployment, marital instability, and an aging population increased the demand for social benefits. Conservative politicians and taxpayers, however, argued that the welfare state was ineffective and costly and would be unable to sustain itself financially.

Advocates of the welfare state have argued that social programs have prevented family poverty from worsening with declining job security and more lone mother families. Critics on the political left sometimes claim that welfare states have been less effective than they could be because most were designed to promote neither class equality nor gender equity. Instead, welfare states were often intended to supplement family income or prevent widespread hunger, which governments hoped would stave off social unrest. Critics from the political right argue that government benefits have enabled people to avoid paid work and family responsibilities, and that people should not be eligible for public benefits before they have first exhausted family resources. Debates continue about whether the state should try harder to assist families or whether families should be expected to show more responsibility for their own welfare.

Welfare Regimes

Political theorists have shown that social program development in different jurisdictions was based on varying assumptions about why some people need government assistance, how the state should help them, and how benefits and services are best delivered. In his well-known categorization of welfare states, Gösta Esping-Andersen (1990) argued that the history of strategic alliances between governments and influential interest groups shaped the development of *welfare regimes*. Welfare regimes are collective agreements about social programs (including services and benefits for families) that endure over time despite changes in government.

Esping-Andersen categorized nations such as the United States and Britain as *liberal* welfare regimes because they focus on individuals and assume that they should provide for their families through paid employment. These governments invest relatively low levels of public money into social programs and rely mainly on social assistance targeted to those without jobs or private resources. Benefits are financed through general taxation and set below the minimum wage to provide incentives to find jobs. Liberal welfare regimes emphasize efficiency rather than equity and individual responsibility rather than collective responsibility. Neoliberal regimes (such as the United States) pay benefits only to those considered deserving.

Esping-Andersen labeled nations such as Germany or Italy as *corporatist* welfare regimes because employers' groups, trade unions, and governments collectively developed social insurance programs to share the risk of income lost due to unemployment, disability, or sickness. These schemes are usually financed through payroll deductions from employees and employers (and sometimes matched with government contributions), and benefits are typically generous for contributors. Corporatist regimes are also called *conservative* because they are not designed to promote equality, but rather to stabilize employee incomes and contribute to social stability and cohesion for employers and governments.

Countries such as Sweden or Denmark have been called *social democratic* because they were designed to use taxes to redistribute income, to maintain full employment, and to prevent poverty. Social democratic welfare states offer benefits to individuals as citizenship rights and attempt to minimize inequalities. Esping-Andersen argued that variation among welfare regimes depends on such factors as the philosophy of the governing party and coalitions between powerful interest groups and political parties. This has been called the *power resource theory*, which is a widely accepted explanation of policy variation among nations, although its details have been criticized.

Feminist Critiques of Welfare Regimes

Feminist scholars, such as Ann Orloff (1993) and Diane Sainsbury (1996, 1999), generally accept the power resource theory. They argue, however, that the analysis of welfare state development by mainstream theorists such as Esping-Andersen has focused too much on men's activities, employment programs, and coalitions between governments and trade unions. They contend that women's

groups, churches, and social reformers also contributed to the development of welfare states, especially to family-related programs (Ursel 1992; Pedersen 1993). By ignoring women's activities, those termed *malestream* theorists have misrepresented the history of social programs and created categorizations of social programs that are not always relevant to family policy. Feminist scholars argue that the power resource theory needs to be refined to incorporate the role of families and voluntary groups in providing for society. Also, women's unpaid caring work should not be ignored because it has upheld both labor market policies and social programs. Many researchers have noted large variations within Esping-Andersen's categories, especially for family policies.

Feminist scholars argue that women's access to benefits from social programs has been shaped more by assumptions about family roles and relationships than welfare regimes (Baker 1995; Lewis 1998; O'Connor, Orloff, and Shaver 1999). As wives and widows, women have often been eligible for relatively generous benefits through their husband's work-related entitlements (Sainsbury 1996). As lone mothers at home, women have been offered minimal support and subjected to moral scrutiny to ensure their eligibility. In contrast, men have typically received state benefits as breadwinners rather than fathers. Their work-related payments are often financed through social insurance and involve higher payments with less personal investigation. Increasingly, women employees are eligible for social insurance, but they receive lower benefits than men because payments are tied to their lower wages. Neither the liberal nor the corporatist welfare states has done much to help women as employees.

In contrast, social democratic countries have experienced some success in resolving conflicts between work and family for employed mothers and reducing family poverty. Social democratic countries have typically supported full employment for men and women and enforced pay equity, but they have also provided public childcare, parental benefits, and leave for family responsibilities to help parents integrate paid work and childrearing. For example, Sweden has one of the lowest child poverty rates for lone parent families among Organization for Economic Cooperation and Development (OECD) nations, at 3 percent compared to about 53 percent in the United States and Australia (Baker and Tippin 1999, p. 22).

Many studies in family policy are based on historical research that indicates that state intervention has evolved over the years, but has been more intrusive for low-income families and mothers in liberal regimes. Social workers have been required to investigate the sexual circumstances and living conditions of lone mothers receiving social benefits, but such investigations would be considered an infringement of privacy for higher income families. The state has intervened most for visible minorities such as indigenous people, sometimes forcibly removing children from their families, placing them in residential schools, or encouraging adoption by white couples.

Although governments have granted more privacy to middle-class families, most researchers and social workers now agree that some aspects of family life should be considered public and of importance to governments. They argue that parents must be required (and helped) to support their children, and that the safety of children, women, and the elderly needs to be protected within the home. Laws must prevent siblings from reproducing together or fathers from raping their daughters. In addition, parents with dependent children (especially mothers) often require help to resolve the growing conflicts between employment and child raising.

Demographic Trends and Family Policy

The 1990s were marked by program cutbacks, the introduction of user fees, and tightened eligibility, especially in neoliberal states. Yet restructuring has been uneven; some programs have been cut while others have been retained or expanded. As more mothers became employed, most jurisdictions improved parental benefits and childcare subsidies. This led some researchers to focus on the demographic trends that provide the impetus for family policy reform, such as declining fertility and increasing maternal employment (Gauthier 1996; Kamerman and Kahn 1997).

Political responses to demographic change, however, can vary: Governments can provide public childcare or encourage the expansion of private childcare. Their programs can be gender-neutral or targeted specifically to women. How do governments decide on policy options? Power resource theorists argue that influential lobby groups and advisors persuade politicians that a particular demographic trend has political consequences and

that a certain policy option is preferable. For this reason, family policy researchers investigate the political context of policy discussions, which interest groups are involved, how the debate is framed, which policy option is eventually chosen, and how program design affects the resolution of the social problem. Sometimes researchers find that policies lead to unintended consequences.

Family policy research often involves comparisons among nations (Bradshaw et al. 1996). Lone mothers and the *postdivorce family* are now the center of attention, especially welfare-to-work programs and policies about child custody and support. Family policy research tends to concentrate on sole mothers because their poverty rates are so high in liberal welfare regimes. When these mothers become employed, they tend to be overrepresented in low-paid jobs, but global labor markets are producing more of these jobs. The income gap is also growing between full-time and part-time workers, but family responsibilities make it difficult for some parents to work full-time without assistance. Family policies clearly need to address labor market issues such as pay equity, parental benefits, childcare services, and leave for family responsibilities.

Many governments now encourage or require beneficiaries to enter paid work sooner than they did in the past. Family policy research indicates that leaving welfare for work often involves taking some risks, such as leaving children with strangers or giving up health care subsidies or concession cards. Furthermore, paid work does not always guarantee a higher income than social benefits (Baker and Tippin 1999). Cross-national research indicates that at least for lone mothers, marriage to a male breadwinner ensures economic well-being more effectively than paid work (Hunsley 1997). States, however, cannot force lone mothers into marriage.

In countries such as Denmark and Italy, sole mothers tend to remain in the full-time workforce throughout their childbearing years, but in Australia and the Netherlands, governments pay sole mothers a benefit to care for their children at home, sometimes while they work part-time. Mothers may experience problems when they try to re-enter the workforce, especially with the growing competitiveness of job markets. Their problems are often exacerbated by workplace practices and assumptions within labor legislation and social programs, including the idea that employees can leave their family concerns at home and that they are of no relevance to employers or governments. These assumptions, as well as structural barriers such as lack of affordable childcare, make it difficult for mothers with young children to compete in the job market despite employability policies.

Redesigning Family Policy

Cross-national research clearly indicates that social programs can counteract the vagaries of labor markets, help to equalize the incomes of two-parent and one-parent families, and more effectively integrate family and employment (Gauthier 1993, 1996; Wennemo 1994). Yet in some jurisdictions, politicians and taxpayers object to prolonged income support and generous family services. Should current programs be maintained, cut back, or expanded to accommodate new family forms?

After the Great Depression of the 1930s, more citizens accepted the idea that individuals should not always be blamed if they were unemployed or poor, and that some beneficiaries have a better chance than others to become self-supporting. Throughout the 1950s and 1960s, growing prosperity encouraged public endorsement of social programs and their expansion. Since then, more people applied for assistance with rising divorce rates and higher unemployment. Furthermore, lobby groups, such as feminists and gay and lesbian groups, argue that social programs must not favor the patriarchal nuclear family, which no longer represents the majority lifestyle. Indigenous people and new immigrants are still arguing that their extended families are ignored. More claims are being made on the welfare state while resources are shrinking.

Most researchers argue that despite economic globalization and the apparent lack of national control over some policy issues, politics matter within family policy. In other words, governments still have the power to develop family policies if they so choose. Research also confirms that family policies cannot be used to induce people to behave in ways that they feel are against their interests. Many factors influence the development of couples' relationships, reproductive behavior, and marital stability. Most governments acknowledge that effective family policies cannot counteract personal choice, labor market forces, or prevailing public opinion, but need to work with them.

Governments in industrialized nations have tried to strengthen families, but they have found new policies difficult to establish, costly, sometimes ineffective, and always controversial. Left-wing groups and those who applaud new family forms are suspicious of the call for *a family policy* because they fear that it could represent a conservative agenda opposing gender equity and personal choice. The political right argues that new programs are expensive and reward the undeserving poor. Creating policies that integrate these two opposing viewpoints has been challenging.

Contemporary governments have therefore focused on less controversial programs and policies: those that assist infant and maternal well-being, that protect women and children from violence, and that enable lone parents to raise infants and toddlers. Most governments have avoided efforts to alter sexual practices, encourage couples to have more children, or reduce reproductive rights. These issues are considered too difficult for governments to influence. To summarize, governments can help maintain family incomes, support healthy child-rearing practices, assist marital partners to stabilize their relationships, and reduce conflicts between work and family. How much public money is invested in these efforts depends on the ideology of the government and the relative power of various lobby groups.

See also: CHILDCARE; CHILDHOOD; CHILDLESSNESS; CHILDREN'S RIGHTS; FAILURE TO THRIVE; FAMILY VALUES; GRANDPARENTS' RIGHTS; GREAT BRITAIN; NEW ZEALAND; POVERTY; RETIREMENT; SEXUAL ORIENTATION; SINGLE-PARENT FAMILIES; UNEMPLOYMENT

Bibliography

Anderson, E. A., and Hulam, R. C., eds. (1991). *The Reconstruction of Family Policy*. New York: Greenwood Press.

Baker, M. (1995). *Canadian Family Policies: Cross-National Comparisons*. Toronto: University of Toronto Press.

Baker, M., and Tippin, D. (1999). *Poverty, Social Assistance, and the Employability of Mothers: Restructuring Welfare States*. Toronto: University of Toronto Press.

Bradshaw, J.; Kennedy, S.; Kilkey, M.; Hutton, S.; Corden, A.; Eardley, T.; Holmes, H.; and Neale, J. (1996). *The Employment of Lone Parents in 20 Countries: A Comparison of Policy*. London: Family Policy Studies Centre and Joseph Rowntree Foundation.

Duncan, S., and Edwards, R. (1999). *Lone Mothers: Paid Work and Gendered Moral Rationalities*. London: Macmillan; New York: St. Martin's Press.

Eichler, M. (1997). *Family Shifts. Families, Policies, and Gender Equality*. Toronto: Oxford University Press.

Esping-Andersen, G. (1990). *The Three Worlds of Welfare Capitalism*. Cambridge, UK: Polity Press.

Gauthier, A. H. (1993). *Family Policies in OECD Countries*. Oxford: Clarendon Press.

Gauthier, A. H. (1996). *The State and the Family: A Comparative Analysis of Family Polices in Industrialized Countries*. Oxford: Clarendon Press.

Hancock, L., ed. (1999). *Women, Public Policy, and the State*. Melbourne: Macmillan.

Hantrais, L., and Letablier, M.-T. (1996). *Families and Family Policies in Europe*. London: Longman.

Hunsley, T. (1997). *Lone Parent Incomes and Social Policy Outcomes: Canada in International Perspective*. Kingston, Ontario: Queen's University, School of Policy Studies.

Kamerman, S., and Kahn, A., eds. (1997). *Family Change and Family Policies in Great Britain, Canada, New Zealand, and the US*. Oxford: Clarendon Press.

Lewis, J., ed. (1998). *Gender, Social Care, and Welfare State Restructuring in Europe*. Aldershot, England: Ashgate.

O'Connor, J. S.; Orloff, A. S.; and Shaver, S. (1999). *States, Markets, Families. Gender, Liberalism, and Social Policy in Australia, Canada, Great Britain, and the United States*. New York: Cambridge University Press.

Orloff, A. (1993). "Gender and the Social Rights of Citizenship: The Comparative Analysis of Gender Relations and Welfare States." *American Sociological Review* 58:303–328.

Pedersen, S. (1993). *Family, Dependence, and the Origins of the Welfare State: Britain and France, 1914–1945*. New York: Cambridge University Press.

Sainsbury, D. (1993). "Dual Welfare and Sex Segregation of Access to Social Benefits: Income Maintenance Policies in the U.K., the U.S., the Netherlands and Sweden." *Journal of Social Policy* 22(1):69–98.

Sainsbury, D. (1996). *Gender, Equality and Welfare States*. New York: Cambridge University Press.

Sainsbury, D., ed. (1999). *Gender and Welfare State Regimes*. Oxford: Oxford University Press.

Ursel, J. (1992). *Private Lives, Public Policy. 100 Years of State Intervention in the Family*. Toronto: Women's Press.

Wennemo, I. (1994). *Sharing the Cost of Children*. Stockholm: Swedish Institute for Social Research.

MAUREEN BAKER

FAMILY RITUALS

Family rituals have been identified as powerful organizers of family life that provide stability during times of stress and transition (Bossard and Boll 1950). Researchers have discovered that rituals provide access to how the family, as a group, is organized and finds meaning in their collective lives. Such studies have found that there is a developmental course to the practice of family rituals (Fiese et al. 1993); rituals serve to protect mental health under high-risk conditions (Bennett et al. 1987) and vary in significant ways across cultures (Martini 1996).

Definitions

Family rituals are practiced in different settings and are multidimensional. Steven J. Wolin and Linda Bennett (1984) have identified three types of family rituals that differ by setting and the degree to which they are connected to cultural practices. *Family celebrations* are holidays practiced and prescribed by the culture, such as Passover Seders, and rites of passage such as weddings. *Family traditions* are linked to family activities such as birthday customs, family vacations, and special anniversaries and are less culture-specific. *Patterned routines,* the third category of family rituals, are the least consciously planned but may occur on a regular basis, for example, dinnertime, bedtime routines, and the types of greetings family members make when they return home.

Barbara Fiese and colleagues make the distinction between routines of daily living and rituals in family life (Fiese et al. 2002). Routines and rituals can be contrasted along the dimensions of communication, commitment, and continuity. Routines typically involve instrumental communication conveying information that "this is what needs to be done." They entail a momentary time commitment, and once the act is completed there is little, if any, afterthought. Routines are repeated over time and recognized by continuity in behavior. Rituals, on the other hand, involve symbolic communication and convey "this is who we are" as a group. There is an affective commitment that leaves the individual feeling that the activity feels right and provides a sense of belonging. Furthermore, there is often an emotional residue where once the act is completed the individual may replay it in memory to recapture some of the affective experience. Rituals also provide continuity in meaning across generations with the anticipation for repeat performance and an investment that this is how the family will continue to be. When routines are disrupted it is a hassle. When rituals are disrupted there is a threat to group cohesion.

To illustrate, consider family mealtimes as an example. A mealtime routine may be an instrumental communication of who needs to pick up milk on the way home from work. Once the milk is procured, there is very little thought about the grocery store. And, often as not, this act may be repeated several times a week. The mealtime ritual, on the other hand, is conversation as a group that may include inside jokes, symbolic objects, and acts meaningful only to the family not easily detected by the outside observer. Once the family is gathered for the meal there is an affective reaction that may be as subtle as a sigh signifying that time has been set aside for the group and that other things are put on hold. There may also be elements of the gathering that have been passed down over generations, including prayers, dishes, and even topics of conversation.

Several authors have proposed typologies of family rituals (Bennett et al. 1988; Roberts, 1988). Janine Roberts (1988) has identified six ways in which families approach rituals. *Under-ritualized* families rarely practice family routines, often ignoring important milestones such as anniversaries or birthdays. *Rigidly ritualized* families prescribe strict rules for conduct and hold high expectations for attendance by all members. *Skewed ritualization* is evident when the ritual practices are linked primarily to one member of the family or one aspect of a family's life such as religion or ethnic heritage. Families who practice *hollow rituals* are characterized by a lack of meaningful affect in their group activities, emphasizing the routine aspect of

family rituals without the symbolic component. Some families experience *interrupted rituals* due to sudden changes in the family such as illness or death. Families who practice *flexible rituals* maintain the symbolically meaningful aspect of family rituals and are able to adapt the roles and routines across the lifecycle.

Assessment of Family Rituals

Family rituals are assessed either through questionnaires, interviews, frequency checklists, or direct observation. The most frequently used self-report questionnaires are the Family Routines Inventory (FRI) (Jensen et al. 1983) and the Family Ritual Questionnaire (FRQ) (Fiese and Kline 1993). Interviews have also been developed where families are asked to identify rituals that are important to them and how frequently they practices such rituals (Fiese et al. 1993; Wolin and Bennett 1984). The practice of family rituals, such as mealtime, has also been directly observed though video-taped recordings (Fiese and Marjinsky 1999) and audio-taped recordings of conversations (Blum-Kulka 1997; Martini 1996).

Research on Family Rituals

Systematic research on family rituals has focused on developmental aspects of the practice of routines and rituals, rituals as a protective factor under high-risk conditions, and cultural variations of ritual practices.

Developmental aspects of routines and rituals. During the childrearing years, creating and maintaining family routines and rituals is a central part of family life. Once children are of preschool age, families report an increase in mealtime and weekend routines (Fiese et al. 1993). When the children are in middle childhood, family routines are adjusted to meet the demands of school and activities outside the home. Families that create predictable routines during these years have children who perform better in school (Brody and Flor 1997; Fiese 2000). During adolescence, children may be less directly involved in family routines, but those who have had the experience of a ritualized household are more socially competent (Fiese, 1992).

Family rituals as a protective factor. Linda A. Bennett and her colleagues were the first researchers to demonstrate empirically the protective role that rituals may play under high-risk conditions. In a study of families with an alcoholic member, it was found that the deliberate planning and preservation of family rituals, specifically dinnertime, protected the offspring from developing problematic drinking patterns (Bennett, et al. 1987). Ellen Bush and Kenneth I. Pargament (1997) studied the relation between rituals and family adjustment in coping with chronic pain. Chronic pain patients reported more satisfaction with family life when predictable and organized routines were part of their daily activities. The patients' spouses reported more satisfaction with family life when there was strong meaning attached to the practice of family rituals. Samia Markson and Barbara Fiese (2000) reported that children with asthma were less likely to experience anxiety symptoms when their families engaged in meaningful rituals.

Cultural variations in family rituals. Family rituals are embedded in the cultural context of family life. In an initial report, Mary Martini (1996) found cultural differences in mealtime conversations: Japanese-American families were more likely to discuss group activities and shared experiences at the dinner table, while Caucasian-American families were more likely to discuss experiences that individuals had outside of the home. Shoshana Blum-Kulka (1997) noted a similar pattern in a comparison of U.S. and Israeli families where the U.S. families paid more attention to individual experiences and the Israeli families focused on group experiences during ritual gatherings. In an observational study of mealtime behaviors, Martini (2002) reported that Japanese-American mealtimes were the most "infant centered," with parents responsive and attentive to their infants during the routine meals. Filipino-American families were somewhat less child-centered, with a greater focus on eating rather than conversing. Hawaiian-American mealtimes were the most adult-focused of the three groups, with children nearby and exploring but less the center of attention. These variations in conversation and interaction patterns across cultures suggest that there may be broad system-level contributions to the practice of family routines and rituals that are at times subtle but also consistent with predominant cultural values and beliefs.

Cultural variations are also observed in ritual practices in societies where elders are revered, where the elderly are often the focus of gift giving and personal attention during family celebrations

(Ingersoll-Dayton 1999). Korean sixtieth-birthday rituals have become more secular in the United States as a result of immigration (Chin 1991). Rather than preparing elaborate feasts in the ancestral home and engaging in ceremonial bowing, contemporary celebrations are conducted in restaurants with less emphasis on bowing and attention to ancestors. Thus, routines and rituals may not only be affected by cultural heritage, but they may also become altered through immigration and the practices of the host country.

Therapeutic Use of Family Rituals

Family rituals have been a form of therapeutic intervention used by family therapists since the 1970s and by human culture at large for a millennia (Imber-Black, Roberts, and Whiting 1988; van der Hart 1983). Family ritual settings, such as dinnertime, can be capitalized on for implementing behavioral interventions. In this regard, the practice of a ritual in its naturally occurring environment is paired with desirable behaviors. Increasing positive interactions during mealtimes have been found to decrease undesirable behavior in children with disabilities (Lucyshyn, Albin, and Nixon 1997) and facilitate good nutrition in infants with failure-to-thrive (Yoos, Kitzman, and Cole 1999).

Couples therapists examine past and current ritual practices to aid in understanding how couples perceive their problems and how they may best address disagreements (Imber-Black 1988). Through a consultation interview, the degree to which couples have either given up or ignored meaningful rituals may illustrate how the couple has lost touch with each other and are in need of a revitalized relationship. The renewal of wedding vows, deliberate planning of a vacation, and creating a ritual to facilitate forgiveness and healing are examples of therapeutic rituals.

Therapeutic rituals have also been used during the transitions associated with remarriage. Maintaining regular routines in divorced and remarried families may foster better adaptation in children, providing them with a sense of security and stability of family life (Henry and Lovelace 1995). As children are faced with moving in with a new parent and siblings, the role of previous rituals may become particularly poignant. How to celebrate holidays and birthdays and even how regular meals are to be conducted is subject to change.

Therapeutic interventions in this case may include an assessment of how rituals were practiced in the past and how different aspects of rituals may be taken from each family (Whiteside 1988).

Conclusion

The steady stream of research and clinical interest in family rituals has been stimulated, in part, because family rituals make sense to families. Family members can identify what rituals they practice and distinguish how important they are to family life. Rituals can be directly observed in their practice. The study of family rituals may allow researchers to break away from the tradition of identifying "good" and "bad" traits and focus on how families find success and meaning in their collective lives.

See also: CIRCUMCISION; FAMILY AND RELATIONAL RULES; FAMILY FOLKLORE; FAMILY STORIES AND MYTHS; HINDUISM; HOME; HONEYMOON; JUDAISM; MARRIAGE CEREMONIES; MARRIAGE, DEFINITION OF; SUBSTANCE ABUSE; THERAPY: FAMILY RELATIONSHIPS; TIME USE

Bibliography

Bennett, L. A.; Wolin, S. J.; Reiss, D.; and Teitelbaum, M. A. (1987). "Couples at Risk for Transmission of Alcoholism: Protective Influences." *Family Process* 2:111–129.

Bennett, L. A.; Wolin, S. J.; and McAvity, K. J. (1988). "Family Identity, Ritual, and Myth: A Cultural Perspective on Life Cycle Transition." In *Family Transitions: Continuity and Change over the Life Cycle,* ed. C. J. Falicov, NY: Guilford.

Blum-Kulka, S. (1997). *Dinner Talk: Cultural Patterns of Socialization in Family Discourse.* Mahwah, NJ: LEA.

Bossard, J., and Boll, E. (1950). *Ritual in Family Living.* Philadelphia: University of Pennsylvania Press.

Brody, G., and Flor, D. L. (1997). "Maternal Psychological Functioning, Family Processes, and Child Adjustment in Rural, Single-Parent, African American Families." *Developmental Psychology* 33:1000–1011.

Bush, E. G., and Pargament, K. I. (1997). "Family Coping with Chronic Pain." *Families, Systems, and Health* 15:147–160.

Chin, S. Y. (1991). "Korean Birthday Rituals." *Journal of Cross-Cultural Gerontology* 6:145–152.

Fiese, B. H. (1992). "Dimensions of Family Rituals across Two Generations: Relation to Adolescent Identity." *Family Process* 31:151–162.

Fiese, B. H. (2000). "Family Matters: A Systems View of Family Effects on Children's Cognitive Health." In *Environmental Effects on Cognitive Abilities,* ed. R. J. Sternberg and E. L. Grigorenko. Mahwah, NJ: LEA.

Fiese, B. H.; Hooker, K. A.; Kotary, L.; and Schwagler, J. (1993). "Family Rituals in the Early Stages of Parenthood." *Journal of Marriage and the Family* 57:633–642.

Fiese, B. H., and Kline, C. A. (1993). "Development of the Family Ritual Questionnaire: Initial Reliability and Validation Studies." *Journal of Family Psychology* 6:1–10.

Fiese, B. H. and Marjinsky, K. A. T. (1999). "Dinnertime Stories: Connecting Relationship Beliefs and Child Behavior." In *The Stories that Families Tell: Narrative Coherence, Narrative Interaction, and Relationship Beliefs. Monographs of the Society for Research in Child Development,* ed. B. H. Fiese, A. J. Sameroff, H. D. Grotevant, F. S. Wamboldt, S. Dickstein, and D. Fravel. Malden, MA: Blackwell.

Fiese, B. H.; Tomcho, T.; Douglas, M.; Josephs, K.; Poltrock, S.; and Baker, T. A. (2002). "Review of Fifty Years of Research on Naturally Occurring Family Routines and Rituals: Cause for Celebration?" *Journal of Family Psychology* (December).

Henry, C. S., and Lovelace, S. G. (1995). "Family Resources and Adolescent Family Life Satisfaction in Remarried Family Households." *Journal of Family Issues* 16:765–786.

Imber-Black, E.; Roberts, J.; and Whiting, R. (1988). *Rituals in Families and Family Therapy.* New York: Norton.

Ingersoll-Dayton, B. S. C. (1999). "Respect for the Elderly in Asia: Stability and Change." *International Journal of Aging and Human Development* 48:113–130.

Jensen, E. W.; James, S. A.; Boyce, W. T.; and Hartnett, S. A. (1983). "The Family Routines Inventory: Development and Validation." *Social Science and Medicine* 17:201–211.

Lucyshyn, J. M.; Albin, R. W.; and Nixon, C. D. (1997). "Embedding Comprehensive Behavioral Support in Family Ecology: An Experimental, Single-Case Analysis." *Journal Consulting and Clinical Psychology* 65:241–251.

Martini, M. (1996). "'What's New?' at the Dinner Table: Family Dynamics during Mealtimes in Two Cultural Groups in Hawaii." *Early Development and Parenting* 5:23–34.

Martini, M. (2002). "How Mothers in Four American Cultural Groups Shape Infant Learning During Mealtimes." *Zero to Three* 22:14–20.

Markson, S., and Fiese, B. H. (2000). "Family Rituals as a Protective Factor for Children with Asthma." *Journal of Pediatric Psychology* 25:471–479.

Roberts, J. (1988). "Setting the Frame: Definition, Functions, and Typology of Rituals." In *Rituals in Families and Family Therapy,* ed. E. Imber-Black, J. Roberts, and R. Whiting. New York: Norton.

Van der Hart, O. (1983). *Rituals in Psychotherapy: Transitions and Continuity.* New York: Irvington.

Whiteside, M. F. (1988). "Creation of Family Identity through Ritual Performance in Early Remarriage." In *Rituals in Families and Family Therapy,* ed. E. Imber-Black, J. Roberts, and R. Whiting. New York: Norton.

Wolin S. J., and Bennett, L. A. (1984). "Family Rituals." *Family Process* 23:401–420.

Yoos, H. L.; Kitzman, H.; and Cole, R. (1999). "Family Routines and the Feeding Process." In *Failure to Thrive and Pediatric Undernutrition: A Transdisciplinary Approach,* ed. D. B. Kessler and P. Dawson. Baltimore, MD: Paul H. Brookes Publishing Co.

BARBARA H. FIESE
KIMBERLY HOWELL

FAMILY ROLES

People throughout history depended on families and the kinship system for their survival. This dependence permitted and required that they conform to expected family roles depending on their living circumstances. This gave a family strong control over its members, a circumstance that is changing in the modern world because people no longer always need families for economic survival.

Intentional and unintentional forces worldwide continue to introduce important changes in family roles, in expectation and practice. For example, recent research in a variety of settings reinterprets women's historical roles in Egypt (Watterson 1998), among the Vikings (Jesch 1996), in medieval Europe (Lewis et al. 1999), and among Native Americans (Klein and Ackerman 1995). Industrialization, urbanization, and the global economy, along with their communication systems, reach into a nation's families, changing where and how men and women live, how often and when they have children, and how they work. World citizenship, global cosmopolitan culture, and international conferences change gender roles. But role change is not unidirectional and may become either narrower or more diverse.

Social roles pivot on assigned and attained places in various social settings, including work, politics, religion, and family activities. Across cultures, gender is an important assigned social location among these (Goody 1996). In the past, *sex role* was the common designation for activities based on being male or female. *Gender role* is more frequently used now because it seems less restrictive than sex role. Both terms continue to be used interchangeably.

Social role applies to family in multiple ways, but examining adult roles is complicated by a family's living arrangement. Family roles vary importantly among one-parent, two-parent, and multiple-parent families depending on the combination of persons by gender. Nations variously prescribe what constitutes the family unit through their laws. Preindustrial cultures more commonly prescribed, or permitted, a marital unit with one male and more than one female (polygyny), and less frequently a unit with one female and more than one male (polyandry). The status of a male or female reflected, in part, how many spouses one would have (Cassidy and Lee 1989). Higher status males tended to have more wives. The social context of these different family living arrangements dictates different rights and responsibilities based on gender (Dodoo 1998). Modernizing societies tend toward equalizing gender status and power.

Several terms identify basic social role dimensions, and an extensive body of literature discusses these dimensions (Farmer 1992). One dimension is role location. Common titles identify family role location such as mother, father, daughter, son, uncle, or aunt. These titles identify the general status and gender of the people within the family. Hence, these titles reflect family rights and responsibilities, duties and privileges, power and authority. Gender is important in making social distinctions because families often transmit wealth and property by gender, making a person's sex a factor in determining family status. Role status and the precision of these terms vary widely among the world's cultures. Increased family mobility and modernization blur traditional kinship statuses, particularly in countries based on traditional agricultural economies.

Cultures and Role Restriction

Cultures vary considerably in their degree of governing gender roles in families. Some cultures closely prescribe male-female roles, and others permit a variety of roles. Worldwide, the male role in early cultures is described as hunter-warrior and the female role as gatherer and childcare giver. However, continuing research suggests that early cultures may have practiced diverse gender roles. Descriptions of wife-husband roles emerging from the nineteenth century Western world assumed a male provider role and a female mediator-nurturant role. Crossing gender lines, such as women doing traditionally male tasks during war, was tolerated and expected, but it followed that with peace, traditional gender roles ought to follow. Deviance from gender roles met with overt and covert punishments and, in some cultures, punishment by death. Generally, punishments were more harshly applied to women than men (Stephens 1963).

Cultures that strictly enforce one role for men and one for women are meeting with considerable criticism. Such countries assume a division of labor based on political and economic conditions no longer suitable amidst economic and industrial change (Ashford 2001). Although loosened roles might focus on lessening female restrictions, both males and females often see personal advantages in moving toward more role options. Some people want to incorporate role dimensions not currently assigned to their gender; males may want to be more expressive and nurturant and females more career-oriented. Extensive research shows that assumptions about roles and actual role behavior do not necessarily coincide.

Industrial and postindustrial cultures tend to permit husbands and wives more role latitude. Cultures ease role restrictions by allowing women to emulate men's greater freedom in the marketplace and inducing men to have greater domestic responsibilities. Single parenting requires even more flexibility in both female and male parenting roles. Although cultures permit multiple parenting roles, parenting is based on gender identity.

There are signs that married roles are becoming even more flexible, as reflected in the individualized ways marriage ceremonies are conducted. Individualized ceremonies and agreements may elaborate traditional norms or reflect innovative lifestyles.

Personal Identity and Roles

People may advocate that married roles ought not to be gender distinctive at all (androgyny) (Singer 1976). Two individuals in a close relationship may have mutual understandings about their responsibilities and privileges, but not base them on gender. This is theoretically possible in all but specific reproductive activities. Females continue to become pregnant and have babies, and males do not. Hence, one may think of cultures aligned along a continuum with one wife and husband role at one end and no gender-based family roles at the other. Role conflict occurs in a single gender role system because of limited role options. However, a lack of clear roles creates role ambiguity. When roles are not clearly delineated, but gender distinctions continue to be made, roles become ambiguous. People respond either by developing new roles or having a confused identity. This latter condition occurs in China where the older Confucian ideals are supplanted by more equalitarian family codes of the Chinese national government (Pimentel 2000).

Elaborate sets of norms, or role prescriptions, delineate behavior appropriate to gender role status. Depending on gender and age, the child differentially defers to the father, mother, or some other designated relative such as an uncle. In the family setting, daughters expect to imitate activities reflecting the mother's status, and sons, the father's. A family often experiences role conflict when children do not conform to their gender status, as occurs in societies undergoing rapid social change, as in Korea (Chun and MacDermid 1997).

Self-identity is an important dimension of social role. Another kind of conflict occurs when cultural norms strictly enforce gender roles that do not match gender identity. Resolution commonly includes finding ways around these prescriptions. In the family setting, the mother or father may reject aspects of their role assignment, as for instance, the father accepting the mother as being a better provider. An extreme resolution includes surgical intervention changing the body's morphology to conform to the self's gender identity, a medical procedure begun in Sweden. Self-identity conflicts arise when a person is unable or unwilling to fulfill societal norms or their partner's expectations.

Societies often have a double standard or different sets of norms for females and males, with the female's behavior usually being more restricted.

Role stereotypes introduce another source of role conflict. Stereotypes are shorthand assumptions about how husbands and wives behave in different social categories. Conflict occurs in the failure to distinguish between stereotypical assumptions and actual behavior, causing misunderstanding and misinterpretation between men and women. An example of such a stereotype is *machismo*, which refers to Latin male forcefulness, vigor, and strength, and which requires deference and obedience. It may be viewed positively or negatively depending on its cultural and gender reference. Machismo may be used to describe emergent behavior in other cultures, such as among the Tewa Pueblo where it is applied to young males (Jacobs 1995). Much literature discusses communication used to diminish marital conflict derived from gender stereotypes.

Role Expectations and Demands

Gender roles, as they pertain to the family, are interactive. Being a daughter implies that there is a mother or father. It suggests that being a daughter entails expectations about a female's behavior vis-à-vis a parent and a parent's behavior vis-à-vis the daughter. A daughter or son reasonably expects physical care and emotional support to a certain age, and parents might expect increasing domestic responsibility and self-direction with their child's physical maturation. Societies usually codify these responsibilities in general terms.

In rural communities around the world, for example, in China and India, kinship responsibilities were well understood without specific laws. With urbanization and industrialization, informal relations weaken, and laws emerge to specify gender-kinship responsibilities. Precise rights and responsibilities are often interpreted by specific cases channeled through the society's legal and welfare systems, particularly for those families needing outside assistance.

Role anticipation is associated with becoming an adult as children mature and leave the family (Nilsson and Strandh 1999). Role anticipation assumes that a particular role will exist in the future, and self-anticipation assumes the person will someday occupy that role. For example, in the fifteen member countries of the European Union (Austria, Belgium, France, etc.), mothers tend to be employed and concomitantly have fewer children (Lesthaeghe and Williams 1999). Role anticipation occurs when the daughter assumes this will be true for her in the future. If she also assumes she will be an employed mother some day with reduced fertility, she engages in self-anticipation. Children emulate the behavior of the parent they identify with, usually the same-gender parent. In this case, the mother becomes an important referent for the daughter's learning the anticipated role.

An assumption is that role learning for the son will be more difficult if the father is absent from the home. Fathers in industrializing countries often leave home, sometimes permanently, to find employment in cities, thereby creating mother-only families. Daughters also have different learning experiences with absent fathers because cross-gender parent experiences are absent or limited. In modern societies, fewer families have absent mothers. A study of people in thirty-nine countries found that the family's national and cultural context may importantly mitigate parental absence through greater social integration (Gohm et al. 1998).

Role compatibility is important in a society that permits multiple role sets for wives and husbands, as when a wife expects her role to include employment outside the home and her husband does not. These kinds of incompatibilities produce role conflict, in this case between the female's self-expectations and the male's role prescriptions. Therefore gender roles become an important part of premarital assumptions and anticipations. Such incompatibilities require varied forms of negotiation, and sometimes counseling, to reduce conflict. Various theories address these negotiations that may include professional mediation and counseling. A study of Australian males, who became primary childcare givers while their wives worked, indicated how difficult it was to shift one's behavior away from traditional role expectations. These men were highly pressured by peers to return to traditional family roles (Grbich 1992).

Role overload and role conflict are closely related. A frequent international phenomenon of role overload occurs when an employed wife also does a large part of the domestic chores traditionally assigned to her. This produces role strain in that not all tasks can be performed in the time available. Consciously acknowledging this imbalance may lead to arguments and, if the issue is not resolved, to marital breakup if the culture permits it.

Work role and other demands outside the family heighten both role strain and conflict. The wife's external employment introduces another set of role demands that increases role strain and conflict through social power adjustments (Standing 1991). Married women's employment outside the home increases stress when they are expected to be primary caregivers to their elderly parents as is expected in traditional extended families. For example, Japan is experimenting with various plans to substitute or supplement the traditional family care of the elderly (Ogawa and Retherford 1997).

When a female enters the marketplace, as is increasingly common worldwide, she derives status benefits from her direct contribution to the family income. However, careful research of past and present cultures indicates that actual family bargaining power is often hidden, though persisting along gender lines. With the wife's greater economic independence, she is more likely to sever the relationship if conflict is unresolved. Dual-earner families may gain greater independence from their employers because dual incomes permit more employment choices. For example, the husband may elect to spend more time in domestic duties while the wife pursues her career goals.

The feminist movement influences gender role change both in and outside the family in multiple ways. Broadly speaking, the movement may be viewed as a social process focusing on female role identities and prescriptions. Its basic premise is that gender ascriptions produce power inequities in family systems where the male is the primary paid earner and the female is confined to domestic duties. Domestic work is viewed as important but is not well rewarded in money or status (Al-Nouri 1993). Feminism identifies inequities and suggests strategies for their modification. Education examines gender role inequities and challenges traditional gender roles (consciousness raising), providing females with greater control over their reproductive functions (McDonald 2000). The 1994 Cairo International Conference on Population and Development specifically addressed women's health issues. Since then, forty countries, including South Africa, Brazil, and Bangladesh, have instituted laws and policies reflecting goals set at this conference (Ashford 2001). Such activities intend to weaken gender role bias by leading to more equitable and individualized family roles.

See also: CHILDHOOD; COHABITATION; DISABILITIES; DIVISION OF LABOR; DUAL-EARNER FAMILIES; FAMILY LIFE EDUCATION; FATHERHOOD; FILIAL RESPONSIBILITY; GAY PARENTS; GENDER; GENDER IDENTITY; GRANDPARENTHOOD; HOUSEWORK; HOUSING; HUSBAND; INDUSTRIALIZATION; LESBIAN PARENTS; LIFE COURSE THEORY; MARITAL QUALITY; MARITAL TYPOLOGIES; MOTHERHOOD; POWER: MARITAL RELATIONSHIPS; RAPE; ROLE THEORY; RURAL FAMILIES; SIBLING RELATIONSHIPS; SOCIAL NETWORKS; STRESS; SYMBOLIC INTERACTIONISM; TIME USE; TRANSITION TO PARENTHOOD; UNEMPLOYMENT; WIDOWHOOD; WOMEN'S MOVEMENTS; WORK AND FAMILY

Bibliography

Al-Nouri, Q. (1993). "Iraqi Rural Women's Participation in Domestic Decision-Making." *Journal of Comparative Family Studies* 24:81–97.

Ashford, L. S. (2001). "New Population Policies: Advancing Women's Health and Rights." *Population Bulletin* 56:3–43.

Cassidy, M., and Lee, G. (1989). "The Study of Polyandry." *Journal of Comparative Family Studies* 20:1–11.

Chun, Y.-J., and MacDermid, S. M. (1997). "Perceptions of Family Differentiation, Individuation, and Self-Esteem among Korean Adolescents." *Journal of Marriage and the Family* 59:451–462.

DoDoo, F. N. (1998). "Marriage Type and Reproductive Decisions: A Comparative Study in Sub-Saharan Africa." *Journal of Marriage and the Family* 60:232–242.

Farmer, Y. (1992). "Role Models." In *Encyclopedia of Sociology,* Vol. 3, ed. E. Borgatta and M. Borgatta. New York: Macmillan.

Gohm, C. L.; Oishi, S.; and Diener, E. (1998). "Culture, Parental Conflict, Parental Marital Status, and the Subjective Well-Being of Young Adults." *Journal of Marriage and Family* 60:319–334.

Goody, J. (1996). "Comparing Family Systems in Europe and Asia: Are There Different Sets of Rules?" *Population and Development Review* 22:1–20.

Grbich, C. (1992). "Societal Response to Familial Role Change in Australia." *Journal of Comparative Family Studies* 23:79–94.

Jacobs, S. (1995). "Continuity and Change in Gender Roles at San Juan Pueblo." In *Women and Power in Native North America,* ed. L. Klein and L. Ackerman. Norman: University of Oklahoma Press.

Jesch, J. (1996). *Women in the Viking Age.* Bury St. Edmunds, UK: St Edmundsbury Press.

Klein, L. F., and Ackerman, L. A., eds. (1995). *Women and Power in Native North America.* Norman: University of Oklahoma Press.

Lesthaeghe, R., and Willems, P. (1999). "Is Low Fertility a Temporary Phenomenon in the European Union?" *Population and Development Review* 25:211–228.

Lewis, K. J.; Menuge, N.; and Phillips, K., eds. (1999). *Young Medieval Women.* New York: St. Martin's Press.

Maccoby, E. E., and Jacklin, C. N. (1974). *The Psychology of Sex Differences.* Stanford, CA: Stanford University Press.

McDonald, P. (2000). "Gender Equity and Theories of Fertility Transition." *Population and Development Review* 26:427–439.

Nilsson, K., and Strandh, M. (1999). "Nest Leaving in Sweden: The Importance of Early Educational and Labor Market Careers." *Journal of Marriage and the Family* 61:1068–1079.

Ogawa, N., and Retherford, R. D. (1997). "Shifting Costs of Caring for the Elderly Back to Families in Japan: Will it Work?" *Population and Development Review* 23:59–94.

Pimentel, E. E. (2000). "Just How Do I Love Thee?: Marital Relations in Urban China." *Journal of Marriage and the Family* 62:32–47.

Singer, J. (1976). *Androgyny: Toward a New Theory of Sexuality.* Garden City, NY: Anchor Press.

Standing, H. (1991). *Dependence and Autonomy: Women's Employment and the Family in Calcutta.* London: Routledge.

Watterson, B. (1998). *Women in Ancient Egypt.* Phoenix Mill, UK: Sutton Publishing Limited.

LAURENCE L. FALK

FAMILY SCIENCE

Family science is a field of study where "the primary goals are the discovery, verification and application of knowledge about the family" (NCFR Task Force on the Development of a Family Discipline 1987, p. 48). Although family science treats contributions from related academic disciplines as vital background information, it has also developed its own unique assumptions, paradigms, methodologies, and world view (Burr, Day, and Bahr 1993).

Historical Background

Prior to the twentieth century, much of the writing about families was characterized by emotion, superstition, speculation, or "revelation." Insights concerning family life were typically gleaned from sources such as family folklore, philosophy, religion, theater, poetry, and the arts. With the rise of Social Darwinism in the second half of the nineteenth century, interest peaked in the social evolution of marriage and family forms. Attempts were made to apply Darwin's concept of biological evolution to social forms and institutions. Harold Christensen (1964) observed that during this period, the occasional scholarship about families became somewhat more systematic. Some of this scholarship was based on assumptions that families pass through natural stages in their evolution, and that this evolutionary trajectory is progressive in nature.

During the first half of the twentieth century, there was a general shift in the academy toward scientific, positivistic modes of inquiry. These approaches employed more rigorous research methodologies, and attempted to maintain a professional, value-free stance. A parallel trend was observed among scholars interested in systematic study of families.

It was during this period that family as a field of inquiry came into its own. Prior to that time, most of the scholarship related to families was imbedded in any number of traditional academic disciplines. Disciplines such as psychology, sociology, political science, anthropology, education, and religion contributed valuable insights into family structure and process. However, each conveyed a limited and fragmented vision of the scope and complexity of family life (Schvaneveldt 1971). No single discipline viewed family as its organizing center or core. None described family in holistic terms, or as a coherent, integrated body of knowledge (NCFR Task Force 1988).

One of the early pioneers to study the family holistically was sociologist Ernest R. Groves. In 1922, while chair of the sociology department at Boston University, Groves launched the first college course with family as its focus, "The Family

FIGURE 1

Interdisciplinary nature of family science

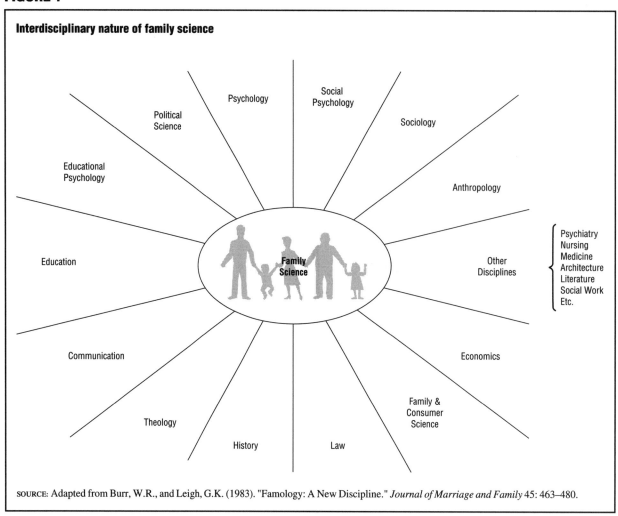

SOURCE: Adapted from Burr, W.R., and Leigh, G.K. (1983). "Famology: A New Discipline." *Journal of Marriage and Family* 45: 463–480.

and Its Social Functions." In 1931 he published the first college textbook in the field, entitled *Social Problems of the Family*. Groves taught the first course on parent education at Harvard University, and from 1937 to 1942 served as special lecturer in marriage and family at Duke University (Dail and Jewson 1986). In 1934 he helped co-found what became the Groves Conference on Marriage and the Family. In 1939 he inaugurated the first three-year graduate training program in marriage and family at Duke (Greene 1986).

The Developing Discipline of Family Science

It might be noted that much of this early work, though family-focused, was interdisciplinary in nature. Some have labeled the initial phase of formal study about families the "Discovery Stage" (NCFR Task Force 1988). During this time, scholars from various disciplines were discovering family to be a

fruitful domain of intellectual inquiry. For example, the premier association of family professionals, National Council on Family Relations (NCFR), was founded in 1938 by law professor Paul Sayre from the University of Iowa, working closely with Ernest Burgess, a sociologist from the University of Chicago, and Sidney Goldstein, a New York rabbi. NCFR's second president was the distinguished Swiss psychiatrist and neurologist, Adolf Meyer, who served as professor of psychiatry at Johns Hopkins University (Dail and Jewson 1986). Many other examples of collaborative activity across disciplines exist from this period.

During the second "Pioneering Stage," Ernest Groves (1946) argued for the formation of a new science of marriage and family.

The establishment of a definite program for the training of specialists in the field of

TABLE 1

Employment Opportunities In Family Science

Career Area	Employment Opportunities	Career Area	Employment Opportunities
Education	Public school teaching in family & consumer sciences (certification) University teaching & research in family science departments Family life and sexuality education Programs in parish & community settings Parent educators Family peace & justice education Children's museum education Marriage & family enrichment facilitators	Business, Consumer and Family Resource Services	Employee assistance specialist Corporate day care administrator Consumer protection agencies Family financial counseling & planning Family resource management Food assistance programs Child and family poverty research Research on work and families Family business consultant
Research	Grant proposal writing Academic and government-related research in family science content areas Population studies & demographic research Community-based research for non-profit family agencies services Program evaluation & assessment	International Education & Development	International family policy analyst Peace corps and NGO leadership Global family planning programs Community & sustainable development International human rights advocacy Immigration & migrant family Cross-cultural family studies programs
Family Intervention	Individual & family therapy Case manager for family treatment plans Crisis & hotline services Court-mandated parent education programs Divorce mediation Abuse protection services Drug & alcohol prevention counselors Residential treatment programs Victim/ witness support services	Community-Based Social Services	Adoption agencies Foster care programs Teen pregnancy counselor Family preservation worker Welfare assistance for low-Income families Vocational rehabilitation & job training Adult day care providers Gerontology programs
Government & Public Policy	Family policy analyst Advocate/lobbyist on behalf of children, women, & family well-being Cooperative extension specialist Aid to dependent children Military family support services Departments of child & family services	Health Care & Family Wellness	Public health programs & services Hospital family support professionals Nutrition education & counseling Prenatal and maternity services Holistic health centers Long-term care administrator Hospice programs
Writing and Communication	Curriculum & resource development in family life education Public service radio and TV programming Newspaper & magazine journalism on social issues affecting children and families	Early Childhood Education	Day care centers Head start programs Montessori schools Child development consultant

marriage and the family means that several sciences must contribute to the instruction. The outcome will be a *science of marriage and the family* carried out by specialists who will draw their data from a wide range of resources. They will not be sociologists, home economists, or social workers, but persons who are committed to the gathering and the giving of information that concerns marriage and the family, who have prepared themselves for such an undertaking, and who approach their task from a background shared by no other science. (p. 26)

Advocates for the emerging field of family science argued that all disciplines have their historic roots and origins. They questioned how commonly recognized *sociology* was in 1839, *psychology* in

1865, or *gerontology* in 1945 (Burr and Leigh 1983). They further reasoned that all other major social institutions have established disciplinary identities. The economic institution has its discipline of *economics*; the religious institution, *religion*; and politics has *political science*. There is a similar need for boundaries around the discipline of family science because "family is one of the most fundamental and complex human institutions, and it is distinct in many ways from other institutions and aspects of reality" (Burr and Leigh 1983, p. 468).

During the Pioneering Stage, family departments generated a variety of names to describe their discipline. A 1982 NCFR (Burr and Leigh 1983) survey indicated that 79 percent of the membership felt that identity ambiguity about the discipline was a "serious problem." In response, a task force was appointed by then NCFR President Bert Adams to reach consensus around the clearest terminology to reflect this emerging field of study. After numerous discussions, open forums, and published essays, the task force brought its final recommendation to the 1985 NCFR Conference in Dallas, Texas. Their recommendation, advocating *family science* as the preferred term for the emerging discipline, was unanimously adopted. "The unanimity of the endorsement was interpreted as a virtual mandate—further justifying subsequent action, such as changing names of courses, majors, and eventually departments around the country" (NCFR Task Force 1987). Around this time a Family Science Section was formed within the NCFR. In 1988, the Family Science Association (FSA), which sponsors an annual conference on Teaching Family Science, was established, and in 1989 the University of Kentucky began hosting an international discussion list for family scientists and researchers called FAMLSCI. The listserv, created and managed by Gregory Brock, had 650 subscribers as of February 2002.

During the "Maturing Stage," family science further consolidated its identity. The result has been a domain of inquiry that is interdisciplinary in nature, yet conceptually unique. It has been suggested that "the family field has entered a unique historical era because it has a bona fide family discipline and also complex interdisciplinary ties. In other words, rather than concluding that it is A rather than B, we conclude that it is A *and* B. It is a discipline and an interdisciplinary area" (Burr and Leigh 1983, p. 470).

Maturity in the field is further seen by the development of professional standards and a professional code of ethics. For example, the Family Science Section of NCFR initiated and developed a code of ethics for family professionals that was endorsed by the broader NCFR membership in 1998 (Adams 2001; Adams et al. 2001; Doherty 1999). The importance of clarifying ethical principles and guidelines for family scientists is reinforced by the fact that one of the Certified Family Life Educator (CFLE) substance areas includes attention to the area of ethics.

Academic Programs in Family Science

Early graduate programs in family science were typically imbedded in related academic disciplines. Selected examples include Columbia University's graduate school of education featuring a doctoral program in Family and Community Education, and the sociology department at the University of Minnesota offering a concentration in Family and Life Course.

In addition to family programs housed in related academic departments, there have been growing opportunities to earn advanced degrees in family-specific programs. In 1981, fifty-four universities offered graduate programs focused on the study of families (Love 1981). By 2002, that number had grown to over 225 family science graduate programs in the United States and Canada (Hans 2002).

The number of family science programs and majors at international universities is growing, as well. Examples include the College of Family Sciences at Zayed University, Dubai, United Arab Emirates; the Department of Family and Consumer Science at Kenyatta University, Nairobi, Kenya; a major in Child and Family Studies at Yonsei University, Seoul, Republic of Korea; the Department of Human Development and Family Studies at the University of Baroda in India; and the Newcastle Centre for Family Studies, University of Newcastle on Tyne in the United Kingdom.

Substance Areas Comprising the Discipline

There have been various attempts to identify the content areas typically falling under the rubric of family science. The preface to the text, *Family Science,* distinguishes family science from related disciplines by noting that it emphasizes concepts such as "generational alliances, differentiation of self, emotional triangles, developmental tasks, analogic messages, boundaries, emotional distance, family paradigms and experiential aspects of mothering" (Burr, Day, and Bahr 1993, p. iii).

The essential concepts most widely recognized are the ten substantive areas required for CFLE status with NCFR. Between 1985 and 2001, the CFLE program has credentialed 1,200 family professionals. Family scientists seeking CFLE certification are required to demonstrate basic competency in the following areas (Powell and Cassidy 2001):

(1) Families in Society;

(2) Internal Dynamics of Families;

(3) Human Growth and Development over the Life Span;

(4) Human Sexuality;

(5) Interpersonal Relations;

(6) Family Resource Management;

(7) Parent Education and Guidance;

(8) Family Law and Public Policy;

(9) Ethics;

(10) Family Life Education Methodology.

The above areas of concentration in family science fall into the broad categories of *family research, policy, practice,* and *education* (Hogan 1995). Many are also distinguished according to whether their focus is primarily *preventative* or *remedial* in nature (Mace and Mace 1974).

Career and Professional Opportunities in Family Science

According to the U.S. Department of Labor, professional opportunities in child and family areas are likely to increase faster than the average for all occupations through 2010 (U.S. Department of Labor 2002). The breadth and availability of such opportunities is related somewhat to the level of one's education (Vance 1989). For example, research with family science graduates indicates that those with master's degrees are more likely to be working with human services organizations, whereas those earning doctorates are more likely to be employed by institutions of higher education (Krasenbaum et al. 1994). Table 1 provides an overview of selected opportunities available to

family scientists in the general areas of family research, education, policy and practice (Burr 1992; Day et al. 1988; Keim 1995).

See also: FAMILY, HISTORY OF; FAMILY LIFE EDUCATION; THERAPY: FAMILY RELATIONSHIPS

Bibliography

Adams, R. (2001). "The Importance of Ethical Guidelines in Family Science." Presentation at the 13th Annual Teaching Family Science Conference, Lewes, DE, June 2, 2001.

Adams, R. A.; Dollahite, D. C.; Gilbert, K. R.; and Keim, R. E. (2001). "The Development and Teaching of the Ethical Principles and Guidelines for Family Scientists." *Family Relations* 50:41–48.

Becker, G. S. (1991). *A Treatise on the Family,* enlarged edition. Cambridge, MA: Harvard University Press.

Benokraitis, N. (1999). *Marriages and Families: Changes, Choices, and Constraints,* 3rd edition. Upper Saddle River, NJ: Prentice Hall.

Berger, P., and Kellner, H. (1964). "Marriage and the Construction of Reality: An Exercise in the Microsociology of Knowledge." *Diogenes* 46:1–25.

Berger, P., and Luckman, T. (1966). *The Social Construction of Reality: A Treatise on the Sociology of Knowledge.* New York: Doubleday.

Bronfenbrenner, U. (1979). *The Ecology of Human Development: Experiments by Nature and Design.* Cambridge, MA: Harvard University Press.

Burr, W. (1993). "Using Theories in Family Science." In *Research and Theory in Family Science,* ed. R. Day, K. R. Gilbert, B. H. Settles, and W. R. Burr. Pacific Grove, CA: Brooks/Cole.

Burr, W. R. (1992). "Family Science." *Peterson's Guide to Graduate Programs in the Humanities and Social Sciences 1993,* 27th edition. Princeton, NJ: Peterson's Guides.

Burr, W. R.; Day, R. D.; and Bahr, K. S., ed. (1993). *Research and Theory in Family Science.* Pacific Grove, CA: Brooks/Cole.

Burr, W. R. and Leight, G. K. (1982). "Identity Problems in the Family Field." *NCFR Report* 27:1–5.

Burr, W. R., and Leigh, G. K. (1983). "Famology: A New Discipline." *Journal of Marriage and the Family* 45: 467–480.

Cherlin, A. J. (1999). *Public and Private Families,* 2nd edition. New York: McGraw-Hill.

Christensen, H. T., ed. (1964). *Handbook of Marriage and the Family*. Chicago: Rand McNally.

Dail, P. W., and Jewson, R. H. (1986). *In Praise of Fifty Years: The Groves Conference on the Conservation of Marriage and the Family*. Lake Mills, IA: Graphic.

Day, R. D.; Gilbert, K. R.; Settles, B. H.; and Burr, W. R., ed. (1995). *Research and Theory in Family Science*. Pacific Grove, CA: Brooks/Cole.

Day, R. D.; Quick, D. S.; Leigh, G. K.; and McKenry, P. C. (1988). "Professional Training in Family Sciences: A Review of Undergraduate and Graduate Programs." *Family Science Review* 1:313–347.

Doherty, W. J. (1999a). "Ethics, Family Science and Family Practice." *NCFR Report* 44:3–4.

Doherty, W. J. (1999b). "Postmodernism and Family Theory." In *Handbook of Marriage and the Family,* ed. M. B. Sussman; S. K. Steinmetz; and G. W. Peterson. New York and London: Plenum Press.

Duvall, E. (1957). *Family Development*. New York: Lippincott.

Greene, J. T. (1986). "Ernest R. Groves: Explorer and Pioneer in Marriage and Family Life Education and Marriage Counseling." In *In Praise of Fifty Years: The Groves Conference on the Conservation of Marriage and the Family,* ed. P. W. Dail and R. H. Gaston. Lake Mills, IA: Graphic.

Groves, E. R. (1946). "Professional Training for Family Life Educators." *Marriage and Family Living* 8:25–26.

Hans, J. D. (2002). *Graduate and Undergraduate Study in Marriage and Family*. Columbia, MD: Family Scholar.

Hogan, J. (1995). *Initiatives for Families: Research, Policy, Practice, and Education*. Minneapolis, MN: National Council on Family Relations.

Keim, R. (1995). "Careers in Family Science." In *Research and Theory in Family Science,* ed. R. D. Day; K. R. Gilbert; B. H. Settles; and W. R. Burr. Pacific Grove, CA: Brooks/Cole.

Krasenbaum, D. N; Pittman, J. F; Bradbard, M. R; and Solheim, C. A. (1994). "Educational and Professional Experiences of Recent Graduates of Four Family Science Master's and Doctoral Programs." *Family Science Review* 7:1–14.

Love, C. J. (1981). *A Guide to Graduate Family Programs*. Minneapolis, MN: National Council on Family Relations.

Mace, D., and Mace, V. (1974). *We Can Have Better Marriages*. Nashville, TN: Abington.

Mead, G. H. (1934). *Mind, Self, and Society*. Chicago: University of Chicago Press.

NCFR Task Force on the Development of the Family Discipline. (1987). "A Recommendation about the Identity of the Family Discipline." *Family Science Review* 1:48–52.

NCFR Task Force on the Development of the Family Discipline. (1988). "What is Family Science?" *Family Science Review* 1:87–101.

Olson, D. H., and DeFrain, J. (2000). *Marriage and Family: Diversity and Strengths*. 3rd edition. Mountain View, CA: Mayfield.

Olson, D. H.; Sprenkle, E. H.; and Russell, C. S. (1979). "Circumplex Model of Marital and Family Systems I: Cohesion and Adaptability Dimensions, Family Types and Clinical Applications." *Family Process* 18:3–28.

Osmund, M. W., and Thorne, B. (1993). "Feminist Theories: The Social Construction of Gender in Families and Society." In *Sourcebook of Family Theories and Methods: A Contextual Approach,* ed. P. Boss, W. Doherty, R. LaRossa, W. Schumm, and S. Steinmetz. New York: Plenum Press.

Parsons, T., and Bales, R. F. (1955). *Family, Socialization, and Interaction Process*. Glencoe, IL: Free Press.

Peterson, G. W., and Hann, D. (1999). "Socializing Children and Parents in Families." In *Handbook of Marriage and the Family,* 2nd edition, ed. M. Sussman, S. Steinmetz, and G. Peterson. New York: Plenum Press.

Powell, L. H., and Cassidy, D. (2001). *Family Life Education: An Introduction*. Mountain View, CA: Mayfield.

Schvaneveldt, J. D. (1971). "Role Problems of the College Family Life Educator and Researcher." *The Family Coordinator* 20:3–10.

Shehan, C., ed. (1999). *Through the Eyes of the Child: Revisioning Children as Active Agents of Family Life*. Greenwich, CT: JAI Press.

Sprey, J. (1969). " The Family as a System in Conflict." *Journal of Marriage and the Family* 31:722–731.

Sussman, M. B.; Steinmetz, S. K.; and Peterson, G. W., ed. (1999). *Handbook of Marriage and the Family,* 2d edition. New York: Plenum Press.

Vance, B. (1989). "The Family Professional Inside and Outside of Academia." *Family Science Review* 2:49–60.

Walker, A. J. (1999). "Gender and Family Relationships." In *Handbook of Marriage and the Family,* 2nd edition, ed. M. Sussman, S. Steinmetz, and G. Peterson. New York: Plenum Press.

Walters, J., and Jewson, R. (1988). *The National Council on Family Relations: A Fifty-Year History, 1939–1987*. Minneapolis, MN: National Council on Family Relations.

Other Resource

U.S. Department of Labor. (2002). "Occupational Outlook Handbook 2002–03 Edition" Available from http://www.stats.bls.gov/oco/ocos060.

MARY ANN HOLLINGER

FAMILY STORIES AND MYTHS

Humans are storytelling beings who, personally and collectively, lead storied lives. The study of stories provides insight into how individuals and families experience the world. Storytelling takes place in families whenever they come together, during ordinary activities such as mealtime and at special occasions such as holiday celebrations and funerals.

Definition of Family Stories and Myths

As raw experiences are transformed into stories, myths, customs, rituals, and routines, they are codified in forms that can be easily recollected (Martin, Hagestad, and Diedrick 1988; Zeitlin, Kotkin, and Baker 1982). Elizabeth Stone (1988, p. 5) observed: "Almost any bit of lore about a family member or experience qualifies as a family story—as long as it is significant and has worked its way into the family canon to be told and retold."

The family canon is the creative expression of a common history transformed into stories for the present and future generations. These stories are as likely to be about the "black sheep" in the family as they are to be about those who led exemplary lives. Despite the fact that the main character is often a man, women in the families are the primary keepers of the canon (Diedrick, Martin, and Hagestad 1986; Martin, Hagestad, and Diedrick 1988; Stone 1988).

Family stories, as with all stories, are told after the fact. This is important because each family can be selective about the events or incidents it chooses to remember and preserve. Steven Zeitlin, Amy Kotkin, and Holly Baker (1982, p. 16) noted that "in this way, each narrative becomes not a rehash of an event but a distillation of experience" unique to each family.

Family myths are the most secret and intimate genre of storytelling. They offer "an explanation and justification of family members' roles, self-images, and shared consensual experience" (Anderson and Bagarozzi 1983, p. 153). Family myths communicate the most idiosyncratic family convictions that families are most reticent to surrender (Stone 1988).

The power of family stories that are allegorical in nature, may be due to the context in which they are told. Elizabeth Stone explains:

> Families believe in their myths for reasons more compelling than respect for versatility of metaphor. What the family tells us has a force and power that we never quite leave behind. What they tell us is our first syntax, our first grammar, the foundation onto which we later add our own perceptions and modifications. We are not entirely free to challenge the family's beliefs as we might challenge any other system of belief. And even when we do challenge, we half disbelieve ourselves. (1988, p. 101)

Myths and stories are meant to offer possible, if not always plausible, explanations for emotional calamities within the family (Stone 1988). They are a blend of fact and fiction preserving important themes, special events, and notable personalities in the history of each family (Anderson and Bagarozzi 1983; Bagarozzi and Anderson 1982). However, to family members, "veracity is never the main point—what's important is what could be rather than what actually was." (Stone 1988, p. 129).

Functions of Family Stories and Myths

Storytelling fulfills many functions in the family. First, stories differentiate a particular family from all other families. The idiosyncratic nature of family stories underscores, in a way invariably clear to the members of a particular family, the essentials of being a part of that family (Stone 1988; Zeitlin, Kotkin, and Baker 1982).

Family stories also help bind the members of the family together by creating a *community of memory,* a chronicle of the way a particular family thinks of itself. Family stories define the family as a unit that encounters numerous transitions together over time (e.g. stories about marriage, family feuds, the welcoming of children into the family fold, and tragic losses). This is called the *transition principle* in family stories (Zeitlin, Kotkin, and Baker 1982). Furthermore, family stories describe "the decorum and protocol of family life—what we are and to whom, what we can expect and from whom, in time and or in money or emotion" (Stone 1988, p. 18). They also enrich the perspectives family members have regarding intergenerational relationships (Zeitlin, Kotkin, and Baker 1982).

Monica Nalyaka Wanambisi of Kenya explains that for her family storytelling is a tool that promotes a sense of communal belonging (Burman 1997). Elaine Reese (1996) supports this idea of stories promoting a sense of communal belonging. The New Zealander Pakeha (European descent) mothers she interviewed viewed birth narratives as a way of introducing their children into their space and the wider family community.

Although most families tell stories, there are some who do not. Michael Sherman (1990) found that when there is an absence of family stories, it led to difficulties for parents' establishment of a comfortable relationship with their child. This is because family stories and myths enable individual family members to make sense of the world and simplify the complexities of family life into an easily remembered, easily communicated narrative (Bagarozzi and Anderson 1982; Zeitlin, Kotkin, and Baker 1982).

Families without stories may have difficulty because stories help relay family values and ideals and thus provide expectations of family members. When analyzing stories of gay, lesbian, and bisexual families, Colette Morrow (1999) found that the stories told by lesbian, bisexual, and gay families had two competing descriptions of sexual identity—one of sexuality as a result of destiny and one of sexuality as a result of free will. This may have been because queer theorists see sexuality as constructed whereas gay political activists legitimize their demands for civil rights by saying sexual identity is biologically determined. Their stories met the demands of both groups.

Family stories function to pass on gender identity. Barbara Fiese and Gemma Skillman (2001) found that sons were more likely to hear stories with themes of autonomy than were daughters. This was especially true of children whose parent adhered to the traditional gender prescriptions. These parents told stories with stronger achievement themes to their sons whereas nontraditional gender-typed parents told stories with stronger achievement themes to their daughters.

In addition to transmitting gender identity, family stories and myths shape the personalities of individual family members. Steven Zeitlin, Amy Kotkin, and Holly Baker (1982) labeled this notion the *character principle* of family stories. Families are complicated, especially in their messages to the individuals who comprise them. Powerful messages about who each person in the family is, what each member is to do, and how each life is to be lived are transmitted through the medium of family stories and myths. In other words, these stories serve as the family's most important instructions (and perhaps covert ground rules) for its members on what they ought to be like. The nature of the family definition of each individual and the stories used to buttress that definition give clues to the family's organization and its power center.

Finally, family stories are interpretive. They offer guidance, based on the collective experience of the family, to individual members as they make sense of the world outside the family. Every family has a vision of what the world is like and a set of implicit and explicit rules for survival. Family stories provide its members a sense of place or position in the larger social world beyond the family (Stone 1988).

Metaphors

Metaphors are embedded in family stories and myths. These metaphors supply meaning for relationships and the relational culture. Leslie Baxter identified four different metaphors dating couples have regarding marriage:

(1) Marriage as work-exchange (marriage involves effort and coordination);

(2) Marriage as journey-organisms (marriage is an ever changing process of growth);

(3) Marriage as force-danger (marriage is a risky undertaking; you can be hurt, you have limited control);

(4) Marriage as game (marriage has a winner and a loser).

Understanding the metaphor used by one's spouse is important because research has shown that those who share similar metaphors toward marriage are more compatible versus those with different metaphors.

Metaphors have also been examined by family counselors. Because the metaphors in reoccurring stories or arguments are often representations of the family's problems, it is believed that if the counselor can help the family change the metaphor, he or she can help the family change (Yerby, Buerkel-Rothfuss, and Bochner 1990).

Using Family Stories as a Research Tool

Family stories and myths are difficult to quantify according to the scientific paradigm (Bruner 1987; Connelly and Clandinin 1990; Reason and Hawkins 1988). This difficulty in quantification is one reason why there has been little research by social scientists. Family therapists, literature and folklore scholars, and others more inclined toward qualitative methods have produced most of what is known about the salience of myths and stories to contemporary family life. Their research has done much to explicate the subtle yet important dynamics at the heart of family interaction.

See also: COMMUNICATION: FAMILY RELATIONSHIPS; FAMILY AND RELATIONAL RULES; FAMILY FOLKLORE; FAMILY RITUALS; GENDER IDENTITY; INTERGENERATIONAL RELATIONS; RELATIONSHIP METAPHORS

Bibliography

Anderson, S., and Bagarozzi, D. (1983). "The Use of Family Myths as an Aid to Strategic Therapy." *Journal of Family Therapy* 5:145–154.

Bagarozzi, D., and Anderson, S. (1982). "The Evolution of Family Mythological Systems: Considerations for Meaning, Clinical Assessment, and Treatment." *Journal of Psychoanalytic Anthropology* 5:71–90.

Bruner, J. (1987). "Life as Narrative." *Social Research* 54:11–32.

Burman, J. (1997). IWP Addresses Kids' Literature. *Spectator,* Spring, 10.

Connelly, F., and Clandinin, D. (1990). "Stories of Experience and Narrative Inquiry." *Educational Researchers* 19:2–14.

Diedrick, P.; Martin, P.; and Hagestad, G. (1986). "Gender Differences as Reflected in Family Stories." ERIC Document Reproduction Service #ED279929. Washington, DC: ERIC Document Reproduction Service.

Fiese, B. H., and Skillman, G. (2001). "Gender Differences in Family Stories: Moderating Influence of Parent Gender Role and Child Gender." *Sex Roles* 43(5–6):267–283.

Martin, P.; Hagestad, G.; and Diedrick, P. (1988). "Family Stories: Events (Temporarily) Remembered." *Journal of Marriage and the Family* 50:533–541.

Morrow, C. (1999). "Family Values/Valued Families: Storytelling and Community Formation among LBG Families with Children." *Journal of Gay, Lesbian, and Bi-Sexual Identity* 4(4):345–356.

Reason, P., and Hawkins, P. (1988). "Storytelling as Inquiry." In *Human Inquiry in Action,* ed. P. Reason. Newbury Park, CA: Sage.

Reese, E. (1996). "Conceptions of Self in Mother-Child Birth Stories." *Journal of Narrative and Life History* 6(1):23–38.

Sherman, M. H. (1990). "Family Narratives: Internal Representations of Family Relationships and Affective Themes." *Infant Mental Health Journal* 11(3):253–258.

Stone, E. (1988). *Black Sheep and Kissing Cousins.* New York: Times Books.

Yerby, J.; Buerkel-Rothfuss, N.; and Bochner, A. P. (1990). *Understanding Family Communication,* 2nd edition. Scottsdale, AZ: Gorsuch Scarisbuck.

Zeitlin, S.; Kotkin, A.; and Baker, H. (1982). *A Celebration of American Family Folklore.* New York: Pantheon.

JAMES J. PONZETTI, JR.
YVONNE KELLAR-GUENTHER

FAMILY STRENGTHS

"Nothing in the world could make human life happier than to greatly increase the number of strong families," according to David R. Mace (1985). *Family strengths* are those relationship qualities that contribute to the emotional health and well-being of the family. Families who define themselves as strong commonly say they love each other, find life together satisfying, and live in happiness and harmony with each other.

Professionals who study families do so for many reasons. Perhaps the most important reason is to help us learn how to get along better with each other in what has been described as our basic social institution and our most intimate environment.

Much of the research on families in the twentieth century focused on family problems in an effort to answer the question, "Why do families fail?" From a family strengths perspective, it is important to also look at families who are doing well in life, and find answers to the question, "How do families succeed?"

Mace was one of the founders of the marriage enrichment movement in Great Britain and the United States. He believed that the study of successful families could yield important knowledge in the quest to help make human life happier by increasing the number of strong families in the world. After researchers have identified the qualities that make families strong, educators can then proceed to develop educational programs for teaching and learning about family strengths. Family therapists can create therapeutic intervention strategies so that family members can develop strengths in their relationships with each other. Family policy makers can design government policies and programs that enhance family well-being rather than diminish it. And family members themselves can put their own very personal approaches to building family strengths in practice in their daily lives together.

Over the years researchers, clinicians, and laypersons have used many different terms to describe families who are doing well together in life: strong families, emotionally healthy families, balanced families, happy families, families with strengths, successful families, optimally functioning families, good families, resilient families, harmonious families, and others. Though the terminology used may differ, the basic notion is that these families believe they are functioning well together, and are satisfied with their relationships with each other.

Researchers studying strong families commonly adopt both "insider" and "outsider" perspectives for their studies. Families who believe they are doing well (the "insiders") are asked to volunteer for a study which measures their strengths; researchers (the "outsiders"), after careful assessment of the family through the process of interviews, observations, and questionnaire data, come to their own conclusions about the family's strengths. Both perspectives are derived from essentially subjective processes.

The Family Strengths Perspective

This is not a theory or conceptual framework, which would imply a set of hypotheses which can be precisely tested through scientific research. The family strengths perspective is a positive, optimistic world-view or orientation toward life and families, grounded in research with more than 21,000 family members in twenty-seven countries. It does not ignore problems, but relegates problems to their proper place in life: as vehicles for testing our capacities as families and reaffirming our connection with each other.

Researchers looking at families from a strengths perspective have developed a number of propositions derived from their work with families that they believe merit serious consideration:

- *All families have strengths.* All families have challenges and all families have areas of potential growth.

- *If one looks only for problems in a family, one will see only problems.* If one also looks for strengths, one will find strengths.

- *It's not about structure, it's about function.* When talking about strong families, it is common to make the mistake of focusing on external family structure rather than internal family functioning. But, there are strong single-parent families, strong stepfamilies, strong nuclear families, strong extended families, strong families with gay and lesbian members, strong two-parent families. For every family structure in the world, there are countless representative strong families. Likewise, every type of family structure in the world also has many families that are not functioning well. Simply knowing the type of family does not tell one anything about the strength of the family.

- *If you grew up in a strong family as a child, it will probably be easier for you to create a strong family of your own as an adult.* However, it's also possible to do so if you grew up in a seriously troubled family.

- *Strengths develop over time.* When couples start out in life together, they tend to have considerable difficulty adjusting to each other, and these difficulties are predictable. Adjusting to each other is not an easy task, but many couples who start out shaky end up creating healthy, happy families.

- *Strengths are tested through normative developmental transitions.* For example, couples commonly face many challenges when their children reach adolescence and young

TABLE 1

Qualities of strong families	
Appreciation and affection	**Commitment**
Caring for each other	Trust
Friendship	Honesty
Respect for individuality	Dependability
Playfulness	Faithfulness
Humor	Sharing
Positive communication	**Time together**
Sharing feelings	Quality time in great quantity
Giving compliments	Good things take time
Avoiding blame	Enjoying each other's company
Being able to compromise	Simple good times
Agreeing to disagree	Sharing fun times
	The ability to cope with stress and crisis
Spiritual well-being	
Hope	Adaptability
Faith	Seeing crises as challenges and opportunities
Compassion	Growing through crises together
Shared ethical values	Openness to change
Oneness with humankind	Resilience

adulthood. These transitions are predictable, and once the period has passed and the younger generation has gained relative independence from the parents, the family settles back into a more emotionally connected and comfortable mode.

- *Good things take time.* A family's strengths are tested by everyday stressors and also by the significant crises that all families face sooner or later. It takes several years before for many couples and families to believe they have become a strong family, but they know this because they have been tested by the significant challenging events that life inevitably brings.

- *Crises can tear families apart. Crises can also make family relationships stronger.* Families in crisis sometimes forget their strengths, and need to remind themselves.

- *A family's strengths are the foundation for growth and positive change.* Families become stronger by capitalizing on their strengths.

- *Most families in the world have considerable strength.* Human beings would not have lasted across countless generations without these qualities. There are many more strong families in the world than families who are deeply troubled. As a global human community, we cannot afford to forget this.

- *Families are about strong emotion.* If family strengths could be reduced to one single quality, it would be the positive emotional connection and sense of belonging with each other. When this emotional bond is present, the family can endure most any hardship.

The Qualities of Strong Families

A number of different conceptions of family strengths, positive family traits, or models of normal family functioning have been proposed (Beavers and Hampson 1990; Curran 1983; Epstein et al. 1993; Krysan, Moore, and Zill 1990; Olson 1996; Stinnett and DeFrain 1985; Stinnett and Sauer 1977). Each model is unique, and this derives from the fact that family strengths and other positive family interaction models are conceptual frameworks. Though the models are derived from observations of real families around the world, the models are subjective constructions based on the perceptions of the researchers and family members. Nevertheless, it is important to point out that the similarities among models of family strengths are more apparent than the differences (Krysan, Moore, and Zill 1990; Olson and DeFrain 2000).

In the same vein, researchers around the world have found remarkable similarities in families in different cultures. Families that describe themselves as strong commonly share a number of broad qualities or traits. What is significant is not how different strong families are in the global community, but how similar they tend to be. In short, people are people, and families are families (Casas et al. 1984; DeFrain, DeFrain, and Lepard 1994; Geggie et al. 2000; Xie et al. 1996).

The Family Strengths Model proposes six clusters of qualities that describe strong families (Stinnett and DeFrain 1985; DeFrain 1999):

- *Appreciation and affection.* People in strong families deeply care for one another, and they let each other know this on a regular basis. They are not afraid to express their love.

- *Commitment.* Members of strong families are dedicated to one another's well-being, investing time and energy in family activities and not letting their work or other priorities take too much time away from family interaction.

- *Positive communication.* Successful families are often task-oriented in their communication, identifying problems and discussing

FIGURE 1

Danger   Opportunity

The Chinese symbol for crisis, a composite of the pictographs for danger and opportunity, suggests that crisis is a time to look for new opportunities.

how to solve them together. Perhaps even more important than this, however, is that strong families spend time talking with and listening to one another just to stay connected. Some of the most important talk occurs when no one is working at connection: open-ended, rambling conversations can reveal important information which helps smooth out the bumps of family life.

- *Enjoyable time together.* One study of 1,500 schoolchildren asked, "What do you think makes a happy family?" Few replied that money, cars, fancy homes, television sets, or Disney World made a happy family. Most children said that a happy family is one that does things together, and that genuinely enjoys the times family members share with each other.

- *Spiritual well-being.* Perhaps the most controversial finding of the family strengths researchers is the importance of religion or spirituality in strong families. We use the phrase spiritual well-being to describe this concept to indicate that it can include organized religion, but not necessarily. People in strong families describe this concept in a variety of ways: some talk about faith in God, hope, or a sense of optimism in life; some say they feel a oneness with the world. Others talk about their families in almost religious terms, describing the love they feel for one another with a great deal of reverence. Others express these kinds of feelings in terms of ethical values and commitment to important causes. Spiritual well-being can be

seen as the caring center within each individual that promotes sharing, love, and compassion. It is a feeling or force that helps people transcend themselves and their day-to-day stressors, and focus on that which is sacred to them in life.

- *Successful management of stress and crisis.* Strong families are not immune to stress and crisis, but they are not as crisis-prone as troubled families tend to be. Rather, they possess the ability to manage both daily stressors and difficult life crises creatively and effectively. They know how to prevent trouble before it happens, and how to work together to meet the inevitable challenges when they occur. (See Figure 1.)

All of the family strengths are interconnected, and are impossible to separate. What unites the strengths is that each is founded upon a sense of *positive emotional connection.* People in strong families feel good about each other and genuinely care for each other's well-being.

Family Strengths and Universal Values

Individuals and families are all unique, and yet there is an apparent paradox: human beings are all also quite similar. Countless people from countless walks of life—novelists, poets, sociologists, anthropologists, singers and songwriters, economists, psychologists, and educators—have remarked upon this.

In the 1930s, cultural anthropologists assumed that every culture was unique. However, over several decades sociologist George Homans (1974) amassed empirical data that contradicted this belief in cultural uniqueness, arguing that certain societal institutions appear in every culture because of the universality of human nature.

Anthropologist Colin Turnbull (1983) devoted his life to studying the nature of human cultures around the world and challenged age-old Western assumptions about differences between so-called "primitive" societies and "modern" societies. Turnbull concluded from his work among the Mbuti of Zaire, the Hindus of Banaras, and middle-class Westerners that the experiences of love, work, loneliness, growing up, and growing old are universal. He concluded that behind all the different

FIGURE 2

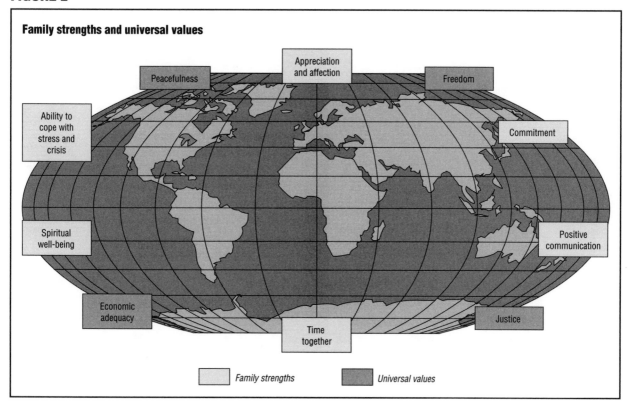

Family strengths and universal values

Designed by Amie DeFrain.

rites, customs, and religions, people in various cultures live in the same eternal, immutable human cycle, governed by the same laws.

Kenneth Boulding (1985), an economist, philosopher, and general systems theorist, wrote that human betterment is the end toward which people, individually and collectively, should strive. Betterment is an increase in the "ultimate good." Four great virtues make up this ultimate good: (1) economic adequacy—wealth in contrast to poverty; nourishment rather than starvation; adequate housing, clothing, health care, and other essentials of life; (2) justice—in contrast to injustice; equality rather than inequality in access to work, education, and health; (3) freedom—in contrast to coercion and confinement; and (4) peacefulness—in contrast to warfare and strife. Boulding proposed that these great virtues may be considered universal values.

Figure 2 combines Boulding's universal values with the Family Strengths Model. From a global perspective, the ultimate good and the strengths that create human happiness in the most intimate institution, the family, are remarkably similar. The human tendency to focus on differences rather than similarities can be divisive and lead to devastating strife. A broader, global perspective emphasizes our common humanity as "citizens of the world." In the words of novelist James A. Michener (1991, p. 249), "We are all brothers [and sisters]. We all face the same problems and find the same satisfactions. We are united in one great band. I am one with all of them, in all lands, in all climates, in all conditions. Since we brothers [and sisters] occupy the entire earth, the world is our home."

See also: COMMUNICATION: FAMILY RELATIONSHIPS; DISABILITIES; FAMILY LIFE EDUCATION; FAMILY LOYALTY; FAMILY VALUES; MARITAL QUALITY; STRESS; TIME USE; TRUST

Bibliography

Beavers, W. R., and Hampson, R. B. (1990). *Successful Families*. New York: Norton.

Boulding, K. (1985). *Human Betterment*. Beverly Hills, CA: Sage.

Casas, C.; Stinnett, N.; DeFrain, J.; Williams, R.; and Lee, P. (1984). "Latin American Family Strengths." *Family Perspective* 18:11–17.

Curran, D. (1983). *Traits of a Healthy Family.* Minneapolis, MN: Winston Press.

DeFrain, J. (1999). "Strong Families Around the World." *Family Matters* 53 (Winter):8–13.

DeFrain, J.; DeFrain, N.; and Lepard, J. (1994). "Family Strengths and Challenges in the South Pacific: An Exploratory Study." *International Journal of the Sociology of the Family* 24(2):25–47.

Epstein, N. B.; Bishop, D. S.; Ryan, C.; Miller, I.; and Keitner, G. (1993). "The McMaster Model of Family Functioning." In *Normal Family Processes,* ed. F. Walsh. New York: Guilford Press.

Geggie, J.; DeFrain, J.; Hitchcock, S.; and Silberberg, S. (2000). "Family Strengths Research Project: Final Report to the Australian Commonwealth Government Ministry of Family and Community Services, Canberra, A.C.T." Callaghan: Family Action Centre, University of Newcastle.

Homans, G. G. (1974). *Social Behavior: Its Elementary Forms,* revised edition. New York: Harcourt.

Krysan, M.; Moore, K. A.; and Zill, N. (1990). "Identifying Successful Families: An Overview of Constructs and Selected Measures." Washington, DC: Child Trends, Inc.

Mace, D. R. (1985). Personal communication cited on book jacket of *Secrets of Strong Families,* by N. Stinnett, and J. DeFrain. Boston: Little, Brown.

Michener, J. A. (1991). *The World Is My Home.* New York: Random House.

Olson, D. H. (1996). "Clinical Assessment and Treatment Using the Circumplex Model." In *Handbook in Relational Diagnosis,* ed. F. W. Kaslow. New York: John Wiley and Sons.

Olson, D. H., and DeFrain, J. (2000). *Marriage and the Family: Diversity and Strengths,* 3rd edition. Mountain View, CA: Mayfield.

Olson, D. H.; Russell, C. S.; and Sprenkle, D. H. (1989). *Circumplex Model: Systemic Assessment and Treatment of Families.* New York: Haworth Press.

Stinnett, N., and DeFrain, J. (1985). *Secrets of Strong Families.* Boston: Little, Brown.

Stinnett, N.; Knorr, B.; DeFrain, J.; and Rowe, G. (1981). "How Strong Families Cope with Crises." *Family Perspective* (Fall):159–166.

Stinnett, N.; Sanders, G.; and DeFrain, J. (1981). "Strong Families: A National Study." In *Family Strengths 3: Roots of Well-Being,* ed. N. Stinnett, J. DeFrain, K. King, P. Knaub, and G. Rowe. Lincoln: University of Nebraska Press.

Stinnett, N., and Sauer, K. H. (1977). "Relationship Characteristics of Strong Families." Family Perspective 11(4):3–11.

Turnbull, C. (1983). *The Human Cycle.* New York: Touchstone/Simon & Schuster.

Xie, X.; DeFrain, J.; Meredith, W.; and Combs, R. (1996). "Family Strengths in the People's Republic of China." *International Journal of Sociology of the Family* 26(2):17–27.

JOHN DEFRAIN
NICK STINNETT

FAMILY SYSTEMS THEORY

Family systems theory's heritage emerged from the work of Ludwig Von Bertalanffy's work on *general systems theory* which offered the world of the mid-twentieth century a different way of viewing science. Instead of the mechanistic models of the time, von Bertalanffy's general systems theory argued that organisms are complex, organized, and interactive. Such an approach shifted from a linear causal model to models that required a broader, *holistic* orientation in order to understand fully the dynamics involved. Von Bertalanffy's work on general systems theory found wide applicability in such fields as community planning, computer science and programming, and the social sciences. By the close of the twentieth century family systems theory had become one of the major theoretical foundations guiding empirical investigations into the study of families and from which clinical interventions and programmatic work with families were being developed.

A general systems perspective examines the way components of a system interact with one another to form a whole. Rather than just focusing on each of the separate parts, a systems perspective focuses on the connectedness and the interrelation and interdependence of all the parts. A systems perspective permits one to see how a change in one component of the system affects the other components of the system, which in turns affects the initial component. The application of the systems perspective has particular relevance to the study of the family as families are comprised of individual members who share a history, have some degree of emotional bonding, and develop strategies for meeting the needs of individual members and the family as a group (Anderson and Sabatelli 1999). *Family systems theory* allows one to understand the organizational complexity of families, as well as the interactive patterns that guide family interactions.

Basic Concepts/Propositions

One of the central premises of family systems theory is that family systems organize themselves to carry out the daily challenges and tasks of life, as well as adjusting to the developmental needs of its members. Critical to this premise is the concept of *holism*. A family systems approach argues that in order to understand a family system we must look at the family as a whole. Two families living across the street from each other may each be comprised of a mother, father, and child. Yet it is in their rules of interacting with each other and their collective history that they are understood as uniquely different. In contrast, a nonsystems approach would attempt to understand each family by looking at the individual members separately. By studying them individually, the way they interact, their communication, or their humor, their uniqueness is lost or clouded. A common analogy often used by family systems theorists and practitioners is found in baking. The cake that comes out of the oven is more than the eggs, flour, oil, baking soda, and vanilla that make up the *parts* or *elements* of the cake. It is how these elements combined to form something larger than the ingredients that makes the cake. Such is true with families as well. It is more than "who makes up a family," it is how they come together that defines that family.

The concept of *hierarchies* describes how families organize themselves into various smaller units or *subsystems* that together comprise the larger family system (Minuchin 1974). Such subsystems are often organized by gender or generation. Practitioners generally have focused on three primary subsystems: *marital* (or *couple*), *parental,* and *sibling.* Each subsystem is distinguished by the members who comprise the subsystem as well as the tasks or focus of the subsystem. Families may organize themselves into subsystems to accomplish the tasks and goals of the family. When the members or tasks associated with each subsystem become blurred with those of other subsystems, families have been viewed as having difficulties. For example, when a child becomes involved in the issues of the marital subsystem, difficulties often emerge that require intervention.

Related to the concept of holism and hierarchies is that of *boundaries*. Families draw boundaries between what is included in the family system and what is external to the system. Boundaries occur at every level of the system and between subsystems. Boundaries influence the movement of people into and out of the system. Boundaries also regulate the flow of information into and out of the family. Although the concept of boundaries as applied to family systems is largely a metaphorical one, the permeability of these boundaries often distinguish one family from another. Some families have very open boundaries where members and others are allowed to freely come and go without much restriction, whereas in other families there are tight restrictions on where family members can go, and who may be brought into the family system. Boundaries also regulate the flow of information about a family. In more closed families the rules strictly regulate what information may be discussed and with whom. In contrast, information may flow more freely in families that have more permeable boundaries. Practitioners working with families often encounter families where they may find themselves being welcomed into the family and information about the family is forthcoming without limitations. In such families the practitioner's ideas and interventions may be accepted with only limited reservation. On the other hand, in more closed families, the practitioner may have a more difficult time being accepted by the family. Information about the family is more difficult to obtain, and ideas and interventions of the practitioner are met with resistance. It is important to also recognize that boundaries exist within the family system and help to distinguish the various subsystems that comprise the larger family system. Finally, the permeability of family boundaries will often change with the developmental age and need of the family members. For example, developmental needs of adolescents and young adults often press the permeability of family boundaries as new ideas and individuals become part of the young person's world.

The concept of *interdependence* is implicit in the discussion of the organizational nature of family systems. Individual family members and the subsystems that comprise the family system are mutually influenced by and are mutually dependent upon one another (Bertalanffy 1975; Whitchurch and Constantine 1993). What happens to one family member, or what one family member does, influences the other family members. This is one of the primary concepts embedded in clinical models emerging from a systems perspective. Clinicians understand that to effectively work with families it is imperative to consider the systemic impact of any intervention.

A second central premise to family systems theory is that families are dynamic in nature and have patterns of rules and strategies that govern the way they interact. The dynamic nature of family helps to ensure that the family can meet the challenges associated with daily living and developmental growth of the family members. The concept of *equilibrium* explains how families strive for a sense of balance between the challenges they confront and the resources of the family. Families are constantly adapting, changing, or responding to daily events as well as more long term developmental challenges and changes. According to family systems theory, families strive for a sense of balance or *homeostasis*. When such balance is not found, the rules or dynamics of the family may need to be adjusted to restore this balance. The concept of *morphostasis* refers to the ability of the family system to maintain consistency in its organizational characteristics despite the challenges that may rise up over time (Steinglass 1987). Patterns of interaction emerge within the family that keeps demands for change in check. In contrast, *morphogenesis* refers to the systems' ability to grow systemically over time to adapt to the changing needs of the family. In all families there is an ongoing dynamic tension between trying to maintain stability and introducing change.

The concept of *feedback loops* is used to describe the patterns or channels of interaction and communication that facilitates movement toward morphogenesis or morphostasis. Negative feedback loops are those patterns of interaction that maintain stability or constancy while minimizing change. Negative feedback loops help to maintain homeostasis. Positive feedback loops, in contrast, are patterns of interaction that facilitate change or movement toward either growth or dissolution. Although the words *negative* and *positive* are used within systems theory, it is not meant to characterize the communication as good or bad. No value is implied in the labels. For example, in the Jones family, the father decides to return to school part time to complete his education now that their youngest child is preschool age. Negative feedback loops are associated with patterns of interaction and communication that keep the family system functioning in its current way. These patterns attempt to maintain the family system in the way it was before the father returned to school. The family members may continue to expect the running of the household and the availability of the father to remain the same, despite the fact that the father is now in the workforce and school. For example, the father may be expected to have the same level of availability to the children and his partner as before. In contrast, positive feedback loops would be patterns of interaction and communication that emerge as a result of the need for change associated with the father being in school. The family may reach an agreement that the father is not to be disturbed during certain hours of the day so that he may study. Alternatively, certain days of the week may be *family time*, whereas other days or times of the week are *studying time*.

As complex interactive systems, families are seen as being goal oriented. Families strive to reach certain objectives and goals. Through patterns of interactions, such as negative and positive feedback loops, the achievement of the goals becomes more or less attainable. The concept of *equifinality* refers to the ability of the family system to accomplish the same goals through different routes (Bertalanffy 1968). Equifinality proposes that the same beginning can result in many different outcomes, and that an outcome may be reached through many paths. For example, the Gonzales family has the goal of having each of the children obtain a college education. Academic scholarships are seen as the primary means of providing access to a college education for the children. Thus, the family may organize itself to foster academic excellence of the children by focusing on homework and providing challenging educational opportunities that push the children to excel. An alternate path may focus on developing the athletic skills of the children, which will provide a different avenue into the academic world. A third focus may be on one or more of the parents working extra hours or jobs to help finance the college education. Families may use one or more of these methods to achieve the same goal.

Challenges and Future Directions

Family systems theory has had a significant impact on the study of families and on approaches to working with families. It has guided research into such areas as understanding traumatic events or chronic health issues and their impact on individuals and families, substance abuse intervention and treatment modalities, and kinship networks. It has provided a useful lens through which a greater understanding of families has emerged. However, as with any lens, critics have challenged the clarity of the lens in certain areas. Some critics have argued that issues of gender inequality are not fully articulated or addressed within family systems theory. For example, in patriarchal societies, where power lies primarily with men, equality of influence between men and women can not be assumed. Critics of family systems theory argue that such inequality is often overlooked or understated (Goldner 1989; Yllo 1993). The application of family systems theory to issues of family violence has been criticized. For example, a systems perspective on family violence will focus on the family dynamics that contribute to the violence, and less attention will be given to the characteristics, motivations, and attitudes of the perpetrator of the violence. Critics argue that the utilization of family systems theory in this area can lead to the perception of a shared responsibility for violence between the victim and perpetrator and less accountability by the perpetrator for his or her actions (e.g. Whitchurch and Constantine 1993; Finkelhor 1984).

Over the years variants in family systems have emerged. The *communications model* focuses on the communication patterns found within family systems, specifically on the role of inputs and outputs in communication and the consistency between these in explaining family communication patterns in functional and dysfunctional families. Such a model was heavily influenced by the work of Gregory Bateson, Don Jackson, Paul Watzlawik, and others at the Mental Research Institute in Palo Alto (Watzlawick, Beavin, and Jackson 1967). In contrast, Salvador Minuchin's (1974) work with family systems theory has focused more on the spatial nature of families. Central to this orientation is an examination of the social contexts and structures in which families find themselves and their interaction with those contexts and structures. In a different area, family systems theory is being challenged to consider and integrate the increasingly important role that genetics and neurobiological structures have on personality traits and individual behavior. Family systems theory is also being challenged to consider cultural and broader contextual issues that influence families. The integration of family systems theory into the medical realm, the study of ethnic and cultural differences, and broader systems is a testament to its continued utility.

See also: BOUNDARY DISSOLUTION; CODEPENDENCY; DEVELOPMENTAL PSYCHOPATHOLOGY; DISABILITIES; FAMILY DEVELOPMENT THEORY; FAMILY DIAGNOSIS/DSM-IV; FAMILY DIAGRAMMATIC ASSESSMENT: ECOMAP; FAMILY THEORY; HUMAN ECOLOGY THEORY; RESOURCE MANAGEMENT; SPOUSE ABUSE: THEORETICAL EXPLANATIONS; THERAPY: COUPLE RELATIONSHIPS; THERAPY: FAMILY RELATIONSHIPS; TRANSITION TO PARENTHOOD; TRIANGULATION

Bibliography

Anderson A., and Sabatelli, R. (1999). *Family Interaction: A Multigenerational Developmental Perspective.* Boston: Allyn and Bacon.

Bertalanffy, L. von. (1968). *General System Theory.* New York: George Braziller.

Bertalanffy, L. von. (1975). *Perspectives on General Systems Theory: Scientific-Philosophical Studies.* New York: George Braziller.

Finkelhor, D. (1984). *Child Sexual Abuse: New Theory and Research.* New York: Free Press.

Goldner, V. (1989). "Generation and Gender: Normative and Covert Hierarchies." In *Women in Families,* ed. M. McGoldrick, C. Anderson, and F. Walsh. New York: Norton.

Minuchin, S. (1974). *Families and Family Therapy.* Cambridge, MA: Harvard University Press.

Steinglass, P. (1987). "A Systems View of Family Interaction and Psychopathology." In *Family Interaction and Psychopathology,* ed. T. Jacob. New York: Plenum Press.

Watzlawick, P. P.; Beavin, J.; and Jackson, D. (1967). *Pragmatics of Human Communication.* New York: Norton.

Whitchurch, G., and Constantine, L. (1993). "Systems Theory." In *Sourcebook of Family Theories and Methods:*

A Contextual Approach, ed. P. Boss, W. Doherty, R. LaRossa, W. Schumm, and S. Steinmetz. New York: Plenum Press.

Yllo, K. (1993). "Through a Feminist Lens: Gender, Power and Violence." In *Current Controversies on Family Violence,* ed. R. Gelles and D. Loseke. Newbury Park, CA: Sage.

WILLIAM M. FLEMING

FAMILY THEORY

Suppose a couple is recently divorced. A friend may wonder why this happened and develop several hunches. Perhaps they argued a lot, and one or both may have frequently seemed upset. The friend may begin thinking about why the couple got married in the first place. Perhaps their dating relationship was unusual, or perhaps their upbringing as children offers clues. Using information about their past, the friend might develop a theory, a speculative argument about factors contributing to the couple's divorce. The word *theory* derives from the Greek verb *theorein,* meaning to behold or contemplate. People have contemplated the nature and operation of human families at least since the ancient Greeks, and they continue to do so today. All individuals may wonder how their own or other families work and about the problems involved.

Theorizing about a particular event or a particular marriage or family seems natural in everyday life. Social scientists, however, are not interested in explaining single events or how one marriage or family works. Instead, social scientists want to know how marriages and families work in general. This does not mean that every divorce will have the same cause, only that the emphasis is on a broad understanding of many marriages and families. If they know what generally is true by examining many different marriages and divorces, they come closer to developing a useful theory about divorce. A useful theory provides a general understanding of what has happened in the past, and it enables the scientists to make predictions about what might happen to other couples in the future.

Furthermore, if social scientists want to help other couples deal effectively with their relationships, they need to have confidence that information about a particular couple is not unique. They need to know what makes marriages similar to one another and especially what makes some marriages different from others.

Why is it impossible to have a scientifically useful theory about one event, such as a particular divorce? Suppose it is strongly believed that certain factors in a couple's past are responsible for their divorce. To be sure of this, the social scientists would have to argue that if the couple's pasts had been different in certain ways then they would not have gotten divorced. Something that actually did not happen might have prevented the divorce. The problem is that scientists cannot know about things that did not happen. Such unknown circumstances are called *counterfactuals.* Theories containing counterfactuals may be plausible, but they cannot be proven true.

Social scientists want to have theories capable of being generally true for as many marriages and families as possible. When exceptions are found, they can explore why the exceptions occur. Good theories also must be capable of disproof. If there is no way to disprove them, outrageous claims can be made, and there is no effective way to argue against them. Because a couple cannot turn back the clock and behave differently, it will never be known what caused their divorce.

Family scientists base their theories on information enabling comparisons across many cases. If many similar couples can be found, and all of them get divorced, scientists might be closer to a general understanding of the causes of divorce. Moreover, if many couples who are similar in all respects but a few are found, and those with the differing circumstances do not divorce, scientists might form an even more useful theory about divorce. Instead of relying on arguments about what did not happen, they compare different couples who have different experiences, some ending in divorce and some staying married.

In this way, family scientists have developed many theories to guide their thinking (Boss et al. 1993). These theories differ from each other in several fundamental ways.

Philosophies of Family Science

Theorizing can be based on different ideas about how a science works. Three primary approaches can be distinguished. A positivistic philosophy of family science makes several assumptions:

(1) There is a real world of family life. This world is a natural one, and it operates according to a set of general principles. Truth is a matter of discovery.

(2) The world of family life is ultimately knowable. Through careful study of how individual families work, scientists can increase their understanding of family life.

(3) The best way to study families is by using standard methods useful in other domains of scientific inquiry. Reliable and valid evidence, or factual information, must be collected, based on observing families.

(4) With increasing knowledge based on the facts, social scientists can intervene or assist others to intervene to improve family life.

This positivistic or optimistic approach was dominant throughout the twentieth century. It arose to help family studies gain stature as a scientific enterprise not unlike the other more established sciences. It also helped to distinguish scientific theories about the family from other kinds of contemplation, based on theological principles or other beliefs about the "appropriate" ways of being a family. Social science should be conducted in a spirit of free inquiry, without interference from governments or other nonscientific authorities.

On the other hand, the critical philosophy of family science starts with the idea that all beliefs and practices are political. Families, as well as the scholars who study them, are engaged in a struggle for domination and respect.

Historically, it can be observed that certain kinds of families and family members have been dominated and oppressed by those who are in more powerful positions in society. The less powerful usually have been females, persons of relatively low socioeconomic status, members of racial and ethnic minority groups, children, and sometimes elderly members of society. Any person or group different from the image of a "normal" family is considered to be abnormal or deviant by members of dominant groups. Those people in power not only control material resources but also intellectual resources, the way society thinks about families. Most members of the scientific "establishment," including family researchers and theorists, have been members of dominating social groups and categories.

The critical perspective challenges not only the content of positivistic theories, but also the assumptions upon which positivism rests. There is no natural world of family life to be discovered. Instead, what seems natural is the product of political forces, and of the domination of thinking and acting by some privileged families, family members, and family scientists. Truth is not a discovery, but a weapon. The proper goals of science are not the accumulation of facts and theories based on them, but instead are enlightenment and emancipation. Theories should be used to expose domination, and to assist the transformation of society and of science itself into more humane entities, resulting in a better world. Such a world will be one in which diversity of both lifestyles and modes of thinking will be equally respected and allowed to flourish. Some feminist theories and social conflict theories of family life rely on a critical philosophy of science (Farrington and Chertok 1993; Osmond 1987; Osmond and Thorne 1993).

A third philosophy of science influencing family theory is the interpretive approach. This view claims that all reality is a human construction. There is no objective truth about families, only a variety of subjective views that are developed through a dialogue with others in an effort to achieve a shared and workable understanding. Whatever is claimed to be known is tentative, always in process, and always just one point of view within a stream of alternative and evolving views. Whatever entity is called a family, the members of that entity are principally engaged in negotiating a sense of meaning, one that enables them to better understand who they are and how they fit into the environment.

Interpretive family theorists tend to reject positivism as naive, as making ideas seem firmer, more factual, or more stable than they really are. Truth is not a discovery, but an invention. The purpose of theorizing about the family is to make a personal statement based on an inevitably limited view. Instead of finding theories that will stand the test of time, the best theories are about the search for meaning in which families participate. These understandings and the processes by which they are created should be part of the content as well as the method used by family theorists. Interpretive theorists and researchers let family members speak and act for themselves and observe how reality is socially constructed. The theories of scholars then emerge and change as the theories created by families emerge and change. Symbolic interaction theory and phenomenological theory usually rely on an interpretive philosophy of science (Gubrium and Holstein 1993; LaRossa and Reitzes 1993).

All three philosophies influenced family scholars throughout the twentieth century. Because they are philosophies, there is no positivistic way of deciding which is best. The preferences of family theorists relate to the way they were trained, the acceptance by their colleagues of the alternatives, and the personal lives and other professional experiences of those in the scientific community (Klein and Jurich 1993; Thomas and Wilcox 1987).

These philosophies do not represent entirely incompatible viewpoints. Some family theorists accept the usefulness of more than one philosophy, even if they rely on only one of their own theories. Others combine features of two or more philosophies of science when they theorize.

Purposes of Family Theory

Theories about the family also differ in terms of the purposes that theorists have in formulating them. The most common goal is to provide a general description of how families work. In order to achieve a useful description, theories contain concepts. These concepts, such as cohesiveness, size, or patriarchy, help to compare families, and commonly have technical definitions. Family theorists usually strive for clear and precise definitions, so that they may measure what happens when families are directly observed or when members report their ideas, feelings, and behaviors. Many concepts are treated as variables, properties with different quantities on some scale. For example, families may be more or less cohesive, larger or smaller, and more or less patriarchal.

Different types of concepts are used in family theories. Some point to the structure of a family, its composition or the way it is organized. Some concepts describe patterns of social interaction, the quality of relationships, or processes that occur in families. Some theoretical concepts show how other concepts are related to each other. For example, if a family has five members and one descriptive concept refers to how flexible each member is, the family itself may be flexible if it meets a certain level of flexibility in its members. Perhaps all members must be at least halfway flexible, or

perhaps some of the five must be very flexible to compensate for the inflexibility of the others. Whatever concepts are used, it is impossible to have a family theory unless there is a fairly detailed vocabulary for describing what makes families similar to and different from each other.

Most family theories go beyond description and provide an explanation. To explain something, it is essential to argue why it occurs. There are two basic ways to explain family life (Burr et al. 1979).

One type of explanation uses a deductive argument. This begins with a small number of premises (or axioms), statements individuals are willing to assume are true. Then, other statements (or theorems) are logically derived from the premises. Consider the following illustration:

(1) All social systems are goal-directed. (Axiom 1)

(2) All families are social systems. (Axiom 2)

(3) One goal of all social systems is survival. (Axiom 3)

(4) All families direct energy toward survival. (Theorem 1)

The theorem may be true, but only if all three axioms are true, in which case an explanation for why families direct energy toward survival exists; they do so because of the meanings inherent in the axioms. If the illustration were a real deductive explanation, additional information would have to be provided. The meaning of social system, goal, family, and energy would have to be defined, and more theorems would be derived. Deductive explanations are usually considered to be powerful if many theorems can be derived from a small set of axioms.

Notice how an explanation is achieved in this example. Families are treated as one type of social system, and survival is treated as one type of goal. Subsuming one phenomenon under a broader phenomenon is a common way of making a deductive argument. Another common way is to link statements in a chain. For example:

(1) If parents encourage their children to explore the environment, children will explore the environment. (Axiom 4)

(2) If children explore the environment, they will have high self-esteem. (Axiom 5)

(3) If children have high self-esteem, they will effectively solve their problems later in life. (Axiom 6)

(4) If parents encourage their children to explore the environment, children will effectively solve their problems later in life. (Theorem 2)

Here, effective problem solving for some people has been explained by referring to a chain of events that produces it. Furthermore, it has been argued that these axioms are transitive. That is, by having a series of statements with *then* in one becoming *if* in the next, it is possible to see a link between two ideas (in this case, what parents do and how children solve problems), a link that previously may have gone unnoticed. The argument may require elaboration before it is satisfactory, however. Simple *if/then* statements may hold only under special conditions. For instance, it may be argued that other things must be present, such as a willingness on the part of children to do what parents encourage them to do, before they will act as Axiom 4 argues.

While deductive explanations tend to be clear about the logic underlying an argument, family theorists have found them to be of limited value. The main reason is that it must be assumed that the premises are true. It often is difficult to make a convincing case that they are true. Different premises might be created that lead to the same conclusions, which would raise doubt about the original premises, or further research might prove that some theorems are false. Either of these situations would indicate that something is wrong with the original deductive explanation, but it would not pinpoint the problem.

The most popular way to explain family life uses a causal argument, which starts by assuming that everything that happens has some cause. The way families are or the actions they take cannot just be accidental. Some actions or conditions in the past exert influence on the current situation. An explanation is achieved by first showing how families are different from each other and then showing how differing prior circumstances are responsible for the differences to be explained.

In its simplest form, a causal argument is deterministic. It is assumed that there is one primary causal factor and it completely determines the result. In practice, however, family scholars have realized that causes are seldom so simple. Causal explanations generally employ several antecedent factors or conditions, working together or as alternatives, and all of them are included in the argument. Each causal element only works to increase the probability that a particular outcome will occur.

Causal explanations may show several factors converging to influence one outcome. They may show several separate paths, with several intervening steps, before an outcome is reached. They may even specify the conditions necessary before one variable can have an influence on another variable. In any case, causal explanations require fairly stable and strong connections between variables. Causal factors must happen chronologically before the effects occur, and the connections must not be just coincidental, byproducts of something else that is the "true" cause.

While causal explanations in family science have been popular, they are often viewed cautiously. Even the best ones tend to explain only a modest fraction of the differences between families. To improve them, there often is a temptation to make causal arguments more complex. If they grow too complex, however, they begin to lose their intuitive appeal. It is a challenge to understand what a very complex causal argument is really claiming. Part of the attraction of causal arguments in family theories is that the technology for using them to conduct empirical research is well developed. This technology involves statistical skills that sometimes seem remote from the family lives the researchers are trying to understand.

One problem with causal explanations is the frequent requirement that scientists follow families over time, because the families are supposed to change due to causal forces. Quite often, however, researchers compare different families at one time, and changes within families are not observed. Thus, researchers may be tempted to think that they have found causes, when they really have only found associations between variables.

Another problem with causal explanations is the mistaken belief that it is possible to explain what usually happens causally. Suppose it is discovered that 30 percent of all children in the

United States are born to single mothers. Researchers may want to know the cause of this percentage. Then, they may identify a possible cause, perhaps the advantages of staying single. When this idea is included, the problem of counterfactuals is faced again. Single mothers may have common experiences suggesting the advantages of singlehood. But social scientists must compare single mothers with other mothers, and they must also compare all of the mothers with regard to the proposed cause. Family scientists can never causally explain what often or always happens in families or the average family experience. Instead, causal explanations can only explain differences, in this example why some mothers are married when they bear children while other mothers are not.

Some critics of causal explanations argue that the entire enterprise is misguided because scientists never can prove that something is a cause or part of a cause. Nevertheless, theories that rely on causal explanations remain popular in the family field, even if they cannot provide complete explanations. Causal explanations provide a useful way to think about family life, and the challenge is to make them better than rival causal explanations, not to assume that they ever will provide the final word or the perfect theory.

Most family theorists who provide descriptions and explanations believe these are the two most important purposes to achieve. Some family theorists, however, want to show how to change families by intervening to do something for their benefit. This goal is based on the idea that some families are not functioning well and that it is important to solve family problems or prevent them from occurring.

Interventions to change families must be based on an evaluation of the current situation and a decision that some families should be altered to reach an objective not now being met. Because people often disagree about goals and standards, any intervention relies on a point of view. Families themselves may determine that they are not meeting their own goals. A theorist may have goals for families that do not correspond with a family's own goals or values. The standard selected may be some notion of what is generally acceptable in society at large.

Whose goals should direct an intervention is often controversial. Consider the discovery that physical abuse of children by parents is fairly common in the United States. A scholar may develop a good theory about why some parents abuse their children and others do not. Perhaps one causal factor in the theory is the extent to which parents feel they have the right to punish children as they see fit. Those parents who feel that severe physical punishment is acceptable then use this form of punishment. A good theory should allow the theorist to determine what needs to be done to reduce the likelihood of child abuse. In this example, what is needed is a change in the belief by some parents that their behavior is acceptable. The problem is that parents may not feel that their punishing behaviors are unacceptable. The only way to avoid controversy surrounding the use of family theories to change families is to identify a goal that everyone accepts.

Even if there is no controversy over goals and values, it may be difficult to implement the desired change. If the theory implies that families must be changed, a program of action must be developed to reach families and change them. Sufficient confidence in the theory must exist so that a change in the causal factors has a good chance of producing the desired effect. This often requires careful research, because undesirable consequences of well-intentioned changes may occur. Finally, the required change in the cause may be difficult in principle to produce. If, for example, a theory argued that the basic fabric of society must be changed in order to reduce child abuse, figuring out how to change the fabric of society would be a tall order.

If a theory explains well what has happened in the past, it should provide a good prediction about the future. Another purpose of family theory is to enable accurate estimates of what families will be like in the future. Therefore, once a theory has been formulated, further research must be conducted to see if the theory remains useful. The connection between past and future, however, depends on a fairly stable environment. Some family theories do not survive events that take place after they have been formulated. This usually means that the original theory must be revised to reflect changes in families and in their environments more accurately. If a theory cannot be revised, it tends to be discarded.

Difficulty predicting family life may not be a serious deficit. The future is difficult to predict in many areas of science. Nevertheless, it is important to notice when a family theory was developed, and to find out what has happened subsequently. If an older theory about the family is encountered that no longer seems popular, newer literature can be examined to see if this loss of popularity is due to faulty prediction or a failure to revise the theory. Family theories usually are not static entities. They tend to change as families and their environments change, and as new theorists with new insights join the field.

Meaning of Family

Another important difference among family theories is in the way their central topic, the family, is defined and used. While all theories have a descriptive purpose, not all family theorists view families identically. In fact, they view families according to four different meanings of the term *family*.

One way to look at families is based on structural features. Families contain varying numbers of persons who are related in particular ways, including such persons as mothers, fathers, and children. This view may be extended to include grandparents, in-laws, step-relations, and perhaps even former relatives. Structural definitions of family focus on the composition of its membership. They may indicate that family members are related by blood, marriage, or some other legal bond such as adoption. Sharing a household may be another structural feature. With a structural definition, the theorist is able to determine which kinds of social groups do not qualify as families and which individuals are in a particular family.

Structural definitions of family also attend to the types of relationships that create social bonds between members. Important bonds are created by communication, power, and affection, as well as the daily work and leisure performed by family members. Scientists can observe how patterns of social interaction among the members are structured, and they can specify the various rules or principles that families use to organize their activities. Families may be structured by such characteristics as gender, age, and generation, as well as their connections to the outside world. These structures also are useful for distinguishing families from other kinds of social groups and organizations.

Theories about the family usually focus on some limited structural form. For example, they may apply only to married couples or to mothers and daughters. Sometimes theories compare different family structures. A theory might deal with how parent-child relations differ when two-parent families are compared to mother-led families.

A second way to look at families is based on functional elements. Why do families exist in the first place? Every human society has families, so they must serve some generally recognized purpose or function. Most functional definitions of the family focus on the importance of human reproduction and the necessity of nurturing dependent children for a relatively long period of time. Functional family theories often address the structural variety of families, with assertions about how effective each structure is in accomplishing the requisite functions that families everywhere have. From this perspective, if a certain structure does not fulfill some family function, families with that structure may be considered to be dysfunctional families.

A third meaning of family is based on interactional features, that is, it emphasizes repeatable processes of social interaction within families. Such interaction may be patterned or structured, but the focus is on the ongoing activity within the family, often conducted jointly by the members or otherwise coordinated. Family theories that rely on an interactional definition include concepts and variables describing what each participant is doing, how the members influence each other, and the quality of their relationships. From this perspective, a group need not have any particular structure to be counted as a family. Any social group that acts like a family would qualify as being a family. Social exchange theories often adopt an interactional view of family relationships (Sabatelli and Shehan 1993).

The fourth meaning of family is based on symbolic elements. Focus is on the meanings, perceptions, and interpretations that people have about family experiences. Only by watching how persons communicate or use dialogue to construct, challenge, and alter meanings do social scientists come to understand what a family is. Often this expression is verbal. The symbols people use to create and recreate family go beyond spoken words, however. Other important symbols are nonverbal intonations, bodily gestures, practices of dress and grooming, written statements, and visual images such as photographs and the spatial arrangement and condition of possessions in the home. Family theories based on the symbolic perspective emphasize various languages used to communicate, as well as the many artifacts with symbolic meaning created by families.

These four meanings of family are not always used separately. Two combinations are especially common. A combined structural and functional perspective informs structure-functional theory (Kingsbury and Scanzoni 1993). A combined interactional and symbolic perspective informs symbolic interaction theory (LaRossa and Reitzes 1993).

Each of the four meanings of family can be used alone, however. For example, it is possible to have a structural theory about some aspect of family life, perhaps offering structural causes of some limited family activity, without implying anything about the functionality of what is explained. For instance, the size of families or the size of communities in which they live might influence the amount of companionship among family members. It is also possible to use patterns of interaction as a cause or as the outcome in a family theory, without incorporating any ideas about the symbolic significance of the interaction to the family's members. For example, how often family members argue may influence how household chores are performed.

Level or Scope of Family Theories

Theories about the family differ in terms of their breadth of vision, level of analysis, and scope. Microscopic theories tend to focus on the internal workings of families, viewed as small groups of people in fairly intense relationships.

Mesoscopic theories focus on the transactions between families and people in the near environment who represent other groups and organizations. At this level, family theories are concerned with such things as friendships between members of different families, and the linkages between families and schools, churches, places of employment, the mass media, retail firms, and other public or private facilities and organizations.

Macroscopic theories concentrate on how the family as a social institution is embedded in society at large or in the nonhuman environment. They may, for instance, address how contemporary ways of family living emerged from significant changes in the economy, in national politics, or in technological developments. Structural and functional theories tend toward the macroscopic end of

the spectrum, while symbolic and interactional theories tend toward the microscopic end.

Scope is a relative matter. For theorists of the human family, the social unit called family is roughly at the center of the spectrum, so that moving outward makes a particular theory more macro and moving inward makes it more micro.

Some family theorists focus on a fairly narrow range of the spectrum and formulate all of their ideas at one level or another. Other family theorists deliberately bridge levels, creating a transcopic theory. These multilevel theories often argue that phenomena at one level are the causes of phenomena at another level. Among such theories, the most common is a top-down approach. Societies affect families, and families in turn affect the individual persons in them. Increasingly popular are bottom-up theories that simply reverse the direction of causation, and reciprocating transcopic theories that emphasize mutual causation between levels in either alternating or simultaneous patterns. Family theories based on ecological principles currently are popular among those that are transcopic (Bubolz and Sontag 1993).

The scope of a theory helps scientists see the amount of causal agency attributed to families, as opposed to other factors outside or inside the family. Some theorists argue that families are primary causal agents. What they do has important consequences, and what makes them act may be important but is not addressed in the theory. Other theorists take exactly the opposite approach. Phenomena at the family level are to be explained by forces external or internal to them. If a theory remains entirely at the family level, it will explain something about family life in terms of causes elsewhere at the family level. A causal theory must have at least some cause or some effect at the family level to really be a theory about families. Some theories are called family theories even if they deal with only parts of a family, such as a theory about divorce or about the relationship between grandparents and grandchildren.

Time Perspectives

All theories about the family deal with the flow of chronological time, and sometimes with the social and psychological organization of time. Four principal time perspectives are common: static, episodic, biographical, and epochal.

In some theories, time is suspended or relegated to the margins. The idea is to craft a theory that is timeless. This static picture may be useful, especially if it is a general description. Given the previously noted problems associated with change, however, static family theories are themselves not very durable.

Often, the image of time is episodic. A process is being described and perhaps explained, and it is temporary. The entire process may last a few moments, a few days, or several months. If scientists trace what is happening over the course of events contained in the theory, everything can be observed with moderate effort when the theory is tested.

Another image of time is biographical. This perspective usually considers the entire span or course of life. Family phenomena begin at birth, develop through time, change along the way, and end when life ends. The idea of a "life" comes from the study of individual organisms, and it must be adjusted to speak meaningfully about the lifetime of a social group containing several organisms.

One adjustment is to consider the "birth" of the group to occur when the group itself forms, with the "death" of the group corresponding to the dissolution of the group. Some of the members will be alive before the group forms, after it dissolves, or both. New members may be added after the family forms, and some may be lost before the family ends. Families may endure even with great turnover in membership, as for example a lineage that survives over many generations. Individual persons may have experiences as members of several different families over the course of their own lives. Becoming a widow, getting divorced, remarrying, and giving birth to or adopting a child are among the events marking the course of both an individual's life and the life of the group.

Because it is usually impractical for one scholar to study large numbers of families from their formation to their dissolution, many theories that deal with biographical time concentrate on a shorter time segment. Some describe and explain what is happening during a particular stage of family life, such as when children are adolescents or after all of the children have become adults and left their parental homes. Another common alternative is to focus on a particular transition period. For instance, some theories focus on the process by which couples get married, or why some get married and others do not, tracing events from first meeting to the early years after marriage or until a breakup before marriage. Other time-limited biographical theories concern the transition to parenthood, the transition to the "empty nest," and so on. Family development is the most common name for the theories that treat families in biographical time (Rodgers and White 1993).

The other image of time is epochal. Fairly broad sweeps of history may be examined and categorized into periods. Families in ancient Greece, families in the American colonies, families during the early industrial era, and families during the Great Depression represent some of the historical categories that may give focus to a family theory. Other theories take a more sweeping historical perspective. Theorists may wish, for example, to explain how human families evolved from primate families, or how the contemporary family emerged from forces at work over several centuries. While many family theories using an epochal image of time are descriptive, evolutionary or biosocial theories of family life usually are explanatory as well (Troost and Filsinger 1993).

Forms of Expressing Theory

One useful way to differentiate theories about the family concerns the way they are expressed by their authors. Some theories are written in narrative form. They use prose expressed in commonly understood language. Other family theories are somewhat more formalized and are called propositional. A theorist identifies a set of well-bounded, declarative statements that serve as the theory's core propositions. Many of the concepts in these statements have technical meanings, and definitions are included. Often, the propositions assert how two or more variables are related, how strong the connections are and when they happen, and whether or not causal influence is implied. Theories that use shorthand, technical expressions are even more formalized. They contain mathematical symbols, diagrams with arrows, flow charts, or figures with classifications into types.

All forms of expression have virtues and limitations. More formalized theories are precise, and they are easy to distinguish from other theories with similar content. If a theory is imprecise or fuzzy, it is difficult for the scientific community to agree on what is meant, and extremely difficult to demonstrate that some of the arguments may be incorrect. Formalized theories require specialized training to be fully interpreted, however. Because technical expressions are arbitrary and may require intricate rules, some family theorists avoid them. Some avoid highly formalized theories because they can dehumanize the subject matter and place more emphasis on the structure of an argument than on its content. A truly good theory may be one that either combines forms of expression or can be translated from one form to another without changing its meaning.

Methods of Creating Theories

Theories about families usually develop over time as theorists incorporate prior knowledge and new experience. At first, there may be only fragments, enough of an argument to share the basic shape of a theory with an audience. If a particular theory has been discussed for a period of time and a consensus has been established, the theory may be named and only brief mention made of its details, on the assumption that colleagues understand what is involved. Working to produce a family theory, however, usually takes place in one of two ways.

Deductive theory is produced by starting with fairly abstract ideas and without particular regard for the way families can be observed to operate in the "real" world. Some of the ideas may be borrowed from other areas of study, and some may represent the integration or modification of existing ideas about family. Portions may be entirely new, but more often the theorist is just reshaping or recombining ideas that have appeared in other scholarly works. Theorists may work deductively even when they are not creating deductive explanations.

Once the new theory is given a clear structure, the theorist or a colleague who is attracted to the theory conducts empirical research to test some of the arguments. If the theory is supported by research data, gathered and analyzed using suitable methods, the theory is provisionally accepted. This acceptance is provisional because it takes repeated tests, often by different groups of researchers using somewhat different methods, before a great deal of confidence in the theory is warranted. If the theory is unsupported or refuted by research data, it is revised or discarded in favor of a superior alternative. Ideally, two rival theories with different explanations and predictions are pitted against each other in a single study or a carefully managed series of studies. This enables scholars to determine which of the two theories is better.

Some family scientists object to the deductive process. While they acknowledge that it is the usual textbook approach, they offer either of two arguments. The *weak theory* objection is that scholars really do not use the deductive method. Instead, they are guided by hunches derived from the direct experiences they have, either as handlers of empirical data or as participants in family life. The *strong theory* objection is that every judgment and decision a scholar makes is based on preconceived ideas to which that scholar has very strong attachments. Because all social scientists have ideas and beliefs about families, the theories they create are biased in ways that escape the attention of even the most impartial theorist.

To take advantage of both objections, some family scientists use an inductive method to create their theories. In its pure form, the scientist disregards all previous knowledge and speculation about the topic of interest. Research with minimal biases is conducted, and the participating families and the results they produce are taken at face value. A useful theory is developed either after the research is concluded or slowly during the process of study. A *grounded* theory emerges.

Much family theorizing is transductive, with elements of both deduction and induction. The two extreme approaches provide models for how to work, but there is room for an intermediate approach.

Many participants are involved in the process of creating any theory. Even if only one author receives credit, that person builds on the ideas of others. If a particular theory has many acknowledged contributors and if it endures sufficiently long, it becomes recognized as a theoretical tradition or school of thought. The family members who participate in the creation of family theory may be recognized as coauthors, but often they are not.

Other Differences

Family theories can be distinguished in additional ways. Some theories are relatively abstract and speculative, while others are more concrete and stated in language closer to observable phenomena.

Some family theories are quite general, while others are much more context-specific. General theories are claimed to hold regardless of time or place, or apply to broadly encompassed times and places. Context-specific theories tend to focus on restricted populations, such as one culture or society, the families in one social class, a segment of families with a narrow age structure, one gender, or one racial or ethnic group. Some family theories entail comparisons across contexts, but without covering all of the possibilities. The context of time also varies between family theories. Whether they adopt episodic, biographical, or epochal images of time, most family theories concerned with processes of change carve out a limited span of time for their arguments.

Theories about the family also differ in terms of the breadth of content they cover and which particular subunits within the family are addressed. Theories may be narrow, middle-range, or broad in their content. Relatively speaking, a theory about the effectiveness of communication by husbands is narrow, while a theory of marital quality is middle-range, and a theory of family functioning is broad. In this example, not only does the subject matter become broader with the move from narrow to broad theories, but the relevant units also become broader.

Family theories differ considerably in complexity. Simple theories may involve no more than two or three concepts and two or three relationships among them. Complex theories contain a large number of concepts or variables, and many links exist among the concepts.

Finally, family theories differ according to how coherent a picture of family life they present. Some theories represent families as fairly atomistic collections of elements; scientists understand families if they understand how their elements work, and understanding is impeded if elements are combined that really do not go together. Other theories are more holistic, because they focus on the family as a totality; while families may have elements or features, scientists do not understand how families work unless they see how the features are connected and how these connections produce something unique. Family systems theory is an example of a popular holistic theory (Broderick 1993; Whitechurch and Constantine 1993).

The ways family theories differ in their abstractness, generality, breadth, complexity, and the coherence of their imagery are all matters of degree. While there is much diversity, there also are unifying efforts. Abstract theories can be made more concrete, context-specific theories can be made more general, and complex theories can be simplified, among other possibilities. Part of the ongoing excitement about theorizing in the family field is that there is an endless array of projects for enterprising theorists.

Conclusion

There are several reasons for the diversity among family theories. One is the growing number of scholars who have taken family life as an area of serious investigation and the rapidly expanding library of works they have produced. Family theorists also represent a large number of academic and applied disciplines, in and beyond the social sciences. Their ideas are shaped by the specialized training they receive and the different missions established in each discipline. Finally, some questions seem to be answered more satisfactorily if one type of theory is used instead of another.

As long as families remain a central domain in the way people think about the world, and as long as family life is sometimes viewed as troubled or problematic, there will be a sense of urgency about increasing understanding of families. The result is predictable: more theories, more research, and more programs proposed to change what can be changed and to accept what cannot.

See also: DIALECTICAL THEORY; FAMILY DEVELOPMENT THEORY; FAMILY SYSTEMS THEORY; FAMILY, DEFINITION OF; FAMILY, HISTORY OF; HUMAN ECOLOGY THEORY; KINSHIP; LIFE COURSE THEORY; PHENOMENOLOGY; ROLE THEORY; SOCIAL EXCHANGE THEORY; STRUCTURAL-FUNCTIONAL THEORY; SYMBOLIC INTERACTIONISM

Bibliography

Boss, P. G.; Doherty, W. J.; LaRossa, R; Schumm, W. R.; and Steinmetz, S. K., eds. (1993). *Sourcebook of Family Theories and Methods: A Contextual Approach.* New York: Plenum.

Broderick, C. B. (1993). *Understanding Family Process: Basics of Family Systems Theory.* Newbury Park, CA: Sage Publications.

Bubolz, M. M., and Sontag, M. S. (1993). "Human Ecology Theory." In *Sourcebook of Family Theories and Methods: A Contextual Approach,* ed. P. G. Boss, W. J. Doherty, R. LaRossa, W. R. Schumm, and S. K. Steinmetz. New York: Plenum.

Burr, W. R.; Hill, R.; Nye, F. I.; and Reiss, I. L., eds. (1979). *Contemporary Theories About the Family,* Vol. 1: *Research-Based Theories.* New York: Free Press.

Farrington, K., and Chertok, E. (l993). "Social Conflict Theories of the Family." In *Sourcebook of Family Theories and Methods: A Contextual Approach,* ed. P. G. Boss, W. J. Doherty, R. LaRossa, W. R. Schumm, and S. K. Steinmetz. New York: Plenum.

Gubrium, J. F., and Holstein, J. A. (1993). "Phenomenology, Ethnomethodology, and Family Discourse." In *Sourcebook of Family Theories and Methods: A Contextual Approach,* ed. P. G. Boss, W. J. Doherty, R. LaRossa, W. R. Schumm, and S. K. Steinmetz. New York: Plenum.

Kingsbury, N., and Scanzoni, J. (1993). "Structural-Functionalism." In *Sourcebook of Family Theories and Methods: A Contextual Approach,* ed. P. G. Boss, W. J. Doherty, R. LaRossa, W. R. Schumm, and S. K. Steinmetz. New York: Plenum.

Klein, D. M., and Jurich, J. A. (1993). "Metatheory and Family Studies." In *Sourcebook of Family Theories and Methods: A Contextual Approach,* ed. P. G. Boss, W. J. Doherty, R. LaRossa, W. R. Schumm, and S. K. Steinmetz. New York: Plenum.

LaRossa, R., and Reitzes, D. C. (1993). "Symbolic Interactionism and Family Studies." In *Sourcebook of Family Theories and Methods: A Contextual Approach,* ed. P. G. Boss, W. J. Doherty, R. LaRossa, W. R. Schumm, and S. K. Steinmetz. New York: Plenum.

Osmond, M. W. (1987). "Radical-Critical Theories." In *Handbook of Marriage and the Family,* ed. M. B. Sussman and S. K. Steinmetz. New York: Plenum.

Osmond, M. W., and Thorne, B. (1993). "Feminist Theories: The Social Construction of Gender in Families and Society." In *Sourcebook of Family Theories and Methods: A Contextual Approach,* ed. P. G. Boss, W. J. Doherty, R. LaRossa, W. R. Schumm, and S. K. Steinmetz. New York: Plenum.

Rodgers, R. H., and White, J. M. (1993). "Family Development Theory." In *Sourcebook of Family Theories and Methods: A Contextual Approach,* ed. P. G. Boss, W. J. Doherty, R. LaRossa, W. R. Schumm, and S. K. Steinmetz. New York: Plenum.

Sabatelli, R. M., and Shehan, C. L. (1993). "Exchange and Resource Theories." In *Sourcebook of Family Theories and Methods: A Contextual Approach,* ed. P. G. Boss, W. J. Doherty, R. LaRossa, W. R. Schumm, and S. K. Steinmetz. New York: Plenum.

Sprey, J., ed. (1990). *Fashioning Family Theory: New Approaches.* Newbury Park, CA: Sage Publications.

Thomas, D. L., and Wilcox, J. E. (1987). "The Rise of Family Theory: A Historical and Critical Analysis." In *Handbook of Marriage and the Family,* ed. M. B. Sussman and S. K. Steinmetz. New York: Plenum.

Troost, K. M., and Filsinger, E. (1993). "Emerging Biosocial Perspectives on the Family." In *Sourcebook of Family Theories and Methods: A Contextual Approach,* ed. P. G. Boss, W. J. Doherty, R. LaRossa, W. R. Schumm, and S. K. Steinmetz. New York: Plenum.

Whitechurch, G. G., and Constantine, L. L. (1993). "Systems Theory." In *Sourcebook of Family Theories and Methods: A Contextual Approach,* ed. P. G. Boss, W. J. Doherty, R. LaRossa, W. R. Schumm, and S. K. Steinmetz. New York: Plenum.

DAVID M. KLEIN (1995)

FAMILY TYPES

See COHABITATION; DUAL-EARNER FAMILIES; EXTENDED FAMILIES; GAY PARENTS: LESBIAN PARENTS; NUCLEAR FAMILIES; SINGLE-PARENT FAMILIES; STEPFAMILIES

FAMILY VALUES

Family values and the value of families are not discrete entities. Rather, like the family, family values exist within social contexts. As such they can be studied in numerous ways including: *intra* (within), *extra* (without), and *cross-cultural* family analysis. An *extra* analysis takes into account the social milieu of families and a cross-cultural might compare attitudinal and systemic aspects of families in two or more countries.

Values are a society's general ideas about what is perceived as good and desirable for a society. For example, liberty and the pursuit of happiness are values that people in the United States hold dear. Thus, family values analysis considers general societal notions about what is beneficial for family life. Yet texts on marriage and family often either fail to include a discussion of family values or fail to specifically define the term. This occurs, in part, because there is a lack of consensus among marriage and family scholars concerning the issue of family values.

When the issue is addressed, it is frequently framed as a debate within the discipline about whether the family is in decline, as some scholars proclaim (Popenoe 1988), or merely changing, as others assert (Coontz 1997; Skolnick 1991; Stacey 1992, 1999). Proponents of the *family in decline* camp cite high divorce rates, a high of rate out-of-wedlock births, an increased proportion of single-parent households, and the continued rise of *individualism* as evidence of the decline of family life and diminished family values. A *New York Times* survey in which respondents ranked independence higher than being a spouse and parent is the type of evidence presented to affirm the decline of family values (Cherlin 2001).

On the other hand, proponents of the *family is changing* perspective argue that the family itself is socially defined and as such acts upon and responds to a society's unique social, economic, and political environment. Those writing from this view, as does Steven Nock (1999), maintain that: "Institutions like the family are bigger than any individual. So when large numbers of people create new patterns of family life, we should consider the collective forces behind such novel arrangements."

Side-stepping a definition of family values, marriage and family texts generally cite indicators or measures of the presence or absence of family values. An *intra* family-values analysis then might include a survey of peoples' attitudes about various aspects of marriage and family life. For example, in a poll of sixteen countries, including India, Singapore, Taiwan, United States, Guatemala, Thailand, Mexico, Canada, Great Britain, Spain, Lithuania, Hungary, Colombia, Germany, France, and Iceland, the vast majority (between 70 and 90%) of those surveyed expressed the attitude that having a child without benefit of marriage is not morally wrong (Gallup Poll 1997). Half of the U.S. respondents said that having a child out-of-wedlock was morally wrong, yet the United States has a higher rate of out-of-wedlock birth than any of the other countries. Asymmetrical attitudes and actions have long been problematic for family-values research, but more important, point to the dilemmas families face as they: ". . . believe in both the traditional and the modern version of the family simultaneously (Wolfe 1998)."

Counter to the *family is declining* thinking, the same poll found that well over a majority of those surveyed in fourteen countries agreed that it was necessary to have a child in order to feel fulfilled (the United States and Germany were the only two countries in which fewer than 50% of the respondents supported this view) yet most respondents in thirteen countries indicated they wanted few children—two or one. A *family in decline* view might argue that limiting the number of children reflects the alarming rise of individualism, whereas a *family is changing* perspective suggests that the material conditions of families (the ability to economically support children), influence decisions about children.

Another *intra* measure of family values is time spent together. A recent survey of 3,155 children ages two to eighteen about their daily exposure to the media found that more than half (53%) had televisions in their room (Roberts et al. 1999). The average child spent almost four and one-half hours in his/her room engaged with media, often using two media forms simultaneously. Four and one-half hours in one's bedroom leaves little time for family interaction—not to mention study time on school nights.

A *family in decline* framework would find the results compelling, whereas the *family is changing* proponents might cite the independence of children as positive. Others might interpret the findings in terms of Arlie Hochschild's work (1996), which suggests that home is not always an emotional refuge where parents and children salve each others' wounds and bolster egos. The study implies that sometimes it is a place of tense relationships with members distancing themselves from each other. Nevertheless, a recent Radcliffe Public Policy study of 1,008 male workers found that 70 percent of men in their twenties and thirties would give up time at work in order to spend more time with their families (Grimsley 2000). The *family in decline* proponents would be interested in whether respondents' attitudes coincided with their behavior.

One study asked parents and children if they thought they spent enough time together (Galinsky 1999). Forty-nine percent of mothers with children aged thirteen through eighteen thought they spend too little time together, whereas only about one-third of children felt the same way. Sixty-four percent of fathers thought they should spend more time, whereas 39 percent of the children responded similarly. A *family is changing* perspective maintains that parents feel both burdened and a sense of ambivalence as they strike a fragile balance between work and family. Parents too often: ". . . are reluctant choosers when it comes to the modern family. . . . They feel not so much liberated by opportunity as weighted down by obligation" (Wolfe 1998).

Cross-Cultural Comparison: Pro Family Policies

The discussion thus far has focused on family values attitudes within families—a debate that shows no signs of abating. However, perhaps most significant to keep in mind when thinking about the family and family values: Is the family valued by society? It is important to examine the value families have for the social system as indicated by pro-family policies. An *extra* and cross-cultural analysis considers a few important measures of family support in five Western industrialized countries, including the United States, France, Great Britain, Italy, and Sweden. Three factors that have an impact on families' well being (especially in light of an increasing proportion of dual-earner couples worldwide) will be addressed: *maternity leave, family leave,* and *childcare.* The information for all countries has been obtained from the Clearinghouse on International Developments in Child, Youth, and Family Policies at Columbia University.

Maternity leave. In France women as mothers are valued by their country in at least two ways: First, they can take advantage of job-protected leave six weeks before and ten weeks after the birth of a child with 80 percent of their pay. Second, medical care related to pregnancy is paid by the state. Great Britain allows more release time from work than does France: eighteen weeks job-protected time off, with 90 percent of wages for six weeks, then twelve weeks at a lower rate of pay. Italy's maternity leave, which was instituted eighty-nine years ago, is more generous than Great Britain. Pregnant women can take a leave from work eight weeks prior to birth and stay out for twelve weeks after the birth with 80 percent of their pay. Another

perquisite that any mother would appreciate: Italian women who work full-time are entitled to a two-hour rest period during the day for the first year after giving birth.

Sweden offers the most generous maternity leave. Swedish women can take up to eighteen months off work with 80 percent of their pay for twelve months. Of the five countries examined, the United States has the least family-friendly maternity policy. The Family and Medical Leave Act of 1993 is useful for those who meet the conditions. First, a worker must be employed by a company with fifty or more employees (companies with fewer than fifty are exempt). Second, the employee must have worked 1,250 hours in the previous year. If those conditions are met, then the employee is entitled to apply for a twelve-week job-protected unpaid leave for birth or adoption of a child or other medical needs of a family. An important caveat: a company is not required to hold the same job the employee held before the leave, only *a* job.

Family leave. What do countries do for families once the child is born? French workers are entitled to job-protected parental leave after one year on the job and can take up to five paid days a year to care for a sick child. An attractive feature is that both parents can take the leave simultaneously. Although not as generous as France, Great Britain also acknowledges the needs of the family concerning this issue. Britons are permitted an unpaid job-protected leave up to thirteen weeks that can be taken until a child reaches 5 years of age. Italy demonstrates its pro-family stance by giving working parents unlimited job-protected leave to care for a sick child less than 3 years old. Sweden's policy is not as generous in terms of time, but it enables parents to take up to sixty days a year to care for an ill child or if the child's caretaker is ill. The United States does not have a policy beyond the Family and Medical Leave Act noted above.

Childcare. Affordable, safe, convenient childcare is one of the most important components for parents to put in place when they are employed outside the home. In France, childcare centers serve children age three months to two years and parents pay about a quarter of the cost. France also has preschool education for children two to six years old. Most parents take advantage of the preschool. Great Britain's childcare support is *means-tested.* That is, it targets children of the poor. Nevertheless, poor parents must pay 30 percent of the cost. On the other hand, Italy's working parents have publicly funded childcare available for children age three months to three years, with working mothers and poor mothers having priority.

Sweden appears to be the most supportive of its families in the area of childcare. It guarantees childcare for children aged one to eleven for parents who work or who are students. Early childhood education centers provide universal coverage for children less than seven years old. In the United States federal subsidies have been instituted that coincide with the Personal Responsibility and Work Opportunity Reconciliation Act that were meant to facilitate the shift from welfare to work for those who need childcare. Then, too, there are Head Start and Early Head Start programs for low-income families. These programs have a dual purpose of preparing poor children for school as well as acting as childcare for their parents who work. Unfortunately, the programs are in danger of being cut because of the U.S. tax cut in early 2001 and the slowdown in the U.S. economy. Other forms of assistance exist for low- to moderate-income parents (parents earning less than $30,000) in the form of the Earned Income Tax Credit and a Dependent Care Tax Credit to assist with childcare expenses.

This cursory comparative overview underscores Cherlin's assessment that: ". . . the U.S. . . . is downright stingy in its family benefits (2001, p. 243)." A concentration of resources for families with young children helps explain why France and Sweden have single digit child poverty rates well below 10 percent. It could explain, too, why the United States has a higher infant mortality rate (higher than twenty-one other industrialized countries).

More U.S. subsidies are means-tested than those in other countries. This correlates with the U.S. ideology of individualism and the notion of family self-sufficiency. It explains, too, why there has been so much resistance to welfare in the United States. As the family-assistance policies are currently written, few are entitled to receive aid. It is instructive to note that the United States, which offers less support for families, outspends all other countries on prisons. In the last decade spending for prisons in the United States has increased in the same proportion that spending for education has decreased.

Family-friendly policies require a collective sacrifice on the part of a citizenry and many countries are currently chafing under the burden of widespread economic stagnation. Nevertheless, the costs are more palatable because the benefits are, for the most part, universal, meaning all can participate to some extent. Thus, in the long run, families have healthier members and states have healthier citizens. The family is changing, but if the family as an institution declines, it does so, in part, because the challenges facing families are not accompanied by supportive family policies.

Conclusion

It is not that some families have values and others do not, or that family values should be placed on the endangered list, or that there is a finite list of values that one can review to determine if a family has values or not. Family discourse about family values requires understanding the social context of families as well as the material conditions of families. Both influence present attitudes as well as expectations about the future. Valuing higher education is not an inherent condition, it is learned from those who have an expectation that its achievement will become a reality. Measuring leisure time spent with loved ones as an indicator of family values has validity only where the conditions provide family members discretionary time.

Although most people prefer to view the family as a private "haven in a heartless" world (Lasch 1977), the family is shaped by its social milieu. The political and economic environment exults or diminishes the family. The family's private troubles are connected to the public issues (Mills 1959). When the state enacts family-friendly policies, it exhibits a reverence for the institution of the family, reinforcing not only family values, but that the family is valued. Where it fails to do so, it contributes to family disintegration. Even at that, the family-values debate will continue.

See also: EVANGELICAL CHRISTIANITY; FAMILY POLICY; FAMILY STRENGTHS; GLOBAL CITIZENSHIP; RELIGION

Bibliography

Cherlin, A. J. (2001). "The Transformation of Motherhood." In *Public and Private Families: An Introduction,* ed. A. J. Cherlin. Boston: McGraw-Hill.

Coontz, S. (2001). "What We Really Miss about the 1950s." In *Family in Transition,* 11th edition, ed. A. S. Skolnick and J. H. Skolnick. Boston: Allyn and Bacon.

Galinsky, E. (1999). "What Children Think about Their Working Parents." In *Ask the Children,* ed. E. Galinsky. New York: HarperCollins.

Grimsley, K. D. (2000). "Making Family a Priority." *Washington Post Weekly,* May 8.

Hochschild, A. R. (1996). "The Emotional Geography of Work and Family Life." In *Gender Relations in Public and Private,* ed. L. Morris and E. S. Lyon. New York: Macmillan.

Lasch, C. (1977). *Haven in a Heartless World: The Family Besieged.* New York: Basic Books.

Mills, C. W. (1959) *The Sociological Imagination.* New York: Oxford University Press.

Nock, S. L. (1999) "The Problem with Marriage." *Society.* (July/August):20–27.

Popenoe, D. (1988). *Disturbing the Nest: Family Change and Decline in Modern Societies.* New York: Aldine de Gruyter.

Roberts, D. L.; Foehr, U. G.; Rideout, V. J.; and Brodie, M. (1999). "Kids and Media @ The New Millennium." Report from the Henry J. Kaiser Family Foundation. Menlo Park, CA.

Skolnick, A. (1991). "The State of the American Family." In *Embattled Paradise: The American Family in an Age of Uncertainty.* New York: Basic Books.

Stacey, J. (1992). "Backward toward the Postmodern Family: Reflections on Gender, Kinship, and Class in the Silicon Valley." In *Rethinking the Family: Some Feminist Questions,* rev. edition, ed. B. Thorne and M. Yalom. Boston: Northeastern University Press.

Stacey, J. (1999). "The Family Values Fable." In *American Families: A Multicultural Reader,* ed. S. Coontz. New York: Routledge.

Wolfe, A. (1998). "The Culture War Within." In *One Nation, After All,* ed. A. Wolfe. New York: Viking Penguin.

Other Resources

Gallup Poll Special Reports. (1997). "Global Study of Family Values." Gallup Poll News Service, Available from http://www.gallup.com/poll/specialReports/pollSummaries/Family.asp.

Kammerman, S. B. (2001). Clearinghouse on International Developments in Child, Youth, and Family Policies at Columbia University. Available from http://www.childpolicyintl.org.

BARBARA A. ARRIGHI

FATHERHOOD

Father is derived from the Latin word *pater*: a man who has engendered a child, a male parent, or a person who takes responsibility for protecting, caring, and rearing. It is only since the early 1980s that there has been a public and professional focus on the more affective use of the term *father*—to protect, care for, and nurture children.

Historical Perspectives

During the seventeenth century, in many Western countries, such as England, France, and the United States, fathers were all-powerful and served as the family's unquestioned ruler (Lamb 1987). Their source of power and authority was the ownership and control of all family property, including land, wives, and children. Men were also charged with the moral and spiritual growth of their children and thus with disciplining them. This early father-child relationship has been described as distant, morally instructive, and condescending, as too much affection was believed to lead to parental indulgence, ruining the character of children (Pleck and Pleck 1997).

In Europe and the United States, the patriarchal style of fathering continued until the mid-eighteenth-century, when a new concept of parenting from England and France began to influence U.S. fathers as well. In this new view, fathers no longer acted as strict authority figures, but increased their roles as moral teachers. Family life continued to shift during the nineteenth century, influenced by the Industrial Revolution and the progressive urbanization of the population. Men went to work in factories, whereas women were stayed at home during the day, in charge of the children and household. The emergence of modern fatherhood began when mothers became the stable core of families, taking over the role as moral teacher and disciplinarian. Despite the decline of patriarchy and the expanded importance of mothers in nineteenth-century family life, middle-class fathers still played a significant role. More than ever before, men were providers for the family, reinforcing their status as heads of households and retaining their place as ultimate disciplinarians of families, but they remained outside the strongest currents of feelings and emotions that flowed within and between family members.

During the nineteenth and twentieth centuries, the rise of industrialism and urbanization in Western Europe and North America helped spread the middle-class phenomenon of emerging modern fatherhood. The separation of the workplace from home life continued to undermine the traditional authority of fathers and spawned two opposing trends: *father-absence* and *father-involvement* (Rotundo 1993). For some men, the lack of a commanding paternal role in modern families made it possible for them to withdraw psychologically and/or physically from their families without immediate disaster. For other men, however, the traditional formality of patriarchy gave way to the enjoyment of more warmth, play, and intimacy with children.

Scholars assert that the interest in fathering roles since 1900 fluctuated between fathers as *providers* (instrumental role) and fathers as *nurturers* (expressive role) (Parke and Stearns 1993). There is a relationship between fertility and the definition of fathering and this is tied to economic conditions. In good economic times, when fathers are able to meet the provider role ideal, fertility increases and fathers' provider roles are emphasized. In nonfavorable economic climates, the alternative definition of fathers as nurturers is more prevalent.

Modern fatherhood lies between these two sets of opposite poles: father-absence versus father-involvement and father as provider (father-provider) versus father as nurturer (father-nurturer). The modern trend of androgynous fatherhood, which includes both feminine and masculine aspects in the father role, is a result of the women's movement and the subsequent reshaping of gender roles. As part of this movement, more fathers became active participants in everyday childcare and were more expressive and nuturant with children. The blurring of the distinction between fatherhood and motherhood has led to a reexamination of *manhood, womanhood,* and *family.* Finally, the level of father-involvement with children has changed since the 1960s. According to a nationally representative study of two-parent families in the United States, there has been an increase in the level of father-involvement between the 1960s and the late 1990s. Although fathers are still not as involved as mothers, father-involvement (measured in time spent with the family) had increased to 67 percent of the time mothers spent

with the family on weekdays and 87 percent of the time mothers spent with the family on weekends in the late 1990s (Yeung et al. 2001). Father-involvement is a hallmark of modern fatherhood, not only in North America, but in Europe, Australia, and the Middle East as well (Lamb 1987). Not all countries have shown a similar increase; fathers in Japan, for example, have increased their involvement more slowly (Ishi-Kuntz 1994).

Fathers Across the Life Span

There is considerable knowledge about the transition to *parenthood,* which occurs during pregnancy and the birth of the child (Cowan and Cowan 2000). Most information on men's transition to parenthood is derived from middle-class white men, but prenatal involvement is also becoming more commonplace among other socioeconomic and ethnic groups. Participating in childbirth education classes is not only found to be supportive for pregnant women, but it also enhances men's knowledge of pregnancy and birth, increases their understanding of the father's role, and elevates their self-confidence and self-esteem relative to carrying out the parental role (Parke 1996). Although the short-term effects of this participation are known, the long-term effects of prenatal and perinatal involvement on marital relationships and fathering behaviors are less clear.

The next phase of fathering, *infancy,* is well researched. Mothers are more involved in caregiving than fathers, but in contrast to commonly held myths, fathers are competent caregivers—even with infants (Parke 1996). Fathers spend a larger proportion of their time in play, whereas mothers tend to divide their time equally between caregiving and play. The styles of play differ for mothers and fathers. Fathers' play is more physically arousing and unpredictable than mothers', who are more verbal, didactic, and use toys in their play interactions (Parke 1996). In spite of these stylistic differences, infants develop attachments to fathers as well as mothers (Lamb 1997).

Is there a universal father play style? Some cross-cultural studies support the assumption of mother-father differences in play style (e.g., England, Australia), but in other cultures (e.g., Sweden, Israel) there are few sex-of-parent differences in level or type of play. Moreover, Chinese, Thai, and Aka pygmy mothers and fathers reported that they

In contrast to commonly held myths, fathers are competent caregivers. Warm, affectionate Latino fathers belie the stereotype of Latino men as cold, distant, and without influence on their children's development. SANDY FELSENTHAL/CORBIS

rarely engage in physical play with their children. These findings suggest that culture may shape fathers' style of interacting with their children.

There is less knowledge about fathers and their school-age children. Mothers continue to spend more time (and more time alone) with children than fathers. However, when both parents and child are together, the interactions initiated by mothers and fathers occur with the same frequency. Studies of Australian school-age children found that a greater proportion of fathers' time is spent in a playful manner whereas mothers' time more often involves caregiving (Russell and Russell 1989). Moreover, fathers participate in instrumental activities, such as scouting and sports, more frequently with sons than with daughters. Relationships with daughters during this period are often

less close, ostensibly because of the increased difficulty men have identifying with the special needs of their daughters (Biller and Klimpton 1997).

In adolescence, parents of both sexes spend less time with children than during earlier developmental periods. Moreover, adolescents continue the trend of spending less time with their fathers than with their mothers. This is qualified by the child's gender, in that adolescents report spending more time alone with their same-sex parent than with the opposite sex parent. Additionally, adolescents are likely to spend more of their free time with fathers, and more work and organized leisure time with mothers (Larson and Richards 1994). During the adolescence phase of the family cycle, the essence of the father-child relationship centers around identity issues in which adolescents struggle with the difficulties of their emergent identity (Brooks-Gunn and Chase-Landsdale 1995).

Little research has focused on the father-child relationship during the postparental transition when children leave home to begin their lives as independent adults. Fathers gradually develop *collegiality* and *mutuality* with their children, are less authoritarian and directive, and children are more receptive to their father's suggestions. Sharing and negotiating emerge as the primary characteristics of their relationship.

Relatively little research has been conducted on the last stage of fathering, *grandfatherhood*. A crucial element of the grandparent-grandchild relationship is that the children's parents—the "in-between" generation—mediate it. Parents determine the frequency of interactions between grandparent and grandchild, and may even determine the quality of the grandparent-grandchild relationship. If parents have negative feelings toward their own fathers, the grandfather-grandchild relationship may be discouraged. The majority of grandfathers derive satisfaction from being a grandfather, and they indulge their grandchildren, because they do not feel they carry the primary responsibility for their grandchildren becoming socially acceptable adults (Smith 1995). Although the strongest bond with grandchildren is likely to be with sons of a son, as men's roles become more androgynous, involving both feminine and masculine qualities, and men's and women's roles become more egalitarian, grandfathers in the future may not make such clear gender distinctions, and granddaughters may receive more of their grandfather's attention.

Determinants of Father-Involvement

Father-involvement is highly variable and determined by a variety of factors including biological, individual, family, and societal influences (Parke 1996). It is not just females who undergo hormonal changes in preparation for parenthood. Human fathers, too undergo hormonal changes during pregnancy and childbirth. In a study men experienced significant prenatal and postnatal changes in several hormones (*prolactin, cortisol,* and *testosterone*)—a pattern which was similar to women. Testosterone levels, for example, were lower in the early prenatal period, which may increase paternal responsiveness to infants, in part, by reducing competitive, nonnurturing behaviors (Storey et al. 2000).

There are individual differences in men's attitudes toward fathering, including the motivation, knowledge, and skill to become involved in childrearing. Men who are more motivated, who value the paternal role, and view themselves as capable are likely to be more involved fathers, not only with infants, but with older children as well.

Family factors are important, and fathers are best understood from a *family systems* perspective. Mothers can either facilitate or inhibit fathers' involvement in their role of gatekeepers in both intact families and postdivorce contexts (Parke 1996). The quality of the marital relationship is a further determinant: when the marital relationship is positive, the level of father-involvement is higher.

A variety of societal and occupational changes have altered father-involvement. Two shifts will be explored: the timing of fatherhood and shifts in patterns of maternal employment.

Men are becoming fathers at earlier and later ages than in earlier eras. Findings show that most teenage males are unprepared to assume the role of parent and provider. Compared to more mature fathers, teenage fathers have unrealistic expectations, lack of knowledge about child development, and are more likely to be abusive. Adolescent fathers often have problems fulfilling their paternal responsibilities as they are unprepared financially and emotionally to undertake the responsibilities of fatherhood. Many leave school, assume low-paying jobs, and live a marginal existence. The detrimental effects of early fatherhood seem less problematic for African-American males even though there is a higher incidence of young, unwed fathers among African-American than Euro-American men.

The stereotypic notion that all teenage fathers are irresponsible, uncaring, and unconcerned about the mother or the infant is incorrect. Many young fathers are deeply involved in the lives of their partners and their babies (Marsiglio and Cohan 1997). Data suggests that half of unwed young fathers visit their children at least once a week and a quarter almost daily. Only 13 percent are reported as never visiting. However, other studies also reveal that as children develop, this contact is likely to decrease. Historically, teenage fathers had no legal rights regarding the children they fathered, but the availability of legal recourse is changing. As rates of adolescent fathering have increased, the social stigma has decreased, paving the way for more social services designed to promote positive father-involvement.

In contrast, men who delay their entry into the fatherhood role until their thirties or forties are more involved with their children than "on time" fathers and contribute more to indirect aspects of childcare such as cooking, cleaning, and doing laundry. Moreover, the style of interaction varies with timing. As fathers age, they are less physically playful and more likely to engage in cognitive stimulatory activities (e.g., reading, verbal games).

One of the major determinants of father-involvement is the shift toward the dual career family. At the beginning of the twenty-first century, over 70 percent of mothers are employed outside the home. Fathers are more likely to increase their level of involvement when mothers' work, a finding that holds for Euro-American, African-American, and Mexican-American fathers. However, this link is complex and may depend on whether mothers work full- or part-time and whether fathers hold traditional or nontraditional views of parenting. When mothers work part-time, fathers increase their involvement only when they hold egalitarian beliefs. Father beliefs are a less important determinant when women work full-time. However, fathers, regardless of maternal employment, still do less than mothers (Pleck 1997).

It is not only maternal employment that influences father-involvement, but the nature of the father's job characteristics as well. The demands and the nature of the fathers' occupations (e.g., travel, hours of work, or proximity to workplace) can facilitate or prohibit their daily involvement in childcare, as can workplace policies for families (e.g., flextime or paternity leaves.) (Parke and Brott 1999). Moreover, aspects of the work environment may carry over into the family environment and influence the quality, as well as the amount, of father-child interaction. For example, Rena Repetti (1994) found that men with high-stress jobs tended to be more withdrawn from their children after returning home from a high-stress shift at work. On the other hand, positive work experiences can enhance the quality of father-involvement.

Divorced and Single Fathers

Fathering occurs not only in nuclear family contexts but when single custodial fathers serve as primary caregivers for their children following divorce or widowhood. Research on this family form indicates that these men and their families function fairly well. Adaptation to the role of primary parent is initially difficult, but once fathers develop routines and children adjust to their fathers being the sole parent, family life usually proceeds smoothly. Initially after divorce or death, children—especially boys—experience adjustment difficulties, such as diminished school performance or behavior problems.

Quality of involvement is critical and not all paternal involvement is good. Some research indicates that involvement with a noncustodial father is associated with positive outcomes for children, whereas other research indicates that there is no association with child outcomes. The parents' relationship is a critical mediating factor. If the parental relationship is conflict-ridden, frequent visitation will be problematic. Many fathers reduce the amount of visitation in order to reduce the amount of conflict with the former spouse. In fact, relationship with the former spouse is the most significant factor in visitation. If the court proceedings are stressful and the relationship with the former spouse is conflictual, then fathers are less likely to remain involved or to provide child support. Moreover, maternal anger or conflict may cause the mother to restrict the amount and type of involvement by fathers as well. There is consistent evidence of maternal gatekeeping in divorced families. However, long-term effects of maternal gatekeeping on children's adjustment are not well understood.

Culture and Fatherhood

Cultural variations and constraints that promote or inhibit men's involvement with families are a relatively new focus of research. Father-involvement is often determined by differences in ethnicity, nationality, occupation, religion, and social class. (see Bozett and Hanson 1991; Lamb 1987 for cross-cultural and international perspectives). To illustrate the impact of culture on fathering, two ethnic groups, African-American and Latino, will be examined.

The persistent image of African-American fathers is one of an invisible figure that is absent from or, at best, peripheral to day-to-day family functioning. This view is challenged by research that finds that African-American fathers are neither absent nor uninvolved in family life, but play essential roles within families (Yeung et al. 2001). What distinguishes the emerging scholarship on African-American families is its emphasis on family unity, stability, and adaptability. Middle-class African-American fathers are involved in the rearing of their children; maintain warm, interpersonal relations with them; and their children are well-adjusted and motivated. A national survey found few differences in the level of father-involvement in intact families or the type of involvement (play versus caregiving) between African-American fathers and fathers of other ethnic groups (Yeung et al. 2001). Clearly, many African-American fathers play an integral role in the family contrary to earlier stereotypes.

Hispanic or Latino men have been depicted as visible, dominant, authoritarian figures who rule their families with an iron hand (Mirande 1991). Research calls into question the notion of Latino fathers as cold, distant authority figures. In the traditional view, fathers made all major decisions and were masters of the household. Fathers were thought to avoid family intimacy, maintain respect by instilling fear in their wives and children, and punish their children severely. Research suggests that the power of males may be less absolute than once believed and that Latino families are not as rigidly structured along age and gender lines as had previously been thought. Latino fathers are found to be warm and affectionate with children and to have significant influence on their children's development (Coltrane 1996). Hence, Hispanic fathers do not conform to the stereotypical portrayals commonly found in the literature.

Although these ethnic families and fathers do not deviate much from Anglo-American families and fathers, they still should not be judged by white middle-class standards. Ethnic minority families are diverse, and there is no single monolithic ethnic family structure among or within them. Internal variation within major ethnic groups prohibits generalization.

Consequences of Fathers for Men Themselves and Their Children

Becoming a father impacts a man's own psychological development and well-being. One avenue of interest is the impact of fatherhood on men's self-identity. Fatherhood is positively related to men's ability to understand themselves, and to understand others sympathetically. In addition, John Snarey (1993) has found that fathers who are highly involved with their children were higher in *societal generativity* (i.e., serving as a mentor, providing leadership in the community, or caring for other younger adults). Fathering may be an important contribution to men's development as adults.

Fathers have an impact on their children as well. In the case of nonresident fathers, there are modest but positive links between fathers' contact with their children and academic success on the one hand and negative links with internalizing problems on the other. Quality matters, too: Adolescents who reported a strong attachment with their nonresidential fathers and whose fathers used authoritative parenting had higher educational attainment, were less depressed, and were less likely to be imprisoned (Amato and Gilbreth 1999). In intact families, similar findings were evident: there is a moderate negative association between authoritative fathering and internalizing and externalizing problems. Moreover, the positive influence of fathers on children's behavior was evident for Euro-American, African-American, and Latino fathers (Marsiglio et al. 2000).

Future of Fatherhood

Fatherhood is changing. However, two distinct bipolar trends—father-absence versus father-involvement and father-provider versus father-nurturer—are still evident in modern fatherhood in many different countries throughout the world. An extreme form of father-absence, resulting from divorce and abandonment, has become such a problem that governments in many Western countries are intervening through child support enforcement agencies to force men to provide financially for their children. On the other hand, there are increased numbers of younger middle-class men moving in the direction of more involvement and nurturance in childcare and family life, as found in family forms such as *househusband* fathers and single adoptive fathers. This androgynous style fits the emerging broader economic and social realities better than older styles of fatherhood. It is believed that these trends will continue despite some people's resistance to the blurring of gender roles. The future will offer fathers multiple options rather than stereotypic roles. With fewer parental prescriptions, modern men are—and will continue to be—freer to choose their own degree of involvement in child rearing and family life. Men will have a broader range of parenthood possibilities from which they can choose the fatherhood model most appropriate for themselves and their circumstances.

The majority of father research has focused on the early part of the family life cycle—pregnancy, birth, and infancy. There needs to be further investigation of the other developmental periods. It is also important to study fatherhood in different social contexts. Scholars need to make finer distinctions between male and female parenting roles and the impact of each gender on the growth and development of children. Examples of questions that need to be answered are: If society values males as parents, how can males be socialized earlier in life to become more nurturing and caregiving with children? What changes are needed in social, economic, legal, educational, and healthcare systems that would enhance men's effective parenting and positive family relationships? Finally, policies and practices need to be placed in international perspective by cross-cultural and cross-national comparisons. Addressing these issues will advance the understanding of fatherhood.

See also: ADOLESCENT PARENTHOOD; ATTACHMENT: PARENT-CHILD RELATIONSHIPS; CHILDCARE; CONFLICT: PARENT-CHILD RELATIONSHIPS; COPARENTING; DUAL-EARNER FAMILIES; FAMILY LIFE EDUCATION; FAMILY ROLES; FERTILITY; GAY PARENTS; GRANDPARENTHOOD; HUSBAND; MOTHERHOOD; PARENTING EDUCATION; PARENTING STYLES; SEPARATION-INDIVIDUATION; SINGLE-PARENT FAMILIES; STRESS; STEPFAMILIES;

SUBSTITUTE CAREGIVERS; SURROGACY; TRANSITION TO PARENTHOOD; WORK AND FAMILY

Bibliography

Amato, P. A., and Gilbreth, J. G. (1999). "Nonresident Fathers and Children's Well-Being: Media Analysis." *Journal of Marriage and the Family* 61:15–73.

Biller, H. B., and Kimpton, J. L. (1997). "The Father and the School-Aged Child." In *The Role of the Father in Child Development,* ed. M. Lamb. New York: Wiley.

Bozett, F. W., and Hanson, S. M. H. (1991). *Fatherhood and Families in Cultural Context.* New York: Springer.

Brooks-Gunn, J., and Chase-Lansdale, L. (1995) "Adolescent Parenthood." In *Handbook of Parenting,* Vol. 2, ed. M. Bornstein. Mahwah, NJ: Lawrence Erlbaum Associates.

Coltrane, S. (1996). *Family Man.* New York: Oxford University Press.

Cowan, C. P., and Cowan, P. A. (2000). *When Partners Become Parents: The Big Life Change for Couples.* Mahwah, NJ: Lawrence Erlbaum Associates.

Ishi-Kuntz, M. (1994). "The Japanese Father: Work Demands and Family Roles." In *Men, Work, and Family,* ed. J. C. Hood. Newbury Park, CA: Sage.

Lamb, M. E. (1987). *The Father's Role: Cross-Cultural Perspectives.* Hillsdale, NJ: Lawrence Erlbaum Associates.

Lamb, M. E. (1997). "The Development of Father-Infant Relationships." In *The Role of the Father in Child Development,* ed. M. Lamb. New York: Wiley.

Larson, R., and Richards, M. (1994) *Divergent Realities.* New York: Basic Books.

Marsiglio, W.; Amato, P.; Day, R. D.; and Lamb, M. E. (2000). "Scholarship on Fatherhood in the 1990s and Beyond." *Journal of Marriage and the Family* 62:1173–1191.

Marsiglio, W., and Cohan, M. (1997). "Young Fathers and Child Development." In *The Role of the Father in Child Development,* ed. M. Lamb. New York: Wiley.

Mirande, A. (1991). "Ethnicity and Fatherhood." In *Fatherhood and Families in Cultural Context,* ed. F. W. Bozett and S. M. Hanson. New York: Springer.

Parke, R. D. (1996). *Fatherhood.* Cambridge, MA: Harvard University Press.

Parke, R. D., and Brott, A. (1999) *Throwaway Dads.* Boston: Houghton-Mifflin.

Parke, R. D., and Stearns, P. N. (1993). "Fathers and Child Rearing." In *Children in Time and Place,* ed. G. H. Elder, J. Modell, and R. D. Parke. Cambridge: Cambridge University Press.

Pleck, E. H., and Pleck, J. H. (1997). "Fatherhood Ideals in the United States: Historical Dimensions." In *The Role of the Father in Child Development,* ed. M. Lamb. New York: Wiley.

Pleck, J. H. (1997). "Paternal Involvement: Levels, Sources, and Consequences." In *The Role of the Father in Child Development,* ed. M. Lamb. New York: Wiley.

Repetti, R. L. (1994). "Short-Term and Long-Term Processes Linking Job Stressors to Father-Child Interaction." *Social Development* 3:1–15.

Rotundo, E. A. (1993). *American Manhood.* New York: Basic Books.

Russell, A., and Russell, G. (1989). "Warmth in Mother-Child and Father-Child Relationships in Middle Childhood." *British Journal of Developmental Psychology* 7:219–235.

Smith, P. K. (1995). "Grandparenthood." In *Handbook of Parenting,* Vol. 2, ed. M. Bornstein. Mahwah, NJ: Lawrence Erlbaum Associates.

Snarey, J. (1993). *How Fathers Care for the Next Generation.* Cambridge, MA: Harvard University Press.

Storey, A. E.; Walsh, C. J.; Quinton, R. L.; and Wynne-Edwards, K. E. (2000). "Hormonal Correlates of Paternal Responsiveness in New and Expectant Fathers." *Evolution and Human Behavior* 21:79–95.

Yeung, W. J.; Sandberg, J. F.; David-Kean, P. E.; and Hofferth, S. L. (2001). "Children's Time with Fathers in Intact Families." *Journal of Marriage and Family* 63:136–154.

ROSS D. PARKE
DAVID J. MCDOWELL

FAVORITISM/DIFFERENTIAL TREATMENT

Parental differential treatment is the degree to which parents treat each child in the family differently. Studies have found that most parents report that they have to be a different parent to each of their children (Dunn and Plomin 1990; McGuire 2002). For instance, parents often indicate that one child needs more attention compared to the siblings. This does not necessarily mean that one child is being favored over the others. Parents who love their children equally may treat them differently to help each child develop properly. *Favoritism* is a specific type of differential treatment; it occurs when one child receives more positive treatment (e.g., more affection or more toys) compared to his or her siblings.

Studies of families in the United States and Great Britain have shown that parental differential treatment is linked to children's temperament characteristics. For instance, emotional children tend to receive more attention from their parents compared to their calmer siblings. Parents also respond to each child's age, sex, and, sometimes, position in the family (that is, birth order). For example, parents do not expect the same degree of obedience from a one-year-old child and her three-year-old brother. It is considered standard for parents to react to children's unique personalities and different developmental levels.

Parental differential treatment is also associated with children's behavior problems, at least in Western societies. Children who receive more parental discipline and less parental warmth relative to their sibling have more adjustment problems compared to children in other family environments. It cannot be assumed that parental differential treatment always causes children's adjustment problems, because children who are disruptive often elicit negative parental behavior. Researchers have examined families over time; findings from these studies suggest that both the parents and the children contribute to this family dynamic (Reiss et al. 2000).

Children's own perceptions of parental differential treatment matter. In fact, siblings' perceptions of fairness are associated with their self-esteem to a greater degree than parental reports or observations of parental differential treatment. Many school-aged children and adolescents report that parental differential treatment is fair. Children and teenagers take into consideration personal differences between the siblings (e.g., age differences and personality factors) and family circumstances when considering the appropriateness of their parents' behavior. It is when children believe that one child is being favored that parental behavior is associated with adjustment problems.

The correlates and consequences of parental differential treatment and favoritism differ by family context. For instance, some studies have investigated parental differential treatment in families in which the younger sibling has a disability compared to families that contained two children with no known handicaps. In these families, older siblings who spent more time with their mothers compared to their disabled siblings showed higher levels of depression and anxiety compared to older siblings in the other family contexts. This is the opposite of the pattern typically found in studies of differential treatment by parents. These findings suggest that the nature of parental differential treatment and favoritism varies across cultures; little research, however, has been conducted comparing children from different countries or subcultures within one country.

See also: BIRTH ORDER; COMMUNICATION: FAMILY RELATIONSHIPS; DEVELOPMENT: SELF; FAMILY AND RELATIONAL RULES; SIBLING RELATIONSHIPS

Bibliography

Dunn, J., and Plomin, R. (1990). *Separate Lives: Why Siblings Are So Different.* New York: Basic Books.

McGuire, S. (2002). "Nonshared Environment Research: What Is It and Where Is It Going?" *Marriage and Family Review* 3. Forthcoming.

Reiss, D.; Neiderhiser, J.; Hetherington, E. M.; and Plomin, R. (2000). *The Relationship Code.* Cambridge, MA: Harvard University Press.

SHIRLEY MCGUIRE

FEMINISM

See WOMEN'S MOVEMENTS

FERTILITY

The conceptions of human life and death are processes full of symbolic and cultural meanings. How the social meaning of human reproduction is constructed depends on the given sociopolitical context. Although the planet as a whole tries to cope with the consequences of overpopulation, in many developed countries governments are worried about the falling birth rates. When studying reproduction and the microprocess of conception, it is important to account for how local and global political tendencies affect population and individual reproductive health (Inhorn and Whittle 2001).

Reproductive health is affected by genetic endowment and by the physical and social environment. Thus it can be improved or undermined by individual behavior, advanced by better socioeconomic living conditions, and changed with medical knowledge and services (Pollard 1994). For example, nutrition during pregnancy affects the health of the fetus and may affect its subsequent viability. Living conditions and access to health care during childhood affects individuals both as children and adults. Education and later work possibilities affect not only individuals' overall life resources and health but also their reproductive health life style and health habits (Davey Smith et al. 2000). Excessive cigarette smoking, alcohol consumption, caffeine intake, obesity—as well as extreme weight loss and physical exercise—have been shown to adversely affect fertility (Feichtinger 1991).

Conception

Conception as a biological matter and a part of human reproduction means *fertilization* in which a sperm makes contact with an egg, fuses with it, and develops into the zygote, embryo, and fetus (Birke, Himmelweit, and Vines 1990). The monthly probability of conception without contraception is called *fecundability,* which for fertile couples is approximately 25 to 30 percent per month (Spira 1986), a remarkably low figure. Nevertheless, among humans fertilization can occur any given month, whereas among many other species fecundity is usually limited only to certain time of the year. An individual woman's *fecundity* varies as a function of her age, menstrual cycle, ovulation, and the functional status of her genital organs. Women in their 20s usually show the highest fecundability, which decreases among those over 35 years old (Day Baird and Strassmann 2000). Both female *oocyte*, or female egg, and uterine quality worsen with age, as do a woman's capacity to become pregnant and deliver a healthy child. In the era of birth control methods, for example, women in the United States and Finland reproduce relatively rarely, because only about 6 percent of them (15–44 years of age) give birth annually. A man's fecundity correspondingly varies with his age and seasonal and environmental factors. There is ample proof that environmental pollutants and occupational exposures to hazardous substances, such as radiation, heat, solvents, and pesticides, have adverse effects on male fertility (Feichtinger 1991). Fewer studies have inquired into the environmental effect on female fertility (Baranski 1993).

Reproductive System

In general, reproduction concerns women more profoundly than men in the physiological and social senses, because conception and development of a fetus happen in woman's body: she gives birth to the child, usually cares for it, and motherhood is culturally more important social and personal identity and institution than fatherhood. However, a woman and a man are both needed for conception (or at least female and male gametes—female egg and male sperm—are needed in *assisted reproduction*). A couple that has achieved a pregnancy is considered *fertile.* A woman and man must be sufficiently healthy to conceive. A healthy, fertile woman has approximately 400,000 immature eggs in her ovaries at the time of her birth. From puberty until menopause a woman's body goes through *ovulation,* in other words, periodic cycles of physical and chemical change during which an egg matures and is released from an ovary into one of the two fallopian tubes (Royal Commission on New Reproductive Technologies 1993). A woman must have at least one functional ovary and her tubes must be open and function to transport the egg to the uterus. The probability of conceiving a surviving pregnancy is highest on the two days before ovulation.

A healthy, fertile man produces 2.4–5 milliliters of *semen* containing between 200 million and 500 million *sperm* at each ejaculation. In order to conceive the anatomies of the man and woman have to be normal and their physiological and hormonal systems must function normally at the right time. The *hypothalamus* at the base of the brain orchestrates the body's hormonal reproductive function. Next, natural conception requires timely oocyte release, sexual intercourse, and the transport of gametes through the female reproductive tract. The woman's hormone level must be sufficient to stimulate the production of eggs and normal cervical mucus. Proper cervical mucus is necessary both near the time of ovulation and later to support implantation of the embryo and maintain pregnancy. Correspondingly, a man must be able to produce an adequate number of normal sperm and must be able to deposit them in the woman's vagina at the appropriate time during the female ovulation cycle (Office of Technology Assessment 1988). Only one sperm is needed to join with an egg in a woman's uterus for fertilization to occur. For this to happen, however, the sperm must be physically and functionally normal, active, and capable of swimming through the woman's reproductive tract.

Infertility

The production and the delivery of eggs and sperm are vulnerable processes that anatomical, genetic, hormonal, behavioral, and environmental problems may interrupt and prevent. *Infertility* is defined in clinical practice as the inability to become pregnant after more than one year of unprotected intercourse. Infertility can be either *primary,* if the couple has never achieved a pregnancy, or *secondary,* if it occurs after a couple has already had one or more pregnancy. Worldwide some form of infertility may affect 8 to 12 percent of couples (Day Baird and Strassman 2000; Spira 1986). Infertility is rarely absolute in nature, whereas *sterility* means the complete, absolute absence of reproductive capacity (the incidence has been estimated to be 3–5% of couples in industrialized countries [Spira 1986]). Female fertility problems may result from disorders in oocyte production, blockage or adhesions of the fallopian tubes, *endometriosis* (presence of endometrial gland tissue outside the uterus), or uterine and cervical abnormalities. Male infertility may be due to the problems in *spermatogenesis* (formation of sperm) and sperm transport and maturation (see Goldman, Missmer, and Barbieri 2000).

In Western countries the majority of women are accustomed to controlling their fertility with effective, accessible, and safe birth control methods and abortion. Likewise, Western women with fertility problems are accustomed to seeking medical help in order to become pregnant (Scritchfield 1989). Not every sterile and infertile couple wishes to have children. Thus, a woman and her partner must desire to have children but be physiologically incapable of becoming pregnant to experience herself as infertile and seek medical help.

Medical Procedures to Increase Fertility

There are *medical procedures* which may increase a person's fertility. Although *sexually transmitted diseases* (STDs, such as *gonorrhea, syphilis,* and *chlamydia*) and, for women, *pelvic inflammatory diseases* (PID), are predominant causes of infertility, preventive actions can decrease the possibility of contracting an STD or PID or suffering adverse environmental and/or occupational effects. *Curative procedures* include gynecological and urological surgery (e.g., surgery to open blocked fallopian tubes in women, or correct varicose veins in men). There are also *infertility-bypassing procedures,* which are called *assisted reproductive technologies* (ARTs), because they do not cure the physiological cause of the infertility. These ARTs include *low-tech therapies,* such as hormone medications and intrauterine insemination using sperm from the woman's partner or from a donor. *High-tech procedures,* which include retrieval of oocytes or fertilization of gametes outside the female body, are referred to as *in-vitro fertilization* (IVF) and related technologies. In IVF, eggs are fertilized outside the female body, and the embryo(s) are cultured in the laboratory; later, fresh or frozen embryo(s) are transferred to the female uterus (Grainger and Tjaden 2000). In IVF, donated gametes and embryos can also be used. When combined with surrogate motherhood, IVF can be used for couples in which the woman is without a womb. Other IVF-related technologies are *zygote intrafallopian transfer* (ZIFT), in which embryos are transferred to the fallopian tubes, and *gamete intrafallopian transfer* (GIFT), in which the egg and sperm are placed in a woman's fallopian tubes (Fidler and Bernstein 1999). The most common micromanipulation technique is *intracytoplasmic sperm injection* (ICSI) where one sperm is inserted into an egg in the laboratory. The access to these high-tech ART procedures depends on the local health care system and insurance coverage. Overall, about half a million children worldwide have been conceived with the help of IVF; and in the United States it has been estimated that approximately 29,000 IVF children are born annually; in Europe, approximately 40,000 IVF children are born annually (Nygren, Andersen, and the EIM 2001; Use of Assisted Reproductive Technology 1999)

IVF has revolutionized reproduction: IVF can be used to treat fertile couples for concerns unrelated to infertility; IVF may be used for embryo biopsy for purposes of sex selection and genetic diagnosis; IVF may be used to store gametes of cancer patients before starting chemotherapy (Lass,

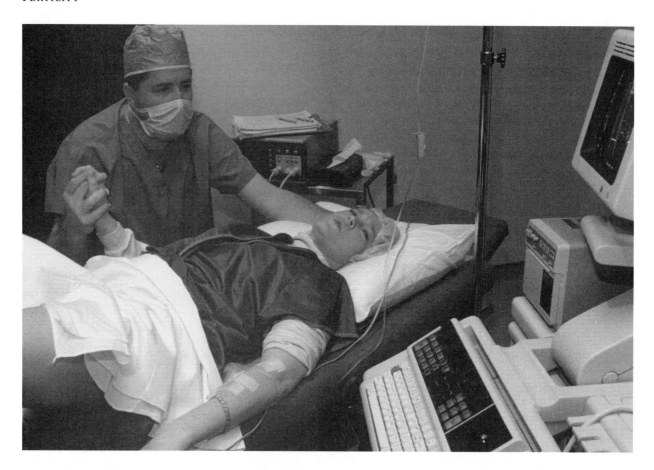

A doctor retrieves eggs from a woman's ovaries. Retrieval of oocytes or fertilization of gametes outside the female body are referred to as in-vitro fertilization (IVF), an infertility-bypassing procedure. ANNIE BELT/CORBIS

Akagbosu, and Brinsden 2001). Insemination can to be used for single women or lesbian couples (Baetens and Brewaeys 2001). IVF with donated eggs is used for postmenopausal women (Sauer, Paulson, and Lobo 1993). *Surrogate motherhood,* combined with IVF, can be used for homosexual male couples. Thus, the ARTs have widened the human possibilities to reproduce.

Conclusion

The social meanings of reproduction phenomena are constructed differently depending on the given sociopolitical context. Local and global political tendencies as well as different social hierarchies have an impact on the reproductive health of populations and individuals (Inhorn and Whittle 2001). Gender, race, and nation mediate individuals' power, personal agency, and choices relating to their reproductive health (Krieger et al. 1993). Genetic endowment and the physical and social environments (for example, environmental pollutants

and occupational exposures) also affect the reproductive health of both women and men. There are various medical procedures that may increase a person's fertility and enable the birth of a wanted child. But emotionally and economically the best solution for infertility is the prevention of infertility at different levels of everyday life.

See also: ABORTION; ASSISTED REPRODUCTIVE
TECHNOLOGIES; BIRTH CONTROL: CONTRACEPTIVE
METHODS; BIRTH CONTROL: SOCIOCULTURAL AND
HISTORICAL ASPECTS; CHILDLESSNESS; FAMILY
PLANNING; FATHERHOOD; INDUSTRIALIZATION;
MENARCHE; MENOPAUSE; MOTHERHOOD;
PREGNANCY AND BIRTH; SEXUALITY IN
ADULTHOOD; SURROGACY

Bibliography

Baetens, P., and Brewaeys, A. (2001). "Lesbian Couples Requesting Donor Insemination: An Update of the Knowledge with Regard to Lesbian Mother Families." *Human Reproduction Update* 7:512–519.

Baranski, B. (1993). "Effects of the Workplace on Fertility and Related Reproductive Outcomes." *Environmental Health Perspectives* 101:81–90.

Birke, L.; Himmelweit, S.; and Vines, G. (1990). *Tomorrow's Child: Reproductive Technologies in the 90s.* London: Virago Press.

Feichtinger, W. (1991). "Environmental Factors and Fertility." *Human Reproduction* 6:1170–1175.

Fidler, A. T., and Bernstein, J. (1999). "Infertility: From a Personal to a Public Health Problem." *Public Health Reports* 114:495–511.

Davey Smith, G.; Chasturvedi, N.; Harding, S.; Nazroo, J.; and Williams, R. (2000). "Ethnic Inequalities in Health: A Review of UK Epidemiological Evidence." *Critical Public Health* 10:375–408.

Day Baird, D., and Strassmann, B. I. (2000). "Women's Fecundability and Factors Affecting It." In *Women and Health,* ed. M. B. Goldman and M. C. Hatch. San Diego, CA: Academic Press.

Goldman, M. B.; Missmer, S. A.; and Barbieri, R. L. (2000). "Infertility." In *Women and Health,* ed. M. B. Goldman and M. C. Hatch. San Diego, CA: Academic Press.

Grainger, D. A., and Tjaden, B. L. (2000). "Assisted Reproductive Technologies." In *Women and Health,* ed. M. B. Goldman and M. C. Hatch. San Diego, CA: Academic Press.

Inhorn, M. C., and Whittle, K. L. (2001). "Feminism Meets the 'New' Epidemiologies: Toward an Appraisal of Antifeminist Biases in Epidemiological Research on Women's Health." *Social Science and Medicine* 53: 553–567

Krieger, N.; Rowley, D. L.; Herman, A. A.; Avery, B.; Phillips, M. T. (1993). "Racism, Sexism, and Social Class: Implications for Studies of Health, Disease, and Well-Being." *American Journal of Preventive Medicine* 9:82–122.

Lass, A.; Akagbosu, F.; and Brinsden, P. (2001). "Sperm Banking and Assisted Reproduction Treatment for Couples following Cancer Treatment of the Male Partner." *Human Reproduction Update* 7:370–377.

Nygren, K.G.; Andersen, A. N.; and the European IVF-monitoring Programme (EIM). (2001). "Assisted Reproductive Technology in Europe, 1998. Results Generated from European Registers by ESHRE. European Society of Human Reproduction and Embryology." *Human Reproduction* 16:2459–2471.

Office of Technology Assessment. (1988). *Infertility: Medical and Social choices.* OTA-BA-358. Washington, DC: Government Printing Office.

Royal Commission on New Reproductive Technologies. (1993). *Proceed with Care: Final report of the Royal Commission on New Reproductive Technologies,* Vol. 2. Ottawa, Canada: Minister of Government Services.

Pollard, I. (1994) *A Guide to Reproduction: Social Issues and Human Concerns.* Cambridge, UK: Cambridge University Press.

Sauer, M. V.; Paulson, R. J.; and Lobo, R. A. (1993). "Pregnancy after Age 50: Application of Oocyte Donation to Women after Natural Menopause." *Lancet* 341: 321–323.

Scritchfield, S. A. (1989). "The Social Construction of Infertility: From Private Matter to Social Concern." In *Images and Issues: Typifying Contemporary Social Problems,* ed. J. Best. New York: Aldine de Gruyter.

Spira, A. (1986). "Epidemiology of Human Reproduction." *Human Reproduction* 1:111–115.

Use of Assisted Reproductive Technology—United States, 1996 and 1998. (1999). *Morbidity and Mortality Weekly Report* 51:97–101.

MAILI MALIN

FICTIVE KINSHIP

The social universe established by kinship cannot be defined solely in terms of biology and marriage alone. Indeed, kinship establishes the base, but not the totality, of what individuals think of as family. The roles that family plays in a society are not complete without the inclusion of fictive kin relationships. They are fictive in the sense that these ties have a basis different from bonds of blood and marriage, not in the sense that these relationships are any less important. In many societies, fictive ties are as important as or more important than comparable relationships created by blood, marriage, or adoption.

Briefly defined, fictive kinship involves the extension of kinship obligations and relationships to individuals specifically not otherwise included in the kinship universe. Godparenthood (or coparenthood), in its many manifestations, is the most commonly cited illustration, but there are numerous other examples. In many societies, people have "aunts" or "uncles" who are merely their parents' closest friends. Members of religious movements may refer to each other as "brother" or "sister" while observing the rules and prohibitions attached to those statuses. Crime networks and youth gangs employ kinship bonds and ideas of "blood brotherhood" as organizing principles. Nontraditional family forms such as gay and lesbian unions may be defined in traditional kinship terms.

Nonetheless, all fictive kin relationships have one element in common: They are defined by criteria distinct from those establishing blood or marriage relationships. Fictive relationships may mimic the ties they copy, but they are defined in their own terms. These terms may have a religious or economic component, be predicated on existing social networks, or manipulate reality to fill gaps in real kinship networks. Fictive relationships serve to broaden mutual support networks, create a sense of community, and enhance social control. In essence, fictive kin ties elaborate social networks and regularize interactions with people otherwise outside the boundaries of family. Unlike true kinship bonds, fictive kin ties are usually voluntary and require the consent of both parties in establishing the bond. The idea that you cannot pick your relatives does not apply to fictive kin.

The concept of godparenthood (sometimes referred to as coparenthood) is certainly the best documented example of a fictive kin relationship. *Compadrazgo,* as it occurs throughout Mexico and Latin America, is an elaboration of the Catholic concept of baptismal sponsorship blended with precolonial religious beliefs. However, it is less a relationship between godparents and godchild than a tie between the parents and the godparents. By linking nonrelated families, *compadrazgo* extends formalized social networks. Individuals often seek to establish ties with wealthier families, establishing a sponsorship and providing the possibility of upward social mobility for the child (Foster 1967; Kemper 1982). Similar relationships exist in many other societies, including *dharma atmyo* in Bangladesh (Sarker 1980), *kumstvo* in the former Yugoslavia (Halpern 1967; Hammel 1968), and *kivrelik* in Turkey (Magnarella and Turkdogan 1973).

Another common form of fictive kinship involves the extension of brotherhood roles and obligations between unrelated males of the same generation. Among the Azande in Africa, for example, the concept of blood brotherhood was well established (Evans-Pritchard 1963). In its strictest sense, blood brotherhood ties are sealed by ingestion or some other "mixing" of each other's blood,

but this need not always be the case. Among the Serbs in Europe, for example, blood brotherhoods (*pobratimstvo*) were traditionally established when a person was seriously ill or believed himself to be near death. The ceremony, performed at a grave site, involved no exchange of blood. *Pobratim* were supposed to behave toward one another as brothers for life, and their children were prohibited from marrying each other (Halpern 1967). Other forms of less rigid brotherhood extension are also common and are better described as partnerships. Among the Netsilik of North America, such partnerships *(niqaitorvigit)* defined an elaborate pattern of sharing relationships. These sharing relationships were a permanent way of distributing meat and helped spread the risk generated by unpredictable food resources (Balikci 1970).

Many important social relationships are established through marriage. In some instances, a tie established through marriage may be crucial to inheritance (providing continuity to a descent group) or maintenance of social bonds. In cases where families do not have children to marry, fictive marriage may serve as a substitute. Among the Kwakiutl of North America, status was passed from grandfather to grandson through the son-in-law. A man without daughters might "marry" a son to another man to create this important link. If he had no children, the marriage tie might be created to a body part as, for example, a marriage between a son-in-law and his father-in-law's leg (Boas 1897). The Nuer of North Africa "marry" a woman to a man who has died without producing heirs (ghost marriage). The woman is actually married to the ghost through a living male relative, and any children resulting from the bond belong to the ghost father and inherit his property (Evans-Pritchard 1951). Another traditional form of fictive marriage existed among the American Plains Indians in the institution of the *berdache*. In the *berdache*, a man might assume both the dress and the role of a woman, often "marrying" another man.

In postindustrial societies, it is possible to argue that fictive kinship ties have taken on increased importance. Social and geographic mobility, soaring divorce rates, and nontraditional family forms have produced social networks based more on voluntary ties than on traditional bonds of blood and marriage. There is, for example, a growing body of literature describing the importance of fictive kin ties in U.S. African-American urban communities and their effects on everything from child care to educational achievement (Fordham 1986; Johnson and Barer 1990). Some researchers have gone so far as to describe ethnicity as being an elaborated form of fictive kinship (Yelvington and Bentley 1991). At the same time, nontraditional families, such as gay or lesbian couples in which children may have two fathers or mothers, can also be characterized as having elements of fictive kinship. Gerontologists and social workers have also emphasized the importance of fictive kin networks to medical treatment and mental health as individuals seek to fill gaps in their existing support networks (Gubrium and Buckholdt 1982; Wentowski 1981).

See also: ETHNIC VARIATIONS/ETHNICITY; EXTENDED FAMILIES; GANGS; GAY PARENTS; GODPARENTS; KINSHIP; LESBIAN PARENTS; NUCLEAR FAMILIES; RELIGION; SOCIAL NETWORKS

Bibliography

Balikci, A. (1970). *The Netsilik Eskimo*. Garden City, NY: Natural History Press.

Boas, F. (1897). *Social Organization and Secret Societies of the Kwakiutl Indians*. U.S. National Museum Annual Report, 1895. Washington, DC.

Evans-Pritchard, E. E. (1951). *Kinship and Marriage Among the Nuer*. Oxford: Clarendon Press.

Evans-Pritchard, E. E. (1963). *Essays in Social Anthropology*. New York: Free Press.

Fordham, S. (1986). "Black Students' School Success: Coping with the 'Burden of "Acting White."'" *Urban Review* 18:176–206.

Foster, G. M. (1967). *Tzintzuntzan: Mexican Peasants in a Changing World*. Boston: Little, Brown.

Gubrium, J. F., and Buckholdt, D. R. (1982). "Fictive Family: Everyday Usage, Analytic, and Human Service Considerations." *American Anthropologist* 84:878–885.

Halpern, J. M. (1967). *A Serbian Village*. New York: Harper & Row.

Hammel, E. A. (1968). *Alternative Social Structures and Ritual Relations in the Balkans*. Englewood Cliffs, NJ: Prentice Hall.

Johnson, C. L., and Barer, B. M. (1990). "Families and Networks Among Older Inner-City Blacks." *Gerontologist* 30:726–733.

Kemper, R. V. (1982). "The *Compadrazgo* in Urban Mexico." *Anthropological Quarterly* 55:17–30.

Magnarella, P. J., and Turkdogan, O. (1973). "Descent, Affinity, and Ritual Relations in Eastern Turkey." *American Anthropologist* 75:1626–1633.

Sarker, P. C. (1980). "Dharma-Atmyo: Fictive Kin Relationship in Rural Bangladesh." *Eastern Anthropologist* 33:55–61.

Sofola, J. A. (1983). "The *Onyenualagu* (Godparent) in Traditional and Modern African Communities: Implications for Juvenile Delinquency." *Journal of Black Studies* 14:21–70.

Wentowski, G. J. (1981). "Reciprocity and the Coping Strategies of Older People: Cultural Dimensions of Network Building." *Gerontologist* 21:600–609.

Yelvington, K. A., and Bentley, G. C. (1991). "Ethnicity as Practice? A Comment on Bentley." *Comparative Studies in Society and History* 33:158–168.

RICHARD A. WAGNER (1995)

FILIAL RESPONSIBILITY

Filial responsibility describes the sense of personal obligation or duty that adult children feel for protecting, caring for, and supporting their aging parents (Schorr 1980). Filial responsibility is evident in both attitudes and behaviors of adult children, frequently finding expression in assistance with household tasks and shopping, maintenance of personal contact, provision of affection and emotional support, shared living arrangements, and help in meeting daily needs. Although typically considered a response to immediate demands or crises, filial responsibility also entails an important preventative dimension that promotes independence among older adults. As such, the filial adult child empowers older parents by enabling them to perform the tasks that they are capable of doing for themselves, discouraging premature dependence. This aspect of filial responsibility is enacted when adult children help their parents to acquire new skills, seek novel and enriching life experiences, and disregard negative stereotypes about aging, and also allow their parents to speak for themselves, and respect their parents' self-determination in making decisions that affect their own lives (Seelbach 1984).

Why Is the Issue Pertinent?

Care of dependent older persons is a salient issue around the world for a number of reasons. Not only are more people surviving to old age due to improved medical care, but greater numbers are living into older age when the incidence of health impairments rises dramatically, increasing the likelihood of the need for support and assistance. Social changes and family lifestyle transformations (e.g., more working women, fewer multigeneration households, more nuclear families, urbanization) have also altered the family's ability to assist older members. Given the likelihood that more adult children will encounter the privileges and demands of filial responsibilities, Victor Cicirelli (1988) coined the concept of *filial anxiety* to capture the "state of worry or concern about the anticipated decline and death of an aging parent as well as worry or concern about the ability to meet anticipated caregiving needs, either prior to any caregiving or during the provision of care and in anticipation of further parental decline and additional needs for care" (p. 478). With a rapidly aging population, the question arises: Should the responsibility for care of older dependent family members lie with the family or be provided by society in general?

Filial Responsibility Laws

Many countries have tried to articulate who is responsible for the welfare of dependent family members via the creation of laws. England's Poor Law of 1601 stated that communities were responsible for meeting the needs of the poor elderly, but only after the resources of adult children were exhausted (Schorr 1980). Although the North American colonies adopted the Poor Laws, the statutes were never really tested. The shift from agrarian-based economies, like those in early North America, to primarily industrial economies led to the possibility that elders would no longer be able to ensure their financial well-being through control of the family farm. Thus, industrialization led to increased independence and individualism, as well as greater vulnerability of dependent elders (Bulcroft, Van Leynseele, and Borgatta 1989).

The interface between private and public sectors for the provision of elder care continues to be defined and shaped by the creation and revision of public policy. For instance, the introduction of the Social Security Act in 1935 in the United States represented a critical federal commitment to the needs of older Americans, decreasing aged persons' dependence on family members. In contrast, however, is the fact that thirty states retain varying types of laws attributing legal responsibilities to the family for the care of elder members. For instance, there is a great deal of variation between the statutes of each state (i.e., definition of need, who is named to support, enforcement procedures, nature of support expected) and the vague and ambiguous language employed, making enforcement difficult, if not impossible (Bulcroft, Van Leynseele, and Borgatta 1989).

Many policies related to the provision of long-term care in the United States offer supplemental assistance to families who are caring for their dependent members, empowering the *natural caregivers,* who offer their services for free (Bulcroft, Van Leynseele, and Borgatta 1989). Governments often attempt to buttress the family's ability to provide for their elderly by offering such incentives as tax breaks for children who claim their parents as dependents. Another example in the United States is the Family Medical Leave Act of 1993 that requires companies with more than fifty employees to grant twelve weeks of unpaid leave per year to any worker requiring time off to care for dependent family members, including parents.

Other countries have also enacted legislative actions and social policies geared toward encouraging filial conduct. China's constitution requires that adult children fulfill their duty to care for aging parents, but the government supplements this aid through public pensions and a state income maintenance program for select elders. Although state programs are increasingly important in enhancing the well-being of elders, expectations from children for support in old age still predominate. This is especially true in rural areas where children, particularly sons, forfeit their right to inherit family property if the obligation to parents is neglected (Pei and Pillai 1999). In 1973, South Korea's Ministry of Health and Social Affairs established a Filial Piety Prize. A major event during *Respect for the Elderly Week,* the prize is awarded to between 150 and 380 of the most filial responsible adult children in Korea each year and serves as one of many incentives for children to provide support to parents (Sung 1990).

In light of the magnitude of the needs required by a growing number of dependent elders, families and governments will benefit from a collaborative approach to meeting the demands. Research on filial responsibility expectations provides some clues as to how government programs can best interface with families in meeting needs of aging members.

Filial Responsibility Expectations

Filial responsibility encompasses attitudes that endorse certain responsibilities or obligations that adult children should assume in addressing their parents' needs and in maintaining their well-being. Researchers examining filial responsibility attitudes have employed a variety of different measures (e.g., vignettes as in Wolfson et al. 1993 and item-scales as in Hamon and Blieszner 1990) with varying sample populations (e.g., grandchildren, college students, elder parents, multigenerational families). Most have also measured filial responsibility expectations in a universal way ("What should children do for parents?"), rather than asking individuals what they expect from themselves or from their own children ("What should my children do for me?") (Lee, Netzer, and Coward 1994a). Some inquire about a few select areas (e.g., shared living arrangements, financial assistance) of filial responsibility, whereas others are more comprehensive in their coverage, including items on instrumental, emotional, and contact norms.

Whether using samples from Canada (Wolfson et al. 1993), the Netherlands (Ikkink, Van Tilburg, and Knipscheer 1999), urban China (Chen and Adamchak 1999), or the United States (Hamon and Blieszner 1990), findings consistently reveal strong and persistent endorsement of filial norms by both adult sons and daughters (Wolfson et al.1993). Greatest support is given to the notion that children should offer emotional support to their parents, with less emphasis placed upon physical assistance and financial support.

Although parents want to maintain their independence and typically do not expect as much from their adult children as children expect from themselves (Hamon and Blieszner 1990; Novero Blust and Scheidt 1988), parents also hope that children will be there for them when called upon to do so. Samples of Floridians and urban Chinese indicated that parents with higher levels of education, more income, and better health have lower filial responsibility expectations (Lee, Netzer, and

The ways in which adult children express filial responsibility for parents include maintaining personal contact, providing affection and emotional support, sharing living arrangements, and helping their parents meet daily needs. PHOTOTEX/CORBIS

Coward 1994a; Chen and Adamchak 1999). In addition, parents may alter their expectations of their children (from high to low) depending upon the characteristics of their children (i.e., how many are female and geographical proximity) rather than on their own personal circumstances (Lee, Netzer, and Coward 1994b). For instance, in South Korea, parents place greatest expectations on eldest sons rather than daughters or daughters-in-law (Won and Lee 1999). However, in many Western countries, because older mothers are more likely to be widowed and survive to older ages, they frequently hope to receive more from adult daughters.

Some cultural differences in expectations emerge. Expectations of shared living arrangements may be greater in Asian cultures (i.e., South Korea), where such practices are more common than in Western cultures (Won and Lee 1999). For Filipinos, respect, warmth and affection were the most strongly endorsed expectations, followed by instrumental support (Novero Blust and Scheidt 1988).

Within the United States, research has shown how racial differences affect norms in filial responsibility. Older African Americans expect more help from their adult children than do their white counterparts (Lee, Peek, and Coward 1998). Expectations for intergenerational coresidence and the exchange of financial assistance are greater among older African Americans and older Hispanics than among older whites (Burr and Mutchler 1999).

Filial Responsible Behavior

Many variables influence what children actually do for their parents. For example, aging parents' life situations influence how much and the types of aid they receive. Parents who need greater assistance (e.g., are widowed and/or are in poor health), expect more help from their children, and actively seek that aid, are more likely to receive support than parents who neither expect nor ask for help (Cicirelli 2000; Hamon 1992; Ikkink, Van Tilburg, and Knipschneer 1999; Litwin 1994; Peek et al. 1998). It is interesting that in both the Netherlands and the United States, mothers are more often recipients of aid from their children than are fathers (Ikkink, Van Tilburg, and Knipschneer 1999).

The circumstances of adult children also influence filial role enactment. Filial concern about the well-being of one's parents positively affects children's inclination to provide emotional support and assistance; conversely, recalled negative family relationship histories negatively affect children's concern and subsequent help (Whitbeck, Hoyt, and Huck 1994).

The child's gender also comes into play. Meeting filial obligations appears to be a gendered activity, with more daughters serving as primary providers and carrying the bulk of filial work, although sons do provide care in many cases (Blieszner and Hamon 1992; Hamon 1992; Lee, Dwyer, and Coward 1993; Matthews 1995). Even in Eastern societies like China and South Korea, which have historically emphasized sons' as primarily responsible for parent care, daughters are increasingly providing more of the elder support (Chen and Adamchak 1999). Among siblings, daughters are more likely to assume nurturing roles and accept tasks related to personal care or domestic support than are sons (Dwyer and Coward 1991; Matthews 1995). In brothers-only sibling networks, sons tend to wait for parents to tell them when they need assistance, work independently of one another in providing for their parents' needs, perform *masculine* tasks (e.g., yard work, attending to plumbing problems), employ outside aid, work to restore and promote their parents' independence, and define their

filial work as relatively inconsequential (Matthews and Heidorn 1998). In a Canadian sample, however, sons who coreside with aging parents are heavily involved in nontraditional forms of care (Campbell and Martin-Matthews 2000). Regardless of whether sons or daughters are providing care, children tend to provide more support to same-sex parents, especially in the realm of personal-care duties (Campbell and Martin-Matthews 2000).

Children's marital status may affect the amount of participation a child assumes in assisting parents. Married and divorced children may have a more difficult time providing *active support* to a parent (Cicirelli 1989; Matthews and Rosner 1988) than those who are single.

Full-time employment and number of dependent children in the home significantly reduced the amount of assistance provided by sons, but not that provided by daughters (Stoller 1983). Geographic location understandably affects the enactment of filial responsibility. Children who live close to or coreside with aging parents are more available to oversee and care for their needs (Matthews and Rosner 1988). As a consequence of economic development and industrialization in Taiwan, however, coresidence between elder parents and their adult sons is declining, but economic transfers and financial help between sons and their parents has increased. This shift may be compensating for the fact that young Taiwanese often must reside far from their parents' home in order to work (Chattopadhyay and Marsh 1999).

The number of siblings present within a family system affects the amount and type of support provided to parents by each individual. For example, in situations where two daughters are present, both appear to share equally for the care of their parent. Although joint responsibility occurs frequently in larger sibling groups, filial responsibilities are less likely to be divided equally. Birth order and a parent's relationship with particular children may also affect the enactment of filial responsible behaviors (Matthews and Rosner 1988).

Motivations For Filial Responsibility

There are a number of theoretical explanations for the existence of filial responsibility. Margaret Blenkner (1965) introduced the concept of *filial maturity* as a unique developmental task of midlife. She observed that a filial crisis occurs when adult children, typically in their forties or fifties, realize that their parents can no longer fulfill the supportive role they once did during economic and emotional hardships and that they must become a reliable source of support for their parents. Corinne Nydegger (1991), on the other hand, believes that the filial role is not the result of a filial crisis, but as the result of gradual change. From her perspective, "filial maturity is a lengthy, complex process, involving children's personal development and their interaction with parents who are also maturing" (p. 107). Although they propose different theories, both views suggest that filial maturity and filial responsibility are the result of a developmental process that occurs during the life course.

Social exchange theory offers another plausible explanation for a strong endorsement of filial norms. According to this theory, human beings are motivated by self-interest and seek to maximize their rewards and minimize the costs that they incur in a relationship. At the same time, the theory asserts that relationships are governed by a norm of reciprocity: "one should reciprocate favors received from others." Because parents provide food, shelter, care, supervision, socialization, and other necessities to their offspring, children should protect and attend to their parents' emotional and material needs when they experience illness and/or are debilitated (Nye 1979). In some cultures, children might even perform rituals for deceased parents in order to contribute to their well-being in the spirit world. Thus, over the life course intergenerational transactions should produce fairly equitable exchanges. Adult children whose own parents were good to them but who fail to feel responsible for maintaining the well-being of aging parents would likely encounter a number of costs (e.g., guilt, social disapproval), whereas those who do acknowledge their part in the interdependent relationship with parents might encounter rewards (e.g., satisfaction, inheritance, affection, gratitude). Some scholars believe that it is impossible for children to restore balance, to ever fully and adequately repay their parents. A sense of indebtedness (Seelbach 1984) or irredeemable obligation (Berman 1987) to parents persists, even in social exchange, because parents give first, voluntarily, and spontaneously. Subsequent gifts, no matter how superior in content, cannot match the first gift. Research by Gary Lee and his colleagues

(1994) supports a *reciprocity effect*: there is a tendency for parents who expect more from their children to also give more to their children. Likewise, those who give more to their children, receive more from them.

Attachment theory poses another explanation for the endorsement of filial norms. The existence of an internal state of attachment, an emotional or affectional bond that adult children have for parents, prompts them to remain in contact and communication with parents, protecting them from harm (Cicirelli 1989; 1993). Thus, a sense of filial responsibility is the result of friendship, mutuality, and positive feelings for one's parents rather than a sense of debt or obligation (English 1979).

A related explanation is that children are inclined to care for aging parents out of a *moral imperative* to do so. Children may perceive that filial norms are morally expected, and demonstrate appropriate or correct behavior toward one's parents. Such beliefs may be rooted in the Judeo-Christian commandment to "honor thy father and thy mother" (Exodus 20:12). In Jerusalem, for instance, the greater the religious observation of the caregiver, the stronger the sense of filial responsibility (Litwin 1994). In many Asian cultures, Confucian moral principles provide a strong ideological basis for filial piety and status of elders as well. Accordingly, filial piety demands that children should love, respect, and serve their parents. The importance of respect and warmth for elders is reflected in the language of Asian cultures (See Ingersoll-Dayton and Saengtienchai 1999). *Utang na loob* (Philippines), *Bunkhun*, (Thailand), and *xiao* (China) respectively refer to the respect, gratitude, and obligation that children should feel toward parents and serves as the basis for the provision of parent care. In fact, among a sample of exceptionally filially responsible children in South Korea, respect for parents was the most important motivator for providing filial support. Respect was indicated by "treating parents with unusual deference and courtesy, showing exceptionally earnest and sincere consideration for the parent, [and] showing extraordinary honor and esteem for parent" (Sung 1990, p. 613).

Children may adopt a responsible filial role because of *socialization*. Most adults acknowledge filial norms, yet filial expectations are not always explicitly delineated in terms of the appropriate or acceptable levels of support and assistance adult children are expected to afford their parents, particularly in light of other role demands (e.g., spouse, parent, employee) (Donorfio and Sheehan 2001). Nonetheless, even though such norms may vary across families, depending upon such things as cultural, racial, or ethnic influences, family structure; socioeconomic status differences; level of embeddedness in social networks; degree of traditionalism; varying geographic locations; and the sense of obligation for one's aging parents persists (Johnson 1996). In South Korea, family harmony, public recognition, and praise from neighbors are all valued outcomes of filial conduct, and as such, are effective incentives for filial role enactment (Sung 1990). Hilary Graham (1983) asserted that women are socialized to care to the extent that it becomes a defining characteristic of their identity and life work. It is through caring that "women are accepted into and feel they belong in the social world" (p. 30), particularly in capitalistic and male-dominated societies. Because women are socialized as kinkeepers, nurturers, and domestic laborers in families, it is not particularly surprising to find that daughters are more likely than sons to be principal caretakers of parents or at least receive more credit for such family work (Blieszner and Hamon 1992; Matthews 1995).

See also: ADULTHOOD; CAREGIVING: INFORMAL; CONFLICT: PARENT-CHILD RELATIONSHIPS; ELDER ABUSE; ELDERS; FAMILY LOYALTY; FAMILY ROLES; GRANDPARENTHOOD; IN-LAW RELATIONSHIPS; INTERGENERATIONAL RELATIONS; LATER LIFE FAMILIES; SANDWICH GENERATION; SOCIAL EXCHANGE THEORY; WIDOWHOOD

Bibliography

Berman, H. J. (1987). "Adult Children and Their Parents: Irredeemable Obligation and Irreplaceable Loss." *Gerontological Social Work With Families* 10:21–34.

Blenkner, M. (1965). "Social Work and Family Relationships in Later Life with Some Thoughts on Filial Maturity." In *Social Structure and the Family: Generational Relations,* ed. E. Shanas and G. F. Streib. Englewood Cliffs, NJ: Prentice Hall.

Blieszner, R., and Hamon, R. R. (1992). "Filial Responsibility: Attitudes, Motivators, and Behaviors." In *Gender, Families and Elder Care,* ed. J. W. Dwyer and R. T. Coward. Newbury Park, CA: Sage.

Bulcroft, K.; Van Leynseele, J.; and Borgatta, E. F. (1989). "Filial Responsibility Laws: Issues and State Statutes." *Research on Aging* 11(3):374–393.

Burr, J.A., and Mutchler, J. E. (1999). "Race and Ethnic Variation in Norms of Filial Responsibility Among Older Persons." *Journal of Marriage and the Family* 61:674–687.

Campbell, L., and Martin-Matthews, A. (2000). "Primary and Proximate: The Importance of Coresidence and Being Primary Provider of Care for Men's Filial Care Involvement." *Journal of Family Issues* 21:1006–1030.

Chattopadhyay, A., and Marsh, R. (1999). "Changes in Living Arrangement and Familial Support for the Elderly in Taiwan: 1963–1991." *Journal of Comparative Family Studies* 30:523–537.

Chen, S., and Adamchak, D. J. (1999). "The Effects of Filial Responsibility Expectations on Intergenerational Exchanges in Urban China." *Hallym International Journal of Aging* 1:58–68.

Cicirelli, V. G. (1988). "A Measure of Filial Anxiety Regarding Anticipated Care of Elderly Parents." *Gerontologist* 28:478–482.

Cicirelli, V. G. (1989). "Helping Relationships in Later Life: A Reexamination." In *Aging Parents and Adult Children,* ed. J. A. Mancini. Lexington, MA: Lexington Books.

Cicirelli, V. G. (1993). "Attachment and Obligation as Daughters' Motives for Caregiving Behavior and Subsequent Effect of Subjective Burden." *Psychology and Aging* 8:144–155.

Cicirelli, V. G. (2000). "An Examination of the Trajectory of the Adult Child's Caregiving for an Elderly Parent." *Family Relations* 49:169–175.

Donorfio, L. M., and Sheehan, N. W. (2001). "Relationship Dynamics between Aging Mothers and Caregiving Daughters: Filial Expectations and Responsibilities." *Journal of Adult Development* 8:39–49.

Dwyer, J. W., and Coward, R. T. (1991). "A Multivariate Comparison of the Involvement of Adult Sons versus Daughters in the Care of Impaired Parents." *Journal of Gerontology: Social Sciences* 46:S259–S269.

English, J. (1979). "What Do Grown Children Owe Their Parents?" In *Having Children: Philosophical and Legal Reflections on Parenthood,* ed. O. O'Neill and W. Ruddick. New York: Oxford University Press.

Graham, H. (1983). "Caring: A Labour of Love." In *A Labour of Love: Women, Work and Caring,* ed. J. Finch and D. Groves. London: Routledge and Kegan Paul.

Hamon, R. R. (1992). "Filial Role Enactment by Adult Children." *Family Relations* 41:91–96.

Hamon, R. R., and Blieszner, R. (1990). "Filial Responsibility Expectations among Adult Child-Older Parent Pairs." *Journal of Gerontology: Psychological Sciences* 45:110–112.

Ikkink, K. K.; Van Tilburg, T.; and Knipscheer, K. C. P. M. (1999). "Perceived Instrumental Support Exchanges in Relationships between Elderly Parents and Their Adult Children: Normative and Structural Explanations." *Journal of Marriage and the Family* 61:831–844.

Ingersoll-Dayton, B., and Saengtienchai, C. (1999). "Respect for the Elderly in Asia: Stability and Change." *International Journal of Aging and Human Development* 48:113–130.

Johnson, C. L. (1996). "Cultural Diversity in the Late-Life Family." In *Aging and the Family: Theory and Research,* ed. R. Blieszner and V. Bedford. Westport, CT: Greenwood Press.

Lee, G. R.; Dwyer, I. W.; and Coward, R. T. (1993). "Gender Differences in Parent Care: Demographic Factors and Same-Gender Preferences." *Journal of Gerontology* 48:S9–S16.

Lee, G. R.; Netzer, J. K.; and Coward, R. T. (1994a). "Filial Responsibility Expectations and Patterns of Intergenerational Assistance." *Journal of Marriage and the Family* 56:559–565.

Lee, G. R.; Netzer, J. K.; and Coward, R. T. (1994b). "Residential Differences in Filial Responsibility Expectations among Older Parents." *Rural Sociology* 59:100–109.

Lee, G. R.; Peek, C. W.; and Coward, R. T. (1998). "Race Differences in Filial Responsibility Expectations among Older Adults." *Journal of Marriage and the Family* 60:404–412.

Litwin, H. (1994). "Filial Responsibility and Informal Support among Family Caregivers of the Elderly in Jerusalem: A Path Analysis." *International Journal of Aging and Human Development* 38:137–151.

Matthews, S. H. (1995). "Gender and the Division of Filial Responsibility between Lone Sisters and Their Brothers." *Journal of Gerontology* 50:S312–S320.

Matthews, S. H., and Heidorn, J. (1998). "Meeting Filial Responsibilities in Brothers-Only Sibling Groups." *Journal of Gerontology* 53:S278–S286.

Matthews, S. H., and Rosner, T. T. (1988). "Shared Filial Responsibility: The Family as Primary Caregiver." *Journal of Marriage and the Family* 50:185–195.

Novero Blust, E. P., and Scheidt, R. J. (1988). "Perceptions of Filial Responsibility by Elderly Filipino Widows and Their Primary Caregivers." *International Journal of Aging and Human Development* 26:91–106.

Nydegger, C. N. (1991). "The Development of Paternal and Filial Maturity." In *Parent-Child Relations throughout Life,* ed. K. Pillemer and K. McCartney. Hillsdale, NJ: Lawrence Erlbaum Associates.

Nye, F. I. (1979). "Choice, Exchange, and the Family." In *Contemporary Theories about the Family,* Vol. 2, ed. W. R. Burr, R. Hill, F. I. Nye, and I. L. Reiss. New York: Free Press.

Peek, M. K.; Coward, R. T.; Peek, C. W.; and Lee, G. R. (1998). "Are Expectations for Care Related to the Receipt of Care? An Analysis of Parent Care among Disabled Elders." *Journal of Gerontology* 53B:S127–S136.

Pei, X., and Pillai, V. K. (1999). "Old Age Support in China: The Role of the State and the Family." *International Journal of Aging and Human Development* 49:197–212.

Schorr, A. L. (1980) . . . *Thy Father and Thy Mother . . . : A Second Look at Filial Responsibility and Family Policy* (DHHS Publication No. 13–11953). Washington, DC: Government Printing Office.

Seelbach, W. C. (1984). "Filial Responsibility and the Care of Aging Family Members." In *Independent Aging: Family and Social Systems Perspectives,* ed. W. H. Quinn and G. A. Hughston. Rockville, MD: Aspen.

Stoller, E. P. (1983). "Parental Caregiving by Adult Children." *Journal of Marriage and the Family* 45:851–858.

Sung, K. (1990). "A New Look at Filial Piety: Ideals and Practices of Family-Centered Parent Care in Korea." *Gerontologist* 30:610–617.

Whitbeck, L.; Hoyt, D. R.; and Huck, S. M. (1994). "Early Family Relationships, Intergenerational Solidarity, and Support Provided to Parents by Their Adult Children." *Journal of Gerontology* 49(2):S85–S94.

Wolfson, C.; Handfield-Jones, R.; Glass, K. C.; McClaran, J.; and Keyserlingk, E. (1993). "Adult Children's Perceptions of Their Responsibility to Provide Care for Dependent Elderly Parents." *Gerontologist* 33:315–323.

Won, Y. H., and Lee, G. R. (1999). "Living Arrangements of Older Parents in Korea." *Journal of Comparative Family Studies* 30:315–328.

RAEANN R. HAMON
KELI R. WHITNEY

FINLAND

See SCANDINAVIA

FOOD

Food and families are two topics in which everyone claims some expertise. *Families* are made up of people who eat food. Both families and food contribute to a person's physical and social well being throughout life.

Dictionary definitions of food include terms such as *nourishing, sustaining growth,* or *furnishing energy.* People recognize that food is necessary for the physical survival of their families. Although sometimes the purpose of food intake is only to satisfy hunger, the role of food in families goes much further than meeting physical needs.

Food structures families' schedules, provides social activity, defines relationships, and represents ethnic identities. Food is part of family celebrations, ceremonies, and rituals. Food-related health concerns such as malnutrition and obesity impact family members' emotions and their relationships with each other. For some families, food is easily accessible. Other families are starving. Through food demands and concerns, families shape societies and societies influence families. The purpose of this entry is to describe the importance of food to families by examining international examples of the many connections between family and food.

Family Meals

People associate food with family relationships. Debra Lupton (1994), an Australian researcher, found that childhood memories of food were related to social relationships rather than to foods themselves. When requested to write about "food," participants in Lupton's study described emotional themes related to belongingness, happiness, control, and disappointment. In most cultures food is linked with group membership, including belonging to a family. Eating together provides opportunities for family members to interact while sharing the same event or eating similar foods. Family members' interests and activities may vary widely in the areas of work, school, and leisure activities; mealtime provides a common focus.

Food does much more than meet family members' physical needs. It structures family schedules, enhances relationships within and between families, and marks cultural and religious identity. INDEX STOCK IMAGERY

Many people recognize the importance of family mealtimes, and many factors, including work schedules, school events, and the convenience of restaurants, make eating together a challenge for some families. Attention to the benefits of family meals is not new. In 1943 James H. S. Bossard indicated that the family meal "holds members of the family together during an extended period of time." During mealtimes, noted Bossard, family members interact, enlarging vocabulary, providing information, developing personality, and socializing children. He acknowledged that because family meals represent "families in action," negative as well as positive interactions occur during meals. Similarly, Lupton noted that the family meal itself is not necessarily positive. When family members cooperate, are valued, and positive interactions predominate during meal preparation and eating, the family meal helps establish a sense of security among family members.

Family mealtimes may be a higher priority for some families than for others, and a possible decline in frequency of family meals is a commonly expressed concern. Social problems, ranging from failure in school to delinquency, have been attributed to the decline in family meals. However, a decline in family meals may not be as extensive as feared. An American Dietetic Association (2000) fact sheet indicates that the average family prepares and eats dinner together five nights a week. Obviously, many people are committed to obtaining the benefits of a family meal.

Parents have an impact on what their children eat and how much they eat. Children prefer foods with which they are familiar (Birch 1996). To develop familiarity with and preference for specific food items, children may need to be exposed to that food ten times. Parents have the responsibility of selecting much of the food eaten by very young children. But children also affect the food behaviors of other family members by influencing what is purchased and prepared. Parents want to serve food that their children will eat. According to Gill Valentine (1999), "the power of children shape[s] the consumption practices of a household." Valentine found that differences in food preferences among family members may lead to negotiation and compromise or to the decision to have meals in which family members eat very differently from one another (e.g., vegetarians and meat-eaters).

Parents and children not only impact one another's food choices. The care and love parents demonstrate by purchasing or preparing food for their children is evident; in addition, children also use food to express care and helpfulness to parents. In interviews conducted in California, adolescents between the ages of eleven and fourteen reported cooking for themselves or siblings in order to be helpful to parents. They viewed preparing food at home as making a contribution to family life (Kaplan 2000). Thus, children and parents alike help to create a sense of family by giving and receiving care demonstrated through food.

The adolescents interviewed by Elaine Bell Kaplan (2000) indicated that their mothers were responsible for preparing the evening meals, but the boys described enjoying cooking as much as the girls did. Boys' enjoyment of cooking follows a trend in which men frequently contribute to preparation of family meals. Women still do most of the cooking for families, but men often participate in food preparation. Lupton (2000) found that among rural Australian heterosexual couples, many enjoyed food preparation, although the men who liked to cook were typically middle-aged or younger. Even though women still took the major responsibility for meals, these couples viewed food preparation as part of the division of labor, which they had negotiated, rather than as the duty of the female. Attitudes toward food and gender role patterns, however, may vary from country to country. More gender role segregation in food practices has been reported in British than in Swedish households (Jansson 1995).

Food preferences and preparation responsibilities are negotiated between husband and wife, as well as between parents and children. People also negotiate and renegotiate food patterns throughout the stages of their own lives. Researchers in Scotland examined changes in eating habits when couples began to live together. Prior to marriage or cohabitation, people shopped for food when they felt like it or needed more food; when they began living together, both meals and shopping became more regular. Women made efforts to improve their husbands' food choices, and men's diets improved. Most couples reported that food was a much more important component of their relationship than they had expected (Kemmer 1998).

As children grow and eventually move out of the household, some parents tend to eat less regular and smaller meals. Parents return to cooking and eating more when children visit. This pattern is particularly characteristic of widowed women, who have experienced loss of social interaction, as well as the satisfaction of providing care through meals (Quandt et al. 1997).

Trends in society include people living longer, an increase in dual-earner and single-parent households, and access to more convenient foods. In addition, many people live alone. Sometimes jobs are located long distances from homes. Therefore, families may have little time or incentive to cook and may choose to eat in restaurants or to bring fully prepared meals into their homes. According to Gisele Yasmeen (2000), few urban Thai families regularly cook meals at home. Because most Thai and Southeast Asian women are in the paid workforce, these families might subscribe to a neighborhood catering network or eat other publicly prepared food. When consumers desire readily available, fully prepared food, industry complies. Increases of fast-food restaurants in Western societies provide an example of both the impact of the consumer on society and society on the consumer. When fully prepared food is available and affordable, families are likely to cook less.

Food content and methods of meal preparation have changed and will continue to change for individuals as they age and for families as their lifestyles change. Nevertheless, meals are an important part of family life in which families experience belonging and continue to pass on culture and traditions to future generations.

Food and Culture

People also connect to their cultural or ethnic group through similar food patterns. Immigrants often use food as a means of retaining their cultural identity. People from different cultural backgrounds eat different foods. The ingredients, methods of preparation, preservation techniques, and types of food eaten at different meals vary among cultures. The areas in which families live—and where their ancestors originated—influence food likes and dislikes. These food preferences result in patterns of food choices within a cultural or regional group.

Food items themselves have meaning attached to them. In many Western countries a box of chocolates would be viewed as an appropriate gift. The recipient of the gift would react differently to a gift of cabbage or carrots than to chocolate. In other countries chocolates might be a less appropriate gift.

Nations or countries are frequently associated with certain foods. For example, many people associate Italy with pizza and pasta. Yet Italians eat many other foods, and types of pasta dishes vary throughout Italy. Methods of preparation and types of food vary by regions of a nation. Some families in the United States prefer to eat "meat and potatoes," but "meat and potatoes" are not eaten on a regular basis, nor even preferred, by many in the United States and would not be labeled a national cuisine. Grits, a coarsely ground corn that is boiled, is eaten by families in the southern United States. A package of grits is only available in the largest supermarkets in the upper Midwest and would have been difficult to find even in large Midwestern supermarkets twenty years ago.

Regional food habits do exist, but they also change over time. As people immigrate, food practices and preferences are imported and exported. Families move to other locations, bringing their food preferences with them. They may use their old recipes with new ingredients, or experiment with new recipes, incorporating ingredients to match their own tastes. In addition, food itself is imported from other countries. Approximately 80 percent of Samoa's food requirements are imported from the United States, New Zealand, or Australia (Shovic 1994). Because people and food are mobile, attempts to characterize a country or people by what they eat are often inaccurate or tend to lump people into stereotypical groups.

Nevertheless, what is considered edible or even a delicacy in some parts of the world might be considered inedible in other parts. Although food is often selected with some attention to physical need, the values or beliefs a society attaches to potential food items define what families within a cultural group will eat. For example, both plant and animal sources may contribute to meeting nutritional requirements for protein; soybeans, beef, horsemeat, and dog meat are all adequate protein sources. Yet, due to the symbolism attached to these protein sources, they are not equally available in all societies. Moreover, even when the foods perceived to be undesirable are available, they are not likely to be eaten by people who have a strong emotional reaction against the potential food item.

Some food beliefs and practices are due to religious beliefs. Around the world, Muslims fast during Ramadan, believed to be the month during which the Qur'an, the Islamic holy book, was given from God to the Prophet Muhammad. During this month, Muslims fast during daylight hours, eating and drinking before dawn and after sunset. Orthodox Jews and some conservative Jews follow dietary laws, popularly referred to as a *kosher* diet, discussed in Jewish scripture. The dietary laws, which describe the use and preparation of animal foods, are followed for purposes of spiritual health. Many followers of Buddhism, Hinduism, and Jainism are vegetarians, in part, because of a doctrine of noninjury or nonviolence. Abstinence from eating meat in these traditions stems from the desire to avoid harming other living creatures. Despite religious food prescriptions, dietary practices vary widely even among those who practice the same faith. Such variations may be due to branches or denominations of a religious group, national variations, and individuals' or families' own degree of orthodoxy or religious adherence.

In addition to impacting food choices, culture also plays a role in food-related etiquette. People in Western societies may refer to food-related etiquette as *table manners,* a phrase that illustrates the cultural expectation of eating food or meals at a table. Some people eat with forks and spoons; more people use fingers or chopsticks. However, utensil choice is much more complicated than choosing chopsticks, fingers, or flatware. Among some groups who primarily eat food with their fingers, diners use only the right hand to eat. Some people use only three fingers of the right hand. Among other groups, use of both hands is acceptable. In some countries, licking the fingers is polite; in others, licking the fingers is considered impolite (and done only when a person thinks no one else is watching). Rules regarding polite eating may increase in formal settings. At some formal dinners, a person might be expected to choose the "right" fork from among two or three choices to match the food being eaten at a certain point in the meal.

The amount people eat and leave uneaten also varies from group to group. Some people from Middle Eastern and Southeast Asian countries might leave a little bit of food on their plates in order to indicate that their hunger has been satisfied (Kittler 2001). Cooks from other locations might be offended if food is left on the plate, indicating that the guest may have disliked the food. Similarly, a clean plate might signify either satisfaction with the meal or desire for more food.

Even the role of conversation during mealtime varies from place to place. Many families believe that mealtime is a good time to converse and to "catch up" on the lives of family and friends. Among other families, conversation during a meal is acceptable, but the topics of conversation are limited. In some Southeast Asian countries it is considered polite to limit conversation during a meal (Kittler 2001).

Food plays an important role in the lives of families in most cultures. However, the degree of importance varies from culture to culture. For example, in American Samoa most family activities and ceremonies center on eating. A host family demonstrates its prosperity or societal rank by providing large quantities of food (Shovic 1994). Among other families in other locations, activities and celebrations include food, but food is not necessarily the center of the event.

Food traditions vary widely throughout the world. Even among people who share similar cultural backgrounds and some of the same food habits, eating patterns are not identical. Further, families vary from their own daily routines on holidays, when traveling, or when guests are present. Men eat differently from women. People of different age groups eat differently. However, in most parts of the world, food is associated with hospitality and expression of friendship. Therefore, sensitivity to food rules and customs is important in building and strengthening cross-cultural relationships.

Food Security
Around the world and across ethnic groups, food security greatly influences the meanings, values, and benefits a family associates with food. A family who has food security is able to obtain enough food to avoid hunger. As income rises, a smaller percent of the income is used for food. Families with lower incomes spend a higher proportion of their incomes on food. Throughout the world, more money is spent on food than on other categories of activities. Sometimes families experience food insecurity; for those families, the primary role of food becomes satisfying hunger.

Hunger has negative consequences for children, including anemia, developmental and behavioral problems, and learning difficulties. Undernourished pregnant women are more likely to have low-birthweight infants who are more likely to experience health and behavior problems. Food insecurity also causes anxiety for parents and children.

Because food is connected with so many social benefits, families who face long-term food insecurity are likely to experience more than physical suffering. Social relationships may be impaired; verbal abilities developed through family mealtime interactions might be less developed; the opportunities to negotiate and compromise food choices may be fewer. Families who are not able to be hospitable may lose social status. Therefore, the impact of food insecurity has far-reaching social, emotional, and developmental consequences for families and children.

Food is part of everyone's life. It affects the structure of family schedules and enhances relationships among family members and between families. Food may be a mark of cultural and religious identity. Culture shapes families' food attitudes and behaviors, and families' needs, beliefs, and behaviors impact culture. Because food is an essential part of families' physical and social lives, examining its role in families helps us to understand families in the context of their cultures.

See also: COMMUNICATION: FAMILY RELATIONSHIPS; DIVISION OF LABOR; EATING DISORDERS; FAILURE TO THRIVE; FAMILY FOLKLORE; HOME; HOUSEWORK; JUDAISM; RELIGION; RESOURCE MANAGEMENT

Bibliography

Birch, L. L. (1996). "Children's Food Acceptance Patterns." *Nutrition Today* 31(6):234-40.

Bossard, J. H. S. (1943). "Family Table Talk: An Area for Sociological Study." *American Sociological Review* 8:295–301.

Jansson, S. (1995). "Food Practices and Division of Domestic Labor: A Comparison between British and Swedish Households." *Sociological Review* 43:462–77.

Kaplan, E. B. (2000). "Using Food as a Metaphor for Care." *Journal of Contemporary Ethnography* 29:474–509.

Kemmer, D.; Anderson, A. S.; and Marshall, D. W. (1998). "Living Together and Eating Together: Changes in Food Choice and Eating Habits during the Transition from Single to Married/Cohabiting." *Sociological Review* 46:48–72.

Kittler, P. G., and Sucher, K. P. (2001). *Food and Culture,* 3rd edition. Belmont, CA: Wadsworth.

Lupton, D. (2000). "'Where's Me Dinner?': Food Preparation Arrangements in Rural Australian Families." *Journal of Sociology* 36(2):172.

Lupton, D. (1994). "Food, Memory and Meaning: The Symbolic and Social Nature of Food Events." *Sociological Review* 42:664–85.

Quandt, S. A.; Vitolins, M. Z.; DeWalt, K. M.; and Roos, G. M. (1997). "Meal Patterns of Older Adults in Rural Communities: Life Course Analysis and Implications for Undernutrition." *Journal of Applied Gerontology* 16(2):152-71.

Shovic, A. C. (1994). "Development of a Samoan Nutrition Exchange List Using Culturally Accepted Foods." *Journal of the American Dietetic Association* 94(5):541-43.

Valentine, G. (1999). "Eating In: Home, Consumption and Identity." *Sociological Review* 47:491–524.

Yasmeen, G. (2000). "Not 'From Scratch': Thai Food Systems and 'Public Eating.'" *Journal of Intercultural Studies* 21(3):341-52.

Other Resource

American Dietetic Association. (2000). "Making the Most of Family Mealtime." Available from http://www.eatright.org/nfs/nfs0900.html.

RENEE A. OSCARSON

FORGIVENESS

Long a topic of discussion and inquiry among theologians and philosophers, forgiveness has attracted the serious attention of scholars within counseling, family studies, and psychology as well. Those interested in understanding this concept, however, will find that there is nearly as much disagreement as agreement among experts about how best to define forgiveness. Numerous definitions of forgiveness exist, and considerable debate continues concerning key components of these definitions.

Despite this debate, most definitions of forgiveness share three elements. First, most describe forgiveness as an active, effortful, and typically difficult process (Enright and Fitzgibbons 2000). Second, most require that the injured party renounce the right to take revenge or exact retribution on the offender (Pingleton 1989). Third, most assume that forgiveness involves cessation, or at least considerable reduction, in negative feeling toward the offending party (North 1998). In an apt summary of these points of agreement, James N. Sells and Terry D. Hargrave (1998, p. 22) describe forgiveness as "the antithesis of the individual's natural and predictable response to violation and victimization."

Apart from the relative consensus on these three basic elements of forgiveness, theorists and scholars disagree on various salient issues concerning what forgiveness involves. For example, although some scholars believe that the reduction of negative feeling toward the offender is sufficient for forgiveness, others (Enright and Fitzgibbons 2000) argue that true forgiveness requires that the injured party endeavor to replace negative feelings with such positive feelings as compassion and respect. Scholars also vary considerably in the extent to which they believe that reconciliation is an integral part of the forgiveness process. Some authors argue that forgiveness without reconciliation is not true forgiveness at all (Hargrave 1994); others contend that reconciliation, although perhaps a desirable goal in many cases, is neither a necessary condition of true forgiveness nor, in every case, advisable (Enright and Fitzgibbons 2000).

Related to the debate concerning reconciliation and its part in forgiving are issues surrounding the role of the offender in the forgiveness process. Those who view reconciliation as an issue separate from forgiveness argue that the offender need not even be aware that the injured party is considering a move toward forgiving (Freedman 1998). Regardless of their perspective on reconciliation, however, most scholars believe that the forgiveness process is facilitated when offenders acknowledge their wrongdoing, express remorse, and are willing to change their behaviors (Enright, Freedman, and Rique 1998). At their roots, these disparate views regarding the importance of reconciliation and the role of the offender may derive from more fundamental disagreements about whether forgiveness is primarily for the benefit of the injured party (Gustafson-Affinito 1999) or the offender (Enright and Fitzgibbons 2000; North 1998; Gordon and Baucom 1999).

Arguments For and Against Forgiving

One interesting theoretical perspective on forgiveness likens forgiving to other pro-social acts such as empathy-motivated helping, accommodation (the process by which individuals choose to inhibit destructive responses to a relationship partner's breach of good conduct and substitute instead constructive responses), and willingness to sacrifice (McCullough 2000). Each of these pro-social behaviors shares the possibility that acting in ways that are beneficial to the other—or the relationship with the other—may come at a personal cost to the individual. From an evolutionary perspective, Michael C. Luebbert (1999) suggests that forgiveness is a pro-social adaptation passed on from generation to generation because of its intrinsic survival value. This view, together with literature that suggests that forgiving may benefit the forgiver in various ways, highlight the possibility that forgiving may be good for both the individual and the larger social group. For example, it can help to restore or maintain supportive caring relationships, which are important for good physical and mental health, as well as help to reduce potentially debilitating emotions such as hostility, bitterness, and resentment, thereby ameliorating their negative effects on health and well-being (see McCullough 2000, for a critical review of the relevant literature).

At the same time, opposing viewpoints emphasize the possibility that serious negative consequences may be associated with a decision to forgive (see Enright and Fitzgibbons 2000 for a review). For example, some authors (Bass and Davis 1994) believe that forgiving gives the offender license to continue the hurtful behavior in which he or she has engaged and, furthermore, that it makes the injured party appear weak, maintaining a power differential that favors the offender over the victim. This sentiment that forgiving keeps the injured party in a subjugated position relative to the offender is echoed by the philosopher Nietzsche (1887) in his claim that forgiveness is a strategy employed by weaklings whose only recourse against injustice is forgiving.

Proponents of forgiveness (Sells and Hargrave 1998) counter this position by arguing that critics who depict forgiveness as detrimental to the individual often base their thinking on underdeveloped concepts of what forgiveness entails—for example, models of forgiveness that confuse forgiving with condoning or excusing the actions of the offender. In Sells and Hargrave's view, such underdeveloped conceptualizations of forgiveness may indeed jeopardize the well being of individuals who have been injured by another's actions. In particular, they argue that mental health professionals who espouse such flawed views of forgiveness may fail to offer their clients a valuable process by which they could overcome the significant and enduring negative effects of the harm they suffered.

At the same time, such criticisms identify the need to distinguish between true or authentic forgiveness and artificial or false forms of forgiveness that either maintain the offender's dominance over the injured party and facilitate continued victimization (Sells and Hargrave 1998) or are used by the injured party as a means of gaining moral superiority over the offender by using forgiveness to induce feelings of guilt and shame. In the first case, such pseudoforgiveness effectively denies the impact of the offender's actions on the injured party and their relationship. In the second case, forgiving is essentially a way of getting even with the offender, an act of condescension rather than of release (Gustafson-Affinito 1999).

Forgiveness as an Intervention in Family/Marital Relationships

Some theorists and practitioners have argued that forgiveness can be used as an effective means of resolving marital and family conflict and promoting healing of the pain associated with the hurtful actions of close family members (Enright and Fitzgibbons 2000; McCullough and Worthington 1994). Some, in fact, have argued that forgiveness is absolutely essential to family and marital relationships because, even when reconciliation may be inadvisable, forgiving enables the hurt individual to move on with his or her life free of the disabling effects of the injury or betrayal (Coleman 1998). There have been several efforts to document specific approaches to conducting forgiveness interventions with spouses and family members (Coleman 1998; DiBlasio 1998; Gordon and Baucom 1999; Safer 1999).

Various unique issues emerge when transgressions occur in the context of extended relationships with kin. For example, sometimes family members may pressure an individual to forgive before he or she is ready or able to consider the possibility or will expect forgiveness to occur within a shorter timeframe than is reasonable. In contrast, family members may sometimes prefer to sweep transgressions under the rug, so to speak, because they would rather not deal with the broader implications of or the fallout from the harm that has been caused. In other cases, family members may choose sides, supporting the offender and perhaps blaming the injured party. Sometimes they may actively discourage forgiving (e.g., in situations involving acts of infidelity, in the case of bitter divorces).

The therapist may often encounter additional challenges when delivering the intervention as part of family as opposed to individual therapy (see Worthington, 1998, for a more detailed discussion). For example, within a family context, transgressions seldom exist as isolated events, but instead as part of chains of events that stretch far back in time and in which the roles of offender and injured party may have been exchanged repeatedly (i.e., often individuals will have both suffered and caused harm themselves). If the offender or other family members are present during therapy, it is unlikely that this point will go unnoticed. In addition, both the offender and the injured party may have their own agendas (as may other family members attending the sessions), some of which may conflict with the

therapist's goal of promoting authentic forgiveness. For example, research by Robert D. Enright and Richard P. Fitzgibbons (2000) has demonstrated that people vary in their developmental understanding of forgiveness. If the offender and injured party differ in their characteristic way of thinking about forgiveness (e.g., differing in their views regarding whether or not the offender must make restitution as a prerequisite to being forgiven), it will be more difficult to establish the common ground during therapy needed to facilitate true forgiving.

Several variables have been identified as potentially influential in determining whether or not an individual will forgive. First, forgiveness is generally facilitated if the injured party experiences—or can be brought to experience—empathy for the offender (McCullough, Worthington, and Rachal 1997). Accordingly, forgiveness interventions typically involve efforts to promote cognitive *reframing* of the hurtful event as a means of separating the offender from his or her hurtful actions (i.e., distinguishing the person from his or her behavior) and thus inducing in the injured party a measure of empathy for the wrongdoer. Forgiving also requires a certain degree of humility on the part of the person who has been harmed (Cunningham 1985; Worthington 1998). Wounded individuals must recognize—or come to recognize—that it is not fair to expect mercy from others in situations when they have done wrong without also extending mercy to those who have hurt them. Therapists will often work with individuals to help them recognize their own fallibility, to acknowledge that they too have needed forgiveness on occasion, and thus to assist them in coming to terms with the paradox that, at some level, being forgiven requires being willing to forgive. Finally, commitment to the forgiveness process is important because it helps to reify the decision to forgive in the forgiver's mind and contributes to the initiation and maintenance of behaviors and changes in attitude that promote continued efforts at forgiving (Worthington 1998). Forgiveness interventions often include real or symbolic gestures that signify in an overt and often public fashion the injured party's (and perhaps the offender's) dedication to the forgiving process.

Unfortunately, there have been relatively few attempts to test the efficacy of forgiveness interventions, whether designed specifically for application within families and marital relationships or for a broader client base. The results of those studies (DiBlasio 1998; Enright and Fitzgibbons 2000; McCullough and Worthington 1995; Worthington 1998) that have sought to empirically validate such interventions have, however, generally been promising. Obviously, there is an urgent need for further research directed toward systematic assessment of the effectiveness of existing forgiveness therapies and the theoretical frameworks upon which they are based.

It is also important to note substantial cultural and religious variation in people's definitions of forgiveness, their ideas concerning whether, when, and under what circumstances it is appropriate; the importance they ascribe to forgiving; and the processes by which forgiving is achieved (for a detailed discussion, see Augsberger 1992). Scientists and practitioners need to be alert to the implications of this variation in conducting their work. Diverse cultural or religious perspectives on forgiveness preclude broad application of forgiveness interventions grounded in one cultural or religious viewpoint. They also proscribe drawing general conclusions from research on forgiveness that is based largely on samples of North American, Judeo-Christian participants.

See also: CONFLICT: COUPLE RELATIONSHIPS; CONFLICT: FAMILY RELATIONSHIPS; CONFLICT: PARENT-CHILD RELATIONSHIPS; DISCIPLINE; THERAPY: COUPLE RELATIONSHIPS; THERAPY: FAMILY RELATIONSHIPS

Bibliography

Augsberger, D. W. (1992). "Reconciliation: The Many Faces of Forgiveness." In *Conflict Mediation Across Cultures: Pathways and Patterns*. Louisville, KY: Westminster/John Knox Press.

Bass, E., and Davis, L. (1994). *The Courage to Heal*. New York: Harper Perennial.

Coleman, P. W. (1998). "The Process of Forgiveness in Marriage and the Family." In *Exploring Forgiveness*, ed. R. D. Enright and J. North. Madison, WI: The University of Wisconsin Press.

Cunningham, B. B. (1985). "The Will to Forgive: A Pastoral Theological View of Forgiving." *The Journal of Pastoral Care* 39:141–149.

DiBlasio, F. A. (1998). "The Use of a Decision-based Forgiveness Intervention Within Intergenerational Family Therapy." *Journal of Family Therapy* 20:77–94.

Enright, R. D., and Fitzgibbons, R. P. (2000). *Helping Clients Forgive: An Empirical Guide for Resolving Anger and Restoring Hope*. Washington, DC: APA.

Enright, R. D., Freedman, S., and Rique, J. (1998). "The Psychology of Interpersonal Forgiveness." In *Exploring Forgiveness*, ed. R. D. Enright and J. North. Madison, WI: The University of Wisconsin Press.

Freedman, S. (1998). "Forgiveness and Reconciliation: The Importance of Understanding How They Differ." *Counseling and Values* 42:200–216.

Gordon, K. C., and Baucom, D. H. (1999). "A Multitheoretical Intervention for Promoting Recovery from Extramarital Affairs." *Clinical Psychology-Science and Practice* 6:382–399.

Gustafson-Affinito, M. (1999). *When To Forgive: A Healing Guide*. Oakland, CA: New Harbinger Publications.

Hargrave, T. D. (1994). *Families and Forgiveness: Healing Wounds in the Intergenerational Family*. New York, NY: Brunner-Mazel.

Luebbert, M. C. (1999). "The Survival Value of Forgiveness." In *Evolution of the Psyche*, ed. D. H. Rosen and M. C. Luebbert. London: Praeger.

McCullough, M. E. (2000). "Forgiveness as Human Strength: Theory, Measurement, and Links to Well-being." *Journal of Social and Clinical Psychology* 19:43–55.

McCullough, M. E., and Worthington, E. L. (1994). "Encouraging Clients to Forgive People Who Have Hurt Them: Review, Critique, and Research Prospectus." *Journal of Psychology and Theology* 22:3–20.

McCullough, M. E., and Worthington, E. L. (1995). "Promoting Forgiveness: A Comparison of Two Brief Psychoeducational Group Interventions with a Waiting-list Control." *Counseling and Values* 40:55–68.

McCullough, M. E.; and Worthington, E. L.; and Rachal, K. C. (1997). "Interpersonal Forgiving in Close Relationships" *Journal of Personality and Social Psychology* 73:321–336.

Nietzsche, F. W. (1887). *On the Geneology of Morals*, trans. W. Kaufman. New York: Vintage Books.

North, J. (1998). "The 'Ideal' of Forgiveness: A Philosopher's Exploration." In *Exploring Forgiveness*, ed. R. D. Enright and J. North. Madison, WI: The University of Wisconsin Press.

Pingleton, J. P. (1989). "The Role and Function of Forgiveness in the Psychotherapeutic Process." *Journal of Psychology and Theology* 17:27–35.

Safer, J. (1999). *Forgiving and Not Forgiving: A New Approach to Resolving Intimate Betrayal*. New York: Avon Books.

Sells, J. N., and Hargrave, T. D. (1998). "Forgiveness: A Review of the Theoretical and Empirical Literature." *Journal of Family Therapy* 20:21–36.

Worthington, E. L. (1998). "An Empathy-Humility-Commitment Model of Forgiveness Applied within Family Dyads." *Journal of Family Therapy* 20:59–76.

SUSAN D. BOON
STACEY L. NAIRN

FOSTER PARENTING

Foster parenting is generally defined as caring for children who cannot remain in their birth homes because their parents are either absent or incapacitated. Throughout history, families and societies have made arrangements for children who were orphaned, abandoned, separated from family by war or epidemic, and, since the mid-nineteenth century, mistreated to the extent that they were unsafe with their parents.

History

It has been the custom of many societies and times for the extended family, or designated relationship kin such as godparents or the child's mother's brothers, to take in orphaned children. In the Old Testament the law requiring a man to marry his brother's widow served to keep children in the home of kin. The story of Moses, abandoned and subsequently found and fostered by the daughter of Pharaoh, is a familiar one, the prototype of many hero stories in which a significant individual was raised by a nonrelative. Medieval Europe made use of monasteries and convents to care for children placed there by their families as a career choice, as a source of education for children of upper-class families, and also to care for a certain number of orphans who had no provision for their upkeep. Following the Reformation, when religious communities were scattered, laws such as the Poor Laws of 1501 in England required communities to make provision for orphans and other destitute persons. Children old enough to be apprenticed or placed to learn a trade (with a farmer, blacksmith, or in domestic service for a girl, for example) were usually dealt with in that manner; younger children or those with a handicap were housed at the Poor Farm or other facility, with no special arrangements made for their education or supervision.

In the early years of the United States, as in Europe and England, this responsibility for a town or county to provide for orphans without resources generally was adhered to and developed in local law. Families, of course, continued to care for their young relatives whose parents were dead or incapacitated, but those without family resources were considered the responsibility of the local authorities, as localities became settled and government developed. Municipalities continued to place older children in apprenticeships, in domestic work, or with families who needed workers on the farm.

During the nineteenth century, a movement to institutionalize and centralize the care of dependent children led to the development of orphanages. Other special populations were also institutionalized at this period—for example, those with mental handicaps and prisoners. Institutions for the hearing- and sight-impaired also developed, as a more efficient and humane way of dealing with this population, incorporating some form of training or education. Following the Civil War, the United States looked to other ways to care for children, as institutionalization proved to be no protection against mishandling and poor outcomes. As mentioned above, efforts to place children in apprenticeships, teaching them a trade, were an approved solution offered by governmental bodies in providing for orphaned or unsupervised children. As industrialization took over the eastern part of the United States, with its more highly trained workforce, there were fewer agricultural and untrained labor jobs available, leading to a concern that children who grew up in orphanages would turn to crime. Another fear at this point was the belief that children of immigrants, particularly from southern and eastern Europe, were somehow by their heritage less likely to have an appropriate work ethic, high personal standards of moral behavior, and resistance to various forms of unlawful life, such as robbery, alcohol use, and prostitution. Charles Loring Brace, a young minister in New York City, appalled by the living conditions of children in the tenements, formed the Children's Aid Society in 1853 to begin modern foster care. He made various efforts to help children in the urban environment—shelters, training programs, and savings banks. However, he felt strongly that children removed from the unsanitary and morally compromised environment of city life to rural life in the West would have a better chance to grow up physically and mentally healthy, with a future in that part of the country where agriculture, construction, and all the other activities of the westward movement would provide a decent and law-abiding living. Brace's *Orphan Trains* (and others following the Children's Aid Society model, which ran until 1929) transported thousands of children to the Midwest and West. His efforts placed children in family homes as the ideal placement for them and were the beginning of foster care as it is now understood.

Even after the advantages of placement in family homes were generally accepted, it was not until the 1980s that child psychology and developmental information began to change the philosophy behind foster homes to consider needs of children beyond their physical care, health, and housing. In 1980 the federal government passed the Adoption Assistance and Child Welfare Act, which spoke to these negative issues of the casual moving of children from home to home and the lack of effort made to prevent the initial removal from the birth family. Although children's physical and medical needs were met, their education provided, and their safety from neglect and abuse assured, they tended to drift in foster care, with few efforts to reunite them with their birth family or initiate efforts towards remediation of the conditions that caused their removal. The uncertainty of being permanently a foster child, having no official determination of length of stay, and no connection with his or her birth family began to be seen as emotionally troubling as the traumatic occurrence that determined the child's entrance into foster care. The term *permanency planning* describes these initiatives to coordinate court efforts, set up rehabilitation services for parents who had lost care of their children, and to review children's situations within the agency in a timely manner to determine whether the services met the needs of both parents and children and helped them reunite if possible. Reunification became the primary permanency planning goal for a child, with relative placement or timely adoption being a secondary goal to give a child a permanent home.

With the passage of the Adoption and Safe Families Act in 1997, efforts to place children with family members, either short term or long term,

spoke to the growing understanding of the need for identification with one's own family. Efforts to encourage extended or fictive family to care for children brought a new term, *kinship care,* to the fore. From the moment that removal from the birth parent is considered, child welfare workers begin the search for individuals related to the child by blood, by marriage, or by family custom (*fictive kin*), who might be a resource for the child. The rationale for kinship placement is that it maintains the connection with the child's extended family and its history and culture, encourages possible ease and naturalness of contact with birth parents, and continues the child's care with as little upset or change as possible. Kinship care also employs the oldest solution for children who cannot be cared for by birth parents—placement with family members. In many cultures the extended family has always had this responsibility, and Americans of Hispanic, Native American, and African American background see kinship care as very much in their cultural tradition.

The Adoption and Safe Families Act also mandated a shortened time in care for children, by setting a calendar for the court to make a decision about the permanent placement of a child—reunification with the parent from whom they were removed, permanent placement with a family member, or termination of parental rights and adoption—by one year from the day a child was removed from his birth home or primary caretaker. Services to facilitate reunification were to be extended very promptly to the birth parents to help changes occur, ensuring that the child could safely be returned to the parental home. And finally, reviews were to take place in a timely manner so that cooperation with the plan of service could be evaluated, and every possible avenue of assistance to the family might be effected.

Modern Trends

At the end of September 1998, there were 568,000 children in foster care in the United States. Of this number, 26 percent were in the homes of relatives, and 48 percent were in family foster homes. (The remainder of children in substitute care were in group and treatment homes, preadoptive placements, and other arrangements, including institutions for children with mental or physical disabilities.) By the end of the reporting period in 1990,

405,743 were in care (Foster Care Statistics, see U.S. Department of Health and Human Services).

However, the same database reflects another trend; children entering substitute care and those leaving care are older, indicating children whose emotional, educational, and therapeutic needs are more serious than the younger children entering care previously. The prevalence of substance abuse is bringing children into substitute care who may have some medical or learning problems from their own drug-positive status at birth or who, being older, have experienced poor supervision, neglect, or abuse for a longer time. Many kinship caregivers are, formally and informally, caring for the children of relatives caught up in the drug world. It is also true that whether or not substance abuse is a factor contributing to families being reported for child abuse or neglect, relatives may refuse to care for children whose behavior problems are so severe that the extended family has already taxed its resources to care for the child before child protective workers intervened. Thus, children entering substitute care to be placed in nonrelative homes are children whose behavior may have already deteriorated to the point that relatives and family friends feel unable to help.

Foster parents not only provide safety, physical care, and access to medical and educational services, but they also remediate the deficits that brought children into out-of-home care. Many people would first think of remediation of nutritional and care deficits, which many neglected children certainly have experienced. Medical check ups, continued monitoring of a chronic condition, and dental care are all immediate needs of children placed in foster homes. Educational needs met in foster care may include regular school attendance, referral of a child for special evaluation for learning or cognitive problems, discovery of an untreated sight or hearing problem, and interaction with the school system to establish and monitor the special education status of a child with learning, behavioral, or emotional problems. In addition, foster parents must work on neglected hygiene, age-appropriate behavior and social interactions, and modeling safe interactions to children who have been sexually abused. Foster parents, even those experienced in childcare through raising their own children or other family members, may encounter situations far outside their expectations of how children are treated. Thus, there

are initial training programs for persons who wish to foster or adopt children, and continuing education in special problems of the individual children in a foster home. States and private agencies that train and certify foster and adoptive parents have extensive curricula and also stringent requirements for those who would care for children. Background checks are done to ensure the prospective parent(s) have an appropriate legal status, with no conviction of crimes against persons. Health standards include safe homes and water supplies, tuberculosis tests for the household, and checks for firearms, medications, and other hazards.

Some of the characteristics seen in successful foster parents are willingness to learn, ability to request and accept help, warmth, acceptance of children and their behavior, a high level of tolerance of frustration, excellent communication skills, good physical and emotional health, and a sense of humor (Jordan and Rodway 1984). Not only must they provide safety and nurturing for children who have been harmed by their previous situations, but they are also part of the team involved in working with the birth parents to reunite the family. Their foster child's own parents may be resentful of the child's attachment to his foster parents and are often deficient in parenting skills and the ability to perceive and act in their child's best interest. For example, foster children often return from parental visits with sadness, resentment, mixed messages ("My real Mom says I don't have to do what you say!"), and emotional instability to the extent that children may experience physical and emotional regression, such as bedwetting, whining, or clinging behavior. Foster parents must then help the child return to his former equilibrium. If parental rights have been terminated, the foster parents are important workers on the team to ready the child for adoption.

Permanency planning also means keeping children, while out of their birth homes, in the least restrictive environment. A family home is indeed the least restrictive placement, with group homes, residential treatment facilities, and hospital settings, both medical and mental health, more restrictive placements. In order to keep children's out-of-home placements as close to family settings as possible, many foster families have obtained specialized training to care for children with unusual physical and emotional needs. Children with substantial physical and mental disabilities and

Foster parents Judith and Phillip Porzel spend time with their adoptive and foster children. Becoming a foster parent in the United States often requires extensive background checks, interviews, training programs, and certification. STEPHANIE MAZE/CORBIS

children with emotional disabilities respond well to family foster homes, where the parents are able to manage their increased needs for physical and medical care—such as a child in a wheelchair or one who requires tube feeding—or therapy sessions, following a behavioral modification regime, or dealing with sexual acting out as examples of increased emotional needs.

Cultural and International Implications

Most of the industrialized nations of the world have formalized arrangements for foster care, although the reasons for implementing out-of-home care may vary widely. Many nations, particularly in war-torn areas, in contrast to the United States, make use of institutionalized care in orphanages, as the most cost-efficient response to

many children suddenly needing care. As noted above, kinship care and the use of a wider definition of family (including tribal connections, godparents, and other fictive kin) is common in other cultures. The widespread acceptance of kinship care for African Americans has its roots in the customs coming from Africa with slaves, honed during slavery when parents and children might be arbitrarily separated, and other relatives would assume responsibility if possible. New Zealand initiatives for the care of Maori children have evolved to encompass the separate constructs of extended family and tribe in planning for placement in a child's best interest. In Oceania relatives have a claim to the care of children; in Hawaii grandparents have a stronger traditional claim than parents to raising children, even with parents available and able to care for their children (Hegar and Scannapieco

1999). Thus, other societies have recognized and adopted into their culture mechanisms for keeping children within the family, societal group, or accepted identity subgroup if at all possible.

The question of caring for children outside their parental homes continues, especially in areas where war and migration during civil unrest or drought have again created the problem. International adoption has been one response to situations in these troubled parts of the world in the twenty-first century. Americans and others have adopted children from Bosnia, Ukraine, Russia, and other nations. A response to the Chinese policy of encouraging one-child families, coupled with traditional high value of a son, has led to international adoption of abandoned female children. Regulation and overseeing of homes where these children are fostered and then adopted is of interest to contemporary child welfare.

The AIDS/HIV epidemic may call for a new kind of fostering in countries where the disease is decimating the population. In many areas of Africa, traditional extended family ties have provided for the care of children orphaned by the virus. However, the prevalence of the disease, as it moves to younger and younger age groups, may overwhelm the traditional systems already in place; aging relatives may not be able to care for the many children whose parents are dying. With infection of women in their earlier childbearing years, more infants will likely be born HIV-positive themselves and be orphaned, with no relatives available to provide the traditional care. The solutions to these problems are daunting for nations already overburdened with the expenses of emerging into the world economy as well as the costs of public health initiatives. These dire developing emergencies in the care of children may well engender new initiatives and supranational cooperation in the best interest of coming generations.

See also: FICTIVE KINSHIP; GAY PARENTS; LESBIAN PARENTS; ORPHANS

Bibliography

Encyclopedia of Social Work. (1995). 19th edition. Washington: National Association of Social Workers Press.

Fahlberg, V. I. (1991). *A Child's Journey through Placement.* Indianapolis: Perspectives Press.

Hegar, R. L., and Scannapieco, M., eds. (1999). *Kinship Foster Care: Policy, Practice, and Research.* New York: Oxford University Press.

Jordan, A., and Rodway, M. R. (1984). "Correlates of Effective Foster Parenting." *Social Work Research and Abstracts* 20:27–31

Kluger, M. P.; Alexander, G.; and Curtis, P. A., eds. (2000). *What Works in Child Welfare.* Washington: CWLA Press.

Pecora, P. J.; Whittaker, J. K.; Maluccio, A. N.; and Barth, R. (2000). *The Child Welfare Challenge: Policy, Practice, Research.* 2nd edition. Hawthorne, NY: Aldine.

Trattner, W. I. (1999). *From Poor Law to Welfare State: A History of Social Welfare in America,* 6th edition. New York: The Free Press.

Other Resources

Jane Addams School of Social Work, University of Chicago. *The Kinship Care Practice Project.* Available from http://www.uic.edu/jaddams/college/kincare.

U.S. Department of Health and Human Services. *National Clearinghouse on Child Abuse and Neglect Information* (2000). Available from http://calib.com/nccanch.

Washington State. Fosterparentscope Training. Available from http://www.dshs.wa.gov/fosterparents/training/index.htm.

ELISABETH KENNY

FRANCE

In France, during the 1960s and 1970s, the family was thought of in terms of its *crisis, decline,* or *rupture.* Some even spoke of its death. The rapid changes brought on by the strong economic, social, and cultural movements of the era explain this phenomenon. Yet the family was ever-present and continued to play a major role in society, as numerous works of the time emphasized (Rémy 1967; Roussel and Bourguignon, 1976; Pitrou 1978). The French have never stopped considering the family an essentially valuable part of society, as shown in the retrospective analysis of about fifty surveys taken between 1968 and 1988 (Chalvon-Demersay 1989). In short, despite the different schools of thought, the French have been and still are attached to the family. This is not only true of adults. A survey taken among a representative sample of people between fifteen and twenty-four years of age (Gurrey and Subtil 1999) shows that more than eight out of ten (82%) consider the family "very important," coming before friendship (75%), work (61%), love (59%), studies (48%), school (39%), money (30%), and sexuality (29%). Yet it must be admitted that the family is no longer that of the 1950s.

Transformations of the Family in France

For more than a century, the marriage rate in France was relatively stable (at around 7.5%), until the beginning of the 1970s. Before that decade, the French believed in the importance of marriage, and nine out of ten people were married before the age of fifty.

In 1972, France recorded the largest number of marriages in its history. Then, to the surprise of the demographers and sociologists of the time—considering that the children of the baby boom were of traditional marriage age—the number of marriages rapidly declined starting in 1973: 395,000 in 1974, 355,000 in 1978, 312,000 in 1982 and 266,000 in 1986, resulting in a marriage rate of less than 5 percent. At first this decline was interpreted to show that people were simply delaying marriage due to the increase in the time spent on education, which seemed logical because the average age of those getting married had increased. This hypothesis was questioned, however, because several years later, the marriage rate did not increase. It was then understood that the younger generation was indeed less infatuated with marriage than their parents had been (Le Bras and Roussel 1982).

Consequently, the number of single people increased. These people were not to be confused with those who were single "despite themselves" (Sullerot 1984), those men, either farmers or farm hands, who were unable to get married due to the lack of perspectives inherent in their economic and social situations. These new single people were made up of urban men and women, of whom most were part of the working community and came from affluent social backgrounds. Culturally and economically privileged, many were more inclined to enjoy their freedom than to rush into marriage and assume the responsibility of a family. Because marriage was not seen as something to aim for, these people deliberately chose to remain single.

This upsurge in the number of single people contributed to an increase in the number of people living alone, which doubled between 1968 and 1990, going from three to six million. However, although living alone, some of them had loving and sexual relationships or found companionship to balance their lives, as in the case of some divorced single parents (Le Gall 1992). This was achieved through noncohabiting duos (one couple, two homes). In short, solitary living or, as J.-C. Kaufmann (1999) called it, "solo" life was not automatically synonymous with solitude because a significant number of single people had intimate, sexual relationships.

Although the new single people hardly find the idea of marriage attractive as an institution, they do not reject living together as couples. For the youth of the 1970s, this was often seen as a transition to marriage, a type of trial marriage that allowed for the least amount of social reprobation. Subsequently, living together gained popularity and was no longer limited to the younger generations. The number of unmarried cohabiting couples went from 1.5 million to almost 2.5 million people between 1990 and 1998. Predictably, the number of births out of wedlock also rose substantially. In 1997, four out of ten children were born to parents who were not married.

The act of getting married has ceased to be the act that establishes a couple in France; that role has been replaced by living together: In 1997, 90 percent of new couples started their life together in this way, and more than half of the women (53%) who give birth to their first child were not married.

Not only do the French marry less, but also, the marriages that do occur are more and more precarious. During the 1950s, the divorce rate was relatively stable and fairly low: one out of ten marriages ended in divorce. Then, in the first half of the 1960s, the divorce rate increased slightly and in 1972, the year when the marriage rate began to fall, it increased dramatically. By the end of the twentieth century, it was no longer one marriage out of ten that ended in a divorce, but one out of three. Evidently, the marriage bond has been weakened. It is nonetheless important to recall that the divorce rate stabilized in the middle of the 1980s. To acquire perspective on the instability of relationships, it is necessary to take into account, along with the increase in the number of families in which couples are not married, the precariousness of the unions of couples who live together, which is proportionately higher than among married couples (Toulemont 1996).

One of the consequences of this conjugal instability has been the increase in the number of single-parent families. Since 1982, divorce has replaced widowhood as the main cause of single-parent families. The increase in this type of family, though, has not been dramatic. Almost one family in ten with children was a single-parent family in 1962; the percentage in 1982 was only 10.2 percent and 13.2 percent in 1990 (INSEE 1994). D. Le Gall and C. Martin note: "The novelty of this phenomenon exists not so much in the increase in the number of single-parent families as in the different evolutions within the category of single-parent families" (1987, p. 20). If the increase in single-parent families is a problem, it is due to the high increase in the divorce rate, coupled with out-of-wedlock births, resulting in an increase of the percentage of single-parent families where only the mother is present. In 1990, 86.2 percent of single parents raising one or more children under the age of twenty-five were women, while 13.8 percent were men. Yet in a society where the family is mainly organized around the couple, having only one parent present can generate certain problems. These hardships differ depending on whether the parent is a man or a woman. Single mothers, more of whom head single-parent families than do men, have more difficulties than single fathers because of past economic inequalities between men and women, which have repercussions on the time period following the break-up of the couple (Lefaucheur 1992).

The instability of couples has increased the number of people who enter a second partnership. Most often, in second marriages or other relationships it is fathers with whom the children do not live on a day-to-day basis. I. Théry notes: "40 percent of children whose parents are separated have a stepmother who lives in a different house while 25 percent have a stepfather (with whom they live on a daily basis)" (1988). In other words, using the terms *daily step-parent* (*beau-parent au quotidien*) or *on-and-off step-parent* (*beau-parent par intermittence*) (Le Gall 1993), children of divorce have a higher probability of having an on-and-off step-mother than a daily stepfather (Le Gall 1996). This

explains why, although almost half of these children have at least one stepbrother or stepsister, only 22 percent live with them.

Finally, another major change that started in the first half of the 1960s is a decrease in the birth rate in France. The rate fell from an average of slightly less than three children per woman in the 1950s to 2.58 in 1968, 1.82 in 1978, and 1.8 in 1988. The decline seems to have stabilized since then and is at about 1.75 children per woman, up from the historic low of 1.65 in 1993 and 1994.

French society, then, has gone through many demographic changes. From the one family model of the 1950s, which was only statistically dominant from the 1920s to the 1960s, private living arrangements in France have become much more diverse. Along with life as a married couple, which has changed only slightly, single living and living together have become more established. At the same time, conjugal instability has increased the number of single-parent families, which itself favors the rapid development of reconstituted families.

Adding further to this list of changes is the increase in the number of families formed either through adoption (Fine 1998), medically assisted procreation using sperm donations (Delaisi and Verdier 1994), or families with same-sex parents (Gross 2000). All of these families, along with reconstituted families, have brought about the notion of *multirelatives* (*pluriparentalité*) (Le Gall and Bettahar 2001). This term is new, but the media began using it quickly. On August 4, 2000, on the front page of the newspaper, *Le Monde,* there was an article entitled "My Half-brother, My Half-sister, My Co-parents, Their Stepchildren and I," which ended with the following sentence: "Don't tell the kids that they are going to spend the vacation with 'the family,' but that they are going to go for a stroll with their multirelatives" (Robert-Diard 2000).

In short, the French family has undergone profound and rapid change, but it has also progressively found a new equilibrium.

The Contemporary Family: Less Statutory and More Relational

The increase of financial autonomy (particularly among women), reinforced social protection, widespread use and mastery of female contraception, and a more permissive atmosphere have all helped to promote people's desire to have more freedom within the family. The family of the 1950s was thus seen as constraining, rigid, and even an obstacle toward self-realization.

For young people in the twenty-first century, family and sexual matters are under less social control from the older relatives and have instead become private issues. Parents are not encouraged to interfere in their child's choice of partner. Feeling is seen as the only legitimate factor for forming a couple. L. Roussel wrote: "The institution [of the family] has stopped being a determinant reality due to the fact that it has not been internalized as a legitimate norm" (1980). The *relational family* implies that the bonds in this type of family are defined less by statute than they are by free consent. "[T]he form of private life that everyone chooses hardly needs any external legitimacy, any conformity to an institution or even any morality. It is structured above all on the mutual recognition and respect of the people living together" (de Singly 1996).

Relationships between men and women within the couple have become more equal. The type of strict authoritarian model has been replaced one in which autonomy and personal fulfillment are favored (Kellerhals et al. 1991). This model is more prominent in middle-class families; parents tend to be more rigid and coercive among the lower classes. Generations living together are less and less common, but living in separate houses does not necessarily exclude "solidarity from a distance." Indeed research on intergenerational solidarity (sometimes four generations, since life expectancy reached 74.6 years for men and 82.3 for women in 1997) unanimously underlines the vitality of family life (Attias-Donfut 1995; Segalen et al. 1998).

This evolution also has its darker side. When the married couple stays together solely because of feelings of love, conjugal differences can more easily lead to a break-up than was formerly the case. Some sociologists have thus spoken of contemporary divorce as "a 'normal' component of the modern marriage model" (Kellerhals et al. 1985). Along these same lines, in an article with the enlightening title "Guilty Love?" ("L'amour coupable?"), F. de Singly writes: "Divorce is an integral part of a marriage based on love" (1992). Yet it is known that, after a divorce, there is almost always a decrease in the standard of living for the person who has custody of the children (Martin 1997), particularly if

This French family sits in the Trocadero Gardens. The number of single-parent families in France has increased slightly since the early 1980s. More significantly, the main cause of single-parent families has changed from widowhood to divorce. CATHERINE KARNOW/CORBIS

this person is a woman, which is usually the case. Also, almost half of the children of divorced parents either no longer see their fathers or see them on a very irregular basis (Léridon et al. 1994). A separation may only slightly affect well-educated single mothers who work, but this is not the case for those women who do not work and who have limited cultural knowledge and academic training. By placing those who were already vulnerable before the separation in an even more precarious position, divorce tends to aggravate the existing social inequalities (Le Gall and Martin 1993).

What seems to be most worrisome is that the family has become little more than a network of emotions and feelings. One result of trying to move away from the collective rules that create and give meaning to the family, individuals may find themselves with a somewhat artificial freedom? According to Théry, "The specificity of the family group as an institution has been completely abandoned. Yet since the dawn of humanity, no society has ever reduced the family to a mere biological reality or a simple question of tastes—the family group is not a group like any other" (1996). What are the society's reference points when the collective framework becomes ephemeral, and the individual believes himself or herself capable of building a sense of self within the intersubjectivity of a group that tends to be a mere emotional network (Le Gall 1997).

Beyond all these changes that have affected the family institution is this evolution, which, for some, seems problematic at a time when the economic crisis makes people more vulnerable and when the conjugal bond is more fragile than before. Reconstituted families are a good illustration of this. If a stepparent, a supplementary social actor in the "family deal," finds it difficult to obtain his role or his place (Le Gall, Martin, 1997), could it not be due to the lack of societal help (Cherlin 1978)? Should this evolution, which satisfies the desire for freedom, continue, delicate problems will arise: "Individuals who must take care of everything themselves no longer have a statutory place which allows them the possibility to free themselves from the here and now of life in order to master their destiny. The ideal of self-government becomes dependence. Private life, when it accepts no reference other than itself, becomes a place of slavery" (Théry 1996). How is it possible to establish an unconditional bond from free mutual choice, since a bond based on choice is revocable by definition?

Conclusion

What seems to be troublesome in France, as in other Western countries, is the contradictory desire of individuals to make the family institution a place that simultaneously and uncompromisingly promotes a regulated status for each person (feeling of belonging, a guaranteed place) and, at the same time, self-fulfillment. Yet, for the French, the desire for more freedom does not seem to exclude the need for ties. As J.-H. Déchaux says, "Individualism does not negate the desire of belonging" (1998). This is why, although many have radically questioned the 1950s family, the overwhelming majority of French people still see the family as an important part of their lives. To get a sense of this

idea, it might be said that the French now want to be *Free Together*—this a paradoxical expression, also the title of the book that F. de Singly published in 2000, best summarizes the idea.

See also: GERMANY

Bibliography

Attias-Donfut, C., ed. (1995). *Les solidarités entre générations. Vieillesse, familles, etat.* Paris: Nathan.

Chalvon-Demersay, S. (1989). "Cette famille toujours indispensable," *Informations Sociales* 4:68–76.

Cherlin, A. (1978). "Remarriage as an Incomplete Institution." *The American Journal of Sociology* 84(3):634–650.

Delaisi, G., and Verdier, P. (1994). *Enfant de personne.* Paris: O. Jacob.

Déchaux, J.-H. (1998). "Dynamique de la famille: Entre individualisme et appartenance." In *La Nouvelle Société Française. Trente Années de Mutation,* ed. O. Galland and Y. Lemel. Paris: A. Colin.

de Singly, F. (1992). "L'Amour coupable?" *Revue Internationale d'Action Communautaire* 27 167:51–55.

de Singly, F. (1996). *Le soi, le couple, et la famille.* Paris: Nathan.

de Singly, F. (2000). *Libres ensemble. L'individualisme dans la vie commune.* Paris: Nathan.

Fine, A., ed. (1998). *Adoptions. Ethnologie des parentés choisies.* Paris: Editions de la Maison des Sciences de l'Homme.

Gross, M., ed. (2000). *Homoparentalités, etat des lieux. Parentés et différence des sexes.* Paris: Editions E. S. F.

Gurrey, B., and Subtil, M.-P. (1999). "Les jeunes critiquent la société mais ne souhaitent pas la bouleverser," *Le Monde,* November 21–22.

Institut National de la Statistique et des Etudes Economiques. (1994). *Les familles monoparentales. portrait social.* Paris: Institute National de la Statistique et des Etudes Economiques.

Kaufmann, J.-C. (1999). *La femme seule et le prince charmant. Enquête sur la vie en solo.* Paris: Nathan.

Kellerhals, J. ; Languin, N. ; Perrin, J.-F. ; and Wirth, G. (1985). "Statut social, projet familial et divorce: une analyse longitudinale des ruptures d'unions dans une promotion de mariages," *Population.* 6:824–825.

Kellerhals, J., and Montandon, C. (1991). *Les stratégies educatives des familles.* Neuchâtel: Delachaux & Niestlé.

Le Bras, H., and Roussel, L. (1982). "Retard ou refus du mariage: L'évolution récente de la première nuptialité en France et sa prévision." *Population.* 6:1009–1044.

Lefaucheur, N. (1992). "Maternité, famille, etat," *Histoire des femmes en occident,* ed. G. Duby and M. Perrot, Volume 5: "Le XXème siècle," ed. F. Thébeaud. Paris: Plon.

Le Gall, D. (1992). "La conjugalité non cohabitante: Du quasi-familial sans co-résidence." In *Du politique et du social dans l'avenir de la famille.* Paris: Haut Conseil de la Population, La Documentation Française.

Le Gall, D. (1993). "Formes de régulation conjugale et familiale à la suite d'unions fécondes." In *Habilitation à diriger des recherches,* ed. F. de Singly. Université de Paris V - Sorbonne.

Le Gall, D. (1996). "Beaux-Parents au Quotidien et par Intermittence." In *Familles et politiques sociales. Dix questions sur le lien familial contemporain,* ed. D. Le Gall and C. Martin. Paris: L'Harmattan.

Le Gall, D., ed. (1997). "Approches sociologiques de l'intime." *Mana,* revue de sociologie et d'anthropologie, Université de Caen Basse-Normandie, no. 3.

Le Gall, D., and Bettahar, Y., ed. (2001). *La Pluriparentalité.* Paris: Presses Universitaires de France.

Le Gall, D., and Martin, C. (1987). *Les familles monoparentales. Evolution et traitement social.* Paris: Editions E. S. F.

Le Gall, D., and Martin, C. (1993). "Transitions familiales, logiques de recomposition et mode de régulation." In *Les recompositions familiales aujourd'hui,* ed. M.-T Meulders-Klein and I. Théry. Paris: Nathan.

Le Gall, D., and Martin, C. (1997). "Fashioning a New Family Tie: Step-Parents and Step-Grandparents." In *Family Kinship in Europe,* ed. M. Gullestad and M. Segalen. London and Washington: Pinter.

Léridon, H., and Villeneuve-Gokalp, C. (1994). *Constance et inconstance dans la famille.* Paris: Ined, travaux and documents [works and documents].

Martin, C. (1997). *L'après-divorce. Lien famial et vulnérabilité.* Rennes: Presses de l'Université de Rennes.

Pitrou, A. (1978). *Vivre sans famille—Les solidarités familiales dans le monde d'aujourd'hui.* Toulouse: Privat. (2nd edition, revised and enlarged, 1992).

Rémy, J. (1967). "Persistance de la famille êtendue dans un Milieu Industriel Urbain." *Revue Française de Sociologie* 4:493–505.

Robert-Diard, P. (2000). "Mon demi-frère, ma demi-súur, mes co-parents, leurs beaux-enfants et moi." Paris, *Le Monde,* August.

Roussel, L., and Bourguignon, O. (1976). *La famille après le mariage des enfants.* Paris: Presses universitaires de France, Ined, Cahiers no. 78.

Roussel, L. (1980). "Mariages et divorces. Contribution à une analyse systématique des modèles matrimoniaux." *Population* 6:1025–1039.

Segalen, M. (1993). *Sociologie de la famille.* Paris: A. Colin.

Segalen, M., and Attias-Donfut, C. (1998). *Grands-parents. La famille à travers les générations.* Paris: O. Jacob.

Sullerot, E. (1984). *Pour le Meilleur et sans le pire.* Paris: Fayard, Paris.

Théry, I. (1996). "Différence des sexes et différences des générations. L'institution familiale en déshérence." *Esprit* 12 (December):65–90.

Théry, I. (1998). *Couple, filiation et parenté aujourd'hui. Le droit face aux mutations de la famille et de la vie privée.* Rapport à la Ministre de l'Emploi et de la Solidarité et au Garde des Sceaux, Ministre de la Justice. Paris: O. Jacob/La Documentation Française.

Toulemont, L. (1996). "La cohabitation hors mariage s'installe dans la durée." *Population* 3:675–716.

DIDIER LE GALL

FRENCH CANADIAN FAMILIES

French Canadian families populate every province and territory in Canada; however, the trends and history of these families are most clearly delineated in Quebec. Like other families in the Western world, the Quebec family has experienced profound transformations since the beginning of the twentieth century. Until this period, the Quebec family had been marked by the historical circumstances of the peopling of New France that led to a natural reproduction regime. This regime, where recourse to voluntary means of reducing fertility did not exist, featured families formed very early in the lives of men and women, resulting in high marriage rates and high fertility levels (Charbonneau et al. 1987). In such a context, French Canadian families' high fertility has been viewed as legendary. However, research shows that although French Canada's fertility level was high compared to that of France, it was comparable to that of other societies in the New World. At the end of the nineteenth century, contraceptive use became much more widespread in other North American regions, but remained rare in Quebec, thus sustaining higher fertility rates (Bouchard and Lalou 1993). Although fertility levels remained high, a decline was under way in some areas and in specific social groups by the end of the nineteenth century (Gauvreau and Gossage 2001).

Sociologists have considered the rural French Canadian family as representative of the stem family described by Frédéric LePlay from European observations. The stem family is characterized by the transmission of the family land to one heir only, who was in charge of assuring the survival of the name and the lineage. But various authors have dismissed the application of this interpretation to the French Canadian family (Gérin 1932; Verdon 1987; Bouchard 1987). Gérard Bouchard's work on the Saguenay families presented the most convincing dismissal of the stem family thesis applied to rural Quebec. Instead, he suggested a family model in which the settlement of as many children as possible served as the basis of the family strategy. This strategy did not aim at protecting the father's patrimony, but rather at enlarging it, exchanging it, or even selling it to assure that all the sons were settled. It also included geographic mobility as an important component, particularly when the territory was fully occupied and where frontier regions were accessible. Even if that theory has not been verified on a provincial scale, it appears to be the most plausible one to apply to the French Canadian family (Bouchard 1992; Dagenais 2000).

Urban families have also been studied. As early as 1921, the majority of Quebec families lived in urban environments. In this context, the family economic cycle was more unstable and precarious than in rural areas, particularly among factory workers' families. "The material and non-material heritage which the family can give to its children is drastically limited" (Falardeau 1953). It is within the urban environment that the Quebec family first changed: "Equalitarian and democratic-minded family units have substituted themselves for families of the traditional authoritarian, quasi-patriarchal type . . ." (Falardeau 1953, p. 117). However, this process happened slowly; according to Philippe Garigue, who studied families in the 1950s, differences between rural and urban families were less pronounced than similarities (1962).

Therefore, it was not until the 1960s, that the effects of industrialization, urbanization, generalized education, and decline of the Catholic-Church influence were felt more intensely. The speed at which changes then took place, as well as their depth, are considered a revolution, often referred to as the Quiet Revolution (Pelletier 1992). Simultaneously profound family changes occurred. These transformations were most easily captured by demographic changes, traditionally considered boundary markers of family life. Not only are these phenomena easily observable and measurable signs, they also have a substantive sociological meaning, revealing the state of social institutions.

The Quebec Family and Marriage

Until the mid 1970s, the Quebec family was based on marriage. Society's norms permitted men and women to live together only if they were bound by a legal union. Moreover, the frequency of marriage before the age of fifty was stable and high: for both men and women, it has remained between 80 and 90 percent among all generations born after 1900 and before 1950. At the same time, for these cohorts, age at marriage decreased from twenty-eight to twenty-five for men, whereas women's average age dropped from twenty-five to twenty-two (Lapierre-Adamcyk and Péron 1983).

Marriage stability was strong; most marriages ended only with the death of one spouse. In Canada, and particularly in Quebec where the Catholic Church's rule prevailed, divorce was practically impossible until 1969, when an important bill was accepted by the Canadian Parliament, making divorce accessible to couples who acknowledged the failure of their marriage. After this, marriage changed from being an irrevocable institution to being a commitment that could be questioned. During the following decades, divorce increased to the point that by the end of the twentieth century, Quebec couples had one of the highest divorce rates in the world, estimated at about 50 percent (Duchesne 2001).

As divorce rates increased, marriage rates declined. In the early 1970s, the total nuptiality rate (indicator analog to the total fertility rate and summarizing current yearly age-specific marriage rates as the proportion of men or women who would get married before age fifty) was about 90 percent. It dropped quickly to less than 50 percent at the beginning of the 1980s and reached 35 percent by the end of the 1990s (Duchesne 2001). This indicator is lower than any marriage rate recorded in other regions of Canada, where legal marriage remained quite popular. By the end of the 1990s, it was lower than in European countries like Denmark and Norway where total nuptiality rates fell as early as 1970 (Duchesne 2001; Sardon 2000).

Nevertheless, because people are not getting married does not mean that they have become uninterested in conjugal life: while marriage was becoming less popular, common-law unions grew as the preferred choice of young couples who wanted to live together. In the early 1990s in Quebec, 80 percent of young women chose cohabitation when they first entered conjugal life. The growing importance of common-law unions is impressive indeed: practically nonexistent before 1970, this type of union included 50 percent of couples in 1996 (among women are aged 15–34). This remarkable evolution has not fully compensated for the decline of marriage; for example, in 1971, among women aged fifteen to thirty-four, 48 percent lived in a union while in 1996 only 44 percent did so. Moreover, the changing nature of conjugal unions has been strongly associated with very low fertility levels.

The Family and Reproduction

With respect to reproduction, Quebec family behavior changed sharply between the beginning and the end of the twentieth century. Although childlessness, due in part to the many men and women who joined celibate Catholic orders, was relatively high at the beginning of the century, the very high proportion of women who had more than six children made up the difference and ensured fast population growth. Quebec families maintained higher fertility levels than other North American families until the end of the 1940s, although the reduction of Quebec family size started as early as the end of the nineteenth century. This decline, although slow, was definitive (Gauvreau and Gossage 2001). During the post-World War II baby boom, Quebec couples adjusted their demographic behavior to resemble that of North America in general. At mid-century, the age at marriage fell, childlessness became less common, and large families became gradually marginalized, to the extent that women born after 1940 in Quebec had

fewer children than those born in Ontario at the same time (Gauvreau and Gossage 2001).

Among cohorts born in the twentieth century, three models summarize the evolution of the distribution of Quebec women by the number of children born. The first model shows a pattern of high childlessness along with a high proportion of women with six or more children (generations born before 1921), which resulted in an average of 3.5 children per woman. The second model is characterized by a marked reduction of the proportion of childless women associated with a decreasing proportion of large families and growth of families with three or four children, leading to an average of 2.5 children (generations 1931–1936). Finally, the third model presents the return of a higher proportion of childless women (this time more related to voluntary childlessness), a domination of the two-child family and a near disappearance of four-child-families, producing an average of 1.6 children (generations born after 1960). Variations in the average age of childbearing are also noticeable. At the beginning of the twentieth century, the mean age at childbearing exceeded thirty years due to the late arrival of the last children. When families started shrinking, the age at childbearing then dropped to between twenty-six and twenty-seven: couples rarely had more than two children, and first and second order children came at an early age following early marriage. Among generations born after 1960, the average age at childbearing grew, to between twenty-eight and twenty-nine, mainly because of the postponement of the first birth.

This transition towards a small family size and lower fertility could not have been possible without effective contraceptive methods. Contraceptive use slowly spread in the population, but at first the main contraceptive method was the rhythm method (periodical abstinence). The influence of the Catholic Church remained a determining factor. Nevertheless, the church gradually lost its influence, and toward the end of the 1960s, women began to use contraceptive pills. Furthermore, in the mid-1970s, a very substantial number of couples turned to sterilization as soon as their desire for children was fulfilled (Marcil-Gratton 2000).

The radical reduction of the family size within the generations born after 1930 resulted from a major decline in the desire for children. How can this be explained? In all likelihood, Quebec, as most Western societies, went through major social and economic reorganizations that profoundly affected society's thinking about families and children. One factor was the influence of structural changes, such as urbanization and industrialization. Generalized education, as well as declining religious values, also had a significant impact, particularly in Quebec. The resulting growth of individualism encouraged both men and women to make decisions based on personal goals rather than social or institutional criteria. Such an evolution necessarily challenged the need or desire for children (Lesthaegue 1988). Second, the declining desire for children was associated with the development of a mentality based on economic rationality: considering their resources, couples compare satisfactions gained from having children with the costs, direct and indirect, they represent; children, especially the third or the fourth, lost in this cost-benefit analysis (Henripin 1989). As this way of thinking became more and more internalized, the desire for children was further reduced. Finally, the entry of married women into the workforce, even though it happened quite late in Quebec, corresponded to one of the most significant transformations associated with family change in Western societies. It provoked an ongoing redefinition of male and female roles in couples' private lives, and major adjustments, still underway, from institutions and labor markets. Numerous authors consider that maintaining a fertility level that is sufficient to ensure social reproduction is founded on the society's capacity to realign its institutions in order to allow men and women to reach equality in their family and professional lives (Chesnais 1996; MacDonald 2000).

Children's New Family Environment

Combined changes in family size and in the nature of conjugal unions greatly modified the environment in which children are raised. In 1951, 32 percent of children lived in families with more than six children; in 1991, this percentage was less than 1 percent. Moreover, in 1951, 27 percent of children were living in families with one or two children; in 1991, this percentage reached 70 percent (Duchesne 1997). The reduction in the number of siblings occurred with a transformation of the family context prevailing at the birth of children. More than 90 percent of children born in the early 1960s

had parents who had not lived together before getting married; among those born in the early 1990s, these children represented less than 25 percent (Marcil-Gratton 1998). Fifty-eight percent of children born in 2000 were born out of wedlock (Duchesne 2001).

New types of unions led to a rise in conjugal instability and, consequently, a growing number of children now experience their parents' separation. This proportion has grown from one cohort to the next, and for recent cohorts; it is almost four times higher for children whose parents were in a common-law union than for children whose parents had married without previously living together (Marcil-Gratton 1998). As a result, more and more children are spending time living with only one parent, as well as life in stepfamilies. For example, 23 percent of children born between 1972 and 1977 (observed at age 10–14) had already lived in a single-parent family, and one-third belonged to step-families when they were observed. Twenty-nine percent of children born five years later had experienced the same situation, with 40 percent belonging to a stepfamily (Duchesne 1997). In the context of this rapid diversification of families, parental roles are undergoing a profound redefinition. In particular, research shows that fatherhood is being shaken by separation and divorce, given the difficulty of maintaining contact between fathers and children in such circumstances (Juby and Le Bourdais 1998). Undoubtedly, these changes are highly significant, and their implications for children's and families' futures remain unknown.

The State and The Family: Family Policies

What is the Quebec family's future? Undoubtedly, the recent evolution, particularly the low fertility level, has provoked public awareness and debate (Dandurand, R.B.; Lefebvre, P.; and Lamoureux, J.P. 1998). The Quebec government, unlike Canada's English-speaking regions, has developed a family policy in the last two decades, following a European trend. During the last half century, Quebec has moved from being the province with the most hostile attitude towards state intervention in the family to being its greatest advocate. When the federal government introduced family allowances in 1946, the Catholic Church and, to some extent, the Quebec government opposed the measure, both because it favored smaller families and because it questioned paternal authority by paying the allowance directly to mothers.

The 1970s, characterized by an increase in women's rights, saw the first measures aimed at reconciling the demands of work and family life; by the end of the decade, the Quebec government confirmed the principle of governmental responsibility in the provision of day care by adopting the *Loi des services de garde à l'enfance* (Law for Child Care Services), and creating the *Office des services de garde à l'enfance* (Office for Child Care Services). In the 1980s, after a broad consultation and years of debates, the government recognized the value of the family to society as a whole and undertook a series of measures to contribute to the cohesion and stability of the family in its diverse forms, and to support parents in their role as the primary caretakers of children. It implemented universal programs of direct financial assistance to families, recognizing the increased needs of larger families, the specific needs of young children, and the equality of all family types. At the end of the decade, measures that favored larger families were included, such as a modest birth allocation for the first and second children and a much more generous one for the third or higher order birth.

However, after years of economic recession and budget cuts as the Quebec government struggled to balance its budget, new legislation adopted in September 1997 changed the face of the programs of direct financial assistance for Quebec families. The dominant universal family policy model was abandoned and replaced by a targeted, selective approach.

Relative to the future of the Quebec family, two questions should be considered in appraising the effects of the family policy: The first addresses the question of promoting a higher birth rate. However, although some studies concluded that the pronatalist measures applied in Quebec in 1988 slightly increased the number of children born (Duclos, E.; Lefebvre, P.; and Merrigan, P. 2002), it remains very difficult to demonstrate without any doubt. The impact of family policy measures on the birth rate remains an open question. The second point concerns the necessity of developing long-lasting measures that complement one another; these measures minimally have to ensure that poor families are supported. At the same time, to the extent that mothers' participation in the labor force is culturally and economically promoted, they have to provide means to reconcile work and family responsibilities.

Conclusion

The evolution of the Quebec family has specific features, but doubtlessly, trends have to be interpreted within the deep transformations of Western families and societies. Greater individualism, weakening of social institutions, increasing individual freedom, rejection of institutional criteria in the decision-making process about family matters, declining influence of religious values, redefinition of male and female as well as parental roles—all of these constitute elements that are intertwined to sustain the frailty of the contemporary family.

See also: CANADA

Bibliography

Bouchard, G. (1987). "Sur la reproduction en milieu rural: Système ouvert et système clos." *Recherches sociographiques* 28(2–3):229–252.

Bouchard, G. (1992). "Les migrations de réallocation comme stratégie de reproduction familiale en terroir neuf." In *Transmettre, hériter, succéder: La reproduction familiale en milieu rural France-Québec XVIIIe-XXe siècles,* ed. R. Bonnain, G. Bouchard, and J. Goy. Lyon: Presses Universitaires de Lyon.

Bouchard, G., and Lalou, R. (1993). "La surfécondité des couples québécois depuis le XVIIe siècle, essai de mesure et d'interprétation." *Recherches Sociographiques* 34(1):9–44.

Charbonneau, H., et al. (1987). *Naissance d'une population. Les Français établis au Canada au XVIIe siècle.* Paris/Montréal: Presses Universitaires de France/Presses de l'Université de Montréal.

Chesnais, J. C. (1996). "Fertility, Family, and Social Policy in Contemporary Western Europe." *Population and Development Review* 22(4)729–739.

Dagenais, D. (2000). *La fin de la famille moderne. Signification des transformations contemporaines de la famille.* Québec: Presses de l'Université Laval.

Dandurand, R.B.; P. Lefebvre; and J.P. Lamoureux, dir., *Quelle politique familiale à l'aube de l'an 2000?,* Montréal/Paris L'Harmattan.

Duchesne, L. (1997). "La situation familiale" and "La mortalité et la fécondité." In *D'une génération à l'autre: évolution des conditions de vie,* ed. by H. Gauthier et al. Sainte-Foy: Bureau de la Statistique du Québec.

Duchesne, L. (2001). *La situation démographique au Québec, Bilan 2001.* Sainte-Foy: Institut de la Statistique du Québec.

Duclos, E.; Lefebvre, P.; and Merrigan, P. (2002). "Quand le gouvernement subventionne la venue des cigognes: résultats d'une 'expérience naturelle' concernant la politique familiale et la fécondité." In *Comprendre la famille, actes du 6e symposium de recherche sur la famille.* Sainte-Foy: Presses de l'Université du Québec.

Falardeau, J-C. (1953). "The Changing Social Structures of Contemporary French Canadian Society." In *Essais sur le Québec contemporain.* English translation in Rioux, M. and Martin, Y. (1964). *French Canadian Society.* Ottawa: Carleton Library No. 18/McClelland and Stewart Limited.

Garigue, P. (1962). *La vie familiale de Canadiens Français.* Montréal/Paris: Université de Montréal, Presses Universitaires de France.

Gauvreau, D., and Gossage, P. (2001). "Canadian Fertility Transitions: Quebec and Ontario at the Turn of the Twentieth Century." *Journal of Family History* 26(2):162–188.

Gérin, L. (1932). "The French-Canadian Family: Its Strengths and Weaknesses." *Revue trimestrielle canadienne* 19(March):37–63. English translation in M. Rioux and Y. Martin. (1964). *French Canadian Society.* Ottawa: Carleton Library No. 18/McClelland and Stewart Limited.

Henripin, J. (1989). *Naître ou ne pas être.* Québec: Institut Québécois de Recherche sur la Culture.

Juby, H., and Le Bourdais, C. (1998). "The Changing Context of Fatherhood in Canada. A Life Course Analysis." *Population Studies* 52(2):163–175

Lapierre-Adamcyk, E., and Péron, Y. (1983). "Familles et enfants au Québec: la toile de fond démographique." In *Santé mentale au Québec.* Montréal: Centre de Santé Mentale Communautaire de Montréal.

LePlay, F. (1871). *L'organisation de la famille, selon le vrai modèle signalé par l'histoire de toutes les races et de tous les temps.* Paris: Téqui.

Lesthaeghe, R. (1988). "Cultural Dynamics and Economic Theories of Fertility Change." *Population and Development Review* 14:1–44.

MacDonald, P. (2000). "Gender Equity in Theories of Fertility Transition." *Population and Development Review* 26:427–439.

Marcil-Gratton, N. (1998). "Growing up with Mom and Dad? The Intricate Family Life Courses of Canadian Children." Statistics Canada, catalogue no. 89-566-XIE.

Marcil-Gratton, N. (2000). "De l'interdiction à la libéralisation: les paradoxes entourant le recours à la stérilisation en Amérique du Nord." In *Les enjeux de la stérilisation,* ed. A. Giami and H. Leridon. Paris: INSERM / INED.

Pelletier, R. (1992). "La révolution tranquille." In *Le Québec en jeu. Comprendre les grands défis,* ed. G. Daigle. Montréal: Presses de l'Université de Montréal.

Sardon, J.-P. (2000). "Évolutions récentes de la démographie des pays développés." *Population* 55(4–5):729–764.

Verdon, M. (1987). "Autour de la famille souche. Essai d'anthropologie conjecturale." *Anthropologie et Sociétés* 11(1):137–160.

EVELYNE LAPIERRE-ADAMCYK
CÉLINE LE BOURDAIS
NICOLE MARCIL-GRATTON

FRIENDSHIP

Friendship is a relationship with broad, ambiguous, and even shifting boundaries. The terms *friend* and *friendship* mean different things to different people and different things to the same people at different times. To think and communicate effectively about the topic, people find it necessary to use distinctions such as true friends, best friends, good friends, casual friends, work friends, social friends, and friendly acquaintances. In spite of friendship's vague and seemingly indefinable quality, friendships contribute in important ways to psychological development and health and well-being from early childhood through the older adult years.

Social and behavioral scientists devoted little attention to friendship prior to the late 1960s. Since that time, however, friendship has become one of the more favored topics among relationship scholars. The study of friendship is interdisciplinary in nature, concerning researchers from various sub-fields within psychology as well as sociology, communications, anthropology, social work, family studies, and psychiatry. It is also international in scope with researchers from many parts of the world making significant contributions to the empirical and theoretical literature. In terms of the sheer number of scholars focusing their work on friendship, countries from North America,

Europe, Asia, and the Middle East (primarily Israel) are especially well represented. Cross-cultural research is common, especially with respect to comparative studies of children's friendships (Schneider et al. 1997). In spite of this disciplinary, geographic, and cultural variety, there is a remarkable degree of agreement about the fundamental meaning of friendship and in documenting its importance.

Definition and Characteristics

Unlike other important relationships, friendship is not defined by kinship, legal ties, or formal social obligations. Normally, there are no ceremonies surrounding the formation of a friendship. In fact, friendships rarely begin with two people declaring that, "from this day forward, we will be friends." Rather, friendships develop gradually and often unwittingly as the partners begin doing "friendship things" together. Once formed, friendships are largely free of clear social norms or expectations that dictate when the partners should get together and how they should interact when they do. When friendships end, they generally do not do so as a result of an announced decision by one or both parties. Occasionally, of course, friendships end abruptly due to obvious breaches of good will such as dishonesty or betrayal. Most often, however, friendships merely fade away as the partners cease doing the things that gave the relationship its meaning.

This lack of social definition gives friendship its vague and intangible character. Nevertheless, it is a relationship that seems to exist almost, but not quite, universally across cultures. This combination of factors led anthropologist Robert Paine (1969) to describe friendship as an *institutionalized non-institution* (Suttles 1970). What, then, verifies a friendship? A friendship exists in the fact that the partners commit time to interaction with one another apart from outside pressures or constraints. In friendship, the partners' lives are interdependent on a voluntary basis. In more structured relationships such as marriage, the partners' lives are also interdependent, but much of the interdependence is based on social norms and expectations obliging them to relate to one another in prescribed ways. Thus, many social and behavioral scientists, in fields ranging from sociology to psychology to anthropology, emphasize voluntariness as an essential feature of friendship.

A second key aspect of friendship is what Gerald Suttles (1970) called the *person-qua-person* factor. That is, friends respond to one another as unique, genuine, and irreplaceable individuals. They do not see one another as mere role occupants or representatives of particular groups or statuses. Friends express this focus on individuality as a personalized interest and concern. Combining these two characteristics provides the following definition: Friendship is a relationship in which the partners respond to one another with an individualized interest and concern and commit time to one another in the absence of constraints toward interaction that are external to the relationship itself. The more these two factors are in evidence, the stronger the friendship.

According to this definition, friendship is a matter of degree rather than an all-or-none proposition. It would undoubtedly be more accurate, even if awkward, to speak of degrees of *friendness* rather than friendship versus non-friendship. Anthropological studies suggest that forms of relating following this pattern are found in most, but not all, cultures (Leyton 1974; Bell and Coleman 1999).

Benefits of Friendship

As part of their unconstrained and personalized interaction, friends benefit one another in innumerable ways. They listen, encourage, give advice, help with chores, loan money, have fun, exchange trivia, share confidences, and simply "are there" for one another. The specifics vary from time to time and from one friendship to another.

Several scholars have suggested ways of grouping these benefits into a manageable number of categories. Many researchers consider just two classes of rewards adequate for most purposes. These two classes are most often labeled as *instrumental* and *expressive*. Instrumental rewards involve receiving tangible resources such as goods or money, and obtaining assistance in completing tasks or reaching goals. Expressive rewards involve receiving emotional support, encouragement, and personal advice from an understanding confidant. Israeli psychologists Mario Mickulincer and Michal Selinger (2001) developed a somewhat different two-way classification, proposing that individuals pursue friendships to fulfill either *affiliative* (companionship) or *attachment* (socioemotional) needs.

Although such two-fold classifications are adequate for many purposes, people sometimes find it useful to consider more specific rewards that are (or are not) present in a friendship, or that are present in one friendship but not another. Some researchers have developed more detailed sets of rewards for exploring such nuances. Robert B. Hayes (1984), for example, formulated a list of four rewarding *friendship behaviors*: *companionship* (sharing activities or one another's company), *consideration* (helpfulness, utility, support), *communication* (discussing information about one's self, exchanging ideas and confidences), and *affection* (expressing sentiments felt toward one's partner).

In a similar vein, Paul H. Wright (1978, 1985) identified five interpersonal rewards or *friendship values*: these are *utility* (providing material resources or helping with tasks), *stimulation* (suggesting new ideas or activities), *ego support* (providing encouragement by downplaying setbacks and emphasizing successes), *self-affirmation* (behaving in ways that reinforce a friend's valued self-characteristics) and *security* (providing a feeling of safety and unquestioned trust).

Voluntariness and Contextual Factors in Friendship

Although most authorities agree that *voluntariness* is the *sine qua non* of friendship (Carrier 1999; Krappmann 1996), it is important to consider what they do and do not mean by this term. Voluntariness indicates only that friendships are non-obligatory, in other words, that they are formed by personal preference and not on the basis of external requirements or expectations. Furthermore, once formed, they are non-obligatory in the sense that friends are much freer to choose what to do or not do with another than partners in more structured relationships. Voluntariness does not mean that a person has either the freedom or possibility of becoming friends with virtually anyone they might choose. Indeed, as sociologists Rebecca G. Adams and Graham Allan (1998) emphasize, both friendship choice and the specific forms of interaction that take place in friendships are affected by contextual factors, in other words, personal, circumstantial, societal, and cultural influences that can be facilitative, limiting, or some of each.

Adams and Graham's point concerning context is illustrated by comparative data on children's friendships collected in East and West Berlin prior to the breakup of the Soviet Union (Little et al. 1999). Eight- to fourteen-year-old children in the two cities were similar in their perceptions of their friendships' quality and reciprocity. Even so, consistent with the restrictive social climate of the time, children in East Berlin reported more conflict, enjoyed fewer mutual visits and sleep-overs, and had less fun in their play. Canadian psychologists Anna Beth Doyle and Dorothy Markiewiscz (1996) documented contextual factors in a different way, reviewing studies showing that children's friendships with other children are enhanced in both number and quality if their parents have high quality relationships between themselves and with friends outside the family.

On a broader social level, given the voluntary and preferential nature of friendship, there are cultures in which such relationships cannot thrive. There are a few cultures, for example, where personal relationships are closely formulated in terms of status and kinship (DuBois 1974), or where speaking taboos are confining and rigidly enforced. In such cultures, friendships are rare or nonexistent. However, as Lothar Krappmann (1996) suggests, individuals in such restrictive cultures often find ways of maintaining ties akin to friendship. Sarah Uhl (1991), for example, found that some women in the Andalusian region of Spain bypassed explicit prohibitions against forming friendships. They established voluntary and personalized non-kin bonds under the guise of interaction required by their domestic chores.

In sum, friendship is a non-obligatory and personalized relationship that is embedded in a context composed of an individual's personal circumstances and social and cultural milieu. Such contextual factors influence the number and specific kinds of friendships an individual has the opportunity and personal resources to form and maintain. Due attention to contextual factors is, therefore, basic to a full understanding of the friendship relationship.

Friendships Throughout Childhood

From an adult perspective, friendship involves voluntary interaction between two persons who relate to one another on a personal and individualized basis. As such, friendship is beyond the capacity of most children until about the age of ten or twelve. Prior to that time, however, children experience friendship in less complete but increasingly sophisticated ways, beginning with a rudimentary conception at about three years of age (Howes 1996; Rose and Asher 2000).

In 1992, William K. Rawlins proposed a means of categorizing children's friendships from toddlerhood through preadolescence with a classification system that has stood the test of time. Following Robert L. Selman (1981), Rawlins describes friends in the first phase (ages three to six years) as *momentary physicalistic playmates*. Children respond to age-mates they meet at, for example, day care or the playground, on the basis of physical characteristics or possessions. The children are "friends" as long as they are participating jointly in some enjoyable activity. They are often inclusive of one another and exclusive of "outsiders" when other children attempt to join them. This exclusiveness is transitory, however, as the children often lose interest in one activity and pick up another with different partners or new "friends." Brief quarrels, usually over toys or space, are common. Although short in duration, these quarrels involve expressing emotions, sometimes having one's own way, and sometimes being compelled to "give in." They often lead to shifts in playmates. During this period, children start developing some of the social skills necessary for forming more enduring friendships. They begin learning, for instance, to take turns and manage their emotions. Moreover, as they become familiar and comfortable with children they meet repeatedly, they start showing some degree of consistency in their preferred playmates.

Friendships of children from about six to nine years of age follow a pattern that Rawlins (1992) describes as *opportunity and activity*. The friends usually live close to one another and are of the same sex and similar in age, social status, and social maturity. They spend most of their time together in physical activities (skating, biking, sports), make-believe games related to domestic or work situations, fantasized athletic accomplishments, and "adventures" modeled after favorite fictional heroes.

Children at this age still tend to describe their friends according to physical characteristics and possessions, but sometimes think of them in more relational terms, such as showing liking and supportiveness. Whereas they realize that different people may see and respond to the same situation

Two young boys in Madagascar display their friendship. Friends between the ages of six and nine spend most of their time together in physical activities, make-believe games, and "adventures" modeled after fictional heroes.
CORY LANGLEY

in different ways, they feel that friends should share points of view. Thus, one child is likely to see another as a friend only during times when their ideas coincide and when they like doing the same things. When they are not, they are not friends. During the "friendship times," they exchange benefits on a tit-for-tat basis. Thus, at this stage, friendships are on-and-off relationships that are largely self-oriented and opportunistic.

Between the ages of roughly nine and twelve years, children increasingly respond to others in terms of internal characteristics (attitudes, beliefs, values). They learn to infer these characteristics by observing the ongoing acts of others, and they are aware that others can, in turn, infer internal characteristics in the same way. With this cognitive ability, a child can "step outside" of the self and take the perspective of the other, including the perceptions the other has of her or him. This enables them to form friendships that Rawlins (1992) labels *reciprocal and equal*.

At this stage, children usually choose friends whose beliefs agree with their own. Such agreement confirms the correctness of their emerging views, thereby providing what psychiatrist Harry Stack Sullivan (1953) called *consensual validation*. To the degree that their perspectives differ, however, friends at this age are able to accommodate some of the differences and arrive at a shared outlook. Although the children still tend to be self-oriented and opportunistic, they realize that their friends are equal to them in the sense of being entitled to benefits from the relationship. Therefore, the exchange of rewards tends to be normative and reciprocal. That is, the child provides benefits when the friend has a need for them because that is what friends are supposed to do. That friend, of course, is expected to return the benefits for the same reason. Thus, friends are people who share ideas, interests and feelings, and who provide rewards on a broadly reciprocal basis. In the reciprocity and equality phase, then, children are on the fringes of a conception of friendship as a relatively stable relationship that transcends occasional disagreements and periods of separation.

At preadolescence (about ten to fourteen years of age), children acquire the ability and inclination to respond to other children in terms of personality traits and styles (nice, easy-going, mean, selfish) and special interests and attitudes. They sometimes see these characteristics as combining to make the other person uniquely admirable and attractive. This sets the stage for what Rawlins (1992) calls the period of *mutuality and understanding* in children's friendships.

According to Sullivan (1953), preadolescent children experience a need for interpersonal closeness in an especially poignant way, and express this need as a strong desire to establish a same-sex "chumship." Research generally confirms the nature of these chumships and the importance Sullivan attaches to them.

As two children come to recognize uniquely attractive features in one another, they are likely to become "real" friends. Such friends consider one another intrinsically worthwhile. They are loyal to one another and provide rewards, not with the expectation of reciprocation, but simply because the

partner is deserving. Preadolescent friends share common day-to-day experiences to which they often react with an intensity and immediacy that either puzzles or amuses important adults such as parents and teachers. Therefore, chums are especially capable of providing empathy and understanding. At this stage, friendships not only build each child's self-esteem, they also provide a context for expressing and trying out personal thoughts and feelings in a free and unguarded manner. Such freedom is possible because friendships, while close and caring, lack the socially mandated responsibilities and inequities present in many relationships, such as that between parents and children.

Thus, children approaching adolescence begin to experience friendship in its full-blown form, that is, as an enduring relationship involving voluntary interdependence and a mutual personalized interest and concern. Through these friendships, they experience and practice empathy, altruism, unselfishness, and loyalty. There is, however, a darker side to preadolescent friendships. Because they are intense and exclusive, they often encourage cliquishness and animosity between sets of friends. At times, too, the friends themselves disagree, become jealous, become competitive, and have an occasional falling out. At this point, however, the partners have a conception of friendship as a relationship that usually persists in spite of episodic difficulties.

Throughout all the phases from toddlerhood through preadolescence, children are generally inclined to select friends of their own sex. Furthermore, girls' and boys' friendships differ, on the average, in several ways. Girls' friendships, for example, are more exclusively pair-oriented whereas boys' are more group- or gang-oriented. Girls tend to talk, "gossip," and exchange secrets more than boys, who concentrate on games, "projects," and shared activities. These contrasts foreshadow overall gender differences that appear in adolescence and persist through adulthood.

Friendships Throughout Adolescence

Adolescence extends from the onset of puberty until the individual begins young adult life by entering the work force or undertaking postsecondary education. Because of the developmental tasks characteristic of this period, the meaning and values of friendship acquired during preadolescence continue and expand (Berndt 1996). Throughout this time, the typical adolescent encounters differing ideologies and values, a variety of activities to pursue or forego, and potential lifestyles to consider. The adolescent's two-fold "task" is to discover which options can and should be committed to, and to integrate them into a personal identity.

Although parents normally remain an important source of guidance and support, part of the adolescent's struggle is to work toward independence from them. Thus adolescents continue to rely on their parents for material support and instrumental rewards, normally respecting their ideals as sources of continuity and stability. They are less likely, however, to see their parents as helpful in developing their views on present and future issues. For their part, parents generally feel an obligation to socialize their adolescents "properly" and, hence, tend to be judgmental as their adolescent children explore different directions. Therefore, close friendships, because they involve nonjudgmental yet caring equals, help the adolescent develop a sense of identity by offering "a climate of growth and self-knowledge that the family is not equipped for" (Douvan and Adelson 1966, p. 174).

As they carry out their friendships, girls are more likely than boys to emphasize expressive rather than instrumental rewards. As in preadolescence, both girls and boys usually form friendships with members of their own sex. Even so, cross-gender friendships are not uncommon, and most adolescents maintain careful distinctions between opposite-sex partners who are friends and those who are romantic or dating partners. Where cross-gender friendships exist, both girls and boys find them valuable sources of information and insight about the opposite sex in a relationally neutral ("safe") context. Boys, especially, find cross-gender friendships advantageous because they provide expressive rewards that are not as readily available in their friendships with other boys. The qualities of cross-gender friendships evident in adolescence tend to persist throughout adulthood (Monsour 2002).

Friendships Throughout Adulthood

Close friendships are possible and, in fact, common at all stages of adulthood. Also, regardless of whether they involve women, men, or cross-gender pairs, close friendships provide benefits

Activities are often the starting point at which friendships begin. By "hanging out" together and sharing interests, these young people are strengthening their relationships.
CHERYL MAEDER/CORBIS

that are similar in kind and degree. There are, however, circumstances at young, middle, and later adulthood that affect typical friendship patterns (Adams and Blieszner 1996; Matthews 1996).

Young adulthood starts with the individual's loosening of emotional ties with parents and family while beginning to explore stable work opportunities or pursue further education. This development includes changes in commitments and activities, and often changes in residence. Such changes usually disrupt the individual's network of non-kin associates, creating the opportunity, if not the necessity, of forming new friendships. Indeed, young adults who succeed in forging new friendships report being happier, less lonely, and better adjusted than those who do not. Individuals at this stage are relatively free of obligations and social roles (e.g., professional advancement, marriage, and parenthood) that might conflict with forming friendships. Consequently, single young adults report more friendships, including cross-gender friendships, than adults at any other stage.

Gender differences in friendships are as much in evidence during young adulthood as at any other time. That is, women are, on average, more expressive and personally oriented in their friendships than men. Moreover, the friendships of women are generally stronger than those of men with respect to both voluntary interdependence and the person-qua-person factor. As in adolescence, males find that their cross-gender friendships provide expressive rewards to a greater degree than do their same-gender friendships.

With such life events as marriage, parenthood, and accelerated career development, young adulthood merges into middle adulthood. Following marriage, both women and men report having fewer cross-gender friends. One obvious reason for this is suspicion and jealousy, but there are other factors. Michael Monsour noted, for example, that "marriage curtails opportunities for cross-sex friendship formation because spouses spend most of their free time together rather than separately in social situations that might lead to cross-sex friendship formation" (2002, p. 156). Furthermore, when people marry, they generally become more dependent on spouses and less so on friends for meeting social needs. Men especially tend to rely on female friends as confidants, but when they marry they find that their wives meet their expressive needs by becoming live-in confidants, that is, "friends."

Also during middle adulthood, men show a drop in the number and intensity of same- as well as cross-gender friendships. This is partly because their preoccupation with career development leaves them little time to cultivate anything but superficial friendships. In addition, men most often meet other men in work settings. Because of this, many of their potential friends are people with whom they compete for raises or advancement, or with whom they are involved either as supervisors or subordinates. Neither of these conditions is conducive to the openness and personalized concern necessary for the development of a close friendship. When friendships do develop between male work associates, they are likely to center around shared activities and camaraderie rather than personal self-disclosure and expressiveness.

The "friendship situation" for women in middle adulthood is complex. Prior to the arrival of children, marriage has little impact on the number, strength, or expressive character of friendships. With the arrival of children, however, women report a decrease in the number of friendships. This is probably due to women's traditionally greater responsibility for the home and family. The fact that many women also work outside the home further limits the time and energy they have to pursue friendships. Even so, the friendships they are able to maintain retain their expressive and highly personalized character. Later in middle adulthood,

presumably as their children become more independent, women report increasing numbers of friends. Women, like men, often form friendships in work settings. However, they are likely to see such relationships as acquaintanceships rather than friendships. They commonly make distinctions among work friends, activity friends, and "real" friends (Gouldner and Strong 1987).

But what about the friendships of adults who never marry? One often hears anecdotally that such never-marrieds cultivate more friendships and treat their friends as special "family." Research, however, does not bear out such a "friends as family" trend. Rather, findings suggest that most unmarried adults increase their contact with relatives rather than forming more or different kinds of friendships.

Older adulthood, usually considered to begin when a person reaches about sixty-five years of age, is marked by two kinds of changes that affect friendships. On the one hand, increasing health concerns, reduced mobility, and declining vigor reduce opportunities for contact with friends and the energy the individual has to devote to them. On the other hand, retirement and reduced social and family obligations increase the free and uncommitted time the individual has to nurture existing friendships and to develop new ones. Not surprisingly, these factors have a different impact on the friendships of older women than those of older men (Field 1999).

For women, the increasing flexibility of middle adulthood continues into older adulthood. Older women are thus able to sustain established friendships and to form new ones as friends die or relocate. Throughout life, women's friendships tend to be more expressive than those of men. In older adulthood, then, women have both the social skills and inclination to continue this pattern. Moreover, women are more likely than men to face the prospect of widowhood and to fill the relationship void by emphasizing their friendships. Whereas widows rely on adult children, especially daughters, for material and practical support, they rely on same aged friends to meet their expressive needs and to maintain their morale.

Because men's friendships are centered mostly around work affiliations and shared activities, when men retire and curtail their activities they often lose their friendships as well. Men are less

Friendship has many different definitions, each unique to an individual's relationship. Women's friendships tend to be more expressive than men's. OWEN FRANKEN/CORBIS

likely than women to form new friendships to replace the ones they lose. Even so, they retain their primary source of personal and emotional support: their wives. In the relatively rare case where a man outlives his wife, he is likely to remarry rather than seek out new friends. With the loss of friends, however, men do lose the stimulation, fun, and camaraderie that goes along with shared interests and activities. Therefore, men who depart from the average and maintain close same-gender friendships throughout life are likely to lead fuller and more satisfying lives in their older adult years.

Conclusion

Friendship is, in many respects, a "comfortable" love relationship. Friendships involve as little or as much intimacy as the partners are inclined to express at any given time. Friends are not normally obligated to exchange benefits, but do so in ways that are often so natural as to be unwitting. The ties that bind them are by unfettered mutual consent. In spite of its being so comfortable, in fact because of it, friendship contributes in unique ways to personal development and well-being.

See also: AFFECTION; ATTRACTION; INTIMACY; LONELINESS; LOVE; PEER INFLUENCE; SELF-DISCLOSURE; SOCIAL NETWORKS; TRUST

Bibliography

Adams, R. G., and Allan, G. (1998). "Introduction: Contextualising Friendship." In *Placing Friendship in Context: Structural Analysis in the Social Sciences,* ed. R. G. Adams and G. Allan. New York: Cambridge University Press.

Adams, R. G., and Blieszner, R. (1996). "Midlife Friendship Patterns." In *A Lifetime of Relationships,* ed. N. Vanzetti and S. Duck. Pacific Grove, CA: Brooks/Cole.

Bell, S., and Coleman, S., eds. (1999). *The Anthropology of Friendship.* Oxford, UK: Berg.

Berndt, T. J. (1996). "Friendship in Adolescence." In *A Lifetime of Relationships,* ed. N. Vanzetti and S. Duck. Pacific Grove, CA: Brooks/Cole.

Carrier, J. G. (1999). "People Who Can Be Friends: Selves and Social Relationships." In *The Anthropology of Friendship,* ed. S. Bell and S. Coleman. Oxford: Berg.

Douvan, E., and Adelson, J. (1966). *The Adolescent Experience.* New York: John Wiley & Sons.

Doyle, A.B., and Markiewiscz, D. (1996). "Parents' Interpersonal Relationships and Children's Friendships." In *The Company They Keep,* ed. W.M. Bukowski, A.F. Newcomb and W.W. Hartup. New York: Cambridge University Press.

Dubois, C. (1974). "The Gratuitous Act: An Introduction to the Comparative Study of Friendship Patterns." In *The Compact: Selected Dimensions of Friendship,* ed. E. Leyton. St. John's, Newfoundland: Institute of Social and Economic Research.

Field, D. (1999). "Continuity and Change in Friendships in Advanced Old Age: Findings from The Berkeley Older Generation Study." *International Journal of Aging and Human Development* 48:325–346.

Gouldner, H., and Strong, M.S. (1987). *Speaking of Friendship.* New York: Greenwood.

Hayes, R. B. (1984). "The Development and Maintenance of Friendship." *Journal of Social and Personal Relationships* 1:75–98.

Howes, C. (1996). "The Earliest Friendships." In *The Company They Keep,* ed. W. M. Bukowski, A. F. Newcomb and W. W. Hartup. New York: Cambridge University Press.

Krappmann, L. (1996). "Amicitia, Drujba, Shin-yu, Philia, Freundschaft, Friendship: On the Cultural Diversity of Human Relationship." In *The Company They Keep,* ed. W.M. Bukowski, A.F. Newcomb, and W.W. Hartup. Cambridge, UK: Cambridge University Press.

Leyton, E., ed. (1974). *The Compact: Selected Dimensions of Friendship.* St. John's, Newfoundland: Institute for Economic and Social Research.

Little, T. D.; Brendgen, M.; Warrner, B.; and Krappmann, L. (1999). "Children's Reciprocal Perception of Friendship Quality in the Sociocultural Contexts of East and West Berlin." *International Journal of Behavioral Development* 23:63–89.

Matthews, S. H. (1996). "Friendships in Old Age." In *A Lifetime of Relationships,* ed. N. Vanzetti and S. Duck. Pacific Grove, CA: Brooks/Cole.

Mickulincer, M., and Selinger, M. (2001). "The Interplay Between Attachment and Affiliation Systems in Adolescents' Same-sex Friendships." *Journal of Social and Personal Relationships* 18:81–106.

Monsour, M. (2002). *Women and Men as Friends: Relationships Across the Life Span in the 21st Century.* Mahwah, NJ: Erlbaum.

Paine, R. (1969). "In Search of Friendship: An Exploratory Analysis of 'Middle-Class' Culture." *Man* 4:505–524.

Rawlins, W. K. (1992). *Friendship Matters.* New York: Aldine.

Rose, A. J., and Asher, S. R. (2000). "Children's Friendships." In *Close Relationships: A Sourcebook,* ed. C. Hendrick and S. S. Hendrick. Thousand Oaks, CA: Sage Publications.

Schneider, B. H.; Smith, A.; Poisson, S. E.; and Kwan, A. B. (1997). "Cultural Dimensions of Children's Peer Relations." In *Handbook of Personal Relationships,* 2nd edition, ed. S. Duck. New York: John Wiley & Sons.

Selman, R. L. (1981). "The Child as a Friendship Philosopher." In *The Development of Children's Friendships,* ed. S. R. Asher and J. M. Gottman. New York: Cambridge University Press.

Sullivan, H. S. (1953). *Interpersonal Theory of Psychiatry.* New York: Norton.

Suttles, G. D. (1970). "Friendship as a Social Institution." In *Social Relationships,* ed. G. J. McCall. New York: Aldine.

Uhl, S. (1991). "Forbidden Friends: Cultural Veils of Female Friendships in Andalusia." *American Ethologist* 18:90–105.

Wright, P. H. (1978). "Toward a Theory of Friendship Based on a Conception of Self." *Journal of Human Communication Research* 4:196–207.

Wright, P. H. (1985). "The Acquaintance Description Form." In *Understanding Personal Relationships: An Interdisciplinary Approach,* ed. S. Duck and D. Perlman. Newbury Park, CA: Sage Publications.

PAUL H. WRIGHT

G

GANGS

The label *gang* has been applied to various groups including outlaws of the nineteenth-century American West, prison inmates, Mafioso and other organized criminals, motorcyclists, and groups of inner city youths. Despite its diverse application, the term gang almost always connotes involvement in disreputable or illegal activities.

Social scientists use the term gang most frequently when describing groups of juveniles. This tendency dates back to Frederic Thrasher's *The Gang: A Study of 1,313 Gangs in Chicago* (1927). According to Thrasher, social conditions in the United States at the end of the nineteenth century encouraged the development of street gangs. In this period, many immigrants settled in ethnic enclaves in inner-city neighborhoods characterized by several features: a large, culturally diverse population; deteriorating housing; poor employment prospects; and a rapid turnover in population. These conditions resulted in socially disorganized neighborhoods where social institutions and social control mechanisms were weak and ineffective. The lack of social control encouraged youths to find other means of establishing social order, which they did by forming gangs.

Thrasher's research has influenced most subsequent theory and research on gangs. Albert Cohen (1955) theorized that gangs emerge from a subculture created by lower socioeconomic youths in response to their exclusion from mainstream middle-class culture. These youths recognize that they are unlikely to obtain the status valued by the middle class and create a gang culture that offers an alternative source of status. According to Walter Miller (1958), lower-class culture includes norms and values that are structured around the focal concerns of trouble, toughness, smartness, excitement, fate, and autonomy. Gangs and criminal activity are behavioral manifestations of these focal concerns. Richard Cloward and Lloyd Ohlin (1960) proposed that delinquency and gang formation stem from differential opportunity structures: the uneven distribution of legitimate and illegitimate means of attaining goals. Lower-class adolescents' limited access to the legal means of achieving goals leaves them frustrated. Gangs can reduce feelings of powerlessness by providing youths access to illegitimate means; that is, with opportunities to learn and be instructed in crime by seasoned offenders.

Interest in gangs declined in the 1970s; however, gangs have increasingly captured the attention of academics since 1980. Many of the efforts since the 1980s focus on the social disorganization perspective from which much of the original gang research originated. For example, Robert Bursik Jr. and Harold Grasmick (1993, p. 147) suggested that expanding the social disorganization model to include "a broader systemic orientation that considers the simultaneous operation of three types of control: private, parochial, and public," is a better approach to studying neighborhood crime and gangs.

Defining Gangs

Gang researchers have suggested several definitions of gangs. Thrasher (1927, p. 46) defined a gang as an interstitial group originally formed spontaneously and then integrated through conflict. It is characterized by the following types of behavior: meeting face to face, milling, movement through space as a unit, conflict, and planning. The result of this collective behavior is the development of tradition, unreflective internal structure, esprit de corps, solidarity, morale, group awareness, and attachment to a local territory.

According to Thrasher, all childhood playgroups are potential gangs. The transformation from playgroup to gang occurs when youths encounter others who oppose or display disapproval for their group. This disapproval may or may not stem from delinquent activities, and Thrasher was careful not to include delinquency in his definition of gangs. Instead, Thrasher argued that gangs *facilitate* delinquency.

In contrast, other scholars distinguish gangs *as* delinquent groups. Malcolm Klein (1995) defines a gang as a group that recognizes itself as a gang, is recognized by the community as a gang, and is committed to a *criminal orientation*. Finn-Aage Esbensen (2000) offers a more precise definition, arguing that a gang has all of the following features: contains more than two members who fall within a specific range of age (commonly, older than eleven and younger than twenty-five); members have some common identity (often accomplished through gang names, symbols, colors, hand signs, and graffiti); the group exhibits stability over time (a year or more); and the group members are involved in criminal activity. Esbensen suggests that the requirement of illegal activity is necessary to distinguish gangs from groups such as school and church clubs.

Other researchers have turned to the individuals who deal with gangs for a definition. Walter Miller (1975) administered a survey to workers in 121 youth-serving agencies in twenty-six areas of the United States. Eighty-five percent of the 309 respondents indicated that six items describe a gang. Miller used these six items to compose the following definition of a gang (see Bursik and Grasmick 1993):

a self-formed association of peers, bound together by mutual interests, with identifiable leadership, well-developed lines of authority, and other organizational features, who act in concert to achieve a specific purpose or purposes, which generally include . . . illegal activity and control over a particular territory, facility or type of enterprise.

The lack of a consensus about the defining features of a gang has made it difficult to generate consistent findings and generalizations. Central to the debate is the issue of criminal activity. The criminality of gangs varies greatly and using criminality to distinguish groups as gangs may be problematic; however, ignoring criminal activity makes it difficult to distinguish gangs from school, church, and youth activity groups.

Gang Formation

Joining a gang generally involves associating with gang members, gaining the acceptance of important members within the gang, and eventually being admitted (Spergel 1995). In many cases, adolescents will hang out with gang members for up to a year before making a commitment to join (Decker and Van Winkle 1996). Initiation rites, which range from being beaten by a row of gang members ("walking the line"), to committing a crime or harming a member of an opposing gang are sometimes required to join a gang, but are often inconsistently applied (Fleisher 1998; Spergel 1995; Miller 2001). Many gangs also actively recruit new members, especially when gang membership is low. Martin Sanchez-Jankowski (1991) offered three typologies of gang recruitment: (1) Fraternity—the gang advertises itself as, "cool, hip, the social thing to be in"; (2) Obligation—the gang appeals to a person's sense of community; and (3) Coercion—the gang uses physical and psychological intimidation.

The youths who join gangs do so for a variety of reasons. Common motives include camaraderie; a sense of belonging; status; new and exciting experiences; access to drugs and alcohol; and monetary opportunities through illegal markets. In most cases, youths believe that the gang will provide them with things they could not otherwise obtain. Many gang members report that they joined gangs because of the protection they offered. Youths who live in areas with gangs may be harassed, assaulted, or even killed if they do not belong to a gang, and friends who are tough and have knowledge of the streets may protect them. However, they may also be harmed if they belong to the *wrong* gang.

Research findings are inconclusive as to whether gangs actually protect their members from violence. Gangs may reduce victimization by encouraging their members to develop a protective group identity, as well as by providing physical protection in dangerous neighborhoods and situations such as confrontations with other gangs (Sanchez-Jankowski 1991). However, as noted earlier, gangs often use violence when initiating new members, and violence is frequently used as a way of controlling members. In addition, female gang members have heightened risks of sexual victimization by the males in their gangs (Miller 2001). Gang disputes, rivalries, and "wars" with other gangs further increase the likelihood that gang members will be victimized, as do conflicts with police and other authorities (Klein 1995; Miller 2001; Sanchez-Jankowski 1991; Venkatesh 2000). In the late 1980s, gang violence increased both in frequency and seriousness as gang-related homicides escalated with the spread of drive-by shootings and other gun attacks (Sanders 1994). Gang homicides have since declined, and by the century's end, youth homicides had declined for several years (Blumstein 2000).

Symbols of Gangs and Gang Membership

Youths often use language, dress, musical tastes, and other symbols to distinguish themselves from other groups of adolescents. Gangs represent a distinct type of relationship and as such have distinct symbols and rituals. These symbols are important in that they serve as a way of identifying fellow gang members and rival gang members. They also function as a means for gaining or maintaining status within the gang.

Nicknames are often used to represent an individual's unique role in the gang (Spergel 1995). For instance, a gang member may earn a nickname for being particularly vicious in a confrontation with another gang, thereby contributing to the gang's reputation as "tough." Alternatively, nicknames may be derogatory, having their basis in individuals' shortcomings (Klein 1995). Graffiti is used to mark territory and to threaten rival gangs. It generally includes the symbolic monikers of gang members and/or a "logo" of the gang's name. Many gangs dress in a manner that sets them apart from nonmembers. Heavily starched, baggy Khaki

pants and Pendleton shirts buttoned only at the collar were at one time the uniform of many Chicano gangs. Other gangs identified themselves by wearing or displaying colored bandanas. Gangs may use hand signs and specific mannerisms, such as a particular way of walking, as symbols of gang identity.

Gangs and Crime

The 1998 National Youth Gang Survey (2000) asked a representative sample of U.S. law enforcement agencies about youth gang crime. According to police, gangs are often involved in entrepreneurial crime, the most common of which are drug sales, theft, burglary, motor vehicle theft, and robbery. Several researchers have identified gangs that are organized around drug sales or other illegal enterprises (Fleisher 1998; Howell and Gleason 2001; Sullivan 1989); however, others doubt that gangs have the organizational structure necessary to conduct drug sales on the scale often described (Klein 1995; Spergel 1995). At the same time, research suggests that most gang members do not reap large profits from drug selling or other illegal activities (Venkatesh 2000).

Although gang members commit more criminal acts than the general population, many gang members report considerable involvement in crime before joining gangs. Thus, it is not clear if gang members' higher rates of offending are a result of belonging to a gang, or because individuals who join gangs are predisposed to crime. Two studies that use longitudinal data from Rochester youths demonstrate that both processes likely contribute to gang crime. Terence Thornberry (2001) noted that although many gang members use violence before joining a gang, gang membership and not prior offending is the better predictor of subsequent involvement in violent crime. However, Beth Bjerregaard and Alan Lizotte (2001) found that youths who owned a gun for protection were more likely to join gangs than were youths who did not own a weapon. These findings suggest that youths who are involved in crime find gangs attractive, and that gangs prefer to recruit seasoned offenders.

Gangs and Neighborhoods

Gangs most often appear in troubled neighborhoods; areas that are socially disorganized, characterized by inadequate social institutions, and whose residents are economically disadvantaged. These areas may be prone to relatively high rates of school dropout, teen pregnancy, public health problems, and may have prostitution and drug sales within their boundaries.

The relationship between gangs and neighborhood residents is complex (Venkatesh 2000). Residents may disapprove of the gang and their activities, particularly their violence and illegal activities. They may form neighborhood organizations or alliances with local law and campaign in order to discourage neighborhood youths from joining gangs and to rid the neighborhood of gangs.

However, residents do not always view gangs as threatening; only about one-third of the gang members in Scott H. Decker and Barrik Van Winkle's (1996) field study of active gang members believed that their neighbors were afraid of them. Gangs may even be accepted as part of the community. If the gang is well established and has existed for some time, residents may simply accept the gang as part of neighborhood life. Residents may also feel that the gang protects the community. This is especially true when rival gangs have been a problem in the community. Gangs may also offer residents other aid: they may help residents with moving, carrying groceries, financial assistance, or providing shelter (Sanchez-Jankowski 1991). Also, neighborhood residents may profit from the illegal activities of gang youths, buying their stolen property or illegal drugs (Sullivan 1989). Sudhir Alladi Venkatesh's (2000) account of a the relationship between the Black King's gang and the tenants of a Chicago housing project illustrates the duality of neighborhood-gang relations:

> Trafficking, extortion, and attempts to bribe tenants, CHA [Chicago Housing Authority] security officers, and law enforcement officials were part of their [the gang's] daily labors; however, the [gang's] leaders also monitored the behavior of strangers who entered the housing development by car and on foot. . . . It was not common, but also not entirely unusual, to see BK's [Black King's] helping tenants in their buildings with a small cash disbursement. During the summer they routinely hosted cook-outs and passed out free food and beer. Throughout the year, they offered the use of a car for errands, and they assisted

tenant leaders in their search for apartment burglars.

Gangs and Ethnicity

Early twentieth-century U.S. youth gangs emerged in ethnic enclaves and formed along ethnic and racial lines. At that time, youth street gangs were ethnically homogenous, and primarily composed of Jewish, Irish, and Italian members (Spergel 1995). In 1975, almost half of all gangs in the six largest cities were primarily composed of African Americans, approximately 36 percent were Hispanic, almost 9 percent were white, and 7.5 percent were Asian (Miller 1975). The 1998 National Youth Gang Survey (2000) revealed a considerable increase in Hispanic gangs: by the late 1990s, 46 percent of gangs were predominantly Hispanic, 34 percent were African American, 12 percent were white, and 6 percent were Asian.

Although ethnic or racial homogeneity within gangs is the norm, gangs are becoming increasingly diverse. The 1998 National Youth Gang Survey reveals that multiethnic/multiracial gangs account for 36 percent of all American gangs (2000). The most common multiethnic gangs involve Hispanics and whites (Klein 1995). Many Asian gangs are also ethnically heterogeneous, involving youths from Chinese, Japanese, Korean, Vietnamese, Cambodian, Filipino and various Pacific Islander backgrounds (Klein 1995).

Some research suggests that the type of crime that members participate in varies with the ethnicity of the gang. Drug offenses appear to be more common among African American gangs, property crimes among white and Asian gangs, and Hispanic gangs appear more involved in territorial violence (Spergel 1990). Territorial violence typically occurs between gangs of the same ethnicity or race; thus gang violence is usually intraracial. However, ethnically or racially divergent gangs may come into conflict as a result of sudden changes in an area's racial or ethnic makeup, or when resources become scarce (Thrasher 1927; Spergel 1995).

Female Gangs

Most early gang research ignores female gang members and female gangs. Indeed, a common approach discusses females only as a means of ending males' gang involvement by encouraging commitments to marriage, fatherhood, and bread-winning. Other studies recognize female involvement in gangs, but identify them as auxiliaries of male gangs. This research describes female gangs as affiliations of a larger, male gang in which males encourage females to develop a gang that adopts a feminized version of the male gang's name, and that provides males with access to female gang members as sex objects.

Anne Campbell's (1984) *The Girls in the Gang* encouraged research to move beyond its traditional focus. Campbell's study focused on three women involved in three different female gangs in New York City in the early 1980s. Campbell concluded that while females generally become involved in gangs through their relationships with males, their role is not merely that of a sex object; moreover, Campbell noted that female "auxiliary" gangs are less tied to their associated male gang than previous research implied. She emphasized the independence of these female gangs, drawing attention to the ways in which females administrate their own gangs, and gain status through their behavior, rather than through their sexuality.

Several scholars have responded to Campbell's challenge, and there is an increasing body of research on female gangs. Jody Miller (2001) interviewed forty-eight gang and forty-six nongang girls in Columbus, Ohio, and St. Louis. She found that most of these young women did not join a gang because of a boyfriend, but formed romantic relationships with gang males after joining a gang. According to Miller, neighborhood exposure to gangs and family contribute more to female gang involvement than do boyfriends. Miller's study, as well as other research, indicates that female gang members commit more crimes than nongang females, as well as nongang males (Curry 2001; Esbensen and Winfree 2001). Moreover, female gang members participate in the same types of offenses committed by male gang members, albeit to a lesser extent.

Recent research notwithstanding, there remains considerable uncertainty about female gangs, including their prevalence. For instance, the 1998 National Youth Gang Survey indicated that only 8 percent of gang members are female (2000). In contrast, the National Evaluation of Gang Resistance Education and Training's (GREAT) 1995 sample of eighth-grade students found that 38 percent of gang members were females (Esbensen and Winfree 2001). The GREAT survey also reports the "mixed gender" gangs far outnumber other gangs: 84 percent of male gang members reported that their gangs had female members (Peterson et al. 2001).

Family, Gangs, and the Gang as Family

The term gang often provokes images of violence, drug use and dealing, and crime. However, youth gangs also have other consequences. Gangs can provide youths with a sense of belonging and identity, social support, and solidarity. Gang youths often compare their gangs to family, and in some respects gangs resemble families.

In some neighborhoods, many members of a family have belonged to the same gang. These multigenerational gangs develop in different settings, but have been most often observed among Hispanics. Sanchez-Jankowski (1991) reported that many gang members told him that their families had a long history of gang involvement that included older brothers, and in a considerable number of cases, fathers and grandfathers. Thirty-two percent of the Los Angeles fathers he interviewed said that they had been members of the same gang to which their children now belonged, while 11 percent reported that four generations of their family had membership in the same gang. Miller (2001) indicated that 79 percent of the forty-eight gang females she interviewed had at least one other family member involved in gangs, and 60 percent had more than one. About half of the gang members in Moore's study (1991) of two Chicano/a gangs in East Los Angeles had a relative in a gang. Moore (1991) suggested that while family members may share the same gang, membership is not inherited, or simply passed on from parent to child.

According to Sanchez-Jankowski (1991), tradition plays an important role in multigenerational gangs. He argues that the long history of multigenerational gangs, coupled with parents' former involvement with the same neighborhood gangs, brings a sense of tradition to the gangs. As indicated in a comment by a gang youth Sanchez-Jankowski interviewed, many youths in these neighborhoods feel that their families and community expect them to join a gang:

> I joined because the gang has been here
> for a long time and even though the name

is different a lot of the fellas from the community have been involved in it over the years, including my dad. The gang has helped the community by protecting it against outsiders so people here have kind of depended on it . . . I feel it's my obligation to the community to put some time helping them out. This will help me to get help in the community if I need it some time.

Occasionally families are split across gangs. Comments from two gang members in Marjorie Zatz and Eduardo Portillo's study (2000, pp. 392, 391) illustrate that these divisions can be particularly devastating when families belong to two feuding gangs:

They [my relatives] are from different gangs, though . . . but I don't care about them because they be trying to shoot at us all the time. My own uncle shot at me, one of them tried to kill me already, but that's all right.

We can't have family reunions or anything because they are always fighting, like my *tios* [uncles] fight. At the funerals they fight, or at the park, or at a picnic when we get together, they just fight. So sometimes the family don't get together, only for funerals, that's the only time.

Thus, families contribute to gangs by modeling gang behavior through previous gang membership, providing a sense of tradition to the gang, and even directly contribute to gang violence against their own families when family conflicts with gang membership.

Families also encourage gang involvement when they fail to provide youths with resources and support typically associated with family life. In many cases, families are simply too poor to provide the economic resources that many gangs are capable of supplying. William Brown's (1998) study of seventy-nine African-American gang members in Detroit reveals that 63 percent of youths lived in a family in which their parents were employed only part-time. A comment by a gang member from Sanchez-Jankowski's (1991) study illustrates the possible consequences of parental poverty:

Before I joined the gang, I could see that you could count on your boys to help in

times of need and that meant a lot to me. And when I needed money, sure enough they gave it to me. Nobody else would have given it to me; my parents didn't have it, and there was no other place to go. The gang was just like they said they would be, and they'll continue to be there when I need them.

Other family characteristics also contribute to gang life. Many gang members report that they live with parents or stepparents who are alcoholics, chronic drug-users, abusive (physical, sexual, and emotional), or involved in illegal activities. These conditions create considerable stress that youths may try to alleviate by joining a gang. Over a quarter of the women in Moore's (1991) study of East Los Angeles gangs reported that a family member had made sexual advances while they growing up. Almost a quarter of the men and about half of the women resided with a heroin addict during their childhood, and about half of the men and over half of the women had a member of the household die during their formative years. Also, more than half of the men and three-quarters of the women witnessed the arrest of a household member when they were children.

These family stresses may encourage youths to create family-like relationships in the groups to which they belong, and as such, these relationships may represent *fictive kin*. According to Stack (1974), fictive kin refers to people who are unrelated biologically or by marriage, but use familial labels (e.g., mother or sister) to signify relationships characterized by trust, reciprocity, and commitment. Fictive kin typically originate in settings where people have limited access to economic resources and familial networks. The insecurity and unexpected crises that characterize these settings may quickly transform a friendship into a deeper, more reciprocal, fictive kin relationship.

Ethnographic research highlights the social and emotional support that gangs can provide. In James Vigil's (1988) study, nearly half of the Chicano gang members he interviewed expressed "familial supportive behavior" when explaining the significance of their gang. Mary G. Harris (1988) found a similar pattern among girls in Chicano gangs: "The girls in this study expressed clearly a strong sense of belonging to the gang, and compared gang membership to a family." Gangs often function similarly to family, providing youths with a sense of belonging and identity, social support, solidarity, excitement, fun and new experiences, a sense of protection, and possible opportunities for economic gain. A young woman from Harris's (1988) study states it succinctly: "It was a family. We protected each other. We took care of each other. We stole for each other."

Gangs may compensate for family by providing members with a sense of belonging. Gang youths often refer to their fellow gang members as brothers or sisters, or use other familial labels to describe relationships. These familiarities stress the group nature of their interactions and provide a sense of personal and group identity. Gangs provide youths an alternate source of identity, and are a place (often the only place) for the youths to experiment with their identity (Vigil 1988). A collective ideology of family can instill a sense of brother/sisterhood, and provide the basis for a common ideology, which aids in maintaining group consciousness (Venkatesh 2000). A comment by a male from Moore's (1991) study reflects this pattern:

> The year that I was there it was like, umm, they were like family, because we could all take care of each other. . . . I think they were like my own family. I think I was more with them than my own family, because I left them for a while.

Gangs Internationally

There is a tendency to view gangs as an American phenomenon. However, youth gangs have been reported across many countries. The literature on international gangs is sparse, most often simply reporting gangs' existence in a certain country. The research that has been conducted abroad generally focuses on the characteristics of gang members and gangs' involvement in criminal activity. Thus, little is known about gangs internationally, and virtually nothing is known about gangs acting as fictive kin abroad. However, gangs in many other countries share many characteristics with American gangs, and thus they may also mirror this aspect of American gangs.

Research in Canada has focused primarily on Asian gangs, describing Chinese gangs in Vancouver and Vietnamese gangs in Toronto (Covey, Menard, and Franzese 1992; Klein 1995). However,

Robert Gordon (1998) highlighted the ethnic diversity of Vancouver gangs, arguing that although these gangs often have ethnic names, a minority are actually composed primarily of members from the same ethnic background. While some discrepancies remain in the research, it is clear that Canadian gangs are not as prevalent as gangs in the United States. Gordon (1998) suggests one reason for this is because Canadian cities' educational, health, and social services are more effective at addressing the underlying problems associated with gangs.

Mexican gangs appear very similar to Cholo culture of the Hispanic gangs of the southwest United States, being similar in territoriality, gang rivalries, graffiti, and delinquent activities (Klein 1995). However, as with American gangs, there also appears to be great variety in their behaviors, especially between gangs in urban and rural areas (Cavan and Cavan 1968).

The limited research on gangs in Asia indicates that youth gangs in Malaysia and Thailand commit a relatively large share of the total crime there (Holyst 1982). Chinese *triads* have garnered much attention from media, however these are mostly composed of adult males, rather than juveniles. Yet the triads may play a role in youth gangs, serving as a blueprint for youth gang structure and activities, as well as providing the triads with new members (Covey, Menard, and Franzese 1992). Chinese youth gangs specializing in theft and drugs have been reported, as well as other gangs that engage in a wider variety of criminal activities and are more varied in age, number of members, and degree of territoriality (Klein 1995). Compared to the United States, adult and youth gangs are responsible for greater portion of crime in Japan, although both adults and youth crime rates are higher in the United States (Spergel 1995).

Youth gangs are also common throughout Europe. Gangs committed a large portion of total offenses in Spain in the 1980s (Holyst 1982), but few gangs exist currently (Klein 1995). After a period of absence, gangs have reemerged in France, although they are still much less prevalent than in the United State. At least in Paris, the re-emergence of gangs is thought to have been spurred by the increase in drug trafficking and the growth of the underclass (Kroeker and Haut 1995). German right-wing youth groups have drawn much attention; however, some researchers suggest they should be distinguished from youth street gangs (Kelin 1995). Neo-Nazi groups resemble youth street gangs in some ways, but they are typically more focused, involved in planning their movement, and spend much more time involved in activities to further their cause, such as writing literature and pamphlets (Klein 1995). Yet their reappearance in the 1990s, and their attacks on immigrant youths are linked to the emergence of gangs more closely resembling the American street gang. For instance, Hermann Tertilt's (2001) field study of a Turkish gang in Frankfort suggests that their violence is a response to the "segregation, degradation and humiliation," inflicted on foreigners in Germany. Others have also noted that territorial youth gangs form in response to extremists' attacks on immigrant youth (Klein 1995).

A broad range of youth groups existed in the former Soviet Union; however, it was not clear that these groups actually constituted gangs. Research since the Soviet Union's demise indicates that contemporary Russian gangs mirror American street gangs in many respects. These gangs emerged in cities with minority populations; they are territorial, and are frequently in conflict with rival gangs (Klein 1995). For the most part, they are large and fairly well organized, and members appear to share a strong sense of solidarity.

Gangs have been a fairly consistent feature of the urban landscape of Britain. In the seventeenth century, British gangs routinely vandalized urban areas, were territorial, and were involved in violent conflict with other gangs (Pearson 1983). Studies of British gangs that existed in the early 1900s suggest that these trends persisted. The research also suggested that British gangs were not as large and structured, nor nearly as violent as American gangs (Cavan and Cavan 1968; Morash 1983; Covey, Menard, and Franzese 1992). However, the 1980s saw the emergence of American-style gangs: ethnic street gangs that populate metropolitan areas, work in the drug trade, and are more violent than previous British gangs (Mares 2001).

Gangs exist in many varieties and forms, across many different countries and cultures. Although their particulars and contexts differ, some trends are apparent. The economic, social, and sometimes violent discrimination immigrants often encounter appears to underpin the formation of gangs in many countries, including the United States. Gangs appear to be much more likely to form in poor, urbanized areas with underdeveloped social institutions. This is consistent with the social disorganization theory that lies at the heart of many theories of gangs. Comparing gangs cross-culturally allows for a greater assessment of the role structure and culture play in gang formation and gang activity.

Conclusion

Gang life and family are fraught with contradictions. The family is idealized as a place for nurturance, support, and protection. However, the majority of gang youths come from families under severe strain; families often unable to provide these things. The gang is often demonized (not without reason) as a source of delinquency and violence. Yet gangs also act as an important source of support for these youths, compensating for what is lacking in their home life. Gangs can act as surrogate families to youths, providing a sense of belonging, identity, status, and protection. Youths who do not receive these things from family or other social institutions may seek them elsewhere, and in the socially disorganized neighborhoods where gangs exist, they are an alternative option.

See also: FICTIVE KINSHIP; JUVENILE DELINQUENCY; NEIGHBORHOOD; RUNAWAY YOUTHS

Bibliography

1998 National Youth Gang Survey: Summary. (2000). Washington, DC: U.S. Dept. of Justice, Office of Justice Programs, Office of Juvenile Justice and Delinquency Prevention.

Bjerregaard, B., and Lizotte, A. J. (2001). "Gun Ownership and Gang Membership." In *The Modern Gang Reader,* 2nd ed., ed. J. Miller, C. L. Maxson, and M. W. Klein. Los Angeles: Roxbury.

Blumstein, A. (2000). *The Crime Drop in America,* ed. A. Blumstein and J. Wallman. New York: Cambridge University Press.

Brown, W. (1998). "The Fight for Survival: African-American Gang Members and Their Families in a Segregated Society." *Juvenile and Family Court Journal* 49:1–14.

Bursik, R. J. Jr., and Grasmick, H. G. (1993). *Neighborhoods and Crime.* New York: Lexington Books.

Campbell, A. (1984). *The Girls in the Gang.* New York: Basil Blackwell.

Cavan, R., and Cavan, J. T. (1968). *Delinquency and Crime: Cross-Cultural Perspectives.* Monterey, CA: Brooks/Cole.

Cloward, R. A., and Ohlin, L. B. (1960). *Delinquency and Opportunity*. New York: Free Press.

Cohen, A. K. (1955). *Delinquent Boys*. Glencoe, IL: The Free Press.

Covey, H. C.; Menard, S.; and Franzese, R. J. (1992). *Juvenile Gangs*. Springfield, IL: Thomas Books.

Curry, G. D. (2001). "Female Gang Involvement." In *The Modern Gang Reader*, 2nd ed., ed. J. Miller, C. L. Maxson, and M. W. Klein. Los Angeles: Roxbury.

Decker, S. H., and Van Winkle, B. (1996). *Life in the Gang: Family, Friends and Violence*. New York: Cambridge University Press.

Esbensen, F. (2000). "Preventing adolescent gang involvement." *U.S. Office of Juvenile Justice and Delinquency Prevention Juvenile Justice Bulletin*, September. Washington: U.S. Department of Justice.

Esbensen, F.; Deschenes, E. P.; and Winfree L. T. Jr. (1999). "Differences Between Gang Girls and Gang Boys: Results from a Multisite Survey." *Youth & Society* 31:27–29.

Esbensen, F., and Winfree, L. T. Jr. (1998). "Race and Gender Differences Between Gang and Non-Gang Youths." In *The Modern Gang Reader*, 2nd ed., ed. J. Miller, C. L. Maxson, and M. W. Klein. Los Angeles: Roxbury.

Fleisher, M. S. (1998). *Dead End Kids*. Madison: University of Wisconsin Press.

Gordon, R. M. (1998). "Street Gangs and Criminal Business Organisations: A Canadian Perspective." In *Gangs and Youth Subcultures: International Explorations*, ed. K. Hazlehurst and C. Hazlehurst. New Jersey: Transaction Publishers.

Harris, M. G. (1988). *Cholas: Latino Girls and Gangs*. New York: AMS Press.

Holyst, B. (1982). *Comparative Criminology*. Lexington, MA: Lexington Books.

Howell, J. C., and Gleason, D. K. (2001). "Youth Gang Drug Trafficking." In *The Modern Gang Reader*, 2nd ed., ed. J. Miller, C. L. Maxson and M. W. Klein. Los Angeles: Roxbury.

Klein, M. W. (1995). *The American Street Gang*. New York: Oxford University Press.

Kroeker, M., and Haut, F. (1995). "A Tale of Two Cities: The Street Gangs of Paris and Los Angeles." *Police Chief* 62:32–38.

Mares, D. (2001). "Gangsters or Lager Louts? Working Class Street Gangs in Manchester." In *The Eurogang Paradox: Street Gangs and Youth Groups in the US and Europe*, ed. M. W. Klein, H. Kerner, C. L. Maxson, And E. Weitkamp. Dordrecht, Netherlands: Kluwer Academic Publishers.

Miller, J. (2001). *One of the Guys: Girls, Gangs, and Gender*. New York: Oxford University Press.

Miller, W. B. (1958). "Lower Class Culture as Generating Milieu of Gang Delinquency." *Journal of Social Issues* 14:5–19.

Miller, W. B. (1973). "The Molls." *Society* 2:23–35.

Miller, W. B. (1975). "Violence by Youth Gangs as a Crime Problem in Major American Cities." National Institute for Juvenile Justice and Delinquency Prevention, US Justice Department. Washington, DC: US Government Printing Office.

Miller, W. B. (1980). "Gangs, Groups, and Serious Youth Crime." In *Critical Issues in Juvenile Delinquency*, ed. D. Schichor and D. H. Kelly. Lexington, MA: DC Health.

Moore, J. W. (1991). *Going Down to the Barrio*. Philadelphia: Temple University Press.

Morash, M. (1983). "Gangs, Groups and Delinquency." *British Journal of Criminology* 23:309–331.

Pearson, G. (1983). *Hooligan: A History of Respectable Fears*. London: MacMillan.

Peterson, D.; Miller, J.; and Esbensen, F. (2001). "The Impact of Sex Composition on Gangs and Gang Member Delinquency." *Criminology* 39:411–439.

Sanchez-Jankowski, M. (1991). *Islands in the Street: Gangs and American Urban Society*. Berkley: University of California Press.

Sanders, W. B. (1994). *Gang-Bangs and Drive-bys: Grounded Culture and Juvenile Gang Violence*. New York: Aldine de Gruyter.

Spergel, I. A. (1990). "Youth Gangs: Continuity and Change." In *Crime and Justice: A Review of Research*, vol. 12, ed. M. Tonry and N. Morris. Chicago: University of Chicago Press.

Spergel, I. A. (1995). *The Youth Gang Problem*. New York: Oxford University Press.

Stack, C. B. (1974). *All Our Kin: Strategies for Survival in a Black Community*. New York: Harper and Row.

Sullivan, M. L. (1989). *"Getting Paid": Youth Crime and Work in the Inner City*. Ithaca, NY: Cornell University Press.

Tertilt, H. (2001). "Patterns of Ethnic Violence in a Frankfurt Street Gang." In *The Eurogang Paradox: Street Gangs and Youth Groups in the US and Europe*, ed. M. W. Klein, H. Kerner, C. L. Maxson, and E. Weitekamp. Dordrecht, Netherlands: Kluwer Academic Publishers.

Thornberry, T. P. (2001). "Membership in Youth Gangs and Involvement in Serious and Violent Offending." In *The Modern Gang Reader,* 2nd ed., ed. J. Miller, C. L. Maxson, and M. W. Klein. Los Angeles: Roxbury.

Thrasher, F. M. (1927). *The Gang: A Study of 1,313 Gangs in Chicago.* Chicago: University of Chicago Press.

Venkatesh, S. A. (2000). *American Project: The Rise and Fall of a Modern Ghetto.* Cambridge: Harvard University Press.

Vigil, J. D. (1988). *Barrio Gangs: Streetlife and Identity in Southern California.* Austin: University of Texas Press.

Zatz, M. S., and Portillos, E. L. (2000). "Voices from the Barrio: Chicano/a Gangs, Families, and Communities." *Criminology* 38:369–401.

BILL MCCARTHY
MONICA J. MARTIN

GAY PARENTS

Research has consistently demonstrated that heterosexual adults retain consistently and overwhelmingly negative attitudes toward lesbians and gay males. Heterosexual adults commonly view this negativity as acceptable despite political rhetoric lauding the contributions and multiple perspectives of an increasingly diverse citizenry (Kite and Whitley 1996). The stigma, prejudice, and discrimination directed at people who identify themselves as homosexual are not confined to individual acts, but have been institutionalized and systematically perpetuated throughout the various levels of the culture. For example, the U. S. legal system does not recognize unions between same-sex partners, nor does it protect relationships between lesbian and gay male parents and their children (Patterson, Fulcher, and Wainright 2000). Despite such obstacles, lesbian and gay male individuals successfully create meaningful family relationships that not only prosper, but thrive (Patterson 2000).

Gay Relationships and Legal Matters

Legal recognition of unions (i.e., marriage) between heterosexual males and females has a long-standing history in the United States, Europe, and other parts of the world influenced by Western cultures. Such recognition has set the standards for acceptable relationships and the benefits that they are believed to bring. One common benefit of marriage relates to the establishment of families and the rearing of children. Most countries in the world deny legal marriage to gay males, including the United States, Canada, and the preponderance of Europe nation-states. The Netherlands stands alone in its legal recognition of same-sex marriage, while Denmark, Sweden, Iceland, and Norway grant domestic partnerships for lesbians and gay males. The state of Vermont in the United States has granted partnership rights and recognition to persons who identify themselves as lesbian or gay.

Because legal marriage is denied to most gay males in the world, however, such individuals who choose to become parents face multiple challenges. These include seeking to adopt children, achieving custody of children from former heterosexual relationships, and gaining access to insurance and other employment benefits routinely offered to heterosexual parents. Notwithstanding these and other issues, many gay men choose to become parents and do so with much success.

Gay Fathers as a Distinct Group

Virtually no data exist on the prevalence of gay parenting among non-Caucasians and non-Western Europeans. Even in the United States, it is difficult to estimate the number of gay male parents due to ongoing prejudice and discrimination that may compel some to mask their sexual identity in certain contexts. In the United States, however, between one and two million gay men are parents, and these men are parenting approximately two to four million children (Patterson and Chan 1996). Gay males who act as parents include a diverse group in terms of age, ethnicity, level of education, socioeconomic status, physical ability, and religious or spiritual background. Their differences notwithstanding, the group contends with issues unique to their sexual orientation. Some of the factors that distinguish gay male parents from heterosexual fathers include the routes through which they become parents, how they negotiate their roles as parents, and the social support that they receive.

Becoming Parents and Negotiating Parenthood

Gay males become parents for a variety of reasons and through a number of means (Patterson and Chan 1996). The largest percentage of gay male

Jon Holden (left), and his partner, Michael Galluccio (right), holding their adopted son Adam. In the United States between one and two million gay men are parents.
AP WIDE WORLD PHOTOS

parents in the United States constitutes divorced men who entered into a heterosexual marriage and had children prior to publicly declaring themselves as gay. Such men report entering into marriage because they loved their spouses, wanted to have children, and desired to live a married life, and because of social and familial expectations or pressures. Some hoped marriage to a woman would diminish or dispel emerging or present homosexual identities and desires. Others became aware of their homosexual identity only after having married. The majority of marriages between gay males and heterosexual females eventually end in divorce, and courts have, in such cases, historically granted child custody to the mother. Cultural beliefs that female and heterosexual parents are more fit parents have dominated custody decisions. Still, gay fathers are sometimes awarded custody of their children and serve as the primary caretakers. Others may live with a variety of visitation arrangements. In instances where gay fathers lose custody of their children, establishing a gay male identity may take place in conjunction with a painful grieving process.

Besides heterosexual marriage or sexual encounters, gay men may become parents through adoption, surrogacy, and joint parenthood with a woman or women (Patterson and Chan 1996). Adoption of children by individuals of a sexual minority status falls into two categories: *stranger*

adoption and *second-parent adoption*. Stranger adoptions occur when unrelated adoptive parents take children in as their own because the biological parents are unable or unwilling to care for offspring. Second-parent adoptions take place when only one member of the couple is the legal or biological parent of a child or children, and the second couple member wishes to pursue adoption of the child(ren) as a means of legally recognizing the relationship between that parent and the child(ren) (Patterson, Fulcher, and Wainright 2000). Internationally, the majority of countries deny legal adoption rights to people who identify themselves as lesbian or gay, and if one member of the couple adopts or has birth children, his partner is not given parental rights (Savin-Williams and Esterberg 2000).

Surrogacy is another avenue to parenthood for some gay males. This method involves fathering a child with a surrogate mother, often through sperm donation by a member of a couple. Frequently, the couple makes a contract with the birth mother to relinquish her parental rights and responsibilities, making the father the legal parent (Patterson and Chan 1996). In gay male couples who become parents through these means, the nonbiological parent may eventually seek adoption of the child via the process described above.

Joint conception and rearing of a child or children with a woman or women is another way for gay males to become parents. Such individuals may enter an agreement in which one member of a gay male couple donates sperm, which is used to inseminate a lesbian or heterosexual woman who is either single or in a committed relationship. In *quadra-parenting,* children brought into the world in this manner may split their time between the two homes (Patterson and Chan 1996). All of the parents together negotiate the specific arrangements.

Gay Males in the Parenting Role

As noted previously, the preponderance of research investigating gay male parents and parenthood has been conducted in the United States using European-American, well-educated, affluent, and urban samples (Patterson 1996). Such research has demonstrated that gay male fathers and heterosexual fathers do not differ in their motives for becoming parents (Bigner and Jacobsen 1989). However, gay male parents reported being more responsive and more likely to exhibit authoritative (e.g., limit setting, open to negotiation), as opposed to authoritarian (e.g., dictatorial), patterns of parenting behaviors than their heterosexual counterparts. Gay fathers also emphasized nurturing in their approach to childrearing and fostered a climate of acceptance and respect for diversity that heterosexual fathers did not as frequently endorse. Future research on parenting quality needs to be conducted with larger and more representative samples of gay and heterosexual fathers before definitive conclusions can be drawn in this regard.

Although a gay man choosing to become a parent within an established, committed relationship with another man faces many of the same adjustment issues that arise for a heterosexual man, issues specific to his stigmatized social status make it imperative that he seek information and support. Specifically, gay male parents need timely information about developmental factors unique to children of gay parents, health concerns, legal matters, and financial planning (Patterson and Chan 1996).

Children of Gay Male Parents

Negative myths, images, and stereotypes about individuals who identify themselves as lesbian or gay and their ability to parent children are created, perpetuated, and maintained at multiple levels of society. One area that has received considerable attention is the impact lesbian and gay parents have on various aspects of development in their children. The results of recent investigations dispel many of these myths.

The home environment. Historically, concerns about the stability of committed gay relationships, the quality of gay parenting, and the nature of the parent-child relationships in households headed by gay males have been raised. However, research has not supported these concerns. On the contrary, the relationship dynamics of gay parents and their children parallel those of heterosexual father-child relationships. For example, gay male and heterosexual couples report similar types and levels of relationship satisfaction, supportive interactions, and conflict (Patterson and Chan 1996). Given comparable environments, the evidence suggests no significant differences in the psychosocial, emotional, and sexual development of children raised by gay and heterosexual couples (Patterson 2000).

Sexual orientation and risk for sexual abuse. Considerable investigative efforts have focused on determining the likelihood that gay parents will have children who are gay due to their exposure to a homosexual home environment. Findings indicate, however, that the majority of children raised by gay men grow up to identify themselves as heterosexual (Patterson and Chan 1996). Furthermore, Bailey, Bobrow, Wolfe, and Mikach (1995) report that the frequency of contact or the length of time children live with their gay fathers does not seem to affect the child's ultimate sexual identity; that is, those who live with gay fathers for long periods of time are no more likely to be lesbian or gay than those who do not.

Another persistent myth about gay male parents is that they are more likely to sexually abuse their children than are their heterosexual counterparts. However, research indicates that children, particularly girls, are at a far greater risk to be sexually abused by adult heterosexual males (Jones and McFarlane 1980). Although some gay males do perpetrate sexual abuse toward children, they are no more likely to do so than are heterosexual males (Jenny, Roesler, and Poyer 1994). The image of gay men as child molesters is a destructive myth that continues to pervade society despite evidence to the contrary.

Conclusion

In many ways, gay fathers are similar to heterosexual fathers. Unique challenges for gay male parents arise from negative societal attitudes toward their intimate relationships, the methods they use to become parents, and the nature of their relationships with their children. Future research efforts should document multicultural and international perspectives, address institutionalized homonegativity that serves to perpetuate discrimination against gay male parents and their children, and provide public policy analyses that will end the discrimination against homosexual parents that effectively reduces the quality of social support they receive.

See also: ADOPTION; CHILDCARE; CHILD CUSTODY; FAMILY ROLES; FATHERHOOD; FICTIVE KINSHIP; FOSTER PARENTS; GENDER; GENDER IDENTITY; LESBIAN PARENTS; PARENTING STYLES; SEXUAL ORIENTATION; SURROGACY

Bibliography

Bailey, J. M.; Bobrow, D.; Wolfe, M.; and Mikach, S. (1995). "Sexual Orientations of Adult Sons of Gay Fathers." *Developmental Psychology* 31:124–129.

Bigner, J. J., and Jacobsen, R. B. (1989). "The Value of Children to Gay and Heterosexual Fathers." In *Homosexuality and the Family,* ed. F. W. Bozett. New York: Harrington Park Press.

Groth, A. N., and Birnbaum, H. J. (1978). "Adult Sexual Orientation and Attraction to Underage Persons." *Archives of Sexual Behavior* 7:175–181.

Jenny, C.; Roesler, T. A.; and Poyer, K. L. (1994). "Are Children at Risk for Sexual Abuse by Homosexuals?" *Pediatrics* 94:41–44.

Kite, M. E., and Whitley, B. E., Jr. (1996). "Sex Differences in Attitudes toward Homosexual Persons, Behaviors, and Civil Rights: A Meta-analysis." *Personal and Social Psychological Bulletin* 22:336–353.

Miller, B. (1979). "Gay Fathers and Their Children." *Family Coordinator* 28:544–552.

Patterson, C. J. (2000). "Family Relationships of Lesbians and Gay Men." *Journal of Marriage and the Family* 62:1052–1069.

Patterson, C. J., and Chan, R. W. (1996). "Gay Fathers and their Children." In *Textbook of Homosexuality and Mental Health,* ed. R. P. Cabaj and T. S. Stein. Washington, DC: American Psychiatric Press.

Patterson, C. J.; Fulcher, M.; and Wainright, J. (2000). "Children of Lesbian and Gay Parents: Research, Law, and Policy." In *Children and the Law: Social Science and Policy,* ed. B. L. Bottoms, M. B. Kovera, and B. D. McAuliff. New York: Cambridge University Press.

Savin-Williams, R. C., and Esterberg, E. G. (2000). "Lesbian, Gay, and Bisexual Families." In *Handbook of Family Diversity,* ed. D. H. Demo, K. R. Allen, and M. A. Fine. New York: Oxford University Press.

TODD A. SAVAGE
MARC E. FRISIELLO
SHARON SCALES ROSTOSKY

GENDER

Gender is a dichotomous social category that prescribes behaviors, attitudes, feelings, and other characteristics as being appropriate for a male or a female. That is, knowing an individual's gender allows us to place him or her in a distinct social category (male or female) and then judge his or her behaviors based on our expectations for that category. This entry introduces the prominent theories and empirical research related to the conceptualization of gender, gender roles and gender stereotypes, gendered power relations, and the interaction of gender with other social categories.

Conceptualization of Gender

The categorization of people on the basis of their biological sex ultimately leads to questions of difference. Theorists debate whether the differences between men and women are extensive enough to merit the common label of *opposite sex*. Maximalists believe that the differences between men and women are large and deeply rooted. Minimalists, in contrast, maintain that differences among men and among women are larger than the differences between men and women (Anselmi and Law 1998).

Another topic of debate is the location of gender. Specifically, are we gendered beings, or do we live in a gendered society? The essentialist stance contends that we are gendered beings; that is, gender is located within the individual. Essentialists argue that the behavioral differences between men and women are fundamental and rooted in biological sex differences. Accordingly, research based on an essentialist stance focuses on finding neurological, hormonal, and evolutionary differences between men and women. Because they emphasize the biological, essentialists often do not differentiate between the terms *sex* and *gender*. Cross-cultural similarities are used to support the essentialist perspective (Anselmi and Law 1998).

Social constructionists offer the contrasting view that gender is located within social arrangements. Specifically, as people relate to one another in a cultural and social context, gender differences arise that are sometimes related to biological sex differences, but are more often viewed as arising from cultural expectations for what are appropriate behavior and characteristics for females and males. Accordingly, research based on a social constructionist stance focuses on identifying conditions that are associated with similarities or differences across gender. From this perspective, sex is treated as a biological category, and gender is treated as a social category. Cross-cultural differences are used to support the social constructionist perspective (Anselmi and Law 1998).

Janice Bohan (1997) offers a useful analogy in understanding the difference between essentialism and social constructionism. After having a conversation with a person, one might either label the individual as friendly or, alternately, label the conversation as friendly. Labeling the person as friendly is analogous to essentialism, as friendly is viewed as a quality of the person. In another view, labeling the conversation as friendly is analogous with social constructionism, as friendly is viewed as a quality of the social interaction,

A third possibility is that gender is located both within individuals and within cultural and societal arrangements. A few biological differences, such as women's ability to bear children, shape social arrangements and influence social interactions. From this perspective, individuals internalize sociocultural expectations for their assigned gender and then behave accordingly. This view integrates essentialism and social constructionism to form an interactionist conceptualization of gender.

Gender Roles and Stereotypes

Gender roles are "socially and culturally defined prescriptions and beliefs about the behavior and emotions of men and women" (Anselmi and Law 1998, p. 195). Many theorists believe that perceived gender roles form the bases for the development of gender identity. Prominent psychological theories of gender role and gender identity development include evolutionary theory (Buss 1995; Shields 1975), object-relations theory (Chodorow 1989), gender schema theory (Bem 1981, 1993) and social role theory (Eagly 1987).

Evolutionary theories of gender development are grounded in genetic bases for differences between men and women. Functionalists (e.g., Shields 1975) propose that men and women have evolved differently to fulfill their different and complementary functions, which are necessary for survival. Similarly, sociobiologists (e.g., Buss 1995) suggest that behavioral differences between men and women stem from different sexual and reproductive strategies that have evolved to ensure that men and women are able to efficiently reproduce and effectively pass on their genes. These evolutionary-based theories share similarities with the essentialist and maximalist perspectives discussed previously.

In contrast, object-relations theorists focus on the effects of socialization on gender development. For example, Nancy Chodorow (1989) emphasizes the role of women as primary caregivers in the development of sex differences. Chodorow asserts that the early bond between mother and child affects boys and girls differently. Whereas boys must separate from their mothers to form their identities as males, girls do not have to endure this separation to define their identities as females. Chodorow (1989) explains that the devalued role of women is a product of the painful process men undergo to separate themselves from the female role.

Gender schema theory (Bem 1981) focuses on the role of cognitive organization in addition to socialization. This theory postulates that children learn how their cultures and/or societies define the roles of men and women and then internalize this knowledge as a gender schema, or unchallenged core belief. The gender schema is then used to organize subsequent experiences (Bem 1993). Children's perceptions of men and women are thus an interaction between their gender schemas and their experiences. Eventually, children will incorporate their own self-concepts into their gender schema and will assume the traits and behaviors that they deem suitable for their gender.

Alice Eagly (1987) offers yet another explanation of gender development that is based on socialization. Eagly's social role theory suggests that the sexual division of labor and societal expectations based on stereotypes produce gender roles. Eagly (1987) distinguishes between the communal and agentic dimensions of gender-stereotyped characteristics. The communal role is characterized by attributes, such as nurturance and emotional expressiveness, commonly associated with domestic activities, and thus, with women. The agentic role is characterized by attributes such as assertiveness and independence, commonly associated with public activities, and thus, with men. Behavior is strongly influenced by gender roles when cultures endorse gender stereotypes and form firm expectations based on those stereotypes (Eagly 1987).

As Eagly suggests, gender roles are closely linked with gender stereotypes. Stereotypes are "overgeneralized beliefs about people based on their membership in one of many social categories" (Anselmi and Law 1998, p. 195). Gender stereotypes vary on four dimensions: traits, role behaviors, physical characteristics, and occupations (Deaux and Lewis 1983). For example, whereas men are more likely to be perceived as aggressive and competitive, women are more likely to be viewed as passive and cooperative. Traditionally, men have been viewed as financial providers, whereas women have been viewed as caretakers. Physical characteristics and occupations have also been considered consistent or inconsistent with masculine or feminine roles.

Traditional gender stereotypes are most representative of the dominant (white, middle-class) culture. Hope Landrine (1999) asserts that although race and social class may not be mentioned when inquiring about gender stereotypes, most people will make assumptions about these categories. Her research suggests that when race and social classes are specified, different gender stereotypes emerge.

Gender roles and stereotypes affect couple and family interaction. Often, for example, the division of household labor is based on gender. Traditionally, white women in heterosexual couples remained at home and completed most of the domestic labor, while their male partners worked outside the home to provide the family income. Although women have increasingly joined the workforce over the past thirty years, they continue to do the majority of the household labor. Lawrence Kurdek (1993) studied white, heterosexual, gay, and lesbian couples without children. He found that heterosexual and gay couples were more likely than lesbian couples to divide household labor so that one partner did the majority of the work. Lesbian couples were most likely to share domestic tasks or take turns doing the tasks (Kurdek 1993).

Gender roles often become more differentiated when men and women become parents. Overall, women provide more direct care for and spend more time with children (Walzer 2001). This care includes taking responsibility for the mental work of gathering and processing information about infant care, delegating the tasks related to infant care, and worrying about infant health and well-being. In sum, the unequal division of both household labor and childcare, with women doing the bulk of the work, is thought to contribute to the reported lower marital satisfaction for women (Walzer 2001).

Gender roles and stereotypes affect men and women in other ways. Specifically, men and women may be judged by how well they conform to traditional stereotypes. In his theory of masculine gender role strain, Joespech Pleck (1976) asserted that boys and men are pressured to fulfill a standard of masculinity. Boys and men, for example, who do not fulfill the standard often suffer from low self-worth (Pleck; Sonnenstein; and Ku1993). Other lifelong consequences befall men who experience traumatic socialization practices such as rites of passage that entail violence. Even men who successfully fulfill the standard of masculinity suffer psychologically or emotionally from rigid constraints on acceptable parenting roles for men (Pleck; Sonnonstein; and Ku 1993). Richard Lazur and Richard Majors (1995) contend that gender role strain is pronounced with men of color. Men of color must balance the dominant standards of masculinity with their cultures' standards of masculinity in an effort to fulfill both satisfactorily. In addition, men of color must overcome prejudice and other obstacles to fulfill the standards of masculinity. The result is increased gender role strain for men of color (Lazur and Majors 1995). Likewise, white women and women of color may be constrained by standards of femininity, such as the pressure to have children.

Gender stereotypes can also affect men's and women's performance. Stereotype threat is defined as "an individual's awareness that he or she may be judged by or may self-fulfill negative stereotypes about her or his gender or ethnic group" (Lips 2001, p. 33). Research indicates that stereotype threat can negatively affect performance by increasing anxiety. For example, Steven Spencer, Claude Steele, and Diane Quinn (1999) found that women performed significantly worse than men on a math test when the participants were led to believe that the test would probably produce gender differences. In contrast, women and men performed equally well when the participants were led to believe that the test did not produce gender differences. These findings suggest that negative stereotypes can and do negatively affect performance even when the stereotype has not been internalized or incorporated into the view of the self.

Interaction between Gender and Power

Differences in male and female gender roles are related to the power differential between men and women. Structural and institutional power reside in the forms of access to educational, economic, and political resources and opportunities. In most societies, access to these structural forms of power are aspects of male privilege.

Education, for example, provides people with the power to gather and process information, thus understanding the world in which they live. Although women in North America receive educations comparable to those of men, women in other nations often lack access to education and the power it affords. The United Nations (2000) reported that females comprise two-thirds of the world's 876 million illiterates. For example, under Taliban religious rule, women in Afganistan were not allowed to attend school, and those who attempted to teach them were harshly punished. One of the first responses when Taliban rule ended was the reinstitution of education for women.

Economies provide people with the power to financially support themselves and their families. The United Nations (2000) stated that women's participation in the workforce, although increasing, tends to be limited to a few occupations. In addition, women continue to occupy lower-status and lower-paying jobs. Women also experience greater unemployment than men (United Nations 2000). Fewer opportunities in the job market may partially explain the recent increases in the proportion of poor women in the United States. The United States 2000 Census data show that, compared to men at 9.9 percent, a higher percentage of women (12.5%) reside below the poverty line in all age categories. The differences are even more dramatic when race is included in the calculations. Whereas 8.3 percent of Caucasian American men fall beneath the poverty line, 24.1 percent of African American women fall beneath the poverty line (US Census Bureau 2001). Whether in the United States, or in other countries, women have less economic power than men.

Similar patterns are apparent in the arena of political power. Governments provide people with the power to voice their needs and wants through voting and holding elected positions. However, women did not have the right to vote in ten of the world's eleven oldest democracies until the twentieth century (Lips 2001). In addition, women are significantly underrepresented in legislative positions. Specifically, in 1998, women filled only 9 percent of the United States Senate seats and 12.9 percent of the House of Representative (Lips 2001).

Some theorists believe that men's greater power and status in societies underlie the differences in gender roles. Social structure theory (Eagly and Wood 1999) postulates that the powerful roles that men hold lead to the development of related traits, such as aggressiveness and assertiveness. Likewise, women who have less access to powerful roles develop traits consistent with their subordinate roles, such as submissiveness and cooperativeness. In sum, the power differential in favor of men may explain why stereotypical male traits are more valued than stereotypical feminine traits.

The existing power differential between men and women can also be manifested within marriages and families. For example, men may actively use their power to avoid sharing the household labor. Women may be relegated to providing more unpaid domestic labor because the gendered structure of their society inhibits their access to economic power.

Findings indicate that men who lack other types of power may compensate by exerting power through violence toward their partners. Women, who often lack economic power and interpersonal power and resources, all too frequently become trapped in increasingly violent relationships. Marital or intimate violence is a worldwide problem. For example, research suggests that one out of four Chilean women are beaten by their partners (McWhirter 1999). Similarly, findings from the National Violence Against Women Survey suggest that almost 25 percent of American women have been sexually and/or physically assaulted by an intimate partner. (Patricia Tjaden and Nancy Thoennes 2000) Unfortunately, social institutions (legal, religious, medical) have historically supported male perpetrators of domestic violence rather than their female victims, effectively maintaining and reinforcing the power differential.

Interaction between Gender and Other Social Categories

Thus far this discussion of gender has focused on the distinction between men and women. However, this complex social category interacts with other social categories, such as race and socioeconomic status. A person is not simply a man or a woman, but is also defined by his or her membership in other social categories.

Too much of the extant literature on gender has been limited to Western, white, middle-class men and women. Pamely Trotman Reid (1999) states that, "for the most part, theory and empirical study in the psychology of women have failed to recognize many distinctions among women" (p. 337). She specifically criticizes the exclusion of poor women in psychological research. Likewise, women of color have often been excluded in the study of women. Despite such limited research samples, researchers frequently interpret their results as if they describe all men and all women, which can lead to false deductions and conclusions (Weber, Higginbotham, and Leung 1999). Certainly a clearer understanding of gender requires careful consideration of the intersections between gender and socioeconomic class, race, ethnicity, and a plethora of other categories that create and perpetuate power differentials in cultures around the globe.

See also: CHILDHOOD; DIVISION OF LABOR; FAMILY ROLES; GAY PARENTS; GENDER IDENTITY; HUSBAND; INTIMACY; LESBIAN PARENTS; NAMES FOR CHILDREN; PLAY; POWER: FAMILY RELATIONSHIPS; POWER; MARITAL RELATIONSHIPS; SEXUALITY; SEXUAL ORIENTATION; STRESS; SEXUALITY IN CHILDHOOD; WIFE; WOMEN'S MOVEMENTS

Bibliography

Anselmi, D. L., and Law, A. L., eds. (1998). *Questions of Gender: Perspectives and Paradoxes.* Boston: McGraw Hill.

Bem, S. L. (1981). "Gender Schema Theory: A Cognitive Account of Sex-Typing." *Psychological Review* 88:354–364.

Bem, S. L. (1993). *The Lenses of Gender: Transforming the Debate on Sexual Inequality.* New Haven, CT: Yale University Press.

Bohan, J. S. (1997). "Regarding Gender: Essentialism, Constructionism, and Feminist Psychology." In *Toward a New Psychology of Gender,* ed. M. M. Gergen and S. N. Davis. New York: Routledge.

Buss, D. M. (1995). "Psychological Sex Differences: Origins Through Sexual Selection." *American Psychologist* 50:164–168.

Chodorow, N. (1989). *Feminism and Psychoanalytic Theory.* New Haven, CT: Yale University Press.

Deaux, K., and Lewis, L. L. (1983). "Assessment of Gender Stereotypes: Methodology and Components." *Psychological Documents* 13:25.

Eagly, A. H. (1987). *Sex Differences in Social Behavior: A Social Role Interpretation.* Hillsdale, NJ: Erlbaum.

Eagly, A. H., and Wood, W. (1999). "The Origins of Sex Differences in Human Behavior: Evolved Dispositions versus Social Roles." *American Psychologist* 54(6):408–423.

Kudek, L. A. (1993). "The Allocation of Household Labor in Gay, Lesbian, and Heterosexual Married Couples." *Journal of Social Issues* 49:127–139.

Landrine, H. (1999) "Race x Class Stereotypes of Women." In *Gender, Culture, and Ethnicity: Current Research about Women and Men,* ed. L. A. Peplau, S. C. DeBro, R. C. Veniegas, and P. L. Taylor. Mountain View, CA: Mayfield.

Lazur, R. F., and Majors, R. (1995). "Men of Color: Ethnocultural Variations of Male Gender Role Strain." In *A New Psychology of Men,* ed. R. F. Levant and S. Pollack. New York: Basic Books.

Lips, H. M. (2001). *Sex and Gender: An Introduction.* 4th edition. Mountain View, CA: Mayfield.

McWhirter, P. T. (1999). "La Violencia Privada: Domestic Violence in Chile." *American Psychologist* 54(1):37–40.

Pleck, J. H. (1976). "The Male Sex Role: Definitions, Problems, and Sources of Change." *Journal of Social Issues* 32:155–164.

Pleck, J. H., Sonnenstein, F. L., and Ku, L. C. (1993). "Masculinity Ideology and Its Correlates." In *Gender Issues in Contemporary Society,* ed. S. Oskamp and M. Costanzo. Newbury Park, CA: Sage.

Reid, P. T. (1999). "Poor Women in Psychological Research: Shut Up and Shut Out." In *Gender, Culture, and Ethnicity: Current Research about Women and Men,* ed. L. A. Peplau, S. C. DeBro, R. C. Veniegas, and P. L. Taylor. Mountain View, CA: Mayfield.

Shields, S. A. (1975). "Functionalism, Darwinism, and the Psychology of Women: A Study in Social Myth." *American Psychologist* 30(7):739–754.

Spencer, S. J.; Steele, C. M.; and Quinn, D. M. (1999). "Stereotype Threat and Women's Math Performance." *Journal of Experimental Social Psychology* 35(1):4–28.

Walzer, S. (2001). "Thinking About the Baby: Gender and the Division of Infant Care." In *Men and Masculinity: A Text Reader,* ed. T. F. Cohen. Belmont, CA: Wadsworth.

Weber, L., Higginbotham, E., and Leung, M. L. A. (1999). "Race and Class Bias in Qualitative Research on Women." In *Gender, Culture, and Ethnicity: Current Research about Women and Men,* ed. L. A. Peplau,

S. C. DeBro, R. C. Veniegas, and P. L. Taylor. Mountain View, CA: Mayfield.

Other Resources

Tjaden, P., and Thoennes, N. (2000). *Extent, Nature, and Consequences of Intimate Partner Violence: Findings from the National Violence Against Women Survey.* Available from http://ncjrs.org/pdffiles1/nij/181867.pdf.

United Nations. *The World's Women 2000: Trends and Statistics.* Available from http://www.un.org/Depts/unsd/ww2000/index.htm.

United States Census Bureau. (2001). *Annual Demographic Survey.* Available from http://ferret.bls.census.gov/macro/032001/pov/new01_000.htm.

KELLY RICE WOOD

SHARON SCALES ROSTOSKY

PAM REMER

GENDER IDENTITY

Gender identity is the private experience of being male or female. *Gender role* is the public expression of gender, everything a person says or does that indicates a status as male or female. Gender role includes social and legal identification. Usually gender identity and gender role correspond like two sides of the same coin, with a unity of gender identity/role.

Gender is a psychological and cultural concept, in contrast to sex, which is a biological term. Sex refers to the physical appearance of the genitals and reproductive organs (gonadal sex or sex phenotype) or in some cases the chromosomes (genotype). Sexual dimorphism refers to the division of sex into two classes, male or female. However, some individuals are born with physical intersex conditions, such as a hermaphrodite whose genitals are ambiguous at birth, so that the person cannot readily be typified as one sex or the other. Usually these people are assigned to one sex for rearing. In some societies they may be assigned and reared as hermaphrodites.

The word *gender* was used primarily to refer to classes of nouns in languages until psychologist John Money adopted the term in 1955 to refer to sexual attributes of people. He first introduced the term gender role to discuss whether hermaphrodites socially disclosed themselves as male or female. Some were reared as boys, others as girls. In most cases, their gender role corresponded to their assigned sex of rearing. The term gender identity was popularized by Money's naming in 1966 of the Gender Identity Clinic at the Johns Hopkins Hospital, which pioneered in evaluation of transsexuals and sex reassignment.

Since the 1970s, the use of the term gender has captured the public imagination in contexts that go far beyond hermaphroditism and transsexualism. Gender has evolved as the term, particularly in feminist usage, to represent the social and cultural characteristics of the sexes as distinct from the biological differences between males and females. Thus, gender is used to imply what is acquired or learned by the sexes, while sex is used to refer to what is thought to be biological and unchangeable. In this framework, sex represents intractable nature, and gender represents malleable nurture. This is a reversal in connotation for the term gender, which Money had used to describe individuals whose physical sex (or intersex) was hormonally and surgically altered to correspond to their psychological gender status.

Development of Gender Identity

Gender identity develops through a process of differentiation: interactions of biological, social, and cognitive-learning factors that occur over time. Differentiation means that a basically similar structure develops differently, depending upon the influence of other factors. Chromosomally female and male human fetuses are undifferentiated (have a similar physical form) until after the second month of prenatal development. As development progresses, various influences increase the difference between the sexes. Changes in sexual and gender development occur (or do not occur) at specific times or sensitive periods, and thereafter may be immutable. The process begins prenatally with the sex-determining chromosomes, the development of fetal gonads, and the influence of hormones on the fetus including influence on the brain. The basic model is female, and something extra has to be added to differentiate a male.

At birth, almost all infants are socially labeled as either a girl or a boy, based on the appearance of the external genitals. Children may be treated

FIGURE 1

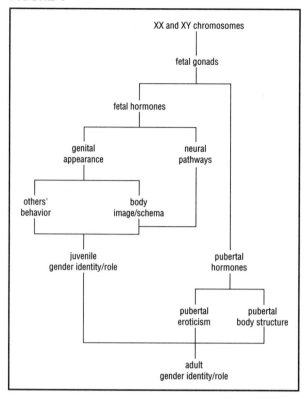

Illustration of the sequential and interactional components of gender-identity differentiation. Money, Principles of Developmental Psychology, *New York: Continuum, 1997.*

differently, depending upon the labeled sex. The child begins to develop a body image of the self as a girl or a boy. After the child acquires language, by eighteen months to two years, the child can label the self as *girl* or *boy*. This is the early expression of gender identity. Learning of some aspects of gender identity occurs at biologically sensitive periods of time; once learned, it is difficult to alter.

All societies partition some aspects of human existence into two distinct roles of male and female. The specific content of female and male gender roles varies among different societies. These characteristics may or may not be closely related to the biological functional differences between females and males: females have a vagina and may bear children; males have a penis and may impregnate. The difficulty that children face in the learning process is determining which characteristics are gender-linked and which are not.

Children develop gender-identity constancy by five to six years of age. Gender constancy is the idea that if a child is a girl, she will always be female and will grow up to be a woman; if a child is

a boy, he will always be male and will grow up to be a man. These continuities are not obvious but must be learned. Before puberty, girls and boys are more like each other than either are like adult women and men. Juvenile gender identity is consolidated through social experiences of exploring sexual and gender characteristics, which may include games such as "show me" and "playing doctor" and sexual rehearsal play.

The hormones of puberty induce changes in the sexual characteristics of the body. Usually these changes are consistent with the gender identity and gender role. Sometimes they are not, as when boys develop breasts, or when the physical changes are delayed or do not meet expectations. These physical changes must be incorporated into the gender identity. Standards of feminine or masculine physical attractiveness change from childhood to adulthood, as do other aspects of gender roles. Social pressures intensify for conformity to female or male gender roles. In addition, the sex hormones fuel romantic and sexual interests. Sexual orientation, as heterosexual, bisexual, or homosexual, also becomes part of an adult gender identity and role, although it originates much earlier in development.

Gender identity is generally consistent from early childhood through adulthood. Although gender identity as man or woman is stable, some of the content of an individual's gender role may change over a lifetime because of changing social norms or a move to another society.

The conceptualization of the self as male or female is a basic part of human identity in all societies. In some societies, however, another gender identity is possible, culturally labeled as a third sex or third gender (Herdt 1994). The Native American *berdache* is accepted as an individual with two spirits, both masculine and feminine. These rare individuals (who are usually genitally male, but may be female) are believed to have supernatural powers. Berdache roles, and associated gender identities, have been documented in North and South America, Oceania, Siberia, Asia, and Africa.

The *hijra* of India are recognized as a special caste, born with male genitals, who live in a neither male nor female gender role (Nanda 1990). They identify themselves as hijra rather than as male or female. Some undergo genital surgery to remove the penis or testicles, but a vagina is not constructed. They engage in sexual relations only with males, but are not labeled as homosexual or as men who have sex with men.

In the Islamic culture of Omani, males who wear clothing that mixes masculine and feminine characteristics and engage in sexual relations with males are called *khanith* and are considered to be a third gender. They are not allowed to wear the veil or certain ritualistic clothing restricted to women.

A distinctive gender identity may be linked to sexual behavior and cross-gender social presentation in different parts of the world. This gender identity includes individuals who do not fit into the society's traditional masculine or feminine sex roles, especially when it involves same-sex relationships, and there is no cultural identity as homosexual (Murray 1999). The *acault* of Burma are socially recognized as males who live as females, and they do not have genital surgery. The *faa fa'fini* (Samoa), the *fakaleiti* (Tonga), and the *mahu* (Hawaii and Tahiti) are males with an effeminate gender identity who dress in feminized styles. In Africa there is great diversity in social roles for nonmasculine males and nonfeminine females, which includes different homosexualities, as well as mixed-gender shaman roles (Murray and Roscoe 1998). Research is only beginning to ascertain which of these roles may correspond to alternative gender identities. Historically, the eunuch males in the Dahomey court (*lagredis*) and Mossi court (*sorones*) were one type of alternative gender identity.

Implications of Changing Social Sex Roles

In some societies sex-role stereotyping is decreasing. Even in traditional two-parent families, distinctions between appropriate tasks, roles, and occupations for women and men are changing. Styles of personal grooming and dress are becoming less differentiated, particularly among younger people.

There is no precedent for a human society without distinction between males and females: no society is sexless or gender neutral. However, societies vary in the content of different sex roles and in the number of characteristics that are sexually differentiated. The irreducible distinction is having a penis or having a vagina. When social differences between males and females are minimized, as in some tribal societies, children are usually exposed to nudity of both sexes. These children can develop gender identities based on physical differences between the sexes and not the social conventions of styles of grooming, dress, or social tasks and roles.

Social learning of new content of gender roles can be as difficult as learning a new language. Changes in the social content of gender roles may be threatening for individuals who developed their gender identities based on superficial gender characteristics.

In marriage and other social relations, interaction and communication are facilitated by a shared sense of gender roles. An individual's own gender identity presupposes a complementary schema for the gender-related behavior of the spouse and individuals of the other sex. Insofar as people do not share the same schema for gender roles, there can be conflict and misunderstood communication. For example, accurate interpretation of the verbal or nonverbal sexual communication of wife and husband presupposes that they each have similar mental schemas for male and female behavior.

Sex, Gender, and Intersex

Intersex individuals (hermaphrodites) do not neatly fit into either the male or female physiological categorization of sex. Truly ambiguous genitalia are a rare condition, but there is a range of variability in all of the physical characteristics that are considered sexual. Historically, the study of intersex individuals has made unique contributions to the understanding of physiological influences on sex differences and gender identity (Money 1997). Some medical historians (Dreger 1998) and biologically trained feminists (Fausto-Sterling 2000) have critically reevaluated the two-sex social categorization system. These theorists present the idea that sex is a socially constructed categorization system, developed particularly with the collusion of medical practitioners. They see the two-sex system as an expression of gender politics, rather than the simple labeling of facts of nature. They raise questions about the conceptualization of gender identity based upon only two sexes, male or female.

Intersex individuals are still raised as either male or female in most societies, and this seems unlikely to change. However, these individuals are challenging medical thinking that they should be surgically or hormonally assigned to one sexual category or the other, particularly during infancy or childhood before they have consolidated their gender identity (Intersex Society of North America). In most societies, intersex individuals do end up living in one gender role or the other and have either a male or a female gender identity.

In a few societies there is a distinct social sex role for some intersex individuals. Two examples of this are the *turnim man* in New Guinea and the *guevodoces* in the Dominican Republic. Newborns with these syndromes (Congenital Adrenal Hyperplasia) may look like girls or boys at birth. However, in some cases the midwives recognize them as intersex, and they are raised in an intersex role. These children masculinize at puberty. They are not marriageable as females and often assume a male role after puberty. The hijra caste in India includes intersex individuals who may be placed there for raising from childhood, although the hijras are predominantly composed of non-intersex males.

Variations in Gender Identity

Some children exhibit many of the gender characteristics of the other sex. This has been mostly studied in Western cultures. Some boys may prefer girls for playmates, avoid rough-and-tumble play and team sports with peer boys, and may identify with female characters and prefer feminine roles in play. Such boys may express dissatisfaction with their male sex and express a desire to be the other sex. Despite considerable rejection and teasing from peers, they persist in their incongruous gender role behavior. Some girls excel in sports and athletics and prefer to engage in these activities with boys. They may avoid domestic play with girls and refuse to wear dresses or skirts. Some also express dissatisfaction with their sex and say they want to be male when they grow up. These girls are subject to peer pressure to be more feminine, but are not usually teased as much as the boys with incongruous gender role behavior.

Extreme manifestations of these characteristics can be considered symptoms of gender identity disorders in children. Parents, teachers, and other professionals may be concerned that these children want to change their sex. However, almost none of these children seek sex reassignment when they grow up. Most of these gender incongruous boys turn out to be homosexual, as do some of the girls. The diagnosis of gender identity disorder in children and the associated benefit of

treatment have become controversial. The outcome of homosexuality is not a disorder, and treatment does not seem to influence this outcome.

Homosexuality is a sexual orientation that is also a variation in gender identity and role. Lesbians and gay men fall in love and are sexually attracted to people of the same sex instead of the other sex. This aspect of a person's gender identity is usually revealed in sexual fantasies in adolescence or young adulthood. This variation may come as a surprise to some; to others it explains the incongruity of gender identity and role that was present from earlier childhood but not understood as sexual orientation. Individuals go through a process of adjusting to this newly revealed component of their gender identity, which is sometimes confusing and upsetting.

Transsexualism represents a severe incongruity of physiological sex, gender identity, and role. Adolescents and adults with a gender identity disorder (transsexuals) know which sex corresponds to their body and the gender in which they were raised. Instead of being comfortable with this gender identity and role, however, they experience discomfort, called gender dysphoria. They believe that the other gender role is more appropriate and consistent with how they feel about themselves (their gender identity). This leads them to seek out medical procedures to alter their body and social presentation to correspond with their gender identity. Transsexuals may be either male-to-female or female-to-male. The frequencies of both of these types of transsexuals vary among different societies.

Some individuals have developed a transgendered identity, rather than identifying as male or female. These individual gender identities do not currently correspond to any specific social gender role. The *International Journal of Transgenderism* shows that this phenomena has been occurring in different societies. Some of these individuals may seek to change only some aspects of their sexual characteristics, or have an identity or social presentation that does not correspond clearly to either the male or female social categories.

Variations in gender identity can cause difficulties of acceptance within families of origin or marriage. In these cases, the traditional gender-role expectations of others have been disappointed. In situations where there is some social tolerance, the individual usually strives to live according to her or his gender identity. Difficulty of acceptance, however, can be associated with a higher suicide rate among gender variant individuals, particularly adolescents and young adults.

Individuals and societies may be hostile toward individuals who manifest variations in gender identity and roles. However, changes in social gender roles have little immediate impact upon the gender identities of members of that society. Gender identity, once established, is remarkably stable and resistant to change.

See also: CHILDHOOD; FAMILY ROLES; FAMILY STORIES AND MYTHS; GAY PARENTS; GENDER; LESBIAN PARENTS; NAMES FOR CHILDREN; PLAY; SEXUALITY; SEXUALITY IN ADOLESCENCE; SEXUALITY IN ADULTHOOD; SEXUALITY IN CHILDHOOD; SEXUAL ORIENTATION; SYMBOLIC INTERACTIONISM; WOMEN'S MOVEMENTS

Bibliography

Dreger, A. D. (1998). *Hermaphrodites and the Medical Invention of Sex*. Cambridge, MA: Harvard University Press.

Fausto-Sterling, A. (2000). *Sexing the Body: Gender Politics and the Construction of Sexuality*. New York: Basic Books.

Herdt, G., ed. (1994). *Third Sex, Third Gender: Beyond Sexual Dimorphism in Culture and History*. New York: Zone Books.

Money, J. (1997). *Principles of Developmental Sexology*. New York: Continuum.

Murray, S. O. (1999). *Homosexualities*. Chicago: University of Chicago Press.

Murray, S. O., and Roscoe, W., eds. (1998). *Boy-Wives and Female Husbands: Studies in African Homosexualities*. New York: Palgrave.

Nanda, S. (1990). *Neither Man nor Woman: The Hijra of India*. Belmont, CA: Wadsworth.

Other Resources
International Journal of Transgenderism. Available from http://www.symposion.com.

Intersex Society of North America. Available from http://www.isna.org.

GREGORY K. LEHNE

GENDER ROLES

See FAMILY ROLES; GENDER; GENDER IDENTITY

GENEALOGY

Genealogy is traditionally defined as the study of a person's ancestry or the study of one's parental lines going back as far as possible in history. Probably the first recorded "genealogy" is that found in the Book of Numbers in the Bible. During the nineteenth century in the United States, genealogy became associated with membership in particular lineage societies. Only those who could prove they were descended from a particular group of people (e.g., Mayflower passengers, participants in the American Revolution) were eligible for membership in specialized societies.

The first genealogical society with membership open to anyone who wished to search for their ancestry, the New England Genealogical Society in Boston, was formed in 1845 and still exists. The National Genealogical Society, located in Arlington, Virginia, formed in 1903 with a national focus in its library collection, publications, and conferences. The National Archives, in Washington, D.C., and its branch record centers throughout the United States hold the federally generated records for public research. By the late twentieth century, many state and local genealogical societies were established where extensive library collections were made available to anyone who wished to research, sometimes for a small membership fee.

After the first U.S. centennial celebration in 1876, the number of published genealogies (often compiled by sources within a family and not always documented by public records) increased. By 1900, Gilbert Cope in Pennsylvania, Colonel Lemuel Chester and Henry F. Waters from New England, and Donald Lines Jacobus in Connecticut began to set a more professional standard for the study of one's family. The study and publication of family histories increasingly involved the use of original documents, evaluation of evidence such as that used in a court of law, standards for documenting sources, local history, and the areas of sociology, economics, and psychology. No longer was the study of genealogy only associated with exclusive organizations.

The study of genealogy has greatly expanded beyond an interest in only parental lines to include relatives who descend from all family members—brothers, sisters, aunts, uncles—across many generations of a family. The general genealogical principle in tracing one's family is to begin with the present and work backward, one generation at a time, collecting information from all living relatives and learning about the locations in and conditions under which they lived. Once that part of the search is completed, the research turns to a vast array of original source material, such as vital, census, land, probate, court, war, church, cemetery, social security, and employment records in the public domain and printed sources.

The U.S. bicentennial celebration and Alex Haley's *Roots* (1976), the saga of an American family with both African slave and Irish immigrant roots, have been credited with the burgeoning interest in family history. Genealogy has become an extremely popular hobby, as well as a growing profession in the United States. Genetic research and computer programs to store, retrieve, and analyze information on multiple generations of a family are both growing aspects of genealogical research.

Standard forms for collecting and documenting the family's history include an ancestral chart tracing paternal lines only, a family group sheet that documents all the details of each nuclear family, and the genogram or family chart diagramming a family's structure and process through multiple generations.

Home-study courses are offered by the National Genealogical Society, which also sponsors an annual conference in various locations around the country. Open to the general public, the conferences provide opportunities for beginning, intermediate, and advanced researchers to learn how to do personal research and use various source materials. College courses on researching genealogy are often offered at the community-college level in larger metropolitan areas. A handful of universities, including Brigham Young University, Vermont College of Norwich University, and New College of the University of Alabama, offer degree-granting programs specializing in family or local history.

By far, the single largest collection of original source material for researching families is that held by the Family History Library (FHL), owned and operated by the Church of Jesus Christ of Latter-Day Saints (the Mormons) in Salt Lake City. The FHL's collection, open to the general public, includes printed and microfilm material from all parts of the world. Hundreds of branch libraries of the FHL are attached to local stakes of the church and provide access to the holdings of the main FHL collection.

Other publicly and privately owned research facilities with large printed and microfilm holdings exist in every region of the country to assist researchers in locating materials of relevance to their families.

The Association of Professional Genealogists, located in Washington, D.C., is the membership organization for professional researchers. Two organizations grant certification or accreditation to professional researchers in the United States: the FHL and the Board for Certification of Genealogists, located in Falmouth, Virginia.

See also: KINSHIP

Bibliography

Bentley, E. P. (1994). *The Genealogist's Address Book,* 3rd edition. Baltimore: Genealogical Publishing.

Doane, G. H. (1992). *Searching for Your Ancestors: The How and Why of Genealogy,* 6th edition. Minneapolis: University of Minnesota Press.

Eakle, A., and Cerny, J., eds. (1984). *The Source: A Guidebook of American Genealogy.* Salt Lake City: Ancestry Publishing.

Eichholz, A., ed. (1992). *Ancestry's Red Book: American State, County, and Town Sources,* revised edition. Salt Lake City: Ancestry Publishing.

Greenwood, V. (1990). *The Researcher's Guide to American Genealogy,* 2nd edition. Baltimore: Genealogical Publishing.

Hey, D. (1996). *The Oxford Companion to Local and Family History.* New York: Oxford University Press.

Jacobus, D. L. (1968). *Genealogy as Pastime and Profession,* 2nd edition. Baltimore: Genealogical Publishing.

Kemp, T. K. (1990). *International Vital Records Handbook.* Baltimore: Genealogical Publishing.

Wright, R. S. (1995). *The Geneologist's Handbook: Modern Methods for Researching Family History*. Chicago: American Library Association.

ALICE EICHHOLZ (1995)
BIBLIOGRAPHY REVISED BY JAMES J. PONZETTI, JR.

GENETIC COUNSELING

Genetic counseling is the process in which a specially trained professional communicates with a person, couple, or family about the occurrence, or chance of occurrence, of a birth defect or genetic condition. Genetic counselors, who have training in both human genetics and counseling, may have an M.D., Ph.D., R.N., or M.S. degree. While many genetic counselors work in university medical centers, others work with private hospitals, state or federal health departments, diagnostic laboratories, or in private practice.

Many individuals, in a variety of situations, may benefit from genetic counseling. Examples of common circumstances in which genetic counseling might be sought are as follows:

(1) A forty-five-year-old pregnant woman and her partner are concerned because her obstetrician has informed them that their pregnancy is at increased risk for Down syndrome and other chromosomal abnormalities because of her age.

(2) A twenty-three-year-old woman has just given birth to a baby with a birth defect called spina bifida, which can cause some paralysis in the lower limbs and may affect bowel and bladder control. She is concerned about a possible genetic contribution to this condition.

(3) A couple in their late twenties is concerned about their two-year-old son's behavior. He is hyperactive and has not yet begun to talk. Their pediatrician recommends a special blood test for the child, which reveals that he has a genetic condition called fragile X syndrome.

(4) A couple in their forties has just learned that the husband's mother has been diagnosed with Huntington's disease, a late-onset, degenerative disorder that is hereditary. They are confused about what this means for the mother, for them, and for their three children.

(5) Sarah and her boyfriend are moving closer to marriage. She is reluctant to be married until she can discover whether the muscular dystrophy that affected her brother and her uncle may be passed along to her own children.

These scenarios illustrate a few of the situations in which people pursue genetic counseling. Although the specific information discussed in each session varies, the genetic counseling process has some common characteristics. A family history is usually taken, and a "family tree" is drawn. Medical information, such as the precise diagnosis, prognosis, and management of the condition, is reviewed in nonmedical, easily understood terms. The way in which heredity contributes to the condition is also discussed. Specialized tests, and their risks and benefits, are described. This is the science-oriented aspect of the practice of genetic counseling.

Just as important to the process are the active listening and counseling skills practiced by the genetic counselor. He or she pays careful attention to words and gestures and notices the way clients interact. The genetic counselor attempts to create an environment in which people feel entirely comfortable expressing the variety of feelings related to having a birth defect or genetic condition, either in themselves or in a family member. These emotions include, among others, anger, sadness, fear, shame, and guilt. By facilitating this type of communication, the genetic counselor assists the clients in adjusting to the condition.

The cornerstone of the practice of genetic counseling is that it is nondirective. The autonomy of the client, and the right of the individual to make decisions based on his or her own values and beliefs, is paramount. Therefore, a genetic counselor must be willing to work with the client to find the path that seems best from the *client's* point of view.

The demand for genetic counseling has grown as knowledge about the human genome has increased. For a growing number of conditions, a person's DNA can be examined to determine whether a malfunctioning gene is present. DNA testing might reveal that someone who is now

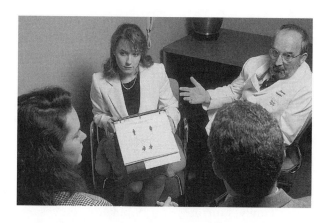

A doctor discusses a couple's genetic information with them during a genetic counseling session. For clients, the chance to openly express feelings related to genetic condition is just as important as the scientific aspects of the process. PHOTO RESEARCHERS, INC.

perfectly healthy will later become affected by a genetic condition, such as Huntington's disease (see example 4), or it might be determined that a healthy woman carries a gene that may cause a genetic disease in her children (such as in example 5).

DNA technology holds remarkable power. Prior to its development, those with a family history of a genetic condition made major life decisions, such as whether to have a child, based on a statistical analysis of the chance that the condition would be passed along. Now, for many conditions, an at-risk person can be tested and can know for sure whether he or she has the gene. Prenatal diagnosis, through methods such as chorionic villus sampling and amniocentesis, allows DNA to be obtained from the fetus to determine whether a pregnancy is affected with a genetic disease. Individuals who learn that they may pass along a genetic condition might choose to avoid this risk by conceiving using artificial insemination or in vitro fertilization with a donor egg. They may, on the other hand, choose to adopt a child. Those who decide to have their own biological children can now do so with a better understanding of their risks and can have the opportunity to prepare for the birth of a child with an inherited condition or a birth defect.

This technology, while increasing the amount of information and the number of options an individual has, can lead to other dilemmas. An issue fraught with ethical, moral, and religious overtones is the question of aborting a pregnancy affected with a genetic condition or birth defect. In this sit-

uation and many others, genetic counselors provide information and support for the individuals to make their own decisions concerning these difficult issues.

Although the day researchers can determine the entire genetic code for any person remains in the future, the field of genetics is providing an ever-increasing number of people with a higher level of understanding and a greater array of choices. It is the role of genetic counseling to assist people as they grapple with these increasingly complex situations.

See also: ABORTION; PREGNANCY AND BIRTH

Bibliography

Applebaum, E. G., and Firestein, S. K. (1983). *A Genetic Counseling Casebook.* New York: Free Press.

Baker, D. L.; Schette, J. L.; and Uhlmann, W. R. (1998). *A Guide to Genetic Counselling.* New York: Wiley-Liss.

Ferrell, J. (1992). "Genetic Counseling." *Vogue,* February, pp. 150–153.

Harper, P. S., and Clarke, A. (1997). *Genetics, Society, and Clinical Practice.* Oxford: BIOS Scientific; Herndon: Distributors, USA and Canada, BIOS Scientific.

Kelly, P. T. (1977). *Dealing with Dilemma: A Manual for Genetic Counselors.* New York: Springer-Verlag.

Kessler, S., ed. (1979). *Genetic Counseling: Psychological Dimensions.* New York: Academic Press.

Otten, A. L. (1989). "Parental Agony: How Counselors Guide Couples When Science Spots Genetic Risks." *The Wall Street Journal,* March 8, pp. A1, A8.

Shiloh, S. (1996). "Genetic Counselling: A Developing Area of Interest for Psychologists." *Professional Psychology: Research and Practice* 27:475–486.

ALICIA CRAFFEY (1995)
BIBLIOGRAPHY REVISED BY JAMES J. PONZETTI, JR.

GERMANY

In modern Western society, family formation is based on (regularly strong) personal emotions, such as romantic love. Moreover, given that *family life* is practically a synonym for *private life,* families are the primordial social contexts of privacy and intimacy, as well as of love and solidarity. Nevertheless, although each family operates in that essentially private manner as an intimate social group, there are public statistical indicators that permit us to observe some of the intimate functioning of families. Family demographers study such indicators, and Dutch demographer Hans van den Brekel (1999) describes the subject of demography as "sex, death and passion, wrapped in indicators," referring to birth and death rates, and marriage or divorce rates, as the visible, measurable, and computable outcomes of the private and intimate human behavior in families. Comparative family demography provides one with information on cross-national and cross-cultural differences, as well as similarities of family development and family life in different places of the world.

The gap between the low fertility in the developed Western world and the high birth rates in Third World countries is well known (Birg 1995). However, even within the West, and even within Europe, there is considerable variation in birth rates, family size, and family structure (Kuijsten and Strohmeier 1997). There is diversity in a cross-sectional perspective (comparing societies) and change in a longitudinal perspective (studying one society over time). Sometimes these two perspectives get intermingled when actual differences between nations are interpreted as indicating different stages in a developmental sequence. The most prominent example of such a fallacy is the concept of the *demographic transition,* which will be dealt with in greater detail below.

Nevertheless, demographic indicators as well as other statistical (family related) indicators, such as female labor force participation, are important tools of historical and international comparison in family research, and such information can be used to characterize the German family and to distinguish it from other types of family life.

In terms of demographic trends, such as changing fertility and marriage behavior, there are some aspects of German family development that are similar to those found in other Western European countries (Hajnal 1983). What is unique about the German case?

In Germany the secular decline of family size began in the nineteenth century—late compared to other western and northern European countries. Germany, in the 1930s and 1940s, experienced an unprecedented period of fascist, racist, and pronatalistic population policy (with increasing births) under the Nazi regime. This period had a long-term impact on family policies in Germany (which in the three post-war decades were characterized by a complete neglect of demographic facts) and on the socially and politically approved model of the German family in the decades after World War II. After the baby boom of the 1950s and 1960s in West Germany, marriage and birth rates decreased after 1965. (Only countries in southern Europe had lower rates.) In 1990, Germany began a unique social, political, and cultural experiment: the merging of two societies with different political systems, different family structure, and population processes. The German Democratic Republic (GDR, a.k.a. East Germany) and the Federal Republic of Germany (FRG, a.k.a. West Germany) were reunited under the rule of the FRG. The former East Germany experienced an unprecedented drop in births, marriages, and divorces, indicating a fundamental shift in the patterns of family formation, with only a slow and hesitant adaptation of the Eastern to the Western pattern.

The Rise of the "Bourgeois Family": The German Family in the Early Twentieth Century

In preindustrial Germany, family formation (through marriage) happened late in the lives of men and women, in line with the European marriage pattern (Hajnal 1983). Family formation was always also an economic decision. Many households included unrelated members, such as manual staff and servants (Laslett 1977), and only in modern times did families lose their function as a place of production, with fundamental changes in individual and social life.

The new model of the *bourgeois family* emerged, with the family as a married couple with children characterized by private, intimate parent-child relationships, and by a strict gender-specific role segregation of men and women. The man, as the sole breadwinner, worked outside the family, whereas his wife was responsible for rearing children, for domestic work, and for the recreation of the family members. One may characterize this family model as a somewhat smaller version of the preindustrial agrarian and aristocratic family—without maids and servants, whose jobs were taken over by the wife.

In the late-nineteenth and early-twentieth century an increasing portion of the population—the

A mother helps her children open a present in the former German Democratic Republic, or East Germany. Government policies in the republic encouraged couples to form families early. OWEN FRANKEN/CORBIS

majority of the middle classes and civil servants—were able to live according to this ideal of the bourgeois family, whereas in rural areas the premodern pattern persisted. The proletarian working classes still lived in family forms different from the bourgeois ideal (Rosenbaum 1992): Poverty and the bare necessities of life forced proletarian women and children to work in factories or otherwise contribute to the family's subsistence. Until the 1920s, many proletarian families in urban centers had to share their small dwellings with nonrelated roomers, and were unable to maintain minimal privacy (according to the bourgeois model).

In the same time, the number of children declined, in urban areas. German women born in 1865 had an average of five live births in their lifetimes, whereas those born in 1900 only had two (Marschalck 1984). This decline of fertility began in the wealthy and educated upper and middle classes. As soon as the economic situation and residential standards improved after World War I the working classes began to reduce the number of their children. John E. Knodel (1974), however, demonstrates persistent differences in family size between the social classes and also among regions. The latter only demonstrated a gap between urban and rural ways of life, but also persistent differences in religious Protestant and Catholic milieus, which held true in the early twenty-first century, to some extent, with considerably larger families in Catholic regions than in the Protestant areas.

After World War I the breadwinner-homeowner model of the bourgeois family was adopted by an increasing part of the population, and became dominant among the working classes. Female labor force participation was low and the family ideal of the majority was a patriarchal, authoritarian type of family (Sieder 1987). Social policy and housing programs improved the living conditions of the urban working class and *familialized* this part of the population. The Great Depression, however, brought severe hardships for a large part of the population and led to high unemployment. It was family solidarity that helped most to survive and it was women that shouldered the burden, working in poorly paid jobs and in informal employment—often earning the families' only income. During the Depression birth and marriage figures tremendously declined. That was the situation when the National Socialists (Nazis) took over in 1933.

As a way out of a perceived national crisis they reemphasized the traditional family, also intending to promote population growth and dominance of what they called the Nordic (*Aryan*) race. Women were removed from the labor market, and state propaganda made them heroines of procreation. Pro-natalistic and racist policies supported marriage (e.g., by offering special loans to young married couples), large families (by means of child allowances, presents and moral incentives), and the male breadwinner model. The mastering of the economic crisis of the early 1930s gave many families, particularly in the lower classes, stable employment (for men) and confidence in their future. The traditional family model dominated and marriage and birth rates grew.

However, the war effort (World War II) needed women as workers in factories and in other positions previously taken by men. Nazi propaganda consequently shifted its focus, and now praised women as mothers *and* heroines of industrial and agricultural production, doing their part in the fight against the numerous enemies of the *Reich*. Thus, Nazi propaganda paradoxically (and unintentionally) supported a modernization of gender roles.

After World War II, when the defeated men returned from war and captivity, the women willingly withdrew again from the labor force and other male positions they had held temporarily. In West Germany, a golden age of marriage and the family began in the 1950s, as the bourgeois family, as in many other European countries, gained unprecedented dominance as virtually the only generally approved pattern of family life. The role of marriage was unquestioned. In this model, only a mother staying at home was a responsible mother, whereas her husband had to provide the financial support of the family. Thus, the improving economy, together with strong (and legally codified) inhibitions as to unmarried cohabitation, worked in favor of early marriage and family formation. The First National Family Report of the German Federal Government (Deutscher Bundestag 1968) devotes a large chapter to teenage marriages. East Germany, at the same time, followed an alternative path incorporating the women into the labor force and building up a system of extra-family day care institutions for children.

From Institution to Choice: Family Change in West Germany since the 1970s

In Germany and in Europe, as well as in the United States, the post-war decades were a golden age of marriage and the family, as marriage rates and then birth rates increased. In 1965, the average West German family had more than 2.3 children. After the mid-1960s, birth rates all over Europe, somewhat unexpectedly, dropped rapidly, and in West Germany, by almost half. (In East Germany this decline did not occur until the early 1970s and it was not as severe.) For the first time in the twentieth century (leaving aside war periods) marriage rates fell: Year by year an increasing share of unmarried young people did not get married. Dutch demographer Dirk van de Kaa (1987) in his booklet on Europe's second demographic transition, describes the behavioral shifts as follows: "from uniform to pluralized families and households," from "the king pair with a child to the king child with parents," from "preventive contraception to self-fulfilling conception." Others (e.g., Strohmeier 1988) refer to the *individualization* of the life cycle and its disentanglement from basic determining factors, such as social class and gender, as the social background of such shifts. This individualization led to an extension of the options available to formerly disadvantaged groups of the age cohorts born after the war, particularly for young women. Policy makers were more than surprised by these changes, and researchers, in fact, did not notice them. Although the birth rates in West Germany had dropped tremendously from 1965 to 1975, the second national government report on the status of the family, *Zweiter Familienbericht,* appearing in 1975, made no mention of this development (Bundesminister für Jugend, Familie und Gesundheit 1975). The first scientific congress of the family sociology section of the German Sociological Association took up the issue only in 1985. Such (somewhat deliberate) neglect of obvious population trends by policy makers and social scientists had reasons that go back to the Nazi period (1933–1945).

Apart from war times and post-war periods, the bourgeois family had been the dominant German family pattern throughout the twentieth century. In the 1940s, U.S. sociologist Talcott Parsons labeled it the *normal family.* The normal family, consisting of a working father, a housewife mother, and children, was the living arrangement most suitable for the mobile life requirements of modern industrial societies.

After the secular fertility decline from an average of more than five children at the end of the nineteenth century, this family pattern was widespread and most common already in the 1930s. Within one decade after 1965, however, this model of the normal family had lost much of its popularity. For the first time since 1965, German families did not shrink in size but in numbers. After 1965 an increasing share of the young birth cohorts of women would remain childless throughout their lives.

Figure 1 shows that the proportion of women with two, three, or more children born throughout their lives are more or less the same as the cohorts from 1940 to 1965. The proportion of mothers of only one child, however, decreased from the older to the younger cohorts, whereas the proportion of permanently childless women increased, reaching values of about one-third in the youngest cohorts, which will most probably persist or even grow. Moreover, permanent childlessness in Germany varies by educational and social status, with more women in the higher status groups remaining childless.

The fertility decline after 1965 (unlike previous decades) is no longer an indication of the reduction of fertility in a predominantly married adult population. On the contrary, it is an indication of a profound de-institutionalization of the family. The

FIGURE 1

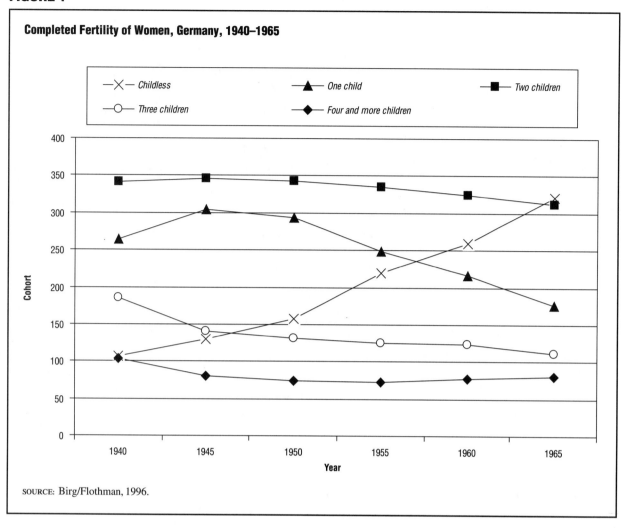

Completed Fertility of Women, Germany, 1940–1965

Legend:
- —X— Childless
- —▲— One child
- —■— Two children
- —O— Three children
- —◆— Four and more children

SOURCE: Birg/Flothman, 1996.

Completed Fertility of Women born 1940–1965.

reasons are all related to the changing life situations and life chances of young women: *individualization* of the life cycle and *pluralization* of life style. The 1960s, in the West, finally brought equality in the legal status of men and women (for example, with the right of a woman to work outside the house without her husband's permission, which was only established in 1958). Moreover, the 1960s and early 1970s brought an enormous educational expansion from which predominantly girls and young women profited. There was a general increase in the standard of living and growing economic prosperity, together with a cultural tendency towards liberalization, and finally there was access to safe contraception.

All these led to an extension of opportunities for women, which, in West Germany, unlike from other countries in Europe, was constrained by a traditional policy profile still enforcing the old *normal family* pattern. The result was that educated, highly qualified young women would rather abstain from family formation. In the last three decades of the twentieth century, the family in Germany has changed from an inevitable institution in everybody's life cycle to an object of rational individual choice, which, particularly among persons of higher educational status, appeared to be losing attraction.

Different Lives in Germany: Families in East and West before and after Unification

After 1950 there were two states in the German territory, the communist German Democratic Republic (GDR) and the Western Federal Republic of

Germany (FRG). The conditions of family life could not have been more different than between these two states, although both were founded on a common cultural heritage and both shared the historical experience of the Nazi period with its particular ideal of the traditional family. Comparing East and West Germany enables one to study the effects of a socialist authoritarian political system with a planned economy and of a pluralist democratic system with a market economy on family life and family development.

Family development in East Germany was affected by three factors: the cultural heritage of the traditional model of the bourgeois family, the shortage of labor supply (a problem that began with the creation of the GDR), so that women were always needed in the labor force, and, in fact, the state was successful with strategies to exhaust this potential, so that lifelong full-time employment became obligatory for women. Finally, the egalitarian socialist ideology had an important effect on gender relations. Consequently, the pattern of family development and family life that emerged in the GDR during the four decades of its existence was marked by considerable modernity and gender equality. But never it did fulfil the promises of an egalitarian model (Trappe 1995). Although the status of working women in most parts of the Western world may be characterized as the *double burden* of paid work and housework, women in East Germany had to bear a *triple burden* of paid work, exclusive responsibility for their household and children, and additional stress imposed on them by an inefficient economy making the acquisition of the goods of daily life an effort (Wendt 1997).

Family formation in East Germany started early, the mean age at first marriage was twenty-one, and it was finished early in the life cycle, usually after the birth of the second child, frequently before age thirty. There were several incentives to start early. Young married couples got a loan from the state, which they did not have to pay back completely if they had children. In a planned non-market-economy with housing shortages married couples with children had special privileges to obtain a flat of their own. One did not take a big risk starting an early family career, even during vocational training or as a student. No one had to fear unemployment and severe economic problems. The earlier women completed the family formation, the longer was the phase of work experience

without any further interruption because of childbirth. Comprehensive day care for children was available everywhere. Falling birth rates in the early 1970s forced the state to provide all-day public day care for children under ten and to introduce one year of parental leave with wage compensation (Huinink and Wagner 1995).

In the GDR incentives to marry and a repression of religious values and institutions in an atheist society resulted in a remarkable decay of the traditional meaning of marriage. The consequence was an increase of divorce rates during the 1980s. whether or not they had children, women were economically independent from their male partners. With an early marriage losing its advantages during the 1980s, an increasing proportion of births took place out of wedlock: by 1989 the figure was 34 percent. Also, the number of cohabiting couples with children rose. In 2002, 50 percent of all cohabiting couples in East Germany live with children; in West Germany this figure is only about 15 percent. However, the proportion of single living men or women in East Germany was considerably lower than in West Germany.

After the breakdown of the socialist regime in East Germany and the reunification of the two German states in the 1990, fertility and marriage rates dropped by more than 50 percent (Conrad, Lechner, and Werner 1996), and divorce rates decreased. Klaus Peter Strohmeier and Hans-Joachim Schulze (1995) interpret these shifts as signs of a *biographic moratorium* of the younger generation avoiding binding decisions in times of rapid change and uncertainty. People wanted to avoid risks, modified their aspirations, and postponed binding decisions. Postponement of family formation made the mean age of women's first birth rise from twenty-two to twenty-six. Family formation of the young women aged fifteen to twenty-four in East Germany approached the West German pattern. In the first years of the twenty-first century, marriage and birth rates in East Germany are far below the West German level, and more couples in East Germany than in West Germany avoid having a second child (Kreyenfeld 2002).

Does all this mean that East German family formation will assimilate to the West German pattern? The adaptation scenario is supported by the fact that the conditions of the transition to adulthood with its uncertainties and risks during early adulthood are now quite similar in East and West Germany—leaving aside the persistent problem of the economic transformation of the East. Demographic indicators, however, support the contradicting thesis of a persisting difference between East and West. Family formation in East Germany still starts earlier and will be completed earlier than in West Germany. Fewer women remain childless in East Germany and the proportion of one-child families in East Germany is higher than in West Germany. The proportion of illegitimate births in East Germany at the beginning of the twenty-first century is 50 percent, whereas in the West it is only 20 percent. This may prove that, indeed, marriage has lost its institutional relevance in East Germany even in the case of motherhood, whereas in West Germany a strong institutional linkage of motherhood and marriage persists. In East Germany we see indications of the establishment of a *postmodern family* without marriage, with only one child. However, maintaining the individual double income strategy under the new restrictive policy profile is difficult. There are severe compatibility problems, although female labor force participation in the East is still considerably higher than in the West.

Change and Diversity: German Family and Family Policy within a European Pattern

If one compares the relationship of family life and family policies in the states of Europe (Kaufmann 1997; Kaufmann et al. 2002) the specific traits of family life and family structure under the West German family policy profile (which is now valid for the united Germany) are evident. In Europe, Germany is the unique case of a society with a traditional family policy profile (still supporting the traditional *bourgeois* family) and a shrinking *family sector* (by increasing lifetime childlessness) which is still mainly traditional. In other words, most families have two or more children, most mothers of these children are not gainfully employed, and an increasing number of women remain childless. Modernization of the forms of private life happens on top of this basic structure.

After the mid-1960s, the *normal family* pattern has lost some of its popularity throughout Europe, and there has been decline of marriages and births, increasing cohabitation, and an increase of single as well as working mothers. Some interpret such cross-national variation as a sign of a *second demographic transition* (van de Kaa 1987). The *first transition,* completed in the 1920s, had led to a balance of births and deaths, the second transition, after the 1960s, has changed the character of the family, from an institution, inevitable in a normal individual life, to a matter of rational individual decisions. The variations in the structures of private life and in family forms in the states in Europe may be understood as indications of different stages of a linear development towards more individualization and self-fulfillment. The end of this process may be the dissolution of the traditional family. Although the traditional *bourgeois family* was the family form optimally adjusted to modern industrial society, Swiss sociologist Hoffmann-Nowotny hypothesizes the family form which will best meet the mobility and flexibility requirements of the individualized postmodern, postindustrial societies of the West will be the unmarried, noncoresident couple sharing a mobile child growing up in two homes with two single parents.

The second demographic transition concept is too superficial. Demographic indicators throughout the countries of Europe do, indeed, move in the same direction over time. Nevertheless, the structures of family life and their development over time are profoundly different. For example, in Denmark, the "land of the vanishing housewife" (Knudsen 1997), the traditional family has practically ceased to exist; whereas in West Germany or Switzerland, where the majority of mothers of two children are housewives, it is still the dominant family type. The Netherlands left this traditional cluster after 1990 and have rapidly been moving towards Scandinavian standards as to mothers' in the labor force. In terms of marriage, there are other remarkable differences. In Scandinavia, the unmarried cohabiting couple with children has become the most common family structure. In Italy and in the other countries of southern Europe there is practically no cohabitation. The majority of young women live with their parents before they get married. In West Germany cohabitation is a premarital arrangement which, with the first child, is transformed into marriage.

There are distinct paths of family development in Europe framed by different national cultural traditions and by different policy profiles. Such national policy profiles are parameters of individual life decisions.

The pro-natalist French profile gives substantial financial support to large families and also supports working mothers by good day-care provisions. The Anglo-Saxon profile (prevalent in Britain and Ireland), on the contrary, regards family life as a private matter and only contains a few rudimentary measures against poverty. The Nordic profile of the Scandinavian countries emphasizes gender equality and the quality of educational standards available to children, provided by the quantitative and qualitative standards of their systems of day care and by flexible parental leave regulations for working parents. The German profile factually supports the traditional family. Germany has the most restrictive policy as to the compatibility of gainful employment and family life (which is only supported in a sequential but not a simultaneous mode), most of the states' expenditures in the area go to the financial support of marriage via tax reductions for married couples, regardless if they have children or not, and into family allowances. In West Germany there is practically no day care for children under three years of age. Finally, the southern European policy profile, like the Anglo-Saxon, is characterized by little state support for families, as the state trusts in functioning extended family networks. Such national policy profiles affect individual life decisions as images of what is considered the normal socially approved mode of family life in the respective countries (Strohmeier 2002). Individual actors and couples treat them as invariant parameters of the irreversible decision to enter parenthood.

In accordance with the German policy profile, a young woman, when she reaches the age at which she may leave school, knows that, if she wishes to have children (which most of them do), she will—irrespective of her vocational training and qualification—almost certainly end up as a housewife after she has given birth to her second child. Her chances of re-entering the labor market are uncertain. She may be better off hiring private support or having her own mother look after her children. If we compare this situation to the one of a Danish or Swedish woman of equal age, the difference is striking. The young Scandinavian can expect a family life with simultaneous life-long employment. The Scandinavian policy profile goes with a different family pattern, characterized by more independence for women and more flexibility in the fulfilment of family tasks and parental

obligations by women and men (Knudsen 1997; Meisaari-Polsa 1997) and it goes with higher average numbers of children, and fewer childless persons.

See also: FRANCE; ITALY; SCANDINAVIA; SWITZERLAND

Bibliography

Birg, H. (1995). *World Population Projections for the 21st Century: Theoretical Interpretations and Quantitative Simulations.* New York: St. Martin's Press.

Birg, H. (2000). "Deutschland wird älter und bunter." *Thema Jugend, Zeitschrift für Jugendschutz und Erziehung* 1:2–6.

Birg, H., and Flöthmann, E.-J. (1996). *Entwicklung der Familienstrukturen und ihre Auswirkungen auf die Belastungs-bzw. Transferquotienten zwischen den Generationen.* Materialien des Instituts für Bevölkerungsforschung und Sozialpolitik (IBS) der Universität Bielefeld. Band 38.

Bundesminister für Jugend, Familie und Gesundheit. (1975). *Zweiter Familienbericht Familie und Sozialisation; Leistungen und Leistungsgrenzen der Familie hinsichtlich des Erziehungs- und Bildungsprozesses der jungen Generation.* Bonn-Bad Godesberg: Author.

Conrad, C.; Lechner, M.; and Werner, W. (1996). "East German Fertility after Unification: Crisis or Adaption?" *Population and Development Review* 22:331–358.

Deutscher Bundestag. (1968). *Erster Familienbericht: Bericht über die Lage der Familien in der Bundesrepublik Deutschland.* Bad Godesberg, Germany: Heger.

Hajnal, J. (1983). "Two Kinds of Pre-Industrial Household Formation System." In *Family Forms in Historic Europe,* ed. R. Wall. Cambridge, UK: Cambridge University Press.

Huinink, J., and Wagner, M. (1995). "Partnerschaft, Ehe und Familie in der DDR." In *Kollektiv und Eigensinn. Lebensverläufe in der DDR und danach,* ed. J. Huinink, K. U. Mayer, et al. Berlin: Akademie Verlag.

Kaufmann, F.-X. (1997). *Herausforderungen des Sozialstaates.* Frankfurt-am-Main, Germany: Suhrkamp.

Kaufmann, F.-X.; Kuijsten, A.; Schulze, H.-J.; and Strohmeier, K. P., eds. (2002). *Family Life and Family Policies in Europe,* Volume II: *Problems and Issues in Comparative Perspective.* Oxford: Clarendon Press.

Knodel, J. E. (1974). *The Decline of Fertility in Germany, 1871–1939.* Princeton, NJ: Princeton University Press.

Knudsen, L. (1997). "Denmark: The Land of the Vanishing Housewife." In *Family Life and Family Policies in Europe,* Volume 1: *Structures and Trends in the 1980s,* ed. F.-X. Kaufmann, A. Kuijsten, H.-J. Schulze, and K. P. Strohmeier. Oxford: Clarendon Press.

Kreyenfeld, M. (2002). "Employment and Fertility—East Germany in the 1990s." Ph.D. diss. Rostock.

Kuijsten, A., and Strohmeier, K. P. (1997). "Ten Countries in Europe: An Overview." In *Family Life and Family Policies in Europe,* Volume 1: *Structures and Trends in the 1980s,* ed. F.-X. Kaufmann, A. Kuijsten, H.-J. Schulze, and K. P. Strohmeier. Oxford: Clarendon Press.

Laslett, P. (1977). "Characteristics of the Western Family Considered over Time." *Journal of Family History* 2: 89–115.

Marschalck, P. (1984). *Bevölkerungsgeschichte Deutschlands im 19. [neunzehnten] und 20. [zwanzigsten] Jahrhundert.* Frankfurt-am-Main, Germany: Suhrkamp.

Meisaari-Polsa, T. (1997). "Sweden: a Case of Solidarity and Equality." In *Family Life and Family Policies in Europe,* Volume 1: *Structures and Trends in the 1980s,* ed. F.-X. Kaufmann, A. Kuijsten, H.-J. Schulze, and K. P. Strohmeier. Oxford: Clarendon Press.

Rosenbaum, H. (1992). *Proletarische Familien.* Frankfurt-am-Main, Germany.

Sieder, R. (1987). *Sozialgeschichte der Familie.* Frankfurt-am-Main, Germany: Suhrkamp.

Strohmeier, K. P. (1988). "Geburtenrückgang als Ausdruck von Gesellschaftswandel. Soziologische Erklärungsversuche der Bevölkerungsentwicklung in der Bundesrepublik." *Bevölkerungsentwicklung und Bevölkerungspolitik in der Bundesrepublik. Bürger im Staat* 1081:55–83.

Strohmeier, K. P. (2002). "Family Policy–How does it work?" In *Family Life and Family Policies in Europe,* Volume II, *Problems and Issues in Comparative Perspective, ed.* F.-X. Kaufmann, A. Kuijsten, H.-J. Schulze, and K. P. Strohmeier. Oxford: Clarendon Press.

Strohmeier, K. P., and Schulze, H.-J. (1995). "Erwerbstätigkeit und Familienbildung im gesellschaftlichen Umbruch." In *Familienbildung und Kinderwunsch. Materialien zur Bevölkerungswissenschaft 82c.* Wiesbaden: BiB.

Trappe, H. (1995). *Emanzipation oder Zwang? Frauen in der DDR zwischen Beruf, Familie und Sozialpolitik.* Berlin: Akademie Verlag.

Van de Kaa, D. (1987). "Europe's Second Demographic Transition." *Population Bulletin* 42(1):3–24.

Van den Brekel, H. (1999), "Sex, Dood en Passie, Vastgepakt in Indices: Dirk van de Kaa: Biografie van een Demograaf" (Sex, Death, and Passion, Wrapped in Indicators: Dirk van de Kaa: A Demographer's biography). In *The Joy of Demography . . . and Other Disciplines: Essays in Honour of Dirk van de Kaa,* ed. A. Kuijsten, H. de Gans, and H. de Fejter. Amsterdam: Thela Thesis.

Wendt, H. (1997). "The Former German Democratic Republic: The Standardized Family." In *Family Life and Family Policies in Europe,* Volume I: *Structures and Trends in the 1980s,* ed. F.-X. Kaufmann, A. Kuijsten, H.-J. Schulze, and K. P. Strohmeier. Oxford: Clarendon Press.

KLAUS PETER STROHMEIER
JOHANNES HUININK

GHANA

With a population of over eighteen million people, Ghana is the second largest country in West Africa. Since the 1960s, Ghana's population has been growing at an annual rate of about 2 to 3 percent (GSS 2000). This increase is a reflection of high birth rates at a time of declining mortality. One consequence of previous decades of high fertility of Ghanaians is that the country's population is quite young, with about 43 percent under fifteen years old (PRB 2000). These patterns of high birth rates, a youthful age structure, and declining mortality (the result of improvements in curative and preventive medicine, advances in sanitation, hygiene, and improved nutrition) indicate momentum for further population growth.

Culturally speaking, the people of modern Ghana comprise more than fifty different ethnic and linguistic groups. The largest of these groups are the Akans, who represent about 50 percent or more of the population and speak a variety of Twi-related dialects. Other major ethnic groups are the Ga-Adangbe, Ewe, and the Mossi-Dagbani. Although a variety of local languages are spoken throughout the country, English is the language used for official communication.

Ghana's contact with the outside world began in the late fifteenth century when the Portuguese arrived on the shores of the country. Over the years, the British ultimately became the dominant power in the area now called Ghana (Gold Coast). British colonial rule lasted more than a century until Ghana became politically independent in 1957, making it the first Black African nation to forgo centuries of British domination. At independence, Ghana was consolidated with the former British trust territory of Togoland, which before then was a German protectorate.

The social and political history of Ghana since its independence has been characterized by turmoil. First, the country's economy deteriorated over the years. Second, beginning in 1966 the country came under a succession of military regimes (briefly interrupted by two civilian administrations). As part of a new democratization process, the country reverted to civilian rule in the early 1990s. In January 2001, a newly elected civilian government was sworn in, making Ghana one of the few African nations with a Western-style democratic government. Although reliable data about the religious composition of the country are not readily available, it has been estimated that more than fifty percent of the people identify themselves as Christians (La Verle 1994) with the rest being either Muslims or believers of African traditional religions.

Family Structure, Family Formation, and Family Life

At the center of Ghanaian society is the institution of family. Sustained through a series of kinship networks and marriages, the family is acknowledged as the bedrock of all social life. The family is not only the basis of Ghanaian social organizations, but is also the main source of social security in old age (emotionally and financially) and the primary or sole caretaker for the young. The family is the basic unit of production and distribution and serves as the main agent for social control. More important, marriage continues to be the main locus of reproduction in a region where marriage is virtually universal (van de Walle and Meekers 1994).

Although the family may be the cornerstone of Ghanaian social life, very little consensus exists on its boundaries. The traditional Ghanaian family is more than the nuclear (conjugal) unit. In everyday usage, the term *family* is used to refer to both the nuclear unit and the extended family. In Ghana, the latter is often based on kinship or lineage ties. On the basis of lineage ties, two main family systems can be identified in Ghana: the matrilineal family and the patrilineal family. Among

the matrilineal Akans, a man's immediate family would include his mother, his own brothers and sisters, and the children of his sisters (maternal nephews and nieces), and his mother's brothers and sisters (maternal uncles and aunts). For a woman, this includes her own children and grandchildren plus all those mentioned above. Apart from the wife's contribution to the household, members of this maternal family traditionally inherited the property of a deceased husband. In contrast to the patrilineal system, under the matrilineal kinship system, children belong to the mother and her family. Thus, kinship ties are more than a system of classification; they involve rights, obligations, and relationships.

As Matthew Lockwood (1995) points out, in many parts of Africa, lineage ties often determine a wide range of behavior, from marriage to the transmission of property. Given its centrality to the lives of many Ghanaians, some researchers have suggested that lineage ties tend to weaken the conjugal family unit (Caldwell and Caldwell 1987). Oppong (1983a, 1983b) has also noted that as a result of the various ways in which family is defined, members of the conjugal unit often do not pool their resources. Some researchers suggest that in Ghana, relatives look askance at a marriage in which the husband and wife develop a close relationship because such a practice tends to reduce the loyalty of the marriage partners to their respective lineage.

Marriage, Family Formation, and Childbearing

Studies of African societies generally indicate that within the whole subregion, men and women are expected to marry. As a result, some researchers indicate that in Africa, marriage is nearly universal. Married life is important to many Africans, including Ghanaians, because it is the basis for assigning reproductive, economic, and noneconomic roles to individuals. Voluntary celibacy is quite rare in traditional African societies. The pro-family and marriage ideology that exists in Ghana also has implications for social relations. Among the various ethnic and linguistic groups, unmarried women are often viewed differently from the married (Takyi and Oheneba-Sakyi 1994). This may explain why by age twenty, a significant proportion of women in Ghana are married (Cohen 1998; GSS, 1999).

Marriage is nearly universal in Ghana, and couples are expected to have children. The family is the basis of social organization, the main source of security in old age and the primary caretaker of the young. CAROLINE PENN/ CORBIS

As shown in Table 1, the proportion of women who have never been married (single) in Ghana ranged from a high of 24 percent in 1998 to a low of 17 percent in 1971. Although a higher proportion of Ghanaians marry, numbers also suggest a new development, changing family processes in the country. For example, since the 1970s, the proportion of women currently married has declined from 72 percent in 1971 to 52 percent by 1998. Accompanying the decline in the number of married people has been a corresponding increase in alternative or nontraditional family forms, especially consensual unions, and single status. Similarly, the proportion of women reporting a divorce or separation is also on the rise, a trend some researchers attribute to the disruptive effects of modernization

and Westernization (Amoateng and Heaton 1989; Boateng 1995). Similarly, it has been reported that women headed about 29 percent of all households in Ghana during the mid-1980s (Bruce, Lloyd, and Leonard 1995).

Childbearing and Childrearing

Not only are Ghanaians expected to marry, but it is unthinkable for married couples to be childless (except for health reasons). In addition, studies show that because Africans value childbearing, they tend to have larger families (Caldwell 1982). Surveys conducted in Ghana indicate that women there bear many children. Between 1960 and the early 1990s, the Total Fertility Rate (TFR) (number of children born per woman aged fifteen to forty-four) averaged six or more. Only during the late 1990s did researchers observe a reduction in fertility levels. Even so, the average family size of nearly five children is considerably higher than what is found in other parts of the world. However, family size varies considerably among women of different social groupings.

Several factors appear to explain why parents in Ghana have more children. One such interpretation is that marriage is nearly universal and also most women marry at an early age. Some also suggest that high fertility is the result of deep-rooted cultural values, norms, and practices that support the existence of large families. In this view, African parents receive more rewards from reproduction than do parents in any other society. Moreover, these upward-wealth flows are guaranteed by interwoven social and religious sanctions. Because children are the main source of old age support, labor, prestige, and marital stability, John Caldwell (1982) and Baffour K. Takyi (2001) suggest that it is suicidal for parents to have no children. Also, parents may want more children because it costs them very little to raise a child; other people help in the provision of childcare through fostering arrangements (Isiugo-Abanihe 1985). After analyzing data from the 1971 post-enumeration survey, Uche C. Isiugo-Abanihe (1985) found that about 20 percent of all children aged ten years and younger were not living with their biological parents. Similarly, the 1998-99 DHS found that about 16 percent of all households included a fostered child.

One important determinant of family size is contraceptive use. In Ghana, because women are

TABLE 1

Percentage distribution of Ghanaians by marital status

| Marital Status | Women | | | | | Men[a] | |
	1971	1979-80	1988	1993	1998	1993	1998
Single	17.4	19.3	19.8	19.5	23.7	35.6	40.9
Married	72	72.4	64.8	58.7	51.9	49.4	52.8
Consensual	na	na	5.5	11.6	12.7	8.1	3.4
Widowed	2.9	1.5	1.5	1.7	1.9	0.8	0.6
Separated/divorce	7.7	6.8	8.3	8.5	9.9	6.2	2.2
Total	100	100	100	100	100	100	100

[a] National level data on men is available since the 1990s.

SOURCE: U.S. Census Bureau, International Data Base.

expected to have many children, few use contraceptives, although this changed in the late twentieth century. Between 1979 and 1999, the proportion of married women using any form of contraceptives increased from 12 percent to about 18 percent for the period (GSS 1999). Some studies also point to the low status of women in the country, while others argue that men's influence and behavior reduce women's ability to make decisions about their reproductive behavior, including their use of contraceptives (Ezeh 1993; Takyi and Oheneba-Sakyi 1997; Dodoo 1993, 1998).

Marital Processes and Types of Marriage

The marriage process itself varies among ethnic groups. Also, the type of marriage consummated by a couple often depends on a host of factors, including their socioeconomic status (e.g., formal education, occupation, income, wealth, place of residence), and their family, religious, and ethnic backgrounds. Ghanaian family law recognizes a plurality of marital forms. Throughout the country, customary law marriages, consensual unions, marriages contracted under Islamic rules, and those contracted under the ordinance (civil or church) are all recognized as legal. Of these four types of marriages, marriage under customary or traditional law accounts for most marriage contracts in the country (Table 2).

Although national-level data on type of marriage are not readily available, evidence from small-scale surveys conducted throughout the country indicate that most marriages in Ghana are the traditional type (Gaisie and de Graft Johnson

TABLE 2

Percentage distribution of Ghanaians by form of marriage contract

Form of union	1969[a] Women	1992/93[b] Couples
Customary only	81.7	69.8
Ordinance only	0.3	na
Ordinance/church/Muslim	5.8	18.0
Mutual consent	11.0	12.2
Other	0.1	na
Not reported	1.1	na

SOURCE: (a) Gaisie and de Graft Johnson (1976). (b) Couples data, Oheneba-Sakyi et al (1995).

1976; Awusabo-Asare 1990; Oheneba-Sakyi et al. 1992; Ardayfio-Schandorf 1995). As indicated in Table 2, although the number of marriages performed under traditional law is declining, they still account for the bulk of all marriages in Ghana. In part, customary law marriages are popular because they are based on traditional norms and beliefs and are often less expensive to contract. Also, unlike marriage under the law, traditional marriage does not have to be monogamous. As a marriage form, the incidence of polygyny varies from somewhere between 20 to 50 percent in the whole of sub-Saharan Africa (Timaues and Reynar 1998). In Ghana during the late 1970s, about one-third of all currently married women were in polygynous unions (Aryee 1985; Gage and Njogu 1994). By the late 1990s, the proportion of women in plural marriages had declined to about 23 percent (Table 3).

TABLE 3

Percentage distribution of married Ghanaian women by their type of union				
	Survey and year			
	GFS 1979[a]	GDHS 1988[b]	GDHS 1993[b]	GDHS 1998[b]
Monogamous unions				
All women	65.4	67.1	72.3	77.3
Urban residents	68.2	71.4	78.5	84.3
Rural residents	64.1	65.2	69.3	74.2
Polygamous unions				
All women	34.6	32.9	27.7	22.6
Urban residents	31.8	28.6	21.5	15.7
Rural residents	35.9	34.7	30.6	25.8

SOURCE: GDHS (a) Aryee (1995, Table 1). (b) GDHS, 1988–1999.

Partner Choice

In traditional Ghanaian society, different ethnic and lineage groups built alliances through the institution of marriage. Marriage contracts were supposed to serve the needs of the larger extended family members as well. As a result, the choice of a marriage partner was not left to the bride and groom alone. In some cases, the marriage was arranged to satisfy the needs of the extended family. Arranged marriages in this context could take any form, including betrothals or marrying someone considered the preferred type. For example, among the matrilineal Akans, who tend to inherit property from the maternal line, marriage between cross-cousins (one's father's sister's child or mother's brother's child) was preferred because it reduced the conflict and tensions that often arose over the distribution of family property. The family's involvement in the marriage negotiations and decision making was also aimed at establishing a series of networks that were viewed as essential to the stability of the relationship. It was assumed that if the partners were compatible, they were less likely to divorce. The evidence on marital trends showed, though, that an increasing number of marriages were being dissolved (Takyi 2001; see Table 1). Similarly, in the urban areas and among the educated elite, parental involvement in mate selection is waning (Takyi et al. 2000; Aryee 1985).

Trends in Family and Marital Processes

Since the 1960s, the Ghanaian family has come under intense stress as a result of contact with the outside world. For example, with increasing levels of education and urbanization has come an increase in the nuclear form of marriage common in North America (Oppong 1983b). Takyi and colleagues (2000) also find that mate selection is increasingly becoming an individual, rather than a family, matter, as it used to be. In terms of property rights, legislation on Intestate Succession (PNDC III) has helped to challenge the existing status quo. Under the law passed in 1985, the majority of marital property (even in the absence of a will) now goes to the nuclear, rather than the extended, family. Increasing urbanization has also been followed by more marriage dissolutions, and it appears that divorce rates in Ghana are on the rise (see Table 1). In terms of household structure, studies increasingly point to an increase in the number of households headed or principally maintained by women (GSS 1989; Lloyd and Gage-Brandon 1993).

Conclusion

As with all institutions, families in Africa have undergone significant transformations over the years (Bledsoe 1990), and the family in Ghana has gone through a series of transformations. For example, HIV/AIDS posed a challenge to the working-age population and fostering and living arrangements. The infection also compromises the family support systems as young adults become afflicted and die before their parents. Also, economic hardship brought a rise in international migration, thus further destabilizing the family. More important, family size will continue to decline as the economy weakens and contraceptive use rises. These changing conditions all represent a challenge to which the Ghanaian family of the twenty-first century must respond.

See also: EXTENDED FAMILIES; KINSHIP

Bibliography

Amoateng, Y., and Heaton, T. (1989). "The Socio-Demographic Correlates of the Timing of Divorce in Ghana." *Journal of Comparative Family Studies* 20:79–96.

Ardayfio-Schandorf, E., ed. (1995). *The Changing Family in Ghana.* Proceedings of the National Conference, Accra, Ghana, January 25–27. Ghana Universities Press.

Aryee, F. "Nuptiality Patterns in Ghana." In *Demographic Patterns in Ghana: Evidence from the Ghana Fertility*

Survey, ed. S. Singh, J. Owusu, and I. Shah. Voorburg, Netherlands: International Statistical Institute.

Bledsoe, C. (1990). "Transformations in Sub-Saharan African Marriage and Fertility." *The Annals of the American Academy of Political and Social Science* 510:115–125.

Boateng, D. (1995). "The Changing Family and National Development in Ghana." In *The Changing Family,* ed. E. Ardayfio-Schandorf. Ghana Universities Press.

Bruce, J.; Lloyd, C.; and Leonard, A. (1995). *Families in Focus: New Perspectives on Mothers, Fathers and Children.* New York: The Population Council.

Caldwell, J. (1982). *A Theory of Fertility Decline.* Canberra: Australian National University Press.

Caldwell, J., and Caldwell, P. (1987). "The Cultural Context of High Fertility in Sub-Saharan Africa." *Population and Development Review* 13(3):409–438.

Cohen, B. (1998). "The Emerging Fertility Transition in Sub-Saharan Africa." *World Development* 26(8):1431-1461.

Dodoo, F. (1993). "Insights into Spousal Differences in Reproductive Dis/agreement." *Sociological Focus* 26(3):257–270.

Dodoo, F. (1998). "Marriage Type and Reproductive Decisions: A Comparative Study in Sub-Saharan Africa." *Journal of Marriage and the Family* 60(1):232–242.

Ezeh, A. (1993). "The Influence of Spouses' Over Each Other's Contraceptive Attitudes in Ghana." *Studies in Family Planning* 24:163–174.

Gage, A., and Njogu, W. (1994). *Gender Inequalities and Demographic Behavior.* New York: The Population Council.

Gaisie, S., and de Graft Johnson, K. (1976). *The Population of Ghana.* Committee for International Coordination of National Research in Demography (CIR-CRED) Series.

Ghana Statistical Service. (1999). *Ghana: Demographic and Health Survey: A Summary Report, 1998.* Accra, Ghana.

Ghana Statistical Service (2000). *2000 Population and Housing Census. Provisional Results.* Accra, Ghana.

Ghana Statistical Service and Macro International, Inc. (1994). *Ghana Demographic and Health Survey 1993.* Accra, Ghana, and Calverton, MD.

Isiugo-Abanihe, U. (1985). "Child Fosterage in West Africa." *Population and Development Review* 11(1):53–73.

Lloyd, C., and Gage-Brandon, A. (1993). "Women's Role in Maintaining Households: Family Welfare and Sexual Inequality in Ghana." *Population Studies* 47(1):115–131.

Lockwood, M. (1995). "Structure and Behavior in the Social Demography of Africa." *Population and Development Review* 21(1):1–32.

Oheneba-Sakyi, Y.; Awusabo-Asare, K.; Gbortsu, E.; and Aryee, F. (1995). *Female Autonomy, Decision Making, and Demographic Behavior Among Couples in Ghana.* Potsdam, NY and Accra, Ghana.

Oheneba-Sakyi, Y., and Takyi, B. (1991). "Sociodemographic Correlates of Breastfeeding in Ghana." *Human Biology* 63(3):389-402.

Oppong, C. (1983a). "Women's Roles, Opportunity Costs and Fertility." In *Determinants of Fertility in Developing Countries,* ed. R. Bulatao and R. Lee. New York: Academic Press.

Oppong, C., ed. (1983b). *Female and Male in West Africa.* London: George Allen and Unwin.

Takyi, B. (2001). "Marital Stability in an African Society: Exploring the Factors that Influence Divorce Processes in Ghana." *Sociological Focus* 34 (1):77–96.

Takyi, B.; Kitson, G.; Miller, N.; and Oheneba-Sakyi, Y. (2000). "Reconsidering the Mate Selection Processes in Ghana." Paper presented at the Annual Meeting of the National Council on Family Relations. Minneapolis, MN, November 11.

Takyi B., and Oheneba-Sakyi, Y. (1994). "Customs, Practices, Family Life and Marriage in Contemporary Ghana, West Africa." *Family Perspectives* 28(4):257–281.

Takyi, B., and Oheneba-Sakyi, Y. (1997). "Gender Differentials in Family Size among Ghanaian Couples." *Journal of African and Asian Studies* 32(3–4):1–11.

Timaeus, I., and Reynar, A. (1998). "Polygynists and Their Wives in Sub-Saharan Africa: An Analysis of Five Demographic and Health Surveys." *Population Studies* 52:(2)145-162.

van de Walle, E., and Meekers, D. (1994). "Marriage Drinks and Kola Nuts." In *Nuptiality in Sub-Saharan Africa: Contemporary Anthropological and Demographic Perspectives,* ed. C. Bledsoe and G. Pison. Oxford: Clarendon Press.

BAFFOUR K. TAKYI

GIFTED AND TALENTED CHILDREN

Gifted children comprise a minority of the population, although not such a small minority as is sometimes thought. Internationally, the most widely used definition of giftedness and talent is that of Françoys Gagné of Quebec. Gagné (1985, 2000) defines gifted children as those who have high levels of *innate ability*, in any domain of human ability, that places them within the top 10 percent of their age-peers—even if their high potential is not yet being demonstrated as high performance. Talented children, by contrast, are those whose abilities have already been translated into achievements, and who are currently performing at a level that places them within the top 10 percent of their age-peers. Gifts are natural abilities whereas talents are systematically developed skills.

Giftedness is not an automatic guarantee of success. A range of environmental variables affect talent development, such as parental encouragement, family relationships, the provisions the child's school makes, or fails to make, to develop his or her gifts into talents, and even the social ethos of the community that can dictate that talents are valued and, therefore, which programs of talent development will be established or funded.

Encouragement and assistance from home and school are essential if gifted children are to develop as talented, but the children themselves must maintain their motivation to succeed. Children, no matter how gifted, will not achieve high levels of talent unless they are prepared to work and study to develop their abilities. A child may be gifted in any domain of ability, intellectual, creative, physical, or social. However, although talent in music, sports, or athletics is valued and actively sought and fostered in many cultures, high intellectual ability is often undervalued (Gross 1999). This can affect how gifted children come to view, or value, their gifts.

Identification of Gifted Children

Contrary to the myth that "every parent thinks her child is gifted," (whether he or she is gifted, or not) parents are highly effective identifiers of high ability in their children (Robinson and Robinson 1992); indeed, they are significantly more accurate than teachers, who are rarely trained in how to identify and respond to gifted students and who may not notice high academic ability if they present the gifted child only with work set at the level and pace of the average child in the class (Jacobs 1971). The majority of parents of intellectually gifted children become aware, in the early years, that their child is very bright (Louis and Lewis 1992).

Intellectual and physical characteristics of young gifted children that parents are likely to notice include unusually early and fluent speech; early mobility (the child crawls, walks or runs earlier than age-peers); early reading (the child spontaneously "picks up" reading from television, street signs, or advertisements); unusually retentive memory; intense curiosity; unusually long attention span; eager desire to learn; unusually mature sense of humor; and less need for sleep than age-peers of average ability (Gross 1993). Of course, not all gifted children display all these characteristics, but the possession of a cluster of the characteristics described above could suggest that the child may indeed be unusually bright.

Furthermore, intellectually gifted children differ from their age-peers in many aspects of their social and emotional development (Silverman 1993). They are often more socially and emotionally mature than other children of their age, their play interests are more like those of children some years older, and they tend to seek out, for companionship, children who are older but of average ability, or age-peers who are also intellectually able. They may be unusually perceptive and sensitive to the feelings of other children or adults and because of this capacity to empathize they may become concerned, much earlier than their age-peers, with ethical or moral issues (Webb, Meckstroth, and Tolan 1983). However, this sensitivity may also make them aware, even in the early years of school, of other students' wariness towards, or even resentment of, their high abilities, and many gifted students deliberately underachieve for peer acceptance (Gross 1989; Colangelo and Assouline 2000).

Standardized testing of ability and achievement can assist in identifying high academic ability in children and adolescents. Used appropriately by qualified professionals (for example, it is important that culturally appropriate tests are used) *IQ (Intelligence Quotient)* tests can provide a wealth of information about a student's intellectual profile, and can assist educators to develop an appropriate educational response to his or her learning needs.

However, a problem that frequently arises in testing academically gifted students is the *ceiling effect*. This occurs when a gifted student is assessed using a teacher-developed or standardized test designed for average ability students of his or her age. Gifted students may score at the upper-

Gifted children are more likely to develop their talents when their parents have interests that require pratice and learning, model a delight in learning, and seek outside assistance for their children from teachers and mentors. STEPHANIE MAZE/ CORBIS

most limits of the test and, although in one sense this affirms their high ability, it also means that there is no way of knowing how much higher these children would have scored if they had been assessed on a test with a higher "ceiling." It is rather like measuring the height of the Harlem Globetrotters on a pole that only goes up to six feet. The Globetrotters all come out at the same height—"six foot plus"—and, unless a longer pole is used, there is no way of measuring their relative heights beyond that point!

To combat the problem of ceiling effect, psychologists working with gifted children recommend *above-level* testing—assessing their achievements using tests designed for students some years older (Assouline and Lupkowski-Shoplik 1997). For example, a third grade students who has "ceilinged out" (made a score at or near the maximum) on a third grade math test may then be assessed on a fifth grade test. Finding that this student scores at the 70th percentile on a test designed for students two years older is much

more meaningful, in terms of curriculum planning, than affirming that she tests at the 99th percentile of her age-peers.

Family Relationships

Because intellectual ability is in part genetically determined (Plomin 1997), children in a family where one child has been identified as intellectually gifted are likely, also, to be highly able (Gross 1993). This does not mean, however, that either the parents or the school will view all children in the family as academically gifted. Teachers, for example, tend to assume that their gifted students are the academically successful teacher pleasers (Betts and Neihart 1988). Additionally, if the "unidentified" sibling has a learning disability or is not motivated to achieve, his or her high abilities may go undetected.

When a child is identified as intellectually gifted, parents sometimes worry about how this will effect the self-esteem of his or her siblings. In making such a comparison, a range of factors needs to be taken into consideration, including birth order, the ages of the children and the gaps between them and the children's gender and levels of intellectual ability, as well as parental values, education, and relationships. Oldest or only children are more frequently identified as gifted, as are children of parents who encourage in their children a love of learning (Pfouts 1980; VanTassel-Baska 1983). However, research suggests that the self-esteem of siblings in a family where at least one child has been identified as gifted, is more dependent on existing family relationships and attitudes towards one another, than on the singling out of a child for special treatment at school or for admission to a gifted program (Cornell and Grossberg 1986). Families where members interact cooperatively, with a respect for each other's differences of personality, opinions, and values, are strongly facilitative of children's healthy self-esteem and acceptance of differences in ability.

Healthy family relationships occur when members are assured that their individual roles are accepted and valued by the others in the family. Sibling rivalry may arise when children compare themselves with siblings, and feel less valued or accepted. If a child who has been identified as gifted receives special attention *at the expense of* the non-identified sibling, then the self-esteem of that sibling is likely to fall. Constant negative comparison with a sibling of perceived superior ability, together with a relative lack of recognition, may damage self-esteem. It is important to remember, however, that it is a result of the family's attitude towards the child who has not been identified as gifted, rather than the school's recognition of the one who has, which results in the sibling's decline in self-esteem (Grenier 1985).

How Families Foster Talent Development

Beginning in the 1960s, research studies have examined the influence of parents and families on young people or adults who have achieved eminence in their fields, for example, Victor Goertzel and Mildred Goertzel's international study (1962), Benjamin Bloom's (1985) study of 120 young Americans, and Miraca Gross's (2000) study of exceptionally gifted young Australians. These studies found parents to be an enormous influence on the degree to which the young people accepted their high abilities and worked to translate them into high achievement. Some of the major findings were:

(1) Even where the parents were not themselves highly educated, they placed a high value on education and learning.

(2) They tended to choose hobbies and interests that required practice and learning, and studied the performance of others to increase their own skill and enjoyment. They modeled, for their children, a delight in learning and a desire to improve their performance.

(3) At least one parent or close relative had a personal interest in the child's area of talent.

(4) The parents encouraged and rewarded the development of the child's talent at home, while seeking outside assistance from teachers or mentors.

The parents did not "push" their children; however, through their pursuit of their own talent areas and, through their encouragement of the children, they provided a model that taught that talent is fostered through accepting one's abilities and striving to fulfill them.

Educational Responses

Educational responses to children with special needs are based not on the "label" that has been given (for example, a child having been diagnosed as hearing impaired, intellectually disabled, or academically gifted) but on the fact that the child differs, in some way that will affect their learning, and that this difference will require a different educational response from the school.

There are different levels of hearing impairment, and the response that a teacher might make to a child with a moderate hearing loss would be of limited effectiveness if it were offered to a child with a severe hearing impairment. Similarly, there are different levels of intellectual or academic giftedness, which require different levels and types of response.

Children of IQ 120 appear in the population at a ratio of one in ten. Gagné's model (2000) would recognize them as gifted, and they are likely to find school rather slow and unchallenging if the teacher does not modify the curriculum, which is designed at the level and pace of their average ability age-peers. They need a curriculum that is faster paced, more academically rigorous and of greater depth (VanTassel-Baska 1998). However, they are likely to find other students in the inclusion classroom who are of approximately the same ability level, and, as long as the curriculum is differentiated to offer them sufficient academic challenge, the inclusion classroom will serve as an appropriate placement.

However, children of IQ 135 appear at a ratio of only 1 in 100 and children of IQ 140 at 1 in 200. If these students are retained in the inclusion classroom, they may pass through several years of elementary school without meeting or working with another child of similar ability. Apart from the intellectual boredom and frustration they may experience if the teacher does not give them material that will interest and challenge them, these children may experience loneliness and even social rejection because their abilities, interests, and ways of thinking are so different from those of their age-peers (Silverman 1993).

A substantial body of research recommends that many gifted students benefit, both academically and socially, from being grouped with children of similar abilities (Rogers 1991; Kulik and Kulik 1997; Gross 1997). This grouping may be full time in a special class for gifted students, or for part of each day when students are grouped by ability in a specific subject, or even for a few hours each week when gifted students are pulled out of their regular classes for enrichment workshops. Contrary to what teachers sometimes fear, ability grouping rarely makes gifted children conceited; actually, conceit is discouraged, rather than fostered, by the experience of working with other students as able, or more able, then oneself.

Acceleration—advancing gifted students to work with students older than themselves—also has substantial research support, showing that, where the acceleration program is well-designed and monitored, accelerated students experience both academic success and social acceptance by their new classmates (Gross 1993; Passow 1996). In the considerable majority of cases the advancement is by a single year, either through allowing students to enter primary, elementary, middle, or high school one year early, or by allowing them to advance a grade within a school building. Students may also be allowed to go to an upper grade for a single subject in which they excel, while remaining with age-peers for the majority of the school day.

Intellectually gifted students are usually advanced for their age in their emotional development as well as their intellectual development (Gross 1993). However, it is essential to ensure that a child who is being considered for acceleration is intellectually, academically, socially, and emotionally ready to work with older students on a more demanding curriculum. Above-level assessment should be used to establish that the student has mastered all, or the majority of, the curriculum of the grade he or she will "skip." It is important that the students themselves should be eager to accelerate and that the teachers with whom they will work have a positive attitude towards the process, allowing them to be accepted as full members of the class they are entering (Feldhusen, Proctor, and Black 1986).

The primary principle of educating gifted and talented children is that schools must acknowledge that these children differ from their age-peers in their learning needs and therefore the provisions the school makes in response should also be different to the provisions made for children of average ability.

See also: ACADEMIC ACHIEVEMENT; DEVELOPMENT: COGNITIVE; DEVELOPMENT: EMOTIONAL; DEVELOPMENT: MORAL; SCHOOL; SELF-ESTEEM; SIBLING RELATIONSHIPS

Bibliography

Assouline, S. G., and Lupkowski-Shoplik, A. (1997). "Talent Searches: A Model for the Discovery and Development of Academic Talent." In *Handbook of Gifted Education,* 2nd edition, ed. N. Colangelo and G. A. Davis. Boston: Allyn and Bacon.

Betts, G. T., and Neihart, M. (1988). "Profiles of the Gifted and Talented." *Gifted Child Quarterly* 32(2):248–253.

Bloom, B. S. (1985). *Developing Talent in Young People.* New York: Ballantine.

Colangelo, N., and Assouline, S. G. (2000). "Counselling Gifted Students." In *International Handbook of Giftedness and Talent,* ed. K. A. Heller, F. J. Monks, R. J. Sternberg, and R. F. Subotnik. Oxford: Pergamon.

Cornell, D. G., and Grossberg, I. N. (1986). "Siblings of Children in Gifted Programs." *Journal for the Education of the Gifted* 9:253–254.

Feldhusen, J. F.; Proctor, T. B.; and Black, K. N. (1986). "Guidelines for Grade Advancement of Precocious Children." *Roeper Review* 9(1):25–27.

Gagné, F. (1985). "Giftedness and Talent: Reexamining a Reexamination of the Definitions." *Gifted Child Quarterly* 29(3):103–112.

Gagné, F. (2000). "Understanding the Complex Choreography of Talent Development through DMGT-Based Analysis." In *International Handbook of Giftedness and Talent,* ed. K. A. Heller, F. J. Monks, R. J. Sternberg, and R. F. Subotnik. Oxford, UK: Pergamon.

Goertzel, V., and Goertzel, M. G. (1962). *Cradles of Eminence.* Boston: Little, Brown

Grenier, M. E. (1985). "Gifted Children and other Siblings." *Gifted Child Quarterly* 29(4):164–167.

Gross, M. U. M. (1989). "The Pursuit of Excellence or the Search for Intimacy? The Forced-Choice Dilemma of Gifted Youth." *Roeper Review* 11(4):189–194.

Gross, M. U. M. (1993) *Exceptionally Gifted Children.* London: Routledge.

Gross, M.U.M. (1997). "How Ability Grouping Turns Big Fish into Little Fish—or Does it? Of Optical Illusions and Optimal Environments." *Australasian Journal of Gifted Education* 6(2):18–30.

Gross, M. U. M. (1999). "Inequity in Equity: The Paradox of Gifted Education in Australia." *Australian Journal of Education* 43(1):87–103.

Gross, M. U. M. (2000). "Issues in the Cognitive Development of Exceptionally and Profoundly Gifted Individuals." In *International Handbook of Giftedness and Talent,* ed. K. A. Heller, F. J. Monks, R. J. Sternberg, and R. F. Subotnik. Oxford, UK: Pergamon Press.

Jacobs, J. C. (1971). "Effectiveness of Teacher and Parent Identification of Gifted Children as a Function of School Level." *Psychology in the Schools* 8:140–142.

Kulik, J. A., and Kulik, C-L. C. (1997). "Ability Grouping." In *Handbook of Gifted Education,* 2nd edition, ed. N. Colangelo and G. A. Davis. Boston: Allyn and Bacon.

Louis, B., and Lewis, M. (1992). "Parental Beliefs about Giftedness in Young Children and their Relation to Actual Ability Level." *Gifted Child Quarterly* 36(1):27–31.

Passow, A. H. (1996). "Acceleration Over the Years." In *Intellectual Talent: Psychometric and Social Issues,* ed. C. P. Benbow and D. Lubinski. Baltimore, MD: Johns Hopkins University Press.

Pfouts, J. H. (1980). "Birth Order, Age Spacing, IQ Differences and Family Relations." *Journal of Marriage and the Family* 42:517–521.

Plomin, R. (1997). "Genetics and Intelligence." In *Handbook of Gifted Education,* 2nd edition, ed. N. Colangelo and G. A. Davis. Boston: Allyn and Bacon.

Robinson, N. M., and Robinson, H. (1992). "The Use of Standardized Tests with Young Gifted Children." In *To Be Young and Gifted,* ed. P. N. Klein and A. J. Tannenbaum. Norwood, NJ: Ablex.

Rogers, K. B. (1991). *The Relationship of Grouping Practices to the Education of the Gifted and Talented Learner.* Storrs, CT: National Research Center on the Gifted and Talented.

Silverman, L. K. (1993). *Counseling the Gifted and Talented.* Denver, CO: Love.

VanTassel-Baska, J. (1983). "Profiles of Precocity: The 1982 Midwest Talent Search Finalists." *Gifted Child Quarterly* 27(3):139–144.

VanTassel-Baska, J. (1998). *Excellence in Educating Gifted and Talented Learners,* 3rd edition. Denver, CO: Love.

Webb, J. T.; Meckstroth, E. A.; and Tolan, S. S. (1983). *Guiding the Gifted Child.* Columbus: Ohio Psychology Publishing.

MIRACA U. M. GROSS

GLOBAL CITIZENSHIP

There was a time when families lived their lives in a very limited space. They grew their own food, made their own clothes, and interacted with their immediate neighbors. Their knowledge of anything more than a day's travel away was sketchy.

In the twenty-first century, families live in a much larger space. They listen to news from around the world, buy products from many countries, and experience entertainment media from all over the world. Transportation, technology, and trade provide often instantaneous connections among the world's people. Because families live in this global environment, they are affected by it, and they necessarily play a role in preparing their members for it, whether they do so consciously or inadvertently. Although much of the discussion about globalization takes place in the fields of economics and politics, families are also intricately interwoven into the international environment.

Families are like musicians creating their own music. Their tunes and lyrics are shaped by the places where they live, the events and changes that occur around them, the songs that they teach to their children, and the songs their children teach them.

Societal Influences

People's attitudes about the world and their abilities to interact with it are colored by their cultures. The values, practices, and conditions that characterize a society create the context in which families live their lives. Families located in different areas of the world tend to hold similar values to the people who live near them. For example, parents in Eastern cultures hope that their children will not someday raise children who are not related to them by blood (e.g., stepchildren, foster children), while parents in Western countries hope their children will not live with their parents when they are grown (Watanabe 2001).

Consistency within a culture helps both people inside that culture and those from other cultures to know what to expect. With increasing amounts of interaction among countries and an accelerated rate of change, however, the consistency of values within cultures is decreasing. Families adopt practices they learn from other cultures, they interact with neighbors who come from other cultures, and they migrate and live in other countries for a variety of reasons. When families change in these ways, they are no longer like their home culture or entirely like the new culture (Sakka and Dikaiou 2001). They may not fit very well anywhere. At the same time, children in migrant families may be especially valuable guides in global living because of their experience in intercultural living and identity (Chisholm 2001). Mobility can be both an asset and a liability.

All families, whether they have been migrants or not, have experienced forces that change their values. Changes in the world create situations that require changes in families. A major force in current global change is modernization. Modernization includes moves toward equality of gender roles, shifts toward individualism, technological advancement, and an increasing tolerance (or at least awareness) of diverse views and lifestyles.

Many people see modernization as being positive for women, children, and economies. Modernization, however, brings some challenges for families and societies. For example, traditions and norms in China and Taiwan have focused on the Confucian value of filial piety and the expectation that individuals will assume the role of caregivers as their parents grow older. Modern education and urban residence have caused that practice to decline (Kung and Yi 2001). This leaves a dilemma for individual families who may feel that they have no alternative but to place the older relatives in group care at the same time that they believe they really should care for them at home. Eastern policy makers struggle to find the appropriate balance between either establishing formal care facilities or helping families to care for their elderly themselves.

Modernization also has changed the way Western family members relate to each other. Families were seen as permanent and inflexible in the past; in contrast, many societies now focus on choices in family membership (du Bois-Reymond 2001). This means that divorce and remarriage are more common than in the past, families are smaller, and the balance of power has shifted. Rather than feeling that the lines of family authority are most important, European families now consider negotiation to be critical. Families may not be aware of the modernization trend, and, even if they are, they may feel helpless in influencing it. Nevertheless, they face its impact daily.

Families, however, are not entirely powerless in their interactions with this global environment. Individuals can be a powerful unit of social change. Families both adjust to changes and redirect them. Research has shown that societies adapt their practices to fit the historical trends (Flanagan 2001; Dai 2001). Parents attempt to prepare their children for the world they think the children will face, while trying to maintain the traditions that they feel are most important. In this way they both react to social change and help to create it.

Global Events

In addition to adjusting to gradual cultural change, families also interact with the global environment when specific events occur around them. These events may range from economic fluctuations to weather to wars and ethnic conflicts. Again, families are affected by the events while also being actors in them. For example, the collapse of the communist systems of Eastern Europe influenced many aspects of family life in those countries. How those economic reforms were enacted, however, was influenced by culture. The economic reforms were colored by conventional views of gender roles in Ukraine, so that women were left with few choices and few resources (Lakiza-Sachuk, cited in

Skalnik et al. 2001). As a result, women began refusing to carry second and third children until better times. International economic events had an unintended impact on family planning and population growth.

Wars have a devastating effect on families. Instability and poverty dominate the lives of people in any war zone. If the war is a communal conflict or civil war, it divides families, and brothers and sisters may take opposing sides. The breakdown of the public sector, including schools, manufacturing, police, banks, and health services, means that families need to assume many new roles to replace those institutions. They also experience monumental internal stressors and losses when dealing with weapon threats, sending family members to the military, and experiencing deaths of loved ones (Milic 2001; Skalník 2001). In ethnic conflicts, it is possible that the family itself was the source of the prejudice and hatred, however. Again, families both respond to wars and become actors in the course of events.

Families do make choices as they react to events such as war, and all individuals in a society do not respond in the same way. Women and mothers have been given special attention in some of this research. Researchers have found that some mothers may focus on the safety and well being of their own children, possibly at the expense of the well being of others, while other mothers focus on the welfare of all children (Azmon 2001).

Parental Teaching

Societal or cultural environments and global events influence families. Adults are responsible in some measure for exposing children to many of those events and for interpreting them to the children. Parents teach children directly or indirectly about the world. Those messages are not, however, always clear and consistent. For example, parents may talk about peace while supporting military conscription, educate their children to believe in human rights while passing on prejudices, and preach environmental protection but are not willing to make the sacrifices necessary to achieve ecologically sound lifestyles (Somlai 2001). Similarly, parents teach their children more about war than peace and describe more of the actions of war than peace, even though all parents purport to believe in peace (Myers-Walls 2001).

In some cases, it is unclear whether the influence of parents on children's globalization skills and attitudes is due to teaching or due to the environments in which they place their children. Only limited research is available about how parents teach their children about global existence, but studies do show that many parental characteristics are linked to children's attitudes. Researchers have found that parents' educational levels and family social status are related to children's attitudes about their own futures and the nature and future of the world (Flanagan 2001; Tóth 2001).

In the areas in which parents do teach their children, their abilities to do so effectively can be compromised by modernization and other changes. For example, traditional African teaching methods in the Sahel were replaced by formal education. As a result, modern farming methods were introduced, and traditional, ecologically sound practices and techniques were lost. This loss of historical wisdom is seen as contributing to droughts and soil erosion in Senegal (Thioune 2001). Innovations in education and family intervention should take into account the perspective of the people and culture that will be affected by them.

Children as Teachers

The leadership in teaching about the global environment is not always from the parent to the child. An interesting artifact of the globalization process and times of rapid change is what the children can teach the parents. Children pick up innovations first and are drawn to new approaches and perspectives. When the children's world is significantly different from what the parents have known in their own childhoods, it is difficult for parents to be the authorities and guides (Obondo, cited in LaHaye et al. 2001). Young people who have migrated to other countries also have an international perspective that may provide the lead for adults.

Not only can children teach adults about some aspects of globalization, but they also can push adults to re-examine what they believe and what they do. Children see the inconsistencies in the world around them and look for explanations. They ask questions about the meaning of traditions, practices, and stated values. "Children's naïve questions become the nagging conscience of an adult society which has lost sight of its values" (Somlai 2001, p. 21).

Challenges for Families and Globalization

As families deal with this process of globalization, they face a number of challenges. One outcome of information dissemination and immediate transmission of news is the concentration of negative messages. News about earthquakes, terrorist attacks, political scandals, and economic disasters are combined from around the world. This situation may create the impression that disasters and threats are increasing and ever-present. It is easy to build a picture of the world as a dangerous place and believe that humanity is racing down the road to destruction. Families are faced with the task of processing the onslaught of international news and international communication technology and putting them in a manageable perspective.

Another challenge for families is the domination of some cultures in the globalization process. This domination could be described as economic, cultural, and intellectual imperialism. Some of the primary economic entities that dominate the international scene are MTV, Coca Cola, Pepsi Cola, McDonald's, Levis, and Microsoft (Qvortrup, cited in Qvortrup et al. 2001). Culturally, domination can lead to a characterization of good parenting or positive family life to be defined as the parenting or family life of the dominant culture (Flanagan 2001). The challenge for families that are not part of the dominant group is to assert themselves and define health and excellence from their own viewpoint. The challenge for those in the dominant group is to become aware of their position of power and take responsibility for the messages they share while developing an openness to and knowledge of others.

Accompanying the inequitable distribution of power is an inequitable distribution of the world's resources. The gap between the standard of living in the United States and Western Europe when compared to Somalia and Nepal is almost incomprehensible. "Even in the United States of America . . . there are probably more poor and illiterate people than in any other nation if we take its economic capacities into consideration" (Qvortrup 2001, p. 45). The increasing interactions and connection among the world's people cannot help but make those inequities evident. The poor and the

rich alike must interpret the contrast, and efforts must be made to reduce the gap if peaceful co-existence is to be possible.

Perhaps the largest challenge is for families to develop a vision of the type of world in which they want to live. Individuals who are interested in and committed to families need to recognize that globalization is a trend relevant to family life. International issues cannot be ignored. Families can simply accept the proclamations and interpretations of the dominant media and politicians; they can ignore the issue and thereby let the dominant forces determine the global agenda unchallenged; or they can explore their values, culture, and dreams and choose to live a life conscious of the global environment.

See also: ACCULTURATION; COMPUTERS AND FAMILIES; FAMILY VALUES; IMMIGRATION; MIGRATION; POVERTY; SOCIALIZATION; TELEVISION AND FAMILIES; TIME USE; WAR/POLITICAL VIOLENCE

Bibliography

Azmon, Y. (2001). "War, Mothers, and a Girl with Braids: Involvement of Mothers' Peace Groups in the National Discourse in Israel." In *Families as Educators for Global Citizenship,* ed. J. A. Myers-Walls and P. Somlai, with R. Rapoport. Aldershot, UK: Ashgate.

Dai Keijing. (2001). "The Tradition and Change of Family Education in Mainland China." In *Families as Educators for Global Citizenship,* ed. J. A. Myers-Walls and P. Somlai, with R. Rapoport. Aldershot, UK: Ashgate.

du Bois-Reymond, M. (2001). "Negotiation Strategies in Modern Families: What Does It Mean for Global Citizenship?" In *Families as Educators for Global Citizenship,* ed. J. A. Myers-Walls and P. Somlai, with R. Rapoport. Aldershot, UK: Ashgate.

Flanagan. C. A. "Families and Globalization: A New Social Contract and Agenda for Research." In *Families as Educators for Global Citizenship,* ed. J. A. Myers-Walls and P. Somlai, with R. Rapoport. Aldershot, UK: Ashgate.

Kung, H. M. and Yi, C. C. (2001). "The Impact of Modernization on Elder-Care: The Case of Taiwan." In *Families as Educators for Global Citizenship,* ed. J. A. Myers-Walls and P. Somlai, P., with R. Rapoport. Aldershot, UK: Ashgate.

LaHaye, W.; Switzer, F.; Obondo, M.; Cohen-Orantes, R.; McCubbin, H., and Wahlström, R. (2001). "Families as Educators: Additional Contributions and Reflections."

In *Families as Educators for Global Citizenship,* ed. J. A. Myers-Walls and P. Somlai, with R. Rapoport. Aldershot, UK: Ashgate.

Milic, A. (2001). "Reflections from a War Zone: A Partial Essay and Memorial Tribute." In *Families as Educators for Global Citizenship,* ed. J. A. Myers-Walls and P. Somlai, with R. Rapoport. Aldershot, UK: Ashgate.

Myers-Walls, J. A. (2001). "The Parents' Role in Educating about War and Peace." In *Families as Educators for Global Citizenship,* ed. J. A. Myers-Walls and P. Somlai, with R. Rapoport. Aldershot, UK: Ashgate.

Qvortrup. J.; Ibrahim, S. E.; Dumon, W.; Chisholm, L.; Flanagan, C. A.; and Rapoport, R. N. (2001). "Families as Educators for Global Citizenship: Additional Contributions and Reflections." In *Families as Educators for Global Gitizenship,* ed. J. A. Myers-Walls and P. Somlai, with R. Rapoport. Aldershot, UK: Ashgate.

Sakka, D, and Dikaiou, M. (2001). "Task Sharing and Sex Role attitudes in Greek Returnees: A Combination of Cross-sectional and Longitudinal Data." In *Families as Educators for Global Citizenship,* ed. J. A. Myers-Walls and P. Somlai, with R. Rapoport. Aldershot, UK: Ashgate.

Skalník, P. (2001). "Globalization, Community Violence and Family: An Anthropologist's Account from Northern Ghana." In *Families as Educators for Global Citizenship,* ed. J. A. Myers-Wallsand P. Somlai, with R. Rapoport. Aldershot, UK: Ashgate.

Skalník, P.; Kusá, Z.; Lakiza-Sachuk, N.; Atchildieva, E.; Myers-Walls, J. A.; Azmon, Y.; Qvortrup, J.; Cohen-Orantes, R.; and Ibrahim, S. E. (2001). "Families, Modernization, and Globalization: Additional Contributions and Reflections." In *Families as Educators for Global Citizenship,* ed. J. A. Myers-Walls and P. Somlai, with R. Rapoport. Aldershot, UK: Ashgate.

Somlai, P. (2001). "Global Citizenship: An Essay on its Contradictions." In *Families as Educators for Global Citizenship,* ed. J. A. Myers-Walls and P. Somlai, with R. Rapoport. Aldershot, UK: Ashgate.

Thioune, O. (2001). "Families as Environmental Educators in the Sahel." In *Families as Educators for Global Citizenship,* ed. J. A. Myers-Walls and P. Somlai, with R. Rapoport. Aldershot, UK: Ashgate.

Tóth , O. (2001). "Hungarian Adolescents' Attitudes Toward their Future, Peace, and the Environment." In *Families as Educators for Global Citizenship,* ed. J. A. Myers-Walls and P. Somlai, with R. Rapoport. Aldershot, UK: Ashgate.

Watanabe, H. (2001). "Transformations of Family Norms: Parents' Expectations of Their Children's Family Lifestyle." In *Families as Educators for Global Citizenship,* ed. J. A. Myers-Walls and P. Somlai, with R. Rapoport. Aldershot, UK: Ashgate.

JUDITH A. MYERS-WALLS

GODPARENTS

The assigning of godparents takes place when a couple selects another couple as sponsors for their child. The couple that accepts the invitation is then responsible for protecting the child and obliged to provide for the physical and spiritual needs of the infant, as well as religious instruction if the parents are absent. Thus, godparents are substitute parents and assume their responsibilities as needed, incorporating their new roles within the extended family (López 1999; Keefe, Padilla, and Carlos 1979).

The origin of godparenting is found in the religious institution of baptism. This ceremony, which usually takes place during the child's first year of life, is aimed at incorporating the child into the larger religious community and is commonly celebrated among Catholics. At the time of baptism, a priest, the child, the parents, and the godparents are present. Although parents customarily choose the godparents, if someone offers to be a godparent, the parents have a hard time not accepting. It is difficult to reject a godparenting request because the offer entails honor, security, social status, and economic well-being for the parties involved. To circumvent any offense derived from the selection process, the family sometimes unofficially has more than one pair of godparents.

Godparents and godchildren, as well as godparents and parents, are bound in a special spiritual kinship with well-established rights and obligations. In Mexico, for example, if the godchild gets sick, the godparents are supposed to take care of him or her, and if the child dies, the godparents prepare the grave (Rojas Gonzalez 1943). Also, frequent cooperation in moral and economic matters is expected. In addition, godparents should act as spiritual guides and authority in times of crisis or need (Pierson 1954). In the past, it was also customary for the children to kiss the hand of the godparents and accept their blessings.

The expectations of parents and godparents, based on the new kinship, have far-reaching consequences. The ground is set for the establishment of special relations as strong as any blood relationship (Rojas González 1943; Lewis 1951). The new relatives should not fight and should treat each other amiably and with respect. If the father dies, then the godfather should fix the corpse for burial, dig the grave (Magallón Junca 1966), and assume the responsibility of the godchild and its family, both spiritually and economically (Rojas González 1943).

The actual functions of godparenting have varied widely from its original purpose. The religious character has weakened and in many cases is confined to the initial baptism ceremony. However, as the religious significance declined, an important social link with many protective characteristics emerged. It has become important to choose godparents whose economic and social status enables them to fulfill their moral and spiritual responsibility to guide the children. Several functional concerns became stronger, creating different types of relationships. When families want to ensure their social position or expand their family network, they search for specific godparents who are more powerful than they are and will allow social climbing (vertical godparenting) (López 1999). At the same time, godparents may be selected from the same social class, a practice termed horizontal godparenting, which gives stability to the family (Foster 1969; Mintz and Wolf 1950). Another form of functional accommodation has been the creation of generational pairings when younger couples select older godparents to help them cope with the stress that accompanies the birth of a first child. Older, experienced godparents guide and reliably support the parents through this process.

European Antecedents

From the Catholic point of view, baptism is a rite of initiation that signifies spiritual rebirth (Rojas González 1943). The biological father plays an important role in the process of conception, and the sponsor (godfather) is introduced as a spiritual father. This notion of sponsorship is not in the New Testament, and Canon Law refers to "custom" as the judicial basis upon which the precept rests (Mintz et al. 1950). Because it is a relic of the Old Testament, sponsorship may derive from the Jewish practice of circumcision, where a witness is required to hold the child undergoing the ritual. The term sponsor itself represents an adaptation of a term current in Roman legal terminology, where *sponsio* signified a contract enforced by religious rather than by legal sanctions (Mintz et al. 1950).

During the era of St. Augustine (354–430 C.E.), parents usually acted as sponsors for their own children. In special cases, like slaves' children or orphans, the sponsor could be a third person (Mintz et al. 1950). Roughly one hundred years later, the Byzantine emperor Justinian, who ruled from 527 to 565 C.E., first issued an edict prohibiting marriages between spiritual relatives. The terms *compater* and *commuter* appeared in 585 and 595 C.E. within the confines of the Western church. Thus, a separate set of sponsors tended to be a later development from a stage in which parents and sponsors were the same people, and this separation must have must have been effected within both Eastern and Western empires roughly between the first quarter of the fifth century C.E. and the end of the sixth century. Nevertheless, full acceptance of this separation and consequent exogamy took place only gradually. From the evidence noted by the Byzantine historian Procopius, we may judge that at the beginning of this period, godparents still actually adopted their children. But the Council of Munich, held in 813 C.E., prohibited parents from acting as sponsors for their own children altogether, and in the books of the Council of Metz of the same year, parents and sponsors are clearly separate terms. In fact, the Western church extended spiritual relationships to cover the officiating priest, the sponsors, the child, and the child's parents. As a result, the number of sponsors permitted was increased to the point of admitting between one and thirty baptismal sponsors (Mintz et al. 1950).

With the start of the feudal period, new rules governed the godparent relationship. The sponsorship of a feudal lord of their serfs included a great deal of manipulation of the labor force and its resources. Ownership of land was vested in the feudal lord. He also owned a share of the labor of the serfs who lived on his land. In return he granted the worker rights to use the land, ownership of certain tools, and the right to consume some goods that he produced. The compadre mechanism and its ritual kin correlates were a functioning part of the class system implicit in this basic relationship. To avoid abuse, Saxons restricted the number of baptismal sponsors to between seven and nine for nobles (i.e., people who belonged to the aristocracy), and to three for burghers (i.e., poor people from the town). Subsequently, the ritual was restricted only to blood relatives, to the baptizing priest, the child, the child's parents, and the child's sponsors.

In Europe, godparenting has generally been retained in its traditional form in areas of Spain, Italy, and the Balkan countries, where the development of industrial capitalism, the rise of a middle class, and the disintegration of the feudal order was slower. In fact, Robert Redfield (1930; in Lynch 1986) refers to godparenthood as a custom of southern rural Europe. These were the areas of Europe involved in the colonization of Latin America; as a result, these customs were transmitted, along with requiring the baptism of indigenous people to bring them into the fold of the Christian community as an addition to the faith and to insure a loyal work force for the Spanish conquerors.

Latin America Background

Godparenthood was imported to the Americas from Europe in the fifteenth century by the Hispanic colonizers as part of the process of domination and conquest. Actually, the Catholic baptism ceremony, mixed with the practical pagan rite of initiation, convinced the conquered, in almost all the towns established by Spain in the New World, of the importance of obedience, and evolved to become a basic institution of social support. In part, the success of the baptism rites grew out of their similarity to some pre-Colombian ceremonies, in which a specific character, sometimes human, some times animal, took charge of the protection of the newborn (Rojas González 1943).

Given the significance that godparenting had for the Europeans and for the New World Indians, and added to the social impact that the bond has in modern Latin America, the present institution is clearly a product of the mixture of Hispanic traditions and indigenous American ideas and practices, as well as their interpretation of Christian precepts. This interactive process made the institution of godparenting strong. It is retained today in many countries, including Brazil, Chile, Colombia, Panama, Peru, Honduras, and Mexico.

The custom, in the case of Mexico, extended to distinguish many people as potential godparents. The possibilities included the woman who cared for the child, a friend, or anyone willing to create a spiritual bond and social relations that would join them together. Also, as an added feature, at the end of the rite, the godfathers comply with the tradition of throwing coins to the children who attend. If this custom is not fulfilled, the belief is that the child will grow unhealthy, and he or she will turn out to be a miserable adult with a bad temper.

To be a godparent in Mexico traditionally included an eight-day ceremony, called *compadre-tlacuas* (banquet of the godfathers), invoking God, so that the child would be healthy and strong. The ceremony was sponsored by the midwife (godmother of lifting), the priest, and the guests (normally in couples), who were invited by the parents. All guests were to wash their hands and put flowers over the child's body and then present some clothes for the godchild. All clothes are then used to dress the child, even if this means putting one garment over many others, as a way of showing gratitude and acceptance of all spiritual relatives. The following act includes a domestic fire (a rustic metal stove, called *anafre* in Spanish) where the mother and godmothers prepare some tortillas filled with meat of which the priest offers four to the fire. While making the offering, the priest prays in *totonaca* (indigenous language), asking for health, well-being, obedience, good luck, and a long life for the infant. The set of rituals is said to achieve the goal of presenting the child to society and obtaining the acceptance of the group. In the days after the ceremony, the family of the godchild feeds all who come to the house (Castro 1986).

Although its basic values and other elements have been sustained, the vitality of the ceremony has diminished because it became prohibitively expensive to hold the banquet of the godparents. Additionally, contact with other customs and cultural groups and the encroachment of modern life explain why, in part, godparents, especially in modern, large, urban areas, no longer adhere to the religious objective of their role. However, the tradition persists as a part of the cultural inheritance that guarantees the protection and care of children.

Bibliography

Castro, C. A. (1986). *Enero y Febrero: Ahijadero, el banquete de los compadres en la Sierra Norte de Puebla.* University of Veracruz Library, Mexico.

Foster, G. M. (1969). "Godparents and Social Networks in Tzintzuntzan." *Southwest Journal of Anthropology* 25:261–278.

Keefe, S. E.; Padilla, A. M.; and Carlos, M. L. (1979). "The Mexican-American Extended Family as an Emotional Support System." *Human Organization* 38(2):144–152.

Lewis, O. (1951). *Life in a Mexican Village. Tepoztlán Restudied.* Urbana-Champaign: University of Illinois Press.

López, R. A. (1999). "Las Comadres as a Social Support System." *Journal of Women and Social Work* 14(1):24–41.

Lynch, J. H. (1986). *Godparents and Kinship in Early Medieval Europe.* Princeton, NJ: Princeton University Press.

Magallón Junca, C. (1966). *El compadrazgo: su función en dos sectores de la población panameña.* Unpublished thesis. National Autonomas University of Mexico.

Mintz, S. W., and Wolf, E. R. (1950). "An Analysis of Ritual Co-parenthood (compadrazgo)." *Southwestern Journal of Anthropology* 6:341–367.

Pierson, D. (1954). "Familia e compadrio numa comunidade rural paulista." *Sociología* 16(4):368–389.

Rojas González, F. (1943). "La institución del compadrazgo entre los indios de México." *Revista Mexicana de Sociología* 5(2):201–213.

ROZZANA SÁNCHEZ ARAGÓN

GRANDPARENTHOOD

Since the mid-1970s, there has been an enormous increase in scholarly interest in grandparenthood. This is largely due to the greater prevalence of grandparents and an increase in the number of years that people experience in the grandparent role.

Prevalence and Increasing Interest

Increases in life expectancy have made grandparenthood more prevalent. Although only about 39 percent of all males and 43 percent of all females born between 1900 and 1902 survived to age sixty-five, projections for those born between 1949 and 1951 are 62 percent for males and 74 percent for females (Anderson 2001). Whereas the number of people aged sixty-five or older was 3.1 million (4.1% of the population) in 1900, it increased to 35 million (12.4%) in 2000, and it is projected to be 70 million (20%) in 2030 (Administration on Aging 2001).

Of children born in 1900, only one in four had all four grandparents alive, and by the time they reached fifteen years, only one in fifty still had all four grandparents alive. In comparison, approximately one-third of those who were twelve years old in the early 1990s had all of the four grandparents alive, and approximately 70 percent had at least two of them alive when they reached adulthood (Szinovacz 1998).

Longer life expectancy has also led to a longer period of grandparenthood. Once someone becomes a grandparent, he or she will have that status for a much longer time than previous generations. It is typical for one to become a grandparent in his or her forties, and some people, particularly women, become grandparents in their thirties (Timberlake and Chipungu 1992). Because some people may be grandparents for several decades, grandparenthood has become a more meaningful stage in one's life course. An increase in the number of single-parent households, resulting from either divorce or birth out of wedlock, has made the role some grandparents fulfill in rearing children more important than it had been previously. Instead of playing merely a supportive role for grandchildren, many grandparents now play an active role in rearing and socializing their grandchildren. Due to prevalence of three-generational households and stronger intergenerational relationships and norms (such as the idea of filial responsibility and familism), grandparenthood appears to be emphasized in foreign countries, particularly in Asia and Latin America.

Grandparenting Styles

Having all of one's grandparents alive was a rare event in the past. It is possible for today's grandparents to be young enough to be in their thirties and for some grandchildren to be old enough to retire. As a result, despite a clearly defined status of grandparenthood, there is not a clearly defined role of grandparenthood. Without good role models or clearly defined social roles, today's grandparents tend to interact with their grandchildren in a more flexible manner, relatively unconstrained by rules and expectations (Johnson 1988).

Traditional literature on grandparenthood focused on how grandparents interact with their grandchildren. Bernice L. Neugarten and Karol K. Weinstein's (1964) pioneering study examined whether grandparents engage in a formal, fun-seeking, or distant-figure style of grandparenting. A *formal* style of grandparenting follows its traditional norms, which are clearly distinct from those of parents. A *fun-seeking* style is characterized by informality and playfulness, whereas a distant-figure style is characterized by infrequent contacts, mostly on ritual occasions.

Using different criteria, Andrew J. Cherlin and Frank K. Furstenberg, Jr. (1985) classified styles of grandparenting into five groups: *detached, passive, supportive, authoritative,* and *influential.* Although both detached and passive grandparents have little interaction with their grandchildren, the detached do not see their grandchildren often whereas the passive do. The supportive type refers to those who have interactions involving helping each other and running errands or chores for each other. The authoritative type refers to those who have high scores on parent-like behaviors such as disciplining, giving advice, discussing problems, correcting behavior, and being asked for advice by grandchildren. Finally, the influential type refers to those who have high scores for both supportive and authoritative dimensions. As for cultural norms about dealing with young grandchildren in the United States, Colleen L. Johnson (1988) states that there are more "should nots" than "shoulds" on enacting a grandmother's role. Grandmothers should not interfere, should not give too much advice, and should not discipline young grandchildren. Grandparents should not overpower, spoil, or buy love from grandchildren. They should not nag, and should not be disappointed if the grandchildren do not return the favors. On the other hand, they should be fun to be with, should be loving, and should make it easier for parents by

A grandmother plays peek-a-boo with her one-year-old grandson. The traditional image of the grandparent is being replaced as increasingly younger people are becoming grandparents, health conditions improve, and the age of retirement increases. LAURA DWIGHT/CORBIS

providing such service as baby-sitting. Other than baby-sitting activities, these "shoulds" are not well delineated.

Quality of Relationship

Quality of relationships between grandparents and young adult grandchildren was assessed by Gregory E. Kennedy (1992). He claims that five elements of the relationship are important to evaluate the quality from the grandchildren's viewpoint. They are *sense of closeness, being known, knowing grandparents, being positively influenced,* and *having an authentic relationship independent of the parents.* In general, the quality of the relationship is better with grandmothers than with grandfathers. The quality is also generally better when grandparents live nearby or with grandchildren, when they are in frequent contact, when the parents experience either divorce or single motherhood, and/or when the grandchild is an only child or a first born child (Roberto, Allen, and Blieszner 2001).

Thomas E. Denham and Craig W. Smith (1989) categorize the nature of grandparental influence into three kinds: *indirect, direct,* and *symbolic.* Indirect influence refers to factors that affect grandchildren only through the effects on the middle-generation parents, such as psychological or financial support and/or stress. Direct influence refers to face-to-face grandparent-grandchild interaction. Grandparents may baby-sit grandchildren.

They may joke, watch television, or go out with grandchildren, thus providing fun. They may give grandchildren advice, teach them skills and games, and even discipline them. They often give grandchildren money and presents. By telling grandchildren what it was like growing up themselves, grandparents serve as observational models for grandchildren. In some cases, grandparents work as "arbitrators" between their children and their grandchildren in confrontations between two different values and personalities.

Symbolic influence, on the other hand, refers to the effect of grandparents just being there without necessarily performing concrete functions. Grandchildren feel good to have grandparents as a *stress buffer,* whom they can go to in case of conflict among family members. Grandparents give grandchildren a sense of family continuity from the past to the present to the future by offering roots for the family. Grandparents may also be considered *family watchdogs* who are there to keep an eye on the family members (Troll 1983). Of the three kinds of influences, symbolic influence seems to be the most important. Although grandparents may be "backstage" most of the time, they are the backbone of the extended family, and they will be available for help if necessary.

In fact, grandparents seem to do very little in the grandparent-grandchildren relationship (Tinsley and Parke 1984). However, having grandparents seems to be important in itself. As such, the presence of grandparents has been found to be very important for the psychological and behavioral development of small children (Tinsley and Parke 1984).

Gender and Relationships

Because more women than men survive into grandparenthood, it is more common for children to have contact with grandmothers than grandfathers. When the differences in the availability of grandmothers and grandfathers are taken into account, studies report that grandchildren have relatively equal and regular contact with grandmothers and grandfathers (Eisenberg 1988). Grandchildren, however, are more influenced by grandmothers than grandfathers in their value development and report a higher degree of psychological closeness with their grandmothers

(Hodgson 1992). Grandmothers are also more satisfied with their relationships with grandchildren, whereas grandfathers are more likely to indulge grandchildren (Thomas 1989).

The grandfather role and the grandmother role are differentiated from each other by gender, just as various other social roles are. Grandfathers often play a "head of the family" or "minister of state" role (Bengtson 1985; Roberto, Allen, and Blieszner 2001), and grandmothers play a "secretary of the interior" role characterized by such activities as child care, "emotion work," and "kinkeeping." Considering the way in which grandparents themselves were raised, stronger gender differentiation of grandparent roles is to be expected.

In the past, grandfathers in the United States adopted either formal, passive, or authoritative styles when dealing with grandchildren, contributing to differences between grandfathers and grandmothers in the intergenerational relationship. Over time, however, more grandfathers seem to have begun adopting fun-seeking and supportive styles. This seems to have decreased, if not completely negated, the differences between grandchild's relationships with grandfathers and grandmothers.

Alice S. Rossi and Peter H. Rossi (1990) reported that percentages of adults who stated that "[Target grandparent] was very important while I grew up" are different not only between grandmothers and grandfathers, but also between the mother's parents and the father's parents. The gender of the middle-generation person is also important for grandparent-grandchild relationships, possibly because women in the middle generation are more likely than men to assume "kinkeeping" roles and to maintain close and affectionate intergenerational relationships (Chan and Elder 2000). In fact, it was reported that grandchildren are most likely to identify maternal grandmothers as their favorite grandparents (Eisenberg 1988; Hodgson 1992).

The gender of grandchildren is also reported to affect the quality of the relationship with grandparents. Merril Silverstein and Jeffrey D. Long (1998) show that grandparents have greater affection for granddaughters than for grandsons in the United States. Robert Strom and his colleagues (1995) show that the quality of grandparent-granddaughter relationships is generally better than that of grandparent-grandson relationships in Japan. Although gender roles are becoming less rigid in developed countries, they remain quite rigid in many countries, emphasizing expressiveness (ability to deal with interpersonal relationships) upon women and instrumentality (ability to deal with the actual task) upon men. In these countries, the nature and quality of grandparent-grandchild relationship may still largely depend on the gender of grandparents, parents, and/or grandchildren.

Demographic Factors and Grandparenthood

The traditional image of grandparents is retired people in rocking chairs—or in the kitchen baking cookies—with all of their time available for family members, including grandchildren. This is no longer the case. Better health conditions have made today's grandparents physically younger and socially more active than the grandparent depicted in traditional images. The retirement age has increased and more women are now in the labor force. As a result, many grandparents are employed. In addition, better health and financial conditions for elderly people have made them less dependent on subsequent generations. Due to a prolonged life expectancy, grandparents are also likely to be caregivers of their own parents.

Maximiliane Szinovacz's (1998) research shows that 35 percent of grandparents work more than 30 hours a week, 12 percent have children age under 19 in the household, 67 percent are currently married, and 34 percent have living parents. Thus, the role of grandparents competes with other responsibilities, such as employment, social life, and family.

Some women become grandmothers very early, often in their thirties. These "off-time grandmothers" tend to be unhappy with their grandmotherhood due to the strains of various roles (grandmother, mother, daughter, granddaughter, employee, and girlfriend) and reluctance to accept grandmotherhood, which symbolizes old age (Timberlake and Chipungu 1992). "On-time grandmothers" seem to cope with this new role relatively better. This pattern also may be due to the prevalent "age norm," or a prescriptive timetable for the ordering of major life events, including becoming a grandparent (Neugarten, Moore, and Lowe 1965). Becoming a grandparent younger than forty-five or

fifty years old is a violation against this age norm and may cause embarrassment.

Due to the increased divorce rate and the increase in single motherhood, many households lack a parent, and grandparents often play a surrogate parent's role. Parents' death and drug and alcohol abuse may also necessitate custodial grandparenting. Esme Fuller-Thomson, Meredith Minkler, and Diane Driver (1997) show that one in ten grandparents have taken primary responsibility for raising their grandchildren for at least six months. The most typical scenario is a single mother, either divorced or never married, living with her children and her mother, which is particularly common among African Americans and low-income families in the United States. Grandmothers usually serve as surrogate parents in place of father figures in these single-mother households. This racial difference seems to be due not only to a larger proportion of single mothers among African Americans, but also to their cultural preferences, including stronger intergenerational relationships (Fuller-Thomson, Minkler, and Driver 1997).

Comparative Aspects of Grandparenthood

The literature on comparative perspectives of grandparenthood is not extensive. Some articles, however, discuss different types of grandparent-grandchild relationships among African Americans, Asians, and Hispanics, focusing on the cultural emphasis on intergenerational relationships.

In terms of the classification developed by Andrew Cherlin and Frank Furstenberg, for example, African American grandparents are more likely to be either authoritative or influential than their white counterparts, suggesting a prevalence of parent-like behaviors among them (1985). Given the emphasis on family traditions and intergenerational relationships, it is expected that grandparents in Asia, Latin America, and Africa are more likely to be authoritative, influential, or supportive, rather than passive or detached.

Elizabeth Timberlake and Sandra Chipungu (1992) show that among African-American grandmothers, those living with their grandchildren tend to value "more highly the grandchild who enabled them to continue to feel useful" (p. 220). This stronger intergenerational relationship will continue after the African-American grandchild grows up (Ashton 1996). Due to slavery and subsequent unfavorable economic circumstances, African Americans are said to depend more upon the intergenerational cooperation involving services, properties, and relationships. This also indicates that African-American grandparents, on the average, play larger roles than their white counterparts.

Latin countries such as Italy, Spain, and those in South America are known to have the idea of *familism*. The family relationships are very important under this idea and the grandparent-grandchild relationship is no exception. Hispanic-American children, for example, are more likely to live with their grandparents than their white counterparts, if less than African Americans (Strom, Buki, and Strom 1997).

There is a strong correlation between the amount of time a grandparent and his/her grandchild spend together and the closeness of the relationship. In Japan, for example, Robert Strom and his colleagues (1995) found that grandparents who spend more than five hours per month with grandchildren and/or who take care of grandchildren daily tend to have a better relationship than others. Three-generational households have been more common among African Americans and Hispanic Americans and in East Asian countries, due to economic circumstances, the notion of familism, and filial responsibility, respectively. Thus, the grandparent-grandchild relationships tend to be stronger among these people than Euro-Americans.

Conclusion

Grandparenthood has received more scholarly attention in the United States due to important demographic changes. Race and gender differences in grandparenthood have been observed. There is not a large body of literature on grandparenthood outside the United States or in cross-cultural contexts, but this topic should gain more attention in the near future. In general, the importance of the grandparent-grandchild relationship is symbolic rather than functional. As the family structure changes, however, this relative importance seems to change in some segments of the population, particularly among the economically disadvantaged.

See also: ADOLESCENT PARENTHOOD; ADULTHOOD; CHILDCARE; DIVORCE: EFFECTS ON PARENTS; ELDERS; EXTENDED FAMILIES; FAMILISM; FAMILY ROLES; FATHERHOOD; FILIAL RESPONSIBILITY; GRANDPARENTS' RIGHTS; IN-LAW RELATIONSHIPS; INTERGENERATIONAL PROGRAMMING; INTERGENERATIONAL RELATIONS; INTERGENERATIONAL TRANSMISSION; LATER LIFE FAMILIES; MOTHERHOOD; RETIREMENT

Bibliography

Ashton, V. (1996). "A Study of Mutual Support between Black and White Grandmothers and Their Adult Grandchildren." *Journal of Gerontological Social Work* 26:87–100.

Bengtson, V. L. (1985). "Diversity and Symbolism in Grandparental Roles." In *Grandparenthood,* ed. V. L. Bengtson and J. F. Robertson. Beverly Hills, CA: Sage Publications.

Chan, C. G., and Elder, G. H., Jr. (2000). "Matrilineal Advantage in Grandchild-Grandparent Relations." *The Gerontologist* 40:179–190.

Cherlin, A. J., and Furstenberg, F. F., Jr. (1985). "Styles and Strategies of Grandparenting." In *Grandparenthood,* ed. V. L. Bengtson and J. F. Robertson. Beverly Hills, CA: Sage Publications.

Denham, T. E., and Smith, C. W. (1989). "The Influence of Grandparents on Grandchildren: A Review of the Literature and Resources." *Family Relations* 38:345–350.

Eisenberg, A. R. (1988). "Grandchildren's Perspectives on Relationships with Grandparents: The Influence of Gender across Generations." *Sex Roles* 19:205–217.

Fuller-Thomson, E.; Minkler, M.; and Driver, D. (1997). "A Profile of Grandparents Raising Grandchildren in the United States." *The Gerontologist* 37:406–411.

Hodgson, L. G. (1992). "Adult Grandchildren and Their Grandparents: The Enduring Bond." *International Journal of Aging and Human Development* 34:209–225.

Johnson, C. L. (1988). *Ex Familia: Grandparents, Parents, and Children Adjust to Divorce.* New Brunswick, NJ: Rutgers University Press.

Kennedy, G. E. (1992). "Quality in Grandparent/ Grandchild Relationship." *International Journal of Aging and Human Development* 35:83–98.

Neugarten, B. L.; Moore, J. W.; and Lowe, J. C. (1965). "Age Norms, Age Constraints, and Adult Socialization." *American Journal of Sociology* 70:710–717.

Neugarten, B. L., and Weinstein, K. K. (1964). "The Changing American Grandparent." *Journal of Marriage and the Family* 26:199–204.

Roberto, K. A.; Allen, K. R.; and Blieszner, R. (2001). "Grandfathers' Perceptions and Expectations of Relationships with Their Adult Grandchildren." *Journal of Family Issues* 22:407–426.

Rossi, A. S., and Rossi, P. H. (1990). *On Human Bonding: Parent-Child Relations Across the Life Course.* New York: Aldine de Gruyter.

Silverstein, M., and Long, J. D. (1998). "Trajectories of Grandparents' Perceived Solidarity with Adult Grandchildren: A Growth Curve Analysis over 23 Years." *Journal of Marriage and the Family* 60:912–923.

Strom, R.; Buki, L.; and Strom, S. (1997). "Intergenerational Perceptions of English Speaking and Spanish Speaking Mexican-American Grandparents." *International Journal of Aging and Human Development* 45:1–21.

Strom, R.; Strom, S.; Collinsworth, P.; Sato, S.; Makino, K.; Sasaki, Y.; Sasaki, H.; and Nishio, N. (1995). "Grandparents in Japan: A Three-Generational Study. " *International Journal of Aging and Human Development* 40:209–226.

Szinovacz, M. (1998). "Grandparents Today: A Demographic Profile." *The Gerontologist* 38:37–52.

Thomas, J. L. (1989). "Gender and Perceptions of Grandparenthood." *International Journal of Aging and Human Development* 29:269–282.

Timberlake, E. M., and Chipungu, S. S. (1992). "Grandmotherhood: Contemporary Meaning among African American Middle-Class Grandmothers." *Social Work* 37:216–222.

Tinsley, B. R., and Parke, R. D. (1984). "Grandparents as Support and Socialization Agents." In *Beyond the Dyad,* ed. M. Lewis. New York: Plenum.

Troll, L. E. (1983). "Grandparents: The Family Watchdogs." In *Family Relationships in Late Life,* ed. T. Brubaker. Beverly Hills, CA: Sage Publications.

Other Resources

Administration on Aging. (2001). *A Profile of Older Americans: 2001.* In *Administration on Aging.* Available from http://www.aoa.gov/aoa/stats/profile/2001.

Anderson, R. N. (2001). "United States Life Tables, 1998." *National Vital Statistics Reports:* 48 (18). Available from http://www.cdc.gov/nchs/products/pubs/pubd/nvsr/48/lifetables98.htm.

YOSHINORI KAMO
CHIZUKO WAKABAYASHI

GRANDPARENTS' RIGHTS

Grandparents' rights is a legal and family issue shaped by changes in society, including the increased number of adults experiencing grandparenthood and the increased number of children raised solely by grandparents (Hill 2000). Grandparents have become a critical source of support to grandchildren who face potentially negative effects of family disruption, such as divorce, illness, or incarceration (Cox 2000).

Grandparent Visitation Rights in the United States

The concept of grandparents' rights is derived from three basic legal approaches. (It is important to note that grandparents' rights only give grandparents the right to file a petition to visit their grandchildren; they do not guarantee that grandparents will be heard before a court of law.) The first approach is *derivative rights theory,* in which grandparents obtain their right to petition to visit their grandchildren by way of their own child. Statutes based on derivative of rights theory allow grandparents to have access to their grandchildren when their own child cannot practice his or her parental rights due to death, divorce, termination of parental rights, incompetence, unfitness, or incarceration. Many states, in line with the second *statutory approach,* also allow grandparents to petition for visitation if family disruptions such as divorce, separation, military duty, and death of parent exist. For example, the government has an interest in maintaining grandparent-grandchild relationships following divorce to reduce the number of children placed in the welfare or foster-care systems. The third approach, using the *best interests of the child,* allows grandparents to petition for visitation against fit, intact families, despite parental objection (Hartfield 1996; Walther 1997). Regardless of the approach, grandparents' rights encompass three specific legal issues: violation of parental rights; promotion of the best interests of the child; and establishment of grandparental rights.

Parental rights. Grandparents' rights legally challenge family law tradition that protects parents' rights to raise their children as they see fit. The rights of biological and adoptive parents have been protected by the U.S. Supreme Court (e.g., *Meyer v. Nebraska* 1923; *Pierce v. Society of Sisters*

1925; *Stanley v. Illinois* 1972; *Wisconsin v. Yoder* 1972) and by common law practices (those practices outside the legislative processes). Some justices, for example, have adhered to common law traditions that historically gave parents ultimate control over the upbringing of their child (e.g., *McMain v. Iowa District Court of Polk County* 1997; *Ward v. Ward* 1987).

Two legal standards may be used in decisions to interfere with the rights of parents: strict scrutiny or rational basis test. *Strict judicial scrutiny* requires a compelling reason to justify government interference in the rights of parents. The *rational basis test,* a lower standard, allows the government to interfere with the fundamental rights of citizens when a reasonable relationship to a justifiable government interest exists (Harvard Law Review 1980). Beginning in 1965, all fifty states began to create statutes that allowed grandparents to petition for visitation with their grandchildren (Segal and Karp 1989). In 1998, the 105th Congress enacted Public Law 105-374, *The Visitation Rights Enforcement Law,* guaranteeing that grandparents can visit their grandchildren anywhere in the United States as long as they have visitation rights in one state. Grandparents' rights reached the U.S. Supreme Court in 2000 with *Troxel v. Granville.* These occurrences brought this family law issue to the center stage of U.S. politics.

In most grandparent visitation cases, including the *Troxel v. Granville* (2000) decision, U.S. Supreme Court and lower court justices largely have ruled in favor of parents over grandparents (Henderson and Moran 2001). In a few cases, state supreme and appellate courts determined that grandparents' rights unfairly interfere with parental rights or do not serve the best interests of the child, unless threat of harm to the child or an unfit parent exists. To protect parental rights, lower court justices frequently cited grandparents' failure to strictly adhere to stipulations in grandparent visitation, child custody, or related statutes.

Best interests of the child. Grandparents' success in acquiring visitation rights also depends on the court's interpretation of what constitutes the best interests of the child or promotes the welfare of the child (the overriding consideration in child custody and visitation decisions) (Harvard Law Review 1980). To protect the interests of children, the government may once again use its *parens patriae* powers, the power to protect the interest of all vulnerable citizens or to become the legal parent

or protector of children (Garner 1999; Harvard Law Review 1980; Mnookin and Weisburg 1993). Following family law traditions that protect the primacy of the parent-child relationship, courts have ruled that protecting the rights of parents serves the best interests of children (e.g., *Brooks et al. v. Parkerson* 1995). In some instances, judges looked at the facts of the case including the economic, psychological, and moral stability of the grandparents or the suitability of the grandparents' home (e.g., *Steward v. Steward* 1995). The quality of the relationship between the parent and grandparent or between the grandparent and grandchild were sometimes considered in determining if grandparental visitation served the best interests of the child. Grandparents' rights have led courts to rethink the legal rights of children (Foster and Freed 1984). In a few cases (*David J. & Rita K. v. Theresa K. et al.* 1993; *Puleo et al. v. Forgue et al.* 1993; *Strouse v. Olson* 1986; *Thompson v. Vanaman* 1986) judges interpreted the best interests of the child to mean promoting the rights of children because children have a right to know their grandparents and to derive benefits from having a relationship with them.

Grandparents' rights. The courts have provided limited legal protections to extended families led by grandparents—except in the case of *Moore v. the City of East Cleveland* (1977), where the grandparent-led family functioned like a traditional family with two parents and children. Consequently, granting grandparent visitation rights showed a slight shift in the legal definition of the family (Bohl 1996; Burns 1991). Because lower court judges knew the facts of the case and had legal authority over custody and visitation decisions, in some instances appellate and state supreme court justices upheld the lower court decisions (e.g., *Hicks v. Enlow* 1989; *In the Matter of Grandparental Visitation of C. G. F.* 1992). State supreme or appellate judges assumed that lower court justices had a better understanding of the facts of the case. In *King v. King* (1992), a Kentucky court made a radical legal decision determining that the grandparent visitation statute sought to promote the rights of parents, children, and grandparents, which is against legal traditions that have protected parental rights and infrequently promoted the rights of children. In other words, the *King v. King* decision implies that grandparents have rights. Despite these trends, parental rights continue to take precedence over the rights of children and grandparents, especially in light of the special weight given to parents in the *Troxel v. Granville* (2000) decision.

Grandparent Visitation Rights in Canada

As early as 1980, Canadian provinces also enacted grandparent access laws based on the best interests of the child (R.S.B.C. 1996 C. 128, s. 24; R.S.B.C. 1996 C. 128, s. 35; R.S.A. 1980, c. P-20, s. 32.1). Factors to be considered when determining if grandparent visitation or access serves the child's best interests involve examining both the wishes and views of the child and the grandparent-grandchild relationship. Other factors to be considered include the child's mental and physical health, the education and training needs of the child, and the ability of the grandparents (or adults seeking access) to adequately care for the child. In Canada, grandparent visitation rights tend to focus more on the child's needs than parental rights. For example, in the case of *Sparks v. Sparks* (2001), the court reasoned "in no case may the father or mother, without grave reasons interfere with personal relations between the child and his grandparents" (p. 6). Despite the statutory and judicial efforts to provide grandparents' access to their grandchildren, Edward Kruk (1995) found that parental divorce, conflictual grandparent-parent relations, and step-parent adoption after remarriage continue to inhibit this access.

Conclusion

Research is needed to determine who petitions for visitation, what problems lead families to petition for grandparental visitation, and what are the long-term consequences of grandparental litigation on family and child development (i.e., family processes, socioemotional development in children, and family economic well-being). Because U.S. grandparents' rights are based on state statutes, social scientists should address the question of what the legal issues are across states. Additional investigation is needed to determine if Canadian courts will follow U.S. courts' tendency toward guarding the rights of parents over that of grandchildren or grandparents. Regardless of the country, if grandparental visitation is awarded, how courts require grandparents to provide for the care and economic support of their grandchildren remains a viable area of study.

See also: CHILD CUSTODY; DIVORCE: EFFECTS ON PARENTS; ELDERS; FAMILY LAW; FAMILY POLICY; GRANDPARENTHOOD; GUARDIANSHIP; INTERGENERATIONAL RELATIONS; REMARRIAGE; SUBSTITUTE CAREGIVERS

Bibliography

Burns, E. M. (1991). "Grandparent Visitation Rights: Is it Time for the Pendulum to Fall?" *Family Law Quarterly* 25:59–81.

Cox, C. B. (2000). "Why Grandchildren Are Going to and Staying at Grandmother's House and What Happens When They Get There." In *To Grandmother's House We Go and Stay,* ed. C. B. Cox. New York: Springer.

Foster, H. H., and Freed, D. J. (1984). "The Child's Right to Visit Grandparents: An Emerging Question of Visitation Rights." *Trial* 18:38–45.

Garner, B. A. (1999). *Black's Law Dictionary,* 7th edition. Eagan, MN: West Group.

Hartfield, B. W. (1996). "Legal Recognition of the Value of Intergenerational Nurturance: Grandparent Visitation Statutes in the Nineties." *Generations* 20(1):53–56.

Harvard Law Review. (1980). *Developments in the Law: The Constitution and the Family.* Boston: Author.

Henderson, T. L., and Moran, P. B. (2001). "Grandparent Visitation Rights: Testing the Parameters of Parental Rights." *Journal of Family Issues* 22:619–638.

Hill, T. J. (2000). "Legally Extending the Family: An Event History Analysis of Grandparent Visitation Rights Law." *Journal of Family Issues* 21:246–261.

Kruk, E. (1995). "Grandparent-Grandchild Loss: Findings from a Study of 'Grandparent Rights' Members." *Canadian Journal on Aging* 14:737–754.

Mnookin, R. H., and Weisburg, D. K. (1993). *Child, Family, and State: Problems and Materials on Children and Law,* 2nd edition. Boston: Little, Brown.

Segal, E. C., and Karp, N. (1989). *Grandparent Visitation Disputes: a Legal Resource Manual.* Washington DC: American Bar Association.

Walther, D. L. (1997). "Survey of Grandparents Visitation Rights." *American Journal of Family Law* 11:95–107.

Cases

Brooks et al. v. Parkerson. (1995). 265 Ga. 189; 454 S.E.2d 769. (1995 Ga. LEXIS 157). 95 Fulton County DR P1103. Available from http://web.lexis-nexis.com.

Grandparental Visitation of C. G. F., H. F., T. F. v. T. F. and D. L, In the Matter of the. (1992). 168 Wis. 2d 62;

483 N.W.2d 803. (1992 Wisc. LEXIS 199). Available from http://web.lexis-nexis.com.

Hicks v. Enlow. (1989). Ky., 764 S.W.2d 68.

King v. King. (1992). 929 S. W. 2d 630.

McMain v. Iowa District Court for Polk County. (1997). 559 N.W.2d 12. (1997 Iowa Sup. LEXIS 60). Available from http://web.lexis-nexis.com.

Meyer v. Nebraska.(1923). 262 U.S. 390.

Moore v. the City of East Cleveland. (1977). 431 U.S. 494; 97 S. Ct. 1932. (1977 U.S. LEXIS 17). 52 L. Ed. 2d 531.

Pierce v. the Society of Sisters. (1925). 268 U S. 510; 45 S. Ct. 571; 1925 U.S. LEXIS 589; 69 L. Ed. 1070; 39 A.L.R. 468.

Sparks v. Sparks. (2001). A. C. W. S. J. LEXIS 15624; 2001 A. C. W. S. J. 613317; 106 A. C. W. S. (3d) 278. Available from http://web.lexis-nexis.com.

Stanley v. Illinois. (1972). 405 U.S. 645; 92 S. Ct. 1208; 1972 U.S. LEXIS 70; 31 L. Ed. 2d 551.

Steward v. Steward. (1995). 111 Nev. 259; 890 P.2d 777; 1995 Nev. LEXIS 17. Available from http://web. lexis-nexis.com.

Troxel v. Granville. (2000). 120 S. Ct. 2054 U. S. LEXIS 3767; 147 L. Ed. 2d 49; 68 U. S. L. W. 4458; 2000 Cal. Daily Op. Service 4345; 2000 Daily Journal DAR 5831; 12 Fla. W. Fed. S. 365. Available from http://web. lexis-nexis.com.

Ward v. Ward. (1987). Del. Fam. Ct., 537 A.2d 1063.

Wisconsin v. Yoder. (1972). 406 U.S. 205.

Other Resource

Bohl, J. C. (1996). "The Unprecedented Intrusion: A Survey and Analysis of Selected Grandparent Visitation Cases." *Oklahoma Law Review* 29:1–18. Available from http://web.lexis-nexis.com.

TAMMY L. HENDERSON

GREAT BRITAIN

Many countries have experienced very significant changes in patterns of family formation and family structure. Great Britain is one of the countries where these changes have been particularly marked, with the result that British families have become less stable and more diverse. The roles of women and men within the family have also changed, especially for women with children, who are now very likely to be combining paid employment with domestic and care work. These trends have led to renewed interest in the family in both the sociological and the policy literature, as well as in popular and political discourse.

The Nature of Family Change in Great Britain

Patterns of family formation and dissolution in Britain changed significantly in the latter half of the twentieth century. This is particularly true since the late 1960s when restrictions on contraception, abortion, and divorce were substantially reduced. The 1964 introduction of the contraceptive pill in Britain made contraception easier to obtain and use and much more reliable. The National Health Service (Family Planning) Act of 1967 allowed doctors to give family-planning advice and to prescribe free contraceptives, initially to married women only. The Abortion Act of the same year allowed the termination of pregnancy if two independent medical practitioners agreed that continuance would cause physical or mental risk to the health of the woman or her existing children. And the 1969 Divorce Reform Act made the "irretrievable breakdown" of the marriage the sole grounds for divorce, although it was necessary to prove this in one of five ways (unreasonable behavior, desertion, adultery, two years separation with consent, five years separation without consent). (It should be noted that there are differences across U.K. countries in the timing and operation of these measures. For example, the 1969 Divorce Reform Act applied to England and Wales, and Scotland did not introduce similar reforms until 1976.)

These measures are still largely in place, with only relatively minor changes, and they have formed the backdrop to widespread change in family structures and the life-course trajectories of individuals. In the immediate postwar period and up to the late 1960s most people experienced a typical life-course pattern of courtship leading to marriage, followed by the birth of children; the woman gave up paid employment during her years of childrearing, and the couple stayed together until "death do us part." But such patterns are increasingly elusive for the late twentieth and early twenty-first century. As figures from the Office of National Statistics show, there is now much more variety and change in the way people in Great Britain move into and out of families:

- The majority of men and women still marry, but nonmarriage is on the increase. Of women born in the early 1960s, 28 percent remained unmarried at the age of thirty-two. Only 7 percent of women born in the early 1940s were still unmarried by that age. This partly reflects later age at marriage but also increased rates of nonmarriage.

- Cohabitation has become increasingly common, usually preceding or following marriage but, for some couples, replacing marriage. The proportion of nonmarried women under sixty cohabiting almost doubled in less than fifteen years—from 13 percent in 1986 to 25 percent in 1998 and 1999. By the early 1990s as many as 70 percent of women cohabited prior to marriage, and so cohabitation seems to have replaced marriage as the first form of co-resident partnership for many couples. There are about 1.5 million cohabiting heterosexual couples in England and Wales.

- The number of marriages has fallen, and the timing of marriage has changed. About 184,000 first marriages took place in 1999 in England and Wales, down from 343,000 in 1971, and the average age at first marriage was twenty-eight for women and thirty for men in 1999, compared with twenty-two and twenty-four, respectively, in 1971.

- Almost one in five conceptions are terminated by legal abortion. Probably about one-fourth of women born in the mid-1970s will remain childless. Those who have children are older and less likely to be married than they used to be. The mean age of women at the time of the birth of their first child was twenty-nine in 1999 compared with twenty-four in 1971. Of all births in 1999, 39 percent were to unmarried women, with the most of these registered by both parents (80 percent, including 60 percent living at the same address).

The numbers and rate of divorce have remained fairly steady since the early 1980s, with about 145,000 divorces per year, a rate of 12.9 per thousand married people. The numbers of divorces involving children under sixteen reached a peak in of 176,000 in 1993, then fell slightly to 150,000 in 1999. One in four children whose parents divorce are under five years old.

The most visible outcome of these changing patterns of family formation and dissolution has been the growth in the number and proportion of families headed by a lone parent. Lone-parent families (i.e., families with one parent, not cohabiting, living with dependent children) now form about 23 percent of all families with children in Britain and number about 1.7 million families with about 2.8 million children. In the 1980s the main growth in lone parenthood came about because of divorce; in the 1990s unmarried motherhood has increased more rapidly. This is mainly a result of rising rates of cohabitation, with women who separate from a cohabiting partner appearing as "single, never-married" in the statistics. About half of all lone parents leave lone parenthood within six years of becoming a lone parent, and many of these go on to form new partnerships, and in some cases to have more children. Stepfamilies are therefore also becoming more common, with about 8 percent of children estimated to be living in such a family in the mid-1990s.

Great Britain has a mainly white population, with the 1991 census counting about three million people as nonwhite (self-definition), about 6 percent of the population. Patterns of family formation and dissolution differ among ethnic minority groups. For example, Caribbean men and women are less likely to be married or cohabiting than their white counterparts, while South Asians have higher rates of marriage and lower rates of cohabitation and marital breakdown.

Family Roles: Men's Work, Women's Work

As Graham Allan and Graham Crow (2001) point out, changes in family life are not only a matter of changing family structures but also changing family roles and relationships. Changing roles are very apparent with respect to paid employment, and one of the most striking trends in Great Britain is the continuing decline of the traditional family model of male breadwinner and dependent wife and the rise of the two-earner family. This is a consequence of changes in women's employment patterns, with much of the employment growth arising from increased employment participation rates among women with children. Women now return to work more quickly after childbirth, with about half of those giving birth in 1998 back at paid work within nine to eleven months (in 1979 this was true for just one-fourth). Overall, about 70 percent of married mothers are economically active, but this varies significantly with the age of the children, 58 percent of women with a youngest child of preschool age (under five) are employed compared with 78 percent of mothers with a youngest child over ten. Part-time work (under thirty hours) is very common, with about two-fifths of mothers in part-time jobs. This does not vary much by age of children, because it is women's full-time work that increases as children get older.

By contrast, becoming a father has little impact on men's employment participation rates—about 85 to 90 percent of fathers are economically active—although fathers do tend to work longer hours than men without children (forty-seven hours per week compared with forty for men in general). But most of the married women who have entered in the labor market over the past decade have been married to employed men rather than unemployed men. Two-earner families increased from about 50 percent of all couples with children in 1985 to about 62 percent in 1995. Two-earner couples are therefore increasingly the norm, particularly among families with school-age children. The most common pattern is for the man to be in full-time work and the women to be in part-time work. If both parents work full-time, the couple is more likely to share domestic work, but if the woman works part-time, she also does the bulk of the domestic work. The higher-paid couples often buy in domestic labor and childcare, and two-earner couples are the family type most likely to use formal childcare. Many, however, also work hours that allow them to shift parent, with fathers providing childcare while mothers are out working, and vice versa. Over one-fourth of two-earner families have at least one parent who regularly works in the evening or at night. The provision of childcare services is relatively low in Great Britain compared with many European countries, and the costs are high, so if both parents are employed, families often have to set up quite complex arrangements using combinations of different sorts of childcare.

For about one in ten couples with children, neither parent is employed, and these families, many suffering from ill-health and experiencing long-term unemployment, form a sharp contrast with the relatively well-off two-earner couples. Lone parents form another sort of contrast. The employment trends for lone mothers have followed a rather different trend from those of married mothers, with no significant growth in employment rates. About half (51%) of lone mothers

are employed, and young, single mothers without educational qualifications are the least likely to be employed, especially if they have young children. Many lone mothers face considerable barriers to paid work, including lack of work experience and qualifications, health problems for themselves or their children, lack of affordable and good-quality childcare, and lack of suitable jobs in the areas where they live. Thus, many lone mothers rely upon government support through social security benefits, and around seven in ten lone parents are receiving Income Support (the means-tested safety net benefit of Great Britain system). Even among those who are employed, low wages mean that there is a heavy reliance upon state financial support, and six in ten employed lone parents are receiving financial support to top up their wages.

One consequence of these family and employment changes has been a polarization between work-rich and work poor households, between those with two earners and those with none. Great Britain has also experienced a large and rapid rise in income inequality and poverty since the 1970s, and this has particularly affected families with children. Government figures show that, between 1979 and 1995-96, average incomes for households with children rose by 35 percent compared with 43 percent for those without children (excluding pensioners). There has been a significant growth in child poverty in Great Britain, with 4.4 million children—one-third of all children—estimated to be living in poor households in the late 1990s (poverty being here defined as households with less than half of the average household income, taking family size into account).

Family Politics and Family Policy

So, as in many other countries, and more so in some respects, Great Britain has experienced a period of rapid family change and widening economic inequality. These trends have been a source of much concern, particularly the rise in lone parenthood, which has been a very political issue in Britain. In the late 1980s and early to mid-1990s lone parenthood was often depicted by British politicians and in the media in a very hostile and negative light. Parents, it was argued, were selfishly putting their own needs before those of children, who suffered as the innocent victims of parental divorce or failure to marry. Thus, the controversial 1991 Child Support Act was presented

A family gathers for breakfast in Northumberland, England. PETER JOHNSON/CORBIS

by the then-Conservative government as a measure that would force absent fathers to face up to their financial responsibilities toward children (without much success, as it turned out, because many men refused to comply, and many others were exempted because of low incomes).

The causes of these family trends have also been debated in the sociological literature on the family, and variously identified as reflecting, for example, women's increased economic independence, the impact of feminism, changing sexual norms and attitudes, and growing individualism and unwillingness to settle for less-than-perfect relationships. Anthony Giddens explored the latter idea in his 1992 book, *The Transformation of Intimacy,* in which he argued that individuals have become more inclined towards pure relationships—relationships freely entered into and continued only as long as they provide the individual with emotional and physical satisfaction. Giddens's work is mainly theoretical, but other leading sociologists, notably Janet Finch (1989) (for families in general) and Carol Smart (1999) (for postdivorce families), have explored the way in which family relationships and obligations are constructed as part of ongoing relationships that are negotiated within families, not absolute but reciprocal, not gifts but exchanges.

There has also been much debate about the relationship between state policies and family behavior. This has mainly been polarized into two camps. In one there are the traditionalists who argue that social and welfare policy has contributed to the problem (by providing financial and housing support to lone parents) and who want to reform policy in order to support the traditional family based on marriage. In the other camp are the pragmatists who argue that government cannot stop these changes and so must reform policies in order to adapt to them. These are not necessarily party political positions, with politicians from both leading political parties, Labour and Conservative, found in either camp. And policy seems to reflect a (perhaps somewhat uneasy) mix of both points of view.

The Labour government took office in Britain in May 1997 promising policy change across a wide range of areas. One of the ten pledges in their 1997 manifesto was the promise that, "we will help build strong families and strong communities" and in October 1998, the Home Office published a discussion document, *Supporting Families,* which, as the foreword pointed out, "was the first time any [British] government had published a consultation paper on the family." The paper proposed two main types of policy intervention. First were measures that are aimed at providing direct support for families in cash or in kind measures to reduce poverty and increase family prosperity, and measures to help parents balance work and home. The former includes a pledge to end child poverty within twenty years, and the latter includes measures such the "national childcare strategy." Both of these are very new in Great Britain—no previous British government has made such a promise about poverty nor has any accepted responsibility for childcare provision, which has previously been seen as falling within the private domain of the family. Other significant new policies include measures to support and encourage lone parents into paid employment with a target set for employment levels (that 70 percent should be employed within ten years). A range of new provisions, national and local, including many pilot or demonstration projects, has been introduced. Benefits for the poorest children (those in families receiving Income Support) have been increased substantially, and there are to be new, more generous tax credits for children.

The second type of policies set out in *Supporting Families* are those that are aimed at changing family behavior in some way. These include, for example, the provision of support and advice services to improve parenting skills, giving local authorities powers to impose child curfews to keep children off the streets at nights in certain areas, setting targets to reduce teenage pregnancy, measures intended to strengthen marriage through information and support to couples when they marry, and mediation and counseling for marital breakdown.

The responses to these sorts of proposals, especially those intended to strengthen marriage, illustrate some of the difficulties inherent in the development of an explicit family policy in postmodern society. As noted above, there are very different and very polarized views about government intervention in family matters, and the measures intended to strengthen marriage have been controversial because they seem to suggest that other family types—lone parents, stepfamilies—are less acceptable and less deserving of support. Other measures, such as the stress on reducing worklessness and increasing levels of employment for all parents, including lone parents, have also been criticized for failing to recognize and value the contribution made by women's unpaid care work within the family.

This lack of consensus about the goals of policy makes family policy potentially a very controversial area, and making policy goals clear and explicit thus risks bringing those disagreements into the open. Family policy has been a growth area of social policy in Great Britain and in many other countries over the past few decades. This reflects the fact that many governments are seeking ways to respond to family trends, either to accommodate to or to try and resist change. But family policy is more directly normative than many other policy areas—it is hard to have neutral policy goals in this area—and so having explicit goals for family policy depends very much on having shared values. The changing family patterns that are pushing governments towards tackling family policy issues are at the same time making it more difficult to reach agreement on these.

See also: FAMILY POLICY

Bibliography

Allen, G., ed. (1999). *The Sociology of the Family: A Reader.* Oxford: Blackwell.

Allen, G., and Crow, G. (2001). *Families, Households and Society,* Basingstoke, UK: Palgrave.

Finch, J. (1989). *Family Obligations and Social Change,* Cambridge, UK: Polity Press.

Ford, R. and Millar, J. eds. (1998). *Private Lives and Public Responses: Lone Parenthood and Future Policy in the UK.* London: Policy Studies Institute.

Giddens, A. (1992). The *Transformation of Intimacy,* Cambridge, UK: Polity Press.

Home Office (1998) *Supporting Families,* London: Stationery Office

Kiernan, K.; Land, H.; and Lewis, J. (1998). *Lone Motherhood in 20th Century Britain.* Oxford: Clarendon Press.

McRae, S., ed. *Changing Britain: Families and Households in the 1990s,* Oxford: Oxford University Press.

Millar, J., and Ridge, T. (2001). *Families, Poverty, Work and Care.* Department for Work and Pensions Research Report No. 153. Leeds, UK: Corporate Document Services.

Millar, J., and Rowlingson, K., eds. (2001). *Lone Parents and Employment: Cross-National Comparisons.* Bristol, UK: Policy Press.

Modood, T., and Berthoud, R. (1997). *Ethnic Minorities in Britain: Diversity and Disadvantage* London: Policy Studies Institute.

Office of National Statistics. (2001). *Social Trends,* Number 31. London: The Stationery Office.

Office of National Statistics. (2001). *Population Trends,* Number 104 (Summer edition), London: The Stationery Office.

Smart, C., and Neale, B. (1999). *Family Fragments,* Cambridge, UK: Polity Press.

JANE MILLAR

GREECE

Greece, the birthplace of Western civilization, has a long history. Philosophy and the humanities have flourished there for more than 2,500 years. Greece is situated at the southeastern end of the European continent and has an area of 132 square kilometers. Now a modern state, it has, according to the 2001 census, approximately 11 million inhabitants. It is a member of the European Union (EU). The country's development has not always followed a clear and balanced direction, which has affected its economical, political, and social structures.

The many and variable migrations of the Greek people have left a significant mark on the country's evolution. Before World War II, Greeks migrated mainly to the United States, Canada, Australia, and countries of the Eastern Mediterranean. After World War II, Greek migration was mainly within the European continent. The majority of migrants ended up in West Germany, Belgium, Holland, and other European countries. Although large numbers of these migrants have now returned to Greece, an equally significant number have remained in the host countries. Thus, many Greek communities exist in countries such as the United States and Canada. After World War II, and especially during the 1960s, a second major migratory movement occurred. Greece lost 20 percent of its population through migration, which had serious consequences for its development. Most of those who migrated were in the most productive phase of their lives and represented the most dynamic part of the labor force.

Between 1971 and 1985, an estimated 625,000 Greeks returned to their homeland. During the same period, an influx of migrants from Third World countries into Greece began. This trend continued into the 1980s and was augmented by an additional flow of migrants from East European countries (Teperoglou and Tzortzopoulou 1996).

Demographic Trends

The economic growth and social development in Greece at the end of World War II, and especially since the 1960s, have changed the form and functioning of Greek society and the Greek family. These developments include massive international migration to the United States, Australia, Canada, and Western Europe, the exodus of rural residents to cities, and the considerable growth of the tourism industry.

The demographic profile of Greece is similar to that of other developed countries: a low birth rate and an increase in the proportion of elderly people. Fertility rates per 1,000 inhabitants are continuously falling in Greece: 18.9 in 1960, 16.5 in 1970, 15.4 in 1980, 10.7 in 1988, and 9.5 in 1998 (Statistical Year Book of Greece). According to the United Nations' population projection, Greece has one of the lowest fertility rates in Europe (1990–1995). The average number (fertility rate) of children per woman between the ages of fifteen and forty-four in Greece was 1.32 in 1995. In all European countries, fertility rates in the same year were 1.43 children per woman. The fertility rates in urban and rural areas of Greece are now the same.

The following is a summary of demographic trends in Greece:

- The average life expectancy was 75.3 for men and 80.5 for women in 1998.

- Contraceptives, especially abortion, are used as methods to interrupt unwanted or unplanned pregnancies.

- Marriage and childbirth now occur later. In 1995 the mean age at which women gave birth to their first child was 28.2 years.

- Infant mortality is dramatically lower, due to improved health conditions for mothers and newborns. In 1960, infant mortality per 1,000 live births was as high as 40.1; in 1998, it was 6.6.

- Internal and international migration are significant factors. The majority of migrants are young people at their most productive age.

The drop in fertility rates, combined with the aging population, poses a serious problem for the country. The ratio of retired people to those who are economically active has increased: In 1977 there was one retired person for every 2.97 people of working age; in 1994 the ratio was 1: 2.09 (Moussourou 1995).

The nondemographic parameters that determine family size in Greece include family income, employment status and level of education of both parents, the status and living conditions of women, and women's labor market participation and their financial independence. Women have made great progress in the various professions and occupations in Greece. They made up 37 percent of the total work force in 1990. Women's employment, however, is not a new development. Women in Greece have always worked either in rural occupations or at home as hairdressers, as dressmakers, or in other service jobs while at the same time being in charge of the household. This type of work has been officially recorded. What is new is an increase in women's occupations that are outside the home.

Women's employment has been considered one of the main causes of low birth rates. Such an inference, though, should be viewed with caution because women who are not employed outside of the home also reported lower birth rates. Families' attitudes towards having a specific number of children are explained by many factors, particularly the economic status of the families. Other factors are industrialization and urbanization (Teperoglou and Tzortzopoulou 1996).

Family income matters not only because it guarantees a family's survival, but also because it determines the social position of the family. A survey by the Consumers' Institute (INKA) has found that a Greek needs to work 18.7 hours to purchase food that a German is able to buy with 9.5 hours of work or an English person with 11.2 hours. The same survey found that the average Greek family needed 378.000 drs ($1,595) per month in 1996 to have an acceptable standard of living (Moussourou 1996).

The incidence of divorce has increased since 1970. In that year the rate was 0.4 per one thousand inhabitants; in 1980, 0.7 per thousand; in 1990, 0.6 per thousand; and in 1995, 1.1 per thousand (Statistical Yearbook of Greece). The main reason is the reform of family law and the legalization of a new form of divorce: divorce by mutual consent, whereby either spouse is entitled to apply for the dissolution of the marriage. Prior to the 1980s, the structure of the Greek family was more traditional, and governments did not approve any initiative for the reform of family law. In the early 1980s reforms were undertaken, and Greek women felt psychologically more liberated to get divorced.

Definition of Family

The term *family* refers to a particular social group whose members are related by blood or marriage at different levels or in different forms or combinations. Each member's role and status within the institution of the family is determined by his or her corresponding position in the family. The forms of family that prevail in Greece refer mainly to the distinction between the conjugal and the extended family. The conjugal family includes the husband and wife and their children. The extended family includes the conjugal family as well as ascendants of the husband and/or wife. Families are further distinguished in complete conjugal and incomplete conjugal families (e.g., one-parent families) and in

A Greek Orthodox wedding in Cyprus. Musicians lead the wedding party back to the couple's new house for a reception. Similar to trends in other developed countries, marriages and childbirth generally occur later than they did for previous generations. JONATHAN BLAIR/CORBIS

extended complete or incomplete families (e.g., one grandparent).

The definition of the family is often confused with other terms—for example, household. The National Statistical Service of Greece considers all people who live under the same roof to be members of the family, regardless of whether they are related.

In Greece, family life and the position of children have changed substantially with the evolution of the traditional rural-agricultural life into an urban industrial-modern system (Moussourou 1994). Anthropological research on Greek rural life suggests that the importance of the Greek family was reflected in the significance attached to the role of the mother. Although the man acted as the family's outside representative, enjoying the social prestige and esteem that this role entailed, the woman was the organizer of the household, the mediator in family disputes, and the guardian of the family's cohesiveness. The family's image rested in large

measure on the woman's ability to carry out her household duties properly (Kyriazis 1995).

The most important characteristic of the family in contemporary society is its fluidity, produced by a combination of three interrelated factors: a) the variety of socially acceptable family patterns according to which one may organize one's private life; b) the possibility of individuals choosing the way in which they wish to organize their private lives; and c) the increased possibility of an individual choosing different, successive patterns during his or her lifetime (Moussourou 1994).

If grandparents who live near their married children are added to families of three generations, the total percentage of daily contacts between the three generations increases. Exchange and assistance between the two adult generations and the young on the one hand, and influence of the elder relatives on the other, are common patterns (Teperoglou 1994).

Role of the Child

The most important result of the contraction of the Greek family is that children become the center of concern and of emotional and financial investment, not only for their parents but for the extended family as well.

The term *child centeredness* means the exclusive and all-inclusive attention that parents and other adult family members pay to the needs of the child. This attention embraces the economic, emotional, developmental, and psychological dimensions of a child's life. The child's overall development is of paramount value to the parents. During this time, family relationships are considerably influenced by the responses parents are trying to give to the problems arising from the child's upbringing.

Greek families need a new way of life and a new way to manage family relationships to address the emotional and financial needs of childhood. In the past, the extended family formed the basis for family and social relationships and the training of the young. Communication was mainly oral. Stories told by grandfathers and grandmothers about their lives and hardships, fairy tales, and nursery rhymes referred to and sustained a value system that had little to do with the modern, competitive society. This way of bringing up the young was made possible not only by the large size of the family, but also by the free time that its members had at their disposal.

Education constitutes the safest basis for social upgrading in the Greek society. Young people spend a considerable amount of time obtaining educational qualifications. School hours—depending on age—and the numerous educational activities outside school (e.g., learning foreign languages, music, or computers) create an exhausting daily schedule for teenagers. Finding a job in the future is connected with qualified knowledge—which is attested by obtained certificates—and not with the quality of knowledge. Unemployment of the young, fear of unemployment, and stiff competition create insecurity and place continuous stress on the family.

The Greek educational system is highly centralized. All decisions concerning staff and curriculum are taken by the Ministry of Education, and there is a national curriculum. Children receive nine years of compulsory education consisting of six years of elementary and three years of secondary schooling (Gymnasium). Compulsory schooling starts at the age of five years and nine months (i.e., when the child will reach the age of six by the December of the current academic year).

The Greek family is determined to suffer whatever hardships necessary to make available all resources and means that their children need for a good education. The majority of parents feel that the way the Greek educational system operates leaves many gaps in their children's education, and so most families pay for extra lessons in foreign languages and activities like ballet, music, and sports. This practice is very common and not directly related to a family's economic background; even when they have limited resources, parents spend a considerable proportion of their income to pay for these supplementary activities.

It is also usual, especially when both parents work, for them to hire private tutors to help children with their homework, or to send their children to *frontistiria* (private evening classes) where the lessons taught in school are repeated and further analyzed in depth; this is especially common with secondary school pupils (Davou and Gourdomichalis 1997).

The Elderly and the Family

The family continues to be very important for the Greek society. Generally, the structure of the Greek family shows a change from the extended family to the nuclear family unit, but close relationships between the two types of family units exist. The younger people respect their elders and still accept them in certain roles. The old male is the connecting bond between the younger people who have left the village in search of better circumstances and those who remain. Beyond this psychological role, he acts as supervisor of the family's wealth in the village. How frequently children visit their parents depends on where they have moved. Nevertheless, because they do not maintain as much close contact as before, parental influence inevitably declines, and with it the influence of the traditional extended family. As a result, parents are left with a feeling of emptiness.

The transition from the extended family to the nuclear family is more prevalent in urban areas than in rural areas. In the nuclear family (the couple and their children, if any), the status of elderly is important as they provide help to the young couple and vice versa. From an economic point of view, life seems better for the elderly in the urban areas, but children still help their parents since pensions are usually insufficient. The medical care offered is also better in the urban areas than in rural ones. Nevertheless, the children, if necessary, take care of their old parents at all stages of illness.

Although the old parents usually live separately from the young couple, the two pairs retain a close relationship. They visit each other often and both take part in family celebrations and festive lunches. In consequence, the elderly people do not suffer from loneliness. Also, the role of the grandmother is extremely important in urban areas. As more women are employed outside the home, related problems have emerged. One of the biggest problems is the shortage of kindergartens, which in turn creates a new role for the grandmother, that of care provider. Many working mothers leave their children in the care of the grandmother.

In conclusion, the customary family care of the elderly is still strong, a situation explained by the traditions, customs, and ethics of Greek people. The elderly must feel that they are still useful and active members of society (Teperoglou 1980).

Conclusion

The economic and social factors that affect Greek society affect the family as an institution and the relations among its members. The economic factors related to unemployment influence interpersonal relations, as employment of family members and the satisfaction coming from it are directly related to peace of mind and communication. The high cost of living puts a serious strain on the family budget, and the financial needs, real or imaginary, lead to additional stress with multiple consequences (Teperoglou and Tzortzopoulou 1996).

Greek society seems to be in step with more developed countries. The difficulty in communicating, which is a result of urbanization, the increasing interest in acquiring material goods, and the wish to become successful lead to isolation, which has a serious impact on the relations within the family. Greek parents are willing to provide their children with the resources that they need to succeed in life. The roles of young couples and grandparents appear to complement each other. In absence of a sufficient number of nursery schools, grandparents are taking care of their grandchildren. On the other hand, in absence of a full-fledged policy on aging, parents take care of their parents.

Bibliography

Davou, B., and Gourdomichalis, R. (1997). "The Athens Report." In *Work and Family life in Five Cities,* ed. W. Scoff. European Commission, Directorate General V.

Demographic Statistics. (1997). Luxembourg: European Commission.

European Commission. (1996). *Employment in Europe.* Brussels: European Commission.

Eurostat (1989, 1990). *Labour Force Surveys.* Luxembourg: European Commission.

Filias, V.; Giselis, G.; Kaftanzoglou R.; and Teperoglou, A. (1984). "Changing Patterns of Cultural Activity within the Greek Family." In *The Family and Its Culture: An Investigation in Seven East and West European Countries,* ed. M. Biskup, V. Filias, and I. Vitanyi. Budapest: Akademiai Kiadò.

Kogidou, D. (1995). *Single Parent Families: Reality, Perspectives, Social Policy.* Athens: Nea Synora-A. A. Livani.

Kyriazis, N. (1995). "Feminism and the Status of Women in Greece." In *Greece Prepares for the 21st Century,* ed. D. Costas and T. Stavrou. Baltimore, MD: The Johns Hopkins University Press.

Lambiri-Dimaki, I. (1983). *Social Stratification in Greece 1962–1982.* Athens: Ant. Sakkoulas Publications.

Moussourou, L. (1985). *Families and Children in Athens,* Athens: Hestia Publications.

Moussourou, L. (1994). "Changes in the Family Life—Repercussions on Child Care and Protection." In *Child Protection: Trends and Perspectives,* ed. D. Kondili. Athens: Papasissis Publications.

Moussourou, L. (1995). "Annual Report on Greece." In *Developments in National Family Policies in 1995,* ed. J Ditch, H. Barnes and J. Bradshaw. Brussels: Commission of the European Communities.

Moussourou, L. (1999). "Family Crisis and Crisis of Values." *The Greek Review of Social Research* 98–99:5–20.

NSSG (National Statistical Service of Greece) (1961, 1966, 1971). Vital Statistics.

Papadakis, M., and Siambos, G. (1995). "Demographic Developments and Perspectives of the Greek Population

1951–1991." In *Greek Society at the End of 20th Century,* ed I. Lambiri-Dimaki and N. Kyriazis. Athens: Papasissis Publications.

Presvelou, C., and Teperoglou, A. (1976). "Sociological Analysis of the Phenomenon of Abortion in Greece, A Study of the Feminine Sample." *The Greek Review of Social Research* 28.

Siampos, G., ed. (1980). *Recent Population Change Calling for Policy Action.* Athens: National Statistical Service of Greece.

Teperoglou, A. (1980). "Open Care for the Elderly—Greece." In *Open Care for the Elderly in Seven European Countries,* ed A. Amann. New York: Pergamon Press.

Teperoglou, A. (1990). *Evaluation of the Contribution of the Open Care Centres for the Elderly.* Athens: National Center of Social Research.

Teperoglou, A. (1990). "Redefinition of Roles in the Greek Urban Family." *Diavazo,* June 24:26–29.

Teperoglou, A. (1994). "Child Centeredness and Its Implications for the Greek Family." In *Changes in Daily Life,* ed. K. de Hoog and J. A.C. van Ophem. The Netherlands: Wageningen Agricultural University.

Teperoglou, A. (1999). "Family, Marriage, Institution. Views and Beliefs of Married Youngsters." *The Greek Review of Social Research* 98–99:221–256.

Teperoglou, A.; Balourdos, D.; Myrisakis, I.; and Tzortzopoulou, M. (1999). *Identity, Particular Characteristics and Needs of Young People in the Prefecture of Thessalonica.* Athens: National Center of Social Research.

Teperoglou, A., and Tzortzopoulou, M. (1996). "Family Theory and Research in Greece 1980-1990." *Marriage and Family Review* 23:487–516.

APHRODITE TEPEROGLOU

GREENLAND

Kalaallit Nunaat, the Greenlanders' Land, is separated from the eastern Canadian Arctic on the west by Davis Strait, Baffin Bay, and Nares Strait, and from Iceland, on the east, by Denmark Strait. Through the ages, peoples from the northern parts of North America, Scandinavia, and Europe have migrated to Greenland, while others, most notably Scottish, English, and Dutch whalers, have frequented the country in times past.

The ancestors of the present-day Inuit, Greenland's indigenous people, first arrived in the country from the Canadian Arctic around 4,500 years ago, hunting land mammals such as musk ox. Successive groups of Inuit migrants continued to harvest the living resources of both land and sea, including caribou, seals, whales, and walrus. Norse farming settlements flourished in south and southwest Greenland, from approximately 985 for almost 500 years. Early English explorers, such as Martin Frobisher and John Davis in the sixteenth century, met with groups of Inuit along the west coast. Pursuing the Greenland right whale, European whalers became regular visitors to the coasts of Greenland starting in the seventeenth century. Greenland was a Danish colony between 1721 and 1953, and an integral part of the Danish Kingdom from 1953 to 1979. During these periods significant numbers of Danes lived and made there homes there, as some 7,000 continue to do today.

As a result of the interactions, intermarriages, and fleeting liaisons between these Inuit, Nordic, and other European migrants and sojourners, a society with a rich cultural heritage has evolved. Greenland is thus situated between the new and old worlds in both a geographical and cultural sense. Today, around 83 percent of Greenland's 58,000 residents are Inuit, a people who share a common language and culture with the Inuit in Canada, Alaska, and the Russian Far East; the remainder are primarily Danes. In 1979, the people of Greenland achieved Home Rule from Denmark. Presiding over an autonomous territory within the Danish Kingdom, the Greenland Home Rule Government has complete legislative power over Greenland's internal affairs.

Importance of Kinship

Anthropologists have generally agreed that kinship is the very foundation of Inuit social organization. In Greenland, kinship is both the basis for social relatedness and social organization, and the key organizing principle for hunting and fishing, which continue to be major activities for many people. However, in Greenland kinship is not simply biologically prescribed. This is immediately apparent to anyone who tries to collect genealogies, work out an individual's kin reckoning and family relationships, or simply listen to the way people use kinship terms in situations of both reference and address. The boundaries of kindred and descent-based groups, as Greenlanders define them, are shifting constantly, as are the interpersonal relationships that are defined in terms of kinship. Kinship and family relationships may appear to have distinct biological roots, but in practice they are flexible and integrate nonbiological social relationships that are considered as real as any biological relationship.

Kinship and family relationships are not always permanent states, and although it may be possible to talk of a kinship *system* in Greenland, it is a system that is inherently flexible and that allows extensive improvisation in that people can choose their kin. Throughout Greenland, social relationships tend to be defined in terms of being either kin or not kin. Kinship is multifaceted, embracing genealogy, consanguinity, affinity, friendship, name-sharing, birthday partners, age-sets, the living, and the dead. Kinship is bilateral, and the term for personal kindred or close extended family is *ilaqutariit*. The root of this word, *ila-*, means *a part,* or *a companion,* and a member of the *ilaqutariit* is called an *ilaqutaq, someone who belongs.* Individual households are suffixed with *-kkut* (e.g. Josepikkut—Josepi's household) and there are usually several -kkut in an ilaqutariit. People often distinguish between an ilaqutaq and an *eqqarleq,* someone who is a genealogical or affinal relative belonging to another ilaqutariit. Eqqarleq derives from *eqqaq,* meaning *the immediate vicinity/area,* or *close to.* As a form of address and reference eqqarleq is not necessarily always applied to distant kin, but its use depends on how a person defines his or her relationship with another person. One vitally important feature of kinship in Greenland is that kin and family relationships can be created if individuals choose to regard a nonkin relationship as something similar to a genealogical or affinal link. Just as people work out and define social relationships in terms of being based on kin or not, they can also decide how closely related they feel to someone. Although it may be rare to hear that somebody regards a sibling as an eqqarleq, an eqqarleq such as a second cousin's spouse may be regarded as a sibling by somebody and referred to as an ilaqutaq, even if those people have no consanguineal or affinal relationship.

Like many other Inuit communities, Greenlanders generally use kin terms in preference to personal names to refer to and address people regardless of any genealogical or affinal connection. To establish and continue a kinship relationship is easy enough—kin terms are simply used for both reference and address, and personal names are avoided in most situations of daily interaction. As forms of address, kin terms are used usually in the possessive: for example, *ataataga* (my father), *paniga* (my daughter). A man or a woman who regards his or her second cousin's (*illuusaq*) wife as a sister will use the appropriate kinship term (a man will call the woman either *aleqa* for older sister, or *najak* for younger sister; a woman will call her *angaju* for older sister, or *nukaq* for younger sister). The woman who is now regarded as a sister will reciprocate by using the appropriate kinship term for brother or sister (*ani* for older brother, or *aqqaluk* for younger brother; *angaju* or *nukaq* for older or younger sister). Such use of kin terms illustrates David Schneider's (1968) argument that the recording and listing of kinship terms does not mean that their designation will follow accordingly. Kin terms are symbols that allow for the imputation of idiosyncratic meaning and form part of a much larger set of symbols and implicit meanings that people use actively and consciously to construct the idea of community (Nuttall 1992).

Kinship and family relationships in Greenland are more accurately described as a complex network and intricate pattern of relationships that includes both the living and the dead (Nuttall 1994). When people die, their names (in Greenlandic *atiit;* singular *ateq*), their kinship relations, and their family relationships carry on in newborn children, so that people retain their social presence despite their physical absence. A person who is named after a dead person is called an *atsiaq* (plural *atsiat*), but the first same-sex child to be born after the death of another person is called that person's *ateqqaataa.* The dead person, who can have more than one atsiaq, is known as the atsiaq's *aqqa.* Aqqa is another word for name. In many Inuit societies in Alaska, Canada, and Siberia, the name is not tied to either gender, and a child can receive the name of a deceased male or female. But in Greenland all personal names are gender-specific (because they are Danish names), and generally a child can only be named after a person of the same sex. This can cause problems if, say, a man whose name is Jens has died, and three girls are then born. Are people to wait until a baby boy is born? There will be concern that Jens's name will be cold, lonely, and homeless for too long. People can get around this potentially disturbing situation by calling one of the girls Jensine (usually the first to be born, if she has not yet received a name). However, a similar improvisation of naming does not occur if a woman dies, and a baby boy is born shortly after.

People continually define and bring into existence real relationships that are not based on biology (Nuttall 1992). Kinship is a cultural reservoir from which individuals draw items they can use to define and construct everyday social interaction. To understand kinship and family relationships in Greenland, it is important to focus on the meanings that individuals attribute to kinship terms and kinship terminologies, rather than accepting at face value that terminologies refer to strict genealogical relationships. Yet, although kinship is flexible, it is not formless. Nor are particular roles without obligation. Kinship in everyday Greenlandic life is all-pervasive: because kinship ties are reaffirmed or created through the naming of children after the deceased, or simply by applying a kin term to someone who may not be a biological relative, almost everyone can trace or establish some kind of kinship relationship with everyone else in their local communities, and often within a wider region. If a relationship does not exist, then one can be created. At the same time, people can deactivate kinship relationships if they regard them as unsatisfactory. Relationships can be created if people regard others as particular categories of kin, and at the same time, genealogical relationships can also be forgotten about if a person regards that relationship as unsatisfactory, uncomfortable, or strained (Guemple 1979; Nuttall 1992). Lee Guemple (1972a) has argued that this is made possible because of the negotiated nature of the Inuit kinship system. In this way genealogical relationships can be rendered obsolete or subordinated to other social relationships. In Greenland it is common to hear people talking about a member of their ilaqutariit as if they were actually an eqqarleq and vice versa. Other people may deny any kin connection whatsoever. In some cases, this may be because two members of an ilaqutariit may have fallen out.

This flexible nature of kinship in Greenland allows individuals the opportunity to move around a complex network of relationships, to reposition themselves and others how they see fit simply by regarding social relationships in term of kinship or nonkinship. The reasons for doing so are various, complex, often intensely personal, and sometimes pragmatic. There may be sexual reasons, or two people who have an especially strong friendship may commemorate it by turning it into a kinship relationship. More practical reasons for choosing one's kin may relate to subsistence activities, where a man may have no brothers but may need to depend on close male kin for participating in hunting and fishing activities. In this way, friends who help out may be regarded as kin and the relationship established with a kinship term. While the flexibility of the kinship system allows individuals to choose whom they want as their relative (or whom they do not want as a relative), it does not give them license to decide how they should behave with that person. An exception would be if two women who are cousins decide to discontinue that kinship connection by dropping the kin term, forgetting about the biological relationship, and using one another's personal name as a form of address; then the obligation to behave in a prescribed way will cease. If two unrelated persons wish to regard themselves as being like cousins, then they can establish that relationship by addressing one another with the kin term for cousin (*illoq*). But by doing so they must recognize that they are expected to behave as if they were cousins and must treat one another with respect and as equals, regardless of any age difference. If the two are men and are both hunters, then there may be certain obligations to share hunting equipment or to give catch-shares from large sea mammals, such as walrus or bearded seals, to each other's households.

To deny a kinship connection is a way for people to disown one another. A. C. Heinrich (1963) distinguished between *optative* and *nonoptative* categories of kinship. Optative kin can include anyone whom an individual wants to consider kin—opting for kinship—while nonoptative kin includes grandparents, parents, and siblings. People can fall in and out of the former category, but it is not really acceptable to deny the existence of one's parents, siblings, grandparents, and possibly aunts and uncles. Optative kinship networks are flexible to the point where incompatible relations between individuals can be remedied by substituting them for more effective and meaningful ones (Guemple

1979). In this way, unlike the situation described by Ernest Burch (1975) in northwest Alaska, biology does not structure kinship relationships and determine how people who are biologically related should behave towards one another. In Greenland, in contrast, kinship is not ascribed but a matter of choice. Unlike Guemple's observation that, for a group of Canadian Inuit, people become relatives if they reside in the same locality, maintain regular contact, and share game according to well-defined rules, Greenlanders do not forget kin if someone moves away from a village or does not share seal meat. Unless an individual decides otherwise, people remain kin despite physical absence and also if they choose not to share meat or fish. (However, although people are not obligated to maintain the same kinship relations if they do not wish, they do have an obligation to share.) People are therefore not constrained by a rigid consanguineal kinship system, but can choose much of their universe of kin. Thus, daily life in Greenland is inextricably bound up with kinship, and people carry out and talk about most social and economic activities—for example, hunting, fishing, other kinds of work, visiting, and gossiping—with reference to kin relationships. But however they construct their own relationships, they are bound to behave in prescribed ways. Kin categories vary in meaning, and their significance lies in the way they give individuals the freedom to employ them in any way they choose. It is in this sense that kinship is symbolic, and it is through kinship that people find expression in their social worlds (Nuttall 1992).

Whatever the particularities of kinship in different parts of Greenland, it nonetheless shapes, informs, influences, and determines how people relate to one another, and is central to the way people conceptualize and define their social worlds (Nuttall 2000). In Greenland social relatedness does not always begin in the local group—for example, children are often named after deceased people who lived in different villages. Once named, they become the kin of the surviving relatives of the deceased.

It is easy to see how an individual's universe of kin can expand to include anyone they wish to consider a relative. These people are not fictive kin; they are real in the same sense as biological kin. Ultimately, people can, if they so wish, distinguish between biological or fictive kinship. The use of the suffix *-piaq*, meaning *one's own, personal, real* can be used to distinguish biological kin from fictive kin, who can be identified by the suffix *-siaq*, meaning *borrowed, bought*, or *found*. The use of a kin term is not usually suffixed as a means of discriminating between categories of biological or fictive kin. Fictive kin are considered to be as real as biological kin and the use of -piaq or -siaq would be making a distinction between categories of kin that people do not necessarily worry about. An adopted son, for example, will be addressed as *erneq*, rather than *ernersiaq*. The use of such terminology suggests that the relationship between parents and son is regarded as real as if the child were the parents' biological offspring. Kinship is a rhetoric of social relatedness, as Guemple argues (1972b), but whether based on biology or affinity, it is real as long as people see it as such.

See also: KINSHIP

Bibliography

Burch, E. S. Jr. (1975). *Eskimo Kinsmen: Changing Family Relationships in Northwest Alaska*. St. Paul, MN: West Publishing.

Damas, D. (1963). *Iglulingmiut Kinship and Local Groupings: A Structural Approach*. Ottawa: National Museum of Canada.

Damas, D. (1964). "The Patterning of the Iglulingmiut Kinship System." *Ethnology* 3:377–88.

Damas, D. (1968). "Iglulingmiut Kinship Terminology and Behaviour, Consanguines." In *Eskimo of the Canadian Arctic,* ed. V. F. Valentine and F. G. Vallee. Toronto: McClelland and Stewart.

Guemple, L. (1972a). "Kinship and Alliance in Belcher Island Eskimo Society." In *Alliance in Eskimo Society,* ed. L. Guemple. Seattle: University of Washington Press.

Guemple, L. (1972b). "Eskimo Band Organization and the 'D. P. Camp' Hypothesis." *Arctic Anthropology* 9:80–112.

Guemple, L. (1979) *Inuit Adoption*. Ottawa: National Museum of Man.

Heinrich, A. (1963). "Personal Names, Social Structure and Functional integration" *Anthropology and Sociology Papers,* no. 27. Montana State University: Department of Sociology and Welfare.

Nuttall, M. (1992). *Arctic Homeland: Kinship, Community, and Development in Northwest Greenland*. Toronto: University of Toronto Press.

Nuttall, M. (1994). "The Name Never Dies: Greenland Inuit Ideas of the Person." In *Amerindian Rebirth: Reincarnation Belief among North American Indians and Inuit,* ed. A. Mills and R. Slobodin. Toronto: University of Toronto Press.

Nuttall, M. (2000). "Choosing Kin: Sharing and Subsistence in a Greenlandic Hunting Community." In *Dividends of Kinship: Meanings and Uses of Social Relatedness,* ed. P. Schweitzer. London: Routledge.

Schneider, D. (1968). *American Kinship: A Cultural Account.* Englewood Cliffs, NJ: Prentice-Hall.

MARK NUTTALL

GRIEF, LOSS, AND BEREAVEMENT

Almost every person in the world, at one time or another, experiences events that can be considered major losses (Harvey and Weber 1998). A *loss* occurs when an event is perceived to be negative by individuals involved, and it results in long-term changes in one's social situations, relationships, or way of viewing the world and oneself. Death is the event most often thought of as a loss, but there are many others. Tangible losses can be *personal* (i.e., loss of one's vision, hearing, sexual activity, or mental capacity; infertility; chronic pain or illness; rape, domestic violence and abuse; or political torture), *interpersonal* (i.e., divorce, ending a friendship, or death of a loved one), *material* (i.e., losing a job, leaving one's country, war-time trauma, changing residence, or becoming homeless), or *symbolic* (i.e., losses related to racism, role redefinition, or reentry adjustment to home culture). *Intangible psychological losses* include changes in self-worth due to harassment at work or job demotion; changes in sense of control and safety due to crime, terrorism, or victimization; changes in identity related to widowhood; or changes in worldview related to experiencing a natural disaster or chemical accident.

Dominant cultures in Western countries tend to define loss dichotomously: an object is either present or absent, a person is either dead or alive. However, coexisting cultural groups in the West and other parts of the world may categorize losses by many levels of gradations—thus, someone from whom we are recently separated (through death or physical separation) may be seen as still communicating and with an active presence, different from someone who has been physically absent for many years (Rosenblatt 1993). There may be a series of stages of transition into nothingness, or to another state. In addition, losses have different meaning between cultures and among individuals within a culture, depending on their life circumstances. For example, in impoverished cultures where infant and child deaths are viewed as inevitable, seriously ill children may be categorized as dead, and their later deaths may not be mourned for more than a few days. Such responses may seem puzzling to outsiders when they learn that those dead children still are considered a part of the nuclear family and are expected to be reunited with the mother in an afterlife (Scheper-Hughes 1985).

Each traumatic or stressful event may cause several losses; and each loss can have multiple consequences. Therefore, when individuals have a severe chronic illness, they and their partners experience multiple losses, including losses each of them experience related to physical or mental deterioration. There can be related losses involving careers, finances, sexual interaction and love life, inability to do normal chores together or participate in activities previously enjoyed. They may experience losses in self-esteem related to having the disease, or the stigma of being with a chronically ill person; and losses related to being ignored by medical personnel discussing one's own condition, or (in the case of unmarried partners) being ignored in medical decision-making because one is not an "official relative."

There are several imprecise terms used to discuss reactions to loss, and it is important to clarify their intent. The usual reaction to a loss of someone or something that was valued is termed *grief.* It consists of emotional, psychological, and physical dimensions (Stroebe et al. 2001) and there has been debate as to whether grief occurs only for individuals, or whether there is such a thing as *family grief* (Gilbert 1996; Moos 1995). In Western cultures grief is typically discussed as a psychological phenomenon—largely as a cognitive challenge, an emotional reaction to loss. In many other cultures, however, grief is viewed as a *somatization*, where "personal and interpersonal distress [is manifested as] physical complaints [and people have learned

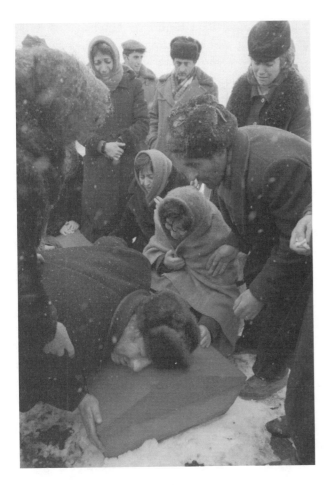

Grieving for the loss of their child, who was killed in an earthquake, this Armenian family crowds around the coffin. Expressions of grief and mourning are shaped by one's cultural group. DAVID TURNLEY/CORBIS

to respond to their losses] through the medium of the body" (Kleinman 1986, p. 51).

The term *mourning* is often used to describe the varied and diverse social expressions of grief. Affects can range from pain and sadness to humor, pleasure, and joy. Actions, rituals, and emotions observed during mourning are shaped and controlled by the beliefs and values of a society or cultural group and are intended to be for the benefit of grievers and/or the community. In countries in which hundreds of cultures are represented (such as the United States and Canada) one might expect that cultural expectations for mourning would evolve in a manner that represents the many co-cultures. However, Paul Rosenblatt and his colleagues (Rosenblatt, Walsh, and Jackson 1976) found that overt expressions of crying, fear, and anger were common, acceptable, and encouraged

in most parts of the world, except for some Western cultural groups. This suggests that the United States and Canada have never truly been "melting pots" beyond some of the early European nationalities in terms of cultural, ethnic, and religious attitudes toward grief, loss, and mourning (Irish 1993).

Bereavement is used to describe the objective situation of someone who has experienced deprivation through the loss of a person or thing that was valued (Corr, Nabe, and Corr 2000). Although bereavement is a factual situation of loss, how individuals respond to loss can be highly varied. The extent to which one grieves, and overt expressions of mourning, will differ from culture to culture, from person to person, and from situation to situation for any one person. For example, the extent to which one grieves for the loss of her parent, colleague, stepchild, pet, partner, homeland, or unfulfilled dream may differ. Level of display of mourning may also differ depending on the societal messages received about one's position in the hierarchy of grievers—that is, how entitled one is to mourn a particular loss. In the United States a bereaved mother is considered more entitled to a high level of grief than are surviving siblings or classmates; and a current spouse is more entitled to grieve than a former spouse. However, the effect of culture on style of grieving may not be "visible" to those within the culture. It is important to remember that there is no one way that an individual "should" react to loss, and that our discomfort with the reactions of others often occurs when their reaction contradicts values and beliefs we have developed in response to our own culture and experiences.

Consequences of Grief

Although loss is a normal event, there can be physical, psychological, and social consequences for survivors, as well as a reduction of individual and family resources, whether personal, material, or symbolic. Over the lifespan, one experiences a buildup of memories associated with losses—some of which may be painful and sad, and some of which may be positive in that we feel we have grown or reacted to situations in ways consistent with our values. These memories are triggered by cues we encounter in daily life, rituals on holidays or anniversaries, familiar places, hearing someone use a word in the same way, or wind blowing the way it did just before the storm that took our home.

Despite attempts by scholars like John Harvey (1998, 2000) to develop an inclusive field called the *social psychology of loss,* most literature on outcomes of loss still comes from research on survivors of the death of a family member, probably because death is viewed as the only type of loss that can never be recovered. Grief related to bereavement can result in negative consequences for physical health, including susceptibility to illness and disease, new symptoms (often similar to those the deceased had endured), aggravation of existing medical conditions, anorexia or loss of appetite, energy loss, sleep disturbances, a drop in the number and function of natural killer cells, and long-lasting changes in both the brain and gene expression (c.f. Murray 2000, 122).

Reported changes in mental health include *affective changes* (i.e., depression, guilt, anxiety, anger, and loneliness), *cognitive manifestations* (preoccupation with thoughts of the deceased, helplessness, hopelessness, lower self-esteem, and self-reproach), and *behavioral changes* (i.e., crying, fatigue, agitation, and social withdrawal) (Stroebe et al. 2001). However, it is not clear to what extent mental and physical health changes occur because of grief and how much change is related to other life changes (i.e., increased consumption of drugs, alcohol, and tobacco, and/or poor nutrition). Individuals with prior personality disorders are more likely to experience complications during grief (Rando 1993). However, neither researchers nor clinicians have done a good job of distinguishing grief from depression, nor of examining traumatic grief separately from "normal" grief.

Dealing with social ramifications of loss can also be problematic. Grieving individuals often report there is a lack of clarity as to their role, and a lack of social or family support. Loss may have resulted in changes in their social status, identity, or income; there may be family or community conflicts related to inheritance or lawsuits—all contributing to a sense of social isolation.

Despite the emphasis on problematic outcomes, literature is emerging that emphasizes growth as an outcome of many types of major losses. *Post-traumatic growth* is said to occur when, at some point following a loss, growth occurs "beyond" one's previous level of functioning (Tedischi, Park, and Calhoun 1998). This growth can include changes in *perception of self* (i.e., as survivor rather than victim, or as self-reliant while recognizing heightened vulnerability), *interpersonal relationships* (i.e., increased ability to be compassionate or express emotions), and *philosophy of life* (i.e., spiritual change or sense of wisdom, gaining a new meaning and purpose in life, or reorganized priorities). However, the experience of trauma alone does not "heal" problematic family relationships; there are other cognitive, motivational, and behavioral changes required as well.

Coping with Loss

Much of what has been written about how people grieve has focused on individual survivors. The Victorian belief that grief was a sign of a "broken heart" resulting from the loss of a love was replaced by the psychodynamic view that grief was painful because it involved letting go of attachment to the deceased. This "letting go" was viewed as essential for "moving on" with one's life, eventual recovery from depression, and a return to "normal" (Neimeyer 2001). Theories of grieving later included an emphasis on differences between *pathological* (complicated) and *normal* (uncomplicated) grief reactions (e.g., Lindemann 1944), and an emphasis on phases, stages, or trajectories of the grieving process. The best-known *stage model* was presented in Elisabeth Kubler-Ross's (1969) book *On Death and Dying.* In discussing anticipatory grief of terminally ill persons she outlines five stages: *shock and denial, anger, bargaining, depression,* and *acceptance.* These stages were viewed by many lay people and professionals as "the" way successful grief is experienced. Many still gravitate to this model for its simple linear approach, using it as a prescription to measure how grief is progressing. Since its publication, this stage model has been applied to other losses including divorce, chronic illness, and infertility.

Although these models have been prominent in the popular media, many scholars have been critical of them (Attig 1991). Studies have failed to find any discernible sequence of emotional phases of adaptation to loss, or any clear endpoint to grieving. Rather than a passive climb up a linear staircase, characteristics of grieving may more closely resemble unsteady twisting and turning paths requiring adaptation and change, but with no specific end. In addition, there is no evidence that someone who deviates from those stages is experiencing pathological grief, so authors have called for a de-emphasis on universal grief syndromes and a recognition of varied practices of subcultural groups.

There also have been many challenges to the concept of *grief work* that underlies these theories—an assumption that one must do cognitive work to confront the loss and that failure to undergo or complete grief work results in pathological grief. The idea that one must "work" at dealing with grief is not a universal concept, and probably is reflective of the broader emphasis in the United States that anything worth having requires hard work.

Newer models of grief tend to focus on context and circumstances of a loss, variability in individuals' grief experiences, meaning of the loss to individual survivors and their families, recognition that rather than a withdrawal of attachment from the deceased (or lost object) there is a continued symbolic bond, and adjusting to the new world that exists after the loss (including new interpretations one has of the environment, and new elements in one's identity). The emphasis appears to have shifted from identifying symptoms to the *process* of grieving. For example, the *Dual Process Model of Coping* developed by Margaret Stroebe and Henk Schut (1999), suggests that active confrontation with loss may not be necessary for a positive outcome. There may be times when denial and avoidance of reminders are essential. Most individuals can expect to experience ongoing oscillation between a *loss orientation* (coping with loss through grief work, dealing with denial, and avoiding changes) and a *restoration orientation* (adjusting to the many changes triggered by loss, changing routines, and taking time off from grief). This reflects a movement between coping with loss and moving forward, but the extent to which one needs either of these dimensions differs for each individual.

Theories about families have been slower to develop elements that address loss and grief. *Family systems theory* (with its emphasis on viewing reactions to loss by the family group as a disruption in the family system's equilibrium and structure requiring reorganization of roles and functions; and the impact of reactions of one family member on another) appears well suited for examining loss. However, its emphasis on the present and current interactions appears to have slowed development along this line. There are a few notable exceptions, including Monica McGoldrick's (1991) elaboration of Murray Bowen's work on the *legacy of loss*.

Bowen (1976) suggested that a family's history and experiences with loss influences how the family adapts to subsequent losses as well as the legacy of viewing themselves as either "survivors" or "cursed" (i.e., unable to rise above the losses) that they pass on to future generations.

Another notable work is that of Ester Shapiro (1994), who integrated individual and family life-cycle development with systems theory to discuss loss as a crisis of identity and attachment, in which grief disrupts the family's equilibrium but makes possible development of new "growth-enhancing stability" (p. 17). In addressing losses related to chronic illness, John Rolland (1994) developed the *Family Systems-Illness Model* to examine the interface of the individual, family, illness, and healthcare team. Rather than focusing on the individual, Rolland views the family or caregiving system as the central resource affected by and influencing the course of the illness.

Differences in Grieving

There are many factors that appear related to differences in nature and intensity of the grief one experiences following a loss. Those who experience losses that are stigmatized by others (e.g., losses that are assumed to have been caused by an individual's disturbed or immoral behavior, or ones where there is a fear of contagion or fear for one's own safety) often feel isolated and pressured to show no grief in public. Grief of someone who recently has experienced an "unusually" high number of losses, as well as that related to the death of a loved one who was a drunk driver, a partner with AIDS, or a son in prison, are not well-acknowledged. Suicide, which is both violent and stigmatized, can provoke feelings of anger and guilt and result in secrecy and blame within the family.

Sometimes what one views as a loss is unrecognized by others, particularly if the loss has been stigmatized. *Disenfranchised grief* occurs when society does not recognize one's "need, right, role, or capacity to grieve" (Doka 1989, 3). Examples of these unacknowledged losses can include divorce after years of being abused; immigration to a "better" place; death of a former spouse, foster parent, stepchild, coworker, companion animal, professional caretaker; or death related to pregnancy. Individuals who may be seen as incapable of, or without a need for, grief include young children, older adults, mentally disabled persons, those who are deaf, masculine grievers, military, police and firefighters, or those in cultures who do not grieve or mourn according to societal norms.

Families may have additional difficulties with loss if they are experiencing other stressful situations at the same time. They may have difficulty if dealing with the stress of typical life-cycle events (e.g., a new marriage, birth of child, changes during adolescence, beginning employment) concurrent with major losses (e.g., illness, death, trauma, loss of employment or homeland). Dealing with life-cycle events and additional losses may tax resources (e.g., money, health, friendship, self-esteem, or sense of mastery).

Vulnerability also is related to centrality of the role and function of the lost item or person, such as items with significant meaning, those that can never be replaced, or losses that are critical to everyday functioning. Complications can also arise with the loss of individuals who played central roles in our lives, or when we lose someone for whom we feel ambivalence, estrangement, or intense continuous conflict. Differences in adjustment often attributed to gender may actually be related to other intertwined cultural factors (Wisocki and Skowron 2000).

To understand how a family perceives a loss, one needs to understand its view of the world. One common family paradigm is known as the *Belief in a Just World* (Lerner 1971). This perspective values control and mastery and assumes there is a fit between one's efforts and outcomes; therefore, one gets what one deserves. This view is only functional when something can be done to change a loss-situation. Otherwise, it results in blaming the griever for the loss. Chronically ill persons are blamed for their condition or lack of recovery, and it is assumed that adolescent deaths are caused by their own reckless behavior or drug use.

Another factor that can influence coping with grief is *boundary ambiguity*—confusion that arises when it is not clear who is in and who is out of the family (Boss 1999). Such a situation can exist in cases where someone is physically absent, but psychologically present in the family (e.g., a soldier missing in action, a missing child, an absent non-custodial parent, or yearning for one's family who remained in the homeland rather than immigrating). It can also exist when someone is psychologically absent but physically present (e.g., a family member with dementia or a brain injury, a parent who spends all her time with work or hobbies, or a depressed adult who has difficulty connecting to his partner). In the case of a sudden traumatic loss, denial and boundary ambiguity may initially be functional, giving the family time to regroup before dealing with the loss, but a high degree of ambiguity over time poses difficulties for coping. Reports that continuing bonds often occur following death (Klass, Silverman and Nickman 1996), with conversations with the dead replacing rituals as the normative way bonds are maintained (Klass and Walter 2001), may challenge the notion of boundary ambiguity, suggesting that conflicting images can coexist within the psychological domain—that one can cognitively recognize the loss and still maintain psychological, emotional, and spiritual connections.

Although the study of what facilitates coping with grief originally tried to classify factors that facilitated grief versus those that inhibited grieving, it appears that some elements may simultaneously complicate and facilitate grieving (Doka 1998). For example, it appears that no single length of time between the first hint of the inevitability of a loss and its actual occurrence is most problematic. Losses that are sudden or unanticipated do not allow one the opportunity to engage in *anticipatory grieving*; losses that are long and drawn-out result in depleted resources, including wearing out one's network of social support. In light of modern technological and medical advances, protracted losses (e.g., chronic illness) can involve a series of improvements and relapses that occur so often that family members begin to expect that with each relapse there will be another recovery. Thus, when death finally occurs, family members may experience it as a sudden unanticipated loss.

Other factors that can simultaneously complicate and facilitate the grieving process include the belief that a loss is "God's will" and the availability of a social support network (Doka 1998). A belief in God's plan can help one in finding meaning in the loss. It can also create anger toward God for being unfair and allowing such an act to happen, leading to guilt and isolation from one's spiritual connection or religious community. A social support network can lend assistance and be there to listen, but it may also place unrealistic expectations on the griever.

Adaptation or Resolution

Questions often arise as to how long grief lasts and how it is resolved. It is a mistaken assumption that grief has an ending point and that one will return to a prior state of "normal." Media-orchestrated *virtual grief* experienced by consumers who go through the rituals of mourning in front of their televisions or computer screens provides an illusion of intimacy and produces an emotional response without the depth of pain experienced in actual grief. Because recovery from virtual grief is quick, individuals may become less sensitive to the extent of time actually required for grieving.

Actual grief can occur as "emotional shock waves" (Bowen 1976) that ebb and flow for years after a loss, and even be transmitted across the generations in a family. Children and adults can experience *regrief* as a revisiting of a significant loss at each new developmental stage (Oltjenbruns 2001) or as reverberating losses in the form of recurrent memories triggered by new major life events. Studies have failed to identify any discernible sequence of emotional phases that lead to adaptation to loss, nor can they identify any clear endpoint to grieving that would constitute a state of recovery (Neimeyer 2001). Rather than a return to a prior state of "normal," one experiences a new normal based on one's new situation, altered identity, and reconstructed meanings of life and loss.

With increased awareness that bonds continue after a loss and that one does not recover from grief, the focus of grief therapy is also shifting away from relinquishing attachments and toward meaning-making and meaning-finding in the loss. There is a growing recognition that grieving is nearly always complicated (Attig 2001), and that some behaviors or thoughts that would be described as pathological at other times may be normal reactions to the abnormal situation of loss. An emphasis on universal syndromes of grieving has been replaced with a recognition of cultural relativity, focus on family patterns and processes by which loss is negotiated, implications of loss for one's sense of identity, and potential for post-traumatic growth.

Conclusion

Although there are some commonalities in response to loss, there is no universally predictable emotional trajectory, and the range of effects, thoughts, and behaviors experienced is quite malleable (Rosenblatt 2001). To understand processes following loss, the dialectic of loss and growth, and meanings one gives to loss-experiences, it is important to consider the individual embedded within the family, family embedded within community, and community embedded within social and cultural systems.

See also: BOUNDARY AMBIGUITY; CHRONIC ILLNESS; DEATH AND DYING; DEPRESSION: ADULTS; DEPRESSION: CHILDREN AND ADOLESCENTS; DISABILITIES; DIVORCE: EFFECTS ON CHILDREN; DIVORCE: EFFECTS ON COUPLES; DIVORCE: EFFECTS ON PARENTS; ELDERS; EUTHANASIA; HEALTH AND FAMILIES; HOSPICE; IMMIGRATION; LATER LIFE FAMILIES; LONELINESS; MISSING CHILDREN; RAPE; RUNAWAY YOUTHS; SUDDEN INFANT DEATH SYNDROME (SIDS); SUICIDE; WIDOWHOOD

Bibliography

Attig, T. (1991). "The Importance of Conceiving of Grief as an Active Process." *Death Studies* 15:385–393.

Attig, T. (2001). "Relearning the World: Making and Finding Meanings." In *Meaning Reconstruction and the Experience of Loss,* ed. R. A. Neimeyer. Washington DC: American Psychological Association.

Boss, P. (1999). *Ambiguous Loss: Learning to Live with Unresolved Grief.* Cambridge, MA: Harvard University Press.

Bowen, M. (1976). "Family Reaction to Death." In *Family Therapy: Theory and Practice,* ed. P. J. Guerin. New York: Gardner.

Corr, C. A.; Nabe, C. M.; and Corr, D. M. (2000). *Death and Dying, Life and Living,* 3rd edition. Belmont, CA: Wadsworth.

Doka, K. J., ed. (1989). *Disenfranchised Grief.* Lexington, MA: Lexington Books.

Doka, K. J. (1998). Introduction to *Living with Grief: Who We Are, How We Grieve,* ed. K. J. Doka and J. D. Davidson. Philadelphia: Brunner/Mazel.

Gilbert, K. R. (1996). "'We've Had the Same Loss, Why Don't We Have the Same Grief?' Loss and Differential Grief in Families." *Death Studies* 20:269–283.

Harvey, J. H. (1998). *Perspectives on Loss: A Sourcebook.* Philadelphia: Brunner/Mazel.

Harvey, J. H. (2000). *Give Sorrow Words: Perspectives on Loss and Trauma.* Philadelphia: Brunner/Mazel.

Harvey, J. H., and Weber, A. L. (1998). "Why There Must Be a Psychology of Loss." In *Perspectives on Loss:*

A Sourcebook, ed. J. H. Harvey. Philadelphia: Brunner/Mazel.

Irish, D. P. (1993). "Introduction—Multiculturalism and the Majority Population." In *Ethnic Variations in Dying, Death, and Grief: Diversity in Universality,* ed. D. P. Irish, K. F. Lundquist, and V. J. Nelsen. Washington, DC: Taylor and Francis.

Klass, D., Silverman, P. R., and Nickman, S. L., eds. (1996). *Continuing Bonds: New Understandings of Grief.* Bristol, PA: Taylor and Francis.

Klass, D., and Walter, T. (2001). "Processes of Grieving: How Bonds are Continued." In *Handbook of Bereavement Research: Consequences, Coping, and Care,* ed. M. S. Stroebe, R. O. Hansson, W. Stroebe, and H. Schut. Washington, DC: American Psychological Association.

Kleinman, A. (1986). *Social Origins of Distress and Disease: Depression, Neurasthenia, and Pain in Modern China.* New Haven, CT: Yale University Press.

Kubler-Ross, E. (1969). *On Death and Dying.* New York: Macmillan.

Lerner, M. (1971). "Justice, Guilt, and Veridical Perception." *Journal of Personality and Social Psychology* 20:127–135.

Lindemann, E. (1944). "Symptomatology and Management of Acute Grief." *American Journal of Psychiatry* 101:141–148.

McGoldrick, M. (1991). "Echoes from the Past: Helping Families Mourn Their Losses." In *Living Beyond Loss,* ed. F. Walsh and M. McGoldrick. New York: Norton.

Moos, N. L. (1995). "An Interactive Model of Grief." *Death Studies* 19:337–364.

Murray, C. I. (2000). "Coping with Death, Dying, and Grief in Families." In *Families and Change: Coping with Stressful Events and Transitions,* 2nd edition, ed. P. C. McKenry and S. J. Price. Thousand Oaks, CA: Sage.

Neimeyer, R. A. (2001). "Introduction: Meaning Reconstruction and Loss." In *Meaning Reconstruction and the Experience of Loss,* ed. R. A. Neimeyer. Washington, DC: American Psychological Association.

Oltjenbruns, K. A. (2001). "Developmental Context of Childhood: Grief and Regrief Phenomena." In *Handbook of Bereavement Research: Consequences, Coping, and Care,* ed. M. S. Stroebe, R. O. Hansson, W. Stroebe, and H. Schut. Washington, DC: American Psychological Association.

Rando, T. A. (1993). *Treatment of Complicated Mourning.* Champaign, IL: Research Press.

Rolland, J. S. (1994). *Families, Illness, and Disability: An Integrated Treatment Model.* New York: Basic Books.

Rosenblatt, P. C. (1993). "Cross-Cultural Variation in the Experience, Expression, and Understanding of Grief." In *Ethnic Variations in Dying, Death, and Grief: Diversity in Universality,* ed. D. P. Irish, K. F. Lundquist, and V. J. Nelsen. Washington, DC: Taylor and Francis.

Rosenblatt, P. C.; Walsh, R. P.; and Jackson, D. A. (1976). *Grief and Mourning in Cross-Cultural Perspective.* New Haven, CT: Human Relations Area Files Press.

Scheper-Hughes, N. (1985). "Culture, Scarcity, and Maternal Thinking: Maternal Detachment and Infant Survival in Brazilian Shantytown." *Ethos* 13:291–317.

Shapiro, E. R. (1994). *Grief as a Family Process: A Developmental Approach to Clinical Practice.* New York: Guilford.

Stroebe, M. S.; Hansson, R. O.; Stroebe, W.; and Schut, H. (2001). "Introduction: Concepts and Issues in Contemporary Research on Bereavement." In *Handbook of Bereavement Research: Consequences, Coping, and Care,* ed. M. S. Stroebe, R. O. Hansson, W. Stroebe, and H. Schut. Washington, DC: American Psychological Association.

Stroebe, M., and Schut, H. (1999). "The Dual Process Model of Coping with Bereavement: Rationale and Description." *Death Studies* 23:197–224.

Tedischi, R. G.; Park, C. L.; and Calhoun, L. G. (1998). "Posttraumatic Growth: Conceptual Issues." In *Posttraumatic Growth: Positive Changes in the Aftermath of Crisis.* Mahwah, NJ: Lawrence Erlbaum.

Wisocki, P. A., and Skowron, J. (2000). "The Effects of Gender and Culture on Adjustment to Widowhood." In *Handbook of Gender, Culture, and Health,* ed. R. M. Eisler and M. Hersen. Mahwah, NJ: Lawrence Erlbaum Associates.

COLLEEN I. MURRAY

GUARDIANSHIP

Guardianship is a legal process that transfers decision-making authority over an individual (a *ward*) deemed incapable of managing his or her personal or financial affairs to another person (the *guardian*). Guardians may be appointed for both minors and adults.

Modern guardianship has its roots in English common law, a legal system which England then transported to its colonies. Under English common law, the doctrine of *parens patriae* (parent of the country) allowed the courts to assume control of and appoint guardians for *infants* (minors) and *incompetents* (incapacitated adults). While the details and terminology vary, guardianship is found not only in the United Kingdom, but also in the United States, Canada, and Australia. In addition, guardianship has been adopted in other countries, such as Japan, whose legal systems are not generally based on the law of England.

In the United States today, state law controls the appointment of guardians, and guardians are appointed by state courts. Because each state is free to enact its own laws, state guardianship laws vary, even on basic terminology. Under the Uniform Guardianship and Protective Proceedings Act, a model act in effect in about one-third of the states, a guardian makes personal-care decisions, while a *conservator* manages property. But in many other states, the court-appointed manager is referred to as either a *guardian of the person* or a *guardian of the property*.

States also vary on procedures for the appointment of guardians. Procedures for appointment of a guardian of a minor are different from and generally less detailed than procedures for an adult appointment. Procedures for minors are less detailed because the incapacity of a minor is presumed, while the incapacity of an adult must be proved.

There are numerous alternatives to guardianship, although many relate only to adults and not to minors. Advising individuals on these alternatives is a major function for professionals such as attorneys and social workers, who counsel individuals on planning for possible incapacity.

Types of Guardianship

There are several types of guardianship. Under a plenary or full guardianship, the guardian is granted comprehensive decision-making authority over an individual's personal care, property, or both. Under a limited guardianship, as its name implies, the guardian is granted only limited and specified powers regarding an individual's personal care or property.

A guardian of the person makes decisions with respect to the ward's personal care. The guardian ordinarily will determine where the ward will live and will arrange for the ward's medical care. The guardian of the property manages the ward's finances. The guardian will disburse funds for the ward's care, will handle the ward's investments, and will determine which assets must be sold.

Guardians are typically appointed for an extended period—until a minor attains the age of majority, or until an adult individual's death or recovery of capacity. Under a temporary or emergency guardianship, however, the guardianship lasts for only a short period of days or months. Because temporary or emergency guardians are appointed for only a short term and often on an emergency basis, the procedures for appointment are usually simpler and more expedited than for a regular, longer-term appointment. Limited and temporary or emergency guardianships are the exception, not the rule, however. The term *guardianship,* without qualification, usually refers to a plenary or full guardianship.

Guardianship, which requires a proceeding before a court before an appointment may be made, must be distinguished from other uses of the term. It is sometimes said that parents, by virtue of their custodial rights, are the natural guardians of their minor children, although this term is falling into disuse. Also, the role of a guardian is very different from that of a guardian ad litem. A guardian ad litem is an individual, usually an attorney, appointed for the sole purpose of representing another person in a particular court proceeding, such as in a dispute over the validity of a will.

Guardianship of Minors

Minors have neither the legal right to manage property nor to make many major life decisions, such as to determine their place of residence or to decide what school they will attend. For most minors, this lack of legal capacity is not an issue; most do not own significant assets. Also, until a minor reaches the age of majority (age eighteen in most states), marries, or is otherwise emancipated, a minor's parents are legally responsible for the minor's custody and care.

Guardianship of a minor's property becomes an issue if the minor acquires significant assets, due to an inheritance or personal injury settlement, for example. A minor's parents do not have the legal right to manage their child's property. For them to do so, they must be appointed as the minor's guardians by a court.

Guardianship of a minor's person becomes an issue whenever there is need for someone other than the parents to assume the child's custody. Guardians must be appointed following the death of both parents unless an adoption can be arranged. This guardian will usually be a close family member. Guardians are appointed following termination of the parents' parental rights, which may occur due to a finding of abuse or other unfitness. Termination of parental rights permanently severs the parent-child relationship, including the parents' right to the child's custody.

Guardians sometimes are appointed with the consent of the parents. Many states authorize the appointment of standby guardians. Standby guardians are appointed for parents with progressive and disabling conditions, such as AIDS, that are likely to render them incapable of caring for their children. The court appoints the guardian while the parent still has capacity. The guardian then stands by, taking office only when the parent's incapacity is certified. Consent guardianships are also frequently used when a child lives with a grandparent or other relative. For example, appointment of the family member as guardian may be necessary to qualify the child for public school attendance.

Guardianship is a concern of many parents with minor children. They are concerned about who will take custody of their children in the event of their deaths. They are also concerned about how property the children may inherit from them will be managed. Many of these concerns can be addressed in the parents' wills. Although wills are primarily directed at the disposition of property after death, they may also be used to nominate guardians for minor children, both for the minor's care and for management of the minor's property. In some states a parental nominee has an automatic right to be appointed guardian upon the parents' death. In other states, a court must approve the parents' choice, although this approval is usually automatic. Also, in many states a parental nomination is ineffective if a minor age fourteen or older objects. In those states, a minor age fourteen or older has the right to nominate his or her own guardian.

Although parents may nominate guardians to manage the minor's property, guardianship of a minor's property may not be the preferred option.

Guardianship of a minor's property terminates when the minor reaches the age of majority, an age at which many parents believe the young adult does not yet have sufficient maturity to manage significant wealth. Creation of a trust is a commonly selected alternative. Under this legal device, which is usually done under the parents' wills, a trustee is named to manage property that would otherwise be placed under guardianship. The responsibilities of the trustee are specified in the will or other trust document. The major advantages of a trust over a guardianship are that court proceedings are avoided, and the parents may designate any age for distribution of the assets to the child.

Guardianship sometimes becomes an issue among divorcing parents. Although custody of children is normally determined by the court granting the divorce, parents or other relatives will sometimes attempt to upset this custody order by moving the child to a different jurisdiction and securing appointment as the child's guardian from a court in the new state. Federal law and international treaties seek to limit the abduction of children to different states or countries and the use of guardianship to facilitate that process.

Guardianship of Adults

Appointment of a guardian for an adult is very different from appointment of a guardian for a minor. A minor, by legal definition, lacks the capacity to manage his or her own personal or financial affairs. An adult, however, is presumed to have such capacity. Before a guardian may be appointed for an adult, it must be established to a court's satisfaction that the adult individual lacks capacity to make his or her own decisions. The procedures for the appointment of a guardian of an adult are therefore more detailed than the procedures for a minor's appointment.

Guardianship of adults is an issue of growing importance, a shift explained by changing demographics. Approximately 80 percent of adult guardianship appointments are made for individuals age sixty or older. This segment of the population is rapidly increasing. In 1987, there were 29.8 million Americans age sixty-five or older. By the year 2020, the number is projected to exceed 52 million. Guardians are also frequently appointed for individuals with developmental disabilities and individuals with serious mental illnesses.

Guardians may be appointed only for adults who are determined to lack capacity. Capacity is a legal standard, not a clinical one. Professionals such as physicians, psychologists, and social workers may be asked to provide evidence concerning the individual's medical condition and ability to perform certain tasks, but the determination of whether an individual lacks legal capacity to make his or her own decisions must be made by a court.

The definition of incapacity was traditionally based on a categorical approach: Did the individual have a specified impairment such as mental deficiency, mental retardation, or infirmity of advanced age? In most states, however, the definitions have moved away from such labels and conclusory statements. The growing trend is to focus on the individual's ability to make decisions with respect to self-care and management of property. If the individual is unable to make such decisions, then a guardian may be appointed if the individual's needs cannot be met by any less restrictive means.

Guardianship of an adult is initiated by filing a written petition with a court, requesting that a guardian be appointed. The petition may request the appointment of a guardian of the person, a guardian of the property, or both. The same person may be appointed as guardian of the person and guardian of the property, or different persons may be appointed. The individual for whom guardianship is sought (the *respondent*) must be given notice of the petition and has the right to contest the requested appointment. In many states an attorney must be appointed to represent the respondent. The court may also appoint a *visitor* to make an independent investigation on whether guardianship is appropriate or order that the respondent be examined by a physician, psychologist, or other qualified professional.

The procedure for appointment of a guardian concludes with a formal hearing before a court. At the hearing, the judge considers the evidence and either makes the appointment, rejects the appointment, or orders that the respondent's needs be met by other means. In some states the respondent may request that this determination by made by a jury. As with minors, the guardian will usually be a close family member. Before making the selection, however, the court will generally consider the ward's preferences.

The role of the appointed guardian has traditionally been to act in the ward's best interests.

Under this model, the guardian must make an objective determination of what is best for the ward and act accordingly. Whether this determination conflicts with the ward's current or prior expressed wishes is not a factor in this situation.

However, other approaches have become increasingly important. Under the least restrictive alternative model, the guardian may exercise authority only to the extent necessitated by the ward's limitations. The guardian must select the alternative least restrictive of the ward's independence and freedom. The guardian must also encourage the ward to participate in making decisions. A third approach is the substituted judgment model. The guardian must make the decision that the ward would have made had the ward still had capacity. Under this approach, the ward's prior expressed wishes and personal values are important factors to be considered.

Many adult guardianships continue for the ward's lifetime and are terminated only by death. Upon the ward's death, the court will discharge the guardian, and the ward's assets will be distributed under the ward's will or to the ward's heirs. Guardianships are not necessarily lifelong, however. The ward may recover capacity, in whole or in part, or other changed circumstances may suggest that guardianship is no longer needed. In all states, a ward may request termination of the guardianship. To protect this right, many states provide that the ward's request need not be made by a formal petition but may be made by informal letter.

The decision to seek guardianship of an adult should never be made lightly. The position of guardian is a heavy responsibility. The ward, because he or she has been found to lack legal capacity, may lose many basic rights, including the right to vote, to travel, to decide where to live, to divorce or marry, to keep and care for children, and even to drive a car.

Similar to children, incapacitated adults are sometimes moved to different states or countries with the appointment of a guardian used to confirm residence in the new locale. Sometimes the move is arranged by a child who disagrees with his or her siblings on what care is best for the parent. Compacts among the states and international treaties attempt to limit use of guardianship to cases where a move to another jurisdiction is in the parent's best interests.

Alternatives to Guardianship

There are numerous alternatives to guardianship. Many require prior planning, which should be done well before the individual's capacity becomes an issue. Perhaps the most important of these alternatives is a durable power of attorney. Under a durable power of attorney, an individual designates another as agent to make decisions when or should the individual no longer be able to do so. Durable powers of attorney may be used for property management and for making health and personal-care decisions.

Another planned alternative is a revocable trust, often referred to as a *living trust*. Under this device an individual transfers his or her assets to a trustee, who holds and administers them as provided in the trust document. Most commonly the individual will act as his or her own trustee until such time as he or she is no longer able to manage the property, at which time a designated successor trustee will assume the responsibility.

Some alternatives do not require prior planning. A representative payee may be named to manage Social Security benefits. Many states have enacted health-care consent statutes allowing family members to make medical decisions for an incapacitated relative. A variety of social services, including assisted living, respite care, and financial counseling may be available to lessen an individual's need to have someone else make decisions. Before initiating the detailed procedure required to secure appointment of a guardian, all alternatives should be explored.

See also: CHILD CUSTODY; FAMILY LAW; GRANDPARENTS' RIGHTS

Bibliography

Anderer, S. J. (1990). *Determining Competency in Guardianship Proceedings*. Washington, DC: American Bar Association.

Commission on the Mentally Disabled/Commission on Legal Problems of the Elderly. (1989). *Guardianship: An Agenda for Reform*. Washington, DC: American Bar Association.

Daniel, C., and Hannaford, P. (1999). "Creating the Portable Guardianship: Legal and Practical Implications of Probate Court Cooperation in Interstate Guardianship Cases." *Quinnipiac Probate Law Journal* 13:351–377.

English, D. (1995). "Minors' Guardianship in an Age of Multiple Marriage." *University of Miami Institute on Estate Planning* 29:5–1 to 5–26.

English, D. and Morgan, R. (1998). "The Uniform Guardianship and Protective Proceedings Act (1997)." *NAELA Quarterly* 11:3–15.

Frolik, L. (1981). "Plenary Guardianship: An Analysis, a Critique, and a Proposal for Reform." *Arizona Law Review* 23:599–660.

Frolik, L. (1998). "Guardianship Reform: When the Best is the Enemy of the Good." *Stanford Law & Policy Review* 9:347–355.

Grisso, T. (1986). *Evaluating Competencies: Forensic Assessments and Instruments*. New York: Plenum Press.

Johns, A. F., and Bowers, V. (1997). "Guardianship Folly: The Misgovernment of Parens Patriae and the Forecast of Its Crumbling Linkage to Unprotected Older Americans in the Twenty-First Century-A March of Folly? Or Just a Mask of Virtual Reality?" *Stetson Law Review* 27:1–90.

Krasik, M. K. (1989). "The Lights of Science and Experience: Historical Perspectives on Legal Attitudes Toward the Role of Medical Expertise in Guardianship of the Elderly." *American Journal of Legal History* 33:201–240.

Parry, J. (1985). "Incompetency, Guardianship, and Restoration." In *The Mentally Disabled and the Law*, ed. S. J Brakel, J. Parry, and B. A. Weiner. Chicago: The American Bar Foundation.

Symposium Issue (2000). "Celebrating Twenty Years: The Past and Promise of the 1980 Hague Convention on the Civil Aspects of International Child Abduction." *New York University Journal International Law & Politics* 22:1–377.

Tor, P., and Sales, B. (1994). "A Social Science Perspective on the Law of Guardianship: Directions for Improving the Process and Practice." *Law and Psychology Review* 18:141.

U.S. Senate Committee on Aging. (1988). *Aging America: Trends and Projections*. Washington, DC: U.S. Department of Health and Human Services.

DAVID M. ENGLISH

GUATEMALA

See LATIN AMERICA

HAITI

See ETHNIC VARIATION/ETHNICITY

HEALTH AND FAMILIES

A growing body of research has shown that family plays an important role, if not the most important role (Doherty 1993), in shaping our health attitudes and behaviors. This is important because positive health behaviors have been shown to significantly affect physical and mental health (Grzywacz and Marks 1999).

Prior to understanding the role the family plays in the adoption of health attitudes and beliefs, it is important to identify what health is. The World Health Organization (1986) defines health as

> . . . the extent to which an individual or group is able, on the one hand, to realise aspirations and satisfy needs; and, on the other hand, to change or cope with the environment. Health is, therefore, seen as a resource for everyday life, not the objective of living; it is a positive concept emphasizing social and personal resources, as well as physical capacities. (p. 73)

The Impact of Marriage and Children on Adults' Health Behaviors

Being married and/or having children affects whether one engages in healthy behavior. Lois Verbrugge (1979) found that married people were healthier than single, widowed, divorced, or separated individuals. She suggested three possible explanations for her findings. First, married and unmarried people have different lifestyles that are associated with higher and lower risk behaviors (e.g., unmarried individuals have a higher number of sexual partners). Second, it is possible that those with poor health are less likely to marry. Third, married people may be less likely to label themselves as ill. Thus, it is unclear whether being married leads to better health or better health leads to marriage.

Debra Umberson's (1987, 1992) research has indicated that the family ties of marriage and parenthood are associated with more positive health behaviors and fewer risk behaviors. Joseph Grzywacz and Nadine Marks (1999) found that having children was associated with a healthier use of alcohol. Moreover, the Israel Ischemic Heart Disease Project found that for men with high levels of anxiety, their wives' love and support appeared to protect them against angina.

Umberson (1987) states that family members influence health behaviors through indirect and direct control mechanisms. Specifically, positive family ties lead to a greater sense of responsibility for one's self and one's family, and thus individuals with positive family ties are more motivated to engage in behaviors that lead to better health. Family members may also directly regulate one's health behavior by physically means (e.g., preparing healthy food), supportive behaviors (e.g., support the adoption of an exercise regime), or social sanctions (e.g., threaten to leave the marriage if spouse continues to smoke) (Orford et al. 1977). It is interesting to note that although married men's health behavior was influenced more by their spouse than married women's health behaviors, married women's health behavior was more influenced by their parents and their children (Umberson 1992).

However, being married and having a family does not always lead to more positive health behaviors. Cathleen Connell (1994) found that taking care of family members is associated with fewer positive health behaviors and more risk behaviors (e.g., smoking) due to the stress associated with being a caregiver. Also, stressful marriages are related to poorer immune functioning (Burman and Margolin 1989). Specifically, Robert Levenson and John Gottman (1983) found that the physiological stress (e.g., nerves, increased heart rate) that accompanied marital conflict predicted a decline in health. Spousal criticism was also found to affect one's health; it has been linked to lower success rates for quitting smoking (Coppotelli and Orleans 1985).

The Impact of Family on Children's Health Behaviors

Family also influences children's health behavior in several ways. Several international studies (see Wold and Anderssen 1992 for references) have found that health programs aimed at decreasing smoking and engaging in dental hygiene were more effective when the parents were involved. Sandra Hunter and her colleagues (1982), however, found that for some ethnic groups in the United States, family members played a more important role in the prevention of smoking than for other ethnic groups. Specifically, they found that close parent-child relationships and the time children and parents spent together were more significant predictors of smoking for African Americans than for Hispanic Americans or white Americans. This finding may be due to the attitudes held about the role of parents in a smoking prevention program. Both African-American children and their parents were more likely than others to think it is important that the parents be involved in a smoking prevention program (Koepke, Flay, and Johnson 1990).

In addition to involvement in health promotions, family members can model appropriate

health behaviors. Albert R. Marston and his colleagues (1988) reported that adolescents who did not use drugs were more likely to have parents who were not drug or alcohol users. Moreover, David Koepke and his colleagues (1990) found that African-American adolescents had a higher rate of smoking than other ethnic groups. They also reported that African-American children and adolescents were more likely to come from a household where others smoked and to live in a household where smoking was permitted.

Family members can support our decision to enact healthier behaviors. Robert Coombs and his colleagues (1991) found that adolescents who abstained from drug use felt better understood by their parents than adolescents who used drugs. Furthermore, those who abstained from drug use reported that their parents influenced them the most, whereas those who used drugs indicated that their friends influenced them the most.

In addition to modeling, families can influence health behaviors by affecting what is available to children. For example, Michael Resnick and his colleagues (1997) found that in the United States, adolescent use of cigarettes, alcohol, and marijuana was associated with how easily accessible these substances were in their own homes. Koepke and his colleagues (1990) found that African-American adolescents were more likely to come from a household where others smoked *and* to live in a household where smoking was permitted.

Jess Alberts and her colleagues (1991) and Michael Hecht and his colleagues (1997) found that occasionally adolescents were offered drugs by family members. Melanie Trost and her colleagues (1999) reported that the adolescent boys in their study found it most difficult to resist a drug offer from an elderly relative (aunts, uncles, or grandparents) and that adolescent girls in their study found it most difficult to resist a drug offer from brothers or male cousins.

Many researchers have found that during adolescence, family, friends, *and* school influence one's health attitudes and behaviors. Resnick and his colleagues (1997), in their longitudinal U.S. study on adolescent health, found that parent-family connectedness and perceived school connectedness were protection against every health risk behavior measured (emotional distress; suicidal thoughts and behaviors; violence; substance use; and sexual-risk behaviors) except the history of pregnancy. Koepke and his colleagues (1990) found that although family influenced whether an adolescent smoked, peers and the adolescent's own attitudes toward risk taking were also significant determinants. Bente Wold and N. Anderssen (1992), who looked at sports participation in ten European countries, also reported that the sport participation of parents, siblings, and peers was related to an adolescent's participation in sports. Also, older siblings who do not take part in sports have a negative influence on sport participation of their young adolescent siblings.

The Impact of Family on Other Family Members' Health Behaviors

Every family member can influence another family member's health attitudes and behaviors through communication. As stated earlier, conflict amongst spouses can affect physical health. Research on mental health has shown that critical comments from family members predicts the chance of relapse in depression, eating disorders, and schizophrenia (Fiscella and Campell 1999; Franks, Campbell, and Shields 1992). This is important because depression and hostility were associated with poor diet, lack of exercise, and a small chance in increased smoking (Fiscella and Campbell 1999). Kevin Fiscella and Thomas Campbell explained that the enactment of these unhealthy behaviors may represent some attempt to cope with these negative feelings (depression and hostility). After controlling for potentially confounding variables such as age, sex, race, marital status, income, education, and physical health, perceived criticism (not actual criticism) was significantly associated with fat consumption and lack of exercise (Fiscella and Campbell 1999). Other researchers have also found that family criticism is associated with physical health problems such as poor glucose control by patients with type 1 diabetes (Koenigsberg et al. 1993), less success with weight loss (Fischmann-Havstad and Marston 1984), and problems with asthma (Hermanns et al. 1989).

Conclusion

The family is the basic social context in which health behaviors are learned and performed (Ford-Gilboe 1997). Research in several different countries has found that families directly or indirectly influence one's mental health, physical health, drug use (including cigarettes and alcohol), diet,

exercise (including participation in sports), dental hygiene habits, and sexual risk-taking behavior. This influence lasts a lifetime.

See also: ACQUIRED IMMUNODEFICIENCY SYNDROME (AIDS); ALZHEIMER'S DISEASE; CAREGIVING: INFORMAL; CHILDREN OF ALCOHOLICS; CHRONIC ILLNESS; DEATH AND DYING; DECISION MAKING; DEMENTIA; DEPRESSION: ADULTS; DEVELOPMENTAL DISABILITIES; DISABILITIES; EATING DISORDERS; FAMILY AND RELATIONAL RULES; GRIEF, LOSS, AND BEREAVEMENT; HOMELESS FAMILIES; HOSPICE; RELIGION; SINGLE-PARENT FAMILIES; SCHIZOPHRENIA; STRESS; SUBSTANCE ABUSE; WIDOWHOOD

Bibliography

Alberts, J. K.; Miller-Rassulo, M. A.; and Hecht, M. L. (1991). "A Typology of Drug Resistance Strategies." *Journal of Applied Communication Research* 19:129–151.

Burman, B., and Margolin, G. (1989). "Marriage and Health." *Advances* 6(4):51–58.

Connell, C. M. (1994). "Impact of Spouse Caregiving on Health Behaviors and Physical and Mental Health Status." *American Journal of Alzheimer's Care and Related Disorders and Research* 9:26–36.

Coombs, R. H.; Paulson, M. J.; and Richardson, M. A. (1991). "Peer vs. Parental Influence in Substance Use Among Hispanic and Anglo Children and Adolescents." *Journal of Youth and Adolescence* 20:73–88.

Coppotelli, H. C., and Orleans, C. T. (1985). "Partner Support and Other Determinants of Smoking Cessation Maintenance Among Women." *Journal of Consulting and Clinical Psychology* 53:455–460.

Doherty, W. J. (1993). "Health and Family Interaction: What We Know." *Family Health: From Data to Policy,* ed. G. Hendershot and F. LeClere. Minneapolis, MN: National Council on Family Relations.

Fiscella, K., and Campbell, T. L. (1999). "Association of Perceived Family Criticism with Health Behaviors." *Journal of Family Practice* 48:128–134.

Fischmann-Havstad, L., and Marston, A. R. (1984). "Weight Loss Maintenance as an Aspect of Family Emotion and Process." *British Journal of Clinical Psychology* 23:265–271.

Ford-Gilboe, M. (1997). "Family Strengths, Motivation, and Resources as Predictors of Health Promotion Behavior in Single-Parent and Two-Parent Families." *Research in Nursing and Health* 20:205–217.

Franks, P.; Campbell, T. L.; and Shields, C. G. (1992). "Social Relationships and Health: The Relative Roles of Family Functioning and Social Support." *Social Science and Medicine* 34:779–788.

Grzywacz, J., and Marks, N. F. (1999). "Family Solidarity and Health Behaviors: Evidence from the National Survey of Midlife Development in the United States." *Journal of Family Issues* 20:243–268.

Hecht, M.; Trost, M. R.; Bator, R. J.; and MacKinnon, D. (1997). "Ethnicity and Sex Similarities and Differences in Drug Resistance." *Journal of Applied Communication Research* 25:1–23.

Hermanns, J.; Florin, I.; Dietrich, M.; and Rieger, C. (1989). "Maternal Criticism, Mother-Child Interaction, and Bronchial Asthma." *Journal of Psychosomatic Research* 33:469–476.

Hunter, S. M.; Baugh, J. G.; Webber, L. S.; Sklov, M. C.; and Berenson, G. S. (1982). "Social Learning Effects on Trial and Adoption of Cigarette Smoking in Children: The Boglusa Heart Study." *Preventative Medicine* 11:29–42.

Koenigsberg, H. W; Klausner, E.; Pelino, D.; and Rosnick, P. (1993). "Expressed Emotion and Glucose Control in Insulin-Dependent Diabetes Mellitus." *American Journal of Psychiatry* 150:1,114–1,115.

Koepke, D.; Flay, B. R.; and Johnson, C. A. (1990). "Healthy Behaviors in Minority Families: The Case of Cigarette Smoking." *Family Community Health* 13(1):35–43.

Levenson, R. W., and Gottman, J. M. (1983). "Marital Interaction: Psychological Linkage and Affective Exchange." *Journal of Personality and Social Psychology* 45:587–597.

Marston, A. R.; Jacobs, D. F.; Singer, R. D.; Widaman, K. F.; and Little, T. D. (1988). "Adolescents Who Apparently are Invulnerable to Drug, Alcohol, and Nicotine Use." *Adolescence* 91:593–598.

Orford, J.; Oppenheimer, E.; Egert, S.; and Hensman, C. (1977). "The Role of Excessive Drinking in Alcoholism Complicated Marriages: A Study of Stability and Change Over a One-Year Period." *International Journal of Addictions* 12:471–495.

Resnick, M. D.; Bearman, P. S.; Blum, R. W.; Bauman, K. E.; Harris, K. M.; Jones, J.; Tabor, J.; Beuhring, T.; Sieving, R. E.; Shew, M.; Ireland, M.; Bearinger, L. H.; and Udry, J. R. (1997). "Protecting Adolescents from Harm: Findings from the National Longitudinal Study on Adolescent Health." *Journal of the American Medical Association* 278:823–832.

Robertson, A., and Minkler, M. (1994). "New Health Promotion Movement: A Critical Examination." *Health Education Quarterly* (Fall):295–312.

Trost, M. R.; Langan, E. J.; and Kellar-Guenther, Y. (1999). "Not Everyone Listens When You 'Just Say No': Drug Resistance in Relational Context." *Journal of Applied Communication Research* 27(2):120–138.

Umberson, D. (1987). "Family Status and Health Behaviors: Social Control as a Dimension of Social Integration." *Journal of Health and Social Behavior* 28:306–319.

Umberson, D. (1992). "Gender, Marital Status and Social Control of Health Behavior." *Social Science and Medicine* 38:907–917.

Verbrugge, L. M. (1979). "Marital Status and Health." *Journal of Marriage and the Family* 41:267–285.

Wold, B., and Anderssen, N. (1992). "Health Promotion Aspects of Family and Peer Influences on Sport Participation" *International Journal of Sport Psychology* 23:343–359.

World Health Organization (1986). "World Health Organization: A Discussion Document on the Concept and Principles of Health Promotion." *Health Promotion* 1:73–78.

YVONNE KELLAR-GUENTHER

HINDUISM

The word *Hinduism* is used to denote the religious beliefs, practices, and social views of people who form the religious majority (approximately 80%) of India. Approximately 90 percent of Hindus live in India, and almost 70 percent of Indians live in its villages. The earliest stages of religious life in India date as far back as between 3000 and 1500 B.C.E. as it was practiced in the Indus Valley civilization. The Aryans, a people who spoke an Indo-European language, invaded India around 1500 B.C.E., conquering and subduing the indigenous inhabitants, and assimilating some elements of the latter's religious worldview into their own. Subsequently, the Vedic religion of the Aryans gained prominence as they settled and spread throughout India. Since then, orthodox Hinduism has evolved for almost 3500 years and has undergone numerous changes in the face of challenges from within (Buddhism and Jainism) and without (Islam and Christianity). These extensive evolutionary developments have kept Hinduism from becoming a homogeneous religious system. Hinduism is complex, and the beliefs and practices of the various traditions within Hinduism are diverse to the extent that they may seem contradictory. However, there are some beliefs that are commonly held by almost all Hindus.

Basic Beliefs of Hindus

Hindus hold to a cyclical view of human life. All sentient beings (human beings and members of the animal world) have an *atman* (*the true self,* or loosely translated as soul), which reincarnates by undergoing a number of births and rebirths. This notion of reincarnation is called *samsara.* An *atman* can reincarnate as an animal or human being, and rebirth as a human being is considered superior to an animal form of life. The bodily form an *atman* assumes in the next life is determined by the totality of one's *karma* (deeds or actions) of the present life. If, as a human being, a person lives a life in which good deeds outnumber bad deeds, then the *atman* reincarnates into a human being with a purer spiritual nature, which enables the possibility of further superior rebirths. The opposite is true if one's bad deeds outnumber one's good deeds. The goal of all human beings is to attain *moksha*—liberation from the endless cycle of births and rebirths. When a person attains *moksha,* he or she is believed to enter into a state where one's *atman* becomes one with *Brahman. Brahman* is the impersonal term referring to the eternal, universal, infinite, spiritual reality, and essence that humanity personally refers to as God (*Brahman* is often confused with the priestly group in Hinduism called *Brahmans.* However, to distinguish between the two, the latter is spelled either as *Brahmin* or without a capital "b").

In Hinduism, there are three *margas* (paths) through which a person can attain *moksha.* The first path is *jnana-marga. Jnana* can be translated as *awareness* or *insight.* When a person becomes aware that he or she is simply a drop in the ocean of *Brahman* and begins to detach him or herself from worldly statuses and possessions, he or she can begin to move towards *moksha* through *jnana-marga.* The second path is *karma-marga,* which entails faithful participation in ritual sacrifices that are often dictated and presided over by a *Brahmin* (priest). The third path is *bhakti-marga. Bhakti* refers to a selfless devotion and commitment to a personal deity.

Most Hindu homes have a shrine or altar. After bathing in the morning, family members devote time to a brief ritual and prayers (puja) *in front of the altar before they begin their daily tasks.* DAVID H. WELLS/CORBIS

The two most commonly worshipped deities in Hinduism are *Vishnu* and *Shiva. Vishnu* is the deity who preserves life, and is also worshipped as *Krishna* or *Rama,* who are believed to be two of *Vishnu's* nine earthly incarnations (*avataras*). *Vishnu* will incarnate for the tenth time when our present age morally deteriorates into injustice and chaos. Unlike *Vishnu, Shiva* does not incarnate into human form. *Shiva* is worshipped based on the variety of attributes he manifests. *Shiva* shows benevolence towards devotees who appeal to him for assistance. *Shiva* is also feared as the deity who takes away human life and destroys the cosmos, and yet, he is also believed to be the one who recreates a new cosmos after destroying the previous one. As the god of death, *Shiva* is believed to frequent cremation grounds. *Shiva* is also the model of an ascetic since he is believed to be sitting in calm meditation in the Himalayan Mountains. Reverence and worship of the female counterparts of *Vishnu* and *Shiva* are equally significant. *Lakshmi* is the divine consort of *Vishnu. Parvati* is that of *Shiva* when she is imaged as a benevolent mother; in her fierce forms, *Parvati* is manifested as the goddesses *Kali* and *Durga.* Devotion to *Durga* and *Kali* is referred to as the *Shakti* tradition. *Shakti* (often translated as *energy*) is the active dimension of the passive ascetic *Shiva.* Apart from these main deities, almost each village in India has its own local *grama-devatas* (village deities). Nevertheless, when a Hindu is questioned about the complexity of multiple deities, the common response is, "there are many names, but God is One."

The oldest scriptures in Hinduism are the *Vedas,* but the three most popular Hindu scriptures are the two great epics, the *Mahabharata* and the *Ramayana,* and the *Bhagavad-Gita,* which is a philosophical section in the *Mahabharata.* The *Puranas* are a collection of stories of the Hindu gods and goddesses, and the lives of the great heroes and heroines of the Hindu faith.

Caste System

The traditional caste system consists of a hierarchy of four castes (*varnas*): *Brahmins* (priests and teachers), *Kshatriyas* (rulers and warriors), *Vaishyas* (merchants and cultivators), and *Shudras* (servants). The non-Aryans who were incorporated into the Aryan society belonged to the *Shudra* caste. Those who were rejected on the grounds of ritual impurity were treated as and called *Untouchables* because members of the four castes did not associate with them. With the expansion and spread of the Hindu worldview throughout India, the division, hierarchy, and names of the traditional castes were not maintained, with the exception of the *Brahmins,* who claimed and were acknowledged as possessing a degree of ritual purity that retained their superiority above the other castes. The word *dharma* is central to Hindu belief. Hindus often refer to their religion as Hindu *Dharma,* basically stating that Hinduism is a way of life rather than a religion.

The key constructors and defenders of the caste system, the *Brahmins,* claimed that the presence of an organized caste system, with its elaborate rules and required caste duty (*dharma*), prevented society from degenerating into chaos. The *Brahmins* thus devised rules for each caste (*varna*) in accordance with the four stages (*ashramas*) in the life of a man (the *Vedic* society was patriarchal): celibate student, married householder, retired forest dweller, and the ascetic stage. This whole system was called *varnashrama dharma*—the duties of each caste in the four stages of a man's life. In the first stage, a boy receives his education by studying under a guru, and in the second stage he marries and has children. In the third stage, he retires with his wife to the forest after handing over the responsibility of the household to his oldest son. In the final stage he sends his wife home to their son and renounces all contact with the society by becoming an ascetic,

and attempting to pursue *moksha* with greater intention. Among the four stages of the *ashramas,* most people only completed the first three. Retired couples usually stayed with their oldest son, and very rarely did a man become an ascetic in his old age. Basically, the concept of the four *ashramas* sought to synthesize the necessity of order in society and the spiritual liberation (*moksha*) of the individual.

With the advent and expansion of modern industries and Western education in the postindependent (after 1947) cities of India, the significance and demands of the caste system has weakened. In the major cities, a person's professional and economic status often determines his or her social standing. The secular constitution of India also outlaws untouchability and recognizes all Indian citizens as equal. Almost all urban Hindus intermingle professionally and socially, and many marry outside their caste. However, in rural areas and smaller towns, the stringent nature of the caste system and its requirements continue to define society and the lives of its members.

Hinduism and the Family

The Hindu view of caste, *ashramas,* and family are inseparable—every person is born into a family belonging to a particular caste, and passes through the four stages of life by practicing *dharma* appropriate to each stage of life.

Among the four *ashramas,* the second stage of the married householder is central because it births and sustains the three other *ashramas.* When a man marries, he pays the three debts he owes to the ancestors, the gods, and his teacher (guru). To the ancestors, a married man pays his debt by having children, especially a male child, to continue the family lineage. Since the surname of the average Hindu is usually the family name, when a son is born the family name continues. This is not the case with daughters, who marry into another family and take up the surname of their husbands. Continuing the family lineage and its *name* is crucial because the memories and integrity of the ancestors are kept alive through these. The *name* (specifically surname) of a family is often synonymous with integrity and respect. Maintaining family integrity is necessary because it reflects the extent to which family members are faithful to their *dharma*. When a son marries a woman from a reputable family, earns a living through a just and honest vocation, and provides for his family, he honors the ancestors. Furthermore, because *dharma* is inclusive of religious traditions and practices relating to *moksha,* when a man imparts family *dharma* to his children, he enables their salvation and that of generations to come.

As a householder, a man pays back debts owed to the gods, the providers of prosperity and comfort, by offering appropriate sacrifices and prayers to them. Giving alms to the poor and religious mendicants, and occasionally feeding *Brahmins* and financially remunerating them for their services, are also deemed as acts symbolizing gratitude to the gods for material benefits enjoyed by a family. A man pays back debts owed to his guru by transmitting knowledge and wisdom received from the guru to his children. However, in the cities and towns of India, and in some villages, the average child rarely studies under a guru. In these contexts, a Western school system is the common mode of education. Furthermore, girls are equal recipients of education in cities and major towns. Urban Indian women who receive a Western form of education hold professional jobs just like their Western counterparts. Many of these women also contribute substantially to household income and have an equal voice in family decisions.

For Hindus, a family is larger than the nuclear family; family includes the extended family—maternal and paternal grandparents, uncles, aunts, and cousins. In India, especially in towns and villages still untouched by a free-market economic structure and modern culture that dominates the cities, many people are born into a joint family system. A joint family basically comprises paternal parents, their sons, daughters-in-law, unmarried daughters, and grandchildren. Here, the oldest male is the head of the entire household. Respect for a family member is based on age because the older a person, the wiser he or she is about family *dharma*. The older men make the financial decisions, and the older women are often informally consulted. In instances where a joint family does not exist, older members as still consulted before important decisions are made, especially in relation to marriage. Among Hindus, the family is the ideal environment through which Hindu *dharma* is passed from one generation to another—a child

begins learning about religious traditions, epic stories, ethics, norms, and values, especially by the example set by family members.

When a person marries in the context of a Hindu family, he or she may literally wed an individual, but on a broader level a person marries into a family. Because a family is the embodiment of *dharma,* a prospective bride is considered a candidate only when the traditions, practices, and economic status of her family match that of the prospective bridegroom's family. Most Hindu marriages are arranged—relatives and friends suggest the name and family of prospective brides or bridegrooms. Before a family considers a person as a candidate for their son or daughter, the family *Brahmin* is consulted to examine the horoscopes of the two individuals concerned, and to suggest whether there is a possible match. In a rural setting, after the approval of the family *Brahmin,* the decision regarding marriage is almost always made by the parents and the extended family of the people involved. In this context, very rarely are the prospective bride or groom's opinions considered. If this process does not result in a wedding, the family search for a bride and bridegroom continues until two families agree that their son and daughter would make a good couple. Among middle class families in Indian cities, depending on the level of conservatism, the man and woman may be allowed to meet alone on one or a number of occasions before a marriage decision is made. Since the 1990s, with the increase of the influence of Western culture, many young men and women in major Indian cities find a prospective bride or bridegroom through the process of a friendship or dating, and then inform their parents of their mutual attraction. However, in the final decision, the families of the man and woman are definitely involved. Unlike in the West, a man and a woman do not get engaged and then inform their families of the "good news."

Household Religious Practice

Almost every Hindu home has a shrine or altar that contains metal, wood, stone, or print images of the family deity and other gods and goddesses. After bathing in the morning, family members, especially married adults, devote time to a brief ritual and prayers (*puja*) in front of the altar before they begin their daily tasks. Prayers are performed at least twice a day, in the morning and at night. In most families, the mothers play a central role in maintaining the religious life of the family. Mothers pray for the well-being of their husbands and children, teach their children about the basic elements of the family faith, lead the family prayers and rituals on significant religious days, and undergo fasts on behalf of the family.

Major Hindu Family Rituals

There are four major *samskaras,* or life-cycle rites, that mark the prominent transitions of a Hindu's life. These are *namakarana* (naming of a child), *upanayana* (initiation thread ceremony for males of the first three castes), *vivaha* (wedding), and *antyeshi samskara* (funeral sacrament). A *Brahmin* is usually involved in conducting these rituals. Along with the nuclear and extended family, relatives and friends attend and participate in these rituals. The death rite has to be performed by the son (preferably the oldest), or the closest male extended family member or relative who is available. In the case of the wedding and funeral rites, the ceremonies can last for many days. The most expensive of these rituals is the wedding ceremony because most families like to celebrate it with pomp and show.

Hinduism Beyond India

There is not one single form of Hinduism practiced outside India. Hindus from all parts of India belonging to various castes have migrated overseas, taking with them the traditions and practices that they were brought up in at home. The social, political, and economic environment of the countries that Hindus have migrated to influence their faith and practices. However, the basic beliefs and practices of Hindus in and outside India do not differ.

Outside India, religious movements devoted to the teachings of a particular guru (religious teacher and usually the founder of the movement) have flourished. Gurus have been instrumental in nurturing the faith of Hindus, functioned as mediators of tradition, and offered advice on how the faith is to be practiced in foreign lands. Many of these gurus and their movements have often attracted followers from other ethnic backgrounds. This has altered the traditional definition of Hinduism as a religion whose members are strictly ethnic Indians. Many Hindus of other ethnic backgrounds founded religious movements that promote Hinduism and make it attractive to mostly non-Indian ethnic groups. These movements follow the basic teachings and practice of Hinduism, but do not contain elements of the faith that are influenced by the Hindu social world in India, such as the caste system. Common practices of these groups are the chanting of *mantras,* meditation, *hatha yoga,* and belief in reincarnation and vegetarianism. These movements have often successfully filled a spiritual vacuum and offer an alternative to Christian and Western ideas and practices.

Among Hindus outside India, the family continues to be the place where children are nurtured in Hindu *dharma.* In this context, women particularly are influential in the spiritual lives of children. For diaspora Hindus, a developed Hindu identity becomes a crucial issue for their children because they live among people of numerous faiths; therefore, efforts are made to inculcate the Hindu faith to their children more deliberately. Children often attend classes (similar to Christian Sunday school) on the Hindu faith at temples and religious centers, where the Hindu community gathers on Sundays and religious holidays. However, Hindu children outside India do not share the same experience as those in India who are surrounded by the Hindu social world, and where Hinduism is the largest religious group. Hindus outside India are always part of a religious minority, which alters some of the dynamics of the social beliefs and practices in which children are brought up. Thus, it is common for families to visit India during vacations to expose their children to Hinduism as family relatives living in India practice it. During such trips, families make pilgrimages to holy sites and make special vows and offerings to the deities.

See also: ASIAN-AMERICAN FAMILIES; FAMILY RITUALS; INDIA; INTERFAITH MARRIAGE; RELIGION

Bibliography

Basham, A. L. (1989). *The Origins and Development of Classical Hinduism.* Boston: Beacon Press.

Brockington, J. L. (1981). *The Sacred Thread: Hinduism in its Continuity and Diversity.* New York: Columbia University Press.

Dasgupta, S. N. (1955). *A History of Indian Philosophy.* 5 vols. Cambridge: Cambridge University Press.

Embree, A. T., ed. (1988). *Sources of Indian Tradition,* 2nd edition. Vol. 1: *From the Beginning to 1800.* New York: Columbia University Press.

Hay, S., ed. (1988). *Sources of Indian Tradition,* 2nd edition. Vol. 2: *Modern India and Pakistan.* New York: Columbia University Press.

Hutton, J. H. (1946). *Caste in India: Its Nature, Function and Origins.* Cambridge: Cambridge University Press.

Kakar, S. (1996). *The Indian Psyche.* New Delhi: Oxford University Press.

Kapur, P. (1970). *Marriage and the Working Woman in India.* New Delhi: Vikas Publications.

Kinsley, D. R. (1987). *Hindu Goddesses.* Delhi: Motilal Banarsidass.

Monier-Williams, Sir M. B. H. (1981). *Brahmanism and Hinduism,* 4th edition. New York: Macmillan.

Michell, G. (1977). *The Hindu Temple: An Introduction to its Meaning and Forms.* New York: Harper and Row.

Miller, B. S., trans. (1986). *The Bhagavad-Gita: Krishna's Counsel in Time of War.* New York: Bantam.

O'Flaherty, W. D., ed. (1975). *Hindu Myths: A Sourcebook Translated from the Sanskrit.* Harmondsworth, UK: Penguin Books.

O'Malley, L. S. S. (1935). *Popular Hinduism: The Religion of the Masses.* New York: Macmillan.

Paul, M. C. (1986). *Dowry and Position of Women in India.* New Delhi: Inter-India Publications.

Pocock, D. (1973). *Mind, Body and Wealth: A Study of Belief and Practice in an Indian Village.* Oxford, UK: Rowman and Littlefield.

Rao, V. V. P., and Nandini, V. (1985). *Marriage, the Family and Women in India.* New Delhi: Heritage Publishers.

Stevenson, M. S. (1971). *The Rites of the Twice-Born.* New York: International Publications Service.

Wolpert, S. (1982). *A New History of India.* New York: Oxford University Press.

Zaehner, R. C. (1962). *Hinduism.* New York: Oxford University Press.

LAJU M. BALANI
SCOTT W. TAYLOR

HISPANIC–AMERICAN FAMILIES

As with any large group, the 7.6 million Hispanic/Latino/Spanish families in the United States comprise a socially diverse population. Thus an analysis of Latino/a group composition and diversity challenges the tendency to use stereotypes. The U.S. Bureau of the Census notes, for example, that Hispanics/Latinos may be of any race—including Asian, Native American, European, African, or Middle Eastern. Moreover, there are numerous mixtures among these groups, some of whom, such as the Mexican *mestizos,* are also formally named. Latino families may be rich or poor, extended or nuclear, and of all social classes. Some families may have arrived from Mexico during the last decade, some may be refugees from the Communist regime in Cuba, whereas the settlement of the *Spanish* in New Mexico antedates the establishment of Jamestown, Virginia in 1609. Even that earliest of Spanish migrations to North America defies preconceptions of colonizing *conquistadores* enslaving native populations, bloody sword in hand. The settler/invaders appear to have included a large component of refugees—Jewish *conversos*—converts to Christianity—fleeing the Spanish Inquisition.

These few examples imply vast differences in cultural attitudes and life choices available to families and their members, and a one-size-fits-all attempt at understanding the social relationships common within and among Hispanic families risks grave misunderstandings. An overview of the Hispanic family must attend to this diversity as well as identifying commonalities. The task of achieving a sensitive understanding of Latino families is rendered even more difficult when it is recognized that social traits shared by Hispanic families with all other U.S. families are likely to be more prevalent than those characteristics one might reasonably identify as *Hispanic.* Even so, the social ascription of a group identity, as well as the commonalities shared by many Hispanics, may have profound and sometimes determining social consequences for an individual or family.

The Hispanic/Latino/Spanish group (the Census Bureau currently uses all three terms) is the fastest growing (in both percentage terms and in raw numbers) of all of the larger social/racial groups—white, African American, Hispanic, and Asian—identified and counted by the U.S. government. In the last census (Census 2000), one in eight of the 281.4 million U.S. residents—35.3 million persons—were enumerated as Latinos. The 1980 census counted only 14.6 million Hispanics, 6.5 percent of the total population. During the twenty years from 1980 to 2000, the 21 million additional Hispanics accounted for more than a third of the 59 million additional residents of the United States the Census counted.

Although the birth rate of Latinos as a whole is high, such astonishing growth can only result from a large net migration into the United States. This immigration, with its ramifying social effects has, perhaps more than any other factor, resulted in profound changes and adaptations for the majority of Hispanic families.

Statistics, mostly collected by the U.S. Bureau of the Census and the Department of Labor, offer crucial information for understanding the status and social conditions challenging the Latino family. In charting the diversity, composition, and social development of Latinos and Latino families, there is at least an entry into the heart of what is most personal and defining. The use of abstract data as a path to the personal is especially ironic for Latinos—more than most people, Latino families are seen as an emotional realm, and the chief sources of warmth and nurturance. Families are seen as providing unfailing support when facing an erratic and threatening world; the family is where one learns what is important, what is not, and the skills and strategies that enable one to survive outside its protective confines. It defines many of the roles one plays in social interactions.

The role of other social institutions as supports—including government agencies, private charities, or corporate employers—may be regarded even more skeptically by Latinos than by other members of U.S. society. In the countries of origin of many Latinos, these institutions of support outside the family are sometimes nonexistent, underdeveloped, corrupt, or, in the case of police and the military, often sources of danger and oppression rather than protection. It is somewhat ironic, therefore, that the primary reason that the Latinos are currently seen, and often see themselves, as members of a single ethnic group arises from the need of a state system, the U.S. government, to develop statistical methodology for collecting data on Hispanics/Latinos/Spanish so that services can be most effectively provided and legal protections administered to those so identified.

In other words, for the Latino, the ultimate source of the social definition that provides his or her group identity—the "I am a Hispanic (or

The Hispanic/Latino/Spanish group is by far the fastest growing (in both percentage terms and in raw numbers) of all of the larger social/racial groups in the United States. A/P WIDE WORLD PHOTOS

Latino/a)"was a government edict. The Latino identity did not arise out of a common perception of shared cultural norms and strategies transmitted (as so many are) from parent to child and from person to person within a community but rather from the needs of the United States federal authorities to more effectively collect statistical data. The vital role of the state in the creation and emergence of group identity is a common phenomenon: Native Americans and African tribal identities, racial ascriptions, Latino subgroup (national) identities, and the "French," but provide few examples (Cohen 1974; Enloe 1981).

The Hispanics/Latinos and Group Definition

The Hispanic ethnic group was created on May 4, 1978, when the U.S. Office of Management and Budget published the following regulation in the *Federal Register*: "Directive 15: Race and Ethnic Standards for Federal Statistics and Administrative Reporting" that defined a Hispanic to be "a person of Mexican, Puerto Rican, Cuban, Central or South American, or other Spanish culture or origin, regardless of race" (p. 19269). This definition (refined, with minor adjustments, in 1997) largely focuses on the countries of origin (which may be generations in the past) and assumes that peoples in these countries share a common "Spanish culture" that is also shared by some people living in the United States.

According to this definition, Hispanics (or after 1997, Hispanic/Latino/Spanish) derive from twenty-six nations that differ in languages, economic resources, educational systems, status structures, and customs. In addition, individual countries are often ethnically diverse. For example, the native language of the majority of Bolivians is either *Quechua* (the language of the Incas) or *Aymara*. *Parana* is spoken by millions of Paraguayans; Mayan dialects by the majority of Guatemalans; and *Garifuna*—a Creole language derived from English, Native American, and African languages—in the coastal areas of Honduras, Guatemala, and Belize. There are a myriad of Native American dialects spoken in Mexico—itself a huge, diverse nation stretching almost 4,000 miles from Tijuana to the Yucatan. English is the official language in Belize and Guyana, French in French Guiana, and Dutch in Suriname.

These language differences are not trivial among Latinos in the United States. There may be hundreds of thousands of native Mayan speakers in the United States, for example, and certainly substantial numbers of Quechua speakers. Garifuna immigrants (comprising perhaps more than 100,000 persons in New York City—they are not differentiated in the census tabulations) stage a large parade in Brooklyn each year.

The U.S. government, however, characterizes Latinos as members of an ethnic group, explicitly noting that "Hispanics may be of any race." In this the Hispanics are not unique. Since its creation, the U.S. government has mandated legal definitions of Native American tribes and the legal ascription of membership in a tribal group. If one is to negotiate and carry out treaties, for example, then the nature of the entity with whom one negotiates (e.g., *Cherokee Nation*) must be defined and the individuals entitled to services required by the treaty must be identified. For example, who is a Cherokee? Likewise, formal, legal racial definitions date to the Colonial era (Enloe 1981).

If one equates ethnicity and ethnic-group identity with cultural traits shared among a population (as few contemporary anthropologists do), then the Hispanic ascription may be confusing; Hispanics are culturally diverse and they did not tend to regard themselves as a collective entity until Regulation 15 was published in 1978. Most contemporary anthropological theorists, however, regard ethnic identity as being established through interactions of groups with other groups or social institutions as

government bureaucracies or the military. The interaction establishes a *we* and a *they,* an *us* and a *them.* Ethnic identity is expressed in a dynamic process among a number of groups (Fredrik Barth [1969]; Abner Cohen [1974]; and Joan Vincent [1974] were pioneers in the rigorous development of this perspective). An entire shared culture is not necessary to define group membership: Sometimes a particular cultural trait may be sufficient. Tragically, religion alone—Roman Catholic versus Eastern Orthodox—defines the ethnic difference between Serbians and Croatians, yet this difference led to war and the establishment of separate nation states.

The Hispanic/Latino as an ethnic group does have a social validity, however, if only because one is required to so identify oneself to many of the society's institutions to receive services and legal protection against discrimination. Furthermore, if the larger society sees one as a member of a group, then persons so ascribed tend to react reinforce common bonds for protection and to achieve common ends.

All too often, Latinos have had to confront stereotyping, discrimination, and oppression from the moment of their first step on U.S. soil (even if as a toddler). Common oppression has thus reinforced the rapid acceptance of the Hispanic/Latino identity following the U.S. government's 1978 ascription. Latino ethnicity is thus a real and valid social category that profoundly affects on the lives of Latinos; this ethnicity should never, however, be regarded as the manifestation of a nearly universal suite of cultural traits. Although Latinos may hold much in common, common traits are rarely universal nor are most sufficient to define an individual as Hispanic, although a Spanish accent would be a sufficient social marker. Persons seeking information about and understanding of the Latino family solely by reference to a list of common traits and behaviors may find themselves doomed to a misunderstanding and misdirection of effort.

In 1978, many newly minted *Hispanics* found this common assumption of cultural/ethnic identity at first confusing, not only because the term *Hispanic* had not previously been used. (If there were any term in common usage for the group as a whole, it was *Latino.*) At that time, most Latinos would have first identified themselves in terms of a nationality, such as Colombian, Dominican, or Argentinian. Exceptions would have included the

Spanish of New Mexico and the *Chicanos,* who were mainly of Mexican derivation, although that ancestry might be traced back as far as the eighteenth century missions of California and Arizona. Eventually, the Hispanic identifier became more popularly accepted, and the sense of group identity was greatly strengthened once the U.S. government added *Latino* and *Spanish* to be used by those who preferred to use these names.

Hispanic/Latino Families: Demographic and Social Indices

Although aggregate statistics should always be interpreted with care to avoid stereotyping, they offer vital insights relating to the situation of Latinos and Hispanic/Latino families at both macro and micro levels. Keeping in mind the proviso that the average is not the individual—although many Hispanics are poor, some are wealthy; communication in Spanish may be common, but some Hispanics may know Spanish poorly or not at all—aggregate statistics do help outline some of the social characteristics of Hispanics as a group.

On the whole, the Latino family in the United States confronts great economic and social challenges, but with relatively few reserves to meet them. The social needs of the Hispanic families are underlined by their standing in five social indices (see Table 1).

Poverty. In 1999, 20.2 percent (one in five) of Hispanic families lived below the poverty level compared with a 9.3 percent poverty rate (one in eleven) for the nation's families as a whole, and 5.5 percent (one in eighteen) for non-Hispanic white families. The situation of married-couple Hispanic families is somewhat better, 14.2 percent, but that of female-headed families can only be described as dire: 39 percent live in poverty and among Puerto Ricans, 47.4 percent. It should also be noted that Puerto Rican residents counted include only those living in the fifty states—residents of the Commonwealth of Puerto Rico (3.8 million persons) are not included in the totals for U.S. residents, although all Puerto Ricans are born as U.S. citizens.

As a point of reference, the U.S. poverty thresholds for families of three and four persons were $13,853 and $18,267 respectively in 2001.

Income. The median income (half make more, half make less) of Latino families is approximately 60 percent that of all U.S. families: $32,000 versus $52,000. The same income differential holds for married-couple families: $37,000 versus $59,000. However, the income levels drop dramatically for single-parent families across all groups, especially for female-headed families: $18,700 for Latinos, $23,700 for all U.S. families and $28,600 for non-Hispanic white female-headed families. Special note should be paid to the $15,600 income of female-headed Puerto Rican families. On the other hand, Cuban female-headed families receive almost as much income, $27,100, as do their non-Hispanic white counterparts. In sum, the majority of female-headed Latino families live in poverty or near poverty conditions (as defined by the U.S. government).

Age. As a group, Latinos are dramatically younger than the rest of the U.S. population. The median age for males is 26.3 and for females 25.5 years versus 34 and 36 years respectively for the total U.S. population. The median age is even higher for non-Hispanic white males, 36.9 years, and females, 38.8 years. Across the board, Latinos' median ages are approximately ten to twelve years younger than those of other groups, with the exception of the Cuban-Latino subgroup, for which the median ages are 40.4 for males and 42.6 for females, higher than any other major group in the United States. The high median ages for Cubans are primarily the result of the erratic nature of Cuban refugee immigration as well as an age bias in the refugee population. Young persons subject to military conscription, for example, have routinely been forbidden exit visas.

Fertility. When the median age of a population is young then the proportion of women in the 15- to 44-year-old age cohorts, and especially in their 20s, will be high. This means that the fertility of the Latino population, with typical median ages a decade younger than the rest of the U.S. population, would be high. However, within all age groups Latina women give birth at much higher rates per thousand (about ninety-five) than those in other groups, which averaged about fifty to sixty-five per thousand women according to a June 2000 Census Current Population Survey (P20–543RV). Latina women accounted for 13.6 percent of the 60.9 million women in the childbearing years and yet gave birth to 19.3 percent of the 3.9 million children born in that period. In addition, the Latina mothers also tended to be younger, raising the likelihood that more of them will have more children.

TABLE 1

Hispanic-American families

(In millions or as a percentage of the total population)

Census Year	U.S. total	Hispanic total	Mexican	Puerto Rican	Cuban	Other Hispanic	White Non-Hispanic	Black Non-Hispanic
2000	281.4	35.3 (12.5%)	20.6 (7.3%)	3.4 (1.4%)	1.2 (0.42%)	10.02 (3.6%)	195.6 (69.5%)	35.4 (12.6%)
1990	248.7	22.4 (9.0%)	13.5 (5.4%)	2.73 (1.1%)	1.04 (0.42%)	5.01 (2.01%)	188.3 (75.7%)	29.3 (11.8%)
1980	222.6	14.6 (6.5%)						
Social Characteristics 1999								
Families (millions)	72.03	7.6	4.8	0.77	0.385	1.6	53.1	
Families, median income	$51,751	$31,663	$31,123	$30,129	38,312		54,121	
Married-couple	$59,346	$37,132	$35,332	$41,776	44,025		59,697	
Male-headed, no spouse present	$37,396	$30,425	$30,710	$29,882	39,811		41,656	
Female-headed, no spouse present	$23,732	$18,701	$19,313	$15,568	27,084		28,627	
Families in Poverty (%)	9.30%	20.20%	21.20%	23%	15%	16.70%	5.50%	
Married-couple	4.80%	14.20%	16.70%	8.10%	10.30%	9.60%	3.30%	
Male-headed	11.70%	16.80%	16%	19%	19.80%	17.60%	9.30%	
Female-headed	27.80%	38.80%	38.40%	47.40%	33.80%	34.60%	18.60%	
Median Age: Males	34	26.3	24	25.4	40.4		36.9	
Median age: Females	36	25.5	24.9	30.2	42.6		38.8	

The future composition of the Hispanic group is likely to be further shaped by another trend that emerges from Census Bureau Data. The fertility of Latina immigrants is far higher than that of those born in the United States. Among native-born women, fertility rates of Latinas were approximately eighty births per year per thousand as opposed to sixty births per thousand for non-Hispanic native-born women. Latina immigrants gave birth at an overall rate of 112 births per thousand. Thus the birth rates of Latina women, although high, are moving toward those of the general population—the trend for immigrant Latinas has not been established, but starts from a far higher level. Thus, the Latino/a child is far more likely to be born of an immigrant mother than would be suggested by the proportion of immigrant mothers in the of child-bearing population as a whole.

Latina immigrant women are thus more likely to bear children, and they are more likely to continue having them than any other group in the U.S. population, although these differences may narrow in the future with acculturation and other social pressures.

Immigration. As enumerated through responses to the Census 2000, at least 16.1 million of the 35.4 million Hispanic/Latinos were born in another country—they immigrated to the United States. Latinos constituted 52 percent of all of the foreign-born U.S. residents counted in the census. (Actually, the number of foreign born may be substantially higher; census counts of the foreign born have been consistently proved inaccurate—low—over the years.) At least 12.5 million Latinos immigrated since 1980, the majority during the 1990s, and these later immigrants now constitute the subgroup of Latinos with the highest fertility rate. Of the 761,000 Latina mothers giving birth last year, 423,000 (or 56%) were foreign born, although the foreign-born Latinas accounted for only 47 percent of the 8 million Latina women of child-bearing age.

Language. Census 2000 tallies indicate that 47.0 million U.S. residents spoke a language other than English in the home. Spanish was the language spoken by 28.1 million, of whom 13.8 million spoke English less than "very well." In a substantial number of families, no member speaks English beyond a level that facilitates the most basic social interactions outside a Spanish language environment. These are called *linguistically isolated families*; data on these families is as yet unavailable, but past experience indicates that there are millions of such isolated families.

In profile, the Latino family is young, poor, and especially in the case of the single-parent family, likely to be living in straitened circumstances. Almost half of Latinos were not born in the United States, with millions having arrived during the last decade. This high volume of immigration is expected to continue. Of course when we speak of the mean income or age, always keep in mind that half of all Latino families exceed the mean. There are many affluent Latinos: doctors, lawyers, skilled craft workers, teachers, executives, and business owners. Latinos as a group have, on the average, low incomes; an individual Latino, however, may have any income, may have lived in North America for fifteen generations, and may still speak Spanish at home.

National Origins: The Component Subgroups

The U.S. Census collects data on various Latino subgroups based on national origins. The primary subgroups are Mexicans (20.6 million), Puerto Ricans (3.4 million), and Cuban (1.2 million)—there were separate boxes to check off for these groups and various categories of *Other Hispanics* (10 million). Most numerous among the latter—the respondent had to write in the group—were 765,000 Dominicans (deriving from the Dominican Republic), 655,000 Salvadorans (El Salvador), and 471,000 Colombians. However, 6.1 million Hispanic respondents only checked off the Hispanic box or wrote in such terms as *Latino*. The origins of about a fifth of the Hispanic/Latino population are a mystery.

Immigration and the Family

The overarching impact of migration upon the structure and relations within individual families cannot be overemphasized. In raw numbers, the fact that 16 million Hispanics are counted as "foreign born" minimizes the scale of Latino immigration: Persons from the Commonwealth of Puerto Rico are not counted as foreign born, for example. They are all U. S. citizens, and Puerto Rico is not counted as a foreign country. Yet in most respects—outside citizenship status—Puerto Ricans have been treated as though they were "foreign" to U. S. society, and the have suffered most of the social dislocations common among immigrants. Furthermore, for all groups the profound effects of migration clearly extend to each family member,

not only those born abroad but also those born in the United States.

Latinos have migrated to the U.S. for many reasons: millions have been refugees, fleeing war-time conditions and political, religious, and racial/social oppression. Some of them were eventually granted refugee status while others were not. And of course, many millions have emigrated to the United States for (sometimes quite desperate) economic reasons and to provide their families with opportunities unavailable in their homelands. These migrations have also taken many forms. Sometimes entire family groups emigrated; sometimes adult workers have migrated first and then reunited with their families later. Almost invariably, emigration disrupted extended family networks and supports.

The conditions leading to emigration and the emigration experience may offer important insights into the dynamics of particular families. For example, consider political refugees: the Cuban migration—particularly during the first twenty years of the Castro regime—is a refugee migration. However, the driving impulse of migration from El Salvador and Nicaragua during the 1980s was the need to escape ongoing wars. Likewise tens of thousands of Guatemalans (particularly Mayan speakers from the highlands), Chileans, and Argentinian immigrants in the 1970s and 1980s were fleeing violence and political repression in those countries. The initial phase of the immigration from the Dominican Republic in the mid-1960s was driven by refugees from political dictatorships and a civil war eventually ended by the occupation of the country by U.S. Marines in 1965.

In addition, since the 1970s, difficult economic conditions and a high population growth rate in parts of Latin America have encouraged emigration to the United States. This has been most dramatically true of immigration from Mexico, with its 2,000 mile-long common border with the United States, long-term historical ties, and recent history of economic mismanagement and recurrent economic crises. The classification of the cause of an emigration from the homeland can sometimes be arbitrary; the disruption caused by war and violent political dictatorships has often wrecked local economies leading desperate inhabitants to leave to obtain the most basic subsistence. The need for workers in the United States offers opportunities that have drawn immigrants north.

Immigrant narratives. Virtually every immigrant family has its narrative of the journey, a narrative that affects the relations among family members and between the family and the external social world. Did the family leave as a unit, or did one or two persons leave first, as pioneers of a sort, and bring others later? What role did/does immigration status play in the narrative and in the continuing structure of opportunities available to family members? Often the narrative of migration is in part a narrative of trauma. The movie *El Norte* offers an extreme example, but millions of Latinos have been, cheated, had to pay bribes, or have been physically threatened or abused during the journey to the United States. Moreover, even if one had not been traumatized, the narrative of immigration trauma is common among most Latinos' acquaintances. If one had to choose a single factor that most directly affects the lives of immigrants, it would be the residence status (legal right to live and work in the United States) of family members. Furthermore, legal status frequently varies among family members, especially if children have been born in the U.S.

There are myriad answers to such questions. For some, immigration brings immediate economic loss—a physician from Chile works as an orderly, for example, or an engineer scrapes by as an automotive mechanic. If these people are middle aged when they arrive, it may be nearly impossible to professionally recertify or to find positions offering equivalent social class status in the United States. For many others, economic benefits may be almost immediate; the United States is a land of opportunity that rewards their labor. For most, the struggle is demanding and the rewards are mixed.

Latino Family Roles

In large part, the Latino family is a family in transition. Within a generation or two the family may not only have immigrated to the United States but may have also migrated from a rural to an urban setting. During this same period, great social and economic changes have been affecting all families in the United States and all social roles within the family. The vast majority of Latinos have been and are being transformed by all of these changes.

Social status may be gained or lost as roles are redefined within the family. Both opportunity and need often encourage females to participate in the workforce resulting in more independence as well as more demands on their time and energy; quick language acquisition for a child may gain him or her sometimes inappropriate power as a translator/ negotiator with the outside world; a husband or father, accustomed to controlling relations between the family and the rest of the social universe may have to adjust to at the least a partial result of this control. Moreover, persons in the community previously regarded as supporting relatives (such as godparents or distant cousins) may no longer regard themselves as having the same responsibilities.

The underdevelopment of state systems in most Latin nations led to the dependence on the family for support of the individual. Family systems tended to be patriarchal, and men were the prime protectors, mediators with an often-hostile world outside the bounds of the family. A number of common cultural strategies developed to protect the family. One was simply an extreme form of patriarchal relations, sometimes called the *machismo/ marianismo* dyad, which served to reinforce the prestige of the male in this difficult mediating role. Another, called *compadrazgo,* served to extend the boundaries of the family through a system of godparent relations—a godparent is a *compadre* or *comadre.* The godparent assumed a certain responsibility to care for and guide the godchild in ways that extended beyond his or her spiritual well-being.

Machismo/marianismo. A man's proper role, at least in the language used in much of Mexico, is to be *macho,* and the ideal of the woman was to be like Mary, the mother of God. The *machismo/ marianismo* dyad has never been a realistic metaphor for the relationship between men and women in the family, and in particular, the concept of *machismo* has been badly distorted as understood in U.S. popular culture. There is historico-cultural truth behind these concepts, however; although patriarchal, they are not as demeaning to either sex as one would infer from the popular stereotype.

The term *macho* has never been universal in Latin culture, and care should be advised when using it; in some places every male would have been offended to be referred to as *muy macho.* In Mexico, however, the word has historically had more positive connotations. A man who was *macho* was one who engendered respect, and not incidentally, also respect for his family; closely allied to that respect was a sense of dignity and often a forcefulness of personality. Therefore, to be *very much a man* is to have a forceful, dignified presence (almost in the Latin sense if *dignitas*), a strong (though not unreasonable) will and sense of purpose, reliability, and courage. These qualities are used in support of, protection of, and defense of the family—this is the ideal. *Machismo* in such a man can be a loving, certainly caring, trait and certainly need not be expressed through sexual conquests; a man could be *muy macho* and faithful to his wife.

American actors Gary Cooper and Humphrey Bogart would have been *muy macho*. A braggart trying to pick up a woman in a bar is definitely not *macho*; indeed, a braggart must have many other fine qualities to overcome such a flaw and make the grade. Regarded in its patriarchal essentials, the male's role outside the home entails a moral sacrifice. In negotiating the family's safe passage through the social world, a man will sometimes be forced to compromise much that he ought not, submit to the will of others who may not be worthy, make mistakes, and even accept that his flaws, errors, and humiliations will be public and reflect on the family. All too often the public life is a series of diminishments for a man who realizes that he alone may not be able to ensure his family's well-being.

The woman/mother, inhabiting a more private sphere, does not need to undergo these humiliations; her ideal—*marianismo*—is to be like Mary, the ultimate source of nurturance and moral authority in the family, free from the need to engage in moral compromises necessary to ensure the family's survival. This is not the role of a weakling. On the contrary, the mother is the moral and practical rock upon which the family is built—she is the source of value. Again, *marianismo* and *machismo* are cultural ideals, not rational expectations to be lived in daily life. And rarely, outside of Mexico, would the terms, as opposed to the underlying concepts, ever be used in an approving context.

While *marianismo* and *machismo,* as used by an anthropologist, never (for example) by an Uruguayan housewife, are linked terms, the concepts are not symmetrical. They are ideological constructs that when put into practice in any modern society tend to reinforce the oppression of women and to perpetuate inequalities of social roles between men and women. In essence, the ideals reflect a need for manipulation resulting from powerlessness. The *macho* man is a presentation, a front, perhaps backed up by other forms of power, perhaps not. The successful patriarchal Latino man is manipulating his social presence for the benefit of his family. In practice, it is but a small step from the self-sacrificing patriarch to the manipulative egotist who uses an ideology of the protective role as a pretext for exercising total control over other family members.

Assuming the moral authority of the mother of God likewise has obvious potential for manipulative abuse within the family. *Marianismo* and *machismo* (even if practiced as habits of thought and not called by those terms) seem to have developed in societies in which relatively few persons were empowered, especially among those who were poor, who were members of groups who suffered racial or even caste-like discrimination, and who had little formal education or opportunities for independent employment. Extreme patriarchal relations may have in part been the result of a dysfunctional colonial socioeconomic system in some Latino homelands. In the United States, whatever the deficiencies in protective social nets, the same conditions do not exist.

Compadrazgo. In religious life the function of the godparent is to ensure that the appropriate spiritual education is provided a godchild. In Latin America acceptance of the godparent role led to the assumption of much broader responsibilities: the godparent ideally would oversee the well-being of the child in all respects. Godparent relations have been referred to as a form of fictive kinship, and networks of godparents certainly helped ensure the safety of family members. The relations are complex; for example, deference and respect is paid to someone who is willing to assume a role as a *compadre* to one's offspring. In some traditional societies there was an aspect of social gamesmanship involved: the higher the social standing of a compadre, the more opportunities available to a child, and indirectly to the entire family.

As in so many other ways, immigration often altered or severed some of these kin bonds. Most commonly, the godparents might be in another country or another part of the United States, or perhaps no longer have supporting resources. Although the social importance of these bonds may be attenuated, some social service agencies have successfully sought out godparents for children in need of foster-care placements, and it is still not unusual for a child to be sent to live with a godparent for a period of time.

The social context of the Latino family is in a constant state of flux. Language acquisition, fluctuating economic conditions, acquisition of residence status and U.S. citizenship, and continued immigration of Latinos—including family reunification—ensure that Latino families will continue to undergo massive transformations. Given the size and birthrate of the Latino group, the ability of these families to provide a physically, emotionally and intellectually healthy environment to raise their families and meet their own needs will do much to determine the social course of the nation in the next generation.

See also: ARGENTINA; ETHNIC VARIATION/ETHNICITY; GODPARENTS; IMMIGRATION; LATIN AMERICA; MEXICO; PERU; SPAIN; UNITED STATES; VENEZUELA

Bibliography

Barth, F. (1969). Introduction to *Ethnic Groups and Boundaries,* ed. F. Barth. Boston: Little, Brown.

Castex, G. M. (1994). "Providing Services to Hispanic/ Latino Populations: Profiles in Diversity." *Social Work* 39:288–296.

Cohen, A. (1974). "Introduction: The Lesson of Ethnicity." In *Urban Ethnicity,* ed. A. Cohen. London: Tavistock.

Enloe, C. H. (1981) "The Growth of the State and Ethnic Mobilization: The American Experience." *Ethnic and Racial Studies* 4:123–136.

McGoldrick, M.; Giordano, J.; and Pearce, J. K., eds. (1996). *Ethnicity and Family Therapy,* 2nd edition. New York: Guilford Press.

Office of Management and Budget. (1978, May 4). "Directive 15: Race and Ethnic Standards for Federal Statistics and Administrative Reporting." *Federal Register* 43:19269.

Stevens, E. P. (1973). "Machismo and Marianismo." *Society* 10(4):57–63.

U.S. Bureau of the Census. (1991). *Race and Ethnic Origin,* Content Determination Report, 1990. Census of Population and Housing, 1990, CDR-6. Washington, DC: Government Printing Office.

U.S. Bureau of the Census. (2001). "Chart Nos.: 37–41, 53: Social and Demographic Characteristics." In *Statistical Abstract of the United States: 2001.* Washington, DC: Government Printing Office.

Vidal, C. (1988). "Godparenting among Hispanic Americans." *Child Welfare* 67:453–459.

Vincent, J. (1974). "The Structuring of Ethnicity." *Human Organization* 33:375–378.

Other Resources

National Center for Children in Poverty [NCCP]. (2002). "Child Poverty Facts." Available from http://www. cpmcnet.columbia.edu/dept/nccp/ycpf-01.html.

U.S. Bureau of the Census. (2001). Various reports. Available from http://www.census.gov.

GRACIELA M. CASTEX

HOME

Home refers to the geographic region, place, or dwelling that family members identify as a familiar residence to which they can return. Home is not a physical structure, but a complex symbolic concept. The symbols of home are constructed from references to physical, temporal, and affective, or emotional, dimensions of everyday acts of dwelling.

Physical Dimension

The physical dimension of home helps to locate what is home. It is inappropriate to use the terms *house* and *home* interchangeably. Families may identify housing as home, but home is not necessarily a domicile (permanent legal residence). Designation of what is home depends on specification and extent of the concept. John Hollander (1993) suggests that home is conceptual concentric circles radiating outward, with the surface of the world as the outermost circle. The smallest central point of the concentricities might be the place of greatest hominess. Moving outward are the broader, public places, such as cities or regions, which are considered home. The notion that home is a community of people in a region comes from the German *heimat* or homeland. This is a collective sense of home rather than the personal and private sense of home of individuals and families.

A place is a home if it is familiar. A place becomes familiar and eventually considered a home through successive interactions with the place. Repeated interactions through organized patterns of routines yield recognition of actions and place.

A home in Arghandab, Afghanistan. The terms house *and* home *should not be used interchangeably. One's sense of home is more complex and develops from significant physical and emotional interactions with a place.* CAROLINE PENN/CORBIS

Frequent and regular family interactions associated with daily acts of living (e.g., food preparation, sleeping, childcare) or repetitive family and community rituals held in a specific place can contribute to familiarity with a residence or a territory.

The place that is home must have a regular physical appearance so that it is recognizable. Too much variation in the place will not elicit enough recognition over time to generate a sense of familiarity. Some stability in the environment may exist, but stability can also be controlled by the family. For example, furnishings in a house are often arranged in patterns and allowed to remain for a period. This regularity permits recognition of the place as familiar rather than strange. Thus, people act as agents in the construction and arrangement of the physical dimension of home (Douglas 1993).

Time Dimension

The idea that a residence becomes familiar through repeated interactions between individuals and a place inherently incorporates the concept of time, the second dimension of home. Time is required to accommodate replicable interactions between individuals in a place (for example, between family members residing in a house) and between individuals and a place (for example, between an individual and a living room). Too much time between interactions will reduce the opportunity to construct a cognitive representation of a familiar and predictable place.

When individuals are absent from home for a long period, the place may be perceived as strange and unfamiliar because the place and/or the individual may have changed during the interim. Alfred Schutz (1945) describes how the homecomer may feel like a stranger in a home territory because the formerly familiar place does not conform to expectations constructed from past experiences.

Affective Dimension

Home is more than a sense of recognition and familiarity with a place. The definition of home also includes the idea that it is a place to which family members intend to return. This symbolic orientation toward a place involves affect, or emotion, the third dimension of home. The feelings associated with the cognitive representation of a place assist in activating the inclination or desire to return and generating a sense of home.

People experience a sense of being *at home* in the inner concentric circles of home. A journey toward the outer circles can elicit feelings of strangeness. At the center of home, the strangeness dissipates and is replaced by ease because the surroundings are familiar. Actions within the place are known or easily remembered (such as knowing the rules for moving about a place) so that less effort is required to understand and interact with the immediate environment. The intimate knowledge about how to act and the behavioral habits or rituals associated with home elicit a sense of control over the home territory (Lyman and Scott 1967). Control does not necessarily mean legal ownership or possession of a physical space; the possession of the territory through habits of daily living is a part of a sense of home.

A sense of control over a territory can include the notion that the place is private or not under surveillance. The idea of privacy has emerged in association with home over the past few centuries (Stone 1991). Some social activities are viewed as public and therefore can be available to be observed by larger groups of people. Surveillance of other activities by the public is less desirable, eliciting a desire for privacy. Peter Wilson (1988) suggests that symbolic boundaries of the home provide indicators of what is private for the household. Territory inside the home that restricts access to nonmembers is considered to have greater privacy than areas that outsiders may more easily enter.

Restricting access to the home is associated with maintaining a sense of safety from the outside world. Home is a retreat from the strange, dangerous, or polluted external world (Rybczynski 1986). Inside the home, the physical setting is treated as private, familiar, and protective of occupants. Interestingly, efforts to create and maintain privacy introduce a lack of freedom. Walling out the outside to gain privacy involves being walled in, with an associated loss of freedom (Schama 1987).

Privacy within the home also emerged from the creation of the need for quiet to accommodate contemplation and concentration; activities such as reading and writing became associated with the need for a private space that is protected from the

noise and chaos of the outside world (Stone 1991). Witold Rybczynski (1986) suggests that the physical and emotional comfort associated with home has emerged in coordination with the development of technology (e.g., sources of heat in colder climates and designs of chairs). Home is a place that is familiar, the physical attributes of the place are coordinated to help the human body feel at ease, and the acts of daily living are fairly convenient. At home, families feel at ease both physically and emotionally.

A place can be designed and decorated to create home as a comfortable place; however, the décor does not make it a home. Some places do not facilitate the ability to feel a sense of privacy or physical comfort, or a sense of emotional ease through esthetics. Joseph Rykwert (1993) notes that the decoration and design of buildings can alienate people by bringing about a feeling of discomfort. Discomfort is also experienced in the strange territories away from home.

Moving far away from the home territory to an unfamiliar place can elicit a longing for home. Sojourns to distant places can be experienced as yearning for the familiar, or nostalgia. Interestingly, nostalgia is derived from the Greek word *nostos*, which means a homeward journey (Hollander 1993). Longing for home may motivate families or family members to enact the familiar rituals of home in an effort to secure a degree of comfort. For example, Arctic explorers recreated family rituals as a way of coping with being in adverse conditions and away from their homes for long periods of time (Johnson and Suedfeld 1996). Additionally, families may use possessions associated with home, such as furniture or decorations, to replicate home in a new place. The possessions help to recreate the familiar place associated with home.

Removal from, or dispossession of, a home may be experienced as a sense of loss. For example, families living in exile may feel deprived of a sense of belonging to a place. The loss, however, may be diminished by efforts to continue of the familiar patterns of family activity in another less familiar place. The study of families who migrate away from their homes reveals the types of efforts to create a place that replicates the former home. For example, Anne-Marie Fortier (2000) describes how Italian migrants to England replicate some aspects of their original home and homeland through rituals, celebrations, and decoration of buildings. Replication of home reduces the distress associated with the loss of home and contributes to a sense of belonging rather than alienation.

Orientation to a place that is considered home may contribute to the social identity of family members. Indeed, Geoffrey Hayward (1975) views home as the manifestation of family identity, which is one type of social identity. Social identity refers to the knowledge of membership in a group and the emotional significance attached to that group (Tajfel 1981). Individuals who recognize a common home are part of a group attached to a place. The emotional significance of the group is associated with the affective dimension of home. Thus, home contributes to a social identity that is defined, to a certain extent, by the physical dimension of the home as well as the affective response to the place.

Social identity associated with home is important for the study of families in an increasingly mobile world. An important related notion is *diaspora,* which is a group of people who have been dispersed from their home for economic, social, or political reasons. Families who are displaced from a home region do not lose their sense of home or homeland, but often are waiting for an opportunity to go home. If they cannot go home, displaced families re-create home in a strange place generating a distinct social identity that is a combination of the new strange land of refuge and the homeland. For these families, daily living is oriented to the homeland but in a place that is not considered home. While some families are dispersed from their homes, other families choose to move because of the increasingly global market economy. What is not clear is how very mobile families manage their social identity and a sense of belonging associated with the familiarity and comfort of home while pursuing an income by moving repeatedly.

See also: COMMUTER MARRIAGES; COMPUTERS AND FAMILIES; FAMILY RITUALS; FOOD; HOMELESS FAMILIES; HOUSEWORK; HOUSING; MIGRATION; TELEVISION AND FAMILIES

Bibliography

Douglas, M. (1993). "The Idea of a Home: A Kind of Space." In *Home: A Place in the World,* ed. A. Mack. New York: New York University Press.

Fortier, A. (2000). *Migrant Belongings: Memory, Space, Identity.* New York: Berg.

Hayward, G. D. (1975). "Home as an Environmental and Psychological Concept." *Landscape* 20:2–9.

Hollander, J. (1993). "It All Depends." In *Home: A Place in the World,* ed. A. Mack. New York: New York University Press.

Johnson, P. J., and Suedfeld, P. (1996). "Coping With Stress Through Creating Microcosms Of Home And Family Among Arctic Whalers And Explorers." *The History of the Family: An International Quarterly* 1:41–62.

Lyman, S. M., and Scott, M. B. (1967). "Territoriality: A Neglected Sociological Dimension." *Social Problems* 15:236–249.

Rybczynski, W. (1986). *Home: A Short History of an Idea.* New York: Penguin Books.

Rykwert, J. (1993). "House and Home." In *Home: A Place in the World,* ed. A. Mack. New York: New York University Press.

Schama, S. (1987). *The Embarrassment of Riches: An Interpretation of Dutch Culture in the Golden Age.* New York: Alfred A. Knopf.

Schutz, A. (1945). "The Homecomer." *The American Journal of Sociology* 50:363–376.

Stone, L. (1991). "The Public and the Private in the Stately Homes of England, 1500-1990." *Social Research* 58:227–253.

Tajfel, H. (1981). *Human Groups and Social Categories: Studies in Social Psychology.* Cambridge: Cambridge University Press.

Wilson, P. J. (1988). *The Domestication of the Human Species.* New Haven, CT: Yale University Press.

SHEILA K. MARSHALL

HOME ECONOMICS

Home economics as a field of study in the United States was formed before the start of the twentieth century by a group of women, most of whom were scientifically educated and reform-oriented, as well as men who were interested in applying science and philosophy to improving everyday life. Frustrated by the lack of opportunity for educated women in the male-dominated disciplines, they met at the Lake Placid Club in upstate New York to create their own interdisciplinary field of study and profession. The Lake Placid Conferences on Home

Economics (1899–1909) culminated in the founding of the American Home Economics Association (AHEA) and the *Journal of Home Economics.* The field's mission has been to improve family well-being by enabling families to be successful in their reciprocal relationships with the environments in which they function. With the industrial revolution, some family functions shifted to factories, hotels, bakeries, restaurants, nursing homes, and schools, making policy concerns relevant. As a result, the field expanded its work, adding development, delivery, and evaluation of consumer goods and services; educating policy makers about concerns of the field; and attempting to shape social and even global change. Consequently, the field has provided many career options for both men and women in not-for-profit organizations, businesses, and government.

Social changes in the United States prompted the creation of specialization in many fields. These changes included exponential knowledge growth, the bustling economy during and after World War II, better public education that prepared more people for higher education, expanding public support for higher education, increasing government support of research, and developing specialized accreditation. Other changes also encouraged specilization within home economics; they included diversification of family structures, the aging population, increases in working women, technological changes, the women's movement, and increases in the number of men in the field.

For the first sixty years of the twentieth century, five specialty areas made up the core of this research-based field, but between 1970 and 2000, more distinct specializations developed (Richards 2000). The five specializations evolved as follows:

(1) Foods and nutrition, and institutional management added dietetics and food science;

(2) Child development and family relations later broadened to human development and family relations, adding family therapy as a specialization;

(3) Clothing and textiles became apparel and textiles and added textile science and merchandising of consumer goods;

(4) Housing and home furnishings developed into interior design of commercial as well as home interiors with particular emphasis on enhancing human well being;

(5) Consumer economics and home management evolved into family resource management, then family management, while consumer economics remained a specialization.

The name, *home economics,* became increasingly inaccurate in describing the work of this discipline with subspecialties studying different family functions and problems. In 1993 the new name, *family and consumer sciences,* was selected at a conference held in Scottsdale, Arizona, entitled *Positioning the Profession for the 21st Century.* Four of the five attending professional organizations (the American Home Economics Association, the American Vocational Association's Home Economic Division, the National Association of Extension Home Economics, and the National Council of Administrators of Home Economics) adopted the name change in 1994. The fifth chose *human sciences* instead. Internationally, the field is referred to primarily as home economics, but other names such as human ecology and home science are also used.

Scholarship and Practice

Family and consumer sciences represents a broader vision, revised conceptual framework, and reconceptualized core body of knowledge for the field. Increases in family and societal problems; ecological concerns and resource limitations; negative, unintended consequences of capitalism; the increasingly global economy; and increases in ethnic and racial diversity called into question the belief that science and its resulting technological developments would solve all our problems. Continuous progress could no longer be considered inevitable. Clearly the step-by-step procedures and sequential problem-solving processes used by laboratory science would not provide predictable results in solving human problems. Even problems themselves were re-conceptualized as opportunities for learning rather than something to be avoided (Richards 2000). These intellectual changes in the field's root disciplines (chemistry, biology, physics, math, philosophy, psychology, sociology, economics, and the arts and humanities) as well as in home economics itself, reinforced a shift away from technical information and procedures toward critical and creative thinking and ethical reasoning.

Traditionally, professionals in the field have studied the everyday lives of individuals in the family as the fundamental social unit, as well as the family's interactions with the larger environments. Over time, the field's increasingly strong specializations became disciplines in their own right, even though they remain vital to the interdisciplinary field as a whole. No other profession or discipline has such a holistic approach to studying and optimizing family life with emphasis on problem prevention.

In the United States and Australia, some professionals embraced Marjorie Brown and Beatrice Paolucci's 1979 definition of the field as a critical science. They question the continuing dominance of scientific reasoning; encourage examination of the field's purposes, assumptions and questions; and urge it to renew its focus on enabling families themselves to foster the development of healthy, responsible, capable and compassionate individuals. Brown and Paolucci also argued that individuals and families should reflectively participate in the critique and formulation of social goals and means of accomplishing them. Using Jürgen Habermas's philosophy as a basis for their new conceptualization, they argued that synthesis of analytical-empirical, interpretive, and emancipatory knowledge (resulting from use of critical theory) was necessary to address practical problems of families politically, ethically, socially, physically, economically, and psychologically. This requires increased critical thinking and moral reasoning; theoretical and interdisciplinary work; evaluation of existing social practices, norms, and assumptions; and emancipation from ignorance and distorted views resulting from such things as prejudice, trauma, repression, oppression, and useless conventions. Critical science emphasizes political-moral action.

International Contributions

Over the years, home economists in other countries have contributed significantly to strengthening programs aimed at women, families, and children (O'Toole and Nelson 1988), and to formally and informally educating women, increasing understanding and appreciation of other cultures, improving public health, and improving the process of introducing change (O'Toole et al. 1988). Home economists in the United States began to become involved outside their country at the start of the twentieth century when mission boards hired graduates to assist in establishing home economics

Ellen Henrietta Swallow Richards was the first president of the American Home Economics Association. THE LIBRARY OF CONGRESS

departments in schools and colleges in other countries to improve the living conditions of the people with whom the missionaries worked (O'Toole and Nelson 1988).

Several professional organizations also have facilitated international involvement. The International Federation of Home Economics, IFHE; the American Home Economics Association (now the American Association of Family and Consumer Sciences, AAFCS; and the American Association of State Universities and Land Grant Colleges, AASULGC (now the National Association of State Universities and Land-Grant Colleges, NASULGC) have been active internationally. The IFHE is the only international nongovernmental professional organization concerned with home economics as a whole. Founded in 1908 in Friburg, Switzerland, IFHE brings together institutions, organizations, associations, and individuals from more than 110 countries worldwide to further the mission of home economics. IFHE has been involved with several United Nations Conferences on Women, including the 1995 Beijing conference. It has consultative status with UCOSOC (United Nations Economic and Social Council), UNESCO (United Nations Education, Scientific, and Cultural Organization), FAO (Food and Agricultural Organization), UNICEF (United Nations International Children's Emergency Fund), and other United Nations and international agencies. IFHE also cooperates with other international nongovernmental organizations related to home economics to strengthen and promote home economics concerns and exchange information (Davis 1999).

The AHEA's affiliation with IFHE began in 1915 (Nelson 1984), only a few years after its own 1909 founding. More extensive involvement began in 1922 when AHEA sent delegates to the Third International Congress in Paris (Davis 1999). This European professional work influenced the early development of home economics in the United States, discouraging emphasis on mere techniques and increasing attention to the thought patterns involved in education for family life. After the 1958 IFHE Congress in Maryland, U.S. memberships, attendance at congresses, and participation on the elected IFHE Council increased (Nelson 1984).

The AHEA published a steady stream of articles in its journals and multiple nonserial publications; it has also adopted almost twenty resolutions on international topics resulting from its members' international work. The association sent teachers to China in 1915, to Europe for home economics teacher exchanges after World War I, and to Turkey in 1920 to facilitate university program development. By 1959 more than 100 home economists were serving overseas (Davis 1999). In the 1960s and 1970s, home economists worked in multilateral efforts in such United Nations agencies as FAO, WHO (World Health Organization), UNICEF, ILO (International Labor Organization), and UNESCO. The AHEA was an invited member of the U.S. National Commission for UNESCO in the 1960s and 1980s.

Work of home economists from the United States with international visitors and students here and abroad has clearly had an impact on families bilaterally. Perhaps the greatest globally has resulted from AHEA/AAFCS sponsorship, beginning in 1930, of hundreds of international students who sought to do graduate study in the United States (Nelson 1984). Recipients have come from a wide variety of countries to study in various institutions, and many returned home to take leadership positions.

Since its creation in 1976, the AHEA/AAFCS International Section has conducted many national and international workshops and international projects. It has cooperated with other association sections and divisions, producing publications, working with many other national and international organizations, and facilitating contacts for members wanting to be internationally involved (Davis 1999). For example, concern about world population growth and hunger prompted AHEA collaboration with USAID (Agency for International Development), UN agencies, and the International Planned Parenthood Federation to initiate the International Family Planning Project that served thirty countries in the 1970s (Davis 1999; O'Toole and Nelson 1988). Other efforts included the Inter-American Commission on Women and foreign government collaborations. The necessity of developing U.S. global appreciation led to the AHEA-USAID Global Connections project. In it, home economists developed *country profiles* on daily life in thirteen countries to teach thousands of students, members, and adult education program participants more about the world. In the 1980s and 1990s the demand for professionals overseas with multi- and bilateral agencies declined, but educational institution study and research opportunities grew (Davis 1999).

As a higher education administrators' organization, AASULGC/NASULGC members encouraged their faculty and extension specialists to do international work. They sponsored conferences funded through U.S. government programs and universities. The early government aid programs influenced the education, role, and status of women in other countries and helped to create an awareness of the meaning of home economics and its value to individuals and families. The Pan American Union (renamed The Organization of American States in 1948) opened opportunities between the 1930s and 1950s for extension home economists to help rural families train local leaders (O'Toole and Nelson 1988). In the 1940s, U.S. foreign aid to Europe and developing countries provided home economists with assignments in Greece and Turkey as consultants and advisors, helping to establish home economics extension and college programs. In post-World War II Europe (1948–1950), home economists were an important part of the Marshall Plan Economic Recovery Program, working in conjunction with the U.S. government, the YWCA, YMCA, and the Fulbright exchange program. Home economists continue to participate in Fulbright programs. During the Kennedy administration home economists were involved in USAID, the Peace Corps, and the Alliance for Progress in Latin America. After 1955 a shift in U.S. foreign aid brought requests for assistance in establishing home economics in schools at all levels and extension community development programs in India and Pakistan.

The strength and vitality of home economics varies worldwide. In Asia, it is strong in higher education. Advances are being made in many Asian countries; research is being conducted, and the discipline is attracting significant numbers of young people. In Latin America there are few units in higher education institutions, but more at the intermediate level in teacher-training programs. However, both Brazil and Colombia have strong higher education programs. In Central and Eastern Europe, home economics training is growing as a result of work done by the IFHE Committee on Outreach.

See also: DIVISION OF LABOR; HOUSEWORK; HUMAN ECOLOGY THEORY; RESOURCE MANAGEMENT

Bibliography

Brown, M. M., and Paolucci, B. (1979). *Home Economics: A Definition*. Washington, DC: American Home Economics Association.

Davis, M. L. (1999). "'International' in AAFCS: A New Perspective." *Journal of Family and Consumer Sciences* 91(5):15–19.

Green, K. B. (1990). "Our Intellectual Ecology: A Treatise on Home Economics." *Journal of Home Economics* 82(Fall):41–47.

Leidenfrost, N. B., ed. (1992). *Families in Transition*. Vienna: International Federation of Home Economics.

Nelson, L. (1984). "International Ventures." In *Definitive Themes in Home Economics and Their Impact on Families 1909–1984*. Washington, DC: American Home Economics Association.

Nickols, S. Y. (2001). "Keeping the Betty Lamp Burning." *Journal of Family and Consumer Sciences* 93(3):35–44.

O'Toole, L.; Mallory, B.; and Nelson, L., eds. (1988). *The International Heritage of Home Economics in the United States*. Washington, DC: American Home Economics Association.

O'Toole, L., and Nelson, L. (1988). "United States Government and Private International Programs and Funding Influencing Involvement of Home Economists in International Programs." In *The International Heritage of Home Economics in the United States*. Washington, DC: American Home Economics Association.

Richards, V. (2000). "The Postmodern Perspective on Home Economics History." *Journal of Family and Consumer Sciences* 92(1):8–11.

Stage, S., and Vincenti, V. B. (1997). *Rethinking Home Economics: Women and the History of a Profession*. Ithaca, NY: Cornell University Press.

VIRGINIA B. VINCENTI

HOMELESS FAMILIES

Homeless families are those that either lack shelter or have shelter that is so inadequate, temporary, or insecure that the situation threatens the social, psychological, or physical health of the family. Homeless families are a departure from the classic homeless image of the single male, detached from society and disaffiliated from kin, friends, and work.

Homeless families receive attention in large part because the presence of children among the homeless confronts society directly with its failure to guarantee a minimum standard of protection. The questions of who these families are, how they became homeless, and how their homelessness can be prevented and ameliorated carry an urgency that contrasts with more blaming attitudes towards the single homeless individual.

Prevalence of Family Homelessness

It is difficult to ascertain the numbers of homeless families. Few countries systematically enumerate the homeless in their national censuses, and unless the families reside in a public shelter, they are difficult to locate. Homeless families may not want to be found for fear of involvement of child welfare authorities. Furthermore, it is not known how many families are doubled up, sleep in vacant buildings, or separate due to lack of housing. At times the single female homeless person may be a woman who has recently lost custody of her children, and this may also mask the true prevalence of homeless families.

What proportion of the homeless population in the United States is comprised of families? Census 2000 counted 170,706 individuals living in emergency and transitional shelters for the homeless, out of a total US population of 281,421,906, or .6 percent of the population (Smith and Smith 2001). Of this number approximately 25.7 percent were under eighteen years old. The 1996 National Survey of Homeless Assistance Providers and Clients (NSHAPC) (Burt et al. 1999) gathered information on homelessness from a statistical sample of homeless-serving agencies in the US and found that 15 percent of all *homeless households* were families consisting of a homeless individual with one or more minor children with them. However, if one considers all *homeless individuals* including minor children, then 34 percent of homeless people found at homeless assistance program were members of homeless families. Of the minor children living with their homeless parent, 20 percent were infants and toddlers (up to age two), 22 percent were preschoolers (ages three to five), 33 percent were elementary school age (six to twelve) and 20 percent were adolescents (twelve to seventeen) (National Survey of Homeless Assistance Providers and Clients NSHAPC 1999).

Most research on homeless families is conducted in emergency shelters for families. This poses the question of whether we are actually studying the *services* for the homeless rather than the phenomenon itself. It then becomes necessary to ask, if many communities are more comfortable in providing services for homeless families than for single people, whether it is correct to conclude that a large proportion of the homeless population are living in families.

Worldwide, the United Nations estimates that one billion people live in conditions of inadequate shelter or literal homelessness. Most of these people are families who are driven to living in squatter settlements due to rural-to-urban migration, severe unemployment and underemployment, and the existence of large numbers of refugees and victims of disasters (United Nations Centre for Human Settlement 1990; Glasser 1994; Bascom 1993).

Causes of Family Homelessness

A major cause of family homelessness in the urban centers of North America and Western Europe is the shortage of affordable housing. Cities have been transformed from manufacturing to service-based economies, and offices, retail complexes, and luxury high-rise apartments have replaced low-rent housing. A widely used word for this process is *gentrification,* a term introduced by Glass (1964), to describe the phenomenon in the 1960s whereby the British gentry bought and renovated old buildings in London.

The problem of the dearth of affordable housing is compounded by the large percentage of family income that poor families spend on rent. According to the National Coalition for the Homeless (1999) and the National Low Income Housing Coalition (1998), a minimum wage earner would have to work eighty-seven hours per week in a median cost state in order to afford a two-bedroom apartment at the 30 percent of one's income that is considered affordable by the U.S. government. If a family receives the financial assistance program Temporary Assistance to Needy Families (TANF), the family will be at or below the federal poverty level and will therefore compete for the limited number of public housing or rent-subsidized housing units available.

One productive method of uncovering causes of family homelessness is to look for two similar societies that have very different rates of family homelessness. Working alone and together in Hartford, Connecticut, and Quebec City, Quebec, Irene Glasser, Louise Fournier, and André Costopolous (1999) found that although both cities have a homeless population, Quebec City has approximately one-tenth the number of people living in its short-term and long-term shelter beds as has Hartford, and no apparent family homelessness.

The most obvious explanation for the absence of family homelessness in Quebec is the larger number of safety net programs in the province of Quebec and in Canada in general. With the greater amount and availability of financial assistance, a family is able to find and keep its housing despite

The presence of children among the homeless gives a sense of urgency to the problem of homelessness and calls attention to society's failure to guarantee adequate protection to families. TONY FREEMAN/PHOTOEDIT

emergencies such as the loss of a job or family separations. An alternative hypothesis is that families with severe problems are separated by the child protection authorities sooner and more frequently in Quebec, and therefore to do not present themselves as homeless families.

In addition to the structural problems of lack of affordable housing and very low income from welfare or work, families also face personal problems that may push them into homelessness. For example, fleeing domestic violence is one path to homelessness. A victim (most often a woman) may first take refuge in a domestic violence shelter, but when the crisis is resolved, and she still has no housing, she may have to move into a homeless shelter (Glasser and Zywiak 2000). Further, addiction to alcohol or drugs may affect parents, severely interfering with their ability to house their family. Moving into a shelter may be considered a first step in treatment, especially if the shelter has the ability to diagnose the addiction and facilitate treatment.

Adaptations to Homelessness

Probably the least researched but most common adaptation to homelessness is that of living with another poor family on a very temporary basis. This is referred to as *doubling-up* and is often a precursor to life on the streets, or in encampments and shelters. The U.S. Census Bureau estimated that in 1999 there were 1,428,000 unrelated *sub-families* or .5 percent of the total family population. These subfamilies are generally thought to be the doubled-up. Their poverty rate was 39 percent in contrast to the 10 percent poverty rate of all families (U.S. Census Bureau 2000).

The pioneering work of Janet Fitchen (1996) on rural homelessness in New York State documented that a frequent response to poverty was to squeeze two families into a trailer or apartment that was already too small for one. These arrangements were often short-lived, as the strain of the situation made life unbearable. Doubling-up was associated with a worsening economy in rural areas due to the large loss of manufacturing jobs and the rise of single motherhood in which income (through work or welfare) was not adequate to pay rent. Fitchen (1992) also found that at times enforcing building codes on a family living in a crumbling farmhouse or a tarpaper-sided shack pushed a family from being a homeowner to being a renter of unaffordable apartments, and eventually, into homelessness.

Anna Lou Dehavenon (1996) documented the relationship between doubling-up and homelessness in New York City's Emergency Assistance Units (EAUs) program, which places homeless families in temporary shelters. The EAUs' policy was to send homeless families back into doubled-up situations, from which 78 percent of them had just come. Although 92 percent of the guest families paid the host families rent, the guest families could not live together in these severely overcrowded conditions.

In the developing world the major adaptation to homelessness for hundreds of thousands of people is to live in squatter settlements. *Squatting,* as a generic term, refers to building a shelter of easily found materials on property to which one has no legal claim. These settlements are known by many terms, including *bidonvilles* (tin cities) in Africa, *favelas* in Brazil, and *pueblos jovénes* (young towns) in Peru, and pavement dwellers in India. The harsh realities of living in a Brazilian *favela* were documented by Carolina De Jesus in the now-classic *Child of the Dark* (1963), one of the few such first-person accounts.

Although squatter settlements were initially thought of as temporary, makeshift arrangements for new rural migrants to urban areas, by the late 1960s, squatter settlements were seen as rational alternatives to the housing shortage for low-income people (Turner 1976). Some governments shifted from a policy of demolishing the settlements to projects bringing them clean water, sanitation, electricity, and security of tenure. Critics of governmental encouragement of self-help point out that this absolves governments from committing significant amounts of money to housing their population and also reduces the wage requirements of workers by giving them access to low-cost housing.

In an in-depth study of the squatters of vacant public housing in and around Paris, Guy Boudimbou (1992) found that most of the squatters were Northern and West African immigrant families who faced significant housing discrimination. One form of adaptation was for a network of squatters to move from one vacant building to another, sometimes with the help of "managers," some of whom collected the rent but were not able to produce an apartment.

Contrasting the Poor-but-Housed with Homeless Families

Further insight into homeless families comes from comparing them to poor-but-housed families. In a study of social relationships, 677 homeless mothers and 495 poor-but-housed mothers were interviewed in New York City (Shinn, Knickman, and Weitzman 1991). The homeless families were interviewed at the time of their request for shelter to avoid confusing characteristics *caused* by residence in the shelter with characteristics of the families themselves. A surprising finding was that the homeless respondents in fact were in greater touch with their social networks than their housed counterparts. However, the homeless respondents were less able to stay with relatives and friends, in large part because they had already worn out their welcome by having stayed with them previously.

Ellen L. Bassuk and John Buchner (1997) contrasted a sample of single mothers and their children living in shelters in Worcester, Massachusetts, with a sample of low-income single mothers who had never been homeless. Mothers of the homeless families were more likely to have been in foster-care placement and to have had a female caregiver who used drugs. In their adult lives they had lived in the area for a shorter period of time. They were also more likely to be African American or Puerto Rican. Factors that prevented homelessness for the poor families were linked with the mother's being a primary tenant (her name was on the lease), receiving monetary housing subsidies, and having a larger social network.

Programs that House Homeless Families

Shelters. Shelters are low-barrier, easy access congregate living for families for a short period of time (two to three months). They are frequently administered by community organizations, and their major form of treatment is case management, which seeks to re-house the family. Family shelters are usually dry—no drug or alcohol use. They may require that the adults be involved in substance-abuse treatment, mental health counseling, education, or job training, or be employed. A real problem for families living in shelters is that many family shelters bar fathers and adolescent boys from staying with the families, in effect splitting up the family (Susser 1993; Friedman 2000).

Transitional and supportive housing. In the United States, by the mid-1980s, a pattern was developing in which at least some of the homeless population experienced repeated episodes of shelter living. Many people were not able to make the transition from shelter to apartment living and were in need of more support in order to maintain permanent housing. This support came in the form of transitional housing, which generally consists of housing with two years of services; and supportive housing, which is housing with the provision of services for an open-ended period of time. Transitional and supportive housing may be provided in one physical space, or they may be provided in scattered apartments in publicly or privately owned buildings, with services brought in to the families. In many communities, these programs are better tolerated than shelters, which are often viewed with fear and suspicion.

An interesting approach to transitional housing is finding foster families for homeless families. Utilizing their experience in providing foster care to children, and noting the lack of social support and sense of isolation that was found in homeless families, the Human Service Associates (HAS), a private, nonprofit, child-placing agency in St. Paul, Minnesota, placed thirty-four families with host

families (Cornish 1992). An evaluation of the project found that 60 percent of the foster families co-resided with the host family for a period of four to six months, then moved into their own housing, and were still in their own housing six months later.

Homesteading. As in the pioneer frontier days of the United States and Canada, urban homesteading represents one strategy for providing housing. An example of contemporary homesteading is Harding Park, located on the waterfront in the Bronx, New York, a twenty-acre community, which now has 250 small homes on it. The area, which had been a weekend campsite for apartment dwellers since the early 1900s, became a refuge for mostly Puerto Rican residents living in high-crime neighborhoods in the Bronx, who found a tract of dilapidated shacks at the water's edge. The area was reminiscent of the fishing villages of Puerto Rico, and through their own labor and materials, and with permission from the City of New York, these modern homesteaders turned the shacks into habitable houses (Glasser and Bridgman 1999).

Eviction prevention. One strategy that prevents homelessness among families is resolving landlord-tenant disputes to avoid evictions. An example is the Tenancy Settlement/Mediation Program in Passaic County, New Jersey, an area with a declining amount of residential housing, a deteriorating economic base, and high rates of poverty and public assistance. The program is staffed by social workers trained in mediation and serves sixteen municipalities with a combined population of 500,000 people. In 1990, approximately 1,300 tenancy disputes were successfully settled, which reflects an 89.5 percent success rate (Curcio 1992).

Community development of squatter settlements. Some developing countries have programs that enable squatter settlements to upgrade their housing, bring in essential services (potable water, sanitation, and electricity), and secure the individual's right to remain in the housing. The World Bank is one of the leaders in the lending of money for squatter upgrading projects, which usually feature a strong self-help component. In some parts of the world, households get together to build each other's houses; in others, the household hires people to work for them; in still others, the household builds the house on its own (Keare and Parris 1982).

One successful example of squatter upgrading has been the Kampung Improvement Programme in Jakarta, Indonesia. A kampung is a village, but in Jakarta it refers to urban settlements on swampy land, subject to serious flooding. The Kampung Improvement Programme provided eighty-seven kampungs (more than one million people) with clean water, canals to mitigate flooding, improved roads and concrete paths, communal sanitation, and a system of garbage disposal. A World Bank Loan in 1974 added schools and health clinics. One major finding of this project was that bringing these services to the community inspired individual householders to improve their dwellings (Oliver 1987).

Conclusion

Examination of homeless families presents a tremendously diverse picture of the face of homelessness. The common thread is that families living in shelters, doubling-up, or in squatter settlements face enormous barriers to being able to nurture and educate their children adequately. Under these circumstances homeless families may eventually lose their ability to function as a family. Therefore, adequate and secure housing is essential in keeping families together; it is the anchor that underlies the very concept of family. Although the problem of homeless families remains substantial, creative approaches to providing permanent housing for families have been discovered in both the industrialized and the developing world. The best of these projects tap into the strengths and active participation of the families.

See also: CHRONIC ILLNESS; HEALTH AND FAMILIES; HOME; HOUSING; MIGRATION; POVERTY; SUBSTANCE ABUSE; UNEMPLOYMENT

Bibliography

Bascom, J. (1993). "Internal Refugees: The Case of the Displaced in Khartoum." In *Geography and Refugees: Patterns and Processes for Change,* ed. R. Black and V. Robinson. London: Belhaven Press.

Bassuk, E. L., and Buchner, J. C. (1997). "Homelessness in Female-Headed Families: Childhood and Adult Risk Factors." *American Journal of Public Health* 87(2):241–248.

Boudimbou, G. (1992). "Les Immigrés Africains et le Squatt des Logements Sociaux dans la Région Parisienne." Paper presented at the Fifth International Research Conference on Housing, Montreal.

Burt, M. R. (1992). *Over the Edge: The Growth of Homelessness in the 1980s.* New York: Russell Sage Foundation.

Burt, M., et al. (1999). *Homelessness: Programs and the People They Serve: Findings of the National Survey of Homeless Assistance Providers and Clients, Summary.* Washington, DC: Urban Institute

Cornish, J. (1992). "Fostering Homeless Children and Their Parents Too: A Unique Approach to Transitional Housing for Homeless Families." *Community Alternatives: International Journal of Family Care* 4(2):43–59.

Curcio, W. (1992). "Mediation and Homelessness." *Public Welfare* (Spring):34–39.

Dehavenon, A. L. (1996). "Doubling Up and New York City's Policies for Sheltering Homeless Families." In *There's No Place Like Home: Anthropological Perspectives on Housing and Homelessness in the United States,* ed. A. L. Dehavenon. Westport, CT: Bergin & Garvey.

De Jesus, C. (1963). *Child of the Dark: The Diary of Carolina Maria De Jesus.* Translated from the Portuguese. New York: New American Library.

Fitchen, J. (1992). "On the Edge of Homelessness: Rural Poverty and Housing Insecurity." *Rural Sociology* 57:173–193.

Fitchen, J. (1996). "Rural Upstate New York." In *There's No Place Like Home: Anthropological Perspectives on Housing and Homelessness in the United States,* ed. A. L. Dehavenon. Westport, CT: Bergin & Garvey.

Friedman, D. H. (2000). *Parenting in Public: Family Shelter and Public Assistance.* New York: Columbia University Press.

Glass, R. (1964). *London: Aspects of Change.* London: Centre for Urban Studies and MacGillion & Kee.

Glasser, I. (1994). *Homelessness in Global Perspective.* New York: G. K. Hall.

Glasser, I. and Bridgman, R. (1999). *Braving the Street: The Anthropology of Homelessness.* New York: Berghahn Books.

Glasser, I.; Fournier, L.; and Costopoulos, A. (1999). "Homelessness in Quebec City, Quebec and Hartford, Connecticut: A Cross-National and Cross Cultural Analysis." *Urban Anthropology and Studies of Cultural Systems and World Economic Development* 28(2):141–164.

Glasser, I. and Zywiak, W. (2000). *Census and Brief Assessment of the Homeless of Hartford.* Hartford, CT: Office of Grants Management.

Keare, D. H., and Parris, S. (1982). *Evaluation of Shelter Programs of the Urban Poor: Principal Findings.*

World Bank Staff Working Papers No. 547. Washington, DC: World Bank.

McChesney, K. Y. (1995). "A Review of the Empirical Literature on Contemporary Urban Homeless Families." *Social Service Review* (September):429–460.

Oliver, P. (1987). *Dwellings: The House Across the World* Austin: University of Texas Press.

Shinn, M.; Knickman, J. R.; and Weitzman, B. C. (1991). "Social Relationships and Vulnerability to Becoming Homeless Among Poor Families." *American Psychologist* 46:1180–1187.

Smith, A. C., and Smith, D. I. (2001). *Emergency and Transitional Shelter Population: 2000.* US Census Bureau, Census Special Reports, Series CENSR/01-2. Washington, DC: US Government Printing Office

Susser, I. (1993). "Creating Family Forms: The Exclusion of Men and Teenage Boys from Families in the New York City Shelter System, 1987–91." *Critique of Anthropology* 13(3):267–283.

United Nations Centre for Human Settlements (Habitat). (1990). *Shelter: From Projects to National Strategies.* Nairobi, Kenya: Author.

Other Resources

National Coalition for the Homeless. (1999). *Homeless Families with Children.* NCH Fact Sheet #17. Available from http://www.nationalhomeless.org/families.html.

National Low Income Housing Coalition. (1998). *Out of Reach: Rental Housing at What Cost?* Available from http://www.nlihc.org/oor98/index.htm.

U.S. Census Bureau. (2000). "Poverty 1999." *March 1999 and 2000 Current Population Surveys.* Available from http://www.census.gov.

U.S. Conference of Mayors. (1998). *A Status Report on Hunger and Homelessness in America's Cites: 1998.* Available from http://www.usmayors.org/uscm/homeless/hhsummary.html.

IRENE GLASSER

HOMESCHOOLING

Homeschooling is a form of education for children and youth that is based mainly in the home and is clearly directed by their parents. Parents retain the main responsibility for and authority over their children's education and training, rather than sending them away to classroom institutions where their education would be controlled and conducted largely by nonfamily state or private teachers.

Homeschool students typically study and learn most of their subjects (e.g., reading, writing, mathematics, science, history, geography, art, music) in their homes using a variety of curriculum materials, such as classic literature, textbooks, periodicals, newspapers, computer software, Internet resources, and common household materials (e.g., kitchen equipment; cooking supplies; and tools for carpentry, gardening, and farming). Research has consistently shown that children who are home educated score fifteen to thirty percentile points higher on standardized academic achievement tests than do public-school students (Ray 2000b; Rudner 1999). They also commonly participate in educational cooperatives with a few other families and in a wide variety of community activities, such as Boy and Girl Scouting organizations, 4-H, political associations, as well as activities associated with churches, synagogues, and temples. A growing body of research shows that homeschool children do well socially, emotionally, and psychologically (Medlin 2000).

Although home-based and parent-led education was the norm throughout many centuries of history in most nations, it waned to near extinction in most countries by the mid-nineteenth century. Homeschooling has experienced a remarkable renewal, however, in several Western nations such as Australia, Canada, Great Britain, and the United States. It is also beginning to increase in such other nations as Japan, South Africa, Russia, and Germany (Ray 1997). It was estimated, for example, that about 1.8 million primary and secondary students were homeschooled in the United States and 78,000 in Canada during the spring of 2002 (Ray 2002).

Many scholars and social commentators think that homeschooling is one of the most notable familial, social, and educational phenomena of the late twentieth century. For example, Patricia M. Lines wrote in *The Public Interest* (2000, pp. 74, 85):

> The rise of homeschooling is one of the most significant social trends of the past half century. . . . It is too early to tell whether homeschooling will establish itself as a major alternative to the modern

school. But some things are clear: Homeschooling is becoming more common and more widely accepted. American families from diverse backgrounds resort to homeschooling because they are dissatisfied with the philosophy, the content, or the quality of American schools. The great majority of homeschooling families are not separatists and isolationists but active members of civil society. They seek to improve this nation, but they want to raise and educate their children in the meantime. Ultimately, they may help to inspire a great renewal of American education, or at least preserve values and ideas that are out of fashion within the education establishment.

Although Lines specifically mentioned homeschooling in the United States, research and popular writings make it apparent that her observations apply internationally to the parents, children, and youth involved in homeschooling.

Family Connectedness and Relationships

Homeschooling clearly puts fathers and mothers in a position of being connected to, responsible for, and having authority over their children. This is because homeschooling returns a critical social function—the education of children—to the family. A long and gradual history of social events and accepted conventions over the past 150 years, however, placed specially trained persons into the role of teachers of children. These events also drew many crucial educational functions out of the home environment, away from parents and into institutions, most state-controlled but some private. Allan C. Carlson, historian and organizer of the international World Congress of Families held in Switzerland, explains much of this in *From Cottage to Work Station* (1993) as he describes ". . . the steady dismantling of the home-centered economy . . ." (p. 17). Institutional schooling places institutionally trained teachers in authority over children and puts these teachers *in loco parentis* (i.e., in place of the parents). Children and youth in schools, therefore, ascribe to these teachers great prestige and influence in their own lives regarding matters of knowledge, values, beliefs, and worldview (Good and Brophy 1987; Blizek 2000; Brophy 1996).

Whereas historically children once accepted their parents as the primary authorities in their lives, increased institutional schooling shifted the locus of authority and control to state and private schools and personnel. Modern home-based and parent-led education reverses this trend because parents continue the education of their children under their own direction (or retrieve them from institutional schools where they had sent them). The parents, therefore, are able to select learning activities, curriculum materials, and community and social activities that are consistent with their own family's values and beliefs and what they think is best for the upbringing of their children. Research shows that institutional school children are more peer-dependent than are homeschooled children; that is, institutional school children exhibit a ". . . significantly greater focus on peers and nonfamily individuals than do the home educated" (Delahooke 1986, p. xiv). Research also indicates ". . . that there are stabilizing forces within home school family systems which allow most of these families to accommodate higher levels of both adaptability and cohesion than the population of families whose children are more conventionally schooled" (Allie-Carson 1990, p. 17).

Many professionals and laypersons today assume, without research evidence, that for normal social and psychological development, children need day-long interaction with same-age peers for five to six days per week. Modern homeschoolers, however, are providing evidence to the contrary and supporting centuries of social history. Research is revealing that due to the increased time together and sharing of experiences between parents and their home-educated children, their social capital (i.e., social relations such as trust and love) is increasing (Coleman and Hoffer 1987; Ray 1990). Their daily increased time, adult-child interaction, and opportunities to reach common goals allow them to establish stronger familial bonds, more trust, and enhanced communication into and through the years of young adulthood than would be possible if the children and youth spent less time with their parents and more with their peers (Allie-Carson 1990; Delahooke 1986; Wartes 1992).

In a similar manner, home-educated children spend more time with their siblings and therefore have more opportunity to develop close ties with them. Rather than focusing large amounts of attention on their nonfamily same-age peers, homeschoolers are able to learn with their brothers and sisters, teach and care for their younger siblings, model after their older siblings, and share in daily real-life experiences with one another. There is evidence that this is leading to stronger life-long bonds among siblings than is likely among siblings who spend about forty hours per week with non-sibling same-age peers (Ray 2002).

Many homeschool families are also integrating multiple generations into the education of the children. Education based at home and in the family increases the likelihood that grandparents, aunts and uncles, and other older community members will participate in the education of the children. The more organic and flexible time schedule and the inviting nature of the home environment are welcoming to extended family members to participate in the educational enterprise. The children and youth then learn from a wider variety of ages of family and local community members. Simultaneously the grandparents and others have an important role to play in the family and society during their senior years of life (Lowe and Thomas 2002; Sheffer 1995).

Finally, research indicates that the overall effect of homeschooling on children and youth is to prepare them for healthy and virtuous relationships within and outside of their families. The psychologist Richard G. Medlin stated in "Homeschooling and the Question of Socialization" (2000), a review of research to date, that several conclusions could be made about homeschooling and socialization, although many unanswered questions remain. The conclusions were, first, that homeschool children are taking part in the daily routines of their communities. Second, they are not socially isolated and, in fact, associate with—and feel close to—many kinds of people. Third, homeschool parents are concerned about their children's long-term social development and actively encourage their children to participate in social opportunities outside the family. Fourth, homeschool children acquire the rules of behavior and systems of beliefs and attitudes that they need for successful living. Fifth, they have healthy self-esteem and are likely to display fewer behavior problems than do those in institutional schools. Sixth, they may have better leadership skills and be more socially mature than others. Finally, they appear to be functioning effectively as members of adult society.

Effects on Marriage

Homeschooling affects marriage in several ways. First, homeschooling provides an opportunity for husband and wife to have much greater authority over the historically most intimate and significant gift and asset in their lives, their children. Modern society, especially in the more developed nations, puts great emphasis on specialization of labor roles. This specialization has removed many roles from the husband/wife unity and the sphere of the family. Husbands/fathers daily go off to the workplace and perhaps a majority of wives/mothers do the same, while their children go off to be taught by specialists over whom the man and woman generally have minimal influence. The married couple has little control over the role models their children will have, the information that they will be taught, and the values and beliefs with which they will be indoctrinated for twelve years, two hundred days per year. Communicating in general, formulating personal philosophical and religious beliefs, and working together to fashion the education of their offspring gives new life to one of the historically most significant functions of marriage—procreation and the nurturing and upbringing of children. In turn, this strengthens the marriage by providing a common goal that the couple has increased potential to achieve. They are empowered as a marriage unity. The shared task of the education of their children brings them together as a duo that is working toward a noble end (Carlson 1995; McDowell 1998).

Second, homeschooling one's children gives adults—parents—something significant to do. This is especially important because many adults in industrialized and technological societies have little they do in life that they consider important in terms of communal, national, or international significance (Carlson 1993, 1995; McElroy 2002; Sheffer 1995). That every society thinks that schooling is a crucial issue and the colloquialism "The hand that rocks the cradle rules the world" together underscore the consequential nature of education. Doing something important together increases the self-confidence and sense of personal value of these adults and therefore enhances the marriage bond.

Third, the homeschooling of children keeps with or returns to the couple a time- and energy-consuming task. Rather than depending on others to teach their children, they must cooperate and

These children are educated by their parents in the same subjects that are taught in public and private schools. Research reveals that homeschooled children outperform public-school students on standardized tests. ED KASHI/CORBIS

develop an effective plan for doing it themselves. Homeschooling may yield long-term benefits (e.g., fewer learning difficulties, fewer social problems with peer pressure) that will save time and energy, but in the short term it is hard work. It is especially hard work for the one parent, usually the mother, who does most of the daily formal teaching. If not maturely approached, this may present stress, imbalance, or tension that will lead to degeneration of the marriage relationship. On the other hand, the husband and wife may use it as an opportunity to work well together and strengthen the marriage bond and reap the long-term benefits of an academically successful and emotionally and socially well-adjusted adolescent (Allie-Carson 1990; McDowell 1998; Page 1997).

Fourth, home-based education generally requires either the husband or the wife to be at home most of the time. Therefore, only one will probably work outside the home, which may reduce the family's income potential. In turn, this may reduce

their standard of living by some physical measures. Many homeschool couples argue, however, that the intangible benefits of improved marriage unity, family cohesiveness, and children's academic and social successes actually increase their holistically viewed standard of living (Lyster-Mensh 2000; McElroy 2002; Ray 2002; Lyman 2001).

Edification of the Natural Family

Carlson directly addresses homeschooling in an essay subtitled "Family Lessons from the New Agrarians" (2001). He explains that although the Agrarians—those writers and thinkers who, grappling with modernity, moved ideas toward decentralization during the twentieth century—understood that the weakness of families largely derived from surrendering key family functions, none of them saw the possibility of restoring home-based education as a first step toward family reconstruction. Several scholars and social, religious, and political leaders, internationally, present parent-led education and upbringing as a key function of the natural family to be protected, if not encouraged, by society (Pruzan 1998; World Congress of Families 2001). Many began during the end of the twentieth century to see home-based education as a robust way to rebuild the natural family. Carlson (1995, pp. 7, 8) argued:

> The education of children must be home-centered, where parents impart *their* visions, values, virtues, and skills to the new generation. These statements reinforce the historical significance of *home schooling*, rising throughout the globe . . . , as *the necessary and powerful step* in family reconstruction. Households, in turn, adhere to kin groups—extended or "stem" families—that give focus to ambition and talent, and grant protection to individuals from the grand ambitions of ideologues. These kin groups, in turn, form communities: villages, towns, or neighborhoods. . . . This sense of close community also offers the only *effective* protection of individuals from pathologies *within* households, . . . without threatening the normative pattern of family living.

State Versus Family

The majority of children worldwide, the future citizens and leaders of the nations, are taught, trained, and indoctrinated in state-controlled schools (World Bank Group 2002). The trend over the past 150 years has been for ever-increasing state education of children. In the United States about 88 percent of all citizens are educated in public schools for their primary and secondary school years. Homeschooling is the antithesis to this arrangement. Home-based education moves the locus of control over academic education, skill training, and indoctrination to the parents and the family system, both nuclear and extended.

Many people who consider themselves advocates of children's rights and of the protection of children from the limitations or abuses of their parents argue that children should regularly be under the supervision of and in contact with agents of the state or otherwise qualified professionals. For example, in some nations, professionals (e.g., teachers, school counselors, school nurses) are required to report to the government any suspected physical or sexual abuse of children. Portions of the state school community and the public think of this reporting capability as an integral and increasingly important function of state-run schools (Fantuzzo et al. 1997; Berkan and Kadushin 1993; Klicka 1995; National Education Association 2000; Skillen 1998). As another example, some scholars argue that state institutional schools provide a forum that frees children from the regressive, selfish, or antipublic influences of their parents and gives the population at large a way to evolve into a more benevolent or broad-minded societal state (Apple 2000). In other words, it is argued that one of the chief functions of state schools is to protect children from the behaviors, beliefs, and worldviews of their parents (Richman 1994).

Most homeschool parents, on the other hand, think it is better for children to remain under their guidance and supervision and be protected from the state (Klicka 1995; Mayberry et al. 1995). The family, they explain, is the natural and nurturing buffer between the child himself and the state and the wider world. They think that they, rather than the state, should be training their offspring, the future citizens and leaders of the nation. These parents would agree with the political scientist James W. Skillen (1998, p. 3; see also Carlson 1993) that free societies should have a high view of the relationship between parents and their children as opposed to the state's intervention in families' and children's lives (Adams, Stein, and Wheeler 1989; Arons 1983; Klicka 1995; Mayberry et al. 1995). He writes that the public should not misidentify the family as a totalitarian place in which parents may do whatever they want to their children. At the same time, however, it is ". . . true that every public-legal attempt to 'liberate' minor children from parents makes the minors subject to whatever legal, medical or other authority is then authorized to direct or influence their actions."

Homeschool parents and advocates argue that parent-led, family-based education retains parental authority and primary influence over a child's education, protects the child from the state, and increases the familial bond between children and their parents, siblings, and kin groups. In contrast, when the state takes power and authority over education for itself and away from parents in the form of state-run schools, children are not only not liberated from all external authorities but one of the most important nongovernmental institutions of society—the family—is weakened by the ample power of the state (Adams, Stein, and Wheeler 1989; Klicka 1995; Apple 2000). Home-based education is consistent with the concept of the natural and strong family with human beings identified, as Skillen explained, ". . . as persons-in-community and the family as the foremost community for children. . ." (p. 5). Home-school parents are reclaiming for the family at large in society, and for their families in particular, the powerful and influential political, social, philosophical, and generational role they once had by reclaiming the education of children (Farris and Woodruff 2000; Lines 1994; Ray 2000a).

Advocates of institutional schooling, state-controlled in particular, continue to promote these schools as the key opportunity of advancement for disadvantaged persons and families (i.e., lower class, poor, minorities). In fact, the largest teachers' union in America, the National Education Association (2001), believes that state-controlled schooling is the cornerstone of social, economic, and political structure, and homeschooling cannot provide students with a comprehensive education experience. Now, however, an increasing number of scholars (Carlson 1995; Loberfeld 2001; Ray 2000a) and parents (Aizenman 2000; National Black Home Educators Resource Association 2001) are considering the proposition that keeping education under the direct authority and control of parents may better ensure an offering of intellectual, social, political, and spiritual freedom to individual children and youth—regardless of class, minority status, or advantage—who will eventually be the political citizens of any nation. For example, although state (public) schools had been desegregated in the United States since 1954, black (African American) students are still far below their white peers in terms of academic achievement in public (state) schools a half-century later. During the early 2000s, a new wave of parents, internationally (Large 2000), are expecting homeschooling to raise their children's academic achievement, improve their social success, increase their thinking skills, and enhance their potential for personal and national freedom.

See also: ACADEMIC ACHIEVEMENT; FAMILY LITERACY; SCHOOL

Bibliography

Adams, B.; Stein, J.; and Wheeler, H. (1989). *Who Owns the Children? Compulsory Education and the Dilemma of Ultimate Authority.* Austin, TX: Truth Forum.

Allie-Carson, J. (1990). "Structure and Interaction Patterns of Home School Families." *Home School Researcher* 6(3):11–18.

Apple, M. W. (2000). "The Cultural Politics of Home Schooling." *Peabody Journal of Education* 75(1–2):256–271.

Arons, S. (1983). *Compelling Belief: The Culture of American Schooling.* New York: McGraw-Hill Book Co.

Berkan, W. A., and Kadushin, A. (1993). *Child Abuse and Neglect Prevention: A Resource and Planning Guide.* ERIC Reproduction Service No. ED368990.

Blizek, W. L. (2000). "Ethics and the Educational Community." *Studies in Philosophy and Education* 19(3):241–51.

Brophy, J. (1996). *Enhancing Students' Socialization.* ERIC Reproduction Service No. ED395713.

Carlson, A. C. (1993). *From Cottage to Work Station: The Family's Search for Social Harmony in the Industrial Age.* San Francisco: Ignatius Press.

Carlson, A. (1995). "Preserving the Family for the New Millennium: A Policy Agenda." *The Family in America* 9(3):1–8.

Carlson, A. (2001). "The Task for Conservatism: Family Lessons from the New Agrarians." *The Family in America* 15(3):1–6.

Coleman, J. S., and Hoffer, T. (1987). *Public and Private High Schools: The Impact of Communities.* New York: Basic Books.

Delahooke, M. M. (1986). "Home Educated Children's Social/Emotional Adjustment and Academic Achievement: A Comparative Study." Ph.D. dissertation. Los Angeles: California School of Professional Psychology. (See also *Dissertation Abstracts International* 47(2):475A.)

Fantuzzo, J. W.; Stevenson, H. C.; Weiss, A. D.; Hampton, V. R.; and Noone, M. J. (1997). "A Partnership-Directed School-Based Intervention for Child Physical Abuse and Neglect: Beyond Mandatory Reporting." *School Psychology Review* 26(2):298–313.

Farris, M. P., and Woodruff, S. A. (2000). "The Future of Home Schooling." *Peabody Journal of Education* 75(1-2):233–55.

Good, T. L., and Brophy, J. E. (1987). *Looking in Classrooms,* 4th edition. New York: Harper and Row.

Klicka, C. J. (1995). *The Right to Home School: A Guide to the Law on Parents' Rights in Education.* Durham, NC: Carolina Academic Press.

Large, T. (2000). "Stay-at-Home Kids Shunning the System." *The Daily Yomiuri,* September 2, p. 7, Tokyo, Japan.

Lines, P. M. (1994). "Homeschooling: Private Choices and Public Obligations." *Home School Researcher* 10(3):9–26.

Lines, P. M. (2000). "Homeschooling Comes of Age." *The Public Interest* 140:74–85.

Loberfeld, B. (2001). "Freedom of Education: A Civil Liberty." *Ideas on Liberty* 51(8):26–32.

Lowe, J., and Thomas, A. (2002). *Educating Your Child at Home*. London: Continuum.

Lyman, I. (2001). "Motherhood Gets a Face-lift." *The New American* 17(9).

Mayberry, M.; Knowles, J. G.; Ray, B. D.; and Marlow, S. (1995). *Home Schooling: Parents as Educators*. Newbury Park, CA: Corwin Press.

McDowell, O. S. A. (1998). *Home Sweet School: The Perceived Impact of Home Schooling on the Family in General and the Mother-Teacher in Particular*. Doctoral dissertation, Peabody College of Vanderbilt University, Nashville, TN.

McElroy, W. (2002). "Can a Feminist Homeschool Her Children?" *Ideas on Liberty* 52(2):8–11.

Medlin, R. G. (2000). "Homeschooling and the Question of Socialization." *Peabody Journal of Education* 75 (1-2):107–23.

Page, R. E. (1997). *Families Growing Together: A Study of the Effects of Home Schooling on the Development of the Family*. Master's thesis, Maryvale Institute, Birmingham, United Kingdom.

Pruzan, A. (1998). *Toward Tradition on Educational Vouchers/School Choice*. Mercer Island, WA: Toward Tradition.

Ray, B. D. (1990). "Social Capital, Value Consistency, and the Achievement Outcomes of Home Education." A paper presented at the Annual Meeting of the American Educational Research Association, April 16–20, Boston, MA. (Available from the National Home Education Research Institute, Salem, Oregon.)

Ray, B. D. (2000a). "Home Schooling for Individuals' Gain and Society's Common Good." *Peabody Journal of Education* 75(1-2):272–93.

Ray, B. D. (2000b). "Home Schooling: The Ameliorator of Negative Influences on Learning?" *Peabody Journal of Education* 75(1-2):71–106.

Ray, B. D. (2002). *Worldwide Guide to Homeschooling*. Nashville, TN: Broadman and Holman.

Richman, S. (1994). *Separating School and State: How to Liberate America's Families*. Fairfax, VA: The Future of Freedom Foundation.

Sheffer, S. (1995). *A Sense of Self: Listening to Home-schooled Adolescent Girls*. Portsmouth, NH: Boynton/Cook Publishers, Heinemann.

Skillen, J. W. (1998). "Justice and Civil Society." *The Civil Society Project* 98(2):1–6.

Wartes, J. (1992). *Effects of Homeschooling upon the Education of the Parents: Comments from the Field*. Woodinville, WA: Washington Homeschool Research Project.

Other Resources

Aizenman, N. C. (2000). "Blacks in Prince George's Join Home-Schooling Trend." *The Washington Post*, October 19, A01. Available from http://washingtonpost.com/wp-dyn/articles/A36262-2000Oct18.html.

Lyster-Mensh, L. (2000). "Is Homeschooling Sexist?" *Home Education Magazine*. Available from http://www.home-ed-magazine.com/HEM/176/ndsexist.html.

"National Black Home Educators Resource Association Offers Services and Information On." (2001). "Who We Are." In the National Black Home Educators Resource Association web site. Baker, Louisiana, USA. Available from http://www.christianity.com/nbhera.

National Education Association. (2000). NEA 2000-2001 resolutions [C-10]: Child abuse, neglect, and exploitation. Available from http://www.nea.org/resolutions/00/00c-10.html.

National Education Association. (2001). *NEA 2000-2001 Resolutions*. Washington, DC: Author. Available from http://www.nea.org/resolutions/.

Ray, B. D. (1999). *Home Schooling on the Threshold: A Survey of Research at the Dawn of the New Millennium*. Salem, Oregon, USA. Available from http://www.nheri.org/.

Rudner, L. M. (1999). "Scholastic Achievement and Demographic Characteristics of Home School Students in 1998." *Educational Policy Analysis Archives* 7(8). Available from http://epaa.asu.edu/epaa/v7n8/.

World Bank Group. (2002). *Private and Public Initiatives: Working Together in Health and Education*. Available from http://www.worldbank.org/html/extdr/hnp/health/ppi/p1curren.htm.

World Congress of Families. (2001). Rockford, Illinois. Available from http://www.worldcongress.org/WCF/wcf_purpose.htm.

BRIAN D. RAY

HOMOSEXUALITY

See GAY PARENTS; GENDER; GENDER IDENTITY; LESBIAN PARENTS; SEXUAL ORIENTATION

HONEYMOON

The *honeymoon* is a peculiarly modern creation. Building on wedding customs of Europe in the late 1800s, the honeymoon has evolved into a ritual that nearly all people in the United States and Canada practice and that has grown in popularity around the world (Bulcroft, Smeins, and Bulcroft 1999). What distinguishes the honeymoon of today from its precursor, the wedding night, is the element of distancing the couple from their social networks by means of traveling to locations that are uniquely unfamiliar or foreign. The term honeymoon first appears in the sixteenth century in Thomas Blount's *Glossographia* (1656), where he defines the honeymoon in terms of the waxing and waning of newlywed emotions. Specifically, "married persons that love well at first, and decline in affection afterwards: it is honey now, but will change as the moon." Contemporary understandings of the honeymoon are far from this original lexicon, and the current emphasis on passion and romance as pivotal aspects of the honeymoon today seem paradoxical in light of Blount's definition of the term.

History

The origins of the honeymoon began in European wedding traditions of the upper class in the nineteenth century, affording the couple the luxury of a bridal tour or wedding trip that often lasted several weeks or months (Gillis 1985). As the middle class grew in industrializing nations, they began to emulate the bridal tour. Middle-class couples could not afford the scale and duration of the bridal tour as practiced by affluent brides and grooms. Thus, the honeymoon trip that lasted a few days to a week provided the semblance of a bridal tour. With the advent of the automobile and train, and later the airplane, couples were able to increases the distance of their honeymoon trips and seek out exotic and popularized locations such as Niagara Falls. By the mid-twentieth century international

sites such as Jamaica, Fiji, and similar tropical locations had become common honeymoon destinations. Resorts that cater exclusively to honeymooning couples were mass-marketed in the later part of the twentieth century.

The Individual and the Post-Industrial Honeymoon

The roles of men and women in the context of the honeymoon have also evolved. Evidence suggests that the honeymoon has become increasingly feminized over time, resulting in the ritual of today, of which the bride is the center (Bulcroft, Bulcroft, Smeins, and Cranage 1997). In America, men were generally responsible for planning and executing the honeymoon until the mid-twentieth century. As marriages increasingly emphasized companionate rather than conjugal roles, romance and individual identities gained in importance. Thus, the honeymoon reflects the emphasis that late-modern societies place on individualism, rationalization, consumption, and creating ritual to alleviate perceptions of risk and uncertainty (Beck 1992; Habermas1970).

The outcomes of modernization are a more complex, depersonalized, and rationalized world. Men and women's lives are freer of regulation such as they used to find in religion and other institutions. Thus, the need for social bonding and intimacy is more to the point than ever. As men and women long for close, intimate relationships, their very identities are based on the establishment of such bonds. The honeymoon is one ritual in the life-course trajectory that helps form individual identities, and the standardization of the honeymoon in recent times suggests that the culturally shared social scripts surrounding such life-course events are increasingly comparable. The paradox results, however, that in their quest for individualism in late-modern societies, people increasingly achieve homogeneity and sameness of experience.

From the 1970s, the honeymoon continued to function as a time of transition between a couple's wedding and married life, but it takes form as an interlude of heightened romance. More than an initiation into marital roles, the postindustrial honeymoon is a ritual that is socially framed as the most romantic juncture in one's life. The honeymoon is about forming one's self-identity as romantic, and couples make honeymoon choices as a means to secure their individual and shared romantic identities. The honeymoon of the twenty-first century requires travel to a destination that can be imagined as having the potential for fulfilling such expectations. Often, the location is imagined as a place where social restraints are eased to permit more uninhibited behavior appropriate to the lore of honeymoon sexual initiation. Tropical islands are preferred, but cities, resorts and hotels in a variety of geographic locations signify romance. Paris and Venice are historically romantic cities and draw couples from around the world. For couples who cannot afford international travel, hotels may provide rooms with such themes ranging from Polynesian timelessness to urban sleek opulence. Two universal activities of this identity-forming ritual are the purchase of souvenirs and romantic artifacts and the documentation of romantic activities with photographs and video films. Couples also post their personal biographies and travel itineraries on Internet home pages. By so doing, they not only assert their romantic identities; they circulate honeymoon practices around the world and contribute to a homogenization of them.

Because identity is at stake, couples seek perfection in honeymoon romance, but travel to unfamiliar places to realize intensified expectations establishes a context for failure. To allay this risk, couples often choose packaged honeymoons, in which hotels, resorts, and cruise lines provide an organized program of rooms, meals, and activities. This desire for a risk-free honeymoon is fueled by guidelines for successful honeymoons found in books, bridal and travel magazines, and Internet web sites, and it contributes to a rapidly growing niche in the global tourism industry.

The Honeymoon as Romantic Consumption

In contrast with traditional sources of identity formation, such as community, family, or national origin, postindustrial identity largely is recognized through commodity choices (Shields 1992). The honeymoon is a cultural production of consumption that expands on modern beliefs in romance (Bulcroft, Smeins, and Bulcroft 1999). Romance is believed to be real, and it is made tangible when couples in everyday life stimulate their personal relationships with rituals in which commodities construct their romance. Flowers, champagne, and candlelight dinners, for example, are becoming universal props for constructing romance (Illouz

1997). The honeymoon comprises an accumulation of these symbolic ingredients and activities over an extended period of time in a tourist setting. Belief in romance is internationally produced in movies and other contemporary media, and the notion of a honeymoon as the occasion for experiencing it intensely is promoted similarly, and especially through advertising. The joining of beliefs in romance, identity through consumption, and an aggressive travel industry has rendered the honeymoon as a social norm not only for heterosexual couples who marry for the first time. Honeymoons mark subsequent marriages, and second honeymoons within marriages are taken to revive remembered romance. Gay and lesbian couples who formalize their unions also plan romantic honeymoons, and many travel agencies, hotels and cruise lines offer specialized packages for them.

The forces of globalization have reduced cultural specificity in honeymoon practices and amplified tendencies toward travel and romantic consumption across cultures. Thus, the study of the honeymoon is better framed in terms of its transmission and assimilation across cultures, rather than looking at cross-cultural differences in the practice of the honeymoon. The mass-marketing of the honeymoon through popular press and visual media has resulted in honeymoon imperialism or the wholesale adoption of the ritual on a global scale. The way in which the honeymoon is practiced today in Japan, Argentina, South Africa, or any other postindustrial nation reflects the standards as practiced in North America.

See also: FAMILY RITUALS; INTIMACY; LOVE; MARITAL
    SEX; MARRIAGE CEREMONIES; REMARRIAGE

Bibliography

Beck, U. (1992). *Risk Society: Towards a New Modernity.* Beverly Hills, CA: Sage.

Blount, T. (1656). *Glosographia.* Menston (York): Scholar Press.

Bulcroft, K.; Bulcroft, R.; Smeins, L.; and Cranage, H. (1997). "The Social Construction of the North American Honeymoon, 1880-1995." *Journal of Family History,* 22(4):462–490.

Bulcroft, K.; Smeins, L.; and Bulcroft, R. (1999). *Romancing the Honeymoon: Consummating Marriage in Modern Society.* Thousand Oaks, CA: Sage.

Gillis, J. (1985). *For Better, For Worse.* New York: Oxford University Press.

Habermas, J. (1970). *Towards a Rational Society.* Boston: Beacon.

Illouz, E. (1997). *Consuming the Romantic Utopia: Love and Cultural Contradictions of Capitalism.* Berkeley: University of California Press.

Shields, R., ed. (1992). *Lifestyle Shopping: The Subject of Consumption.* New York: Routledge.

KRIS BULCROFT
LINDA SMEINS
RICHARD BULCROFT

HOSPICE

Hospice programs have the mission of supporting a meaningful quality of life for terminally ill people and their families. What exactly is a hospice program? How and why did these programs begin? What kind of assistance do they provide? How can terminally ill people and their families make informed decisions about seeking the hospice option? Questions such as these have been raised with increasing frequency in recent years as both the general public and health care professionals have demonstrated a willingness to discuss the once-taboo topic of dying and death (Feifel 1959; Becker 1973).

Origins and Development of the Hospice Approach

Modern hospice programs have ancient roots (Phipps 1988; Stoddard 1978). Greek temples of healing offered a soothing environment, encouragement, and a spectrum of services that included bathing, massage, music, and therapeutic serpents. The belief that the whole person should be supported by a team of skilled and compassionate people would later become a core principle of the hospice movement. This promising beginning was overwhelmed by "progress" as the Roman Empire gained ascendance. The rulers established hospitals whose bureaucratic organization anticipated the modern health care system. The emphasis was on repairing wounded soldiers so they could fight again—the mutilated and the dying were far down the priority list.

Compassionate care for the sick and the dying continued to be provided in several monasteries. An exceptional woman of fourth century Rome observed their practices. Sorrowing over the death of her husband, Fabiola devoted herself to providing comfort to other people in their last days. Fabiola's personal example and her powers of persuasion persuaded others to take up this cause as well. The hospice movement would go through periods of both advance and decline through the centuries, but Fabiola's example had set the process in motion: the living could and should comfort the dying.

By the fifth century hospice was a part of medieval society. The word itself derives from the Latin *hospitium,* which also has given us host and hostess. In those years the hospice was a dwelling that functioned under the auspices of a religious order. Pilgrims were afforded the opportunity to rest, replenish their energies, and receive encouragement before they resumed their long, wearying, and dangerous journeys to sacred destinations. Some travelers were literally at death's doorstep. They were welcomed across the threshold, given bedding, food, and compassionate companionship by keepers of the faith. In the great age of pilgrimage, life itself became viewed as a journey (Cole 1992) with hospice serving as a final way station. In and around the Holy Land, crusader knights also operated hospice facilities and were known on occasion to provide care for people of other faiths as well.

Many hospice programs fell victim to social upheavals throughout the ensuing centuries. It proved difficult and often impossible to maintain a charitable service in the midst of warfare, religious conflicts, and economic and ecological disasters. The subsequent rise of technology and mass society was also inhospitable to hospice. Nevertheless, throughout these dark years there were still some small houses in which a few caregivers provided comfort for the sick and dying. Work houses and other large institutions provided shelter for the homeless and destitute, but closed their doors to "incurables" (Gilmore 1989).

Modern hospice care made its appearance in 1879 with the establishment of Our Lady's Hospice in Dublin, operated by the Irish Sisters of Charity. The mission was specifically to care of dying people and support for their families. Relief of pain was a high priority, and the staff quickly became experts in this art. Medical practice had become more ambitious as part of nineteenth burgeoning industrial, commercial, and scientific development. "Incurables" were increasingly regarded as people who stubbornly failed to respond to medical interventions and were therefore of little interest. Our Lady's Hospice would bequeath to the international hospice movement its emphasis on symptom relief and welcoming attitude toward family involvement. Just as significantly, the dying person was not regarded as a throwaway or a failed machine but as a unique and valuable individual. Several other institutions followed the lead of Our Lady's Hospice, but compassionate and effective care for the dying remained an endeavor well beyond the fringe of mainstream medicine.

The situation started to change dramatically in 1963 with the establishment of St. Christopher's Hospice. Dame Cicely Saunders, a nurse and a physician, had been inspired by the courage and insight of David Tasma, a man she had cared for in his last year of life (Saunders 1997). Under Saunder's innovative and charismatic leadership, St. Christopher's became the model for hospice care throughout the world. Saunders and her colleagues faced the challenge not only of developing improved methods of symptom control, but also of persuading the medical establishment that people could and should be given effective assistance in the end-phase of life.

The news traveled fast throughout the United Kingdom and to the United States and Canada where many people had become distressed by the perceived impersonality of medical care in general and the abandonment of the terminally ill person in particular. "Death with dignity" had become the rallying cry. The first North American hospice program was established in New Haven, Connecticut in 1974. Hospice made rapid strides, although not without resistance, conflicts, and misunderstandings that often arise when tradition is challenged. Studies soon confirmed that the hospice alternative did produce benefits such as pain relief and the ability to spend more time at home rather than in hospital (Mor, Greer, and Kastenbaum 1984). Convinced that this approach also reduced the costs of end-of-life services, the federal government enacted legislation enabling terminally ill people to select either hospice or traditional medical care. This program has been a qualified success. Provisions of the federal program are often criticized (e.g., Beresford and Connor 1999; Hoefler 1997), but more than 3,000 hospices serve nearly half a million patients a year.

The term *hospice* was problematic in bilingual Canada. Physician Balfour Mount (1997) introduced the term *palliative care* in the mid-1970s. This term not only eased the acceptance of hospice services in Canada, but has also gained widespread usage throughout the world. Palliative care in Canada is offered primarily as an in-hospital service. In the United States many programs emphasize home care with access, however, to in-hospital units when necessary. To think of hospice as a place is often an oversimplification. Hospice is an approach to terminal care that can be carried out in a variety of settings.

Hospice programs are now flourishing in many nations (Saunders and Kastenbaum 1997). Each society has had to find its own way to integrate hospice care into its family and religious values as well as its political, economic, and environmental circumstances. Nations as diverse as China, Colombia, Japan, Jordan, and Saudi Arabia have learned how to introduce palliative care into cultures that differ in many ways from the United Kingdom and North America. This is often a difficult process as in Colombia, for example, where the government and medical establishment strongly resisted prescribing morphine for dying people even though the sale of illegal drugs is rampant there. One major obstacle in some nations has been the deeply rooted attitude that death should not be discussed, even if this means systematically trying to deceive the dying person that all is well. Even in these circumstances, however, people have come to recognize the value of open communication and the possibility of significant pain relief (e.g., Smith and Zhu 1997).

The Hospice Option

Most patients served by hospice have either a form of cancer that is not responding to treatment or a progressive neurological condition such as *amyotropic lateral sclerosis* (ALS, also known as *Lou Gehrig's disease*). Hospice has been proving itself more flexible, however, by adapting its programs to serve children, people with acquired immunodeficiency syndrome (AIDS), and, so far to a limited extent, people with end-stage dementia.

Hospice care is intended as an alternative, not a replacement for management of terminal illness within the mainstream medical system. Several factors are important in making the choice.

Awareness of impending death. Eligibility for the Medicare Hospice Benefit requires medical certification that the patient has a life expectancy of six months or less. Just as significant, however, is the patient's own judgment and attitude. One might feel like fighting all the way, seeking additional treatment even though the odds seem against recovery or remission. Families also might refuse to accept the terminal prognosis and urge physicians to do everything, no matter how slim the chances. Occasionally a person judged to be terminally ill does recover. Unreadiness to acknowledge that the patient is nearing death can be based upon actual glints of hope that remain in the medical situation or anxious denial, to mention only the extremes. The decision to select the hospice alternative generally requires that the individual understands that his or her life is nearing its end. The individual might have this understanding and nevertheless decide to remain within the traditional medical care system, but hospice care is intended primarily for those who, in fact, are dying and who are cognizant of this fact.

Accurate knowledge of hospice care. There is still the lingering misconceptions that entering a palliative care program is an act of despair that consigns the person to a death-obsessed isolation. However, Balfour Mount (1997) speaks for many other palliative care physicians when he observes that "[a]ctually, effective symptom control and the presence of those who are there because they *choose* to care for the dying, frequently produces a liberation that enables the patients to focus on living and the quality of each day rather than on dying" (pp. 79–80).

Much that has been learned about effective symptom control has come from hospice care (Muir et al. 1999). The mistaken assumption that patients would be exposed to less competent medical and nursing care in hospice programs has kept some people from exploring this alternative. Furthermore, the development of palliative care was motivated in large part by the concern that the psychological, social, and spiritual needs of dying people were being neglected by mainstream medical practices. Hospice programs encourage continued interactions with family and friends and the support of the patient's own preferences and values.

There has also been some misunderstanding about the role of religion in hospice programs. As already noted, hospice programs from the early middle ages onward were usually offered under the auspices of a religious organization. St. Christopher's, the first center of the modern hospice movement, was also under Christian auspices and staffed primarily by nuns. Many—but not all—hospice programs today are associated with a particular religious faith. Does this mean that people who are not religious or belong to the "wrong" faith are not welcome in hospice programs or would be pressured to convert? Some terminally ill people have shied away from hospice programs because of this concern. In actuality, hospice programs have long been open to people regardless of their religious beliefs. David Tasma, the man who inspired Dame Cicely Saunder's work, was Jewish, and St. Christopher's set the example of providing compassionate care without attempting to impose their own faith. Studies have shown that most hospice staff and volunteers have a strong religious faith to sustain their efforts, but do not infringe on the patient's own beliefs (Schneider and Kastenbaum 1993).

Family communication and participation. Palliative care is intended as a cooperative endeavor characterized by open communication and mutual trust. In the ideal situation a skilled hospice team works with a close and caring family. A primary family caregiver is identified and provided with ongoing instruction and support by hospice experts. Other family members also participate in the care process in various ways and provide relief for the primary caregiver. Hospice experts make themselves available to answer questions and respond to problems as they emerge so that the family as well as the patient never feel abandoned, neglected, or misunderstood. When decision points arise there is consultation within the hospice team, within the family, and between both units. The patient participates in this process to the extent of his or her ability and inclination.

Unfortunately, situations often are less than ideal. The family might have other significant burdens and obligations that must continue to be managed. For example, the person theoretically in the best position to serve as primary family caregiver might be a spouse with physical disabilities of his or her own or a teenager struggling with issues that require intensive family support. The family might also be having difficulty even in talking about the situation and experiencing a pattern of withdrawal or confrontation with each other because of the tensions generated by the illness. Furthermore, the family may not have a physician who knows them well, or a physician who is knowledgeable about hospice and willing to make a referral. Whatever encourages open communication within the family and between family and human service professionals will help to make the wisest and most timely decision about the hospice alternative.

Availability, access, and appropriateness. Although palliative care programs are available throughout much of North America, some areas and some populations are underserved. Information can be obtained through state and county health departments, as well as from websites of such organizations as Hospice Foundation of America, Hospice Nurses Association, and the National Hospital and Palliative Care Organization. Coverage for hospice expenses is provided through Medicare. Four requirements have been established:

- The patient is eligible for Medicare Part A.

- The patient's physician and the hospice medical director certify that the patient has a terminal illness with a life expectancy of six months or less. (The hospice medical director can also serve as the patient's own physician, if circumstances warrant.)

- The patient signs a statement choosing hospice care instead of standard Medicare benefits for the terminal illness.

- Care is provided by a Medicare-approved hospice program.

Regulations are always subject to change, so it is useful to check with local health, social work, or Medicare agencies before applying. Availability and access can also depend on the nature and course of the illness (Stuart 1999). It is useful to inquire of local health agencies to learn whether or not hospice care is a practical alternative for a person with a particular condition.

Useful information about hospice care is provided by books for the general public such as those by Michael Appleton and Todd Henschell (1994) and M. Catherine Ray (1997). Health care professionals can learn of new developments in books such as *Improving Care for the End of Life* by Joanne Lynn, Janice Lynch Schuster, and Andrea Kabcenell (2000).

Hospice is often and accurately characterized as a grassroots movement. Society—including many health care professionals—decided it was time to become more than alert consumers: We could also be compassionate and effective caregivers to each other in the final phase of life. The future of hospice depends on many factors, but none greater than society's continued commitment to compassionate care.

See also: ACQUIRED IMMUNODEFICIENCY SYNDROME (AIDS); CAREGIVING: FORMAL; CAREGIVING: INFORMAL; CHRONIC ILLNESS; DEATH AND DYING; DECISION MAKING; DEMENTIA; EUTHANASIA; GRIEF, LOSS, AND BEREAVEMENT; HEALTH AND FAMILIES; SUBSTITUTE CAREGIVERS

Bibliography

Appleton, M., and Henschell, T. (1994). *At Home with Terminal Illness: A Family Guidebook to Hospice in the Home.* Upper Saddle River, NJ: Prentice-Hall.

Becker, E. (1973). *The Denial of Death.* New York: Free Press.

Beresford, L., and Connor, S. R. (1999). "History of the National Hospice Organization." In *The Hospice Heritage,* ed. I. B. Corless and Z. Foster. Binghamton, NY: Haworth.

Cole, T. R. (1992). *The Journey of Life.* Cambridge, UK: Cambridge University Press.

Feifel, H., ed. (1959). *The Meaning of Death.* New York: McGraw-Hill.

Gilmore, A. (1989). "Hospice Development in the United Kingdom." In *Encyclopedia of Death,* ed. R. Kastenbaum and B. Kastenbaum. Phoenix, AZ: Oryx.

Hoefler, J. M. (1997). *Managing Death.* Boulder, CO: Westview.

Lynn, J.; Schuster, J. L.; and Kabcenell, A. (2000). *Improving Care for the End of Life: A Sourcebook for Health Care Managers and Clinicians.* New York: Oxford University Press.

Mor, V.; Greer, D. S.; and Kastenbaum, R., eds. (1988). *The Hospice Experiment.* Baltimore, MD: Johns Hopkins University Press.

Mount, B. (1997). "The Royal Victoria Hospital Palliative Care Service: A Canadian Experience." In *Hospice Care on the International Scene,* ed. C. Saunders and R. Kastenbaum. New York: Springer.

Muir, J. C.; Krammer, L. M.; Camerson, J. R.; and von Gunten, C. F. (1999). "Symptom Control in Hospice—State of the Art." In *The Hospice Heritage,* ed. I. B. Corless and Z. Foster. Binghamton, NY: Haworth.

Phipps, W. E. (1988). "The Origin of Hospices/Hospitals." *Death Studies* 12:91–100.

Ray, M. C. (1997). *I'm Here to Help: A Guide for Caregivers, Hospice Workers, and Volunteers.* New York: Bantam.

Saunders, C. (1997). "Hospices Worldwide: A Mission Statement." In *Hospice Care on the International Scene,* ed. C. Saunders and R. Kastenbaum. New York: Springer.

Saunders, C., and Kastenbaum, R., eds. (1997). *Hospice Care on the International Scene.* New York: Springer.

Schneider, S., and Kastenbaum, R. (1993). "Patterns and Meanings of Prayer in Hospice Caregivers." *Death Studies* 17:471–481.

Smith, A., and Zhu, D. Z. (1997). "Hospice Development in China: 'Like Green Bamboo Shoots in the Spring.'" In *Hospice Care on the International Scene,* ed. C. Saunders and R. Kastenbaum. New York: Springer.

Stoddard, S. (1978). *The Hospice Movement.* New York: Stein and Day.

Stuart, Brad. (1999). "The NHO Medical Guidelines for Non-Cancer Disease and Local Medical Review Policy: Hospice Access for Patients with Diseases Other than Cancer." In *The Hospice Heritage,* ed. I. B. Corless and Z. Foster. Binghamton, NY: Haworth.

ROBERT KASTENBAUM

HOUSEWORK

Housework is the term used to describe the physical and emotional labor performed in the household, generally in the service of family and typically accomplished by women.

History of Housework

Before the Industrial Revolution, economic production was organized in and through homes. All household members, resident servants, and apprentices contributed to the upkeep of the home and to the production of goods that sustained the family. The household served several functions, acting also as educational institution and factory. Within this productive unit, housework contributed to the production of goods for internal use as well as for sale to others.

As the Industrial Revolution altered the economic landscape, productive work moved from homes into factories, and the character of housework changed. Men and unmarried women left home in increasing numbers to work in the waged labor force, while housewives found themselves doing less productive and more family-related labor. This unpaid work, also referred to as *social reproduction,* included bearing and raising children, as well as preparing other family members for work in the paid labor force by cooking, cleaning, and tending to their physical and emotional needs.

As men began to specialize in paid work, housework became increasingly linked to women. In the early nineteenth century, the ideology of separate spheres, associating men with the (public) workplace and women with the (private) home, became popular. According to this ideology, the home was viewed as pure, serene, and secure, as opposed to the impure, unsympathetic, and uncertain work world. Women, perceived as pious, virtuous, and submissive, became the rightful guardians of the domestic haven, even as their role in productive labor declined. Although more fantasy than reality, particularly in poor and working-class families, the "cult of true womanhood" linked women's "nature" with the performance of family work.

By the middle of the nineteenth century, many chores previously performed in the home had moved into the public sphere. Fabrics, soaps, candles, and other household items formerly manufactured in the household were increasingly factory-made and purchased by women for use in the home. By the late nineteenth century, households that once produced their own goods had begun to consume the products of U.S. industry (Strasser 1982). In the process, women's unpaid housework came to be seen as less important than men's paid labor, which financed this burgeoning household consumerism.

In the latter part of the nineteenth century and into the twentieth century, the declining importance of housework was countered by the rise of home economics, which advocated industrial-like efficiency in running households. Technological developments, including the spread of electricity and running water, encouraged invention of a number of "labor-saving" household appliances, including electric irons and washing machines. However, these appliances actually saved little time because the early twentieth century also saw a substantial increase in standards of household care (Cowan 1983). Since then, continuous innovation in household appliance technology has increased the efficiency of many tasks, but these innovations have also promoted higher standards of cleanliness, hygiene, and fashion, which in turn have encouraged women to perform selected household tasks more frequently (such as bathing, laundry, ironing, vacuuming, and dusting). Newer market-based "conveniences"—such as fast-food restaurants, supermarkets, and Internet shopping—have reduced the time that women spend on housework, but only slightly. In the modern era, labor markets and economic conditions have increased women's paid labor force participation and reduced the time that they have available to perform domestic labor. At the same time, cultural expectations that housework is "women's work" have persisted.

What is Housework?

Housework encompasses different tasks, the amounts and types of which depend on household size, composition, and cultural expectations. If children are present, caring for them is a primary household duty that brings with it a range of other housework tasks. Similarly, caring for aging parents is common and includes supplemental domestic responsibilities. People hire domestic help to do housework or to care for the young or old when they can afford to, but in most homes, the women of the household do these tasks without financial reward. Routine household tasks necessary to sustain individuals and maintain homes include meal preparation and clean-up, house cleaning, grocery shopping, and laundry. These tasks tend to be obligatory, repetitive, and boring, and they have historically been women's responsibility. Occasional tasks that need less frequent attention—gardening and yard care, bill paying, household repairs, and auto maintenance—are typically performed by men and tend to be more time-flexible, discretionary, and enjoyable than routine housework.

Housework Performance

Women in most developed nations still do at least two-thirds of the family's routine housework and take responsibility for monitoring and supervising the work, even when they pay for domestic services or assign tasks to other family members (Coltrane 2000; Thompson and Walker 1989). Moreover, married women and those with children tend to perform an even greater proportion of housework than do single women and those without children. Married women in the United States do about three times as much routine housework as do married men. This pattern is consistent across many countries, with wives doing approximately 70 to 80 percent of the routine housework (Baxter 1997).

International studies of housework show that although women do far more housework than their male partners, their hours of housework are declining, and men are increasing their contributions slightly compared to earlier decades (United Nations 2000). Canadian, Australian, and Swedish men do slightly more housework than U.S. men, while Japanese men do less. Data from seven countries (Australia, France, Japan, Latvia, Netherlands, New Zealand, and Republic of Korea) indicate that in the 1990s women performed more than twice as many hours of housework as men, with men in Korea and Japan reporting the least unpaid labor, and those in Latvia reporting the most. In most countries, women devote well over half of their work time to unpaid labor. Men, in contrast, spend about one-third or less of their work time on unpaid labor. Moreover, when small children are present, unpaid labor increases substantially more for women than for men. Averaging reports from three countries (Australia, the Netherlands, and New Zealand) show an increase in women's unpaid labor of twelve hours per week when children are present, as opposed to an increase of less than two hours per week for men (United Nations 2000).

Developed countries have long used time-use surveys to assess what men and women do on a daily basis, but developing countries are only starting to use such surveys. At least twenty-two countries in Africa, Asia, Latin America, and the Caribbean have begun work on national time-use surveys since 1995, but results are not yet widely available (United Nations 2000). Thus, few comparisons have been made to less developed countries, though it has been found that three out of five Asian countries have greater rates of sharing housework than does the United States (Sanchez 1994).

Predictors of Men's Sharing

Studies have identified multiple consistent predictors for men's relative share of housework, including employment, ideology, and earnings, and, to a lesser extent, age, marital status, and children. Men share more housework when women are employed more hours, and sometimes when the men themselves are employed fewer hours. When wives earn more income than their husbands, husbands also generally share more housework. Younger and more highly educated women do less housework, while men with more education tend to do more. Women's (and sometimes men's) egalitarian gender attitudes also predict more sharing. Conversely, being married is associated with more housework for women but less for men. Finally, when couples have children, women tend to do substantially more housework, whereas men's housework hours tend to remain about the same or decrease slightly (Coltrane 2000).

Fairness in Housework Allocation

In the United States, both women and men say they should share housework equally when both are employed, but neither evaluates fairness based on an ideal of equal sharing. Only when wives do about twice as much housework as their husbands do they agree that the division of labor is fair (Lennon and Rosenfield 1994). Most women continue to feel responsible for the upkeep of homes and well-being of family members and are thus more likely than men to adjust their work and home schedules to accommodate others. Judging unbalanced divisions of labor as fair is related to cultural ideals of gender that, in turn, are shaped by economic, political, and legal institutions that value men's time over women's.

Children's Housework

Although considered primarily recipients of care, children are also substantial contributors to housework performance, often supplying up to seven hours or more per week of unpaid family work, mostly on routine indoor tasks (Blair 1992). Younger children's housework is less typed by gender than that of adults or teenagers, but as they become teens, they take on more gender-segregated tasks. Adolescent girls do about twice as much household labor as adolescent boys, with girls doing more routine chores like cooking and cleaning, and boys doing occasional outside chores like yard care. This division of adolescent chores socializes young people into accepting marriage and family roles that are bifurcated by gender.

Consequences of an Unbalanced Division of Labor

Many people—especially women—derive satisfaction from doing housework for family members because these activities symbolize love (DeVault 1991). At the same time, because housework continues to be relegated to wives and daughters, it is typically analyzed as part of a larger system of gender inequality. Although they may find some tasks enjoyable, most people do not like housework and, when financially able, most hire others to do the work. Because many hired domestic workers are poor women of color, this system also perpetuates class and race inequalities and socializes privileged children to expect to be waited on by disadvantaged women (Glenn, Chang, and Forcey 1994).

The amount of time that working-class women spend doing paid domestic work detracts from time they might spend with their own families. The time that all women spend doing housework detracts from the amount of time they might otherwise spend in paid labor, thus increasing their financial dependence on husbands and extended kin, and potentially reducing their relative power in society. Moreover, women who spend significant time in both unpaid labor and the paid workforce find themselves shouldering a "second shift" (Hochschild 1989), working in paid employment all day and doing housework and childcare when they come home. Employed wives enjoy less leisure and experience more stress than husbands (Schor 1991). When women bear a disproportionate share of responsibility for housework, their perceptions of fairness and marital satisfaction decline, and depending on gender attitudes and other factors, marital conflict and women's depression increase (Coltrane 2000).

Housework in Diverse Family Types

With the late twentieth century proliferation of diverse family forms, the potential has increased for different divisions of housework. Unmarried cohabiting couples, for instance, have more egalitarian gender attitudes and show more flexibility than married couples in how they divide family labor (Seltzer 2000). Cohabiting women do less housework than married women, and cohabiting men do more than their married counterparts, although cohabiting women continue to do more housework than their male partners. Similarly, attitudes in lesbian and gay couples may be more egalitarian than in most heterosexual couples, but equal sharing is still difficult to attain, and partners with more financial resources in homosexual unions, as in heterosexual ones, tend to perform less routine housework (Carrington 1999). Finally, remarried couples also share more egalitarian attitudes, decisions, and sometimes, chores than do couples in their first marriage, but housework generally continues to be governed by traditional gender roles and remains, essentially, the wife's duty (Coleman, Ganong, and Fine 2000).

Future of Housework

Women do most of the unpaid labor around the world, although their housework hours have declined, and their husbands' proportionate contributions have increased. Women still bear a double burden of work inside and outside the home. To ease this burden, families with adequate incomes are increasingly purchasing goods and services. Families with wives employed full-time are more likely to eat at restaurants, and employed wives are more likely than nonemployed wives to purchase cleaning services (Oropesa 1993). Women's labor force participation may be fueling an expanded global service economy, but workers in service positions are relatively disadvantaged themselves and are typically forced to accept minimum wage jobs and to forego providing direct daily care to their own children and families. Patterns of housework allocation are thus linked to patterns of gender, class, and race stratification in the larger society (Coltrane and Collins 2001). Ultimately, relieving the negative consequences of unbalanced divisions of housework for women will require men to assume equal responsibility in the home, as women assume equal responsibility for earning income.

See also: CAREGIVING: INFORMAL; CHILDCARE; COMPUTERS AND FAMILY; DIVISION OF LABOR; DUAL-EARNER FAMILIES; EQUITY; FAMILY ROLES; FOOD; HOME; HOME ECONOMICS; HOUSING; INDUSTRIALIZATION; RETIREMENT; TIME USE; WORK AND FAMILY

Bibliography

Baxter, J. (1997). "Gender Equality and Participation in Housework: A Cross-National Perspective." *Journal of Comparative Family Studies* 28:220–247.

Blair, S. L. (1992). "Children's Participation in Household Labor: Child Socialization Versus the Need for Household Labor." *Journal of Youth and Adolescence* 21:241–258.

Carrington, C. (1999). *No Place Like Home: Relationships and Family Life Among Lesbians and Gay Men.* Chicago: University of Chicago Press.

Coleman, M.; Ganong, L.; and Fine, M. (2000). "Reinvestigating Remarriage: Another Decade of Progress." *Journal of Marriage and the Family* 62:1288–1307.

Coltrane, S. (2000). "Research on Household Labor: Modeling and Measuring the Social Embeddedness of Routine Family Work." *Journal of Marriage and the Family* 62:1208–1233.

Coltrane, S., and Collins, R. (2001). *Sociology of Marriage and the Family: Gender, Love, and Property.* Belmont, CA: Wadsworth.

Cowan, R. S. (1983). *More Work for Mother.* New York: BasicBooks.

DeVault, M. L. (1991). *Feeding the Family: The Social Organization of Caring as Gendered Work.* Chicago: University of Chicago Press.

Glenn, E. N.; Chang, G.; and Forcey, L. R. (1994). *Mothering: Ideology, Experience, and Agency.* New York: Routledge.

Hochschild, A. R. *The Second Shift: Working Parents and the Revolution at Home.* New York: Viking.

Lennon, M. C., and Rosenfield, S. (1994). "Relative Fairness and the Division of Housework: The Importance of Options." *American Journal of Sociology* 100:506–531.

Oropesa, R. S. (1993). "Using the Service Economy to Relieve the Double Burden." *Journal of Family Issues* 14:438–473.

Sanchez, L. (1994). "Material Resources, Family Structure Resources, and Husband's Housework Participation: A Cross-National Comparison." *Journal of Family Issues* 15:379–402.

Schor, J. B. (1991). *The Overworked American: The Unexpected Decline of Leisure.* New York: BasicBooks.

Seltzer, J. A. (2000). "Families Formed Outside of Marriage." *Journal of Marriage and the Family* 62:1247–1268.

Strasser, S. (1982). *Never Done: A History of American Housework.* New York: Pantheon Books.

United Nations. (2000). *The World's Women 2000: Trends and Statistics.* New York: United Nations Publications.

MICHELE ADAMS
SCOTT COLTRANE

HOUSING

Housing is a built form, or dwelling, where people engage in daily activities that sustain residents, such as eating, sleeping, economic activities, and socialization. Housing comes in many architectural forms, including single-family detached houses, apartments, or row housing. Housing refers here to the various forms of shelter used by families.

The study of housing can be approached from nearly all the scientific and humanistic fields. Disciplines such as physics and engineering can contribute to the study of physical aspects of housing, such as how certain air contaminants can enter a dwelling. Aesthetics and artistic expression assist in understanding the design of housing and how it affects human behavior. The relationship between families and their houses is described in this entry through social and psychological terms.

Families rely on their housing for shelter from the elements and adversity. Variations in form, which range from local folk structures to high-style architecture, (Ennals and Holdsworth 1998) suggest that housing is more than shelter. Witold Rybczynski (1992) notes that the arrangement, amenities, and adornment of houses are symbols of public and private cultural notions of family life. Symbols are shared meanings, and the built form of housing is endowed with meaning as an indicator of social organization and social, legal, and economic status. Family housing is both shelter and symbol.

Housing as Shelter

Housing provides shelter and protection from the elements for people and their resources, such as food, clothing, and possessions. Local weather and geography contribute to the form and permanence of family housing. Requirements for protection from the elements vary according to local conditions such as minimum and maximum temperatures, susceptibility to flooding or snowfall, and

Brick row houses in Haarlem, Netherlands. MICHAEL S. YAMASHITA/CORBIS

other adverse conditions such as animals and wind. However, housing forms may be influenced by cultural differences in interpretations of human vulnerability and physical comfort (Rybczynski 1986), the quantity and quality of household resources requiring protection, and the advancement and diffusion of housing technology (Doucet and Weaver 1991; Ennals and Holdsworth 1999).

The view that shelter from the elements is critical for human well-being has implications for housing policy and research. The provision of housing requires resources such as land and building supplies. Therefore, housing can be incorporated into an economic market and considered a commodity. In this view, resources to procure housing are more often the responsibility of individual households. The inability to purchase housing may result in homelessness, a condition that is often socially denounced with the blame for the inability to purchase housing focused primarily on individuals or families (Hopper 1993). In contrast, a rights-based view of housing provision argues that access to adequate housing is an international human right. Centrally planned economies can provide publicly subsidized housing to ensure shelter is accessible to all households. The two contradictory views of housing—commodity and right—are frequently central issues in developing research and policy agendas. For example, housing was explicitly described as a human right at the 1996 United Nations Conference on Human Settlements (Habitat II) in Istanbul, Turkey. In the same document that declared shelter as a human right, housing was recognized as a productive economic sector. This declaration recognizes the need to find remedies for reconciling access to shelter among populations with very few financial resources without diminishing the benefits of generating incomes through the housing economy in impoverished regions.

In addition to providing shelter from the elements, housing can be employed by household members as a shelter from people outside of the built unit. For example, household members can control access to information about themselves (Wilson 1988). In this sense of shelter, the house is employed as a symbol of social group organization.

Housing as Symbol

Social organization. In many cultures housing is indivisible from family. For example, the common Greek word for family is *oikoyenia,* which means *relatives of the house* (Sutton 1999). Related to house and family is *household,* which is a group of people associated with a particular physical unit, or dwelling, through productive and reproductive activities over a particular period of time (Wallerstein and Smith 1992). A household differs from family in that it may be composed of both family and nonfamily members. However, it is important to note how some family-related social groupings such as household are defined by tenure in a certain physical unit or housing form. Thus, housing is central to family life.

Housing is frequently a symbol of home (Gurney and Means 1993), but family housing differs from the notion of home. Housing or dwelling implies a physical unit, whereas home is the cognitive representation of a familiar place of retreat.

Housing contributes to the social organization and dynamics of kin groups because it "defines and delimits space for the members of a household" (Lawrence 1987, p. 155). Dwellings contribute to patterns of social organization because households are defined by the set of people who co-reside or use the physical unit over a particular period.

Human interactions with the built form of the dwelling are founded upon spatial meanings such as cues for behavior (e.g., staircase indicates methods of ascent and descent). The built unit plays a dual role of communicating the appropriate behaviors to employ and accommodating the behaviors (Birdwell-Pheasant and Lawrence-Zúñiga 1999). Amos Rapoport (1982) describes how built forms act as a memory device for cueing appropriate behavior. Behavioral regularities emerge from the rules affiliated with spaces within houses (e.g., "don't slam the screen door") and household objects (Wood and Beck 1994). Meanings for spaces include the rules for the individuals who are allowed access to specific areas.

Peter Wilson (1988) suggests that the boundaries of domestic spaces allow household members some control over access to themselves. Behaviors and information can be concealed from, or displayed to, individuals outside the built unit, thus creating a symbolic division between public and private spaces. Consequently, in addition to providing shelter from the elements, housing can be employed by household members as a shield from public attention.

Boundaries within domestic spaces are symbolic indicators of the organizational patterns among household members. Features of dwellings are used to convey a system of meanings about the spaces that establish the control over private spaces within the home. Houses can incorporate doorways, or other architectural details, that facilitate certain household members' control over the use of areas. Control over areas within the house is important for understanding the notion of privacy among family members. Historical overviews of housing forms demonstrate how the shape of housing and designation of control over spaces is associated with the promotion of the idea of privacy and individualism in family life in Europe and North America (Johnson 1993; Ward 2000). Separate spaces assigned to specific activities (such as

A small house in Gorstan, Scotland. BJORN BACKE; PAPILIO/CORBIS

bathrooms for bathing) have replaced large multi-functional spaces. Privacy is accomplished through the adoption of specialized enclosed spaces.

Although the built form contributes to the ordering of family and community interactions, it should not be considered the cause of interpersonal interactions because individuals would be assumed to lack the capacity to decide for themselves how to interact. Families and households contribute to shaping housing through adaptation of space utilization (Werner 1987) and changing of existing structures or construction of new structures in an effort to adjust to familial, social, and political changes (Birdwell-Pheasant and Lawrence-Zúñiga 1999).

Households engage in a process of adjusting their housing to fit their needs over the life-cycle while being constrained by the availability of household resources and the economic, social, and cultural environments. Change processes normally begin with a household's assessment of current conditions against housing norms. Housing norms, a type of symbol, are defined as social pressures in the form of rules for behavior and life conditions that are accompanied with related sanctions (Dillman; Tremblay; and Dillman 1979; Morris and Winter 1975). These include societywide norms, but a household may have special group norms depending on the household's background. The family itself may also develop its own unique set of housing norms. A difference between a housing

condition prescribed by a norm and the actual condition presents a deficit (Beyer 1949; Nickell et al. 1951; Morris et al. 1990; Morris and Winter 1975, 1978; Rossi 1955). For example, if a household has five bedrooms but the norms prescribe six, the household has a deficit of one bedroom. Dissatisfaction with current housing deficits may lead to intentions for change. For example, Irit Sinai (2001) found that the degree of satisfaction with housing in Kumasi, Ghana, predicted change, although shelter characteristics, tenure, and the use of housing for income were associated with the decision to either move or modify housing. If the layout of a dwelling is not well suited to the resident family, the family may either make changes in the dwelling, move, or compensate for the dwelling by making changes in other aspects of family life. However, adaptation of the dwelling is not entirely controlled by the members of the household because housing is a resource that is embedded in a context of external constraints such as government building regulations and economic markets.

Social status. Housing is produced and used, in part, to convey social status. Association with a certain dwelling affords individuals the status of membership in a household. Nonmembership in a household is a state of homelessness, which is usually considered a very low social status. Social status is also conveyed through housing design and adornments. Vernacular architecture, or ordinary local housing, often emulates sophisticated housing such as high-style architecture designed by architects (Ennals and Holdsworth 1998), suggesting that housing forms and amenities are efforts to communicate material wealth and status to those outside the household.

Houses are encoded with symbolic meanings (Birdwell-Pheasant and Lawrence-Zúñiga 1999) that include assignment of status to internal spaces. Social status of activities associated with spaces help to define areas within housing as well as familial roles. For example, the recreation room in North American homes during the mid-1900s was assigned to the basement because children's play was a rough and physical activity preferably hidden from the outside world, while the living room, located on the main floor of the house with large windows, was reserved for important adult socializing (Rybczynski 1992). Other research has shown how laundry is a low status activity afforded very

A row of Tongkona, traditional houses in the Toraja village of Palawa, Indonesia. ALBRECHT G. SCHAEFER/CORBIS

little space or low status areas in European housing (Laermans and Meulders 1999).

Status assignment of household spaces has been studied in relation to gendered patterns of family roles. Gilman (1903) was one of the first authors to identify that the private activities of the home were of lower status than the public activities outside the home. She described a gendered pattern of familial roles in which private household activities, such as cooking and childcare, were viewed as the responsibility of women. Household activities were held in lower esteem than men's participation in the public world. More recent cross-cultural research suggests that the degree of accessibility to both men and women to socially valued information and space, such as the workplace, is associated with the degree of gendered spatial segregation (Spain 1992).

Legal status. The social status of belonging to a dwelling, or membership in a household, is also a form of legal status. The family residence can be recognized by a legal system to represent a fixed place that contributes to the recognition and identification of a household and/or person. Thus, association with a domicile provides individuals with citizenship.

Homeless families are viewed as not belonging to a legal residence or dwelling and therefore have a low status with respect to the rights associated with citizenship. They may live in a dwelling such as temporary shelter in a detention camp, but homeless families are not viewed as existing, by operation of the law, in a permanent dwelling. Historically, homelessness has come to be viewed as a social problem (Keyssar 1993) often associated with economic status.

Economic status. Economic status is attributed to housing when durable dwellings and the land they are situated on are considered commodities. Families buy, sell, or rent housing to gain the legal and social right to access and control dwellings. The ability to acquire housing is associated with the balance between household resources and the cost and availability of housing. For example,

Houses in a Tata village in Togo. DANIEL LAINI/CORBIS

when housing costs are high relative to income, household formation rates are lower, and the age of individuals purchasing housing (household head) is higher (Skaburski 1994).

The economic value of commodity housing is also interpreted as an indicator of social status. The great houses and courts of England and France were constructed as public displays of wealth and power (Stone 1991). Michael Doucet and John Weaver (1991) describe how the promotion of house ownership in North America has historically been used as an indicator of family success and stability. Ownership is an indicator of freedom from subordination and the attainment of financial and familial security.

The economic value of housing reflects social meaning (Lawrence 1987) such as power or poverty. Further, the ability to acquire commodity housing is associated with attaining the legal right to reside in a permanent domicile and citizenship. Thus, the economic status of housing is integrally related to aspects of the household members' social and legal status. Housing is a pervasive symbol of the status of households and families while operating as physical protection from the environment.

See also: FAMILY AND RELATIONAL RULES; FAMILY FOLKLORE; FAMILY ROLES; HOME; HOMELESS FAMILIES; HOUSEWORK; POVERTY; RESOURCE MANAGEMENT; SELF-DISCLOSURE; SINGLE-PARENT FAMILIES; SOCIOECONOMIC STATUS; WIDOWHOOD; WORK AND FAMILY

Bibliography

Beyer, G. H.; Mackesey, T. W.; and Montgomery, J. E. (1955). *Houses Are for People: A Study of Home Buyer Motivatiors.* Ithaca, NY: Cornell University Housing Research Center.

Birdwell-Pheasant, D., and Lawrence-Zúñiga, D. (1999). "Introduction: Houses and Families in Europe." In *House Life: Space, Place and Family in Europe,* ed. D. Birdwell-Pheasant and D. Lawrence-Zúñiga. New York: Berg.

Crankshaw, O.; Gilbert, A.; and Morris, A. (2000). "Backyard Soweto." *International Journal of Urban and Regional Research* 24:841–857.

Dillman, D. A.; Tremblay, K. R.; and Dillman, J. J. (1979). "Influence of Housing Norms and Personal Characteristics on Stated Housing Preferences." *Housing and Society* 6:2–19.

Doucet, M., and Weaver, J. (1991). *Housing the North American City*. Montreal and Kingston: McGill-Queen's University Press.

Ennals, P., and Holdsworth, D. W. (1998). *Homeplace: The Making of the Canadian Dwelling Over Three Centuries*. Toronto: University of Toronto Press.

Gilman, C. P. (1903). *The Home: Its Work and Influence*. New York: McClure, Phillips.

Gurney, C., and Means, R. (1993). "The Meaning of Home in Later Life." In *Ageing, Independence, and the Life Course,* ed. S. Arber and M. Evandrou. London: Jessica Kingsley Publishers.

Hopper, J. (1993). "A Poor Apart: The Distancing of Homeless Men in New York's History." In *Home: A Place in the World,* ed. A. Mack. New York: New York University Press.

Johnson, M. (1993). *Housing Culture: Traditional Architecture in an English Landscape*. Washington, DC: Smithsonian Institution.

Keyssar, A. (1993). "Introduction." In *Home: A Place in the World,* ed. A. Mack. New York: New York University Press.

Laermans, R., and Meulders, C. (1999). "The Domestication of Laundering." In *At Home: An Anthropology of Domestic Space,* ed. I. Cieraad. New York: Syracuse University Press.

Lawrence, R. J. (1987). "What Makes a Home?" *Environment and Behavior* 19:154-168.

Leckie, S. (1992). *From Housing Needs to Housing Rights: An Analyses of the Right to Adequate Housing Under International Human Rights Law*. London: International Institute for Environment and Development.

Morris, E. W.; Winter, M.; Whiteford; M. B.; and Randall, D. C. (1990). "Adjustment, Adaptation, Regeneration, and the Impact of Disasters on Housing and Households." *Housing and Society* 17:1–29.

Morris, E. W., and Winter, M. (1975). "A Theory of Family Housing Adjustment." *Journal of Marriage and the Family* 37:79–88.

Morris, E. W., and Winter, M. (1978). *Housing, Family, and Society*. New York: John Wiley & Sons.

Nickell, P.; Budolfson, M.; Liston, M.; and Willis, E. (1951). *Farm Family Housing Needs and Preferences in the North Central Region*. Ames: Iowa State University Press.

Rapoport, A. (1982). *The Meaning of the Built Environment: A Non-verbal Communication Approach*. Beverly Hills, CA: Sage.

Rossi, P. H. (1955). *Why Families Move*. New York: Free Press.

Rybczynski, W. (1986). *Home: A Short History of an Idea*. New York: Penguin.

Rybczynski, W. (1992). *A Journey Through Architecture*. New York: Penguin.

Sinai, I. (2001). "Moving Or Improving: Housing Adjustment Choice in Kumasi, Ghana." *Housing Studies* 16:97–114.

Skaburski, A. (1994). "Determinants of Canadian Headship Rates." *Urban Studies 31*:1377–1389.

Spain, D. (1992). *Gendered Spaces*. Chapel Hill, NC: University of North Carolina Press.

Stone, L. (1991). The Public and the Private in the Stately Homes of England, 1500–1990. *Social Research* 58:227–252.

Sutton, S. B. (1999). "Fleeting Villages, Moving Households: Greek Housing Strategies in Historical Perspective." In *House Life: Space, Place, and Family in Europe,* ed. D. Birdwell-Pheasant and D. Lawrence-Zúñiga. New York: Berg.

Wallerstein, I., and Smith, J. (1992). "Introduction: Households as an Institution of the World-Economy." In *Creating and Transforming Households: The Constraints of the World-economy,* ed. I. Wallerstein and J. Smith. Cambridge: Cambridge University Press.

Ward, P. (2000). *A History of Domestic Space: Privacy and the Canadian Home*. Vancouver: University of British Columbia Press.

Werner, C. M. (1987). "Home Interiors: A Time and Place for Interpersonal Relationships." *Environment and Behavior* 19:169–179.

Wilson, P. (1988). *The Domestication of the Human Species*. New Haven, CT: Yale University Press.

Wood, D., and Beck, R. J. (1994). *Home Rules*. Baltimore: Johns Hopkins University Press.

SHEILA K. MARSHALL

HUMAN ECOLOGY THEORY

Theories of human interaction should provide a way of making sense of events that have happened in the past, and then allow us to make predictions about what may happen in the future. *Human ecology theory* is a way of looking at the interactions of humans with their environments and considering this relationship as a system. In this theoretical framework, biological, social, and physical aspects of the organism are considered within the context of their environments. These environments may be the natural world, reality as constructed by humans, and/or the social and cultural milieu in which the organism exists.

Human ecological theory is probably one of the earliest theories of the family and yet, it also contains many new and evolving elements that have emerged as we have begun to realize how the natural and human created environments affect our behavior, and how individuals and families in turn, influence these environments. In human ecology, the person and the environment are viewed as being interconnected in an active process of mutual influence and change.

The Origins of Human Ecological Theory

The origin of the term *ecology* comes from the Greek root *oikos* meaning "home." As a result, the field of home economics, now often called human ecology, has produced much of the contemporary research using this theoretical perspective. Margaret Bubolz and M. Suzanne Sontag (1993) attribute the concept of an ecological approach to the work of Aristotle and Plato, and then to the evolutionary theory of Darwin. They trace the word ecology to Ernest Haeckel, a German zoologist who, in 1869, proposed that the individual was a product of cooperation between the environment and organismal heredity and suggested that a science be developed to study organisms in their environment. Early home economists were major proponents of this theory as their field developed in the early twentieth century applying various disciplines to the study of the family. The theory has since been used by sociologists, anthropologists, political scientists, and economists. This work continues, with the human ecological framework being a major perspective in research and theory development in the twenty-first century.

The Family as a System

The application of systems theory is a basic tenet of human ecological theory. The family is seen as a system, with boundaries between it and other systems, such as the community and the economic system. Systems have inputs that drive various processes and actions, such as the finite amounts of money or time that families possess. They also have throughputs, which are the transformation processes that occur within the system, such as the exchange of money for the provision of an essential service, such as food, by eating in a restaurant. In addition, systems have outputs, which affect other systems, such the production of waste materials, which are byproducts of activity in the family, being returned to the larger environment. There are feedback loops from the end of the system back to the beginning, to provide both positive and negative comment back into the process and allow the system to adapt to change. In an ecosystem, the parts and the whole are interdependent.

Most theorists outline an ecosystem, most particularly a human ecosystem or a family ecosystem, as being composed of three organizing concepts: humans, their environment, and the interactions between them. The humans can be any group of individuals dependent on the environment for their subsistence. The environment includes the natural environment, which is made up of the atmosphere, climate, plants, and microorganisms that support life. Another environment is that built by humans, which includes roads, machines, shelter, and material goods. As Sontag and Bubolz (1996) discuss, embedded in the natural and human-built environments is the social-cultural environment, which includes other human beings; cultural constructs such as language, law, and values; and social and economic institutions such as our market economy and regulatory systems. The ecosystem interacts at the boundaries of these systems as they interface, but also can occur within any part of an ecosystem that causes a change in or acts upon any other part of the system. Change in any part of the system affects the system as a whole and its other subparts, creating the need for adaptation of the entire system, rather than minor attention to only one aspect of it.

There are also systems nested within systems, which delineate factors farther and farther from individual control, and that demonstrate the effects of an action occurring in one system affecting several others. Urie Bronfenbrenner's analysis of the systems such as the *microsystem, mesosystem, exosystem,* and *macrosystem* are an integral part of the theory. The microsystem is our most immediate context, and for most children, is represented by their family and their home. Young children usually interact with only one person until they develop and their world expands. The mesosystem is where a child experiences reality, such as at a school or childcare setting. Links between the institutions in the mesosystem and the child's family enhance the development of academic competence. The exosystem is one in which the child does not participate directly, but that affects the child's experiences. This may be a parent's workplace and the activities therein, or bureaucracies that affect children, such as decisions made by school boards about extracurricular activities. Our broadest cultural identities make up the macrosystem. This system includes our ideologies, our shared assumptions of what is right, and the general organization of the world. Children are affected by war, by religious activities, by racism and sexist values, and by the very culture in which they grow up. A child who is able to understand and deal with the ever-widening systems in his or her reality is the product of a healthy microsystem.

Bubolz and Sontag (1993) outline five broad questions that are best answered using this theory, which is helpful in deciding areas where the theory can make a useful contribution to our knowledge. These are:

(1) To understand the processes by which families function and adapt—how do they ensure survival, improve their quality of life, and sustain their natural resources?

(2) To determine in what ways families allocate and manage resources to meet needs and goals of individuals and families as a group. How do these decisions affect the quality of life and the quality of the environment? How are family decisions influenced by other systems?

(3) How do various kinds and levels of environments and changes to them affect human development? How does the family system adapt when one or more of its members make transitions into other environmental settings, such as day care, schools, and nursing homes?

(4) What can be done to create, manage, or enhance environments to improve both the quality of life for humans, and to conserve the environment and resources necessary for life?

(5) What changes are necessary to improve humans' lives? How can families and family professionals contribute to the process of change?

Research Framework

The studies and concept development based upon human ecological theory range from very abstract to concrete. Bronfenbrenner (1979), one of the first researchers to rely extensively on human ecology theory in studies of children and families, defined an ecological perspective by focusing on development as a function of interaction between the developing organism and the enduring environments or contexts in which it lives out its life. He applies the theory in a practical way to explain quality factors in day care for children, the value of flexible employment schedules for parents, and improving the status of women. Bronfenbrenner argues that the child always develops in the context of family relationships and that development is the outcome of the child's genetic attributes combined with their immediate family and eventually with other components of the environment. This work stands in contrast to many psychological studies that explain individual behavior solely by considering individual traits and abilities.

James Garbarino (1997) uses human ecological theory to explain abuse in families, especially toward children. He considers the nature-or-nurture dilemma–whether the powerful influence of the environment can override the conditions of our biology. The interactions between these factors are difficult to research, because often one is held constant in order to assess variations in the other. For example, studying genetically identical twins reared separately to show the effect of nature or nurture on intelligence, or seeing how different newborns react to the stimulus of a smiling human face, are one-dimensional perspectives. Garbarino has collaborated with other authors in 1994 and 1996 in considering the effects of the political environment in Palestine on children's behavior problems.

The model has been used by researchers to investigate problems in various cultural contexts. Bengt-Erik Andersson (1986) shows how different social environments of children in Sweden influence their development, especially environments represented by their peer group, their neighborhood, and whether they had been *latch-key* children. Amy Avgar, Urie Bronfenbrenner, and

Charles R. Henderson (1977) consider childrearing practices in Israel in three different community settings—the communal kibbutz, the cooperative moshav, and the city. The study surveys preadolescents, asking them to respond on behalf of their mother, father, peer, and teacher. It finds that the traditional family structure exerts a major effect on the predicted socialization patterns, although it also notes the effect of the larger society, with significant differences among the three communities.

Sontag and Bubolz (1996) use the ecosystem model to conceptualize the interaction between farm enterprises and family life. The family, the farm, and other components are mutually interdependent and cannot be considered separately. For example, they consider production, as well as decision-making and management activities, from the perspective of both agricultural and home production. Margaret Bubolz and Alice Whiren (1984) use an ecological systems model for analysis of the family with a handicapped member. They show that these families are vulnerable to stress because of the demands placed on them for physical care, attending to emotional needs, and locating and obtaining access to support services. They conclude that the total needs of the family must be considered when policy decisions and programs are devised rather than focusing only on the handicapped family member.

Conclusion

A basic premise of a human ecological theory is that of the interdependence of all peoples of the world with the resources of the earth. The world's ecological health depends on decisions and actions taken not only by nations, but also by individuals and families, a fact that is increasingly being realized. Although the concept of a family ecosystem is not a precise one, and some of the terms have not been clearly and consistently defined, a human ecological theoretical perspective provides a way to consider complex, multilevel relationships and integrate many kinds of data into an analysis. As new ways of analyzing and combining data from both qualitative and quantitative dimensions of interconnected variables develop, this theoretical perspective will become more precise and continue to enhance understanding of the realities of family life.

See also: FAMILY SYSTEMS THEORY; FAMILY THEORY; HOME ECONOMICS; NEIGHBORHOOD; RESOURCE MANAGEMENT

Bibliography

Andersson, B. E. (1986). "Research on Children: Some Thoughts on a Developmental-Ecological Model." *Forskning-om-Utbildning* 13(3):4–14.

Andrews, M. P.; Bubolz, M. M.; and Paolucci, B. (1980). "An Ecological Approach to the Study of the Family." *Marriage and Family Review* 3(1/2):29–49.

Avgar, A.; Bronfenbrenner, U.; and Henderson, C. R. (1977). "Socialization Practices of Parents, Teachers, and Peers in Israel: Kibbutz, Moshav, and City." *Child Development* 48(4):1219–1227.

Bronfenbrenner, U. (1975). "Reality and Research in the Ecology of Human Development." *Proceedings of the American Philosophical Society* 119(6):439–469.

Bronfenbrenner, U. (1979). *The Ecology of Human Development.* Cambridge, MA: Harvard University Press.

Bubolz, M. M., and Sontag, M. S. (1993). "Human Ecology Theory." In *Sourcebook of Family Theories and Methods: A Contextual Approach,* ed. P. Boss, W. J. Doherty, R. LaRossa, W. R. Schumm, and S. K. Steinmetz. New York: Plenum Press.

Bubolz, M. M.; and Whiren, A. P. (1984). "The Family of the Handicapped: An Ecological Model for Policy and Practice." *Family Relations* 33:5–12.

Garbarino, J. (1997). *Understanding Abusive Families: an Ecological Approach to Theory and Practice.* San Francisco: Jossey-Bass.

Klein, D. M. (1995). "Family Theory." In *Encyclopedia of Marriage and the Family,* ed. David Levinson. New York: Simon & Schuster Macmillan.

Klein, D. M., and White, J. M. (1996). *Family Theories.* Thousand Oaks, CA: Sage.

Sontag, M. S., and Bubolz, M. M. (1996). *Families on Small Farms.* East Lansing: Michigan State University Press.

RUTH E. BERRY

HUNGARY

Early marriages, a relatively small proportion of single men and women, and a high level of fertility have historically characterized the Hungarian population. The family has traditionally played an important role in Hungarian society. The sociological and demographic analyses carried out during the 1990s have shown that the family is more important for people than other areas of life (e.g., work, recreation, and other social contact). The notion of family had a positive connotation in general; married people were considered happier than others; and public opinion held that the family was and remained the most important point of stability (Szalai 1991). The Hungarian people see the ideal family as a married couple bringing up one or two children.

Certain signs indicate a change in the generally positive view of the family and marriage, and the family as a social institution is struggling with a number of crises. The crises are evident in such trends as the decreasing ratio of those who live in a traditionally ideal family. The decreasing number of new marriages, the high ratio of divorces, and the decreasing fertility rate are other indicators, as is the increasing number of children born outside marriage. Beyond these, other phenomena, such as the high numbers of alcoholics, people suffering from psychiatric illnesses, neglected children, children living in poverty, and suicides are all closely linked with the crisis of family life.

Marriage

The high value that Hungarians put on marriage showed in the marriage data until 1989 (when the political system changed); until then, the proportion of people who had not married by the age of fifty remained below 5 percent. At the same time, the gradual decrease in the number of marriages began in the early 1980s (Tóth 1999). In the 1970s there were 9.2 marriages per 1,000 inhabitants, a figure that had dropped to only 4.5 by 1999. Demographics explain the higher rate of marriage in the 1970s; by this time the many people born in the 1950s reached the age of marriage. Young people in large numbers were encouraged to marry early because of their financial interests, the dominant ideology, and the norms of their families.

From the beginning of the 1980s, however, the marriage trend reversed, and the number of marriages started to decrease. As a result, fewer marriages have taken place since 1980—that is, every year more marriages ended than began. Many factors acting together explain this trend and the low rate of marriages. Of these, first is the change in the timing of marriage. In 1975 men first married, on average, at the age of 23.4, while women did so at the age of 21.3. In this time 40 percent of the women married before reaching their twentieth year. By 1999 the mean age at first marriage was 26.8 for men and 24.2 for women. That women are marrying later is connected to the rise of their educational level. In the middle of the 1990s, more women than men were enrolled in secondary and postsecondary education. Education improves women's chances in the labor market, increases their choices, and even makes it possible for them eventually not to accept the traditional form of marriage.

During the 1990s, the number of those remarrying also decreased in Hungary. In the 1970s there were 129 marriages per 1,000 divorced men; by 1999 this ratio had dropped to 27.4. The number of marriages per 1,000 divorced women decreased from 115 in the 1970s to 18.6 by 1999. This means, first, that men and women have more equal chances for remarrying. Second, those divorced show much less willingness to remarry, compared to several decades earlier.

The decline of marriage as a preferred partner relationship can also be related to economic factors. First, those that have benefited most from the 1989 political changes may choose to remain unmarried. In its lifestyle, this group resembles the young middle class in Western countries; members of this group earn good incomes. The delay or eventual failure to marry at all has another economic cause at the other end of society: those who are poor and getting poorer. Unemployment burdens those beginning their careers at a much higher rate than the average; thus, because these young people lack an income, the founding of a family is uncertain.

Cohabitation

The decline in the popularity of marriage is also related to major changes in beliefs about and acceptance of cohabitation. The number of people living together without being married and the share of lasting partner relationships that they represent is still lower in Hungary compared to Western European countries, but this was especially true in previous decades. For a long time, this type of partner relationship belonged to the lower levels of the society. The number of people cohabiting was negatively affected by economic factors (first of all, the possibilities of getting a place to live), legal factors, and social factors—society still did not accept nonmarital cohabitation in lieu of marriage. However, during the years since the 1989 political changes,

A Hungarian family in Budapest takes a break from ice-skating. Hungarians see the ideal family as a married couple bringing up one or two children. PETER TURNLEY/ CORBIS

the effect of these factors weakened. Cohabitation gradually became an accepted partner relationship in the case of young people who had not yet married. According 1996 data from the Microcensus, the number of unmarried couples living together grew from 125,000 in 1990 to 180,000 in 1996—a figure that represents 7 percent of the marriage-type partner relationships. In the 1990s, the ratio of cohabitation increased in the younger age groups. In 1994, among women between the ages of fifteen and nineteen who lived with partners, one-third were not married to their partner; in 1980, this figure in the same type of group was 3 percent. In the same year, among women between the ages of twenty and twenty-four who lived with partners,

15 percent were not married; this figure was 1 percent in 1980 (Klinger 1996).

Divorce

The number of divorces has been relatively stable over the past three decades. It peaked in the 1980s, when an average of 28,000 marriages were dissolved each year. This figure shows that in the 1980s, there was a kind of dualism in the way society looked at the family. On the one hand, society expected young people to marry, but on the other it accepted that a significant proportion of the marriages ended in divorce.

The 1989 changes in the political system coincided with smaller changes in the number of divorces. Until 1992, the number of divorces decreased, and then the yearly absolute number of divorces fell below 22,000. After 1992, the trend again shifted, and in 1999 the number of divorces rose to 25,600 (563 per 1,000 new marriages). If the divorce rates remain steady, it would be expected that close to one-third of the marriages contracted in the end of the 1990s will end in divorce. In three-quarters of the marriages that end in divorce, the couples have children.

Thus, the political changes, at least temporarily, increased the stability of existing marriages. During this time of change in family life, several contradictory factors were affecting the situation. The social and economic processes that began in 1989 supposedly increased solidarity and kept individuals in families. These included, first, unemployment and impoverishment. The same trend is visible in the increasing number of family-run small businesses as a means to escape unemployment. At the same time, the increased educational level of women pushed the indicators toward what has remained a high divorce rate.

Fertility

The Hungarian society kept its traditional character in the area of marriage until the end of the 1980s. Trends in childbirth, however, showed radical changes much earlier. Compared to the fertility situation in the 1970s, when the age group born in the middle of the 1950s was at peak child-bearing years, a gradual decline can be found. The turning point was in 1981, when the number of deaths exceeded the number of birth each year. However, the proportion of women who were childless at age fifty-one remained below 10 percent in different age cohorts. The total fertility rate was 1.29 in 1999. These trends mean that, concerning fertility, Hungary does not show the signs of a non-European marriage type (in which the age at first marriage is low, few people remain unmarried, and a high fertility rate exists). A new phenomenon is that the proportion of live births outside marriage is rapidly increasing. In 1990 13.1 percent of children were born out of wedlock. In 1999 this proportion reached 28 percent.

Encouraging families to have more children was one of the key issues of the prevailing Hungarian policy-makers. Different financial incentives and moral-ideological pressure were used in past decades to encourage Hungarian families to have more children. These efforts had little or only temporary success. The majority of Hungarian families have one or two children. As the number of the families without a child was low, so was the number of families with three or more children.

Attitudes

In Hungarian society in the 1990s, behavior moved away from the traditional family forms. Attitudes, in contrast, moved in the opposite direction in some areas (Tóth 2000). In 1994, the adult population valued the advantages of marriage more than they did in 1988. Significantly more adults found that the most important function of marriage was to ensure financial security. Significantly more men than women believe that married people are happier. What is becoming more important for women is that marriage serve as a secure framework for raising children. At the same time, however, young, highly qualified women believe substantially less both in the ability of marriages to create happiness automatically and in their function of childrearing. This is in comparison with men with similar qualifications, as well as compared with other women or with the 1988 data.

Given that Hungary lacks services and institutions to help couples resolve disputes, divorce is the most accepted way of treating martial conflict. Women—as the divorce statistics also show—are willing to accept divorce at a higher rate than are men. After the divorce, children usually stay with the mother; thus the role of the parent raising her child alone is known and accepted for women. Maintaining a deteriorated marriage relationship is not appealing to women, not even in the (eventual) interest of the child. In this area, attitudes and real demographic behavior are moving into the same direction.

The decrease in the number of children per family started decades ago in Hungarian society. In sharp contrast with their numbers, children held a high position in the society's value system, and their importance increased during the 1990s. Nevertheless, the stated love for children, documented by various surveys (Pongrácz and Molnár 1999), is contrary to other evidence. The adult population spends much time working, so they cannot interact with their children as much as they would like to. Parent-child relationships involve a lot of tension, and force and thrashing are accepted tools of raising children. An exception to this is the case of the youngest, most educated male and female classes; this group is less likely than average to place the raising of children above all other values. The temporary or permanent decision not to have children and the change of attitudes go together in the case of this group.

Bibliography

Hajnal, J. (1965). "European Marriage Patterns in Perspective." In *Population in History,* ed. D. V. Glass and D. E. C. Eversley. London: Arnold.

Klinger, A. (1996). "Magyarország népesedésfejlodése" (Population growth in Hungary). *Statisztikai Szemle* 8–9:325–348

Mikrocenzus. (1996). "A népesség és a lakások jellemzoi" (Characteristics of the population and homes). Budapest: Central Statistics Office.

Pongrácz, T., and Molnár, E. S. (1999). "Changes in Attitudes Towards Having Children." In *The Changing Role of Women,* ed. K. Lévai and I. G. Y. Tóth. Budapest: Social Research Informatics Center.

Szalai, J. (1991). "Some Aspects of the Changing Situation of Women in Hungary." *Signs* 1:152–170.

Tóth, O. (1999). "Marriage, Divorce and Fertility in Hungary Today. Tensions between Facts and Attitudes." In *Construction. Reconstruction. Women, Family and Politics in Central Europe. 1945-1998,* ed. A. Peto and B. Rásky. Budapest: Open Society Institute—Central European University.

Other Resource

Tóth, O. (2000). "Marriage and Child: Attitudes and Behaviour in Comparative Perspective." The Tokyo Woman's Christian University, Cross Cultural Study on Women in the World Program. Available from http://www.twcu.ac.jp.

OLGA TÓTH

HUSBAND

A *husband* is a male partner in a marriage. Most cultures recognize this common social status with a specific affinal kinship term. In most times and places, men have been expected to become husbands at some point in their adulthood. The stage at which this happens varies greatly, however, as does the social role a husband may play in a family and the legal rights and constraints of his status. Much depends on the typical form of marriage itself, gender role conventions, economic conditions, and religious and political edicts concerning marital roles. Despite such diversity, people often hold very strong opinions on the proper role of husbands in marriages. This is notably so at the present time when marital roles have become the subject of often acrimonious debate between cultural and religious conservatives, feminists, social liberals, and sexual minorities pushing for legal recognition of alternative marriage styles (Coontz 1992).

Most males in contemporary Western countries enjoy a great deal of freedom in choosing when to get married or whether to marry at all. (Statistics reveal that most do by their late twenties, somewhat older than women.) In most societies, where marriages are arranged between families, men have far less choice (Fox 1967). In cultures practicing infant betrothals, a boy may become identified as a *husband* while still very young at the start of a long period of preparation for the full adult role. In other circumstances, for example, where divorces are prohibited or marriages require a large payment to the bride's family (*bride-wealth*), men may delay becoming husbands until quite late in life. Among the Maasai of eastern Africa, for instance, men cannot marry until they go through initiation rituals making them into "warriors" and then acquire cattle from their fathers, around the age of

thirty. Older men who own many cattle often marry several wives.

The marital roles assumed by husbands also depend upon the general conception of the family. After the Industrial Revolution in Europe, an idealized form of middle-class family life emerged in which an husband was seen as the breadwinner, working outside the household in wage labor, while the wife was confined to raising children and taking care of the private domestic sphere. This ideal came under increasing pressure in the course of the twentieth century as large numbers of women entered the work force and, over time, challenged the disparity in wages and opportunities between men and women. Still favored by social conservatives, the image of the patriarchal nuclear family now competes with an equally popular idealization of the family as a partnership between equals. Both of these versions of marital relations differ from those in cultures where marriages are arranged by and supported in extended families. Here the role of a husband is usually subservient to rules of seniority and gender in the extended household as a whole. In the joint families of rural northern India, for instance, husbands come under the authority of the senior male in the household—usually their father or an older brother—until and unless they survive to take that role themselves.

The role of husband is also a legal status, with rights and obligations set by local convention, religious edicts, and state laws. These often parallel rights to property and its disposal. Among the matrilineal Hopi Indians of the southwestern United States, for example, husbands form rather marginal adjuncts to households in which women and their brothers (if present) own the land. In contrast, for most of Christian and Islamic history, husbands have exercised legal control over wives, often including the right to beat them and to dispose of the property they bring into a marriage either in dowries or by inheritance. Religious fundamentalists have tended to insist on a sharp differentiation on the roles of husband and wife and the requirement that wives submit to their husband's authority. Secular states have tended to move in the opposite direction in modern times, passing and enforcing laws that bring the rights of husbands and wives over children and property more into balance (Ruether 2000).

See also: BRIDE-PRICE; DIVISION OF LABOR; FAMILY ROLES; FATHERHOOD; GENDER; KINSHIP; MATE SELECTION; WIFE

Bibliography

Coontz, S. (1992). *The Way We Never Were: American Families and the Nostalgia Trap.* New York: Basic Books.

Fox, R. (1967). *Kinship and Marriage.* Harmondsworth, UK: Penguin.

Ruether, R. R. (2000). *Christianity and the Making of the Modern Family.* Boston: Beacon Press.

JOHN BARKER

HUTTERITE FAMILIES

The Hutterites are an Anabaptist group, along with the Amish and the Mennonites. Jacob Hutter founded the religion in central Europe in the middle 1500s. The official name of the religion is the Hutterian Brethren. Today, they total about 45,000 members living in more than 400 colonies. They are the oldest family communal group in the Western world, but they consider the community to be more important than the family. They believe that salvation is found in total submission to the group, which is more important than the individual. One of their original basic tenets was that believing Hutterites must separate from nonbelieving spouses (Huntington 1997).

Continually persecuted, many Hutterites moved to Russia in 1770 where they were promised tolerance of their beliefs and practices. This lasted for about a century before the czars forced them into the national schools and the military. Between 1874 and 1877, all 800 surviving Hutterites immigrated to the United States. About half of them were not practicing communal living and eventually joined the Mennonites. The others settled in South Dakota into three colonies, each with a different leader. From then to the present day each of these groups, or *Leut,* maintains its own council of elders, has minor differences in customs, and seldom intermarries, although relations are friendly across groups. From most to least conservative in their practices, they are called the *Lehrerleut,* the *Dariusleut,* and the *Schmeideleut.*

World War I brought persecution from the U.S. government because the Hutterites refused to serve in the military, so as a group they made arrangements with the Canadian government, which granted them immunity from the draft. As a result, almost all of them moved to western Canada. They now have colonies in Montana and eastern Washington as well.

Originally craftsmen, they turned to agriculture when the Industrial Revolution made their skills obsolete (Peter 1971). The Hutterites live together in communities and speak a German dialect as well as English. Unlike the Amish, they do accept and use modern devices such as automotive equipment and electricity. Each community, or *Bruderhof* (a colony within a Leut), is administered by a council of six men, usually elected for life. The preacher is the spiritual leader. There is also a business manager, a farm boss, and a German teacher (Kephart 1976). They live in apartment buildings of their own making.

Kinship Structure

All Hutterites are descended from eighteen families. Four names have since died out, so only fourteen Hutterite surnames remain. The society is patriarchal, and kinship is patrilineal and patrilocal, so men have lifelong association in the same community while women usually leave their colony of birth at marriage. They have maintained the extended family, with three or four generations in the same community, but not necessarily under the same roof.

They believe in a hierarchy of relationships that is ordained by God. Men have higher status than women, and the elderly deserve the respect of the young. The gender and age ranking is seen in all settings, be it church, school, work, or meals. Men typically are assigned to the outdoor farm work; women are in charge of the kitchen and the nursery. Males sit on one side of the room and the females on the other, with the oldest in the back. After church services, for instance, the males file out first, with the oldest woman following the youngest boy (Hofer 1991, 1998).

Due to the high intermarriage that occurs, a colony might have only one or two family names, but consist of eight to fourteen extended families all related to each other to some degree. Others may have as many as seven family names. The three Leut have been endogamous—marrying only within the group—since 1879. However,

Hutterite children stand in a field on the Forest River Colony near Fordville, North Dakota. Members of the colony live a communal life and share the responsibilities of their farm. KEVIN FLEMING/CORBIS

within these groups, an incest taboo is maintained that includes up to first cousins on both sides (Peter 1971).

The House Child

The sequence and details of childcare were originally described by Hutterite leader Peter Riedemann in 1545 and are basically still followed. Because Hutterites generally adhere to the old rules, their childcare has changed far less than that of the outside world and remains generally untouched by Freudian psychology and other thinking (Huntington 1997). However, since about 1980, some modernizing influences have been noted. Parents now toilet-train their children at about age two rather than at three months; nursing may go all the way to the second birthday, but solid foods are introduced somewhere between six and twelve months (Ingoldsby 2001), whereas it used to be as early as one month after birth (Hostetler 1974).

When the child is an infant, the mother's female relatives commonly visit and care for both the new mother and the infant. The mother is allowed time off from her regular duties to attend to the needs of her newborn infant and to recover from the pregnancy.

The late infancy stage is a time for the house child to venture beyond the mother to a greater range of peers and associations within the colony. When the child gets a little older, the mother is reassigned back to her original job, and so the rest of the community helps to raise the child. In effect, the colony becomes a large extended family tending to the needs and welfare of the young Hutterite (Stanton 1989).

In the Middle Ages the Hutterites believed that "as soon as the mother hath weaned the child she giveth it to the school." Today the nuclear family is not so limited in its functions, but the schools do play a large part in the lives of Hutterite youth (Hostetler 1974).

Kindergarten

Children stay with their families until they are three, at which time they go to the community kindergarten, which usually lasts from seven or eight in the morning to four in the afternoon. Throughout their six-day-a-week program, the children are separated from the rest of the colony, including parents and siblings, from early in the morning to mid- or late afternoon. The children sing together, memorize together, eat together, and even take their mid-morning and mid-afternoon naps together.

Young children are considered to be willful, and strict punishment, including strapping, is used. They are expected to learn to obey, pray, share, and sit properly. The three Leuts have different practices in the area of toys. For the most conservative Lehrerleut, none are permitted. The Dariusleut will tolerate small toys brought from home, and the Schmiedeleut provide them in the school (Hostetler 1974).

However, many Dariusleut colonies have stopped running kindergartens. Although the kindergartens have been a key element in the philosophy of putting the community over the family in the raising of children throughout most of Hutterite history, these colonies are simply not organizing them. This means that small children are now spending those years with their families (Ingoldsby 2001).

School

Following kindergarten comes a ten-year period from ages six to sixteen that is a time of intensive preparation for embracing the Hutterian way of life. A large part of this period is spent in the *big school*. The local school board instructor teaches from the normal provincial curriculum, and their German teacher provides the moral and religious instruction. The instruction takes place in a one-room classroom with children from the first to the tenth grade in attendance.

The English school is staffed by a teacher provided by the government, who teaches at the colony. Before and after those classes, the Hutterites run their own, in which the children are taught German and the Hutterian way of life. This way, the colony meets government requirements, and the children get a minimal education for interacting in the larger world, but they are not corrupted from their way of life (Kephart 1976).

The education system successfully separates Hutterite children from the outside world. Having close primary, intimate, concrete relations with the colony and only a secondary generalized relationship with the outside world, Hutterites find it hard to interact with and relate to the outside world, so defection is rare (Peter 1971).

Adolescence

Adolescence is from age fifteen to baptism (which is around age twenty), where adult work is learned and begun. Corporal punishment stops here. Termed *the foolish years,* this is a time when adults expect minor deviations—smoking, having a radio, dating—and tolerate them. Serious problems like suicide, drug addiction, arson, or sexual immorality are virtually nonexistent (Kephart 1976). At this point, adolescents begin to eat with the adults in the dining hall.

The young adult occupies an apprentice position. The boys in this group do most of the colony's hard labor and enjoy the opportunity to demonstrate their strength and stamina. Almost all the boys in this age group find ways to generate cash of their own. They may share it with their sisters in exchange for having the sisters sew them clothes that depart from the accepted pattern in some small way. This is, however, against the expectations of the good basic communal commitments of the Hutterites. Young adults are still considered to be immature emotionally and in need of more religious instruction, but moodiness or poor work performance is not tolerated (Hostetler 1974).

Hutterite preachers condemn dating as a carnal or romantic activity, but it occurs anyway. Parents will usually veto a child's choice that they do not like, or colony leaders will intervene if the partner is considered inappropriate (such as a first cousin). John A. Hostetler quotes a sixteen-year-old girl speaking on relationships:

> When boys or girls from other colonies come and visit we all go together in the evening. If the visitors have never been here before, one of our group does the introducing (so the boys know what the girl's name is when he wants her for a

date). Then we sit and talk or play. If a boy wants a date, he goes out with one of our guys and tells him; then he calls out the girl he wants. If she wants, she goes along with him. If not, she says no. Sometimes the boys don't like it if we refuse, but you can't tell a girl to go along if she doesn't want to. It's only in leap year that the girls call the boy for a date. Otherwise the boy has to do the calling. In wintertime we really get a lot of visitors because there's not much work to do. In all the colonies each boy gets a two-week vacation. Then they can go and visit whenever they please. (1974, p. 223)

A later description of Hutterite dating involves more physical contact:

A date could be as simple as going for a walk or sitting in a dark corner holding hands, talking, and kissing. On a typical date however, a couple meets in a private room, preferably with a cot or bed on which to sit or lie on (most Hutterites don't have sofas in their homes). Sometimes several dating couples will use the room simultaneously, each minding their own business, on separate cots. And so, usually with the lights off, the couple "dates" often in horizontal position. I was told that this is not universally practiced among the Schmiedeleit, but I do know it is among the Lehrerleit. I suspect that most young people of all three Leit date this way. (Hofer 1998, p. 51)

Hutterite leaders are uncomfortable with the dating style, and they hide it from outsiders, which is not surprising given the strong religious stance they have of confining sexual relations to marriage. Hutterite dating, then, although still conservative, has become romantic. Love and sexual attraction may be as important as orthodoxy in mate selection.

Marriage

The Hutterites invented a matching procedure during which once or twice a year the marriageable youth were assembled, and the preacher gave each male a choice of three females from which to select a wife. The man had to wait for the next time if he did not want to marry any of the three.

This changed to personal choice in 1830 following the uproar caused when a young girl refused to marry an older man (Peter 1971). However, one must marry a Hutterite, and interfaith marriages never occur in the Hutterite church (Hofer 1998). Most colonies are like a large extended family where everyone is either a relative or feels like one, so one usually goes outside the colony to find a spouse. Because Hutterites cannot marry until after baptism and because visiting across colonies is relatively infrequent (for weddings, funerals, and the like), courtships of three or four years are not uncommon (Kephart 1976).

After it is informally known that a couple wishes to marry, and any objections with the families or the colony are worked out, the formal procedure begins the Sunday before the actual wedding. First, the boy asks the preacher's help, which is granted. Next, the elders consider his request and lecture him on proper behavior, and he is encouraged to confess his sins. The next day father and son travel to the girl's colony to get her parent's permission. The day after they are *put together* in the girl's church. Following this are two days of celebration in the girl's colony and the rest of the week in the boy's. They are married on Sunday and lectured on submissive role of the wife and the kind protective role of the husband. They do not have a honeymoon, but rather immediately return to the normal routine. Marriages are durable due to the strong community relations, and divorce is unknown (Kephart 1976).

Weddings should not take place right before Christmas or Easter, and rarely occur during the planting or harvest seasons. Half of all Schmiedeleut marriages occur in November or December (Hostetler 1974). The bride typically wears a blue brocade wedding dress, along with her usual kerchief head covering instead of a veil. The groom wears a black suit (made for him by his fiancée) with a white shirt and black tie. Wedding cakes seem to be getting fancier, and pictures are now usually taken. It is a happy time, with much to eat and drink (Hofer 1998).

Men are under pressure to marry because they cannot grow beards until they are married, and a beardless male is visibly set apart and not allowed to move into the upper authority levels. The marriage bond is relatively weak in that the couple is generally together only at night. In some colonies their bedroom is next to the husband's parents during the first year. Overt affection is discouraged, but romantic love is filtering in from Canadian society. Wives have a sense of loyalty and devotion to their husbands, but the men are more concerned with other males, as they are the ones who vote on advances in the occupational hierarchy (Peter 1971). Since about 1980 an increase in love and affection in marriage has been noted, with a resulting focus of family over work structure (Ingoldsby 2001).

In 1950 the median age at marriage was 22.0 years for women and 23.5 years for men. Only 1.9 percent of the men and 5.4 percent of the women over the age of thirty had never been married, and only one divorce and four desertions had been reported since 1875 (Hostetler 1974).

Fertility

In 1954, Joseph W. Eaton and Albert J. Meyer published their landmark study on Hutterite fertility. They documented that from 1880 to 1950, the Hutterites grew from 443 to 8,542 persons. This represents an annual increase of 4.12 percent, which appears to be the world's fastest natural growth rate. Documenting an average family size of slightly over ten children, Eaton and Meyer established the Hutterites as the demographic standard and estimated that maximum fertility for humans is twelve to fourteen children.

Because Hutterites do not marry when a woman first becomes fertile and because there is virtually no premarital sex, the actual number of children is lower than the theoretical maximum. Birth control is considered to be murder, and Eaton and Meyer noted that it was often not used when medically recommended. Natural methods, such as coitus interruptus, are considered sinful. These sexual beliefs and practices have been substantiated in other research (Lee and Brattrud 1967).

Since that time a 33-percent drop in their birthrate has been confirmed. K. Peter (1966, 1980) attributed the decline to later age of marriage and speculated that the purpose was to delay colony divisions or to save money and avoid having idle workers. Although it is true (Laing 1980) that age of marriage is increasing and colony size decreasing, others (Boldt and Roberts 1980) believe that some forms of birth control must be practiced,

which could represent a weakening of church authority and a change in core values.

In 1985 access was given to the medical records of all Hutterites treated at a clinic in a small southern Alberta town. Six colonies (three Lehrerleut and three Dariusleut) patronize that clinic for treatment. The clinic had medical records on forty-eight married Hutterite women. Of these 12.5 percent of the women had used oral contraceptives, IUDs, or both. An additional 25 percent had tubal ligations or hysterectomies, meaning that over one-third of the sample made use of some form of birth control. Other physicians and Hutterite leaders confirmed this (Ingoldsby and Stanton 1988).

Later Life

The Hutterites believe that the aged are to be respected and deserving of rest. Women are usually relieved of regular colony jobs in their late forties. Most will continue with food preparation because they prefer that to being alone in their apartments. Men will move to council positions. Having a large family is seen as *grandchild insurance* against loneliness in old age, and a grandchild may be assigned to run errands for someone with health problems.

Hostetler used a short survey based on Myers-Briggs categories to assess personality. Results indicated that Hutterites are generally extraverted rather than introverted, sensing rather than intuitive, feeling rather than thinking, and judgmental rather than perceptive. They believe that God controls the time of death, and they envy children who die young for having avoided life's temptations and struggles. Most colonies have cemeteries, but funerals are quiet and simple (Hostetler 1974).

Conclusion

Superficially, Hutterite society may appear unchanging. Many colonies hold firmly to the traditional rules concerning dress, food, and recreation, but at the same time important shifts have been occurring in family size and relations. Although still very communal by outside standards, some evidence suggests that individualism is on the rise (Huntington 1997).

In visiting a Dariusleut colony, one gets the feeling of an extended family sharing an inherited farm. The atmosphere is not so much one of communalism as it is of togetherness. Rather than living in the apartment rows, every nuclear family has its own home. This includes mobile homes brought onto the property. Families do their own laundry, and furniture stays in a family from one generation to the next rather than going back to the community.

Although there is the community dining hall, each house has a kitchen with a microwave and refrigerator, and people can eat at home if they chose to. The groups use many store-bought goods in addition to those the colony produces. Each adult is given a personal monthly allowance, and everyone has personal knick-knacks. They are comfortable with picture taking. One sees children's books, soda cans, and toys in the rooms. Unlike the Lehrerleut households, their furniture is soft and comfortable.

Most important is the family interaction, which reminds one of the idealized American family of the 1950s. Families are still technically patriarchal with occasional blustering on the part of the father, but the mother does what she wants in most cases. There is a real affection that leads to greater gender equality in decision-making. Without televisions, families engage in easy, happy conversations. Word games and jokes are common, with extended kin dropping in and out throughout the evening.

The center of life seems to be the family, with the colony as a shared business extended family. Hutterites remain faithful to key tenets and are not threatened by societal incursion in minor areas. They are still conservative enough to be set apart and are less individualistic than are members of the greater society. But the family is now psychologically more important than the community, which has become a support rather than the center (Ingoldsby 2001).

See also: ANABAPTISTS (AMISH, MENNONITE); EXTENDED FAMILIES; FAMILY PLANNING; INTENTIONAL COMMUNITIES

Bibliography

Boldt, E., and Roberts, L. (1980). "The Decline of Hutterite Population Growth: Causes and Consequences—A Comment." *Canadian Ethnic Studies* 12(3):11–117.

Eaton, J. W., and Meyer, A. (1954). *Man's Capacity to Reproduce: A Demography of a Unique Population.* Glencoe, IL: The Free Press.

Hofer, S. (1991). *Born Hutterite.* Winnipeg: Hofer Publishers.

Hofer, S. (1998). *The Hutterites: Lives and Images of a Communal People.* Winnipeg: Hofer Publishers.

Hostetler, J. (1974). *Hutterite Society.* Baltimore: John Hopkins University Press.

Huntington, G. (1997). "Living in the Ark: Four Centuries of Hutterite Faith and Community." In *America's Communal Utopias,* ed. Donald Pitzer. Chapel Hill: University of North Carolina Press.

Ingoldsby, B. (2001). "The Hutterite Family in Transition." *Journal of Comparative Family Studies* 32(3):377–392.

Ingoldsby, B., and Stanton, M. (1988). "The Hutterites and Fertility Control." *Journal of Comparative Family Studies* 19(1):137–142.

Kephart, W. (1976). *Extraordinary Groups: The Sociology of Unconventional Life Styles.* New York: St. Martins Press.

Laing, L. M. (1980). "Declining Fertility in a Religious Isolate: The Hutterite Population of Alberta, Canada, 1955–71." *Human Biology* 52(May):288–310.

Lee, S. C., and Brattrud, A. (1967). "Marriage Under a Monastic Mode of Life: A Preliminary Report on the Hutterite Family in South Dakota." *Journal of Marriage and the Family* 29(3):512–520.

Peter, K. (1966). "Toward a Demographic Theory of Hutterite Population Growth." *Variables* 5(Spring):28–37.

Peter, K. (1971). "The Hutterite Family." In *The Canadian Family,* ed. K. Ishwaran. Toronto: Holt, Rinehart, and Winston.

Peter, K. (1980). "The Decline of Hutterite Population Growth." *Canadian Ethnic Studies* 12(3):97–109.

Stanton, M. (1989). "The Maintenance of the Hutterite Way: the Family and Childhood Life-Cycle in the Communal Context." *Family Science Review* 2(4):373–388.

BRON B. INGOLDSBY

I

IMMIGRATION

Immigration is the term used to describe the process of a person entering and settling as a permanent resident in another country; *emigration* is the process of leaving one's country of origin. When the term immigration is used, emigration is assumed to have occurred first. Emigrating is the beginning and immigrating is the end of the process of international migration. International migration is when people move voluntarily (immigrants) or involuntarily (refugees) from one country to another, settling permanently or temporarily (sojourners) in another country.

The process of international migration has a profound effect on families. Family, economic, and political situations all influence reasons for immigrating. A country's immigration policies determine who is admitted and its approach to integration of newcomers. The decision to emigrate is made by one or more family members, and may be viewed initially as a permanent or temporary move. The tendency is to look at the effect of the immigration process on those who settle in a new country, although the effect extends to those who remain in the home country. Families also play a role in immigrant adaptation.

Reasons for Immigration

Researchers from diverse disciplines focus on slightly different but interrelated reasons for the decision to immigrate. Economists identify *push* and *pull* factors, both of which emphasize employment opportunities. For example, if the economy in the other country compared to the home country offers better chances for job advancement, wages, and employment, the individual is pushed to emigrate. In a pull situation, a country is actively recruiting new workers for specific jobs, and the opportunities are sufficient to entice the person to immigrate (Suarez-Orozco and Suarez-Orozco 2001). Countries of origin may encourage people to leave for economic reasons. If some family members emigrate but others remain behind, the family and the country both benefit from the financial support sent back to family members (Rumbaut 1997).

Sociologists describe a chain migration process in which migration begets additional migration. The first person emigrating from the area sends information to those in the home country about jobs, housing, and schools in the new setting. Others immigrate and are assisted by those who preceded them. Eventually, within a geographic area in the new country, there are a number of immigrants from the same area in the home country.

Anthropologists focus on changes in the standard of living and cultural reasons for immigration. First-hand accounts from new immigrants as well as media accounts of the country's standard of living entice people to immigrate to the new country for a better way of life. Parents place their children's interests before their own; immigration is worthwhile because it betters the lives of their children even if the parents' situation is not as good as they anticipated (Suarez-Orozco and Suarez-Orozco 2001).

Psychologists suggest that personality factors are important in the desire to emigrate. Those who want to emigrate are more work-oriented, consider the family less central, are lower on affiliation motivation, and have higher achievement and power motivation. These personality factors are most salient for those who are not family-sponsored immigrants (Boneva and Frieze 2001).

Political scientists emphasize ethnopolitical reasons for emigration. Countries may encourage emigration to ease ethnic conflict, or to establish presence in another country, by resettling particular ethnic groups voluntarily or involuntarily. Whether one is allowed to emigrate may depend upon payment to or permission of authorities in the country of origin.

Policy

Immigration policy encompasses criteria for qualifying as an immigrant, through an independent application or family reunification. Policies vary over time based on the types of workers that are needed, definitions of family used in family reunification, and assessment of the impact of such policies on the country's social, political, and economic systems.

In an independent application, the immigrant is applying based on the country's employment admission criteria. Family reunification occurs when an immigrant applies to bring family members into the country. Priority for admission is given to spouses and children. Close relatives such as siblings and parents are included during periods of more openness in immigration policy.

In describing nine industrialized democratic nations' approaches to immigration policy at the end of the twentieth century, Wayne Cornelius, Philip Martin, and James Hollifield (1994) classified the countries as follows: countries of immigration (United States and Canada), reluctant countries of immigration (France, Germany, Belgium, and Britain), and latecomers to immigration (Italy, Spain, and Japan).

Australia, like the United States and Canada, is a country of immigration. All three countries are proud of being nations of immigrants and lands of opportunity for newcomers. Until the mid-1960s and 1970s, immigration to these countries was primarily from Europe; after that, larger-scale immigration of visible minorities from Asia, Latin America, and the Caribbean began. Western nations are experiencing increased ethnic diversity because of the general movement of people in the last half of the twentieth century from developing to industrialized nations (Zlotnic 2001).

At the start of the twenty-first century, some Western countries wanted to limit admittance under family reunification and to place more controls on immigration. Controls involve sanctions against employers and immigrants. The government fines employers who hire immigrants who are in the country illegally, and family-sponsored immigrants are limited in eligibility for public resources such as welfare.

There are three primary reasons for needing controls. First, Western countries do not have the ability to provide employment for more newcomers and permanent residents. Second, immigration from developing nations affects national culture, language, and identity of the country of immigration. Finally, more immigrants strain already overburdened government-funded health, education, and welfare systems (Cornelius et al. 1994).

Critics suggest that the need for controls is overstated, and that the controls are based on ethnocentrism, reflecting Western views of marriage, family, and way of life. Such controls potentially have an impact on arranged marriages, adoption, extended family, and homosexual relationships. Marriages may be viewed as a way to enter a country—a marriage of convenience rather than a legitimate marriage (Cohen 2001).

Controls have an impact on families adjusting to their new country. If controls restrict the reuniting of family members, families remain separated by national boundaries or they enter as illegal immigrants. If family members are admitted, families remain responsible for them financially. This places a burden on the family, and also reinforces dependence, keeping spouses in an untenable marriage (violence, abuse) and limiting opportunities (Cohen 2001). Controls are based on the idea that family reunification is a drain on public resources. Some research suggests that this is not the situation (Jasso and Rosenzweig 1995).

Pathways to Immigration

The path taken to become an immigrant varies and affects subsequent adjustment and opportunities in the new country. Two common patterns are for the family to immigrate at the same time or for the primary wage earner to immigrate first and sponsor the rest of the family later. The primary wage earner is usually the most employable family member, either a man or woman, depending upon job opportunities and who meets the criteria for immigration. This wage earner is expected to support family members back home financially while also saving enough money to sponsor their immigration.

Carola and Marcelo Suarez-Orozco (2001), in their study of children of immigrants in fifty schools in Boston and San Francisco, noted that only 35 percent of their sample immigrated at the same time as their parents. Typically, the child stays in the home country with one parent or other relatives, with the separation lasting months or years. The child remains behind because the home country is the best place to raise the child, or the immigrant parent's work hours limit ability to care for the child. When further schooling is not available in the country of origin, the child immigrates. Whether detrimental effects occur depend upon how the parties involved view the situation. If it is considered acceptable in the child's native culture, and if positive relationships exist with parents and temporary caregivers, the effects are less negative. Shorter periods of separation, knowledge of when the separation will end, and frequent communication through letters, gifts, phone calls, and visits, result in less negative outcomes. Once the child is reunited with parents, there are additional adjustments—loss of not being with caregiver and friends in the home country, adjusting to the new country, specifically to school, to parent(s), and to siblings born in the interim.

Family sponsorship rather than employment is the major route of recent immigration to the United States, but not to Canada and Australia. In the year 2000, 71 percent of U.S. immigrants were family sponsored compared with 31 percent of Canadian and 45 percent of Australian immigrants (Dovidio and Esses 2001). Under family sponsorship, marriage to a citizen is the major route of entry in the United States. There is a multiplier effect of family reunification on immigration among legal immigrants. Individuals sponsored by family become permanent residents and are able to sponsor additional family members. Many recent immigrants have kin already living in and knowledgeable about life in the new country, facilitating their adjustment (Rumbaut 1997).

Illegal or undocumented immigration is another route. Legal immigration is critical for full access to public benefits and opportunities afforded to legal residents. Illegal or undocumented immigrants may also be deported, splitting up the family unit if it contains citizens born in the country as well as non-documented members (Suarez-Orozco and Suarez-Orozco 2001). Experts suggest that limits on family sponsorship result in additional illegal immigrants because they do not see a chance to reunite otherwise (Donato, Durand, and Massey 1992).

Not all immigration involves a permanent move to another country. There are three types of temporary immigration: (1) A *target earner* goes to another country for employment, returning to the home country when a targeted amount of earnings have been saved. One or both parents may be such earners, but the children remain with relatives in the home country. Months or even years later, the earner has achieved the goal and reunites with family in the home country. (2) Sojourners are temporarily in the country. They may be executives or employees of multinational corporations, or seasonal workers in agriculture or construction. Spouse or children may go with them or remain behind in the home country. (3) Binationals work and live in two countries, having the legal status (work permits, citizenship) to do so. This pattern is not common, possibly because it requires proximity or ease of travel between the two nations and considerable financial resources (Suarez-Orozco and Suarez-Orozco 2001).

Immigration's Effect on Families

Family ties are maintained across national boundaries. Some family members may not want to immigrate, others may not be allowed to immigrate, and the immigrant may have insufficient finances to sponsor relatives. Immigrants show considerable ingenuity in providing food, clothing, medical items, and money to relatives with less access to such resources in the home country. Items are shipped directly, or more complex exchanges are done to ensure that items reach the intended relatives. For example, an immigrant family might give money to another family in the country of immigration; in turn, that family instructs their relatives in the home country to give an equivalent amount of money to the other immigrant's relatives in the home country (Gold 1992).

Immigrants who reside in the new country begin to create a new family life, one that is influenced by both past cultural customs and the ways of the new country, but is also different from both (Foner 1997; Kibria 1997). Such families exemplify integration or bicultural adjustment rather than assimilation. Assimilation (a *melting pot* approach) means giving up one's home culture to adopt the ways of the dominant culture. Integrated or bicultural families are possible if there are sufficient numbers in the ethnic community, if immigration continues from the country of origin, and if the ethnic community has links with the country of origin (Kibria 1997).

Nancy Foner (1997) summarizes research on how the immigrant family's cultural background, social and economic circumstances in the new country, and the legal system, help create an integrated or bicultural family. Although traditions change over time in the country of origin, the immigrant may continue to think that such customs are timeless, and interpret the present based upon the remembered past. Such cultural understandings are critical in reinforcing traditional family values and behaviors. Social influences, such as the availability of close kin and a balanced sex ratio, also help maintain traditional family life. For example, the absence of appropriate close kin such as older relatives to care for the children and to do housework results in nontraditional patterns of husbands assisting wives in such activities. An imbalance of men to women affects who gets married and whether spouses are from another ethnic group or are sought from the home country (Foner 1997). Even when there are sufficient numbers of women, a man may seek a marital partner from the home country because he wants a traditional wife, not one who exemplifies Western values (DeLaet 1999).

Young immigrants compared to their parents, and women more than men, may incorporate Western values (less patriarchy and more egalitarian views) because they represent independence or freedom from some traditional roles (Foner 1997). Women are expected to raise their children to understand cultural traditions as well as to fit into the new setting. Although there are pressures to retain specific gender roles, women have multiple opportunities for changing roles, especially when they are separated from extended families and receive limited reinforcement of cultural roles from the ethnic community. Olivia Espin (1999) suggests that "the degree of integration of the women of a given immigrant group in the host society—rather than the integration and/or success of men—indicates the significance of the transformation occurring in the immigrant community. It signals their adaptation to the new life" (p. 4).

The legal system identifies certain cultural practices as illegal (e.g., polygamy) and makes it possible for other practices to be challenged or prosecuted (e. g., physical abuse of wife or child). Legitimate children and legal but not common-law spouses can be sponsored under family reunification. Government agencies interact with women, not only the men in the household, thus increasing the woman's potential influence in the family (Foner 1997).

Economic circumstances shape family life: men's earnings may be insufficient, and women's earnings become essential for the family. Women's employment brings some economic independence, potentially altering traditional patterns of authority in the family (Foner 1997). When women work outside the home, men are expected to share household responsibilities (Suarez-Orozco and Suarez-Orozco 2001). Postmigration, Vietnamese immigrants have shown additional sharing in household tasks even though considerable sharing had been done traditionally. The pattern of sharing shifted from performance of tasks by several members of the household to husband and wife sharing the tasks (Johnson 1998). If the elderly do not have financial resources, their authority may be weakened. On the other hand, access to public support such as welfare may provide the elderly with independence from their grown children (Foner 1997). Because it is easier for children than their parents to learn the country's language, children become the interpreters and serve as the family's contact with the outside world, undermining parental authority and status (Suarez-Orozco and Suarez-Orozco 2001).

Assistance of family members is often important for ensuring economic viability of new immigrants, especially for those who have limited financial resources. When extended family members are not available, substitute family networks are created. Newcomers form households of all unrelated individuals, or of related and unrelated individuals, who view each other as family. They also marry to create kinship ties that are helpful if difficult financial times occur; sponsor relatives, even distant and less known ones, to ensure that kin are available to help out in the future; and form kin networks in which in-laws are treated as substitutes for siblings or parents. Reciprocal help, inherent in the kin-based households, is expected in these variant households (Kibria 1993). Sharing resources, such as pooling income earned by all household members, reduces the chance of the household being in poverty (Caplan, Whitmore, and Choy 1989) and provides the opportunity to own a home or other possessions more quickly (Gold 1993).

Family or ethnic businesses may be viewed as an optimal solution for new immigrants who have difficulty obtaining employment in nonethnic labor markets that require language fluency and other skills (Gold 1992). Ethnic businesses serve several functions: economic support for the family, employment of others in one's ethnic group or family, and autonomy that is not readily available with low- or minimum-wage employment. Other advantages of ethnic businesses are provision of in-kind wages such as food, clothing, or a chance to bring children to the work setting instead of hiring a caretaker (Gold 1992). In her study of Chinese restaurants in Britain, Miri Song (1999) noted that older children play an integral role in the business when parents need translation assistance and unpaid labor for the survival of the business. The children consider helping out in the family business as expected and done out of good will rather than for wages. In return, parents provide material and emotional support, exemplifying the importance of intergenerational exchanges.

Reading first-hand accounts enhances understanding the daily lives of immigrants as they adapt to life in the new country. Thomas Dublin (1993) provided a sampling of such stories and an extensive bibliography covering U.S. immigration from 1773–1986. He noted the similarities across the ethnically diverse waves of immigrants: similar motivations (economic and war dislocations) for immigrating and similar processes of becoming part of the new country. Common experiences included cultural differences that separate them from the existing population, resulting in discrimination, exclusion, and the formation of ethnic communities for mutual economic and social support. Cultural conflicts between generations and within one's beliefs were evident when immigrants were caught between the values of two cultures. The successes of immigrants—working hard and succeeding financially and academically, and contributing to their new country—were portrayed.

In *Immigration and the Family,* edited by Alan Booth, Ann Crouter, and Nancy Landale, a strong case was made for expanding the role of families in future immigration research and policy. As stated by Rubén Rumbaut, "the family is perhaps *the* strategic research site . . . for understanding the dynamics of immigration flows (legal and illegal) and of immigrant adaptation processes." (1997, p. 4; emphasis in original).

See also: ACCULTURATION; FAMILISM; GLOBAL CITIZENSHIP; GRIEF, LOSS, AND BEREAVEMENT; MIGRATION; URBANIZATION

Bibliography

Boneva, B. S., and Frieze, I. H. (2001). "Toward a Concept of a Migrant Personality." *Journal of Social Issues* 57:477–491.

Booth, A.; Crouter, A. C.; and Landale, N., eds. (1997). *Immigration and the Family: Research and Policy on U.S. Immigrants.* Mahwah, NJ: Lawrence Erlbaum Associates.

Caplan, N.; Whitmore, J. K.; and Choy, M. H. (1989). *The Boat People and Achievement in America.* Ann Arbor: The University of Michigan Press.

Cohen, S. (2001). *Immigration Controls, the Family, and the Welfare State.* London: Jessica Kingsley Publishers.

Cornelius, W.; Martin, P. L.; and Hollifield, J. F., eds. (1994). *Controlling Immigration: A Global Perspective.* Stanford, CA: Stanford University Press.

DeLaet, D. L. (1999). "Introduction: The Invisibility of Women in Scholarship on International Migration." In *Gender and Immigration,* ed. G. A. Kelson and D. L. DeLaet. London: Macmillan.

Donato, K. M.; Durand, J.; and Massey, D. S. (1992). "Stemming the Tide? Assessing the Deterrent Effects of the Immigration Reform and Control Act." *Demography* 29:139–157.

Dovidio J. F., and Esses, V. M. (2001). "Immigrants and Immigration: Advancing the Psychological Perspective." *Journal of Social Issues* 57:375–387.

Dublin, T., ed. (1993). *Immigrant Voices: New Lives in America 1773–1986.* Urbana: University of Illinois Press.

Espin, O. M. (1999). *Women Crossing Boundaries: A Psychology of Immigration and Transformations of Sexuality.* New York: Routledge.

Foner, N. (1997). "The Immigrant Family: Cultural Legacies and Cultural Changes." *International Migration Review* 31:961–974.

Gold, S. J. (1992). *Refugee Communities: A Comparative Field Study.* Newbury Park, CA: Sage.

Gold, S. J. (1993). "Migration and Family Adjustment: Continuity and Change among Vietnamese in the United States." In *Family Ethnicity: Strength in Diversity,* ed. H. P. McAdoo. Newbury Park, CA: Sage.

Jasso, G., and Rosenzweig, M. R. (1995). "Do Immigrants Screened for Skills Do Better Than Family Reunification Immigrants?" *International Migration Review* 29:85–111.

Johnson, P. J. (1998). "Performance of Household Tasks by Vietnamese and Laotian Refugees." *Journal of Family Issues* 19:245–273.

Kibria, N. (1993). *Family Tightrope: The Changing Lives of Vietnamese Americans.* Princeton, NJ: Princeton University Press.

Kibria, N. (1997). "The Concept of 'Bicultural Families' and Its Implications for Research on Immigrant and Ethnic Families." In *Immigration and the Family. Research and Policy on U.S. Immigrants,* ed. A. Booth, A. C. Crouter, and N. Landale. Mahwah, NJ: Lawrence Erlbaum Associates.

Rumbaut, R. (1997). "Ties that Bind: Immigration and Immigrant Families in the United States." In *Immigration and the Family: Research and Policy on U.S. Immigrants,* ed. A. Booth, A. C. Crouter, and N. Landale. Mahwah, NJ: Lawrence Erlbaum Associates.

Song, M. (1999). *Helping Out: Children's Labor in Ethnic Businesses.* Philadelphia, PA: Temple University Press.

Suarez-Orozco, C., and Suarez-Orozco, M. M. (2001). *Children of Immigration.* Cambridge, MA: Harvard University Press.

Zlotnik, H. (2001). "Past Trends in International Migration and their Implications for Future Prospects." In *International Migration into the 21st Century,* ed. M. A. B. Siddique. Northampton, MA: Edward Elgar.

PHYLLIS J. JOHNSON

INCEST

Incest is the sexual exploitation of a person who is legally unable to give informed consent due to age, intellect, and/or physical impairment by an older person having a close family blood tie (e.g., parent, grandparent, sibling, aunt, uncle, or cousin) or a substitute for such a blood tie (e.g., stepparent, stepbrother, or stepsister). In short, incest can be defined as the sexual exploitation of a child by a relative with more power. Incest includes sexual contact, exhibitionism, masturbation, anal intercourse, exposure to sexually oriented media, or any acts that have a sexually stimulating component for either the victim or the perpetrator (Renvoize 1993). Sexual contact includes touching, kissing, fondling, or overt sexual contact such as intercourse, manual stimulation of genitals, and oral-genital contact (Trepper and Barrett 1989).

Incest often involves collusion of the nonperpetrating parent and/or siblings and occurs in an inclusive system (Glasser et al. 2001). Psychological preparation for incest often occurs within a family by way of dissolving healthy generational boundaries. Some victims are manipulated by withdrawal of love or affection or with rewards of money, objects, and/or time with the perpetrator. Incest perpetrators often use elaborate methods of persuasion to manipulate victims. Isolation and secrecy is part of the *grooming* period that often comes before actual incest. Perpetrators use trust, favoritism, alienation, secrecy, and boundary violations to prepare children to participate in sexual activities (Christiansen and Blake 1990).

Prevalence of Incest

Prevalence rates for incest vary widely due to differences of definition, methods of study, and the population source of the data (Glasser et al. 2001). Commonly, studies report prevalence rates of child abuse in general and do not break the abuse into familial and nonfamilial. In the United States in the 1990s, it was estimated that 100,000 to one million cases of incest occur annually, but only about 10 percent of them are reported (Johnson 1983). Although some research estimates that less than 2 percent of the general population experiences sexual abuse (Kutchinsky 1992), other studies estimate that incest is experienced by 10 to 20 percent of children in the general population (Briere and Runtz 1989; Finkelhor et al. 1990; Russell 1983). A few other countries have published research in English on the prevalence of incest. In Brazil, for example, prevalence estimates range widely from 0.05 percent to 21 percent (Flores, Mattos, and Salzano 1998).

It is not unusual to find very different prevalence rates of incest for males and females, as in the study conducted by Renvoize (1993) who reported that as many as one-third of all girls and one-fifth of boys have experienced incest. Researchers agree that girls are much more often the victims of incest. Others report that the incidence for males is less than half of that for females because a higher proportion of males are sexually abused by adults outside the home by strangers (Carlstedt, Forsman, and Soderstrom 2001; Finkelhor et al. 1990; Gonsiorek, Bera, and LeTourneau 1994). Male incest victims may also report less frequently because they are socialized not to express feelings of helplessness and vulnerability (Nasjleti 1980).

Estimates of the prevalence of incest have risen steadily since the late 1960s as knowledge of child sexual abuse and incest has increased. There is some controversy, however, over the validity of the reported prevalence of incest. The often painful and shameful aspects of sexual abuse within the family make the collection of data very difficult. It is generally thought by professionals that the underreporting of incest is common due to the secrecy, shame, the tendency to blame the victim, and criminal ramifications surrounding incest. However, false reports by children of nonoffending parents, especially in divorce-custody situations, may account for an increase in reported incidents. There has been criticism that therapists may encourage reports through a process of recovering memories forgotten by the patient. Even considering false reporting and misuse of recovering memories, it is still very likely that the number of incest cases is underreported.

Recidivism among incest offenders is estimated at around 8.5 percent, though up to the late 1990s, very few studies had been conducted on this issue, and recidivism is as underreported as are first reports of incest (Quinsey et al. 1995). A study of the sexual recidivism of 251 convicted adult male incest perpetrators in a clinical setting in Ottawa, Canada, found that 6.4 percent had committed another sexual offense six-and-a-half years after their incest conviction (Firestoneet et al. 1999).

Effects on Victims

Sexually abused children report and/or display affective, cognitive, physical, and behavioral symptoms (Shaw et al. 2000). Symptoms may include general behavior problems, delinquency, anxiety, regressive behaviors, nightmares, withdrawal from normal activities, internalizing and externalizing disorders, cruelty and self-injury, posttraumatic stress disorder, poor self-esteem, and age-inappropriate sexual behavior. A review of forty-five studies indicated two common patterns of psychological response to incest (Williams and Finkelhor 1993). The first are those associated with posttraumatic stress symptomology. The second is an increase in sexualized behaviors, including sexualized play with dolls, putting objects into anuses or vaginas, excessive or public masturbation, seductive behavior, and age-inappropriate sexual knowledge and behavior.

Long-term psychological sequelae of incest include depression, anxiety, psychiatric hospitalization, drug and alcohol use, suicidality, borderline personality disorder, somatization disorder, and eroticization (Schetky 1990; Silverman, Reinherz, and Giaconia 1996). Common, too, are learning difficulties, posttraumatic stress disorder, dissociative disorders and conversion reactions, running away, prostitution, re-victimization, poor parenting, and an increased likelihood of becoming a perpetrator. The frequency and severity of psychological sequelae secondary to sexual abuse has been related to frequency and duration of the abuse, relationship to the perpetrator, use of force, type of sexual abuse, penetration, age of the victim, age difference between victim and offender, and the parental support variable (Schetky 1990). Most incest victims experience confusion about their own reactions to the incest experience. It is this betrayal of innocence and resultant confusion, along with the loss of control and power over one's own behavior, that lead to the emotional and psychological impact on the victim. Victims often experience, both at the time of the incestuous act and later as adults, a sense of shame, a feeling of powerlessness, and a loss of their childhood.

Sibling incest is often thought to be the least harmful form. Although one of the key aspects of incest is the difference in power between the perpetrator and the victim, sexual behavior between two siblings of equal power, where touching, looking, and exploring are mutual decisions, can still pose problems for the participants and/or parents. What Diana Russell (1986) calls the *myth of mutuality* in relation to sibling incest may put the victim in a psychologically and physically vulnerable position. In her research with adult women, she found that 78 percent of her subjects who had had childhood sexual experiences reported that their sexual behavior with brothers was abusive. When the reported sexual behavior was with a sister, 50 percent of the female subjects experienced the behavior as abusive. Approximately one-half reported sibling incest as extremely upsetting, and another one-fourth as somewhat upsetting. The degree of coercion and the emotional harm in sibling incest may be more underestimated than incest in general.

The effects of sexual abuse on children and their later development into adulthood depend on at least five important factors: the age of the child, the duration of the abuse, the type of the abuse, the manner in which the child frames the abuse, and the ability of the child to heal. It is likely that there are important gender differences in how girls and boys make sense out of incest experiences. Girls tend to view the incest experience within the larger context of the child-adult relationship and are likely to be more concerned with the perpetrator's feelings and family stability. In contrast, a boy may focus more on his own sexual experience. All children, whether male or female, attempt to make sense of or to create an explanation for the incestuous relationship as a part of the healing process.

The ability of people to heal from a damaging experience is related to their ability to confront their own feelings of fear, terror, anger, rage, confusion, helplessness, and vulnerability. A common report of adult victims of childhood incest is a clear sense of removing oneself from the event. A sense that it was being done to someone else and/or a sense of leaving the body during the sexual contact are common reports. The danger is that denial becomes the *preferred* or most common behavior to deal with stress. Moving beyond denial to healing requires that the incest victims allow themselves to experience the feelings of confusion, rage, and helplessness.

To manipulate the victim, most incest perpetrators foster in the child a set of behaviors that help the child maintain the denial and self-deception needed to survive an ongoing incestuous relationship. The effects of this on the victim can be manifested in multiple ways, including fear of violence, sex, intimacy, and people of the same sex as the perpetrator. Confusion of gender identity, as well as uncontrolled sexual activity, may also result. There is often a need to care for and control others, at home, school, and work. Feelings of isolation, shame, and guilt, often not associated with any specific activity, help to foster a poor self-image, which may lead to suicidal behavior. There is also a tendency for victims of incest to suffer from other disorders, such as sleep disturbances, nightmares, depression, and eating disorders. Incestuous relationships are at a minimum a contributing factor to the above effects, and for countless victims, they are the primary contributor.

Part of the process of healing is the victim's awareness of the context within which he or she made choices. Often, in treatment, victims gain a sense of empowerment when they can begin to trace the development of the incestuous relationship over time. Typically, victims can account for a gradual increase in their ability to make choices and implement them. Victims have often stated that at a certain time, they were able to stop the incest perpetrator's manipulations with the threat of breaking secrecy.

Profile of Offenders

Efforts to conceptualize incest before 1980 led to it being categorized as a subcategory of pedophilia (Stoller 1975). Since then, the trend is to describe incest in terms of interaction factors in the family context (Bentovim 1992; Trepper and Barrett 1986). Some researchers believe that incest does not have a single cause; rather it develops from a combination of influences (Finkelhor 1986; Friedrich 1990; Maddock and Larson 1995; Trepper and Barrett 1989). Incest is a complex and varied family dynamic, although at the same time some patterns of sexual abuse may be predictable and reflective of general disturbances in family patterns of interactions (Maddock and Larson 1995). Some of the systemic factors that influence whether or not incest will occur in a family include intrapsychic influences, relational variables, developmental variables, and situational or circumstantial that make incest more or less likely to occur.

Researchers agree that perpetrators of incest are more likely to be males than females, although plenty of evidence has emerged since the 1980s that shows that some mothers do sexually abuse their children. Fewer female offenders are willing to admit to committing incest (Allen 1991), and society may consider women to be sexually harmless. But it is important to recognize the increased opportunity that women have to perpetrate incest as primary caretakers of children (Jennings 1993). Women in all societies are given a great deal of responsibility of raising children, and with that comes control over their dependents. They are more often in charge of many intimate activities surrounding the care of the child, including things such as breastfeeding, putting to bed, and bathing. Some cultures where mother-son closeness is the norm may have more occurrences of incest. For example, some Japanese mothers initiate sexual acts with their sons after witnessing their sons masturbate for the first time in order to teach him about sex (Katahara 1989). One very small Australian study of a clinical sample of male incest survivors found a number of factors most likely to influence the occurrence of sexual abuse of young males (Harper 1993). Those include living in a single-parent family headed by a woman of low socioeconomic status where the mother suffers from a schizophrenic illness and/or abuses drugs or alcohol, and where there is a history of violent parental behavior.

Women may commit incest for different reasons than do males. Gender expectations and socializations may vary for males and for female perpetrators, but this does not mean that one form of incest is less harmful to the victim than the other. Regardless of the type of perpetrator, incest perpetrators commit incest for a variety of reasons. They often have poor skills in dealing with their emotions, demonstrate poor empathy skills, and display a marked inability to observe the behavior of others. These perpetrators are often emotionally in a developmental stage equivalent to that of the child they are assaulting.

In a study of seventy-five male and sixty-five female sexual abuse perpetrators, the men and women showed no difference in educational levels, both reported that their marriages as less stable than their parents', and both reported their need for emotional fulfillment is greater than their need for sexual fulfillment (Allen 1991). Both offenders report the least intrusive form of offending (exhibitionism, voyeurism, touching) to be more frequent than oral, vaginal, or anal intercourse. At the same time, women offenders were less likely to report committing sexual activities with children, more likely to report their own experience as victims of sexual abuse, and reported lower marital satisfaction. Women reported greater satisfaction with the relationship with their children, more sexual satisfaction with their spouses/partners, and reported having more sexual partners than the male perpetrators. Women offenders reported significantly higher *need* for both emotional and sexual fulfillment. Women offenders report more physical abuse by their partners and family of origin. Many more women than men sexually abuse with another (usually male) person whereas men are more likely to commit their offense alone (Jennings 1993). Females tend to use violence less often than males during their offending (Krug 1989). Females are more likely to know their victims; the abuse is usually less frequent and shorter in duration; and female offenders usually have fewer victims (Jennings 1993).

Men as incest perpetrators are not a homogeneous group. In a study funded by a grant from the National Center on Child Abuse and Neglect, researchers identified five distinct types of incestuous fathers: sexually preoccupied, adolescent regressive, instrumental sexual gratifiers, emotionally dependent offenders, and angry retaliators (Williams and Finkelhor 1992). This typology helps to foster better understanding of the motivations for abuse and may enable better treatment for incest perpetrators. It should be kept in mind that an offender may not fit perfectly into one type; most offenders are a combination of one or more types.

The first type, the sexually preoccupied offenders, is characterized by a sexual interest in their victim, usually from an early age. This offender usually begins molesting the child before age six and continues the molestation past puberty. The second type, the adolescent regressive offenders, has a conscious sexual interest in their victims but usually do not begin molesting until the victims approach or reach puberty. The third type of offenders, the instrumental sexual gratifiers, uses the victim as a vehicle for sexual fantasy. These offenders are more sporadic in their offending, and they often associate the action with remorse. The fourth type, the emotionally dependent, is often lonely and depressed, sex is not a primary motivator, and they often romanticize their need for closeness and intimacy. Fifth, angry retaliators demonstrate low sexual arousal toward their victims but instead use the sexual assault to focus their anger. Often, the assault on the victim is in retaliation for a real or imagined infidelity or abandonment by a spouse.

Besides there being some risk factors for becoming an incest perpetrator, the authors of one Swedish research study suggested there may be protective factors that prevent some victims from entering the victim-to-abuser cycle (Glasser et al. 2001). Those include: (1) positive self esteem; (2) the presence of other important adults in the child's life; (3) religious education stressing positive development and forgiveness rather than sin and damnation; (4) success in school, sports, or other activities; (5) personality, strengths, and social situations that promote long-term goals; (6) parental monitoring reducing the frequency of abuse; and (7) age-appropriate sexual knowledge prior to abuse.

Treatment

Using trial and error, clinicians now see the necessity for systemic rather than linear interventions for the treatment of incest (Gil 1996). The characteristics of a healing environment are openness, honesty, support, and worthiness. Incestuous families are characterized by secrecy, deception, isolation, and worthlessness. Early in treatment, offenders will commonly protest society's and the criminal justice system's *overreaction* to their behavior. Offenders will often believe that the child liked the behavior, never objected, and was already sexually active and therefore not harmed by it. Other family members may participate in this pattern of denial as well. As the perpetrator and family begin to understand the effects on the victim of the secrecy and deception the incestuous relationship requires, they begin to break through the denial and rationalizations.

In general, early treatment should be designed to protect society from the offender and the offender from a recurrence of the abuse during the beginning of treatment (Conte 1990). Treatment should include careful assessments and well-informed treatment plans that are directive, cautious, comprehensive, and full of measurable and attainable goals and objectives (Gil 1996). No research has been published that definitively proves one mode of treatment is superior to others. Eliana

Gil (1996) notes that clinical interventions focused on the offender were unsuccessful because they did not take into account the interactions between parents and children. She states that treatment carries with it the responsibility to alter harmful behaviors while making an effort to preserve the family without compromising the child's safety. Treatment often includes individual, family, couple, or group therapy for the offender, the victim, the nonoffending parent, and other family members. Finally, the perpetrator and other family members need to be evaluated for co-existing problems such as substance abuse, domestic violence, and psychiatric disorders.

See also: CHILD ABUSE: SEXUAL ABUSE; INCEST/INBREEDING TABOOS; POSTTRAUMATIC STRESS DISORDER (PTSD); SEXUALITY IN ADULTHOOD

Bibliography

Allen, C. M. (1991). *Women and Men Who Sexually Abuse Children*. Orwell, VT: Safer Society Press.

Beitchman, J. H.; Zucker, K. J.; Hood, J. E.; DaCosta, G. A.; Akman, D.; and Cassavia, E. (1992). "A Review of the Long-Term Effects of Child Sexual Abuse." *Child Abuse and Neglect: The International Journal* 16:101–118.

Bentovim, A., and Davenport, M. (1992). "Resolving the Trauma Organized System of Sexual Abuse by Confronting the Abuser: A Focal Family Therapy Approach with a Woman Who Was a Childhood Victim of Sexual Abuse." *Journal of Family Therapy* 14(1):29<en>50.

Briere, J., and Runtz, M. (1989). "The Trauma Symptom Checklist (TSC-33): Early Data on a New Scale." *Journal of Interpersonal Violence* 4:151–163.

Carlstedt, A.; Forsman, A.; and Soderstrom, H. (2001). "Sexual Child Abuse in a Defined Swedish Area 1993-97: A Population-Based Survey." *Archives of Sexual Behavior* 30:483–493.

Christiansen, J. R., and Blake, R. H. (1990). "The Grooming Process in Father-Daughter Incest." In *The Incest Perpetrator: A Family Member No One Wants to Treat*, ed. A. L. Horton, B. L. Johnson, L. M. Roundy, and D. Williams. Newbury Park, CA: Sage.

Conte, J. R. (1990). "The Incest Offender: An Overview and Introduction," in *The Incest Perpetrator: A Family Member No One Wants to Treat*. ed. Horton, A. L. et al. Thousand Oaks, CA: Sage.

Finkelhor, D. (1986). *A Sourcebook on Child Sexual Abuse.* Newbury Park, CA: Sage.

Finkelhor, D.; Hotaling, G.; Lewis, I. A.; and Smith, C. (1990). "Sexual Abuse in a National Survey of Adult Men and Women: Prevalence, Characteristics, and Risk Factors." *Child Abuse and Neglect* 14:19–28.

Firestone, P.; Bradford, J. M; McCoy, M.; Greenberg, D. M.; Larose, M. R.; and Curry, S. (1999). "Prediction of Recidivism in Incest Offenders." *Journal of Interpersonal Violence* 14:511–531.

Flores, R. Z.; Mattos, L. F. C.; and Salzano, F. M. (1998). "Incest: Frequency, Predisposing Factors, and Effects in a Brazilian Population." *Current Anthropology* 39:554–558.

Gil, E. (1996). *Systemic Treatment of Families Who Abuse.* Rockville, MD: Jossey-Bass.

Glasser, M.; Kolvin, I.; Cambell, D.; Glasser, A.; Leitch, I.; and Farrelly, S. (2001). "Cycle of Child Sexual Abuse: Links Between Being a Victim and Becoming a Perpetrator." *British Journal of Psychiatry,* 179:482–494.

Gomes-Schwartz, B.; Horowitz, J.; and Cardarelli, A. (1990). *Child Sexual Abuse.* Newbury Park, CA: Sage Publications.

Gonsiorek, J. C.; Bera, W. H.; and LeTourneau, D. (1994). *Male Sexual Abuse: A Trilogy of Intervention Strategies.* Thousand Oaks, CA: Sage.

Harper, J. (1993). "Prepuberal Male Victims of Incest: A Clinical Study." *Child Abuse and Neglect* 17:419–421.

Jennings, K. T. (1993). "Female Child Molestation: A Review of the Literature." In *Female Sexual Abuse of Children: The Ultimate Taboo,* ed. M. Elliott. Essex, UK: Longman Group UK.

Johnson, M. S. (1983). "Recognizing the Incestuous Family." *Journal of the National Medical Association* 75:757–61.

Krug, R. S. (1989). "Adult Male Report of Childhood Sexual Abuse by Mothers: Case Descriptions, Motivations and Long Term Consequences." *Child Abuse & Neglect* 13:111–119.

Kutchinsky, B. (1992). "Pornography and Rape: Theory and Practice? Evidence From Crime Data in Four Countries Where Pornography is Easily Available." *International Journal of Law and Psychiatry* 14:47–64.

Maddock, J. W., and Larson N. R. W. (1995). *Incestuous Families: An Ecological Approach to Understanding and Treatment.* New York: W. W. Norton.

Nasjleti, M. (1980). "Suffering In Silence: The Male Incest Victim." *Child Welfare* 59:269-275.

Quinsey, V. L.; Lalumiere, M. L.; Rice, M. E.; and Harris, G. T. (1995). "Predicting Sexual Offenses." In *Assessing Dangerousness: Violence By Sexual Offenders, Batterers, and Child Abusers,* ed. J. C. Campbell. Thousand Oaks, CA: Sage.

Renvoize, J. (1993). *Innocents Betrayed.* London: Routledge.

Russell, D. E. H. (1986). *The Secret Trauma: Incest in the Lives of Girls and Women.* New York: Basic Books.

Russell, D. E. H. (1983). "The Incidence and Prevalence of Intrafamilial and Extrafamilial Abuse of Female Children." *Child Abuse and Neglect* 7:133–146.

Shaw, J. A.; Lewis, J. E.; Loeb, A.; Rosado, J.; and Rodriguez, R. A. (2000). "Child On Child Sexual Abuse: Psychological Perspectives." *Child Abuse and Neglect* 24:1591–1600.

Trepper, T., and Barrett, M. J. (1986*). Treating Incest: A Multiple Systems Perspective.* New York: The Haworth Press.

Trepper, T. S.; and Barrett, M. J. (1989). *Systemic Treatment of Incest: A Therapeutic Handbook.* New York: Brunner/Mazel.

Vander Mey, B. (1988). "The Sexual Victimization of Male Children: A Review of Previous Research." *Child Abuse and Neglect* 12:61–72.

Williams, L. J., and Finkelhor, D. (1992). *The Characteristics of Incestuous Fathers.* Report in partial fulfillment of a grant from the National Center on Child Abuse and Neglect, Washington, DC.

JENNIFER L. MATHESON

INCEST/INBREEDING TABOOS

The incest taboo is one of the oldest and most perplexing mysteries encountered by students of human society. Historically, western scholars believed that the incest taboo—long proposed as a *cultural universal*—is vital to understanding the human condition. Thus, interest in the incest taboo has an extensive history.

Although the incest taboo varies in meaning by society, it is frequently an important rule of prohibition, commonly encompassing religious sanctions, and usually forbidding sexual contact between particular categories of relatives and family members. Closely related to the incest taboo are the *rules of exogamy* that usually prohibit marriage between the same categories of kin forbidden by incest rules (Murdock 1949). Typically included in the taboo are nuclear (parents and children) and immediate (e.g., grandparents, aunts and uncles, nieces and nephews, and first cousins) family members. In societies composed of unilineal descent groups (e.g., lineages, clans, and moieties), the incest rule often includes all or most of a person's descent (kinship) group. This includes distantly related individuals to which an actual genealogical connection cannot be made (Murdock 1949). A thorough understanding of the incest taboo necessarily recognizes this rule as an important part of a larger system of sexual regulations. In turn, these sexual regulations are an important component of the extensive normative structure regulating family, marriage, and kinship systems, and ultimately the larger society.

There are many cross-cultural variations in the incest taboo. Whereas it appears that most societies have some sort of incest prohibition, the rule is not strictly universal. Likewise, many societies deem the incest taboo extremely serious, whereas other groups view the taboo more casually. Sanctions for taboo violations reflect a similar cross-cultural diversity. In some societies, members simply express disapproval or distaste when incest occurs, as might be expected in the presence of bad manners. In other communities, the act of incest is considered horrifying or unthinkable, and transgressors may be put to death or expelled from the society. In many instances, the incest taboo is intricately entwined with religious tenets and proscribes supernatural sanctions against violators or against the society as a whole. In technologically advanced societies scientific explanations have commonly replaced religious beliefs, and religious sanctions have been replaced by legal penalties and concerns about genetic harm to progeny.

Historical Review

Plutarch (C.E. 46–120?) was one of the earliest Western scholars interested in the incest taboo. His writings anticipated two modern theories: *alliance theory* and *familial conflict theory*. Alliance theory concludes that the incest taboo exists to create an outward reaching network of cooperative kin, which is a primary social structure essential for human survival. This network works because rules of incest force individuals to find sexual and marriage partners outside their own families. Familial conflict theory argues that incest restrictions exist to prevent destructive conflicts within the family. If family members were to engage in sexual relationships with each other, role conflicts and jealousies would destroy the effectiveness of the family institution.

The Roman historian Tacitus (C.E. 56–120) offered a theoretical framework similar to Plutarch's, suggesting alliance networks as the reason for the incest prohibitions in Roman society (Honigmann 1976). In addition to alliances, Augustine (C.E. 354–430) proposed a natural aversion to incest and an "inherent sense of decency" that prevents incestuous relationships. Thomas Aquinas (C.E. 1225–1274) advocated alliance theory and asserted that incest hindered child development. Aquinas believed that close kin marriages encourage lust and result in disruptive role conflicts that could destroy the family (Honigmann 1976).

The development of the social sciences in the nineteenth and twentieth centuries continued these themes. George Murdock (1949) and Yehudi Cohen (1978) accepted alliance theory, whereas Sigmund Freud (1950) and Talcott Parson (1954) continued the argument that incestuous relations are destructive to the family.

In *The Descent of Man* (1871), Charles Darwin acknowledged the family conflict model but proposed an evolutionary foundation by hypothesizing that inheritable traits allowing incest would be selected against in the evolutionary process.

Edward Westermarck, in *The History of Human Marriage* (1891), employed Darwinian evolutionary theory and posited that incest avoidance emerged as an instinct to prevent the genetic harm produced by inbreeding. Westermarck hypothesized that this instinct was activated when people were raised in close proximity, such as in families. He believed that this aversion would be evident most commonly among siblings, but Westermarck also proposed that sexual repugnance would develop when unrelated children were reared together. This same thesis (*Westermarck's hypothesis*) is currently asserted by sociobiologists of human behavior (*human sociobiologists*), who assume that many complex social behaviors are grounded in genetic inheritance shaped by natural selection.

Beyond these historical accounts, notable explanations of the incest taboo include *demographic theory,* proposed by Mariam Slater (1959) and elaborated by Charles Case (1969). It is these theorists' contention that the demographic characteristics of human breeding populations (e.g., life expectancy, birth order, and the distribution of sex among siblings) make incestuous activity in the immediate family unlikely and, at best, short-lived.

Talcott Parsons's (1954) *socialization theory* asserts that the incest taboo is part of a normative structure employing eroticism—and its withdrawal—as a system of sanctions in the socialization of children. The affection offered by parents and other adults (often relatives) acts as a powerful reward for "proper" behavior in children, just as its withdrawal acts as a forceful punishment. Parsons claimed that this is an effective socialization process because of the deeply social nature of the human species.

For Parsons, the incest taboo is part of the system of sexual regulations that draws a boundary beyond which the family may not wander when imparting erotic rewards. Withholding erotic rewards forces the adolescent child to participate in the larger society in order to find greater sexual fulfillment. This ties the society together through marriage and kin relationships.

Nature versus Nurture

In current incest taboo literature, the most pronounced dispute reflects the *mind/body* debate. Scholars prescribing inheritable social behavior, as opposed to those postulating that social behavior is produced through environmental experiences, presently dominate much of the discussion. With the publication of Edward O. Wilson's *Sociobiology* (1975), the extension of Darwin's natural selection theory to complex human behaviors experienced a zealous revival. Central to this revival is the assertion by human sociobiologists that because of the universal character of the incest taboo, and the prevalence of inbreeding avoidance in other species, incest/inbreeding avoidance in humans represents the best example of a naturally selected behavior.

Sociobiologists of human behavior have supported their theory of incest/inbreeding avoidance by employing research from four major areas.

These include research exploring the universal nature and compliance with incest rules; studies of inbreeding harm; ethological and animal research on inbreeding avoidance; and investigations of marriage practices among children raised together (Ruse 1981–1982; Leavitt 1990). A critical look at these research areas, however, raises significant questions regarding their support for human sociobiological hypotheses. Specifically, the *deleterious hypothesis* of inbreeding, which underlies the sociobiology thesis on incest avoidance, has been called into question.

Incest/Inbreeding Harm

Sociobiologists believe that life—and its evolution—results from the competition between individual species members to spread their genes by producing the most progeny. (Progeny, by definition, carry parental genes to future generations.) The central sociobiological thesis concerning incest/inbreeding avoidance simply states that natural selection favors outbreeding behavior because inbreeding more often results in genetically debilitated offspring—in other words, inbreeding is not the best adaptive strategy for producing the most descendants. Although the deleterious thesis is widely accepted, and has taken on a law-like stature, a careful examination of the simple Mendelian mathematics involved quickly refutes this notion (Shields 1982; Livingstone 1969).

Almost all harmful genes are recessive, requiring that both parents carry the gene to produce offspring that manifest the deleterious effect. Since relatives share some common ancestry, they are more likely than nonrelatives to share the same harmful recessive genes. In this respect, the more closely related the mates, the more common their ancestry, and hence the more likely they will share the same deleterious genes. Thus, mating between relatives is thought to more readily produce genetically harmed descendants.

However, if a society customarily practices inbreeding, such as first and second cousin marriage, harmful recessive genes will quickly pair up and wash out of the gene pool. This occurs because deleteriously effected individuals are far less likely to reproduce and pass along the harmful genes to descendants. The result of systematic and recurring inbreeding in a population is to reduce the "genetic load" (the number of harmful recessive in the gene pool). Thus, inbreeding is no more harmful than outbreeding. Indeed, the advantage of an inbreeding system, especially for slow breeding mammals like humans, is that it preserves genotypes that have already proven successful in the environment.

Inbreeding is no more harmful than outbreeding unless inbreeding is practiced erratically in an otherwise outbreeding population. In outbreeding populations, mates are less likely to share close ancestry and thus the same harmful recessives traits. In this kind of reproductive system, recessive genes do not wash out of the population and thus accumulate as a large genetic load. The result can be the manifestation of harmful characteristics in the offspring of mating relatives.

For most of human history, breeding populations were small and isolated, and the community often practiced cousin marriage. The results were a relatively homogenous population of inbred individuals. Such homogenous populations are also common in other species (Shields 1982). It is unlikely, therefore, that a naturally selected mechanism would evolve to prevent incest/inbreeding.

Sibling Marriage and Human Isolates

There are several reliable examples of human communities where incest and/or close inbreeding have occurred on a regular and systematic basis. These examples include not only the well known cases of royal family incest but also incestuous practices among commoners. This social class distinction is important to note because human sociobiologists have dismissed the many instances of royal incest as exceptional and of no consequence to the debate. Cases involving commoners, where sibling or other incestuous marriages are usual and systematic, strongly challenge sociobiological suggestions that a selection mechanism exists to prevent inbreeding.

One of the more conspicuous examples of incestuous marriage involves the Roman Egyptians of the first three centuries C.E. A great deal of documentary evidence with genealogical information (mostly census records, but also personal letters, marriage contracts and other types of contracts, petitions, and documents addressed to the administrative authorities) has been unearthed and reveals that Egyptian commoners frequently practiced full brother-sister marriage (Scheidel 1996; Middleton

1962). Russel Middleton argues that there is little uncertainty in these documents. "Unlike some of the earlier types of evidence which may be subject to differing interpretations, these documents of a technical character have an 'indisputable precision'" (1962, p. 606).

It is evident that full sibling marriages accounted for 15 to 21 percent of all unions. When considering how many sibling marriages were demographically possible and socially acceptable (i.e., some families would not have children with siblings of the opposite sex that survived to marriageable age; or have children with opposite sexed siblings; or have children with siblings with the customary age differences—Egyptian marriages conventionally occurred between an older man and younger woman), we find that almost all possible brother-sister marriages were, in fact, contracted. This strongly suggests that sibling marriages were not only common but the preferred norm.

The documents also demonstrate that sibling marriages sometimes continued through two and three generations, and that the overwhelming majority of brother-sister marriages produced children. This practice lasted for at least three centuries and ended only when the Romans discouraged the custom by withholding Roman citizenship from persons continuing the practice.

Another example of a brother-sister incest custom is presented by Edward E. Evans-Pritchard when writing about the African Azande. "[W]hen a boy reaches puberty he may take his sister and with her build their little hut near his mother's home and go into it with his sister and lay her down and get on top of her—and they copulate" (1974, p. 107). Middleton (1962, p. 603) also notes that Azande kings married their daughters and that father-daughter incest was common among the Thonga.

Among the Greeks, Keith Hopkins notes that "[t]he Athenians allowed marriage between half-siblings of the same father but different mothers; the Spartans allowed marriage between half-siblings of the same mother and different fathers" (1980, p. 311). The ancient Hebrews permitted a similar practice as noted in the Old Testament by Abraham's marriage to his half-sister Sara.

John M. Goggin and William C. Sturtevant (1964) list eight other societies that allowed sibling marriage among commoners as well as thirty-five societies that allow sibling marriage between persons of high status.

In addition to cases of sibling marriage, there is abundant evidence of close inbreeding provided by human isolates—small isolated communities where the degree of inbreeding is determined by the size, extent, and length of isolation of the population (Leavitt 1990). These small isolated communities were numerous in the past and represent the norm for preagricultural Paleolithic societies.

A well-documented illustration of a human isolate is the Samaritans of the Middle East. From about 200 B.C.E., when the Samaritans broke completely from Jewish society, until the twentieth century, the Samaritan population declined dramatically (largely due to persecution by more powerful neighbors). At the end of World War II, the Samaritan population numbered 146 individuals, and this population had remained relatively stable for 100 years. By the 1980s, however, the population had increased and the Samaritans consisted of two communities of about 250 individuals (Bonne-Tamir 1980; Jamieson 1982; Talmon 1977).

Inbreeding in the Samaritan communities has been intense, not only because of their small population, but because of three other well established customs. First, Samaritan religion prohibits marriage with individuals outside of their faith. Second, the Samaritans limit their marriages to extended family lineages. Third, they prefer cousin marriage. Batsheva Bonne-Tamir (1980) has observed that nearly 85 percent of all Samaritan marriages are between first and second cousins. However, over a long period of time, the Samaritans have revealed neither a higher rate of genetic disease nor lower fertility than other populations.

Westermarck's Hypothesis: The Israeli Kibbutzim and Chinese *sim pua* Marriage

To support the deleterious theory of incest/inbreeding avoidance, human sociobiologists have repeatedly emphasized Edward Westermarck's hypothesis (1891) that children raised in close proximity will develop an aversion to sexual relationships with each other. Sociobiologists assume that this aversion originated as a naturally selected mechanism. Human sociobiologists site evidence from two case studies of human communities in support of Westermarck's hypothesis.

One group, the Israeli *kibbutzim,* separate children from their parents' household at birth and raise them in age-graded cohorts. In these cohorts boys and girls are raised without segregation, even sharing sleeping, bathing and toilet facilities; the proximity and intimacy of their upbringing is greater than what would usually be expected among siblings. Joseph Shepher (1983) studied these *kibbutzim* as a test of Westermarck's hypothesis and reported that of the nearly 3,000 *kibbutzim* marriages he examined there was not one case of intra-cohort marriage.

However, several other researchers reported compelling research results which demonstrate that there are numerous social structural and ideological reasons why individuals of the same *kibbutzim* cohort might not marry (Talmon 1964; Spiro 1965). Mordecai Kaffman (1977), on the other hand, reported that by the late 1970s sex and marriage between cohort members had become common. John Hartung (1985), in re-analyzing Shepher's research, reported that not only did cohort members from Shepher's samples marry but did so at a disproportionately higher rate than would be expected for marriages involving non-cohort members.

A second case study, often sited in support of Westermarck's hypothesis, was published by Arthur Wolf (1995). Wolf studied a form of Chinese marriage known as *minor* marriage (or *sim pua* marriage). In this marriage custom a family adopts a young girl and raises her as a sister to their son. This adopted sister will eventually be the son's wife. Because these marriages had a higher divorce rate and produced fewer children than Chinese "major" marriage, Wolf and the human sociobiology community presented this research as primary evidence in support of Westermarck's hypothesis.

Wolf makes it clear, however, that the Chinese consider *sim pua* unions to be low-status marriages for the poor, and these marriages are often the object of public ridicule and scorn. Adopted daughter-in-laws are frequently mistreated and unhappy, and given the suggestion of incest in a sibling relationship, it is a wonder that such marriages worked at all. In other words, there is no need to invent a complicated Darwinian mechanism to understand why the Chinese minor marriages more often failed.

Another area of research that refutes Westermarck's hypothesis is from studies of nudist communities. Dennis Craig Smith and William Sparks (1986) found that nudist children experience more sexual play with siblings and have more incestuous relations with immediate family members than non-nudists even though their early associations are quite intimate.

Sociocultural Factors in the Development of Incest Regulations

The incest taboo is better understood when examined in the context of the sociocultural development of human systems (Leavitt 1989). This development is best understood in light of the general organizational framework of human kinship groups (or descent systems) that comprise a fundamental component of many human communities.

In general, descent systems are either *bilateral* or *unilineal*. Bilateral systems, like American society, are diffused and include equally the relatives of both an individual's parents. In this system, a person is not usually acquainted with relatives beyond first or second cousins, and ritual or formal activities beyond the most immediate family are typically absent.

In a unilineal kinship system, all members of the kinship group trace their ancestry to a common ancestor (either mythical or actual). If this founder was male, descent is traced through the male line (*patrilineal*); if the founder was female, ancestry is traced through the female line (*matrilineal*). In a few rare instances, there are societies of *double* or *dual* descent in which each individual inherits two descent group memberships. Because membership in unilineal descent groups is determined by an individual's descendancy from a single ancestor, only some of a person's relatives will belong to their kinship group.

Societies with unilineal descent systems are commonly organized around lineages or clans, in other words, kinship organizations, which include hundreds of people recognized as blood relatives. These groups are the organizational backbone of the society and orchestrate most societal activities, including political, economic, military, religious, and educational functions.

The earliest, simplest societies (*hunting and gathering* or *foraging* societies) typically consisted of a tribe incorporating a number of small nomadic bands organized through bilateral descent. *Band exogamy* was practiced to ensure that the bands remained unified, even though they ranged far apart and saw each other only occasionally. This meant that a person had to marry and have sex with a partner outside of the immediate family and band. Thus, the survival of the tribe was ensured through bonds of blood and marriage (Johnson and Earle 1987). When bands, which consisted normally of twenty-five to fifty people, found themselves in trouble their marriage and blood ties ensured that they could seek aid from other groups.

At the end of the Ice Age (10,000 B.C.E.), the earth's climate, flora, and fauna changed sufficiently to begin moving human communities toward agriculture (Harris 1977). With this change came a need for more sophisticated social structures, especially for politico-military and economic activities. As life became increasingly sedentary and communities grew in size, access to resources became increasingly crucial, as did the need to defend relatively scarce fertile farmland. These structural and institutional changes encouraged the appearance of unilineal descent groups.

By extending the incest taboo to encompass lineage or clan members, the kinship group compelled its children into marriages of alliance with other descent groups. Such marriages carried reciprocal obligations for economic and military assistance essential for survival. These marriage bonds were so important that parents and other kin commonly determined whom their young would marry (*arranged marriage*). Frequently, kin group associations were made strong and stable through an exchange of gifts between family groups (*bride price, dowry, groom wealth*) and the encouragement of the couple to have many children (Johnson and Earle 1987).

As human societies continued to grow and evolve technologically and structurally (including larger settlements), the incest taboo began to contract, encompassing fewer relatives. New organizational structures not based on kinship ties or descent became increasingly common, and these structures were more efficient for operating larger, more complex societies. These new institutions were part of the development of the *state,* which ensured political and economic alliances through its own bureaucratic agencies.

With the appearance of modern industrial societies, the incest taboo contracted to encompass only the nuclear family and a few other immediate relatives (Cohen 1978). Punishments for violating the incest taboo have followed a similar evolutionary path. Where the incest taboo has been extended to ensure survival, its violation has generally been punished more severely. As the incest prohibition became less essential for enhancing alliances, it contracted to include fewer categories of relatives, and sanctions for violations of the incest proscriptions have become less severe (Leavitt 1989).

By understanding human sociocultural and environmental conditions, it is possible to understand the incest taboo, as well as its many variations, without tortuous allusions to genetic evolution.

See also: INCEST; KINSHIP; SEXUALITY IN CHILDHOOD; SEXUALITY IN ADOLESCENCE; SEXUALITY IN ADULTHOOD

Bibliography

Bonne-Tamir, B. (1980). "The Samaritans: A Living Ancient Isolate." In *Population Structure and Genetic Disorders,* ed. A.W. Eriksson, H.R. Forsius, H.R. Nevanlinna, P.L. Workman, and R.K. Norio. London: Academic Press.

Case, C. C. (1969). "Comments." *Current Anthropology* 10:50–51.

Cohen, Y. (1978). "Disappearance of the Incest Taboo." *Human Nature* 1:72–78.

Darwin, C. (1871). *The Descent of Man.* London: John Murray.

Evan-Pritchard, E. E. (1974). *Man and Woman Among the Azande.* New York: Free Press.

Freud, S. (1950). *Totem and Taboo.* London: Routledge & Kegan Paul.

Goggin, J. M., and Sturtevant, W. C. (1964). "The Calusa: A Stratified, Nonagricultural Society." In *Explorations in Cultural Anthropology,* ed. Ward H. Goodenough, 179–291. New York: McGraw-Hill.

Harris, M. (1977). *Cannibals and Kings: The Origins of Cultures.* New York: Random House.

Hartung, J. (1985). Book Review of *Incest: A Biosocial View,* by J. Shepher (1983). *American Journal of Physical Anthropology* 67:169–171.

Honigmann, J. J. (1976). *The Development of Anthropological Ideas.* Homewood, IL: Dorsey Press.

Hopkins, K. (1980). "Brother-Sister Marriage in Roman Egypt." *Comparative Studies in Society and History* 22:303–354.

Jamieson, J. W. (1982). "The Samaritans." *Mankind Quarterly* 23:141–148.

Johnson, A. W., and Earle, T. (1987). *The Evolution of Human Societies: From Foraging Group to Agrarian State.* Stanford, CA: Stanford University Press.

Kaffman, M. (1977). "Sexual Standards and Behavior of the Kibbutz Adolescent." *American Journal of Orthopsychiatry* 47:207–217.

Leavitt, G. C. (1989). "Disappearance of the Incest Taboo: A Cross-Cultural Test of General Evolutionary Hypotheses." *American Anthropologist* 91:116–131.

Leavitt, G. C. (1990). "Sociobiological Explanations of Incest Avoidance: A Critical Review of Evidential Claims." *American Anthropologist* 92:971–993.

Livingstone, F. B. (1969). "Genetics, Ecology, and the Origins of Incest and Exogamy." *Current Anthropology* 10:45–61.

Middleton, R. (1962). "Brother-Sister and Father-Daughter Marriage in Ancient Egypt." *American Sociological Review* 27:603–611.

Murdock, G. P. (1949). *Social Structure.* New York: Free Press.

Parsons, T. (1954). "The Incest Taboo in Relation to Social Structure and the Socialization of the Child." *British Journal of Sociology* 5:101–117.

Ruse, M. (1981–1982). "Is Human Sociobiology a New Paradigm?" *Philosophical Forum* 13:119–143.

Scheidel, W. (1996). "Brother-Sister and Parent-Child Marriage Outside Royal Families in Ancient Egypt and Iran: A Challenge to the Sociobiological View of Incest Avoidance?" *Ethology and Sociobiology* 17:319–340.

Shepher, J. (1983). *Incest: A Biosocial View.* New York: Academic Press.

Shields, W. M. (1982). *Philosophy, Inbreeding, and the Evolution of Sex.* Albany: State University of New York Press.

Slater, M. K. (1959). "Ecological Factors in the Origin of Incest." *American Anthropologist* 61:1042–1059.

Smith, D. C., and Sparks, W. (1986). *The Naked Child: Growing Up Without Shame.* Los Angeles: Elysium Growth Press.

Spiro, M. (1965). *Children of the Kibbutz.* New York: Schocken.

Talmon, S. (1964). "Mater Selection in Collective Settlements." *American Sociological Review* 29:491–508.

Talmon, S. (1977). "The Samaritans." *Scientific American* 236:100–108.

Westermarck, E. A. (1891). *The History of Human Marriage*. London: Macmillan.

Wilson, E. O. (1975). *Sociobiology: The New Synthesis*. Cambridge, MA: Belknap Press.

Wolf, A. P. (1995). *Sexual Attraction and Childhood Association: A Chinese Brief for Edward Westermarck*. Stanford, CA: Stanford University Press.

GREGORY C. LEAVITT

INDIA

The Indian subcontinent covers an area of 1,269,346 square miles (3,287,590 square kilometers). It is the seventh largest country in the world, with a population that exceeds 1 billion, making it the second most populous country in the world after China. The Himalayan Mountains, the highest range in the world, separate most of northern India from the rest of Asia. The southern half is a triangular peninsula that stretches southward to the Tropic of Cancer and extends into the Indian Ocean. The Arabian Sea lies to the west of India, and the Bay of Bengal to the east of India (Census of India 2001) India has a rich cultural, social, historical, and religious heritage. The Indus Valley civilization that was established around 2500 B.C.E. was a rich, advanced, and prosperous civilization. Since that time, the Greeks, Persians, Turks, Mughals, and Europeans have collectively enhanced the religious beliefs, traditions, spirituality, and culture of India.

India is a secular and pluralistic society characterized by tremendous cultural and ethnic diversity. It is made up of twenty-eight states and seven union territories. There are eighteen different languages and more than 300 dialects spoken by the Indian people. Indians practice many religions. Hinduism is the dominant religion in India, but through the centuries Indians have learned to coexist with people of other faiths. A majority (83%) of Indians are Hindus, about 14 percent are Muslims, 2.4 percent are Christians, 2 percent are Sikhs, .7 percent are Buddhists, .5 percent are Jains, and there are smaller numbers of Bahai, Jews, and Zoarastrians (Observer Research Foundation 2001; India at a Glance 2001).

India is distinctive in the proportion of people living in rural and urban communities. In 1999, 72 percent of the residents lived in rural areas and 28 percent lived in urban communities. The proportion of rural-to-urban residents is high, although India is the tenth most industrialized country in the world (World Development Report 2002). The literacy profile of Indians has greatly changed from a mere 5.3 percent in 1901 to 36.13 percent in 1981, to 52 percent in 1991, to 65.38 percent in 2001. The literacy rate is higher (73%) in urban areas as compared to rural areas (44%). Also, males have a higher literacy rate (76%) compared to females (54%) (Mullatti 1995; Census of India 2001).

Indians identify themselves with a particular religion but also affiliate themselves with a specific geographical region or state in India. Religion specifies the form of worship and guides their day-to-day behavior, while the specific region generally identifies the language one speaks, the literature, art, music one prefers, the food one eats, and the clothing one wears (Segal 1991).

Because India is a secular and ethnically diverse society, there are religious, regional, cultural, social, and educational variations in structural and functional patterns of family life. Hence, it is difficult to generalize values, behaviors, attitudes, norms, mores, practices, traditions, and beliefs about family life from one community to all Indian communities. Because the large majority of Indians are Hindus, this chapter will primarily focus attention on family life in the Hindu community.

The Hindus believe in a multitude of gods and goddess that are an integral aspect of Hindu mythology. Hinduism is a major world religion, has approximately 800 million followers, and also has had a profound influence on many other religions during its long history that dates back to 1500 B.C.E. The ideal Hindu lifestyle is influenced by the teachings in the Upanishads, Vedas, Bhavadgita, Ramayana, and Mahabharata. These scriptures stress the importance of work, knowledge, sacrifice, and service to others and finally, the renunciation of worldly goods in later life (Chekki 1996). Hinduism is not an organized religion like Western religions (Nandan and Eames 1980), but rather a way of life. According to the Hindu ideology, a person's life consists of four stages that correspond with the human life-cycle stages. The first stage is the Brahamacharya ashram (apprenticeship)—this is the period of discipline and education. The second stage is the Grihastha ashram (household and family), devoted to marriage, parenthood, family, and establishment of a household. Stage three is the Vanaprastha ashram (gradual retreat) and is characterized by a gradual retreat and loosening of social, emotional, and material bonds. Finally, the goal of the fourth and final stage, the Sanyasa ashram (renouncement), is to seek solitude, indulge in meditation, prepare for death, and strive for salvation and wisdom (Chekki 1996; Seymour 1999).

Most Hindu households have a prayer platform or room that is considered the most sacred place in the home. Most devout Hindus are vegetarians. They pray, fast, and worship their deity at least once a day, especially on holy days and days of festivities. As part of the religious activities, Hindus take regular morning baths, recite and chant certain mantras, light incense, prepare specific food items, offer flowers to the deities, and worship ancestors.

Caste System

The rigid caste system, in existence for more than 1,500 years, is a unique social institution. The caste system has religious elements and is interwoven with the Hindu faith. Each member of the Hindu community belongs to one of the more than 2,000 castes and subcastes (O'Malley 1975; Vohra 1997). This caste system puts people into endogamous groups and different social strata. The people belonging to the highest caste are the Brahmins (the priestly class), followed by the Kshatriyas (the warriors and farmers), then the Vaishyas (the merchants, traders, and businessmen), and the Shudras, (the servants, workers, and laborers), who are considered the lowest caste. Below the Shudras are those people commonly known as *untouchables,* who are considered inherently impure and unholy (Seymour 1999).

The social position of each individual is fixed by heredity, not by personal qualifications, accomplishments, or material acquisitions. Membership in a caste dictates one's occupation, religious beliefs, alliances, and friendships (Mullatti 1992). Consequently, the caste system divides people into groups, and its most salient feature is mutual exclusiveness, because each caste considers other castes as separate communities. The caste system bonds people of the same caste together but at the same time splits up a society into divisions in which people eat, drink, socialize, and expect to marry within their own caste. Although the caste system was officially abolished, it continues to play a crucial role and is unchangeable in most of its essential features (Mullatti 1995).

Family Life and Family Values

In India the family is the most important institution that has survived through the ages. India, like most other less industrialized, traditional, eastern societies is a collectivist society that emphasizes family integrity, family loyalty, and family unity. C. Harry Hui and Harry C. Triandis (1986) defined collectivism, which is the opposite of individualism as, "a sense of harmony, interdependence and concern for others" (p. 244). More specifically, collectivism is reflected in greater readiness to cooperate with family members and extended kin on decisions affecting most aspects of life, including career choice, mate selection, and marriage (Hui and Triandis 1986; Triandis et al. 1988).

The Indian family has been a dominant institution in the life of the individual and in the life of the community (Mullatti 1992). For the Hindu family, extended family and kinship ties are of utmost importance. In India, families adhere to a patriarchal ideology, follow the patrilineal rule of descent, are patrilocal, have familialistic value orientations, and endorse traditional gender role preferences. The Indian family is considered strong, stable, close, resilient, and enduring (Mullatti 1995; Shangle 1995). Historically, the traditional, ideal and desired family in India is the joint family. A joint family includes kinsmen, and generally includes three to four living generations, including uncles, aunts, nieces, nephews, and grandparents living together in the same household. It is a group composed of a number of family units living in separate rooms of the same house. These members eat the food cooked at one hearth, share a common income, common property, are related to one another through kinship ties, and worship the same idols. The family supports the old; takes care of widows, never-married adults, and the disabled; assists during periods of unemployment; and provides security and a sense of support and togetherness (Chekki 1996; Sethi 1989). The joint family has always been the preferred family type in the Indian culture, and most Indians at some point in their lives have participated in joint family living (Nandan and Eames 1980).

With the advent of urbanization and modernization, younger generations are turning away from the joint family form. Some scholars specify that the *modified extended family* has replaced the traditional joint family, in that it does not demand geographical proximity or occupational involvement and does not have a hierarchal authority structure (Nandan and Eames 1980; Mullatti 1995; Shangle 1995). This new family form encourages frequent visits; financial assistance; aid and support in childcare and household chores; and involvement and participation in life-cycle events such as births, marriages, deaths, and festival celebrations. The familial and kinship bonds are thus maintained and sustained. Even in the more modern and nuclear families in contemporary India, many functional extensions of the traditional joint family have been retained (Nandan and Eames 1980), and the nuclear family is strongly embedded in the extended kinship matrix. In spite of the numerous changes and adaptations to a pseudo-Western culture and a move toward the nuclear family among the middle and upper classes, the modified extended family is preferred and continues to prevail in modern India (Chekki 1996; Mullatti 1995; Segal 1998).

India is an extremely pronatalistic society, and the desire to have a male child is greatly stressed and is considered by some to be a man's highest duty, a religious necessity, and a source of emotional and familial gratification (Kakar 1981). Because male children are desired more than female children, they are treated with more respect and given special privileges. Male children are raised to be assertive, less tolerant, independent, self-reliant, demanding, and domineering (Kumar and Rohatgi 1987; Pothen 1993). Females, in contrast, are socialized from an early age to be self-sacrificing, docile, accommodating, nurturing, altruistic, adaptive, tolerant, and religious, and to value family above all (Kumar and Rohatgi, 1987; Mullatti, 1995). In rural areas, low-income women have always worked outside the home. In urban areas, there has been a substantial increase in the number of middle- and upper-class women working to supplement their husbands' incomes. In a traditional Indian family, the wife is typically dependent, submissive, compliant, demure, nonassertive, and goes out of her way to please her husband. Women are entrusted with the responsibility of looking after the home and caring for the children and the elderly parents and relatives.

Childrearing practices in India tend to be permissive, and children are not encouraged to be independent and self-sufficient. The family is expected to provide an environment to maximize the development of a child's personality and, within the context of the Hindu beliefs and philosophy, positively influence the child's attitudes and behaviors.

Adolescence and young adulthood are particularly stressful and traumatic stages in the lives of Indian youths. In one way, they desire emancipation and liberation from family but residing in the matrix of the extended family makes it difficult for them to assert themselves and exhibit any independence in thought, action, or behavior. Social changes are gradually occurring but arranged marriages are still the norm, and dating generally is not allowed. Furthermore, sex and sexuality issues are not openly discussed, sex education is not readily available, interrelationships with the opposite sex are discouraged, and premarital sex is frowned upon. In the traditional Indian family, communication between parents and children tends to be one-sided. Children are expected to listen, respect, and obey their parents. Generally, adolescents do not share their personal concerns with their parents because they believe their parents will not listen and will not understand their problems (Medora, Larson, and Dave 2000).

Life expectancy for both Indian men and women is increasing. According to the 2001 Census of India, life expectancy was 61.9 years for men and 63.1 years for women (Census of India 2001). This has led to a significant increase in the population of elderly individuals. The elderly in India are generally obeyed, revered, considered to be fountains of knowledge and wisdom, and treated with respect and dignity by family and community members. Old age is a time when a person is expected to relax, enjoy solitude, retirement, pray, enjoy spending time with the grandchildren, and not worry about running the household or about finances because the oldest son is now in charge of the finances and family matters, and the oldest daughter-in-law is generally running the household. In most instances, the elderly care for their grandchildren and assist with cooking and household chores. Even adult children continue to consult their parents on most of the important aspects of life.

Mate Selection and Marriage

Marriage in India is regarded as one of the most significant life-cycle rituals and is a familial and societal expectation for Hindus. In traditional Hindu society, marriage was considered a sacrament and not a contract and therefore was expected to be for life. It is important to point out that *vivaha* (wedding) is generally obligatory for all individuals. According to Kanailal Kapadia (1966), the primary aim of a Hindu marriage is *dharma praja* (progeny, particularly sons) and *rati* (pleasure). Furthermore, marriage is regarded not only as a union of two individuals, but also as the union of two families, making them almost like blood relatives. Marriages are religiously, economically, politically, and socially oriented and they are generally arranged by the elders and extended family members (Chekki 1996; Sureender, Prabakaran, and Khan 1998).

Even in contemporary Indian society, Hindus consider marriage as a social and cultural obligation and a contract for life. Marriage is not viewed as a means to attain personal happiness nor as a means of sharing your life with a person you love. Instead, the basic qualities of family unity, family togetherness, family harmony, family cohesiveness, and sharing of common family goals, values, and a way of life are of significant importance, and personal considerations are secondary. That the couple is not in love with each other or that the two partners are not physically attracted to one another or the possibility that the two do not have too much in common are not considerations because love is expected to come after marriage (Medora 2002). It is customary for individuals to marry within their religion, caste, and subcaste.

Most marriages in India are arranged to a greater or lesser extent. Even among the educated middle- and upper-class families from urban areas, marriage is as much a concern of the families as it is of the individual (Mullatti 1995; Nanda 1995). Most Indian youths do not believe that they have the experience, knowledge, or wisdom to select a prospective mate. They also do not believe that it is essential to date many partners to pick the right spouse. The type of family that the prospective spouse comes from is given primary consideration, along with occupational and cultural compatibility. Educational and social class homogamy of the family are also qualities taken into consideration by the respective parents on both sides (Nanda 1995).

A Hindu bride and groom in traditional Indian dress with flower garlands during the wedding ceremony. Hindus consider marriage a social and cultural obligation and a contract for life. NILUFER MEDORA

The last decades of the twentieth century brought an increasing trend to consult and get input from the children regarding their marriage. Typically, parents or kin select a prospective pool of eligible partners who have been screened by them first to ensure a similar social, cultural, educational, and economic background. One of the most common ways in which the partners are often selected is from among the children of friends and extended family who have a similar socioeconomic background (Medora 2002).

The use of matrimonial advertisements is increasing and thus becoming an integral part of the mate selection process (Banerjee 1999; Das 1980; Nanda 1995). Advertisements are placed in the newspaper because it is likely to attract a wide readership. Screening is first done on the basis of photographs. Next, the young adults are allowed to meet and talk over the phone, and occasionally go out with a chaperone who is usually an adult family member who accompanies the young couple while they are trying to determine the person with whom they are most compatible. While this exchange is occurring, marriage is foremost on the minds of both partners and all forms of premarital sex are discouraged (Medora 2002). After the couple go out a few times, the male generally proposes to the woman. If the woman accepts the proposal, the respective parents are informed about their children's decisions.

Before the engagement is announced to friends and the marriage finalized, most Hindu families consult an astrologer to ensure that the two prospective partners are well suited for each other (Sureender, Prabakaran, and Khan 1998). The astrologer matches the two horoscopes and predicts whether the couple will be compatible and happy, enjoy good health, enjoy financial success, and, most importantly, have children. Indians are fatalistic and believe their lives are predestined, their fates preordained, and that they are helpless as far as choice is concerned, and therefore they must succumb to the celestial forces of the universe (Gupta 1976).

Dowry System

An important consideration in the mate selection process is the giving of the dowry by the girl's parents to the boy's family. According to Leela Mullatti (1992), "the custom of dowry has taken the form of a market transition in all classes and castes irrespective of the level of education" (p. 99). The dowry system was initiated with the intention of providing security for a girl in case of adversity and unexpected circumstances after marriage. The parents gave whatever they could to their daughter (consequently to the groom's family) for this purpose. By the beginning of the twenty-first century, however, the custom had deteriorated to a point whereby the prospective groom and his family had become very greedy. They made tremendous demands, which if not met after marriage result in dowry deaths—burning girls alive if the dowry is insufficient, so that the boy can remarry another girl for a higher or better dowry (Mullatti 1995). The more educated a man is, the higher the family is in the caste and social hierarchy, the better his employment prospects, the higher is the expectation for dowry at the time of marriage. This makes

A Hindu bride dressed in a red wedding sari, wearing traditional gold jewelry. NILUFER MEDORA

it difficult for families with daughters who are highly educated to arrange marriages because the girls are required to have even more educated husbands (Seymour 1999).

Status of Single and Divorced Persons in India

An individual who remains single and never marries feels out of place, socially and culturally. Traditionally, single persons were supposed to be the responsibility of the extended family, and this tradition still continues. Remaining single is more acceptable for men than it is for women. When a woman is not married, it is assumed that there is something wrong with her; she may be very difficult to get along with, she may be uncompromising, and therefore she is single. Single men and women are not allowed to participate in religious festivities and marriage celebrations because it is considered unlucky, unholy, and inauspicious

(Rao and Rao 1976). Traditionally, parents who could not find a suitable match for their daughters were ostracized and looked down on.

Divorce was not even a remote possibility or even thought of until recent times (Kakar 1998; Mullatti 1995). In India, there is a cultural, religious, and social stigma associated with divorce. Community disapproval is stronger for divorced women than it is for divorced men (Lessinger 2002).

Studies of divorced, separated, and deserted women show that a majority of them experience serious financial problems, and as a result, many of them are unable to provide food, clothing, and shelter for themselves and their children (Kumari 1989; Mullatti 1995; Pothen 1989).

After a divorce, Indian women also experience a multitude of problems in the social arena. Because there are very few divorced, separated, or single-parent families, minimal or little social support is available to them. Divorced Indian women encounter greater social barriers to dating and re-marriage (Amato 1994; Mullatti 1995). Moreover, they are hesitant to make friends with men (either single or married) because the friendliness might be misinterpreted to mean that the woman is friv-olous, immoral, and sexually permissive. As a mat-ter of fact, a large proportion of divorced women reported problems with sexual harassment, in the workplace and on the social scene (Amato 1994; Mehta 1975; Pothen 1986). According to Paul Amato (1994), most Indians consider sexual rela-tions outside of marriage as unacceptable for women, so most divorced women's sexual needs are unfulfilled unless she remarries, and remarriage for an Indian woman is relatively uncommon. It is, therefore, not surprising that a majority of Indian divorced women experience problems with loneli-ness (Choudhary 1988; Pothen 1986).

As a result of social stigmatization and familial ostracism, a majority of divorced women in India set up their own households and become self-sufficient (Choudhary 1988; Mehta 1975; Pothen 1989). Satya Leela (1991) found that one-fourth of separated and widowed mothers lived with rela-tives and only 5 percent were economically de-pendent on their families.

The doctrine of *pativratya* also makes it diffi-cult for a woman to leave her husband; instead, an unhappily married woman is expected to accept her destiny—a notion strongly supported by the Hindu concept of predestination (Amato 1994). Amato further added that a divorcee with children generally was forced to make demands upon other male kin within the joint family, and this may in-terfere with a man's primary role obligation, that is, the economic support of his own spouse, chil-dren, and perhaps elderly parents. Hence, a woman without a husband (with the exception of a widowed mother) cannot be accommodated over the long term within the framework of the joint family structure without considerable com-promise and tension.

Conclusion

Gradual changes have been ushered in by reli-gious, social, and cultural reforms. Industrializa-tion, urbanization, and technological advances have been instrumental in changing family struc-tures, values, and lifestyles. Ganeswar Misra (1995) emphasized that middle- and upper-class families in urban areas were undergoing a dramatic trans-formation because the younger generation is ques-tioning power issues, traditional roles, hierarchical relationships, obligations, loyalty, and deference for kinsmen and elderly.

With changing times, Indian family structure, functions, traditional division of labor, and author-ity patterns have altered, favoring more egalitarian relations between the husband and the wife and also a move toward more shared decision-making patterns between parents and children. Despite these changes, the fact remains that most individu-als continue to value and give top priority to the family, and families continue to maintain strong kinship bonds and ties.

See also: ASIAN-AMERICAN FAMILIES; HINDUISM; ISLAM; SIKHISM

Bibliography

Amato, P. (1994). "The Impact of Divorce on Men and Women in India and the United States." *Journal of Comparative Family Studies* 25:208–221.

Banerjee, K. (1999). "Gender Stratification and the Con-temporary Marriage Market in India." *Journal of Fam-ily Issues* 20:648–676.

Chekki, D. (1996). "Family Values and Family Change." *Journal of Comparative Family Studies* 27:409–413.

Choudhary, J. N. (1988). *Divorce in India Society.* Jaipur: Rupo Books.

Das, G. (1980). "Matrimonial Advertisements: An Examination of its Social Significance in Mate Selection in Modern India." *Man in India* 60:187–200.

Gupta, G. (1976). "Love, Arranged Marriage, and the Indian Social Structure." *Journal of Comparative Family Studies* 7:75–85.

Hui, C. H., and Triandis, H. C. (1986). "Individualism-Collectivism: A Study of Cross-Cultural Researchers." *Journal of Cross-Cultural Psychology* 17:22–248.

Kakar, S. (1981). *The Inner World: Psychoanalytic Study of Childhood and Society in India*. Bombay: Oxford University Press.

Kakar, S. (1998). "Asian Indian Families." In *Minority Families in the United States: A Multicultural Perspective*, ed. R. L. Taylor. Englewood Cliffs, NJ: Prentice Hall.

Kapadia, K. M. (1966). *Marriage and Family in India*. Bombay: Oxford University Press.

Kumar, P., and Rohatgi, K. (1987). "Value Patterns as Related with High and Low Adjustment in Marriage." *Indian Journal of Current Psychological Research* 2:98–102.

Kumari, R. (1989). *Women-Headed Households in Rural India*. New Delhi: Radiant Publishing.

Leela, D. S. (1991). "Women-Headed Family-Problems, Coping Patterns, Support System, and Some Related Policy Matters." In *Research on Families with Problems in India*, ed. S. Bharat. Bombay: Tata Institute of Social Sciences.

Lessinger, J. (2002). "Asian Indian Marriages: Arranged, Semi-Arranged, or Based on Love?" In *Contemporary Ethnic Families in the United States: Characteristics, Variations, and Dynamics*, ed. N.V. Benokraitis. Englewood Cliffs, NJ: Prentice Hall.

Medora, N. P. (2002). "Mate Selection and Marriage Practices in Contemporary India: Love Marriages vs. Arrange Marriages." *In Couple Formation in Contemporary International Contexts*, ed. R. R. Hamon and B. B. Ingoldsby. Thousand Oaks, CA: Sage.

Medora, N. P.; Larson, J. H.; and Dave, P. B. (2000). "East-Indian College Student's Perceptions of Family Strengths." *Journal of Comparative Family Studies* 31:408–424.

Mehta, R. (1975). *Divorced Hindu Women*. Delhi: Vikas Publishing.

Misra, G. (1995). "Reflection on Continuity and Change in the Indian Family System." *Trends in Social Science Research* 2:27–30.

Mullatti, L (1992). "Changing Profile of the Indian Family." In *The Changing Family in Asia: Bangladesh,*

India, Japan, Philippines, and Thailand, ed. UNESCO. Bangkok: Principal Regional Office for Asia and the Pacific.

Mullatti, L. (1995). "Families in India: Beliefs and Realities." *Journal of Comparative Family Studies* 26:11–25.

Nanda, S. (1995). "Arranging a Marriage in India." In *India and South Asia,* ed. J. K. Norton. Guilford, CT: Brown and Benchmark.

Nandan, Y., and Eames, E. (1980). "Typology and Analysis of the Asian-Indian Family." In *The New Ethnics: Asian Indians in the United States,* ed. P. Saran and E. Eames. New York: Praeger.

Observer Research Foundation. (2001). *India: 2001–2002 Observer Statistical Handbook*. New Delhi: Rekha Printers Pvt. Ltd.

O'Malley, L. S. S. (1975). *India's Social Heritage*. New York: Octagon Books.

Pothen, S. (1986). *Divorce: Its Causes and Consequences in Hindu Society*. New Delhi: Shakti Books.

Pothen, S. (1989). "Divorce in Hindu Society." *Journal of Comparative Family Studies* 20:377–391.

Pothen, S. (1993). "Divorce in Hindu Society." In *Next to Kin,* ed. L. Tepperman and S. J. Wilson. Englewood Cliffs, New Jersey: Prentice Hall.

Rao, V. V., and Rao, V. N. (1976). "Arranged Marriage: An Assessment of the Attitudes of the College Students in India." *Journal of Comparative Family Studies* 7:433–453.

Segal, U. A. (1991). "Cultural Variables in Asian Indian Families." *Families in Society* 74:233–242.

Segal, U. A. (1998). "Career Choice Correlates: An Indian Perspective." *Indian Journal of Social Work* 69:338–348.

Seymour, S. C. (1999). *Women, Family, and Child Care in India: A World in Transition*. New York: Cambridge University Press.

Sethi, B. B. (1989). "Family as a Potent Therapeutic Force." *Indian Journal of Psychiatry* 31:22–30.

Shangle, S. C. (1995). "A View into the Family and Social Life in India." *Family Perspective* 29:423–446.

Sureender, S.; Prabakaran, B.; and Khan, A. G. (1998). "Mate Selection and its Impact on Female Marriage Age, Pregnancy Wastages, and First Child Survival in Tamil Nadu, India." *Journal of Social Biology* 45:289–302.

Triandis, H. C.; Bontempo, R.; Villareal, M. J.; Asai, M.; and Lucca, M. (1988). "Individualism and Collectivism: Cross-Cultural Perspective on Self—In Group

Relationships." *Journal of Personality and Social Psychology* 16:187–205.

Vohra, R. (1997). *The Making of India a Historical Survey.* Armonk, NY: M.E. Sharpe.

World Development Report. (2002). Building Institutions for Markets. New York: Oxford University Press.

Other Resources

"Census of India." (2001). In the Census of India web site. Available from http://www.censusindia.net/.

"India at a Glance." (2001). In the Census of India web site. Available from http://www.censusindia.net/religion.html.

"Land and the People." (2002). In the Consulate General of India web site. Available from http://www.indianconsulate-sf.org/.

NILUFER P. MEDORA

INDONESIA

The Republic of Indonesia, the world's fourth most populous nation, has 203 million people living on nearly 1,000 permanently settled islands. Java and Madura hold about 60 percent of the nation's population. Some 200–300 ethnic groups with their own languages and cultures inhabit the nation, some numbering in the millions, some in the thousands. The national motto, *Unity in Diversity,* expresses a hope that the multicultural nation can build a common national culture overlaying ethnic and regional ones.

For more than 2,000 years trading ships have sailed between India and China via the equatorial *spice islands*. From about 100 C.E. to 1400 C.E., Indian culture was spread widely and deeply by traders and others, though there was never imperialism from India. Kingdoms developed, whose rulers adopted Hinduism and Buddhism. From about 1200 C.E. to 1600 C.E., Islam was brought by traders and teachers from India and the Middle East, and today Indonesia has the most Muslims of any nation. The Portuguese and Dutch came to trade in the sixteenth and seventeenth centuries. By the nineteenth century the Dutch colonial government controlled Java and had links to rulers on other islands. In the early twentieth century Netherlands Indies expanded from Sumatra to West New Guinea, the present borders of Indonesia. Nationalist movements arose, led by intellectuals and religious leaders representing various cultures of the archipelago. The Dutch remained in control until 1942 when the Japanese occupied the archipelago. They attempted to return in 1945 when Indonesians declared independence, but they met armed resistance and the Indonesians and Dutch for five years. The Dutch withdrew in 1950 and the Republic of Indonesia was born (Rickleffs 1993).

Kinship is a primal loyalty of great importance throughout Indonesia. Obligations to kin can be onerous, but they provide vital support in various aspects of life. Government provides little social security, unemployment insurance, or elder care: these are provided by family and kin networks. This also leads to familial and ethnic nepotism, patronage, and paternalism in public and private sectors. Many Indonesian ethnic groups have clans and lineages based upon descent. *Patriliny* is most common, though *matriliny* is found in a few societies, such as the Minangkabau of West Sumatra (Blackwood 2000). Some societies, such as the Javanese, have bilateral kinship systems of the type found in the United States.

Marriage and Parenthood

Marriage and parenthood give people full adult status. In Indonesian, one does not ask, "Is he/she married?" but "Is he/she married yet?" to which the correct response is, "Yes" or "Not yet." The same is true in questions about whether a person has children. Unmarried adults are uncommon, though urban people are marrying at later ages than in the past or in rural society. Even homosexuals are under family pressure to marry, whether or not their orientation is known.

Marriage in many Indonesian societies commonly involves protracted negotiation and gift exchanges, often involving middle persons. Certain societies in Sumatra and Eastern Indonesia practice *affinal alliance,* by which marriages are arranged between persons in patrilineages who are related (near or distantly) as cross-cousins. In these societies the relationship between wife-giving and wife-taking lineages is basic to the structure of society and involves lifelong obligations for exchange of goods and services between kin (Singarimbum 1975). For Batak, a prominent Sumatran example of such a people, clan membership and marriage alliances between lineages are important whether they live in their mountain homeland or have migrated to distant cities. Though marriages may be made to perpetuate relationships between lineages, love between young people also may be considered by their families and kinsmen, as may education, occupation, religion, and wealth among urbanites. Newly married couples are usually expected to live with the parents of one spouse, especially before a child is born, and many societies require the husband to serve the wife's parents during that time.

In societies without lineal descent groups, love is more prominent in leading people to marry, but again class, education, occupation, religion, or wealth (in cities), or the capacity to work hard, be a good provider, and have access to land or other resources (in villages), are also considered. Among stratified societies such as Javanese or Bugis, higher status families are more likely to arrange marriages (or veto potential relationships). Marriage can be an important means of maintaining, advancing, or losing family social status, and extravagant marriage ceremonies with Hindu-derived ritual are used to display status (Koentjaraningrat 1985).

Among Muslims divorce is governed by Muslim law and may be settled in Muslim courts or, as with non-Muslims, in government civil courts. Initiation of divorce and its settlements favor males in Muslim courts and also much customary law. Divorce also may be handled by local elders and officials according to customary law, and terms for settlements may vary considerably by ethnic group. Societies with strong descent groups, such as the Batak, eschew divorce and it is rare (Rodenburg 1997). Such societies may also practice the *levirate* (requiring widows to remarry a brother or cousin of their deceased spouse). In societies without descent groups, such as the Javanese, divorce is reportedly frequent and is initiated by either spouse. Divorce among upper-class and wealthy Javanese is rarer (Brenner 1998).

Polygamy is recognized among Muslims, some immigrant Chinese, and some traditional societies, but not by Christians. Such marriages are probably few. Marriages between members of different religions are rare, and those between members of different ethnic groups remain relatively uncommon, though they are increasing in urban areas and among the better educated.

Family and Gender

The nuclear family of husband, wife, and children is the most common domestic unit, though elders and unmarried siblings may be added to it in various societies and at various times. It is found among remote peoples and city dwellers, and is unrelated to the presence or absence of clans in a society. An exception is the rural matrilineal Minangkabau, for whom the domestic unit still comprises co-resident females around a grandmother (or mothers) with married and unmarried daughters and sons in a large traditional house. A husband comes only as a visitor to his wife's hearth and bedchamber. Some societies, such as the Dayak of Kalimantan, live in long houses with multiple hearths and bedchambers belonging to related or even unrelated nuclear families.

Inheritance

Inheritance patterns are diverse even within single societies. Muslim inheritance favors males over females as do the customs of many traditional societies (an exception being matrilineal ones where rights over land, for example, are passed down between females.) Inheritance disputes may be settled in Muslim or civil courts, or by customary village ways. Though custom generally favors males, actual practice often gives females inheritances. Many societies distinguish between inherited and acquired property: the former is passed on in clan or family lines, the latter goes to children or the spouse of the deceased. In many areas land is communal property of a kin or local group, whereas household goods, personal items, or productive equipment are familial or individual inheritable property. With changing economic conditions, newer ideas about property, and increasing demand for money, rules and practices regarding inheritance are changing, and this can produce conflicts that a poorly organized legal system and weakened customary leaders cannot easily manage.

Though Indonesia is predominantly Muslim, the status of women is considered to be relatively high, though their position and rights vary considerably in different ethnic groups, even Muslim ones. Nearly everywhere gender ideology, both by custom and national reinforcement, views men as community leaders and decision makers (even among matrilineal Minangkabau) whereas women are the backbones of the home and teachers of values to the children.

An elementary school teacher helps a young pupil with an assignment. Many teachers in elementary schools are women, while most teachers at the secondary and university levels are men. SERGIO DORANTES/CORBIS

Women and men share many tasks in village agriculture across the archipelago, though plowing is more often done by men and harvest groups composed only of women are commonly seen. Gardens may be tended by either sex, though men more commonly tend orchards. Men hunt and fish, which may take them away for a long time. If men do long-term work outside the village, women may do all aspects of farming and gardening. Women are found in the urban work force in stores, small industries, and markets, as well as in upscale businesses, but usually in fewer numbers and lower positions than men. Many elementary school teachers are women, but men are more frequently teachers in secondary schools and universities. Men dominate all levels of government, though some women are found in various subordinate positions. The 2001–2004 president's cabinet has thirty-two ministers, only two of whom are women. President Megawati Sukarnoputri is a woman, though her following derives mainly from respect for her father, Sukarno, the leading nationalist and first president, rather than any of her achievements. She was opposed, unsuccessfully, by many Muslim leaders because of her gender.

Increasing urbanization and interregional migration in the 1980s and 1990s, the need felt by rural people to seek money in the city, weak urban infrastructure, and poor employment opportunities for many school graduates, put strains on families and marriages. After 1998, the fall of President Suharto, political instability, economic deterioration, decreasing law and order, and communal and religious violence in some areas added strain to family and kin networks in both urban and rural areas. However, they continue to be vital resources for supporting people in Indonesia.

See also: ETHNIC VARIATION/ETHNICITY; ISLAM; KINSHIP

Bibliography

Blackwood, E. (2000). *Webs of Power: Women, Kin, and Community in a Sumatran Village.* Lanham, MD: Rowman & Littlefield.

Brenner, S. A. (1998). *The Domestication of Desire: Women, Wealth, and Modernity in Java.* Princeton, NJ: Princeton University Press.

Geertz, H. (1989). *The Javanese Family: A Study of Kinship and Socialization.* Prospect Heights, IL: Waveland.

Geertz, H., and Geertz, C. (1975). *Kinship in Bali.* Chicago: University of Chicago Press.

Koentjaraningrat. (1985). *Javanese Culture.* Singapore: Oxford University Press.

Rickleffs, M. C. (1993). *A History of Modern Indonesia since c. 1300,* 2nd edition. Stanford, CA: Stanford University Press.

Rodenburg, J. (1997). *In the Shadow of Migration: Rural Women and Their Households in North Tapanuli, Indonesia.* Leiden, The Netherlands: KITLV Press.

Singarimbun, M. (1975). *Kinship, Descent and Alliance among the Karo Batak.* Berkeley: University of California Press.

Williams, W. L. (1991). *Javanese Lives: Women and Men in Modern Indonesian Society.* New Brunswick, NJ: Rutgers University Press.

CLARK E. CUNNINGHAM

INDUSTRIALIZATION

Industrialization refers to the mechanization of production, and particularly the substitution of human and animal labor by mineral power, such as coal, water, and steam. Two other processes, however, that preceded mechanization had a major impact on family life: *agrarian reform* that made the production of food more efficient, at once increasing the quantity of food and releasing human labor from its production; and *proto-industry,* a system in which rural workers, operating as family units, purchased raw materials from contractors, worked them into semi-finished or finished products, and sold them back to the urban manufacturer. In some regions and countries this type of production, particularly in the case of certain textiles, persisted along with full-scale factory production into the twentieth century. Output expanded through the multiplication of production units—families—rather than through mechanized tools of production, thus making the family an agent of economic development (Mendels 1972; Tilly 1983; Berg 1986). Ultimately mechanized production in factories became the dominant form of production, creating new social classes and a new ideology about family life.

A number of factors caused England to industrialize first, beginning around 1750. Rapid population growth acted as a catalyst for increased production of food and manufactured goods, and England had the advantages of abundant raw materials, colonial possessions, and advanced transportation systems on sea and land. The social impacts of industrialization in England were in many ways brutal, particularly when rural laborers were forced off the land and when the skills of artisans became obsolete. Although the case of England was long thought to be the "classic" model of industrialization, no other country had exactly the same conditions and patterns of development. Industrialization in France began later and far more slowly than in England, with large-scale industry developing only in the 1850s. Germany and parts of central Europe followed in the 1860s, the United States in 1870s, and Russia only at the end of the century (Blackwell 1968; Henderson 1969; Landes 1969; Trebilcock 1981).

Although the timing, pace and social impacts of industrialization varied, it had similar impacts everywhere on marriage and family life. One of the most important consequences was the removal of work from the home. Second, it promoted migration from the countryside to the city, and between towns, as well as to other countries, particularly across the Atlantic. Third, it promoted a decline in marital fertility, and families became much smaller. Fourth, it created two new social classes, the *industrial proletariat* and the *bourgeoisie,* each of which experienced change in family life very differently. The bourgeoisie gave rise to a new model of family life that came to dominate

social mores as well as social policy in the nineteenth and twentieth centuries (Moch 1983; Accampo 1989; Levine 1984).

Marriage

Prior to industrialization and during its early phases, economic considerations determined the choice of marriage partners, leaving little room for romantic love. Among the upper classes, marriages were contracted to consolidate landholdings and political power through dowries, patrimony, and social alliances, and with the aim of preserving bloodlines. Among the lower classes, mere survival necessitated marriage, and men often chose wives on the basis of their potential productive contribution as well as their reproductive capacities. Peasant farmers needed strong women who could help with labor, especially during harvests, as well as cultivate gardens, run a household, and sell products in the local market. Artisans needed partners who could help with their craft, and often chose wives from families of the same occupation. Even middle class wives provided essential assistance to their husbands in running businesses, as shopkeepers and accountants, in purchasing and selling products, and in negotiating prices. Romantic love may have affected choice of a partner, but parents and other kin actually feared its subversive influence on the broader economic community. Because marriage involved so many economic and familial considerations, couples wed at a late age through the beginning of the nineteenth century. On the average, men married at about age twenty-nine, and women at about age twenty-six. Many couples married only after one or both of their parents had died; parental death not only released patrimony, it released young people from the need for parental consent (Stone 1977; Davidoff and Hall 1987; Smith 1981; Gillis 1985).

The more intensified development of industrial *capitalism* in the nineteenth century undermined the restrictions on marriage among all classes, though economic concerns continued to prevail. In certain circumstances industrial wage labor encouraged earlier marriage because the contributions of a wife and children could increase chances for survival or for a higher standard of living. But in other circumstances low wages made marriage impossible; Michael Mitterauer and Reinhard

Sieder (1983) discovered that in the Viennese district of Gumpendorf, up to a third of all workers in the mid-nineteenth century could never afford to marry or have a family. Others formed consensual unions and had children out of wedlock. Migration resulting from industrial change also disrupted marriage patterns, but far less than might be expected. Numerous studies have shown that young people rarely migrated alone, and when they did, it was to join relatives and neighbors who had preceded them to their destinations (Moch 1983; Anderson 1971). *Marital endogamy* thus persisted: people married others who were from similar occupations or similar origins, whether they had traveled twenty-five miles from their native village, or across the Atlantic. In Europe, and particularly in the United States, which received Europeans of so many different backgrounds, people married within their own ethnic groups, and specific ethnic groups concentrated in certain trades. In this manner, marriage countered the disruptive effects of geographical displacement, and continued to be the product of survival more than the result of romantic love.

Industrial capitalism and complex cultural factors associated with its impacts also influenced bourgeois marriages, but in a manner different from those of the lower classes. The accumulation of wealth that produced the bourgeoisie also fostered an ethic of *individualism* and created cultural freedom for the development of intimacy. The era of *Romanticism* in the early nineteenth century associated with art and literature also reflected and encouraged the development of romantic love (Perrot 1990; Kern 1992). Although economic considerations continued to play a crucial role in choosing a spouse, romantic love at least as an ideal began to compete with the traditional ethic, and gave rise to what historians have called the *companionate marriage* in which mutual affection was considered necessary for a successful union. Indeed, love between spouses became a moral duty among the middle classes (Stone 1977; Mitterauer and Sieder 1983).

Family

Industrialization changed the family by converting it from a *unit of production* into a *unit of consumption,* causing a decline in fertility and a transformation in the relationship between spouses and between parents and children. This change occurred unevenly and gradually, and varied by social class and occupation. Through the nineteenth century industrial workers continued to have relatively large families; women tended to have children about every two years from marriage to age forty. Most types of workers had little motivation for limiting family size because children continued to contribute to the family economy and infant and child mortality rates remained high in industrial cities, sometimes reaching fifty percent in the first year of life. Usually women stopped working outside the home once they became mothers, but often their husbands' wages were too low to support a family, so they took in tasks such as sewing to supplement the family income; but earnings were so low, and hours so long, that households suffered even more than they did when women left the home to work (Accampo, Fuchs, and Stewart 1995). In France especially, the practice of sending children out to wet-nurses continued to be widespread, and hygiene reports blamed infant mortality on women who did not breastfeed their own children (Fuchs 1992; Cole 2000).

Industrialization disrupted the traditional relationship between generations, as well as the relationship between spouses. Fathers could no longer pass on skills to their children—often the only patrimony workers had—when skills became obsolete. During times when the father was unemployed, family roles could be dramatically reversed: children and wives would bring home wages while the husband tended to the household. In conditions of severe poverty, "family life" could barely exist when multiple families and individuals crowded into tiny dwellings to save on rent.

The conditions of working class families varied widely, however, according to region and economic activity, and the family often became a means to resist change or soften its worst impacts. Particularly in textiles, male weavers went to great lengths to preserve their craft, avoid factory work, and preserve the family domestic economy. For example, French handloom weavers in the region around Cholet managed to preserve their craft for a century after linen production had become mechanized. As their own earnings declined from factory competition, they sent their wives and children into unskilled work in the local shoe and linen factories (Liu 1994). Where textiles did become completely industrialized in France, England,

and the northern United States, historians have shown that entire families would become reconstituted in workshops, keeping the family unit together with fathers often supervising the work of their children. Families most affected by industrial change had a remarkable ability to adjust and survive (Smelser 1959; Hareven 1977, 1982; Hareven and Langenback 1978).

The nineteenth-century bourgeoisie experienced a fundamental transformation in family life as well. In the early phases of industrial capitalism, bourgeois women helped manage family businesses; little separation existed between private household affairs and the family enterprise, and their attitude about the latter extended to all aspects of life. As mothers they concentrated on alleviating themselves of childcare responsibilities and sent their infants to wet-nurses. When the mechanization of production and the professionalization of commerce removed work from the home, however, gender roles and ideals about family life changed dramatically. Men left the home to work and to socialize with other men, whereas women devoted themselves to domesticity and motherhood. Wives were to establish a moral haven from the unethical capitalist world to which their husbands could return. They supervised and instructed servants and elaborately decorated their households and themselves as symbols of their husbands' success. A *cult of domesticity* and a new ideology about motherhood emerged, dictating that women devote themselves exclusively to the nurturing function, breast-feeding their children themselves and rearing them according to strict rules of moral and religious discipline (Smith 1981; Davidoff and Hall 1987).

Although servants remained in bourgeois households until after World War I as domestics, nursemaids, and governesses—undermining the prescribed role of motherhood—family life among the bourgeoisie grew more private and closed in on itself, and affective relationships intensified. Ironically, the much higher expectations about marriage and childrearing emerged at a time when male and female worlds were becoming increasingly separate and differentiated. It was this family model that provided the basis upon which Sigmund Freud developed his psychoanalytic theory (Weeks 1985); it is difficult to imagine the theory's appropriateness to previous family forms.

The Bourgeois Family as a Model

Although workers generally did not embrace the same family ideology as that of the middle classes during the period of industrialization, the bourgeois model did spread to lower-middle and working-class families in the early twentieth century. As the male wage rose, and legislation restricted children's work, large families became impractical. Realizing that their populations were a national resource, governments throughout the industrializing world became deeply concerned with infant and child mortality, fertility decline, and marriage. They sought means to improve the health of the population and to guarantee a high growth rate. They feared that birth rates in competing nations and among their own immigrants and ethnic minorities would outpace their own "native stock" (Gordon 1977; Weeks 1981). Reform often meant intervening in family life through restricting women's and children's labor and attempting to encourage women to have more children and to breast-feed them rather than sending them to wet-nurses (Accampo, Fuchs, and Stewart 1985). Birth control generally remained difficult to obtain, if not illegal, until after World War I; it then became a part of *family planning* rather than individual reproductive freedom when it finally became legal (Gordon 1977; Weeks 1981).

The family that industrialization made possible, however, also created the very conditions that would undermine it, because political democratization accompanied economic modernization in Europe and North America. Although motherhood had gained a new status that gave women more dignity, many women began to seek the individual social and political rights that their brothers, husbands, and sons enjoyed, and became critical of their complete economic dependence and lack of education. Over the course of the twentieth century there has been an enormous rise in all industrial countries of married women in the labor force as well as a continuing decline in fertility, suggesting that women do not think of motherhood as their only purpose. Martine Segalen (1996) notes that by the late twentieth century, an increasing number of women with young children were entering the labor force throughout the industrial world. She suggests that the modern family, rather than representing the bourgeois "traditional" family, is a fusion of several models, including that of the working class where women never had the leisure or economic resources to make a "cult" of domesticity. High divorce rates and a sharp rise since 1970 of the number of unmarried, cohabiting couples suggest that the post-industrial family is continuing to reinvent itself (Segalen 1996; Burguière et al. 1996).

See also: CHRONIC ILLNESS; DIVISION OF LABOR; FAMILY ROLES; FERTILITY; HOUSEWORK; MIGRATION; POVERTY; RURAL FAMILIES; TIME USE; URBANIZATION; WORK AND FAMILY

Bibliography

Accampo, E. (1989). *Industrialization, Family Life and Class Relations: Saint Chamond, 1815–1914*. Berkeley: University of California Press.

Accampo, E.A.; Fuchs, R.; Stewart, M. L. (1995). *Gender and the Politics of Social Reform in France, 1870–1914*. Baltimore, MD: Johns Hopkins University Press.

Anderson, M. (1971). *Family Structure in Nineteenth-Century Lancashire*. Cambridge, UK: Cambridge University Press.

Berg, M. (1986). *The Age of Manufacturers: Industry, Innovation and Work in Britain, 1700–1820*. New York: Oxford University Press.

Blackwell, W. L. (1968). *The Beginnings of Russian Industrialization, 1800-1860*. Princeton, NJ: Princeton University Press.

Burguière, A.; Klapisch-Zuber, C.; Segalen, M.; and Zonabend, F. (1996). "The Family: What Next?" In *A History of the Family,* Vol. 2: *The Impact of Modernity,* ed. A. Burguière, C. Klapisch-Zuber, M. Segalen, and F. Zonabend. Cambridge, MA: Harvard University Press.

Cole, J. (2000). *The Power of Large Numbers: Population, Politics, and Gender in Nineteenth-Century France*. Ithaca, NY: Cornell University Press.

Davidoff, L., and Hall, C. (1987). *Family Fortunes: Men and Women of the English Middle Class, 1780–1850*. Chicago: University of Chicago Press.

Fuchs, R. G. (1992). *Poor and Pregnant in Paris*. New Brunswick, NJ: Rutgers University Press.

Gillis, J. (1985). *For Better, for Worse: British Marriages, 1600 to the Present*. New York: Oxford University Press.

Gordon, L. (1977). *Woman's Body, Woman's Right: Birth Control in America*. New York: Penguin Books.

Hareven, T. (1977). *Family and Kin in Urban Communities, 1700–1930*. New York: New Viewpoints.

Hareven, T. (1982). *Family Time and Industrial Time*. Cambridge, UK: Cambridge University Press.

Hareven, T., and Langenback, R. (1978). *Amoskeag: Life and Work in an American Factory-City*. New York: Pantheon.

Henderson, W. O. (1969). *The Industrialization of Europe, 1780-1914*. New York: Harcourt Brace.

Kern, S. (1992). *The Culture of Love: Victorians to Moderns*. Cambridge, MA: Harvard University Press.

Landes, D. (1969). *The Unbound Prometheus: Technological Change and Industrial Development in Western Europe from 1750 to the Present*. London: Cambridge University Press.

Levine, D. (1977). *Family Formation in an Age of Nascent Capitalism*. New York: Academic Press

Levine, D., ed. (1984). *Proletarianization and Family History*. New York: Academic Press.

Liu, T.P. (1994). *The Weaver's Knot: The Contradictions of Class Struggle and Family Solidarity in Western France, 1750–1914*. Ithaca, NY: Cornell University Press.

Mendels, F. (1972). "Proto-Industrialization: The First Phase of the Industrialization Process." *Journal of Economic History* 32:241–261.

Mitterauer, M., and Sieder, R. (1983). *The European Family: Patriarchy to Partnership from the Middle Ages to the Present*. Chicago: University of Chicago Press.

Moch, L. (1983). *Paths to the City: Regional Migration in Nineteenth-Century France*. Arlington, TX: A&M University Press.

Perrot, M, ed., (1990). *A History of Private Life: From the Fires of Revolution to the Great War*. Cambridge, MA: Harvard University Press.

Segalen, M. (1996). "The Industrial Revolution: From Proletariat to Bourgeoisie." In *A History of the Family,* Vol. 2: *The Impact of Modernity,* ed. A. Burguière, C. Klapisch-Zuber, M. Segalen, and F. Zonabend. Cambridge, MA: Harvard University Press.

Smelser, N. (1959). *Social Change and the Industrial Revolution*. Chicago: University of Chicago Press

Smith, B. (1981). *Ladies of the Leisure Class: TheBourgeoises of Northern France in the Nineteenth Century*. Princeton, NJ: Princeton University Press.

Stone, L. (1977). *The Family, Sex and Marriage in England, 1500–1800*. New York: Harper & Row.

Tilly, C. (1983). "Flows of Capital and Forms of Industry in Europe, 1500–1900." *Theory and Society* 12:123–142.

Trebilcock, C. (1981). *The Industrialization of the Continental Powers, 1870-1914.* London and New York: Longman.

Weeks, J. (1981). *Sex, Politics and Society: The Regulation of Sexuality since 1800.* London: Longman.

Weeks, J. (1985). *Sexuality and its Discontents: Meanings, Myths, and Modern Sexualities.* London: Routledge.

ELINOR ACCAMPO

INFANTICIDE

Infanticide is the deliberate killing of infants under the age of one year. This restricted definition conceptualizes infanticide as a postnatal abortion procedure rather than as a type of child abuse. Infanticide and abortion are often used as family planning mechanisms, carried out to protect the health of unweaned children, the family economy, or the mother's social standing. Information on the killing of children older than one year is given in this entry only when it pertains to other issues being discussed or when the ages of the victims seem to include infants less than a year old.

In modern societies, where infants are born in hospitals, their birth certificates confer citizenship. However, throughout most of human history, babies were born at home and infanticide was a private action done by family members. For this reason, reports about infanticide are often absent or inaccurate, particularly in places having laws against the act.

A number of authors infer infanticide from family size and female infanticide from sex ratios. These indirect measures have been criticized because small family size may result from long postpartum sex taboos, high child mortality, selling unwanted children, or giving them up for adoption. Skewed sex ratios may result from neglect of daughters or underreporting females to census takers.

Prevalence

Marvin Harris (1977) calls infanticide the most widely used method of population control during much of human history. Infanticide, like abortion, seems to occur in virtually all contemporary tribal societies, although the frequency of infanticide varies considerably. The practice has been described in hunter-gatherer, horticulturist, and agrarian societies (Dickemann 1975), as well as among Australian Aborigines (Cowlishaw 1978) and Eskimos (Chapman 1980). It is relatively infrequent in Africa, probably because of the value of large families to agricultural and pastoral people and the high infant mortality rates (Williamson 1978).

Infanticide has been documented in the ancient civilizations of Greece, Rome, Egypt, Israel, China, and Western Europe. Infanticide, particularly female infanticide, was common among the classical Greeks and Romans. Spartans exposed unfit infants of both sexes. Infanticide was so common in Greece and Rome that the average family was small and seldom had more than one daughter (Boswell 1988).

Infanticide and infant abandonment occurred throughout Europe, despite Christian prohibitions against it. Its frequency increased during the Black Death plague in the fourteenth century and became a widespread problem in the eighteenth century, an age of rapid population growth. In the eighteenth and nineteenth centuries, servants were not permitted to marry or have children, forcing many servant girls to kill or abandon their infants, who were often fathered by their masters. In nineteenth-century Europe and in other technologically advanced nations, the introduction of the condom and increased public concern for children began to decrease infanticide rates (Boswell 1988; Langer 1974).

In most twentieth-century nations, the increase of adoption, the spread of contraception, and the legalization of abortion, allowing for safe abortions under medical supervision, increasingly have made infanticide an unnecessary and outdated method of birth control.

Time of Occurrence

Infanticide is usually carried out at birth or in the first month, before the performance of the infant's birth ceremony. These ceremonies, which incorporate the infants into their kin groups and give them identity and legal status, often take place between the second and fourth weeks and may be delayed if the infant is sickly. In some societies, infants are not considered human or members of the family and community until after their birth ceremonies. The performance of infanticide *before* the birth ceremony indicates that it is conceptualized as a postnatal abortion (Daly and Wilson 1984; Minturn 1989a, 1989b).

In the sample studied by Leigh Minturn and Jerry Stashak (1982), infanticide was performed by mothers or midwives in 79 percent of societies and by fathers or other men in only 15 percent. Birth ceremonies, on the other hand, were performed by fathers and other men in 69 percent and by women only in 22 percent of the societies, with adults of both sexes participating in the ceremony for the remaining societies. These results suggest that unwanted newborns are killed by women before they are presented to the lawgiving men for the birth ceremonies.

Methods

Infanticide is sometimes done quickly by strangling, crushing the skull, smothering, or poisoning. Other common methods of infanticide include exposure, abandonment, and overlaying.

Exposure. Exposure relieves parents and midwives of the responsibility of actually killing infants. The exposed infant is placed somewhere away from the community where the elements or animals will kill it. The prevalence of legends about the survival and subsequent good fortune of exposed infants (Moses, Oedipus, Romulus and Remus, Tom Jones) suggests that this method reduced the guilt of child killing. A singular modern exception to distant exposure occurs in modern hospitals, where legal constraints prohibit any method of killing a seriously handicapped infant except via the withholding of food and water, which amounts to exposing the infant in the presence of his or her caregivers (Lund 1985).

Urban exposure. Urban exposure of infants was common throughout Europe until the nineteenth century. In medieval Europe, infants were left in the streets, on trash heaps, and at church steps. European urban exposure became most frequent during the eighteenth century, when numerous poor women abandoned infants in streets or foundling homes and Parisian garbage collectors picked up abandoned infants on their rounds. However, urban exposure was not confined to Europe. During the seventeenth century, Jesuit missionaries to China found that babies were thrown into the streets and collected with the trash (Boswell 1988; Langer 1974).

Foundling homes. Public outrage over urban exposure of infants led to the establishment of foundling homes in Europe. The mortality rates of infants in these homes was as high as 90 percent. Wet nurses employed in foundling homes neglected infants and sometimes killed them so frequently that they were called "killer nurses" or "angel makers." In effect, consigning infants to these homes amounted to institutionalized urban exposure. Foundling homes allowed parents to abandon unwanted infants without fear of prosecution. As this practice became openly acceptable in the eighteenth century, attitudes toward outright infanticide became more lenient (Boswell 1988; Breiner 1990; Langer 1974). Foundling homes proved to be so ineffectual that, in the late nineteenth century, France and Britain passed laws requiring them to be licensed. Government support for unwed mothers began to replace foundling homes and orphanages in a number of countries (Langer 1974).

Overlaying. Infant death by overlaying—the accidental smothering of a baby by rolling over on it in bed—was common in Europe from the early Middle Ages through the nineteenth century. It is not always clear from the records whether overlaying occurred before or after birth ceremonies, but most overlay victims seem to have been less than one year old. Overlaying was recognized in law and religion. Sleeping with infants was discouraged and sometimes illegal (Kellum 1974). It has been suggested that some overlaying deaths in nineteenth-century England were due to Sudden Infant Death Syndrome (SIDS), which is related to nutritional tetany, and that the upper classes blamed such deaths on overlaying to disassociate themselves from the poor (Hansen 1979). Ethnographies report numerous societies where mothers or both parents routinely sleep with infants, often with older children in the bed, but do not report overlaying. It seems that this belief was, in large part, a legal fiction that allowed infanticide deaths to be declared accidental.

Vctims of Infanticide

Two studies of folk and tribal societies drawn from the Human Relations Area Files (HRAF) at Yale University report similar results to each other (Daly and Wilson 1984; Minturn and Stashak 1982). The most frequently killed infants are illegitimate (57%, 53%); weak or deformed (60%, 53%); twins and triplets (40%, 40%); or excess because of family size or circumstances of birth spacing (31%, 23%). Minturn and Stashak (1982) also found infants are killed because they are the results of abnormal births (20%); unwanted, usually because the mothers are too old or too young to raise children (27%); or females (17%).

Comparison of these results with those of a study done by George Devereux (1976) of abortion in tribal societies indicates that the victims of abortion and infanticide are the same types of infants, not surprising since the motive in both is the elimination of unwanted infants.

Infrequently, ethnographers report infanticide because of incest, kinship considerations, quarrels between parents, sacrifice, or war (Daly and Wilson 1984; Williamson 1978).

Female Infanticide

Female infanticide is the only type of infanticide still widely practiced. Female infanticide at birth and indirect female infanticide through neglect are still widespread in Third World countries.

Ethnographic reports of female infanticide, however, are relatively rare. Minturn and Stashak (1982) report it in 17 percent of their societies, Martin King Whyte (1978) in only 6 percent. Female infanticide has also been estimated from sex ratios, with a note that some societies reporting the absence of this custom have suspiciously skewed sex ratios favoring boys (Divale and Harris 1976). When reporting twin infanticides, ethnographers often note that if only one twin of a dual-sex pair is kept, it is usually the boy (Granzberg 1973).

In India and China, this custom of female infanticide dates back centuries. Female infanticide in India is most common in the northwestern states (Miller 1981; Minturn 1993), but it has also been reported for groups in the south. The poverty of China's peasants and its frequent famines are two reasons for female infanticide. In both India and China, female infanticide is increasingly being replaced by female feticide after amniocentesis to determine fetal sex. The one-child policy of Communist China and the two-child policy of India

have increased the prevalence of sons (Jefferey, Jefferey, and Lyon 1984).

Theories

Sarah B. Hrdy and Glenn Hausfater (1984) cite five functional categories of reasons for infanticide in animals in general: (1) exploitation of the infant as a resource, usually cannibalism; (2) competition for resources; (3) sexual selection; (4) parental increase of their own lifetime reproductive success by eliminating particular offspring; and (5) social pathology. Human infanticide includes examples of all of these functions (Daly and Wilson 1984; Dickemann 1984; Hrdy and Hausfater 1984; Scrimshaw 1984).

Resource competition is a popular theory of human infanticide. The threat of famine has been cited as the explanation for infanticide among Eskimos, Australian Aborigines, and Yanomamö. In Imperial China, Japan, and Europe, infanticide was used to control population and avoid starvation and social disruption. This was especially true for female infanticide, since eliminating females is a much more efficient form of population control than eliminating males.

Other theories of reasons for female infanticide include hypergymous marriage and large dowries (Dickemann 1979); differential values of children for their potential contributions to the parental kin groups (Hughes 1981); and high mortality rate of men in hunting (Riches 1974). The theory that female infanticide is a form of population control in warrior societies (Divale and Harris 1976) has been challenged by several authors who note many flaws in the original study (Fjellman 1979; Hirschfeld, Howe, and Levin 1978; Kang, Horan, and Reis 1979).

Acceptability and Legality

It has been suggested that infanticide and abortion may be underreported in tribal societies because of the presence of missionaries and colonial governments who deem these practices to be illegal (Divale and Harris 1976). Reports of infanticide prosecution by colonial governments are virtually absent in HRAF records. When babies are born at home, infanticide laws are seldom enforceable.

Ethnographic reports of abortion and infanticide are considerably more frequent than reports of punishments for either action, suggesting that tribal law was frequently permissive about both practices. A study of seventy-eight societies found no information on punishment of abortion for sixty-seven of them, and information on punishment of infanticide was so rare that it could not be coded. The absence of punishment may be viewed as recognition of parental rights to dispose of unwanted infants. Some tribal societies explicitly recognize this right until the cord is cut, until after the birth ceremony, or in a few societies, until the infant is weaned (Minturn 1989a).

Although infanticide was a capital offense in many countries for centuries, there is evidence that courts frequently took measures to avoid or mitigate punishment and that a variety of beliefs supported acquittals. In many courts, infanticidal mothers might successfully plead insanity. Eighteenth-century courts greatly extended the scope of the insanity plea by citing, as reason for dismissal of infanticide cases, the belief that pregnancy itself may make women deranged (Boswell 1988). As infanticide became more frequent, courts became more lenient, particularly when defendants were poor, unwed mothers.

Penalties also varied according to the method of killing. In the early Middle Ages, infanticide by exposure, a widespread practice of poor parents, was not a criminal offense. Overlaying was punished by one year on bread and water and two more years without wine or meat. This three-year penance, which became the standard punishment for overlaying, was shorter than the penalty for the accidental killing of adults (Kellum 1974).

Conclusion

There are four ways to avoid conceiving or to eliminate unwanted children: abstinence, contraception, abortion, and infanticide. Although abstinence was and is practiced in some societies by customs of late marriage, postpartum sex taboos, and customary periods of celibacy, it has never prevented all unwanted pregnancies. When these occurred in the past, infanticide was the safest method for disposing of the unwanted children. As medical advancements have been made, however, contraception and abortion have become more widely used and have replaced abstinence and infanticide as forms of birth control.

See also: ABORTION; BIRTH CONTROL: CONTRACEPTIVE METHODS; BIRTH CONTROL: SOCIOCULTURAL AND HISTORICAL ASPECTS; CHILD ABUSE: PHYSICAL ABUSE AND NEGLECT; DEATH AND DYING; EUTHANASIA; FAMILY PLANNING

Bibliography

Birdsell, J. B. (1968). "Some Predictions for the Pleistocene Based on Equilibrium Systems Among Recent Hunter-Gatherers." In *Man the Hunter,* ed. R. B. Lee and I. De-Vore. Chicago: Aldine.

Boswell, J. (1988). The *Kindness of Strangers: The Abandonment of Children in Western Europe from Late Antiquity to the Renaissance.* New York: Pantheon.

Breiner, S. J. (1990). *Slaughter of the Innocents: Child Abuse Through the Ages and Today.* New York: Plenum.

Chagnon, N. A.; Flinn, M. V.; and Melancon, T. F. (1979). "Sex-Ratio Variation Among the Yanomamö Indians." In *Evolutionary Biology and Human Social Behavior: An Anthropological Perspective,* ed. N. A. Chagnon and W. Irons. North Scituate, MA: Duxbury Press.

Chapman, M. (1980). "Infanticide and Fertility Among Eskimos: A Computer Simulation." *American Journal of Physical Anthropology* 53:317–327.

Cowlishaw, G. (1978). "Infanticide in Aboriginal Australia." *Oceania* 48:262–283.

Daly, M., and Wilson, M. (1984). "A Sociobiological Analysis of Human Infanticide." In *Comparative and Evolutionary Perspectives on Infanticide: Introduction and Overview,* ed. S. B. Hrdy and G. Hausfater. New York: Aldine.

Denham, W. W. (1974). "Population Structure, Infant Transport, and Infanticide Among Pleistocene and Modern Hunter-Gatherers." *Journal of Anthropological Research* 30:191–198.

Devereaux, G. (1976). *A Study of Abortion in Primitive Societies,* revised edition. Madison, CT: International Universities Press.

Dickemann, M. (1975). "Demographic Consequences of Infanticide in Man." *Annual Review of Ecology and Systematics* 6:107–137.

Dickemann, M. (1979). "Female Infanticide, Reproductive Strategies, and Social Stratification: A Preliminary Model." In *Evolutionary Biology and Human Social Behavior: An Anthropological Perspective,* ed. N. A. Chagnon and W. Irons. North Scituate, MA: Duxbury Press.

Dickemann, M. (1984). "Concepts and Classification in the Study of Human Infanticide: Sectional Introduction and Some Cautionary Notes." In *Comparative and Evolutionary Perspectives on Infanticide: Introduction and Overview,* ed. S. B. Hrdy and G. Hausfater. New York: Aldine.

Divale, W. T. (1972). "Systemic Population Control in the Middle and Upper Paleolithic." *World Archeology and Anthropology* IV:65–68.

Divale, W. T., and Harris, M. (1976). "Population, Warfare, and the Male Supremacist Complex." *American Anthropologist* 78:521–538.

Fjellman, S. M. (1979). "Hey, You Can't Do That: A Response to Divale and Harris's 'Population, Warfare, and the Male Supremacist Complex.'" *Behavior Science Research* 14:189.

Fukasaku, M. (1975). "The Psychology of Infanticide." *Japan Interpreter* 10:205–208.

Granzberg, G. (1973). "Twin Infanticide: A Cross-Cultural Test of a Materialistic Explanation." *Ethos* 1:405–412.

Hansen, E. (1979). "'Overlaying' in 19th-Century England: Infant Mortality or Infanticide?" *Human Ecology* 7:333–352.

Harris, M. (1977). *Cannibals and Kings: The Origins of Culture.* New York: Random House.

Hirschfeld, L. A.; Howe, J.; and Levin, B. (1978). "Warfare, Infanticide, and Statistical Inference: A Comment on Divale and Harris." *American Anthropologist* 80:110–115.

Hrdy, S. B., and Hausfater, G. (1984). *Comparative and Evolutionary Perspectives on Infanticide: Introduction and Overview.* New York: Aldine.

Hughes, A. L. (1981). "Female Infanticide." *Ethnology and Sociobiology* 2:109–111.

Jefferey, R.; Jefferey, P.; and Lyon, A. (1984). "Female Infanticide and Amniocentesis." *Social Science and Medicine* 19:1207–1212.

Kang, G.; Horan, S.; and Reis, J. (1979). "Comments on Divale and Harris's 'Population, Warfare, and the Male Supremacist Complex.'" *Behavior Science Research* 14:201–211.

Kellum, B. (1974). "Infanticide in England and in the Later Middle Ages." *History of Infanticide Quarterly* 1:367–388.

Kunz, J., and Bahr, S. J. (1996). "A Profile of Parental Homicide Against Children." *Journal of Family Violence* 11(4):347–362.

Lancaster, C., and Lancaster, J. (1978). "On the Male Supremacist Complex: A Reply to Divale and Harris." *American Anthropologist* 80:115–117.

Langer, W. (1974). "Infanticide: A Historical Survey." *History of Childhood Quarterly* 1:353–365.

Lund, N. (1985). "Infanticide, Physicians, and the Law: The 'Baby Doe' Amendments to the Child Abuse Prevention and Treatment Act." *American Journal of Law and Medicine* 11:1–29.

Miller, B. D. (1981). The *Endangered Sex.* Ithaca, NY: Cornell University Press.

Minturn, L. (1989a). "The Birth Ceremony as a Rite of Passage into Infant Personhood." In *Abortion Rights and Fetal Personhood,* ed. E. Doerr and J. W. Prescott. Long Beach, CA: Centerline Press.

Minturn, L. (1989b). "This Child Is Ours: A Cross-Cultural Study of Definitions of Personhood." In *Heterogeneity in Cross-Cultural Psychology,* ed. D. M. Keats, D. Munroe, and L. Mann. Rockland, MA: Swets and Zeitlinger.

Minturn, L. (1993). *Sita's Daughters: Coming Out of Purdah.* Oxford, UK: Oxford University Press.

Minturn, L., and Stashak, J. (1982). "Infanticide as a Terminal Abortion Procedure." *Behavior Science Research* 17:70–90.

Neel, J. V. (1970). "Lessons from a 'Primitive' People." *Science* 170:815–822.

Pitt, S. E., & Bale, E. M. (1995). "Neonaticide, Infanticide, and Filicide: A Review of the Literature." *Bulletin of the American Academy of Psychiatry and the Law* 23(3):375–386.

Richards, C. E. (2000). *The Loss of Innocents: Child Killers and Their Victims.* Wilmington, DE: Scholarly Resources.

Riches, D. (1974). "The Netsilik Eskimo: A Special Case of Active Female Infanticide." *Ethnology* 13:351–361.

Schrire, C., and Steiger, W. L. (1974). "A Matter of Life and Death: An Investigation into the Practice of Female Infanticide in the Arctic." *Man* 9:161–184.

Schwartz, L. L., & Isser, N. (2000). *Endangered Children: Neonaticide, Intanticide, Filicide.* Boca Raton, FL: CRC Press.

Scrimshaw, S. C. M. (1984). "Infanticide in Human Populations: Societal and Individual Concerns." In *Comparative and Evolutionary Perspectives on Infanticide: Introduction and Overview,* ed. S. B. Hrdy and G. Hausfater. New York: Aldine.

Smithey, M. (1998). "Infant Homicide: Victim/Offender Relationship." *Journal of Family Violence* 13(3):285–297.

Whyte, M. K. (1978). "Codes Dealing with the Relative Status of Women." *Ethnology* 17:211–237.

Williamson, L. (1978). "Infanticide: An Anthropological Analysis." In *Infanticide and the Value of Life,* ed. M. Kohl. Buffalo, NY: Prometheus.

LEIGH MINTURN (1995)
BIBLIOGRAPHY REVISED BY JAMES J. PONZETTI, JR.

INFERTILITY

See CHILDLESSNESS; FAMILY PLANNING; FERTILITY

INFIDELITY

Infidelity is a breach of trust that signifies a lack of faithfulness to a moral obligation to one's partner. Infidelity usually implies *sexual* infidelity, although some people, particularly women, regard an intense emotional relationship as an unfaithful extramarital involvement, even when there is no physical component. In short, infidelity is feelings or behavior that go against a partner's expectations for the exclusivity of the relationship. Some couples are comfortable with having relationships outside their union. These liaisons do not constitute infidelity unless they violate the couple's shared understandings about discretion, partner choice, and sexual conduct—understandings that are designed to protect their relationship from disruption.

In the United States, open marriages that tolerate extramarital sex are the exception. Most U.S. husbands and wives say that sexual fidelity is very important to a marriage (Blumstein and Schwartz 1983; Greeley 1991). Ninety-nine percent of married people in the United States say that they expect sexual exclusivity of their spouse, and 99 percent report their spouse expects the same of them (Treas and Giesen 2000). Cohabitors are only slightly less likely (94%) to say they expect fidelity from a partner. Although males in same-sex couples tend to be more tolerant of multiple sexual partners, few heterosexuals in the United States are indifferent to their mate's sexual activities.

Cross-Cultural Perspectives

It has been argued that limiting sex to socially sanctioned partnerships like marriage contributes to the stability of the relationship, because it makes the union the unique focus of self-disclosure and sexual pleasure. The emphasis on sexual fidelity, however, varies from culture to culture. Around the globe, about half of societies have strong prohibitions against extramarital sex for women, and about a quarter object strongly to extramarital sex for men (Frayzer 1985). Extramarital sex is permissible for men in half of societies, but it is permissible for women in only one quarter. This double standard—controlling female sexuality more than male sexuality—has been traced to the desire to insure the paternity of heirs. It has also been attributed to the unequal power between the genders—inequality that supports a man's sense of ownership over a woman. Masculine roles, by contrast, often encourage sexual adventuring. For example, brothel visits are a common ritual of male camaraderie in Thailand and elsewhere.

Monogamy, the institutional form of marriage permitting only one spouse at a time, still confronts extramarital relationships, particularly for husbands. *La casa chica,* or *little house,* is an established Latin American custom whereby married men maintain a second partner and family. Although polygamy, the custom of taking multiple wives and concubines, is illegal in China, the tradition has made a comeback among businessmen, who can afford to maintain a young mistress in her own apartment. These institutions, of course, still serve to protect the family and the marital relationship by minimizing the intrusion of secondary partnerships. Even in societies where extramarital relationships are casual and fleeting, a degree of secrecy and discretion usually surrounds the activities to minimize marital disruptions.

In honor-based Arab societies, which place a high value on female chastity, relatives may feel obliged to put an unfaithful wife to death. In other societies, casual sexual liaisons outside marriage are widely accepted both for men and for women. This is the case in parts of Africa. Where children are regarded as belonging to broad kinship groups, there may be less concern with paternity and with controlling female sexuality. Where financial responsibility for offspring falls to women, they often rely on supportive sex partners in order to provide for themselves and their children. In urban Nigeria, for example, two-thirds of men and one-third of women in monogamous marriages reported that their *most recent* sexual encounter was with someone besides their legal spouse.

The less tolerant attitudes in Western nations may be traced to Christian teachings on marriage and sexuality. In the twenty-four largely Western and industrial countries in the 1994 International Social Survey Program, most people stated that extramarital sex was "always wrong" (Widmer et al. 1998). Fully 80 percent of U.S. respondents condemned extramarital relations as being always wrong, a figure comparable to conservative Catholic populations like Ireland (80%), Northern Ireland (81%), and the Philippines (88%). The "always wrong" response found less favor in other countries: Australia (59%), Austria (67%), Bulgaria (51%), Canada (68%), Czech Republic (43%), Germany (data reported separately: East Germany, 60%, and West Germany, 55%), Great Britain (67%), Hungary (62%), Israel (73%), Italy (67%), Japan (58%), Netherlands (63%), New Zealand (75%), Norway (70%), Poland (74%), Russia (36%), Slovenia (57%), Spain (76%), and Sweden (68%). On average, however, only 4 percent of survey respondents believed that extramarital sex was "not at all wrong." Thus, moral judgments in Western countries continue to support sexual exclusivity between husbands and wives.

Although people in the United States have become increasingly tolerant of premarital sex and homosexual sex, they voice stronger disapproval of extramarital sex. Disapproval has actually increased in recent decades. According to data from the General Social Surveys, extramarital sex was condemned as "always wrong" by 70 percent of U.S. respondents in 1973. Following a sharp increase in disapproval at the end of the 1980s, perhaps in response to the AIDS crisis, views on extramarital sex largely stabilized and stood at 81 percent strongly disapproving in 1998.

Permissive sexual values reflect liberal religious and political ideologies. Men are more permissive than women. People with more schooling are more tolerant than people with less education. African Americans and people who live in big cities are also more tolerant of extramarital sex. Not surprisingly, people with permissive sexual values are more likely to have adulterous relationships. Only 10 percent of U.S. respondents who

say extramarital sex is "always wrong" report having extramarital sex, as compare to 76 percent of respondents who say extramarital sex is "not at all wrong" (Smith 1994).

Studying Sexual Infidelity

The scientific study of sexuality has faced the problem of finding a neutral terminology to describe behavior that often elicits strong moral sentiments. *EMS,* the abbreviation of extramarital sex, is a common convention used in scholarly papers. Philip Blumstein and Pepper Schwartz (1983) employ a nonjudgmental term, *non-monogamy,* which they apply to married and cohabiting couples, heterosexual or same-sex, who have sex outside of their union. *Adultery* is a narrower, legal concept. Adultery refers to voluntary sexual intercourse, either between a *married* man and someone who is not his wife or between a *married* woman and someone who is not her husband. Although an unmarried partner may have an adulterous relationship with a married person, only married people have *extramarital sex.* The epidemiological literature in public health focuses on the number of sexual partners. This approach to measuring sexual behavior distinguishes *secondary sex partners,* who are defined by reference to a *primary sex partner* (i.e., the person reported to be the most important or frequent sexual partner). The primary partner is typically a spouse, cohabitor, or steady date. Married people who have *multiple* or *secondary* sex partners are assumed to have had extramarital sex.

The accuracy of sex data depends on the respondents' recall and candor. People have difficulty remembering sexual activities from the distant past. Also, because sexual infidelity is what survey experts describe as "sensitive" behavior, people may be embarrassed or reluctant to admit infidelities, particularly if an infidelity is not really characteristic of their usual patterns. This reporting bias could mean that survey estimates of extramarital sex and secondary partners are understated. Critics of sex surveys have challenged the validity of data, because men, on average, report a higher number of partners than women do. This pattern is seen in the United States, Great Britain, Norway, and Canada. Close examination of sex data does not suggest widespread problems. The problem is limited to a few men who skew the results by reporting extremely high numbers of sex partners.

Data quality is not a new concern. To discourage under-reporting of sexual behavior, Alfred Kinsey's pioneering sex studies of the 1930s and 1940s used complex cross-checks and aggressive interviewing techniques. Kinsey's estimates of the population engaging in extramarital sex—half of married men at some point and a quarter of married white women by age 40—were startlingly high. As statistical experts of the day noted, it is impossible to determine the validity and reliability of Kinsey's findings. His figures may have resulted from his biased volunteer sample, which was skewed toward prisoners, divorcees, and others whose sexual experiences were not representative of the U.S. population at large. The limitations of the historical data make it impossible to determine with much confidence whether the incidence of sexual fidelity has changed over time for U.S. husbands and wives.

Because of the sensitive nature of their topics, sex studies, including recent ones, have encountered heated political opposition. As a consequence, much research on extramarital sex has been based on dubious sources, such as readers who are sufficiently motivated to mail back a magazine questionnaire on sex. Largely in response to the AIDS crisis, however, several countries fielded large, nationally representative sample surveys of sexual behavior in the 1990s. In the English-speaking world, two surveys in 1992—the British National Survey of Sexual Attitudes and Lifestyles (Wellings et al. 1994) and the U.S. National Survey of Health and Social Life (Laumann et al. 1994)—have contributed to our understanding of sexual partnering.

Contemporary interview surveys have devoted considerable attention to improving the quality of sex data. Researchers go to great lengths to develop, pretest, and refine their questionnaires. To insure the integrity of their scientific samples, they work hard to secure interviews with sample persons who are difficult to locate or reluctant to be interviewed. They make special efforts to conduct confidential interviews out of earshot of other household members. Anonymous, self-administered questionnaires that work well for sensitive questions are combined with face-to-face interviews where clarification is needed. For example, interviewers collect complicated rosters for the start and end dates of sexual relationships; these can be used to determine if there are overlaps in time that would indicate sexual infidelity.

Data are analyzed for consistency and compared to results from other surveys.

How Common Is Infidelity?

The U.S. media perpetuates the belief that extramarital sex is widespread. Television programs, for example, are nearly as likely to feature extramarital sex as marital sex. Even serious newspapers report on extramarital affairs if they involve a breach of public trust or an instance of personal hypocrisy. In their own lives, most people in the United States know somebody who has had extramarital sex. This may explain why two-thirds of married people are prepared to believe that fidelity is more important in their own marriage than in the marriages of other people (Greeley 1991). Research on sexual behavior, however, does not sustain the impression that sexual infidelity is the behavioral norm in the United States. Most married people do not have sex outside marriage. Although sexual infidelity may be habitual behavior for some people, most married people who do have extramarital sex do not have it very often or with very many partners. Extramarital sex is atypical behavior.

Surveys find that between 1.5 and 3.6 percent of married people in the United States had multiple sex partners in the preceding year. Similar figures are reported in British surveys. Although few people are engaged in extramarital sex at any particular point in time, the numbers who have had sex outside marriage *at some point while they were married* are, of course, higher. Nonetheless, only a minority of men and women report ever having had other sex partners while they were married or cohabiting with a partner. Whether one considers older or younger generations, more than 90 percent of women and more than 75 percent of men say that they have always been faithful (Laumann et al. 1994). The low incidence of extramarital sex underscores the importance of sexual exclusivity as a condition of committed heterosexual relationships in the United States.

What Are the Origins of Infidelity?

Gender differences in sexual attitudes and behavior are striking. Compared to men, women are less accepting of extensive sexual experience, nonmarital coitus, and casual sex outside a committed relationship. Sexual behavior is consistent with

Sexual exclusiveness is strongly related to marriage stability. Women consider infidelity to be a greater threat to marriage than do men. HELEN KING/CORBIS

sexual values. Wives are less likely than husbands to engage in extramarital sex. Apparently, this is due largely to attitudes: Controlling for permissiveness of sexual values and for the frequency of sexual thoughts largely eliminates the gender difference in the likelihood of sexual infidelity (Treas and Giesen 2000). Although men are willing to consider sex without emotional commitment, women view romantic attachment as a prerequisite for sex. Hence, women regard sexual infidelity as a greater threat to marriage than do men (Blumstein and Schwartz 1983; Wellings et al. 1994). When asked what might justify extramarital sex, women are more likely than men to invoke falling in love and less likely to cite sexual gratification.

One explanation for gender differences in sexual behavior frames an evolutionary argument: Men's genetic legacy is maximized when they impregnate many women while women's optimal reproductive strategy calls for breeding *selectively* with men who will help to raise the children. Other explanations emphasize social roots of monogamy such as the gendered nature of learned scripts explicitly motivating sexual activity.

For both men and women, normative beliefs and behavioral patterns seem to be established by late adolescence and early adulthood. In the early teen years, girls' peer groups are already reinforcing monogamous feeling norms (e.g., don't have romantic feelings for a boy who has a girlfriend or for more than one boy at a time). Even in adulthood, sexual attitudes continue to reflect the values of the community in which one was raised. Early experience foretells later behavior. According to French survey data, the younger the age at first intercourse, the more likely an individual living in a couple relationship is to have multiple sexual partners (Bozon 1996). In the United States, having had more sexual partners before the first marriage or cohabitation also increases the likelihood of infidelity (Treas and Giesen 2000). The implication seems to be that premarital sexual lifestyles encourage infidelity in marriage, but some unidentified common factor (e.g., a preference for risk-taking behavior) may account for sexual behavior both before and during marriage.

Individuals who strongly disapprove of extramarital sex are not likely to be unfaithful. The personal discomfort in violating deeply held values discourages infidelity, although those who are unfaithful may also work to bring their values in line with their behavior (Lawson 1988). Most organized religions teach values that emphasize sexual fidelity. People who attend religious services are less likely to engage in infidelity, even when the individual's sexual values are taken into account (Treas and Giesen 2000). Belonging to a community that is supportive of sexual fidelity seems to discourage extramarital sex—above and beyond any influence on individual moral beliefs.

Is the Marriage the Problem?

Sexual infidelity leads people to question whether the primary relationship is somehow lacking and whether having a new sexual partner implies dissatisfaction with the old one. There is evidence that more committed partners are less likely to be unfaithful. People who are merely dating are at greater risk for infidelity than those living in cohabiting relationships. Cohabitors, in turn, are more likely than married people to have sexual affairs—a pattern that cannot be fully explained by their more permissive sexual values (Treas and Giesen 2000). The implication is that married people, who have made a bigger commitment, are less willing to put their relationship at risk by violating expectations for sexual exclusivity. Infidelity declines as people grow older: This may reflect the fact that older people have had the time to make bigger investments in their relationship, or it may simply signify more general biological declines in sexual activity with aging.

Is extramarital sex evidence of an unhappy marriage or a bad sex life? Certainly, people sometimes begin sexual affairs in order to register a complaint or force a spouse to end an unhappy union, but many people who engage in extramarital sex are quite satisfied with their marriages. Research has not found a consistent association between marital satisfaction and the risk of sexual infidelity. On the one hand, various studies report no significant association between sexual infidelity and marital happiness, the quality of marital sex (for whites), or physical satisfaction with sex (for men). Other studies show that sexual infidelity is positively associated with marital unhappiness, low emotional satisfaction with the union, women's reports of marital inequity, and men's sexual dissatisfaction. Unfortunately, there are no large, longitudinal studies to sort out whether unhappiness comes before or after infidelity. The causal direction of the association remains unclear. Although an unhappy relationship may lead to sexual infidelity, infidelity may make people unhappy with their relationship. Ironically, married people report that marital problems led them to have extramarital sex, but they blame their *spouse's* infidelities for marital problems.

Couples who take pleasure in one another's family and friends are less likely to be unfaithful (Treas and Giesen 2000). Shared social circles may validate the couple's relationship. They may foster a satisfying union so that the partners have more to lose from infidelity. Certainly, couples who share many activities have fewer opportunities for sex outside their marriage than do couples who lead separate lives (Blumstein and Schwartz 1983). In other words, more opportunities for sex outside marriage may lead to more sex outside marriage. The workplace is one place where people meet potential sexual partners. In Britain, people who work away from home overnight are not as likely to be sexually monogamous (Wellings et al. 1994). In the United States, a job that involves intimate interpersonal contact—being alone with, touching, and discussing personal concerns of clients, coworkers, and customers—is associated with a greater risk of sexual infidelity (Treas and Giesen 2000). The risk is also greater in large cities that offer greater anonymity and more potential partners than do small towns. More generally, communities that have more potential partners have been found to have more divorce.

What Are Secondary Sexual Relationships Like?

Except for studies of commercial sex workers, secondary sex partners have not been much studied. U.S. researchers find that married, cohabiting, and dating persons choose secondary partners who are very much like their spouse, cohabiting partner, or usual date. There is only limited evidence that people are actually able to improve on their current partner by having a sexual affair. Compared to their usual partner, women's secondary sex partners are a bit more likely to be college graduates. Men's secondary partners are more likely than their primary partner to be enrolled in school, suggesting that they are perhaps younger.

If both types of sex partners are quite similar, it is because people find their sex partners—primary and secondary—in the social world they inhabit.

To be sure, married and cohabiting men are less likely to have met their secondary sex partner through friends and family members. They are more likely to have met at work and to have introduced themselves. The implication seems to be that men meet secondary sex partners outside the watchful eye of wife, family, and friends—a hardly surprising finding since adulterers usually go to great lengths to keep their affairs secret. The finding also points up that secondary sexual relationships lack the public commitment and stabilizing social networks of marriages and cohabiting unions.

Although a breach of fidelity may undermine a marriage, secondary sex partners do not usually displace primary ones. Some extramarital affairs are long lasting, but most secondary sexual relationships are casual and short-lived. Many people do not even expect to have sex with the secondary partner ever again. In fact, at least for women, the secondary relationship is not as satisfying sexually as the primary one.

This may reflect the fact that secondary sexual relationships are often short-term relationships: Men and women in short-term relationships say sex is less satisfying, emotionally and physically, than married and cohabiting people do. Of course, sexual practices differ between short-term and long-term relationships. Short-term sexual relationships are characterized by greater condom usage, more oral sex, and more alcohol use than is the case for long-term relationships, cohabitations, and marriages (Laumann et al. 1994). Secrecy and deceit also characterize sexual infidelity. Sexual affairs, for example, are apt to involve clandestine meetings in out of the way places and elaborate ruses to cover absences from home. Although some people find the intrigue exciting, others experience guilt and anxiety.

What Are the Consequences?

The social and economic costs of sexual infidelity have declined, because the government has largely stopped regulating noncommercial sex between consenting adults. Before no-fault divorce laws were passed in the 1970s, an adulterer might expect to lose custody of children, suffer in the division of marital property, or fare poorly in alimony orders. In removing adultery as grounds for marital dissolution, no-fault laws also eliminated sexual infidelity as a justification for favoring one spouse over the other. Similarly, so-called *heart balm torts* once permitted a betrayed spouse to sue the third party on grounds like alienation of affection. These torts have almost disappeared from U.S. law, too. Of course, half of the U.S. states still have laws against adultery on the books. These laws would prevent an adulterer from voting, serving alcohol, practicing law, adopting children, or residing with a former spouse. Adultery laws, however, are virtually never enforced. Many states have quietly repealed the obsolete statutes. Where the laws have not been repealed, they serve largely symbolic purposes, embodying the state's support for conventional morality and family life.

How sexual infidelity affects relationships is a question that demands further study. Although a secondary involvement is sometimes meaningful to the participants, it usually does not generate lasting commitment. Nonetheless, marriage counselors testify that extramarital sex is destabilizing to a marriage. Domestic violence is one known consequence of sexual jealousy; divorce may be another. Divorced people are more likely than still-married people to report having had extramarital sex at one time or another (Laumann et al. 1994). Unfortunately, we do not know to what extent preexisting personal or marital problems lead both to infidelity and to the divorce. In short, we do not know how important sexual infidelity is as a cause of divorce.

Theoretically, infidelity is thought to destabilize marriage. It negates the couple's closed network of intimacy, undermines assumptions of mutual "ownership," and short circuits the solidarity that comes when one's partner is the sole source of a valued (sexual) service. Sexual affairs divert time, energy, and money away from the marital relationship. Perhaps because they are more likely to involve an emotional component, women's affairs are argued to be more likely than men's to result in divorce and to lead to a new committed relationship (Lawson 1988).

Only longitudinal data following individuals over time can clarify the causal relationships. The assumption that infidelity actually causes divorce rests on tenuous inferences. Although 15 percent of newly divorced people in the United States admitted to being involved with someone else just before their marriage ended, 40 percent accused their ex-spouse of being involved with someone else. It is not known, however, whether these extramarital affairs precipitated the divorce or were only initiated after the married couple began the divorce. Whatever the chain of events, the betrayal of norms of sexual exclusivity is condemned by most people in the United States.

See also: COHABITATION; COMMUNICATION: COUPLE RELATIONSHIPS; INTIMACY; JEALOUSY; MARITAL QUALITY; MARITAL SEX; RELATIONSHIP DISSOLUTION; RELATIONSHIP MAINTENANCE; RELIGION; SEXUALITY; SOCIAL NETWORK; SEXUAL COMMUNICATION: COUPLE RELATIONSHIPS; THERAPY: COUPLE RELATIONSHIPS; TRUST

Bibliography

Blumstein, P., and Schwartz, P. (1983). *American Couples: Money, Work, Sex.* New York: Morrow.

Bozon, M. (1996). "Reaching Adult Sexuality: First Intercourse and Its Implications." In *Sexuality and the Social Sciences,* ed. M. Bozon and H. Leridon. Aldershot, UK: Dartmouth.

Frayzer, S. G. (1985). *Varieties of Sexual Experience: An Anthropological Perspective on Human Sexuality.* New Haven, CT: HRAF Press.

Greeley, A. M. (1991). *Faithful Attraction: Discovering Intimacy, Love, and Fidelity in American Marriage.* New York: TOR Books.

Laumann, E. O.; Gagnon, J. H.; Michael, R. T.; and Michaels, S. (1994). *The Social Organization of Sexuality: Sexual Practices in the United States.* Chicago: University of Chicago Press.

Lawson, A. (1988). *Adultery: The Analysis of Love and Betrayal.* New York: Basic Books.

Smith, T. W. (1994). "Attitudes Toward Sexual Permissiveness: Trends, Correlates, and Behavioral Connections." In *Sexuality Across the Life Course,* ed. A.S. Rossi. Chicago: University of Chicago Press.

Treas, J., and Giesen, D. (2000). "Sexual Infidelity Among Married and Cohabiting Americans." *Journal of Marriage and the Family* 62:48–60.

Wellings, K.; Field, J.; Johnson, A. M.; and Wadsworth, J. (1994). *Sexual Behavior in Britain: The National Survey of Sexual Attitudes and Lifestyles.* London: Penguin Books.

Widmer, E. D.; Treas, J.; and Newcomb, R. (1998). "Attitudes Toward Nonmarital Sex in 24 Countries." *Journal of Sex Research* 35:349–358.

JUDITH TREAS

INHERITANCE

See KINSHIP; PRIMOGENITURE; RICH/WEALTHY FAMILIES

IN-LAW RELATIONSHIPS

Relationships with in-laws are a special category within kinship systems that has not been widely studied. Generally, kin relationships are defined by either blood (consanguine) ties or marriage (affinal) ties. Blood relationships are bound together by genetic lines, but relationships based on marriage are bound together by law and a code of conduct that accompanies them. In-law relationships are unique in that they are defined through a third party by both a marriage and a blood relationship. Some anthropologists have argued that in-law relationships are important to societies, both past and present, because they represent an alliance between two groups of blood relations (Wolfram 1987). In these cultures, in-law relationships are clearly defined and circumscribed by explicit institutional arrangements and prescribed and proscribed behaviors (Goetting 1990). In Western ideology, however, the husband-wife marital bond is the central family tie and supersedes claims of the extended family. Despite agreement about the rules of membership, the codes of conduct associated with in-law relationships remain nebulous. The actual interactions and sentiments assigned to these relationships are subject to individuals' definitions (Goetting 1990). The few patterns that do exist and have been observed are restricted to relationships between parents-in-law and children-in-law. Other in-law relationships, such as that between sisters- or brothers-in-law, appear to be solely based on friendship or idiosyncratic relations (Finch 1989).

Very little research has been conducted on affective relationships between parents and children-in-law, but there is ample evidence in the popular culture of negative attitudes toward mothers-in-law. These negative attitudes have also been documented in psychological studies wherein children report a perception of greater interpersonal distance and more negative attitudes toward mothers-in-law than mothers (Denmark and Ahmed 1989). The problematic nature of the relationship is also underscored in studies of early years of marriage that focus on adjustment of in-laws and the influence of in-laws on the marital relationship.

The bulk of research on in-law relationships has focused on assistance and support patterns. These patterns reflect the distinctive feature of in-law relations, which is that they are generally conducted through and, in a sense, for the sake of a third party (Finch 1989). Children-in-law primarily receive support from parents-in-law as indirect beneficiaries of parental aid to married children. Hence, the primary patterns of contact and support between children-in-law and their parents-in-law reflect customary patterns of parent-child relationships.

Studies demonstrate that over the life cycle, aid between parents and children tends to be unidirectional, from parents to children, and that parental aid is most concentrated in the early years of children's marriages and decreases over time (Goetting 1990). Although financial aid most often begins and is concentrated in early years of marriage, aid in the form of services reaches a peak during preschool years of grandchildren. Both gender and class differences have been observed in provision of parental aid (Adams 1964). The wife's parents tend to be a source of greater aid in

In Western cultures, in-law relationships are subject to voluntary definitions and individual interpretations. Studies of the early years of marriage have shown the problematic nature of these relationships. ELKE HESSER/CORBIS

terms of service, while sons' parents tend to provide financial aid. More frequent financial help is given to middle-class than to working-class children and children-in-law. Working-class parents, when they live close by, give what they can in terms of services.

The presence of grandchildren also appears to influence in-law relationships. The birth of the first child has been reported to transform the mother-in-law–daughter-in-law relationship into one involving significant support patterns. Lucy Fischer (1983) notes that daughters with preschool children needed and received more help from both mothers and mothers-in-law. Mothers-in-law were more likely to give things, whereas mothers were more likely to do things. Daughters-in-law tended to seek help and advice more frequently from their mothers than from their mothers-in-law and were more likely to express ambivalence about help from their mothers-in-law.

Just as there is little evidence of direct support from parents-in-law to their children-in-law, so research is consistent in demonstrating that children-in-law make a minimal direct contribution to the care of their elderly parents-in-law. The flow of support for in-laws from the child generation to the parent generation is indirect and reflects patterns of gender differences associated with parental care. Parents are more likely to turn to daughters and, thereby, sons-in-law for help than to sons and daughters-in-law. However, help to the elderly, which does not usually entail financial support, is more restricted to services and help with household tasks and personal care (Powers and Kivett 1992; Schorr 1980). This type of support is primarily performed by daughters, not sons or sons-in-law.

Although daughters are the preferred caregivers for elderly parents, geographic proximity also influences parental care. When daughters are not available or geographically close, parents turn to sons and daughters-in-law for help when there is illness (Powers and Kivett 1992). In these situations, daughters-in-law often provide more direct service than their husbands, reflecting women's role as kin keepers (Finch 1989). In the hierarchy of sources of support for the elderly, daughters-in-law take precedence over sons (Schorr 1980). Moreover, children-in-law are often more functional in the kin network than are consanguine kin who are more distantly related, such as grandchildren or siblings (Kivett 1985). There is some evidence, however, that caring for mothers-in-law is perceived as more stressful and requiring more tasks than caring for a mother (Steinmetz 1988).

Support for parents-in-law can also take place in the form of coresidence. Again, the stronger kinship tie of women appears to dictate a greater number of mothers living with daughters and sons-in-law than with sons and daughters-in-law. Social class also has been observed to be associated with different patterns of support. There is a greater flow of financial aid from middle-class children to parents and parents-in-law than is true of working-class families, but a greater flow of service and coresidence exists among the working class.

The requirement of a third party as a defining factor for an in-law relationship makes these relationships uniquely vulnerable to dissolution when the marriage of the third party is dissolved by divorce or death. Along with gender differences, the presence or absence of children from the dissolved marriage appears to influence the continuance of in-law-relationships. Once a marriage has produced offspring, in-laws become affinal relatives who are defined not only by the order of law but also by their recognition of a biological link to the child. Hence, when the legal basis of the relationship is dissolved, there remains a relationship based on a common biological link (Johnson 1989). It is this tie, combined with the tendency in Western culture for mothers rather than fathers to retain custody of the children after a divorce, that appears to influence in-law relationships after divorce. Overall, divorce decreases in-law contact and support to various degrees. The extent of these decreases differs by gender and the presence or absence of grandchildren. There is greater interaction and support given between divorced women and their former in-laws than is true for men (Goetting 1990; Johnson 1989). It has been suggested that this greater contact may be motivated by the desire of grandparents to maintain access to grandchildren. Maternal grandparents have less contact with ex-sons-in-law than do paternal grandparents with ex-daughters-in-law, and the extent of contact between the paternal grandparents and ex-daughters-in-law tends to diminish over time as grandchildren grow and their needs diminish (Johnson 1989).

In-law relationships are perhaps the kin relationships most subject to voluntary definitions and individual interpretations. Most often, "in-laws serve as a reservoir of supplemental resources to be tapped as social norms dictate and practicalities allow" (Goetting 1990, p. 86). It must be underscored, however, that research focused on in-law relationships has been limited, and the patterns reported here apply mainly to mainstream U.S. culture. Although researchers have observed and reported variation by social class, they have virtually ignored other demographic factors, such as ethnicity and regional residence.

See also: CHILD CUSTODY; DIVORCE: EFFECTS ON PARENTS; FILIAL RESPONSIBILITY; GRANDPARENTHOOD; INTERGENERATIONAL RELATIONS; KINSHIP; WIDOWHOOD

Bibliography

Adams, B. N. (1964). "Structural Factors Affecting Parental Aid to Married Children." *Journal of Marriage and the Family* 26:327–331.

Anderson, T. B. (1984). "Widowhood as a Life Transition: Its Impact on Kinship Ties." *Journal of Marriage and the Family* 46:105–114.

Brody, E. M., and Schoonover, C. B. (1988). "Patterns of Parent-Care when Adult Daughters Work and When They Do Not." *Gerontologist* 5:372–381.

Denmark, F. L., and Ahmed, R. A. (1989). "Attitudes Toward Mother-in-Law and Stepmother: A Cross-Cultural Study." *Psychological Reports* 65:1194.

Finch, J. (1989). *Family Obligations and Social Change.* Cambridge, UK: Polity Press.

Fischer, L. R. (1983). "Mothers and Mothers-in-Law." *Journal of Marriage and the Family* 45:263–290.

Goetting, A. (1990). "Patterns of Support Among In-Laws in the United States: A Review of Research." *Journal of Family Issues* 11:67–90.

Johnson, C. L. (1989). "In-Law Relationships in the American Kinship System: The Impact of Divorce and Remarriage." *American Ethnologist* 16:87–99.

Kivett, V. R. (1985). "Consanguinity and Kin Level: Their Relative Importance to the Helping Network of Older Adults." *Journal of Gerontology* 40:228–234.

Lopata, H. Z. (1970). "The Social Involvement of Widows." *American Behavioral Scientist* 14:4–57.

Powers, E. A., and Kivett, V. R. (1992). "Kin Expectations and Kin Support Among Rural Older Adults." *Rural Sociology* 57:194–215.

Schneider, D. (1968). *American Kinship: A Cultural Account.* Englewood Cliffs, NJ: Prentice Hall.

Schorr, A. L. (1980). *Thy Father and Thy Mother: A Second Look at Filial Responsibility and Family.* Washington, DC: U.S. Government Printing Office.

Serovich, J. and Price, S. (1994). "In-Law Relationships: A Role Theory Perspective." *International Journal of Sociology of the Family* 24:127–146.

Spicer, J., and Hempe, C. (1975). "Kinship Interaction After Divorce." *Journal of Marriage and the Family* 37:113–119.

Steinmetz, S. K. (1988). *Duty Bound: Elder Abuse and Family Care.* Newbury Park, CA: Sage Publications.

Townsend, A. L., and Poulshock, S. W. (1986). "International Perspectives on Impaired Elders' Support Networks." *Journal of Gerontology* 41:101–109.

Wolfram, S. (1987). *In-Laws and Out-Laws: Kinship and Marriage in England.* London: Croom Helm.

RHONDA J. V. MONTOGOMERY (1995)
BIBLIOGRAPHY REVISED BY JAMES J. PONZETTI, JR.

INTENTIONAL COMMUNITIES

Intentional communities, utopian communities, communes, alternative communities, collectives, cooperatives, experimental communities, communal societies, and communitarian utopias are some of the more popular terms used to describe what many consider to be nonconventional living arrangements. The definitions of these terms vary from study to study but, for the most part, the term *intentional community* is broad enough to encompass all of those listed above. These terms are often used interchangeably.

According to Geoph Kozeny, "An 'intentional community' is a group of people who have chosen to live together with a common purpose, working cooperatively to create a lifestyle that reflects their shared core values. The people may live together on a piece of rural land, in a suburban home, or in an urban neighborhood, and they may share a single residence or live in a cluster of dwellings" (1995, p. 18). Lyman Tower Sargent defines an intentional community as a "group of five or more adults and their children, if any, who come from more than one nuclear family and who have chosen to live together to enhance their shared values or for some other mutually agreed upon purpose" (1994, p. 15). Timothy Miller identified the following seven criteria as necessary ingredients to be considered an intentional community: "(1) A sense of common purpose and of separation from the dominant society; (2) some form and level of self-denial, of voluntary suppression of individual choice for the good of the group; (3) geographic proximity; (4) personal interaction; (5) economic sharing; (6) real existence; and (7) critical mass" (1998, p. xx).

Contemporary intentional communities come in many different varieties including communes, ecovillages, urban housing cooperatives, residential land trusts, student co-ops, co-housing developments, monasteries, kibbutzim, and spiritual communities. The nature of intentional communities varies depending on the criteria selected to define the community and the group's mission. Housing cooperatives, ecovillages, and co-housing developments are the most popular types of intentional communities listed in *Communities Directory: A Guide to Intentional Communities and Cooperative Living* (Fellowship for Intentional Community 2000).

Intentional communities are not new phenomena nor are they transitory or ephemeral. Those who seek to live in community mirror, in many ways, the essence of early utopian thought which stated that human beings had the potential for goodness and that they could attain that goodness if they lived in the proper kind of society. Philosophers and writers throughout the centuries have shared their thoughts on how these societies should be constructed. In his book *Utopia,* Thomas More ([1516] 1965), a sixteenth-century British humanist, attacked the economic and social conditions as well as the other evils affecting the society of his time. He was particularly critical of the ruling elite in the government and the church officials who were abusing their powers at the expense of the commoners. More designed an imaginary society based on a shared life and called this society Utopia. His book, which is a critique of the Elizabethan social order and status quo, has become one of the most read and cited works in literature. More's *Utopia* inspired hundreds of other thinkers throughout the centuries to share their visions of an ideal society.

Benjamin Zablocki (1980) identifies three varieties of utopias: exhorted, imposed, and communitarian. *Exhorted utopias,* such as those discussed in More's *Utopia* and B. F. Skinner's *Walden Two,* are fictional places. These utopias have been created with no practical plans for implementation. *Imposed utopias* are actual attempts sovereign powers have made to provide citizens with a better-functioning communal structure. Examples of imposed utopias include Calvin's City of Geneva, the Jesuit order in seventh-century Paraguay, and the New Town movement in England and the United States. The Chinese communes are probably the most ambitious of these utopias. In 1949, after the defeat of Chiang Kaishek and the ascendancy of Mao Tse-tung, 80 percent of the Chinese were peasants. Mao organized 500 million peasants into 24,000 communes. His goal was to create a socialist utopia through collective agricultural communes. In 1977, Deng Xiaoping came to power in China and revealed that Mao's experiment with communes had failed (McCord 1989). *Communitarian utopias* are those that develop from the combined interests and intentions of their participants. The majority of utopian experiments have been communitarian utopias.

Rosabeth Moss Kanter (1972) believes the origins of American utopias and intentional communities, in particular, can be traced to one of three major themes: a rejection of the established order and a desire to follow religious and spiritual values; a willingness to reform society from corruption, injustice, inhumanity, and evil, especially within the realms of economics and politics; and a rejection of the alienation and isolation of society by promoting the psychosocial growth of the individual within community. These three themes compare favorably with the three historical waves of development and growth among communitarian utopias. The first wave of communitarianism began in the early years of the United States and lasted until approximately 1845. Religious themes were popular during this time. The second wave began in 1820, peaked in the 1840s, and continued until 1930. It emphasized economic and political issues. The third wave, or the psychosocial period, emerged following World War II and peaked in the late 1960s.

Historic Commual Utopias

Donald E. Pitzer (1997) provides examples of historic communal utopias. The United Society of Believers in Christ's Second Appearing, more commonly known as the Shakers, began during the depression and millenarian upsurge following the American Revolutionary War. The Shakers built twenty-four communities, and scholars estimate that overall membership was about 17,000 persons. The Shakers were founded by Ann Lee, a charismatic woman who made celibacy a central tenet of Shakerism.

German Pietists groups found the United States very appealing, at first because of religious freedom. The Community of True Inspiration, or Amana, rejected Lutheranism and believed in biblical prophecy. The Community of True Inspiration was founded by Christian Metz, who settled near Iowa City, Iowa, and created seven villages. Communal living was eventually eliminated, and members separated economic functions from religious functions and formed a joint-stock company (a business whose capital is held in transferable shares of stock by its joint owners) in 1932.

John Humphrey Noyes founded the Oneida Community in Oneida, New York, and preached a theology of perfectionism. Noyes was a charismatic leader who introduced his community to mutual criticism, complex marriage, and male continence. Noyes's ideas and practices eventually forced him into hiding, and the community eventually disbanded into a joint-stock company similar to Amana. One of the Oneida Community's many successful business ventures was the manufacture of silverware.

Michael Barkun (1984) reports that the United States experienced four periods of communitarian utopianism (1842–1848, 1894–1900, the 1930s, and the 1960s), and he believes that history strongly suggests the presence of a utopian cycle in the United States. Barkun hypothesized that utopian development occurs in approximately fifty to fifty-five year waves that follow accelerations and decelerations of prices.

Brian J. L. Berry agrees with Barkun's assessment of utopian cycles but carries the argument one step further. His central hypothesis states that "utopian surges embedded within upwellings of millenarian excitation, have been triggered by the long-wave crises (economic fluctuations) that periodically have affected American economic development. A corollary is that the utopias that have been built have been critical reactions to the moving target of capitalism; as capitalism has been transformed, so have the utopian alternatives" (1992, p. xv).

Contemporary Intentional Communities

Even though William Kephart and William Zellner (1991, p. ix) believe the modern communal movement is dead or dormant, conservative estimates by scholars indicate that there are 3,000 to 4,000 intentional communities in the United States. The Fellowship for Intentional Community (2000) has data which include the names and addresses of over 600 North American intentional communities and over 100 intentional communities on other continents. One such group is Twin Oaks of Louisa, Virginia, a community originally based, in part, on the principles of Skinner's *Walden Two*. Twin Oaks celebrates its thirty-fifth anniversary in the spring of 2002.

In addition to these communal groups there are over 425 Hutterite colonies in North America (75% are in Canada and 25% in the United States) with a combined population of over 40,000. There is also a colony in Japan, started by a group of Japanese who admired the Hutterite lifestyle. The Hutterites are the oldest communal group in North America. They trace their roots back to Europe and the Anabaptist movement of the 1500s. They arrived in the United States in the 1870s and settled in the Dakota Territory. They operate large farms, and their colonies are largely self-sufficient. Hutterites practice *Gelassenheit,* which means self-surrender (Kraybill and Bowman 2001).

The largest communal movement outside North America is the Israeli kibbutzim. Significant changes have occurred among some of the kib-butzim. Fewer of them have collective dining rooms and children now tend to reside with their parents. Collectivism and egalitarianism have waned under the pressure of modernism and indi-vidualism (Ben-Rafael 1997, p. 77). There are 270 kibbutzim in Israel, and together they have 125,000 members (Oved 1999, p. 67).

The *Communities Directory: A Guide to Inten-tional Communities and Cooperative Living* has listings for twenty-eight countries outside North America including locations in Europe, Asia, Africa, South America, Australia, and Mexico. England, Australia, and Germany have the largest number of intentional communities. Communal living is alive and well at the beginning of the twenty-first cen-tury. In a survey completed by 600 of the 728 com-munities listed in the directory, 255 were formed in the 1990s, 133 in the 1980s, 164 in the 1970s, 46 in the 1960s, and 48 before 1960 (Fellowship for In-tentional Community 2000).

Zablocki (1980) developed a useful classifica-tion system of intentional communities based on his study of 120 communes (60 urban and 60 rural, of which 37 were religious and 83 secular) from 1965–1978. The communal groups were placed in one of eight classifications (Eastern, Christian, psy-chological, rehabilitative, cooperative, alternative family, countercultural, and political) depending on their strategic philosophy (consciousness or direct action) and their locus of attention (spiritual world, individual self, primary group community, or secu-lar society). Zablocki found the most significant dif-ferences regarding membership and social struc-ture to be between the religious communes and the secular communes, not between consciousness-oriented groups and direct-action-oriented groups.

Much has been written on the success and fail-ure of contemporary intentional communities. Kanter (1972) developed a theory of commitment and concluded that those groups that were able to incorporate as many commitment-producing mechanisms (sacrifice—abstinence and austerity; investment—physical and financial; renunciation—of relationships outside the community; communion—shared characteristics; mortifica-tion—deindividuation; and transcendence—ideol-ogy) as possible were more likely to survive and be successful. She identified three types of commitment that bind people to organized groups:

continuance (sacrifice and investment), cohesion (renunciation and communion), and control (mor-tification and transcendence). Kanter wanted to un-cover the structural arrangements and organiza-tional strategies that promote and sustain commitment. She found that nineteenth-century groups used transcendence and communion mech-anisms the most, followed by sacrifice, renuncia-tion, investment, and mortification. William L. Smith (1986) investigated contemporary urban religious communities and found that communion, mortifi-cation, and transcendence mechanisms were used at moderate or high rates, while sacrifice, invest-ment, and renunciation were not widely used.

In a study of communalists from the 1960s and 1970s, Angela A. Aidala and Benjamin Zablocki (1991) found that communalists came from a vari-ety of social class backgrounds. Approximately one-quarter of them were from working-class or lower-middle class origins, while the remaining members were predominantly from the upper-middle and middle-middle classes.

Family and Intentional Communities

Yaacov Oved (1993) states that communal scholars generally agree that family life and community life are usually incompatible with one another. The major assumption is that family ties tend to be a source of conflict in communal groups. Barry Shenker (1986) argues that familial relationships can enhance one's satisfaction and commitment to communal life. Smith (1999) writes that families are an essential component of communal life unless a reliable substitute is found to replace them and their functions. Most communal groups, historical and contemporary, have not abolished the family. Only a minority of groups have adopted celibacy, monasticism, or some type of complex marriage such as pantagamy (every husband is married to every wife) as exhibited by the Oneida commu-nity. The Shakers abolished the nuclear family but they substituted for it by creating multiple commu-nal families at each of their villages. Historic groups such as Amana incorporated nuclear fami-lies into the community and contemporary groups like the Hutterites and Jesus People USA do like-wise. Some intentional communities are better suited for marriage and family life than others.

Aidala and Zablocki (1991) found that few communalists saw themselves involved in building new family forms, and they did not reject the nuclear family in favor of communal alternatives. The reason most often given by communal members for joining communes is to live with people who have similar values and goals. Smith (2001) studied a group of intentional communities who were listed in the 1995 edition of the *Communities Directory*. These groups stated their primary purpose or focus was family-related. He found that while the stated purpose of the community was family-related only a small minority of communalists ranked family as the most important communal goal or purpose. The majority of communalists ranked consensual community (living with those who share similar values and beliefs) as their top priority.

See also: ANABAPTISTS (AMISH, MENNONITE); FAMILY, DEFINITION OF; HUTTERITE FAMILIES; ISRAEL; MARRIAGE, DEFINITION OF

Bibliography

Aidala, A. A., and Zablocki, B. D. (1991). "The Communes of the 1970s: Who Joined and Why?" *Marriage and Family Review* 17:87–116.

Barkun, M. (1984). "Communal Societies as Cyclical Phenomena." *Communal Societies* 4:35–48.

Ben-Rafael, E. (1997). "Crisis and Transformation: The Kibbutz at the Turn of the Century." *Communal Societies* 17:75–102.

Berry, B. J. L. (1992). *America's Utopian Experiments: Communal Havens from Long-Wave Crises.* Hanover, NH: University Press of New England.

Fellowship for Intentional Community. (2000). *Communities Directory: A Guide to Intentional Communities and Cooperative Living.* Rutledge, MO: Fellowship for Intentional Community.

Kanter, R. M. (1972). *Commitment and Community: Communes and Utopias in Sociological Perspective.* Cambridge, MA: Harvard University Press.

Kephart, W., and Zellner, W. (1991). *Extraordinary Groups.* New York: St. Martin's Press.

Kozeny, G. (1995). "Intentional Communities: Lifestyles Based on Ideals." In *Communities Directory: A Guide to Cooperative Living.* Langley, WA: Fellowship for Intentional Community.

Kraybill, D. B., and Bowman, C. F. (2001). *On the Backroad to Heaven: Old Order Hutterites, Mennonites, Amish, and Brethren.* Baltimore, MD: John Hopkins University Press.

McCord, W. (1989). *Voyages to Utopia: From Monastery to Commune, the Search for the Perfect Society.* New York: Norton.

Miller, T. (1998). *The Quest for Utopia in Twentieth-Century America.* Syracuse, NY: Syracuse University Press.

More, T. ([1516] 1965). *Utopia,* trans. P. Marshall. New York: Washington Square Press.

Oved, Y. (1993). *Two Hundred Years of American Communes.* New Brunswick, NJ: Transaction Publishers.

Oved, Y. (1999). "Communes in the Twentieth Century." *Communal Societies* 19:67–72.

Pitzer, D. (1997). *America's Communal Utopias.* Chapel Hill, NC: University of North Carolina Press.

Sargent, L. T. (1994). "The Three Faces of Utopianism Revisited." *Utopian Studies* 5:1–37.

Shenker, B. (1986). *Intentional Communities: Ideology and Alienation in Communal Societies.* London: Routledge & Kegan Paul.

Skinner, B. F. (1976). *Walden Two.* New York: Macmillan.

Smith, W. L. (1986). "The Use of Structural Arrangements and Organizational Strategies by Urban Communes." *Communal Societies* 6:118–137.

Smith, W. L. (1999). *Families and Communes: An Examination of Nontraditional Lifestyles.* Thousand Oaks, CA: Sage Publications.

Smith, W. L. (2001). "Families in Contemporary Intentional Communities: Diversity and Purpose." *Communal Societies* 21:79–93.

Zablocki, B. (1980). *Alienation and Charisma: A Study of Contemporary American Communes.* New York: Free Press.

WILLIAM L. SMITH

INTERFAITH MARRIAGE

Religious intermarriage as it reflects interaction in an open society is a gauge of changing social structures and norms. The extent to which interfaith marriage is possible and the degree of social and religious institutions' acceptance of interfaith couples indicate the breadth and depth of such changes.

Prevalence

Generally, members of religious minorities are increasingly likely to marry out of their religious traditions as the unavailability of same-faith prospective partners combines with sociopsychological pressures toward becoming part of the majority. For example, a *US Catholic Study of Catholics in the United States* (Official Catholic Directory 1997) found that although only 18 percent of Roman Catholics married non-Catholics in dioceses with greater than 50 percent Catholic populations, the rate of intermarriage by Catholics rose to 51 percent in dioceses with less than 10 percent Catholic populations. This phenomenon might also reflect the possibility that those who live in areas with low numbers of individuals who share their religious faith already identify less strongly with their religious faith and so more likely to intermarry.

In the early 1970s, about 7 percent of married American Jews had unconverted non-Jewish spouses; by 1990 this figure had risen to 28 percent, while the figure for all marriages involving American Jews between 1985 and 1990 was as high as 52 percent. This exponential growth rate has been attributed to several factors, such as: the disappearance of social and economic barriers against Jews, the later age of marriage (in which presumably couples are less influenced by childhood training and parental guidance), the geographic shift from areas of high Jewish concentration, the increased presence of women in the labor force with accompanying opportunities for outgroup contact, and the increased incidence of divorce and remarriage (Jewish Outreach Institute 2001). However, the 52 percent figure should be dissected to make it clear that Jews who marry out tend to be older than those who marry in. For many of these older couples, the interfaith marriage is a second or later marriage, in which children are not expected or where there are preexisting children whose religious identities have already begun to be formed. As of 2001 about 40 percent of children of American Jews married to non-Jews were being raised with no clear religious identity, that is, not as formal members of a religious institution. Interfaith marriages are of particular concern to Jewish communities because of the great losses incurred through the *Shoah* (Holocaust) and other persecution, and, ironically, because of attrition resulting from greater freedom and toleration in pluralistic societies.

India has a state policy of freedom of worship, not favoring any particular denomination. However, by 2000, tensions between Hindus and both Muslims and Christians had risen to a point of creating some alarm in proponents of maintaining the secular state (U. S. Department of State 2000). Within the context of official religious pluralism, furthermore, are practical obstacles to the interfaith couple. In India, Muslim law controls Muslim marriage, and provisions for divorce and polyandry/polygamy are applied with vastly different consequences for men and for women in Muslim marriages.

There is a similar gender-based inequity in Indian laws regarding divorce among Christians. In 1994 in Bombay, 10 percent of weddings conducted in Catholic churches involved a non-Catholic partner (Association of Interchurch Families 2000). The Indian Christian Marriage Act, 1872, made no mention of intermarriage. However, the Indian Divorce (Amendment) Act passed in 2001, mandates that no marriage between a Christian and a non-Christian may be conducted in a church (U. S. Department of State 2001).

In 1999, there were more than 150,000 intercultural couples in Malaysia (Melwani 1999). These are not strictly interfaith, since by Malaysian law, a non-Muslim spouse must convert to Islam. However, the Malaysian Hindu community sees this phenomenon as a direct loss. The Malaysian intermarriage situation is further complicated by the government's fear that intermarriage will lead to an influx of foreign workers demanding citizenship by right of marriage. Therefore, the government in 1997 enacted a ruling restricting such marriages by limiting opportunity and benefits available to interfaith couples, for example, by denying the foreign spouse an extended stay, a permanent residence visa, or citizenship (Ragataf 2000).

The population of Israel in 1996 comprised 4.6 million Jews, 840,000 Muslims, 180,000 Christians, and 100,000 Druze (plus 80,000 people who fell into the "Other" category) (Israeli Central Bureau of Statistics 1996). Interreligious marriage of all sorts is illegal in Israel, partly because of the disproportionate political power wielded by the Jewish Orthodox minority and partly because of the historic spheres of influence of the other religious faiths, which tend to cling to their own separatist and exclusivist policies. However, Israeli law recognizes marriages contracted in other countries. Because Israeli couples wishing to intermarry often do so abroad, and because a number of interfaith couples who married elsewhere have immigrated to Israel (for example, from the former Soviet Union), intermarried couples are by no means unknown there.

The political friction between Palestinians and Israelis, and between Muslims and Jews within Israel, makes marriages particularly problematic; however, they do exist. As for Christian/Jewish marriage in Israel, it has reached sufficient proportions that at least one networking group for such couples was operating in 2002 (Rosenbaum 2002).

Special Considerations: Challenges and Benefits

Interfaith marriages are subject to challenges, both internal and external. The primary internal challenge may derive from differing notions of the nature of marriage itself. Some examples follow.

Buddhist. Marriage is a social, rather than a religious undertaking. Maintaining the proper relations and duties between the partners will aid them in following the Eightfold Path to enlightenment (the set of beliefs and actions that govern the Buddhist belief system). However, the nature of those relations and duties will vary with the culture.

Hindu. Marriage is a sacrament binding man and woman to a lifelong commitment. It is seen as both fulfilling a sacred obligation to one's ancestors and as a means of spiritual growth. In some ways, this can lead to greater difficulty gaining the acceptance of the extended family and the broader society, particularly in India. In other ways, some Hindu religious leaders consider that intermarriage does not necessarily compromise the religious identity of the Hindu partner.

Islamic. Strictures against intermarriage may be mitigated by the opinion that Muslims are enjoined only against marrying unbelievers, that is, polytheists. In this view, Christians and Jews are acceptable partners for Muslims, with the provision that any children will be raised in Islam.

Jewish. Marriage is understood as the ideal human state, established by God, for the purposes of companionship and procreation. The primary context is that of human society, rather than of a heavenly or sacramental ground; still, marriage is held to configure the relationship of God to Israel, and as such bears both a divine and a socioethnic component. In this context, some rabbis feel that a Jewish intermarriage is a contradiction in terms. (Studies indicate a softening in general in American rabbinic attitudes, however [Jewish Outreach Institute 2000]).

Orthodox Christian. Marriage is not a human construction and does not depend on human social institutions for its character and essential nature. The sacramental essence of marriage makes a union of two people into a *monad,* simultaneously two and one, united in God. This formulation restricts Orthodox marriage by definition to that between two baptized Christians.

Protestant Christian. Marriage is not a sacrament, but Christians are called to marriage as a positive good in God's gift. As a result, most Protestant denominations will allow interfaith marriage.

Roman Catholic Christian. Marriage between two baptized partners constitutes a sacramental ongoing mutual bond as a sign of the bond between Christ and the church. Ecumenical or interchurch marriage has become increasingly acceptable since the Second Vatican Council (1962–1965) Interfaith marriage in which there is what Canon Law terms *disparity of cult* may be undertaken with episcopal permission, subject to varying restrictions.

External pressures on interfaith couples vary according to the level in which tolerance and pluralism are considered positive values by the larger society. The incidence of intermarriage among Hindus ranges from very rare in rural India to increasingly acceptable in the United States and other countries, such as Malaysia, in which Hindus are in the minority. However, Hindus who marry out, particularly those whose partners are members of Western religions or cultures, may find greater difficulty in adjustment. Differing attitudes toward polygamy, the role of women, and extended family are among those most likely to create friction. When it is the woman who is the Hindu, however, traditional ideas of gender-related submission and cooperation may result in less overt stress than in marriages involving a Hindu man and a Christian or Jewish woman. Theologically, polytheistic (belief in multiple gods) elements of Hinduism may cause the greatest conflict in marriages to Christians, Jews, or Muslims. This potential can be ameliorated by the Hindu partner's focusing on the underlying concept of Brahman as Universal Being. Similarly, Hinduism's traditional multiplicity of approaches to the divine can result in greater tolerance for a non-Hindu spouse's faith, and in less feeling of confusion or alienation for children, than intermarriages between partners who each believe in a single divinity but identify this being differently.

Another external factor in the relative difficulty faced by partners in an interfaith marriage is the socioeconomic position of each of the groups represented by the partners. The change in U.S. Jewish marriage patterns can partially be attributed to Jewish upward mobility in economic and educational status, and to the concomitant tendency for the Jewish population, particularly those born in the United States, to disperse out of primarily Jewish urban settings into more heterogeneous situations. These phenomena, coupled with reduced anti-Semitism and the population pressures known as the Baby Boom that took place after World War II, have led to increased tolerance for intermarriage both inside and outside the Jewish community.

Central difficulties experienced by interfaith couples, aside from the initial ones involved in planning and implementing the wedding ceremony itself, rotate around issues involving children: welcoming and other life-passage rituals, family holiday observances, and dealing with extended family. As the interfaith family resolves these issues, however, focus shifts onto the spiritual and religious lives of the marital partners. It is at this point that the fruits of interreligious understanding may begin to be felt (Rosenbaum 1998, 2000).

Cultural and ethnic patterns also play a primary role in forming the interfaith marriage. Catholic emphasis on family bonds meshes with that of traditional Jewish culture. Catholics and Jews, further, tend to have strong attachments to ritual and tradition in framing religious identities. In addition, the importance Catholics and Jews typically place on strength of religious identity may make them more tolerant of a spouse's maintaining connection to a family of origin's faith than a Protestant or a nonreligious person might be. These suppositions are at least partially borne out by a 1999 study indicating that individuals born into Protestant households who then marry Jews are twice as likely to convert to Judaism as are those born into Catholic households (Rebhun 1999). At the same time, the same study found that Jews married to Catholics were less likely to have strong institutional ties or affiliations to Jewish institutions than were those married to Protestants. This seeming anomaly may be explained by the actual or perceived level of greater exclusion from the Jewish group of those intermarrieds whose spouses maintain active ties to their parents' faiths (more likely to be Catholics).

Interchurch Marriage

In Ireland, ongoing political strife is demarcated along religious denominational lines, though the underlying issues are not religious in nature. Indeed, with the disappearance of linguistic and other distinctive cultural markers over the past three centuries, members of Unionist and Nationalist factions can be differentiated only by religious allegiance. This can make intermarriage between Catholic and Protestant literally a life-and-death matter.

The tension is exacerbated by the fact that the proportion of Protestants in the Republic of Ireland had fallen by some 40 percent between 1911 and 1981, partly because of emigration, partly because of the lower Protestant birth rate. But the major cause of the decline in Protestant population has been interchurch marriages (25 percent of all marriages of Protestants), coupled with the Irish Catholic Church's demand that children of these marriages be raised Catholic.

In Northern Ireland, the proportion of 57-to-43 Protestant-to-Catholic population remained fairly constant between 1981 and 1991, primarily because of the tremendous societal pressure to in-marry, and because the population of each group is large enough to provide an ample pool of prospective partners from within the group. There is also anecdotal evidence that, in Northern Ireland, even when mixed partners promise to raise children as Catholics, perhaps as many as half in fact raise them Protestant (Association of Interchurch Families 2000).

The former Yugoslavia is another area where ethnic animosities contribute to extreme difficulties for interchurch couples. Interchurch families in this region are subject to extraordinary political and social pressures, particularly people with Catholic/Serbian Orthodox partners (Association of Interchurch Families 2000).

Positive Prospects

Jewish institutions have tended to focus on the question of membership for interfaith families. Rela Mintz Geffen and Egon Mayer (1998) recommend, rather, shifting the emphasis to the needs of the families involved in such a way as to develop meaningful outreach services for such families.

Although the Christian Orthodox Church has some of the most restrictive policies on intermarriage, the rate has risen steadily around the world.

The Orthodox response has been to focus on the opportunities offered by the possibility of pastoral flexibility expressed in guidelines known as *economia*.

The Presbyterian Church (U.S.A.) guidelines emphasize sensitivity to cultural differences and advise negotiating legal issues within the context of the non-Presbyterian community.

As intermarried populations grow worldwide, children, particularly, may feel less isolated; they will have specifically interfaith communities to identify with. In the United States, on the cutting edge of intermarriage trends, the end of the twentieth century and the beginning of the twenty-first has seen an exponential growth of nondenominational networking groups for interfaith couples and the beginnings of schools and curricula specifically designed for children of interfaith couples (Rosenbaum 2002).

Relatively high involvement and commitment of interchurch couples can be viewed as an opportunity for ecumenical understanding rather than a threat to traditional values (Association of Interchurch Families 2000). They may even provide a foundation for future reconciliation among Christian denominations. This opportunity may be extrapolated to other sorts of intermarriage to improve pluralistic tolerance. In North America particularly, the growth of the non-Christian population coupled with an emphasis on individual rather than communal identity may promote interfaith understanding, with intermarriage as at least one vehicle of communication.

See also: BUDDHISM; CATHOLICISM; EVANGELICAL CHRISTIANITY; HINDUISM; ISLAM; JUDAISM; PROTESTANTISM; RELIGION

Bibliography

Crohn, J. (2000). *Mixed Matches: How to Create Successful Interracial, Interethnic, and Interfaith Relationships.* 2d edition. New York: Fawcett Columbine.

Geffen, R. M., and Mayer, E. (1998). "The Ripple Effect: Interfaith Families Speak Out." New York: B'nai B'rith Center for Jewish Identity and the Jewish Outreach Institute.

Hawxhurst, Joan C. (1998). *The Interfaith Family Guidebook: Practical Advice for Jewish and Christian Partners.* Kalamazoo, MI: Dovetail Publishing.

Interfaith Marriage. (1992). Louisville, KY: Office of Ecumenical and Interfaith Relations, Presbyterian Church U.S.A.

Israeli Central Bureau of Statistics (ICBS). (1996). "Israel by Religion." Tel Aviv, Israel: Government Publishing House.

Jewish Outreach Institute. (2000). "Survey of the American Rabbinate." New York: Author.

Jewish Outreach Institute. (2001). "Interest in and Awareness of Outreach." New York: Author.

Joanides, C. (2000). "Orthodox Perspective on Marriage." Originally presented at the 1998 Clergy & Laity Conference, Orlando, FL. Syosett, NY: Greek Orthodox Archdiocese of America.

Lazerwitz, D. (1980). "Current Jewish Intermarriages in the United States." In *Papers in Jewish Demography,* ed. U. O. Schmelz. Proceedings of the Demographic Sessions held at the 7th World Congress of Jewish Studies, Jerusalem, August 1977. Jerusalem: Institute of Contemporary Jewry, Hebrew University of Jerusalem.

Lee, R. M. (1994). *Mixed and Matched: Interreligious Courtship and Marriage in Northern Ireland.* Lanham, MD: University Press of America.

Mayer, E. (1983). *Children of Intermarriage: A Study in Patterns of Identification and Family Life.* New York: American Jewish Committee, Institute of Human Relations.

Mayer, E. (1985). *Love and Tradition: Marriage Between Jews and Christians.* New York: Plenum Press.

National Jewish Population Study (NJPS) (1990). New York: Council of Jewish Federations.

Official Catholic Directory. *Anno Domini 2001.* New York: P. J. Kennedy & Sons.

Oriental Orthodox-Roman Catholic Interchurch Marriages: and Other Pastoral Relationships. (1995). Washington, DC: United States Catholic Conference.

Phillips, B. A. (1997). *Re-examining Intermarriage: Trends, Textures, and Strategies: Report of a New Study.* Los Angeles: Susan and David Wilstein Institute of Jewish Policy Studies : American Jewish Committee, William Petschek National Jewish Family Center.

Rebhun, U. (1999). "Jewish Identification in Intermarriage: Does a Spouse's Religion (Catholic vs. Protestant) Matter?" *Sociology of Religion: A Quarterly Review* 60(1):71–88.

Romain, J. (1998). *Till Faith Us Do Part: Couples Who Fall in Love across the Religious Divide.* London: Fount.

Rosenbaum, M. H., ed. (1992–2002). *Dovetail: A Journal by and for Jewish-Christian Families*. Boston, KY: Dovetail Institute for Interfaith Family Resources (DI-IFR).

Rosenbaum, M. H., and Rosenbaum, S. N. (1999). *Celebrating Our Differences: Living Two Faiths in One Marriage,* 2nd edition. Shippensburg, PA: Ragged Edge Press.

Schneider, S. W. (1989). *Intermarriage: The Challenge of Living with Differences between Christians and Jews.* New York: Free Press.

U.S. Department of State (USDOS). (2000). *2000 Annual Report on International Religious Freedom: India.* Bureau of Democracy, Human Rights, and Labor, September 5.

Other Resources

Association of Interchurch Families (AIF). (2000). *Interchurch Families,* Spring 2000. Available from http://www.aifw.org/aif.htm.

Fitzgerald, G. (1991). "From an Irish Perspective." London: Association of Interchurch Families. Available from http://www.aifw.org/aif.htm.

Melwani, L. (1999). "Mixed Marriages Part III: Two Religions, One Marriage—The Gamble, the Costs." *Hinduism Today.* Available from http://www.vivaaha.org/mixed.htm.

Ragataf, I. (2000). "Malaysia Curbs Intermarriage, Tightens Migration Policies." *Politics, Society Geo-Scope.* Available from http://www.islam-online.net/.

MARY HELÉNE ROSENBAUM

INTERGENERATIONAL PROGRAMMING

Intergenerational programs refer to social service programs that provide opportunities for different generations to come together to share experiences, knowledge, and skills that are mutually beneficial and foster positive long-term relationships. These experiences typically involve interactions between the generations at the opposite end of the human life span—the young and the old. Integral to all these programs are interactions that meet the needs of both populations by fostering growth, understanding, and friendship between the generations (Adapted from National Council on Aging 1981).

The notion that a special synergy exists between the young and the old and that caring for each other is natural, appropriate, and timely is fundamental to intergenerational work and has been integrated into social service programs that address a diverse range of issues affecting today's families and communities (Newman et al. 1997). Intergenerational programs involve planned, ongoing interactions that extend over periods of time between nonbiologically linked children, youth, and older adults and engage the generations in activities that benefit both the young and the old. The young participants may be mainstream, at risk, special needs, or the gifted, ranging from infants through college age. Participating older persons include high functioning independent older adults, as well as older persons who are dependent, lower functioning, frail, or at risk.

Rationale—Why Now?

Intergenerational programs have been evident in the United States since the late 1970s in response to emerging social issues and problems that have affected the quality of relationships between children, youth, older adults, and their families as well as the quality of life within our communities. These issues and problems are a function of some social, demographic, and economic conditions in the United States that have impacted society as a whole, but particularly the two most vulnerable populations—the young and the old. Examples of these conditions include:

- An increase in the number of two working parent or single parent families that are over 70 percent of families with young children (Morrison 1995);

- Nearly 500,000 teenage girls becoming parents each year—roughly 40 percent are below eighteen years of age, three-quarters of whom are unmarried and a majority are poor (U.S. Department of Health and Human Services 2000);

- An increase in the older adult population, (persons over sixty years of age), which is approximately 15 percent of the total population in the United States, with the most rapidly growing population over eighty-five years of age (Williams 1995); and

- The geographic separation of nuclear families and their grandparents, a condition experienced by between 30 and 40 percent of U.S. families, all of whom live more than 200 miles from their extended family members (Newman 1997).

Researchers and practitioners in child development, education, mental health and gerontology have suggested that there is a relationship between these social conditions and specific problems that are confronting our young and old (Newman et al. 1997). These problems include:

- Isolation, low self-esteem, infrequent and inconsistent familial contact, and feelings of abandonment for older adults;

- Poor school attendance, school drop out, lack of motivation, antisocial behaviors, and disconnection from the family for children and youth; and

- Inadequate care giving, limited support systems, substance abuse, and poverty for both populations.

Intergenerational programs have been developed to bring together a community's young and old and to empower them by combining their assets, skills, interests, and backgrounds to address some of the societal issues that significantly affect their lives.

Program Models

Intergenerational programs, as a response to social conditions and problems, have been developing in the United States since the 1970s. From their grass roots beginnings and local origins, these programs have expanded into diverse program models that are available across the United States. They are evident in small and large educational and social service systems such as K-12 schools, libraries, child and adult day care, mental health systems, multipurpose community centers, long-term care and residential communities, and institutions of higher education. There are four basic types of program models. These models have a specific structure that enables them to be replicated in a variety of settings and to have similar and measurable successful outcomes. This structure includes several components:

- Partnerships between systems serving children and youth and systems serving older adults;

- A formalized set of goals and objectives;

- Planned program implementation procedures that include orientation and training of the professional staff and participants, and defined intergenerational activities;

- Staff and administrative commitment;

- Support from diverse groups in the community; and

- An ongoing evaluation plan.

The most common intergenerational program model involves older adults providing service to children, youth, and families in the community. Represented in this model are programs in which older adults are:

- Rockers for HIV positive infants in hospital settings (border babies);

- Caregivers for preschool age children in childcare (infants through kindergarten);

- Mentors, tutors, special subject coaches, and resource persons for K-12 students in school or after school programs;

- Special friends to families whose children have disabilities;

- Counselors to pregnant teens or other at-risk youth;

- Cultural support persons for immigrant families; and

- Advisors and mentors to students in higher education.

There are an estimated two million older adults involved in intergenerational programs in which older adults serve children, youth, and families.

The second most frequently reported intergenerational program model involves children and youth serving older adults. Programs representative of this model include:

- Small groups of young children, prekindergarten through grade three, engaging in activities such as arts and crafts, reading and music with frail elderly in long-term care or adult care settings;

TABLE 1

```
Intergenerational program models

• Older adults serve children, youth, and families

• Children/youth serve older adults

• Children/youth/older adults serve others

• Children/youth/older adults share sites
```

- Groups of school age children in grades four through nine visiting individual or groups of residents in long-term care or personal care environments to talk, or participate in activities such as board games, exercises, music and crafts; and

- Youth from grades ten through twelve, as well as college students, visiting individually with older adults in their own homes or apartments or in their personal care or long-term care environments. During these visits the old and young may talk, write letters, share hobbies or a meal, take walks, shop together, or go on an outing (i.e., to the museum or library).

These visits frequently occur over a period of several years with relationships continuing after students graduate from high school or college. Several hundred thousand children and youth are involved in serving the elderly in their communities.

The third intergenerational model demonstrates partnership activities between a community's children and youth and older adults. Typically, these programs involve groups of youth and older adults who plan and execute activities that benefit the community. Teams of youth and older adults engage in environmental or gardening projects, community fundraising initiatives, collaborative musical or theatrical performances, or discussion groups. The participants in these projects may be members of youth and elder clubs, school classes joining older adult agencies, or young and old individuals from the community who come together to plan a service activity.

The fourth intergenerational model consists of interactions between older adults, children, and youth who share a physical environment and who engage in informal and formal planned or spontaneous interactions. Examples of this model, referred to as *shared sites,* may be adult and child

care in a shared space, long-term care and child care in the same building, a senior center housed at a school, or a multigenerational community center in which interactive intergenerational activities such as computer training, folk dancing, and cooking ethnic foods lend themselves to cross-age scheduling at the site.

Though intergenerational program models differ in size, location and frequency of interactions, and number and ages of participants, they embrace several common characteristics. All intergenerational programs:

- Benefit the younger and older participants;

- Strive to meet specific intergenerational needs of the community;

- Require the commitment and collaboration of multiple agencies;

- Are designed to improve relationships between the community's young and old; and

- Enhance the quality of life in the community and among its families.

Intergenerational Interactions

An anticipated outcome of intergenerational programs is the creation of new and positive relationships. These relationships evolve over time and are a function of behaviors that occur during intergenerational interactions. The behaviors typically reported in intergenerational interactions are supportive and positive. They are referred to in the literature by a variety of researchers and include: helping, encouraging, agreeing, instructing, giving, showing affection, talking calmly, complimenting, reinforcing, smiling, hugging, being spontaneous, sharing tasks, and building group solidarity (Kuehne 1989; Newman, Morris, and Streetman 1999; Penninx 1996; Larkin and Newman 2001).

Many of these behaviors are fundamental to Erik Erikson's developmental theory that explains a process of interdependence and independence across the life span. In later life this process encourages the purposeful effort to leave a legacy of ideas, skills, and values for one's family, community, and society (Erikson, Erikson, and Kivnick 1986).

Included in the literature about the development, structure, outcomes, and implications of intergenerational programs are references to concepts that have a direct impact on family relationships. Valerie Kuehne (1989) discusses the basic social nature of an intergenerational culture in school classrooms as preparation for a meaningful description of the interactions taking place between group members of vastly different ages (and in different settings). "Groups of adults and children in intergenerational programs may be seen as small societies in which certain behaviors are evident that help to create solidarity and minimize conflict among group members" (Kuehne 1989).

Intergenerational groups involving older adults and youth of all ages may exhibit behaviors, interactions, or relationships that correspond to those found in other familiar social groups (e.g., families and educational institutions) (Hare, Borgatta, and Bales 1955; Kuehne 1989). It is therefore of interest to examine relationships between the behaviors reported in intergenerational programs and those evident in intergenerational familial settings.

Impact on Families

The behaviors that have been demonstrated over time in intergenerational programs have not systematically been examined in the context of family settings. However, there is increasing anecdotal information reported by caregivers, teachers, intergenerational program participants, and families that the behaviors described in intergenerational programs are being observed within the family. This section, therefore, will present some of the observed behaviors of participants within an intergenerational program setting and show how they translate into relationships within the family.

For the young child, prekindergarten through grade three, it has been observed that participation in intergenerational programs often results in an increase in the ability to stay on task, a decrease in anxiety, less crying, more smiling, and overall more relaxed, happy, and cooperative behaviors (Larkin and Newman 2001). Within the family, the young child seems more secure in relationships with older siblings and less fretful in new situations and with new people. The child seems more willing to wait and less prone to moments of "I want and I need now" behaviors. This is perhaps because the child feels more confident that his/her needs will be met.

For the school age child as a result of intergenerational experiences there is an increase in social and academic skills, added competence and self-confidence, and evidence of values that demonstrate caring for others. The impact on family relationships of these experiences for school age children, as reported by parents, includes an increase in cooperation and understanding, a decrease in sibling conflict, more sibling cooperation, and greater willingness to be helpful in household responsibilities. Often, a child with intergenerational experiences is viewed as more accepting and respectful of parents, grandparents, and older generations in the neighborhood.

For teenagers, the intergenerational experience can motivate a willingness to talk with parents about problems, a willingness to be part of the family, and an acceptance of differences in the family and in the community. Additionally, those teens with experience in intergenerational service activities (i.e., visiting with older adults) often develop a sense of social responsibility that converts into a social activism and involvement in community projects. Many youth develop leadership skills that enable them to help solve family problems and assist siblings with difficult personal or academic issues. The intergenerational service experience helps a youth recognize differences and inequities in society that can prompt an acceptance of family differences. Teenagers involved in providing intergenerational community service or in being the recipient of mentoring or tutoring by older adults speak about an increased willingness to communicate with parents and grandparents. These youth refer to increased compassion and understanding of the plight of older generations. "I never realized that Mr. G is a survivor of two wars, the Depression, and the loss of his wife and home. He is amazing and I have tremendous respect for him. I bet there are many other people like him in his generation," states a sixteen-year-old friendly visitor of a ninety-year-old man living at home.

For college youth the intergenerational experience as a mentor or as a service provider to frail or isolated older adults has created a career direction in aging. It often elicits memories of special childhood experiences with elder family members. Triggered by these memories, many youth reconnect with their families' older members and restore the bonds that may have been lost during adolescence.

For the single parent mother whose experience with an older adult may be as a family friend, as a caregiver for her child in childcare, or as a mentor or tutor in school classrooms, there are dramatic stories of a greater ability to cope with family stress, reduced personal anxiety, and more confidence in talking with friends and family rather than paid professionals. These mothers typically refer to the older adult caregiver as a friend who listens to their problems, loves their children, and from whom advice is accepted. Working mothers report increased energy and comfort in knowing that someone acknowledges their plight, encourages them and helps them address some of their social, financial, and family problems. Mothers often refer to the caring and experienced older adult as a friend who helps them enjoy their role as mother. "I now feel confident enough to talk with my son's teacher without feeling defensive and frightened. M., our family friend, has helped me see that my learning impaired child has lots to give," explains the mother of a learning-disabled seven-year-old son.

From the older adults who have been involved in intergenerational experiences as the receiver or provider of intergenerational services we learn of an increased ability to understand and accept the behaviors and motivations of young people in their own families and communities. There is a decrease in their stereotypes about youth and an increase in their awareness of problems confronting the young. Older adults often report on how being aware of the positive effect they have on young people often boosts their own self-esteem and improves their interaction with their own families, especially grandchildren. Many familial interactions for older adults have assumed new meaning as they share some of their intergenerational experiences and insights.

For frail older adults, typically in institutional settings, who are recipients of youth services, there are reduced feelings of isolation, an improvement in activities of daily living, (the ability to care for oneself), and a rebirth of interest in socializing and communicating with family members. The relationship with a visiting young person often ignites their interest in socialization and stimulates cognitive functioning that yields a higher level of communication with their family. "I think I understand my teenage granddaughter better now that K. has become my teenage friend. I am learning a lot about these kids and it is fun," claims an eighty-five-year-old resident in a long-term care residential setting who has a weekly teenage friendly visitor.

International Intergenerational Programming Efforts

The value of intergenerational programs as a forum for social change is being explored as a global phenomenon. In countries around the world there are local and national intergenerational programming initiatives that are being developed to study and address specific social issues. Global intergenerational programs concern education, literacy, housing, and unemployment of the young and old. They address issues of violence, poverty, the environment, and technology in their societies and, in particular, the impact on communities' elderly and younger members. A special focus of international intergenerational initiatives is the revitalization of communities. This focus, evident in countries as varied as the Netherlands, the United Kingdom, South Africa, and Uganda is frequently related to rebuilding the family. In the Netherlands, intergenerational programs are being developed to solve some of the problems related to the integration of immigrant families into the Dutch culture. In these programs where the grandparents have been left behind, the youth (i.e., Moroccan and Croatian) are linked with older Dutch mentors and tutors. In South Africa and Uganda, in communities where HIV has all but decimated a generation of parents the grandparents, and other older adults collaborate in caring for the communities' children. Informal intergenerational programs are providing supplies and education to these caregivers who are trying to rebuild both the family structure and the sense of community.

Intergenerational programs are evident at different stages of development in countries within Europe, Asia, Africa, Australia, North and South America (Hatton-Yeo and Ohsako 2000). Fundamental to many of the international intergenerational initiatives are concerns related to the changing families in these countries and the role of children and older adults within the family and within the community at large. Many countries need to share ideas and problems related to the family and seek cross-national solutions.

A growing global interest in intergenerational initiatives has given rise to the creation of the International Consortium for Intergenerational Programmes (ICIP), an organization dedicated to supporting the development of intergenerational programs and practices as agents for social change.

ICIP will foster intergenerational approaches to issues of community revitalization, crossgenerational learning, generational cohesiveness, and quality of life for a nation's old and young. This nascent organization hopes to become the vehicle for networking, program development and exchange of information and research to facilitate intergenerational initiatives that meet the social needs of diverse countries across the world.

Conclusion

Conclusive data reporting on the outcomes of intergenerational programs in the context of relationships within families is not yet available. However, a growing body of qualitative and quantitative information on intergenerational interactions between nonbiologically connected older and younger adults reports on universally positive behaviors that are evident in diverse intergenerational programs (Kuehne 1989; Penninx 1996; Larkin and Newman 2001). These behaviors seem also to be manifest in families whose members have experienced ongoing intergenerational interactions. These limited qualitative studies use anecdotal reports, interviews, surveys, and case studies that show the positive relationships being developed through nonbiological interactions in intergenerational programs that can also impact on the quality of relationships in families. With intergenerational programming being developed as a vehicle for positive social change in the larger community it will be important for researchers throughout the world to systematically examine the process for transferability of positive behaviors from formal intergenerational program models to encourage more stable and positive informal family systems.

See also: CHILDCARE; ELDERS; INTERGENERATIONAL RELATIONS; INTERGENERATIONAL TRANSMISSION; NEIGHBORHOOD; SANDWICH GENERATION; SCHOOL

Bibliography

Erikson, E.; Erikson, J.; and Kivnick, H. (1986). *Vital Involvement in Old Age.* New York: Norton.

Hare, A. P.; Borgatta, E.; and Bales, R., eds. (1955). *Small Groups: Studies in Social Interaction.* New York: Knopf.

Hatton-Yeo, A., and Ohsako, T., eds. (2000). *Intergenerational Programmes: Public Policy and Research Implications: An International Perspective.* Hamburg, Germany: UNESCO Institute for Education; Stoke-on-Trent, UK: Beth Johnson Foundation.

Kaplan, M. (1996). "A Look at Intergenerational Program Initiatives in Japan: A Preliminary Comparison with the United States." *International Journal of Aging and Human Development* 44(3):205–219.

Kuehne, V. (1989). "Younger Friends/Older Friends: Study of Intergenerational Interactions." *Journal of Classroom Interaction* 24(1):14–21.

Larkin, L., and Newman, S. (2001). "Benefits of Intergenerational Staffing in Preschools." *Educational Gerontology* 2(5):373–385.

Morrison, G. (1995). "Interest and Issues." In *Early Childhood Education Today.* Englewood Cliffs, NJ: Prentice Hall.

National Council on Aging. (1981). "Report of the Mini-Conferences on Intergenerational Cooperation and Exchange." Washington, DC: White House Conference on Aging.

Newman, S.; Ward, C.; Smith, T.; Wilson, J.; and McCrea, J. (1997). *Intergenerational Programs: Past, Present, and Future.* Washington, DC: Taylor and Francis.

Newman, S.; Morris, G.; and Streetman, H. (1999). "Elder-Child Interaction Analysis: An Observation Instrument for Classrooms Involving Older Adults as Mentors, Tutors, or Resource Persons." In *Intergenerational Programs: Understanding What We Have Created,* ed. V. Kuehne. New York: Haworth Press.

Ng, S. H.; Liu, J. H.; Weatherall, A.; and Loong, C. S. F. (1997). "Younger Adults' Communication Experiences and Contact with Elders and Peers." *Human Communication Research* 24(1):82–108.

Penninx, K. (1996). *The Neighborhood of All Ages: Intergenerational Neighborhood Development in the Context of Local Social Policy.* Utrecht, Netherlands: Dutch Institute for Care and Welfare.

Pitts, J. (1961). "Introduction: Personality and the Social System." In *Theories of Society: Foundations of Modern Sociological Theory,* ed. T. Parsons, E. Shils, K. Naegele, and J. Pitts. New York: Free Press.

U.S. Department of Health and Human Services. (2000). *Second Chance Homes: Providing Services for Teenage Parents and Their Children.* Washington, DC: Government Printing Office.

Williams, J. (1995). *The U.S. Population: A Fact Sheet.* Congressional Research Service Report for Congress. Washington, DC: Government Printing Office.

Other Resource

International Consortium for Intergenerational
    Programmes (ICIP). Web site. Available from
    http://www.centreforip.org.uk/about.htm.

SALLY NEWMAN

INTERGENERATIONAL RELATIONS

Intergenerational relations refer to the ties between individuals or groups of different ages. Family circumstances and the decisions made by members of one generation within the family have implications for the development of members within the same generation and for members of other generations.

Family Structure

Family structures changed considerably in the twentieth century. There were changes in patterns of living arrangements, divorce and remarriage, decreases in fertility, and increases in women's labor force participation. Each of these has the potential to affect intergenerational relations.

Many individuals have delayed both marriage and childbearing in order to spend more time pursuing educational goals. Starting a family later, coupled with decreased fertility, means that families are smaller today than at any point in the past, and the typical pattern is fewer children spaced more closely together in age than in previous generations. This results in what Vern Bengtson, Carolyn Rosenthal, and Linda Burton (1990) refer to as the *beanpole family,* in which each generation is smaller, with more years between each generation, but more generations are alive at any one time. The rise in rates of teenage pregnancy and out-of-wedlock births has, to some extent, mitigated this trend, which Bengtson and his colleagues (1990) refer to as *age-compressed families.* It is unclear how the nature of intergenerational ties may be affected by these changing family structures, and whether fewer and more enduring ties might lead to increased closeness between generations or serve instead to accentuate any conflict between generations (Bengtson, Rosenthal, and Burton 1996).

The changing structure of intergenerational relationships in the United States is further complicated by increases in rates of divorce and remarriage. Divorce rates roughly doubled between 1970 and 1990 (Cherlin 1992; Martin and Bumpass 1989) and have remained consistently high; more than half of all first marriages end in divorce. Most individuals who divorce eventually remarry, and divorce rates among subsequent marriages are even higher than for first marriages. Marital dissolution and reconstitution affect intergenerational ties in ways that are only now beginning to be fully appreciated. For example, due to the cumulative effects of families being formed, dissolved, and reconstituted an older adult may find himself or herself embedded in a complex web of ties with biological children, stepchildren, and children-in-law. Given that a majority of baby boomers can expect to find themselves in one of these complex family forms, it is important to learn more about how these marital transitions affect the availability of support for future generations of older adults.

One final trend in families is the increase in women's labor force participation. Women now work outside of the home in the vast majority of households. This labor force participation has implications for the individual's or couple's timing of retirement, wealth upon retirement, parent-child relationships, and the availability of family caregivers for frail older adults (e.g., Zarit and Eggebeen 1995).

Heng-Wei Chen and Merril Silverstein (2000) remark that modifications in family and household structures resulting from economic development in contemporary China have broken down the extended family living households. With smaller households and an increase in nuclear families, a new type of living arrangement has evolved—the *network family*—in which married adult children, rather than coresiding, tend to live near their older parents so as to provide assistance to the older adults. Cross-national work on the relationship between family and state systems of care reveals families are likely to continue to provide high levels of assistance to older adults through adaptations of family functioning (Davey and Patsios 1999; Davey et al. 1999).

Living Arrangements

Changes in demography and family structure have shaped the living arrangements of both the elderly and adult children. Although these changes vary across countries and cultures, the latter half of the twentieth century was characterized by declining household size and an increase in nuclear families.

Lower fertility and increased migration have shrunk the average household size in both developed and developing countries and led to more dispersed family networks, whereas the proportion of people living alone in single-person households is mounting. The sources for these trends include normative changes, such as delayed marriage and changing gender roles, as well as higher rates of marital dissolution and growing numbers of elderly persons whose spouses have died.

The most striking change in household arrangements in developed countries has been a drift towards single-person households. Tracing the historical trends in family living arrangements, Gerdt Sundstrom (1993) found that Western countries and Japan have shown declines in the proportion of older people living with their children since 1950. This is particularly true for the older people in Sweden, who are more likely to live alone than elders in the United States (40% compared to 30%). In the early 1950s, for example, 27 percent of elderly Swedes lived with their children compared to 33 percent in the United States. Now, the rate of cohabitation of older people with their children had fallen to roughly 5 percent in Sweden compared with 15 percent in the United States.

The probability of living alone increases with age, even though there might be a decline for the oldest ages. Because women on average outlive men and tend to be younger than their spouses, it is not surprising to find that in all older age groups the percentage of women living alone is usually higher than that of men. It has been recognized that older men in the United States almost certainly live with a spouse, even in very late life. In contrast, women are most likely to live alone or with their children (Himes, Hogan, and Eggebeen 1996).

Despite the high proportion of the elderly who live alone in developed countries, a majority of those aged sixty-five and over live with others. Recent cohorts of young adults have postponed nest-leaving and an increasing number of adult children return to the parental home during periods of transition, economic hardship, or marital problems. Obviously, in these cases coresidence is a response to the needs of adult children, rather than caregiving for parents. Sons are found to be more likely than daughters to delay nest-leaving or to return to the parental home (Goldscheider and Goldscheider 1994). Moreover, Alwin Duane (1996) found that there is a trend towards the acceptability of coresidence and that the younger cohorts were more approving of coresidence with aged parents as compared to the elders themselves. This could be because coresidency comes across as a more positive experience for the adult children (Ward and Spitze 1996). Parental coresidence is more prevalent among men and women raised by single or remarried mothers and men living with single fathers, and less common among individuals living with remarried fathers (Szinovacz 1997).

Living patterns are important because they affect the exchange of help and support and also reflect cultural preferences. For instance, parent-child proximity in the United Kingdom may be more likely to arise from the needs of the older generation, whereas in Italy strong cultural norms pertaining to mutual aid between parents and children may be the rationale for cultural proximity and—often—coresidence (Glaser and Tomassini 2000).

An examination of living arrangements of the elderly in developing countries shows that relatively few elderly individuals live alone. Nearly three out of four Koreans aged sixty years and over live with their children. Korean parents are more likely to live with sons than daughters, and are also more likely to live with married children (Won and Lee 1999). Akiko Hashimoto (1991) examined seven different developing countries—Brazil, Egypt, India, South Korea, Singapore, Thailand, and Zimbabwe—and found that older parents maintained coresidence with their adult children despite changing socioeconomic and demographic conditions. Among these countries, India, Singapore, Thailand, and South Korea showed the highest incidence of coresidence between older parents and married children and lowest in Egypt and Brazil.

Intergenerational Norms and Exchanges

Bengtson's theory of intergenerational solidarity (Mangen, Bengtson, and Landry 1988) points to the many ways in which generations relate to one another in terms of living arrangements (*structural*), shared values (*normative*), norms (*consensual*), contact (*associational*), closeness (*affectual*), and instrumental support (*functional*). Older generations are generally perceived to invest in younger generations (*generational stake*) because resources are often seen to flow down from an older to younger generations. More recent explanations of intergenerational relations have focused on differences in needs and resources of each generation, emerging perspectives recognizing positive and negative, conflictual and consensual, aspects of intergenerational relationships are further advancing our understanding of the variability in ties between generations. For instance, Adam Davey and Joan Norris (1998) studied younger and older adults' perceptions of the availability of support from specific members of their social support network, along with the perceived costs of seeking support from those individuals. Within close relationships, individuals reported expecting to receive support contingent on need. Likewise, expectations for short-term reciprocity, considered as the costs of seeking assistance, were low. Findings also indicated that expectations for support and reciprocity differed between close relationships and those that were not as close. There is also evidence that older adults make distinctions along these dimensions in close relationships to a greater extent than younger adults. Because individuals' social resources may decline with age, it has been suggested that they will place greater importance on their closest relationships, compared with those that are not as central in their social networks.

Important differences in filial expectations were found among African Americans, who have higher filial responsibility expectations than European Americans (Lee, Peek, and Coward 1998). Likewise, in many Asian countries, the flow of intergenerational financial support and personal assistance is expected to come from the adult children to older parents. Lee Lillard and Robert Willis (1997) found that the dominant direction of monetary transfers between non-coresident parents and children in Malaysia is from younger to the older generations. Traditional familial norms of filial piety among the Chinese reinforce the obligation adult children have to their older parents.

Understanding individuals' perceptions of support in close relationships is certainly important, but is there evidence that, in times of need, adult children do in fact provide assistance in a manner consistent with the contingent exchange perspective? David Eggebeen and Adam Davey (1998) examined this question by bringing longitudinal data to bear on the issue. Beyond midlife (over age fifty), individuals commonly experience transitions such as loss of spouse, decreases in health status, increases in functional limitations, and substantial drops (i.e., greater than 50%) in income. In the U.S. National Survey of Families and Households, nearly two-thirds of individuals over age fifty experienced one or more such events over a five-year period. In addition, each transition (27% of the total sample experienced more than one) was associated with an increased probability that parents would receive assistance from at least one adult child. This was true for any form of assistance (i.e., help with shopping, help with the activities of daily life [ADLs], and the hours of help received). Only receipt of help around the house and receipt of advice were not associated with the number of transitions. These results speak to the power of social norms for the intergenerational provision of support contingent on need. In addition, these norms seem more powerful than either beliefs or expectations regarding intergenerational support.

Similar findings were seen in a cross-cultural study by Karen Glaser and Cecilia Tomassini (2000), who found that parent-child proximity in the United Kingdom may be more likely to arise from the needs of the older generation, especially health. In comparison, parent-child proximity in Italy may reflect a cultural preference regardless of need. Similarly, in China the network family that emerged due to demographic, economic, and housing changes is another example of where married children tend to live near their older parents not because of needs but because of norms and culture.

How support is given and received may have consequences for the mental health and well-being of older adults—over and above the effects of the events that elicit such support. Davey and Eggebeen (1998) found that older adults who were overbenefited in relationships with an adult child reported greater depression than would be expected based on their previous levels of functioning. This is in direct contrast to the predictions of *social exchange theory* and only partially consonant with the predictions of *equity theory* (which suggests that both underbenefit and overbenefit will be psychologically detrimental). In contrast, Davey and Eggebeen (1998) found evidence for the importance of contingent exchange. Although receipt of contingent assistance is beneficial, there may be negative psychological consequences of providing assistance around one's own needs.

In developing countries (e.g., China), the opportunity for receiving support in old age from adult children is crucial for parental happiness. Older parents benefit from receiving both emotional and financial support from children, whereas only the provision of instrumental support—but not financial support—to adult children improved the morale of the two generations (Chen and Silverstein 2000). Moreover, providing support to adult children was shown to be important for psychological health in later life. This could be because it boosts the parents' power in the family and reinforces their ability to reciprocate in exchanges with children. The childcare and household services that older parents are able to provide to the adult children can serve as reciprocity for financial resources derived from children.

There is consistent evidence that marital disruption leads to a decrease in contact, diminishes the quality of relationships, and decreases the support exchanged between the two generations. These effects differed for mothers and fathers. Paul Amato, Sandra Rezac, and Alan Booth (1995) used longitudinal data to examine the effect of marital quality, divorce, and remarriage on the exchange of assistance. They found that divorce reduced helping between fathers and offspring, but not between mothers and children. Although single mothers received more help, they gave less to their children than mothers in first marriages. It is interesting to note that remarried mothers gave as much assistance as first-married mothers, but they received significantly less help. A study by Frank Furstenberg, Saul Hoffman, and Laura Shreshta (1995) confirms that it is essential to take the timing of the divorce into account when studying the differences between men and women in this context. Parental divorce when children are young adults does not predict differences in intergenerational ties by gender of the parent, although the effects of divorce could be stronger for fathers than mothers.

The existence of grandchildren also affects exchange relationships between aging parents and their adult children, and the position of the generations in the life-course plays an important role in understanding the pattern of exchanges. Merril Silverstein and Anne Marenco (2001) found that younger grandparents are more inclined to live closer to and have greater contact with grandchildren. Younger grandparents often baby-sit and share recreational activities with them. Older grandparents tended to provide financial assistance and more strongly identified with the role. In a recently completed review of the literature about grandparents who care for grandchildren, Anne Pebley and Laura Rudkin (1999) stated that in 1995 approximately 5.6 percent of children lived in their grandparents' households. (These figures include grandchildren living in grandparents' homes with one or both parents present.) The probability is higher for African Americans, Hispanics, and the poor to be in a custodial care household with grandparents bearing most of the responsibility in raising of the grandchildren. Although most grandparents report that they enjoy the experience, the grandparents who considered themselves as "off time" or "non-normative" experienced the strain of role overload (Burton 1996).

Intergenerational ties remain important throughout the life-course. They play an important role in developed and developing nations, Eastern and Western cultures, and have implications for the health and well-being of each generation involved. The structure of intergenerational ties suggests that they are highly adaptive across sweeping demographic and social structural changes.

See also: CLAN; DIVORCE: EFFECTS ON PARENTS; ELDER ABUSE; ELDERS; EXTENDED FAMILIES; FAMILY STORIES AND MYTHS; FILIAL RESPONSIBILITY; GRANDPARENTHOOD; GRANDPARENTS' RIGHTS; INHERITANCE; IN-LAW RELATIONSHIPS; INTERGENERATIONAL PROGRAMMING; INTERGENERATIONAL TRANSMISSION; KINSHIP; LATER LIFE FAMILIES; RETIREMENT; SOCIAL EXCHANGE THEORY

Bibliography

Amato, P. R.; Rezac, S. J.; and Booth, A. (1995). "Helping between Parents and Young Adult Offspring: The Role of Parental Marital Quality, Divorce and Remarriage." *Journal of Marriage and the Family* 57:363–74.

Bengtson, V.; Rosenthal, C. J.; and Burton, L. (1990). "Families and Aging: Diversity and Heterogeneity." In *Handbook of Aging and the Social Sciences,* 3rd edition, ed. R. H. Binstock and K. George. New York: Academic Press.

Bengtson, V.; Rosenthal, C. J.; and Burton, L. (1996). "Paradoxes of Families and Aging." In *Handbook of Aging and the Social Sciences,* 4th edition, ed. R. H. Binstock and L. K. George. New York: Academic Press.

Burton, L. M. (1996). "Age Norms, the Timing of Family Role Transitions, and Intergenerational Caregiving among Aging African American Women." *Gerontologist* 36:199–208.

Chen, X., and Silverstein, M. (2000). "Intergenerational Social Support and the Psychological Well-Being of Older Parents in China." *Research on Aging* 22:43–65.

Cherlin, A. J. (1992). *Marriage, Divorce, and Remarriage.* Cambridge, MA: Harvard University Press.

Davey, A., and Eggebeen, D. J. (1998). "Patterns of Intergenerational Exchange and Mental Health." *Journal of Gerontology: Psychological Sciences* 53:P86–P95.

Davey, A.; Femia, E. E.; Shea, D. G.; Zarit, S. H.; Sundstrom, G.; Berg, S.; and Smyer, M. A. (1999). "How Much Do Families Help? A Cross-National Comparison." *Journal of Aging and Health* 11:199–221.

Davey, A., and Norris, J. E. (1998). "Social Networks and Exchange Norms across the Adult Life-Span." *Canadian Journal on Aging* 17:212–33.

Davey, A., and Patsios, D. (1999). "Formal and Informal Care to Older Citizens: Comparative Analysis of the United States and Great Britain." *Journal of Family and Economic Issues* 20:271–300.

Duane, A. (1996). "Coresidence Beliefs in American Society—1973 to 1991." *Journal of Marriage and the Family* 58:393–404.

Eggebeen, D. J., and Davey, A. (1998). "Do Safety Nets Work? The Role of Anticipated Support in Times of Need." *Journal of Marriage and the Family* 60:939–50.

Furstenberg, F. F.; Hoffman, S. D.; and Shreshta, L. (1995). "The Effect of Divorce on Intergenerational Transfers: New Evidence." *Demography* 32:319–34.

Glaser, K., and Tomassini, C. (2000). "Proximity of Older Women to Their Children: A Comparison of Britain and Italy." *Gerontologist* 40:729–37.

Goldscheider, F., and Goldscheider, C. (1994). "Leaving and Returning Home in Twentieth-Century America." *Population Bulletin* 48(4):1-35.

Hashimoto, A. (1991). "Living Arrangements of the Aged in Seven Developing Countries: A Preliminary Analysis." *Journal of Cross-Cultural Gerontology* 6:359–81.

Lee, G.; Peek, C. W.; and Coward, R. T. (1998). "Race Differences in Filial Responsibility Expectations among Older Parents." *Journal of Marriage and the Family* 60:404–12.

Lillard, L. A., and Willis, R. J. (1997). "Motives for Intergenerational Transfers: Evidence from Malaysia." *Demography* 34:115–34.

Mangen, D. J.; Bengtson, V. L.; and Landry, P. H. (1988). *Measurement of Intergenerational Relations.* Newbury Park, CA: Sage.

Martin, T. C., and Bumpass, L. L. (1989). "Recent Trends in Marital Disruption." *Demography* 26:37-51.

Pebley, A. R., and Rudkin, L. L. (1999). "Grandparents Caring for Grandchildren." *Journal of Family Issues* 20:218–42.

Silverstein, M., and Marenco, A. (2001). "How Americans Enact the Grandparent Role across the Family Course." *Journal of Family Issues* 22:493–522.

Sundstrom, G. (1993). "Care by Families: An Overview of Trends." In *Caring for Frail Elderly People.* Paris: Organization of Economic Co-operation and Development.

Szinovacz, M. (1997). "Adult Children Taking Parents into Their Homes: Effects of Childhood Living Arrangements." *Journal of Marriage and the Family* 59:700–17.

Ward, R., and Spitze, G. (1996). "Will the Children Ever Leave? Parent-Child Coresidence History and Plans." *Journal of Family Issues* 17:514–39.

Won, Y., and Lee, G. (1999). "Living Arrangements of Older Parents in Korea." *Journal of Comparative Family Studies* 30:315–28.

Zarit, S. H., and Eggebeen, D. J. (1995). "Parent-Child Relationships in Adulthood and Old Age." In *Children and Parenting,* vol. 1 of *Handbook of Parenting,* ed. M. H. Bornstein. Mahwah, NJ: Lawrence Erlbaum Associates.

ADAM DAVEY
JYOTI "TINA" SAVLA
LISA M. BELLISTON

INTERGENERATIONAL TRANSMISSION

Intergenerational transmission is one dimension of the larger concept of intergenerational relations. The term *intergenerational relations* describes a wide range of patterns of interaction among individuals in different generations of a family: for example, between those in *older* generations, such as parents and grandparents, aunt, uncles, and those in *younger* generations, such as children and grandchildren, nieces and nephews. The term is also frequently used to describe behaviors involving older and younger people in society at large, even if they are unrelated to one another. For example, media accounts describe potential issues between the attitudes and behaviors of older members of the *baby boom generation* and younger *generation Xers.*

In the context of family lives, intergenerational transmission refers to the movement, passage, or exchange of some *good* or *service* between one generation and another. What is transmitted may be intangible and include beliefs, norms, values, attitudes, and behaviors specific to that family, or that reflect sociocultural, religious, and ethnically relevant practices and beliefs. Intergenerational transmission can, however, also include the provision of resources and services or assistance by one generation to another. One example of this, illustrated by Barry McPherson (1998) is the issue of transferring the ownership and operation of the family farm from one generation to the next.

Family roles may also be transmitted from generation to generation. For example, Carolyn Rosenthal (1985) describes the roles of headship, kin keeper, confidante, and financial adviser as roles within families. This work documents how not only are these roles in themselves mechanisms for the transmission of information, advice, beliefs, values, and resources between generations, but that the roles are passed through the generations, in a form of *generational succession.* Rosenthal and Victor Marshall (1988) also examine the intergenerational transmission of ritual in families in a study across three generations of Canadian families.

The concept of intergenerational transmission is also used by social scientists who conduct research on family violence. For example, Ann Duffy and Julianne Momirov (2000) utilize the concept of *intergenerational transmission* to explain the social learning of violence within families. In this context, intergenerational transmission refers to the socialization and social learning that helps to explain the ways in which children growing up in a violent family learn violent roles and, subsequently, may play out the roles of victim or victimizer in their own adult families.

Family researchers have also studied the intergenerational transmission of difficult life course transitions like marital dissolution or divorce. In particular, studies in the United States have found that parental divorce increases the likelihood that adult children will experience separation or divorce (Glenn and Kramer 1987; Keith and Finlay 1988; Amato 1996). Even when factors such as the socioeconomic status of both parents and children are controlled for, Nicholas Wolfinger (2000) concludes that the children of parents who have had more than one marriage tend to replicate these patterns of marital instability. Multiple family structure transitions have a negative effect on children; that is, the experience of numerous parental relationship transitions is likely to result in the reproduction of these behaviors by adult children.

Cultural Transmission: Values, Norms, and Beliefs

The intergenerational stake hypothesis (Bengtson and Kuypers 1971) maintains that children and parents have different expectations and understandings of the filial relationship. While parents are concerned with the continuity and intergenerational transmission of values they have found important in life, children focus on the differences in the two generations' value systems in an attempt to establish independence from their parents.

The importance of gender differences in the intergenerational transmission of roles is highlighted in Alice Rossi's (1993) study on the application of the intergenerational stake hypothesis in a study comparing men and women. Rossi notes two key reasons why women have a greater investment in maintaining relationships with their children than do men. First, women function as primary family caregivers in later life. Second, different socialization experiences result in motherhood assuming a more central role in the lives of women than fatherhood does in the lives of men; that is, as women are socialized to be more expressive than men and are more likely to assume the "kin-keeper" role in the family.

In addition to gender, ethnicity is another important factor in the investigation of intergenerational transmission over the life course. For example, much research on Asian immigrant family values has been based on the conception of Asian North Americans as having ideal families. This conception has emerged from the "model minority" myth, a stereotype that attributes the educational and occupational success of Asian North Americans to adherence to traditional Asian cultural value systems (Takaki 1989). The ideal family myth

Research on intergenerational transmission has yet to fully explore grandparent-grandchild relationships, which may have a greater potential for the transfer of generation-distinct information. MICHAEL S. YAMASHITA/CORBIS

assumes that Asian North Americans, regardless of generation or ethnocultural group, greatly revere older family members and feel strongly obligated to provide support to them (Ishii-Kuntz 1997; Osako 1979). Asian–North American families are believed to have been particularly successful in the intergenerational transmission of the values associated with reverence for elders and filial piety.

Yoshinori Kamo and Min Zhou (1994) attributed the prevalence of Asian-American co-residence among married adult children and older parents to the strong influence of filial obligation. Co-residence, however, is only an example of behaviorally oriented and intergenerationally transmitted values of filial piety (Sung 1995); that is, co-residence alone does not provide support for the hypothesis that Asian–North American adult children necessarily provide more love and affection

(emotionally oriented filial piety) to their aging parents than do adult children in other ethnic groups. In addition, these findings do not take into account generational differences in the intergenerational transmission and retention of traditional values in post-immigrant Asian–North American families.

An early example of intergenerational value transmission research, Minako Maykovich's (1980) study of acculturation and familism in three generations of Japanese Canadians, found significant intergenerational differences in the retention of traditional family values. Her conclusions support Gordon's theoretical proposition that acculturation is a multiphase process, whether it is measured by the retention of traditional familism or the adoption of "new world" values. Similarly, Pamela Sugiman and Harry Nishio's (1983) study of socialization and cultural duality among aging Japanese Canadians concludes that, in contrast to the traditional age-related norms of the *issei* (first generation), middle-aged *nisei* (second generation) parents demonstrate a decreased dependence on their children for support in later life. Victor Ujimoto (1987) attributes this change in support expectations to generational differences in the retention of traditional first generation values.

In a study on intergenerational relationships in Japanese-Canadian families, an exploration of the factors affecting social support from children to parents, Karen Kobayashi (2000) finds that adherence to the traditional issei value of *oya koh koh* (filial obligation) has a significant effect on children's provision of emotional support to parents in later life families. She concludes that despite the cultural transformation of values such as oya koh koh by successive generations of nisei and sansei children, filial obligation still remains important in the decision-making process around support for aging parents.

According to Tamara Hareven (1994), generational differences in value perceptions are due to changes in the timing of life-course events for parents and children. Instead of timing events in concert with the family's collective needs, children now display a more individualized timing regulated to their specific age norms. Hareven's (1994) research indicates that if parents and children have a strong filial relationship characterized by satisfaction on the part of both parties, it is more likely that children will use the collective needs of the family to guide the timing of their life-course events and hence, minimize the differences in value system perceptions. This may be especially true in adult children's adherence to filial obligation.

Social Support

Much of the mainstream literature on family relationships in later life has examined the intergenerational transmission of the tangible services or support that adult children, particularly daughters, provide to older parents as caregivers (e.g., Burton 1996; McMullin and Marshall 1995). Given this focus, it is not surprising that many studies report a negative relationship between parental dependency and quality of the parent-child relationship (Baruch and Barnett 1983; Brody 1985; Mindel and Wright 1982). In a study on the factors that predispose adult sons and daughters to provide support to older parents, Merril Silverstein and colleagues (1995) found that intergenerational affection was the factor that most motivates daughters, while sons are primarily motivated by filial obligation, legitimation of inheritance, and frequency of contact.

Research on the transmission of support in ethnic minority families has focused on varying issues depending on the ethnic group(s) under study. For example, many studies on African- and Hispanic-American intergenerational relations in later life families have examined social support according to such demographic indicators as socioeconomic status (Mindel et al. 1988; Moynihan 1965; Mutran 1986). This focus has excluded the exploration of key intergenerational issues, such as the impact of changing value systems on supportive attitudes and behaviors in adult children. A growing body of comparative research on later life support in Asian-Canadian families is promising in that it acknowledges intergenerational differences in the intergenerational transmission of, and adherence to, values such as filial obligation (Sugiman and Nishio 1983; Ujimoto 1987).

Most of the support literature on the later life family focuses on the one-way flow of support from adult children to older parents, neglecting issues around the intergenerational transmission of support that parents provide to children (Connidis et al. 1996; Ishii-Kuntz 1997; Kahn and Antonucci 1981). In an attempt to address this imbalance,

Teresa Cooney and Peter Uhlenberg (1992) examined the changes in three types of parent-to-child support (emotional, financial, and service) that occur as parents and adult children age over the life course. They report a decline in transmission of support from parents to children after children reached the age of thirty, but that the pattern of decline varied according to the type of support. In addition, they stated that while parents, "may not assume active, regular supportive roles in their children's lives, they are widely viewed by their children as valued and dependable sources of support should a need for help arise" (Cooney and Uhlenberg 1992, p. 82). This view holds true for adult children across the life course, and reflects a difference between actual versus potential or latent intergenerational transmission of support.

Intergenerational Solidarity

The concept of family solidarity or cohesion, as proposed by Vern Bengtson and his colleagues (1985), has been the focus of much research into intergenerational transmission over the past two decades. Theoretically grounded in the life-course perspective, it focuses on six dimensions of solidarity: family structure; associational solidarity (the degree to which members of a lineage are in contact with one another and engage in shared behavior and common activities); affectual solidarity (the degree of positive sentiment expressed in the intergenerational relationship); consensual solidarity (the degree of consensus or conflict in beliefs or orientations external to the family); functional solidarity (the degree to which financial assistance and service exchanges occur among family members); and normative solidarity (the norms of familism held by family members, in terms of expectations of proximity and assistance.

A number of studies have attempted to address some of the shortcomings of the original solidarity model. Robert E. Roberts and Bengtson's (1990) examination of intergenerational family relationships includes a number of additional dimensions of family cohesion. In adding filial responsibility, dependency needs, experiences not shared across generations, residential propinquity, gender linkage of pair, and helping behavior, they acknowledge the complexity of parent-child relationships in later life. The results indicate that intergenerational solidarity in later life is not a unidimensional construct, and that each component is determined by different variables. Also, Leora Lawton and her colleagues (1994) use a gendered analysis to examine family solidarity in intergenerational pairs of family members. Their study finds that gender, marital status of parent, education, and race are key factors in cohesion between parents and children, and that the influence of a grandparent during childhood is "associated with more frequent contact, emotional closeness, and shared opinions in the child's adult years" (Lawton, Silverstein, and Bengston 1994, p. 42). Inasmuch as these studies attempt to explain later life patterns of intergenerational family solidarity, however, they are limited by their inattention to the historical, cultural, and social structural forces that shape family relationships and patterns of intergenerational transmission along solidarity dimensions.

Limitations

As it is often used in the literature, the concept of intergenerational transmission is frequently narrow in its application. For example, it is often used to imply a one-way flow: the transmission of resources *from* an older generation *to* a younger, or the intergenerational transmission of beliefs and attitudes *of* one generation *to* another. This is by no means the case, however. While reciprocity is a distinct concept, it is an integral part of intergenerational relations and intergenerational transmission.

A second limitation is that the concept of intergenerational transmission is almost exclusively applied to flows and transfers, particularly financial, *down* the generations, from older to younger generations. Except in the extensive gerontological literature on caregiving (which focuses almost exclusively on what family members in mid-life do to assist their frail and aging parent or parents), there is little consideration of the intergenerational transmission of values *up* the lineage from younger to older generations.

A third limitation is the infrequency with which the concept of intergenerational transmission is utilized to describe relations between generations that are non-contiguous, or that represent "skipped" generations. For example, while there is considerable research on parent-child relations, there is much less research on grandparent-grandchild relations (although there is some literature on the role of grandparents in raising grandchildren in families where the middle generation is, for reasons of divorce, addiction, or disability, unable to do so).

See also: ACCULTURATION; ELDERS; ETHNIC VARIATION/ETHNICITY; FAMILY FOLKLORE; GRANDPARENTHOOD; INTERGENERATIONAL PROGRAMMING; INTERGENERATIONAL RELATIONS; SOCIOECONOMIC STATUS

Bibliography

Amato, P. R. (1996). "Explaining the Intergenerational Transmission of Divorce." *Journal of Marriage and the Family* 58:628–641.

Baruch, G., and R. C. Barnett. (1983). "Adult Daughters' Relationships With Their Mothers." *Journal of Marriage and the Family* 45:601–606.

Bengston, V. L.; Cutler, N. E.; Mangen, D. J.; and Marshall, V. W. (1985). "Generations, Cohorts, and Relations between Age Groups." In *Handbook of Aging and the Social Sciences,* ed. R. H. Binstock and E. Shanas. New York: Van Nostrand Reinhold.

Bengtson, V. L., and Kuypers, J. A. (1971). "Generational Differences and the Developmental Stake." *International Journal of Aging and Human Development* 2:249–260.

Brody, E. M. (1985). "Parent Care as a Normative Family Stress." *The Gerontologist* 25:19–29.

Connidis, I. A.; Rosenthal, C. J.; and McMullin, J. A. (1996). "The Impact of Family Composition on Providing Help to Older Parents: A Study of Employed Adults." *Research on Aging* 18:402–429.

Cooney, T. M., and Uhlenberg, P. (1992). "Support from Parents over the Life Course: The Adult Child's Perspective." *Social Forces* 71:63–84.

Duffy, A., and Momirov, J. (2000). "Family Violence: Issues and Advances at the End of the Twentieth Century." In *Canadian Families,* 2nd ed., ed. N. Mandell and A. Duffy. Toronto: Harcourt Brace Canada.

Giarusso, R.; Stallings, M.; and Bengtson, V. L. (1995). "The 'Intergenerational Stake' Hypothesis Revisited: Parent-Child Differences in Perceptions of Relationships 20 Years Later." In *Adult Intergenerational Relations: Effects of Societal Change,* ed. V. L. Bengtson, K. W. Schaie, and L. M. Burton. New York: Springer.

Glenn, N. D., and Kramer, K. B. (1987). "The Marriages and Divorces of the Children of Divorce." *Journal of Marriage and the Family* 49:811–825.

Hareven, T. K. (1994). "Aging and Generational Relations: A Historical and Life Course Perspective." *Annual Review of Sociology* 20:437–461.

Ishii-Kuntz, M. (1997). "Intergenerational Relationships Among Chinese, Japanese, and Korean Americans." *Family Relations* 46:23–32.

Kahn, R. L. and Antonucci, T. C. (1981). "Convoys of Social Support: A Life Course Approach." In *Aging: Social Change*, ed. S. B. Kiesler, J. Morgan, and V. K. Oppenheimer. New York: Academic Press.

Kamo, Y., and Zhou, M. (1994). "Living Arrangements of Elderly Chinese and Japanese in the United States." *Journal of Marriage and the Family* 56:544–558.

Keith, V. M., and Finlay, B. (1988). "The Impact of Parental Divorce on Children's Educational Attainment, Marital Timing, and Likelihood of Divorce." *Journal of Marriage and the Family* 50:797–809.

Kobayashi, K. M. (2000). "The Nature of Support from Adult *Sansei* (Third Generation) Children to Older *Nisei* (Second Generation) Parents in Japanese Canadian Families." *Journal of Cross-Cultural Gerontology* 15:185–205.

Lawton, L.; Silverstein, M.; and Bengtson, V. L. (1994). "Affection, Social Contact, and Geographic Distance Between Adult Children and Their Parents." *Journal of Marriage and the Family* 56:57–68.

Maykovich, M. K. (1980). "Acculturation versus Familism in Three Generations of Japanese Canadians." In *Canadian Families: Ethnic Variations,* ed. K. Ishwaran. Toronto: McGraw-Hill Ryerson.

McMullin, J. A., and Marshall, V. M. (1995). "Social Integration: Family, Friends, and Social Support." In *Contributions to Independence over the Life Course,* ed. V. W. Marshall, J. A. McMullin, P. J. Ballantyne, J. F. Daciuk, and B.T. Wigdor. Toronto: Centre for Studies in Aging, University of Toronto.

McPherson, B. D., (1998). *Aging as a Social Process,* 3rd ed. Toronto: Harcourt Brace Canada .

Mindel, C. H., and Wright, R., Jr. (1982). "Satisfaction in Multigenerational Households." *Journal of Gerontology* 37:483–489.

Mindel, C. H.; Habenstein, R.W.; and Wright, R., Jr., eds. (1988). *Ethnic Families in America,* 3rd edition. New York: Elsevier.

Moynihan, D. P. (1965). *The Case for National Action: The Negro Family.* Washington, D.C: U.S. Department of Labor.

Mutran, E. (1986). "Intergenerational Family Support Among Blacks and Whites: Response to Culture or to Socioeconomic Differences." In *Family Issues in Current Gerontology,* ed. L. E. Troll. New York: Springer.

Osako, M. (1976). "Intergenerational Relations as an Aspect of Assimilation: The Case of Japanese Americans." *Sociological Inquiry* 46:67–72.

Roberts, R. E. L., and Bengston, V. L. (1990). "Is Intergenerational Solidarity a Unidimensional Construct? A Second Test of a Formal Model." *Journal of Gerontology* 45:S12–20.

Rosenthal, C. J. (1985). "Kinkeeping in the Familial Division of Labor." *Journal of Marriage and the Family* 47:965–974.

Rosenthal, C. J., and Marshall, V. W. (1988). "Generational Transmission of Family Ritual." *American Behavioral Scientist* 31:669–684.

Rossi, A. S. (1993). "Intergenerational Relations: Gender, Norms, and Behavior." In *The Changing Contract across Generations,* ed. V. L. Bengston and W. A. Achenbaum. New York: Aldine de Gruyter.

Silverstein, M., and Bengtson, V. L. (1997). "Intergenerational Solidarity and the Structure of Adult Child-Parent Relationships in American Families." *American Journal of Sociology* 103:429–460.

Silverstein, M.; Parrott, T. M.; and Bengtson, V. L. (1995). "Factors That Predispose Middle-aged Sons and Daughters to Provide Social Support to Older Parents." *Journal of Marriage and the Family* 57:465–475.

Sugiman, P., and Nishio, H. K. (1983). "Socialization and Cultural Duality among Aging Japanese Canadians." *Canadian Ethnic Studies* 15:17–35.

Sung, K. (1995). "Measures and Dimensions of Filial Piety in Korea." *The Gerontologist* 35:240–247.

Takaki, R. (1989). *Strangers from a Different Shore.* New York: Penguin.

Ujimoto, K. V. (1987). "Organizational Activities, Cultural Factors, and Well-being of Aged Japanese Canadians." In *Ethnic Dimensions of Aging,* ed. D. E. Gelfand and C. Barresi. New York: Springer.

Wolfinger, N. H. (2000). "Beyond the Intergenerational Transmission of Divorce." *Journal of Family Issues* 21:1061–1086.

ANNE MARTIN-MATTHEWS
KAREN M. KOBAYASHI

INTERPARENTAL CONFLICT–EFFECTS ON CHILDREN

Few parent-child relationships are conflict-free. In fact, some parents argue with heated emotion, but also clearly love each other. Thus, arguing may be an element of their communication style and may be productive for them. When interparental conflict is more frequent, intense, and longer-lasting, however, studies show that children are at increased risk for emotional and behavioral difficulties (Cummings and Davies 1994). In fact, interparental conflict is a better predictor of child adjustment problems than divorce or global indices of marital functioning (such as satisfaction). The extent to which marital conflict accounts for differences in psychological functioning in children has been estimated at 4 percent to 20 percent (Cummings and Davies 1994). When the family environment includes additional stressors such as poverty or violence, marital conflict can be expected to have even more significant effects (Cummings, Davies, and Campbell 2000).

Witnessing anger or conflict can be aversive for children and it is often associated with increased arousal, distress, and aggression as well as long-term adjustment difficulties including behavioral, emotional, social, and academic problems. Children from homes characterized by high conflict appear to be vulnerable to externalizing problems such as verbal and physical aggression, noncompliance, and delinquency, as well as internalizing problems such as depression and anxiety (Cummings and Davies 1994). Typically, however, stronger associations are found with externalizing rather than internalizing problems. Living with marital conflict also increases the risk of children displaying poor interpersonal skills and low levels of social competence (Cummings, Davies, and Campbell 2000).

Cultural differences exist with respect to what is normative in the expression and management of conflict. Thus, the meaning and impact of conflict may vary across families. The conditions under which children from different cultural or racial groups respond to marital conflict, as well as the various ways in which they respond, are areas of ongoing research. Some authors suggest that ethnic minority youth may be less vulnerable to the effect of conflict whereas others find similar results across different ethnic or racial groups (see McLoyd, Harper, and Copeland 2001). Research on culture, ethnicity, and race is limited, however, and is an area in need of further exploration.

Negative secondary affects of exposure to marital conflict have been shown for boys as well as girls, though the results are sometimes stronger for boys. Some studies find different patterns of reactivity between boys and girls, though it has been proposed that the variability in functioning within each gender is probably greater than the variability in functioning across the two sexes (see Davies and Lindsay 2001). Although no clear patterns have consistently emerged across studies, some interesting findings have begun to appear with respect to interactions between sex of parent and sex of child. There are some indications that marital conflict may be more likely to affect opposite-sex parent-child relationships than same-sex parent-child relationships (Cox, Paley, and Harter 2001).

Theoretical Models

Since 1990, there has been an increased emphasis in the literature on a search for mechanisms whereby marital processes might affect children. Three of the more compelling theoretical models are outlined below.

Cognitive-contextual theory. Rooted in information processing and stress and coping theories, John Grych and Frank Fincham (1990) developed the cognitive-contextual theory to help explain children's responses to interparental conflict. This model hypothesizes that children's appraisals mediate the impact of conflict and guide children's coping efforts (Grych and Cardoza-Fernandes 2001). Appraisals are defined as children's attempts to understand the conflict and its implications for themselves and are affected by the manner in which the conflict is expressed and contextual factors such as previous exposure to conflict and the quality of the parent-child relationships. Appraisals occur in a two-stage sequence. *Primary processing* refers to children's initial determination of the relevance and level of threat posed by the conflict. *Secondary processing* represents attempts to understand why the conflict has occurred. For example, children may look for someone to blame for the conflict and those that tend to blame themselves are at higher risk for depressive symptomatology and for becoming involved or triangulated into the conflict, a situation that is linked with adverse outcomes (Grych et al. 2000). Children's appraisals of their own coping efforts also are important to consider. According to this theory, the more confident children feel in their ability to cope with the conflict, the less likely they are to be threatened (Grych and Cardoza-Fernandes 2001).

Emotional security hypothesis. Patrick Davies and Mark Cummings (1994) proposed the emotional security hypothesis as a means of understanding the impact of marital conflict on children. This theoretical model focuses on the meaning children ascribe to marital conflict and the extent to which children perceive the conflict as threatening to their level of emotional security and the integrity of their family system. Children's emotional security is hypothesized to be a function of three regulatory systems, each of which may be disturbed by interparental conflict: *emotion regulation* (i.e., emotional reactivity and arousal), *internal representations of family relationships* (i.e., interpretations of the meaning and the potential consequences of the conflict for one's own well-being), and *regulation of exposure to family affect* (i.e., level of involvement in or withdrawal from conflict). There is some suggestion that children who engage in the conflict exhibit higher levels of difficulty than those who withdraw (Kerig 2001).

Parenting. In addition to the potential mediating effects of the cognitive processes as outlined in the cognitive-contextual theory and the emotional regulatory processes of the emotional security hypothesis, marital conflict has also been hypothesized to indirectly affect children through its impact on parenting. Studies have found marital conflict prior to the birth of a child predicts insecure attachment (Howes and Markman 1989) through its association with insensitive parenting (Owen and Cox 1997). Cross-sectional studies support the findings from longitudinal work, and marital conflict has been found to be associated with poorer quality parent-child relationships. Marital conflict has been shown to be associated with less emotionally available and less sensitive and responsive parenting as well as with more rejecting, hostile, and aggressive parenting (see Cox, Paley, and Harter 2001). Inconsistency in discipline, both within and across parents, has been linked with interparental conflict. A number of studies have found parents from more conflictual marriages to be more likely to triangulate (or involve) a child in the conflict (Kerig 1995; Lindahl, Clements, and Markman 1997), in essence forming a coalition with the child against the other parent.

Parenting findings are inconsistent with respect to sex and scarce with regard to ethnicity. Although Ross Parke and Barbara Tinsley (1987) and Susan Crockenberg and Susan Covey (1991) both concluded that marital functioning was more closely related to fathers' than mothers' parenting,

Osnat Erel and Bonnie Burman (1995) did not find sex to moderate the association between quality of the marriage and parenting. In a later review focusing specifically on marital conflict, Mary Jo Coiro and Robert Emery (1998) found that the behavior of both parents was adversely affected, with slightly stronger effects found for fathering than mothering. Others have suggested that destructive levels of marital conflict are likely to overwhelm mothers as well as fathers and that the impact on parenting may be different for parents, but is likely to be present for both sexes (Crockenberg and Covey 1991). Limited cross-cultural data are available, but marital conflict has been associated with more critical and domineering parenting in Anglo- and African-American families and more disengagement in Hispanic families (Malik and Lindahl 2001; Shaw, Winslow, and Flanagan 1999).

Dimensions of Marital Conflict

Not all marital conflict is created equal with respect to the impact on children's adjustment. Conflict that is more frequent, intense, and of longer duration tends to be associated with more negative child outcomes. None of these factors act in isolation, however, and significant interdepedence is the norm rather than the exception. How each dimension might impact child development is likely related to other dimensions of the family context in which marital conflict is embedded.

Frequency and intensity. Numerous studies have shown a positive association between the frequency of parental arguments and level of maladjustment in children. Frequency has been linked to conduct problems, anger and insecurity, and academic difficulties (Cummings and Davies 1994). Although a majority of the studies in this area rely exclusively on self-report measures, the data are supported by results from studies utilizing laboratory and observational methodologies. Exposure to interadult anger under controlled, laboratory-based settings has been linked with increased distress and aggression in children. Parental monitoring of conflict at home also has been found to be associated with behavioral and emotional difficulties in children. In a series of studies, mothers were taught how to keep a daily diary of conflict events at home. Reports of more frequent interparental conflict were associated with greater distress, insecurity, and anger in children (Cummings and Davies 1994). Similarly, intensity of arguments has been shown to be linked to more anger, sadness, concern, and helplessness in children as well as to higher levels of behavior problems (Grych and Fincham 1993; Kerig 1996).

Content. The content or topic of parental disputes is another important domain of marital conflict. Conflict that is child-related has been associated with children's report of higher levels of shame, self-blame for the conflict, and fear of being drawn in to the conflict (Grych and Fincham 1993). Parental arguments or disagreements about childrearing policies and strategies have been shown to better predict child difficulties than other dimensions of marital dysfunction, including global marital distress and or nonchild-related fights (Jouriles et al. 1991).

Resolution. In addition to how parents express their anger, the extent to which disagreements are resolved also matters. Resolution is probably best described as residing along a continuum, from no resolution to complete resolution (Cummings and Davies 1994). Higher degrees of resolution have been shown to be associated with reduced levels of distress in children. In fact, even partially resolved disputes are associated with reductions in children's anger as compared to unresolved fights. Laboratory studies have found children's responses to background anger (from unknown adults) that is followed by a complete resolution are comparable to reactions to entirely friendly interactions (see Cummings and Davies 1994).

Individual Protective Factors

Protective factors refer to the processes that reduce the probability of negative developmental outcomes occurring despite the presence of some psychosocial or biological hazard, or risk factor (Margolin, Oliver, and Medina 2001). The marital conflict literature has identified several individual child characteristics that serve not only to reduce a child's level of vulnerability to a stressor such as marital conflict, but in many cases to lead to adaptive outcomes. Some of these characteristics include cognitive appraisals, coping responses, intelligence, and emotional responsiveness. Children who report less self-blame, less threat, and more resolution have better outcomes, as do children who utilize emotion-focused (how to regulate stressful emotions within oneself), rather than problem-focused coping (trying to manage or alter the conflict) (Margolin, Oliver, and Medina 2001).

More effective coping strategies appear, in particular, to reduce the likelihood of anxiety and depression symptoms (Kerig 2001). As is the case with other risk factors, children with higher levels of intelligence tend to fare better in the context of marital conflict than do children with lower levels of intelligence (Katz and Gottman 1997), though this may be due its association with the development of more effective coping resources. In addition, several lines of research suggest that focusing on children's emotional responses to conflict is important. How children evaluate the conflict, their emotional reaction to it, and how they regulate affect all play a role in determining children's adjustment (Crockenberg and Langrock 2001).

Conclusion

Although the magnitude of the relationship is not always large, an association between interparental conflict and child maladjustment is a robust finding in the literature. Exposure to conflict by parents, however, though it increases the probability of adjustment difficulties in children, appears to lead to serious maladaptive outcomes in a relatively small percentage of children (Fincham 1998). Goals of future research include developing a better understanding of how demographic variables such as sex and ethnicity/race and individual differences in cognition and emotion intersect with each other and with other elements of family functioning (e.g., parenting) in determining the impact of marital conflict on children.

See also: ATTACHMENT: PARENT-CHILD RELATIONSHIPS; CONFLICT: COUPLE RELATIONSHIPS; CONFLICT: FAMILY RELATIONSHIPS; CONDUCT DISORDER; COPARENTING; DEPRESSION: CHILDREN AND ADOLESCENTS; DEVELOPMENTAL PSYCHOPATHOLOGY; DIVORCE: EFFECTS ON CHILDREN; INTERPARENTAL VIOLENCE—EFFECTS ON CHILDREN; JUVENILE DELINQUENCY; MARITAL QUALITY; REMARRIAGE; TRIANGULATION

Bibliography

Coiro, M. J., and Emery, R. E. (1998). "Do Marriage Problems Affect Fathering More than Mothering? A Quantitative and Qualitative Review." *Clinical Child and Family Psychology Review* 1:23–40.

Cox, M. J.; Paley, B.; and Harter, K. (2001). "Interparental Conflict and Parent-Child Relationships." In *Interparental Conflict and Child Development,* ed. J. H.

Grych and F. D. Fincham. Cambridge, UK: Cambridge University Press.

Crockenberg, S. L., and Covey, S. (1991). "Marital Conflict and Externalizing Behavior in Children." In *Models and Integrations,* vol. 3 of *Rochester Symposium on Developmental Psychopathology,* ed. D. Cicchetti and S. Toth. Rochester, NY: University of Rochester Press.

Crockenberg, S. L., and Langrock, A. (2001). "The Role of Emotion and Emotional Regulation in Children's Responses to Interparental Conflict." In *Interparental Conflict and Child Development,* ed. J. H. Grych and F. D. Fincham. Cambridge: Cambridge University Press.

Cummings, E. M., and Davies, P. (1994). *Children and Marital Conflict: The Impact of Family Dispute and Resolution.* New York: Guilford Press.

Cummings, E. M.; Davies, P. T.; and and Campbell, S. B. (2000). "Children and the Marital Subsystem." In *Developmental Psychopathology and Family Process: Theory, Research, and Clinical Implications,* ed. E. M. Cummings, P. T. Davies, and S. B. Campbell. New York: Guilford Press.

Davies, P. T., and Cummings, E. M. (1994). "Marital Conflict and Child Adjustment: An Emotional Security Hypothesis." *Psychological Bulletin* 116:387–411.

Davies, P. T, and Lindsay, L. L. (2001). "Does Gender Moderate the Effects of Marital Conflict on Children?" In *Interparental Conflict and Child Development,* ed. J. H. Grych and F. D. Fincham. Cambridge, UK: Cambridge University Press.

Erel, O., and Burman, B. (1995). "Interrelatedness of Marital Relations and Parent-Child Relations: A Meta-Analytic Review." *Psychological Bulletin* 118:108–132.

Fincham, F. (1998). "Child Development and Marital Relations." *Child Development* 69:543–574.

Grych, J. H., and Cardoza-Fernandes, S. (2001). "Understanding the Impact of Interparental Conflict on Children: The Role of Social Cognitive Processes." In *Interparental Conflict and Child Development,* ed. J. H. Grych and F. D. Fincham. Cambridge, UK: Cambridge University Press.

Grych, J. H., and Fincham, F. D. (1990). "Marital Conflict and Children's Adjustment: A Cognitive-Contextual Framework." *Psychological Bulletin* 108:267–290.

Grych, J. H., and Fincham, F. D. (1993). "Children's Appraisals of Marital Conflict: Initial Investigations of the Cognitive-Contextual Framework." *Child Development* 64:215–230.

Grych, J. H.; Fincham, F. D.; Jouriles, E. N.; and McDonald, R. (2000). "Interparental Conflict and Child Adjustment: Testing the Mediational Role of Appraisals in the Cognitive-Contextual Framework." *Child Development* 71:1648–1661.

Howes, P., and Markman, H. J. (1989). "Marital Quality and Child Functioning: A Longitudinal Investigation." *Child Development* 60:1044–1051.

Jouriles, E. N.; Murphy, C. M.; Farris, A. M.; Smith, D. A.; Richters, J. E.; and Waters, E. (1991). "Marital Adjustment, Parental Disagreements about Child-Rearing, and Behavioral Problems in Boys: Increasing the Specificity of the Marital Assessment." *Child Development* 62:1424–1433.

Katz, L. F., and Gottman, J. M. (1997). "Buffering Children from Marital Conflict and Dissolution." *Journal of Clinical Child Psychology* 26:157–171.

Kerig, P. K. (1995). "Triangles in the Family Circle: Effects of Family Structure on Marriage, Parenting, and Child Adjustment." *Journal of Family Psychology* 9:28–43.

Kerig, P. K. (1996). "Assessing the Links between Interparental Conflict and Child Adjustment: The Conflicts and Problem-Solving Scales." *Journal of Family Psychology* 10:454–473.

Kerig, P. K. (2001). "Children's Coping with Interparental Conflict." In *Interparental Conflict and Child Development,* ed. J. H. Grych and F. D. Fincham. Cambridge, UK: Cambridge University Press.

Lindahl, K. M.; Clements, M.; and Markman, H. (1997). "Predicting Marital and Parent Functioning in Dyads and Triads: A Longitudinal Investigation of Marital Processes." *Journal of Family Psychology* 11:139–151.

Malik, N. M., and Lindahl, K. M. (2001). "Relations among Family Subsystems: Marital Power, Family Processes, and Ethnicity." Paper presented at the 109th annual meeting of the American Psychological Association, 24–28 August, San Francisco, California.

Margolin, G.; Oliver, P. H.; and Medina, A. M. (2001). "Conceptual Issues in Understanding the Relation between Interparental Conflict and Child Adjustment: Integrating Developmental Psychopathology and Risk/Resilience Perspectives." In *Interparental Conflict and Child Development,* ed. J. H. Grych and F. D. Fincham. Cambridge, UK: Cambridge University Press.

McLoyd, V. C.; Harper, C. I.; and Copeland, N. L. (2001). "Ethnic Minority Status, Interparental Conflict, and Child Adjustment." In *Interparental Conflict and Child Development,* ed. J. H. Grych and F. D. Fincham. Cambridge, UK: Cambridge University Press.

Owen, M. T., and Cox, M. J. (1997). "Marital Conflict and the Development of Infant-Parent Attachment Relationships." *Journal of Family Psychology* 11:152–164.

Parke, R. D., and Tinsley, B. J. (1987). "Family Interaction in Infancy." In *Handbook of Infant Development*, ed. J. Osofsky. New York: Wiley.

Shaw, D. S.; Winslow, E. B.; and Flanagan, C. (1999). "A Prospective Study of the Effects of Marital Status and Family Relations on Young Children's Adjustment among African American and European American Families." *Child Development* 70:742–755.

KRISTIN LINDAHL

INTERPARENTAL VIOLENCE– EFFECTS ON CHILDREN

Exposure to violence in the home provides a major threat to children's development worldwide where it is estimated that 33 percent of women have been assaulted or abused by a male spouse or family member (Heise, Ellsberg, and Gottemoeller 1999). As shown in a sampling from different countries, estimates of incidence vary: China, 29 percent (Family Violence Prevention Foundation 2001b); Chile, 60 percent; Japan, 59 percent (Family Violence Prevention Foundation 2001h); Peru, 90 percent (Human Rights Watch 2001); South Africa, 25 percent (Family Violence Prevention Foundation 2001f); United States, 31 percent (Commonwealth Fund 1999); Russia, 81 percent of domestic crimes were against women (Family Violence Prevention Foundation 2001e); and Canada, 48 percent (Rodgers 1994).

Children's exposure to woman abuse is not assessed in most countries. However, in Australia 23 percent of young people surveyed had witnessed an incident of physical or domestic violence against their mothers or stepmothers (Indermaur 2001). In the United States it is estimated that as many as 10 million children are exposed to violence between their parents each year (Straus 1992), and that slightly more than half of female victims of intimate violence live in households with children under age 12 (U.S. Department of Justice 1998).

The Impact of Exposure

Research suggests that exposed children are, on average, at greater risk for school, social and behavioral problems (see reviews in Jaffe, Wolfe, and Wilson 1990; Rossman, Hughes, and Rosenberg 2000). Exposure is defined as children's seeing, hearing, or perceiving the effects of physical aggression between their parenting figures, and perhaps should also include the psychological abuse and verbal hostility that often accompany it. Greater frequency and duration of exposure and whether children have also been personally abused are associated with greater child problems. In addition, children's perceptions of the properties of the conflict and associated attributions appear to play a role in their reactions (Cummings and Davies 1996; Grych, Sied, and Fincham 1992; Laumakis, Margolin, and John 1998). Conflicts that are unresolved, involve threats to leave or of physical aggression, are about the child, seem more severe and frequent, and elicit more self-blame are linked to greater distress. Though much work has been done with shelter-resident children who experience additional stresses of relocation, major findings have been replicated with exposed community children.

Children exposed to violence demonstrate emotional and behavioral problems at both ends of the spectrum, including symptoms of *internalizing* (e.g., depression, anxiety, somatic complaints) and *externalizing* (e.g., aggression, misbehavior, impulsivity) more than similar nonexposed children do. Teachers also reported these differences (Sternberg, Lamb, and Dawad-Noursi 1998). Exposed preschoolers and toddlers are thought to be at greater risk due to their greater likelihood of exposure (Fantuzzo et al. 1997), their less well-developed cognitive and emotion regulation skills for coping, and their dependence on the reactions of family members for information about the meaning of the conflict. However, they tend to show lower levels of behavioral problems, more of which are internalizing types of problems. There may be an age-by-gender interaction for older children wherein school-age boys and adolescent girls are showing greater externalizing problems.

Research of the trauma status of exposed children has revealed that 20 to 50 percent of children are diagnosable with Posttraumatic Stress Disorder (PTSD) (Rossman and Ho 2000). Additional risks come from children's frequent exposure to reminders of marital aggression, as well as ongoing parental violence that is associated with poorer child outcomes a year later (e.g., Rossman 2000).

Research also identifies possible information processing and social cognition problems for exposed children. For example, although cognitive strengths are seen as a protective factor (Masten 2001), this may be problematic for exposed children who perform significantly lower on math and reading achievement tests than similar nonexposed children (Pepler and Moore 1989). Associated with greater exposure history, one study (Medina, Margolin, and Wilcox 2000) found that children scored better on *attention,* but poorer on *delayed recall* following the eliciting of emotional arousal by having children listen to tapes of adult conflict. Using a similar conflict tape exposure priming paradigm, Mary O'Brien and Calvin Chin (1998) showed that older school-age children in high-conflict families were more accurately able to recognize aggressive words they had heard previously, but also more likely to misidentify new aggressive words, suggesting a memory bias or sensitization to marital conflict. Similarly, more children from violent families residing in shelters than controls expected taped ambiguous adult and peer interactions to end in aggression, displaying an aggressive bias (Mallah, West, and Rossman 2001) that could constitute a risk for social development.

Social support is often considered a protective factor, yet extant research suggests that social relationships and problem-solving strategies are problematic for exposed children who have fewer social problem-solving strategies (and most of those strategies are aggressive [e.g., Margolin 1998]). Sandra Graham-Bermann and colleagues (1996) found that greater positive relationships in or outside the family were associated with fewer behavior problems for exposed children, whereas Laura McCloskey and colleagues (1995) did not. Thus, the role of social support is unclear.

Effects on Parent-Child Relationships

Parental well-being and parenting practices could constitute protective factors for exposed children. E. Mark Cummings and Patrick Davies (1996) speculate that the negative effects of parental conflict result from challenges to children's sense of emotional security. These seem likely in violent families, because poverty, emotional distress, parenting stress, and negative life events are generally greater for battered than nonbattered mothers (e.g., Holden et al. 1998). Battered mothers report

being less emotionally available to their children than do nonbattered mothers (Holden et al. 1998). However, battered mothers do not report greater corporal punishment, but are less proactive in avoiding power struggles (Holden et al. 1998). Battered mothers do report being less consistent in their discipline (Holden and Ritchie 1991), and endorse a mixture of parenting practices that are internally inconsistent (Rossman and Rea 2001), likely being impacted by their partner's violence. Nonetheless, observations of battered mothers' warmth and authority-control were predictive of children's prosocial behaviors (Levendosky and Graham-Bermann 2000), suggesting that warmth and consistency in parenting may act as a protective factor for children.

Longer-Term Effects

Although most studies are of concurrent impact, a few short-term prospective studies have been done. George Holden and colleagues (1998) found some improvement in behavior problems at six months following shelter stay, and Robert Emery (1996) also found improvement at twelve months for children in families where violence ceased. B. B. Robbie Rossman (2000) found violence cessation and modest services (6–12 sessions) were predictive of better child outcome one year later. It appears that violence cessation and intervention may be protective factors for children. Longer-term retrospective studies (e.g., Maker, Kemmelmeier, and Peterson 1998) do suggest that exposure effects may be carried into adult relationships.

One complication in interpreting impact research is that most participants have been from lower-income families, meaning that exposure often covaries with poverty and family stressors. A family's economic distress appears to provide a risk for children, because poverty may make it more likely that parents will be distressed, depressed, or nonsupportive, or provide harsh and inconsistent discipline (e.g., Harnish, Dodge, and Valente 1995).

Cultural Diversity

A further limitation of existing impact research is that it is based on work with Caucasian or mixed ethnicity families where cultural differences are not targeted (although see Sternberg et al. 1993 for Israeli youth). However, children's reactions to parental violence may vary from culture to culture. It is important to note that within a particular cultural background there are also large individual differences among families in acculturation or biculturation (e.g., Dana 1993), and that, for many families of color, the nuclear family and extended family may play a more central role than for Caucasian families. Many factors besides domestic violence, including poverty and immigrant status, affect ethnically diverse women and their families (Kanuha 1997), which makes the picture complex.

Although information specific to interparental violence is lacking, it appears that the way in which children express distress may vary somewhat from culture to culture. To summarize, there may be a tendency for Asian and American-Indian children and Latino girls to express distress in internalizing ways and for African-American children and Latino boys to show greater externalizing behavioral difficulties (e.g., Allen and Majidi-Ahi 1989; Ramirez 1989; Weisz et al. 1993). Nonetheless, the school problems and suicide rates that mark distress across ethnic backgrounds suggest that non-Caucasian children experience adversity, including interparental conflict, at equal if not higher rates than their Caucasian peers.

In other words, exposure to marital conflict and aggression can be traumatic and is associated with poorer academic, behavioral, and social outcomes for many children. More knowledge is needed about underlying mechanisms and risk and protective factors associated with outcomes for exposed children of all nationalities and ethnicities in the short and longer term.

Prevention and Intervention Programs

Fortunately, many professionals worldwide have been working on the development of prevention and intervention programs. These efforts raise several issues: who receives services; what programs are available; what are program goals; and how effective are the programs.

Primary prevention efforts, by definition, assume that all children and adults can benefit from programs designed to reduce domestic violence by promoting skills and understandings that facilitate forming nonviolent relationships. For school age children such programs are often psychoeducational and delivered through the schools. Successful programs have typically included topics such as identification of feelings, anger management, family roles, friendship skills, and self-esteem enhancement (Wolfe and Jaffe 2001). Trauma-oriented treatment may be delivered in individual sessions (e.g., Kerig et al. 2000) through trauma play, systematic desensitization, or cognitive behavioral therapy.

For prevention among high risk families with children below school-age, home-based intervention programs with maternal support and parenting training have been successful in reducing child abuse and improving children's adaptive functioning (e.g., Olds et al. 1997). Some preventive programs have targeted primarily adults and provided community resources designed to reduce family violence by decreasing parental stress and increasing parental skills (e.g., Braden and Hightower 1998).

Multifaceted intervention programs may be the most useful, and typically provide services for exposed children and their battered mothers (see review by Graham-Bermann 2001), and sometimes for abusive fathers (e.g., Peled and Edleson 1995). Many intervention programs for exposed children and mothers have been developed through clinical necessity and delivered through community shelters and domestic violence agencies. These ten- to twelve-week programs are usually offered to small groups (six to nine) of children of approximately the same age, and are intended for mild to moderately distressed children. Research suggests that there is substantial variability in the severity of exposed children's problems, meaning that intervention plans need to include assessment and treatment additional to or preceding children's participation in group programs for the 35 to 50 percent of exposed children with problems in the clinically significant range (Carlson 1996).

Peter Jaffe and his colleagues (1990) and Einat Peled and Diane Davis (1995) have developed programs that serve as prototypes for many existing group programs for children. Group programs for children typically cover the following topics: education about interparental violence, gender role stereotypes, and attributions of responsibility for the violence; emotion identification, expression and management skills, particularly for anger and fear; social skills, social problem-solving and the building of support systems; self-esteem enhancement; safety planning; and understanding children's schemas about others and their wishes for their family.

A new and promising form of intervention for exposed children involves taking services to families in their homes (Rossman, Hughes, and Rosenberg 2000), which facilitates extended service provision. A successful home-based intervention for battered mothers of oppositional defiant or conducted disordered boys, ages four to nine, found that these boys' conduct problems were reduced over eight months of follow-up for families receiving home-based versus only typical services (Jouriles et al. 2001). Such results are promising and dictate the need for further program delivery and evaluation efforts.

Initial prevention efforts to combat domestic violence are underway in many countries. Some examples include the Project Against Domestic Violence in Cambodia (Family Violence Prevention Foundation 2001a); Harmony House Limited in Hong Kong (Family Violence Prevention Foundation 2001c); Jagori in India (Family Violence Prevention Foundation 2001d); the Russian Association of Crisis Centers for Women (Human Rights Watch World Report 2001) and, the Agisanang Domestic Abuse Prevention and Training clinic in South Africa (Family Violence Prevention Foundation 2001f). Although these initial efforts are often directed toward education, legislation, public awareness, and the needs of battered women, such programs provide the promise of a brighter future for their children.

See also: CHILD ABUSE: PSYCHOLOGICAL MALTREATMENT; CONDUCT DISORDER; CONFLICT: COUPLE RELATIONSHIPS; CONFLICT: FAMILY RELATIONSHIPS; DEPRESSION: CHILDREN AND ADOLESCENTS; DEVELOPMENT: COGNITIVE; DEVELOPMENT: EMOTIONAL; DEVELOPMENTAL PSYCHOPATHOLOGY; DIVORCE: EFFECTS ON CHILDREN; INTERPARENTAL CONFLICT—EFFECTS ON CHILDREN; MARITAL QUALITY; POSTTRAUMATIC STRESS DISORDER (PTSD); SPOUSE ABUSE: PREVALENCE; SPOUSE ABUSE: THEORETICAL EXPLANATIONS

Bibliography

Allen, L., and Majidi-Ahi, S. (1989). "Black American Children." In *Children of Color: Psychological Interventions with Minority Youth,* ed. J. T. Gibbs and L. N. Huang. San Francisco: Jossey-Bass.

Braden, J. P., and Hightower, A. D. (1998). "Prevention." In *The Practice of Child Psychotherapy,* 3rd edition, ed. R. J. Morris and T. R. Kratochwill. Needham Heights, MA: Allyn and Bacon.

Carlson, B. E. (1996). "Children of Battered Women: Research, Programs, and Services." In *Helping Battered Women: New Perspectives and Remedies,* ed. A. R. Roberts. New York: Oxford University Press.

Commonwealth Fund. (1999, May). Health Concerns Across a Woman's Life Span: 1998 Survey of Women's Health.

Cummings, E. M., and Davies, P. T. (1996). "Emotional Security as a Regulatory Process in Normal Development and the Development of Psychopathology." *Development and Psychopathology* 8:123–139.

Dana, R. H. (1993). *Multicultural Assessment Perspectives for Professional Psychology.* Needham Heights, MA: Allyn and Bacon.

Emery, R. E. (1996). "A Longitudinal Study of Battered Women and Their Children: One Year Following Shelter Residence." Paper presented at the First International Conference on Children Exposed to Family Violence, June 1996, Austin, Texas.

Fantuzzo, J. W.; Boruch, R.; Beriana, A.; Atkins, M.; and Marcus, S. (1997). Domestic Violence and Children: Prevalence and Risk in Five Major Cities. *Journal of the American Academy of Child and Adolescent Psychiatry* 36:116–122.

Graham-Bermann, S. A. (2001). "Designing Intervention Evaluations for Children Exposed to Domestic Violence: Applications of Research and Theory." In *Domestic Violence in the Lives of Children: The Future of Research, Intervention, and Social Policy,* ed. S. A. Graham-Bermann and J. L. Edleson. Washington, DC: American Psychological Association.

Graham-Bermann, S. A.; Banyard, V.; Coupet, S.; Egler, L.; and Mattis, J. (1996). "The Interpersonal Relationships and Adjustment of Children in Homeless and Economically Distressed Families." *Journal of Clinical Child Psychology* 25:250–261.

Grych, J. H.; Sied, M.; and Fincham, F. D. (1992). "Assessing Marital Conflict from the Child's Perspective: The Children's Perception of Interparental Conflict Scale." *Child Development* 63:558–572.

Harnish, J. D.; Dodge, K. A.; and Valente, E. (1995). "Mother-Child Interaction Quality As a Partial Mediator of the Roles of Maternal Depressive Symptomatology and Socioeconomic Status in the Development of Child Behavior Problems." *Child Development* 66:739–753.

Heise, L.; Ellsberg, M.; and Gottemoeller, M. (1999, December). "Ending Violence against Women." The Commonwealth Fund: Population Reports, Series L, No. 11.

Holden, G. W., and Ritchie, K. L. (1991). "Linking Extreme Marital Discord, Child Rearing, and Child Behavior Problems: Evidence from Battered Women." *Child Development* 62:311–327.

Holden, G. W.; Stein, J. D.; Ritchie, K. L.; Harris, S. D.; and Jouriles, E. N. (1998). "Parenting Behaviors and Beliefs of Battered Women." In *Children Exposed to Marital Violence: Theory, Research, and Applied Issues,* ed. G. W. Holden, R. Geffner, and E. N. Jouriles. Washington, DC: American Psychological Association.

Jaffe, P. G.; Wolfe, D. A.; and Wilson, S. K. (1990). *Children of Battered Women.* Newbury Park, CA: Sage Publications.

Jouriles, E. M.; McDonald, R.; Spiller, L.; Norwood, W. D.; Swank, P. R.; Stephens, N.; Ware, H. S.; and Buzy, W. M. (2001). "Reducing Conduct Problems among Children of Battered Women." *Journal of Clinical and Consulting Psychology* 69:774–785.

Kanuha, V. (1997). "Women of Color in Battering Relationships." *Woman of Color: Integrating Ethnic and Gender Identities in Psychotherapy,* ed. L. Comas-Diaz and B. Greene. New York: Guilford Press.

Kerig, P. K.; Fedorowicz, A. E.; Brown, C. A.; and Warren, M. (2000). "Assessment and Intervention for PTSD in Children Exposed to Violence." In *Children Exposed to Domestic Violence: Current Issues in Research, Intervention, Prevention, and Policy Development,* ed. R. A. Geffner, P. G. Jaffe, and M. Sudermann. Binghamton, NY: Haworth Press.

Laumakis, M.; Margolin, G.; and John, R. S. (1998). "Children's Emotional, Cognitive and Coping Reactions to Specific Dimensions of Marital Conflict." In *Children Exposed to Marital Violence: Theory, Research, and Applied Issues,* ed. G. W. Holden, R. Geffner, and E. N. Jouriles. Washington, DC: American Psychological Association.

Levendosky, A. A., and Graham-Bermann, S. A. (2000). "Behavioral Observations of Parenting in Battered Women." *Journal of Family Psychology* 14:1–15.

Maker, A. H.; Kemmelmeier, M.; and Peterson, C. (1998). "Longterm Psychological Consequences in Women of Witnessing Parental Physical Conflict and Experiencing Abuse in Childhood." *Journal of Interpersonal Violence* 13:574–589.

Mallah, K.; West, J.; and Rossman, B. B. R. (2001). "The Concurrent and Prospective Relationship of Aggressive Expectations to Adaptive Functioning for Children Exposed to Family Conflict and Violence." Denver, CO: University of Denver, Department of Psychology (under review).

Margolin, G. (1998). "Effects of Domestic Violence on Children." In *Violence Against Children in the Family and Community,* ed. P. K. Trickett and C. Schellenbach. Washington, DC: American Psychological Association.

Masten, A. S. (2001). "Ordinary Magic: Resilience Processes in Development." *American Psychologist* 56:227–238.

McCloskey, L. A.; Figueredo, A. J.; and Koss, M. P. (1995). "The Effects of Systemic Family Violence on Children's Mental Health." *Child Development* 66:1239–1261.

Medina, A. M.; Margolin, G.; and Wilcox, R. R. (2000). "Family Hostility and Children's Cognitive Processes." *Behavior Therapy* 31:667–684.

O'Brien, M., and Chin, C. (1998). "The Relationship Between Children's Reported Exposure to Interparental Conflict and Memory Biases in the Recognition of Aggressive and Constructive Conflict Words." *Personality and Social Psychology Bulletin* 24:647–656.

Olds, D.; Kitman, H.; Cole, R.; and Robinson, J. (1997). "Theoretical Foundations of a Program of Home Visitation for Pregnant Women and Parents of Young Children." *Journal of Community Psychology* 25:9–25.

Peled, E., and Davis, D. (1995). *Group Work with Child Witnesses of Domestic Violence: A Practitioner's Manual.* Thousand Oaks, CA: Sage Publications.

Peled, E., and Edleson, J. L. (1995). "Process and Outcome in Small Groups for Children of Battered Women." In *Ending the Cycle of Violence: Community Responses to Children of Battered Women,* ed. E. Peled, P. G. Jaffe, and J. L. Edleson. Newbury Park, CA: Sage Publications.

Pepler, D. J., and Moore, T. E. (1989). "Children Exposed to Family Violence: Home Environments and Cognitive Functioning." Paper presented at the meeting of the Society for Research in Child Development, March 1989, Kansas City, Missouri.

Ramirez, O. (1989). "Mexican-American Children and Adolescents." In *Children of Color: Psychological Interventions with Minority Youth,* ed. J. T. Gibbs and L. N. Huang. San Francisco: Jossey-Bass.

Rodgers, K. (1994). "Wife Assault: The Findings of a National Survey." *Juristat* 14:9

Rossman, B. B. R. (2000). "Time Heals All: How Much and for Whom?" *Journal of Emotional Abuse* 2:31–50.

Rossman, B. B. R., and Ho, J. (2000). "Posttraumatic Response and Children Exposed to Parental Violence." In *Children Exposed to Domestic Violence: Current Issues in Research, Intervention, Prevention, and Policy*

Development, ed. R. A. Geffner, P. G. Jaffe, and M. Sudermann. Binghamton, NY: Haworth Press.

Rossman, B. B. R.; Hughes, H. M.; and Rosenberg, M. S. (2000). *Children in Violent Families: The Impact of Exposure.* Washington, DC: Taylor and Francis.

Rossman, B. B. R., and Rea, J. (2002, accepted for publication). "The Relation of Parenting Styles and Inconsistencies to Adaptive Functioning for Children in Conflictual and Violent Families." *Journal of Family Violence.*

Sternberg, K. J.; Lamb, M. E.; and Dawud-Noursi, S. (1998). "Using Multiple Informants to Understand Domestic Violence and Its Effects." In *Children Exposed to Marital Violence: Theory, Research, and Applied Issues,* ed. G. W. Holden, R. A.Geffner, and E. N. Jouriles. Washington, DC: American Psychological Association.

Sternberg, K. L.; Lamb, M. E.; Greenbaum, C.; Cicchetti, D.; Dawud, S.; Cortes, R. M.; Krispin, O.; and Lorey, F. (1993). "Effects of Domestic Violence on Children's Behavior Problems and Depression." *Developmental Psychology* 29:44–52.

Straus, M. A. (1992). "Children as Witness to Marital Violence: A Risk Factor for Life Long Problems among a Nationally Representative Sample of American Men and Women." In *Children and Violence* (Report of the 23rd Ross Roundtable on Critical Approaches to Common Pediatric Problems), ed. D. F. Schwarz. Columbus, OH: Ross Laboratories.

U.S. Department of Justice. (1998). Violence by Intimates: Analysis of Data on Crimes by Current or Former Spouses, Boyfriends, and Girlfriends. Washington, DC: National Institute of Justice.

Weisz, J. R.; Suwanlert, S.; Chaiyasit, W.; Weiss, B.; Achenbach, T.; and Eastman, K. L. (1993). "Behavioral and Emotional Problems among Thai and American Adolescents: Parent Reports for Ages 12–16." *Journal of Abnormal Psychology* 102:395–403.

Wolfe, D. A., and Jaffe, P. G. (2001). "Prevention of Domestic Violence: Emerging Initiatives." In *Domestic Violence in the Lives of Children: The Future of Research, Intervention, and Social Policy,* ed. S. A. Graham-Bermann and J. L. Edleson. Washington, DC: American Psychological Association.

Other Resources
Family Violence Prevention Foundation. (2001a). *Global Frontlines: Cambodia. Document No. 98.* Available from http://www.endabuse.org/programs.

Family Violence Prevention Foundation. (2001b). *Global Frontlines: China. Document No. 100.* Available from http://www.endabuse.org/programs.

Family Violence Prevention Foundation. (2001c). *Global Frontlines: Hong Kong. Document No. 75.* Available from http://www.endabuse.org/programs.

Family Violence Prevention Foundation. (2001d). *Global Frontlines: India. Document No. 102.* Available from http://www.endabuse.org/programs.

Family Violence Prevention Foundation. (2001e). *Global Frontlines: Russia. Document No. 106.* Available from http://www.endabuse.org/programs.

Family Violence Prevention Foundation. (2001f). *Global Frontlines: South Africa. Document No. 108.* Available from http://www.endabuse.org/programs.

Family Violence Prevention Foundation (2001g). *Global Solutions.* Available from http://www.endabuse.org/newsflash./index.

Family Violence Prevention Foundation. (2001h). *International Programs: Global Frontlines Catalogue.* Available from http://www.endabuse.org/programs/international

Human Rights Watch World Report. (2001). *Violence against Women.* Available from http://www.hrw.org/wr2k1/women/women2.html.

Indermaur, D. (2001). *Young Australians and Domestic Violence. Publication No. 195.* Available from http://www.aic.gov.au.

B. B. ROBBIE ROSSMAN

INTERRACIAL MARRIAGE

Interracial marriage is the term used to describe marriages that take place between people who are from different racial or ethnic groups. *Intercultural marriages* are defined as marriages between people who come from two different cultural backgrounds. A marriage between a woman from China, whose culture emphasizes the needs of the family over the needs of the individual, and a man from the United States, whose culture emphasizes individual autonomy, would be an example of a intercultural marriage. Whereas relationships between people from different ethnic and cultural groups are becoming increasingly common, there are substantial increases in the number of individuals engaging in interracial or intercultural marriages.

However, even though the number and societal acceptance of interracial marriages is growing, little has been written about these marriages, the reasons for their increase, or their strengths and liabilities.

Growth of Interracial Marriage

The United States has historically promoted the concept of purity, or the separation of the races. Laws were enacted to keep the races separate and to prohibit marriages between members of different races, especially between people who by virtue of marriage would not maintain the purity of racial-ethnic groups. These laws were often specifically worded to make marriages illegal between Caucasians and African Americans (Davis 1991). In 1664 Maryland enacted the first anti-miscegenation law in the United States, and by the 1700s five additional states had enacted such laws. Between 1942 and 1967, fourteen states repealed these laws through legislative action. In 1967 the Supreme Court of the United States (*Loving v. Virginia*) declared anti-miscegenation laws unconstitutional. However, due to the stigma associated with these unions, the court's decision resulted in little increase in the numbers of interracial marriages.

The number of interracial marriages has steadily grown since the 1980s and has increased rapidly in the early twenty-first century. The U.S. Census Bureau reported that in 1990 there were 1,348,000 interracial marriages, compared to 651,000 in 1980. The growth of interracial marriages is even more pronounced when one notes that the 1960 statistics indicated only 149,000 interracial marriages. The rise in interracial marriages in the United States coincides with changes in the legal status of interracial marriages and in the changing attitudes of Americans towards individuals engaged in interracial marriages and relationships. In U.S. Census Bureau (2000) data, the number of interracial marriages rose to slightly more than 3,000,000 and comprised approximately 5.5 percent of all marriages. Some of the growth can be accounted for by declining societal prejudice towards—and less shame experienced by—people in interracial marriages. In addition, changes in the census forms encourage individuals to identify all parts of their racial composition.

The growth in interracial marriages is not occurring only in the United States. For example, the number of interracial marriages in China between Shanghainese (individuals who live in Shanghai, China) and individuals from other countries increased 67 percent from 1991 to 1992. In 1996, 3.5 percent of the marriages in Shanghai took place between Shanghainese with foreigners.

The growth in interracial marriages is not uniform. In other words, interracial marriages have become more common for some racial and ethnic groups, but not for others. In the United States it is estimated that 40.6 percent of Japanese Americans and 53.7 percent of Native Americans engage in interracial marriages. However, only 1.2 percent of black women and 3.6 percent of black males engage in interracial marriages. According to Anita Foeman and Teresa Nance (1999), these small percentages are due in part to the continued condemnation of black-white intermixing.

Difficulties in Interracial Marriages

The problems encountered by interracial couples are often the result of negative societal attitudes about interracial relationships. Black-Caucasian unions have the lowest frequency of occurrence because of longstanding negative beliefs about these marriages. Studies have indicated that, in general, Caucasians tend to disapprove of interracial marriages, and blacks tend to approve. Other research suggests that people engage in interracial relationships due to self-hate or rebelliousness. In addition, there is some question as to whether or not partners in interracial relationships reciprocate love (Gaines et al. 1999). Given that the dominant culture tends to disdain black-Caucasian unions, it is difficult to imagine how these couples are able to maintain their relationships.

Asian Americans have also experienced difficulties in their interracial marriages. Asian Americans engage in more interracial relationships than any other racial or ethnic group in the United States. Laws forbidding interracial marriages between Asians and Caucasians were common in the United States. For example, in 1901 California extended the 1850 Marriage Regulation Act to include Mongolians (i.e., Chinese, Japanese, Koreans), and in 1933 the law was further extended to include Malays (i.e., Filipinos) (Kitano, Fugino, and Sato 1998). These laws, like all other anti-miscegenation laws, were overturned following a state judicial decision in California (*Perez v. Sharp* 1948) and a 1967 U.S. Supreme Court decision

(*Loving v. Virginia*). Even though the results of these cases made interracial marriages legal, the negative societal perspective on such unions has been slow to change.

Bok-Lim Kim (1998) points out that since World War II, marriages between Asian women (specifically women from Japan, South Korea, the Philippines, and Vietnam) and U.S. military men have become a legacy of United States military involvement. He notes that many of those marriages took place because of the low socioeconomic status of many of the women who lived near U.S. military bases, and the low self-esteem experienced as a result of their low economic conditions. He also points out that these interracial marriages displayed undaunted courage and optimism in spite of the obstacles they faced due to language and cultural differences and the lack of support from their families and communities in both countries. However, Kim also points out that the Asian women often carry the burden of cultural norms that provide severe penalties for marriage outside their ethnic group (out-marriages). Even though there has been improvement in the acceptance of Asian out-marriages by their families, there continue to be difficulties because of cultural differences.

Interracial relationships and marriages remain controversial for several additional reasons. Many Asian Americans are alarmed because of the rising number of interracial unions, which they believe reduces the pool of eligible men and women who could otherwise engage in same-culture unions. Some Asian Americans are concerned that, because of the high number of out-marriages, distinct groups of Asians may disappear within a few generations. Additionally, whereas so many Asian women are out-marrying, there is the fear that many Asian-American men will remain unmarried because of the dwindling number of available Asian-American women (Fujino 1997). A similar fear is expressed by African-American men and women. As African-American men and women increase their level of education and move to higher economic levels, fewer and fewer members of their race are available for marriage. This often leads to frustration on the part of African Americans who seek to marry someone of their own race, and also leads to increased levels of out-marriage, as increases in income and educational levels occur.

Some of the difficulties experienced by interracial couples are unique and a direct result of the interracial experience. The myths that surround interracial couples can also be stumbling blocks to a healthy marriage. In a study conducted by Richard Watts and Richard Henriksen (1999), Caucasian females report that, when engaged in interracial marriages with black males, they often receive the following messages: "Black men belong with black women because they will treat them better than white women" and "Biracial children will always be referred to as black and, therefore, should have a black mother." The Watts and Henriksen (1999) study also found that problems and difficulties are also experienced because of the mythical messages received from the Caucasian culture. These include: "Black men only marry white women for status symbols or upward mobility," "Interracial marriages do not work; therefore, you will lose your spouse to someone else," "Those who engage in interracial marriages must hate their parents," and "Those who engage in interracial relationships or marriages must have psychological difficulties." The problems faced by couples involved in black-Caucasian unions are also experienced by those involved in other interracial unions. However, many couples state that the reasons they got married are not that much different than same-race couples.

Reasons for Entering into Interracial Marriages

Like other couples deciding to spend their lives together in marriage, interracial couples have many reasons for their choice to marry. The words of a Caucasian female engaged in an interracial marriage point out the importance of recognizing that interracial couples are attracted to each other for the same reasons as homogeneous couples.

> People should first look inside themselves before they look at others and judge them. They should remember that a couple is made up of two people, not two races or cultures. Like other women, I was attracted to my husband because he is considerate, caring, and someone I enjoy spending time with. . . . Healthy families raise healthy children no matter the race or culture of the parents. (Watts and Henriksen 1999, p. 70)

Research supports this woman's perspective. Interracial couples tend to marry because of four important facts: shared common interests, the attractiveness of the partner, shared similar entertainment interests, and socioeconomic similarity. Racial selection factors tend to be less important in selecting an interracial partner for marriage than nonracial factors (Lewis, Yancey, and Bletzer 1997). In other words, as with other couples, interracially married couples are typically attracted to each other based on similarities rather than differences.

Interracial dating is affected by propinquity, attractiveness, and acculturation. Research involving Asian-American out-dating demonstrates that propinquity is the strongest predictor of whether or not the individual will engage in interracial dating. Acculturation and assimilation have also been shown to be positively related to the incidence of interracial marriages. When removed from the demand for intraethnic relationships imposed on Asian Americans by family and the community, Asian Americans are more likely to explore relationships with partners of different racial and ethnic backgrounds, often resulting in interracial marriages (Fujino 1997). These factors are true for other racial and ethnic groups as well.

Resiliency in Interracial Marriages

Many of the people engaged in stable, well-functioning interracial marriages tend to be older, more educated, and have higher incomes, all factors seen as increasing marital stability. Interracial couples that appear to be more vulnerable to marital difficulties tend to have lower incomes, less education, and limited residence in the United States of a foreign-born partner. The length of residence can amplify cultural differences in the relationship and generate or exacerbate marital discord. Marital stability is also affected by the particular racial combination. Racial prejudice is often cited as a main reason why, in some racial groups, out-marriages are rare and in others are more common. In addition, racial prejudice has been shown to affect the resiliency of the marriage based on the partner's ability to cope with the prejudice (Chan and Wethington 1998).

Anna Y. Chan and Elaine Wethington (1998) identified several factors that could facilitate resiliency in interracial marriages. First, interracial marriages tend to be more stable and involve fewer conflicts than other types of interracial relationships. Second, whereas interracial couples and families face unique challenges, they tend to develop mature coping and conflict-resolution styles. Third, given that well-functioning interracial couples often have higher levels of education, they tend to have superior resources for coping with the problems they encounter. Finally, interracial couples tend to build support networks of like-minded people and build strong bonds with each other as a means to overcome adversity.

Conclusion

Any view of interracial marriages must be taken in light of the current worldview of interracial relationships. In the current global climate, there is both increased tension and greater openness. People are more likely to engage in activities that cross racial and ethnic boundaries. However, there also continues to be prejudice and fear about racial ethnic groups with whom many people have little contact. Nevertheless, when people strive to understand the traditions, values, and beliefs that are endemic to the many groups that make up our global societies, then they will be better able—and, it is hoped, more inclined—to work together for the good of all.

Bibliography

Chan, A. Y., and Wethington, E. (1998). "Factors Promoting Marital Resilience Among Interracial Couples." In *Resiliency in Native American and Immigrant Families*, ed. H. I. McCubbin and E. A. Thompson. Thousand Oaks, CA: Sage Publications.

Davis, F. J. (1991). *Who Is Black? One Nation's Definition*. University Park: Pennsylvania State University Press.

Foeman, A. K., and Nance, T. (1999). "From Miscegenation to Multiculturalism: Perceptions and Stages of Interracial Relationship Development." *Journal of Black Studies* 29:540–57.

Fujino, D. C. (1997). "The Rates, Patterns and Reasons for Forming Heterosexual Interracial Dating Relationships Among Asian Americans." *Journal of Social and Personal Relationships* 14:809–28.

Gaines, S. O., Jr.; Rios, D. I.; Granrose, C. S.; Bledsoe, K. L.; Farris, K. R.; Youn, M. S. P.; and Garcia, B. F. (1999). "Romanticism and Interpersonal Resource Exchange among African American-Anglo and Other Interracial Couples." *Journal of Black Psychology* 25:461–89.

Kim, B-L. C. (1998). "Marriages of Asian Women and American Military Men: The Impact of Gender and

Culture." In *Re-visioning Family Therapy: Race, Culture, and Gender in Clinical Practice,* ed. M. McGoldrick. New York: Guilford Press.

Kitano, H. H. L.; Fujino, D. C.; and Sato, J. T. (1998). "Interracial Marriages: Where are the Asian Americans and Where Are They Going?" In *Handbook of Asian American Psychology,* ed. C. Lee and N. W. S. Zane. Thousand Oaks, CA: Sage Publications.

Lewis, R., Jr.; Yancey, G.; and Bletzer, S. S. (1997). "Racial and Nonracial Factors that Influence Spouse Choice in Black/White Marriages." *Journal of Black Studies* 28:60–78.

Watts, R. E., and Henriksen, R. C., Jr. (1999). "Perceptions of a White Female in an Interracial Marriage." *The Family Journal: Counseling and Therapy for Couples and Families* 7:68–70.

Cases

Loving v. Virginia, 388 US 1, 18 L ed 2d 1010, 87 S Ct 1817, (1967)

Perez v. Sharp, 32 Cal.2d 711 [L. A. No. 20305. In Bank. Oct. 1, 1948.]

Other Resource

United States Census Bureau (2000). "America's Families and Living Arrangements." Available from http://www.census.gov/population/socdemo/hh-fam/p20-537/2000/tabFG4.txt.

RICHARD C. HENRIKSEN JR.
RICHARD E. WATTS

INTIMACY

Intimacy is a cornerstone of a good couple relationship and facilitates the health and well-being of the partners. In an intimate interaction, partners reveal their private selves to one another, sharing parts of themselves that are ordinarily hidden. Ideally, they receive one another's personal revelations with nonjudgmental acceptance and continued interest, attraction, and caring, and validate one another by indicating that they too have had such thoughts, feelings, and experiences.

Intimacy is beneficial for individual health and well-being. Individuals who perceive their spouses to be supportive confidantes are buffered from the pathogenic effects of stress. This buffering effect can be observed with a variety of stressors (e.g., births, illnesses, deaths), and with various stress-related outcomes (e.g., depression, anxiety, illness). In contrast, people whose intimacy needs are not met feel lonelier (Rubenstein and Shaver 1982) and their relationships are more prone to dissolution (Hendrick 1981).

Intimacy is beneficial, but attaining a style of intimate relating that meets both partners' needs is a challenge. Intimacy entails risks: People expose their most vulnerable selves to the other and may not receive a sensitive response. Worse, partners sometimes hurl previously whispered confidences at one another as weapons in a struggle for control. For these reasons and more, partners seek a fine-tuned communication process by which they seek, decline, and regulate intimate contact in their relationship.

There is very little research on conceptions of intimacy internationally. The focus of this entry, therefore, is on North America.

Conceptions of Intimacy

A dilemma for scholars who study intimacy is deciding on the best way to conceptualize it. Conceptions of intimacy usually address one (or more) of three phenomena: intimate interactions, intimate relationships, or intimate experiences. Intimate interactions are communicative exchanges between people. In line with the etymological origins of the word *intimacy,* most definitions of intimate interaction converge on a notion of sharing the personal (i.e., innermost, private) aspects of the self. Verbal sharing can involve self-disclosure of personal facts, opinions, and beliefs, and the verbalization of feeling and emotion. Nonverbal sharing can include a shared meaningful glance, affectionate touching, or shared expressions of emotion such as tears or laughter, and sexual encounter. Sharing the personal means sharing vulnerable aspects of the self.

Intimate relationships, in contrast, "impl[y] a series of interactions between two individuals known to each other . . ." (Hinde 1981, p. 2). Intimate experiences are the feelings and thoughts people have during, and as a result of, their intimate interactions. Intimate relationships are those in which partners know each other well and who maintain positive, loving feelings towards the partner who they know so well.

Intimate Interactions

Intimate interactions can be characterized on the basis of the behavior, feelings, and thoughts that participants have during and following their interaction. Intimate behavior includes openness and self-disclosure, especially the sharing of personally vulnerable aspects of the self; sensitive, empathic responses to partner openness and vulnerability; communication of positive regard and respect; emotional support; touching and physical affection; and sexual activity. Positive feelings that accompany these intimate behaviors include pleasure, love, gratification, pride, security, comfort, and safety.

Openness and Self-Disclosure

Self-disclosure is a vital component of intimacy, and it is related to greater emotional involvement, fulfillment of needs and relationship satisfaction (Prager and Buhrmester 1998). Self-disclosure facilitates the development of new intimate relationships (Altman and Taylor 1973) and helps to maintain ongoing ones (Haas and Stafford 1998). Although some theorists have suggested that there could be too much self-disclosure in a relationship, there is little evidence that a high degree of intimacy is associated with the presence of relationship problems.

Partners' self-disclosures vary in personalness and in emotional content, and each of these dimensions is positively associated with intimacy. When interaction participants reveal more personal, vulnerable aspects of themselves through self-disclosure, and when they express feelings about what they have disclosed (Lippert and Prager 2001), they perceive their interactions to be more intimate. Self-disclosure is also more intimate when it addresses issues that are immediate to the time and place of the interaction and salient to the discloser and recipient.

Partner Responsiveness

The extent to which relationship-partners actively attend and convey interest (Miller and Berg 1984), understanding (Reis and Shaver 1988), and empathy for the other's perspective is *partner responsiveness*. In Harry Reis and Philip Shaver's (1988) model of intimate interactions, intimacy is a process that begins when one person communicates personally relevant and revealing information to

A couple's intimate interaction is captured as they sit in a park. Sharing vulnerable aspects of oneself—opinions, beliefs, and emotions—is just as much a part of intimacy as physical affection. PETER TURNLEY/CORBIS

another person, and the second person responds to the speaker in a sensitive manner. According to Reis and Shaver, an interaction is intimate if a discloser perceives that his/her listener conveyed understanding, acceptance, validation, and caring towards the discloser and her/his communication.

Research supports the notion that responsiveness contributes to daily experiences of intimacy in couple relationships, over and above the effects of self-disclosure. In one study of college students, Jean-Paul Laurenceau, Lisa Barret, and Paula R. Pietromonaco (1998) found that self-disclosure was not as intimate when partners were insensitive or unresponsive to that disclosure.

Responsive behavior is both nonverbal and verbal. Intimate nonverbal behaviors are sometimes called involvement behaviors, and they include smiling and maintaining a forward lean, eye contact, and close physical proximity during an interaction. Behaviors such as mutual gaze and forward lean have been associated with positive affect during an interaction and are more visible when partners are romantically involved. Involvement behaviors are critical to people's perceptions of intimacy during interactions (Burgoon et al. 1984).

Communication of Positive Regard

The expression of positive, loving feelings towards one's partner is an important aspect of intimate communication, both as a disclosure and as a response to disclosure (Lippert and Prager 2001). Perceiving one's partner as having a positive view of oneself, especially a partner who knows one very well, helps partners maintain a high self-esteem (Murray, Holmes, and Griffin 2000).

Partners who communicate positive regard to one another may be in a better position to sustain intimacy in their relationship. Work by Sandra Murray and her colleagues (2000) suggests that people determine how much vulnerability they will risk with their partners, in part, on the basis of how positively they believe their partner perceives them. Expressions of positive feelings contribute uniquely to couple-relationship partners' daily experiences of intimacy (Lippert and Prager 2001).

Reassurance and Emotional Support

Some intimate interactions are characterized by emotional support, in which one partner shares a difficulty, and the other offers comfort, reassurance, confidence building, and alternative (i.e., more benign) perspectives for thinking about the problem. Adults who perceive that others, especially their spouses, are available to provide emotional support if and when they need it enjoy many positive outcomes, including better physical and mental health and improved immune functioning.

Effective provision of emotional support is important for a relationship as well as for the individual partner. Partners who are agile providers of emotional support in the early stages of their relationships have less marital distress later on. People can acquire the ability to provide effective emotional support (e.g., Johnson and Greenberg 1994) but its acquisition requires sensitivity to the partner because there is no single means of providing emotional support that is effective for everyone.

Touch and Affectionate Expression

Touches eliminate the space between people, and can intensify experiences of intimacy in verbal communication or stand on their own as intimate behaviors. Stanley E. Jones and Elaine A. Yarbrough (1985) identified three types of touch that nearly always elicited intimate experience in one sample of college students. Inclusion touches, such as legs, knees, or shoulders that touched, conveyed tactile statements of togetherness. Sexual touches involved extended holding and caressing. Affectionate touches covered the widest range of touches, and were neither inclusion nor sexual touches.

Not surprisingly, some touches are more intimate than others. Face touching, for example, is more personal than handshakes, arm touches, or arms around the shoulder or waist. Jones and Yarbrough distinguished between "nonvulnerable" body parts (in the United States, this includes hands, arms, elbows, shoulders, and upper-middle back) and "vulnerable" body parts (all others). Touches on the latter are usually confined to the couple relationship and may, if done in public, signal the couple's level of intimacy (Jones and Yarbrough 1985). Any touch is more intimate if it is prolonged.

Sexuality

Sexuality is one of the most important types of intimacy couples share. Sexuality involves the sharing of very private, personal aspects of the self—one's nude body, expressing to a partner what feels good, and experiencing an orgasm in the presence of the partner.

Positive experiences with sexual intimacy are associated with relationship success: heterosexual couples who remain married report that their sexual relationships are better after marriage, whereas those who divorce report, in retrospect, that theirs were worse. Although satisfied relationship partners engage in more frequent sexual relations, sex frequency is an imperfect gauge of relationship intimacy. Sexual contact is less frequent in more enduring relationships, when partners are older or less educated, and when relationships are less equitable.

Less frequent sexual contact does not always signal a relationship in trouble. Desire or lack thereof may be an even more significant indicator of a relationship's functioning than coital frequency. Pamela C. Regan (1998) found that sexual desire is more closely associated with feelings of love than sexual behavior in the minds of college students as well. Couples in therapy with sexual desire problems have a poorer prognosis than those whose problems are more centered around lack of shared gratification.

Intimacy and the Couple Relationship

Most writers argue that intimacy is more than a type of interaction. It is also a "detailed knowledge or deep understanding" of the other, acquired over time within the context of a loving relationship

(Bargarozzi 1999). Across repeated interactions, relationship partners form general perceptions that reflect the degree to which the relationship is intimate. Over time, these perceptions take on an emergent property that extends beyond the experiences contained within any particular interaction (Chelune, Robison, and Krommor 1984). These perceptions, or intimacy schemas, encapsulate each partner's experience with the other over time, and mediate the impact of individual interactions.

Intimacy schemas, if they represent mostly positive experiences, can result in a back-drop of loving, positive feelings about the partner that buffer the relationship from the inevitable negative emotions that arise. This positive sentiment override (Weiss 1980) can sustain the relationship even when shared intimate experiences are not immediately forthcoming. A similar pattern exists with partners' perceptions of support availability, which persist during times when the partners are not seeking support from one another and, in turn, reliably distinguish between more and less satisfied couples.

Finally, the information gleaned from intimate interactions becomes a base of knowledge and understanding of the partner that goes beyond understanding a particular message or communication. As two people become more intimate, partners come to perceive one another as each perceives her- or himself, yet in a more positive light (Murray, Holmes, and Griffin 2000). When a deeper, richer knowledge of the other is accompanied by acceptance and respect for the partner's interests, preferences, and proclivities, the partners have by definition formed an intimate relationship.

Arthur Aron and colleagues (1991) suggest that increased intimacy leads to the psychological inclusion of the other within the self, so that the boundaries of the self extend to include the other's well-being and her or his desirable and undesirable characteristics. Perhaps as a result of this inclusion, more intimate partners may project themselves onto the other and perceive the other as more similar to themselves than he or she actually is (Ruvolo and Fabin 1999). Ann P. Ruvolo and Lisa A. Fabin argue that it is validating to perceive others as having similar values and characteristics to oneself, especially when it comes to one's intimate partner. Further, through mutual influence, partners may actually become more similar as a result of confiding in and listening to one another.

More intimate partners do not necessarily idealize one another, but relative to those who are less intimate, they do tend to see the other as more similar to the self.

Trajectories for Intimacy over Time

All types of long-term couple relationships, regardless of sexual orientation or marital status, have demonstrable declines in frequency of intimate interactions over time. Sexual intimacy declines most precipitously within the first to second years of a relationship (Blumstein and Schwartz 1983). There are documented declines in affectionate expression, in the number of pleasing things partner do for one another, and in the time partners spend in joint leisure activities (Huston, McHale, and Crouter 1986; Kurdek 1995). Possibly, as couples become more secure with one another they no longer need to "touch base" as frequently and may even take each other for granted.

Intimate interactions appear to become less emotionally intense over time, perhaps leading partners to conclude that they are less intimate than they once were. Some writers have argued that emotional intensity is a critical part of intimate experience (e.g., Sternberg 1988) whereas others have argued that it is only the *memorable* intimate experiences that are emotionally intense (Lippert and Prager 2001). Emotional intensity may signal the newness of intimacy between partners because new relationships are characterized by uncertainty and novelty, each of which add excitement and anxiety to intimate experience. As partners get to know and become increasingly predictable to one another, the emotional intensity of their interactions may wane even though they are still sharing and responding sensitively to one another and are therefore still engaging in intimate interactions (Berscheid 1983).

Intimacy, Vulnerability, and Risk

Relative to the intimate relationship, there are few adult relational contexts in which the possibility of another's rejection is more threatening to the self and in which the possibility of acceptance is more self-affirming. Such stakes seem to necessitate a certain degree of caution. Intimates balance their experiences of closeness with experiences of felt security, and prevent themselves from risking more vulnerability than they can tolerate. Partners' tolerance for the risks of intimacy are related to their level of confidence in their partner's admiration, reciprocated affections, and commitment (Prager 1999). More secure partners may well be willing to risk more.

In established relationships, a climate of safety, which comes from each partner's sensitivity and positive regard of the other, allows partners to continue sharing their vulnerability with one another in intimate interactions. Taking risks—of being hurt, exposed, or made to feel foolish—is an integral part of intimate relating. The result of risk taking in the absence of negative consequences is trust, which fosters further intimacy. Supporting this notion is a study by Paul Robert Appleby, Lynn Carol Miller, and Sadina Rothspan (1999), who found that the most common reason given by gay men for engaging in sexually risky behavior was, ironically, that the behavior demonstrated the love, trust, and commitment shared by the partners.

Individual Differences and Intimacy

Given the inevitable balance of pleasures and risks that intimacy offers, it is not surprising that individual differences exist in the strength of people's intimacy needs and in their tolerance for the anxiety associated with its risks. Some people appear to be content with much less openness, emotional support, sexual contact, and/or affectionate expression than others (Prager 1995). Disagreements and unresolvable conflicts about intimacy create thorny problems in couple relationships.

Dan McAdams's (1988) research on intimacy motivation has supported the notion that some people desire and seek out opportunities for intimate interaction more frequently than others. High intimacy motivation may be an advantage, as individuals high in intimacy motivation experience greater satisfaction in their dating and marital relationships, and provide more social support to their partners (Sanderson and Evans 2001).

Partners whose intimacy needs are compatible are more likely to have their needs met and less likely to encounter conflict. Karen J. Prager and Duane Buhrmester (1998) discovered that partners whose needs are met more frequently have more intimate contact and less conflict. Conversely, people whose partners do not meet their expectations or standards (Vangelisti and Daly 1997) report

lower levels of relationship satisfaction. Partners who argue about intimacy-related issues, such as how much each should express to the other about his and her private feelings and thoughts, or how often partners should have sexual relations, report higher levels of marital distress than those who have other kinds of incompatibilities

Research on individual differences in working models of attachment suggests that people's expectations for a secure (or insecure) attachment in a romantic relationship are associated with different levels of tolerance for the risks of intimacy. Couple relationships share many of same characteristics as parent-child relationships when it comes to attachment and may serve a similar function for adults, providing them with a home-base within which they feel secure and giving them a stable base from which to explore new environments and opportunities (Ainsworth 1989).

The quality of attachments varies from one relationship to another, and there is evidence that these variations are due, in part, to different expectations, or working models, that adults bring into their romantic relationships. Working models reflect adults' earlier relationship experiences, with the result that most adults have emotionally charged preconceived notions about how their relationships will turn out (e.g., happy, secure, abandoned, or smothered).

Individual differences in working models of attachment are associated with individual differences in intimacy needs and preferences (e.g., Collins and Read 1990). For example, recent research indicates that people with insecure attachment expectations (i.e., dismissing) appear to have little tolerance for intimacy (Brennan and Morris 1997) and are more likely than others to have multiple, nonexclusive relationships thereby keeping their partners at a distance (Stephan and Bachman 1999). In contrast, secure individuals are more sexually exclusive and least likely to engage in behavior destructive to their relationships. This research, combined with evidence from McAdams's earlier research on intimacy motivation, suggests that individual differences in intimacy-related needs and fears do exist and affect people's behavior. Further, it seems that working models of attachment are systematically associated with these individual differences.

Intimacy and Gender

Every couple relationship exists in a broader context that affects their opportunities for intimacy and the quality of their intimate interactions. Gender is a contextual variable that is both present within the dyad (such as the gender of the partners and the nature of their relationship) while being simultaneously reflected in the broader culture within which the couple lives (i.e., sets of roles and sociocultural norms).

Intimacy has come to be associated with females and femininity in modern U.S. culture. Women are believed to be "relationship experts," and are encouraged to place more emphasis upon becoming skillful at relating intimately than are men (Steil 1997). Perhaps, as a result, men disclose less and describe themselves as less concerned with meeting emotional intimacy needs than women (Prager 1995). That this is a sociohistorical phenomenon is supported by research showing that men are more open and affectionate with one another in some non-Western cultures than in Western ones (Berman, Murphy-Berman, and Pachauri 1988). Unfortunately, there is a paucity of research on couple intimacy in cultures other than the United States.

Overall sex differences are mitigated in heterosexual romantic relationships where women and men report similar patterns of self-disclosure (e.g., Antill and Cotton 1987). Despite these similarities in women's and men's self-reported disclosure levels with their romantic partners, women are more lonely in their romantic relationships than are men (Rubenstein and Shaver 1982), initiate more separations, and report more problems (Fletcher 1983). Anita L. Vangelisti and John A. Daly (1997) found that women and men have similar standards for their romantic relationships, but that women are more likely to report that their standards are not being met by their partners. Either women's socialization to be relationship experts causes them to be more aware of relationship problems, or women are more effective relationship partners than men are, resulting in men experiencing fewer relationship problems (Steil 1997).

Intimacy Regulation in Couple Relationships

In order to reap the rewards of intimacy without experiencing undo anxiety and rejection, couples look for ways to regulate intimate contact in their relationships. Each couple seeks their own balance between intimate encounter and risk, based on their respective individual intimacy capacities and preferences and on the other strengths of their relationship (Fitzpatrick 1988).

One way that couples regulate the risk of rejection and relationship dissolution is through selective disclosure and withholding of disclosure. Leslie A. Baxter and William W. Wilmot (1985) found that disclosure regarding certain topics (e.g., extra-relationship activity, relationship norms, conflict-inducing topics) was avoided in college student dating relationships because these topics were perceived as threatening to the relationship. Secrecy may also be used to prevent some of intimacy's risks (Finkenauer and Hazam 2000).

Couples also need to regulate intimacy in order to preserve each partner's perception of himself or herself as a distinct individual. Because intimacy involves some blurring of individual boundaries in the interest of each knowing the other and maintaining the bond between them, intimate times need to be balanced with time alone or time for separate interests. Intimacy and autonomy may exist in a dialectical tension in relationships, in which neither needs to conflict with the other but both can and must coexist for a relationship to function well (Baxter and Wilmot 1985). In support of this notion, Karlein M. G. Schreurs and Bram P. Buunk (1996) found that, in lesbian relationships, intimacy and autonomy were both positively related to satisfaction. Emotional dependency, in contrast, was not, nor was it positively correlated with autonomy; it was, however, to intimacy. Perhaps intimacy can coexist with either autonomy or emotional dependency, but the highest levels of satisfaction accompany intimacy and autonomy in combination.

See also: AFFECTION; ATTACHMENT: COUPLE RELATIONSHIPS; COMMUNICATION: COUPLE RELATIONSHIPS; COMMUNICATION: FAMILY RELATIONSHIPS; FRIENDSHIP; GENDER; HONEYMOON; INFIDELITY; LOVE; MARITAL SEX; MARITAL TYPOLOGIES; RELATIONSHIP INITIATION; RELATIONSHIP MAINTENANCE; SELF-DISCLOSURE; SEXUAL DYSFUNCTION; SEXUALITY; TRUST

Bibliography

Ainsworth, M. D. S. (1989). "Attachments Beyond Infancy." *American Psychologist* 44:709–716.

Altman, I., and Taylor, D. A. (1978). *Social Penetration: The Developmental of Interpersonal Relationships.* New York: Holt, Rinehart, and Winston.

Antill, J. K., and Cotton, S. (1987). "Self-Disclosure between Husbands and Wives: Its Relationship to Sex Roles and Marital Happiness." *Australian Journal of Psychology* 39:11–24.

Appleby, P. R.; Miller, L. C.; and Rothspan, S. (1999). "The Paradox of Trust for Male Couples: When Risking is a Part of Loving." *Personal Relationships* 6:81–93.

Aron, A.; Aron, E. N.; Tudor, M.; and Nelson, G. (1991). "Close Relationships as Including the Other in the Self." *Journal of Personality and Social Psychology* 60:241–253.

Bagarozzi, D. A. (1999). "Marital Intimacy: Assessment and Clinical Considerations." In *The Intimate Couple,* ed. J. Carlson and L. Sperry. Philadelphia, PA: Brunner/Mazel.

Baxter, L. A., and Wilmot, W. W. (1985). "Taboo Topics in Close Relationships." *Journal of Social and Personal Relationships* 2:253–269.

Berman, J. J.; Murphy-Berman, V.; and Pachauri, A. (1988). "Sex Differences in Friendship Patterns in India and in the United States." *Basic and Applied Social Psychology* 9:61–71.

Berscheid, E. (1983). "Emotion." In *Close Relationships: Development and Change,* ed. H. H. Kelly, E. Berscheid, A. Christensen, J. H. Harvey, T. L. Huston, G. Levinger, E. McClintock, L. A. Peplau, and D. R. Peterson. New York: Freeman.

Blumstein, P., and Schwartz, P. (1983). *American Couples: Money, Work, Sex.* New York: Morrow.

Brennan, K. A., and Morris, K. A. (1997). "Attachment Styles, Self-Esteem, and Patterns of Seeking Feedback from Romantic Partners." *Personality and Social Psychology Bulletin* 23:23–31.

Burgoon, J. K.; Buller, D. B.; Hale, J. L.; and deTurck, M. A. (1991). "Relational Messages Associated with Nonverbal Behaviors." *Human Communication Research* 10:351–378.

Chelune, G. J.; Robison, J. T.; and Krommor, M. J. (1984). "A Cognitive Interactional Model of Intimate Relationships." In *Communication, Intimacy, and Close Relationships,* ed. V. J. Derlega. Orlando, FL: Academic Press.

Collins, N. L., and Read, S. J. (1990). "Adult Attachment, Working Models, and Relationship Quality in Dating Couples." *Journal of Personality and Social Psychology* 58:644–663.

Derlega, V. J.; Metts, S.; Petronio, S.; and Margulis, S. T. (1993). *Self-Disclosure.* London: Sage Publications.

Finkenauer, C., and Hazam, H. (2000). "Disclosure and Secrecy in Marriage: Do Both Contribute to Marital Satisfaction?" *Journal of Social and Personal Relationships* 17:245–263.

Fitzpatrick, M. A. (1988). *Between Husbands and Wives.* Newbury Park, CA: Sage Publications.

Fletcher, G. J. O. (1983). "Sex Differences in Causal Attributions for Marital Separation." *New Zealand Journal of Psychology* 12:82–89.

Haas, S. M.; and Stafford, L. (1998). "An Initial Examination of Maintenance Behaviors in Gay and Lesbian Relationships." *Journal of Social and Personal Relationships* 15:846–855.

Hendrick, S. S. (1981). "Self-Disclosure and Marital Satisfaction." *Journal of Personality and Social Psychology* 40:980–988.

Hinde, R. A. (1981). "The Bases of a Science of Interpersonal Relationships." In *Personal Relationships,* ed. S. W. Duck and R. Gilmour. London: Academic Press.

Huston, T. L.; McHale, S. M.; and Crouter, A. C. (1986). "When the Honeymoon's Over: Changes in the Marriage Relationship over the First Year." In *The Emerging Field of Personal Relationships,* ed. R. Gilmour and S. W. Duck. New York: Academic Press.

Johnson, S. M., and Greenberg, L. S. (1994). "Emotion in Intimate Relationships: Theory and Implications for Therapy." In *The Heart of the Matter,* ed. S. H. Johnson and L. S. Greenberg. New York: Brunner/Mazel.

Jones, S. E., and Yarbrough, E. (1985). "A Naturalistic Study of the Meanings of Touch." *Communication Monographs* 52:19–56.

Kurdek, L. A. (1995). "Developmental Changes in Relationship Quality in Gay and Lesbian Cohabiting Couples." *Developmental Psychology* 31:86–94.

Laurenceau, J-P.; Barret, L. F.; and Pietromonaco, P. R. (1998). "Intimacy As an Interpersonal Process: The Importance of Self-Disclosure, Partner Disclosure, and Perceived Partner Responsiveness in Interpersonal Exchanges." *Journal of Personality and Social Psychology* 74:1238–1251.

Lippert, T., and Prager, K. J. (2001). Daily Experiences of Intimacy: A Study of Couples. *Personal Relationships.*

McAdams, D. P. (1988). "Personal Needs and Personal Relationships." In *Handbook of Personal Relationships: Theory, Relationships, and Interventions,* ed. S. W. Duck. New York: Wiley.

Miller, L. C., and Berg, J. (1984). "Selectivity and Urgency in Interpersonal Exchange." In *Communication, Intimacy, and Close Relationships,* ed. V. J. Derlega. Orlando, FL: Academic Press.

Murray, S. L.; Holmes, J. G.; and Griffin, D. W. (2000). "Self-Esteem and the Quest for Felt Security: How Perceived Regard Regulates Attachment Processes." *Journal of Personality and Social Psychology* 78:478–498.

Prager, K. J. (1995). *The Psychology of Intimacy.* New York: Guilford Press.

Prager, K. J. (1999). "The Multi-Layered Context of Intimacy." In *The Intimate Couple,* ed. J. Carlson and L. Sperry. Philadelphia, PA: Brunner/Mazel.

Prager, K. J., and Buhrmester, D. (1998). "Intimacy and Need Fulfillment in Couple Relationships." *Journal of Social and Personal Relationships* 15:435–469.

Regan, P. C. (1998). "Of Lust and Love: Beliefs about the Role of Sexual Desire in Romantic Relationships." *Personal Relationships* 5:139–157.

Reis, H. T., and Shaver, P. (1988). "Intimacy as Interpersonal Process." In *Handbook of Personal Relationships: Theory, Relationships, and Interventions,* ed. S. Duck. New York: Wiley.

Rubenstein, C. M., and Shaver, P. (1982). *In Search of Intimacy.* New York: Delacorte Press.

Ruvolo, A. P., and Fabin, L. A. (1999). Two of a Kind: "Perceptions of Own and Partner's Attachment Characteristics." *Personal Relationships* 6:57–79.

Sanderson, C. A., and Evans, S. M. (2001). "Seeing One's Partner through Intimacy-Colored Glasses: An Examination of the Processes underlying the Intimacy Goals-Relationship Satisfaction Link." *Personality and Social Psychology Bulletin* 27:463–473.

Schreurs, K. M. G., and Buunk, B. P. (1996). "Closeness, Autonomy, Equity, and Relationship Satisfaction in Lesbian Couples." *Psychology of Women Quarterly* 20:577–592.

Steil, J. M. (1997). *Marital Equality: Its Relationship to the Well-Being of Husbands and Wives.* Thousand Oaks, CA: Sage Publications.

Stephan, C. W., and Bachman, G. F. (1999). "What's Sex Got to Do with It? Attachment, Love Schemas, and Sexuality." *Personal Relationships* 6:111–123.

Sternberg, R. J. (1988). "Triangulating Love." In *The Psychology of Love,* ed. R. J. Sternberg and M. L. Barnes. New Haven, CT: Yale University Press.

Vangelisti, A. L., and Daly, J. A. (1997). "Gender Differences in Standards for Romantic Relationships." *Personal Relationships* 4:203–219.

Weiss, R. L. (1980). "Strategic Behavioral Marital Therapy: Toward a Model for Assessment and Intervention." In *Advances in Family Intervention: Assessment and Theory,* vol. 1, ed. J. P. Vincent. Greenwich, CT: JAI Press.

KAREN JEAN PRAGER

INUIT FAMILIES

See CANADA FIRST NATIONS FAMILIES; GREENLAND

IRAN

Iran (also known as Persia) is a Middle Eastern country in Southwest Asia. The country's official name became the Islamic Republic of Iran after the Islamic revolution of 1979, which abolished the monarchy of the Pahlavi dynasty and established a theocratic republic regime. The population of Iran is approaching 66 million (49% female), with 40 percent being younger than fifteen years of age in 1996. The area of the country is 1,648,000 square kilometers (38% rural). Infant mortality rate is twenty-nine per 1,000 live births, and life expectancy is sixty-nine years. The literacy rate for the total population is close to 80 percent (Marandi 1996).

Iran is a multiethnic country. The majority are *Fars;* other groups include *Aazari, Kurds, Baloochi, Turkman, Lurs,* and *Arabs.* The official language is *Persian* (or *Farsi*). The ethnic groups also speak their own languages or dialects. About 98 percent of the total population are Moslems (of the Shi-e sect, different from the Sunni sect to which a great majority of Arab Moslems belong), and the rest are Zoroastrians, Jews, Christians (officially recognized and represented by elected deputies in the national legislative body), and Bahais (Sanasarian 2000).

Iranian culture and social institutions have been shaped by Islamic values, blended with traditions inherited from the pre-Islamic national religion (Zoroastrianism) and ancient customs. Many Iranian nationalists identify themselves more with the Persian culture—and feel national pride as the

Women voting in Iran, some in traditional Muslim chadors and others in modern secular clothes. Iranian women were given the right to vote and hold office in 1963. Despite the influence of Western ideas, women still have a low social status. A/P WIDE WORLD PHOTOS

inheritors of a great ancient civilization with a history of more than 2,000 years (Mackey 1996)—than with a particular religious faith or ethnic group (Amanat 1993).

Marriage

Marriage in Iranian culture is viewed not only as the sole socially acceptable pathway to sexual access, but also as a permanent commitment to lifelong companionship, bonding not only the married couples, but also their families (Shapurian and Hojat 1985).

In Iranian culture, procreation is a primary goal of marriage. Some Iranians consider infertility an adequate justification for divorce. It has been

reported that about 2 percent of all divorces in Iran occur because one spouse is unable to have children (Aghajanian 1986). The choice of a spouse in traditional families is often made or supervised by parents and older family members. Even in modern families, parental approval of the prospective spouse is an important factor.

Men and women each have marital pledges. Marital undertakings by the man include a bride-price *sheer bahaa* (literally *milk price,* or an agreed upon money or gift given to the bride's family), and *mahri-eh* (an agreed-upon sum of money, gold coins or property that women are entitled to receive at any time after marriage; more often, it is a source of financial security for married women in case of divorce or widowhood). Also, the groom's family pays the expenses for the marriage reception and ceremony. In return, the girl's family provides the dowry (*jehizi-eh*), which usually includes basic household items (e.g., rugs, bedding, furniture, cookware) needed by the newly wed couple to start their new lives in their new home.

In the rapidly urbanizing contemporary Iranian society, however, most people view the bride-price as demeaning to women (Afkhami 1994; Haeri 1994), although *mahri-eh* and *jehizi-eh* in some cases have become important status symbols. In more educated intellectual and religious families, these two customs are also considered demeaning and indicative of a lack of trust between the bride and the groom and their families. In these families, often spiritually valuable but inexpensive items such as a volume of the holy Qur'an are exchanged instead of *mahri-eh,* and the bride and groom mutually agree to share the expenses for purchasing the *jehizi-eh*.

Endogamy and Polygamy

Endogamy, especially marriage between parallel and cross-cousins, is common in Iran. An Iranian stating that marriage between cousins is summoned in Heaven indicates the popularity of this practice. According to a 1977 survey, about one-fourth of marriages reported in rural areas were endogamous (Givens and Hirschman 1994). The rate of such marriages is estimated to be about 50 percent among some ethnic minorities (Nassehi-Behnam 1985).

A man can have more than one wife. Although the Shi-e marriage law, now dominant in Iran, allows a man to simultaneously have up to four wives, polygamy lacks popular support and is rarely practiced in Iran.

Arranged Marriages

In traditional Iranian families, arranged marriage proceedings begin with *khaastegaari,* or formal marriage proposal, by a delegation (usually of parents and elders) from the man's side. During the initial meeting, various aspects of the marital contract (e.g., the bride-price and dowry) are discussed.

In modern families, particularly among the upper and middle-class urban families, the couple intending to marry usually takes the initial steps based on mutual choice and leaves the formalities of *khaastegaari* to their parents. Arranged marriages in the form known in other Asian countries such as India or Pakistan (marriage decisions made by parents at an early age of their children) are rare, except among very traditional families.

Temporary Marriage (*Sigheh*)

A man (married or not), and an unmarried woman (virgin, divorced, or widowed) can enter a temporary marriage contract (*sigheh* or *nekah-e mong-hate'e*) in which both parties agree on the period of the relationship and the amount of compensation to be paid to the woman. This arrangement requires no witnesses, and no registration is needed. This form of temporary marriage, according to its proponents, is a measure for curbing free sex and controlling prostitution.

A man can have as many *sigheh* wives as he can afford, but the woman can be involved in no more than one such temporary relationship at any given time and cannot enter another contract before a waiting period (*edda*) of three months or two menstrual cycles elapse. This obligatory waiting period also applies to divorced women in permanent marriage and is intended to determine paternity in case the woman becomes pregnant (Haeri 1989). Sigheh has been very unpopular, particularly among the educated middle-class families and among women who tend to associate it with legalized prostitution. It is known to be practiced mainly by widowed or divorced women and is believed to be more common in theological seminaries and among the clergy (Haeri 1989).

The Family

The family has been valued as the main social institution in the Islamic and pre-Islamic cultures of Iran. In the constitution of the Islamic Republic of Iran, the family is defined as the fundamental unit of society and the major center for the growth and advancement of human beings (Tabari and Yeganeh 1982). In traditional Iranian culture, as in any other collectivist society, the kinship and family (*khanevadeh, khanevar, tayefeh, eel-o-ashireh*) is a closely linked network in which the highest priority is assigned to the welfare of the members, rather than to individual goals (Triandis 1995). The family in Iran is considered the most important factor in bonding people, and family ties take precedence over all other social relationships (Hojat et al. 2000).

Sociopolitical changes in Iran have affected young people's marital aspirations, preferences, and the function and structure of the family. Some indicators of this change are the marked rise in the age at first marriage; the tendency of many to remain unmarried until relatively late in life when they become financially independent; the widespread use of contraceptives and the consequent sharp decline in fertility rate and family size; and the gradual rise in divorce rates.

According to the majority of Shi-e theologians, the minimum ages for marriage for women and men are from seven to nine and twelve to fifteen years, respectively. At the close of the twentieth century, the age of marital consent for women was thirteen in Iran (Tohidi 1994). The emphasis on early marriage is partly based on the extremely negative attitude toward premarital sex and a belief that men and women who remain unmarried after early puberty risk engaging in forbidden sexual gratification.

Ironically, although the Islamic regime encouraged early marriage, the average age at first marriage during the period between 1976 and 1996 actually increased from 19.7 to 22.4 for women, and from 24.1 to 25.6 for men. Also, the proportion of women who married before age 19 decreased drastically during this period, from 34 to 18 percent (the corresponding proportions for men are 7% and 3%). Despite these tends, according to population statistics, over 90 percent of Iranian men and women are married by age 30.

Premarital Sex and Extramarital Relationships

Popular culture demands that a bride be a virgin for her first marriage. Mohammadreza Hojat and colleagues (1999) showed that the majority of Iranians believe that men seek to marry a virgin. Virginity, (*bekaarat, dooshizegi*), chastity (*nejaabat*), and authenticity or originality (family with good reputation, *esaalat*) are among the standards employed when men embark on a search for a spouse (Hojat et al. 2000). Women can ruin the family honor by not maintaining their virginity prior to marriage, or by involving themselves in extramarital affairs. Men, in contrast, may engage in premarital sex because of the double standards that prevail in many aspects of sexual and social life in Iran (Hojat et al. 1999; Mir-Hosseini 1999).

Sexual intercourse with person who is married to someone else can carry a harsh penalty according to the Islamic criminal code. Moreover, extramarital intercourse by women is viewed among traditional Iranians as a social disgrace and a grave insult to the whole family. Fornication (*zena*) by women can be punished by stoning to death. At the same time, although the penalties for nonmarital sex included in the current Islamic criminal code also apply to men (if the female partner is not married), they incur little or no social disgrace for illegitimate sex. If caught in such relationships, men can often escape punishment by producing evidence of temporary marriage to their partner.

Divorce

Although not prohibited, divorce is strongly discouraged in Islam and disapproved by Iranian culture. A religious saying (*hadith*) attributed to the Prophet Mohammad says: "Of all things permissible, divorce is the most reprehensible" (Haeri 1989). Because of the low economic activity and social status of Iranian women and their dependence on the men for sustenance and social protection, divorce carries particularly heavy costs and consequences for women. Their situation is made worse because Islamic laws give men the right to custody of their children after age three (in the case of sons) or seven (in the case of daughters).

Nevertheless, married couples who find it inconvenient to live together have the option of getting a divorce. According to Islamic law, a man can in principle divorce his wife at any time by uttering the phrase "I divorce you" in the presence of one or more adult observers. In such cases, women are only entitled to their *mahri-eh*. In practice, the amount of *mahri-eh* is often not enough to support the divorced woman for a long time and, unless it is in the form of gold or property, it can easily be eroded by inflation. This has made some women's families seek very expensive *mahri-eh,* in the form of property or gold coins (which do not erode with inflation). This quest has also emerged as one of the main barriers to marriage by young people.

Before the Islamic revolution, the Family Protection Law (*ghanoon-e hemaayat-e khanevadeh,* enacted in 1967 and revised in 1975) curtailed some of the unilateral rights of men in divorce (Aghajanian 1986). After the Islamic revolution, this law was suspended and replaced by a Special Civil Court (*daadgaah-e madani-e khaas*) that restored some of men's exclusive rights in divorce. After they had noted widespread abuse of this right by men, the state authorities modified the law by providing women with more protection. Under this system, women could include any conditions in the written marital contract (e.g., the right to choose place of residence, study, work, travel abroad), and can take away the unilateral right to divorce from her husband or to make it conditional. In this case the court would decide if the conditions specified in the marital contract have been met to file for divorce.

Although Iranian men can still easily obtain a divorce, the rate of marital dissolution is relatively low, hovering around 10 percent (Sanasarian 1992). Marital dissolution is particularly rare in rural and tribal communities. In urban communities and metropolitan areas, the situation is different, and the rate of divorce is reported to be higher and rising (Nassehi-Behnam 1985). Nevertheless, in a survey of a sample of educated Iranians in Tehran, only a small minority of women (24%) agreed that divorce should be made easier, despite their very limited right of obtaining it (Hojat et al. 1999). This finding indicates the cultural disgrace associated with divorce. Research on divorce in Iran, however, shows that the rate of divorce is increasing among employed women, compared to women who are not employed outside the home (Aghajanian 1986).

Conclusion

In summary, marriage in contemporary Iran is looked upon as an important institution for the purposes of procreation, and it is undertaken as a permanent union. Marital relationships serve as resources to share happiness and enjoyment and as buffers to alleviate suffering and grief. Husband and wife, according a to a popular saying, are *shareek-e shadi va gham* (share their happy and sad moments).

The family is viewed as a secure haven, built upon marriage, and is valued as being a center for warmth and affection (*kanoon-e garm-e khaanevadeh*). Iranians believe that both marriage and the family have survival value for the society by satisfying biological, emotional, social, and financial needs.

See also: ARRANGED MARRIAGE; ETHNIC VARIATION/ETHNICITY; ISLAM; KURDISH FAMILIES

Bibliography

Afkhami, M. (1994). *In the Eye of the Storm: Women in Post-Revolutionary Iran*. Syracuse, NY: Syracuse University Press.

Aghajanian, A. (1986). "Some Notes on Divorce in Iran." *Journal of Marriage and the Family* 48:749–755.

Amanat, M. (1993). "Nationalism and Social Change in Iran." In *Irangeles: Iranians in Los Angeles,* ed. R. Kelly, J. Friedlander, and A. Colby. Berkeley, CA: University of California Press.

Givens, B. P., and Hirschman, C. (1994). "Modernization and Consanguineous Marriage in Iran." *Journal of Marriage and the Family* 56:820–834.

Haeri, S. (1989). *Law of Desire: Temporary Marriage in Shi'e Iran*. Syracuse, NY: Syracuse University Press.

Hojat, M.; Shapurian, R.; Foroughi, D.; Nayerahmadi, H.; Farzaneh, M.; Shafieyan, M.; and Parsi, M. (2000). "Gender Differences in Traditional Attitudes Toward Marriage and the Family: An Empirical Study of Iranian Immigrants in the United States." *Journal of Family Issues* 21:419–434.

Hojat, M.; Shapurian, R.; Nayerahmadi, H.; Farzaneh, M.; Foroughi, D.; Parsi, M.; and Azizi, M. (1999). "Premarital Sexual, Child Rearing, and Family Attitudes of Iranian Men and Women in the United States and Iran." *The Journal of Psychology* 133:19–31.

Mackey, S. (1996). *The Iranians: Persia, Islam, and the Soul of a Nation*. New York: Dutton.

Marandi, A. (1996). "Integrating Medical Education and Health Services: The Iran Experiences." *Medical Education* 3:4–8.

Mir-Hosseini, Z. (1999). *Islam and Gender: The Religious Debate in Contemporary Iran*. Princeton, NJ: Princeton University Press.

Nassehi-Behnam, V. (1985). "Change and the Iranian Family." *Current Anthropology* 26:557–662.

Sanasarian, E. (1992). "The Politics of Gender and Development in the Islamic Republic of Iran." *Journal of Developing Societies* 13:56–68.

Sanasarian, E. (2000). *Religious Minorities in Iran*. New York: Cambridge University Press.

Shapurian, R. and Hojat, M. (1985). "Sexual and Premarital Attitudes of Iranian College Students." *Psychological Reports* 57:67–74.

Tabari, A., and Yeganeh, N. (1982). *In the Shadow of Islam*. London: Zed Press.

Tohidi, N. (1994). "Modernity, Islamization, and Women in Iran." In *Gender and National Identity: Women and Politics in Moslem Societies, ed.* V. M. Moghadam. London: Oxford University Press.

Triandis, H. C. (1995). *Individualism & Collectivism*. Boulder, CO: Westview Press.

MOHAMMADREZA HOJAT
AMIR H. MEHRYAR

IRELAND

The most striking feature of the family in Ireland during the last decades of the twentieth century is the rapid rate at which it has changed. From around the late 1960s the Irish family, in response to a national program of economic development, changed from a traditional rural form typical of economies based on agriculture to a postmodern form typical of postindustrial societies. Although the changes that occurred are common to most Western European societies, the rate of change in Ireland was exceptional. In less than one generation, the Irish family was transformed.

Demographic Change

Since the time of the Great Famine in 1847, the population of Ireland steadily decreased until the time of economic expansion in the 1960s. The principal causes of this decline were high emigration and low marriage rates due to a stagnant economy and large-scale unemployment. Ireland did not experience the demographic transition typical of most Western European countries in the post-World War II period. It was not until much later that Ireland manifested the characteristics of this transition, giving rise in the 1970s to a baby boom. The effects of this baby boom have been a major influence on Irish families since then, with Ireland having the youngest population in the European Union.

With an upsurge in the economy in the 1960s, birth rates increased. By 1971 the birth rate had reached a high of 22.7 per 1000 of population, giving a total period fertility rate of four, which is almost twice the replacement level. Since then, birth rates have declined, and by the 1990s they were below replacement level. By 2000 the birth rate had fallen to 14.3 and the total period fertility rate to 1.89 (Vital Statistics 2001). However, due to an increase in net immigration, largely because of the return of Irish workers and their families to take up employment in Ireland's new booming economy of the 1990s, the population continued to increase.

These changes were also accompanied by changes in marriage rates, age at time of marriage, age at the time of first maternity, family size, the number of out-of-wedlock births, marital separation, and cohabitation. By the end of the twentieth century Ireland had caught up with the demographic trends in most Western European countries and, apart from some differences, the overall pattern is much the same. The biggest difference is that while most of Europe experienced these changes over a period of two generations, Ireland went through them in one.

Family Change

Change over time is also evident in the internal structure and dynamics of the family. This is seen when comparing the findings of two classical anthropological studies of the rural Irish family. The first of these studies was carried out by Conrad Arensberg and Solon Kimball (1940) in the 1930s. This study showed that there was a single family type in rural Ireland that was characterized as having a dominant patriarchal authority system with a rigidly defined division of labor based on gender. In contrast, the second study carried out by Damian Hannan and Louise Katsiaouni (1977) in the 1970s, when the process of change had begun, found a wide variety among farm families, including the socialization experiences of spouses and family interaction patterns. They also found that families were more democratic in structure and that there was a move towards a division of labor based on competence rather than gender. The authors concluded that the family was going through a process of change from a traditional to a modern form, and they linked these changes to the changes taking place in the economic, social, and cultural environments in Ireland at the time.

Changes in the family are also associated with the decline in the influence of the Catholic Church on Irish family life, especially in the area of sexual morality. The traditional family in Ireland has long been characterized as highly conservative, reflecting the dominant value system of the Catholic Church. Although religious practice continues to be high, evidence shows that the influence of Catholic teaching on family life has greatly diminished. This is seen, for example, with the widespread use of contraception and the extent of sexual activity outside marriage. These behavioral changes were also accompanied by the introduction of extensive new legislation on family matters in the 1980s and 1990s, including the passage of a referendum on divorce that led to the introduction of no-fault divorce. Much of this legislation challenged the traditional ideology of the Catholic Church that promoted the privatization of the family and was strongly opposed to state "interference" in family matters.

Marriage

Under Article 41 of the Irish Constitution, the state pledges to "guard with special care the institution of marriage, on which the family is founded." This position of marriage as the basis of the family was further reinforced in 1966 when the Supreme Court interpreted this Article to mean that the family as structurally defined is based on the institution of marriage. Although this Article in the Constitution reflects the ideology of Ireland in the 1930s and does not represent the reality of Irish family life today, marriage has remained relatively stable when compared to other European countries.

Although the marriage rate has decreased from a high of 7.4 per 1,000 of population in the early

Children continue to be an important pat of Irish families, even though the birth rate is below replacement level. The importance of children is underscored by the National Children's Strategy, launched by the Irish government in 2000 to protect children from poverty and abuse. DAVID TURNLEY/CORBIS

1970s, to a low of 4.3 by 1997, marital break-up has remained relatively low. For example, the divorce rate in the European Union for the year 1998 was 1.8 per 1,000 of population, while in Ireland it was 0.6 (Census 1996). However, divorce rates alone are misleading in Ireland because most couples who break up tend to separate rather than divorce. Trends seem to indicate a pattern of people using separation as an exit from marriage and divorce as an entry to a new relationship. In addition, divorce has only been available in Ireland since 1996. In the 1996 census 78,005 people reported themselves as separated, compared to fewer than 10,000 divorced. Nonetheless, even taking account of the numbers reported, marital break-up is comparatively low, and there has been a slight upward turn in the marriage rate, which in

2000 was 5.1 per 1,000 of population (Vital Statistics 2001).

Attitude studies also show a strong commitment to marriage, with companionship more highly valued than personal freedom outside of marriage (MacGreil 1996). These attitudes are further reflected in a Eurobarometer study (1993) that showed that 97.1 percent of Irish respondents placed the family highest in a hierarchy of values. In addition, alternatives to marriage, such as cohabitation, are not a strong feature of Irish families, with only 2 percent of couples living in consensual unions.

Single-Parent Families

The typical family type is that of two parents and their children, but there has been an increase in single-parent families. In the year 2000 nonmarital births accounted for 31.8 percent of all births (Vital Statistics 2000). These births were to women in their twenties and older, not to teenagers. (Teenage births are not a significant proportion of nonmarital births in Ireland.) The average age of nonmarried mothers is twenty-five. Nonmarital births reflect a diversity of family forms that includes cohabiting couples, reconstituted families following marital separation that have not been legally regulated, and single-parent families.

It is not known to what extent these nonmarital births reflect a trend towards increased single-parent households or simply a prelude to marriage. In the year 2000 single-parent families represented 10 percent of all households, and the largest group of these consisted of widows and their children.

Children

The presence of children still continues to be an important part of Irish families, even though the birth rate is below replacement level. The traditional large family consisting of four or more children has been replaced by smaller families. In 1968, for example, 37.4 percent of births were to mothers with three or more children. By 1998 this had fallen to 12.7 percent (Health Statistics 1999, p. 28). The trend is for more women to have children, but to have fewer of them. Only 15 percent of couples live in households where there are no dependent children (Social Situation in the EU 2000). This strong positive attitude towards having children is supported by attitude surveys, which show that the Irish adult population places great value on having children for their own sake (Mac-Grail 1996).

Although children are highly valued, they are still at risk of poverty; studies consistently show that single-parent families and families with three or more children are most at risk (Johnson 1999). In an attempt to combat this, successive governments in the 1990s introduced a range of measures, including significant increases in child benefit and employment incentives for unemployed parents. In an effort to protect children from poverty and abuse, the government launched a National Children's Strategy in 2000 and established an Ombudsman for Children.

Mothers and Employment

A relatively new feature of family life in Ireland is the increased participation of mothers in the active labor force outside the home. In 1987 only 32.7 percent of mothers with children under the age of fifteen years and at least one child under five were active in the paid labor force (Labour Force Survey 1987). Ten years later in 1997, this had risen to 53.1 percent (Labor Force Survey 1997). Of particular significance is that the highest percentage of mothers in full-time employment are mothers of children under age two. In contrast, the highest percentage of mothers in part-time employment is of mothers with children over age ten.

This trend poses difficulties in balancing work and family responsibilities. For example, a 1998 study (National Childcare Strategy 1999) found that 22 percent of mothers of children from infants to four-year-olds, and 68 percent of mothers of children aged five to nine years who were in full-time employment, did not use any form of paid childcare. The study assumed that the younger age group of children were cared for by their fathers and other nonpaid relatives, such as grandparents, but made no comment on who cares for the much larger group of children aged five to nine. These findings seem to support other studies that suggest that the provision of affordable quality childcare, and not attitudes towards paid employment of mothers, is the crucial factor influencing mothers to take up paid employment.

The increased participation of mothers in the paid labor force is not, however, matched by any significant increase in the amount of work undertaken by fathers in the home. The only major study on the division of household tasks of urban Irish families (Kiely 1995) found that, while more than 80 percent of mothers in the study thought that husbands should share housework equally, the reality was that mothers not only did most of the housework but also provided most of the care for the children. Fathers were generally inclined to participate in the more pleasurable aspects of childcare such as playing with the children and going on outings with them, while the mothers did most of the less glamorous tasks like changing diapers and putting the children to bed. The study did, however, show that young, educated, middle-class fathers whose wives were also employed had higher rates of participation than other fathers, although this was still relatively low.

Household Composition

A reflection of the position of the family in Irish life can be seen by the composition of households. Although many factors influence household composition, the relatively low percentage of households consisting of one adult and no children (7% of all households), compared to households with children (66% of all households), shows the dominance of families composed of one or more adults with dependent children.

Only 15 percent of households are composed of two adults without children. The remainder of households are composed of three or more adults without dependent children. When the number of persons living in family households is calculated as a percentage of people living in all private households, the dominance of family households is all the more striking—with almost 88 percent of the population living in such households (Census 1996).

With rising house prices in the late 1990s, more young adults appear to remain in their parents' home for longer periods, including young mothers and their children. This probably accounts for the increase in households consisting of three or more generations. These households also include families where an adult child cares for a dependent parent. In both of these three or more generation family types, the key caretakers are women in their midlife, caring either for a parent or a grandchild. These are also the people who have the least attachment to the paid labor force.

Family Diversity

Family diversity is found not only in family composition, but also in its structure and functions. Thus, while studies show a movement from a traditional to a modern form of the family, this movement is in no way uniform. Some families, for example, are democratic in structure, while others are hierarchical. Also, some continue to fulfill a variety of functions, while others are more specific. Again, some families place a higher value on relationships over the importance of the family as an institution. These variations are consistent with the patterns found in most countries that have gone through a modernizing process and reflect a blend of traditional and modern value positions. Diversity, not uniformity, is the hallmark of modernity, and this is now also the hallmark of Irish families.

See also: WAR/POLITICAL VIOLENCE

Bibliography

Arensberg, C. and Kimball, S. (1940). *Family and Community in Ireland.* Cambridge, MA: Harvard University Press.

Central Statistics Office. (1996). *Census 1996: Household Composition and Family Units.* Dublin: Stationery Office.

Central Statistics Office. (1987) *Labour Force Survey.* Dublin: Stationery Office.

Cleary, A.; NicGhiolla Phádraig, M.; and Quin, S. eds. (2001). *Understanding Children in Ireland.* 2 vols. Dublin: Oaktree Press.

Colgan McCarthy, I., ed. (1995). *Irish Family Studies: Selected Papers.* Dublin: Family Studies Centre, University College Dublin.

Commission on the Family. (1998). *Strengthening Families for Life.* Dublin: Stationery Office.

Department of Health and Children. (1999). *Health Statistics 1999.* Dublin: Stationery Office.

Department of Health and Children. (2000). *Vital Statistics, 4th Quarter.* Dublin: Stationery Office.

Eurostat. (2000). *The Social Situation in the European Union: 2000.* Brussels: European Commission.

Hannan, D., and Katsiaouni, L. (1997). *Traditional Families? From Culturally Prescribed to Negotiated Roles in Farm Families.* Dublin: Economic and Social Research Institute.

Johnson, H. (1999) "Poverty in Ireland." In *Irish Social Policy in Context,* ed. G. Kiely, A. O'Donnell, S. Kennedy, and S. Quin. Dublin: University College Dublin Press.

Kiely, G. (1995). "Fathers in Families." In *Irish Family Studies: Selected Papers,* ed. I. Colgan McCarthy. Dublin: Family Studies Centre, University College Dublin.

MacGréil, M. (1996). *Prejudice in Ireland Revisited.* Maynooth, Co. Kildare: Survey and Research Unit, St Patrick's College.

McKeown, K.; Ferguson, H.; and Rooney, D. (1998). *Changing Fathers? Fatherhood and Family Life in Modern Ireland.* Cork: The Collins Press.

Malpas, N., and Lambert, P. (1993). *Europeans and the Family. (Eurobarometer* 39). Brussels: Commission of the European Communities.

Partnership 2000 Expert Working Group on Childcare. (1999). *National Childcare Strategy.* Dublin: Stationery Office.

GABRIEL KIELY

ISLAM

The religion of Islam is practiced by people from different ethnicities and nationalities throughout the world. People who adhere to the faith and practice of Islam are called Muslims. Traditional Muslims who practice as Sunnis and Shiites follow the teachings of the prophet Muhammad. From regions (e.g., North and Central Africa, Middle East) to various ethnic groups (e.g., Iranian, Egyptian, Malaysian), Islam encompasses vast multicultural groups of people (Al Faruqui 1978).

Background and Beliefs of Islam

The Islamic faith has served as the foundation for the moral and spiritual development of many generations of people. The word *Islam* literally means *submission to Allah* (Higab 1983). Islam is a monotheistic religion. Any person who makes a pledge to submit to Allah is referred to as a Muslim. Muslims display their Islamic beliefs through everyday practices, guided chiefly by the teachings in the Qur'an. The Qur'an is the holy book that serves as the blueprint for the life that Muslims believe Allah prescribed. The Qur'an, along with the Sunnah, and the Hadith, practices and traditions of the prophet Muhammed, provides guidance and direction for daily living. Each person is obliged to live his or her life in accordance with these traditions and practices (Al-Hali and Khan 1993). The Prophet Mohammed is believed to be the one true prophet who received the word of God in the seventh century as recorded in the sacred writings of the Qur'an. The religion of Islam has less formal structure than does Judaism or Christianity; there are no rabbis, priests, or ministers, for example. The imam of a mosque, the closest parallel to these roles, is considered to be more like a teacher than a leader or mediator. The other chief divergence between Islam and Judeo-Christian religions lies in the six articles of faith and the five pillars of Islam listed below. In addition to worshipping Allah (God), the practicing Muslim must pray five times a day, fast yearly during Ramadan, contribute to the poor, and make a pilgrimage to Mecca at least once in his or her lifetime. Due to the nature of these practices, Islam tends to be more visible, more daily, and more ritualized than other religions may appear to be (El-Amin 1991).

The Six Articles of Faith represent the necessary beliefs that undergird the religion of Islam. These beliefs support the core of Islamic faith. They are:

(1) Belief in the Oneness of God (Allah). This view stems from the belief that God is one being, and there are no other creators but God. Muslims believe in various prophets who were sent divine messages from God, but they worship only one God.

(2) Belief in the Holy Book. This concept pertains to Muslims' belief in the Holy Qur'an. This book serves as the blueprint for a way of life. Muslims believe that it contains all of the necessary elements for a productive life here on earth.

(3) Belief in the angels. This is the belief that angels are messengers sent from God. However, they should not be worshipped by humans and should only be viewed as messengers from God.

(4) Belief in the Prophet. Muslims believe that Muhammad was the last prophet sent by Allah. However, Muslims also believe that other persons such as Abraham and Jesus are prophets.

(5) Belief in the day of judgment. This stems from the Islamic belief that there is life after death and that one's actions as an earthly being shall be judged by the Creator (Allah).

(6) Belief in predestination. Muslims believe that Allah predestines one's life in reference to good versus evil.

The Five Pillars of Faith represent the fundamental practices necessary to incorporating Islam into a way of life. The five pillars are:

(1) Worship of Allah (God). This basic pillar incorporates the other four. To acknowledge Allah is to adhere to the messages sent to Muhammad as the Holy Word.

(2) Prayer. This pillar is viewed as one of the most fundamental practices of Islam. Muslims believe that praying five times a day serves as a daily vow of submission to Allah. Prior to prayer, cleansing is done (i.e., washing of hands/body) as a sign of purifying one's self in preparation for giving praise to Allah.

(3) Fasting. This Islamic principle serves as Muslims' vow of abstinence from food, drink, or sexual behavior for a period of time. This serves as a test of one's willingness to submit to Allah.

(4) Zakat. This principle refers to the donating of a portion of one's property/income to various areas of need within the Muslim community. These may include donations to the poor and maintenance of public facilities.

(5) Pilgrimage. When possible, this pillar is viewed as a sacred voyage back to the holy city of Mecca. It is believed that Mecca is the city where the Prophet Muhammad received his revelation from Allah. It is at this time when all Muslims can come together to pay homage to Allah.

Gender Relations

Relationships between men and women vary slightly by country of origin and governmental regulations but are nonetheless for all Muslims guided by Islamic law and practice, as specified in the Qur'an. The Qur'an sets the ideals that describe the relationship between men and women. It states, "[A]nd for women are rights over men similar to those of men over women" (2:226). This Surah (Qur'anic passage) supports the act of mutual submission of women and men to each other. The interpretation of this teaching varies. The independence and rights of women were originally supported by the prophet Muhammed, but Muslim scholars and governments have interpreted these rights in a variety of ways. History also notes that Muhammed began the practice of taking multiple wives and the obligatory veiling of women in public. Polygamy has fallen out of general practice and acceptance in most parts of the Muslim world but the obligatory veiling of women—called *hijab*—has remained. This veiling or hijab is practiced to some degree by virtually all Muslim women around the world. In some countries, such as Saudi Arabia, hijab is interpreted and regulated by the government as a total covering with black cloth of a woman's face, head, and body. In other countries, such as Iran, hijab is interpreted as a head covering with modest clothing to cover the body. The hijab is an identifying characteristic of Muslim women that renders them more visible in societies such as the United States, where head covering is not routinely practiced. Unfortunately, some Muslim women have experienced harassment or refusal of employment because of this visible requirement to cover their head or person.

Traditionally women and men are not free to date or intermingle, so the choice of a spouse is a more deliberate process. The vast majority of marriages are arranged marriages; that is, parents or guardians select appropriate mates for their offspring and bring them together for matrimony. The amount of choice and acceptance of these potential partners varies by culture and sometimes by class and educational status. Important characteristics in choosing a worthy mate are faith and chastity as demonstrated in this Surah (Qur'an 33:35): "For Muslim men and women, for believing men and women, for true men and women, for men and women who are patient and for men and women who guard their chastity, and for men and women who engage much in Allah's praise, for them has Allah prepared forgiveness and great reward."

As in most religions and cultures, marriage in Islam is a legal contract promoting love and harmony as well as procreation between a woman and a man (Higab 1983). This concept of commitment is strongly rooted in the Qur'an. The Qur'an gives a detailed account of the marital relationship and the responsibilities of each partner. Accordingly, it is stated that Allah believes that men and women are equal with no one person having precedence over the other. Nevertheless, it is believed that there are different functions of wives and husbands in regards to marriage. Note this Surah from the Qur'an (4:34): "Men are protectors and maintainers of women, because Allah has given them more physical strength than the other, and because they support them from their means. Therefore, righteous women are devoutly obedient, and guard in the husband's absence what Allah have them guard." Therefore, in Islam, the concept of marriage is viewed as a partnership with each person complementing the other (Lemu 1978). This means that the obedience required from Muslim women complements the role of the husband as the provider of the family. In other words, as long as the husband adheres to the proper Islamic teachings regarding his family, the woman's loyalty is supposed to be maintained.

Additionally, some basic fundamental ideas are recognized as central to a Muslim marriage (Sakr 1991). The family is recognized as the foundation of Islamic society. Husbands and wives are expected to produce offspring and maintain close relations with extended family members. Individuals are strongly encouraged to marry, and there is pressure on all single men and women to marry as soon as possible. Connected with this notion that Allah has established a mate for each individual. It is understood that these two persons should live together harmoniously in pursuit of a productive life. Premarital or extramarital sexual intercourse is prohibited. Men and women are expected to enter marriage in a virginal state and remain faithful. Marriage is regarded as an aspect of the Islamic faith that should be fulfilled with various benefits to the individuals involved (i.e., earthly and heavenly). Central is the custom that a groom provide a dowry (sum of money) to the bride or her family prior to marriage as a sign of commitment to the family. This dowry varies with cultures and traditions but is fairly universal in practice. Wives should expect to be supported by their husbands financially and are not expected to work outside of the home. In return, husbands can expect procreative and sexual access to their wives. When a couple marries, marriage should be publicized with a *waleemah* (reception) offered in celebration of the new marriage. Marriages should be celebrated publicly to announce to the world the beginning of a sacred commitment.

From an ecological perspective, Muslims believe that the marital dyad is crucial to the survival of the ecology of the family and the community. It is believed that these systems (i.e., family and community) are dependent upon the unity that is maintained in Muslim marriages (Sakr 1991). Additionally, the extended kinship established through marriage creates an even larger network that should enhance marital quality (Ninji 1993). Thus, the Islamic view of marriage identifies this institution as the central element of Muslim communities.

Family Relations

In addition to the responsibilities that men and women have in marriage, parenthood is central to Muslim identity and faith. As an Islamic parent, it is necessary to follow certain criteria when rearing children. These include maintaining an Islamic environment, especially in the home, and adhering to Islamic teachings regarding dress, diet, and prayer that are essential components of a household. The couple must educate the children with the understanding that Allah's teachings are the only acceptable principles for practicing a proper way of life. Providing religious education is the core responsibility of the parents. Often the father also takes on this more formally with older children, especially males. Parents must also serve as examples of the correct way of life according to Allah, and they must establish a sense of open communication among family members. The couple is expected to expose children to other Muslim families and children. This is especially important in countries in which Islam is only one of multiple practicing religions.

The role of motherhood is highly esteemed. Women as mothers are at the center of the family (Sherif 1999). The duties of motherhood are highly respected and considered a major responsibility and privilege of womanhood. Traditionally, the Muslim family is an extended rather than nuclear unit. The Qur'an supports respect for parents and elders and the necessary interdependence and mutual responsibility of young and old for the good of everyone. Extended family members offer guidance on childrearing and marriage and also provide support and mediation in times of need. Extended family participation and support is a welcome and common part of daily life.

Conclusion

Muslim individuals and families live around the world in many different countries and practice their faith in similar ways. Cultural variations such as type of dress and rituals for weddings may vary, but fundamentally Muslims are governed by the same principles found in the Qur'an. Of note is the fact that in the year 2000, the number of Muslims surpassed the number of Christians in the world. This may mean that Islam will be more visible in years to come in Western cultures. Insights and information about religions and practices can be a helpful way to facilitate more visibility and understanding.

See also: AFGHANISTAN; BEDOUIN-ARAB FAMILIES; CIRCUMCISION; EGYPT; ETHNIC VARIATION/ETHNICITY; INDIA; INDONESIA; INTERFAITH MARRIAGE; IRAN; ISRAEL; KURDISH FAMILIES; KYRGYZSTAN; MALAYSIA; RELIGION; SENEGAL; TURKEY

Bibliography

A-Hali, T., and Khan, M. (1993). *Interpretation of the Meanings of the Noble Quar'an in the English Language*. Kingdom of Saudi Arabia: Maktaba Dar-us-Salam.

Al Faruqi, L. I. (1978). "An Extended Family Model from the Islamic Culture." *Journal of Comparative Family Studies* 9:243–256.

Cooper, M. H. (1993). "Muslims in America." *CQ Researcher* April 30, 363–367.

El-Amin, M. M. (1991). *Family Roots: The Quaranic View of Family Life*. Chicago: International Ummah Foundation.

Higab, M. (1983). *Islam Is the All-Divine Messages in One*. Lagos, Nigeria: Islamic Publications Bureau. Lemu, Aisha (1978). "Women in Islam." In *The Challenge of Islam*, ed. Altaf Gauher. London: Islamic Council of Europe.

Ninji, A. A. (1993). "The Muslim Family in North America: Continuity and Change." In *Ethnic Families: Strength in Diversity*, ed. H. P. McAdoo. Newbury Park, CA: Sage.

Sakr, A. H. (1991). *Matrimonial Education in Islam*. Chicago: Foundation for Islam Knowledge.

Sherif, B. (1999). "Islamic Family Ideals and Their Relevance to American Muslim Families." In *Ethnic Families: Strength in Diversity,* ed. H. P. McAdoo. Newbury Park, CA: Sage.

MARSHA T. CAROLAN
MONICA MOUTON-SANDERS

ISRAEL

Compared to other industrialized countries, Israel is a familistic society. The country's small size permits relatives to live in close geographic proximity and have frequent personal contact. Holidays and life-cycle events are generally celebrated through ceremonies and customs that bring family members together. Intrafamilial involvement and assistance (from baby sitting through major financial help) are the norm. Key indicators of Israel's familism include relatively high marital and fertility rates and low divorce rates, compared to other postindustrial countries. In 1999, for every 1,000 persons in the population of 6.4 million, there were 6.7 marriages, 21.9 births, and 1.7 divorces. The downside of this familism is that people without family may suffer social isolation, lack of social support, and a sense of not belonging.

At the same time, the traditional Israeli family shares many features of the modern family. Marriage is based more on emotional bonds than on economic or social considerations. Family functions such as childcare and caring for the elderly have been transferred to the community. Independence from the family of origin is encouraged from an early age. The monogamous nuclear family is increasingly becoming one model among others. The major values that people expect to realize within the family are less the good of the family than the good of the individual. The Israeli family also shares the stresses of other modern families: spousal tension over roles and tasks brought about by increasing gender equality, and difficulties, especially among mothers, in balancing childcare, work, and personal interests and goals.

Declining marital rates, rising divorce rates, and falling birth rates point to decreasing familism in the last quarter of the twentieth century. The decrease is most salient in the Jewish population (81% of the total), which saw substantial falls in the marital and birth rates and a doubling of the divorce rate. The Muslim (15.6%), Christian (1.8%), and Druse (1.6%) communities have remained more strongly family oriented, but cracks have begun to appear. Among the Muslims, marital rates have risen slightly, but the birth rate has fallen, and the divorce rate has more than doubled. Among the Christians and Druse, marital rates have risen or remained high, and divorce is virtually nonexistent, but birth rates have declined substantially.

Factors Affecting the Israeli Family

Key factors that have shaped the Israeli family are Israeli family law, the country's history of immigration, and the prevalence of trauma and war.

Family law. Family law in Israel comes under both religious and secular jurisdiction, with two parallel legal systems working in tandem. People who want to marry and divorce in Israel must obtain the authorization of the court of their religion. These state-supported courts rule in accord with religious laws, which restrict interfaith marriage, encourage family stability, and place obstacles in the way of divorce. Jewish religious law forbids marriage between relatives or between divorcees and descendants of the ancient priesthood. Divorce requires that the husband give his wife a writ of divorce and that she accept it.

The rulings of the religious courts are subject to the laws passed by Israel's parliament. These forbid child marriage, polygamy, and the husband's one-sided, nonjudicial divorce of his wife, which are permitted by Muslim religious law. They allocate legal guardianship for the children of a union (whether in or out of wedlock) to both parents. In divorce, custody is to be awarded on the basis of the best interests of the child, and noncustodial parents receive visiting rights and pay child support.

The religious courts' control over marriage may be circumvented by wedding abroad or by cohabitation. After a stipulated period of time, cohabiting couples become *known in public* and are legally entitled to full spousal rights. Their control of divorce is reduced by provisions permitting either partner to file for divorce in a religious or civil court (which may rule on all matters other than the writ of divorce) and to appeal to the civil court against religious court rulings.

TABLE 1

Marital, birth, and divorce rates in Israel: 1975–1999

Number of marriages, births, and divorces a year for every 1,000 people

	Marriages	Births	Divorces
Jews 81%	9.6–6.1	24.3–18.7	0.9–1.9
Muslims 15.6%	7.3–7.9	39.5–34.5	0.5–1.1
Christians 1.8%	4.5–5.7	19.9–16.4	0.1
Druse 1.6%	9.3	36.8–22.7	0.6

SOURCE: Central Bureau of Statistics 2000.

Immigration. Israel is a country built by successive waves of immigration. In 1995, only 61 percent of Israelis were native born (Good and Ben-David 1995). The pattern for the mainstream Israeli family developed from the meeting of the European and Afro-Asian immigrants whose descendants compose in about equal portions most of Israel's Jewish population.

The European Jews who arrived in Israel in the first half of the twentieth century separated themselves from the ramified, closely knit European Jewish family that had served as a haven and support in Europe's hostile, anti-Semitic environment. The first group to arrive was made up of young, unmarried idealists, who came from Eastern Europe at the turn of the century with the dream of creating an entirely new Jewish society, free of the faults of their Eastern European Jewish communities. They viewed marriage and family as secondary to this task. They rejected the traditional norms and customs of European Jewish family life, including prearranged marriage, rigid sex roles, and high fertility, and sought to replace them with equality and freedom (Katz and Peres 1986). These immigrants were followed in the 1930s by Jews fleeing Hitler's Europe and in the 1940s and 1950s by survivors of the Nazi Holocaust. The new arrivals did not share the radical ideology of their predecessors. But they too were mostly young, without parents and relatives, and distanced both geographically and psychologically from their former family model.

The European immigrants established in Israel a Western, liberal family model, of small to medium-sized, isolated nuclear units, characterized by various degrees of closeness and the ideal, if not always the practice, of gender equality. Family relations were influenced by two contrary pulls:

(1) the prevailing ideal of the *sabra,* or native-born Israeli, which touted toughness and autonomy, and (2) the strong needs of the refugees and survivors, most of whose families of origin had been eradicated in Europe. The survivors generally infused their new families with intense emotional significance and vested in their children their aspirations for renewal.

The European model was modified by the arrival in the 1950s of the Afro-Asian immigrants from the Arabic-speaking countries of North Africa and the Middle East. Arriving in whole communities, these immigrants introduced into Israel the conservative, patriarchal family structure and values of the countries from which they came. They had large households (five or more children), and large extended family networks. Most marriages were arranged; girls married young; fertility was high. The family was held together by a clear structure of authority and reciprocal obligations between genders and generations (Katz and Peres 1986). These immigrants and their descendants bolstered the familism that had been weakened by the immigrants from Europe.

Over time, the two models converged. The Afro-Asian Jewish family loosened its hold; arranged marriage is unacceptable in both communities; and the age of first marriage, fertility rates, and the allocation of conjugal tasks are similar for similar socioeconomic levels. Because the European culture of the early immigrants was the dominant one in Israel, most of the changes were made by the Afro-Asian family. The European family, however, which had been enlarged by the natural addition of grandparents and other relatives, also adapted in the encounter, with a renewed valuation of marriage and childrearing.

The immigrants who followed added to the diversity of the Israeli family. Two groups, from the Soviet Union, who arrived in the 1970s and 1990s, and from Ethiopia, who arrived in the 1990s, are of particular interest.

The Soviet immigrants can be divided into those from the Muslim republics and those from Russia's urban areas. The former came with large, traditional families, much like those of the Afro-Asian immigrants two decades earlier. The latter have small but tightly knit families, often with only one child. Thirty percent of them are headed by single mothers, with the father remaining in Russia.

The grandmother is an important family member and major source of support, taking care of the home and children while the parents work. The outcome is a high degree of interdependence among family members. Many Russian immigrants live in three-generational households. They generally place considerable emphasis on education. The upbringing of the children tends to be strict and the parents to be highly involved in the children's lives (Poskanzer 1995).

The Ethiopians came largely from closed rural communities, where core families lived alongside one another in multigenerational extended family groups, which cooperated socially and economically. Authority was vested in the oldest male, and the father was the undisputed head of the family; women were considered the property of their husbands. In Israel, this structure has been undermined: by the high death rate of immigrant males en route to the country, the fact that different parts of the family-community immigrated at different times, and the economic dependence of the formerly self-supporting family group on the Israeli government. More than 30 percent of the Ethiopian core families in Israel are headed by single mothers, whose husbands died or abandoned them (Ben-David 1993).

Immigration has had a strong impact on the families of all the immigrant groups. As among immigrants elsewhere, the children became the agents of socialization, standard intergenerational conflict was intensified, and parental authority was weakened as the children learned the language and adopted the identity and values of the new land. Moreover, in its encounter with Israel's Western culture, which stressed individualism, the close relatedness of the traditional Jewish family of all extractions yielded to increased emotional distance between generations.

The transition has been particularly wrenching for the immigrants from traditional cultures. These immigrants faced discrimination and lacked the means to compete in Israel's technologically advanced society. Men who had provided adequately for their families in their countries of origin, where they worked as farmers, artisans, or tradesman, found it difficult to earn a living in Israel, and their wives, who were formerly confined to the home, had to go out to work. The result was that the father lost his status and authority as the patriarchal head of the family. As elsewhere, these developments sometimes exacted a high social price in alienation, street gangs, and crime among the descendants of the immigrants (Halpern 2001)

Successive Israeli governments have viewed immigration both as a way of rescuing Jews and of building a new Israeli society. Large numbers of children and adolescents in certain immigrant groups were thus brought to Israel before their parents. In Israel, many immigrant children were sent to boarding facilities for their education and acculturation. The practice was particularly widespread among Ethiopian children at the beginning of the twenty-first century, some 90 percent of whom study in publicly supported religious boarding facilities. The practice stresses immigrant absorption and the acculturation of young immigrants over family closeness and continuity.

Recurrent traumas. The legacy of the Nazi Holocaust, multiple wars stemming from the protracted Arab-Israeli conflict; and decades of terrorism have fostered familism in Israel, while placing great burdens on Israeli families. These events produced a perpetual, underlying anxiety, which has intensified Israelis' needs for the affiliation and belonging that the family can provide (Malkinson; Rubin; and Witztum 2000). They also engendered a realistic concern with losing a child to war or terror, which has led most Israeli couples to have more children than their counterparts in other Western countries and Israeli society to encourage childbirth.

At the same time, these events have caused enormous stress for Israeli families. Hardly a family in Israel is untouched by loss and bereavement. Many Israeli families cope with the myriad emotional, practical, and financial difficulties of caring for a family member who has been physically injured or psychologically traumatized by these events.

Family Patterns

Several overlapping family patterns may be found in Israel.

The mainstream family. Among Israeli Jews, the great majority of families, of both European and Afro-Asian origin, combine traditional Jewish family values and norms with modern features. These are medium-size families with an average of three children. Marriage is seen primarily, though not only, as a framework for raising children. The man is expected to be the major breadwinner and the woman to fulfill the duties of wife and mother. Although 70 percent of the women work outside the home, work is secondary to childrearing. Divorce is viewed as a failure, not as an opportunity for growth. At the same time, under the impact of feminism and Israel's egalitarian ideology, the men in these families are increasingly involved in childcare, decisions are made jointly, and resources are divided democratically.

The ultra-orthodox family lives by literal adherence to Jewish religious law and at a remove from what they view as the corruption of Israel's secular society. It emphasizes personal modesty (married women must cover their heads); the separation of men and women in education, worship, and public places; early marriage; and clear role divisions. The woman's task is to be a wife and mother, responsible for making a Jewish home. The man's task is to pursue religious studies. The commandment to be fruitful and multiply is taken literally, resulting in a high birth rate. At the same time, ultra-orthodox women have always worked (in feminine occupations, such as secretary and teacher) so as to enable their husbands to study. In addition, there is increasing cooperation with the secular authorities to deal with family problems that were traditionally kept within the community.

Postmodern and single parent families. Israel has a small percentage of postmodern families. These include double-career families, in which the husband and wife are financially autonomous, as well as cohabiting couples, same-sex couples, some of them with children, and unmarried parents by choice.

In 1998, 11 percent of all Israeli families were headed by single parents, 90 percent of them by mothers. Of these mothers, 68 percent were divorced, 17 percent widowed, and 15 percent unmarried (Central Bureau of Statistics 1999). The unmarried mothers are mostly middle- and upper-middle-class college-educated women of European origin, who first gave birth in their mid- to late thirties. Their choice reflects both the high valuation of having children in Israeli society and the legitimacy it accords to the individual's strivings for self-actualization.

The kibbutz family. The kibbutz family today falls into the mainstream family pattern, but it was once a daring social experiment. The kibbutz is a collective community that was created in Israel on the basis of egalitarian, Marxist principles. For ideological and economic reasons, the family took second place to the community. The legal and ceremonial aspects of marriage were de-emphasized, meals were taken in the communal dining room, and community pressure was exerted on people to spend their leisure time in communal activities rather than with their families. Children were raised with their age mates in separate children's houses. They were cared for by child minders and spent only leisure time, two to three hours daily, with their parents. Their physical, social, and emotional needs were to be met by the kibbutz.

Although kibbutz members have contributed beyond their numbers to the defense and leadership of Israeli society, the psychological impact of this communal upbringing and loosened family ties was always a matter of debate. Beginning in the 1970s, one kibbutz after another returned the children to their parents' homes and care. Moreover, extended families now constitute a recognized part of the kibbutz social landscape.

The Arab family. The traditional Arab family is hierarchical, patriarchal, partrilineal, and collectivist. Individuals are expected to subordinate their wishes to the needs of their families, and wives their wishes to those of their husbands. The nuclear family nests within the *hamula,* an extensive kinship network formed by ties of marriage and blood, whose traditional function was to provide its members with cohesion and financial support (Haj-Yahia 1995).

Over the latter part of the twentieth century, the Arab family in Israel has been undergoing a process of modernization. The *hamula* has been whittled down in size and the status and the authority of its elders undermined (Smooha 1989). Arab men have seen their traditional role as head of the family eroded and their authority over their wives and children diminished. Arab women have become increasingly educated and, to help carry the economic burden, have started to work outside the home. Nonetheless, women are generally still expected to be deferential to their husbands, parents-in-law, and parents (Haj-Yahia 1995). Divorce, though on the rise, is strongly stigmatized (Cohen and Savaya 1997; Al-Krenawi and Graham 1998).

Public Support for Families

Familism in Israel is encouraged by the availability of extensive public supports, which are anchored in law and provided by a combination of state and voluntary bodies.

Families benefit from mandatory health insurance with universal access and from a guaranteed minimal income contingent on the number of dependents.

Israel's many laws and services on behalf of children reflect the society's positive attitudes towards children. Employers are forbidden to fire pregnant women. Prenatal care, hospitalization, and delivery are included in the national health package, as is artificial insemination. New mothers receive a monetary grant to pay for the newborn's needs and are entitled to a twelve-week maternity leave, paid for by the National Insurance Institute.

Direct financial support is provided to assist parents to care for their children. Every family receives a monthly child allowance for each child deposited directly into the mother's bank account. Single parents are entitled to a discount on municipal taxes and to financial assistance for such things as purchasing school supplies. The National Insurance Institute pays child support where the father, whether divorced or not, defaults on his obligations.

A ramified system of prenatal and well-baby clinics run by state-supported HMOs and other public bodies is dispersed throughout the country. Day care centers run by state-subsidized voluntary organizations liberally dot Israel's towns and cities. So do community centers, which provide low-cost activities for children, teens, and adults.

Most municipalities in Israel offer state-funded family services that include instrumental services, family counseling, and educational testing and counseling. Shelters for battered women and children have been established by a variety of women's organizations.

The elderly receive National Insurance payments. Indigent elderly who have difficulties taking care of themselves are entitled to home care.

In sum, although Israel is a relatively familistic society, Israeli families, hailing from many parts of the world, are highly diverse and still changing.

See also: BEDOUIN-ARAB FAMILIES; FAMILISM; IMMIGRATION; INTENTIONAL COMMUNITIES; ISLAM; JUDAISM; WAR/POLITICAL VIOLENCE

Bibliography

Al-Krenawi, A., and Graham, J. R. (1998). "Divorce among Muslim Arab Women in Israel." *Journal of Divorce and Remarriage* 29:103–119.

Ben-David, A. (1993). "Culture and Gender in Marital Therapy with Ethiopian Immigrants: A Conversation in Metaphors." *Contemporary Family Therapy: An International Journal* 15:327–339.

Central Bureau of Statistics. (1998). *Statistical Abstract of Israel,* no. 49. Jerusalem.

Central Bureau of Statistics. (1999). *Statistical Abstract of Israel,* no. 50. Jerusalem.

Cohen, O., and Savaya, R. (1997). "Broken Glass: The Divorced Woman in Moslem Arab Society in Israel." *Family Process* 36: 225–245.

Good, I. J., and Ben-David, A. (1995). "Family Therapy in Israel: A Review of Therapy Done under Unusual Circumstances." *Contemporary Family Therapy: An International Journal* 17:353–366.

Haj-Yahia, M. (1995). "Toward Culturally Sensitive Intervention with Arab Families in Israel." *Contemporary Family Therapy: An International Journal* 17:429–447.

Halpern, E. (2001). "Family Psychology from an Israeli Perspective." *American Psychology* 56:58–64.

Katz, R., and Peres, Y. (1986). "The Sociology of the Family in Israel: An Outline of Its Development from the 1950s to the 1980s." *European Sociology Review* 2:148–159.

Malkinson, R.; Rubin, S. S.; and Witztum, E. (2000). *Traumatic and Nontraumatic Loss and Bereavement: Clinical theory and Practice.* Madison, CT: Psychosocial Press.

Poskanzer, A. (1995). "The Matryshka: The Three-Generation Soviet Family in Israel." *Contemporary Family Therapy: An International Journal* 17:413–428.

Smooha, S. (1989). *Arabs and Jews in Israel: Conflict and Shared Attitudes in a Divided Society.* San Francisco: Westview Press.

ORNA COHEN

ITALY

As in other southern European countries, in Italy, new family structures are coming into being more slowly and in a smaller measure than in northern

European countries and North America. These new structures include such patterns as cohabitation, extramarital births, single parenthood, and one-person households. These countries are examples of the so-called Mediterranean model (Laslett 1983). At the same time, Italian families, as well as those of the other Mediterranean countries, have been experiencing important transformations both in dimensions and in the relationships among their members (Barbagli and Saraceno 1997).

Since 1970, Italy has witnessed great changes in family size, age at marriage, marriage stability, and birthrate (among the lowest, if not the lowest, in the world), although the pace of change has differed by region: family behaviours in north-central regions are more like those of western European countries than of southern Italian regions. People marry later and less frequently, have fewer children, divorce more often, and create new family models such as cohabitation, extramarital births, single parenthood, and one-person households.

Beyond the traditional differences between north and south are other relevant regional variations: The so-called *Third Italy* (Umbria, Marche, Abruzzo, Toscana, Emilia, Veneto, and Friuli) was characterized in the past by patrilocal residence and by multiple or extended family structures, while southern regions were characterized by neolocal independent residence and nuclear families, even if women married very young. The nuclear structure of southern families may be connected to the concentration of property in fiefs, and to the settling of peasants in rural towns. This is unlike Tuscany or Lombardy in the north, where peasants lived in "poderi" or "cascine" located in the fields. Both patterns were traditionally evident in north-western regions, with nuclear families in the urban areas and extended families in the countryside. The situation changed in the last half of the twentieth century, as multiple and extended families steadily decreased all over the country. Regional differences remain, although they are less marked than before (Barbagli 2000).

Italian families maintain strong bonds over generations. Children, after leaving home to establish new families, maintain strong relationships with their parents. Usually they live very near to one of the two parental families, make daily telephone calls to their parents (mainly the mother),

and visit them weekly. Their relationships with their parents typically display strong reciprocal support and exchanges, including childcare, care of the elderly and ill, help with economic troubles, loans, and advice. One of the main characteristics of Italian families is the strong intergenerational solidarity that allows Italians to overcome difficulties, find jobs, look after children, and ask for loans in situations in which the family network provides what, in other Western countries, is granted by public or private institutions. This sense of connectedness explains the great relevance that family as an institution assumes in Italian culture. To be a member of a family is what gives the individual a guarantee against any serious trouble in life, more so than being a member of any other group (C. E. R. 1999).

Marriage and Children

People in modern Italy marry less frequently and at an older age than in the past. Women get married at age twenty-seven, on average, and men at almost thirty. By the end of the twentieth century, Italians faced a new model of marriage that caused a shift forward of all the different phases of the family life cycle: later exit from the family, later achievement of independence, and later experience of parenthood.

In 1999, separations and divorce increased in the north (respectively, 5.1% and 3%) more than in the south of Italy (2.7 percent and 1.2 percent per 1,000 married couples). When couples separate or divorce, more than 90 percent of minors live in the custody of their mothers, 94 percent of those under six years of age.

Civil marriages have increased as well, (16.8 percent in 1990 and 20.3 percent in 1996), mainly because second marriages have become more common, and one cannot marry twice in the Catholic Church. Consequently, new models of cohabitation, in which one or both spouses have had a previous marriage and children, become less unusual.

The number of marriages in which one of the members of the married couple is not an Italian doubled in the 1990s, from 2.2 percent in 1989 to 5 percent in 1999. These marriages take place mainly in the north of Italy, and most involve Italian men who marry women from Eastern Europe or Latin America. Very few Italian women marry

TABLE 1

Italian families per number of members, by percentage			
Members	1989/90	1993/94	1998
One	20.3	21.5	21.7
Two	23.7	24.7	26.1
Three	23.2	23.4	23.4
Four	22.6	21.5	21.1
Five	7.7	6.5	5.9
Six or more	2.4	2.3	1.8

SOURCE: Istat, Indagini Multiscopo, 1990, 1993, 1994, 1998.

foreigners, and in these cases they marry mainly European men and men from North Africa, above all Morocco.

These processes and transformations of Italian families have been accompanied by a dramatic drop in the birthrate caused by the postponement of the birth of the first child, delayed marriages, and a new trend in deciding when one wants to become a parent. In 1971 the average age of women having their first child was 25.1; in 1998 it was 28.4. Only a small minority of Italian women have more than three children, and the majority have one or two. The average number of children per woman dropped from 2.4 in 1981 to 1.2 in 1998. In 1993-94 one-child families represented 43.8 percent of the total of all families with children; in 1997–98 they represented 45.2 percent.

To understand these changes in Italian family structures, it is important to consider the changes in the relationship of women to education and employment.

Education and Gender Roles

Italian women attend high school more successfully than do Italian men, and also more frequently. In 1950 only 7 percent of girls between the ages of fourteen and seventeen went to school, while 12 percent of boys did. In 1998-99 84 percent of the girls and 81 percent of the boys attended high schools. At university level women outnumbered men by the late 1990s. The increased level of education of Italian women helps to explain the greater presence of women in the labor market. However, Italian women are still well below the levels of other European and American countries (in 1999, 35.3% of Italian women aged fifteen and older were employed outside the home).

Women's traditional role of wife and mother is no longer appealing, and young housewives perceive their situation more as a necessity than as a choice. Working mothers declare themselves more satisfied than housewives and mothers, although they are weighed down by an enormous amount of work when one adds the work in the house to the work outside: 35 percent of young working mothers spend more than seventy hours working per week, and more than half, including those who work more than seventy, work more than sixty hours per week.

Italian men contribute very little to housework and childcare. The relations between husband and wife within the family are still very traditional, with a rigid separation of gender roles. Even children are asked to do very little housework, and gender differences are still present in the expectations of sons and daughters in helping with the housework: Boys are asked and expected to do less housework, have more freedom, and are less controlled by parents than are girls.

That Italian men contribute very little to housework and childcare may partially explain why Italy is experiencing a strong reduction in the number of children per couple among young couples. Italian mothers, unlike those of other western European and Western countries, do not leave the labor market even temporarily after having a child. The rigidity of the Italian labor market makes it extremely difficult, if not impossible, for mothers with young children to re-enter the job market, even after only a few years out. These mothers are not attractive to employers, who prefer men or childless women. Furthermore, part-time jobs are not common, and families have serious difficulties in living on only one salary. Therefore, the reproductive strategies of Italian families have changed, drastically reducing the number of children. This is compounded by the limited participation of the husband in childrearing and housework. Typically, a woman waits to get a good job, and after which it becomes very complicated to have more than one child without giving up the job.

Marriage and maternity are delayed to accomplish different goals: graduation from high school and university and the attainment of a stable occupation. These deep transformations are visible in the data from the Italian National Institute of Statistics (Istat 1998) on mothers with small children.

The majority of women who have at least one small baby (0-2 years old) are working mothers (47.4 percent) while 42.8 percent are housewives. In the north of Italy 63.1 percent of mothers of young children are working; in the center 54.95 percent; while in the south the figure is only 31 percent, with 53.7 percent of the mothers as housewives.

Young People Living in the Parental Family

The rise in the age at first marriage means that young people spend a longer time living in the parental family, which is favored over alternatives such as premarital cohabitation.

According to the data from the Multiscope survey "Family, Social Subjects, and Childhood Conditions" carried out in 1998 by ISTAT, only 2 percent of youths (4% of males compared to 2.5 percent of females) between the age of eighteen and thirty-four are living with a partner, 3.8 percent are living alone, and roughly 60 percent are living in the parental family, a higher percentage than in earlier years. In fact, in 1990 about 52 percent of youths in the same age group were living with their families. The experimenting of alternative family models, such as cohabitation and living alone, does not seem to attract Italian young people, who traditionally leave the parental home at the time of marriage. Prior to this, they rarely have the opportunity to live alone both because students usually attend university in the town in which their family lives and because of a lack of social policies that promote an early departure from the parental family (absence of unemployment benefits and grants to students). To this one must add the difficulty in obtaining housing caused by a lack of subsidized loans or government financing. The growth in new family structures is due, therefore above all to marital instability, and in fact one-person households are made mainly of divorced men and women.

The 1990s showed some evidence of change. There was a slight increase in the percentage of one-person households among the young. Living alone, though, involved mainly people between the ages of thirty-five and fifty-four, while the percentage of lone elders (55-75 years) decreased because both men and women were living longer.

Gender differences are striking: the great majority of nonwidowed singles are males (29.4%

TABLE 2

Italian singles living alone, for age classes, by percentage			
Age	1989/1990	1993/1994	1997/1998
15-24	1.2	1.1	1.2
25-34	4.7	5.1	5.3
35-44	3.6	5.6	5.1
45-54	4.5	5.9	5.1
SOURCE: Multiscopo Surveys 1990, 1993, 1994, 1997, 1998.			

compared to 24.3% of females) living in central and northern towns, where the percentage of divorces and separation is higher. This is because in Italy, mothers usually receive custody of their children. In the south there is a smaller percentage of singles (16.7%). Marriages are more stable in this region, which also has the highest percentage of families that include an elderly member (Cer 1999). The larger number of elderly people, mainly women, that live alone in the north does not imply an absence of family ties. Usually the single elder is well-placed in the family solidarity network, giving and receiving both material help and solidarity from younger family members. In this light, the intensity and frequency of family relationships is a forced response (Saraceno 1998) to the lack of adequate government family policies.

The need for adequate social family policies is growing. In Italy more than in other European countries, two great demographic changes are underway: a marked fertility decrease (1.2 children per woman) and a progressive aging of the population. The decrease in young people and the increase of the elderly pose serious questions on the future of health and retirement policies. In 2050 there will be two elderly citizens per young person (Cer 1999). This forecast represents a threat to·the persistence of family solidarity networks: the dwindling younger generations will have difficulties meeting the needs of an increasing number of elderly family members. Presumably the increase in single elderly citizens will be a cause of increased government expenditure on health and retirement benefits, and the growth in numbers of the nonactive (those retired, or too young or old to work) versus the active population will pose a problem for the pension system.

See also: GERMANY

Bibliography

Barbagli, M. (2000). *Sotto lo stesso tetto* (Under the same roof). Bologna: Il Mulino.

Barbagli, M., and Saraceno, C., eds. (1997). *Lo stato delle famiglie in Italia* (The characteristics of Italian families). Bologna: Il Mulino.

C. E. R (1999). *La solidarietà intergenerazionale nell'ambito familiare* (Intergenerarional solidarity within the family). Rome: Quaderni Cer.

Laslett, P. (1983). "Family and Household as Work Group and Kin Group." In *Family Forms in Historic Europe*, ed. R. Wall, J. Robin, P. Laslett. Cambridge, UK: Cambridge University Press.

Saraceno, C. (1998). *Mutamenti della famiglia e politiche sociali in Italia* (Family's change and social policies in Italy). Bologna: Il Mulino.

ISTAT (Istituto Nazionale di Statistica). (1998). "Family, Social Subjects and Childhood Conditions." In *Indagine multiscopo,* Roma.

ISTAT (Istituto Nazionale di Statistica). (2000). *Rapporto annuale* (Annual report, 1999). Roma.

Other Resource

Sabbadini, L. L. (1999). "Modelli di formazione e organizzazione della famiglia" (Formation and organization patterns of Italian families). Conference *Le famiglie interrogano le politiche sociali.* Bologna, 29-31 March. Available from http://www.Istat.it.

LUISA LEONINI

J

JAMAICA

See CARIBBEAN FAMILIES; ETHNIC VARIATION/ETHNICITY

JAPAN

The concept of the modern family—one in which biological parents give birth to, love, and nurture children—was introduced in Japan in the early twentieth century, after the nation opened itself up to international diplomacy under Emperor Meiji in 1868. A nationwide registration system was established at the end of the nineteenth century under the Meiji government. Until that time, people who did not belong to aristocratic, warrior, or landlord families did not register with the state or regional legal systems. Most of the people who did not fall in these categories were registered in the Buddhist temples of the local area.

Before the Meiji government, the term *family* did not include only biologically related people, but was far broader. Workers who lived in and subsisted on their labor in one village were regarded as one family. This changed after Japan entered the international scene; the Japanese Imperial Constitution of 1889 legally defined family in a written law as formed by blood lineage, with a father as head of the household.

Until 1945, when Japan was defeated in World War II and a new constitution was promulgated,

polygamy was still legal. Multiple wives, their children by one father, and their relatives were regarded as one family. After World War II, a reconstruction of Japanese society occurred under the new constitution, and a nationwide family registration system was established. The concept of family was understood in a modern way. However, the registration system that existed since the nineteenth century was preserved as *koseki* (family registration), with the individual registered under the family line headed by the father. *Koseki* still functions in the same way as the previous feudalistic system. People's origins can be traced back to the late nineteenth century. In this patriarchal system, a woman is supposed to enter the husband's family line and separate from her original family.

Under the democratic constitution, marriage was supposed to be based on equal relations between the man and woman. Polygamy was prohibited, and a family was formed under the father as a head of household. The contemporary Japanese family, however, is changing rapidly because of lower birth rates, longer life expectancies, an increase in the number of one-person households, and later age at marriage. In 2000, the average number of children for women in their reproductive years was 1.35. The average life expectancy in 1999 was 84 for women and 77 for men. The second most predominant household (after household with parents and unmarried children) is the single household. The percentage of single households among total households increased from 18.2 percent in 1975 to 24.1 percent in 2000. Among one-person households, those made up of older women and unmarried youths are increasing in number. The average age of first marriage for women in 2000 was 27 years, for men 28.8 years; the age of marriage in general, including second and third marriages, was 28.2 for women and 30.4 for men (White Paper on Women 2001).

Mating and Marriage

The typical ways in which marriage partners first meet are at work, through introduction by friends and siblings, and through marriage arrangement agencies. Since 1965, there have been more marriages based on love than arranged marriages. Women consider personality, economic stability, and occupation important characteristics in a potential mate. Men seek good personality, physical attractiveness, and shared hobbies.

Many people pay large amounts of money to have luxurious wedding ceremonies. The cost can range from 3,000,000 to 10,000,000 yen (US $30,000–$100,000). Typically, 100 to 200 guests will be invited to hotel ballrooms. Both Shinto-style weddings and more Western-style ceremonies are popular. A Shinto-style wedding is held in a shrine with traditional Japanese wedding costumes; a Western-style ceremony is held in a church, and the bride typically wears a white wedding dress, but wears both a traditional Japanese kimono and Western-style dress for the party after the ceremony. Most hotels in Japan have facilities for both. Newly married couples often honeymoon in Europe or North America, paying 1,500,000 yen (US $15,000) for a week or so.

According to research by the National Institute for Population and Social Welfare (1998), premarital sexual relations are increasing among the younger generation. The research shows that 80 percent of people, especially in urban areas, think it acceptable to have sex outside of marriage, if the partners love each other. The rate of premarital sex for women in 1987 was 30.2 percent; in 1992, 38.2 percent; and in 1997, 50.5 percent. The rate for men in 1987 was 53.0 percent; in 1992, 54.9 percent; and in 1997, 60.1 percent. Reports by the popular media suggest that young people get married when the woman gets pregnant, although there is no concrete research on this issue.

Legal marriage accounts for more than 85 percent of adult relationships. *Jijitsukon,* defined as a situation in which the partners live together for

A Japanese bride and groom hold champagne glasses during a traditional Shinto wedding ceremony. JERRY COOKE/CORBIS

more than a few months essentially as a married couple but without a formal marriage procedure, is not common. If the couple lives this way for two years or more, they are given the same rights as if they were legally married. Ninety-five percent of women take their husbands' family name upon marriage and are registered under the men's family name and lineage under the *koseki* system. More and more women, however, are keeping their maiden family names to continue their careers. The use of different family names among married couples is practiced in daily life, but legal registration still only permits the same family name for a married couple.

Gender Roles

The traditional gender roles—men as breadwinners and women as homemakers—are only supported by only 40 to 50 percent of people (NHK 1994; Ministry of Public Management 1995). Among younger couples, more flexible gender roles are becoming popular. Although attitudes are changing, actual behaviors are not: Japanese men do only twenty to thirty minutes' worth of domestic work per day, while women spend three and a half hours in household chores.

Husbands and wives report very little communication and conversation, as little as ten to fifteen minutes per day. The writer Iku Hayashi first coined the term *kateinai rikon* (domestic divorce) in 1983 to describe this situation. It means that there is no conversation, communication, and sexual relations between a husband and wife, but they do not divorce.

Roles for mothers and fathers are segregated. Childcare is regarded as the mother's responsibility; the father's domestic role is limited to small household repairs and playing with children on weekends. Full-time working wives also have the burden of housekeeping without help. Domestic help is not popular in Japan. When women need help in housekeeping work and childcare, their mothers help them, and working mothers prefer living close to their mothers' house for this reason. Husbands and wives call each other *father* and *mother,* even when children are not around. Japanese couples regard parental roles as more important than couple roles when they have children.

Masculinity and Men's Suicide

Data from the daily time budget survey (1990) suggest that men perform very limited housekeeping work and women spend seven times as much as men spend on housekeeping on weekdays. The data show that men work seven-and-a-half hours per day outside the home, although actual working hours may be longer than nine hours and commuting time one to two hours. Wives do almost 90 percent of chores such as cooking, shopping, cleaning, and laundry. Young men seem willing to take part in domestic tasks, yet the data reveal that they do so for only thirty minutes or less per day.

Because of the economic stagnation that has began in 1995, Japanese employment customs such as lifelong employment and seniority have been abolished. More middle-aged men are unemployed in a society that is highly geared towards information technology. The suicide rate among these men is increasing. There is a deep preconception that men should be strong, reliable breadwinners for family. If they cannot take this role and responsibility, men think they are less than men and lose the traditional identity of fathers. This loss is large enough to cause some men to commit suicide. If the man has insurance, family members can receive a settlement after his death, depending on the case. Recent scholarship has focused on children who have lost fathers by suicide, as the number is increasing.

Decreasing Number of Children

On average, Japanese women have 1.35 children, one of the lowest birth rates in the world, as of 2000. The decline in birth rates has brought a drastic decrease in the younger population. The major reasons that women do not have children are financial: the high cost of childcare, education, and housing of an adequate size. Another factor has to do with the isolation women feel from the outside society once they are mothers. They are expected to quit their jobs to bring up children. In Japanese society, childcare, especially for children under six, is considered the mother's role. This social norm is called *Bosei shinwa.* The increase of child abuse by parents (more often by mothers) is a sign of this isolation. Social services for children are not sufficient, and the sole responsibility for childcare is a heavy burden by women.

Many women have only one or two children, few enough so that they are able to stay home to nurture and educate them adequately. Many parents want their children to excel in academic endeavors and pass the rigorous examinations to get into distinguished universities.

Adult children often continue to live with their parents even after they have completed their education. Those adults who stay with parents as dependents are called *parasite singles,* a phrase coined by Masahiro Yamaguchi of Tokyo Metropolitan University. They are supported by their parents and given a place to live and money for food, clothes, and entertainment. Eighty percent of women and 60 percent of men in their twenties fit this category. Parents prefer children to live at home; because they have a small number of children, they are uneasy to about living by themselves, and children can take care of them when they get sick.

Seniors

The increase in the number of older people is another important trend in Japanese society. According to the 2000 census, the number of people aged sixty-five or over is 21,860,000, or 17.4 percent of the total population. The number of older women above sixty-five who are living by themselves is 1,922,000; the number of men older than sixty-five who are living single is 556,000. The majority of older women (80 percent) live by themselves. The heavy burden of seniors' care is on women. The eldest son's wife is expected to take care of older parents at home in the traditional Japanese manner. Elder abuse by family members occurs in some households. As elders are taken care of in a private space by family members, the abuse is hidden and not discovered until the situation becomes serious.

Public services for seniors are not sufficient. In 1998, The Ministry of Labor and Health established a new senior care management system and the qualifying examination. Senior care service in Japan is family based. Seniors are taken care of at private homes. The national senior care system produced many caregivers for older people, but the working conditions and wages are not good enough to obtain high-quality professional services.

Divorce

Compared with other developed countries, the rate of divorce in Japan is still very low. Among 1,000 people, 20 (2%) are divorced, according to a study conducted by the Ministry of Labor and Welfare, Statistics and Information Division in 2000. The rate has been slowly increasing—in 1997 it was 1.78 percent, and in 1998 it was 1.94 percent. The divorce rate is higher in urban areas such as Osaka, Japan's second largest city, which had a 2.42 percent divorce rate in 1998. The divorce rate increased up to 4.6 times from 1965 to 1995.

Divorce is not a serious stigma among young people. But in general, especially in when a divorced couple lives in a local area with close neighborhood relations, divorce is viewed as detrimental to the family and a tragedy for children. The discriminatory attitude is often seen in communities and in schools. Divorced mothers find it hard to support themselves. Middle-aged divorced women have problems finding stable jobs. Single fathers find that the childcare role and housekeeping chores that they have to assume are heavy burdens.

Women's Vulnerable Economic Base

The younger generation is more likely to divorce than the older one. Couples divorce for various reason. The most common is mismatched personalities and values; the second is inadequate support by the husband; and the third is violence by the husband. Wives propose the majority (70%) of divorces. The primary reason for the low divorce rate in Japan compared to other developed countries is that women lack an economic base to live by themselves: 75 percent of middle-aged married women have no job or are unstable part-time workers. The second reason is that the Japanese wage system is based on a family wage system, and the major income earner is the husband. Men get additional fringe benefits for supporting wives and children; women who are full-time workers only get their wages. A woman can require the employer to pay fringe benefit to support children only when she makes more money than her husband and is approved by a local government to be head of the household. The third reason for the low divorce rate is the expectation that women should stay home with children combined with the long working hours typical in Japan. These factors make it too heavy a burden for a woman to both work full time and take care of children. Thus, most of women leave the workplace when they have children. When women's economic base is provided by her husband, divorce means that she has no way to support herself and her children.

Single Mothers at the Poverty Level

The rate of single-mother households was 1 percent in 1999—that is, among the total of 44,923,000 households, there were 448,000 single-mother households. Among all single mothers, 85.1 percent are widows, 7.5 percent are divorced, and 1.6 percent have never been married.

The standard of living for single mothers is lower than that of two-parent households. Average annual income decreases by almost one-third to 2,150,000 yen (approximately US $21,500), compared to a household with both husband and wife at an annual income of 6,480,000 (approximately US $64,800). Given the high cost of living in Japan, many single mothers need social welfare support.

Family Wage System

The Japanese wage system is base on family wage. When a man has a wife and children, he receives additional payment to support them. The family wage is paid only when the wife has no income or income less than 1,030,000 yen (about US $10,300) per year. If she earns this amount or less, she need not pay state tax and local government tax, and she is also exempted from the pension reserve fund. In addition, she can get 70 percent of husband's estate, if he had any fortune, after his death. Although the system was originally gender neutral, in almost all cases, women have lower wages or no income. This system eventually supports full-time housewives with no income. The taxation and wage system strengthens the attitude that women need not work full-time or at all because their husbands should support them. This system is based on the recognition of women's role in the family and their nonpaid work at home. The results are a wider gender gap in wage and fixed social roles for women and men. This system also rationalizes the lower wage for women in workforce.

Domestic Violence

In April 2001, an antidomestic-violence law was promulgated in Japan. Since 1995, spousal violence by husbands became a social issue. In 1997, the Tokyo metropolitan office did research on the situation of domestic violence in the Japanese family. Women who suffered any kind of violence by their husbands constituted 33 percent of the sample. This rate was unexpectedly high. The kinds of violence vary greatly and include physical and psychological violence and verbal dehumanization. Forced sexual relations and nonuse of condoms are common forms of domestic violence. Complaining about the way housekeeping is done another way that it manifests itself.

Japan lacks sufficient counseling services and shelters for the women who have experienced domestic violence. As of 1999, there were only thirty private women's shelters available in Japan. (At the local government level, each prefecture established an anti-prostitution facility in the late 1950s, but these are not for married women who are victims of domestic violence.) Public service by local governments does not show an understanding that women are vulnerable when they are not economically independent. Even if women are sheltered from abusive husbands for several weeks, they have no house to return to other than their husbands'.

Birth Control and Abortion

Abortion is legal in Japan as long as it is done within twenty-two weeks of conception. In 1997, a total of 337,799 abortions were reported. Among these, 23.8 percent were among women between the ages of twenty and twenty-four, and 20.4 percent were among twenty-five- to thirty-year-olds. The number of abortions overall has decreased since the 1960s, but the teenage abortion rate is increasing. This increase is occurring because teenage girls lack knowledge of birth control and their reproductive function and rights. When women have abortions, they have strong feelings of guilt and fear of taking a life.

In Buddhist temples there is a special way of mourning an aborted baby's soul, called *mizuko-jizou*. Often temples ask women to donate a large amount of money to mourn her aborted baby, claiming that otherwise, the women will be possessed by the evil spirits of aborted babies. This kind of superstition is still alive in some rural and urban areas. Some temples profit greatly from this superstition.

The most common method of birth control is the condom (77.8% in 1998). Use of the birth control pill (1.1%) is not widespread because it is available only through gynecologists and can not be purchased without a prescription.

Leave for Working Parents

In 1998, the revised Equal Employment Opportunity Law included parental leave for one year for fathers and mothers. Mother can take paid maternal leave for childbirth, but leave for childcare is not covered and wages are not paid by the employer. In 99 percent of the cases, mothers take parental leave to stay home for the children. Fathers rarely take parental leave.

Conclusion

The Japanese family is changing rapidly. More women want to be economically independent. Men are showing some flexibility toward taking part in domestic activities. In the twenty-first century, the Japanese family is developing into a more individualistic, gender-equal family.

See also: ANCESTOR WORSHIP; ASIAN-AMERICAN FAMILIES; BUDDHISM; CONFUCIANISM; ETHNIC VARIATION/ETHNICITY

Bibliography

Higuchi, K., et al., eds. (1999). *Genndai Jyosei.* (Women of Modern Days). Tokyo: Toyo Keizai Shinpousha Japan.

Huber, K. R. (1992). *Women in Japanese Society, An Annotated Bibliography of Selected English Language Materials.* New York: Greenwood.

Inoue, T., et al. (1999). *Jyosei no Data Book* (Data book on women). Tokyo: Yuhikaku.

International Comparative Research on Family and Work. (1994). Tokyo: NHK (Japan Broadcasting Association).

Ishida, A. (1989). "Women and the Family: Post-Family Alternatives." *Review of Japanese Culture and Society* 3(1):79–95.

Japan Statistical Yearbook. (2002). Tokyo: Ministry of Public Management, Home Affairs.

Jyoseino Kurashi To Seikatsu Ishiki Data Shu (Women's Living and Attitude Research Result Data). (2001). Tokyo: JYOUHOU SENTAA.

Kokuminn Seikatsu Hakusho (White paper nation's life). (1999). Tokyo: Gyousei.

Nihon Rodo Kyokai, ed. *Problems of Working Women. 1981 and 1986.* Tokyo: Japan Institute of Labor.

Ministry of Public Management. Home Affairs, Statistics Bureau. (1995). *Youth and Their Life, Basic Attitudinal Research.* Tokyo: Ministry Report.

Ueno, C. (1988a). "Genesis of the Urban Housewife." Japan Quarterly 34(2):130–142.

Ueno, C. (1988b). "The Japanese Women's Movement: The Counter-Values To Industrialism." In *The Japanese Trajectory: Modernization and Beyond,* ed. Gavan McCormack and Yoshio Sugimoto. New York: Cambridge University Press.

Yokohama Women's Forum, ed. (1997). *Zuhyou Demiru onna no Gennzai* (Data on women of today). Kyoto: Minerva Shobou.

JUNKO KUNINOBU

JEALOUSY

Often called the "green-eyed monster," jealousy has been a literary theme for centuries. However, it was not until the 1970s that jealousy became the focus of systematic, social science research.

Most contemporary conceptualizations of jealousy define it by focusing on situational antecedents. This makes it possible to distinguish jealousy from envy because different situations evoke them. Jealousy is precipitated by a threat from an agent to a person's relationship with someone, whereas envy is a negative reaction that is precipitated when someone else has a relationship to a person or object (Bringle and Buunk 1985).

Distinguishing between jealousy and envy does not mean they cannot occur in the same situation; they can. However, the overlapping occurrence of the two phenomena does not suggest that one can be reduced to the other.

Jealousy is best viewed as a compound emotion resulting from the situational labeling of one or more of the primary emotions such as fear or anger. Society teaches us to label the primary emotions we experience in specific situations that threaten significant relationships as *jealousy*. In other words, the primary emotion words such as *anger* and *fear* describe the emotional state, whereas the compound emotion word *jealousy* explains the emotional state (Hupka 1984).

Because individuals learn "explanations" during the socialization process, this conceptualization of jealousy assumes that jealousy is a social phenomenon. It is at least partially learned and it is manifested in response to symbolic stimuli that have meaning to the individual. The social aspects of jealousy have been noted by a number of writers. Kingsley Davis (1936), who is among the most prominent, argues that a comprehensive conceptualization of jealousy must include the public or community element.

The distinction between primary emotions and the compound emotion of jealousy is illustrated by the following example of sexual jealousy. A husband confesses to his wife that he recently had a one-time sexual relationship with another woman while away from home on a trip. Depending upon a variety of cultural, personal, and relational factors, the wife may experience either anger, fear, disgust, sadness, or a combination of such primary emotions. If the woman is typical of most individuals in Western society, she will interpret her husband's extramarital relationship as a threat to their marriage and will have learned that people experience jealousy in such situations. As a result, she will explain her anger, fear, and other primary emotions in terms of jealousy. Because extramarital sex is incompatible with many people's moral values, this example illustrates Eugene Mathes's (1991) point that the situations in which jealousy is experienced are determined by a person's beliefs about morality as well as by social expectations.

Jealousy is defined in a variety of ways in the literature. Gordon Clanton (1981) defines it as a protective reaction to a perceived threat to a valued relationship. Gerald McDonald (1982), taking a *structural exchange* perspective, views marital jealousy as the perceived threat of diminution or loss of the valued resources of the spouse. Robert Bringle and Bram Buunk (1985) define it as an aversive emotional reaction that occurs as the result of a partner's extradyadic relationship that is real, imagined, or considered likely to occur. Ira Reiss (1986) presents a sociological or group perspective by defining jealousy as a boundary-setting mechanism for what the group feels are important relationships. Finally, Gary Hansen (1991) expands upon Clanton's definition and views jealousy as a protective reaction to a perceived threat to a valued relationship, arising from a situation in which the partner's involvement with an activity and/or another person is contrary to the jealous person's definition of their relationship.

Dual-Factor Conceptualization

These definitions imply that two factors are necessary for a person to be jealous. First, the person must perceive his or her partner's actual or imagined involvement with an activity and/or another person as contrary to his or her definition of their relationship (Factor 1). Second, the person must perceive the relationship as valuable (Factor 2). Factor 1 acknowledges the fact that how one subjectively defines a relationship is important in understanding jealousy. As Carolyn Ellis and Eugene Weinstein state (1986, p. 343), "Jealousy occurs when a third party threatens the area of identification that *specifically defines the relationship* (emphasis in original)." The partner's behavior referred to in Factor 1 need not be sexual. Jealousy can arise from one's partner's involvement with children, professional colleagues, or solitary activities if such behavior is contrary to the jealous person's definition of their relationship and the relationship is valued. Factor 2, the importance of viewing the relationship as valuable, is demonstrated by cross-cultural work that finds that the importance of marriage or the value society places on it is related to jealousy.

This conceptualization focuses on the social psychological and sociological aspects of jealousy.

In addition, there is the psychoanalytic speculation that early sibling conflicts may increase the intensity of jealousy in adult romantic relationships (Freud 1955). There also is John Bowlby's (1969, 1973, 1980) *attachment theory* that postulates that ill-formed or disrupted attachments with early caretakers often results in *anxious attachment*. The anxiously attached person remains excessively sensitive to the possibility of separation or loss of love and is especially susceptible to adult jealousy. A study by Clanton and David Kosins (1991) designed to test these two perspectives found little support for them and concluded that a sociological view emphasizing jealousy's role as a protector of valued relationships is a theoretical framework with greater utility.

Types of Jealousy

Various attempts have been made to distinguish between different types of jealousy. One important distinction is between *normal* and *abnormal jealousy* (Pines 1992). Normal jealousy has its basis in a real threat to a person's relationship with another. Most "normal" people experience intense jealousy when a valued relationship is threatened. On the other hand, jealousy is abnormal in two circumstances. First, jealousy is abnormal when it is not related to a real threat to a valued relationship, but to some inner trigger of the jealous individual. Such jealousy is also called *delusional jealousy*. Second, jealousy is abnormal when the jealous response is dramatically exaggerated or violent.

A similar distinction is made by Gerrod Parrott (1991), who believes the most important distinction concerns the nature of the threat to the relationship. Jealousy may occur when the threat is only suspected and its nature is unclear. On the other hand, it may occur when the threat is unambiguously real and its effects are known. When the threat is unclear or only suspected, the result is *suspicious jealousy,* and the predominant reactions concern fears and uncertainties. When the threat to the relationship is unambiguous and damaging, the result is a fait accompli: jealousy and the reactions are an accomplished fact.

Finally, Gregory White and Paul Mullen (1989) differentiate three major classes of jealousy. *Symptomatic jealousy* is a consequence of a major mental illness such as paranoid disorder, schizophrenia, substance abuse, or organic brain disorders. Because of personality disorder or strong sensitizing experiences, some people are especially sensitive to self-esteem or relationship threat and experience *pathological jealousy*. *Normal jealousy*, on the other hand, occurs in people who are neither sensitized nor suffering from a major mental illness. These three classes of jealousy differ according to the relative influences of biology, personality, and relationship on the development of jealousy; in the jealous person's capacity for reality testing; and in suggested treatment approaches.

Correlates of Jealousy

Research has identified a number of factors associated with jealousy. Although both women and men experience jealousy, there are differences in the ways they experience and react to it. Men are more reactive to sexual involvement or threats, whereas women are more distressed by emotional involvement, loss of time and attention, and the prospect of losing a primary relationship (Buss et al. 1992; Teismann and Mosher 1978). *Evolutionary psychology* explains these sex differences in terms of the different adaptive problems men and women have faced. Because fertilization occurs internally within women, men have faced the problem of uncertainty in their genetic parentage of offspring. Therefore, men's jealousy is triggered by cues to sexual infidelity. Although women do not face the uncertainty of parentage, infidelity of a regular mate can be damaging. The man's time, energy, commitment, parental investment, and resources can be channeled to another woman and her children. Therefore, women's jealousy is more likely to be triggered by the possibility of the long-term diversion of such commitments as the mate's emotional involvement with another woman.

A cross-cultural study conducted in the Netherlands, Germany, and the United States lends support to this explanation (Buunk et al. 1996). It found that men in all three societies tend to become more upset over a partner sharing purely sexual interest in a third person whereas women demonstrate more upset over a partner's desire for romantic and emotional involvement with another person. This doesn't mean that culture is unimportant, however. The same study found that the magnitude of sex differences clearly vary across cultures.

When it comes to reacting to jealousy, women are more likely to try to change to please their partners in order to avoid the threat of another relationship, whereas men are more likely to seek solace or retribution in alternative relationships (White and Mullen 1989). In addition, women are more likely to test a relationship by deliberately attempting to make their partners jealous (Adams 1980).

Researchers have consistently found gender-role traditionalism to be related positively to jealousy for one or both sexes. The division of labor in traditional gender roles may foster dependency and a sense of personal inadequacy. The resulting fear of facing the world alone increases jealousy. Similarly, positive associations have been found between jealousy and low self-esteem, insecurity, relationship dependency, and/or lack of alternatives for one or both sexes.

There is evidence that jealousy is negatively related to post-conventional moral reasoning among women (Mathes and Deuger 1985). This means that women who evaluate actions in terms of individual rights and abstract ethical principles are less likely to experience jealousy. In addition, males in heterosexual relationships are more sexually jealous than males in homosexual relationships (Hawkins 1990). Other findings are of interest for what they fail to show. Both *romanticism* and *trust* have been found not to be related to jealousy (Hansen 1982, 1985). These results fail to support the belief that jealousy and romantic love are intimately linked as well as the assumption that trust decreases the probability of jealousy.

Responses to and Coping with Jealousy

People respond to jealousy-producing situations in a number of ways. One of the more comprehensive attempts to classify them comes from Jeff Bryson (1991), who identified eight modes of response: *emotional devastation, reactive retribution* (get even), *arousal* (intensify ardor or interest in partner), *need for social support* (more intensive interaction with friends), *intropunitiveness* (blame and punish oneself for being jealous), *confrontation* (confront the situation directly), *anger,* and *impression management* (make others think don't care/get drunk or high). These eight responses comprise a variety of cognitive, emotional, and behavioral reactions that are independent of each other. A person may experience all of them, some of them, or only a single reaction in response to a particular jealousy-producing situation.

In addition to identifying the ways in which people respond, research also has focused on how people cope with jealousy. Buunk (1982) examined the ways people cope with their spouses' extramarital relationships and identified three strategies: *avoidance* (of the spouse), *reappraisal* (of the situation), and *communication*. Avoidance includes such things as considering the possibility of leaving the spouse and retreating. Reappraisal refers to cognitive attempts to reduce one's jealousy and includes developing a critical attitude toward one's own jealousy as well as direct attempts to get the jealousy under control by relativizing the whole situation. Communication, the most common strategy, can reduce jealousy if it results in a redefinition of the relationship or a changed perception of the partner's behavior. Buunk (1982) found that communication is positively related to marital satisfaction whereas avoidance is negatively related to it. Janice L. Francis (1977) reached a similar conclusion when she identified the development of communication skills as the appropriate treatment mode for sexual jealousy.

There is evidence that some people also cope with jealousy by devaluing their relationship. Peter Salovey and Judith Rodin (1985) found that *selective ignoring,* defined as simply deciding that the desired object is not that important, is a coping strategy used by some.

Although many studies of jealousy do not investigate the extreme techniques of coping with jealousy such as the use of physical force or homicide, studies of family violence leave little doubt that they occur frequently. Martin Daly, Margo Wilson, and Suzanne Weghorst (1982) reviewed several studies of spousal homicide that used data beyond those found in police files and concluded that male sexual jealousy may be a major source of conflict in an overwhelming majority of spousal homicides in North America. In addition, young males experiencing intense sexual jealousy are among the most common perpetrators of murder and suicide (Marzuk, Tardiff, and Hirsch 1992). Similarly, studies have noted the prevalence of jealousy as a motive in nonfatal wife abuse (Dobash and Dobash 1979) and courtship violence (Bookwala et al. 1992).

It is interesting to note that culture appears to contribute to the severity of aggression in sexual jealousy situations among males. Hupka and James M. Ryan (1990) studied ninety-two preindustrial societies and found that importance attached to being married, limitations placed on nonmarital sexual gratification, and emphasis placed on private ownership of property are associated with more aggressive responses in jealousy situations.

Further evidence for the importance of culture comes from the work of Ana R. Delgado, Gerardo Prieto, and Roderick A. Bond (1997) who examined whether people consider jealousy justification for wife battery. They found striking differences between Britain where the harmdoer was seen as more guilty and Spain where the victim was seen as more guilty.

Finally, a number of social-psychological studies provide some insight into some of the cognitive processes that may be involved as people cope with jealousy by changing their perceptions of their partners' behavior. Studies by White (1981) and Buunk (1984) indicate that perceived motives or attributions for the partner's behavior are related to jealousy. Therefore, changes in perceived motives or attributions can reduce jealousy. In addition, Bernd Schmitt (1988) found that jealous people derogate their rival on attributes they perceive to be important to their partners, but not on attributes they perceive as less important to their partners.

Conclusion

Jealousy has emerged as a legitimate area of social scientific study since the 1970s. Considerable progress has been made in understanding the nature of jealousy, identifying factors associated with it, and examining some of the ways people respond to and cope with jealousy. However, because there is much more to learn, jealousy, which is a major issue in many intimate relationships, should remain a significant focus of scientific investigation. Considering the fact that most contemporary empirical work has been done in North America and Europe, there is an obvious need for additional work focusing on jealousy in non-Western societies.

See also: CONFLICT: COUPLE RELATIONSHIPS; INFIDELITY; THERAPY: COUPLE RELATIONSHIPS

Bibliography

Bringle, R., and Buunk, B. (1985). "Jealousy and Social Behavior: A Review of Person, Relationship, and Situational Determinants." In *Self, Situations, and Social Behavior,* vol. 6 of *Review of Personality and Social*

Psychology, edited by P. Shaver. Beverly Hills, CA: Sage.

Bryson, J. B. (1991). "Modes of Response to Jealousy-Evoking Situations." In *The Psychology of Jealousy and Envy,* edited P. Salovey. New York: Guilford Press.

Buss, D.; Larsen, R. J.; Westen, D.; and Semmelroth, J. (1992). "Sex Differences in Jealousy: Evolution, Physiology, and Psychology." *Psychological Science* 3:251–255.

Buunk, B. (1982). "Strategies of Jealousy: Styles of Coping with Extramarital Involvement of Spouse." *Family Relations* 31:13–18.

Buunk, B. (1984). "Jealousy as Related to Attributions for the Partner's Behavior." *Social Psychology Quarterly* 47:107–112.

Buunk. B.; Angleitner, A.; Oubaid, V.; and Buss, D. M. (1996). "Sex Differences in Jealousy in Evolutionary and Cultural Perspective: Test From the Netherlands, Germany, and the United States." *Psychological Science* 7:359–363.

Clanton, G. (1981). "Frontiers of Jealousy Research: Introduction to the Special Issue on Jealousy." *Alternative Lifestyles* 4:259–273.

Clanton, G., and Kosins, D. J. (1991). "Developmental Correlates of Jealousy." In *The Psychology of Jealousy and Envy,* edited P. Salovey. New York: Guilford Press.

Daly, M.; Wilson, M.; and Weghorst, S. J. (1982). "Male Sexual Jealousy." *Ethology and Sociobiology* 3:11–27.

Delgado, A. R.; Prieto, G.; and Bond, R. A. (1997). "The Cultural Factor in Lay Perception of Jealousy as a Motive for Wife Battery." *Journal of Applied Social Psychology* 27:1824–1841.

Ellis, C., and Weinstein, E. (1986). "Jealousy and the Social Psychology of Emotional Experience." *Journal of Social and Personal Relationships* 3:337–357.

Francis, J. L. (1977). "Toward the Management of Heterosexual Jealousy." *Journal of Marriage and Family Counseling* 3:61–69.

Freud, S. (1955). "Some Neurotic Mechanisms in Jealousy, Paranoia and Homosexuality." In *The Standard Edition of the Complete Psychological Works of Sigmund Freud,* vol. 18, ed. and trans. J. Strachey. London: Hogarth Press.

Hansen, G. L. (1982). "Reactions to Hypothetical, Jealousy-Producing Events." *Family Relations* 31:513–518.

Hansen, G. L. (1985). "Perceived Threats and Marital Jealousy." *Social Psychology Quarterly* 48:262–268.

Hawkins, R. O., Jr. (1990). "The Relationship between Culture, Personality, and Sexual Jealousy in Men in Heterosexual and Homosexual Relationships." *Journal of Homosexuality* 19:67–84.

Hupka, R. B. (1984). "Jealousy: Compound Emotion or Label for a Particular Situation." *Motivation and Emotion* 8:141–155.

Hupka, R. B., and Ryan, J. M. (1990). "The Cultural Contribution to Jealousy: Cross-Cultural Aggression in Sexual Jealousy Situations." *Behavior Science Research* 24:51–71.

Mathes, E. W. (1991). "A Cognitive Theory of Jealousy." In *The Psychology of Jealousy and Envy,* ed. P. Salovey. New York: Guilford Press.

Pines, A. M. (1992). *Romantic Jealousy: Understanding and Conquering the Shadow of Love.* New York: St. Martins Press.

Schmitt, B. H. (1988). "Social Comparison and Romantic Jealousy." *Personality and Social Psychology Bulletin* 14:374–387.

Teismann, M. W., and Mosher, D. L. (1978) "Jealous Conflict in Dating Couples." *Psychological Reports* 42:1211–1216.

White, G. L. (1981). "Jealousy and Partner's Perceived Motives for Attraction to a Rival." *Social Psychology Quarterly* 44:24–30.

White, G. L., and Mullen, P. E. (1989). *Jealousy: Theory, Research, and Clinical Strategies.* New York: Guilford Press.

GARY L. HANSEN
ZHENG ZENG

JOINT CUSTODY

See CHILD CUSTODY

JUDAISM

According to Jewish tradition, the family and home make up a *mikdash me'at,* or a small sanctuary, like a synagogue. However, as fewer twenty-first century Jewish families can be called traditional, there are different interpretations of what sanctifies them now and what will sanctify them in the future. No longer shaped primarily by religious laws, the Jewish family today defines itself in many ways.

Tradition and Change

Halakhah is the branch of rabbinical writing outlining the laws of Jewish religious and ethical behavior. A proposal for new Jewish family values in a *post-halahkic* time (Ackelsberg 1992) suggests that Jewish families can live outside traditional religious ideals and the demands they make on personal, family, and social life. Such families construct their values according to the forms of Judaism that fit their experience and reflect their desires for traditional observance. Competing accounts of contemporary Jewish experience insist on the need for religious and historical norms for Jewish family life, and particularly so at a time when modern society is increasingly pluralistic and relativistic in matters of behavior and ethics. Even those favoring the traditional Jewish family acknowledge the need to recognize variations in commitment and practice as legitimate adaptations to modern life (Wertheimer 1994).

However one feels about contemporary values, any general account of the Jewish family is likely to overstate its commonalties (just as the historical image of the Jewish family can obscure important differences [Kramer 1989]). What can be said of the Jewish family is perhaps best put in the form of contrasts, choices, and adaptations of tradition. If, as two authoritative studies of Jewish life have recently proposed, it is "the Jew within"—the Jew who interprets for himself or herself the meaning and practice of Judaism—who matters more than halakhic conformity and synagogue membership, then the family too will represent the possibilities for change and Jewish adaptation as much as it does tradition (Cohen and Eisen 2000; Fishman 2000).

For much of its history the Jewish family has been guided by religious rules and practices, as represented in the Hebrew Bible (including the Torah, or the Five Books of Moses) and the commentaries of the rabbis in the compilations known as the *Talmud* and the *Mishnah*. With the destruction of the Temple in Jerusalem by the Babylonians in 586 BCE and then again by the Romans in 70 BCE, Jews have been a people in exile. Their books, laws, and other habits of society they represent, became an essential source of education and continuity. Thus, the story of the Jewish family begins in Genesis, where it is written that God blessed the first man and woman, and instructed them to have children and to raise them in a family. To do so would be a primary way, because God had created humans in his image, of also living in a divine world. In Exodus (20:12) the Jews are commanded to "Honor your father and your mother in order that your days may be prolonged on the soil that your God is giving you." With the core impulse and relational code in place, Judaism provided a strong ethical bond for the family. *Shalom bayit*—respect for every member of the family, recognition of the different needs of every member, and mutual responsibility for each other's physical and emotional well being—is the guiding historical principle. It is accomplished by fulfilling the *mitzvoth* and observing the rituals of the Jewish week and year. Mitzvoth are the 613 religious commandments in the Torah and also ordinary good deeds.

Throughout the Jews' long history, the family and the home, incorporating the desires of private rather than public life, provided identity and security. Until they gained legal rights, during the period of *emancipation* in eighteenth century Europe, Jews had little reason to identify with the state. The classic Jewish texts, and the social habits they had prompted and sustained, were an essential source of high rates of marriage and childbearing among Jews in the premodern world. However, traditional control of the family began to decline as Jewish thought and society made way for new ideas, science, and democracy. With emancipation and then the *Jewish Enlightenment* the Jewish family, like other institutions, changed in response to greater social and economic opportunities. Less bound by religion, the family became more adaptive—a scene of growth and development, particularly for life in the large cities. Nevertheless, its traditional structure still prompted many to see it as the source of authentic Judaism. Thus, a French writer said in 1886 that "It is neither the rabbis, nor the synagogue, nor the Talmud, nor even the law or persecution which preserved the Jewish religion. It is the love of parents for children, the love of children for parents—it is the family" (cited in Hyman 1989).

Indeed, lighting the Sabbath candles and making the blessings over the bread and wine, and enjoying the Sabbath dinner, remain universal and durable expressions of Jewish family identity. Jewish holidays and celebrations—like Channukah and

Purim—are typically centered in the home for observance and celebration as well as in the synagogue. For many Jews today the Passover Seder represents the meaning of the Jewish family. There is the ancient distribution of roles in the meal-based service. Women light the candles and men make the blessing over the wine. The youngest child recites the *Four Questions,* in effect guiding the entire family toward recognition of what is unique about the biblical events the holiday records.

As is often noted, Jewish celebrations all have their special foods, reflecting too the role of eating Jewish dishes among those whose claim Jewish identities but have only occasional interest in Judaism as a religion. Lionel Blue vividly tells us:

> The changes of the liturgical year are marked out for the Jew by smell and taste, by the aromas of the kitchen. Through the most basic senses, he feels the changing moods of the spirit. Theologies alter and beliefs may die, but smells always remain in his memory, calling him back to his own childhood. . . . Whatever prayers he may forget, the gastronomic cycle remains. (cited in DeLange 2000)

Thus, Jewish family memory can be intense even when an individual lives a largely secular and assimilated life.

Migration from Europe

With increasing anti-Semitism and violence against Jews in Europe and Russia, from the Russian pogroms of the 1880s through the Holocaust, the Jewish population center shifted from Europe to the United States and Israel. After World War II, the Jewish family in the United States prospered. U.S. Jews have been particularly successful in education and the professions and have claimed many of the advantages of middle class life. Even so, virtually every account of contemporary Jewish life registers uneasiness about its status and future, including the fate of the family. "Once perhaps the most predictably normative of American family types, contemporary Jewish-American families now seem to be the epitome of change" (Fishman 2000). For with prosperity, as is the case with other groups, has come a high degree of assimilation, and among many Jews, the feeling that they are at least as much "Americans" as they are Jews.

The increasing influence of the modern Jewish denominations has meant changing ideas about the individual and the family. *Conservative* and *Reform* Jews, although differing in attitudes toward Jewish tradition, are both less categorically tied to traditional family practices than the *Orthodox.* For example, the laws and ritual practices of *kashrut* still govern Orthodox and sometimes Conservative family life, whereas they are unevenly observed or ignored among Reform Jews. A fourth denomination, *Reconstructionism,* is widely understood to fall between Conservatism and Reform, and families who identify with it also blend traditional and modern features of Jewish living.

Jewish identity—for individuals and within the family—represents a combination of religion and ethnicity, the latter being the dominant factor for many Jews in the years since World War II. The family is the crucible of Jewish identity, the place where commitments to Jewish ideas, values, and ways of living are encountered and expressed. But the Jewish family, like other institutions in the United States has responded to pressures that both reduce difference, late artifacts of the famous *melting pot,* and strengthen it, like the ethnic revivals of the 1960s and 1970s when racial and then ethnic minorities found it satisfying to accentuate what made them different from others. Thus, as Charles Liebman (1990) has argued, the Jewish family should be seen against the historical choices posed by loyalty to *universalism,* or the values Jews share with others, in contrast to *particularism,* or those values Jews believe are unique to their history and faith. Even so, with the increasing individualism of Jewish life, either choice can mean a weaker connection to traditional religious observance.

In the latest study of the U.S. Jewish community (Cohen and Eisen 2000), the family is presented ideally as a chain of influence across generations. Thus, "Those who are nearest exert the greatest influence upon Jewish observance and supply its greatest meaning, serving as both stimulus and audience to the enactment of convictions, which might otherwise have remained within the self." Grandparents are identified as being crucial and beloved role models for many Jews who came to adulthood in the later decades of the twentieth century. However, as wealth and mobility have increased during this time, the extended Jewish family became less common, and nostalgia for the roles of family elders has replaced the experience

A Jewish family celebrating Seder. For many Jews today the Passover Seder represents the meaning of the Jewish family. The ancient distribution of roles is represented in the meal-based service. ROGER RESSMEYER/CORBIS

of family life with them. The success of Allegra Goodman's collection of short stories, *The Family Markowitz* (1996), illustrates the transition in intergenerational roles. Gathered for the family's Passover *seder,* the Markowitz's four children offer competing images of Jewish commitment. Their parents and grandmother accept them all as signs of the inevitable breakup of tradition and of the Jewish future in which the family will house (generally) tolerant varieties of contemporary Judaism reflecting generational, ideological, educational, and experiential difference. Whether Judaism can in fact hold a family together, and whether a family can maintain a unified view of religious belief and practice, is precisely what worries a middle class professional who understands the tensions of contemporary Jewish family life:

> I hope [my children] become practicing and believing Jews. In other words that there is a consistency there, that they are not just practicing. It's because they actually believe the prayers and it's important.

And somehow I would approach that question by saying that all these other qualities that I want for them are the things that instigate whatever their Jewish practice is. I don't particularly care if they want to join an Orthodox congregation; that doesn't bother me. If they become Jews in such a way that it excludes me or any other members of their family, that's a different story (Cohen and Eisen 2000).

Holding the Jewish family together has been seen—in history and in popular U.S. culture—the primary responsibility of the Jewish mother. There is an old Jewish proverb, "God could not be everywhere, so mothers were created." Even so, like other groups around the world, Jews maintained a patriarchal family structure throughout most of their history. However, feminism and the women's movement have had a major impact on what Jews think about family life, with new roles for women in ritual life at home and in the synagogue. Thus, the famous *Jewish mother,* a domineering if loving fixture of the suburban American-Jewish family, can give way to a mother who is no less loving but who contributes less by control of the household (especially the kitchen table) and more in terms of a her unique grasp of the spiritual and of the meaning of community (see Hendler 1999 for a personal account of this transformation).

Intermarriage and the Jewish Future

Nothing could guarantee, however, that the Jewish family would maintain the reputation it has had for stability and durability. In this century, Jews have maintained high rates of marriage and childbearing (even if at a low birth rate) and relatively low rates of divorce. By nearly every measure, Jews have exemplified U.S. ideas of the normal family (see Fishman 2000 for a compact account of recent statistics). Yet, near the end of the twentieth century, survey research prompted one scholar to claim that U.S. Jewish life had "progressively weakened demographically as a result of low fertility, high intermarriage, significant dispersion, and assimilatory losses." In the 1990s there was intense debate about the meanings of these changes. In particular, there has been significant attention to the question of intermarriage, which increased dramatically in the decades after World War II—over 50 percent according to some interpretations of statistics. The consequences for *Jewish continuity,* a widely used phrase toward the end of the twentieth century, signifying as much fear as optimism, were the subject of increasing attention. "The majority of all new Jewish households formed in the United States in recent years involved a non-converted non-Jewish spouse. . . . [And] while only 16% of households established before 1965 consisted of a born Jew with a non-Jewish spouse, this percentage increased to 69 for those families established between 1985 and 1990. Thus, in less than one-third (31%) of the households are there children who are exposed to parents who were both born into the Jewish religion" (Klaff 1995).

Accordingly, for many scholars, and religious and lay leaders in Jewish life, intermarriage poses the most significant single threat to the Jewish family and to the prospects for Jewish continuity altogether. Although intermarriage among ethnic groups generally tends to yield little family conflict, religious differences are a likely source of tension, particularly so in the matter of childrearing and

what is to be provided for children in religious education and other resources for identification with Judaism. In any case, empirical studies of the family consequences of intermarriage are often limited by the difficulties in establishing consistency among research subjects' expressed views about religious beliefs and observance, and the meaning of Judaism for their day-to-day lives (e.g., Heller and Wood 2000).

Although Jews might regret increasing intermarriage, they do not see it necessarily as a threat to Judaism and the Jewish family. Indeed, in the popular film *Keeping the Faith* (1999) even though the cosmopolitan young rabbi marries a non-Jewish woman, the title appears to be anything but an irony. For many Jews, intermarriage is not as great a threat to the Jewish future as is a general decline in U.S. spirituality and the inability of many Jews—particular those in the first half of life—to relate to religion. What is called *Jewish Renewal* (Lerner 1994) offers a vision of Judaism that accepts an adaptive role for the Jewish family in regulating behavior on behalf of rededication to Jewish social and communal values including recognition of new family *styles* in our *post-halahkic* time.

Loyalty to the traditional Jewish family can "result in the fear that as traditional families change, and as more and more people live in alternative, or non-traditional, structures, individuals will become isolated, community weakened, and the Jewish future threatened" (Ackselberg 1992). Because only a minority of U.S. Jews live in the traditional nuclear family, there must be recognition of the legitimacy of other forms: "Giving the nuclear family first class status makes everyone else second class . . . [and] those whose intimacy constellations differ from the norm need not be on the margins of organized Jewish communities" (Ackselberg 1992). The goal is a more egalitarian and democratic Jewish community, with women participating fully not only in leading the family but in matters of spirituality and religious ritual in the home and the synagogue. Moreover, in the most liberal views of the future of the Jewish family, new structures, including single women bearing children (or raising them as adoptees) or homosexual unions of men or women should have the advantage of *holy purpose* in their households.

Critics of the newest ideas about the Jewish family, although accepting change, offer the success of traditional values, or the durability of Jewish history and culture as the best argument for keeping the past active in the present. Thus: "We will educate our children and adults to be understanding of other configurations and considerate of the people in them, but the Jewish [family] ethic will be what it has been in the past—not because of its historical roots, but because of the real personal and communal needs it serves" (Dorff 1992). Seen from another perspective, the twenty-first century Jewish family will continue to be a location for different ideas about what it means to be Jewish and to be a part of a Jewish household and family. Neither the decline in traditional Jewish beliefs shaping Jewish family life nor ideas about family structure representing radical breaks with tradition should be understood as defining the future. Not surprisingly, the Jewish past can still be invoked on behalf of its contributions to finding what new forms of family life can be made in the image of Judaism (Harman 1999).

See also: CIRCUMCISION; FAMILY RITUALS; FOOD; INTERFAITH MARRIAGE; ISRAEL; RELIGION

Bibliography

Ackselberg, M. A. (1992). "Jewish Family Ethics in a Post-Halakhic Age." In *Imagining the Jewish Future: Essays and Responses,* ed. David Teutsch. Albany: State University of New York Press.

Cohen, S., and Eisen, A. (2000). *The Jew Within: Self, Family, and Community in America.* Bloomington: Indiana University Press.

De Lange, N. (2000). *An Introduction to Judaism.* Cambridge: Cambridge University Press.

Dorff, E. A. (1992). "Response." In *Imagining the Jewish Future: Essays and Responses,* ed. David Teutsch. Albany: State University of New York Press.

Fishman, S. B. (2000). *Jewish Life and American Culture.* Albany: State University of New York Press.

Hartman, D. (1999). "Memory and Values: A Traditional Response to the Crisis of the Modern Family." *A Heart of Many Rooms: Celebrating the Many Voices within Judaism.* Woodstock, VT: Jewish Lights.

Heller, P., and Wood, B. (2000). "The Influence of Religious and Ethnic Differences on Marital Intimacy: Intermarriage versus Intermarriage." *Journal of Marital and Family Therapy* 26(2): 241–252.

Hendler, L. M. (1999). *The Year Mom Got Religion: One Woman's Midlife Journey into Judaism.* Woodstock, VT: Jewish Lights.

Klaff, V. (1995). "The Changing Jewish Family: Issues of Continuity." In *American Families: Issues of Race and Ethnicity,* ed. C. K. Jacobson. New York: Garland.

Kraemer, D., ed. (1989). *The Jewish Family: Metaphor and Memory.* New York: Oxford University Press.

Lerner, M. (1994). *Jewish Renewal: A Path to Healing and Transformation.* New York: Putnam.

Wertheimer, J. (1994). "Family Values and the Jews." *Commentary* 97(January):30–34.

STEVEN WEILAND

JUVENILE DELINQUENCY

Society places a heavy burden on families by assigning responsibility for childrearing to parents. Families must transmit values so as to lead children to accept rules that they are likely to perceive as arbitrary. It should be no surprise, therefore, to find that family life bears a strong relation to juvenile delinquency.

Family life can be viewed from three general perspectives. The first is structure: Who lives within a household? The second is interaction: How do the family members treat one another? And the third is social setting: What is the nature of the community in which the family can be found? Each of these perspectives contributes information relevant to understanding the impact of family life on juvenile delinquency.

Juvenile delinquency is defined differently in different cultures, and responses to juvenile delinquents differ also. For example, in Germany, assault is considered a violent crime only if a weapon is used during the commission of the crime, whereas in England and Wales, the degree of injury to the victim determines whether or not an assault is considered a violent crime. Crime is also measured differently in different countries. For example, the United States and Great Britain commonly rely on numbers of arrests to measure crime. In Germany, Austria, and Italy, crime is measured by the number of cases solved by police, whether or not the offender has been apprehended. Although rates for property crimes are higher in Canada, England and Wales, and the Netherlands than in the United States, in comparison with other Western countries, the United States has a higher rate for violent crimes committed by juveniles. The Federal Bureau of Investigation reported an arrest rate for violent crimes (aggravated assault, robbery, and rape) among thirteen- to seventeen-year-olds in the United States of nearly 800 per 100,000 in 1994. In the same year, in England and Wales, approximately 600 per 100,000 fourteen- to sixteen-year-olds were convicted or cautioned by the police for violent crimes. In Germany, 650 per 100,000 fourteen- to seventeen-year-olds, and in the Netherlands, 450 per 100,000 twelve- to seventeen-year-olds were suspects for violent crimes in 1994 (Pfeiffer 1998).

Comparing how countries deal with juvenile offenders presents a challenge because countries differ in the ages during which young people are considered legal juveniles, in the types of institution used to sanction juvenile offenders, and in the sanctions available for them. In Switzerland, for example, a child as young as seven can have criminal responsibility as determined through special juvenile courts. In Belgium, a child under the age of sixteen would not be held criminally responsible for any action and under the age of eighteen could not be incarcerated. In Japan, criminal responsibility can begin at age fourteen, but full criminal responsibility is not assumed until the age of twenty. In New Zealand, since 1989, Family Group Conferences have been used to replace or supplement youth courts for serious criminal cases. In the Netherlands, an offender can be charged as a juvenile between the ages of twelve and eighteen and can be given a lifetime sentence. Sweden and Denmark have no juvenile courts, and juveniles under the age of fifteen in Denmark may not be punished, although they may be referred to a social welfare agency. In the United States, states differ regarding the ages for partial and full criminal responsibility. Most states stipulate no minimum age. Some states grant full criminal responsibility at age fifteen, almost a dozen consider an offender an adult at age sixteen, and the remaining states give full criminal responsibility to an offender after the age of seventeen. Although many jurisdictions in the United States permit capital punishment for juveniles, few other countries allow the execution of minors.

Most research focused on identifying how socialization practices affect the behavior of children has been carried out in the United States. There are, however, some relevant studies about the impact of socialization practices in Great Britain, Scandinavia, Japan, Colombia, and the Netherlands.

Family Structure

When anthropologists discuss family structures, they consider normative patterns. That is, they consider ideal households—or at least widely respected households—in terms of membership. Societies that idealize households with one adult man and woman plus their offspring, nuclear family societies, can be contrasted with those in which one man lives with several women and their children (called *polygynous*) or several men live with one woman and their children (called *polyandrous*).

Nuclear families and single-parent households. Increasingly, among contemporary industrial societies, a nuclear family structure has been idealized. Conversely, deviations from this structure have been blamed for a variety of social problems, including delinquency. Although both the popular press and participants in the legal system blame broken homes for failures to socialize children as willing participants in an ordered social system, this conclusion goes well beyond the facts.

Claims that single-parent households produce delinquents fit well with several theories. Some assume that children learn how to become adults by association with parents of their own sex. Boys reared without a resident father, according to this assumption, would be deprived of the association necessary for appropriate maturation. As a result, children are said to overreact by asserting masculinity through delinquent behavior. This opinion has been buttressed by reports suggesting that typical delinquents lack the guidance of a father.

The conviction that lack of paternal guidance causes delinquency dominated early research in the field. High rates of broken homes among incarcerated youths were taken as evidence supporting this assumption. In the 1920s, for example, boys in New York State reformatories were shown to be twice as likely to come from broken homes as boys in New York City public schools. Studies in London, Chicago, rural California, and Boston followed. These, too, showed that broken homes were more common among incarcerated delinquents than among unselected populations. In 1965, convinced that broken homes cause crime, Daniel Moynihan suggested that crime could be reduced by altering family structure among African Americans. Despite the publicity given to the Moynihan Report, however, research has not shown a causal connection.

If poverty causes crime and the incidence of broken homes is greater among the poor, then broken homes might be incorrectly blamed for causing crime. In addition, official records for delinquency may inflate a connection because they reflect decisions by authorities regarding how to treat delinquents. When deciding what to do with a delinquent, representatives of the criminal justice system who believe that broken homes cause crime are more likely to place those from single-parent families in institutions.

Simple comparisons of the proportions of delinquents from single-parent homes with the proportions of nondelinquents from such homes confound many factors associated with family structures in the comparisons. Both social class and ethnicity are among the confounding factors.

Untangling the complexities. Several studies that went beyond comparing the incidence of broken homes among criminals with the incidence in the general population failed to show a link between broken homes and delinquency. For example, among blacks in St. Louis, boys from broken homes were not more likely to become delinquent than those from two-parent homes (Robins and Hill 1966). Careful analyses of juvenile court cases in the United States during 1969 showed that economic conditions rather than family composition influenced children's delinquency (Chilton and Markle 1972). In studies of London schoolboys and of American school children of both sexes, within social class, delinquency was not more prevalent among children from single-parent homes.

Children in single-parent families are likely to have been exposed to such crime-promoting influences as parental conflict and alcoholism. To detect effects on sons' criminality, one study divided both broken and united families according to whether or not the father was an alcoholic or a criminal (McCord 1982). The study showed that alcoholic or criminal fathers were more likely to have sons convicted of serious crimes, whether or not the father was present. There was no association between criminal behavior and single-parent families, regardless of whether the sons had alcoholic or criminal fathers.

Single parents often find it hard to get assistance. If they must work to support themselves and their families, they are likely to have difficulty providing supervision for their children. Poor supervision, like alcoholism and criminality, seems to generate delinquency.

Careful study of the impact of differences in household composition shows that in homes that lack fathers, grandmothers and other adult relatives are protective against delinquency. This evidence further undermines theories that rely on same-sex adults as explanation for successful socialization in families.

Knowledgeable observers have concluded that the evidence fails to support a conclusion that single-parent families cause crime. Asking whether broken homes are good or bad is misleading; the answer must depend in part on the available alternatives. Family conflict is particularly likely to promote criminal behavior, and the choice to divorce must typically be made by parents who do not get along. Convincingly, David Farrington found that among boys who had not been previously aggressive, marital disharmony of parents when the boys were fourteen predicted subsequent aggressive behavior. Furthermore, effects of living with a single parent vary in relation to the emotional and economic climate in the home. Indeed, in their longitudinal study of family disruption among London boys, Heather Juby and David Farrington (2001) found that those who stayed with their mothers following disruption had delinquency rates that were almost identical to those reared in intact families with low conflict. And in their study of inner-city minority youths living in Chicago, Deborah Gorman-Smith, Patrick Tolan, and David Henry (1999) showed that single-parent status had little impact on delinquency.

Family interaction. Whatever characteristics individuals may have inherited, resulting personalities and behavior are influenced by the social environments in which they are raised. Genetic transmission does not occur without environmental influences. Perhaps the best grounds for believing that family interaction influences conduct comes from those programs that alter parental management techniques and thereby benefit siblings. Consistent and reasonable guidance forms the foundation for such programs.

Social control theory postulates that bonds between parents and children provide a basis for children to give up their immediate pleasures in exchange for receiving distal rewards attached to socialized behavior. Consistent discipline and supervision add social control to the internalized bonds on the route toward forming well-socialized adolescents. The theory gains support from a series of studies showing absence of parental affection to be linked with delinquency. Furthermore, reductions in delinquency between the ages of fifteen and seventeen years appear to be related to friendly interaction between teenagers and their parents, a reduction that seems to promote school attachment and stronger family ties (Liska and Reed 1985).

Warm family relationships appear to reduce the risk of delinquency in a variety of cultures other than those found in the United States. For example, Danish adolescents having warm family interactions were less likely to shoplift or commit vandalism than their peers (Arnett; Jeffrey; and Balle-Jensen 1993). In the Netherlands, adolescents between the ages of fourteen and twenty-one who had positive relations with their mothers were considerably less likely to have been engaged in delinquent behavior than those who had negative relationships (Terlouw and Junger-Tas 1992). Similarly, the likelihood that Colombian adolescents would engage in delinquency was reduced by close bonds with parents (Brook; Brook; De La Rosa; Whiteman; and Montoya 1999). In Japan (Harada 1995) and in Sweden (Martens 1992), close emotional ties within the family also appeared to reduce the likelihood that children would become delinquents.

Parental rejection may affect the ways in which children regard both themselves and others. Parents who fail to provide consistent guidance deprive their children of opportunities to gain approval by choosing to behave in accordance with parental rules. If parents treat their offspring with disdain, the offspring are likely to regard themselves as unworthy of care and may come to believe that the way they are treated is how they should treat others.

Symbolic interaction theories suggest that roles assigned within families can have an important effect on how children define others with whom they are likely to have contacts. A variety of types of evidence suggests that delinquents have little self-esteem. Other studies suggest that delinquents lack empathic responses to those around them.

Whether family rejection or neglect affects tendencies toward delinquency through failures in attachment or through role concepts may appear to be merely an interesting academic debate. Yet designs for intervention strategies have depended on these theories in order to decide what approaches to take.

Prevention programs that successfully develop bonds between counselors and youths have failed to prevent delinquency, as have some carefully designed programs aimed toward building self-esteem. The Cambridge-Somerville Youth Study successfully established close bonds between young boys and counselors over a period of several years. Nevertheless, boys who formed such bonds were not less likely to become delinquents than matched boys who were not assigned to program counselors.

One of many programs aimed at improving self-esteem identified aggressive boys in sixth grade and provided a randomly selected group of the vulnerable children with special classes in remedial reading and lessons that provided models for behavior the next school year. Although the boys in these special classes reported that the program had been helpful, neither school nor police records supported a judgment that the program had reduced delinquency (Reckless and Dinitz 1972). Similarly discouraging results come from attempts to build self-confidence among adjudicated delinquents between the ages of fifteen and seventeen (Empey and Erickson 1972) and students in public schools (Gottfredson 1987).

Programs that help parents become adequate guides for their children seem to be more effective when begun before kindergarten (Weikart and Schweinhart 1992), and changes in self-esteem appear more likely to reduce aggressive behavior when begun in primary grades (Tremblay et al. 1992). Once personalities have become fairly stable, the evidence suggests, intervention programs may be ineffective if they rely either on attempts to establish internal bonds or to increase self-esteem.

In sum, parental affection and reasonable parental control have been shown to promote socialized behavior. Yet when children fail to receive these early in their lives, substitutions have typically been ineffective. Of course temperamental, physical, and intellectual differences sometimes influence parenting. Therefore, children's characteristics may affect the relationship between early parenting and later child problems. Parents who are themselves aggressive and antisocial are the most likely to use harsh punishments and to have children who are at heightened risk for aggressive, antisocial behavior.

When children misbehave, parents (or their substitutes) are the first line of control. How they discipline can influence not only immediate behavior, but also their future influence on the child's values. Several longitudinal studies investigating effects of punishment on aggressive behavior have shown that punishments are more likely to result in defiance than compliance.

One study identified toddlers one month after they had started walking unassisted and studied them again a month later. The sample, drawn from Lamaze classes, was middle class, with mothers at home. Among them, "Infants of physically punishing mothers showed the lowest levels of compliance and were most likely to manipulate breakable objects during the observations" (Power and Chapieski 1986, p. 273). Six months later, those who had been physically punished showed slower development as measured by the Bayley mental test scores.

In an investigation of two-year-olds, mothers described their techniques for discipline and various features about family life. Their infants were asked to respond to directions in the laboratory. The same mother-child pairs were studied one month later in their homes during meal preparation and mealtime. After controlling other types of maternal behavior, the observers' ratings indicated that negative control was related to defiance in both settings (Crockenberg and Litman 1990).

Similarly, spanking seems counterproductive for children preparing to enter school. Parents in three cities reported on family disciplinary practices over the prior year as they registered their children for kindergarten. The children were subsequently observed in their classrooms. Children spanked by their mothers or fathers displayed more angry, reactive aggression in the kindergarten classrooms than did those who did not receive physical punishments (Strassberg et al. 1994).

Long-term effects of corporal punishment have been identified in a study based on biweekly observation of 224 parents and their sons over an average period of five-and-one-half years. In addition to measuring the use of corporal punishment in the home, the researchers rated each parent in terms of warmth expressed toward the child. At the time of these ratings, the sons were between the ages of ten and sixteen. Thirty years later, the criminal records of the subjects were traced. Even after statistically controlling for paternal warmth, the father's use of corporal punishment predicted an increased likelihood that the son would subsequently be convicted for a serious crime. After statistically controlling for maternal warmth, the mother's use of corporal punishment predicted an increased likelihood that the son would subsequently be convicted for a serious crime of violence (McCord 1997a).

Taking into account the wide variety of studies on the use of physical punishments, the American Academy of Pediatrics together with the Albert Einstein College of Medicine/Montefiore Medical Center Division of Adolescent Medicine held a conference in 1996 to decide on policy. After two days of debates and consideration of a variety of studies, the conference attendees who had been selected to incorporate widely disparate points of view endorsed the following: "Currently available data indicate that corporal punishment, as previously defined, when compared with other methods of punishment, of older children and adolescents is not effective and is associated with increased risk for dysfunction and aggression later in life."

Community

Where a family lives affects the nature of opportunities that will be available to its members. In some communities, public transportation permits easy travel for those who do not own automobiles. Opportunities for employment and entertainment extend beyond the local boundaries. In other communities, corner gatherings open possibilities for illegal activities. Lack of socially acceptable opportunities leads to frustration and a search for alternative means to success. Community-based statistics show high correlations among joblessness, crime, household disruption, housing density, infant deaths, and poverty.

Community variations may explain why some types of family life have different effects in terms of delinquency in different communities. In general, consistent friendly parental guidance seems to protect children from delinquency across neighborhoods, with the exception of the most disrupted and deprived (Gorman-Smith, Tolan, and Henry 1999). Poor socialization practices, however, seem to be more potent in disrupted neighborhoods.

Neighborhoods influence children's behavior by providing the values that lead them to perceive how to act. The theory of differential association suggests that people acquire their behavioral orientations by learning to define experiences through the eyes of their associates. This theory and the related Construct Theory of Motivation (McCord 1997b) place a premium on the idea that peer groups can shape the behavior of adolescents.

Communities in which criminal activities are common tend to establish criminal behavior as acceptable. Tolerance for gang activities varies by community. In neighborhoods in which gangs are respected, gang membership may generate loyalties that increase the likelihood of violence. Friendships among delinquents seem to involve closer ties as well as greater mutual influence than do friendships among nondelinquents. Through ties of friendship, communities have multiplying effects.

Conclusion

This brief review of research indicates that a popular opinion about family impact is wrong: parental absence is *not* importantly related to juvenile delinquency. Family interactions have greater influence on delinquency. Children reared by competent, affectionate parents who avoid using physical forms of punishment are unlikely to commit serious crimes either as juveniles or as adults. On the other hand, children reared by parents who neglect or reject them are likely to be greatly influenced by their community environments, which may offer opportunities and encouragement for criminal behavior.

See also: CHILD ABUSE: PHYSICAL ABUSE AND NEGLECT; CHILDHOOD, STAGES OF: ADOLESCENCE; CHILDREN OF ALCOHOLICS; CONDUCT DISORDERS; CONFLICT: FAMILY RELATIONSHIPS; DISCIPLINE; DIVORCE: EFFECTS ON CHILDREN; GANGS; INTERPARENTAL CONFLICT—EFFECTS ON CHILDREN; NEIGHBORHOOD; OPPOSITIONALITY; POVERTY; RUNAWAY YOUTHS; SELF-ESTEEM; SINGLE-PARENT FAMILIES; SPANKING; SUBSTANCE ABUSE; TEMPERAMENT

Bibliography

Arnett, J., and Balle-Jensen, L. (1993). "Cultural Bases of Risk Behavior: Danish Adolescents." *Child Development* 64(6):1842–1855.

Brook, J. S.; Brook, D. W.; De la Rosa, M.; Whiteman, M.; and Montoya, I. D. (1999). "The Role of Parents in Protecting Colombian Adolescents from Delinquency and Marijuana Use." *Archives of Pediatric and Adolescent Medicine* 153:457–464.

Chilton, R. J., and Markle, G. E. (1972). "Family Disruption, Delinquent Conduct and the Effect of Subclassification." *American Sociological Review* 37:93–99.

Crockenberg, S., and Litman, C. (1990). "Autonomy as Competence in Two-Year-Olds: Maternal Correlates of Child Defiance, Compliance, and Self-Assertion." *Developmental Psychology* 26:961–971.

Empey, L .T., and Erickson, M. L. (1972). *The Provo Experiment: Evaluating Community Control of Delinquency*. Lexington, MA: Lexington Books.

Gorman-Smith, D.; Tolan, P. H.; and Henry, D. (1999). "The Relation of Community and Family to Risk among Urban-Poor Adolescents." In *Where and When: Historical and Geographical Aspects of Psychopathology*, ed. P. Cohen, C. Slomkowski, and L. N. Robins. Mahwah, NJ: Lawrence Erlbaum Associates.

Gottfredson, G. D. (1987). "Peer Group Interventions To Reduce the Risk of Delinquent Behavior: A Selective Review and A New Evaluation." *Criminology* 25(3):671–714.

Harada, Y. (1995). "Adjustment to School, Life Course Transitions, and Changes in Delinquent Behavior in Japan." In *Current Perspectives on Aging and the Life Cycle*, Vol. 4: *Delinquency and Disrepute in the Life Course*, ed. Z. S. Blau and J. Hagan. Greenwich, CT: JAI Press.

Juby, H., and Farrington, D. P. (2001). "Disentangling the Link Between Disrupted Families and Delinquency." *British Journal of Criminology* 41:22–40.

Liska, A. E., and Reed, M. D. (1985). "Ties to Conventional Institutions and Delinquency: Estimating Reciprocal Effects." *American Sociological Review* 50 (August):547–560.

Martens, P. L. (1992). *Familj, Uppvaxt Och Brott* (Family, environment and delinquency). Stockholm, Sweden: Brottsforebyggande radet.

McCord, J. (1982). "A Longitudinal View of the Relationship Between Paternal Absence and Crime." In *Abnormal Offenders, Delinquency, and the Criminal Justice System,* ed. J. Gunn and D. P. Farrington. Chichester, UK: John Wiley and Sons.

McCord, J. (1997a). "On Discipline." *Psychological Inquiry* 8(3):215–217.

McCord, J. (1997b). "He Did It Because He Wanted To . . . ." In *Motivation and Delinquency,* ed. W. Osgood. Vol. 44. *Nebraska Symposium on Motivation.* Lincoln: University of Nebraska Press.

Pfeiffer, C. (1998). "Juvenile Crime and Violence in Europe." In *Crime and Justice: A Review of Research,* ed. M. Tonry. Vol. 23. Chicago: University of Chicago Press.

Power, T. G., and Chapieski, M. L. (1986). "Childrearing and Impulse Control in Toddlers: A Naturalistic Investigation." *Developmental Psychology* 22(2):271–275.

Reckless, W. C., and Dinitz, S. (1967). "Pioneering with Self-Concept as a Vulnerability Factor in Delinquency." *Journal of Criminal Law, Criminology, and Police Science* 58:515–523.

Robins, L. N., and Hill, S. Y. (1966). "Assessing the Contribution of Family Structure, Class, and Peer Groups to Juvenile Delinquency." *Journal of Criminal Law, Criminology, and Police Science* 57:325–334.

Strassberg, Z.; Dodge, K. A.; Pettit, G.; and Bates, J.E. (1994). Spanking in the Home and Children's Subsequent Aggression toward Kindergarten Peers. *Development and Psychopathology* 6(3):445–461.

Terlouw, G., and Junger-Tas, J. (1992). "The International Juvenile Self-Report Delinquency Study: Design and First Results of the Dutch Survey." Paper presented at the 44th annual meeting of the American Society of Criminology, New Orleans, LA.

Tremblay, R. E.; Vitaro, F.; Bertrand, L.; LeBlanc, M.; Beauchesne, H.; Boileau, H.; and David, L. (1992). "Parent and Child Training to Prevent Early Onset of Delinquency: The Montreal Longitudinal-Experimental Study." In *Preventing Antisocial Behavior: Interventions from Birth through Adolescence,* ed. J. McCord and R. E. Tremblay. New York: Guilford Press.

Weikart, D. P., and Schweinhart, L. J. (1992). "High/Scope Preschool Program Outcomes." In *Preventing Antisocial Behavior,* ed. J. McCord and R. E. Tremblay. New York: Guilford Press.

Other Resources

American Society of Criminology. Web site. Available from http://www.asc41.com.

International Society for Criminology. Web site. Available from http://perso.wanadoo.fr/societe.internationale. de.criminologie/index_ang.htm.

JOAN MCCORD

ISBN 0-02-865674-1

90000